FOURTH EDITION

# STRATEGIC MANAGEMENT
## CONCEPTS AND CASES

### Peter Wright
*The University of Memphis*

### Mark J. Kroll
*University of Texas at Tyler*

### John A. Parnell
*Texas A & M University Commerce*

D1417978

Prentice Hall, Upper Saddle River, NJ 07458

Acquisitions Editor: David Shafer
Associate Editor: Lisamarie Brassini
Editorial Assistant: Chris Stogdill
Editor-in-Chief: Natalie E. Anderson
Marketing Manager: Tammy Wederbrand
Senior Production Editor: Cynthia Regan
Production Coordinator: Carol Samet
Managing Editor: Dee Josephson
Manufacturing Supervisor: Arnold Vila
Manufacturing Manager: Vincent Scelta
Senior Designer: Ann France
Design Director: Patricia Smythe
Interior Design: Suzanne Behnke
Cover Design: Amanda Kavanaugh
Illustrator (Interior): TSI Graphics
Composition: TSI Graphics
Cover Art/Photo: Letraset Phototone

**The Library of Congress has cataloged the Combined Volume as follows:**
Wright, Peter.
    Strategic management : concepts and cases / Peter Wright, Mark J.
Kroll, John A. Parnell. — 4th ed.
        p.     cm.
    Includes bibliographical references and index.
    ISBN 0-13-681750-5
    1. Strategic planning.   2. Strategic planning—Case studies.
I. Kroll, Mark J.      II. Parnell, John A. (John Alan)
III.  Title.
HD30.28.W75        1998
658.4′012—dc21                                              97-36699
                                                                CIP

Printed in the United States of America
10   9   8   7   6   5   4   3

PRENTICE-HALL INTERNATIONAL (UK) LIMITED, *LONDON*
PRENTICE-HALL OF AUSTRALIA PTY. LIMITED, *SYDNEY*
PRENTICE-HALL CANADA INC., *TORONTO*
PRENTICE-HALL HISPANOAMERICANA, S.A., *MEXICO*
PRENTICE-HALL OF INDIA PRIVATE LIMITED, *NEW DELHI*
PRENTICE-HALL OF JAPAN, INC., *TOKYO*
PEARSON EDUCATION ASIA PTE. LTD., *SINGAPORE*
EDITORA PRENTICE-HALL DO BRASIL, LTDA., *RIO DE JANEIRO*

# Brief Contents

## GLOBAL ENVIRONMENT

## SMALL BUSINESS

## NOT-FOR-PROFIT ORGANIZATIONS

## ETHICS AND SOCIAL RESPONSIBILITY

# Contents

## PART II ■ CASES IN STRATEGIC MANAGEMENT

## GOODS PRODUCERS

## SERVICE PROVIDERS

# Preface

This fourth edition reflects the truth of one of our book's basic tenets: environmental change is inevitable. In fact, changes in the business environment and developments in the academic field of strategic management drove us to begin revising *Strategic Management Concepts* less than a year after the third edition first appeared on the market. This new edition not only contains those changes, but it also benefits significantly from the perceptive feedback of our reviewers and the adopters of the first, second, and third editions.

The text portion synthesizes and builds upon the most recent strategy-related literature from numerous fields. And virtually every concept, theory, or idea is illustrated with examples from real organizations. The cases represent the works of knowledgeable and discerning authors who have provided highly readable information on enterprises ranging from small, local businesses to huge, global corporations.

## GOALS OF THE TEXT

Our purpose in writing this text was twofold: to provide students with the most current, comprehensive, state-of-the-art analysis of the field of strategic management, and to promote student understanding of the material with applied, innovative learning features.

To accomplish our first goal, we incorporated the most up-to-date coverage of the strategic management literature into the text in a clear, easy-to-read style. The coverage includes the most relevant and exciting multidisciplinary contributions to the field. Strategic management is a relatively young discipline that has borrowed from, built upon, and contributed to such business fields as economics, management, marketing, finance, operations management, and accounting, among others. In recent years, however, exciting developments from such diverse fields as psychology, sociology, and anthropology have also broadened and enriched the knowledge base of strategic management. Students will gain new insights from these cutting-edge, integrative developments.

The strategic management and business policy course is designed to help students integrate and apply what they have learned in their separate functional business courses and to help them gain experience in using the tools of strategic analysis. To facilitate this process and promote student learning—the second major goal of this text—we have developed a number of innovative learning tools. You will find this book rich with applied material—realistic business examples carefully woven throughout the text, provocative discussions of strategic management conducted by well-known companies, and experiential exercises to help students think strategically. Since the core of the course is case analysis, our text provides an excellent, diverse collection of up-to-date cases depicting meaningful decision situations.

## STATE-OF-THE-ART COVERAGE

Along with traditional coverage, this text incorporates a number of innovative topics and provides several unique chapters that give it a distinct competitive advantage over other textbooks in strategic management. Some of that coverage includes the following material:

- Diverse theories that have influenced our approach to strategic management are briefly presented in Chapter 1. These include biological and Schumpeterian theories of evolution and revolution; theories based upon the fields of industrial organization and Chamberlinian economics; and contingency and resource-based theories.

- Chapter 3 presents not only the traditional viewpoint that a firm's strategy should be shareholder-driven, but also the competing perspectives that strategy should be customer-driven or, more broadly, stakeholder-driven. Resource-based theory is used to analyze a firm's strengths and weaknesses.

- Our S.W.O.T. portfolio framework is introduced in Chapter 5, along with more traditional approaches. New material analyzing corporate strategies and returns is also included in Chapter 5.

- Chapter 6, a unique chapter on business unit strategies, relates generic strategies to such concepts as total quality management (TQM), product/process innovations, leverage through organizational expertise and image, market share, industry life cycle stages, value analysis, and strategic groups.

- Unique coverage of how functional activities can be integrated to help a business attain superior product design, customer service, speed, and product/service guarantees is contained in Chapter 7.

- A framework is presented in Chapter 8 for helping top management assess the effectiveness of the organization's structure.

- Chapter 9 offers innovative discussion of how strategy is implemented through managerial leadership, the appropriate use of power, and the molding of organizational culture.

- A unique approach to strategic control in Chapter 10 presents multiple control standards and several different and useful ways of exerting strategic control.

- Global issues are not only integrated throughout the text but are comprehensively covered in Chapter 11. This unique chapter revisits the strategic management processes covered in Chapters 2 through 10 in the context of the world marketplace.

- Chapter 12 is devoted exclusively to strategic management in not-for-profit organizations.

- Differences in strategic management processes in large and small companies are examined in separate sections throughout the chapter portions of the text.

## NEW TO THIS EDITION

New to the Fourth Edition is the coverage of the following material:

- Although the traditional industry analysis is presented in Chapter 2, it is also argued in this Chapter that the pressure for enhanced firm efficiency and innovation during the last two decades has increased to such an extent that analyzing any one industry may not fully reflect what impacts an enterprise's performance. Rather, the performance of a firm may be determined by its competitive and cooperative interactions with other firms across different industries. Thus, what is newly examined is exchanges among an assemblage of firms across various industries.

- Updated Strategic Insight Boxes and examples.

- In Chapter 6, value chain analysis is presented as a series of internal and external agency relationships. An agency relationship exists when one party (an agent) acts on behalf of another party (a principal) to increase the value of the principal's resources or activities.

- In Chapter 7, an expanded coverage of cross functional teams and process management takes place.

- In Chapter 8, an expanded coverage of the assessment of organizational structure is presented.

- In Chapter 9, leadership, power, and culture are depicted with a focus on each as components of strategy implementation.

- In Chapter 10, more recent developments on strategic control are covered.

## SPECIAL LEARNING FEATURES OF THIS TEXT

We have consistently integrated theory with practice throughout the chapter portion of the book. You will find that strategic management concepts are liberally illustrated with examples from actual, well-known organizations.

To promote student learning further, we built into the text a number of special features to help students understand and apply the concepts presented. Each chapter of the text provides the following learning features:

- *A strategic management* model helps to portray visually the important stages in the strategic management process. This model is introduced and explained in Chapter 1, then reappears at the beginning of each chapter, with the portion to be discussed in a given chapter highlighted. The model serves as a student's road map throughout each chapter of Part I.

- *Key concepts* are boldfaced in the text when first introduced and are immediately defined. A list of key concepts with definitions appears at the end of each chapter.

- *Strategic Insight* boxes throughout the chapter portion of the book illustrate successful and unsuccessful applications of strategic management concepts in such companies as Southwest Airlines, IBM, Coca-Cola, and Sears, Roebuck and Company. Each of the boxes illustrates a major point in the text.

- A *chapter summary* helps reinforce the major concepts that the student has learned in the chapter.

- End-of-chapter *discussion questions* test the student's retention and understanding of important chapter material and can be used as a tool for review and classroom discussion.

- *Strategic Management Exercises* unique to this text appear at the end of each chapter. These experiential exercises offer students the opportunity to apply their knowledge of the chapter material to realistic strategic business situations.

- *Internet Exercises* are located at the end of each chapter to help students learn how to use the WWW as a strategic resource. These can be found at **http://www.prenhall.com/wrightsm**.

## CASES

Part II: *Cases in Strategic Management.* In this edition, we have reduced the number of case offerings in the combined Concepts and Cases version of the text in order to offer a higher degree of flexibility and lower costs to students. The 23 cases, organized around the areas of Goods Producers, Service Providers, Global Environment, Small Business, Not-for-Profit Organizations, and Ethics and Social Responsibility, offer a broad range of companies and issues. Additional cases can be ordered through the *Prentice Hall Custom Case Program.* Visit us at **http://www.prenhall.com/phbusiness** for more information. An alternative "Cases only" text

is also available that contains an additional 17 cases for a total of 40.

A special introductory section preceding the cases, "Strategic Management Case Analysis," is designed to help students prepare written and oral case analysis by offering specific guidelines and methodologies. Concluding this section are several suggestions for enhancing student performance in the strategic management course and for working within a group.

We have selected cases that students and instructors should find interesting and thought-provoking to read. Our case selection includes some of the largest, best-known businesses in the world as well as small, developing organizations. The companies examined include huge multi-divisional corporations, mid-size firms competing in only one or two markets, and small sole-proprietorships.

We have sought out cases which provide students an opportunity to be exposed to great diversity, both in terms of the industries covered as well as location. A vast array of industries are represented in the case selection. The global breadth of the cases is also extensive with cases covering firms in such locations as Poland, France, and Mexico. However, we have also included cases which involve organizations as familiar as the nearest fast-food restaurant or department store. The case selection also reflects a conscious effort to expose students not only to a diversity of enterprises but also to the diversity of the individuals who manage those enterprises. The following are key features of our case selection:

- In keeping with the increasing globalization of business and AACSB's concern for the internationalization of the business curriculum, we have selected cases that provide a more global perspective of business. These cases include enterprises based outside the United States and U.S. based firms with multinational operations.

- A concerted effort was made to include cases that not only detail the history and present condition of organizations, but also present the future issues that managers must face if the enterprises are to survive and prosper. Whether the issues involve exploiting new opportunities in the environment or taking steps to avoid threats, the student analyzing the case must make critical decisions regarding the future of the organizations examined.

- The extensive case selection gives students an opportunity to make strategic management decisions at the corporate level, the business unit level, and the functional level.

- Several small business cases are included, addressing such issues as confronting competition from much larger organizations, making a small business acquisition decision, and managing the growth of a successful small business.
- Not-for-profit cases range from Presque Isle State Park to The University of Texas Health Center at Tyler.

As in the earlier editions of this text, our primary criterion for our case selection was the overall quality of the cases. Special attention was also given to finding cases that were not only well written and interesting but also contained ample information for analysis.

## SUPPLEMENTS

*Internet Support Site—**StratPlus**—*a Web site that supports all of Prentice Hall's publications in Strategic Management, contains additional information on Value Chains, Industrial Chains, Porter's Five Factors, SWOT Analysis, Industrial Organization, and Environmental Analysis. In addition, there is an on-line annotated "How To Do a Case" section along with Internet resources and bimonthly new updates.

*Instructor's Resource Manual—*includes test items and extensive case notes containing a synopsis, a mini-S.W.O.T. analysis, and transparency masters for each case.

*Computerized Instructor's Resource Manual—*offers all the features of the IRM on a 3.5" disk.

*Overhead Transparencies—*covering the major concepts for the first 12 chapters.

*PowerPoint Transparencies—*Electronic version of the Overhead Transparency program available on 3.5" disk.

## ACKNOWLEDGMENTS

We are deeply indebted to our colleagues who have so generously permitted us to use their high quality cases in this text. The selection process was lengthy and rigorous, and we take considerable pride in presenting these cases. The author(s) of each case is identified on the first page of the case. A list of case contributors appears below:

**Gary Bridges,** *University of Southern Colorado*
**Julius S. Brown,** *Loyola Marymount University*
**William D. Chandler,** *University of Southern Colorado*
**Casey Donoho,** *Northern Arizona University*
**Julie Driscoll,** *Bentley College*
**W. Jack Duncan,** *University of Alabama at Birmingham*
**Andrew D. Dyer,** *Georgetown University*
**David R. Frew,** *Gannon University*
**Cynthia V. Fukami,** *University of Denver*
**Ronald P. Garrett,** *United States Air Force*
**Peter M. Ginter,** *University of Alabama at Birmingham*
**Walter Greene,** *University of Texas Pan American*
**W. Harvey Hegarty,** *Indiana University*
**Todd E. Himstead,** *Georgetown University*
**Alan N. Hoffman,** *Bentley College*
**John Holm,** *The University of Texas at Tyler*
**Mark Kroll,** *University of Texas at Tyler*
**Jeffrey A. Krug,** *The University of Memphis*
**Sharon Ungar Lane,** *Bentley College*
**Angela R. Lanning,** *University of Guelph*
**Donald L. Lester,** *Union University*
**Robert C. Lewis,** *University of Guelph*
**Daniel O. Lybroo,** *Purdue University*
**Zbigniew Malara,** *Technical University of Wroclaw, Poland*
**Michael D. Martin,** *Healthsouth Corporation*
**Robert P. McGowan,** *University of Denver*
**Robert N. McGrath,** *Embry-Riddle Aeronautical University*
**Michael L. Menefee,** *Purdue University*
**Albert J. Milhomme,** *Southwest Texas State University*
**Mary Mulligan,** *Loyola Marymount University*
**John Noland,** *University of Alabama at Birmingham*
**Godwin Osuagwa,** *Jarvis Christian College*
**Jon Ozmun,** *Northern Arizona University*
**John A. Parnell,** *North Carolina Central University*
**Charles Rarick,** *Transylvania University*
**Paul Reed,** *Sam Houston State University*
**Dr. Woodrow D. Richardson,** *University of Alabama at Birmingham*
**Patrick Asubonteng Rivers,** *University of Alabama at Birmingham*
**Alison Rude,** *Bentley College*
**Carol Rugg,** *Bentley College*
**C. Louise Sellaro,** *Youngstown State University*
**Bonnie Silveria,** *Bentley College*

**Douglas L. Smith,** *University of Alabama at Birmingham*
**N. Craig Smith,** *Georgetown University*
**Kellie F. Snell,** *HealthSouth Corporation*
**John J. Vitton,** *University of North Dakota*
**Donna M. Watkins,** *University of South Colorado*
**Joan Winn,** *University of Denver*

We are also deeply indebted to many individuals for their assistance and support in this project. We especially wish to thank our manuscript reviewers for the first, second, third, and fourth editions. These colleagues were particularly able and deserve considerable credit for their helpful and extensive suggestions. They include:

**William P. Anthony,** *Florida State University*
**B.R. Baliga,** *Wake Forest University*
**Robert B. Brown,** *University of Virginia*
**William J. Carner,** *University of Texas at Austin*
**Peng Chan,** *California State University, Fullerton*
**Edward J. Conlon,** *University of Notre Dame*
**Halil Copur,** *Rhode Island College*
**George B. Davis,** *Cleveland State University*
**Louis R. Desfosses,** *State University of New York, Brockport*
**Pierre E. Du Jardin,** *Bentley College*
**Kamal Fatchi,** *Witchita State University*
**Lawrence K. Finley,** *Western Kentucky University*
**Philip C. Fisher,** *University of South Dakota*
**Len Frey,** *Nicolls State University*
**Joseph J. Geiger,** *University of Idaho*
**Manolete V. Gonzalez,** *Oregon State University*
**Donald Harvey,** *California State University, Bakersfield*
**Marilyn M. Helms,** *University of Tennessee at Chattanooga*
**Stevan R. Holmberg,** *The American University*
**Tammy G. Hunt,** *University of North Carolina at Wilmington*
**William Jackson,** *Stephen F. Austin State University*
**Michael J. Keeffe,** *Southwest Texas State University*
**Daniel G. Kopp,** *Southwest Missouri State University*
**Augustine Lado,** *Cleveland State University*
**Don Lester,** *Crichton University*
**William Litzinger,** *University of Texas, San Antonio*
**James Logan,** *University of New Orleans*
**Michael Lubatkin,** *University of Connecticut*

**John E. Merchant,** *California State University, Sacramento*
**Omid Nodoushani,** *University of New Haven*
**Tim Pett,** *University of Memphis*
**Bevalee Pray,** *Union University*
**Elizabeth Rozell,** *Missouri Southern State College*
**Hael Y. Sammour,** *East Texas State*
**Daniel A. Sauers,** *Louisiana Tech University*
**Charles W. Schilling,** *University of Wisconsin, Platteville*
**Louise Sellaro,** *Youngstown State University*
**Jeffery C. Shuman,** *Bentley College*
**Carl L. Swanson,** *University of North Texas*
**James B. Thurman, Ph.D.,** *George Washington University*
**Howard Tu,** *University of Memphis*
**Philip M. Van Auken,** *Baylor University*
**Robert P. Vichas,** *Florida Atlantic University*
**Richard J. Ward,** *Bowling Green State University*
**Marion White,** *James Madison University*
**Carolyn Y. Woo,** *Purdue University*
**David C. Wyld,** *Southeastern Louisiana University*

Special thanks are due to our editor, David Shafer, and our production editor, Cynthia Regan, for overseeing this project from inception to completion. We are deeply indebted to Professor Charles "Hemingway" Pringle for the quality he imputed to the development of the first two editions of this text. His brilliance will live on and carry us through the subsequent revisions.

Administrators at each of our universities have been most supportive of our work. We particularly wish to thank Dean Donna Randall and Management Chairman Robert Taylor, University of Memphis; and President George F. Hamm, Vice President of Academic Affairs Bill Baker, and Dean Jim Tarter of the University of Texas at Tyler.

Finally, but certainly not least, the support, patience, and understanding of special family members—William, Mahin, and Teresa Wright; Nghi Kroll; and Denise Parnell—were not only helpful but essential in making this book a reality.

## ABOUT THE AUTHORS

Peter Wright is a Professor of Management who holds the University of Memphis Endowed Chair of Excellence in Free Enterprise Management. He received his M.B.A. and his Ph.D. in management from Louisiana State University. He has acted as a consultant to many business organizations and was president/owner of an international industrial trading firm. Professor Wright is widely published in journals such as the *Harvard Business Review, Strategic Management Journal, Academy of Management Journal, Journal of Management, Journal of Business Research, Journal of Banking and Finance, Long Range Planning, British Journal of Management, Journal of the Academy of Marketing Science, Business Horizons, Planning Review,* and *Managerial Planning,* among others. Some of his academic publications have been reported in the media such as *The CBS Television Evening News, The Washington Post, Business Week, The Economist,* the *Wall Street Journal,* and *Smart Money.*

Mark J. Kroll is Professor Chair of the Management and Marketing Department at the University of Texas at Tyler. He received his M.B.A. from Sam Houston State University and his D.B.A. in management from Mississippi State University. His articles on strategic management topics have appeared in many journals including the *Academy of Management Executive, Academy of Management Journal, Academy of Management Review, Journal of Business Research, Journal of the Academy of Marketing Science* and *Strategic Management Journal.* He has also authored a number of cases, which have appeared in various strategic management textbooks and in the *Case Research Journal.* Professor Kroll consults for a wide variety of business organizations and teaches the capstone strategic management course at both the undergraduate and graduate levels.

John A. Parnell is Professor and Head of the Marketing and Management Department at Texas A & M University-Commerce. He received his M.B.A. from East Carolina University, his Ed.D. from Campbell University, and his Ph.D. from The University of Memphis. He served three years as president/owner of a direct-mail firm and is the author of over 100 journal articles, published cases, and conference proceedings. His works appear in such leading journals as *Administration and Society, British Journal of Management, Human Resource Management Review, International Journal of Organizational Analysis,* and *International Journal of Value-Based Management.* Professor Parnell teaches the capstone strategic management course at the undergraduate and graduate levels.

# I THE CONCEPTS AND TECHNIQUES OF STRATEGIC MANAGEMENT

# STRATEGIC MANAGEMENT MODEL

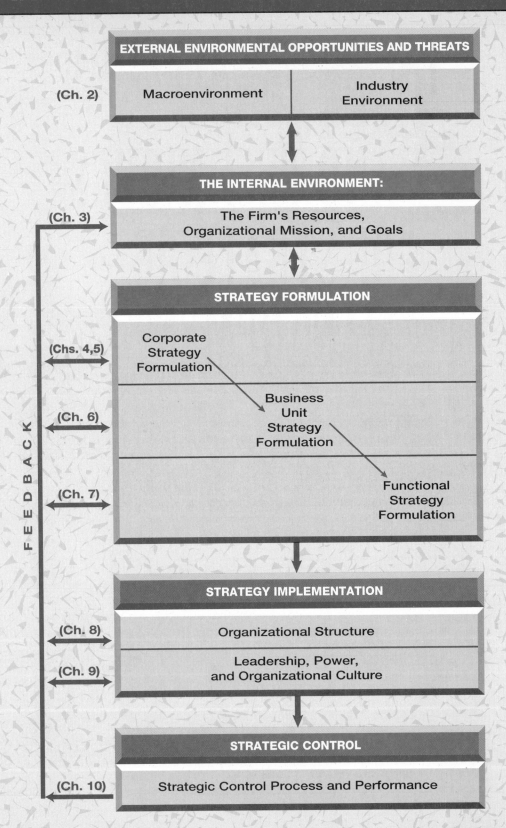

**EXTERNAL ENVIRONMENTAL OPPORTUNITIES AND THREATS**

(Ch. 2)

| Macroenvironment | Industry Environment |
| --- | --- |

**THE INTERNAL ENVIRONMENT:**

(Ch. 3)

The Firm's Resources, Organizational Mission, and Goals

**STRATEGY FORMULATION**

(Chs. 4,5) Corporate Strategy Formulation

(Ch. 6) Business Unit Strategy Formulation

(Ch. 7) Functional Strategy Formulation

**STRATEGY IMPLEMENTATION**

(Ch. 8) Organizational Structure

(Ch. 9) Leadership, Power, and Organizational Culture

**STRATEGIC CONTROL**

(Ch. 10) Strategic Control Process and Performance

FEEDBACK

# 1 Introduction to Strategic Management

Managers face no greater challenge than that of strategic management. Guiding a complex organization through a dynamic, rapidly changing environment requires the best of judgment. Strategic management issues are invariably ambiguous and unstructured, and the way in which management responds to them determines whether an organization will succeed or fail.

Strategic management is challenging because it is far more than simply setting goals and then ordering organization members to attain those goals. An organization's strategic direction depends upon a variety of considerations. Among them are top management's assessment of the external environment's opportunities and threats, and management's analysis of the firm's internal strengths and weaknesses. Senior executives are authorized to determine the mission and goals of the firm in the context of external opportunities or threats and internal strengths or weaknesses. Simultaneously, the top management team must take into account the competing desires and needs of the organization's various stakeholders (or interested parties) because their support is essential to successful strategy implementation. Stakeholders include not only the organization's managers and employees but also the firm's owners (stockholders), suppliers, customers, creditors, and community members.

This text focuses on strategic management. The issues and processes discussed are real ones that are directly relevant to all types of organizations—large or small, international or domestic, diversified or single-product, and profit or nonprofit. The material contained herein should provide keen insight into strategic management and an appreciation of its vital role in enhancing organizational effectiveness.

## WHAT IS STRATEGIC MANAGEMENT?

### ■ Strategic Management Defined

Because the word *strategy* or some variation of it is used throughout the text, its definition should be clear. **Strategy** refers to top management's plans to attain outcomes consistent with the organization's mission and goals. One can look at strategy from three vantage points: (1) strategy formulation (developing the strategy), (2) strategy implementation (putting the strategy into action), and (3) strategic control (modifying either the strategy or its implementation to ensure that the desired outcomes are attained).

**Strategic management** is a broader term that encompasses managing not only the stages already identified but also the earlier stages of determining the mission and goals of an organization within the context of its external and internal environments. Hence, strategic management can be viewed as a series of steps in which top management should accomplish the following tasks:

1. Analyze the opportunities and threats or constraints that exist in the external environment.
2. Analyze the organization's strengths and weaknesses in its internal environment.
3. Establish the organization's mission and develop its goals.
4. Formulate strategies (at the corporate level, the business unit level, and the functional level) that will match the organization's strengths and weaknesses with the environment's opportunities and threats.
5. Implement the strategies.
6. Engage in strategic control activities to ensure that the organization's goals are attained.

Although the various steps in this process are discussed sequentially in this book, in reality they are highly related. Any single stage in the strategic management process must be considered in conjunction with the other stages because a change at any given point will affect other stages in the process.[1] These stages are discussed sequentially throughout the text only to make them more understandable.

In its broadest sense, strategic management consists of managerial decisions and actions that help to ensure that the organization formulates and maintains a beneficial fit with its environment. Thus, strategic managers evaluate their company's evolving strengths and weaknesses. Maintaining a compatible fit between the business and its environment is necessary for competitive viability. Because both the environment and the organization change with the passage of time, this process is an ongoing concern for management.

### ■ Strategic Management Model

To help one envision the strategic management process, a schematic model is presented in Figure 1.1. At the top, the model begins with an analysis of external environmental opportunities and threats. In the next stage, the organization's internal environment (firm resources, mission, and goals) is linked to the external environment by a dual arrow. This arrow means that the mission and goals are set in the context of external environmental opportunities and threats as well as of the internal strengths and weaknesses of the firm (its resources).

**Figure 1.1**                     **Strategic Management Model**

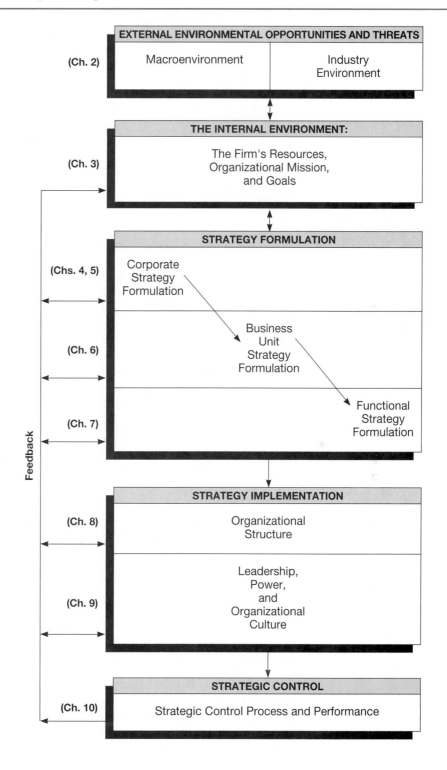

The organization is affected by external environmental forces. But the organization can also have an impact upon its external environment.[2]

> Federal legislation, for instance, can be influenced by lobbying activities; the ecological environment can be improved through corporate social responsibility actions; customer behavior can be swayed through advertising and sales promotion; large, economically powerful retailers can affect the actions of suppliers; and pricing strategy and product improvements certainly influence the activities of competitors.[3]

The mission and goals of the acquisitions drive strategy formulation at the corporate, business unit, and functional levels. However, the present and potential strengths and weaknesses of the organization (firm resources at corporate, business unit, and functional levels) also influence the mission and goals of the firm. This is demonstrated by the two-way arrow between the internal environment and strategy formulation. At the corporate level, the decision makers are the chief executive officer (CEO), other top managers, and the board of directors. Most of the strategic decisions at the business unit level are made by the top manager of the business unit and his or her key executives, and the decision makers at the functional level are the heads of the functional areas (the managers of such departments as production, finance, marketing, and research and development). In some organizations, instead of functional departments, there are core process centers (such as materials handling center rather than purchasing and manufacturing functional departments).

The next arrow depicts the idea that strategy formulation sets strategy implementation in motion. Specifically, strategy is implemented through the organization's structure, its leadership, its distribution of power, and its culture. Then, the final downward arrow indicates that the actual strategic performance of the organization is evaluated. To the extent that performance fails to meet the organization's goals, strategic control is exerted to modify some or all of the stages in the model in order to improve performance. The control stage is demonstrated by the feedback line that connects strategic control to the other parts of the model.

More details on the strategic management model are provided in the next nine chapters. At the beginning of each chapter, the part of the model that is to be featured is highlighted. In chapters 11 and 12, the entire model is revisited through a focus, respectively, on international and not-for-profit organizations.

## ■ Importance of Strategic Management

Current events covered in such business publications as *Fortune*, *Business Week*, and the *Wall Street Journal* involve strategic management concepts. Hence, an understanding of the business world requires familiarity with the strategic management process. As domestic and foreign competition intensifies, and during those periods when government's influence on business operations expands, an understanding of strategic management becomes even more essential.

Employees, supervisors, and middle managers must be familiar with strategic management. An appreciation of their organization's strategy helps them relate their work assignments more closely to the direction of the organization, thereby enhancing their job performance and opportunity for promotion and making their organization more effective.

### ■ Evolving Study of Strategic Management

During the 1950s the Ford Foundation and the Carnegie Corporation funded an analysis of business school curricula and teaching. From this research came the Gordon-Howell report, which concluded that formal business education at universities should be broadened and should conclude with a capstone course that would integrate students' knowledge from such courses as accounting, finance, marketing, management, and economics.[4] Most business schools accepted the conclusions of this report and developed a capstone course that became known as "Business Policy."

The initial thrust of the business policy course was to integrate the functional areas within an enterprise so that it could attain a consistent direction. The direction would be one that capitalized upon its strengths while deemphasizing its weaknesses, relative to the opportunities and threats presented by the organization's external environment.

Over time, the parameters of this capstone course expanded to include more formal analyses of the organization's macroenvironment, industry environment, mission and goals, strategy formulation, strategy implementation, and strategic control. This expanded conception of the field began to be referred to as *strategic management*, as opposed to the more narrow term *business policy*.[5]

In strategic management, it can be argued that the ideal executive of the future will be a leader, not a mere administrator.[6] This ideal executive will be a master servant for the organization's various constituencies. He or she will be a visionary, a team player, and a coach who is global in perspective and capable of capitalizing on diversity.

## INFLUENCE ON STRATEGIC MANAGEMENT

As a field of study, strategic management is eclectic, drawing upon a variety of theoretical frameworks. This section examines some of the diverse roots that have influenced our approach to strategic management.

### ■ Evolution and Revolution Theories

Charles Darwin, the naturalist, proposed a theory of evolutionary change of biological species.[7] In its most basic form, Darwin's theory suggested that environmental change forces each species into incremental, but continuous, mutation or transformation. Through such a change, a living entity can adapt to its environment and survive. A species that cannot conform to its environmental requirements is doomed, eventually becoming extinct.

This perspective of evolutionary change has influenced many management thinkers.[8] As a result, they believe that organizations are influenced by the environment; that environmental change is gradual, requiring concomitant organizational change; and that effective organizations are those that conform most closely to environmental requirements. Firms that cannot or do not adapt to gradual external change eventually find themselves outpaced by their competitors and forced out of business.

A different view of environmental change was proposed by certain natural historians and by the economist Joseph Schumpeter.[9] According to this view, environmental change is not gradual but occurs in revolutionary and abrupt forms. Natural historians in this school of thought believe that species can exist in unaltered form for a lengthy period of time. Then, as a result of sudden, revolutionary environmental change, old species might be destroyed and novel species created. The resultant species then exist for many decades or centuries until the environment again changes abruptly, prompting the creation of still newer species.

Likewise in the field of social science, Schumpeter proposed that an economic environment is characterized by a relatively long period of stability, punctuated by brief periods of discontinuous and revolutionary change. These revolutions are generated by the advent of new entrepreneurial enterprises with novel technologies. The new industries created by these entrepreneurial ventures destroy existing firms and industries by making them obsolete.

Some views of revolutionary change are more moderate, proposing that at least some of the existing firms would be able to adapt to the abrupt environmental change.[10] These adaptive organizations allow the innovative firms to absorb the costs and risks of creating new products and services and then imitate those successful innovations.[11] Even Schumpeter, in 1950, changed from his earlier (1934) position by arguing that some existing firms could survive revolutionary change.[12] Survival, he believed, could come reactively through imitating the revolutionary products or services of newer enterprises or proactively by originating new products or services.

## ▪ Industrial Organization Theory

Industrial organization, a branch of microeconomics, emphasizes the influence of industry environment upon the firm. Implicit in industrial organization theory is the premise of evolutionary change. A firm must adapt to its particular industry's forces to survive and prosper (these forces are discussed in detail in the following chapter), and thus its financial performance is determined by that industry in which it competes. Industries with favorable structures, or forces, offer the opportunity for high returns, whereas the opposite is true for firms operating in industries with less favorable forces.[13]

Industrial organization theory is deterministic because it assumes that an organization's survival depends upon its ability to adapt to industry forces. A firm's strategies, resources, and competencies are reflections of the industry environment.[14] Because the focus of this field is on industry forces, the organizations within an industry are viewed as possessing similar strategies, resources, and competencies. Hence, competing firms in an industry operate in relatively homogeneous ways. If one firm should develop a superior strategy or operating competency, its uniqueness would be short-lived. Less successful firms could imitate the higher-performing firm by purchasing the resources, competencies, or management talent that have made the leading firm so profitable.[15] Recent developments in industrial organization theory have given increased prominence to firm strategy, which not only might affect the strategy of rivals but also might modify the structure of the industry.[16]

The areas that we have briefly examined—theories of evolution and revolution and industrial organization theory—enhance our understanding of how primarily environmental forces can affect organizations. The following theories take a somewhat different perspective by looking not only at the environment but also at the competitive status of the firm. These ideas will complement those theories that we have just discussed.

## ■ Chamberlin's Economic Theories

Economist Edward Chamberlin, representing another branch of microeconomics, presented his ideas within the context of evolutionary environmental change. He proposed that a single firm could clearly distinguish itself from its competitors:

> [A] general class of product is differentiated if any significant basis exists for distinguishing the goods (or services) of one seller from those of another. Where such differentiation exists, even though it might be slight, buyers will be paired with sellers, not by chance . . . but according to their preferences.[17]

Differentiation can exist for quite some time because of such legal protection as trademarks or patents or because a firm's unique strategies, competencies, and resources cannot be easily duplicated by its competitors.

The premise that buyers will be paired with sellers, not by chance but according to their preferences, emphasizes the need for the firm to structure a compatible fit between its competitive status (its strengths and weaknesses relative to those of its competitors) and the opportunities and threats within its environment. This emphasis on the fit between a firm and its environment is reflected in recent contingency theories.

## ■ Contingency Theory

Contingency theory also exists within the context of evolutionary environmental change. The basic premise of contingency theory is that higher financial returns are associated with those firms that most closely develop a beneficial fit with their environment. Unlike the earlier theories on evolutionary and revolutionary change and industrial organization, which were framed at a high level of abstraction, contingency theory can be used to view environment-organization interaction at any level of analysis—industry, strategic group (discussed in chapter 6), or individual firm.[18] And, whereas those earlier theories were deterministic, contingency theorists view organizational performance as the joint outcome of environmental forces and the firm's strategic actions. Firms can become proactive by choosing to operate in environments in which the opportunities and threats match the firms' strengths and weaknesses.[19] Should the industry environment change in a way that is unfavorable to the firm, the firm could perhaps leave that industry and reallocate its resources and competencies to other, more favorable industries.

So both Chamberlin and contingency theorists view organizations as heterogeneous firms that can choose their own operating environments. Organizational performance is determined by the fit between the environment's opportunities and threats and the firm's strengths and weaknesses.

## ■ Resource-Based Theory

Resource-based theory accords even more weight to the firm's proactive choices. Although environmental opportunities and threats are important considerations, a firm's unique resources comprise the key variables that allow it to develop and sustain a competitive strategic advantage. "Resources" include all of a firm's tangible and intangible assets (such as capital, equipment, employees, knowledge, and information).[20] As can be inferred, resource-based theory focuses primarily on individual firms rather than on the competitive environment.

If a firm is to use its resources for sustained competitive advantage, those resources must be valuable, rare, and subject to imperfect imitation, and they must have no strategically relevant substitutes.[21] Valuable resources are those that contribute significantly to the firm's effectiveness and efficiency. Rare resources are possessed by few competitors. Imperfectly imitable resources cannot be fully duplicated by rivals. And resources that have no strategically relevant substitutes enable the firm to operate in a matchless competitive fashion.

Resource-based theory can be framed in the context of either evolutionary or revolutionary change.[22] A firm that possesses unique advantages within an evolutionary environment can continue to compete effectively by making incremental improvements to its resource base. Alternatively, resources that give a firm a competitive advantage within a revolutionary environment do not become irrelevant in newly created settings.

The ideas that we have just examined have important philosophical influences on the field of strategic management. As will become evident, these theories form the basic conceptual underpinnings of the remainder of this textbook.

## STRATEGIC DECISIONS

### ▪ Who Makes the Decisions?

The CEO is the individual ultimately responsible for the organization's strategic management. But except in the smallest companies, the CEO relies on a host of other individuals, including members of the board of directors, vice presidents, and various line and staff managers. Precisely who these individuals are depends upon the type of organization. For instance, businesses with centralized decision-making processes generally have fewer managers involved in strategic decisions than do companies that are decentralized. Businesses that are organized around functions (production, marketing, finance, personnel) generally involve the vice presidents of the functional departments in strategic decisions. Firms with product divisional structures (e.g., the home appliance division, the lawn mower division, the hand tool division) usually include the product division managers along with the CEO. Very large organizations often employ corporate-level strategic-planning staffs to assist the CEO and other top managers in making strategic management decisions.

Inputs to strategic decisions can be generated in a number of ways. For example, an employee in a company's research and development department may attend a conference where a new product or production process idea that seems relevant to the company may be discussed. Upon returning from the conference, the employee may relate the idea to his supervisor, who, in turn, may pass it along to her boss. Eventually, the idea may be discussed with the organization's marketing and production managers. As it moves from one area to another, the idea becomes increasingly clear and specific. Ultimately, it may be presented to top management in a formal report. The CEO will eventually decide to adopt or to reject the idea. But can we actually say that this strategic decision was made solely by the CEO? In a sense, the answer is yes because it is the CEO's responsibility to decide which alternative the company will adopt. But from a broader perspective, the answer is no because most strategic decisions result from the streams of inputs, decisions, and actions of many people. Top management is ultimately responsible for the final decision, but its decision is the culmination of the ideas, creativity, information, and analyses of others.

## ■ Characteristics of Strategic Decisions

In addition to involving more than one area of an organization, strategic decisions usually require obtaining and allocating sizable resources (human, organizational, and physical). Further, strategic decisions involve a lengthy time period, anywhere from several years to more than a decade. Consequently, strategic decisions are future-oriented, with long-term ramifications. In other words, strategic decisions require commitment.[23]

---

### S T R A T E G I C   I N S I G H T

## *Strategic Decisions*

Strategic decisions, by their very nature, are characterized by considerable risk and uncertainty. Dynamic and largely unpredictable environmental changes can quickly transform even the most well-conceived plans into ineffectual strategies. Most strategic decision makers clearly recognize this danger and learn to live with it. Some examples:

- Designing and producing a large commercial aircraft costs as much as $5 billion before any sales revenue is realized. Boeing has taken this enormous risk with its new 777 airliner. The 777 is designed to transport 328 passengers and has a range of 5,000 miles. The design phase began in 1986 when Boeing planners probed the ideas of numerous pilots, passengers, and mechanics about a new type of airliner. As Dean Thornton, head of Boeing's Commercial Airplane Group, puts it: "The 777 causes me to sit bolt upright in bed periodically. It's a . . . gamble. There's a big risk in doing things totally differently."
- American Airlines, the largest airline in the Western Hemisphere, faces—like all major airlines—a number of challenges: steadily rising costs, unstable national economies, uncertain volumes of do-

mestic traffic, and protectionist threats to international traffic. In the face of these threats, CEO Robert Crandall suggests that: "you have to accept the notion at the senior levels of any big company, you rarely know what the outcome of any decision is going to be. . . . Most people at big corporations are rarely certain of what they ought to do. . . . If it were clear what should be done, these jobs wouldn't be nearly so hard."

- Many companies develop "basic beliefs" or "key principles" to guide strategic decision makers through turbulent times. For years, IBM relied on three basic beliefs: the pursuit of excellence, provision of the best customer service, and respect for the individual. However, when outsider Louis V. Gerstner Jr. became IBM CEO, he established new principles for Big Blue, ones emphasizing the marketplace, technology, and entrepreneurial vision. Several top managers noted that modifying the basic philosophy intended to steer decision makers through uncertainty was needed if the company were to see the fruits of its labor. Gerstner put it bluntly: "When it comes to a results-oriented culture, we're not there yet, not by a long shot. . . . There are still a couple of four-minute miles that have to be run."

---

SOURCES: E. A. Robinson, "America's Most Admired Companies," *Fortune*, 3 March 1997, p. F2; W. M. Carley, "GE and Pratt Agree to Build Engine for Boeing Jumbo Jet," *Wall Street Journal Interactive Edition*, 9 May 1996; J. Cole and C. S. Smith, "Boeing Loses Contest to Become China's Partner in Building Plane," *Wall Street Journal Interactive Edition*, 2 May 1996; B. Ziegler, "IBM Is Growing Again; 'Fires Are Out,' Chief Says," *Wall Street Journal Interactive Edition*, 1 May 1996; L. Hayes, "Gerstner Is Struggling as He Tries to Change Ingrained IBM Culture," *Wall Street Journal*, 13 May 1994, pp. A1, A8 (quotation from p. A1); J. Main, "Betting on the 21st Century Jet," *Fortune*, 20 April 1992, pp. 102–117 (quotation from p. 102); D. Moreau, "From Big Bust to Big Blue: IBM and Its Vigorous Rebirth," *Kiplinger's Personal Finance Magazine*, July 1995, pp. 34–35; J. Sager, "We Won't Stop until We Find Our Way Back," 1 May 1995, pp. 116–118 (quotation from p. 116).

## Strategy in the Automobile Industry:
## European and Japanese Inroads

Contrary to popular belief, the world's first workable cars were not manufactured in the United States but in France and Germany. In fact, automakers in these two countries dominated car manufacturing until Henry Ford began producing cars through assembly line techniques. By 1920, Ford alone produced almost half of the cars in the world. The U.S. leadership in car production continued for the next several decades.

By the 1950s, however, U.S. carmakers were becoming complacent. They routinely produced large, heavy cars with powerful engines. Following their policy of "planned obsolescence," U.S. manufacturers gave these cars annual cosmetic changes, designed to make it clear which consumers were driving the latest models. While U.S. car companies were concentrating on styling and sales, European producers were developing an impressive array of technological improvements, including disc brakes, rack-and-pinion steering, front-wheel drive, unitized bodies, and fuel injection systems. By 1970 European automobile exports were 25 times those of the United States.

When the first oil price shock hit the United States in 1974, American carmakers were virtually unprepared. American consumers began to turn to more fuel-efficient European models and, increasingly, to Japan's small economical vehicles. Detroit's carmakers grudgingly began to manufacture smaller cars. But their attitude was best summed up by the comment of Henry Ford II: "Minicars mean miniprofits."

By the late 1970s American consumers were turning to Japanese cars in record numbers. Not only were the cars more economical, but most buyers felt that they were of higher quality than American-made cars. Frightened, U.S. automakers sought government protection. At the behest of the U.S. government, the Japanese "voluntarily" agreed to import restrictions in the early 1980s.

Ironically, however, these restrictions provided Japanese automakers with the impetus to construct plants in the United States to avoid restrictions. Although they originally only assembled cars in America, today Honda, Toyota, and Nissan have established research and development, engineering, and design centers in the United States. In fact, by 1990 Honda was producing cars that were totally planned and built in America—mostly by Americans. More than a million Japanese cars were produced in the United States by 1990, compared with about 1,000 eight years earlier. Honda's Accord even began to vie with Ford's Taurus for the title of best-selling car in the United States.

In the early 1990s the U.S. auto industry had declined to its lowest point, posting record losses. However, cost-cutting programs, quality improvements, attractive new models, and a brighter economy resulted in a resurgence of profits by late 1992. But some analysts believe that overhaul of the Big Three is still only half completed. When the strong yen pushed up Japanese car prices in the mid-1990s, the Big Three responded by raising prices of their own cars instead of gaining market share. As a result, Japanese manufacturers have made significant inroads into the once U.S.-dominated light truck segment.

The Big Three—particularly GM—have begun to experience success marketing their vehicles in Japan. However, the overall success of the Big Three may also be tied to the lucrative European market, where trade barriers are coming down and Ford and GM own over one-third of the market. However, most analysts believe that quality—as perceived by the consumer—will ultimately determine the industry's winners and losers.

*Strategy in the Automobile Industry: European and Japanese Inroads*

SOURCES: E. A. Robinson, "America's Most Admired Companies," *Fortune*, 3 March 1997, p. F2; "Japan Car Imports Rise 24% on Gains in Overseas Plants," *AP-Dow Jones News Service*, 8 May 1996; M. M. Boitano, "Japan Current Account Fall Seen Hurting GDP," *Dow Jones News Service*, 13 May 1996; H. Sender, "On the Chin: No One Rules Endaka More Than Japan's Carmakers," *Far Eastern Economic Review*, 8 June 1995, pp. 40–41; E. Updike, "Japan's Auto Shock," *Business Week*, 29 May 1995, pp. 44–47; R. L. Simison, D. Lavin, and J. Mitchell, "With Auto Prices Up, Big Three Get a Major Opportunity," *Wall Street Journal*, 4 May 1994, pp. A1, A16; J. Mitchell and N. Templin, "Ford's Taurus Passes Honda's Accord As Best-selling Car in a Lackluster Year," *Wall Street Journal*, 7 January 1993; P. Ingrassia and T. Appeal, "Worried by Japanese, Thriving GM Europe Vows to Get Leaner," *Wall Street Journal*, 27 July 1992; K. Kerwin, J. B. Treece, T. Peterson, L. Armstrong, and K. L. Miller, "Detroit's Big Change," *Business Week*, 29 June 1992; D. Cordtz, "The First Hundred Years: How the U. S. Auto Companies Blew Their Stranglehold on the Industry," *Financial World*, 22 August 1989, pp. 54–56.

## STRATEGIC MANAGEMENT: A CONTINUOUS PROCESS

Once a planned strategy is implemented, it often requires modification as environmental or organizational conditions change. These changes are often difficult or even impossible to forecast. In fact, it is a rare situation indeed in which top management is able to develop a long-range strategic plan and implement it over several years without any need for modification.

Hence, an **intended strategy** (what management originally planned) may be realized in its original form, in a modified form, or even in an entirely different form. Occasionally, of course, the strategy that management intends is actually realized, but usually, the intended strategy and the **realized strategy** (what management actually implements) differ.[24] The reason is that unforeseen environmental or organizational events occur that necessitate changes in the intended strategy. The full range of possibilities is illustrated in Table 1.1.

---

**Table 1.1**        **Intended Strategy, Realized Strategy, and Results: Range of Possibilities**

1. What is intended as a strategy is realized with desirable results.
2. What is intended as a strategy is realized, but with less than desirable results.
3. What is intended as a strategy is realized in some modified version because of an unanticipated environmental or internal requirement or change. The results are desirable.
4. What is intended as a strategy is realized in some modified version because of an unanticipated environmental or internal requirement or change. The results are less than desirable.
5. What is intended as a strategy is not realized. Instead, an unanticipated environmental or internal change requires an entirely different strategy. The different strategy is realized with desirable results.
6. What is intended as a strategy is not realized. Instead, an unanticipated environmental or internal change requires an entirely different strategy. The different strategy is realized with less than desirable results.

## STRATEGIC MANAGEMENT AND WEALTH CREATION

The ultimate purpose of strategic management is to create wealth for the owners (shareholders) of the firm through the satisfaction of the needs and expectations of other stakeholders (e.g., customers, suppliers, employees, discussed in chapter 3). One measure of wealth creation is Tobin's Q. Tobin's Q measures the market's assessment of a firm's value normalized by the replacement cost of its assets.[25]

When Tobin's Q is greater (less) than one, it reflects the market's positive (negative) perception that the combined value of a firm's tangibles and intangibles is greater (less) than the replacement cost of its existing assets (i.e., the cost the firm has to incur to acquire the assets that have the same productive capacity as existing assets).[26]

Currently, many leading firms measure wealth creation through what is referred to as market value added (MVA). This measure of wealth creation has been developed by the New York consulting firm Stern Stewart.[27] The concept is intuitively appealing—the market value of the firm (market value of its outstanding common stock, preferred stock, and long-term debt) less the book value of the capital that has been invested in the firm (such factors as the amount invested by stockholders, what has been lent by banks, and retained earnings). If the firm's market value is greater (less) than the book value of the capital invested in it, then the firm has a positive (negative) MVA, which means that wealth is expected to be created (destroyed) by strategic managers. We believe that a better way to measure MVA is to divide the market value of the firm (market value of its outstanding securities) by the book value of what has been invested in it. This would control for scale differences when one firm's performance is evaluated relative to its smaller or larger rivals.

Many leading firms, such as Quaker Oats, Coca-Cola, and AT&T, use some modified version of MVA to measure their performance.[28] While such firms as Wal-Mart, Intel, Microsoft, Coca-Cola, and Rubbermaid have been wealth creators, others, notably Kmart, TWA, and Morrison Knudsen, have been wealth destroyers in recent years.

Alternatively, a simple measure of wealth creation, and one that we recommend, is the market-to-book ratio. This represents the firm's current stock price divided by its book value per share. If investors view the prospects of the firm positively (negatively), then this ratio should be greater (less) than one.

The reason we argue that the purpose of strategic management is to create wealth for shareholders through the satisfaction of the needs of the various stakeholders is that the support of all stakeholders is needed to create wealth. To maximize shareholder wealth at the expense of other stakeholder groups is myopic. The financial gains of stockholders at the expense of the monetary needs of personnel, for instance, will only alienate the employees, eventually harming the company's financial prospects. Although the maximization of wealth for stockholders has been traditionally proposed as a normative goal in the financial literature, select financial scholars more recently have discussed the importance of being stakeholder-driven.[29]

Professor G. Donaldson of Harvard, for instance, has argued that General Mills has been correct to take an extensive time to restructure (rather than to do so abruptly) in order to be stakeholder-driven. The benefits of taking a longer time to restructure include lowering the number of personnel through a freeze on hiring and accelerated voluntary retirement rather than through abruptly firing people and demoralizing the entire organization; changing suppliers and channels of distribution gradually with longer time notices, thereby avoiding damage to the company's reputation; and selling assets gradually rather than under time pressure, which puts the seller in an unfavorable bargaining position. Professor Donaldson concludes that General Mills has also created more wealth for the shareholders by being stakeholder-driven.

Directors of McKinsey and Company, a leading consulting firm, also argue that firms must be stakeholder driven in order to create wealth for their stockholders.[30] Moreover, many corporations have mission statements that explicitly state their obligations to employees, suppliers, customers, and the community as well as to stockholders. Finally, there is empirical evidence that being stakeholder-driven contributes to competitiveness and an increase in stock price valuation.[31] For instance, firms with quality affirmative action programs are supportive of their human resources and, in turn, may gain through their human resources contributing to lower costs and higher differentiation. Such firms tend to have more committed and productive human resources who have lower absenteeism and turnover—and thereby a reduced cost structure. These corporations also tend to have better problem-solving capabilities and are more creative. Consequently, they are better able to enhance their differentiation. Lower costs and higher differentiation positively impact stock prices.

## TEXTBOOK OVERVIEW

This presentation of the strategic management process begins with an analysis of the external environment in which a firm operates. All firms are concerned with two levels of the external environment. The broader of the two is the macroenvironment, which is comprised of political-legal, economic, technological, and social forces that affect all organizations. But each organization also has a more specific external environment(s), known as an industry environment(s), in which it operates. The industry defines the firm's set of customers, suppliers, competitors and so on. The first step in strategic management is analysis of these two levels of the external environment. Chapter 2 provides a framework for understanding and analyzing the macroenvironment and industry environment.

Because strategic management consists of structuring a compatible fit between the organization and its external environment, the reason for the existence of the firm (i.e., its mission) must be defined within its environmental forces as well as in the context of firm resources (strengths and weaknesses). Once the firm's identity is clearly understood, top management must formulate goals to give the organization direction. Establishing the organization's mission and goals through S. W. O. T. (strengths, weaknesses, opportunities, threats) analysis is the subject of chapter 3, which focuses on the internal environment of the firm.

After its mission and goals are established, the organization's strategy must be addressed. Strategy formulation occurs at three organizational levels: corporate, business unit, and functional. Chapters 4 and 5 focus on corporate-level strategy formulation. At this level, the essential question is, In what businesses or industries should we be operating? Chapter 4 presents corporate restructuring and the strategic alternatives that are available to top management. Chapter 5 introduces several analytical frameworks that may be used by corporations that operate multiple businesses.

At the business unit level, the question that must be answered is, How should we compete in each of the businesses or industries in which we have chosen to operate? (The difference between corporate-level and business unit strategies is illustrated via two questions in Figure 1.2.) Chapter 6 identifies the alternative generic business unit strategies that are available to management and explains under what circumstances each is appropriate.

Chapter 7 analyzes the formulation of functional strategies (strategies in production, marketing, research and development, finance, etc.). It emphasizes the interdependence of an organization's functional strategies and their relationship to the company's business unit strategies.

After the examination of strategy formulation at these three levels, the discussion turns to how these strategies can be implemented. The organizational structure adopted by a company plays a key role in strategy implementation. Chapter 8 identifies the structures available to management and discusses the circumstances under which each is likely to lead to effective implementation of the organization's strategies.

Other essential aspects of strategy implementation are presented in chapter 9. How the CEO and the top management team secure the cooperation of the organization's members by exercising leadership and informal power is discussed in some detail. Then, the key role played by organizational culture in implementing strategy is analyzed.

As strategies are implemented, the process of strategic control begins. Strategic control consists of determining the extent to which the organiza-

---

**Figure 1.2**      **Corporate- and Business Unit-Level Strategic Questions**

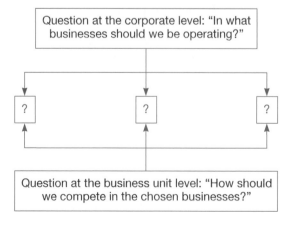

tion's goals are being attained. This process often requires management to modify its strategies or implementation in some fashion so that the company's ability to reach its goals will be improved. Strategic control is the subject of chapter 10.

Strategic management is discussed in the context of the world marketplace in chapter 11. Here, the contents of chapters 2 through 10 are revisited through a distinctly international perspective.

The process of strategic management is applied to not-for-profit organizations in chapter 12. Although the basic principles of strategic management apply equally to profit and not-for-profit organizations, there are some differences that require examination. A diagrammatic overview of chapters 2 through 12 is shown in Figure 1.3.

**Figure 1.3**              **Overview of the Book**

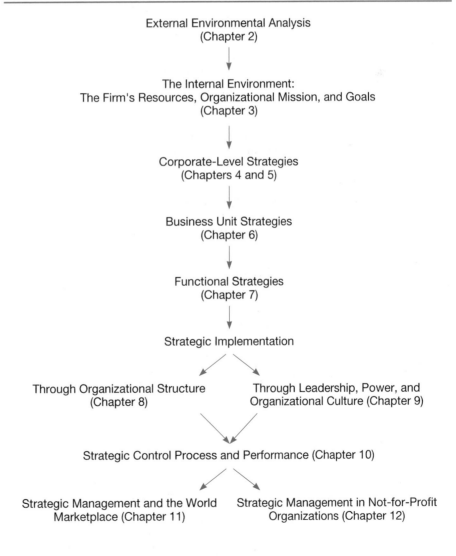

External Environmental Analysis
(Chapter 2)

The Internal Environment:
The Firm's Resources, Organizational Mission, and Goals
(Chapter 3)

Corporate-Level Strategies
(Chapters 4 and 5)

Business Unit Strategies
(Chapter 6)

Functional Strategies
(Chapter 7)

Strategic Implementation

Through Organizational Structure
(Chapter 8)

Through Leadership, Power, and
Organizational Culture (Chapter 9)

Strategic Control Process and Performance (Chapter 10)

Strategic Management and the World
Marketplace (Chapter 11)

Strategic Management in Not-for-Profit
Organizations (Chapter 12)

Finally, the second section of the text begins by presenting an overview of strategic management case analysis. The methodology discussed will help in analyzing the cases contained in the latter part of the text.

Cases, which present the strategies and operations of real companies, provide the opportunity to apply the knowledge gleaned from chapters 1 through 12 to analyses of real situations. Case analysis encourages active, involved learning rather than passive recall of the book's contents.

Some of the cases are narrow, primarily involving single issues. These cases provide opportunities to apply knowledge to a specific issue, problem, or situation. Most, however, are broad, encompassing many different aspects of an organization and its environment. The advantages of such cases are several. First, they encourage the application and integration of what has been learned in this text with knowledge gained from other courses and even from one's work experience. Second, they provide a vehicle for analyzing a total organization versus one narrow aspect or functional area of that company. Third, they promote the awareness that varied aspects of the organization and its environment, and their interrelationships, must be examined to formulate and implement strategies effectively.

## SUMMARY

Strategic management refers to the process that begins with determining the mission and goals of an organization within the context of its external environment and its internal strengths and weaknesses. Appropriate strategies are then formulated and implemented. Finally, strategic control is exerted to ensure that the organization's strategies are successful in attaining its goals.

Strategic management, as a field of study, has been influenced by such diverse disciplines as biology (in theories of evolution and revolution) and economics (particularly the views of Schumpeter and Chamberlin and the perspective of industrial organization theory). More recently, the views of contingency theory (that high financial returns are associated with those firms that most closely develop a beneficial fit with their environment) and resource-based theory (that a firm's unique resources are the key variables that allow it to develop and sustain a competitive strategic advantage) have provided useful frameworks for analyzing strategic management.

Determining organizational strategy is the direct responsibility of the CEO, but he or she relies on a host of other individuals, including the board of directors, vice presidents, and various line and staff managers. In its final form, a strategic decision is molded from the streams of inputs, decisions, and actions of many people.

Strategic management is a continuous process. Once a strategy is implemented, it often requires modification as environmental or organizational conditions change. Because these changes are often difficult or even impossible to predict, a strategy may, over time, be modified so that it bears only a slight resemblance to the organization's intended strategy. This realized strategy is the result of unforeseen external or internal events that require changes in the organization's intended strategy. Thus, strategies need to be examined continuously in the light of changing situations. Finally, the reason for strategic management is to create wealth for the owners (shareholders) through the satisfaction of the needs and expectations of other stakeholders.

## TAKE IT TO THE NET

We invite you to visit the Wright page on the Prentice Hall Web site at:

**http://www.prenhall.com/wright**

for this chapter's World Wide Web exercise.

## KEY CONCEPTS

**Intended strategy**   The original strategy that management plans and intends to implement.

**Realized strategy**   The actual and eventual strategy that management implements. The realized strategy often differs from the intended strategy because unforeseen environmental or organizational events occur that necessitate modifications in the intended strategy.

**Strategic management**   The continuous process of determining the mission and goals of an organization within the context of its external environment and its internal strengths and weaknesses, formulating appropriate strategies, implementing those strategies, and exerting strategic control to ensure that the organization's strategies are successful in attaining its goals.

**Strategy**   Top management's plans to attain outcomes consistent with the organization's mission and goals.

## DISCUSSION QUESTIONS

1. In what sense does the CEO alone make the company's strategic decisions? In what sense does the CEO *not* make the company's strategic decisions alone?

2. Explain the difference between an intended strategy and a realized strategy. Relate an example of a company whose ultimate realized strategy differed from its original intended strategy.

3. How can an understanding of strategic management be beneficial to your career?

## NOTES

1. A. E. Singer, "Strategy as Moral Philosophy," *Strategic Management Journal* 15 (1994): 191–213.

2. See J. B. Barney, "Types of Competition and the Theory of Strategy: Toward an Integrative Framework," *Academy of Management Review* 11 (1986): 791–800; J. Child, "Organizational Structure, Environment, and Performance: The Role of Strategic Choice," *Sociology* 6 (1972): 1–22; J. A. Schumpeter, *The Theory of Economic Development* (New York: Oxford University Press, 1934).

3. J. G. Longenecker and C. D. Pringle, "The Illusion of Contingency Theory as a General Theory," *Academy of Management Review* 3 (1978): 682.

4. R. A. Gordon and J. E. Howell, *Higher Education for Business* (New York: Columbia University Press, 1959).

5. M. Leontiades, "The Confusing Words of Business Policy," *Academy of Management Review* 7 (1982): 46.

6. B. O'Reilly, "Reengineering the MBA," *Fortune*, 24 January 1994, pp. 37–47.

7. S. J. Gould, *Ever Since Darwin* (New York: Norton, 1977).

8. D. A. Gioia and E. Pitre, "Multiparadigm Perspectives on Theory Building," *Academy of Management Review* 15 (1990): 584–602.

9. N. Eldredge and S. J. Gould, "Punctuated Equilibria: An Alternative to Phyletic Gradualism," in T. J. M. Schopf, ed., *Models in Paleobiology* (San Francisco: Freeman, Cooper, 1972), pp. 82–115; Schumpeter, *The Theory of Economic Development*.

10. M. L. Tushman, W. H. Newman, and E. Romanelli, "Convergence and Upheaval: Managing the Unsteady Pace of Organizational Evolution," *California Management Review* 29, no. 1 (1986): 29–44; J. D. Utterback and W. J. Abernathy, "A Dynamic Model of Product and Process Innovation," *Omega* 3 (1975): 639–656.

11. Barney, "Types of Competition and the Theory of Strategy"; R. R. Nelson and S. G. Winter, *An Evolutionary Theory of Economic Change* (Cambridge, Mass.: Harvard University Press, 1982); O. Nodoushani, "The End of the Entrepreneurial Age," *Human Systems Management* 10 (1991): 19–31.

12. J. A. Schumpeter, *Capitalism, Socialism, and Democracy* (New York: Harper & Row, 1950).

13. M. E. Porter, "The Contributions of Industrial Organization to Strategic Management," *Academy of Management Review* 6 (1981): 609–620.

14. J. S. Bain, *Industrial Organization* (New York: Wiley, 1968); F. M. Scherer and D. Ross, *Industrial Market Structure and Economic Performance* (Boston: Houghton-Mifflin, 1990).

15. A. Lado, N. Boyd, and P. Wright, "A Competency-Based Model of Sustainable Competitive Advantage: Toward a Conceptual Integration," *Journal of Management* 18 (1992): 77–91; J. B. Barney, "Strategic Factor Markets: Expectations, Luck, and Business Strategy," *Management Science* 42 (1986): 1231–1241; J. B. Barney, "Firm Resources and Sustained Competitive Advantage," *Journal of Management* 17 (1991): 99–120.

16. A. Seth and H. Thomas, "Theories of the Firm: Implications for Strategy Research," *Journal of Management Studies* 31 (1994): 165–191.

17. E. H. Chamberlin, *The Theory of Monopolistic Competition* (Cambridge, Mass.: Harvard University Press, 1956), p. 231.

18. R. S. Dooley, D. M. Fowler, and A. Miller, "The Benefits of Strategic Homogeneity and Strategic Heterogeneity: Theoretical and Empirical Evidence Resolving Past Differences," *Strategic Management Journal* 17 (1996): 293–305.

19. L. G. Hrebiniak and W. F. Joyce, "Organizational Adaptation: Strategic Choice and Environmental Determinism," *Administrative Science Quarterly* 21 (1985): 41–65.

20. J. B. Barney, "Looking Inside for Competitive Advantage," *Academy of Management Executive* 19 (1995): 49–61.

21. Ibid.

22. R. Rumelt, "Towards a Strategic Theory of the Firm," in R. Lamb, ed., *Competitive Strategic Management* (Englewood Cliffs, N. J.: Prentice Hall, 1984), pp. 556–570; R. Rumelt and R. Wensley, "In Search of the Market Share Effect," in K. Chung, ed., *Academy of Management Proceedings* (1981): 2–6; S. Winter, "Schumpeterian Competition in Alternative Technological Regimes," *Journal of Economic Behavior and Organization* 5 (1984): 287–320.

23. P. Ghemawat, *Commitment: The Dynamic of Strategy* (New York: The Free Press, 1991).

24. H. Mintzberg, "Opening Up the Definition of Strategy," in J. B. Quinn, H. Mintzberg, and R. M. James, eds., *The Strategy Process* (Englewood Cliffs, N. J.: Prentice Hall, 1988), pp. 14–15.

25. See B. H. Hall, *The Manufacturing Sector Master File Documentation: 1959 1967*, Mimeo (University of California at Berkeley, 1990) for computational details.

26. B. C. Reimann, *Managing for Value* (Cambridge, Mass.: Basil Blackwell, 1989).

27. L. Walbert, "America's Best Wealth Creators," *Fortune*, 27 December 1993, pp. 64, 76.

28. B. Cornell and A. Shapiro, "Corporate Stakeholders and Corporate Finance," *Financial Management* 16 (1987): 5–14; G. Donaldson, "Voluntary Restructuring: The Case of General Mills," *Journal of Financial Economics* 27 (1990): 117–141.

29. Donaldson (1990).

30. K. P. Coyne and R. W. Ferguson, "Real Wealth," *The McKinsey Quarterly* 4 (1991): 69–80.

31. P. Wright, S. P. Ferris, J. S. Hiller, and M. Kroll, "Competitiveness through the Management of Diversity: The Effect on Stock Price Valuation," *Academy of Management Journal* 38 (1995): 272–287.

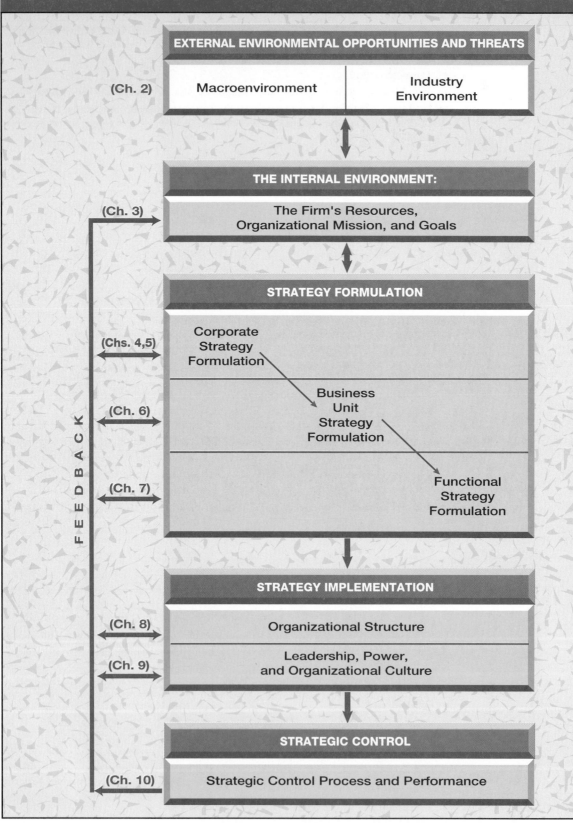

# STRATEGIC MANAGEMENT MODEL

**EXTERNAL ENVIRONMENTAL OPPORTUNITIES AND THREATS**

(Ch. 2)

| Macroenvironment | Industry Environment |
|---|---|

**THE INTERNAL ENVIRONMENT:**

(Ch. 3)

The Firm's Resources, Organizational Mission, and Goals

**STRATEGY FORMULATION**

(Chs. 4,5)  Corporate Strategy Formulation

(Ch. 6)  Business Unit Strategy Formulation

(Ch. 7)  Functional Strategy Formulation

**STRATEGY IMPLEMENTATION**

(Ch. 8)  Organizational Structure

(Ch. 9)  Leadership, Power, and Organizational Culture

**STRATEGIC CONTROL**

(Ch. 10)  Strategic Control Process and Performance

FEEDBACK

# 2 External Environmental Opportunities and Threats

S trategic management involves three levels of analysis: the organization's macroenvironment, the industry in which the organization operates, and the organization itself. These levels are portrayed in Figure 2.1 on page 24. This chapter focuses upon the first two levels—the macroenvironment and industry. Then, chapter 3 begins our analysis of the firm.

Every organization exists within a complex network of environmental forces. All firms are affected by political-legal, economic, technological, and social systems and trends. Together, these elements comprise the **macroenvironment** of business firms. Because these forces are so dynamic, their constant change presents myriad opportunities and threats or constraints to strategic managers.

Each business also operates within a more specific environment termed an **industry:** a group of companies that produce competing products or services. The structure of an industry influences the intensity of competition among the firms in the industry by placing certain restrictions upon their operations and by providing various opportunities for well-managed firms to seize the advantage over their competitors. As we shall see in this chapter, successful management depends upon forging a link between business and its external environment through the activities of environmental analysis.

## ANALYSIS OF THE MACROENVIRONMENT

All organizations are affected by four macroenvironmental forces: political-legal, economic, technological, and social. Although very large organizations (or several firms in association with one another) will occasionally attempt to

**Figure 2.1**              **Three Levels of Analysis**

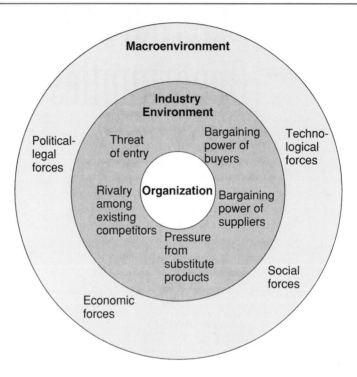

influence legislation or, through research and development, will pioneer technological or social changes, these macroenvironmental forces are generally not under the direct control of business organizations. Hence, the purpose of strategic management is to enable the firm to operate effectively within environmental threats or constraints and to capitalize on the opportunities provided by the environment. To accomplish this purpose, strategic managers must identify and analyze these national and global macroenvironmental forces, which are described in the following sections.

## ■ Political-Legal Forces

Political-legal forces include the outcomes of elections, legislation, and court judgments, as well as the decisions rendered by various commissions and agencies at every level of government. As an example of the impact of these forces, consider the automobile industry. The U.S. government's insistence on legislating gradually increasing fuel economy standards for cars has affected the size and design of cars, their engine size, and their horsepower. Although American automakers have viewed these regulations as a constraint upon the types of models that they can make and sell, Japanese car manufacturers perceived it as an opportunity to make inroads into the prosperous American market.

On the other hand, the U.S. government's imposition of import fees on automobiles and its success in convincing Japanese manufacturers to restrict "voluntarily" their exports to the United States have provided opportunities for American firms to increase their car sales. Unfortunately, the U.S. car producers have not taken advantage of all of these opportunities to increase their market share. But some Japanese carmakers successfully adapted to these constraints by building manufacturing plants in the United States.

As another example, consider the U.S. defense industry. Both the Bush and Clinton administrations and the Congress recommended huge cuts in defense spending through 1998. These reductions resulted in massive layoffs and restructurings among some of the nation's largest corporations. Affected, to some extent, were such prominent firms as General Dynamics, Northrup, LTV, Martin Marietta, McDonnell Douglas, and Lockheed. But an even greater impact was felt by the thousands of small suppliers and subcontractors whose businesses depended almost entirely on defense contracts. We can see, then, that the U.S. political-legal system can have a major impact on business

On a more global scale, the 1985 decision by the Commission of the European Community to form a single European market for the twelve-nation European community presents both opportunities and threats to U.S.-based firms. One of the major opportunities is the attractive nature of this large, affluent market, which some U.S. firms may have avoided up until now because they considered the market too fragmented and its trade regulations overly complicated. However, a possible threat is that a consolidated market may allow European firms to build a solid base upon which they can develop into much stronger world competitors.

A nation's political-legal system greatly influences its business operations and the standard of living of its citizens. Historically, higher standards of living have been associated with nations whose economic systems are pro-business. In the United States, capitalism has contributed significantly over the past two centuries to America's unparalleled economic growth. But even free enterprise has its weaknesses. By the beginning of the twentieth century, such undesirable social consequences as unsafe working conditions, child labor, low wages, monopolistic competition, deceptive advertising, and unsafe products made it clear that some degree of governmental regulation was necessary. Examples of some of the more significant regulations are shown in Table 2.1 on page 26.

Not all of the legislative and judicial movement in American society, however, has been in the direction of greater regulation of business. In the late 1970s and the 1980s, a major shift in national policy occurred, which reversed this trend in several industries. This "deregulation" movement eliminated a number of legal constraints in such industries as airlines, trucking, and banking.

However, while some industries were being deregulated, overall regulation was increasing. The federal government employs approximately 125,000 regulators to oversee this process. The U.S. Chamber of Commerce predicted a 25 percent increase in business regulatory costs during the 1990s, bringing the total cost of regulation to $600 billion annually.[1]

Deregulation presented both new opportunities and new threats to organizations in the affected industries. Airline deregulation, for instance, offered opportunities to entrepreneurs to start companies such as Southwest Airlines. For some established firms, though, like Eastern and Pan Am, the reduction of regulation posed a threat by creating intense cost and price competition, resulting in their eventual demise. In banking, deregulation presented vast opportunities for expansion in services and geographic scope. Banks began offering brokerage services, for example, and mergers across state lines became common. On the other hand, deregulation intensified competition for banks because non-banking firms, such as money market funds and brokerage houses, began competing directly with banks for consumers' savings.

**Table 2.1**    **Examples of Government Regulation of Business**

| Legislation | Purpose |
|---|---|
| Sherman Antitrust Act (1890) | Prohibits monopoly or conspiracy in restraint of trade |
| Pure Food and Drug Act (1906) | Outlaws production of unsanitary foods and drugs |
| Clayton Act (1914) | Forbids tying contracts, which tie the sale of some products to the sale of others |
| Federal Trade Commission Act (1914) | Stops unfair methods of competition, such as deceptive advertising, selling practices, and pricing |
| Fair Labor Standards Act (1938) | Sets minimum-wage rates, regulations for overtime pay, and child labor laws |
| Wheeler-Lea Amendment (1938) | Outlaws deceptive packaging and advertising |
| Antimerger Act (1950) | Makes the buying of competitors illegal when it lessens competition |
| Equal Pay (1963) | Prohibits discrimination in wages on the basis of sex when males and females are performing jobs requiring equal skill, effort, and responsibility under similar working conditions |
| Occupational Safety and Health Act (1970) | Requires employers to provide a working environment free from hazards to health |
| Consumer Product Safety Act (1972) | Sets standards on selected products, requires warning labels, and orders product recalls |
| Equal Employment Opportunity Act (1972) | Forbids discrimination in all areas of employer-employee relations |
| Magnuson-Moss Act (1975) | Requires accuracy in product warranties |
| Americans with Disabilities Act (1992) | Protects the physically and mentally disabled from job discrimination |
| Family and Medical Leave Act (1993) | Offers workers up to twelve weeks of unpaid leave after childbirth or adoption, or to care for a seriously ill child, spouse, or parent |

## ■ Economic Forces

Like political-legal systems, economic forces also have a significant impact on business operations. As prime examples, we will consider the impact of growth or decline in gross domestic product and increases or decreases in interest rates, inflation, and the value of the dollar. These changes present both opportunities and threats to strategic managers.

### Gross Domestic Product

Gross domestic product (GDP) refers to the value of a nation's annual total production of goods and services and serves as a major indicator of economic growth. Moderate, consistent growth in GDP generally produces a healthy economy in which businesses find increasing demand for their outputs because of rising consumer expenditures. Opportunities abound for both established and new businesses during such prosperous times.

On the other hand, a decline in GDP normally reflects reduced consumer expenditures and lower demand for business outputs. When GDP declines for two consecutive quarters, the national economy is considered to be in a recession. During such times, competitive pressures on businesses increase dramatically; profitability suffers and business failure rates increase. However, even recessions provide opportunities for some firms. Movie theaters are normally strong performers during hard economic times, providing escape from financial worries for their patrons. Likewise, trade school enrollments often increase as unskilled laborers attempt to learn trades to improve their job marketability.

## Interest Rates

Short- and long-term interest rates significantly affect the demand for products and services. Low short-term interest rates, for instance, are particularly beneficial for retailers such as Sears and Kmart because such rates encourage consumer spending. For other businesses, such as construction companies and automobile manufacturers, low longer-term rates are especially beneficial because they result in increased spending by consumers for durable goods.

Interest rate levels greatly affect strategic decisions. High rates, for instance, normally dampen business plans to raise funds to expand or to replace aging facilities. Lower rates, by contrast, are more conducive to capital expenditures and to mergers and acquisitions. But some businesses may buck these trends. For example, firms that own apartment buildings usually benefit when long-term interest rates rise, because potential homebuyers find that they cannot qualify for mortgage loans and are forced to rent until rates decline significantly.

## Inflation Rates

High inflation rates generally result in constraints on business organizations. High rates boost various costs of doing business, such as the purchase of raw materials and parts and the wages and salaries of employees. Consistent increases in inflation rates will constrict the expansion plans of businesses and cause the government to take action that slows the growth of the economy. The combination of government and business restraints can create an economic recession.

Of course, inflation can present opportunities for some firms. For instance, oil companies may benefit during inflationary times if the prices of oil and gas rise faster than the costs of exploration, refining, and transporting. Likewise, companies that mine or sell precious metals benefit because such metals serve as inflation hedges for consumers.

## Value of the Dollar

As we have seen, the value of the dollar relative to other major world currencies can be affected by international agreements and the coordinated economic policies of governments. Currency exchange rates, however, can also be affected by international economic conditions. When economic conditions boost the value of the dollar, U.S. firms find themselves at a competitive disadvantage internationally. Foreign customers are less inclined to buy American-made goods because they are too expensive relative to goods produced in their own home markets. Likewise, U.S. consumers find that their strong dollars can be stretched by buying foreign-made products, which are less expensive than goods produced domestically.

For example, in the early 1990s, Caterpillar was in the midst of a major cost-cutting program designed to maintain its position as the world leader in heavy machinery. Yet even as it reduced its cost structure, its efforts were being undermined by the rise in the value of the dollar vis-à-vis the Japanese yen. The resultant difference in exchange rates gave Caterpillar's chief Japanese competitor, Komatsu, such a substantial price advantage in the U.S. market that it completely negated Caterpillar's extensive cost-cutting program. Komatsu even merged its U.S.-based manufacturing and engineering facilities with Dresser Industries, headquartered in Dallas, as a hedge against future currency fluctuations.[2] Subsequently, when the dollar weakened relative to the Japanese yen, Caterpillar benefited.

The dollar's value affects the strategic decisions of managers. When it is strong, American manufacturers tend to locate more of their plants abroad, make purchases from foreign sources, and enter into strategic alliances with firms in other countries. However, when the dollar is relatively weak, less financial incentive exists for American companies to purchase from foreign sources or to build new plants overseas.

## ■ Technological Forces

Technological forces include scientific improvements and innovations that provide opportunities or threats for businesses. The rate of technological change varies considerably from one industry to another. In electronics, for example, change is rapid and constant, but in furniture manufacturing, change is slower and more gradual.

Changes in technology can affect a firm's operations as well as its products and services. Recent technological advances in computers, robotics, lasers, satellite networks, fiber optics, and other related areas have provided significant opportunities for operational improvements. Manufacturers, banks, and retailers, for example, have used advances in computer technology to perform their traditional tasks at lower costs and higher levels of customer satisfaction.

From another perspective, however, technological change can decimate existing businesses and even entire industries, since it shifts demand from one product to another. Examples of such change include the shifts from vacuum tubes to transistors, from steam locomotives to diesel and electric engines, from fountain pens to ballpoints, from propeller airplanes to jets, and from typewriters to computer-based word processors. Interestingly enough, these new technologies are often invented outside of the traditional industries that they eventually affect.

## ■ Social Forces

Social forces include traditions, values, societal trends, and a society's expectations of business. Traditions, for instance, define societal practices that have lasted for decades or even centuries. For example, the celebration of Christmas in many countries in the Western Hemisphere provides significant financial opportunities for card companies, toy retailers, turkey processors, tree growers, mail-order catalog firms, and other related businesses.

Values refer to concepts that a society holds in high esteem. In the United States, for example, major values include individual freedom and equality of opportunity. In a business sense, these values translate into an emphasis on entrepreneurship and the belief that one's success is limited only by one's ambition, energy, and ability. These values, over the past century, have attracted millions of immigrants to the United States in search of economic and political freedom. We can expect, therefore, to find a more vibrant and dynamic business environment in the United States than in countries that place less value on the freedom of the individual and equality of opportunity.

Societal trends present various opportunities and threats or constraints to businesses. For example, the health-and-fitness trend that began several years ago has led to financial success for such companies as Nike (sport shoes) and Nautilus (exercise equipment) and the makers of diet soft drinks, light beer, and bottled water. This trend, however, has financially harmed businesses in other industries such as cattle raising, meat and dairy processing, tobacco, and liquor.

For example, over the past ten years, the consumption of hard liquor by the 18-to-34-year-old segment of the U.S. population fell significantly. This trend is of considerable concern to distillers because that age group comprises 40 percent of the U.S. population. The reasons include not only the health-and-fitness trend but also a growing nationwide revulsion toward drunk driving, the increased legal liability of hosts who serve alcohol to their guests, and a general increase in "sin taxes" (taxes on alcohol and tobacco products) at the federal and state levels. As a result, many alcohol makers are diversifying into nonalcoholic drinks.[3]

Societal trends also include demographic changes. Fast-food chains, for instance, are currently wrestling with a pressing problem. Teenagers, who comprise 85 percent of the fast-food work force, declined in number by 5 million in total between 1981 and 1995, while the number of preteen children (primary customers for fast food) increased by 4 million. The result is more customers for fast-food restaurants with fewer people to serve them. These pressures are resulting in increased hiring of the elderly, attempts to reduce turnover among teenage employees, and improvements in productivity.[4]

Demographic trends can dramatically affect business opportunities. The baby boom, which lasted from 1945 through the mid-1960s, initially provided opportunities for such businesses as clothing and baby apparel manufacturers, private schools, record companies, candy and snack makers, and so on. Later, as the baby boomers entered the job market, businesses were blessed with a tremendous pool of job applicants. As they continue to age, the baby boomers will shop at home more and will spend vast sums of money for health care needs, leisure activities, and vacation alternatives.[5] Further, this population segment may not be as brand loyal as older Americans.[6]

Finally, a society's expectations of business present other opportunities and constraints. These expectations emanate from diverse groups referred to as **stakeholders.** These groups affect and, in turn, are affected by the activities of companies. Stakeholders include a firm's owners (stockholders), members of the board of directors, managers and operating employees, suppliers, customers, creditors, distributors, and other interest groups.

At the broadest level, stakeholders include the general public. Increasingly, in recent decades, the general public has expected socially responsible behavior from business firms. Although social responsibility will be discussed in chapter 3, consider just one element of social responsibility—pollution. The public's concern about pollution has resulted in various forms of legislation that have constrained the operations of firms in such industries as automobiles, energy, and mining. On the other hand, this legislation has provided an opportunity for firms such as Waste Management to sell its services in reducing pollution.

In a more limited sense, stakeholder groups may hold conflicting expectations of business performance. For example, stockholders and unionized employees may have financial goals that clash. Chapter 3 will elaborate further on this topic.

### ■ Environmental Scanning

The preceding sections were able to examine only a few of the important macroenvironmental forces that affect organizations. Examples of other significant forces are identified in Table 2.2.

How do managers recognize the various opportunities or threats that arise from changes in the political-legal, economic, technological, and social arenas?

S T R A T E G I C     I N S I G H T

## *Capitalizing on Technological and Social Forces at Knight-Ridder*

Environmental analysis helps a company take advantage of the changing technological and social forces. One such example is Miami-based Knight-Ridder, a firm that has achieved annual sales of $2.3 billion in the information industry.

Founded in 1903, Knight-Ridder was originally a newspaper company. Its first major newspapers were the *Miami Herald* and the *Akron Beacon Journal*. Since that time, it has purchased numerous newspapers and today owns such well-known publications as the *Detroit Free Press*, the *Philadelphia Inquirer*, and the *San Jose Mercury News*. Its newspaper business, which includes a news syndication service, a newsprint mill, and newspaper printing plants in twenty-nine cities, provides 86 percent of its sales revenue.

Increasingly, however, Knight-Ridder is taking advantage of technological innovations to expand its information network. The company owns an on-line newswire service for financial markets, a cable/pay television channel, and an electronic information retrieval service. Its various information services reach more than 100 million people in 129 countries.

The company has also been cognizant of changing social forces. According to its CEO, James Batten, the firm successfully capitalized upon an opportunity provided by demographic changes in Miami several years ago. Observing that the Miami area was becoming home to more than 250,000 residents of Cuban origin, management believed that the time was right to introduce a Spanish-language daily newspaper. The paper, *El Nuevo Herald*, became an instant success and is now the largest of its kind in the United States.

Knight-Ridder may go even further in taking advantage of the opportunities presented by demographics. Management is currently studying the feasibility of tailoring newspapers to specific groups of readers, such as the elderly, households with children, and so on.

**Table 2.2**      **Examples of Additional Macroenvironmental Forces**

| Political-Legal Forces | Social Forces | Economic Forces | Technological Forces |
|---|---|---|---|
| Tax laws | Attitudes toward product innovations, lifestyles, careers, and consumer activism | Money supply | Expenditures on research and development (government and industry) |
| International trade regulations | Concern with quality of life | Monetary policy | Focus of research and development expenditures |
| Consumer lending regulations | Life expectancies | Unemployment rate | Rate of new-product introductions |
| Environmental protection laws | Expectations from the workplace | Energy costs | Automation |
| Enforcement of antitrust regulations | Shifts in the presence of women in the work force | Disposable personal income | Robotics |
| Laws on hiring, firing, promotion, and pay | Birth rates | Stage of economic cycle | |
| Wage/price controls | Population shifts | | |

They engage in **environmental scanning**—the gathering and analysis of information about relevant environmental trends.

Responses to a survey of Fortune 500 firms that were asked to identify the major payoffs of their environmental-scanning activities included an increased general awareness of environmental changes, better strategic planning and decision making, greater effectiveness in governmental matters, and sound diversification and resource allocation decisions. However, the respondents also indicated that the results of their environmental analysis were often too general or uncertain for specific interpretation.[7]

There is also some evidence that top managers may use "selective perception" in scanning the environment; that is, their scanning activities may be influenced by their organization's strategy. One study concluded that the heads of financial institutions that use a "low-cost" strategy (one that focuses upon being the low-cost provider of products or services) emphasize monitoring activities of competitors and regulators. By contrast, scanning activities in financial institutions that use a "differentiation" strategy (one that emphasizes superior products or services) are likely to focus upon opportunities for growth and ways of satisfying customer needs.[8]

Although macroenvironmental forces influence the operations of all firms in a general fashion, a more specific set of forces within an industry directly and powerfully affects the strategic-planning activities of the firms within that industry. Figure 2.2 on page 32 presents a diagrammatic representation of the impact of macroenvironmental and industry forces. These industry forces are discussed in the following section.

**Figure 2 .2**                    **Macroenvironmental and Industry Forces That Present Opportunities and Threats to Firms**

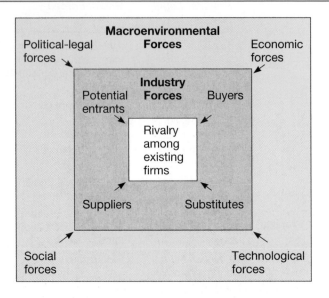

# ANALYSIS OF THE INDUSTRY

Professor Michael E. Porter of Harvard University is a leading authority on industry analysis; the following overview of industry forces is based on his work.[9] Porter contends that an industry's profit potential (the long-run return on invested capital) depends on five basic competitive forces within the industry:

1. The threat of new competitors entering the industry
2. The intensity of rivalry among existing competitors
3. The threat of substitute products or services
4. The bargaining power of buyers
5. The bargaining power of suppliers

These forces can be quite intense in industries such as tires or steel, where returns are generally low, but may be relatively mild in such industries as cosmetics and toiletries, where returns are often high.

The key to competing effectively is for the company to find a position in the industry from which it can influence these five forces to its advantage or can effectively defend itself against them. Such a strategy requires an understanding of these competitive forces, which are described in the following sections.

## ■ Threat of Entry

As new competitors enter an industry, its productive capacity expands.[10] Unless the market is growing rapidly, a new entry intensifies the fight for market share, thereby bidding prices down and lowering industry profitability. The likelihood that new firms will enter an industry rests on two factors: barriers to entry and the expected retaliation from existing competitors. Each factor is discussed in the sections that follow.

### Barriers to Entry

High barriers and/or expectations of sharp retaliation reduce the threat of entry. There are seven major **barriers to entry,** that is, obstacles to entering an industry. Each barrier is described next.

**Economies of Scale.** **Economies of scale** refer to the decline in unit costs of a product or service (or an operation, or a function that goes into producing a product or service) that occurs as the absolute volume of production per period of time increases. Substantial economies of scale deter new entrants by forcing

---

### S T R A T E G I C  I N S I G H T

## *Enormous Barriers to Entry in the Airline Industry*

One of the major purposes of deregulating the airline industry in 1978 was to encourage new start-up ventures, thereby increasing the amount of competition in the industry. For a while, deregulation worked; new companies such as Southwest Airlines, Midway Airlines, and People Express helped to lower ticket prices significantly.

But over time, the major airlines have succeeded in erecting enormous barriers to entry. Consider the following obstacles:

- Major carriers hold 20- to 40-year leases on almost all of the passenger-loading gates at big airports.
- They have 95 percent of the landing rights (i.e., permission to take off and land in certain time slots) at four key airports.
- They own the computer reservation systems, pay travel agents (who book 85 percent of all tickets) extra commissions for bringing business to them, and charge small carriers hefty fees for tickets sold through those systems.
- They operate frequent-flier programs that are far too costly for a new airline to offer and that encourage passengers to avoid switching airlines.
- Their computer-pricing systems enable them to selectively offer low fares on certain seats and to cer-

tain destinations, thereby wiping out a start-up airline's pricing edge.
- Most have a large number of U.S. hub airports, a feeder system to those hubs, and international routes that tie into the hubs. Such systems take decades and hundreds of millions of dollars to acquire.
- The dominant major carriers are willing to match or beat the ticket prices of smaller, niche airlines. Most have proved themselves capable of absorbing losses until weaker competitors are driven out of business.

As a result of these obstacles, even two decades after deregulation, the airline industry's best routes and markets are concentrated in the hands of a few carriers. Many analysts predict that newly formed carriers will likely be limited to less desirable routes or small geographical coverage. However, there are signs that many of the barriers to entry are beginning to erode. Surpluses of nonunionized pilots, airplanes, and investors have led to the launching of about a dozen new airlines each year. Although many fail in their first year or two of operation, others like Reno Air have been successful and are filling viable niches in the industry.

SOURCES: S. McCartney, "Conditions Are Ideal for Starting an Airline, and Many are Doing It," *Wall Street Journal*, 1 April, 1996, pp. A1, A7; L.A. *Times* Wire Services, "Boeing 1st-Quarter Profit Off 34%," 30 April 1996; A. L. Velocci Jr., "USAir Defends Aggressive Pricing," *Aviation Week & Space Technology*, 21 August 1995, p. 28; T. K. Smith, "Why Air Travel Doesn't Work," *Fortune*, 3 April 1995, pp. 42–49; D. Greising, P. Dwyer, and W. Zellner, "A Destination But No Flight Plan," *Business Week*, 16 May 1994, pp. 74–75; J. A. Byrne, "The Pain of Downsizing," *Business Week*, 9 May 1994, pp. 60–68; M. J. McCarthy, "Airlines Squeeze Play," *Wall Street Journal*, 18 April 1994, pp. B1, B8; W. Zellner, A. Rothman, and E. Schine, "The Airline Mess," *Business Week*, 6 July 1992, pp. 50–55.

them either to come in at a large scale, thereby risking a strong reaction from existing firms, or to come in at a small scale, with its accompanying cost disadvantages. For example, Xerox and General Electric failed in their attempts to enter the mainframe computer industry some years back, probably because of scale economies in production, research, marketing, and service.

**Product Differentiation.**   Established firms may enjoy strong brand identification and customer loyalties that are based on actual or perceived product differences, customer service, or advertising. New entrants must spend a great deal of money and time to overcome this barrier. Product differentiation is particularly important in baby care products, over-the-counter drugs, cosmetics, and public accounting. Large brewers, such as Anheuser-Busch, have gone even further by coupling their product differentiation with economies of scale in production, marketing, and distribution.

**Capital Requirements.**   The need to invest large financial resources to compete creates a third type of entry barrier. Large amounts of capital may be necessary for production facility construction, research and development, advertising, customer credit, and inventories. Some years ago, Xerox cleverly created a capital barrier by renting its copiers rather than only selling them. This move increased the capital needs for new entrants.

**Switching Costs.**   **Switching costs** refer to the one-time costs that buyers of the industry's outputs incur if they switch from one company's products to another's. Changing from an established supplier to a new supplier may require the buyer to retrain employees, purchase new ancillary equipment, and/or hire technical help. Most customers are reluctant to switch unless the new supplier offers a major improvement in cost or performance. For example, nurses in hospitals may resist buying from a new supplier of intravenous (IV) solutions and kits, since the procedures for attaching solutions to patients and the hardware for hanging the IV bottles differ from one supplier to another.

**Access to Distribution Channels.**   To enter the distribution channels already being used by established firms, a new firm must often entice distributors through price breaks, cooperative advertising allowances, or sales promotions. Each of these actions, of course, reduces profits. Existing competitors often have distribution channel ties based on longstanding, or even exclusive relationships, meaning that the new entrant must create a new channel of distribution. Timex was forced to do exactly that decades ago to circumvent the channels dominated by the Swiss watchmakers.

**Cost Disadvantages Independent of Scale.**   Established firms may possess cost advantages that cannot be replicated by new entrants regardless of their size or economies of scale. These advantages include proprietary product technology (e.g., Polaroid's monopoly on instant photography), favorable access to raw materials (e.g., Texas Gulf Sulphur's control of large salt dome sulphur deposits), favorable locations (e.g., McDonald's locations at interstate highway exits), and the learning or experience curve (the tendency for unit costs to decline as a firm gains experience producing a product or service; an example is Federal Express's efficient operations or Toyota's production process).

**Government Policy.**   Governments can control entry to certain industries with licensing requirements or other regulations. For instance, entry into the taxicab business in most large cities is controlled by licensing, and entry into the liquor retail business is heavily regulated by states. Even pollution control requirements can serve as an entry barrier because of the need for a certain level of technological sophistication.

### Expected Retaliation

Entry may well be deterred if the potential entering firm expects existing competitors to respond forcefully. These expectations are reasonable if the industry has a history of vigorous retaliation to new entrants or if the industry is growing slowly. Retaliation may also be expected if the established firms are committed to the industry and have specialized fixed assets that are not transferable to other industries, or if the firms have sufficient cash and productive capacity to meet customer needs in the future.[11]

## ■ Intensity of Rivalry Among Existing Competitors

Competition intensifies when one—or more—of the firms in an industry sees the opportunity to improve its position or feels competitive pressure from others. It manifests itself in the form of price cutting, advertising battles, new-product introductions or modifications, and increased customer service or warranties.[12] The intensity of competition depends on a number of interacting factors, as discussed in the following sections.

### Numerous or Equally Balanced Competitors

The number of companies in the industry or how equally balanced they are in terms of size and power may determine intensity of rivalry. Industries with few firms tend to be less competitive, but those that contain a few firms that are roughly equivalent in size and power may be more competitive because each firm will fight for dominance. Competition is also likely to be intense in industries with large numbers of firms, since some of those companies believe that they can make competitive moves without being noticed.[13]

### Slow Industry Growth

Firms in industries that grow slowly are more likely to be highly competitive than companies in fast-growing industries. In slow-growth industries, one firm's increase in market share must come at the expense of other firms' shares.

### High Fixed or Storage Costs

Companies with high fixed costs are under pressure to operate at near-capacity levels to spread their overhead expenses over more units of production. This pressure often leads to price cutting, thereby intensifying competition. The U.S. airline industry has experienced this problem periodically. The same is true of firms that have high storage costs. For that reason, profits tend to be low in industries such as lobster fishing and hazardous-chemical manufacturing.

## Lack of Differentiation or Switching Costs

When products are differentiated, competition is less intense because buyers have preferences and loyalties to particular sellers. Switching costs have the same effect. But when products or services are less differentiated, purchase decisions are based on price and service considerations, resulting in greater competition.

## Capacity Augmented in Large Increments

If economies of scale dictate that productive capacity must be added only in large increments, then capacity additions will lead to temporary overcapacity

---

### S T R A T E G I C   I N S I G H T

## Two Equally Balanced Competitors: PepsiCo and Coca-Cola

Consolidated industries that contain only a few companies can be highly competitive. One of the best examples is the soft-drink industry, where Coca-Cola and PepsiCo have been fighting for dominance for many years. Although most consumers probably consider these two fierce competitors to be similar types of firms, they were actually quite different.

A distinction was that most of Coca-Cola's sales came from the soft-drink market, but PepsiCo was more diversified. Over the past twenty years, Coca-Cola has made several attempts at diversification (e.g., motion pictures, coffee, tea, and wine), but none was particularly successful. PepsiCo, on the other hand, consisted of three major product divisions: soft drinks, snack foods (e.g., Frito-Lay), and fast-food restaurants (Pizza Hut, KFC, and Taco Bell). Although in the 1970s and 1980s diversification seemed like a good idea for PepsiCo, by the latter 1990s it was evident that fast food was not going to continue to generate much profits. PepsiCo's restaurants, known for their creativity, began to stall. This was partially due to a proliferation of fast-food stores which had opened for business in the 1990s. Note that opening fast-food restaurants requires relatively low investments. By 1997 PepsiCo made the decision to spin off its three fast-food restaurant chains. Thus, similar to Coca-Cola, PepsiCo found that diversification was not advantageous.

Currently, the battle arena for the two firms is the soft-drink market. Most of their competition has taken the form of advertising, attempting to maximize shelf space in retail outlets, waging price wars, and introducing new products. PepsiCo and Coca-Cola will likely continue to wage new battles. For instance, U.S. demand for cola drinks has recently declined in favor of such New Age drinks as flavored seltzers, juice drinks, and iced teas. Although Snapple was an early dominating force in this segment, PepsiCo and Coca-Cola countered with naturally brewed versions of their respective Lipton and Nestea brands. Both giants control massive geographical distribution channels and soft-drink machines. Hence, the intensity of rivalry between the two leading soft-drink producers is likely to continue.

SOURCES: "Pepsi Readies Promotion Giving Beepers to Teens," *Wall Street Journal Interactive Edition,* 13 May 1996; M. Wallin and D. Lytle, "PepsiCo Moves to Shore Up S. American Bottler," *Dow Jones News Service,* 9 May 1996; "Hardee's Food Systems Renews Contract With Coca-Cola," *Dow Jones News Service,* 8 May 1996; R. Frank, "Pepsi to Take Control of Latin American Bottler," *Wall Street Journal Interactive Edition,* 10 May 1996; P. Sellers, "PepsiCo's New Generation," *Fortune,* 1 April 1996, pp. 110–118; "The Fortune 500 Largest U.S. Industrial Corporations," *Fortune,* 16 April 1996; G. Collins, "Juice Wars: The Squeeze Is On; Snapple Looks Back to See Coke and Pepsi Gaining", *New York Times,* 15 July 1995, p. 17; N. Deagun, "Pepsi Has Had Its Fill of Pizza, Tacos, Chicken," *Wall Street Journal,* 24 January 1997; G. W. Prince and E. Sfiligoj, "New Age Flourishes," *Beverage Industry Supplement,* March 1994, pp. 21–23; L. Zinn, "Does Pepsi Have Too Many Products?" *Business Week,* 14 February 1994, pp. 64–66; M. J. McCarthy, "Soft-Drink Firms Search for Answers as Volumes Drop," *Wall Street Journal,* 27 July 1992.

in the industry and resultant price cutting. This problem characterizes the manufacture of chlorine, vinyl chloride, and ammonium fertilizer.

### Diverse Competitors

Companies that are diverse in their origins, cultures, and strategies will often have differing goals and differing ways of competing. These differences mean that competitors will have a difficult time agreeing on a set of "rules for the game." Industries with foreign competitors and industries with entrepreneurial owner-operators may, therefore, be particularly competitive.

### High Strategic Stakes

Rivalry will be quite volatile if firms have high stakes in achieving success in a particular industry. For instance, Sony or Toyota may have perceived a strong need to establish a solid position in the U.S. market to enhance its global prestige or technological credibility. These desires can even involve the willingness to sacrifice profitability.

### High Exit Barriers

**Exit barriers** can be economic, strategic, or emotional factors that keep companies from leaving an industry even though they are earning a low—or possibly negative—return on their investment. Examples of exit barriers are fixed assets that have no alternative uses, labor agreements, strategic interrelationships between that business unit and other business units within the same company, management's unwillingness to leave an industry because of pride, and governmental pressure to continue operations to avoid adverse economic effects in a geographic region.

## ■ Pressure From Substitute Products

Firms in one industry may be competing with firms in other industries that produce **substitute products,** which are alternative products that satisfy similar consumer needs but differ in specific characteristics. Substitutes place a ceiling on the prices that firms can charge. For instance, the products of fiberglass insulation were unable to raise their prices despite unprecedented demand during a severe winter because of the availability of insulation substitutes such as cellulose, rock wool, and Styrofoam. And movie theaters are coming under increasing competition from pay-per-view cable channels, which show first-run movies at less than half the theater ticket price. In contrast, firms that produce products that have no substitutes are likely to be highly profitable.

## ■ Bargaining Power of Buyers

The buyers of an industry's outputs can lower that industry's profitability by bargaining for higher quality or more services and playing one firm against another. Buyers are powerful under the following circumstances:

- Buyers are concentrated or purchase large volumes relative to total industry sales. If a few buyers purchase a substantial proportion of an industry's sales, then they will wield considerable power over prices.

- The products that the buyers purchase represent a significant percentage of the buyers' costs. If the products account for a large portion of the buyers' costs, then price is an important issue for the buyers. Hence, they will shop for a favorable price and will purchase selectively.
- The products that the buyers purchase are standard or undifferentiated. In such cases, buyers are prone to play one seller against another.
- The buyers face few switching costs. Switching costs, of course, lock buyers to particular sellers.
- The buyers earn low profits. Low profits create pressure for the buyers to reduce their purchasing costs.
- Buyers can engage in backward integration (they become their own suppliers). General Motors and Ford, for example, use the threat of self-manufacture as a powerful bargaining lever.
- The industry's product is relatively unimportant to the quality of the buyers' products or services. When the quality of the buyers' products is greatly affected by what they purchase from the industry, the buyers are less likely to have significant power over the suppliers.
- Buyers have full information. The more information buyers have regarding demand, actual market prices, and supplier costs, the greater their bargaining power.

### ■ Bargaining Power of Suppliers

Suppliers can squeeze the profitability out of an industry that is unable to recover cost increases in its own prices. The conditions that make suppliers powerful basically mirror those that make buyers powerful. Hence, suppliers are powerful under the following circumstances:

- The supplying industry is dominated by a few companies and is more concentrated than the industry to which it sells. Selling to fragmented buyers means that concentrated suppliers will be able to exert considerable control over prices, quality, and selling terms.
- There are no substitute products. If buyers have no alternative sources of supply, then they are weak in relation to the suppliers that exist.
- The buying industry is not an important customer of the suppliers. If a particular industry does not represent a significant percentage of the suppliers' sales, then the suppliers have considerable power. If the industry is an important customer, however, suppliers' fortunes will be closely tied to that industry, and they will find that reasonable pricing and assistance in such areas as research and development are in their best interests.
- The suppliers' product is an important input of the buyers' business. If the product is a key element in the buyers' manufacturing process or product quality, the suppliers possess significant power.
- The suppliers' products are differentiated or they have built-in switching costs. Product differentiation or switching costs reduce the buyers' ability to play one supplier against another.
- The suppliers pose a credible threat of forward integration (they can become their own customers). If suppliers have the ability and resources to operate their own manufacturing facilities, distribution channels, or retail outlets, they will possess considerable power over buyers.

We can see, then, that—at one extreme—a company could operate quite profitably in an industry with high entry barriers, low intensity of competition among member firms, no substitute products, weak buyers, and weak suppliers. On the other hand, a company doing business in an industry with low entry barriers, intense competition, many substitute products, and strong buyers and/or suppliers would be hard-pressed to generate an adequate profit. The key, of course, is for management to scan and understand the industry in which it operates and to position its company as favorably as possible within that industry. In fact, the next few chapters are devoted to an examination of this key issue in strategic management.

## S T R A T E G I C   I N S I G H T

### *Supplier Power: The Case of NutraSweet*

In 1901, John Francisco Queeny was unable to persuade the wholesale pharmaceutical company for which he worked to produce saccharin, the low-calorie sweetener, rather than to continue to import it from Germany. He took $5,000 and started his own company in St. Louis, calling it Monsanto Chemical Works after his wife's family name.

Some eighty-four years later, Monsanto returned to its roots by acquiring G. D. Searle, the pharmaceutical company known for its extremely successful low-calorie sweetener, NutraSweet. Now a separate business unit of Monsanto, NutraSweet manufactures aspartame for beverages, dessert products, and tabletop sweeteners (under the brand name Equal). Its sales represented 10 percent of Monsanto's annual revenues of $9 billion, and, in 1992, it controlled 75 percent of the U.S. sweetener market. Furthermore, aspartame's operating margins were an impressive 20 percent.

The secret to this success was NutraSweet's patent protection on aspartame. In fact, for two decades, NutraSweet was the world's only supplier of this artificial sweetener. Its monopoly sometimes resulted in a reputation for high-handedness among its customers. For instance, NutraSweet insisted that its logo be displayed in a certain way on all products that contained aspartame. Its power was further demonstrated through its high prices.

But the days of unilateral power are over. NutraSweet's patent expired in 1992, opening the market for aspartame to numerous competitors. To adapt to its declining clout with customers, top management lowered prices by one-third and pledged its $20 million advertising budget to support customer products that contained NutraSweet.

Shortly before the patent expired, Coca-Cola and PepsiCo, NutraSweet's two largest customers, again signed contracts to buy aspartame from NutraSweet, although Coke also signed a similar contract with Holland Sweetener of The Netherlands. Industry observers suggested that neither of the soft-drink giants wanted to take the risk of replacing an ingredient that already had such high consumer acceptance.

Monsanto's Searle unit is continuing to fund efforts aimed at creating an even better sweetener. The company is committed to developing Sweetener 2000, an artificial sweetener that is hundreds of times sweeter than sugar and yet contains no calories.

SOURCES: M. Wilke, "Sweetener Battle Could Fizz Up," *Advertising Age*, 1 May 1995, p. 39; "America's Most Valuable Companies," *Business Week*, 28 March 1994, pp. 72–127; "Monsanto Posts Sales and Net Gains," *Chemical Marketing Reporter*, 26 July 1993, p. 5; L. Therrien, P. Oster, and C. Hawkins, "How Sweet It Isn't at NutraSweet," *Business Week*, 14 December 1992, p. 42; M. J. McCarthy, "Pepsi, Coke Say They're Loyal to NutraSweet," *Wall Street Journal*, 22 April 1992.

## ASSEMBLAGE OF PLAYERS

In the previous section, five industry forces that can have an impact on a firm's profitability were identified. A study of these forces promotes an understanding of firm performance within industries. However, four assumptions are implicit in the preceding section:

- Firms tend to compete in industries with distinct parameters.
- In an industry, the boundaries and identities of each of the five forces are relatively clear-cut.
- The gain of one industry force may result in a loss to another (e.g., one firm gains at the expense of its rivals; a buying organization benefits at a cost to its suppliers).
- Each force may develop independently of other forces (e.g., existing firms develop independently of the buyers they serve).

Although examining the five forces simplifies one's understanding of the performance of firms in an industry, the preceding assumptions are largely violated in many of today's highly complex industries. The pressure for enhanced efficiency and innovation during the last two decades has increased to such an extent that analyzing any one industry does not fully reveal what determines a firm's performance. We can at times benefit by departing from the assumptions of the five-force model and instead examine firm performance in the context of an assemblage of players, which are not confined to a single industry.

The economic prospects for any one firm may in some circumstances be better understood in terms of its interactions with an assemblage of competitive and cooperative firms, called players. For instance, rather than viewing Coca-Cola and PepsiCo as competitors only in the soft-drink industry, we can examine their competition and cooperation with other firms across several industries (Our examination relates to PepsiCo prior to the spin-off of its fast food restaurants). This does not mean that the soft-drink industry classification is irrelevant, but that firm performance may be better understood if factors not solely confined to a specific industry are examined.

### ■ Exchanges with Cooperative Players

Exchanges with cooperative players refer to the mutually beneficial relationships that develop among firms across different industries, although such exchanges are not always obvious. For instance, a carbon dioxide supplier, a chicken processor, and a soft-drink company might engage in mutually supportive, cooperative exchanges. Liquid Carbonic, Airco, or Air Liquide might supply carbon dioxide to PepsiCo for carbonation. These firms might also provide carbon dioxide to chicken processors such as Tyson Foods for freezing the birds. Moreover, Tyson might supply PepsiCo's KFC and Taco Bell units with frozen chicken.

Exchanges among these firms could be mutually advantageous. Higher demand for frozen chicken by PepsiCo's KFC and Taco Bell businesses might benefit Tyson by enabling the chicken processor to enhance its scale economies. This might make it feasible for Tyson to pass along a portion of its cost savings to KFC and Taco Bell. Moreover, higher demand for carbon dioxide by PepsiCo and Tyson might allow the producers of carbon dioxide to reduce their operating costs, making it possible for Airco, Liquid Carbonic, or Air Liquide to transfer a percentage of the cost savings back to PepsiCo and Tyson.

## ■ Exchanges with Competitive Players

Examining interactions among competitors can also be instructive. Competition among PepsiCo, McDonald's, Burger King, Wendy's and Disney exists in various markets. PepsiCo has been prevented from selling its soft drinks to the latter businesses because PepsiCo's restaurants—Pizza Hut, Taco Bell, and KFC—are rivals of McDonald's, Burger King, Wendy's, and Disney-owned establishments. PepsiCo is also excluded from co-branding and merchandising ventures with Disney, whereas Coca-Cola is Disney's partner in such ventures. Alternatively, Coca-Cola cannot bid for the soft-drink needs of Pizza Hut, Taco Bell, and KFC.

Some firms beneficially anchor one competitor to another. For instance, a carbon dioxide supplier such as Airco, Liquid Carbonic, or Air Liquide could serve as an anchor by supplying both PepsiCo and Coca-Cola. Alternatively, Tyson Foods could supply chicken to PepsiCo's units as well as to units of its competitors. In this way competitors may indirectly engender mutual benefits through anchor firms. The heavy demands of Coca-Cola and PepsiCo for carbonation may enable a producer of carbon dioxide to reduce costs and ultimately share a portion of the cost savings with the two firms. Similarly, Tyson, as an anchor firm may simultaneously lower the cost of chicken for PepsiCo's restaurants and for the restaurants owned by McDonald's, Burger King, and Wendy's, because the combined demand of these restaurants provides greater economies of scale for Tyson.

## ■ Existence of Cooperation and Competition

Whereas exchanges among mutually supportive firms are cooperative as they interact to create value, the relationship turns competitive over the division of spoils. Thus, both cooperative and competitive behavior may exist among mutually supportive firms, although they will be more interested in cooperation than in competition. In some situations, adversaries may collaborate for mutual gain, such as in setting technical standards or by sharing research, as the U.S. automakers have done in developing battery technology for electric vehicles.

## ■ Changing Nature of Exchanges and Roles

The nature of exchanges and the roles of competitors or collaborators may change over time. For instance, cooperative exchanges once existed between PepsiCo and Burger King. Before PepsiCo diversified into three restaurant chains, Burger King sold Pepsi products through its outlets. However, after PepsiCo became one of Burger King's prime competitors, the nature of their exchange shifted from cooperation to competition; their roles changed from being mutually supportive to being adversarial (The nature of their exchanges may again change due to the spin-off).

Moreover, the interactive roles some firms play may not be clear-cut. For example, Novell has performed well by consistently converting rivals into partners or customers through the development and use of its NetWare software.

Alternatively, on any given day AT&T finds Motorola to be simultaneously a competitor, partner, supplier, and customer.[14] In this context, only firms capable of cooperating and competing simultaneously will be top performers.[15]

### ■ The Process of Mutual Development

The conceptualization of an assemblage of players may help shed light on the process of mutual development through cooperative and competitive firm behavior.[16] In many respects, behavior among firms is analogous to activity in the animal kingdom. For instance, lions, hyenas, and zebras develop together in the wild. The lion culls the weak and slow zebras, thus strengthening the herd of zebras over time. But to prevail over a stronger and faster herd, the lion must also become more adept. Similarly, the hyena, which competes for the zebra, must become stronger and faster in order to feast on the zebra.

Interactions in the animal kingdom, however, also entail both competitive and cooperative behaviors. Although male zebras compete with each other for mates, their herd behavior to evade predators protects their potential mates as well as their male rivals. Also, although lions (or hyenas) may cooperate in hunting the zebra, they inevitably compete over the kill. Additionally, hyenas may chase the zebra herd toward the lions (or lions toward hyenas), demonstrating an unintentional but effective cooperation between the lion and the hyena.

Competitive or cooperative behavior is instinctive in the animal kingdom, but firms tend to cooperate or compete intentionally. Mutual development among organizations may be based on their competitive or cooperative behavior. Enterprises confronted with strong rivalry may develop into more efficient and innovative units. Alternatively, without viable rivals, firms may lack the incentive to advance, causing them to become less efficient and productive. Such was the case in the 1960s and 1970s when U.S. automakers lacked strong international rivals and became complacent.

Mutual development can occur not only through rivalries, but also through interactions such as between suppliers and buyers. For example, IKEA provides research assistance to its suppliers and leases equipment to them, allowing the supplier firms to keep pace with technological developments. The assistance IKEA provides to its suppliers not only strengthens the suppliers but benefits IKEA by allowing it to produce outputs with reliable components that facilitate operational efficiencies. As firms develop efficiencies and innovations, competitive pressure is even exerted on firms that produce substitute products or services. For instance, the enhanced efficiency of airlines, resulting in lower prices, has exerted pressure on bus and railroad companies to emphasize efficiencies.

## FORECASTING THE ENVIRONMENT

Macroenvironmental and industry scanning and analyses are only marginally useful if all they do is reveal current conditions. To be truly meaningful, such analyses must forecast future trends and changes. Although no form of forecasting is foolproof, several techniques can be helpful: time series analysis, judgmental forecasting, multiple scenarios, and the Delphi technique. Each method is described in the following sections.

## ▪ Time Series Analysis

**Time series analysis** attempts to examine the effects of selected trends (such as population growth, technological innovations, changes in disposable personal income, or changes in number of suppliers) on such variables as a firm's costs, sales, profitability, and market share over a number of years. This methodology also enables management to relate such factors as seasonal fluctuations, weather conditions, and holidays to the firm's performance. Likewise, time series analysis can reveal the effect of economic cycles on the organization's sales and profits. The purpose is to make a prediction about these variables.

Because time series analysis projects historical trends into the future, its validity depends upon the similarity between past trends and future conditions. Any significant departure from historical trends will weaken the forecast dramatically. Unfortunately, departures from historical trends seem to be occurring with increasing frequency.

A second potential weakness in time series analysis is that it provides quantitative answers. Managers must take care that they do not place too much confidence in these results. The use of numbers and equations often gives a misleading appearance of scientific accuracy.

## ▪ Judgmental Forecasting

When the relationships between variables are less clear than they are in time series analysis or when they cannot be adequately quantified, judgmental forecasting may be used. In **judgmental forecasting,** an organization may use its own employees, customers, suppliers, or trade association as sources of qualitative information about future trends. For instance, sales representatives may be asked to forecast sales growth in various product categories from their knowledge of customers' expansion plans. Survey instruments may be mailed to customers, suppliers, or trade associations to obtain their judgments on specific trends.

For example, Allied Corporate Investments, a Los Angeles broker for buyers and sellers of businesses, originally specialized in relatively low-priced small businesses. In 1984, however, it conducted a judgmental forecast, asking its research staff, sales force, and outsiders (such as banks, customers, and the chamber of commerce) to forecast what business opportunities might be available in the future. The consensus of the forecast was that the Los Angeles economy would expand and the value of businesses would be substantially bid up. In response, Allied opened several more offices, contacted commercial sections of foreign embassies to inform them of business opportunities, and brokered more expensive businesses. As a result of its judgmental forecast, its volume of business increased by ten times. Judgmental forecasting should be done periodically to ensure that recent events are taken into account. Unfortunately, Allied did not update its forecast. The recession of the early 1990s, the bankruptcy of Orange County in 1994, and natural disasters severely impacted its operations, leading to a reduced business base and layoffs.

## ▪ Multiple Scenarios

The increasing unpredictability of environmental changes makes it incredibly difficult to formulate dependable assumptions upon which forecasts can be based. One means of circumventing this troublesome state is to develop multiple scenarios about the future. In **multiple scenarios,** the manager formulates several alternative descriptions of future events and trends.[17]

One scenario, for example, may specify the economic conditions thought most likely to occur at some future point. Alternative scenarios may use a more optimistic assumption and a more pessimistic assumption. The same process can just as easily be used to express differing assumptions about technology, political elections, environmental regulation, oil prices, strikes, and other events.

For example, Royal Dutch/Shell Group, the world's second largest corporation, with annual sales exceeding $103 billion, currently uses two scenarios to formulate strategy. One assumes that European economic unification is successful, Japan and the United States avoid a trade war, and stable economic growth occurs throughout most of the world. In such a case, the physical environment will receive increasing attention, meaning governments will formulate additional emission restrictions and natural gas will take precedence over oil as a source of energy. The second scenario assumes international trade wars and widespread recession. Under such conditions, environmental regulations will be de-emphasized and oil consumption will increase dramatically. The point is not to predict which outcome will occur but to encourage managers to analyze a variety of "what if" possibilities.[18]

In formulating scenarios, strategic managers must identify the key forces in the macroenvironment and industry, assess their likely interrelationships, and estimate their influence upon future events. Contingency plans can then be prepared to cover the various conditions specified in the multiple scenarios. These plans may be general statements of action to be taken, without completely specifying the intended operational details. Contingency plans usually specify trigger points—events that call for implementing particular aspects of a plan.[19]

## ■ Delphi Technique

In certain cases, the **Delphi technique** may be used to forecast the future.[20] If the trend to be forecasted lies within a particular field of study, then experts in that field can be identified and questioned about the probability of the trend's occurring. For instance, if a home building firm would like to know when it will become feasible to build entire housing developments with solar energy as the sole source of electricity, heating, and cooling, the firm would compile a list of experts in the field of solar energy. Each expert would then be mailed a questionnaire asking for his or her judgments as to when knowledge of solar energy will be sufficiently advanced to rely solely on it for home energy needs. The respondents will fill out the questionnaires, without communicating with one another, and return them to the home building company.

The company will compile a summary of the results and send it to each respondent along with a second questionnaire. After reviewing the summary and observing the other experts' judgments, each respondent will fill out and mail in the second questionnaire. Some respondents may alter their judgments on this questionnaire after reviewing the judgments of the other members. This process of responding–receiving–feedback–responding continues until consensus is reached. The home builder will then rely, at least partially, on this consensus in formulating the firm's plans for the future.

In the previous paragraphs, several forecasting techniques were presented. Examples of others are shown in Table 2.3.

**Table 2.3**

**Other Forecasting Techniques**

| Technique | Description | Weakness |
|---|---|---|
| Econometric forecast | Simultaneous multiple regression systems | Assumes past relationships will continue into the future |
| Sales force forecast (judgmental) | Aggregate sales force estimate | Potential bias in opinions |
| Managerial forecast (judgmental) | Aggregation of estimates made by research and development, production, finance, and marketing managers | Potential bias in opinions |
| Consumer survey (judgmental) | Aggregate preferences of consumers | Potential bias in opinions |
| Brainstorming (judgmental) | Idea generation in supportive group interaction | Potential bias in opinions |

## SUMMARY

Each organization exists within a complex network of environmental forces comprised of (1) the national and global macroenvironment and (2) the industry in which the organization competes. Because these forces are dynamic, their constant change presents numerous opportunities and threats to strategic managers.

Four macroenvironmental forces affect an organization. Political-legal forces, in the broadest sense, include a government's basic stance toward business operations and, more narrowly, the outcomes of elections, legislation, and court judgments, as well as the decisions of various commissions and agencies at all levels of government. Economic forces comprise elements such as the impact of growth or decline in GDP and increases or decreases in interest rates, inflation, and the value of the dollar. Technological forces include scientific improvements and innovations that affect a firm's operations and/or its products and services. Social forces include traditions, values, societal trends, and a society's expectations of business. To identify and understand changes and trends in these forces, managers engage in environmental scanning.

A more specific set of forces within a firm's industry directly and powerfully affects management's strategic planning. Professor Porter has identified five basic competitive industry forces: the threat of new entrants in the industry, the intensity of rivalry among existing competitors in the industry, the pressure from producers of substitute products or services, the bargaining power of buyers of the industry's outputs, and the bargaining power of suppliers to the industry's companies. The goal of a competitive strategy for a firm is to find a position in the industry from which it can best defend itself against these competitive forces or can influence them to its advantage.

An alternative way we can examine firm performance is in the context of an assemblage of competitive as well as cooperative players. Exchanges among cooperative firms refer to the mutually supportive interactions of an assemblage of firms across different industries. Exchanges with competitive players consist of interactions of adversarial firms in various industries. Both cooperative and competitive firm behavior may prevail among supportive or adversarial players. The nature of exchanges and the roles of players, however, may change over time. Also, the roles played by some firms as they interact with each other may not always be clear-cut. Moreover, mutual development may occur among cooperative or competitive organizations.

Strategic planners must not only understand the current state of the macroenvironment and their industry but must also be able to forecast the future states. Although forecasting is an inexact science, four techniques can be particularly helpful: time series analysis, judgmental forecasting, multiple scenarios, and the Delphi technique.

---

## TAKE IT TO THE NET

We invite you to visit the Wright page on the Prentice Hall Web site at:

### http://www.prenhall.com/wright

for this chapter's World Wide Web exercise.

---

## KEY CONCEPTS

**Barriers to entry**   Obstacles to entering an industry. The major barriers to entry are economies of scale, product differentiation, capital requirements, switching costs, access to distribution channels, cost disadvantages independent of scale, and government policy.

**Delphi technique**   A forecasting procedure in which experts in the appropriate field of study are independently questioned about the probability of some event's occurrence. The responses of all the experts are compiled, and a summary is sent to each expert, who, on the basis of this new information, responds again. Those responses are then compiled and a summary is again sent to each expert, with the cycle continuing until consensus is reached regarding the particular forecasted event.

**Economies of scale**   The decline in unit costs of a product, an operation, or a function that goes into producing a product, which occurs as the absolute volume of production per period of time increases.

**Environmental scanning**   The gathering and analysis of information about relevant environmental trends.

**Exit barriers**   Obstacles to leaving an industry. Exit barriers can be economic, strategic, or emotional.

**Industry**   A group of companies that produces products or services that are in competition.

**Judgmental forecasting**   A forecasting procedure in which employees, customers, suppliers, and/or trade associations serve as sources of qualitative information regarding future trends.

**Macroenvironment**   The general environment that affects all business firms. Its principal components are political-legal, economic, technological, and social systems and trends.

**Multiple scenarios**   A forecasting procedure in which management formulates several plausible hypothetical descriptions of sequences of future events and trends.

**Stakeholder**   An individual or group who is affected by—or can influence—an organization's operations.

**Substitute products**   Alternative products that may satisfy similar consumer needs and wants but that differ somewhat in specific characteristics.

**Switching costs**   One-time costs that buyers of an industry's outputs incur if they switch from one company's products to another's.

**Time series analysis**   An empirical forecasting procedure in which certain historical trends are used to predict such variables as a firm's sales or market share.

## DISCUSSION QUESTIONS

1. Give an example, other than those in the text, of how political-legal forces have presented an opportunity or a threat to a particular industry or business organization.

2. Explain how changes in the value of the dollar affect the domestic and international sales of U.S.-based companies.

3. Give an example, other than those in the text, of how technological forces have presented an opportunity or a threat to a particular industry or business organization.

4. Select a specific business organization and identify the stakeholders of that particular firm.

5. Using your university as an example, explain how political-legal, economic, technological, and social forces have affected its operations over the past decade.

6. Identify an industry that has low barriers to entry and one that has high barriers. Explain how these differences in barriers to entry affect the intensity and form of competition in those two industries.

7. Give some specific examples of exit barriers. How do they affect competition in those industries?

8. Aside from the examples given in the text, identify some products whose sales have been adversely affected by substitute products.

9. Identify an industry in which the suppliers have strong bargaining power and another industry in which the buyers have most of the bargaining power.

10. What are the strengths and weaknesses of time series analysis as a forecasting technique?

# STRATEGIC MANAGEMENT EXERCISES

1. Select a specific company with which you are somewhat familiar. From your recollection of current events (events you may have read about in newspapers or magazines or have heard about on television or radio), identify some of the important macroenvironmental opportunities and threats for this company.

2. From your recollection of current events (events you may have read about in newspapers or magazines or have heard about on television or radio), identify and analyze the industry forces for an automobile company of your choice.

3. Select a major company for which there is considerable information available in your university library. Conduct a macroenvironmental analysis for that company. Your analysis should contain four sections: political-legal forces, economic forces, technological forces, and social forces. (See Appendix 2A for help in locating sources of macroenvironmental information.) Worksheet 1 may help to structure your analysis.

   You need not limit yourself to the terms listed under "Important Information." In some cases, other items that you discover in your research will be of equal or greater importance.

   Once you have identified the important components of each macroenvironmental force, you should determine whether each presents an opportunity or a threat to your company. You might assign a "+" to opportunities and a "−" to threats, or you might list each item under the subheadings "Opportunities" and "Threats." (You can refer to the beginning of the case section, "Strategic Management Case Analysis," for further details.)

4. Conduct an industry analysis for the company that you selected in Exercise 3. Your analysis should contain information in five areas: threat of entry, intensity of rivalry among existing competitors, pressure from substitute products, bargaining power of buyers, and bargaining power of suppliers. (See Appendix 2A for help in locating sources of industry information.) Worksheet 2 should help you to organize your work.

5. Assume that you have been asked to develop an environmental forecast for the bookstore at your university, using the judgmental forecasting technique. Attempt to forecast the environment of the bookstore by writing a summary report based on questions that you ask several employees and customers of the bookstore. Inasmuch as you may not have access to suppliers or trade associations, include your own judgment of what opportunities and threats the environment holds for the bookstore.

**Worksheet 1**     **Macroenvironmental Analysis**

| Macroenvironmental Force | Important Information |
| --- | --- |
| Political-legal | Outcomes of elections, legislation, court judgments, and decisions rendered by various federal, state, and local agencies |
| Economic | GDP, short- and long-term interest rates, inflation, and value of the dollar |
| Technological | Scientific improvements, inventions, and the rate of technological change in the industry |
| Social | Traditions, values, societal trends, consumer psychology, and the public's expectations of business |

**Worksheet 2**     **Industry Analysis**

| Industry Sector | Important Information |
| --- | --- |
| Threat of entry | Extent to which the following factors prevent new companies from entering the industry: economies of scale, product differentiation, capital requirements, switching costs, access to distribution channels, cost disadvantages independent of scale, government policy, and expected retaliation |
| Intensity of rivalry among existing competitors | Number and relative balance of competitors, rate of industry growth, extent of fixed or storage costs, degree of product differentiation and switching costs, size of capacity augmentation, diversity of competitors, extent of strategic stakes, and height of exit barriers |
| Pressure from substitute products | Identification of substitute products, and analysis of the relative price and quality of those products |
| Bargaining power of buyers | Concentration of buyers, their purchase volume relative to industry sales and to the buyers' costs, product differentiation, buyers' switching costs, buyers' profits, possibility of buyers integrating backward, importance of the product to the quality of the buyers' products, and amount of information possessed by the buyers |
| Bargaining power of suppliers | Number and concentration of suppliers, availability of substitute products, importance of the buying industry to the suppliers, importance of the suppliers' product to the buyer's business, differentiation and switching costs associated with the suppliers' product, and possibility of suppliers integrating forward |

# NOTES

1.  J. Sadler, "Small Businesses Complain that Jungle of Regulations Jeopardize Their Futures," *Wall Street Journal*, 11 June 1992; R. W. Duesenberg, "Economic Liberties and the Law," *Imprimis* 23 (April 1994): 1–4.

2.  K. Kelly, "A Dream Marriage Turns Nightmarish," *Business Week*, 29 April 1991, pp. 94–95; R. L. Rose, "Caterpillar Sees Gains in Efficiency Imperiled by Strength of Dollar," *Wall Street Journal*, 6 April 1990.

3.  T. Y. Wiltz, "It's Enough to Drive the Distillers to Drink," *Business Week*, 25 June 1990, pp. 98–99; M. Charlier, "Youthful Sobriety Tests Liquor Firms," *Wall Street Journal*, 14 June 1990.

4.  A. Miller, "Burgers: The Heat Is On," *Newsweek*, 16 June 1986, p. 53.

5.  K. J. Marchetti, "Customer Information Should Drive Retail Direct Mail," *Marketing News*, 28 February 1994, p. 7.

6.  S. Ratan, "Why Busters Hate Boomers," *Fortune*, 4 October 1993, pp. 56–69; B. W. Morgan, "It's the Myth of the '90s: The Value Customer," *Brandweek*, 28 February 1994, p. 17.

7.  J. Diffenbach, "Corporate Environmental Analysis in Large U.S. Corporations," *Long Range Planning* 16, no. 3 (June 1983):109, 112–113.

8.  D. F. Jennings and J. R. Lumpkin, "Insights Between Environmental Scanning Activities and Porter's Generic Strategies: An Empirical Analysis," *Journal of Management* 18 (1992): 791–803.

9.  M. E. Porter, *Competitive Strategy* (New York: Free Press, 1980), pp. 3–4, 7–14, 17–21, 23–28. Reprinted with permission of The Free Press, a division of Macmillan, Inc., from *Competitive Strategy for Analyzing Industries and Competitors*, by Michael E. Porter. Copyright © 1980 by The Free Press.

10. See A. Taylor III, "Korea Revs Up for Jeep Country," *Fortune*, 10 January 1994, p. 20.

11. M. J. Chen and D. Miller, "Competitive Attack, Retaliation, and Performance: An Expectancy-Valence Framework," *Strategic Management Journal* 15 (1994): 85–102.

12. J. R. Graham, "Bulletproof Your Business Against Competitor Attacks," *Marketing News*, 14 March 1994, pp. 4–5; J. Hayes, "Casual Dining Contenders Storm 'Junior' Markets," *Nation's Restaurant News*, 14 March 1994, pp. 47–52.

13. See A. Taylor III, "Will Success Spoil Chrysler?" *Fortune*, 10 January 1994, pp. 88–92.

14. G. Hamel and C. K. Prahalad, *Competing for the Future* (Cambridge: Harvard Business School Press, 1994).

15. See A. A. Lado, N. G. Boyd, and S. C. Hanlon, "Competition, Cooperation and the Search for Economic Rents: A Syncretic Model," *Academy of Management Review*, 22 (1997): 110–141.

16. See J. F. Moore, "Predators and Prey: A New Ecology of Competition," *Harvard Business Review*, 71 (1993): 75–86.

17. L. Fahey and V. K. Narayanan, *Macroenvironmental Analysis for Strategic Management* (St. Paul, Minn.: West, 1986), p. 215.

18. C. Knowlton, "Shell Gets Rich by Beating Risk," *Fortune*, 26 August 1991, p. 82.

19. C. D. Pringle, D. F. Jennings, and J. G. Longenecker, *Managing Organizations: Functions and Behaviors* (Columbus, Ohio: Merrill, 1988), p. 114.

20. N. C. Dalkey, *The Delphi Method: An Experimental Study of Group Opinion* (Santa Monica, Calif.: Rand Corporation, 1969).

# *Appendix 2A: Sources of Environmental and Industry Information*

Much valuable information on environmental and industry conditions and trends is available from published or other secondary sources. Managers should consult these sources prior to gathering expensive primary data.

Local libraries, for instance, contain introductory information on the political-legal, economic, technological, and social components of the macroenvironment in almanacs and encyclopedias. University libraries provide government publications that are rich with political-legal and economic data. Additional information can be obtained from business literature indexes, business periodicals, and reference services. Regularly published periodicals and newspapers such as *Business Week*, the *Wall Street Journal*, and *Fortune* provide excellent, timely macroenvironmental and industry information. More specific sources of information that may be found in many libraries are listed in Table 2A.1 on page 52.

Other highly specific information may be obtained from the annual reports of companies, reports of major brokerage firms (such as Merrill Lynch), and trade publications (examples include *American Paints and Coatings Journal, Modern Brewery Age, Quick Frozen Foods*, and *Retail Grocer*).

Information on the macroenvironment and industries may also be assimilated from radio business news, television shows (such as "Wall Street Week" and "Money Line"), and suppliers, customers, and employees within the industry. And a visit to a branch office of the U.S. Commerce Department can be helpful. The Commerce Department has an extensive bibliography of its own publications, which is available at the branch offices.

Managers can use these sources of information along with assistance from consultants to forecast changes so that the firm can modify its strategy appropriately. Professional consulting firms are available in all major cities and many midsize locales. University professors in all areas of business administration and other disciplines such as sociology, psychology, engineering, and the sciences can also provide expert counseling in relevant areas.

**Table 2A.1**　　　　**Major Sources of Information on the Business Environment**

| Name of Index | Breadth of Information | Description |
|---|---|---|
| Business Periodicals Index | Political-legal<br>Economic<br>Technological<br>Social<br>Industry | Identifies periodicals in all aspects of business and industry. Its "Book Review" covers publications on a variety of topics. |
| Funk & Scott Index of Corporations and Industries | Industry<br>Economic<br>Suppliers<br>Competitors | Identifies periodicals and brokerage reports on all SIC (Standard Industrial Classification) Industries. Its yellow pages provide weekly updates, its green pages provide lists of articles and dates, and its white pages list information on articles about specific companies. |
| New York Times Index | Political-legal<br>Economic<br>Technological<br>Social<br>Industry | Provides an index of articles published in the *New York Times.* |
| Public Affairs Information Service Bulletin | Social<br>Economic<br>Political-legal | Provides a subject listing on national and international journals, books, pamphlets, government publications, and reports of private and public agencies. |
| Reader's Guide to Periodical Literature | Political-legal<br>Economic<br>Technological<br>Social<br>Industry | Provides an author and subject index on periodicals and books. |
| Social Science Index | Political-legal<br>Economic<br>Social | Provides an author and subject index on periodicals and books. |
| Wall Street Journal/ Barron's Index | Political-legal<br>Economic<br>Technological<br>Social<br>Industry | Provides an index of articles published in the *Wall Street Journal* and *Barron's.* Also includes a list of book reviews. |
| U.S. Industrial Outlook | Political-legal<br>Economic<br>Technological<br>Social<br>Industry | Gives the U.S. Department of Commerce's annual forecasts for over 350 industries. |
| Predicasts Forecasts | Political-legal<br>Economic<br>Technological<br>Social<br>Industry | Provides forecasts (as a quarterly service) of products, markets, and industry and economic aggregates for the United States and North America. Forecasts are grouped by SIC numbers and many go into the twenty-first century. |

**Table 2A.1**          **Major Sources of Information on the Business Environment (cont'd.)**

| Name of Index | Breadth of Information | Description |
|---|---|---|
| *Standard and Poor's Industry Surveys* | Political-legal<br>Economic<br>Technological<br>Social<br>Industry | Profiles and analyzes thirty-three basic industry groups. Trends and projections are detailed. Also contains analyses of each industry's leading performers. |
| *Corporate & Industry Research Reports* | Political-legal<br>Economic<br>Technological<br>Social<br>Industry | Provides analyses and forecasts of 8,000 U.S. companies and 600 industries from analytical research reports of 68 securities and institutional investment firms. |

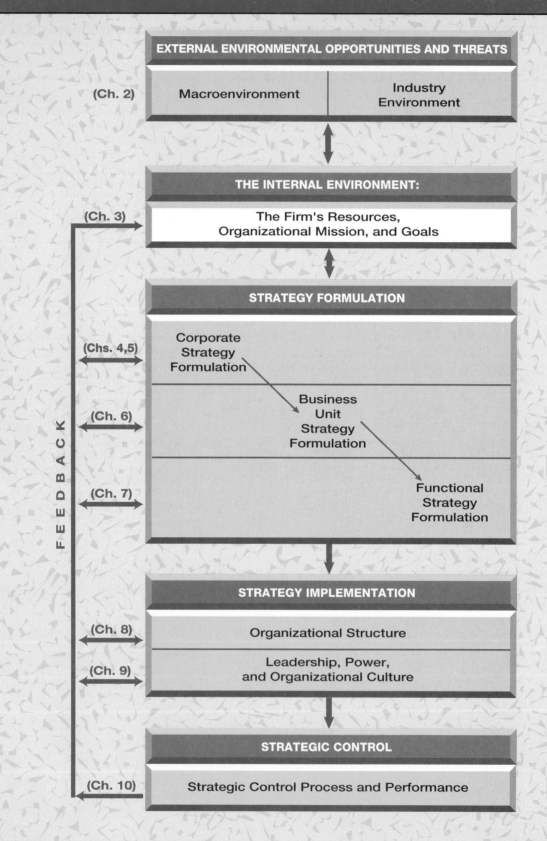

# STRATEGIC MANAGEMENT MODEL

**EXTERNAL ENVIRONMENTAL OPPORTUNITIES AND THREATS**

(Ch. 2)

| Macroenvironment | Industry Environment |

**THE INTERNAL ENVIRONMENT:**

(Ch. 3)

The Firm's Resources, Organizational Mission, and Goals

**STRATEGY FORMULATION**

(Chs. 4,5)

Corporate Strategy Formulation

(Ch. 6)

Business Unit Strategy Formulation

(Ch. 7)

Functional Strategy Formulation

FEEDBACK

**STRATEGY IMPLEMENTATION**

(Ch. 8)

Organizational Structure

(Ch. 9)

Leadership, Power, and Organizational Culture

**STRATEGIC CONTROL**

(Ch. 10)

Strategic Control Process and Performance

# 3 The Internal Environment: The Firm's Resources, Organizational Mission, and Goals

A s we saw in the preceding chapter, an assessment of the opportunities and threats in the organization's external environment is essential in formulating strategy. In this chapter, we turn from the external environment to take an inward look at the firm. This step in the strategy process—establishing the organization's mission and goals—requires management to determine the direction in which the organization is to move within its external environment.

Organizational direction is difficult to determine unless management and the board of directors, with input from diverse stakeholders, have clearly delineated the firm's purpose. The purpose of a firm is delineated in order to strategically create wealth for the shareholders through the satisfaction of the needs and expectations of various stakeholders. According to H. B. Fuller's top manager, Tony Anderson, a firm "exists to make money for its shareholders, but if you have happy customers and employees . . . , the payoff to stockholders will work itself out."[1] A firm's purpose may be conceptualized in the context of **S.W.O.T. analysis** (the strengths and weaknesses of the firm relative to its competitors as well as the opportunities and threats in the external environment). Hence, this chapter begins with a discussion of S. W.O. T. analysis and more specifically the firm's resources, which comprise its strengths and weaknesses, before we examine the organization's mission, its reason for existing. Goals and objectives, as well as other related topics, are subsequently examined.

## S.W.O.T. ANALYSIS

Underlying the organization's mission is an analysis of its internal strengths and weaknesses and the opportunities and threats that are posed in the external environment. The framework presented in Table 3.1 identifies many of the variables that management should analyze. The point of the analysis is to enable the firm to position itself to take advantage of particular opportunities in the environment and to avoid or minimize environmental threats. In doing so, the organization attempts to emphasize its strengths and moderate the impact of its weaknesses. The analysis is also useful for uncovering strengths that have not yet been fully utilized and in identifying weaknesses that can be corrected. Matching information about the environment with a knowledge of the organization's capabilities enables management to formulate realistic strategies for attaining its goals.

A firm's resources constitute its strengths and weaknesses.[2] They include **human resources** (the experience, capabilities, knowledge, skills, and judg-

---

**Table 3.1**          **Framework for S.W.O.T. Analysis**

### *Sources of Possible External Environmental Opportunities and Threats*

| | | | |
|---|---|---|---|
| Economic forces | Political-legal forces | Social forces | Technological forces |
| Industry forces | | | |

### *Possible Organizational Strengths and Weaknesses*

| | | | |
|---|---|---|---|
| Access to raw materials | Distribution | Management | Purchasing |
| Advertising | Economies of scale | Manufacturing and operations | Quality control |
| Board of directors | Environmental scanning | Market share | Research and development |
| Brand names | Financial resources | Organizational structure | Selling |
| Channel management | Forecasting | Physical facilities/ equipment | Strategic control |
| Company reputation | Government lobbying | Product/service differentiation | Strategy formulation |
| Computer information system | Human resources | Product/service quality | Strategy implementation |
| Control systems | Labor relations | Promotion | Technology |
| Costs | Leadership | | |
| Customer loyalty | Location | Public relations | Inventory management |
| Decision making | | | |

ment of all the firm's employees), **organizational resources** (the firm's systems and processes, including its strategies, structure, culture, purchasing/materials management, production/operations, financial base, research and development, marketing, information systems, and control systems), and **physical resources** (plant and equipment, geographic locations, access to raw materials, distribution network, and technology). In an optimal setting, all three types of resources work together to give a firm a **sustained competitive advantage,** as illustrated in Figure 3.1. Sustained competitive advantage refers to valuable strategies that cannot be fully duplicated by the firm's competitors and that result in high financial returns over a lengthy period of time.

Just as chapter 2 explored the external environmental opportunities and threats, the following paragraphs will briefly examine each of the three types of resources that comprise a firm's internal strengths and/or weaknesses.

## ■ Human Resources

Because even the most superb organizational and physical resources are useless without a talented work force of managers and employees, we place most of our emphasis on a firm's human resources. These resources can be examined at three levels—the board of directors; top management; and middle management, supervisors, and employees.

### *Board of Directors*

At the top of the human resource hierarchy sits the board of directors. Because board members are becoming increasingly involved in corporate affairs, they can materially influence the firm's effectiveness. In examining their strengths and weaknesses, the following questions may be asked.

- What contributions do the board members bring to the firm? Strong board members possess considerable experience, knowledge, and judgment, as well as valuable outside political connections.
- Are the members internal or external, and how widely do they represent the firm's stakeholders? Although it is common for several top managers to be board members, a disproportionate representation of them diminishes

**Figure 3.1**           **Route to Sustained Competitive Advantage**

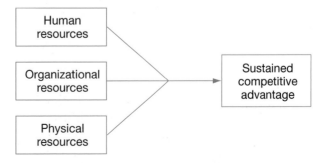

the identity of the board as a group apart from top management. Ideally, board members should represent diverse stakeholders, including minorities, creditors, customers, and the local community. A diverse board membership can contribute to the health of the firm.

- Do the members own significant shares of the firm's securities? Significant stock ownership may increase the board's responsiveness to stockholders, while significant bond holdings may enhance its concern with the firm's creditworthiness.
- How long have the members served on the board? Long-term stability enables board members to gain knowledge about the firm, but some turnover is beneficial because new members often can bring a fresh perspective to strategic issues. More is stated on boards of directors subsequently.

## Top Management

The organization's top executives must establish and communicate a vision for the firm that encompasses the needs and desires of the firm's various stakeholders. Strategic leadership will be discussed further in chapter 9. Ideally, then, top managers should assume the role of "selfless stewards" concerned primarily with attaining stakeholders' goals.[3] Several questions might be asked in assessing the strengths and weaknesses of any firm's top management.

- Who are the key top managers, and what are their strengths and weaknesses in job experience, managerial style, decision-making capability, team building, and understanding of the business? There are advantages, for instance, in having executives who have an intimate knowledge of the firm and its industry. On the other hand, managers from diverse backgrounds may generate innovative strategic ideas. And, of course, an organization's management needs may change as the firm grows and matures. For instance, start-up firms are often headed by entrepreneurs who are innovative but may be weak in administrative abilities. More mature firms need strong administration but must continue to be innovative.
- How long have the key top managers been with the firm? Lengthy tenure can mean consistent and stable strategy development and implementation, yet low turnover may breed conformity, complacency, and a failure to explore new opportunities.
- What are top management's strategic strengths and weaknesses? Some executives may excel in innovative strategy formulation, for instance, but may be weak in implementing strategy. Some may spend considerable time interacting with external constituents, whereas others concentrate on internal stakeholders and operations.

## Middle Management, Supervisors, and Employees

A firm can have brilliant top managers and board members but if its work force is less than top-notch, even the most ingenious strategies cannot be implemented effectively. Each firm's human resources are unique. That uniqueness stems not only from the fact that every organization employs a different set of human beings, but also from the specific synergies that result from combining each firm's human resources with its particular organizational and physical resources. In this context, a firm's personnel and their knowledge, abilities, commitment, and performance tend to reflect the firm's human resource programs. These factors can be explored by asking several key questions about those programs to ascertain the strengths and weaknesses of the organization's managers and employees.

- Does the organization have a comprehensive human resource planning program? Developing such a program requires that the firm estimate its personnel needs, including types of positions and requisite qualifications, for the next several years based on its strategic plan. Many organizations do little planning in this area, and such short-term thinking rarely results in effective operations.
- How much emphasis does the organization place on training and development programs? Firms that ignore personnel training and development are virtually doomed to stagnation.
- What is the organization's personnel turnover rate compared to the rest of the industry? High turnover rates, compared to those of competitors, generally reflect personnel problems, such as poor management–employee relations, low compensation or benefits, weak personnel policies, or low job satisfaction due to other causes.
- How much emphasis does the firm place on performance appraisal? Effective programs provide accurate feedback to managers and employees, link rewards to actual performance, show managers and employees how to improve performance, and comply with all equal employment opportunity programs.
- How well does the organization manage a work force that increasingly reflects society's changing demographics? Many firms have begun to evaluate and adjust practices that were designed for yesterday's more homogeneous work force. Those firms that lead the way in promoting diversity have a decided advantage in attracting and retaining a highly qualified work force. Human resources are further discussed in chapter 7.

## ■ Organizational Resources

The assessment of organizational resources basically hinges on the question of whether the resources are properly aligned with the firm's strategies and whether they are sufficient for the strategies' implementation. Although the issues are too numerous to cover completely here, some of the key questions are discussed.

- Are the corporate, business unit, and functional strategies consistent with the organization's mission and goals? The mission, goals, and strategies must be compatible and reflect a clear sense of identity and purpose.
- Are the organization's corporate, business unit, and functional strategies, discussed in chapters 4, 5, 6, and 7 respectively, consistent with one another? These three levels of strategy must be closely intertwined and highly consistent. Hence, managers at the corporate, business unit, and functional level should be represented at each level of strategic planning. Recall that corporate strategies should influence business unit strategies, which, in turn, should influence functional strategies. But, at the same time, functional strategies affect business unit strategies, which then affect corporate strategies.
- Is the organization's formal structure appropriate for implementing its strategy? The content of chapter 8 is entirely devoted to this topic.

- Are the organization's decision-making processes effective in implementing its strategies? Issues of centralization versus decentralization are covered in chapter 5 and chapter 9. Chapter 9 also includes an analysis of leadership team processes.
- Is the organization's culture consistent with its strategy? A part of chapter 9 focuses on the role of culture in strategy formulation and implementation.
- How effective are the organization's strategic control processes? Chapter 10 examines this crucial issue.

## ■ Physical Resources

Although the types of physical resources possessed by firms differ considerably from one organization to another (consider, e.g., the different physical plants required by an automobile maker versus a management consulting firm), some general questions assessing the strengths and weaknesses of physical resources might take the following form.

- Does the organization possess up-to-date technology? Whereas cutting-edge technology is no guarantee of success, competitors who have superior technology and know how to use it have a decided advantage in the marketplace.
- Does the organization possess adequate capacity? Although a continual backlog of orders indicates market acceptance of a firm's product, it may conceal the lost business and declining customer goodwill that accompany insufficient capacity. We emphasize that numerous firms have restructured their operations in recent years, eliminating excess capacity.
- Is the organization's distribution network an efficient means of reaching customers? Note that distribution networks do not apply only to firms that manufacture products. American Airlines' domination of passenger gates at Dallas–Fort Worth Airport and United's similar control at O'Hare Field give both of these service companies a competitive advantage.
- Does the firm have reliable and cost-effective sources of supply? Suppliers who are unreliable, do not have effective quality control programs, or cannot control their costs well put the buying firm at a decided competitive disadvantage.
- Is the organization (and its branches) in an optimum geographic location? Appropriate location may depend on cost factors (land, building, and labor); the availability of skilled labor, natural resources, and sources of supply; customer convenience; and shipping costs.

What should be emphasized, according to resource-based theory, is the unique combination of human, organizational, and physical resources possessed by a firm. As the firm acquires additional resources, unique synergies occur between its new and existing resources. Because each firm already possesses a distinct combination of human, organizational, and physical resources, the particular types of synergies that occur will differ from one firm to another. For example, if the quality of a new resource in the external environment is represented by Z, once that resource is acquired by organization A the quality of the resource is transformed to ZA. If this resource were instead purchased by organization B, then Z's resultant quality would be transformed to ZB. ZB, of course, represents a qualitatively different value than ZA.

## ■ The Organization's Mission

Having examined the firm's external environment in the previous chapter and its potential resource strengths and weaknesses in the preceding paragraphs, we now examine the organization's mission. Organizations are founded for a purpose. Although this purpose may change over time, it is essential that stakeholders understand the reason for the organization's existence, that is, the organization's **mission.** Often, the organization's mission is defined in a formal, written **mission statement**—a broadly defined but enduring statement of purpose that identifies the scope of an organization's operations and its offerings to the various stakeholders.[4]

As suggested before, a firm's mission should evolve in the context of S.W.O.T. analysis.[5] In the following section, we examine the organization's mission at both the corporate and business unit levels. Changes in the organization's mission over time are then discussed, followed by an overview of the relationship between the organization's mission and its strategy. Goals and objectives, as well as other related topics, are subsequently probed.

### Mission and Organizational Level

The mission of an organization, at the corporate level, is stated in fairly broad terms. For instance, the management of General Motors (GM) has stated the firm's overall mission as follows:

> The fundamental purpose of General Motors is to provide products and services of such quality that our customers will receive superior value, our employees and business partners will share in our success, and our stockholders will receive a sustained, superior return on their investment.[6]

Certainly, a large number of activities can be covered by such a broad statement. Such disparate GM undertakings as manufacturing vehicles, producing electronics and defense products, and providing technology can all be included in this mission statement. However, in each of these cases, the statement indicates that GM intends to furnish superior value to customers, to have employees and business partners share in the firm's success, and to provide a sustained, superior return to stockholders on their investment. So even though very broad, this corporate-level statement does provide direction to the company.

At the business unit level, the mission becomes narrower in scope and more clearly defined. For example, the mission of the Chevrolet business unit would include manufacturing safe and reliable economy cars, sport cars, sedans, and trucks. The Hughes Aircraft subsidiary's mission would be to produce electronic components and systems for defense and industrial customers.

The mission of some business units even specifies in which country the products will be manufactured and strategically links the business unit to the corporate level in some manner—such as through the transfer of knowledge and technology. For example, GM's Saturn business unit has the following mission statement:

> The mission of Saturn is to market vehicles developed and manufactured in the United States that are world leaders in quality and customer satisfaction through the integration of people, technology and business systems and to transfer knowledge, technology and experience throughout General Motors.[7]

## Mission and Change

Corporate and strategic business-level missions will generally change over time. In many cases, the change will be slow and gradual, but in some instances, the change may take place very rapidly. As an example of a firm whose mission changed gradually, consider Primerica. At one time, Primerica was known as American Can Company and was engaged in the container manufacturing and packaging businesses. Over the years, the company diversified into financial services and specialty retailing. When it finally sold its can and packaging operations, its name no longer fit its businesses, and it was renamed Primerica. Obviously, its mission had also gradually changed from manufacturing to services. Now its mission is to provide life insurance to individual consumers, originate home mortgages, provide mutual and pension fund management and brokerage services, and offer retail services for recorded music and audio and video products.

UAL, Inc. (United Airlines), serves as a classic example of a firm whose mission changed quickly. In 1987, UAL's chief executive officer, Richard Ferris, decided to broaden the company's mission. Rather than only provide air travel, UAL would become an integrated travel service company with operations encompassing the total service requirements of travelers. The firm would expand into rental cars (to provide customers transportation to and from airports) and hotels (where customers could stay while on trips). To reflect this broadened mission, the firm's name was changed from United Airlines to Allegis. The new mission was quite controversial, and various groups that had vested interests in the company believed that those interests would be better served by the firm's original mission—passenger and cargo air transportation. Within four months, Ferris was fired and the company's name and mission reverted to their previous forms.

Boston Consulting Group's Jeanie Duck has argued that change is very personal. For change to occur in any firm, each person and group must adopt a different attitude and perform an aspect of his or her job differently. This argument may be extended to change and stakeholder groups. If a mission of a firm is to change, stakeholder groups must be positively predisposed toward the change. Otherwise, the change will not occur successfully or will be short-lived, as was the case with United Airlines.[8]

## Mission and Strategy

An organization with a keen sense of its own identity is far more likely to be successful than one that has no clear understanding of its reason for existence. For example, Armco diversified widely more than a decade ago in an attempt to shelter itself from fluctuations in the steel industry. But it found itself in alien territory when it moved into financial services and insurance. After acquiring an insurance holding company, Armco's managers discovered that they "had very few people in [their] management group who could ask the right questions and trouble shoot in that part of [their] operations."[9] They determined to limit future diversification to markets with which they were familiar. Sears, another example of a firm with a blurred mission, is discussed in the Strategic Insight box.

By contrast, Wal-Mart transformed the discount retailing industry by identifying itself as a general merchandiser, committed to low-cost operations with

## STRATEGIC INSIGHT

### A Blurred Mission at Sears

Prior to 1975, Sears, Roebuck was the dominant national force in U. S. retailing. As a full-line general merchandiser with 850 stores, Sears was a regular shopping stop for most of America's families. That dominance ended abruptly, however, as the retail industry experienced rapid and dramatic changes. Sears' private-label business was eroded by the growing popularity of specialty retailers, such as Circuit City and The Limited, and its cost structure was successfully challenged by such low-overhead discounters as Wal-mart and Best Buy.

Initially, Sears reacted by attempting to emphasize fashion with such labels as Cheryl Tiegs sportswear. But high-fashion models did not mesh well with Sears' middle-America image. In fact, Sears allowed the key post of women's fashion director to remain vacant from 1980 until 1989. Turning next to diversification, Sears tried to convert its dowdy image into a "financial supermarket" by purchasing Dean Witter Financial Services and Coldwell Banker Real Estate. But in-store kiosks never caught on with customers, and the expected synergy between these two subsidiaries and Sears' Allstate Insurance Business unit and its Discover Card failed to materialize. Eventually, Sears decided to spin off its Dean Witter Financial Services Group and its Coldwell Banker real estate holdings to permit the firm to sharpen its focus on its core retailing business.

Next, management modified the store's image to one that sold nationally branded merchandise along with private-label brands at "everyday low prices." The idea was to create individual "superstores" within each of the Sears outlets to compete more effectively with powerful niche competitors. Sears' original intent, which was widely publicized, was to depart from its traditional practice of holding weekly sales in order to save on advertising expenses and inventory handling while offering stable, everyday low prices. But the "everyday low prices" turned out to be, in some cases, higher than Sears' old sale prices, advertising expenses climbed rather than declined, and Sears continued to run special sales. By this time, customers were totally confused. Sears' response was to announce that, once again, it was going to emphasize women's fashions and would advertise them in such magazines as *Vogue* and *Mademoiselle*. But, in 1992 alone, Sears lost $3.9 billion, its worst performance ever.

In 1993, Sears terminated its big catalog operations, began spinning off some of its businesses unrelated to general merchandising, overhauled its clothing lines, eliminated more than 93,000 jobs, and closed 113 stores. In 1995, Sears reentered the catalog business. This time, instead of a big book Sears catalog, it set up joint ventures to provide smaller catalogs. Sears provides its name and its 24 million credit card customers database. Its partners select the merchandise, mail catalogs, and fill orders. By 1998, Sears had begun to benefit from its strategic shift to moderately priced apparel and home furnishings. If Sears can maintain a clear mission and present a consistent image during the late 1990s, the retail giant may sustain profits once again. As CEO Arthur Martinez put it, "We've established our platforms for future growth. They're in home stores, home services, credit, and automotive. Sears will stay close to things we're known for and things we're good at."

SOURCES: E. A. Robinson, "America's Most Admired Companies," *Fortune*, 3 March, 1997, p. F3; A. Ward, "Sears 'On Course' Despite Hard Retail Conditions, CEO Says," *Wall Street Journal Interactive Edition*, 9 May 1996 (source of quotation); K. Fitzgerald, "Sears, Ward's Take Different Paths," *Advertising Age*, 31 July 1995, p. 27; S. Chandler, "Sears' Turnaround is For Real—For Now," *Business Week*, 15 August 1994, pp. 102-104; D. Longo, "Kmart Can Learn Some Lessons From Sears," *Discount Store News*, 21 February 1994, p. 9; J. Kirk, "Sears' 'Many-Sided' Look," *Adweek*, 14 February 1994, p. 3; A. Markowitz, "Sears Takes Steps to Strengthen and Revitalize," *Discount Store News*, 7 February 1994, pp. 2, 91; J. A. Parnell, "Strategic Change Versus Flexibility: Does Strategic Change Really Enhance Performance?" *American Business Review*, Vol. 12(2) (1994): 22–30; "Sears Loses $3.93 Billion in '92, *Harrisonburg* (VA) *Daily News-Record*, 10 February 1993.

"everyday low prices." Through concentrating its efforts on discount retailing, Wal-Mart Stores developed its innovative logistics system, known as *cross-docking*. Products are continuously delivered to its warehouses, where they are normally repacked and transferred to stores within two days, maximizing inventory turnover. The products purchased by Wal-Mart cross from an incoming loading dock to an outgoing dock, enabling this firm to have the lowest cost operation in the discount retailing industry. Wal-Mart's low-cost strength has matched well an external opportunity—customers' demand for low-priced general merchandise.[10]

Hence, effective management requires not only an understanding of the environment, but also a focus on the organization's mission (in the context of its strengths and weaknesses). A clear sense of purpose is necessary in establishing goals, because it is difficult to know where one is going if one does not first know who one is. Firms with a clear sense of their mission are able to determine which activities fit into their strategic direction and which ones do not.

Management consultant C. K. Prahalad emphasizes that organizations should spend more time understanding what proficiencies they possess. For instance, Sony has used its skills in miniaturizing audio, video, and electronics products as its particular strategic competence. Likewise, AT&T's diversification into the credit card field was an application of its strategic competence in transaction processing, based on its extensive billing experience in the telephone industry.[11] Figure 3.2 summarizes the discussion up to this point.

**Figure 3.2**          **The Role of the Organization's Mission**

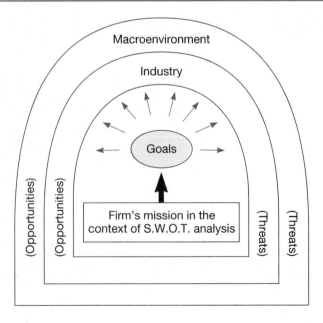

# THE ORGANIZATION'S GOALS AND OBJECTIVES

This section focuses on organizational goals and objectives. On the surface, it appears that establishing organizational goals is a fairly straightforward process. As will become evident, however, this process is actually quite complex. Various stakeholder groups have different goals for the firm. The organizational goals that eventually emerge must balance the pressures from the different stakeholder groups so that the continuing participation of each is assured.

## ■ Goals and Objectives Defined

Whereas the mission is the reason for the existence of the firm, the organization's **goals** represent the desired general ends toward which efforts are directed. **Objectives** are specific, and often quantified, versions of goals. For example, management may establish a goal "to expand the size of the firm through internal growth." From this goal, a number of specific objectives may be derived, such as "to increase sales by 10 percent each year for the next eight years." As another example, management's goal may be "to become the innovative leader in the industry." On the basis of this goal, one of the specific objectives may be "to have 25 percent of sales each year come from new products developed during the preceding three years."

As you can see, objectives are verifiable and specific. That is, with the objectives in the preceding paragraph, management will be able to answer the question: "Has this objective been attained?" Without verifiability and specificity, objectives will not provide a clear direction for managerial decision making, nor will they permit an assessment of organizational performance.

## ■ Goals and Stakeholders

Various stakeholders will have different goals for the firm. Each stakeholder group—owners (stockholders), members of the board of directors, managers, employees, suppliers, creditors, distributors, and customers—views the firm from a different perspective. To illustrate this point, Table 3.2 on page 66 delineates the goals of selected stakeholders for Kellogg Company.

Rationality suggests that stakeholders establish goals from the perspective of their own interests. Because of the diversity of these interests, top management faces the difficult task of attempting to reconcile and satisfy each of the stakeholder groups while pursuing its own set of goals. Because the interests of various stakeholder groups are quite different, a close examination of some of their interests can be enlightening.

## ■ Influence on Goals

Who has the most influence on a firm's goals and who determines what the organization does? The traditional view is one of a shareholder-driven corporation. From this perspective, both top management and the board of directors are primarily accountable to the owners (the shareholders) of the corporation. Top management is responsible for enhancing the financial value of the firm, and the board of directors is charged with overseeing top management's decisions to ensure that those decisions enhance firm value.

**Table 3.2**  **General Goals of Kellogg's Stakeholders**

| Stakeholders | Goals |
|---|---|
| Customers | Customers would likely want Kellogg's goals to include providing healthy, quality foods at reasonable prices. |
| General public | The general public would likely want Kellogg's goals to include providing goods and services with minimum costs (i.e., pollution), increasing employment opportunities, and contributing to charitable causes. |
| Suppliers | Suppliers would likely want Kellogg's goals to include remaining with them for the long term and purchasing from them at prices that allow the suppliers reasonable profit margins. |
| Employees | Employees would likely want Kellogg's goals to include providing good working conditions, equitable compensation, and promotion opportunities. |
| Creditors | Creditors would likely want Kellogg's goals to include maintaining a healthy financial posture and a policy of on-time payment of interest and principal. |
| Distributors | Wholesalers and retailers would likely want Kellogg's goals to include remaining with them for the long term and selling to them at prices that allow for reasonable profit margins. |
| Stockholders | Stockholders would likely want Kellogg's goals to be the enhancement of returns on their equity. |
| Board of directors | Directors would likely want Kellogg's goals to be to keep them as directors and to satisfy the demands of the other stakeholders so that the directors would not be liable to lawsuits. |
| Managers | Managers would likely want to benefit personally from Kellogg. Other management goals are to expand Kellogg's market share in the cereal business, to make compatible growth-oriented acquisitions, to boost capacity, to improve productivity, and to launch new cereals worldwide. |

An argument exists, however, that if owners are to experience enhanced financial returns, the corporation must be customer-driven. Consumer advocate Ralph Nader, for instance, has argued for more than thirty years that large corporations must be more responsive to customers' needs.[12] In addition, the marketing strategy literature emphasizes the necessity for firms to maintain strategic adaptability based on changes in customer desires.[13]

A broader viewpoint recognizes that, because corporations are complex and depend upon environmental resources, they cannot maximize any single stakeholder group's interests. Rather, corporation must be broadly stakeholder-driven, attempting to balance the desires of all stakeholders.[14] Maximizing any one stakeholder group's interests at the expense of other groups can seriously jeopardize the corporation's effectiveness. A firm cannot emphasize the financial interests of shareholders over the monetary needs of employees, for example, without alienating the employees and eventually harming the firm's financial returns. Likewise, raising prices to please stockholders will cause customers to take their business elsewhere.

Because various stakeholders' desires may conflict, management must resolve these opposing demands.[15] Fortunately, however, some stakeholders may have more than a unidimensional self-interest. For instance, although some stockholders may desire high financial returns, they may be unwilling to invest in corporations that produce tobacco products, even though higher returns may be associated with such investment opportunities. Moreover, some consumers may be willing to pay higher prices for products that do not harm the environment.

Ideally, top managers recognize that the corporation must be managed to balance the pluralistic demands of various stakeholder groups. Obviously, this requirement poses a considerable challenge. A careful reading of the goals in Table 3.2 illustrates this point. In the following paragraphs, select stakeholder groups are discussed in the context of their paramount goals.

## ■ Goals of Top Management

Ideally, the goals of top management should be attempts to enhance the return to stockholders on their investment while simultaneously satisfying the interests of other stakeholders. However, the motivation of top management to enhance profits has been questioned for many years. In fact, for as long as absentee owners (stockholders) have been hiring professional managers to operate their companies, questions have been raised concerning the extent to which these managers actually attempt to increase the wealth of the absentee owners. On the one hand, it has been argued that management primarily serves its own interests. On the other hand, some have proposed that management shares the same interests as the stockholders.

### Management Serves Its Own Interests

The argument of researchers adhering to this viewpoint is that hired top managers tend to pursue strategies that ultimately increase their own rewards.[16] In particular, top executives are likely to increase the size of their firms since larger rewards usually accompany larger organizational size and its greater responsibilities.

Perhaps the major work in this area can be traced to Herbert A. Simon,[17] who won the 1978 Nobel Prize in economics for his research on managerial decision-making behavior. Building on Roberts's study of executive compensation, Simon suggests that a reward differential exists at each managerial level in an organizational hierarchy.[18] That is, first-level supervisors receive the lowest managerial salaries, but salaries increase with each succeeding level in the organization up through the chief executive officer's (CEO's) salary. The larger the organization and the greater the number of levels in its hierarchy, the greater the rewards will be for top-level executives. Hence, top managers have a powerful incentive to increase the size of their firms. Other researchers have empirically demonstrated that larger firm size is positively associated with greater rewards.[19] One study concluded that "the size/pay relation is causal and . . . CEOs can increase their pay by increasing firm size, even when the increase in size reduces the firm's market value."[20]

Top managers may also be selfishly motivated to increase the size of their firms through diversification, by acquiring companies in other industries. Diversification not only increases a firm's size but may also reduce the top managers' job risks, for when an organization falters, its top managers often lose their jobs. Diversification should spread this risk and help upper-level managers preserve their positions. Although diversification can benefit top management, it may not similarly advance stockholders' interest. They can more effectively reduce their financial risks by diversifying their personal financial portfolios.[21]

This interest in organizational growth does not necessarily mean that top management is unconcerned with the firm's profitability or market value, but it does suggest to researchers that top managers are likely to emphasize business performance only to the extent that it discourages shareholder revolts and hostile takeovers. Simon suggests, for instance, that the difference between what a firm's profits can be and what its profits actually are represents "organizational slack," which will only be reduced if outside pressure is applied.[22]

### Management Shares the Same Interests as Stockholders

A second viewpoint contradicts the preceding view by proposing that the interests of top management are the same as those of the stockholders. Indeed, some studies do reveal positive associations between business performance and managerial rewards. One study, for example, found that profits, not the size of firms, can determine top management rewards.[23] Also, there can be a significant relationship between common stock earnings and the rewards of top executives.[24]

In a widely cited theoretical work, Eugene F. Fama argues that the self-interest of top managers requires that they behave in ways that benefit the stockholders.[25] His argument is based on the premise that the market for managerial talent provides an effective disciplining force. If top managers do not promote the interests of stockholders, this information will result in a lowering of their value in the managerial labor market. This lowered value will adversely affect the managers' alternative employment opportunities.[26] Managerial performance may also be indirectly evaluated by the stock market, because it implicitly judges top management's performance by bidding the firm's stock price either up or down.[27]

From a different perspective, John Child proposes that stock option plans and high salaries bring the interests of top management and stockholders closer together.[28] According to his reasoning, top executives wish to protect their salaries and option plans and can do so only by striving for higher business performance.

This concept of congruent interests has gained support from other scholars, but for different reasons.[29] They suggest that managerial jobs contain "structural imperatives" that force managers to attempt to enhance profits.

> Before the rise of the large stock corporation, individuals who filled the roles of entrepreneur were probably motivated to realize profits. If they did not act as if they were so motivated, however, the failure of their firms would eventually remove them from their positions. . . . The behavior exhibited by entrepreneurs was a structural requirement of the position of entrepreneur itself rather than merely a function of the motivation of individuals who became entrepreneurs.[30]

Similarly, managers would be removed from their positions if they failed to increase profits. Therefore, these scholars reason that top managers will be

## STRATEGIC INSIGHT

# CEO Compensation

Excessive CEO compensation has been roundly criticized in recent years. Although no firm standards exist for defining what is "excessive," a number of CEOs have come under fire for their annual compensation. For example, over the past several years, angry shareholders have noted that Champion Paper's annual return has been less than the average annual return on risk-free U. S. treasury notes. Yet Champion's CEO, Andrew Sigler, receives more than $1 million in annual compensation and has been awarded a bonus for more than twenty consecutive years.

Consider also that AT&T Chairman and CEO Robert Allen earned about $11 million in 1995 but drew heavy criticism when he announced 40,000 layoffs as part of the firm's restructuring plan. Since Allen's appointment, AT&T shares have appreciated at the same rate as the S&P 500.

The stock prices of H. J. Heinz, Masco, and Torchmark all fell behind the S&P 500 annual average return over the past five years, yet their CEOs earned $120 million, $38 million, and $37 million, respectively, over the period. And even defenders of high salaries called it excessive when Gibson Greetings fired its CEO, Benjamin Sottile, in early 1996, but agreed to pay his salary and benefits through 1998.

According to several recent surveys, most managers believe CEOs earn too much. During the 1980s, CEO compensation rose by 212 percent, compared to 54 percent for factory workers, 73 percent for engineers, and 95 percent for teachers. After a brief decline in the early 1990s, CEO salaries have begun to climb once again. In 1997, chief executives of American firms with more than $2.5 billion in annual revenues averaged $950,000 in salary alone. Their counterparts in Germany, Great Britain, and Japan earned $775,000, $580,000, and $450,000, respectively.

While cash compensation has risen considerably, CEOs also typically receive stock options and bonuses, revenues from profitsharing plans, retirement benefits, interest-free loans, and the like. As a result, CEOs in America's largest publicly held corporations average more than $4 million in earnings annually.

Numerous studies have demonstrated that CEO salary is more closely tied to company size than to performance. Part of the reason for the historically low correlation between CEO pay and performance is the way in which the typical CEO's compensation is set. Determining that compensation is the responsibility of the compensation committee of the board of directors. The board is usually appointed by the CEO and guided by a compensation consultant appointed by the CEO. Often, the CEO does not even leave the room when his or her compensation is discussed.

Recently, however, firms have begun to tie compensation more closely to corporate performance. DSC Communications Chairman James Donald earned more than $25 million in 1994, but the majority of that came from stock gains. Between 1992 and 1994, Green Tree Financial's CEO, Lawrence Coss, took home more than $55 million, most of which was attributed to a twelvefold increase in the company's stock price. While GE's John Welch was the highest paid CEO in 1995, netting more than $22 million, including benefits and stock options, his earnings were accompanied by strong performance throughout the company. Most firms appear willing to continue to pay large sums to chief executives, provided the corporation performs equally well.

SOURCES: G. Burns, "Fat Wallets," Business Week, 3 March 1997, p. 6; C. Duff, "Top Executives Ponder High Pay, Decide They're Worth Every Cent," Wall Street Journal Interactive Edition, 13 May 1996; W. Bounds, "Ousted Chairman of Gibson to Get Pay Until April 1998," Wall Street Journal Interactive Edition, 29 April 1996; "Is Chairman Allen of AT&T Overpaid?" Wall Street Journal, 29 February 1996, p. B1; C. Farrell, "Why Some Compensation Is Clean Outta Sight," Business Week, 4 September 1995, p. 60; J. Flynn, "Continental Divide over Executive Pay," Business Week, 3 July 1995, pp. 40–41; "Random Numbers: Executive Pay," Economist, 3 June 1995; E. S. Hardy, "America's Highest Paid Bosses," Forbes, 22 May 1995, pp. 180–182; P. G. Wilhelm, "Application of Distributive Justice Theory to the CEO Pay Problem: Recommendations for Reform," Journal of Business Ethics, 12(1993): 469–482; J. A. Byrne, L. Bongiorno, and R. Grover, "That Eye-Popping Executive Pay," Business Week, 25 April 1994, pp. 52–58.

motivated to enhance profitability, and "even if they are not so motivated, they must act as if they are if they wish to remain in their positions of authority."[31]

As we can see from the preceding discussion, the issue of whether top managers will attempt to enhance their firms' returns or whether they will pursue a more narrow goal of self-enrichment has not been satisfactorily resolved. Compelling evidence and logic exist on both sides of the controversy. Also unresolved is how motivated top managers are to satisfy the interests of stakeholders beyond the owners of the firm. We turn now to another controversial area—the goals of the board of directors.

### ▪ Goals of Boards of Directors

Legally, boards of directors are responsible for such aspects of corporate leadership as selecting (and replacing) the chief executive officer, setting his or her rewards, advising top management, and monitoring managerial and company performance in order to promote the interests of shareholders. There is evidence, however, that board members have, in many cases, failed to fulfill their legal roles.[32] A common explanation for this failure is that boards have long

---

## STRATEGIC INSIGHT

### *The Growing Responsiveness of Boards*

For years, corporate boards have been referenced as "rubber stamps" for top managers. However, the directors of many prominent corporations have become increasingly responsible to stockholder interests in recent years. Leading the charge has been the increased influence of institutional shareholders, which now control the majority of shares of publicly traded companies. These large investment companies hold substantial numbers of shares in various firms and have the savvy and clout necessary to pressure board members for change.

But many analysts and executives believe that there is still a long way to go. According to David Leighton, former chairman of the board at Nabisco Brands, Ltd., companies need to seek out more independent and better qualified board members. Further, companies make fewer mistakes and earn greater profits when they are governed by active boards. Too often, Leighton claims, the critical issues of strategy and firm growth are not aggressively considered by boards.

In some instances, boards of directors, pressured by institutional investors, have forced the turnover of top managers. For example, GM experienced poor performance during the 1980s and the early 1990s. Between 1981 and 1992, GM's market share declined from 44 to 33 percent. Its 1991 and 1992 losses were record-setting. In 1992, the California Public Employees Retirement System, a significant shareholder, pressured the eleven outside board members (a majority of the fifteen-member board) to reassert strategic control over the firm. As a result, a complete overhaul of senior executives was forced at GM, the first since 1920. GM generated profits in subsequent years.

This incident illustrates that the system of corporate governance many not need overhauling. Rather, the system simply needs to be made to work as intended.

SOURCES: C. Torres, "Firms' Restructuring Often Hurt Foreign Buyers," *Wall Street Journal Interactive Edition*, 13 May 1996; M. L. Weidenbaum, "The Evolving Corporate Board," *Society*, March–April 1995, pp. 9–16; J. W. Lorsch, "Empowering the Board," *Harvard Business Review*, (1995) 73(1): 107–117; *General Motors 1995 Annual Report* (Detroit: General Motors Corporation); R. Litchfield, "Conversation: Board Games," *Canadian Business*, October 1993, pp. 53–55; P. G. Stern, "The Power and the Process," *Directors and Boards*, Spring 1993, pp. 6–9.

been considered "creatures of the CEO."[33] Often, board members are nominated by the CEO, who, in turn, expects the directors to support his or her strategic decisions. For their support, the directors receive generous compensation. One British member of several corporate boards once described board membership as follows:

> No effort of any kind is called for. You go to a meeting once a month in a car supplied by the company. You look both grave and sage, and on two occasions say "I agree," say "I don't think so" once, and if all goes well, you get 500 [pounds] a year. If you have five of them, it is total heaven, like having a permanent hot bath.[34]

Directors sometimes behave in this fashion, not only because they wish to show their loyalty to the CEO, who appoints and compensates them (average annual compensation is more than $50,000 for serving on the board of a major corporation), but also because they often make decisions based primarily on information provided by the CEO.[35] As one CEO put it: "[My board members] often have to have blind faith in management. It would take them a month to really understand some of the decisions they make."[36]

In theory, the primary goal of the board is to safeguard the interests of the stockholders. Technically speaking, board members are elected by the stockholders. In reality, however, stockholders are limited to casting a yes or no vote for each individual nominated to the board by top management. Each nominee's credentials are briefly stated in management's mailed "notice of annual meeting of shareholders," and few stockholders will have much knowledge regarding the nominees beyond these basic facts. Hence, most stockholders will simply follow the recommendations of top management.

Therefore, it is not surprising to find that board members are often beholden to top management for their positions. In such cases, the directors' basic loyalties lie with the CEO rather than with the stockholders. Frequently, this loyalty takes the form of approval of lavish compensation packages for top management. In some cases, these packages may even conceal the actual amounts that top managers receive. For example, stockholders did not know that F. Ross Johnson was granted 40,000 shares of stock before RJR Nabisco was acquired by Kohlberg Kravis Roberts. One account described it as follows:

> Johnson received around $20 million, most of which the shareholders didn't know he had coming until the takeover. . . . Shareholders may not always have a legal right to override the decisions of their own board of directors. But they surely have a right to know what their boards have decided.[37]

Ignoring the stockholders' interests has begun to diminish in recent years, however. The turning point was the 1985 decision by the Delaware Supreme Court that Trans Union Corporation's directors had accepted a takeover bid too quickly. They were accused of failing to read the sales contract before approving it, not soliciting an independent, outside opinion on the fairness of the sales price, and approving the sale of the company in a hasty, two-hour meeting dominated by the CEO. They were held personally liable for the difference between the offer they accepted and the price the company might have received in an open sale. The directors had to pay $13.5 million of the $23.5 million settlement—the excess over their liability insurance coverage.[38]

The pressure on directors to acknowledge stockholder wishes continues to increase. For instance, stockholder suits against directors rose by almost 70 percent over the past fifteen years.[39] But the major source of pressure in recent years has come from institutional investors. These stockholders—chiefly pension funds, mutual funds, and insurance companies—own $1 trillion of stock in U. S. corporations. By virtue of the size of their investments, they wield considerable power and are becoming more active in using it. For example, the California Public Employees' Retirement System and the Pennsylvania Public School Employees' Retirement System recently launched a proxy battle that led Honeywell's management to restructure the company. Considering that institutional investors own large chunks of many major companies (e.g., 82 percent of Lotus Development, 81 percent of Southwest Airlines, and 80 percent of Whirlpool), their potential power is quite impressive.[40]

On the other side, however, it should be emphasized that some board members have played effective stewardship roles. Many directors promote strongly the best interests of the firm's shareholders and various other stakeholder groups as well. Research indicates, for instance, that board members are invaluable sources of environmental information.[41] By conscientiously carrying out their duties, directors can ensure that management does not solely pursue its own interests by focusing management's attention on company performance.[42] Directors do exist who believe that their job is to represent shareholders. For example, the chairman of the board of Compaq Computer states that "the owners of the company should be represented by the directors. That has ceased to happen at lots of companies where management dominates the board."[43] Murray Weidenbaum, an economist who serves on three corporate boards, does not "view the director's role as helping the CEO. The role of the director, the legal obligation, is to represent the shareholders."[44]

## ■ Goals of Creditors

Creditors of a corporation include bondholders, banks, and other financial institutions. Their primary goal is to influence the firm to maintain a healthy financial posture in order to safeguard both the principal and interest on their loaned funds. Recent trends toward acquisitions and mergers that involve financial leverage have given creditors increasingly powerful roles in corporate America. In cases in which heavy debt financing exists, an increasing number of business decisions may be transferred to creditors. Such decisions could include choices as crucial as the selection of top management, the identification of acquisition targets, and the determination of which products to produce and where and how to produce them. Furthermore, as mergers and acquisitions continue, fewer competitors will remain in the marketplace, and many of those who do remain will be heavily financed by creditors.

The increased power of creditors can result in market distortions. For example, now-defunct Pan Am Corporation, which operated one of the oldest fleets of airplanes in the airline industry, was on the brink of bankruptcy for years. Yet in 1989, after losing $2.5 billion over the preceding decade, it tried (but failed) to buy Northwest Airlines—a much larger and more profitable competitor. It could only attempt this through the strong support of a group of creditors—such as Bankers Trust, Morgan Guaranty, Citicorp, and Prudential-Bache—that was willing to provide financing of $2.7 billion.

## ■ Conflicting Goals

It is evident from the preceding discussion that the goals of top managers, boards of directors, and creditors are not always congruent with the goals of the firm's shareholders or other stakeholder groups. Broadly speaking, of course, the goals of all stakeholders are best served when the firm functions as a viable entity. It is then able to supply goods to customers, contribute to society's standard of living, provide employment, and channel financial and nonfinancial benefits to all stakeholders.

We must realize, however, that a viable firm has the power to benefit each stakeholder group differently. For instance, tough bargaining with suppliers will transfer benefits from suppliers to stockholders, managers, and customers. Shirking responsibility for controlling environmental pollution transfers benefits from society (because the general public bears the costs of pollution) to a number of stakeholders who benefit from the financial savings. Bestowing extremely generous compensation on top management transfers benefits from stockholders, employees, and customers to upper-level managers.

Perhaps the most common suggestion for making the goals of top management and stockholders more congruent is to award shares of stock or stock options to top management. The rationale is that significant stock ownership would align the interests of top management with the interests of shareholders. Select scholars have theoretically argued[45] and empirically found[46] that as managerial ownership rises, the interests of managers and shareholders begin to converge. Other scholars have concluded that interests of top managers and shareholders have become more congruent with managerial ownership only up to a point.[47] When managers are major shareholders, however, they become entrenched and may adopt strategies that are beneficial to themselves but not necessarily to the shareholders.[48] Attempts to align the interests of upper-level management with those of other stakeholder groups have also been negatively imposed through lawsuits—that is, fines imposed on the firm by various public agencies and court decisions.

## CORPORATE GOVERNANCE

Although top managers are charged with creating wealth for shareholders through strategies that are meant to satisfy the needs of the various stakeholders, these managers may not always comply with their responsibilities. Consequently, publicly traded firms have **corporate governance** systems. Corporate governance refers to the board of directors, institutional investors (e.g., pension and retirement funds, mutual funds, banks, insurance companies, among other money managers), and blockholders (individuals or families with significant shareholdings) who monitor firm strategies to ensure managerial responsiveness.

Boards of directors and institutional investors should be the most influential in the governance systems. Boards of directors represent the owners of the firm and are legally authorized to monitor firm strategies. They are also responsible for the selection, evaluation, and compensation of top managers. Institutional investors own more than half of all shares of publicly traded firms; therefore, they are influential because of their substantial ownership. Although blockholders are significant shareholders, they are less influential because their ownership ordinarily is less than 20 percent and some of them are passive investors.[49]

Professor Walter Salmon of Harvard has observed that prior to the 1990s, boards of directors normally tolerated mediocre management.[50] Board members were reduced to damage control in response to demands for restructuring and objections of shareholders against unworthy acquisitions through corporate assumption of substantial debt.[51] Moreover, from the 1960s through the middle of the 1970s, senior management comprised the majority of board membership. From the mid-1970s to the 1990s, however, the presence of senior managers on boards of directors has been reduced—from an average of five insiders (senior managers who are board members) and eight outsiders (board members from outside the firm) to an average of three insiders and nine outsiders. This has enabled board members to more effectively oversee managerial decisions.[52]

Because institutional investors are majority owners of publicly traded firms, on the one hand they face increased pressure to influence managerial strategies in order to push for national competitiveness and social causes as well as to promote the enhancement of firm value. On the other hand, institutional investors have been criticized for becoming too involved in influencing managerial strategies. The CEO of Contel, Charles Wohlstetter, for instance, has argued that although institutional investors are increasingly in control of large firms, they have no managerial skills, "no experience in selecting directors, no believable judgment in how much should be spent for research and marketing—in fact, no experience except that which they have accumulated controlling other people's money."[53]

A working group of experts, representing both large publicly traded corporations and leading institutional investors, has made a number of recommendations on how to promote an effective governance system. For the board of directors, the recommendations include that outside directors should be the only ones to evaluate the performance of top managers against established mission and goals; that all outside board members should meet alone at least once annually; and that boards of directors should establish appropriate qualifications for board membership (and shareholders should be informed of these qualifications). For institutional shareholders, the suggestions include that institutions (and other shareholders) should act as owners and not just investors; that they should not interfere with day-to-day managerial decisions; that they should evaluate the performance of the board of directors regularly; and that they should recognize that the prosperity of the firm benefits all shareholders.[54]

## STAKEHOLDERS AND TAKEOVERS

What happens when top managers of a firm with ineffective board members continue to mismanage the firm? In such cases of mismanagement, institutional investors, blockholders, and other shareholders may sell their shares, depressing the market price of the company's stock. Depressed prices often attract takeover attempts, as is discussed in the following paragraphs.

### ■ An Overview

Any firm whose stock is publicly traded faces the possibility of a takeover. Depending upon the form in which a takeover occurs, different groups of stakeholders will be affected in various ways.

A **takeover** refers to the purchase of a significant number of shares of a firm by an individual, a group of investors, or another organization. Takeovers may be attempted by outsiders or insiders.

Attempts to take over a company by those outside the organization may be friendly or unfriendly. A friendly takeover is one in which both the buyer and seller desire the transaction. In recent years, General Electric's takeover of RCA, Disney's takeover of Capital Cities/ABC, and Greyhound's takeover of Trailways illustrate friendly takeovers. An unfriendly takeover is one in which the target firm resists the sale. Examples of unfriendly takeovers include Carl Icahn's successful bid for TWA and Sir James Goldsmith's unsuccessful bid for Goodyear.[55]

Unfriendly takeovers are sometimes precipitated by **raiders**—individuals who believe that the way a company is being managed can be significantly improved. Raiders purchase a large number of shares in the target firm either to force a change in top management personnel or to manage the firm themselves.

Other reasons for takeovers by outsiders include acquisitions by investors or creditors for financial purposes or acquisitions by another firm for strategic reasons. For example, Chrysler's takeover of American Motors several years ago provided Chrysler with immediate expansion of product lines, production capacity, and market share.

Transfer of ownership to organizational insiders, such as employees or top managers, may occur gradually through special types of takeovers known as **employee stock ownership plans (ESOPs).** Since the enactment of a tax law in 1974 that encouraged ESOPs, many closely held firms (those with only a few stockholders whose shares are not traded publicly) have been partially turned over to their managers and employees. This process usually begins when the principal owner of the closely held firm retires or when an ESOP plan is developed as a benefit or motivational incentive for the firm's employees. As the employees receive more and more shares of stock over a period of time, the ownership of the firm is gradually turned over to them.

The transfer of ownership to insiders may also occur suddenly through a takeover by the firm's employees or top managers. In one of the most publicized takeover attempts in American business, F. Ross Johnson, the CEO of RJR Nabisco, and his top management group attempted to take the firm private (concentrate its ownership in their hands). However, their bids were topped by the investment firm of Kohlberg Kravis, which paid about $25 billion for the firm.

Sudden takeover attempts often (but not always) rely heavily on borrowed funds to finance the acquisition. Borrowing funds to purchase a firm is referred to as a **leveraged buyout (LBO).** When a takeover is financed in this fashion, the company is burdened with heavy debt, which must be paid back either by funds generated from operations or by the sale of company assets, such as subsidiaries or product divisions.

## ■ Pros and Cons

Takeovers have been both defended and criticized. Their defense generally consists of pointing out the useful role that takeovers play in replacing ineffective management. For instance, T. Boone Pickens Jr., a renowned corporate raider, has argued:

After decades of sovereign autonomy, the professional managers of many large, publicly held corporations are finding themselves on the firing line. They are being asked to justify lackluster performance and questionable strategies. They are being called on to address the chronic undervaluation of their securities.[56]

Takeovers have been criticized from several perspectives. One argument is that the primary goal of some takeover attempts is for the raider to make short-term profits. Even the bidder who ultimately loses out to a higher bidder usually pockets a considerable profit because of the increase in the stock's price brought about by the bidding. In some cases, management will attempt to take the firm private, usually through an LBO, to prevent the unfriendly takeover. This action will limit the firm's future strategic options because it must make heavy interest payments on its newly acquired debt for many years. These payments make it difficult for the firm to finance research and development activities, to explore new markets, and to promote and advertise its goods and services.

Bondholders, too, suffer from LBOs. As company debt increases following an LBO, the firm's bonds become more risky, since their ultimate redemption is less certain. This increase in risk results in a deterioration of the credit rating of the firm's bonds and a loss of value to the bondholders.

Finally, most takeovers are followed by layoffs of employees and managers. But more than those employees and their families are affected. For example, when Gulf Oil was taken over by Chevron, Gulf's Pittsburgh headquarters was closed. Nearly 6,000 employees either were transferred from Pittsburgh or were fired. This move had a significant negative impact on the many Pittsburgh-area firms that supplied various products and services to Gulf. Additionally, the city suffered because of lower tax revenues, and the price of real estate throughout the city declined.

For these reasons, some states have passed laws that protect their firms from takeovers. For example, when T. Boone Pickens attempted, in 1987, an unfriendly takeover of Boeing, the largest employer in the state of Washington, a bill was passed by state legislators that put a five-year ban on the sale of Boeing's assets to pay off creditors. This act effectively nullified Pickens's bid, because his only way to repay the debt he would incur in buying the company was to sell off some of its assets.

## SOCIAL RESPONSIBILITY AND ETHICS

One of an organization's primary goals is its obligation to operate in a socially responsible manner. This section examines corporate social responsibility and the related area of managerial ethics.

### ■ Corporate Social Responsibility

Our society grants considerable freedom to business organizations. In return, businesses are expected to operate in a manner consistent with society's interests. **Social responsibility** refers to the expectation that business firms should act in the public interest. Certainly, businesses have always been expected to provide employment for individuals and to provide goods and services for customers. But social responsibility implies more than that. Today, society expects business to help preserve the environment, to sell safe products, to treat its employees equitably, to be truthful with its customers, and, in some cases, to go even further by training the hard-core unemployed, contributing to education and the arts, and helping revitalize urban slum areas.

Some observers, ranging from Adam Smith to Milton Friedman, have argued that social responsibility should not be part of management's decision-making process.[57] Friedman has maintained that business functions best when it sticks to its primary mission—profitably producing goods and services within society's legal restrictions. Indeed, its sole responsibility is to attempt to maximize returns. When it goes further than that by tackling social problems, business is spending money that should more properly be returned to its stockholders. The stockholders, who have rightfully earned the money, should be able to spend that money as they see fit, and their spending priorities may differ from those of business.

In reality, however, business is part of society, and its actions have both economic and social ramifications. It would be practically impossible to isolate the business decisions of corporations from their economic and social consequences. For instance, Federal Express's insistence that its South African partners, XPS Services, employ a 50/50 ratio of minority and white managers and Microsoft's development of an internship program for South Africans at its U.S. headquarters advance the social aims of both the South African and the U.S. governments.[58]

In fact, top managers may find a number of areas where their interests, various stakeholders' interests, and society's interests are mutually compatible.[59] For example, a firm that pollutes the atmosphere because it fails to purchase costly antipollution equipment is harming not only society but also, ultimately, its own stakeholders. With a polluted environment, the quality of life of the firm's stockholders, directors, managers, employees, suppliers, customers, and creditors suffers. As another example, if businesses do not contribute to the education of young people, their recruitment efforts will suffer and they will eventually experience a decline in the quality of their work force. This result benefits no group of stakeholders.

Many government regulations over business operations came into being because some firms refused to be socially responsible. Had organizations not damaged the environment, sold unsafe products, discriminated against some employees, and engaged in untruthful advertising, laws in these areas would not have been necessary. The threat of ever more government regulation exists unless companies operate in a manner consistent with society's well-being.

Ideally, then, firms that are socially responsible are those that are able to operate profitably while simultaneously benefiting society. But realistically, it is not always clear exactly what is good for society. For example, society's needs for high employment and the production of desired goods and services must be balanced against the pollution and industrial wastes that are generated by these operations. Despite these difficulties, however, many firms in their annual reports express, at least in general terms, how they are socially responsible. General Motors, for instance, has published an annual *Public Interest Report* for more than twenty years. A recent issue described GM's efforts in such areas as clean air, ozone depletion, global warming, waste management, automotive safety, minority programs, philanthropic activities, higher quality products, and greater operating efficiency.

---

S T R A T E G I C     I N S I G H T

## Social Responsibility at GM

Each year, GM publishes a *Philanthropic Annual Report* and an *Environmental Report* detailing its corporate activities in the area of social responsibility. A few of the more noteworthy activities in which GM is involved are listed here:

- In 1995, GM made charitable contributions in excess of $55 million, including $4.4 million to United Way chapters.
- In 1994, GM provided 842 scholarships, totaling more than $1.8 million, to outstanding business and engineering students.
- GM has entered into a partnership with The Nature Conservancy, an international environmental organization, in which GM will spend $1 million annually to assist in the preservation of land and water systems in North America, Latin America, the Caribbean, and the Asia/Pacific region.
- Under the GM Mobility Program for Persons with Disabilities, GM will reimburse up to $1,000 of the cost of any aftermarket adaptive driving equipment or passenger aids installed in a GM vehicle.

GM works in conjunction with the University of Michigan and local public schools to implement the Global Rivers Environmental Education Network (GREEN) in GM plant cities worldwide. GREEN is designed to teach students to monitor water quality, analyze watershed usage, and identify the socioeconomic determinants of river degradation.

GM contributed more than $600,000 to assist victims of the Midwest floods in the summer of 1993, and (with the United Auto Workers) contributed more than $1.4 million to the American Red Cross and Salvation Army to assist victims of the January 1994 earthquake in Southern California.

All of GM's Mexican operations support local charities to improve education and health care.

SOURCES: G. Collins, "G.M. to Sponsor AIDS Supplement," *New York Times*, 26 April 1995, p. D9; *General Motors Environmental Report 1995* (Detroit: General Motors Corporation); *GM Philanthropic Annual Report 1994* (Detroit: General Motors Corporation); *General Motors Public Interest Report 1994* (Detroit: General Motors Corporation).

---

## ■ Managerial Ethics

Closely related to issues of corporate social responsibility are the ethics of individual managers. **Ethics** refers to standards of conduct and moral judgment—that is, whether managers' decisions and behaviors are right or wrong. (Table 3.3 presents two companies' views of ethical behavior.) What is morally right or wrong, of course, has been argued since the beginning of civilization, and as we might expect, there are few generally accepted global standards of ethical behavior. Even in the same nation, various people may look at ethical issues from different perspectives. Over the past several years, for example, many American corporations have "restructured" to become more competitive. Part of the restructuring process inevitably involves mass layoffs of employees. Is it right to lay off employees so that a company can compete more effectively with foreign firms and—in essence—assure its survival, or is it wrong to put people with family and financial responsibilities and obligations out of work?

Ethical behavior can be viewed in several different ways. First, it may be considered from the perspective of self-interest. Adam Smith proposed that if each individual pursued his or her own economic self-interests, society as a whole would benefit. Milton Friedman, as mentioned earlier, believed that

**Table 3.3**                    **Codes of Ethics**

---

*A Large Business: Electronic Data Systems (EDS)\**

---

We conduct EDS' business in accordance with both the letter and spirit of the applicable laws of the United States and of those foreign countries in which EDS does business. We will conduct our business in the center of the field of ethical behavior—not along the sidelines, skirting the boundaries. . . . We must be honest in all our relationships and must avoid even the appearance of illegal or unethical conduct. For example, no employee of EDS will give or receive bribes or kickbacks; make improper political contributions; abuse proprietary or trade secret information, whether EDS' or our suppliers', business partners' or customers'; or misuse the company's funds and assets. . . .

The success of EDS rests directly on the quality of our people and our services. The integrity of all our people is an essential part of this quality that we offer to our customers. If our integrity ever became suspect, the future of EDS would be in jeopardy. . . .

When in doubt, measure your conduct against this Golden Rule of Business Ethics: Could you do business in complete trust with someone who acts the way you do? The answer must be YES.

*A Small Business: Schilling Enterprises (operates automobile dealerships in Tennessee and Arkansas and a heating/air-conditioning distributorship in Alabama)\*\**

---

Schilling's Guiding Principles:

- Practice honesty, integrity and fairness in everything we do.
- Assure every customer receives value, quality, and satisfaction.
- Create an environment in which our employees can succeed.
- Return to the community a share of the success we experience.
- Consistently promote these principles through our Christian behavior.

---

*\*Excerpted from EDS Code of Conduct.*

*\*\*Excerpt from statements made to the authors by Harry Smith, chairperson of the board, and Rex Jones, president of Schilling Enterprises.*

firms that attempt to maximize their returns within the legal regulations of society behave ethically.

Smith and Friedman viewed ethics economically, but Charles Darwin approached the issue from a biological perspective. In this sense, ethics can be explained implicitly in terms of survival of the fittest. Some species survive at the expense of other species. The survivors are those who are either instinctively or deterministically able to structure compatible fits with their environments. Ethical behavior, in a Darwinian sense, then, may encompass survival of one at the expense of the destruction of another. Hence, self-interest is at the heart of the approaches of Darwin, Smith, and Friedman. It is ethical to take care of oneself.

A second way of viewing ethics also involves the concept of self-interest, but in a broader sense. From this perspective, if an individual always promotes his or her interests at the expense of others, eventually the individual will be isolated by others. Selfish children find themselves without playmates, just as selfish managers are unable to fully secure the cooperation of their employees, peers or supervisor. Hence, individuals should be concerned with the welfare of others because it serves their own interests in the long run.

A third common perspective of ethics bases the concepts of right and wrong on religious beliefs. In the United States, the strongest religious tradition is the Judeo-Christian heritage, although other religious viewpoints also prevail. From this perspective, it is "God's will" for individuals to behave in ways that benefit others. Behaving in a correct manner involves treating other people as one would wish to be treated. The concept of selfishness is frowned upon, and individuals are cautioned against ignoring the plight of others who are less fortunate.

Another view of ethics differs from all of the preceding by holding that human beings are inherently concerned with others. This concern is not based on either selfish or religious reasons but is simply a natural condition of humankind. In wars, soldiers help the wounded at the expense of their own lives. In natural disasters, individuals sacrifice their own lives in attempts to save others. Such naturally unselfish behavior is not without precedent, for it also occurs outside the domain of human beings. Certain species of animals, such as elephants, dolphins, and bison, routinely show great concern for the welfare of their family members, even to the point of protecting them with their own lives.

However ethical behavior is viewed, evidence exists that ethical operations may be related to organizational success. For instance, in certain parts of the country, Quaker and Mennonite entrepreneurs are often successful because of their reputations for being conscientious, reliable, trustworthy, and willing to stand behind their firms' products or services. And some institutional investors invest only in stocks that represent firms known for their high social and ethical standards. In brief, behavior that is ethically considerate of other stakeholders and socially responsible makes good business sense.

## SUMMARY

Underlying the organization's mission is an analysis of its internal strengths and weaknesses in the context of the external opportunities and threats. A firm's strengths and weaknesses reside in its human, organizational, and physical resources. Ideally, these resources work together to give the firm a sustained competitive advantage.

Organizations are founded for a particular purpose, known as the organization's mission. The mission, at the corporate level, is stated in fairly broad terms but is sufficiently precise to give direction to the organization. At the business unit level, the mission is narrower in scope and more clearly defined. It is essential that an organization carefully understand its mission, because a clear sense of purpose is necessary for an organization to establish appropriate goals.

Goals represent the desired general ends toward which organizational efforts are directed. From the organization's goals, management formulates objectives—specific, verifiable versions of goals. However, various stakeholder groups, because of their own interests, will desire different goals for the firm. Because of the diversity of these interests, top management faces the difficult task of attempting to reconcile and satisfy the interests of each of the stakeholder groups while pursuing its own set of goals.

Controversy exists over the extent to which top management actually attempts to enhance return on the stockholders' investment. One viewpoint argues that top managers pursue strategies, such as increasing the size of their firm, that ultimately increase their own rewards. Another proposes that top management's interests coincide with those of the firm's stockholders for various reasons.

Controversy also exists over the extent to which boards of directors serve as "creatures of the CEO" versus the degree to which they represent the interests of the stockholders. Certainly, recent legal trends have emphasized the boards' stewardship of the stockholders' interests. Publicly traded firms have corporate governance, which monitors firm strategies to ensure managerial responsiveness. Components of corporate governance are the board of directors, institutional investors, and blockholders.

Stakeholder groups are affected by corporate takeovers. Their impact differs, depending upon whether the takeover is friendly or unfriendly and whether it is engineered by outsiders or insiders. Takeovers, from a societal viewpoint, have both defenders and critics.

Of considerable concern in the strategic decision-making process are the concepts of corporate social responsibility and managerial ethics. Social responsibility refers to the extent to which business firms should act in the public interest while conducting their operations. Ethical considerations involve questions of moral judgment in managerial decision making and behavior. Society today demands that companies operate in a socially responsible manner and that managers exhibit high ethical behavior.

## TAKE IT TO THE NET

We invite you to visit the Wright page on the Prentice Hall Web site at:

**http://www.prenhall.com/wright**

for this chapter's World Wide Web exercise.

## KEY CONCEPTS

**Corporate governance**  The board of directors, institutional investors, and blockholders who monitor firm strategies to ensure managerial responsiveness.

**Employee stock ownership plan (ESOP)**  A formal program, administered by a trust, that transfers ownership of a corporation—through shares of stock—to its employees. The program is usually initiated by the organization's owners for financial, tax, and/or motivational reasons.

**Ethics**   Standards of conduct and moral judgment.

**Goals**   Desired general ends toward which efforts are directed.

**Human resources**   The experience, capabilities, knowledge, skills, and judgment of the firm's employees.

**Leveraged buyout (LBO)**   A takeover in which the acquiring party borrows funds to purchase the firm. The resulting interest payments and principal are paid back by funds generated from operations and/or the sale of company assets.

**Mission**   The reason for an organization's existence.

**Mission statement**   A broadly defined but enduring statement of purpose that identifies the scope of an organization's operations and its offerings to the various stakeholders.

**Objective**   A specific, verifiable, and often quantified version of a goal.

**Organizational resources**   The firm's systems and processes, including its strategies, structure, culture, purchasing/materials management, production/operations, financial base, research and development, marketing, information systems, and control systems.

**Physical resources**   An organization's plant and equipment, geographic locations, access to raw materials, distribution network, and technology.

**Raider**   An individual who attempts to take over a company because he or she believes that its management can be significantly improved. Raiders purchase a large number of shares in the target firm either to force a change in top management personnel or to manage the firm themselves.

**Social responsibility**   The expectation that business firms should act in the public interest.

**Sustained competitive advantage**   A firm's valuable strategies that cannot be fully duplicated by its competitors and that result in high financial returns over a lengthy period of time.

**S.W.O.T. analysis**   An analysis intended to match the firm's strengths and weaknesses (the $S$ and $W$ in the name) with the opportunities and threats (the $O$ and $T$) posed by the environment.

**Takeover**   The purchase of a significant number of shares in a firm by an individual, a group of investors, or another organization. Takeovers may be friendly—in which both the buyer and the seller desire the transaction—or unfriendly—in which the target firm resists the sale.

# DISCUSSION QUESTIONS

1. Do corporate-level missions and business unit missions usually change over time? Why or why not?

2. Explain the relationship between an organization's mission and its strategy.

3. Explain the difference between a goal and an objective. Give an example of each, different from those given in the text.

4. Why is it essential that objectives be verifiable?

5. Why do various groups that are stakeholders in the same organization have different goals? Should they not all be pulling together in the same direction?

6. How might the goals of top management differ from those of the firm's board of directors? How might they be similar?

7. What might be the impact of a takeover on various stakeholder groups?

8. What are the risks for the acquiring party in a leveraged buyout?

9. Explain the relationship between managerial decisions and social responsibility.

10. Explain the relationship between managerial decisions and ethics.

# STRATEGIC MANAGEMENT EXERCISES

1. Select a well-known company about which there is a considerable amount of published information. Using Table 3.1 and the question on human, organizational, and physical resources as your outline, conduct a S.W.O.T. analysis for this firm. (Note that you may be unable to address all of the issues covered in the chapter because of a lack of information, and as you conduct your research, you may be able to identify factors not addressed in the chapter.) Explain your rationale.

2. Select a particular type of business that you may wish to start.

   a. Develop a written mission statement for that business.
   b. Construct a set of goals for the business.
   c. From the set of goals developed in part (b), formulate specific, verifiable objectives.
   d. Devise a statement of social responsibility for the business.

3. Select a company that has a written mission statement. Evaluate its mission statement along each of the following criteria:

   a. Is the mission statement all-encompassing yet relatively brief?
   b. Does the mission statement delineate, in broad terms, what products or services the firm is to offer?
   c. Does the mission statement define the company's geographical operating parameters (whether it will conduct business locally, regionally, nationally, or internationally)?
   d. Is the mission statement consistent as it moves from the corporate level to the business unit level?
   e. Is the mission statement consistent with the company's actual activities and competitive prospects at the corporate level? (For instance, Chrysler's mission of using its technology to operate both in the automobile industry and in the defense industry failed to match its competitive stance. Facing powerful international competition in the automobile industry required Chrysler to concentrate totally on that industry. As a result, it was forced to sell its nonvehicle businesses.)
   f. Is the mission statement consistent with the company's actual activities and competitive prospects at the business unit level? (For instance, GM's mission of providing quality outputs matches the operation of its Electronic Data Systems business unit, but the quality of its vehicle products has been questioned over the years by many industry observers and customers.)

# NOTES

1. P. Sellers, "Who Cares About Shareholders?" *Fortune*, 15 June 1992, p. 122.

2. J. Barney, "Firm Resources and Sustained Competitive Advantage," *Journal of Management* 17 (1991): 99–120; A. Lado, N. Boyd, and P. Wright, "A Competency-Based Model of Sustainable Competitive Advantage: Toward a Conceptual Integration," *Journal of Management* 18 (1992): 77–91.

3. R. Jacob, "The Search for the Organization of Tomorrow," *Fortune*, 18 May 1992, p. 93. Also see O. Nodoushani, "The Professional Ideal in Management History," *Human Systems Management* 14 (1995): 335–345.

4. J. A. Pearce II, "The Company Mission as a Strategic Tool," *Sloan Management Review* 23 (Spring 1982): 15.

5. See A. Davidson, "Frank Barlow," *Management Today*, February 1994, pp. 50–54.

6. J. K. Clemens, "A Lesson from 431 B.C." *Fortune*, 13 October 1986, p. 164.

7. G. Fuchsberg, "Visioning Mission Becomes Its Own Mission," *Wall Street Journal*, 7 January 1994, p. B1.

8. J. D. Duck, "Managing Change: The Art of Balancing," *Harvard Business Review* 71 (1993): 109–118. See also P. Strebel, "Why Do Employees Resist Change?" *Harvard Business Review* 74 (1996): 86–92.

9. G. Brooks, "Some Concerns Find That the Push to Diversify Was a Costly Mistake," *Wall Street Journal*, 2 October 1984, p. B1.

10. G. Stalk, P. Evans, and L. E. Shulman, "Competing on Capabilities: The New Rules for Corporate Strategy," *Harvard Business Review* 70 (1992): 57–69.

11. M. Schrage, "Consultant's Maxim for Management: Ignore Markets, Build on Competence," *Washington Post*, 17 May 1991, p. 12.

12. For an example of his early work, see R. Nader, *Unsafe at Any Speed: Design and Dangers of the American Automobile* (New York: Grossman, 1964).

13. D. O. McKee, R. Varadarajan, and W. M. Pride, "Strategic Adaptability and Firm Performance: A Market Contingent Perspective," *Journal of Marketing* 53 (1989): 21–35.

14. H. A. Simon, "On the Concept of Organizational Goal," *Administrative Science Quarterly* 9 (1964): 1–22; J. Pfeffer and G. Salancik, *The External Control of Organizations* (New York: Harper & Row, 1978).

15. R. M. Cyert and J. G. March, *A Behavioral Theory of the Firm* (Englewood Cliffs, N.J.: Prentice Hall, 1963); J. G. March and H. A. Simon, *Organizations* (New York: John Wiley & Sons, 1958).

16. M. Kroll, P. Wright, L. Toombs, and H. Leavell, "Form of Control: A Critical Determinant of Acquisition Performance and CEO Rewards," *Strategic Management Journal* (in press).

17. H. A. Simon, "The Compensation of Executives," *Sociometry* 20 (1957): 32–35.

18. D. R. Roberts, "A General Theory of Executive Compensation Based on Statistically Tested Propositions," *Quarterly Journal of Economics* 20 (1956): 270–294.

19. K. J. Murphy, "Corporate Performance and Managerial Remuneration: An Empirical Analysis," *Journal of Accounting and Economics* 7 (1985): 11–42; Aoki, *Co-Operative Game Theory of the Firm*; A. A. Berle and G. C. Means, *The Modern Corporation and Private Property*, rev. ed. (New York: Harcourt, Brace & World, 1968).

20. G. P. Baker, M. C. Jensen, and K. J. Murphy, "Compensation and Incentives: Practice vs. Theory," *Journal of Finance* 43 (1988): 609.

21. D. J. Teece, "Towards an Economic Theory of the Multiproduct Firm," *Journal of Economic Behavior and Organization* 3 (1982): 39–63.

22. H. A. Simon, *Administrative Behavior* (New York: Macmillan, 1957).

23. M. Kroll, P. Wright, L. Toombs, and H. Leavell, "Form of Control: A Critical Determinant of Acquisition Performance and CEO Rewards," *Strategic Management Journal* 18(1997): 85–96.

24. Ibid.

25. E. F. Fama, "Agency Problems and the Theory of the Firm," *Journal of Political Economy* 88 (1980): 288–307.

26. Y. Amihud, J. Y. Kamin, and J. Romen, "Managerialism, Ownerism, and Risk," *Journal of Banking and Finance* 7 (1983): 189–196.

27. Fama, "Agency Problems and the Theory of the Firm."

28. J. Child, *The Business Enterprise in Modern Industrial Society* (London: Collier-Macmillan, 1969).

29. D. R. James and M. Soref, "Profit Constraints on Managerial Autonomy: Managerial Theory and the Unmaking of the Corporation President," *American Sociological Review* 46 (1981): 1–18.

30. Ibid., p. 3.

31. Ibid.

32. J. Bacon, *Corporate Directorship Practices: Membership and Committees of the Board* (New York: The Conference Board, 1973); J. C. Baker, *Directors and Their Functions* (Cambridge: Harvard University Press, 1945); Berle and Means, *The Modern Corporation and Private Property*; B. K. Boyd, "Board Control and CEO Compensation," *Strategic Management Journal* 15 (1994): 335–344; C. C. Brown and E. E. Smith, *The Director Looks at His Job* (New York: Columbia University Press, 1957); E. J. Epstein, *Who Owns the Corporation? Management vs. Shareholders* (New

York: Priority Press, 1986); J. M. Juran and J. K. Louden, *The Corporate Director* (New York: American Management Association, 1966); H. Koontz, *The Board of Directors and Effective Management* (New York: McGraw-Hill, 1967); J. K. Louden, *The Director: A Professional's Guide to Effective Board Work* (New York: Amacom, 1982); M. L. Mace, *Directors: Myth and Reality* (Cambridge: Harvard University Press, 1971); O. E. Williamson, *The Economics of Discretionary Behavior: Managerial Objectives in a Theory of the Firm* (Englewood Cliffs, N.J.: Prentice Hall, 1964); S. G. Winter, "Economic Natural Selection and the Theory of the Firm," *Yale Economic Essays* 4 (1964): 225–231.

33. A. Patton and J. C. Baker, "Why Won't Directors Rock the Boat?" *Harvard Business Review* 65, no. 6 (1987): 10–18.

34. L. Herzel, R. W. Shepro, and L. Katz, "Next-to-the-Last Word on Endangered Directors," *Harvard Business Review* 65, no. 1 (1987): 38.

35. C. Loh, "The Influence of Outside Directors on the Adoption of Poison Pills," *Quarterly Journal of Business and Economics* 33, no. 1 (1994): 3–11.

36. S. P. Sherman, "Pushing Corporate Boards to Be Better," *Fortune*, 18 July 1988, p. 60.

37. G. S. Crystal and F. T. Vincent Jr., "Take the Mystery Out of CEO Pay," *Fortune*, 24 April 1989, p. 220.

38. M. Galen, "A Seat on the Board Is Getting Hotter," *Business Week,* 3 July 1989, p. 72; Sherman, "Pushing Corporate Boards to Be Better," p. 62.

39. W. E. Green, "Directors' Insurance: How Good a Shield?" *Wall Street Journal*, 14 August 1989.

40. B. D. Fromson, "The Big Owners Roar," *Fortune,* 30 July 1990, pp. 66–78.

41. J. Pfeffer, "Size, Composition, and Function of Hospital Boards of Directors: A Study of Organization-Environment Linkage," *Administrative Science Quarterly* 18 (1973): 349–364; Pfeffer and Salancik, *External Control of Organizations*; and K. G. Provan, "Board Power and Organizational Effectiveness Among Human Service Agencies," *Academy of Management Journal* 23 (1980): 221–236; J. Goldstein, K. Gautum, and W. Boeker, "The Effects of Board Size and Diversity on Strategic Change," *Strategic Management Journal* 15 (1994): 241–250.

42. M. S. Mizruchi, "Who Controls Whom? An Examination of the Relation Between Management and Board of Directors in Large American Corporations," *Academy of Management Review* 8 (1983): 426–435.

43. Sherman, "Pushing Corporate Boards to Be Better," p. 58.

44. Ibid., p. 60.

45. M. C. Jensen and W. H. Meckling, "Theory of the Firm: Managerial Behavior, Agency Cost and Ownership Structure," *Journal of Financial Economics* 3 (1976): 305–360.

46. S. L. Oswald and J. S. Jahera, "The Influence of Ownership on Performance: An Empirical Study," *Strategic Management Journal* 12 (1991): 321–326.

47. J. J. McConnell and H. Servaes, "Additional Evidence on Equity Ownership and Corporate Value," *Journal of Financial Economics* 27 (1990): 595–612; R. A. Morck, A. Shleifer, and R. Vishny, "Managerial Ownership and Market Valuation: An Empirical Analysis," *Journal of Financial Economics* 20 (1988): 293–315.

48. P. Wright, S. P. Ferris, A. Sarin, and V. Awasthi, "Impact of Corporate Insider, Blockholder, and Institutional Equity Ownership on Firm Risk Taking," *Academy of Management Journal* 39 (1996): 441–463.

49. J. J. McConnell and H. Servaes, "Additional Evidence on Equity Ownership and Corporate Value," *Journal of Financial Economics* 27 (1990): 595–612; A. Shleifer and R. Vishny, "Large Shareholders and Corporate Control," *Journal of Political Economy* 94 (1986): 461–488.

50. W. J. Salmon, "Crisis Prevention: How to Gear Up Your Board," *Harvard Business Review* 71 (1993): 68–75.

51. Ibid.

52. *Harvard Business Review*, The Working Group on Corporate Governance, "A New Compact for Owners and Directors," *Harvard Business Review* 69 (1991): 141–143.

53. C. Wohlstetter, "Pension Fund Socialism: Can Bureaucrats Run the Blue Chips?" *Harvard Business Review* 71 (1993): 78.

54. *Harvard Business Review* (1991).

55. T. B. Pickens Jr., "Professions of a Short-Termer," *Harvard Business Review* 64, no. 3 (1986): 75.

56. Ibid.

57. A. Smith, *An Inquiry into the Nature and Causes of the Wealth of Nations* (Chicago: Encyclopedia Britannica, 1952); M. Friedman, "The Social Responsibility of Business Is to Increase Its Profits," *New York Times Magazine*, 13 September 1970, pp. 33, 122–125.

58. B. Bremmer, A. Fine, and J. Weber, "Doing the Right Thing in South Africa?" *Business Week*, 27 April 1992, pp. 60, 64.

59. C. Smith, "The New Corporate Philanthropy," *Harvard Business Review* 72 (May/June 1994), 105–116; For further discussion, see M. B. E. Clarkson, "A Stakeholder Framework for Analyzing and Evaluating Corporate Social Performance," *Academy of Management Review* 20 (1995): 92–117.

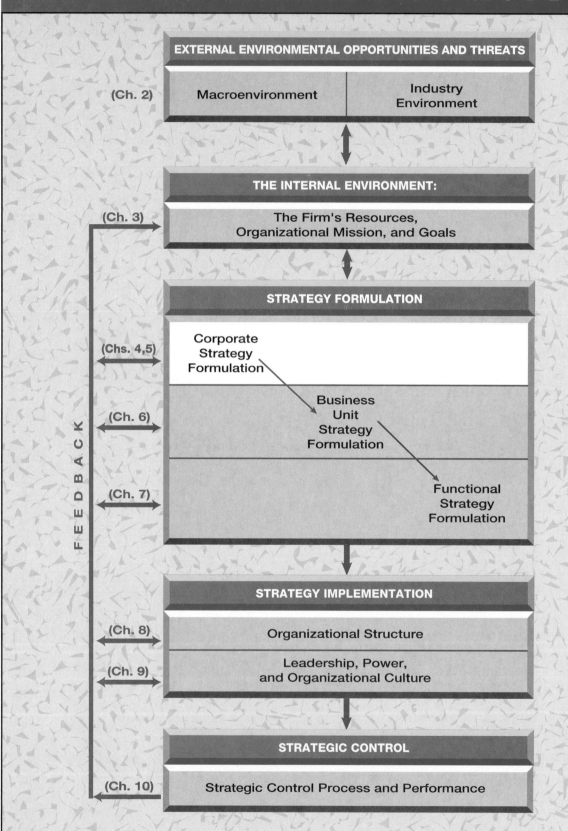

# STRATEGIC MANAGEMENT MODEL

**EXTERNAL ENVIRONMENTAL OPPORTUNITIES AND THREATS**

(Ch. 2)  Macroenvironment | Industry Environment

**THE INTERNAL ENVIRONMENT:**

(Ch. 3)  The Firm's Resources, Organizational Mission, and Goals

**STRATEGY FORMULATION**

(Chs. 4,5)  Corporate Strategy Formulation

(Ch. 6)  Business Unit Strategy Formulation

(Ch. 7)  Functional Strategy Formulation

**STRATEGY IMPLEMENTATION**

(Ch. 8)  Organizational Structure

(Ch. 9)  Leadership, Power, and Organizational Culture

**STRATEGIC CONTROL**

(Ch. 10)  Strategic Control Process and Performance

FEEDBACK

# 4 Corporate-Level Strategies

Once the organization's mission, goals, and objectives are delineated, as was discussed in the preceding chapter, top management can formulate the firm's strategy. Strategy exists at three levels: the corporate level, the business unit level, and the functional level. The focus of this chapter and the one following it is **corporate-level strategy**—the strategy top management formulates for the overall corporation. The subsequent two chapters will discuss business unit and functional strategies. Although each of these chapters emphasizes strategy at a separate level, in reality, all three levels are closely intertwined.

At the corporate level, the basic strategic question facing top management is, In what particular businesses or industries should we be operating? The answer to this question depends upon the firm's particular strengths and weaknesses and the opportunities and threats posed by the external environment. This chapter explores strategic alternatives at the corporate level.

Although in this and the next chapter we primarily focus on strategic alternatives and portfolio management at the corporate level, we initially discuss a phenomenon that has been in vogue in the 1980s and the 1990s—corporate restructuring. The study of corporate restructuring goes back several decades although it has received greater emphasis since the 1980s.

## CORPORATE RESTRUCTURING

**Corporate restructuring** may include a broad set of decisions and actions, such as changing the organization of work itself in the firm, reducing the amount of cash under the discretion of senior executives (through the assumption of higher corporate debt or an increase in dividend payments or the declaration of a special one-time dividend or corporate share buybacks), and acquiring or divesting business units. Ideally, the purpose of corporate restructuring is to enhance the wealth of the shareholders by satisfying the needs of various stakeholders.

Firms that manage shareholder value through voluntary restructuring as needed ordinarily do not have to be concerned with hostile takeover bids and externally forced, involuntary restructuring. For instance, General Mills has voluntarily restructured a number of times. The benefits of voluntary restructuring for General Mills have included lowering the number of personnel through a freeze on hiring and accelerated voluntary retirement rather than through abruptly firing people and demoralizing the entire organization; changing suppliers and channels of distribution gradually with longer time notices, so as not to gain a poor corporate reputation; and selling assets gradually rather than under a time pressure that puts the seller in an unfavorable bargaining position. This stakeholder approach to restructuring has also created more wealth for the shareholders of General Mills.[1] Firms that do not manage for value may eventually be forced to restructure by outsiders. Involuntary restructuring normally is costly and creates trauma for the stakeholders. Corporate restructuring has three interrelated dimensions. They are organizational, financial, and portfolio dimensions.[2]

**Organizational restructuring** refers to fundamentally changing the organization of work itself at the corporate level or radically reconfiguring activities and relationships at the business unit level (discussed in chapter 6). Organizational restructuring was studied by Alfred Chandler more than three decades ago.[3] His conclusion was that as corporate strategy changes, organization of the corporate entity must also change in order to get the work done efficiently. For instance, a functional organization (discussed in chapter 8) may be appropriate if a firm is in a single business. With diversification, however, the functional organization may not serve as an efficient means of organizing the firm's work. Thus, an organizational restructuring may be required.

Organizational restructuring may be undertaken in parts of the corporation or in its entirety. The goal, in either case, is to heighten effectiveness and efficiency. For instance, Paramount Publishing Group at one time had two divisions—Prentice Hall and Allyn & Bacon—which sold a variety of textbooks to universities. Subsequently, Paramount also acquired MacMillan Publishing, with its own variety of books. Rather than having each publisher sell a variety of books, the publishing work was reorganized so that Prentice Hall could concentrate on business texts and Allyn & Bacon on social science, health, education, and the physical sciences. MacMillan was dissolved, and its titles were transferred to Prentice Hall or Allyn & Bacon.

Organizational restructuring may be done proactively, as was the case with Paramount, or in response to changes in the environment. For instance, colleges and universities have had to organizationally restructure because students have progressively become more interested in specialized areas of education rather than in a traditional liberal arts education.[4]

**Financial restructuring** refers to reducing the amount of cash available to senior executives so that they are not tempted to waste shareholders' wealth on unprofitable projects that may be personally appealing to the managers. Reducing the amount of cash also puts pressure on the executives to emphasize efficiency as financial slack is reduced. Cash at the disposal of executives may be reduced by channeling it to the stockholders through stock buybacks or special dividends. An increase in regular dividends also takes away cash from managerial discretion and gives it to the stockholders.

Financial restructuring is driven by agency theory. The premise of agency theory is that top managers are often compensated and rewarded on the basis of strategies that are self-serving and do not necessarily benefit the shareholders. For instance, managerial rewards may be increased more through growth and diversification than through enhancement of firm value. Some scholars have even argued that managerial rewards may be independent of their incentives.[5] Thus, financial restructuring is instituted in order to reduce agency costs. Emphasis should be made that financial restructuring has become more prominent as the number and size of institutional investors and blockholders have increased. Since the 1980s institutional investors and blockholders have become significant shareholders and, because of this substantial ownership, can force management to financially restructure to enhance firm value.

**Portfolio restructuring** refers to the acquisition or divestment of business units to enhance corporate value. Portfolio restructuring is comprehensively addressed in the next section through a discussion of strategic alternatives, and in chapter 5 under corporate portfolio frameworks.

## STRATEGIC ALTERNATIVES

Most firms begin their existence as single-business companies. Some enterprises continue to thrive while remaining primarily a single industry. Examples of such companies include Federal Express, Wal-Mart, Wrigley, Xerox, Campbell Soup, McDonald's, Anheuser-Busch, and Timex.

By competing in only one industry, a firm benefits from the specialized knowledge that it derives from concentrating on a limited business arena. This knowledge can help firms offer better products or services and become more efficient in their operations. McDonald's, for instance, has been able to develop a steadily improved product line and maintain low per-unit cost of operations over the years by concentrating exclusively on the fast-food business. Wal-Mart has also benefited from operating primarily in the retailing industry. And Anheuser-Busch has limited its scope of operations largely to the brewing industry, from which it derives more than 80 percent of its sales and 90 percent of its profits.

Operating primarily in one industry, however, may increase a firm's vulnerability to business cycles. Also, should industry attractiveness decline, through a permanent decrease in consumer demand for the firm's products or an onslaught of severe competition from existing or new competitors (in the same industry or substitute industries), the firm's performance is likely to suffer.

These disadvantages can be overcome by operating in different industries through diversification. In fact, senior executives often justify diversifying their firms (having corporate presence in more than one industry) by claiming that it reduces uncertainties associated with being tied to only one industry. Note should be made that the majority of U.S. firms today are active in more than one industry.

Firms may diversify into unrelated or related businesses. Unrelated diversification is driven by the desire to capitalize on profit opportunities in any industry. Unrelated diversification often involves the corporation in businesses that typically have no similarities or complementarities (along important strategic dimensions) among them.

Related diversification involves diversifying into other businesses that have similarities or complementarities along important strategic dimensions. More is stated on related and unrelated diversification throughout this chapter. We emphasize, however, that although executives justify diversification by arguing that it reduces uncertainties associated with being involved in one industry, in reality, diversifying wildly into numerous unrelated businesses also presents its own set of uncertainties. The uncertainties of being in one industry may be compared to putting all of one's eggs into a single basket, whereas being in numerous unrelated businesses may result in uncertainties associated with losing touch with the fundamentals of each business and the difficulty of analyzing the numerous disaggregate external opportunities and threats inherent in unrelated industries. In fact, select authors have empirically concluded that an important way for firms to minimize uncertainties is to diversify into similar industries, rather than remain in just one industry, or to diversify into very different industries.[6] Broadly speaking, senior managers have three corporate-level strategies from which to choose. They may elect to pursue a strategy of growth, stability, or retrenchment. The available strategies are listed in Table 4.1.

## ■ Growth Strategies

Ideally, a firm should select a **growth strategy** that results in an increase in sales or market share only if that growth is expected to result in an increase in firm value. Growth may be attained in a variety of ways. In the following subsections, we describe key growth strategies firms can adopt.

### *Internal Growth*

**Internal growth** is achieved through increasing a firm's sales, production capacity, and work force. Some companies consciously pursue this route to growth rather than the alternative route of acquiring other firms. Their belief is

---

| Table 4.1 | Corporate-Level Strategies |
|---|---|

1. Growth strategies
   a. Internal growth
   b. Horizontal integration
   c. Horizontal related diversification
   d. Horizontal unrelated diversification (conglomerate diversification)
   e. Vertical integration of related businesses
   f. Vertical integration of unrelated businesses
   g. Mergers
   h. Strategic alliances
2. Stability strategy
3. Retrenchment strategies
   a. Turnaround
   b. Divestment
   c. Liquidation

that internal growth better preserves their organizational culture, efficiency, quality, and image. McDonald's, for instance, has never purchased other fast-food restaurant chains. To maintain its high standards for cleanliness, service, and product consistency, it has grown by granting franchises only to people who are willing to be trained in the McDonald's way.

Likewise, American Airlines prefers to grow internally. American was the only U.S.-based airline to expand its services to three continents (Europe, Asia, and South America) at once, and its chairman, Robert L. Crandall, was asked why American did not buy ailing Pan Am or TWA as a quick way to enter these overseas markets. He responded:

> We've always said we don't want to buy another airline. We don't want to acquire another airline's airplanes. We don't want another airline's people. . . .[7]

Internal growth not only includes growth of the same business but also the creation of new businesses, either in a horizontal or vertical direction. **Horizontal internal growth** may involve creating new companies that operate in related or unrelated businesses. Recall that Blockbuster was initially in the video-rental business. Subsequently, it created its music stores, which sell CDs and tapes. This demonstrates Blockbuster's horizontal internal growth. **Vertical internal growth** refers to creating related or unrelated businesses within the firm's vertical channel of distribution and takes the form of supplier-customer relationships. For example, airlines normally purchase their in-flight meals from outside suppliers, such as Dobbs International, that prepare and deliver meals to the air carriers. However, United Airlines has created its own in-flight food service; hence its food service business serves as a supplier to its in-house customer, the airline.

As already emphasized, internal growth helps preserve the organization's culture, efficiency, quality, and image. The chief disadvantages to internal growth, however, are the rising bureaucratic and coordinating costs that generally accompany internal growth. United's in-flight food service, for example, requires its own management team, personnel procedures, and accounting systems. Moreover, its operations need to be coordinated with those of the airline. Therefore, creating new businesses should only be undertaken when their benefits exceed their costs. Note should be made that cost-benefit analysis, in a strategic context, involves important decision components that are difficult to quantify. For instance, a firm may elect to grow internally to maintain its employment level rather than to subcontract its needs to suppliers who may be able to provide their work at marginally lower costs. This may obviate reducing the number of employees (and the costs associated with lower organizational morale).

## Horizontal Integration

Some firms expand by acquiring other companies in the same line of business, a process called **horizontal integration.** ConAgra, for instance, has acquired Banquet Foods, Armour Foods, RJR Nabisco Frozen Foods (Morton, Patio, and Chun King), Beatrice (Hunt's, Wesson, Swift, Eckrich, Butterball, and Orville Redenbacher's), and Golden Valley Microwave Foods (Act II).[8] There are several reasons for engaging in horizontal integration. One of the primary reasons is to increase market share. Along with increasing revenues, larger market share provides the company with greater leverage to deal with its suppliers and customers.[9] Greater market share should also lower the firm's costs through scale economies. Increased size enables the firm to promote its products and services more efficiently to a larger audience and may permit greater access to channels of distribution. Finally, horizontal integration can result in increased operational flexibility.

An example of horizontal integration is Chrysler's purchase of American Motors some years ago. The combination of these two firms is a greater competitive threat to other automobile manufacturers than were the two firms owned and operated separately. The combined firm is larger and financially stronger and can appeal to a broader group of customers through its more diverse product line.

Antitrust legislation, of course, restricts some forms of horizontal integration. The Chrysler purchase of American Motors was approved because Chrysler was far smaller and weaker than either General Motors (GM) or Ford and because American Motors was close to being forced out of business. But many horizontal integrations that would substantially lessen competition in an industry—such as a hypothetical one between GM and Ford—are usually prohibited by the U.S. Justice Department.

---

### S T R A T E G I C     I N S I G H T

## *Horizontal Integration in the Paper Industry: Union Camp and Georgia-Pacific*

The horizontal growth of one major firm in an industry is likely to affect all of its competitors. Consider the U. S. paper industry. For decades, the industry was characterized by nonantagonistic competition. Even when horizontal integrations occurred, they were considered friendly. Because competition was not cutthroat, firms like the $2.75 billion Union Camp Corporation were able to survive even during economic downturns.

Then in 1990, Union Camp's largest competitor, Georgia-Pacific, changed the rules of the game by acquiring Great Northern Nekoosa in a hostile takeover. The purchase gave Georgia-Pacific annual sales of more than $10 billion, placing it thirty-fourth on the 1990 Fortune 500. Overnight, Georgia-Pacific became the world's largest paper products producer. Its new size and efficient fit with Great Northern Nekoosa gave it such economies of scale that Georgia-Pacific became the lowest-cost producer of several major liens of paper products.

Georgia-Pacific's low-cost position, combined with an economic recession, placed significant pressure on Union Camp and other companies in the industry to reduce their costs dramatically. As price pressures and discounting increased, these firms faced the unpleasant prospect of being underbid in the industry's price competition.

Union Camp, however, did enjoy some advantages. Its strong balance sheet enabled it to continue expanding aggressively, primarily through internal growth. Georgia-Pacific, on the other hand, found that its acquisition of Great Northern Nekoosa increased its interest expense substantially, forcing it to reduce capital spending and sell more than $2 billion in assets, as well as close sixty distribution centers in 1996.

SOURCE: "Georgia-Pacific to Close 60 Distribution Centers," *New York Times*, 30 June 1995, p. 3D.

## *Horizontal Related Diversification*

When a corporation acquires a business that is in an industry outside of its present scope of operations (through a payment of cash or stock or some combination of the two) but is related to the corporation's core competencies, the corporation has engaged in **horizontal related diversification.** Relatedness suggests that similar or complementary core competencies may be transferred or shared between the corporation and the acquired business. **Core competencies** are the major resource strengths (human, organizational, physical—present or potential) of organizations. Broadly speaking, core competencies can include, among others, operations excellence, superior technology, cutting edge research and development, and effective marketing. For example, one firm acquiring another with **similar core competencies** in marketing may strengthen both of their overall competitive positions.

Alternatively, two firms may combine **complementary core competencies.** A firm, for instance, that possesses a competency in its product distribution network but limited competence in research and development may acquire a firm that is a leader in research and development but weak in distribution. Each firm would presumably benefit from the acquisition.

Coca-Cola is a good example of shared or transferred competencies. Coca-Cola's expertise in promoting consumer products could be transferred from its soft-drink business to the fruit-juice business (Minute Maid) that it acquired. Also, Coca-Cola's sales force competency may be shared by these two units by a common sales force that simultaneously sells Coca-Cola and Minute Maid products. Examples of two other consumer products companies that have undertaken a number of horizontal related diversifications are shown in Table 4.2.

As is evident, the primary impetus for acquiring horizontal related businesses is to achieve synergy and to strengthen a firm's core competencies.[10] Synergy is attained when the combination of two firms results in higher effectiveness and efficiency than the total yielded by them separately. Three major

**Table 4.2** **Examples of Corporations That Have Undertaken Horizontal Related Diversifications**

| *Johnson & Johnson* | *Gillette* |
|---|---|
| Dental products | Razors and blades |
| Oral contraceptives | Toiletries |
| Wound care products | Electrical shavers, curlers, toothbrushes, alarm clocks, coffee makers |
| Prescription drugs | |
| Hospital products | Stationery products and writing instruments |
| Over-the-counter drugs | |
| Diapers | |
| Feminine hygiene products | |
| Infant products | |

synergistic advantages may be associated with horizontal related acquisitions: horizontal scope economies, horizontal scope innovations, and a combination of the two. Each of these possible advantages is discussed next.

**Horizontal scope economies** occur when a firm's multiple business units are able to share purchasing, research and development, marketing, or other functional activities at a lower total or per-unit cost than would be available if the business units did not share. For instance, a firm that has several business units, each producing a type of major appliance, could reduce its total or per-unit advertising expenses by spreading those costs over a broad range of appliances. Similarly, a corporation may receive a quantity discount by purchasing common parts or supplies for several of its business units.

**Horizontal scope innovations** refer to improvements or innovations that can be transferred or shared across the corporation's business units. Consider Daimler-Benz, for example. This producer of Mercedes-Benz vehicles has, over the past decade, acquired business units in defense electronics, aerospace, automation systems, appliances, and financial services. Together, Daimler-Benz's business units share research and development innovations that help each of them offer superior, state-of-the-art products.

Daimler-Benz also illustrates the **combination of horizontal scope economies and scope innovations.** By acquiring those business units, Daimler-Benz not only benefits from technological and product innovations but also lowers its total research and development costs by spreading them among the business units.

Horizontal related diversification is often accompanied by two disadvantages: increased bureaucratic costs and greater costs of coordinating the activities of the multiple business units. As a result, such diversification should be preceded by a careful cost-benefit analysis.

## Horizontal Unrelated Diversification (Conglomerate Diversification)

When a corporation acquires a business in an unrelated industry, it has undertaken a **horizontal unrelated diversification** or **conglomerate diversification.** Whereas horizontal related diversification is based on the premise of strategically managing and coordinating related businesses to create synergy and value, conglomerate diversification decisions are made primarily for financial investment reasons. The assumption, in the latter case, is that structuring a portfolio of businesses based on their potential financial benefits will create value.[11] Thus, whereas diversifying into related industries is strategically driven, diversifying into unrelated industries is largely financially driven.[12]

In one sense, conglomerate diversification is simpler than horizontal related diversification because it is based on financial analysis without concern for the potential synergistic effects of combining core competencies. Also, since the acquired business units are unrelated to the firm's existing businesses, the costs of coordination are relatively few. Bureaucratic costs, however, tend to increase with unrelated diversification. Again, firms are well advised to undertake a cost-benefit analysis before acquiring unrelated businesses.[13]

USX provides an example of horizontal unrelated diversification. Formerly known as U.S. Steel, this firm began to diversify out of the declining steel industry and into the more attractive energy industry by acquiring Marathon Oil. The firm hoped to increase its financial returns by entering an industry with greater opportunities.

## STRATEGIC INSIGHT

### *Horizontal Related Diversification at Daimler-Benz*

Sometimes acquisitions do not appear to be in related areas, but, upon more careful examination, common attributes become evident. Take, for example, Daimler-Benz. One of the world's largest companies with $62 billion in annual sales, Daimler-Benz conducts manufacturing and marketing operations around the world. Almost two-thirds of its sales stem from transactions outside its home base of Germany.

This corporate giant operates four distinct business units: Mercedes-Benz cars and trucks, Deutsche Aerospace defense and military electronics, AEG nondefense electronics and consumer products, and Debis financial services. At first glance, washing machines, coffee makers, luxury cars, and military electronics seem to share few attributes. But closer inspection

reveals that these businesses have a common technological core.

For instance, developments in technology at Deutsche Aerospace are helping engineers at the Mercedes-Benz car and truck division to design vehicles that can detect road hazards and improve the driver's vision. In fact, Daimler-Benz has formed a centralized research and development center charged with creating innovations that can be transferred from one business unit to another. Daimler's chief executive officer insists that every product line, from washing machines to jet fighters, incorporate innovations using microelectronics and new materials. The central research and development facility is responsible for helping transfer these new technologies from one product or service to another.

SOURCES: "Germany Daimler Releases Unit-By-Unit Plan for 1996/1997," *AP-Dow Jones News Service*, 26 April 1996; "Le Shuffle," *Economist*, 8 July 1995, p. 7; "Cap Gemini Sogeti: Genesis or Exodus?" *Economist*, 26 February 1994, p. 67; "Daimler-Benz: A Slow Recovery," *Economist*, 18 December 1993, pp. 60–61; J. Templeman, D. Woodruff, and S. Reed, "Downshift at Daimler," *Business Week*, 16 November 1992, pp. 88–90.

A desire to reduce risk may lead to conglomerate diversification for firms operating in volatile industries that are subject to rapid technological change. However, financial economists argue that, from the perspective of the owners, risk reduction should not drive acquisition strategies. Their point is that individual stockholders can reduce their financial risk more efficiently by diversifying their personal financial portfolios rather than by owning stock in diversified firms.

Some conglomerates are managed quite effectively. TRW, for instance, has generally demonstrated successful financial performance. This firm, which began in Ohio as The Steel Products Company in 1916, now produces such diverse products and services as spacecraft, software and systems engineering support services, electronic systems, original and replacement automotive equipment, consumer and business credit information services, computer maintenance, pumps, valves, and energy services.

Another conglomerate that has performed well throughout the years is Dover Corporation. This firm has more than 70 different businesses, which produce elevators, valves and welding torches, and garbage trucks, among others. According to Dover CEO Thomas Reece, making a conglomerate a winner requires giving near-total autonomy to heads of business units, buying good companies at reasonable prices and retaining their existing managers, keeping headquarters staff and overhead at a minimum, and not being concerned with synergy.[14]

## Carlson Companies: From Conglomerate to Horizontal Related Diversification

In the 1960s, Carlson Companies operated in a single business, trading stamps, as the Gold Bond Trading Stamp Company. However, it followed the path of many other enterprises in the 1970s, diversifying into unrelated businesses. By the end of that decade, Carlson Companies had become a conglomerate involved in eleven different business lines. Carlson soon learned the lesson, however, that many other conglomerates did: It is difficult to manage divergent businesses profitably. Consequently, Carlson Companies sold most of its businesses to concentrate in only three related areas—travel, hospitality, and marketing services.

Today, Carlson is one of the nation's largest privately owned firms, with about $10 billion in annual sales and about 70,000 employees. Curtis L. Carlson serves as chairman of the board and CEO.

Management describes the firm as "synergistically diversified." Its individual business units complement, support, and create business for one another. For instance, its travel agents and tour companies book reservations in its hotels, resorts, motels, and inns. One of its hotel chains, Radisson Hotels, hosts conventions and meetings often arranged by one of Carlson's marketing services. Next door to the Radisson

may be a TGI Friday's or a Dalts, two of the restaurant chains owned by Carlson. Even more synergy should flow from Carlson's superluxury cruise ship, SSC Radisson Diamond. Designed to serve the most upscale segment of the market, the huge ship has fully equipped meeting facilities.

To take advantage of the falling trade barriers in Europe, Carlson bought a London-based marketing group. The firm already provides twenty-eight different marketing services to businesses in the United States, Australia, and Japan. It is now expanding those services to France, Germany, Italy, and Spain.

Carlson Companies is extremely aggressive, continuing to expand its operations. The firm has grown at an annual rate of about 20 percent during the past decade. Leading the way is the Radisson Hotel chain, with locations in the United States, Russia, Eastern Europe, Australia, India, Mexico, Switzerland, Spain, Thailand, Canada, and the Caribbean. Carlson plans to add a new hotel every ten days until the year 2000; it is presently adding one every six days. Over the past decade, the number of hotel units has increased more than tenfold, making Radisson one of the top hotel companies in the world.

SOURCES: "Radisson Expands into Asia," *New York Times*, 31 March 1995, p. C5; M. Torchia, "How Twin Cities Employers Are Reshaping Health Care," *Business and Health*, February 1994, pp. 30–35; P. Grant, "Bringing Claims Administration Home," *Business and Health*, September 1993, pp. 54–60; R. Donoho, "Lofty Ambitions," *Successful Meetings*, August 1993, pp. 80–86; S. Pesmen, "Bad Times Good for Carlson," *Business Marketing*, July 1993, p. 48.

### Vertical Integration of Related Businesses

**Vertical integration** refers to merging into a functional whole various stages of activities backward into sources of supply or forward in the direction of final consumers. Vertical integration may be partial or full. Performing all stages of activities ranging from raw materials to final outputs may be referred to as full integration. Performing some of these activities comprises partial integration. Acquiring a company with similar or complementary core competencies in the vertical distribution channel may be referred to as **vertical integration of related businesses.** Here also, relatedness suggests that pertinent organizational competencies or strengths may be transferred or shared.

Vertical integration may be either backward or forward in the distribution channel. Backward vertical integration occurs when the companies acquired supply the firm with products, components, or raw materials. An example of backward vertical integration is DuPont's purchase several years ago of Conoco. Conoco, an oil company, supplies petroleum products that DuPont uses in manufacturing its chemicals. By buying its suppliers, a firm assures itself of a steady source of supply.

A firm engages in forward vertical integration when it acquires companies that purchase its products. The acquired companies are closer to the end user. For example, when a manufacturer of navigation and guidance systems purchases an aircraft manufacturer, it has engaged in forward vertical integration.[15] The navigation and guidance systems are installed in the aircraft before it is sold to the airlines.

Four principal advantages are associated with vertical integration of related businesses. **Vertical chain economies** may result from eliminating production steps, reducing overhead costs, and coordinating distribution activities to attain greater synergy. **Vertical chain/horizontal scope economies** can occur when a corporation's horizontally related business units purchase from one of the corporation's business units that serves as a supplier. If sufficiently large, such purchases can improve the supplier's economies of scale while reducing purchasing costs for the horizontal business units. Take, for example, a corporation with horizontal business units that produce hair dryers, industrial fans, cooling systems for electronic equipment, and electric pencil sharpeners. The electric motor parts for all these products are produced by another of the corporation's business units in its vertical chain. As a result of the large combined internal demand for these motor parts, the supplier business unit benefits from scale economies, which lower its per-unit costs of operations. These lower costs are then passed along to the purchasing business units, which, in turn, can subsequently sell their products at highly competitive prices.

**Vertical chain innovations** refer to improvements or innovations that may be transferred or shared among the corporation's business units in the distribution channel. For example, firms such as IBM, Ford, and Digital Equipment acquire suppliers that conduct research and development on promising technology.[16] Vertical chain innovations not only can promote the development of technologically superior outputs, but they can also help the firm differentiate its outputs through improved design, faster delivery, or better marketing practices.

A final advantage is a **combination of vertical chain economies and chain innovations.** As an example, consider Admiram Corporation. One of its business units produces electric switches and plugs, for which it purchases plastic fasteners from another of Admiram's business units. Several years ago that same supplier produced steel fasteners for switches and plugs. As a result of extensive communication between the managers of the two business units, the fastener unit developed sturdy plastic fasteners to replace those made of steel. The business unit that produced the switches and plugs then redesigned its products around the new plastic fasteners. The shift from steel to plastic parts and the subsequent redesigned products resulted in substantial cost savings in supplies, production, and assembly. Customers benefited from redesigned products not only because of the improved design but also because of the product's lighter weight, which led to reduced transportation and handling costs.

Although vertically integrated firms with related businesses in the distribution channel may be better positioned to gain on efficiency and innovation potentials internally, their disadvantage is that they are not predisposed to capitalize on such potentials developed in the external environment.[17] The reason is that such firms focus on internal coordination of activities meant to promote efficiencies and innovations. Firms with vertically unrelated business units, discussed next, are not as strictly subject to internal coordination needs. For instance, the activities of brewing beer and producing aluminum cans need not be coordinated for gains in efficiency or innovation. A brewer of beer with its own aluminum can production may seek external ideas to improve its brewing as well as its aluminum can operations. Note that this points out the disadvantage of being in vertically related businesses and, on the other hand, the advantage of being in vertically unrelated businesses.

We should also point out that firms that adhere to vertical integration of related businesses tend to have more complex patterns of integration. Although the uncertainty of suppliers and customers may have been the motivation to structure complex patterns, the complexity may lead to increased risk, especially in more dynamic environments.[18] Thus, outsourcing for suppliers and distributors may be beneficial in more dynamic environments.

Certain other disadvantages are also associated with vertical integration of related businesses. When market demand varies unpredictably over time, it becomes difficult to coordinate vertically integrated activities. Another disadvantage is that a technological innovation in the vertical channel may require all of the vertically linked businesses to modify their operations. Next, a firm that buys all of its needs internally may pay more if less expensive external sources of supply exist. Finally, the longer the chain, the greater will be the costs associated with increased coordination and bureaucracy. Obviously then, potential costs and benefits must be compared before engaging in vertical integration of related businesses.

### Vertical Integration of Unrelated Businesses

Whereas vertical integration of related businesses centers on transferring or sharing pertinent complementary or similar core competencies, **vertical integration of unrelated businesses** is undertaken with limited possibilities for transferring or sharing core competencies.[19] The purchase by American Agronomics (a producer of citrus juices) of Precision Plastics (a manufacturer of plastic containers) is an example of vertical integration of unrelated businesses. Some juices, of course, can be marketed in plastic containers, but these containers also have multiple other uses. Also, the combination of a juice producer and a plastics company allows limited possibilities for transferring or sharing core competencies. Thus, there are limited potentials for achieving synergy.

Emphasis should be made that some stages of vertical integration may be related while others may be unrelated, as suggested by a number of scholars.[20] For instance, operational technology, managerial approaches, and organizational formats may be much more similar between wholesaling and retailing but quite different from those for manufacturing and processing. A firm that is vertically connected in two stages—component production and manufacturing—may be vertically related in these stages. If this firm additionally acquires its own wholesaling or retailing, however, then it will have vertically integrated into an unrelated business.

As already suggested, one advantage of vertically unrelated businesses is that they are normally more likely to adopt improvements and innovations of outsiders. This leads to a second advantage. Particularly in dynamic industry environments, they face lower risk of technological obsolescence because they are externally oriented.

Managing vertically unrelated businesses can be associated with two major disadvantages: The more vertical businesses the firm owns, the higher the costs of bureaucracy—and perhaps coordination—are likely to be, and a firm that commits itself to buying all of its needs internally may pay higher costs by failing to seek competitive bids from outside suppliers.

Note that some acquisitions do not fall neatly into either a horizontal or a vertical category. For example, PepsiCo's purchase of KFC, Pizza Hut, and Taco Bell can be viewed as horizontal related diversification. Their common core would be the marketing of fast food and soft drinks within the restaurant industry. But these same purchases can also be viewed as forward vertical integration of related businesses in that PepsiCo supplies soft drinks to KFC, Pizza Hut, and Taco Bell. Recall that relatedness did not pay off for PepsiCo so it spun-off these business units.

As is evident, some of the growth strategies discussed consist of acquiring other companies—either in a horizontal or a vertical direction. Growth may also be pursued through the voluntary merging of two independent companies.

## Mergers

Many firms elect to grow through mergers. A **merger** occurs when two or more firms, usually of roughly similar sizes, combine into one through an exchange of stock. Mergers are undertaken to share or transfer resources and gain in competitive power. For example, Sperry and Burroughs merged to form Unisys several years ago in an attempt to compete more effectively in the computer industry.

The overall reason for a merger is to take advantage of the benefits of synergy. When the combination of two firms results in greater effectiveness and efficiency than the total yielded by them separately, then synergy has been attained. Synergy can result from either horizontal mergers, such as that between NCNB and C&S/Sovran (now named NationsBank), or from vertical mergers. The merger of Ocean Drilling and Exploration (an oil exploration and drilling firm) with Murphy Oil (a refiner) illustrates a vertical merger.

Because either type of merger usually results in increased bureaucratic and coordination costs, they should be undertaken only when the projected benefits exceed the merger's estimated costs.

## Strategic Alliances

**Strategic alliances** are partnerships in which two or more firms carry out a specific project or cooperate in a selected area of business. The firms comprising the alliance share the costs, risks, and benefits of exploring and undertaking new business opportunities.[21] Such arrangements include joint ventures, franchise/ license agreements, joint research and development, joint operations, joint long-term supplier agreements, joint marketing agreements, and consortiums. Strategic alliances can be temporary, disbanding after the project is finished, or long term. Ownership of the firms, of course, remains unchanged.

Strategic alliances may be undertaken for a variety of reasons—political, economic, or technological. In certain countries, for instance, a foreign firm may be permitted to operate only if it enters into a strategic alliance with a local partner. In other cases, a particular project may be so large that it would strain a single company's resources. Thus that company may enter into a strategic alliance with another firm to gain the resources to accomplish the job. Other projects may require multidimensional technology that no one firm possesses. Hence, firms with different, but compatible, technologies may join together. Or in other cases, one firm may contribute its technological expertise while another contributes its managerial talent.

There are many examples of strategic alliances. IBM and Apple Computer recently agreed to exchange technology in an attempt to create a new computer operating system that would dominate the industry. The major U.S. automakers—GM, Ford, and Chrysler—are jointly conducting research, with the assistance of $120 million from the U.S. Department of Energy, to develop battery technology for electric cars. And GM, Lockheed, Southern California Edison, and Pacific Gas & Electric have formed a consortium to speed the development of widely used electric vehicles and advanced mass transportation systems.

Strategic alliances have two major advantages. The first, due to the companies' remaining separate and independent, is little increase in bureaucratic and coordination costs. Second, each company can benefit from the alliance without bearing all the costs and risks of exploring new business opportunities on its own. On the other hand, the major disadvantage of forming a strategic alliance is that one partner may take more than it gives. That is, some partners in the alliance possess less knowledge and less advanced technology than other partners and may, in the future, use their newly acquired knowledge and technology to compete directly with their more progressive partners. In addition, the profits from the alliance must be shared.

## ■ Stability Strategy

Corporate growth strategies may be adopted for a period of time but inevitably the firm may choose to adopt the stability strategy, or perhaps one of the retrenchment strategies discussed in the next section. It needs to be emphasized that when a firm is in different businesses, corporate strategy addresses what businesses to be in, and business unit strategy, discussed in chapter 6, emphasizes how to compete in those businesses. However, when a firm is in a single business, corporate strategy and business unit strategy become synonymous.

The **stability strategy** for a firm (that has operations in more than one industry) is the maintenance of the current array of businesses. There are two reasons for adopting the corporate stability strategy. First, this strategy enables the corporation to focus managerial efforts on the existing businesses with the goal of enhancing their competitive postures. That is, rather than continuing to add new businesses to the corporation and working hard to manage numerous different business units, management can concentrate on improving the productivity and innovation of existing businesses. Second, senior managers may perceive that the cost of adding new businesses may be more than the potential benefits. With the passage of time, however, the corporation may forgo the stability strategy and under favorable circumstances again adopt one of the growth strategies or, under less favorable conditions, one of the retrenchment strategies.

For a single-industry firm the stability strategy is one that maintains approximately the same operations without seeking significant growth in revenues or

S T R A T E G I C    I N S I G H T

## International Strategic Alliances

Strategic alliances between firms headquartered in different countries have become increasingly popular in recent years. Consider the following examples:

### Nestlé and General Mills

Nestlé, the world's largest food company, headquartered in Switzerland, has joined with U. S.-based General Mills to form Cereal Partners Worldwide (CPW). Using Nestlé's powerful channels of distribution, General Mills is penetrating such markets as Europe, Asia, Africa, and Latin America with its Wheaties and Cheerios brands.

### General Motors and Toyota

In 1984, General Motors and Toyota established a joint production venture in California known as the New United Motor Manufacturing, Inc. (NUMMI). Although some GM executives were skeptical, CEO Roger Smith recognized that GM lacked the technology—from research and development through sales—to produce a high-

quality small car. Toyota sought the joint venture because it wanted a production facility in the United States without going it alone. Much of the Saturn philosophy that has contributed to its present success—from long-term relationships with supplies to just-in-time manufacturing—was gleaned from the GM–Toyota alliance.

### Northwest and KLM

U.S.-based Northwest Airlines teamed up with Netherlands-based KLM to make Northwest more competitive in the North Atlantic market and to give KLM access to critical U. S. routes. The alliance allowed both carriers to act as a single airline. However, such alliances can bring about strained relationships between the participating firms. KLM has considered dissolving the alliance in part because of a Northwest shareholders-rights plan that caps KLM's stake in Northwest.

SOURCES: C. Goldsmith, "KLM Considers Dissolving Tie with Northwest Airlines," *Wall Street Journal Interactive Edition*, 2 May 1996; "Nestle Lays Off 43 Workers at Fulton, NY Chocolate Plant," *Dow Jones Business News*, 9 May 1996; E. H. Phillips, "Northwest Calls KLM Pact 'Strategic Asset'," *Aviation Week and Space Technology*, 31 October 1994, pp. 56–57; W. Webb, "Partnering with New Media Companies," *Editor and Publisher*, 15 April 1995, pp. 29–30; J. Bleeke and D. Ernst, "Is Your Strategic Alliance Really a Sale?" *Harvard Business Review*, January–February 1995, pp. 97–105; T. Sasaki, "What the Japanese Have Learned from Strategic Alliances," *Long Range Planning*, 26(3) (1994): 41–53; C. Knowlton, "Europe Cooks Up a Cereal Brawl," *Fortune*, 3 June 1991, pp. 175, 179.

in the size of the business. Why might a firm in a single business adopt this strategy? In some cases, it may be forced to do so if it operates in a low-growth or no-growth industry. Second, it may find that the cost of expanding its market share or of entering new-product or new-market areas is higher than the benefits that are projected to come with that growth. Third, a firm that dominates its industry through its superior size and competitive advantage may pursue stability to reduce its chances of being prosecuted for engaging in monopolistic practices. And finally, smaller enterprises that concentrate on specialized products or services may choose stability because of their concern that growth will result in reduced quality and customer service.

As an example of the last reason, consider Peet's Coffee and Tea, a group of eight coffeehouses that employs 170 people in the San Francisco Bay area. These establishments serve only the finest freshly roasted coffee to the accompaniment of piped-in classical music. Although the owner of Peet's, Gerald Baldwin, has received numerous lucrative offers to franchise his business nationwide, he has always refused. His concern is that with growth, quality may suffer. He fears, for instance, that some franchisees might serve coffee that was not freshly roasted in order to cut their costs and to increase their profits.

## ■ Retrenchment Strategies

Growth strategies and the stability strategy are normally adopted by firms that are in satisfactory competitive positions. But when the performance of a firm's business units is disappointing or, at the extreme, when its survival is at stake, then **retrenchment strategies** may be appropriate. Retrenchment may take one of three forms: turnaround, divestment, or liquidation.

### Turnaround

The intent of a **turnaround** is to transform the corporation into a leaner and more effective firm. Turnaround includes such actions as eliminating unprofitable outputs, pruning assets, reducing the size of the work force, cutting costs of distribution, and rethinking the firm's product lines and customer groups.[22]

Take, as an example, what may be the most famous turnaround in American history. Chrysler Corporation, by the late 1970s, was on the verge of bankruptcy. Its newly hired CEO, Lee Iacocca, implemented a dramatic turnaround strategy. Large numbers of blue- and white-collar employees were laid off, the remaining workers agreed to forgo part of their salaries and benefits, and twenty plants were either closed or consolidated. These actions lowered the firm's break-even point from an annual sales level of 2.4 million cars and trucks to about 1.2 million. Iacocca also implemented a divestment strategy (discussed in the following section) by selling Chrysler's marine outboard motor division, its defense business, its air-conditioning division, and all of its automobile manufacturing plants located outside the United States. By 1982, Chrysler began to show a profit, after having lost $3.5 billion in the preceding four years.

Unfortunately, the turnaround failed to last. By 1991, Chrysler was losing over $2 million a day and had been replaced by Honda as the third-largest seller of cars in the United States. Chrysler once again energetically began to cut costs by closing plants and firing employees, by selling its 50 percent share in its strategic alliance with Mitsubishi Motors, and by modifying its operating systems. For instance, Chrysler began assigning engineers to teams that design a single car rather than continuing to place them in functional groups (such as engine design). This change cut product development time from $4\frac{1}{2}$ to $3\frac{1}{2}$ years. Chrysler also began implementing ways to cut the delivery time of cars to dealers. As a result, Chrysler had record profits in 1994 of $3.7 billion, and its cash position in 1994 and 1995 was enviable in the auto industry. This firm's superior performance continued through the latter 1990s.

### Divestment

When a corporation sells or "spins off" one of its business units, as Chrysler did, it is engaging in **divestment.** Divestment usually occurs when the business unit is performing poorly or when it no longer fits the corporation's strategic profile. The business unit may be sold to another company, to its managers and employees, or to an individual or group of investors. Such sales are fairly common. For instance, General Electric, Westinghouse, and Singer have all sold their computer businesses. Singer also sold its original core business unit that produced sewing machines and began to concentrate on high-technology electronics.

Note that divestment may be necessary in a number of situations—where a business unit drains resources from more profitable units, where the business unit is not as efficient as alternatives in the marketplace, or where the unit's interdependence with other units is not synergistic. Divestments in the 1980s and the 1990s have been motivated by the underperformance of many of the business units acquired in the 1960s and the 1970s. Moreover, select authors have suggested that the underperformance of some corporations has been due to the unrelatedness of their units.[23] Consequently, the takeovers of the 1980s and the 1990s have often been characterized as acquisitions that were followed by sell-offs of previously acquired unrelated businesses or leveraged takeovers by the managers themselves that were then pruned by substantial sell-offs of assets.[24]

As suggested above, divestment can also occur through a spin-off. In this case, shares of stock in the business unit that is to be spun off are distributed. The stock of the parent corporation and the spun-off business unit then begin to trade separately. For example, the Adolph Coors Company has spun off business units that sell ceramic multilayer computer boards, packages for soaps and dog food, vitamins for animal feed, and automobile parts in order to concentrate more fully on the highly competitive beer industry.

### Liquidation

A strategy of last resort is **liquidation.** When neither a turnaround nor a divestment seems feasible, liquidation occurs through termination of the business unit's existence by sale of its assets. Most stakeholder groups suffer in liquidations. Stockholders and creditors lose, some of the managers and employees lose their jobs, suppliers lose a customer, and the community suffers an increase in unemployment and a decrease in tax revenues.

## S U M M A R Y

In choosing a strategy, top management may adopt any one of three general corporate profiles: The firm may compete in a single business, in several related businesses, or in several unrelated businesses. A recent phenomenon related to the corporate profile decision is corporate restructuring. The purpose of corporate restructuring is to enhance the wealth of the shareholders through the satisfaction of needs of various stakeholders. Corporate restructuring has organizational, financial, and portfolio dimensions.

Given the corporate portfolio, top managers have three corporate-level strategies available: growth, stability, or retrenchment. Growth can be attained through internal growth or the creation of new businesses. New businesses can be created horizontally or vertically. Growth is also possible through horizontal integration—acquiring other companies in the same line of business.

Diversification (acquiring another company through a payment of cash and/or stock) can be either horizontal or vertical. Horizontal diversification may take the form of horizontal related diversification, or horizontal unrelated diversification. Vertical integration may be related or unrelated. Mergers involve the voluntary combination of two or more firms into one through an exchange of stock. A final form of growth is the strategic alliance—a partnership in which two or more independent firms carry out a specific project or cooperate in a selected area of business.

Some firms adopt a stability strategy in which they attempt to maintain their size and current lines of business. Firms in less satisfactory competitive positions are forced to adopt a retrenchment strategy. Retrenchment may take one of three forms: turnaround (transforming the organization into a leaner and more effective business), divestment (selling or spinning off one or more business units), or liquidation (terminating a business unit's existence by sale of its assets).

## TAKE IT TO THE NET

We invite you to visit the Wright page on the Prentice Hall Web site at:

**http://www.prenhall.com/wright**

for this chapter's World Wide Web exercise.

## KEY CONCEPTS

**Combination of horizontal scope economies and scope innovations**   When a firm's multiple business units share or transfer competencies at a lower total cost than would be available if the business units did not share or transfer and, at the same time, they share or transfer improvements or innovations.

**Combination of vertical chain economies and chain innovations**   When a firm, within its vertical distribution channel, is able to attain economies through its internal supplier-customer relationships while sharing or transferring improvements or innovations among its multiple vertical business units.

**Complementary core competencies**   When one firm's competency (such as strength in the research and development area) fits, in a complementary fashion, with another firm's core competency (such as strength in manufacturing).

**Conglomerate diversification**   See Horizontal unrelated diversification.

**Core competency**   A major strength of an organization—present or potential.

**Corporate-level strategy** The strategy that top management formulates for the overall company.

**Corporate restructuring** A process that may include a broad set of decisions and transactions, such as changing the organization of work itself in the firm, reducing the amount of cash under the discretion of senior executives, and acquiring or divesting business units.

**Diversification** A corporate-level growth strategy in which one company acquires another company in an industry outside of its present scope of operations through a payment of cash or stock or some combination of the two.

**Divestment** A corporate-level retrenchment strategy in which a firm sells one or more of its business units.

**Financial restructuring** Reducing the amount of cash available to senior executives so that they will not be tempted to waste shareholders' wealth on unprofitable projects that may be personally appealing to them.

**Growth strategy** A corporate-level strategy designed to increase profits, sales, and/or market share.

**Horizontal integration** A form of acquisition in which a firm expands by acquiring other companies in its same line of business.

**Horizontal internal growth** A type of internal growth strategy in which a firm creates new companies that operate in the same business as the original firm, in related businesses, or in unrelated businesses.

**Horizontal related diversification** A form of diversification in which a firm expands by acquiring a business that is in an industry outside of its present scope of operations but is related to its core competencies.

**Horizontal scope economies** Economies that occur when a firm's multiple business units are able to share functional activities at a lower total cost than would be available if they did not share.

**Horizontal scope innovations** Improvements or innovations that can be transferred or shared across a corporation's business units.

**Horizontal unrelated diversification** A form of diversification in which a firm expands by acquiring a business in an unrelated industry.

**Internal growth** A corporate-level growth strategy in which a firm expands by internally increasing its size and sales rather than by acquiring other companies.

**Liquidation** A corporate-level retrenchment strategy in which a firm terminates one or more of its business units by the sale of their assets.

**Merger** A corporate-level growth strategy in which a firm combines with another firm through an exchange of stock.

**Organizational restructuring** A change in the organization of work in the corporation to improve effectiveness and efficiency.

**Portfolio restructuring**   The acquisition or divestment of business units in order to enhance corporate value.

**Retrenchment strategy**   A corporate-level strategy undertaken by a firm when its performance is disappointing or when its survival is at stake. A retrenchment strategy tends to reduce the size of the firm.

**Similar core competencies**   When one firm's core competency or resource strengths (such as strength in the research and development area) is the same as another firm's core competency.

**Stability strategy**   A corporate-level strategy intended to maintain a firm's present size and current lines of business.

**Strategic alliance**   A corporate-level growth strategy in which two or more firms form a partnership to carry out a specific project or to cooperate in a selected area of business.

**Turnaround**   A corporate-level retrenchment strategy intended to transform the firm into a leaner and more effective business by reducing costs and rethinking the firm's product lines and target markets.

**Vertical chain economies**   Scale economies in a firm's distribution channel that result from eliminating production steps, reducing overhead costs, and coordinating distribution activities to attain greater synergy.

**Vertical chain innovations**   Improvements or innovations that may be transferred or shared among a firm's business units in the distribution channel.

**Vertical chain/horizontal scope economies**   Scale economies that occur when a firm's horizontally related or unrelated business units purchase from one of the firm's business units that serves as a supplier in sufficiently large quantities to improve the supplier's economies of scale while reducing purchasing costs for the horizontal business units.

**Vertical integration**   Merging into a functional whole various stages of activities backward into sources of supply or forward in the direction of final consumers.

**Vertical integration of related businesses**   A form of integration in which a firm expands by acquiring a company with similar or complementary core competencies in the distribution channel.

**Vertical integration of unrelated businesses**   A form of integration in which a firm expands by acquiring a company that will provide limited synergy in its distribution channel.

**Vertical internal growth**   A type of internal growth strategy that generally takes the form of supplier-customer relationships within the firm's channel of distribution.

# DISCUSSION QUESTIONS

1. Explain the distinction between horizontal and vertical internal growth.

2. What do you believe are the advantages that internal growth has over growth through mergers and acquisitions? What particular advantages might mergers and acquisitions have over internal growth?

3. Explain the distinction among horizontal integration, horizontal related diversification, and horizontal unrelated diversification.

4. Discuss the major advantages and disadvantages of horizontal related diversification.

5. Explain the following statement: "While diversifying into related industries is strategically driven, diversifying into unrelated industries is largely financially driven."

6. Discuss the major advantages and disadvantages of vertical integration of related businesses.

7. Why would a firm prefer to engage in a strategic alliance over a more permanent arrangement?

8. Why would management adopt a stability strategy? Do you feel that such a strategy is viable over a lengthy period of time? Why or why not?

9. When is a retrenchment strategy appropriate? Identify some criteria that will help determine what particular retrenchment strategy should be used.

# STRATEGIC MANAGEMENT EXERCISES

1. Using information in your library, identify three firms: one that is in a single business, one that is in two or more related businesses, and one that is in unrelated businesses. Now, insofar as information permits, explain the advantages and disadvantages of the corporate profile that each company has selected.

2. Identify a particular type of business that you might wish to start, assuming that you have the necessary financial resources. Furthermore, assume that after some period of time during which the business is successful, you wish to adopt a growth strategy for your company. Explain how your firm might expand through each of the following strategies: internal growth, horizontal integration, horizontal related diversification, horizontal unrelated diversification, merger, and strategic alliance.

3. Identify a well-known company with which you are reasonably familiar. Explain how it might expand either through vertical integration of related businesses or vertical integration of unrelated businesses. What are the potential benefits and risks associated with the form of growth that you have selected for this particular company?

# NOTES

1. G. Donaldson, "Voluntary Restructuring: The Case of General Mills," *Journal of Financial Economics* 27 (1990): 117–141.

2. J. E. Bethel and J. Liebeskind, "The Effects of Ownership Structure on Corporate Restructuring," *Strategic Management Journal* 14 (1993): 15–31; E. H. Bowman and H. Singh, "Corporate Restructuring: Reconfiguring the Firm," *Strategic Management Journal* 14 (1993): 5–14.

3. A. D. Chandler, *Strategy and Structure*, Cambridge: MIT Press, 1962.

4. E. J. Zajac and M. S. Kraatz, "A Diametric Forces Model of Strategic Change: Assessing the Antecedents and Consequences of Restructuring in the Higher Education Industry," *Strategic Management Journal* 14 (1993): 83–102.

5. M. C. Jensen and K. J. Murphy, "Performance Pay and Top-Management Incentives," *Journal of Political Economy* 98 (1990): 225–264.

6. M. Lubatkin and S. Chatterjee, "Extending Modern Portfolio Theory into the Domain of Corporate Diversification: Does It Apply?" *Academy of Management Journal* 37 (1994): 109–136.

7. B. O'Brian, "American Air Expands into Three Continents, Flexing Its U.S. Muscle," *Wall Street Journal*, 8 June 1990, p. A1.

8. L. Therrien, "ConAgra Turns Up the Heat in the Kitchen," *Business Week*, 2 September 1991, p. 59.

9. B. Kelley, "A Day in the Life of a Card Shark," *Journal of Business Strategy*, March/April (1994): 36–39.

10. M. Lubatkin and S. Chatterjee, "Extending Modern Portfolio Theory into the Domain of Corporate Diversification: Does It Apply?" *Academy of Management Journal* 37 (1994): 109–136.

11. M. S. Salter and W. S. Weinhold, "Diversification Via Acquisition: Creating Value," *Harvard Business Review* 56, no. 4 (1978): 166–176.

12. M. Lubatkin, "Merger Strategies and Stockholder Value," *Strategic Management Journal* 8 (1987): 39–53; J. B. Barney, "Returns to Bidding Firms in Mergers and Acquisitions: Reconsidering the Relatedness Hypothesis," *Strategic Management Journal* 9 (1988): 71–78.

13. G. Samuels, "Learning by Doing," *Forbes*, 14 March 1994, pp. 51–54.

14. L. Zweig, "Who Says the Conglomerate is Dead?" *Business Week*, 23 January, 1995, p. 92.

15. R. Davis and L. G. Thomas, "Direct Estimation of Synergy: A New Approach to the Diversity-Performance Debate," *Management Science* 39 (1994): 1334–1346.

16. K. Kelly, "Learning from Japan," *Business Week*, 27 January 1992, p. 53.

17. R. D. Buzzell, "Is Vertical Integration Profitable?" *Harvard Business Review* 61 (January–February 1994): 92–102.

18. R. A. D'Aveni and A. Y. Ilinitch, "Complex Patterns of Vertical Integration in the Forest Products Industry: Systematic and Bankruptcy Risks," *Strategic Management Journal* 35 (1992): 596–625.

19. B. B. Pray, "Types of Vertical Acquisitions and Returns to Acquiring Firms," unpublished manuscript, University of Memphis, 1992.

20. R. D. Buzzell, "Is Vertical Integration Profitable?" *Harvard Business Review* 61 (January–February 1994): 92–102; M. Gort, *Diversification and Integration in American Industry*, (Princeton: Princeton University Press, 1962); G. J. Stigler, "The Division of Labor Is Limited by the Extent of the Market," *Journal of Political Economy* (June 1951): 185–193.

21. J. Mohr and R. Spekman, "Characteristics of Partnership Success: Partnership Attributes, Communication Behavior, and Conflict Resolution Techniques," *Strategic Management Journal* 15 (1994): 143–152; A. A. Lado, "The Role of Strategic Intent in the Choice of Modes of Cross-Border Alliances: An Investigation of Select U.S. Multinational Companies," unpublished manuscript, University of Memphis, 1992.

22. See M. Garry, "A&P Strikes Back," *Progressive Grocer*, February 1994, pp. 32–38.

23. A. Shleifer and R. W. Vishny, "Takeover in the '60's and the '80's: Evidence and Implications," *Strategic Management Journal* 12 (1991): 51–59.

24. S. N. Kaplan, "The Staying Power of Leveraged Buyouts," Working Paper, 1990, University of Chicago.

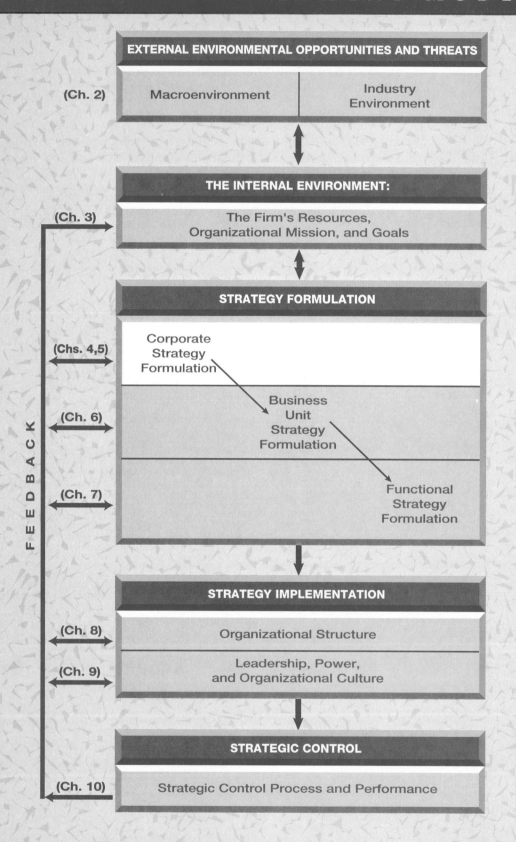

# STRATEGIC MANAGEMENT MODEL

**EXTERNAL ENVIRONMENTAL OPPORTUNITIES AND THREATS**

(Ch. 2)

| Macroenvironment | Industry Environment |
|---|---|

**THE INTERNAL ENVIRONMENT:**

(Ch. 3)

The Firm's Resources, Organizational Mission, and Goals

**STRATEGY FORMULATION**

(Chs. 4,5) — Corporate Strategy Formulation

(Ch. 6) — Business Unit Strategy Formulation

(Ch. 7) — Functional Strategy Formulation

**FEEDBACK**

**STRATEGY IMPLEMENTATION**

(Ch. 8) — Organizational Structure

(Ch. 9) — Leadership, Power, and Organizational Culture

**STRATEGIC CONTROL**

(Ch. 10) — Strategic Control Process and Performance

# 5 Corporate Portfolio Management and Related Issues

M any firms operate multiple business units in different industries. Such firms may often use portfolio frameworks as a guide to corporate strategy formulation. This chapter will initially examine a number of corporate portfolio frameworks. Then, discussion will focus on corporate involvement in business unit operations and on the financial returns associated with corporate-level strategies. Finally, the role that top managers' motives may play in corporate acquisitions is discussed.

## CORPORATE PORTFOLIO FRAMEWORKS

It is essential to note, as the various corporate portfolio frameworks are presented, that although each provides useful guidelines for the strategist, unique firm-specific conditions may require exceptions to the guidelines. This section examines select analytical frameworks that can be used in corporate management: our S.W.O.T. portfolio framework, the original and revised Boston Consulting Group frameworks, and the General Electric (GE) framework. Discussion then turns to the extent to which corporate-level top management may be involved in managing the firm's business units.

### ■ S.W.O.T. Portfolio Framework

Our **S.W.O.T. portfolio framework** is designed along two dimensions: the competitive status of the corporation's business units (their resource strengths and weaknesses relative to those of competitors, as discussed in chapter 3) and the state of the external environment (environmental opportunities and threats). By external environment we mean the macroenvironmental or industry factors discussed in chapter 2. From this perspective, the corporation's business units can be classified as having strong, average, or weak competitive status, and the environment of the corporation's business units can contain critical threats, moderate opportunities and threats, or abundant opportunities. The resultant matrix, showing the competitive status of the corporation's business units on the horizontal axis and the state of the environment on the vertical axis, is presented in Figure 5.1.

Recall that corporate, business unit, and functional strategies are intertwined. Hence, the strengths and weaknesses of each of these strategies can enhance or inhibit the organization's overall effectiveness. For instance, lower costs may be attained at the corporate level through scope economies, as discussed in the preceding chapter. Then the business unit level may further reduce costs by adopting its own low-cost strategy, discussed in the following chapter, and by adopting appropriate functional strategies (e.g., mass purchasing and mass production), as presented in chapter 7. The strengths or weaknesses of strategies at any level, then, will affect the organization's overall performance. Thus, while the discussion that follows emphasizes the corporation's business units, it should be evident that the firm's strengths and weaknesses evolve collectively from corporate, business unit, and functional levels.

Understanding of the matrix in Figure 5.1 can be enhanced by looking at some examples. A corporation's business unit may be categorized to be in compartment A, for instance, if it has impressive competitive strengths with few weaknesses and competes in an environment with abundant opportunities and relatively few threats. On the other hand, a corporation's business unit may be categorized to be in compartment F if it has average competitive strengths and weaknesses and operates in an environment full of critical threats and few opportunities. And a firm's business unit that is categorized to be in compartment H possesses more weaknesses than strengths and does business in an environment with moderate opportunities and threats.

Our S.W.O.T. portfolio framework offers strategy guidelines for the corporation's business units that are categorized to be in any one of the framework's nine compartments. Each of these compartments will now be examined.

## Compartment A

Compartment A is obviously a desirable category. The corporation's business units that are evaluated to be in this compartment possess impressive competitive strengths and few weaknesses and operate in an environment with abundant opportunities and few significant threats. In such a setting, a number of strategies may be appropriate. Internal growth can be an effective strategy if top management believes that it would best preserve the business unit's organizational culture, efficiency, quality, and image. Vertical integration of related businesses may be more suitable for business units that wish to assure themselves of predictable sources of supply or of outlets for their outputs, especially in stable environments.[1] This strategy may also be appropriate if management feels that it will help reduce systemwide costs or improve output innovations. Mergers or horizontal integration may be appropriate, provided antitrust laws do not impede those strategies, if the business unit desires a larger market share and increased competitive clout.

**Figure 5.1**                    **S.W.O.T. Portfolio Framework**

**Competitive Status of the Corporation's Business Units**

| | Strong | Average | Weak |
|---|---|---|---|
| **Abundant environmental opportunities** | **Compartment A**<br>1. Internal growth<br>2. Vertical integration of related businesses<br>3. Mergers<br>4. Horizontal integration | **Compartment D**<br>1. Mergers<br>2. Horizontal integration<br>3. Strategic alliances | **Compartment G**<br>1. Turnaround<br>2. Divestment |
| **Moderate environmental opportunities and threats** | **Compartment B**<br>1. Vertical integration of related businesses<br>2. Horizontal related diversification | **Compartment E**<br>1. Stability<br>2. Mergers<br>3. Horizontal integration<br>4. Strategic alliances<br>5. Divestment | **Compartment H**<br>1. Turnaround<br>2. Divestment |
| **Critical environmental threats** | **Compartment C**<br>1. Horizontal related diversification<br>2. Horizontal unrelated diversification (conglomerate)<br>3. Vertical integration of unrelated businesses<br>4. Divestment | **Compartment F**<br>1. Divestment<br>2. Horizontal related diversification<br>3. Horizontal unrelated diversification<br>4. Stability | **Compartment I**<br>1. Liquidation |

*State of the External Environment*

Corporate growth need not always result in an expanding business unit. An alternative method is to divide the business unit into smaller, semiautonomous business units, with each concentrating on a growing, but narrower, market. For example, Johnson & Johnson (J&J) divides any of its business units that grow beyond what top management believes is optimal. As a result, J&J now has 166 highly decentralized businesses, each concentrating on a specific market for health and personal care products. Because the optimal size for a J&J business unit differs from one market to another, J&J's businesses range in size from $100,000 in annual sales to $1 billion.[2]

## Compartment B

The corporation's business units that possess significant competitive strengths and that operate in environments with moderate opportunities and threats may find that a vertical integration of related businesses or horizontal related diversification strategy is appropriate. Because the environment is only moderately promising, a compartment B firm may enhance its success by diversifying into a related industry that has better prospects.

Consider PepsiCo as an example. The soft-drink industry at one time presented only moderate opportunities. Although this industry has reasonable growth prospects, particularly outside the United States, this opportunity was dampened by the immense competitive threat posed by Coca-Cola. By diversifying into a related industry, fast-food restaurants, PepsiCo reduced its

## STRATEGIC INSIGHT

### Gaylord Entertainment's TNN and CMT: Operating in Compartment B

Gaylord Entertainment—once primarily entrenched in the publishing industry—presently operates businesses in entertainment, cable television, and broadcasting, including Opryland U. S.A. Theme Park. In recent years, Gaylord's strategy of growth through related diversification has proven successful, due in part to the country music phenomenon. Gaylord's cable television business consists of TNN—The Nashville Network—and CMT—Country Music Television.

The Nashville Network, launched in 1983, is an advertiser-supported cable television network focusing on Nashville-type entertainment that is on the air eighteen hours a day and is available throughout the United States and Canada. Its programming focuses on country music entertainment, variety and talk shows, news, and sports. Popular TNN shows include Nashville Now, Crook and Chase, On Stage, Country Kitchen, and American Music Shop. Currently, TNN is the tenth-largest cable network in terms of subscribers, serving approximately 57 million subscribers (approximately 93 percent of all cable households and 61 percent of all television households in the United States).

Country Music Television was acquired in partnership with Group W Satellite Communications, a Westinghouse subsidiary. Country music's answer to MTV, CMT is a 24-hour country music video channel with approximately 20 million subscribers. Gaylord provides a satellite uplink (or alternative means of transmission) to the cable systems.

The Nashville Network and Country Music Television are performing very well as Gaylord management develops expertise in its relatively new line of business. Although competition for cable adoption is intense, few cable alternatives exist in the country/western niche. According to published reports, Gaylord is presently considering further expansion in this area. Hence, the future for this firm appears promising.

SOURCES: "Gaylord Entertainment Names E. K. Gaylord II Vice Chairman," *Dow Jones News Services*, 8 May 1996; M. Burgi, "Cable's Promised Land: Networks Discover Original Programming Can Achieve Broadcast-Quality Ratings," *Mediaweek*, 27 March 1995, pp. 26–34; R. Brown, "The Nashville Network," *Broadcasting and Cable*, 20 February 1995, pp. 34–35; B. Battle, "Gaylord CEO: We are Going to Grow," *Nashville Banner*, 16 April 1994, p. A1; A. Sharpe, "Country Music Finds New Fans and a Firm in Nashville Prospers," *Wall Street Journal*, 19 January 1994, pp. A1, A8; "Opryland Music Has Fertile Roots," *Nashville Banner*, 26 June 1993; P. Stark, "Country Ratings Streak Ends as Format Reaches Plateau," *Billboard*, 15 June 1993, pp. 87–89; D. A. Fox, "Gaylord is Stretching Its Muscles," *Tennessean*, 30 May 1993, p. A1.

dependence on the soft-drink industry. Simultaneously, PepsiCo used its core competence in marketing to expand its fast-food business units. This growth, in turn, helped protect an increasing amount of PepsiCo's soft-drink sales, because Taco Bell, KFC, and Pizza Hut served only soft drinks produced by PepsiCo. (Recall that the preceding chapter suggested that PepsiCo's purchase of fast-food businesses can be considered both horizontal related diversification and vertical integration of related businesses.) Subsequently, PepsiCo spun-off these businesses to again concentrate on soft drinks.

### Compartment C

A business unit in compartment C has distinct competitive strengths but faces critical environmental threats. For some firms, the appropriate strategy may be to diversify into more attractive related industries. Some tobacco firms, for instance, perceive that increasing social and political-legal threats reduce their opportunities for profit and growth. Philip Morris, as one example, has diversified into such related businesses as brewing (Miller) and consumer foods (Kraft General Foods). Such diversification has benefited from Philip Morris's core competence in consumer marketing.

In other cases, the desirable strategy could be to diversify horizontally into unrelated industries, or, by vertical integration of unrelated businesses, to enter into more promising opportunities, or to adopt a divestment strategy. Philip Morris's purchase of a packaging company for its tobacco and food products represents a vertical integration of unrelated businesses. On the other hand, Primerica at one time manufactured containers and packaging materials. Declining opportunities in those industries caused Primerica to diversify horizontally into such unrelated businesses as financial services and specialty retailing. Eventually, it divested itself entirely of its manufacturing businesses and became heavily involved in service industries.

### Compartment D

In compartment D, abundant opportunities face a business unit that has average competitive strengths and weaknesses. In such a situation, management generally prefers to remain in the industry, because of its rich opportunities, but attempts to improve the business unit's competitive strengths.

Moderate competitive strength can take either of two forms: The business unit may have only moderate core competencies, or its strengths may be offset by equivalent weaknesses. In either case, a firm can try to improve its competitive prospects by adopting strategies—merger, horizontal integration, and/or strategic alliance—that link the business unit to organizations that can provide synergistic core competencies. For example, both Nike and Reebok are considered to possess strengths in design and marketing but weaknesses in manufacturing. Consequently, both have forged strategic alliances with low-cost, high-quality manufacturers in Southeast Asia.[3]

### Compartment E

Compartment E business units—those with average strengths and weaknesses that face environments with moderate opportunities and threats—have several strategic alternatives available to them. If the business is reasonably profitable, it may elect a stability strategy. Alternatively, it may attempt to improve its competitive position through a strategy of merger, horizontal integration, or strategic alliance. Should the business unit not become more competitive, the firm might consider divestment, which is also an option for firms that cannot find compatible partners for a merger, horizontal integration, or strategic alliance. Some leading corporations, such as General Electric, for example, divest any business unit that does not become one of the top two performers in its industry within a reasonable period of time.

### Compartment F

Although a business unit in compartment F has moderate competitive strengths, it faces critical environmental threats. If the threats are anticipated to be relatively permanent, divestment may be an appropriate strategy for the

---

STRATEGIC INSIGHT

## *Delta Air Lines: Operating in Compartment E*

By many standards, Delta Air Lines, Inc.'s airline business has been one of the most successful airlines since the deregulation process began in 1978. During the 1980s, the number of passengers served by the airline increased twentyfold while revenues quadrupled to approximately $13 billion. Some possible explanations for Delta's success include its informal corporate culture, its strong service orientation, and the high commitment to its employees.

But regardless of its historically solid competitive position, not all is currently well at Atlanta-based Delta. The carrier lost more than $1.2 billion over three years in the early 1990s. Low-cost airlines such as Southwest have chipped away at Delta's business for a decade. Delta's pilots earn about $100,000 more per year

than do pilots at some of the upstart low-cost airlines.

In an effort to become more cost-competitive by making the carrier more efficient, CEO Ronald W. Allen is slashing everything from advertising budgets to fuel expenses. Delta plans to reduce its work force by 20 percent or 15,000, cut annual labor costs by $640 million, and trim marketing expenses by $400 million by the late 1990s. Allen projects that with these changes, Delta will become profitable.

Allen expects the periodic price competition to continue into the foreseeable future. He believes that the airline can become cost-competitive. Although some analysts are skeptical about Delta's prospects, most agree that Delta will improve and survive as a carrier into the twenty-first century.

SOURCES: "U. S. Okays Delta Air Lines, Korean Air Code-Sharing Pact," *Dow Jones Business News*, 29 May 1996; A. Bryant, "Three Airlines Chart Austerity Course; Delta and Two Small Carriers Are Thriving by Cutting Costs," *New York Times*, 14 June 1995, p. D1; "Delta Achieves Strong Results in Cost-Cutting," *New York Times*, 28 July 1995, p. C4; D. Greising, P. Dwyer, and W. Zellner, "A Destination, But No Flight Plan," *Business Week*, 16 May 1994, pp. 74–75; P. M. Swiercz, "Delta Airlines, Inc.: Taking the Family Global," in P. Wright, J. A. Parnell, and M. Kroll (eds.), *1993 Edition of Cases in Strategic Management* (Boston: Allyn & Bacon, 1993), pp. 53–68.

---

firm because transforming a business unit into a top performer is extremely challenging in the face of critical threats. Alternatively, a firm may diversify out of the present industry into horizontally related or unrelated industries with more promising opportunities. If the environmental threats are deemed temporary, a stability strategy can be appropriate. For instance, some financial institutions with savings and loan businesses chose stability in the latter 1980s and early 1990s because the environmental threats of economic recession and intense competition were expected to be relatively short-lived.

### Compartment G

A turnaround strategy is particularly appropriate for business units in compartment G. They have few strengths and many weaknesses and operate in an environment with plentiful opportunities. The firm might eliminate or outsource any activities in which it lacks competence. Simultaneously, management should attempt to cultivate the business unit's potential strengths. In some cases, granting the business unit significant autonomy from the corporate bureaucracy can unleash latent strengths.

Another alternative is to divest the business through a spin-off. For example, when Lexmark was a business unit of giant IBM, its needs were often neglected. Its printer and typewriter business was represented by IBM salespeople who were more interested in selling computers that brought higher sales commissions; typewriters and printer sales were no more than afterthoughts. Eventually, Lexmark was spun off by IBM. After eliminating 2,000 jobs, Lexmark's management divided the business into small, semiautonomous units, with each concentrating on one product line such as printers, keyboards, printer supplies, or typewriters. Operating procedures were also modified. For instance, Lexmark's CEO, who had been the business unit's top manager when it was under IBM's centralized control, indicated that, whereas IBM had encouraged managers to acquire large budgets and then spend every cent of them, Lexmark would reward managers for coming in under budget.[4]

Divestment can be an appropriate strategy for firms operating business units in compartment G for another reason. Because the environment's opportunities are ample, a business already in the industry can be attractive to other firms desiring to enter the industry on the belief that the business can be turned around. The proceeds from the divestment can be used to strengthen the corporation's remaining business units. Although other strategies—such as mergers, horizontal integration, and strategic alliance—are possible, they are unlikely choices. Other firms are rarely desirous of becoming partners with a business unit that has critical weaknesses.

## Compartment H

A business unit in compartment H has critical competitive weaknesses and faces moderate environmental opportunities. In this case, the turnaround and divestment strategies seem most appropriate, although they are more challenging to implement than in compartment G, where opportunities are more prevalent. A turnaround would take more time and effort, and divestment would be more difficult because fewer potential buyers are interested in acquiring a business in a less-promising industry. Even if divestment were possible, the proceeds from the business's sale would be relatively small.

## Compartment I

The worst case scenario exists for a business unit in compartment I, where the business's critical weaknesses are overwhelmed by extreme environmental threats. In such situations, liquidation is usually the most feasible strategy. Neither a turnaround nor a divestment strategy is practicable because the business's precarious position provides a poor foundation for either strengthening its operations or attracting outsiders.

Because liquidation is distasteful to virtually all of the firm's stakeholders, top management may delay in closing the business. Unfortunately, a delay can jeopardize the health of the entire corporation because the profits of some business units must be used to offset the losses of the business unit that should already have been liquidated. If overall losses exceed profits, the entire firm may have to declare bankruptcy. With some forms of bankruptcy, a firm can continue operating under the supervision of the courts in return for the settlement of the firm's financial obligations.

LTV Corporation is an example of such a firm. For years, its defense and aerospace business subsidized its unprofitable steel business. By 1986, its corporate operating loss amounted to $3 billion. In declaring bankruptcy, LTV's top management indicated that the corporation would liquidate its steel business to concentrate on its more attractive defense and aerospace business.[5]

The following three sections present other portfolio frameworks—two developed by the Boston Consulting Group and one by General Electric.

## ■ Original BCG Framework

The framework discussed in this section was developed in 1967 by the Boston Consulting Group (BCG), a firm that specializes in strategic planning. Originated by Alan J. Zakon of BCG and William W. Wommack of Mead Corporation, the framework has since been elaborated upon by Barry Hedley, a director of BCG.

The **original BCG framework** is illustrated by the matrix shown in Figure 5.2. The market's rate of growth is indicated on the vertical axis, and the firm's share of the market is indicated on the horizontal axis. Each of the circles represents a business unit. The size of the circle reflects the business unit's annual sales, the horizontal position of the circle indicates its market share, and its vertical position depicts the growth rate of the market in which it competes. For instance, the circle in the lower left corner of the matrix symbolizes a business unit with relatively large sales and a very high share of its market. Its market, however, is stagnant, exhibiting little growth. Using this framework, management can categorize each of its different businesses as stars, question marks, cash cows, or dogs, depending upon each business unit's relative market share and the growth rate of its market.[6]

---

**Figure 5.2**                    **The Original BCG Framework**

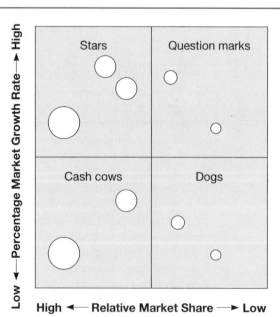

Source: Reprinted from *Long Range Planning*, Vol. 10, B. Hedley, "Strategy and the 'Business Portfolio,'" pp. 9–15, Copyright (1977), with permission from Pergamon Press Ltd., Headington Hill Hall, Oxford OX3 OBW, UK.

A star is a business unit that has a large share of a high-growth market (one with an annual growth rate of 10 percent or more). Although stars are profitable businesses, they usually must consume considerable cash to continue their growth and to fight off the numerous competitors that are attracted to fast-growing markets. Question marks are business units with low shares of rapidly growing markets. Many question marks are new businesses just entering the market. If they are able to grow and become market leaders, they evolve into stars; but if they are unable eventually to command a significant market share despite heavy financial support from corporate headquarters, they will usually be divested or liquidated.

Turning to the lower half of the matrix, a cash cow is a business unit that has a large share of a slow-growth market (one growing at an annual rate of less than 10 percent). Cash cows are normally highly profitable because they often dominate a market that does not attract many new entrants. Because they are so well established, they need not spend vast resources for advertising, product promotions, or consumer rebates. The excess cash that they generate can be used by the corporation to support its stars and question marks. Finally, dogs are business units that have small market shares in slow-growth (or even declining) industries. Dogs are generally marginal businesses that incur either losses or small profits.

Ideally, a corporation should have mostly stars and cash cows, some question marks (because they represent the future of the corporation), and few, if any, dogs. To attain this ideal, corporate-level managers can use any of the four alternative strategies described in the following paragraphs.

---

## STRATEGIC INSIGHT

### *Neglecting a Cash Cow at Diamond International*

From the perspective of the original BCG portfolio framework, U. S. Playing Card was a cash cow for its parent company, Diamond International. Although cash cows do not require vast expenditures for advertising or product promotions, they must still be managed carefully so that they will generate as much excess cash as possible to invest in stars and promising question marks. But Diamond International neglected its U. S. Playing Card subsidiary by allowing the number of highly paid unionized employees to grow without corresponding increases in productivity and by failing to maintain and replace aging machinery and equipment.

Over time, the cash cow became a dog and was divested by Diamond International. The business, however, continued to perform poorly until it was purchased in 1986 by Ronald Rule. Rule engaged in a successful turnaround through such actions as cutting labor costs by one-third, replacing the company's union labor with nonunion employees, and purchasing state-of-the-art machinery and equipment. Today, U. S. Playing Card produces 220,000 decks of cards daily and holds a 70 percent share of the U. S. market and a worldwide market share of 45 percent. Its annual sales amount to $83 million.

U. S. Playing Card is now owned by the Jesup Group of Stamford, Connecticut, although Rule remains its CEO. It accounts for over a quarter of Jesup's annual revenues and serves as a cash cow for some of Jesup's other product lines: laminated plastics, plastic materials and resins, adhesives and sealants, and synthetic rubber.

## Build Market Share

One of the strategies is to build market share. To accomplish this end, managers must identify promising business units that currently fall into the question mark category. Management then attempts to transform these businesses into stars. This process of increasing market share may involve significant price reductions, even if that means incurring losses or marginal profitability in the short run. The underlying assumption of this strategy is that once market share leadership is attained, profitability will follow.

## Hold Market Share

Another strategy is to hold market share. In this situation, cash cows are managed so as to maintain their market shares, rather than to increase them. Holding a large market share generates more cash than building market share does. Hence, the cash contributed by the cash cows can be used to support stars and selected question marks.

## Harvest

Harvesting means milking as much short-term cash from a business as possible, usually while allowing its market share to decline. The cash gained from this strategy is also used to support stars and selected question marks. The businesses harvested are usually dogs, question marks that show little promise of growth, and perhaps some weak cash cows.

## Divest

Divesting a business unit usually provides some cash to the corporation (from the sale) and stems the cash outflow that would have been spent on the business in the future. As dogs and less promising question marks are divested, the cash provided is reallocated to stars and to question marks with the potential to become stars.

As is evident, the BCG framework heavily emphasizes the importance of market share leadership. Cash cows and stars are market share leaders. Some question marks are cultivated to become leaders as well, but less promising question marks and dogs are usually targeted either for harvesting or divestiture. This emphasis on market share has been heavily criticized, leading the BCG to reformulate its portfolio framework.

## ■ Revised BCG Framework

The **revised BCG framework** is illustrated in Figure 5.3. In place of the star, question mark, cash cow, and dog categories are volume, specialization, fragmented, and stalemate business units. Only the volume business is targeted for market share leadership. The volume business generates high profitability through large market share and its accompanying economies of scale. Business units denoted by specialization, however, are those able to yield high profits even though they have a low market share. Because they have selected a market niche in which to operate, they are able to distinguish themselves from their

**Figure 5.3**                    **The Revised BCG Framework**

| Maintain and Support | Divest |
|---|---|
| Volume (emphasize market share leadership) | Stalemate (regardless of relative market share) |
| Specialization (emphasize maintenance of low market share) | |
| Profitable fragmented (do not emphasize market share) | Unprofitable fragmented (regardless of relative market share) |

competitors in the market. The appropriate strategies for these two types of business units, according to the BCG, are for the volume business unit to attempt to gain an even greater market share and for the specialization unit to maintain its low market share.

The next category is fragmented businesses. This term refers to business units operating in fragmented industries. A fragmented industry is one in which numerous firms, perhaps even thousands, exist. Examples include the motel, restaurant, and retail clothing industries. Fragmented industries are characterized by low barriers to entry. (By contrast, a consolidated industry, such as the U. S. automobile manufacturing industry, has high barriers to entry, and, therefore, contains only a few very large competitors.) Businesses in this category can be highly profitable—or unprofitable—regardless of their market share. A local motel or restaurant, for example, can be quite successful, as can Holiday Inn or McDonald's. So fragmented business units should be cultivated for profitability while the importance of market share is de-emphasized. The BCG recommends that profitable fragmented business units be maintained and supported and that unprofitable units be divested.

In the final category, a stalemate business is one that has low, or no, profitability because its industry offers poor prospects. Again, market share is not a consideration in this category. The recommendation for stalemate businesses is that they be divested.

These strategic recommendations are reflected in Figure 5.3. Business units shown on the left side of the figure should be maintained and supported, but those on the right side should be divested.

■ **GE Framework**

Another well-known framework was developed by GE with the help of McKinsey and Company, a consulting firm. As shown in Figure 5.4, the **GE framework** categorizes business units according to industry attractiveness (low, medium, or high) and business unit strength (weak, average, or strong). The ideal business unit is one that is strong relative to its competitors and operates in an industry that is attractive. Some of the criteria used to determine industry attractiveness and business strength are shown in Table 5.1.

**Table 5.1**                    **Criteria for Determining Industry Attractiveness and Business Unit Strengths**

| Industry Attractiveness Criteria | Business Unit Strength Criteria |
| --- | --- |
| Annual industry growth rate | Market share |
| Cyclicality of the industry | Firm profitability |
| Historical profitability of the industry | Per-unit cost of operation |
| Macroenvironmental opportunities and constraints particularly relevant to the industry | Process research and development performance |
| Overall industry size | Product quality |
| Seasonality of the industry | Managerial and personnel talent |
| Intensity of competition | Market share growth |
| Industry predisposition to unionization | Operation capacity |
| Rate of innovation in the industry | Technological know-how |
| | Product research and development performance |
| | Brand reputation |

As shown in Figure 5.4, a corporation's most successful business units fall in the top left section of the diagram, and its least successful ones are in the bottom right section. Average business units fall in between. Strategically, the corporation should divest itself of the business units in the bottom right section while supporting those in the top left area. The average business units will receive less support than those in the upper left unless they are perceived as candidates that have the potential for becoming highly profitable operations.

**Figure 5.4**                    **The GE Framework**

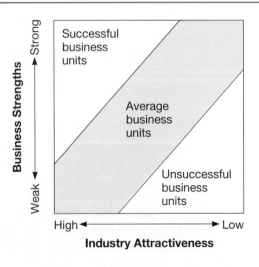

The S.W.O.T., BCG, and GE frameworks may be used by corporate-level management to evaluate each of their business units, to make strategic decisions, and to reallocate resources. Although our discussion has focused on large firms with multiple business units, some small, privately held companies are also active in a number of businesses. These frameworks may be used by their top managers to evaluate their businesses as well.

## ■ Corporate Involvement in Business Unit Operations

We have seen that corporations may have multiple business units in related or unrelated industries. How closely corporate-level managers become involved in the strategy formulation and operation of those business units varies from one firm to another. Historically, corporations that have diversified into unrelated businesses operate in a relatively decentralized fashion.[7] In **decentralization,** firms tend to employ small corporate staffs and allow the business unit managers to make most strategic and operating decisions. These decisions involve functional areas such as purchasing, inventory management, production, finance, research and development, and marketing. Examples of decentralized corporations are Viacom, Litton Industries, and Textron.

Alternatively, corporations whose business units are in the same industry or in related industries usually operate in a relatively centralized fashion. Under **centralization,** many major decisions affecting the business units are made at corporate headquarters, so these companies have larger corporate staffs. Examples include GE and Daimler-Benz.

Corporate involvement in business unit operations can be conceptualized as shown on the continuum below. Involvement can range from being highly centralized to being almost completely decentralized.

Centralized corporations ◄━━━━━━━━► Decentralized corporations

Corporations, of course, may be found at literally any point on this continuum. Decisions regarding centralization and decentralization are not of the either-or variety. Instead, a firm's decision-making processes are termed *relatively centralized* or *relatively decentralized*. Most companies, therefore, are not located at either of the extreme ends of the continuum.

Companies that are relatively centralized make many functional decisions—such as those in purchasing, marketing, finance, and production—at the corporate level. The more commonality in those functional activities across the firm's business units, the greater the tendency is to coordinate those activities at the corporate level. Such centralized decisions can result in efficiencies and consistencies across all business units.

For instance, quantity discounts are larger if the same products are purchased at the corporate level for all business units than if each business unit purchases them separately. As another example, a corporation can borrow more funds at a lower interest rate than separate business units can. Also, central coordination can encourage business units to buy components, if possible and economically feasible, from other business units within the same corporation instead of buying them from outside the company.

Centralization, however, also incurs costs. As the organization grows, larger and larger corporate staffs are required. As the staff increases, so does the distance between top corporate management and the business units. Top managers are forced to rely increasingly on their staff for information, and they communicate downward to the business units through their staff. These processes result in obvious problems in communication and coordination and in the proliferation of bureaucratic procedures.

Decentralized corporations are able to eliminate these problems since highly decentralized firms maintain only skeletal corporate staffs. But they are seldom able to benefit from coordinated activities across their business units, since each operates as at least a semi-independent entity. Therefore, synergy may be lower in a decentralized organization than in one that is centralized.

## CORPORATE STRATEGIES AND RETURNS

In the preceding chapter, we discussed the advantages and disadvantages of various growth strategies. Because most corporations adopt growth strategies of one or more types, considerable research has been conducted on the financial returns associated with these strategies. In this section, we examine the returns generated by corporate growth strategies that involve acquisitions (The following chapter will look at the returns associated with businesses that confine their activities to a single industry.)

Despite the volume of research on this topic, little consensus has been reached. Although numerous studies have concluded that the stockholders of target businesses (those being acquired) benefit financially from the takeover,[8] to what extent the acquiring firms' shareholders benefit is not clear.

One reason for this lack of clarity may be that if competitive rivalry erupts among several acquirers for bidding on a target company, the price of the target company may rise until all above normal profits are eliminated for the corporation that ultimately wins the bidding war. On the other hand, when private and unique synergistic potentials exist between an acquirer and a target company, other bidders may not enter into a competitive bidding for the target company.[9] Thus, in this situation, above normal profits may accrue to the acquiring corporation. Whether competitive bidding occurs or not may explain why the evidence is not clear on the benefits of acquisitions to the shareholders of the acquiring firms.

Another reason for lack of clarity might be that sources of synergy may change over time. What will yield a positive synergy between a bidder and a target company at one point in time may yield a negative synergy at another point in time.[10] Yet another reason may hinge on whether stock ownership of an acquiring corporation is concentrated or diffused.[11] In a diffusely held firm, no one shareholder may find it worthwhile to monitor the corporate executives to make sure that they manage the target company efficiently. Moreover, whether the acquisition is made with cash or stock (or a combination) may influence returns given that cash offerings normally have more positive impacts in financial markets.[12]

Adding a final note to the confusion is the different theoretical paradigms that drive empirical investigations. This is discussed next.

### ▪ Acquisitions Are Not Beneficial

In microeconomics—as well as in one of its research streams, industrial organization—and in select financial theories, it is suggested that acquisitions do not benefit the shareholders of acquiring firms. According to the microeconomics perspective, markets are characterized by perfect competition. (A perfectly competitive market contains a large number of firms, none of which can affect price or supply on its own; each firm has complete knowledge of the activities of all the other firms, including their profitability; there are many customers, none of whom can affect price on their own; all customers have complete knowledge of all products and prices; all of the industry's products are homogeneous; there are many identical potential acquiring firms, none of which on its own can affect the share price of target companies; all shareholders possess perfect information; and no shareholder alone can affect stock prices.) If there were such a setting, all of the firms in a single industry would be identical in their attributes and strategies because, as soon as one attempted to differentiate its product or lower its price to attract more customers, the others would follow suit.

In such a setting, acquisitions could offer only above average returns to the shareholders of the target companies. The acquiring firm's stockholders would receive only "normal returns" because, when the acquiring firm made a bid for another company, its competitors would also recognize the value of the target company and, hence, would engage in competitive bidding to drive up the price of the target company's stock until only normal returns could be realized. Within this context, firms should not make acquisitions because such takeovers will not benefit the shareholders of the acquiring firms. Scholars influenced by this perspective have generally found empirical support for their theories.

In traditional organization theory it is pointed out that the external environment determines the firm's strategy and returns. According to this theory, industry environments differ in their potential returns.[13] Firms that operate business units in favorably industry environments will have higher returns than those operating in unfavorable industry environments.

Select financial theories also emphasize the financial market environment rather than the firm. Because these theories assume that markets are competitive, acquiring attractive target companies would be costly. Therefore, the acquisition strategies of potential acquiring firms would be identical, and the market would set the price of any acquisition. Under such circumstances, these theories do not necessarily recommend acquisitions because they are not thought to be particularly beneficial to the acquiring firms' shareholders.

All of these streams of thought attribute importance to environmental or external factors rather than to the relative strategic strengths and weaknesses of the corporation and its business units. In summary, because acquisitions are viewed as identical strategies that yield only normal returns in competitive markets, scholars in these areas do not consider acquisitions to be advantageous to the shareholders of acquiring firms.

### ■ Acquisitions May Be Beneficial

Advocates of contingency theory and of resource-based theory suggest that acquisitions may benefit the acquiring firms' shareholders. Contingency theorists argue that returns are influenced not only by the environment but also by the strategic fit between the firms' business units and their environments. This school of thought more realistically views markets as imperfectly competitive (markets in which individual suppliers and/or customers can influence price or supply, where firms do not have complete knowledge of all products and prices, where products are differentiated, and where potential acquiring firms may benefit differentially from purchasing a target company so that they would submit dissimilar bids for the same company). Under this scenario, corporations may pursue different acquisition strategies and, hence, would earn different returns.

Implicit in contingency theory is the assumption that related acquisitions may create shareholder value. Related acquisitions are those in which the acquiring and target firms are in related industries and have similar core competencies (such as both in research and development) or complementary core competencies (such as one in manufacturing and one in marketing). The results of research on acquisitions, relevant to this field of thought, are mixed. Some studies show that related acquisitions may be associated with relatively high returns to the acquiring firm's stockholders.[14] Other studies, however, have questioned the value of relatedness in acquisitions. Some have found no significant differences in the returns to the acquiring firm's shareholders whether the acquisition was related or unrelated. Others have found that unrelated acquisitions are associated with higher returns to the acquiring firm's owners than are related acquisitions.[15]

According to advocates of resource-based theory, although the environmental opportunities and threats do matter, they are not the prime influences on an organization's performance, because they change so frequently. A more stable basis for developing strategy would be the firm's unique attributes or strengths. Resource-based theory, therefore, gives less emphasis to the externally imposed bounded opportunities for the firm than does the previously discussed contingency theory. Hence, from this perspective, the firm can behave in a highly proactive fashion. Similar to contingency theory, this school of thought also views markets as imperfectly competitive.

Implicit in resource-based theory is the assumption that related acquisitions might create shareholder value due to the synergies created by similar or complementary core competencies. Although few empirical investigations are based strictly on resource-based theory, the contention that synergies are possible due to similarities or complementarities in core competencies does have empirical support.[16]

So we have seen that, although the stockholders of target companies generally benefit from acquisitions, the evidence is mixed on the extent to which the shareholders of acquiring firms benefit. The question arises, therefore, as to why corporations continue to acquire other businesses in the face of this mixed evidence. Some researchers have argued that top managers may be motivated to acquire other companies because of certain benefits that may accrue to themselves, but not necessarily to the firm's owners.

## MANAGERS' MOTIVES FOR ACQUISITIONS

Although, ideally, the interests of top management and the firm's owners should be congruent, they often are not.[17] In fact, according to numerous studies, the compensation of top-level managers appears unrelated to the financial success of their organizations.[18] Since their compensation often is not closely tied to bottom line results, top managers may select corporate strategies that could enrich them without necessarily benefiting their stockholders. This potential for conflict of interest is termed an **agency problem**—that is, a situation in which the owners' agents, the corporation's top managers, fail to act in the best interests of the owners.

Agency problems may be particularly prevalent in acquisition situations. Since an acquisition immediately increases the size of the acquiring firm and since higher compensation for top management can be related to the size of the firm,[19] top managers may well be encouraged to acquire other companies. However, increased firm size is not always beneficial to shareholders. Acquisitions often involve taking on significant amounts of debt to finance the purchase, which can, at least for several years, depress profits. Depressed profits generally translate into lower stock prices and sometimes even reduced dividends.

Additionally, acquisitions of companies in other industries may also benefit the acquiring firm's top management but not its stockholders. Diversification may reduce the risk that top executives will lose their jobs[20] because it reduces the firm's overall risk by spreading risk across more than one industry. But, as suggested earlier, shareholders can better reduce their financial risk by diversifying their own investments (through buying stocks in companies in different industries or purchasing mutual funds) rather than by having top management do it for them.

# SUMMARY

Because managing several businesses concurrently is quite complex, a number of corporate portfolio frameworks are available to assist top managers. The S.W.O.T. portfolio framework helps corporate-level managers assess the strengths and weaknesses of each of their business units in light of the opportunities and threats presented by the business unit's environment. Based upon the relative match between the environment and the business unit, this framework suggests which corporate-level strategy or strategies are appropriate for each of the firm's business units.

Other frameworks, by the Boston Consulting Group and by General Electric, can assist corporate-level managers to evaluate the performance of each of their business units, to make strategic decisions for each unit, and to reallocate resources from one unit to another.

Corporate-level managers must decide on the extent to which they will be involved in strategic and operational decision making at the business unit level. Usually, corporations that have diversified into related businesses remain fairly centralized, whereas conglomerates operate in a relatively decentralized fashion.

Because of the prevalence of growth strategies, considerable research has been conducted on the financial returns associated with these strategies. To date, studies indicate that, in general, the stockholders of target businesses benefit financially from the takeover, but the extent to which shareholders of the acquiring firm benefit is not entirely clear. In some cases, acquisitions appear to yield no benefits, whereas in other cases, they do. Yet, even when takeovers do not benefit the acquiring firm's shareholders, top managers are often encouraged to acquire other firms because, by so doing, they can reduce the risk of losing their jobs while they increase their compensation.

## TAKE IT TO THE NET

We invite you to visit the Wright page on the Prentice Hall Web site at:

**http://www.prenhall.com/wright**

for this chapter's World Wide Web exercise.

## KEY CONCEPTS

**Agency problem**   A situation in which a corporation's top managers (who serve as the agents of the firm's owners, the stockholders) fail to act in the best interests of the owners.

**BCG portfolio framework (original)**   A corporate portfolio framework developed by the Boston Consulting Group that categorizes a firm's business units by the market share that they hold and the growth rate of their respective markets.

**BCG portfolio framework (revised)**   The more recent framework developed by the Boston Consulting Group that categorizes a firm's business units as volume (generates high profitability through large market share), specialization (yields high profits by operating in a market niche), fragmented (operates in a fragmented industry in which market share is unrelated to profitability), and stalemate (incurs low or no profits because its industry offers poor prospects).

**Centralization**   An organizational decision-making process in which most strategic and operating decisions are made by managers at the top of the organization structure (at corporate headquarters).

**Decentralization**   An organizational decision-making process in which most strategic and operating decisions are made by managers at the business unit level.

**GE portfolio framework**   A corporate portfolio framework developed by General Electric Company that categorizes a corporation's business units according to industry attractiveness and business unit strength.

**S.W.O.T. portfolio framework**   Our corporate portfolio framework that categorizes each of a corporation's business units according to its strengths and weaknesses and its environment's opportunities and threats. It goes on to provide guidelines as to which corporate strategies may be appropriate under particular situations.

## DISCUSSION QUESTIONS

1. Explain the purpose of corporate portfolio framework analysis.

2. Discuss how the S.W.O.T. portfolio framework can help corporate-level managers develop strategies for multiple business units.

3. Which corporate-level strategies are most viable for a business unit operating in compartment E in the S.W.O.T. portfolio framework? Under what circumstances might each of these strategies be appropriate? Which ones would you recommend for a corporation of your own choosing and its business units?

4. Which corporate-level strategies are most viable for a business unit operating in compartment G of the S.W.O.T. portfolio framework? Under what circumstances might each of these strategies be appropriate?

5. Compare and contrast the S.W.O.T. portfolio framework with the original BCG portfolio framework.

6. What are the differences and similarities between the original and revised BCG frameworks?

7. Explain the differences and similarities between the original BCG framework and the GE framework.

8. What types of organizations are likely to operate in a relatively centralized (versus a relatively decentralized) fashion? Why?

9. When one firm acquires another, which group of stockholders—those of the acquiring firm or those of the target firm—is more likely to benefit financially? Why?

10. Even though the evidence is mixed on the extent to which the stockholders of acquiring firms benefit from acquisitions, the top managers of many firms continue to engage in acquisitions. Why?

# STRATEGIC MANAGEMENT EXERCISES

1. Choose a real corporation that has multiple business units (either related or unrelated). Attempt to place each of the firm's business units into the appropriate compartment (A, B, C, etc.) in the S.W.O.T. portfolio framework.

2. Now place each business unit (Exercise 1) into the appropriate category in the original BCG framework (star, cash cow, question mark, or dog).

3. Place each of the business units (Exercise 1) into the appropriate category in the revised BCG portfolio framework (volume, specialization, fragmented, or stalemate).

4. Place each of the business units (Exercise 1) into the appropriate category in the GE portfolio framework (successful, average, or unsuccessful).

5. Now take one of these business units (Exercise 1) and compare the strategies that are recommended for it by the S.W.O.T. framework, the

original BCG framework, the revised BCG framework, and the GE framework. Discuss why different frameworks have recommended different strategies for the same business unit (if they have).

# NOTES

1. R. A. D'Aveni and A. Y. Ilinitch, "Complex Patterns of Vertical Integration in the Forest Products Industry: Systematic and Bankruptcy Risks," *Strategic Management Journal* 35 (1992), 596–625.

2. B. Dumaine, "Is Big Still Good?" *Fortune*, 20 April 1992, p. 51.

3. Ibid., p. 53.

4. P. B. Carroll, "Story of an IBM Unit That Split Off Shows Difficulties of Change," *Wall Street Journal*, 23 July 1992; Dumaine, "Is Big Still Good?" p. 56.

5. M. Schroeder and A. Bernstein, "A Brawl with Labor Could Block LTV's Rebirth," *Business Week*, 16 March 1992, p. 40.

6. B. Hedley, "Strategy and the Business Portfolio," *Long Range Planning*, 10, no. 2 (1977): 9–14.

7. D. K. Datta and J. H. Grant, "Relationships Between Type of Acquisition, the Autonomy Given to the Acquired Firm, and Acquisition Success: An Empirical Analysis," *Journal of Management* 16 (1990): 29–44.

8. J. B. Barney, "Returns to Bidding Firms in Mergers and Acquisitions: Reconsidering the Relatedness Hypothesis," *Strategic Management Journal* 9 (1988): 71–78.

9. Ibid.

10. R. Davis and L. G. Thomas, "Direct Estimation of Synergy: A New Approach to the Diversity-Performance Debate," *Management Science* 39 (1993): 1334–1346; S. Huddart, "The Effect of a Large Shareholder on Corporate Value," *Management Science* 39 (1993): 1407–1421.

11. S. Huddart, "The Effect of a Large Shareholder on Corporate Value," *Management Science* 39 (1993):1407-1421.

12. O. Nodoushani, "The Legitimacy of Management," *Scandinavian Journal of Management* 9 (1993): 225–240; A. A. Lado, N. G. Boyd, and P. Wright, "A Competency-Based Model of Sustainable Competitive Advantage: Toward a Conceptual Integration," *Journal of Management* 18 (1992): 77–91; J. B. Barney, "Returns to Bidding Firms."

13. L. Everett, "Past Returns, Acquisition Strategies and Returns to Bidding Firms," unpublished manuscript, the University of Memphis, 1992; R. P. Rumelt, *Strategy, Structure, and Economic Performance* (Cambridge: Division of Research, Graduate School of Business Administration, Harvard University Press, 1974); C. K. Prahalad and R. A. Bettis, "The Dominant Logic: A New Linkage Between Diversity and Performance," *Strategic Management Journal* 7 (1986): 485–501; R. M. Grant, "On Dominant Logic, Relatedness, and the Link Between Diversity and Performance," *Strategic Management Journal* 9 (1988): 639–642; C. K. Prahalad and G. Hamel, "The Core Competence of the Corporation," *Harvard Business Review* 68, no. 3 (1990): 79–91.

14. R. A. Bettis and W. K. Hall, "Diversification Strategy, Accounting Determined Risk, and Accounting Determined Return," *Academy of Management Journal* 25 (1982): 254–264; M. Lubatkin, "Merger Strategies and Stockholder Value," *Strategic Management Journal* 8 (1987); 39–53.

15. P. T. Elgers and J. J. Clark, "Merger Types and Stockholder Returns: Additional Evidence," *Financial Management* 9 (1980): 66–72; P. Dubofsky and P. Varadarajan, "Diversification and Measures of Performance: Additional Empirical Evidence," *Academy of Management Journal* 30 (1987): 597–608.

16. J. S. Harrison, M. A. Hitt, R. E. Hoskisson, and R. D. Ireland, "Synergies and Post-Acquisition Performance: Differences versus Similarities in Resource Allocations," *Journal of Management* 17 (1991): 173–190; H. Singh and C. A. Montgomery, "Corporate Acquisition Strategies and Economic Performance," *Strategic Management Journal* 8 (1987): 377–386.

**17.** P. Wright, S. P. Ferris, A. Sarin, and V. Awasthi, "Impact of Corporate Insider, Blockholder, and Institutional Equity Ownership on Firm Risk Taking," *Academy of Management Journal* 39 (1996): 441–463; G. P. Baker, M. C. Jensen, and K. J. Murphy, "Compensation and Incentives: Practice vs. Theory," *Journal of Finance* 43 (1988): 593–616; M. C. Jensen and K. J. Murphy, "CEO Incentives—It's Not How Much You Pay, But How," *Harvard Business Review* 14, no. 3 (1990): 138–153.

**18.** Jensen and Murphy, "CEO Incentives—It's Not How Much You Pay, But How."

**19.** M. Kroll, P. Wright, L. Toombs, and H. Leavell, "Form of Control: A Critical Determinant of Acquisition Performance and CEO Rewards," *Strategic Management Journal*, 18 (1997): 85–96.

**20.** Y. Amihud and B. Lev, "Risk Reduction as a Managerial Motive for Conglomerate Mergers," *Bell Journal of Economics* 7 (Autumn 1981): 605–617.

# STRATEGIC MANAGEMENT MODEL

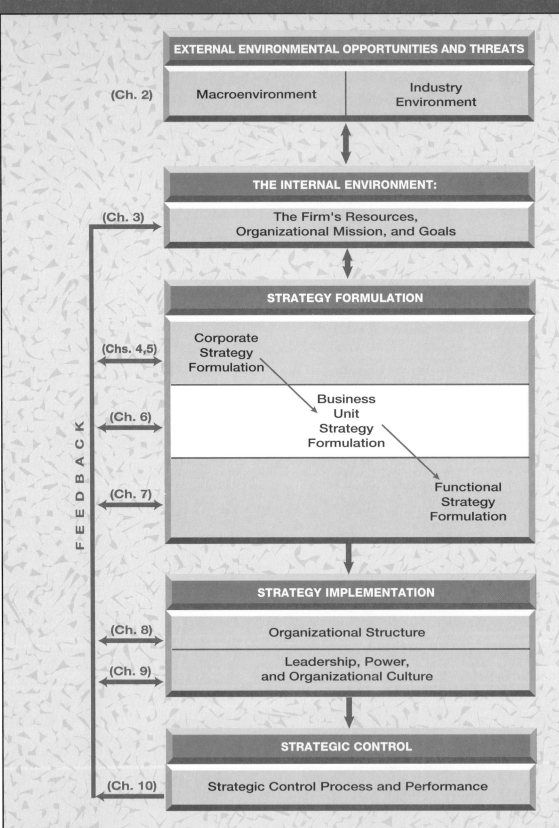

**EXTERNAL ENVIRONMENTAL OPPORTUNITIES AND THREATS**

(Ch. 2)

| Macroenvironment | Industry Environment |

**THE INTERNAL ENVIRONMENT:**

(Ch. 3)

The Firm's Resources, Organizational Mission, and Goals

**STRATEGY FORMULATION**

(Chs. 4,5) Corporate Strategy Formulation

(Ch. 6) Business Unit Strategy Formulation

(Ch. 7) Functional Strategy Formulation

**STRATEGY IMPLEMENTATION**

(Ch. 8) Organizational Structure

(Ch. 9) Leadership, Power, and Organizational Culture

**STRATEGIC CONTROL**

(Ch. 10) Strategic Control Process and Performance

FEEDBACK

# 6 Business Unit Strategies

While the strategic question at the corporate level is, In what industries or businesses should we be operating?, the appropriate question at the business unit level is, How should we compete in the chosen industry or business? A **business unit** is an organizational subsystem that has a market, a set of competitors, and a mission distinct from those of the other subsystems in the firm. The concept of the strategic business unit was pioneered by General Electric Company (GE). At GE, for example, one business unit manufactures and markets major appliances such as ranges, refrigerators, dishwashers, and clothes washers and dryers. Another business unit is responsible for producing and selling jet engines to airplane manufacturers. In total, GE contains more than 200 strategic business units. Each of these business units adopts its own strategy consistent with the organization's corporate-level strategy. Because each business unit serves a different market and competes with different companies than do the firm's other business units, it must operate with its own mission, goals, and strategy.

A single company that operates within only one industry is also considered a business unit. For instance, an independent company that builds and sells swimming pools is considered a business unit. In such an organization, corporate-level strategy and business unit strategy are the same. Hence, the focus of this chapter is on organizational entities that contain their own functional departments, such as production and sales, and operate within a single industry.

Managers of these business units can choose from a number of **generic strategies** to guide their organizations. These strategic alternatives are termed *generic* because they can be adopted by any type of business unit, whether it be a traditional manufacturing company, a high-technology firm, or a service

135

organization. Of the seven strategies available and discussed in this chapter, three are most appropriate for small business units; the remaining four are used by large business units.

## GENERIC STRATEGIES FOR SMALL BUSINESS UNITS

This section presents the generic strategies that are most appropriate for small business units: the niche–low cost, niche–differentiation, and niche–low-cost/differentiation strategies.

### ■ Niche–Low-Cost Strategy

The **niche–low-cost strategy** emphasizes keeping overall costs low while serving a narrow segment of the market. Business units that adopt this strategy produce no-frills products or services for price-sensitive customers in a market niche. The no-frills outputs of one business differ little from those of competing businesses, and market demand for these outputs is elastic.

Depending upon the prevailing industry forces, customers generally are willing to pay only low to average prices for no-frills products or services. Hence, it is essential that businesses using this strategy keep their overall costs as low as possible. Therefore, they emphasize keeping their initial investment low and holding operating costs down. For instance, these organizations will purchase from suppliers who offer the lowest prices, and they will emphasize the function of financial control. Research and development efforts will be directed at improving operational efficiency, and attempts will be made to enhance logistical and distribution efficiencies. Such businesses will de-emphasize the development of new or improved products or services that might raise costs, and advertising and promotional expenditures will be minimized.

**Figure 6.1**          **A Business Competing with the Niche–Low-Cost Strategy**

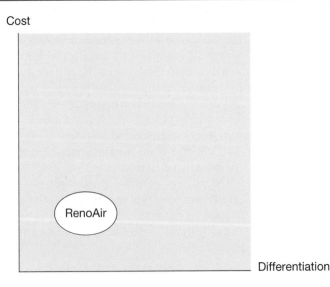

Figure 6.1 portrays the strategic position of a business unit (Reno Air) that competes using the niche–low-cost strategy. Its location on the chart reflects its strategy of low costs and minimal product/service differentiation.

Ideally, the small business unit that adopts the niche–low-cost strategy competes only where it enjoys a cost advantage relative to large low-cost competitors. For example, small short-line railroads are able to make a profit by serving shippers whose business is too insignificant for the large railroads. The small railroads do not have to hire union labor, so their wage rates are lower and they can use smaller crews than their larger rivals.[1]

Businesses that compete using the niche–low-cost strategy might deliberately avoid creating successively new outputs for fear of increasing their costs.

---

### S T R A T E G I C   I N S I G H T

## *Reno Air's Niche–Low-Cost Strategy*

Reno Air, Inc. is a Reno-based, publicly held short-haul passenger carrier. It offers daily jet service to destinations throughout the western United States and Canada for low fares. The company is led by airline veteran Robert Reding, president and CEO. Reno Air, which began operations in 1992, employs a niche–low-cost strategy. The company appeals to price-sensitive and time-conscious travelers, and, management places a heavy emphasis on intensive aircraft use and high employee productivity.

By keeping its costs low, Reno Air is price-competitive not only with other airlines but also with such alternative modes of transportation as personal automobiles and rental cars. For instance, Reno Air once charged $39 for a flight from Reno to Seattle, less than half the fare of its competitors. Moreover, Reno Air does not require that passengers purchase round-trip tickets. Fares are based on advance purchase only. It is not surprising that a U. S. Department of Transportation study found that 48 million new passengers took to the skies in 1996 because of low-cost airlines such as Reno Air.

Although Reno Air has adopted some of the successful strategies of Southwest Airlines, there are some fundamental strategic differences as well. Unlike Southwest, which is committed to increasing its market share nationally, Reno Air management intends to pursue controlled growth while keeping the airline fairly small and limiting flights to its twenty or so destinations, primarily located in the western United States. Further, whereas some low-cost carriers like Southwest attempt to dominate the routes they serve with more than ten daily flights, Reno Air has chosen to concentrate on few departures between cities, partly to avoid head-on competition with the large carriers.

Reno Air's niche–low-cost strategy is not without its challenges. In the airline industry, low-price firms are under constant scrutiny by the media, organized labor, and larger airlines concerning pilot training, flight hours, and safety issues. After the May 1996 ValuJet crash near Miami that killed more than 100 people, larger airlines and government officials called for federal investigations into safety standards. Safety records released after the crash revealed that small, low-cost airlines experience four times as many accidents as major airlines, although the Federal Aviation Administration's subsequent investigation of low-cost airlines revealed a spotless record for Reno Air.

SOURCES: J. Stearns, "Winning Industry Respect," *Reno Gazette-Journal*, 25 February 1996, pp. 1E, 2E; H. Robertson, "Boss Pilots Reno's Inaugural Flight to Fairbanks," *Fairbanks Daily News-Miner*, 5 April 1996, pp. B1, B2; E. deLisser, "Low-Fare Airlines Mute Their Bargain Message," *Wall Street Journal*, 22 May 1996, pp. B1, B7; "Conditions Are Ideal for Starting an Airline, and Many Are Doing It," *Wall Street Journal*, 1 April, 1996, pp. A1, A7; J. Stearns, "Federal Report Shows Reno Air with Flawless Record for Safety," *Reno Gazette-Journal*, 25 May 1996, pp. 1A, 5A; A. Bryant, "Three Airlines Chart Austerity Course; Delta and Two Small Carriers Are Thriving by Cutting Costs," *New York Times*, 14 June 1995, p. D1; G. Delaplane, "Flyin' High on Low Fares," *Reno Gazette-Journal*, 11 July 1996, pp. 1C, 6C; *Reno Air 1995 Annual Report*.

Such businesses may value technological stability in their organizations. Stable technologies enable them to produce no-frills outputs at low costs.

An important vulnerability of the niche–low-cost strategy is that intense price competition periodically occurs in markets with no-frills outputs. For instance, several years ago Laker Airways used the niche–low-cost strategy successfully by providing a first in the airline industry: no-frills, low-priced trans-Atlantic passenger service. However, the major airlines eventually responded by offering virtually identical service. The resulting price war drove Laker Airways out of business. The large competitors, because of their greater financial resources, were able to survive the shakeout even though many of them incurred financial losses.

Another important vulnerability of this strategy may be technological obsolescence. Businesses that may value technological stability, and consequently might avoid responding to new product and market opportunities, may eventually find that their products have become obsolete and are no longer desired by their customers.

## ■ Niche-Differentiation Strategy

The **niche-differentiation strategy** is appropriate for business units that produce highly differentiated, need-fulfilling products or services for the specialized needs of a narrow range of customers or a market niche. Because these outputs are intended to fulfill a deeper set of customer needs than either no-frills goods or differentiated goods (discussed later under the differentiation strategy), and because the market demand for these outputs tends to be inelastic, these goods or services can command high prices. Hence, cost reduction efforts are not often emphasized by businesses competing with the niche-differentiation strategy.

In fact, these businesses may be deliberately inefficient because they continuously attempt to create new product and market opportunities or to respond to them. Both actions are costly. Therefore, they may highly value technological and organizational fluidity in order to create or keep pace with new developments in their industries.

Broadly speaking, high prices are acceptable to certain customers who need product performance, prestige, safety or security. For instance, some customers may be willing to pay high prices for state-of-the-art stereo component systems that perform at a wide range of frequencies and low sound distortions (performance needs). Another cluster of customers will pay very high prices for designer clothes (prestige needs). Yet another group of industrial buyers will pay significantly more to suppliers who continuously improve the reliability of the nuts and bolts they produce to fasten the wings of an airplane to its body (safety or security needs). Figure 6.2 shows the strategic position of a business unit (Bijan) that serves the specialized needs of select customers. Note that high costs and high product/service differentiation characterize the niche-differentiation strategy.

The exclusive Beverly Hills retailer Bijan demonstrates this strategy. Bijan buys specialized, quality products only for customized needs that tend to change frequently and carries one-of-a-kind, costly merchandise. Shopping at Bijan is done only through personal appointment.

The chief vulnerability of this strategy is that competitors who also emphasize lowering of costs may in some situations be able to offer similar products

**Figure 6.2**  **A Business Competing with the Niche-Differentiation Strategy**

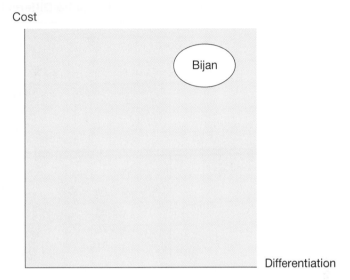

at predatory prices. In fact, using niche–differentiation in conjunction with lower costs can be a particularly effective strategy for a number of, but not all, small business units in select industries.

### ▪ Niche–Low-Cost/Differentiation Strategy

Business units that compete using the **niche–low-cost/differentiation strategy** produce highly differentiated, need-fulfilling products or services for the specialized needs of a select group of customers or of a market niche while keeping their costs low. Figure 6.3 on page 140 reflects the strategic position of a business unit (Porsche) that has adopted this strategy. Note that this business has low costs relative to Rolls-Royce, for instance, while offering a high degree of output differentiation.

How can a business simultaneously differentiate its products or services and lower its costs? The following discussion presents several ways these dual goals can be attained. These methods are listed in Table 6.1. (Note that although these routes are discussed in the context of small business units, they also pertain to large business units that adopt the low-cost–differentiation strategy, which is discussed later in this chapter.)

**Table 6.1**  **Ways Organizations Can Simultaneously Differentiate Their Products/Services and Lower Their Costs**

Dedication to quality

Process innovations

Product innovations

Leverage through organizational expertise and image

**Figure 6.3**

**A Business (Porsche) Competing by Using the Niche–Low-Cost/Differentiation Strategy and Another Business (Rolls-Royce) Competing by Using the Niche-Differentiation Strategy**

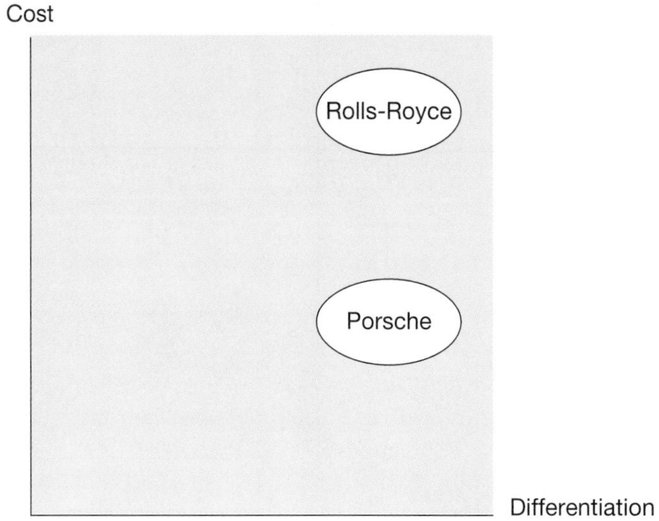

## Dedication to Quality

A consistent, continual dedication to quality throughout the business not only improves outputs but also reduces costs involved in scrap, warranty, and service after the sale. **Quality** is defined as "the totality of features and characteristics of a product or service that bear on its ability to satisfy stated or implied needs."[2] Hence, a high-quality product or service conforms to a predetermined set of specifications and satisfies the needs of its users. In this sense, quality is a measure of customer satisfaction with a product over its lifetime, relative to customer satisfaction with competitors' product offerings.[3] Note that the customer's perception of quality is the key criterion. While conformance to a predetermined set of specifications is necessary, perceived quality by the buyer provides the sufficient condition.

Quality consultant Philip B. Crosby states that building quality into a product does not cost a company more, because the costs of rework, scrap, and servicing the product after the sale are reduced, and the business benefits from increased customer satisfaction and repeat sales. Simultaneous emphasis on quality and low costs is feasible not only in manufacturing but also in service businesses.[4] For example, improved information systems allow banks to offer higher-quality services to their customers at lower costs.

In a broader sense, numerous companies in recent years have adopted **total quality management (TQM)** programs. Such approaches attempt to improve product and service quality and increase customer satisfaction by modifying a company's management practices. An essential attribute of TQM programs is that the customer is the final arbiter of quality. A U. S. General Accounting Office study of twenty companies that adopted TQM programs concluded that, in most cases, quality improved, costs fell, customer satisfaction increased, and profitability grew.[5]

## Process Innovations

Activities that increase the efficiency of operations and distribution are termed **process innovations.** Although these improvements are normally thought of as lowering costs, they can also enhance product or service differentiation.

> A computer manufacturer invested $20 million in a flexible assembly system. The investment made good operational sense because it paid for itself in less than a year. Strategically, the investment was even more attractive. Production time was cut by 80%, and product quality improved tenfold.[6]

In this case, costs were lowered, and the significant increase in product quality helped differentiate the product from those of the organization's competitors.

## Product Innovations

Although it is common to think of **product innovations** in the context of enhancing differentiation, such improvements can also lower costs. For instance, over the years Philip Morris developed a filter cigarette and then, later, cigarettes with lower tar and nicotine levels. Although these innovations differentiated its product, they also helped lower its costs. The techniques used to produce these cigarettes (freeze drying and reconstituted tobacco sheets) allowed the company to use less tobacco per cigarette to produce a product perceived as higher quality at a dramatic reduction in per-unit costs.[7]

## Leverage Through Organizational Expertise and Image

There are other ways to lower costs and heighten differentiation. For instance, small manufacturers normally suffer from a disadvantage in purchasing relative to their larger competitors, because big firms can obtain quantity discounts and often receive substantial engineering support from their suppliers. However, Porsche, a relatively small manufacturer of sports cars, has overcome this problem.

> Even though Porsche purchases small quantities of goods for its operations, it gets competitive prices and significant technical support from its suppliers. The reason is that Porsche does quite a bit of outside engineering for giants such as General Motors, Ford, Volkswagen, etc. Suppliers wish to be a part of Porsche's outside engineering developments in order to have the inside track for future orders forthcoming from those larger companies. Hence, it is to the benefit of suppliers to keep Porsche a very satisfied customer.[8]

Porsche, then, is able to use its **organizational expertise**—a business's ability to do something particularly well in comparison with its competitors—in engineering to persuade its suppliers to discount their prices, which lowers Porsche's costs. At the same time, Porsche has obtained high-quality supplier support.

Porsche has also creatively lowered its costs and heightened its differentiation in the area of promotion. Rather than spend substantial sums on mass advertising, Porsche has concentrated its efforts on public relations. Knowing that automobile enthusiasts perceive a certain image or mystique associated with Porsche cars, the company has used this leverage (organizational image) to cultivate a close relationship with such magazines as *Road and Track, Motor Trend,* and *Car and Driver.* These magazines report extensively on Porsche cars, at no cost to Porsche.

## GENERIC STRATEGIES FOR LARGE BUSINESS UNITS

This section presents the generic strategies that are most appropriate for large business units. These are the low-cost, differentiation, and low-cost–differentiation strategies. Finally, in some instances, large business units may employ some combination of generic strategies. This approach is termed *multiple strategies*[9] and is discussed subsequently.

### ▪ Low-Cost Strategy

Large businesses that compete by using a **low-cost strategy** produce no-frills products and services industrywide. That is, they address a mass market comprised of price-sensitive customers. The outputs of one business differ little from those of other businesses, and the market demand for the outputs is elastic. Consequently, companies using this strategy attempt to lower their costs in their functional areas. For instance, purchases are made from suppliers that offer quantity discounts and the lowest prices. Mass production is pursued whenever possible to lower production costs per unit. Finance plays an influential role since cost control is a high priority. Research and development efforts are directed at improving operational efficiency, and attempts are made to improve logistical and distribution efficiencies. Such businesses de-emphasize the development of new or improved products or services that may raise costs, and advertising and promotional costs are minimized. Figure 6.4 portrays the

**Figure 6.4**　　　　**A Business (Wal-Mart) Competing by Using the Low-Cost Strategy and Another Business (Nieman-Marcus) Competing by Using the Differentiation Strategy**

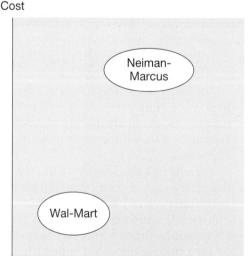

strategic position of a large business unit (Wal-Mart) that competes with the low-cost strategy. As may be seen, Wal-Mart offers low-differentiated services at low costs relative to Neiman-Marcus, for instance. Wal-Mart's purchasing costs are generally the lowest in the industry, and as in other discount department stores, its services are minimal.

Pursuing a low-cost strategy is consistent with acquiring a large share of the market.[10] A large market share allows scale economies in such areas as purchasing (quantity discounts), manufacturing (mass production), financing (lower interest rates are usually available to large firms), and distribution (mass wholesaling and merchandising).

Small business units using the niche–low-cost strategy keep their costs down through a low initial investment and low operating expenses, but large business units that pursue a low-cost strategy rely on large market shares and scale economies. For example, a small bank offering no-frills services benefits from operating in a small, unpretentious building (low initial investment). Its fixed and variable costs are relatively low because it operates with few employees and limited assets relative to large banks with head offices, bank branches, and many employees. By contrast, a large bank offering no-frills services benefits from the economies of scale that can be gained through large-volume operations. So even though both the niche–low-cost strategy and the low-cost strategy rely on keeping costs down, the means of attaining this goal are different.

Examples of companies that compete by pursuing the low-cost strategy can be found in the commodities industries, where firms produce and sell no-frills products. As a case in point, Hanson PLC's business units compete with the low-cost strategy. For instance, one of Hanson's business units—Peabody—produces coal, another one—Quantum Chemical—is a maker of polyethylene, used in packaging, and yet another one—Cavenham—is in the forest products and lumber business. A well-known historical example in the manufacturing arena is the Ford Motor Company, which used to compete using the low-cost strategy. The Model T, a no-frills automobile, was mass-produced and sold at a low price to a large and growing market.

Some manufacturers that choose to use a low-cost strategy, however, may be vulnerable to intense price competition, which drives profit margins down.[11] Under these circumstances, their ability to improve outputs, augment their products with superior services, or spend more on advertising and promotion may be severely limited.[12] If they begin to lose customers to competitors with superior products, they might, in response, lower their prices, which would put even more pressure on their profit margins. The prospect of being caught in this vicious cycle keeps many manufacturers from adopting the low-cost strategy.

Another important vulnerability of this strategy may be technological obsolescence. Manufacturers that value technological stability, and consequently avoid responding to new product and market opportunities, may eventually find that their products have become obsolete and are no longer desired by their customers.

## ■ Differentiation Strategy

Businesses that employ the **differentiation strategy** produce distinct products or services industrywide. That is, they address a large market with a relatively inelastic demand. Their customers are generally willing to pay average to high prices for distinct outputs. Because customers are relatively price-insensitive, businesses emphasize quality in each of their functional areas. For instance, purchases are made from suppliers that offer high-quality raw materials, parts, and components, even if the cost is relatively high. The production department emphasizes quality over cost considerations. Research and development activities focus on developing new or improved products and services, and the company's sales efforts are generously supported with advertising and promotion. Although the finance function is important, it does not dominate organizational decision making.[13] If a business suddenly finds itself faced with a competitor's superior products, it may well borrow money immediately to improve its products, even if the prevailing interest rate is high.

Businesses that compete by pursuing the differentiation strategy attempt to create new product and market opportunities or respond to them,[14] although these actions are costly. Such organizations value technological fluidity so that they may create or keep pace with new developments in their industries.[15]

Figure 6.5 portrays the strategic position of a business unit (Sony Engineering and Manufacturing, maker of televisions, video and audio hardware) that uses the differentiation strategy; note its high costs and high differentiation. Such a company requires a large market share so that it may establish a distinct image throughout the industry. To attain this end, the business may either acquire patent protection or develop strong brands that create consumer loyalty. Sony is an example of a successful differentiator.

Others have not been as fortunate and have had to change their strategy. Xerox is an example of such a business. For years, Xerox copiers were made with costly, internally produced components, and they were heavily advertised and promoted. And for years, the company was able to pass along its high costs to its customers in the form of high prices.[16] However, Xerox, like other businesses using a differentiation strategy, found itself vulnerable to new competitors with similar products at lower costs and prices.[17] As Japanese competitors began to offer high-quality copiers that were produced more efficiently and priced significantly lower than Xerox products, Xerox saw its earnings and

**Figure 6.5**          **A Business Competing by Using the Differentiation Strategy**

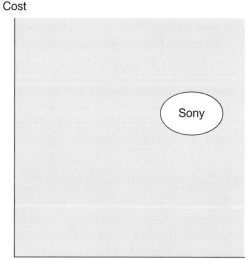

Cost

Sony

Differentiation

market share decline significantly. To rebound, it cut its manufacturing costs by 30 percent, reduced the time needed to develop new products by 50 percent, and greatly improved the quality of its copiers.[18] Xerox now follows the generic strategy, discussed next.

### ■ Low-Cost–Differentiation Strategy

Organizations that compete by pursuing a **low-cost–differentiation strategy** serve, for the most part, the same large, relatively price-insensitive market for distinct products or services that was already discussed. This strategy is illustrated in Figure 6.6. The business (Anheuser-Busch) shown in the figure maintains low costs while offering differentiation.

This particular strategy is relatively controversial. Some theorists believe that competing simultaneously with low costs and differentiation is inconsistent. That is, a business that emphasizes differentiation cannot also maintain low costs, and a business that keeps costs low cannot produce differentiated outputs.[19] However, a growing volume of theoretical and empirical work demonstrates that a dual emphasis on low costs and differentiation can result in high performance.

We believe that the low-cost–differentiation strategy is possible to attain and can be quite effective. This strategy begins with an organizational commitment to quality products or services. Thus, the organization is active technologically in order to improve output quality. By providing high-quality outputs, the business differentiates itself from its competitors. Because customers for particular products or services are drawn to high quality, the business unit that offers such quality will experience an increasing demand for its outputs. This increasing demand results in a larger market share, providing economies of scale that permit lower per-unit costs in purchasing, manufacturing, financing, research and development, and marketing. Such businesses as Wrigley, Campbell Soup,

---

**Figure 6.6**      **A Business Competing by Using the Low-Cost–Differentiation Strategy**

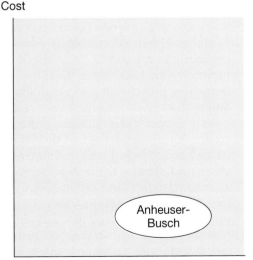

and many of the large business units of GE differentiate their outputs through high quality while they simultaneously maintain low per-unit-cost operations.

For instance, Anheuser-Busch is the largest producer of beer in the United States, with a market share of 42 percent. Because of its size, the company bene-fits from quantity discounts in purchasing and from other scale economies in its processing operations, its research and development activities, and its mar-keting functions. Even with its low costs, however, Anheuser-Busch differenti-ates itself through its taste and its advertising ("This Bud's for you" and "The night belongs to Michelob") and by emphasizing its high-quality raw materials ("choicest hops, rice and best barley") and its production process ("brewed by our original process"). Additionally, this business keeps pace with market de-velopments and introduces new products periodically, with Ice Draft being a recent example.

In the service area, Federal Express used the differentiation strategy to create the overnight delivery industry two decades ago. But, as competitors entered the industry and began to duplicate Federal Express's superb service, cus-tomers began shopping for companies with lower prices. By 1992, Federal Ex-press was rapidly adopting the low-cost–differentiation strategy to stay com-petitive. It shut down many of its European operations, purchased more efficient aircraft, and developed new technology and productivity methods to lower its costs. Simultaneously, it differentiated its services by offering just-in-time shipments for customers' manufacturing and distribution processes and by installing computer terminals in large customers' offices so that they could track their own shipments.[20]

■ **Multiple Strategies**

In some cases, large business units employ **multiple strategies,** or more than one of the strategies identified in the preceding sections. For instance, a busi-ness that uses the differentiation strategy or the low-cost–differentiation strat-egy may also adopt one of the niche strategies used by small companies. Figure 6.7 on page 148 portrays the strategies of two hotels: Hyatt uses both the differ-entiation strategy and the niche-differentiation strategy; Holiday Inn employs a combination of low-cost–differentiation and niche-differentiation strategies.

Large business units may compete with multiple strategies for either proac-tive reasons (attempting to modify some segment of their operations to en-hance their effectiveness) or reactive reasons (reacting to environmental change to maintain their effectiveness). For example, Holiday Inn, a business unit of the British firm Bass PLC, and one of the largest companies in the hotel/motel industry with 1,600 hotels worldwide, maintains its preeminent position by competing proactively using both low-cost–differentiation and niche–differen-tiation strategies.

Its low-cost–differentiation strategy is revealed through its use of scale economies in purchasing and financing and its nationwide reservation system, which keeps cost low, and its differentiation through its quality rooms and ser-vices. Additionally, the company heavily advertises and promotes its quality accommodations. But to appeal to more than one customer group, this business reserves a small section of some of its inns for the more discriminating cus-tomer. In these sections, spacious suites with plush furnishings, wet bars, re-frigerators, and hair dryers are provided, along with complimentary food, newspapers, and beverages. As might be expected, the price that Holiday Inn

## The Low-Cost–Differentiation Strategy: A Giant Success at Giant Foods

Perhaps no business has used the low-cost–differentiation strategy with more success than the $3.3 billion Giant Foods supermarket chain, one of the largest retailing companies in the nation. The chain has differentiated itself by being among the first to offer gourmet meals to go, fresh pizza made in-house, and a "frequent-buyer" program that rewards customer loyalty with credits toward future shopping trips. Further differentiation efforts include offering more Asian goods in areas with substantial Vietnamese and Thai populations and stocking extensive lines of vegetarian foods in neighborhoods where many Seventh-Day Adventists live.

Yet Giant has managed to keep its costs at rock bottom through such innovations as providing its own house brands, milk, soda, ice cream, ice cubes, and plastic packaging; pioneering efficient replenishment technology that uses point-of-sale scanning data to reorder merchandise automatically when needed; employ-ing electronic article surveillance (EAS) systems to reduce shoplifting; developing many of the shopping centers in which its stores are located; producing its own television ads; and even doing its own pest exterminating. These operations make Giant one of the nation's more versatile supermarket chains.

The chain, whose after-tax profit margins are triple the industry average, is highly competitive. When Safeway restructured, Giant responded by cutting its own prices further and by increasing its coupon offerings. When wholesale clubs invaded Giant's territory, the supermarket initiated its own "club pack" program for health and beauty care items, dog food, laundry detergents, frozen foods, and other grocery items.

Few cost-saving possibilities are overlooked. When its shopping center construction crews are not building the chain's own centers, they are earning more than $20 million annually from outside contracts.

SOURCES: M. Garry, "Efficient Replenishment: The Key to ECR," *Progressive Grocer*, December 1993, pp. 5–8; M. Garry, "The Electronic Cop," *Progressive Grocer*, August 1993, pp. 113–118; S. Bennett, "Niche Jumping," *Progressive Grocer*, June 1993, pp. 97–100; K. Swisher, "Giant Plans 1st Expansion Outside Local Sales Region," *Washington Post*, 28 January 1993; "The Service 500: The 50 Largest Retailing Companies," *Fortune*, 1 June 1992, p. 188; R. A. Pyatt Jr., "Giant's Expansion Plans Made with Refreshing Optimism," *Washington Post*, 29 November 1990; D. Foust, "Why Giant Foods Is a Gargantuan Success," *Business Week*, 4 December 1989, p. 80.

charges for these suites is significantly higher than its price for ordinary rooms. This niche-differentiation strategy requires a higher initial investment per suite and higher operating costs. By using multiple strategies, Holiday Inn appeals to different groups of customers.

Likewise, Hyatt offers special suites in each of its hotels to elite customers. However, even its regular rooms are advertised to discriminating customers who are willing to pay higher-than-average prices for a hotel room.

R. J. Reynolds provides an example of a large business that reactively competes with multiple strategies. For years, Reynolds employed a low-cost–differentiation strategy for its cigarette brands. But as the Liggett Group and other smaller firms began to produce generic (no-brand) cigarettes in the early 1980s, Reynolds responded by also adopting a niche–low-cost strategy. The company positioned its otherwise slow-selling and lackluster-performing brand, Doral, against generic cigarettes by reducing its costs of production and its price.[21]

**Figure 6.7**

**Businesses Competing by Using Multiple Strategies: Hyatt Uses the Differentiation and Niche-Differentiation; Holiday Inn Uses the Low-Cost–Differentiation and Niche-Differentiation**

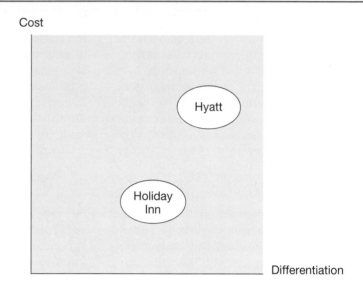

It is important to note several exceptions to the preceding discussion. First, a large business unit that uses a low-cost strategy is unlikely to employ multiple strategies. A combination of the low-cost strategy with a niche–low-cost strategy is redundant, since both strategies concentrate on no-frills outputs at low costs. Combining the low-cost strategy with either of the other niche strategies is probably unworkable because it is difficult for an organization to operate primarily on the foundation of a no-frills philosophy (and all that it implies) while simultaneously producing highly differentiated products.[22]

Additionally, a large business unit that competes by pursuing a differentiation strategy is unlikely to employ a niche–low-cost strategy or a niche–low-cost/differentiation strategy because low costs are not emphasized by its managers.

Also, large business units will not adopt as their sole strategy any of the three niche strategies identified earlier as being appropriate for small business units. A small market share with relatively low sales figures cannot justify sizable expenditures on research and development, operations, and marketing.[23] Of course, enlightened managers of small business units and entrepreneurs are well aware of these restrictions on the operations of large business units. Hence, small enterprises are often strategically buffered from head-to-head competition with large firms. The market that small companies have carefully chosen is simply too small to attract large organizations as major competitors.

The seven generic strategies that have been discussed in this chapter are summarized in Table 6.2. The emphasis of each strategy, its market coverage, the characteristics of its products and services, its market demand, and its pricing are all identified.

**Table 6.2**           **Generic Business Unit Strategies and Their Ramifications**

| Generic Business Unit Strategy | Emphasis of Business Unit | Market Coverage | Characters of Products and Services | Market Demand | Pricing |
| --- | --- | --- | --- | --- | --- |
| Niche–low-cost | Lower overall costs | Market niche | No frills | Elastic | Depending on industry forces, low to average |
| Niche-differentiation | Fulfilling specialized customer needs | Market niche | Highly differentiated | Inelastic | High |
| Niche–low-cost/ differentiation | Fulfilling specialized customer needs and low costs | Market niche | Highly differentiated | Inelastic | High |
| Low-cost | Lower overall costs | Marketwide | No frills | Elastic | Depending on industry forces, low to average |
| Differentiation | Higher quality | Marketwide | Differentiated | Relatively inelastic | Depending on industry forces, average to high |
| Low-cost–differentiation | Higher quality and low cost | Marketwide | Differentiated | Relatively inelastic | Depending on industry forces, average to high |
| Multiple strategies | Mixed | Mixed | Mixed | Mixed | Mixed |

## SELECTING A GENERIC STRATEGY

In theory, an industry progresses through certain stages during the course of its life cycle: embryonic, growth, shakeout, maturity, and decline. If so, then the appropriate generic strategy for a business unit would depend, at least to some extent, upon the particular stage of its industry's life cycle.

Of course, not all industries follow these exact stages. For instance, some industries, following their decline, may be revitalized into new growth because of changes in the macroenvironment. For example, the bicycle industry fell into decline some years ago. It has now, however, been rejuvenated by society's interest in health and physical fitness.

The following paragraphs will demonstrate how generic strategies for business units are related to industry life cycle stages.[24] This discussion is appropriate for those industries that follow the traditional life cycle, but it can also be useful for business units operating in industries that deviate from the traditional life cycle. First, we will examine the industry life cycle stages and then present a framework that integrates the business generic strategies with these life cycle stages.

## STRATEGIC INSIGHT

### A Change in Strategy at Compaq Computer

Founded in 1982 by three ex-employees of Texas Instruments, Compaq Computer quickly rose to prominence by adopting the niche–differentiation strategy. Its personal computers (PCs) were characterized by innovative technology, high quality, and premium prices. Compaq's corporate culture was one of "sparing no expense to launch only the very best PCs on the market."

But by the late 1980s Compaq's industry environment was changing. New low-cost clone producers such as Dell Computers and AST Research entered the market, driving prices down. At first Compaq took little notice of these changes, continuing to operate in its customary fashion. But financial losses, a decline in its market share, and a fall in Compaq's stock price roused the company's board of directors. Co-founder and CEO Rod Canion was ousted and replaced by Eckhard Pfeiffer, the company's chief operating officer, who had been pressing for cost and price cuts.

Less than a year later Compaq introduced a new line of desktop and laptop PCs to the market. Priced to compete directly with Dell and AST, these machines were to be marketed, not through the traditional network of Compaq dealers, but through mass merchandise outlets, computer stores, and direct mail.

Supporting these new products was a massive cost-cutting program. Compaq eliminated 25 percent of its work force, forced suppliers to engage in competitive bidding, replaced some in-house production of components with outside contractors, shifted some production from Texas to Singapore, and even abolished its tradition of offering free soft drinks to employees. At the same time Compaq increased its U. S. advertising by 60 percent and set up a toll-free telephone number for its customers. Compaq managed to lower prices while raising margins by squeezing excess from its once-bloated infrastructure.

Although Compaq has lowered prices, its products are still priced higher than its rivals because they are more innovative. Compaq had switched to a niche–low-cost/differentiation strategy.

In 1994 Compaq built up an estimated $1 billion worth of inventory in anticipation of industry growth. The gamble paid off. In 1995 Compaq became the market leader for personal computers in the United States and has moved aggressively to restructure its operations and remain customer-focused. In 1996 Compaq continued to expand volume.

SOURCES: "H-P and Compaq to Invest in Silicon Video, a Start-Up," *Wall Street Journal Interactive Edition*, 14 May 1996; "Compaq Continues Strategy of Chopping Computer Prices," *Dow Jones News Service*, 7 May 1996; N. Templin, "Compaq Watches Its Users to Improve Their Computers," *Wall Street Journal Interactive Edition*, 8 May 1996; M. Fitzgerald, "Compaq Refocuses on Customers," *Computerworld*, 15 May 1995, p. 32; D. McGraw and A. Bernstein, "A Hard Drive to the Top: Compaq Is Now the U. S. Leader in Personal Computers," *U. S. News and World Report*, 9 January 1995, pp. 43–44; L. Zuckerman, "Compaq Cuts Its Prices in Effort to Widen Its Lead," *New York Times*, 17 August 1995, p. C3; P. Burrows, "Where Compaq's Kingdom Is Weak: In Laptops and Home PCs, the Monarch Doesn't Rule," *Business Week*, 8 May 1995, pp. 98–99; C. Arnst, S. A. Forest, K. Rebello, and J. Levene, "Compaq: How It Made Its Impressive Move Out of the Doldrums," *Business Week*, 2 November 1992, pp. 146–151.

## ■ Industry Life Cycle Stages

The traditional stages in an **industry's life cycle** are shown in Figure 6.8. A young industry that is beginning to form is considered to be in the *embryonic stage*. Consumer demand for the industry's outputs is low at this time because many consumers are not yet aware of these products or services. Virtually all purchasers are first-time buyers. At this stage in the industry's development, choice of technology is often not yet settled. For instance, at the beginning of the automobile industry, various small manufacturers experimented with electric, steam, and internal combustion technologies.

Normally, once the choice of technology is made and increasing numbers of consumers begin to desire the industry's outputs, the industry enters the *growth stage*. In the car industry, this stage began when the internal combustion engine became the accepted technology. Simultaneously, Henry Ford installed the assembly line to produce a single model car that many customers could afford. At this stage, most buyers are still first-time purchasers of the industry's outputs.

Over time, growth of the industry begins to slow as market demand approaches saturation. Fewer first-time buyers remain; most purchases are now for replacement purposes. As growth in demand begins to slow, some of the industry's weaker competitors may go out of business. This stage, therefore, is known as the *shakeout stage*. In the U. S. auto industry, the shakeout stage resulted in the demise of such independent car producers as Hudson, Packard, Studebaker, and American Motors, leaving General Motors, Ford, and Chrysler as survivors.

When the market demand for the industry's outputs is completely saturated, the *maturity stage* has been reached. Virtually all purchases are limited to replacement demand, and industry growth may be low, nonexistent, or even negative. The U. S. car industry is currently in the maturity stage.

Finally, market demand begins to fall steadily. This *decline stage* is often ushered in when consumers begin to turn to the products or services of substitute industries. These substitutes may have lower costs or greater convenience (such as mass transportation over car travel), they may be safer (such as chewing gum over tobacco products), or they may be technologically superior (such as the personal computer over the typewriter).

**Figure 6.8**          **Industry Life Cycle Stages**

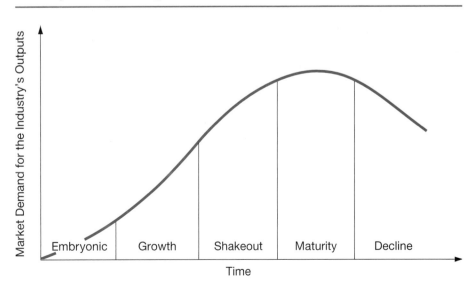

## ■ An Integrative Framework

How appropriate a generic strategy is for a given business unit depends upon the business's competitive status and the external forces in its industry life cycle stage. Recall that a business unit's competitive status is derived from the combined strengths and weaknesses of corporate-level, business unit, and functional-level strategies. For instance, a business unit's ability to differentiate its outputs may depend upon corporate scope innovations (discussed in chapter 4) and functional strength in research and development (discussed in the following chapter).

Figure 6.9 presents general guidelines for choosing a generic strategy in light of a business unit's particular industry life cycle stage. The vertical axis represents the life cycle stage, and the size of the business unit is shown on the horizontal axis.

**Figure 6.9**    **Generic Strategies in the Context of Industry Life Cycle and Size of Businesses**

**Size of Businesses**

| | Smaller Businesses | Larger Businesses |
|---|---|---|
| **Decline** | **Cell 5**<br>Niche–low-cost<br>Niche–low-cost/differentiation | **Cell 9**<br>Low-cost<br>Low-cost–differentiation<br>Multiple |
| **Maturity** | **Cell 4**<br>Niche–low-cost<br>Niche-differentiation<br>Niche–low-cost/differentiation | **Cell 8**<br>Low-cost<br>Differentiation<br>Low-cost–differentiation<br>Multiple |
| **Shakeout** | **Cell 3**<br>Niche–low-cost<br>Niche-differentiation<br>Niche–low-cost/differentiation | **Cell 7**<br>Low-cost<br>Differentiation<br>Low-cost–differentiation<br>Multiple |
| **Growth** | **Cell 2**<br>Niche–low-cost<br>Niche-differentiation<br>Niche–low-cost/differentiation | **Cell 6**<br>Low-cost<br>Differentiation<br>Low-cost–differentiation<br>Multiple |
| **Embryonic** | **Cell 1**<br>Niche-differentiation | |

Stage of Industry Life Cycle

## Cell 1

Virtually all businesses are small during an industry's embryonic stage since there has not yet been much opportunity for growth.[25] In this situation, the niche-differentiation strategy is appropriate because businesses in cell 1 are attempting to create new product or market opportunities. Their costs tend to be high and the number of first-time buyers to whom their outputs appeal is limited. Such businesses value organizational and technological fluidity so that they can either create or keep pace with state-of-the-art developments in the new industry. Those customers who purchase the industry's outputs are willing to pay high prices because these products or services fulfill their particular needs.

## Cells 2 and 6

As the industry grows, some businesses grow with it (those in cell 6) while others remain relatively small (those in cell 2). In cell 2, any of the generic strategies for smaller businesses may be appropriate, depending upon the particular business's strengths and weaknesses and the external opportunities and threats its management identifies. If a business can keep its costs down while serving price-sensitive customers, the niche–low-cost strategy can be appropriate. For instance, while the personal computer industry grew quickly during the 1980s, Kaypro remained small by serving the no-frills needs of certain price-sensitive customers.

Businesses that can produce highly differentiated, need-fulfilling outputs, however, may use the niche-differentiation strategy. For example, the industry for stereophonic products has grown significantly during the last three decades, but small companies such as Ampax have thrived by producing exclusive, top-of-the-line products. Likewise, a small business that is able to control its costs while producing highly differentiated outputs may use the niche–low-cost/differentiation strategy.

Similarly, among those businesses that choose to grow along with the industry, any of the strategies available to larger businesses may be appropriate. A company can choose to grow at a rapid pace by emphasizing low costs and no-frills outputs, by differentiating its outputs to a large market, by simultaneously emphasizing low costs and differentiated outputs, or by employing multiple strategies.

## Cells 3 and 7

The same strategies that were appropriate in the two preceding cells would also be suitable as the industry begins to "shake out" its less effective competitors. Although the growth in market demand is slowing, the industry is still expanding, and well-managed companies can thrive by following any of the generic strategies that best suit their strengths and weaknesses and their environment's opportunities and threats.

## Cells 4 and 8

As the industry approaches zero or even negative growth, emphasis is placed on cutting costs and/or differentiating products/services to maintain sales levels. Without market expansion, competing successfully with high costs becomes increasingly difficult. Hence, the more viable smaller companies can normally be expected to adopt either the niche–low-cost or niche–low-cost/differentiation strategy in cell 4, and most viable larger businesses are likely to adopt either the low-cost or low-cost–differentiation strategies in cell 8.[26] Some businesses with unique products or services may still be able to compete successfully with either the niche-differentiation or differentiation strategies, but there will be fewer of them than in cells 3 and 7.

### Cells 5 and 9

As demand for the industry's outputs declines significantly, high-cost businesses find themselves unable to compete as companies slash prices to try to maintain their market shares. Virtually all surviving smaller business units will have adopted the niche–low-cost or niche–low-cost/differentiation strategies, whereas those larger companies that remain will be following the low-cost, low-cost–differentiation, or multiple strategies.[27]

## ■ Generic Strategies and Business Unit Size

The preceding sections identified generic strategies appropriate for small and large business units. Midsized business units were not discussed because these organizations normally perform poorly in comparison with small or large competitors.[28] The reason is that midsize businesses often do not possess the advantages of their smaller or larger counterparts. Whether the business unit is considered small, midsize, or large, of course, depends upon its size relative to the size of its competitors in the industry.

The competitive superiority that small businesses enjoy over midsize business units includes their flexibility in meeting specific market demands and their potentially quicker reaction to environmental changes. Additionally, because of their lower investments, they can pursue small orders that would be unprofitable for midsize businesses. Finally, they can capitalize on their small market shares by creating an image of exclusivity. Customers who buy products for prestige purposes do so only if the market has relatively few of those products.[29] For instance, consumers who purchase Rolls-Royce automobiles would be alienated if they began to see a Rolls-Royce on every block, because the prestige of exclusivity is the primary reason for their purchase. Management at Rolls-Royce is satisfied with this situation, because nearly three months is required to build each car. The company's image is enhanced by the fact that 60 percent of the 115,000 cars it has produced can still be driven.[30]

The crucial advantage that a large business has over the midsize company lies in its ability to translate its economies of scale into lower costs per unit. Also, larger businesses may be better able to bargain with their suppliers or customers.

Therefore, since midsize business units may not have the advantages of either small or large firms, they have two strategic options to increase their effectiveness. First, they may, over time, expand their operations to take advantage of scale economies. Second, they may retrench in order to avail themselves of the advantages possessed by small companies. The feasibility of expansion or retrenchment depends upon various competitive and industry forces.[31]

# VALUE CHAINS AND BUSINESS UNIT RECONFIGURATION

Traditionally, each business unit has been conceived as a link in a **value chain.** That is, an enterprise receives inputs from suppliers of resources, transforms them into outputs (thus adding value to the inputs through their transformation), and channels the outputs to buyers (whether the buyers are other enterprises or the final consumers). Each enterprise, then, serves as a link in the value chain, in which raw materials are provided (by some enterprises); these are subsequently transformed into semifinished goods and components (by other companies); and these semifinished goods and components are then transformed into finished goods and services (by yet other businesses).

Moreover, each business unit has been viewed as having its own internal value chain. That is, the business unit is conceived as a progression of activities that incrementally add value in the context of an organizational continuum. For example, purchasing and materials management, production and operations management, and marketing all add incremental value in the organization's transformation of inputs into outputs. [32]

Each business unit has its own vulnerabilities and core competencies. Recall that core competencies are the major resource strengths (human, organizational, and physical) of a firm. In creating and delivering value to customers, business units with a competitive advantage are those that undertake functional or process activities that are based on their core competencies while leaving to others those functions or processes in which they do not excel. Thus, executives need to analyze the value chain by looking at the firm internally as well as assessing outside suppliers, potential partners (strategic allies), and customers in order to structure a superior system of value creation and delivery.

As shown in Figure 6.10, supplier organizations create and deliver value in terms of provision of goods or services. These goods and services are subsequently purchased by another organization as inputs. More specifically, purchasing and materials management plans and coordinates the procurement of these inputs, thus adding and delivering further value (by locating and contracting appropriate suppliers). As shown, other functions are also involved in this process of value creation and delivery. However, although a business may perform the functions of managing purchasing and materials, production/operations, finance, human resources, and marketing (because of its own strengths in these functions), it may leave to other organizations the functions of information systems management as well as research and development (in which the outside firms excel).

Value chain examination should be undertaken periodically because conditions tend to change over time. For instance, in the past numerous firms found it more economical to perform many functions internally. More recently, however, a number of companies have switched to outsiders for some of their functions because the outsiders are more efficient in those functions. Indeed, some firms, such as Reebok, only design and market their outputs, leaving such functions as purchasing and materials management and production/operations management to outsiders.

The value chain may be perceived as a series of internal and external agency relationships. An **agency relationship** exists when an individual, group, or organization, called an **agent,** acts on behalf of another individual, group, or organization, identified as a **principal,** to increase the value of the principal's

**Figure 6.10**          **A Chain of Creating and Delivering Value**

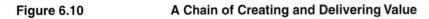

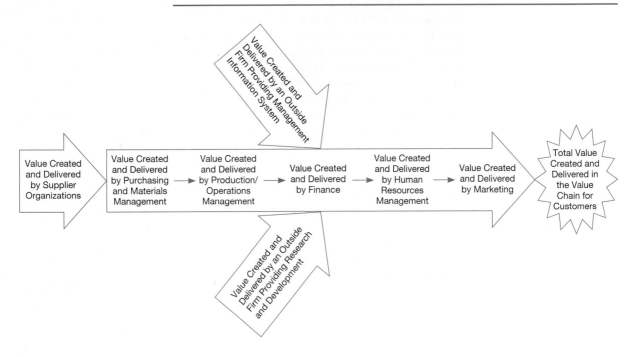

resources or activities. For instance, production/operations management may act as a principal and the purchasing and materials management as an agent within a firm. An agency relationship may also exist between the firm and an outside organization. Note that the business in Figure 6.10, as the principal, has contracted outside agents to perform the functions of managing information systems and research and development. By performing these functions, the outside agents add value to the overall value chain of the principal organization.

We emphasize that functions do not necessarily determine who is the principal and who is the agent. A manufacturer may be a principal and a marketing organization an agent in one situation. (Ford, for instance, is a principal and its dealers are agents.) In another situation, however, a marketer may be the principal and the manufacturer the agent. (Recall that Reebok is a marketer and the principal, leaving manufacturing to an outside agent.)

The value chain and its examination is meant to improve the effectiveness and efficiency of the system of value creation and delivery. In the preceding discussion, the value chain is portrayed as a point-to-point process of value creation. A periodic examination of this process is normally necessary for incremental and continuous improvements. Although in some situations this conception of value chain may be appropriate, in other situations it may be limiting.

Management consultants Richard Normann and Rafael Ramirez have criticized the concept of a value chain, calling it "as outmoded as the old assembly line that it resembles."[33] Hammer and Champy have argued that none of the business fads in the last two decades, including value chain analysis, has reversed the deterioration of competitiveness of U. S. businesses.[34] We emphasize that some of the winning enterprises base their strategic advantage on **reconfiguring** their business practices around nontraditional options to create and deliver value, rather than on using value chain analysis, which focuses on predetermined, point-to-point, incremental improvements. Simply put, reconfiguring the business is the fundamental changing of business activities and relationships internally or externally to achieve desired performance outcomes.

Reconfiguring the business unit is motivated by the idea that many existing enterprises are locked into predetermined, point-to-point sequencing of activities that deliver value, when in fact their commitment to the conventional value chain may be their competitive vulnerability. Other businesses can attack this vulnerability by reconfiguring the way value is created and delivered, thus significantly improving their competitive prospects. Reconfiguring the business unit involves making radical changes in conventional business practices. Radical change may be needed internally or in the way the enterprise interacts with external variables. Also referred to as reengineering or process redesign, reconfiguring the business starts with a clean sheet of paper on which alternative answers to the following question may be explored: "How do we better satisfy the needs and expectations of the buyers through reconfiguring our business internally and perhaps changing its relationships with outsiders, such as suppliers and even the customers themselves?"

When businesses perform poorly, asking this question becomes necessary and meets with less resistance from an organization's personnel. As explained by John Thorbeck, CEO of the Geo E. Keith shoe company, "One of the few good things about companies in trouble is that they're nervous about the status quo and primed for change."[35] The same question, however, may need to be asked periodically by executives whose businesses are currently performing well. In this scenario, the managers may face more opposition from personnel. That is, the personnel may subscribe to the notion that "if it ain't broke, don't fix it!" According to John Welch, GE's CEO, a business that is performing well simply cannot maintain the status quo: "Somebody's always coming from another country with another product, or consumer tastes change, or the cost structure does, or there's a technology breakthrough."[36] The following are a number of examples of business reconfigurations. Note that in every case reconfiguration of the business unit involves adopting business practices that are substantially different from "business-as-usual" norms prevalent in the industry. This radical change is what may enable an enterprise to turn competitive disadvantages into advantages or to build on the competitive advantage the business unit already possesses.

## ▪ Southwest Airlines

Southwest began its operations in 1971 as a small, short-haul airline between the older in-town airports of Dallas and Houston. At the time, leading airlines had a number of strategic advantages in the industry, including, for example, ownership of their computer reservation systems, meals-on-board service, and the capability to transfer baggage to other carriers. Southwest reconfigured the conventional way of doing business in the airline industry, turning what might have been competitive disadvantages into advantages. First, its city-to-city, short-haul flight strategy made a computer reservation system unnecessary. Not owning a computer reservation system saved Southwest $25 million annually, contributing to its strategy of keeping costs down. Second, since serving a meal on short-haul flights was not considered crucial by customers, a no-frills airline did not have to provide meals. This helped Southwest maintain its low costs and undercut fares offered by competitors. Finally, being a city-to-city, short-haul airline, Southwest did not have to provide baggage transfer, again contributing to its cost savings and its capability of offering low prices relative to its rivals.

## ■ Savin Business Machines

This company has reconfigured the conventional approach to competing in the office products industry. The major players are vertically integrated; thus they manufacture their own components and parts. They then mass produce the office products and market them through their own sales representatives. Moreover, they offer lease options to their customers. Contrarily, Savin Business Machines purchases components and parts from reliable suppliers that offer low prices. It has developed a more efficient and flexible method of manufacturing its products. Rather than hiring a costly sales force to parallel that of its rivals, it has entered into long-term contracts with select office products dealers, some of whom offer their own lease options to the customers.

## ■ IKEA

Furniture retailing has traditionally consisted of stores purchasing finished furniture from manufacturers or wholesalers and displaying it in their retail outlets. What the customers purchase is ordinarily delivered to them. IKEA, a Swedish furniture retailer, has become the largest firm of its kinds in the world, with operations across Europe, the Far East, and North America, through reconfiguring the way value is created and delivered. Note that its reconfiguration represents a radical change from the conventional practice in furniture retailing. The radical change is evident by observing IKEA's internal operations as well as its interactions with external variables, such as suppliers and customers.[37]

IKEA enables its suppliers to gain access to the world marketplace by selling the goods of the suppliers in the global arena. Moreover, IKEA provides technical and research and development assistance to the suppliers and even leases needed equipment to them. The purpose of providing such supplier support is to ensure that IKEA's goods will keep pace with world standards in design and efficiencies that will then assure IKEA of a low cost structure.

In order to provide items for as much as 50 percent below competitors' prices, IKEA links its customers to its operations by helping them become partners in furniture assembly and distribution. That is, customers purchase furniture kits that can easily be assembled at home and are often provided in smaller packings that can be transported by the customers themselves. Finally, the company's internal operations are fundamentally different, offering a unique experience to the customer that varies from what is normally associated with a furniture store. The buyers not only are provided with notepaper, pencils, and tape measures to facilitate their purchases, but also with such augmented services as supervised child care as well as playgrounds for the children. Reconfiguration has also enabled management to further empower personnel while flattening the organizational structures not only at IKEA, but at other organizations.[38]

We emphasize that corporate and business unit mission and strategy tend to influence how the business is reconfigured. For instance, if the mission of a corporation is to be in high-technology, innovative businesses, corporate strategy may answer the question, "In what high-technology businesses should we be operating?" Business unit strategy, in this context, may emphasize select differentiation dimensions instead of, or in conjunction with, low cost considerations. In this situation, reconfiguration of the business may be explored with the intention of enhancing differentiation through innovations.

Contrarily, the mission may emphasize being in commodity businesses in which low costs are important. For instance, Union Carbide's mission emphasizes commodity chemicals as opposed to specialty, high-technology chemicals. Union Carbide's business units, consequently, have adopted the low-cost strategy and emphasize efficiencies as opposed to differentiation dimensions. This firm has reconfigured its businesses so that the entire corporation can "seek its competitive advantage in the lowest possible manufacturing costs."[39] Union Carbide's polyethylene business unit, as an example, developed a low-cost process in the early 1970s and has continued to improve upon it. Polyethylene is the most widely used basic plastic. Not only does this company receive fees from licensing others to use its patented technology, it also maintains its competitive edge by a series of reconfigurations, yielding further enhancements and keeping "some enhancements all to itself—a still cheaper way of making polyethylene . . . or low-cost extensions of the technology to make plastic for TV and phone casings."[40]

## VALUE ANALYSIS AND STRATEGIC GROUPS

This concluding section of the chapter analyzes how generic strategies are related to what customers value and strategic groups. First, the strategies that are most likely to provide value to buyers are discussed. Then the concept of strategic groups is examined.

### ■ Generic Strategies and Value Analysis

The marketplace rewards business units that are able to offer better **value** to buyers, which is the worth of a good or service in terms of its perceived usefulness or importance to consumers in relation to its price. The ultimate judge of value is the customer. Customers compare the price and quality of any one business unit's outputs with the price and quality of competitors' outputs. Business units that offer poor value to their customers in the form of relatively high prices and relatively low quality face negative prospects. If they hold to their price level, they will lose market share and profitability. Likewise, if they maintain their market share by discounting their prices, they will also suffer lower profits. In either case, they will be hard-pressed to generate the necessary funds to increase their product quality so that their value might be maintained or improved.

On the other hand, business units that offer good value (competitive prices and high quality) to their customers face bright prospects. If they increase their prices, they may be able to maintain their market share if consumers perceive that the new price–quality relationship is still fair relative to competitors' outputs. The worst that can happen is that they will lose market share but will be able to maintain or even increase their overall profits on the reduced sales through their higher prices. Alternatively, these businesses may reduce their prices, which will increase their market share and allow them to lower their costs through economies of scale. The result will be increased profitability.

Depending on the strengths and weaknesses of a business and the opportunities and threats in the external environment, any of the generic strategies may be associated with creating and delivering value, particularly if the strategy involves reconfiguration of the business unit, discussed in the previous section. For instance, Reno Air, competing with a niche–low-cost strategy, delivers value through the adoption of a set of business practices substantially different from what is prevalent in the airline industry—as did Southwest Airlines when it was a start-up company. Likewise, IKEA, while competing with the low-cost strategy, nonconventionally creates and delivers value in the furniture retailing industry.

## ■ Generic Strategies and Strategic Groups

Most industries are comprised of a number of business units that compete more directly with certain businesses in the industry than with others.[41] Groups of direct competitors are identified by the similarity of their strategic profiles, and each collection of direct competitors is termed a **strategic group.**

**Figure 6.11**        **Groups of Business Units in an Industry Competing by Using Different Generic Strategies**

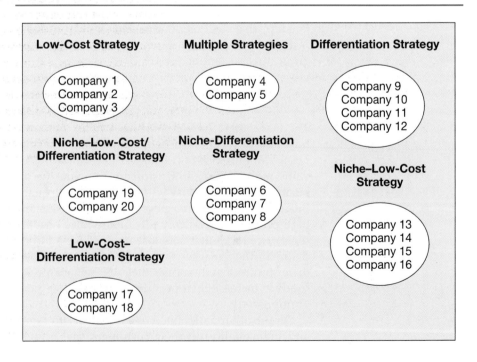

As an example, assume that an industry contains many businesses, each of which employs one of the seven generic strategies that has been discussed. Such an industry can be portrayed as shown in Figure 6.11. All twenty business units in this industry compete with one another. But business units within each strategic group engage in more direct and intense competition with one another.

Businesses normally experience difficulty in moving from one strategic group to another. In fact, strategic groups are quite stable and remain distinct from one another because of this relative immobility. Group-specific mobility barriers arise because the businesses in each group make strategic decisions that cannot easily be duplicated by enterprises outside the group. Such decisions require "outsiders" to incur significant costs, elapsed time, and/or uncertainty about the outcome of their decisions.[42] Thus, businesses in a lower-performing strategic group find it difficult and costly to switch to a higher-performing strategic group.

Note should be taken that controversy exists over the strategic group concept. For instance, strategic groups have been identified in ways that differ from our definition,[43] and some observers even question the existence of strategic groups.[44]

# SUMMARY

While the strategic question at the corporate level is, In what industries or businesses should we be operating?, the appropriate question at the business unit level is, How should we compete in the chosen industry or business? Three generic strategies are available for small business units: the niche–low-cost strategy, the niche-differentiation strategy, and the niche–low-cost/differentiation strategy. Large business units may choose from among the low-cost strategy, differentiation strategy, low-cost–differentiation strategy, and multiple strategies.

While the niche-differentiation strategy is most appropriate for businesses in the embryonic stage of an industry's life cycle, any of the three generic strategies for smaller businesses or any of the four generic strategies for larger businesses may be appropriate during the growth, shakeout, or maturity stages of the industry life cycle. The choice of a particular strategy depends upon the strengths and weaknesses of each company and the environment's threats and opportunities. In the decline stage of the industry's life cycle, however, the industrywide emphasis on price competition renders the niche-differentiation and differentiation strategies ineffective.

Analysis of these strategies leads to the conclusion that either small or large business units are likely to be more effective than midsize business units. Small businesses have the advantages of flexibility and/or the ability to produce outputs that fulfill customers' particular needs for prestige, performance, or safety, and large companies possess the advantage of economies of scale.

Some of the winning enterprises base their strategic advantage on reconfiguring their business practices around nontraditional options in creating and delivering value. Reconfiguring the business is the fundamental changing of activities and relationships to achieve desirable performance outcomes.

The marketplace rewards business units that are able to offer better value to buyers. The ultimate judge of value is the customer.

Within most industries, certain business units compete more directly with some businesses than with others. Businesses that engage in very direct and intense competition with one another are considered to be a strategic group. Most industries contain several strategic groups, each of which is composed of members possessing similar strategic profiles.

## TAKE IT TO THE NET

We invite you to visit the Wright page on the Prentice Hall Web site at:

**http://www.prenhall.com/wright**

for this chapter's World Wide Web exercise.

## KEY CONCEPTS

**Agency relationship**   A relationship that exists when an individual, group, or organization, called an agent, acts on behalf of another individual, group, or organization, identified as a principal, to increase the value of the principal's resources or activities.

**Agent**   The individual, group, or organization in an agency relationship that acts on behalf of another individual, group, or organization, identified as a principal, to increase the value of the principal's resources or activities.

**Business unit**   An organizational subsystem that has a market, a set of competitors, and a mission distinct from those of the other subsystems in the firm.

**Differentiation strategy**   A generic business unit strategy in which a larger business produces distinct products or services industrywide for a large market with a relatively inelastic demand.

**Generic strategies**   Strategies that can be adopted by business units to guide their organizations.

**Industry life cycle**   The temporal stages (embryonic, growth, shakeout, maturity, and decline) through which many—but not all—industries pass.

**Low-cost–differentiation strategy**   A generic business unit strategy in which a larger business unit maintains low costs while producing distinct products or services industrywide for a large market with a relatively inelastic demand.

**Low-cost strategy**   A generic business unit strategy in which a larger business produces, at the lowest cost possible, no-frills products and services industrywide for a large market with a relatively elastic demand.

**Multiple strategies**   A strategic alternative for a larger business unit in which the organization simultaneously employs more than one of the generic business strategies.

**Niche-differentiation strategy**   A generic business unit strategy in which a smaller business produces highly differentiated, need-fulfilling products or services for the specialized needs of a narrow range of customers or a market niche. Because the business's outputs are intended to fulfill a deep set of customer needs, prices are high and demand for the outputs tends to be inelastic.

**Niche–low-cost/differentiation strategy**   A generic business unit strategy in which a smaller business produces highly differentiated, need-fulfilling products or services for the specialized needs of a select group of customers or a market niche while keeping its costs low.

**Niche–low-cost strategy**   A generic business unit strategy in which a smaller business keeps overall costs low while producing no-frills products or services for a market niche with elastic demand.

**Organizational expertise**   An organization's ability to do something particularly well in comparison with its competitors.

**Principal**   In an agency relationship, an individual, group, or organization on whose behalf an agent acts to increase the value of the principal's resources or activities.

**Process innovations**   A business unit's activities that increase the efficiency of operations and distribution.

**Product innovations**   A business unit's activities that enhance the differentiation of its products or services.

**Quality**   The totality of features and characteristics of a product or service that bear on its ability to satisfy stated or implied needs.

**Reconfiguring the business unit**   Fundamentally changing businesses' practices and relationships to achieve desirable performance outcomes.

**Strategic group**   Within an industry, a select group of direct competitors who have similar strategic profiles.

**Total quality management (TQM)**   A broad-based program designed to improve product and service quality and to increase customer satisfaction by modifying a company's management practices.

**Value**   The worth of a good or service in terms of its perceived usefulness or importance to a consumer. Value is usually judged by comparing the price and quality of one business's outputs with those of its competitors.

**Value chain**   The notion that an enterprise receives inputs from suppliers of resources, transforms them into outputs, and channels the outputs to buyers, adding value at each point in the process.

## DISCUSSION QUESTIONS

1. How does a business unit strategy differ from a corporate-level strategy?

2. Small business units have a choice of three generic strategies. Explain each of these strategies and give an example of a business unit that competes with each strategy.

3. Large business units have a choice of four generic strategies. Explain each of these strategies and give an example of a business unit that competes with each strategy.

4. Explain the difference between a niche–low-cost/differentiation strategy and a low-cost–differentiation strategy.

5. How is it possible for a business to differentiate its outputs and, simultaneously, lower its costs?

6. What strategy or strategies are most appropriate for business units in the embryonic stage of an industry's life cycle? Now identify the strategies that are most effective in the decline stage of an industry's life cycle. Explain why.

7. Why might we expect the performance level of midsize business units to be lower than the performance level of either small or large business units?

8. What does reconfiguring the business unit mean?

9. What is a strategic group? Select an industry and identify, by name, some of the business units that comprise two of the strategic groups within that industry.

## STRATEGIC MANAGEMENT EXERCISES

1. Assume that you have conducted market research that indicates the need for a bookstore close to your campus. Further assume that you believe that either of two generic strategies could be successful for the bookstore: the niche–low-cost strategy or the niche–differentiation strategy. Respond to the following questions for *each* of these two strategies. Note that your responses for the two strategies will be quite different.

   - What type of physical store should you create?
   - What kinds of books would you carry in your inventory?
   - What in-store services would you provide?
   - Would you generally charge low, average, or high prices?

   Now, answer these same questions for a small business and a generic strategy of your own choosing.

2. Assume that you have the financial resources to own a national chain of video stores. Further assume that you believe that either of two generic strategies could be successful for this chain: the low-cost strategy or the differentiation strategy. Describe the physical aspects of your stores, their services, their advertising programs, and so on, for *each* of these two strategies.

3. Select an actual business and analyze its strategic profile (i.e., which generic strategy has it adopted?). Please justify your answer.

# NOTES

1. S. D. Atchison, "The Little Engineers That Could," *Business Week*, 27 July 1992, p. 77.

2. ANSI/ASQC, *Quality Systems Terminology, American National Standard* (1987), A3-1987.

3. D. A. Garvin, *Managing Quality* (New York: Free Press, 1988).

4. M. Helms, M. Ahmadi, and R. Driggans, "Quality and Quantity Goals in Service Industries: Compatible or Conflicting Strategies," *Journal of Business Strategies* 7 (1990): 120–133; S. Cappel, P. Wright, M. Kroll, and D. Wyld, "Competitive Strategies and Business Performance: An Empirical Study of Select Service Businesses," *International Journal of Management* 9 (1992): 1–11.

5. United States General Accounting Office, "Management Practices: U. S. Companies Improve Performance Through Quality Efforts," GAO/NSIAD-91-190, May 1991.

6. E. A. Haas, "Breakthrough Manufacturing," *Harvard Business Review* 65, no. 2 (1987): 76.

7. A. Farnham, "America's Most Admired Companies," *Fortune*, 7 February 1994, pp. 50–54; R. H. Miles, *Coffin Nails and Corporate Strategies* (Englewood Cliffs, NJ: Prentice Hall, 1982).

8. P. Wright, "Winning Strategies for Small Manufacturers," *Planning Review* 14 (1986): 20.

9. K. Kelley, "Suddenly, Big Airlines Are Saying: 'Small Is Beautiful,'" *Business Week*, 17 January 1994, p. 37.

10. H. Rudnitsky, "The King of Off-Price," *Forbes*, 31 January 1994, pp. 54–55; J. A. Parnell, "New Evidence in the Generic Strategy and Business Performance Debate: A Research Note," *British Journal of Management*, in press.

11. W. J. Abernathy and K. Wayne, "Limits of Learning Curve," in Harvard Business School, eds., *Survival Strategies for American Industry* (New York: Wiley, 1983), pp. 114–131; R. Luchs, "Successful Businesses Compete on Quality–Not Costs," *Long Range Planning* 19, no. 1 (1986): 12–17.

12. R. D. Buzzell and B. T. Gale, *The PIMS Principles* (New York: Free Press, 1987).

13. N. Paley, "Post These Notes," *Sales & Marketing Management*, February 1994, pp. 49–50.

14. J. Trout and A. Ries, "Don't Follow the Leader," *Sales & Marketing Management*, February 1994, pp. 25–26; P. Wright, "A Refinement of Porter's Strategies, *Strategic Management Journal* 8 (1987), 93–101.

15. P. Wright, M. J. Kroll, C. D. Pringle, and J. A. Johnson, "Organization Types, Conduct, Profitability, and Risk in the Semiconductor Industry," *Journal of Management Systems* 2 (1990): 33–48.

16. R. Buaron, "New Games Strategies," *The McKinsey Quarterly* 3 (1981): 24–40.

17. W. D. Vinson and D. F. Heany, "Is Quality Out of Control?" *Harvard Business Review* 55, no. 6 (1977): 114–122.

18. C. Willis, "Wall Street," *Money*, April 1992, p. 70.

19. M. E. Porter, *Competitive Advantage: Creating and Sustaining Superior Performance* (New York: Free Press, 1985).

20. C. Hawkins, "FedEx: Europe Nearly Killed the Messenger," *Business Week*, 25 May 1992, pp. 124–126.

21. Wright, "A Refinement of Porter's Strategies."

22. P. Wright, "The Strategic Options of Least Cost, Differentiation and Niche," *Business Horizons* 22 (1986): 21–26.

23. Wright, "A Refinement of Porter's Strategies."

24. Industry and organizational life cycles may not be correlated. For a discussion of organizational life cycles, see H. R. Dodge, S. Fullerton, and J. E. Robbins, "Stage of the Organizational Life Cycle and Competition as Mediators of Problem Perceptions for Small Businesses," *Strategic Management Journal* 15 (1994): 121–134.

25. L. R. Watts, "Degrees of Entrepreneurship and Small Firm Planning," *Journal of Business and Entrepreneurship* 2, no. 2 (1992): 59–67.

26. Many brewers attempt to differentiate while keeping their costs down. See E. Sfiligoj, "Ice Beers Give Stroh Another Excuse to Keep Coming Out with New Brews," *Beverage World*, 31 January 1994, p. 3.

27. See L. Zinn, "The Smoke Clears at Marlboro," *Business Week*, 31 January 1994, pp. 76–77.

28. S. Schoeffler, R. Buzzell, and D. Heany, "Impact of Strategic Planning on Profit Performance," *Harvard Business Review* 52 (1974): 137–145; M. E. Porter, *Competitive Strategy* (New York: Free Press, 1980); Wright, "A Refinement of Porter's Strategies"; L. Feldman and J. Stephenson, "Stay Small or Get Huge—Lessons from Securities Trading," *Harvard Business Review* 66, no. 3 (1988): 116–123; M. T. Hannan and J. Freeman, "The Population Ecology of Organizations," *American Journal of Sociology* 82 (1977): 946–947.

29. P. Wright, "Systematic Approach in Finding Export Opportunities," in Harvard Business School, eds., *Managing Effectively in the World Marketplace* (New York: Wiley, 1983), pp. 331–342.

30. T. Aeppel, "Rolls-Royce Tries to Restore Luster as Car Sales Fade," *Wall Street Journal*, 26 May 1992.

31. P. Chan and T. Sneyoski, "Environmental Change, Competitive Strategy, Structure, and Firm Performance: An Application of Data Development Analysis," *International Journal of Systems Science* 22 (1991): 1625–1636.

32. The concept of value chain was developed by McKinsey and Company and refined by Professor Michael Porter.

33. R. Normann and R. Ramirez, "From Value Chain to Value Constellation: Designing Interactive Strategy," *Harvard Business Review* 71 (1993): 65.

34. M. Hammer and J. Champy, *Reengineering the Corporation* (New York: Harper Business, 1993).

35. J. Thorbeck, "The Turnaround Value of Values," *Harvard Business Review* 69 (1991): 54.

36. J. E. Davis, "A Master Class of Radical Change," *Fortune*, 13 December 1993, p. 82.

37. Normann and Ramirez, "From Value Chain to Value Constellation: Designing Interactive Strategy," p. 65.

38. R. Heygate and G. Breback, "Corporate Reengineering," *McKinsey Quarterly* 2 (1991): 44–55; R. B. Kaplan and L. Murdock, "Core Process Redesign," *McKinsey Quarterly* 2 (1991): 27–43.

39. T. A. Stewart, "Reengineering: The Hot New Managing Tool," *Fortune*, 23 August 1993, p. 43.

**40.** M. Magnet, "Let's Go for Growth," *Fortune*, 7 March 1994, p. 62.

**41.** W. T. Jackson, L. R. Watts, and P. Wright, "Small Businesses: An Examination of Strategic Groups," *Journal of Business and Entrepreneurship* 5, no. 1 (1993): 86–96.

**42.** J. McGee and H. Thomas, "Strategic Groups: Theory, Research and Taxonomy," *Strategic Management Journal* 7 (1986): 141–160.

**43.** Ibid.

**44.** J. B. Barney and R. E. Hoskisson, "Strategic Groups: Untested Assertions and Research Proposals," *Managerial and Decision Economics* 11 (1990): 187–198.

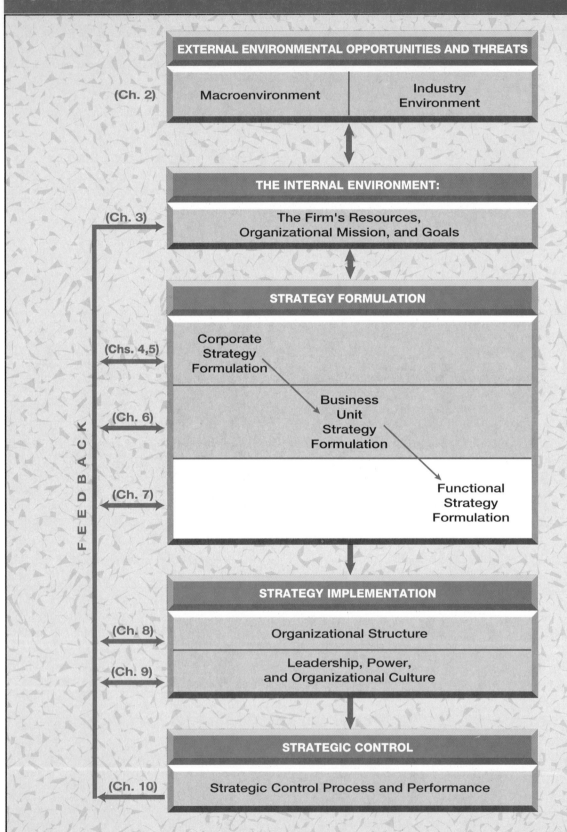

# STRATEGIC MANAGEMENT MODEL

**EXTERNAL ENVIRONMENTAL OPPORTUNITIES AND THREATS**

(Ch. 2)

| Macroenvironment | Industry Environment |

**THE INTERNAL ENVIRONMENT:**

(Ch. 3)

The Firm's Resources, Organizational Mission, and Goals

**STRATEGY FORMULATION**

(Chs. 4,5)

Corporate Strategy Formulation

(Ch. 6)

Business Unit Strategy Formulation

(Ch. 7)

Functional Strategy Formulation

**STRATEGY IMPLEMENTATION**

(Ch. 8)

Organizational Structure

(Ch. 9)

Leadership, Power, and Organizational Culture

**STRATEGIC CONTROL**

(Ch. 10)

Strategic Control Process and Performance

FEEDBACK

# 7 Functional Strategies

Recall from the previous chapter that the marketplace rewards businesses that are able to offer value to buyers, that is, the perceived usefulness or importance of a good or service to customers in relation to its price. In fact, the ultimate judge of value is the customer. To create and deliver value to customers, all businesses rely on the performance of certain functions—production, finance, research and development, marketing, and so on. Moreover, proper use of generic strategies (chapter 6) requires that considerable attention be given to the business unit's functional areas.

In formulating **functional strategies**—the strategies pursued by the functional areas of a business unit—managers must be aware that these functions are interrelated. Each functional area, in attaining its purpose, must mesh its activities with the activities of the other functional departments, as shown in Figure 7.1. A change in one department will invariably affect the way other departments operate. Hence, the strategy of one functional area cannot be viewed in isolation; rather, the extent to which all of the business unit's functional tasks mesh smoothly determines the effectiveness of the unit's generic strategy.

Unfortunately, in some companies, personnel in each functional area tend to view their operations introspectively and independently of other functions. If the ultimate judge of value is the customer, such a view is unlikely to result in customer satisfaction, since the needs and expectations of the customer are ordinarily fulfilled through the interaction of a number of functional areas. Many companies are learning this lesson. Boeing's unsettling experience, for instance, with discontinuities among its production, human resources, and marketing functions in the manufacture and delivery of its 747-400 airline has resulted in

169

**Figure 7.1**        **Interrelationships among Functions**

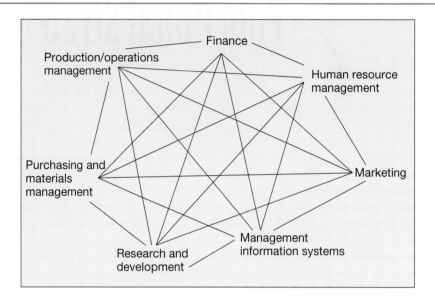

significant changes. Its new 777 airplane is designed and built by teams of marketing, engineering, manufacturing, finance, and service representatives so that each functional area will always know what the other is doing.[1]

This chapter examines functional strategies in the areas of purchasing and materials management, production/operations, finance, research and development, human resources, information systems, and marketing. Then the ways in which these functional strategies can be integrated are analyzed.

## PURCHASING AND MATERIALS MANAGEMENT

All organizations have a purchasing function. For example, in manufacturing companies, the purchasing department buys raw materials and/or parts so that the production department may process them into a finished product for the marketing department to sell. In retailing organizations, individual buyers purchase clothing, toys, furniture, and other items from manufacturers for resale to the ultimate consumer. The tasks of purchasing are to identify potential suppliers, evaluate them, invite bids and price quotations, negotiate prices and terms of payment, place orders, follow up on those orders, inspect incoming shipments, and pay suppliers.

A business unit's purchasing strategy will differ, depending upon which generic strategy it adopts. Companies that use either the niche–low-cost strategy or the low-cost strategy emphasize purchasing at the lowest costs possible. Large organizations are able to purchase at low costs through their ability to demand quantity discounts. [The terms *large* and *small* are relative ones referring to an organization's size (usually measured in annual sales or total assets) in relation to the size of its competitors in the industry.] And buyers that are larger than their suppliers and whose purchases represent a significant percentage of their suppliers' sales also possess considerable negotiating clout.

Small companies, however, must attain low-cost purchasing in other ways. A recent purchasing trend for small business is to form industry networks—that is, to band together with other small businesses in the same industry—to pool their purchasing requirements. Such a network is able to wield as much power as a single large business in demanding quantity discounts and exerting negotiating clout. Other small businesses may attempt to develop contacts with domestic and foreign suppliers that are able to offer limited supplies at low prices. In many cases, an extensive search can locate such suppliers.

We wish to emphasize that low costs are not the only consideration in purchasing activities. It is more accurate to state that businesses using niche–low-cost or low-cost generic strategies should seek out the "best cost." The best cost is as low as possible consistent with the quality of the purchased good or service. A low price is useless if the item breaks in the production process or fails to perform for the customer. On the other hand, excessive quality unnecessarily raises costs and prices.[2]

Organizations that use the generic strategy of niche-differentiation or differentiation emphasize the procurement of high-quality inputs, even if they cost more than alternative offerings. In these cases, the quality of the parts or products takes precedence over cost considerations.

When management pursues a niche–low-cost/differentiation or low-cost–differentiation generic strategy, however, emphasis is placed on buying high-quality inputs at low costs. As pointed out in the preceding chapter, even small businesses that adopt niche–low-cost/differentiation may be able to attain this purchasing goal through the development of organizational expertise and image, as Porsche has done.

Using multiple strategies, of course, requires a mixture of purchasing plans. At Holiday Inn, for instance, cost is a consideration in purchasing furnishings and accessories for the Inn's regular rooms. But the company buys higher-quality items—at higher costs—for its top-of-the-line suites. These suites feature more expensive linens, towels, soaps, shampoos, and beverages, which are provided free of charge.

The purchasing function is the first step in the materials management process. From the materials management perspective, purchasing, the operation of storage and warehouse facilities, and the control of inventory are interrelated functions;[3] consequently, they can only be efficiently and effectively conducted if they are viewed as parts of a single task.[4]

As an example of how these functions are interrelated, consider the **just-in-time inventory system (JIT).** This system of inventory management was popularized by Japanese manufacturers to reduce materials management costs. Using this technique, the purchasing manager asks suppliers to ship parts just at the time they are needed by the company to use in its production process. Such a system, of course, holds inventory, storage, and warehousing costs to a minimum.

Although American manufacturers are turning to this system in growing numbers, it is important to realize that just-in-time deliveries work particularly well in Japan because large Japanese manufacturers buy many of their inputs from small local companies. Hence, the giant buyers have considerable bargaining power over their much smaller suppliers. (In fact, some Japanese manufacturers own controlling interests in their suppliers, giving them even more power to control deliveries.) Such a system is likely to work well in the United States when the manufacturer has greater bargaining power than its suppliers. However, in the reverse situation, a just-in-time system is unlikely to evolve. Another hindrance to its use is that some suppliers, owing to the high demand for their products, are occasionally late in their deliveries by weeks or even months. However, most American-based suppliers are small concerns, with under $5 million in annual sales and fewer than thirty employees.[5]

Another potential difficulty with the JIT system is the possibility that labor strikes can shut down a supplier. A few years ago, for example, one of the plants that supplies parts to GM's Saturn manufacturing operations shut down—fortunately, for a short time—due to a local labor dispute. Saturn, which uses the JIT system, suddenly found itself unable to produce cars—in a time of overwhelming consumer demand—because it had no inventory of the more than 300 metal parts that it purchased exclusively from the supplier whose plant was struck.[6]

Most large U.S. manufacturers are currently reducing the number of suppliers they use from a dozen or more to two or three to control delivery times and quality.[7] These companies then attempt to build strong and enduring relationships with their suppliers and provide them with detailed knowledge of their requirements and specifications. Buyers and suppliers work together to improve the quality and lower the costs of the purchased items.

> This involves taking a *long* term view of the buyer/supplier relationship and also involves commitment to building an enduring cooperative relationship with individual suppliers where information is readily shared and both organizations work to meet shared goals.[8]

# PRODUCTION/OPERATIONS MANAGEMENT

Although production/operations management (POM) is most often associated with manufacturing processes, operations management is crucial to all types of organizations.[9] Credit card companies, for instance, must satisfy customers' desires for timeliness, accuracy, and company responsiveness. Hospitals must diagnose medical problems and attempt to heal patients. Prisons must house prisoners and try to rehabilitate them. Insurance companies must meet their clients' demands for fast, responsible, thorough coverage. Each of these POM examples from service organizations requires a careful analysis of their operations.

The following sections describe POM strategies for small and large business units and discuss the quality considerations emerging currently in POM.

## ■ Production/Operations Management Strategies for Small Business Units

Strategies for POM differ, of course, depending upon which generic strategy the business unit adopts. Small business units that compete with the niche–low-cost strategy emphasize low initial investments in their plants, equipment, and outlets to hold their fixed costs down, and they attempt to keep their variable operations costs as low as possible. Because of technological in-

---

### S T R A T E G I C   I N S I G H T

## *Improving Supplier Quality Across Several Industries*

Never before has there been such emphasis on the purchasing and materials management function. The primary impetus for this movement is the increasing intensity of foreign competition. The results to date have been a reduction in the number of suppliers used by most companies and growing pressure on those that remain to meet high-quality, cost, and delivery time standards.

As a buyer begins to pressure its suppliers, they, in turn, must convince their own suppliers to improve. For example, Ford influenced its suppliers to improve their quality and cost levels. One of those suppliers, Motorola, has lowered its defect rate from 3,000 per million parts to fewer than 200 per million parts as a result. In fact, Motorola's emphasis on "doing it right the first time" has cut its waste, inspection time, and warranty costs by $250 million in two years. Now Motorola has urged its 3,000 suppliers (down from 10,000) to improve their quality by asking them to enter the competition for the Malcolm Baldrige National Quality Award (won by Motorola in 1988). Those that have chosen not to enter have been dropped as suppliers by Motorola.

Although more is being demanded from suppliers, the best ones become "partners" with their buyers. Their employees may receive training in new manufacturing and quality techniques from buyers, may become involved in the design of the buyers' new products, may receive free consulting assistance from their buyers, and may become privy to the strategic plans of the buyers. In some cases, such suppliers are even able to become the sole supplier of a particular part to a buyer.

These principles have been adopted by retail organizations as well as manufacturers. Dillard's, a fast-growing and highly profitable department chain in the South, Southwest, and Midwest, works closely with its venders and is amazingly loyal to them. The company has discovered, like many others, that building stronger relationships and improving dialogue with fewer suppliers can serve its needs more effectively in the long run.

---

SOURCES: A. L. Adler, "Ford Suppliers Take On More Design, Engineering Costs," *Automotive News*, 7 August 1995, pp. 3–4; J. Carbone, "Improving Delivery Performance," *Electronic Business Buyer*, February 1994, p. 79; T. Stundza, "More Dialogue, Fewer Suppliers," *Purchasing*, 13 January 1994; J. R. Emshwiller, "Suppliers Struggle to Improve Quality As Big Firms Slash Their Vendor Rolls," *Wall Street Journal*, 16 August 1991; A. Gabor, "The Front Lines of Quality," *U. S. News and World Report*, 27 November 1989, pp. 57–59; S. Camaniti, "A Quiet Superstar Rises in Retailing," *Fortune*, 23 October 1989, pp. 167–174.

---

novations, some industries, such as steel manufacturing and film developing, can create small physical plants that are cost-competitive with much larger companies.

An example of this comparison is shown in Figure 7.2. The graph on the left depicts the per-unit production cost of a small business; the graph on the right shows the per-unit production cost of a large company. Note that the small business has achieved low per-unit costs similar to those of the larger organization because of its use of modern technology. Because the emphasis of business units that compete with the niche–low-cost generic strategy is on holding costs down, production/operations strategies are continuously scrutinized to make them more efficient. In some cases, production facilities may even be moved abroad to lower costs significantly.

**Figure 7.2**          **Per-Unit Cost of Production in a Small and in a Large Firm**

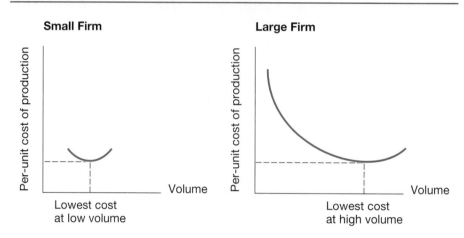

Small business units that compete with the niche-differentiation strategy stress POM strategies that yield superior quality. In some instances, such strategies may involve hand-crafting processes versus the mass production operations of much larger businesses. Rolls-Royce, for example, stresses the hand crafting of many automobile components, and each component can be traced to the individual worker who took part in its creation. As is evident, low costs are not the primary concern of this niche-differentiation strategy.

Small business units competing with the niche–low-cost/differentiation strategy emphasize POM strategies that simultaneously lower costs and heighten differentiation. This strategy may initially involve higher costs, but over time, cost savings and quality improvements evolve. For instance, one American manufacturer of electronic products realized that moving its metal production processes overseas would result in a 15 percent cost reduction. But switching to plastics in place of metal would lower costs by 20 percent and could be accomplished in the United States. In addition, plastic materials would offer better value for electronic products because of their lighter weight. Elizabeth Haas, a consultant in manufacturing strategy and advanced technology, has documented businesses in a variety of industries that have managed both to lower costs and heighten differentiation.[10]

### ■ Production/Operations Management Strategies for Large Business Units

Large business units can take advantage of a number of factors that accompany their larger size. Each factor falls under the concept of the **experience curve:** the reduction in per-unit costs that occurs as an organization gains experience producing a product or service. The Boston Consulting Group has popularized this concept, noting that production/operations costs may be systematically reduced through larger sales volume.[11] That is, each time a company's output doubles, POM costs decline by a specific percentage, which varies from one industry to another. For instance, with a sales volume of 1 million units, per-unit costs may be $100 in a particular industry. With a doubling of volume to 2 million units, per-unit costs may decline by 30 percent. Another doubling of volume to 4 million units may lower per-unit costs another 30 percent. In other industries, however, each doubling of volume will reduce costs by other amounts. The experience curve has been observed in a wide range of industries, including automobiles, long-distance telephone calls, airlines, and life insurance. Note that both manufacturing and service industries are represented.

The experience curve concept is based on three underlying variables: learning, economies of scale, and capital-labor substitution possibilities. Learning refers to the idea that the more an employee performs a task, the more efficient he or she should become at the job. Increases in volume, therefore, permit the employee to perform the task more often, resulting in greater expertise. This reasoning holds for all jobs—line and staff, managerial and nonmanagerial— and at all levels—corporate, business unit, and functional. Learning does not occur automatically, however. For instance, as experience is gained with a particular product, production managers, operative employees, and design engineers have the opportunity to learn more about how to redesign the product for manufacturing and assembly. By taking advantage of this opportunity, a business is able to conserve material, gain greater efficiencies in the manufacturing process, and substitute less costly materials, while simultaneously improving the product's performance. Such techniques, for example, allowed Ford Motor Company's business units to trim their manufacturing costs significantly. For instance, Ford plants can manufacture such midsize models as the Taurus and Mercury Sable in fewer than 17.2 hours, whereas such comparable models as the Chevrolet Lumina and Pontiac Grand Prix require 32.2 to 36.3 hours.[12]

Economies of scale at the business unit level refer to reductions in per-unit costs as volume increases. Capital-labor substitution means that as volume increases, an organization may be able to substitute labor for capital, or capital for labor, depending upon which combination produces lower costs and/or greater effectiveness. For example, a car manufacturer may operate highly automated factories in economically advanced nations because of the high cost of labor. But the same manufacturer may employ more labor and less automation in its factories located in developing nations to take advantage of the lower cost of labor in those areas.

Putting all three of these variables together, Figure 7.3 portrays how the overall experience curve promotes lower unit costs as volume increases. Hence, as a business gains greater market share, its per-unit costs can decrease as it takes advantage of the experience curve. However, investing in greater plant capacity is not necessarily an automatic route to lower unit costs. As can be seen from the curve in Figure 7.3, the experience curve flattens at point *A* on the graph. Production beyond that point will not lower unit costs any further.

Although large business units benefit from the experience curve, the particular generic strategy adopted by a given business unit will have different ramifications for success. For instance, many (but not all) businesses that compete with the low-cost strategy tend to buy their way to lower costs. In other words, they sell their products or services at low prices, even if those prices are initially below their costs. The low prices increase their volume, thereby permitting them to lower their costs through use of the experience curve. These businesses, however, are particularly vulnerable to business units that are also able to attain low costs but offer better-quality products and services.[13]

A different approach is taken by business units that compete with the differentiation and low-cost–differentiation generic strategies. Instead of charging

**Figure 7.3**                **Experience Curve**

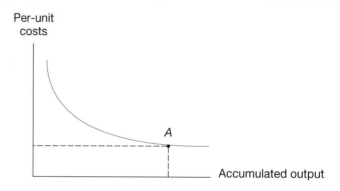

average or low prices, they charge average to high prices, seeking to gain market share by offering higher-quality outputs. The increase in sales may also allow them to lower their costs. But the managers of the business units that adopt differentiation as their strategy do not actively capitalize on the opportunities presented by low costs, whereas managers of businesses that compete with low-cost–differentiation do.[14] Hence, adopters of differentiation as a generic strategy are vulnerable to competitors that offer alternative products, but at lower, or even predatory, prices. The low-cost–differentiation adopter is less vulnerable than businesses using either of the preceding strategies, however, because this strategy emphasizes lower costs (as protection against low-cost companies) and high-quality outputs (to protect against differentiated businesses).

Regardless of the generic strategy adopted, large business units that use the experience curve take a significant risk. Increases in volume often involve substantial investments in plant and equipment and a commitment to the prevailing technology. However, if technological innovations should make the plant's production processes obsolete, millions of dollars in capital equipment may have to be written off. How may this need to invest in plant and equipment be balanced against the risk that technology will change? History provides a partial answer.

Virtually any technology is improved upon over time. But at some point, further improvement becomes prohibitively expensive.[15] At such times, emphasis should be placed on developing innovations, even at the risk of rendering obsolete the company's prevailing technology. A major vulnerability in using the experience curve is that managers become psychologically dependent upon the organization's technology both because they are familiar with it and because they have committed so much in resources to it. Consequently, when a competitor develops a new technology, the company can quickly become technologically obsolete.

As an example, consider NCR, a business that once had the lowest costs (through the experience curve) in the mechanical cash register industry. When Burroughs and other competitors developed a fully integrated electronic cash register that was superior in performance, the market demand quickly shifted from the technologically obsolete mechanical cash register to the new product. As a result, NCR lost its competitive edge.

### ■ Quality Considerations

An issue of increasing importance in production/operations management in recent years is quality or total quality management (TQM). This concept, introduced in chapter 6, refers to the totality of features and characteristics of a product or service that bear on its ability to satisfy stated or implied needs. Historically, quality has been viewed largely as a controlling activity that takes place somewhere near the end of the production process, an after-the-fact measurement of production success. Over the years, however, more and more managers have come to realize that quality is not something that is measured at, or near, the end of the production process but is an essential ingredient of the product or service being provided. Consequently, quality is part of the overall approach to doing business and becomes the concern of all members of the organization. When quality comes to be viewed in this way, the following conditions prevail:

- Making a quality product decreases the quantity of defects, which causes yield to increase.
- Making a product right the first time reduces the number of rejects and time spent on rework.
- Making the operative employees responsible for quality eliminates the need for inspection.

These conditions also apply to service quality, whether the service is performed for the customer or for some other department in the same organization. The ultimate result is that quality is viewed as reducing, rather than increasing, costs.[16] As quality consultant Philip B. Crosby points out:

> Every penny you don't spend on doing things wrong, over, or instead of, becomes . . . [a savings] right on the bottom line. . . . If you concentrate on making quality certain, you can probably increase your profit by an amount equal to 5% to 10% of your sales.[17]

W. Edwards Deming, the world-renowned consultant, argued that improvement of quality converts the waste of employee hours and machine time into the manufacture of good product and better service. Management in some Japanese companies observed as early as the late 1940s that improvement of quality naturally and inevitably begets improvement of productivity.[18] This process is illustrated in Figure 7.4. As you can see, such a process is essential to businesses that use the niche–low-cost/differentiation or low-cost–differentiation generic strategies. If below-average industry prices are charged, the business benefits because it may increase its market share and, subsequently, may reduce its costs. If average or above-average industry prices are charged, the business benefits from greater profit margins. Even companies that adopt differentiation as their strategy can develop a distinct competitive advantage by focusing on the quality of their products and services.

In fact, quality improvements in virtually any type of company seem to yield attractive results. A U.S. General Accounting Office study of twenty companies—including both large and small businesses in manufacturing and service industries—that had adopted TQM programs concluded that quality improvements enhanced profitability, increased market share, decreased customer complaints, and improved customer satisfaction. These results occurred on average two and a half years after the TQM programs were adopted.[19] Although the

**Figure 7.4**                    **The Deming Chain Reaction**

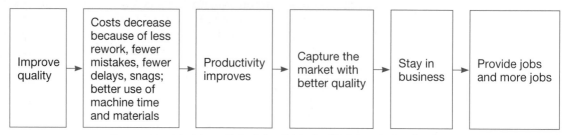

*Source*: Reprinted from *Out of the Crisis*, by W. Edwards Deming by permission of MIT and W. Edwards Deming. Published by MIT, Center for Advanced Engineering Study, Cambridge, Mass. 02139. Copyright 1986 by W. Edwards Deming.

exact form of each program differed from one company to another, these programs did contain the following common features:

- Corporate attention was focused on meeting customer requirements.
- Top management took the lead in emphasizing quality.
- All employees were trained, empowered, and involved in organizational efforts to improve quality and to reduce costs.
- Systematic processes were integrated throughout the organization to foster continuous improvement.[20]

## FINANCE

The finance function encompasses not only cash management but also the use of credit and decisions regarding capital investments. Ideally, each business would like to have a surplus of internally generated cash, beyond what is needed for expenditures, to allow it to reinvest the cash back into the business. In this way, the future viability of the enterprise is assured. However, a company resorts to borrowing funds when strategic decisions require cash beyond what can be generated from operations. Long-term capital investment decisions focus on the allocation of resources and, hence, are linked to corporate and business unit strategies in an obvious fashion.

Business units that use niche–low-cost or low-cost generic strategies pursue financial strategies that are intended to lower their financial costs. Insofar as possible, they attempt to keep their costs within the limits of the funds they are able to generate from operations. If borrowing becomes necessary, they try to borrow during times when credit costs are relatively low. If they sell common stock to generate additional funds, they time the sale carefully to coincide with a bull market (a market in which stock prices, on the average, are rising). Their capital investment decisions center on plant and equipment, technology, and research and development efforts that can lower their cost positions even more. Furthermore, they attempt to time major equipment purchases from foreign producers when the dollar is strong relative to the foreign currency.

Business units that adopt the niche-differentiation or differentiation generic strategies pursue financial strategies that fund quality enhancements. To stay in step with their competitors' product improvements or innovations, they direct their financial efforts toward upgrading their present and future outputs. If internal funds are insufficient, then they will attempt to raise money either through selling common stock or borrowing funds. Stock may be sold even though stock prices in general are relatively low, and funds may be borrowed even if interest costs are relatively high. In other words, these business units place the highest strategic priority on quality maintenance and enhancement rather than on financial considerations.

Finally, those business units that compete with the niche–low-cost/differentiation, low-cost–differentiation, or multiple strategies use their financial function, on the one hand, to lower costs and, on the other hand, to promote quality enhancements. Because such business units ordinarily perform well, they tend to have stronger financial positions than other business units, which allow them greater flexibility. These business units often have cash surpluses, can borrow funds at competitive rates, and are able to command high prices for new stock offerings. Hence, their investment strategies revolve around financial considerations that attempt to lower costs and heighten differentiation simultaneously. Further specifics on financial considerations are offered in Exhibit 1 of "Strategic Management Case Analysis."

## RESEARCH AND DEVELOPMENT

Research and development (R&D) has two basic components: product/service R&D and process R&D. **Product/service R&D** refers to efforts that ultimately lead to improvements or innovations in the company's outputs. **Process R&D** aims at reducing the costs of operations and making them more efficient. The more dynamic the industry environment, the more important R&D efforts of both kinds become.

Business units that compete with the niche–low-cost and low-cost strategies emphasize process R&D to reduce their operations costs. However, those business units that use the niche-differentiation and differentiation strategies place more importance on product/service R&D to produce improved and innovative outputs. Finally, adopters of the niche–low-cost/differentiation, low-cost–differentiation, and multiple strategies simultaneously stress both product/service R&D and process R&D efforts.

Organizations with effective R&D departments are, in essence, lowering their risks by making themselves more competitive. Product/service R&D focuses on market competitiveness, and process R&D emphasizes cost competitiveness. But R&D efforts also involve risks of another kind.

Process innovations, for instance, may be too technologically sophisticated to be implemented effectively, or they may not even be used at all. For example, consider the U.S. Postal Service's experience with expensive, high-technology mail sorting machines. The use of these machines achieved only about a third of the expected productivity improvements. At 91 percent of the post office sites reviewed by the Postal Inspection Service, mail that was supposed to have been processed by the new machines was still being processed in the traditional way.[21]

Product/service innovations also involve risks. Once they are introduced, new products or services may find little market demand. RJR Nabisco, for example, spent millions of dollars to develop and produce its "smokeless" cigarette, Premier. Although introduced to the market with considerable fanfare, smokers refused to switch to the new product, and it was canceled within a few weeks of its introduction.

This example illustrates the problems inherent in **technology transfer,** the process whereby a company transforms its scientific discoveries into marketable products. Some companies accomplish this transfer exceedingly well. Hewlett-Packard, for example, estimates that about 60 percent of its research results in product applications. In fact, over 50 percent of its sales come from products developed within the past three years. This remarkable record results from a two-tier arrangement in which corporate R&D operations work on projects with three-to-seven-year time horizons, while each business unit has its own R&D function that concentrates on shorter-range product applications.[22] But no one method is best. General Electric, another highly innovative firm, operates through a corporate-level R&D department that then demonstrates its inventions to each of its business units. This system has resulted in some unexpected applications; for instance, a device that was invented to protect coal-spraying nozzles in a locomotive was subsequently used to create a new generation of energy-saving light bulbs. Likewise, a medical diagnostic instrument invented for human body imaging is now also used as a cost-saving tool for inspecting jet engines.[23]

Noted management consultant Peter Drucker emphasizes the importance of both process and product R&D. He stresses that Japanese companies "abandon" their new products as soon as they reach the market. This decision to minimize the life cycle of each new product forces the Japanese to develop new products immediately to replace the ones currently on the market. Such a swift cycle, they believe, gives them a considerable advantage.[24] U.S. companies are responding by increasingly forming direct research links with their domestic competitors (GM, Ford, and Chrysler, e.g., are jointly developing new battery technology for electric automobiles), asking their suppliers to participate in new-product design programs, and taking ownership positions in small start-up companies that have promising technologies.[25]

## HUMAN RESOURCE MANAGEMENT

The human resource management functions include such major activities as planning for future human resource needs, recruiting personnel, placing people in jobs, compensating them, evaluating their performance, developing them into more effective employees, and enhancing their work environment. Overall, the aim is to build a work force that enables the organization to achieve its goals.[26] Moreover, the human resource function may facilitate the development and utilization of organizational competencies.[27]

One of the major detriments to effective human resource management practices over the past decade was an unprecedented wave of mergers and acquisitions. This massive restructuring of American business resulted in widespread layoffs and disillusioned formerly loyal employees. Before this time, many workers assumed that as long as they performed well, they would have a job for as many years as they wished. The past decade not only ended that dream for those who were laid off but also created anxiety among those who survived

---

## Importance of Human Resources at Merck and Motorola

Merck, the New Jersey-based pharmaceutical company that has topped *Fortune*'s "Most Admired Corporations" list for several consecutive years, attributes its success to "attracting, developing, and keeping good people." And, indeed, companies in virtually every industry are becoming increasingly aware of the importance of their human resources.

Perhaps the biggest change in attitude has occurred in American factories. The unskilled, single-task job that typified factory work for most of this century is rapidly disappearing. Its replacement is a position on an empowered cross-functional team in which each member must be a generalist who is able to participate in a variety of decisions. Many of these decisions are technical, involving computer-operated machinery and other manufacturing processes.

This need for technically sophisticated employees clashes with the public school system in the United States, where 27.8 percent of the students over the age of 15 drop out before finishing high school and students who have not yet mastered the skills in their current grade are routinely promoted. Examples of this conflict abound. For instance, several years ago, as Motorola was beginning to use empowered teams,

management discovered that only half of its work force could solve the equation $4 + x = 10$. Programs to remediate this deficit cost Motorola $30 million over a five-year period—a cost, its management points out, that did not have to be borne by its major competitors in Japan and Sweden.

A National Association of Manufacturers poll revealed that 50 percent of the 360 companies surveyed reported serious deficiencies among their employees in fundamental math and reading skills. As *Business Week* concludes, "The issue is one of a growing gap between the skills people have and the skills that jobs demand."

Although the root of the problem may be in America's educational system, businesses—and American competitiveness—suffer from it. Consequently, many companies that are upgrading their technological processes or are moving to empowered cross-functional teams are investing sizable amounts of money in remedial math, reading, and writing programs. Observers report that employees tend to pay more attention to their teachers than they did in junior high or in high school because what they are learning is directly relevant to their continued employment.

SOURCES: "Enter the 'New Hero': A Boss Who Knows You Have a Life," *Wall Street Journal Interactive Edition*, 8 May 1996; K. Ludeman, "Motorola's HR Learns the Value of Teams Firsthand," *Personnel Journal*, June 1995, pp. 117–120; K. Kelley and P. Burrow, "Motorola: Training for the Millenium," *Business Week*, 28 March 1994, pp. 158–162; C. Milloy, "Teaching Failure By Example," *Washington Post*, 17 March 1993; F. Swoboda, "A New Breed on the Line," *Washington Post*, 2 August 1992; T. Segal, K. Thurston, and L. Haessly, "When Johnny's Whole Family Can't Read," *Business Week*, 20 July 1992, pp. 68–70; K. Ballen, "America's Most Admired Corporations," *Fortune*, 10 February 1992, p. 43.

---

the cutbacks. It is difficult for a company to eliminate as much as 20 percent of its work force and still retain a commitment among those who remain.

Hence, a priority for business units, regardless of their particular generic strategy, is to develop commitment among their employees to the organization and to the job. Companies that wish to foster that commitment and develop a strong, competitive work force must create—and maintain—certain working conditions for their employees. And progressive organizations consider human resources their most precious asset. Consequently, such companies give their employees' needs for customized benefits, child day care, parental leave, and flexible working hours equal consideration with such traditional needs as training and development, job enrichment, and promotional opportunities.

The modern work force is frequently characterized as "diverse." In rapidly increasing numbers, women, African Americans, Hispanic Americans, Asian Americans, and disabled persons are transforming the traditional white, male image of many American corporations. As a result, managers must learn to help persons of diverse backgrounds and perceptions to work closely together. This necessity for teamwork, of course, is further impelled by the need for closer cooperation among the employees of the organization's functional areas. The success of such cooperative endeavors as cross-functional teams, quality circles, and just-in-time inventory systems requires a unity of action that can be achieved only through the mutual respect and understanding of others.

This increased diversity in today's work force requires changing organizational policies and practices to mesh with its needs. Attracting the best from the new work force is a prerequisite for reducing costs and/or heightening differentiation. Valuable human resources may contribute to efficiencies through cost-cutting ideas and by lower absenteeism and turnover. Likewise, valuable human resources could promote differentiation via their innovative ideas and excellence in job performance.

In a more narrow sense, a business unit's generic strategy also influences specific components of its human resource program. Take, for example, a company's reward system. Rewards—in the usual sense of recognition, pay raises, and promotions—should be tied to employee behavior that helps the business attain its goals. Hence, business units that follow a niche–low-cost strategy or a low-cost strategy must reward employees who help reduce operating costs. Businesses adopting the niche-differentiation or differentiation strategy should establish reward systems that encourage output improvements or innovations. Finally, those companies that use the niche–low-cost/differentiation strategy or a low-cost–differentiation strategy should have broad-based reward programs that foster activities that either lower costs or promote output improvements or innovations.

## INFORMATION SYSTEMS MANAGEMENT

A well-designed information system can benefit all of a business unit's functional areas. A computer-based decision support system can permit each functional area to access the information it needs and to communicate electronically with the other functional departments to enhance interdepartmental coordination.

This advantage is not the only benefit of an effective information system, however. Such a system can cut internal costs (essential to business units pursuing the niche–low-cost, niche–low-cost/differentiation, low-cost, or low-cost–differentiation strategy) while promoting differentiation and quality through a faster response to the market's needs (vital to companies that follow the niche-differentiation, niche–low-cost/differentiation, differentiation, or low-cost–differentiation strategy). In fact, some businesses owe their high performance to their information systems. In the overnight package delivery industry, for example, the chairman and CEO of United Parcel Service (UPS), Kent Nelson, believes that "the leader in information management will be the leader in international package distribution—period."[28] Hence, UPS and such competitors as Federal Express use their core competencies in managing information to keep their costs low while giving their customers superb service (differentiation).

Leading retailers, such as The Limited, have also developed sophisticated information systems to manage their vertically integrated distribution channels. The Limited's system links its hundreds of retail stores throughout the United States to its Columbus, Ohio, headquarters and to its textile mills in Hong Kong. Sales information from each of the stores is gathered and analyzed in Columbus. Based on that analysis, within a few days, the Hong Kong textile mills are producing more fast-selling items and fewer slow-turnover goods.[29]

Because of the rapidity of change in information technology, some companies are increasingly *outsourcing*, or farming out, their information systems function. Kodak, for instance, has turned over to IBM its information processing through 1999. Kodak's management believed that it should concentrate on its core competencies and concluded that running computers was not one of those competencies. Enron, the Houston-based natural gas producer, likewise outsourced its information processing to EDS (the world's largest provider of information services) in order to focus on its goal to become the leading natural gas company in the nation. Says its CEO, "Nothing in [our mission] says we want to be a provider of information systems."[30]

Although other functional areas—such as marketing, human resources management, or POM—may be outsourced, contracting out the information systems management function is more prevalent because many companies simply are unable to keep up with the frequent technological information changes in this area. Additionally, outsourcing can lower a company's information costs because such information systems providers as EDS, IBM, or Andersen Consulting can process data from several client companies through a single mainframe, thereby passing along the lower costs achieved through economies of scale.[31]

Whether it is conducted in-house or farmed out, an information system is effective not because of its sophisticated nature but because it helps the business carry out its strategy. Far too many companies emphasize the hardware and software components of their functional system rather than the system's ability to satisfy customer needs.[32] For that reason, some managers oppose outsourcing of information systems. Computer programmers, these managers maintain, are the key to creating software that can set a company apart from its competitors. They recommend that a business outsource only standard tasks, such as payroll processing or accounts receivable or payable, while retaining technologically creative information systems experts.[33]

# MARKETING

Marketing consists of four dimensions: products/services, pricing, channels of distribution/location of outlets, and promotion. The particular generic strategy adopted by the business unit influences how these various dimensions are planned and executed.

As we saw in the preceding chapter, business units that compete using the niche–low-cost and low-cost generic strategies produce no-frills products/services. Although these outputs are undifferentiated or minimally differentiated with respect to those of their competitors, they are by no means unreliable or shoddy. For example, Motel 6 Inc. offers no-frills rooms. They are clean and contain comfortable, but low-priced, furniture and beds. Motel 6 offers few services; for instance, it has no restaurants or conference rooms. Its simple brand name, Motel 6, is intended to convey the impression of economy services.

Consistent with its no-frills outputs, Motel 6 normally charges low prices. In particular circumstances, it may be able to charge average prices, but only when competitors are either few or far removed. Because it is a service company, channels of distribution are not relevant, but geographic location is. Motel 6 has been successful in choosing locations, primarily near interstate highway exit ramps. Promotion efforts are undertaken at low costs and attempt to convey to the traveling public that Motel 6 offers satisfactory economy lodging.

Different marketing strategies are pursued by businesses that use the generic strategies of differentiation and low-cost–differentiation. Marketing quality products and services that are distinguishable from the outputs of rivals requires approaches considerably at variance from those described in the preceding two paragraphs.[34] For example, Holiday Inn offers larger rooms with better-quality furnishings than Motel 6. Holiday Inns also contain such

---

## STRATEGIC INSIGHT

### The Importance of Distribution and Production Capacity at Colgate-Palmolive and Compaq Computer

The role of distribution is often overlooked amid the more glamorous marketing activities of advertising, selling, and designing products and packages. Although less visible, distribution is certainly as important as these other aspects of marketing.

Consider a company that has used distribution to its distinct advantage: Colgate-Palmolive. This multiunit company's most profitable business is not toothpaste or soap; it is, surprisingly, pet food. Part of the secret to the success of its Hill's Pet Products division is distribution. Unlike better-known and much larger competitors such as Ralston Purina, Hill's sells its pet food almost exclusively through veterinarians. Its premium-priced product (a single can of dog food costs about $2) comes in several formulations, ranging from diet food for overweight pets to low-sodium meals for animals with heart conditions. Although Ralston Purina has

similar products, it faces considerable difficulty breaking into Hill's long-established distribution channel.

On the one hand, a good product can be ruined by limited production capacity. Compaq Computer at one time developed an additional computer line called ProLinea. This entry into the inexpensive, low-profit-margin market was enormously successful at building consumer demand. However, Compaq greatly underestimated demand, leading to widespread shortages of the much-desired ProLinea computer within a month of its introduction. While it took Compaq over a year to add shifts at manufacturing plants in order to meet the influx of demand, disappointed consumers turned to such competitors as Dell and Hyundai. Compaq has secured the production capacity necessary and is now also performing well with this product line.

SOURCES: H. W. Jenkins Jr., "That Old-Time Religion," *Wall Street Journal Interactive Edition*, 23 April 1996; "Helping Two Companies Form a Third," *Personnel Journal*, January 1994, p. 63; R. Blackburn and B. Rosen, "Total Quality and Human Resources Management: Lessons Learned from Baldridge Award-Winning Companies,"*Executive*, August 1993, pp. 49–66; C. Milloy, "Teaching Failure by Example," *Washington Post*, 17 March 1993; F. Swoboda, "A New Breed on the Line," *Washington Post*, 2 August 1992; K. Ballen, "America's Most Admired Corporations," *Fortune*, 10 February 1992, p. 43.

features as restaurants, shops, swimming pools, and conference rooms. The brand name Holiday Inn is intended to give the impression of quality. Average to high prices are charged for Holiday Inn rooms, depending upon the competitive situation, and promotional efforts convey a differentiated quality image.

Still other marketing strategies are followed by business units that adopt the niche-differentiation and niche–low-cost/differentiation generic strategies. These businesses tend to offer specialized, highest-quality products and services to meet the particular needs of a relatively small market. Holiday Inn Suites, featured in some Holiday Inns, offer spacious rooms, wet bars, hair dryers, and complimentary food, beverages, and newspapers. The brand name attempts to convey the impression that in addition to having access to Holiday Inns' restaurants, shops, swimming pools, and conference rooms, customers will be further pampered by these extra features. High prices are charged for these suites, and promotional campaigns address the relatively few potential customers who desire the suites' extra features.

A summary of our discussion to this point is shown in Table 7.1 (see pages 186–87). The entries in the left column represent the generic strategy that a given business unit is following. The horizontal entries to the right indicate the particular strategy that should be used by each of the business unit's functional areas.

# BENCHMARKING

Buyers everywhere look for value. In Lima, Peru, Coke is preferred to the locally produced Inca Cola. Customers across Latin America, Europe, Africa, Asia, and Australia demand Levis and Toyotas. What is the ramification of creating and delivering value for the functional areas? The answer is that in order to provide value to buyers, the business must have superior functional and cross-functional performance. **Benchmarking,** in this context, refers to the comparison of functional and cross-functional performance of one business relative to desirable standards.

Traditionally, U.S. businesses benchmarked their performance relative to superior rivals in the same American industry. This worked well particularly during the post–World War II years when the plants of overseas competitors were struggling to emerge from being bombed into rubble. During the 1970s, however, the game changed dramatically as "lean and mean" European and Japanese competitors began to challenge U.S. businesses not only globally but also in the American market. By the latter 1970s and throughout the 1980s, U.S. companies began to benchmark against the best global competitors in the same industry. This allowed many of the American enterprises to achieve competitive parity with their global rivals.

What is emerging during the 1990s and what will drive superior performance into the next century is the realization that achieving competitive parity (or even a marginal advantage) is not enough and will not last long. According to McKinsey and Company, a leading global consulting firm, a business and its functional areas must strive not for competitive parity but for "stimulating new ways of competing that dramatically surpass competitors' capabilities."[35] This involves benchmarking functional and cross-functional performance of one business against the best in any industry anywhere in the world. Indeed, each

| Table 7.1 | The Link Between Business Unit Strategies and Functional Strategies | | |
|---|---|---|---|
| *Strategy* | *Purchasing & Materials Management* | *Production/ Operations Management* | *Finance* |
| Niche–low-cost | Purchase at low costs through networks and contacts with domestic and foreign suppliers. Operate storage and warehouse facilities and control inventory efficiently. | Emphasize low initial investments in plants, equipment, and outlets. Emphasize low operation costs. | Lower financial costs by borrowing when credit costs are low, selling common stock during a bull market, etc. |
| Niche-differentiation | Purchase high-quality inputs, even if they cost more. Conduct storage, warehouse, and inventory activities with utmost care, even if at higher costs (e.g., fine wine must be kept in high-cost storage with correct lighting and air-conditioned space). | Emphasize specialized quality in operations even at high cost, such as the hand crafting of products. | Emphasize obtaining resources and funding output improvements or innovations. Emphasize innovations even when financial costs may be high. |
| Niche–low-cost/ differentiation | Purchase high-quality inputs, if possible, at low costs. This may be done through the development of organizational expertise, as Porsche has done. Conduct storage, warehouse, and inventory activities with utmost care, if possible, at low costs. | Emphasize specialized quality of operations, if possible, at low costs. | Emphasize obtaining resources and funding output improvements or innovations, if possible, at low costs. |
| Low-cost | Purchase at low costs through quantity discounts. Operate storage and warehouse facilities and control inventory efficiently. | Emphasize operation efficiencies through learning, economies of scale, and capital-labor substitution possibilities. | Lower financial costs by borrowing when credit costs are low, selling common stock during a bull market, etc. |
| Differentiation | Purchase high-quality inputs, even if they cost more. Conduct storage, warehouse, and inventory activities when extensive care, even if at higher costs. | Emphasize quality in . operations, even if at high cost. | Emphasize obtaining resources and funding output improvements or innovations. Emphasize innovations even when financial costs may be high. |
| Low-cost– differentiation | Purchase high-quality inputs, if possible, at low costs. Conduct storage, warehouse, and inventory activities with care, if possible, at low costs. | Emphasize quality in operations, if possible, at low costs. | Emphasize obtaining resources and funding output improvements or innovations, if possible, at low costs. |
| Multiple | Mixed | Mixed | Mixed |

| Research & Development | Human Resource Management | Information Systems | Marketing |
|---|---|---|---|
| Emphasize process R&D aimed at reducing costs of operations and distribution. | Emphasize reward systems that encourage lowering of costs. | Emphasize timely and pertinent information on costs of operations. | Emphasize low-cost distribution and low-cost advertising and promotion. |
| Emphasize product and service R&D aimed at enhancing the outputs of the business. | Emphasize reward systems . that encourage output improvements or innovations. | Emphasize timely and pertinent information on the ongoing specialized processes that yield highly differentiated outputs. | Emphasize specialized distribution and targeted advertising and promotion. |
| Emphasize product and service R&D as well as process R&D. | Emphasize reward systems that encourage lowering of costs and output improvements or innovations. | Emphasize timely and pertinent information on costs of operations and on the ongoing specialized processes that yield highly differentiated outputs. | Emphasize specialized distribution and targeted advertising and promotion, if possible, at low cost, as Porsche has done. |
| Emphasize process R&D aimed at reducing costs of operations and distribution. | Emphasize reward systems that encourage lowering of costs. | Emphasize timely and pertinent information on costs of operations. | Emphasize low-cost distribution and low-cost advertising and promotion. |
| Emphasize product and service R&D aimed at enhancing the outputs of the business. | Emphasize reward systems that encourage output improvements and innovations. | Emphasize timely and pertinent information on the ongoing processes that yield differentiated outputs. | Emphasize differentiated distribution and emphasize advertising and promotion on a broad scale. |
| Emphasize product and service R&D as well as process R&D. | Emphasize reward systems that encourage output improvements or innovations and the lowering of costs. | Emphasize timely and pertinent information on costs of operations and and on the ongoing improvement or innovation processes that are meant to yield differentiated outputs. | Emphasize differentiated distribution and emphasize advertising and promotion, on a broad scale, if possible, at low costs. |
| Mixed | Mixed | Mixed | Mixed |

business and its functional personnel need to answer the question, Are we as good as the best in the world marketplace? According to one expert, "If you're not better than the best on a worldwide basis, you're not going to make a living."[36] Although benchmarking may start with competitor analysis, it should be extended to other businesses outside the industry. Benchmarking only against the rivals tends to encourage personnel to "fight the last war" or to develop competencies to beat competitors "as they exist today, rather than as they will exist tomorrow."[37]

# INTEGRATING THE FUNCTIONS

For a business unit's generic strategy to be successful, each functional area must do more than simply operate effectively. Overall strategic success requires that all functional activities be tightly integrated so that their operations mesh smoothly with one another. Those businesses that are best able to achieve functional integration are those most likely to attain the competitive advantages detailed in the following paragraphs.

## ■ Superior Product Design

Although product design has been recognized as an important competitive dimension for years, only in the past few years has it received increased attention. Until recently, design was primarily associated with product appearance. But now, the concept is being broadened to include such features as designing a product for easy manufacturability so that fewer parts have to be purchased. Additionally, increased emphasis is being put on improving the product's functionality (its ability to perform its purpose) and quality. Overall, today good design addresses aesthetics as well as "the consumer's every concern—how a product works, how it feels in the hand, how easy it is to assemble and fix, and even, in this era of environmental concern, whether it can be recycled."[38]

Gaining a competitive advantage through superior product design involves all functional areas. Even in those companies where POM has been the dominant function, the revised emphasis is on the interrelationships of all functional areas. For instance, when Caterpillar reorganized so that it could compete more effectively with heavy-equipment manufacturers from Japan, it first "intended to move only its design engineers to the plants to work more closely with the production people. . . . [Then the question became] why just the manufacturing and the engineering people . . . so marketing and pricing folks [also moved] into the plants."[39]

A well-designed product is attractive and easy to build, market, use, and maintain. Simplicity drives the best-designed products. But superior product design alone is not sufficient to gain a substantial competitive edge; design must be combined with superior service.

## ■ Superior Customer Service

Developing and maintaining the quality of customer service is often more challenging than improving product quality.[40] The reason is that the consumer perceives service value primarily at the time the service is either rendered or not rendered. As one manager put it:

## S T R A T E G I C   I N S I G H T

### Concurrent Engineering at Chrysler and Caterpillar

Impressive increases in manufacturing productivity in Japan and in Germany over the past twenty years and the deepening U. S. trade deficit have placed growing pressure on U. S. factories to become more efficient. Although there are a number of ways to increase industrial productivity, the process of concurrent engineering seems to hold particular promise.

During the 1980s, American manufacturers spent billions of dollars on factory automation, with no dramatic increase in productivity. Some experts believe the poor result was due to misplaced priority: The emphasis should have been on product design rather than on the production process. Even the most sophisticated automation equipment cannot compensate for a poorly designed product, in that design decisions "lock in" up to 90 percent of production costs long before the first item is ever produced. As a result, U. S. manufacturers are beginning to adopt concurrent engineering, a technique in which the product and its production processes are designed simultaneously.

Traditionally, an organization's R&D department came up with a new product idea. Then the idea went to design engineers who built a prototype, which was then turned over to the production department. Production had to develop a process for manufacturing the product, which usually meant that they had to give the blueprints back to design for revision. Further transfer of the blueprints back and forth between design and production could occur several times. Finally, purchasing would get copies of the finalized plans and ask for bids from suppliers. Then eventually, actual production of the product would begin. If problems occurred during the production process, the product might have to be reworked in each of the preceding departments.

By contrast, concurrent engineering brings together personnel from R&D, design engineering, purchasing, production, and marketing, as well as from the company's suppliers, to work side by side and compare notes constantly from the very inception of the project. Using concurrent engineering, Chrysler was able to bring its Viper, Neon, Intrepid, and Grand Cherokee models to market in only three years—versus Chrysler's normal five-year development time. And adoption of concurrent engineering has helped Caterpillar cut its new product development time in half. One expert estimates that the use of concurrent engineering can save a company anywhere from 20 to 90 percent of its usual time to market, while its quality improves by 200 to 600 percent and its return on assets increases from 20 to 120 percent.

SOURCES: "Caterpillar: Exports to Make Up 75% of Sales within 10 Years," *Dow Jones News Service*, 13 May 1996; K. Jackson, "Chrysler's Next Task: Update the Product," *Automotive News*, 21 August 1995, pp. 18–19; F. AitSahlia, E. Johnson, and P. Will, "Is Concurrent Engineering Always a Sensible Propositions?" *IEEE Transactions on Engineering Management*, May 1995, pp. 166–170; E. Raia, "IH Story," *Purchasing*, 18 February 1993; K. Kelley, A. Bernstein, and R. Neff, "Caterpillar's Don Fites: Why He Didn't Blink," *Business Week*, 10 August 1992; O. Port, Z. Schiller, and R. W. King, "A Smarter Way to Manufacture," *Business Week*, 30 April 1990, pp. 110–117.

You can tell me how awful someone's behavior was, but there is nothing for me to go back and look at. There aren't any artifacts, like broken gizmos I can go back and test.[41]

All functional areas must work together to provide the customer with product and service value. For example, a supermarket must fulfill several customer needs. First, it must offer value to customers in their shopping. Carrying the products that customers desire, at competitive prices, means that the purchasing, inventory, information systems, and finance functions must communicate with one another and cooperate closely. Next, the store must make certain that its employees are able to respond to customer inquiries. This capability requires effective human resource management practices in hiring and training. Then, the supermarket must ensure that it stocks sufficient quantities of the items that it advertises. Meeting this objective requires interaction among the purchasing, inventory, information systems, and marketing functions. Finally, the store must provide the means for customers to check out their purchases accurately and quickly, requiring the close cooperation of information systems and human resource management.

The importance of service cannot be overemphasized. In a recent survey, over one-third of the respondents indicated that they choose businesses that charge high prices but provide excellent service over companies that offer low prices but mediocre service.[42] As one observer points out:

> Despite all the talk these days about quality and customer satisfaction, most companies provide more lip service than customer service. Companies that really do provide service can command premium prices for their products. . . . [For example,] at Premier's [a business that provides hard-to-find fasteners and other related items] . . . charges are typically between 10% and 15% more than competitors' prices—and sometimes as much as 200% higher.[43]

Personal attention is an important way that some businesses provide superior service. Personal attention involves paying heed to details, addressing customers' concerns, answering technical questions, and providing service after the sale.[44] Such attention often plays an important psychological role as well. For example, the top managers of one industrial products supplier routinely visit plants to which the company has sold its products. In speaking of the psychological aspect of those visits, one manager indicated:

> We know our machine products are reliable and do not require visits. But when our clients see us physically inspecting their machines, sometimes merely dusting them off, they derive a sense of security and comfort that our products are in their plants, albeit at higher costs to them. When they are asked for a reference on suppliers, they usually suggest our firm.[45]

Recall that TQM not only involves producing a high-quality product, but it also implies quality in all of the services that accompany the product. In this regard, a TQM orientation means that a company must be willing to perceive the world from the customer's viewpoint and that the company can move quickly to satisfy the customer.[46] Consequently, we now examine the importance of superior speed.

### ■ Superior Speed

Speed in developing, making, and distributing products and services can give a business a significant competitive advantage.[47] In fact, a survey of fifty major U.S.-based companies revealed that speed (alternatively referred to as "time-based strategy") was a top priority.[48] To illustrate the point, consider the comments of two managers:

> We can design, produce, and deliver before our big competitors get the paperwork done.

> We have a lock on our customers. You see, it may take some of our big buyers several weeks [to complete a purchase order], during which time their engineers request an order, their purchasing department receives the request and commu-

nicates it to the suppliers. We are in constant touch with the plant engineers, and normally we know what their next purchases are before their own purchasing departments. Consequently, we can normally deliver their needs overnight or within a few days.[49]

Some companies have taken these lessons to heart. Motorola, for instance, cut the time it takes to produce a cellular radio telephone from 14 hours to 90 minutes. Concomitantly, the retail price of the phone dropped from $3,000 to $600 in three years.[50] Today, Coleman Company can produce and ship an order of camping stoves or lanterns in a week, versus two months just a few years ago. At the same time, it significantly reduced new product development time. Citibank estimates that Coleman's increased speed has enhanced the company's value by about $100 million.[51]

The importance of superior speed in serving customers cannot be exaggerated. For example, Premier, the fastener company mentioned earlier, received a call one day from one of its customers, Caterpillar. A $10 electrical relay had malfunctioned, bringing one of Caterpillar's assembly lines to a halt. A Premier representative located a replacement part in a Los Angeles warehouse and had it placed immediately on a plane bound for St. Louis. When it arrived, a Premier employee picked the part up and delivered it to Caterpillar. As might be expected, Caterpillar and other firms are willing to pay significantly higher prices for Premier's products because of the speed and superior service they receive.[52]

## ■ Superior Guarantee

Even in the best-managed businesses, problems occasionally arise that result in less-than-acceptable product or service quality. Hence, companies must take steps to guarantee an acceptable level of quality. Highly successful companies often go to great lengths to back their guarantees. For example, the famous retailer and mail-order house L. L. Bean accepts customer returns of its products for any reason, even after several years. A pair of hunting boots that was returned after ten years would be immediately replaced by a new pair with no questions asked.[53]

Many companies, however, ignore this competitive advantage. Often, guarantees lapse after a very short time period or contain too many exceptional conditions to be effective competitive weapons. For instance, some companies guarantee their electronic products for only ninety days; others are sufficiently confident of their product quality to offer one-year guarantees. Some airlines guarantee that their passengers will make connecting flights on time if no delays are caused by air traffic control problems or poor weather conditions. Unfortunately for the passengers, the majority of flight delays are due to these two factors.

Because of its intangible nature, a service guarantee is even more challenging to provide than a product guarantee. Christopher W. L. Hart, a business researcher and consultant, suggests that the following five desirable characteristics be included in service guarantees.[54]

- The guarantee should be unconditional, with no exceptions.
- It should be easily understood and written in simple language.
- The guarantee should be meaningful by guaranteeing what is important to the customer and making it worth the customer's time and effort to invoke the guarantee, should he or she be dissatisfied.

- The guarantee should be convenient to invoke and not require the customer to appeal to several layers of bureaucracy.
- The customer should be satisfied promptly, without a lengthy waiting period.

These characteristics, of course, should also be included in product guarantees.

## CROSS-FUNCTIONAL TEAMS AND PROCESS MANAGEMENT

Satisfying the customer may require that instead of functional managers, the organization adopt **process managers** who supervise teams of people representing various functional areas. Consequently, the parameter of activities would shift from independent functions to key processes containing interdependent functions. This may not only improve operations, but also permit the flattening of the organizational structure (further discussed under horizontal structure in chapter 8).

The advantage of process management and cross-functional teams over independently operating functions can be demonstrated by a product-improvement example. Traditionally, the marketing manager could authorize market research studies. The market research group may ask customers through a number of methods what they might desire in products and services. When the results of the market research are brought back, they are submitted to the marketing manager, who may discuss the results with a vice president. Once the vice president gives her approval, the results are typically presented to the production manager. This manager normally asks the production engineers to develop a prototype for testing. If the prototype is acceptable to marketing, the manager of purchasing is contacted and asked for an analysis of costs associated with the procurement of parts and components necessary for the product. The personnel in purchasing are subsequently charged with determining such costs through their interaction with various suppliers. If supplier prices are too high, then the production people may be asked to revise product specifications that might permit the use of less costly components and parts. The revised product specification must then be approved by the marketing personnel.

As is evident, much effort (going up and down as well as laterally in the organization) is expended in the above product improvement example to coordinate activities among independently operating functional areas. Note that if a process manager were in charge of the same activities, while having in her group personnel from the various functions, that effectiveness and efficiency might improve. As an example, let us scrutinize how Thermos developed its breakthrough product for the charcoal barbecue grill market[55] through a cross-functional team.

Thermos assigned the job to develop a superior grill to its product development process manager. The members of this process group were composed of people from various functional areas. This enabled the group to simultaneously consider multiple functional issues (such as marketing, production, and purchasing issues) relevant to the product development effort rather than in sequence. The process group members, similar to many people, presumed that the barbecue grill was typically used by men. Moreover, they assumed that grilling might be an enjoyable alternative to cooking in the kitchen. In order to gather further information, Thermos's cross-functional team made trips to various parts of the country attending and videotaping barbecues at home.

Several surprising conclusions were drawn. First, cooks were often found to be women rather than men. Second, grilling seemed to require substantial effort. That is, the charcoal must be purchased and brought to the house, where it has to be put into the grill and lighted. After the cookout, cleaning the grill is arduous and time consuming. Third, rather than being an enjoyable experience, the cooks were visibly uncomfortable with the dirty chores involved in preparing, grilling, and cleaning afterwards. Fourth, barbecuing seemed to take place on expensive decks in attractive backyards, and a dirty, ash-ridden grill detracted from the appearance of the residence.

The cross-functional team members decided on the development of a non-traditional product in response to their first-hand observations. The consensus was that the product needed to be attractive and low maintenance while producing a charcoal taste. This meant that the product must use electricity and have a nonstick cooking grid (for easy cleaning). Moreover, the warm-up time had to be less than for charcoal.

To produce a charcoal taste with conventional electrical grill models was not possible because they used heat rods built several inches away from the grill surface, which baked the meat instead of grilling it. To obtain a cookout taste, it was necessary to sear the meat with electricity. Consequently, electrical heat rods needed to be structured within the surface of the grill. Also, a double-walled insulated dome was necessary to keep moisture, smoke, and the heat inside. The parts and components needed for manufacture of such a new product were determined to be reasonably priced by select suppliers.

This is how Thermos developed its thermal electric grill. The grill preheats within five minutes and produces the barbecue lines on the surface of the meat. Moreover, the meat tastes as if it were prepared on charcoal. The grill is not only attractive but it also is easy to clean.

## S U M M A R Y

Once corporate-level and business unit generic strategies are developed, management must turn its attention to formulating strategies for each business unit's functional areas. Here, the manager should not view the strategy of one functional area in isolation, because it is the extent to which all of the functional tasks mesh smoothly that determines the effectiveness of the unit's generic strategy.

A business unit's purchasing strategy will differ depending upon which generic strategy it adopts. Companies that use the niche–low-cost strategy or the low-cost strategy emphasize purchasing at the lowest costs possible. Those that use niche-differentiation or differentiation stress the procurement of high-quality inputs, even if they cost more than alternative offerings. Organizations that pursue niche–low-cost/differentiation or low-cost–differentiation attempt to buy high-quality inputs at low costs, and those that employ multiple strategies use a mixture of purchasing plans. Purchasing is the first step in the materials management process, followed by storage and warehousing functions and inventory control. The latest trend in materials management, the just-in-time inventory system, ties these functions together.

The next functional strategic area is POM. Small business units that compete with the niche–low-cost strategy emphasize low initial investments in their plants, equipment, and outlets to hold their fixed costs down, and they attempt to keep their variable operations costs as low as possible. Small businesses competing with niche–differentiation stress POM strategies that yield superior quality, and those that use niche–low-cost/differentiation emphasize POM activities that simultaneously lower costs and heighten differentiation. Large business units, on the other hand, are able to take advantage of the experience curve by using learning, economies of scale, and capital-labor substitution possibilities to their advantage. To gain market share so that they may enjoy the experience curve, large business units that compete with the low-cost strategy may sell at low prices to increase volume. Large enterprises that use differentiation or low-cost–differentiation may attempt to gain market share by offering higher-quality outputs. But using the experience curve entails risks, such as becoming wed over time to an obsolete technology.

One of the primary considerations in any POM strategy is product or service quality. Businesses that build quality in, rather than attempt to inspect for quality after production has occurred, are able to enhance both productivity and profitability. Well-designed TQM programs, in particular, have yielded positive results.

In the finance function, business units that compete with the niche–low-cost and low-cost strategies pursue financial strategies intended to lower their financial costs. Companies that adopt niche–differentiation and differentiation strategies develop financial strategies that fund quality enhancements. And those that use niche–low-cost/differentiation, low-cost–differentiation, and multiple strategies use their financial function both to lower costs and to promote quality enhancements.

Research and development (R&D) has two basic components: product/service R&D and process R&D. Business units competing with the niche–low-cost and low-cost strategies emphasize process R&D to reduce their operations costs; those that use niche-differentiation or differentiation place greater importance on product/service R&D; and adopters of niche–low-cost/differentiation, low-cost–differentiation, and multiple strategies simultaneously stress both types of R&D.

Effective organizations will manage their human resource function so as to maintain a strong, competitive work force. This goal requires attention to personnel needs and the development of strategies that strengthen organizational and job performance commitment and teamwork across functional areas.

Tying all of these functions together is the organization's information system. Well-designed information systems are capable of cutting internal costs while they promote differentiation and quality through faster responses to the market's needs.

In marketing, the particular generic strategy adopted by a business unit influences the types of products or services the business offers, its prices for those products or services, the channels of distribution it uses, the location of its outlets, and its advertising and promotional policies. The key is to strive for consistency among these elements.

How well the functional areas perform may be evaluated through benchmarking. This involves the comparison of functional performance of one business relative to desirable standards.

Finally, it is essential that the business's functional activities be tightly integrated. An organization that is able to mesh its functional strategies smoothly is more likely to gain a competitive advantage based on superior product design, customer service, speed, and/or guarantee. In some situations, satisfying the customer may require that instead of functional managers, the organization adopt process managers who supervise teams of people representing various functional areas.

## TAKE IT TO THE NET

We invite you to visit the Wright page on the Prentice Hall Web site at:

**http://www.prenhall.com/wright**

for this chapter's World Wide Web exercise.

## KEY CONCEPTS

**Benchmarking**   The comparison of functional and cross-functional performance of one business relative to desirable standards.

**Experience curve**   The reduction in per-unit costs that occurs as an organization gains experience producing a product or service. The experience curve concept is based on three underlying variables: learning (the more an employee performs a task, the more efficient he or she should become at the job), economies of scale (the decline in per-unit costs of a product or service as the absolute volume of production increases per period of time), and capital-labor substitution possibilities (as volumes increase, the organization may be able to substitute labor for capital, or capital for labor, depending upon which combination produces lower costs and/or greater effectiveness).

**Functional strategy**   The strategy pursued by each functional area of a business unit. Functional areas are usually referred to as "departments" and include purchasing/materials management, production/operations, finance, research and development, marketing, human resources, information systems, and marketing. Their strategies may take various forms, depending upon which generic strategy the business unit adopts.

**Just-in-time inventory system (JIT)**   An inventory system, popularized by the Japanese, in which suppliers deliver parts just at the time they are needed by the buying organization to use in its production process. Used properly, such a system holds inventory, storage, and warehousing costs to a minimum.

**Process managers**   Managers who supervise teams of people representing various functional areas.

**Process R&D**   Research and development activities that concentrate upon reducing the costs of operations and making them more efficient.

**Product/service R&D**   Research and development activities that are intended to lead to improvements or innovations in the firm's products or services.

**Technology transfer**    The process whereby a company transforms its scientific discoveries into marketable products.

# DISCUSSION QUESTIONS

1. What is the relationship among corporate-level, business unit, and functional strategies?

2. Explain the linkage that a just-in-time inventory system provides between the purchasing and production functions. What are the implications for quality?

3. Production/operation management concepts are equally applicable to manufacturing and service organizations. Explain the POM process at a university.

4. What are some of the more important relationships among the POM, finance, and R&D functions?

5. What sorts of POM strategies might a small business unit adopt to compete effectively with a large business unit?

6. Relate the concept of the experience curve to the production operations of an automobile assembly plant.

7. Explain the relationship between quality and productivity.

8. What is the linkage between long-term capital investment decisions and the organization's corporate and business unit strategies?

9. Give, and explain, an example of (a) a business that emphasizes product/service R&D, and (b) another business that emphasizes process R&D.

10. What are some of the major relationships among marketing, information systems, and human resources management?

# STRATEGIC MANAGEMENT EXERCISES

1. Assume that two groups of investors are each planning to start a restaurant in the same city. The first group wishes to appeal to family meal needs, and the second wants to appeal to the needs of people who prefer gourmet food in particularly nice surroundings on special occasions. As is evident, different functional strategies will need to be adopted by the two restaurants. How would you suggest that each restaurant plan and implement its functional strategies? Be specific in your suggestions. If you need further information, either conduct relevant research or make reasonable assumptions.

2. Assume that you are asked to consult for a top-of-the-line restaurant in New York City that competes with the niche-differentiation strategy. While attending management's strategic-planning session, you learn that the managers would like to broaden their appeal in the New

York City market. One way of doing that, they believe, is to reduce their prices. To attain that end, they must cut costs. Therefore, one manager suggests that to reduce costs, they should make some of their purchases locally instead of purchasing from the highest-quality suppliers worldwide. (Currently, the restaurant flies in certain foods from foreign countries at considerable cost.) Another manager believes that the restaurant should use less expensive tablecloths and napkins. Finally, another wishes to cancel the restaurant's live musical entertainment to save money. Through these cost-cutting measures, the managers believe that they can reduce their prices and become more competitive.

What advice would you give these managers regarding their functional strategies?

3. Contrast the functional strategies that are followed by two automobile manufacturers: (a) Ford, which, as one of the world's largest producers, competes with the low-cost–differentiation strategy, and (b) Rolls-Royce, a relatively small company, which uses the niche-differentiation strategy. Specifically, how might you expect these two companies to differ in carrying out each of the following functional strategies: purchasing/materials management, production/operations, finance, research and development, human resources, information system, and marketing?

4. Select a specific company on which you will be able to obtain information.

   a. Determine which generic business unit strategy this company has adopted.
   b. Analyze the company's functional strategy in purchasing/materials management, production/operations, finance, research and development, human resources, information systems, and marketing.
   c. Analyze the extent to which these functional strategies mesh smoothly with one another and with the business's generic strategy.
   d. Make suggestions for improvements in the company's functional strategies.
   e. If you were asked to form cross-functional teams and have process managers for these teams, what would be your suggestions?

# NOTES

**1.** J. Cole, "Boeing's Dominance of Aircraft Industry Runs into Bumpiness," *Wall Street Journal*, 10 July 1992; D. J. Yang, M. Oneal, S. Toy, M. Maremont, and R. Neff, "How Boeing Does It," *Business Week*, 9 July 1990, pp. 46–50.

**2.** E. E. Scheuing, *Purchasing Management* (Englewood Cliffs, N. J.: Prentice Hall, 1989), p. 4.

**3.** T. H. Hendrick and F. G. Moore, *Production/Operations Management*, 9th ed. (Homewood, Ill.: Irwin, 1985), p. 336.

**4.** J. G. Miller and P. Gilmour, "Materials Managers: Who Needs Them?" *Harvard Business Review* 57, no. 4 (1979): 145.

**5.** S. P. Galante, "Distributors Bow to Demands of 'Just-in-Time' Delivery," *Wall Street Journal*, 30 June 1986.

**6.** F. Swoboda, "GM's Saturn Plant Closed by Strike," *Washington Post*, 28 August 1992.

**7.** J. Dreyfuss, "Shaping Up Your Suppliers," *Fortune*, 10 April 1989, p. 116.

**8.** J. Browne, J. Harhen, and J. Shivnan, *Production Management Systems: A CIM Perspective* (Workingham, England: Addison-Wesley, 1988), pp. 158–159.

**9.** W. T. Neese, "Food for Thought: Should We Teach More about Operations?" *Marketing News*, 17 January 1994, p. 4.

**10.** E. A. Haas, "Breakthrough Manufacturing," *Harvard Business Review* 65, no. 2 (1987): 75–81.

**11.** See Boston Consulting Group, *Perspectives on Experience* (Boston: The Boston Consulting Group, 1976); G. Hall and S. Howell, "The Experience Curve from an Economist's Perspective," *Strategic Management Journal* 6 (1985): 197–212.

**12.** A. Taylor III, "Can GM Remodel Itself?" *Fortune*, 13 January 1992, p. 33.

**13.** T. Peters and N. Austin, *A Passion for Excellence* (New York: Random House, 1985), p. 53.

**14.** R. D. Buzzell and B. T. Gale, *The PIMS Principles* (New York: Free Press, 1987), chap. 6.

**15.** B. Saporito, "Behind the Tumult at P & G," *Fortune*, 7 March 1994, pp. 74–82.

**16.** R. Johnson, W. O. Winchell, and P. B. DuBose, *Strategy and Quality* (Milwaukee: American Society for Quality Control, 1989); B. Jones, "Formula for Success," *Progressive Grocer*, February 1994, pp. 117–118.

**17.** P. Crosby, *Quality Is Free* (New York: McGraw-Hill, 1979), p. 1.

**18.** W. E. Deming, *Out of the Crisis* (Cambridge, Mass.: Massachusetts Institute of Technology, Center for Advanced Engineering Study, 1986).

**19.** United States General Accounting Office, "Management Practices: U.S. Companies Improve Performance Through Quality Efforts," GAO/NSIAD-91-190, May 1991.

**20.** Ibid., p. 4.

**21.** M. Lewyn, "The Post Office Wants Everyone to Pay for Its Mistakes," *Business Week*, 5 March 1990, p. 28.

**22.** G. Bylinsky, "Turning R&D into Real Products," *Fortune*, 2 July, 1990, pp. 72–73; J. Benson, "A Far Different Competitive Landscape," *Directors and Boards* (Winter 1994): 12–13.

**23.** A. K. Naj, "GE's Latest Invention: A Way to Move Ideas from Lab to Market," *Wall Street Journal*, 14 June 1990.

**24.** P. F. Drucker, "Japan: New Strategies for a New Reality," *Wall Street Journal*, 2 October 1991.

**25.** K. Kelly, O. Port, J. Treece, G. DeGeorge, and Z. Schiller, "Learning from Japan," *Business Week*, 27 January 1992, p. 53.

**26.** P. M. Wright and G. C. McMahan, "Theoretical Perspectives for Strategic Human Resource Management," *Journal of Management* 18 (1992): 298.

**27.** A. A. Lado and M. C. Wilson, "Human Resource Systems and Sustained Competitive Advantage: A Competency Based Perspective," *Academy of Management Review* 19 (1994): 699–727; J. A. Parnell, "Functional Background and Business Strategy: The Impact of Executive Strategy Fit on Performance," *Journal of Business Strategies* 11, no. 1, pp. 49–62.

**28.** P. Coy, "The New Realism in Office Systems," *Business Week*, 15 June 1992, p. 128.

**29.** R. B. Chase and D. A. Garvin, "The Service Factory," *Harvard Business Review* 67, no. 4 (1989): 67.

**30.** J. W. Verity, "Let's Order Out for Technology," *Business Week*, 13 May (1996), p. 47.

**31.** Ibid.

**32.** P. Coy and C. Hawkins, "UPS: Up from the Stone Age," *Business Week*, 15 June 1992, p. 132; Coy, "The New Realism in Office Systems," pp. 129–130.

**33.** Kirkpatrick, "Why Not Farm Out Your Computing?", p. 112.

**34.** M. McCarthy, "Mazda Earmarks $30 Million to Ring in Millenia," *Brandweek*, 7 March 1994, pp. 1, 6.

**35.** A. S. Walleck, J. D. O'Halloran, and C. A. Leader, "Benchmarking World-Class Performance," *The McKinsey Quarterly* 1 (1991): 8, 9.

**36.** S. Sherman, "Are You as Good as the Best in the World?" *Fortune*, 13 December 1993, p. 95; B. Dumaine, "Design That Sells and Sells and . . . ," *Fortune*, 11 March 1991, p. 86.

37. Walleck, O'Halloran, and Leader, "Benchmarking World-Class Performance," pp. 8, 9.

38. Dumaine, "Design That Sells and Sells and . . . ," p. 86.

39. J. Main, "Manufacturing the Right Way," *Fortune*, 21 May 1990, p. 54.

40. A. G. Perkins, "Manufacturing: Maximizing Service, Minimizing Inventory," *Harvard Business Review* 72, no. 2: 13–14.

41. A. Bennett, "Making the Grade with the Customer," *Wall Street Journal*, 12 November 1990.

42. A. Bennett, "Many Consumers Expect Better Service and Say They Are Willing to Pay for It," *Wall Street Journal*, 12 November 1990.

43. D. Milbank, "Service Enables Nuts-and-Bolts Supplier to Be More Than Sum of Its Parts," *Wall Street Journal*, 16 November 1990.

44. L. Dube, L. M. Renaghan, and J. M. Miller, "Measuring Customer Satisfaction for Strategic Management," *Cornell Hotel and Restaurant Administration Quarterly* (February 1994): 39–47.

45. P. Wright, "Competitive Strategies for Small Businesses," in A. A. Thompson Jr., A. J. Strickland III, and W. E. Fulmer, eds., *Readings in Strategic Management* (Plano, Tex.: Business Publications, 1984), p. 90.

46. F. Rose, "New Quality Means Service Too," *Fortune*, 22 April 1991, pp. 97, 100.

47. W. M. Bulkeley, "Pushing the Pace," *Wall Street Journal*, 23 December 1994, pp. 1, 5.

48. B. Dumaine, "How Managers Can Succeed Through Speed," *Fortune*, 13 February 1989, p. 54.

49. Wright, "Competitive Strategies for Small Businesses," p. 89.

50. J. D. Burge, "Motorola's Transition to a High Performance Workforce," an Executive Lecture at James Madison University, 20 February 1992.

51. B. Dumaine, "Earning More by Moving Faster," *Fortune*, 7 October 1991, pp. 89, 94.

52. S. Phillips, A. Dunkin, J. Treece, and K. Hammonds, "King Customer," *Business Week*, 12 March 1990, p. 88.

53. B. Uttal, "Companies That Serve You Best," *Fortune*, 7 December 1987, p. 98.

54. C. W. L. Hart, "The Power of Unconditional Service Guarantees," *The McKinsey Quarterly* (Summer 1989): 75–76.

55. B. Dumaine, "Payoff from the New Management," *Fortune*, 13 December 1993, pp. 103–104.

# STRATEGIC MANAGEMENT MODEL

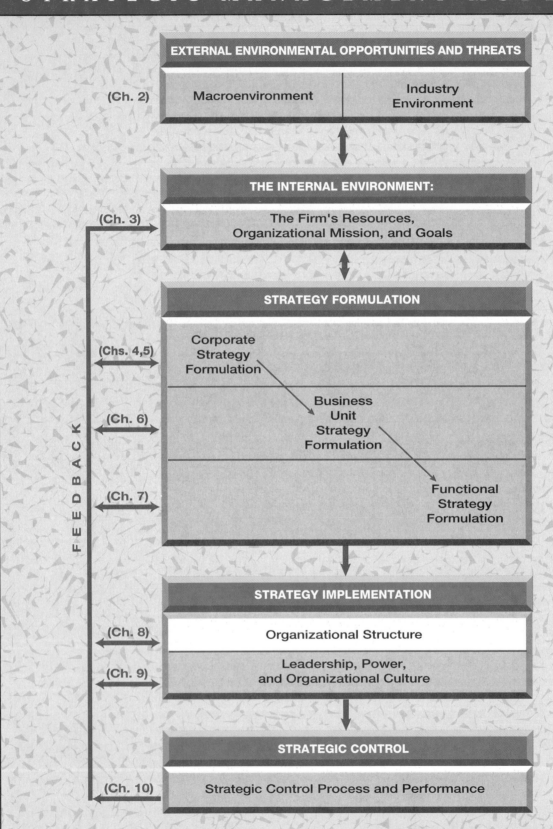

**EXTERNAL ENVIRONMENTAL OPPORTUNITIES AND THREATS**

(Ch. 2)

| Macroenvironment | Industry Environment |
|---|---|

**THE INTERNAL ENVIRONMENT:**

(Ch. 3)

The Firm's Resources, Organizational Mission, and Goals

**STRATEGY FORMULATION**

(Chs. 4,5) Corporate Strategy Formulation

(Ch. 6) Business Unit Strategy Formulation

(Ch. 7) Functional Strategy Formulation

**STRATEGY IMPLEMENTATION**

(Ch. 8) Organizational Structure

(Ch. 9) Leadership, Power, and Organizational Culture

**STRATEGIC CONTROL**

(Ch. 10) Strategic Control Process and Performance

FEEDBACK

# 8 Strategy Implementation: Organizational Structure

T he four preceding chapters dealt with strategy formulation at the corporate, business unit, and functional levels. This chapter and the following one address the implementation of these strategies. Successful strategies not only must be well formulated but also must be carried out effectively.

Effective strategy implementation requires managers to consider a number of key issues. Chief among them are how the organization should be structured to put its strategy into effect and how such variables as leadership, power, and organizational culture should be managed to enable the organization's employees to work together in carrying out the firm's strategic plans. This chapter deals with the first of these key issues—structuring the organization. Leadership, power, and organizational culture will be addressed in the following chapter.

## ORGANIZATIONAL GROWTH

**Organizational structure** refers to the ways that tasks and responsibilities are allocated to individuals and the ways that individuals are grouped together into offices, departments, and divisions. The structure, which is reflected in an organization chart, designates formal reporting relationships and defines the number of levels in the hierarchy.[1]

Normally, when small businesses are started, they consist of an owner-manager and a few employees. Neither an organization chart nor formal assignment of responsibilities is necessary at this stage. Structure is fluid, with each employee often knowing how to perform more than one task and with the owner-manager involved in all aspects of the business. If the organization survives those crucial first years and becomes successful, it is because of the increased demand that it has created for its products or services. To meet this increased demand, the business must grow. With growth, the organization of the business begins to evolve from fluidity to a status of more permanent division of labor. The owner-manager, who once was involved in all functions of the enterprise on a hands-on basis, now finds that his or her role is becoming more managerial and less operational. As new employees are recruited, each is assigned to perform a specialized function.

As Figure 8.1 illustrates, growth expands the organization's structure, both vertically and horizontally. In this figure, the owner-manager's hands-on activities have been taken over by managers who specialize, respectively, in manufacturing and marketing. Each of them manages employees who work only in one specialized functional area. The organization has now added one vertical level—a managerial one—and has expanded horizontally into two separate departments. The following sections discuss these two types of organizational growth.

## ▪ Vertical Growth

**Vertical growth** refers to an increase in the length of the organization's hierarchical chain of command. The **hierarchical chain of command** represents the company's authority-accountability relationships between managers and employees. Authority flows down the hierarchy from the highest levels in the organization to those at the bottom, and accountability flows upward from bottom to top. In Figure 8.1, the organization on the right has three levels in its hierarchy. Employees at each level report to the manager who is in charge of their specific operations. The number of employees reporting to each manager represents that manager's **span of control.**

Figure 8.2 illustrates two extremes in organizational configuration. At the left is a **tall organization,** comprised of many hierarchical levels and narrow spans of control. The other structure is a **flat organization,** which has few levels in its hierarchy and a wide span of control from top to bottom. It is important to note that each of these configurations represents an extreme. Rather than being at either extreme, many organizations fall somewhere in between. Hence, we speak of organizations as being "relatively tall" or "relatively flat."

**Figure 8.1**          **Organization of the Enterprise at Start-up and with Growth**

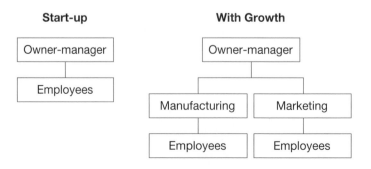

**Figure 8.2**                    **Tall and Flat Organizational Structures**

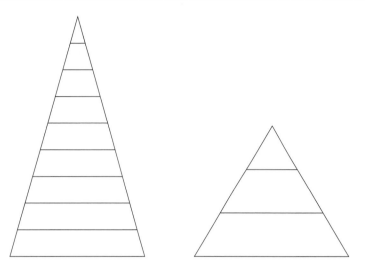

Tall organization, with nine levels     Flat organization, with three levels

According to John Child, a management researcher, the average number of hierarchical levels for an organization with 3,000 employees is seven.[2] Consequently, we might consider an organization with about 3,000 employees and four hierarchical levels to be relatively flat, but another of similar size with nine levels to be relatively tall.

Because relatively tall organizations have a narrow span of control, the managers in such organizations have a relatively high degree of control over their subordinates. The opposite, of course, is true in relatively flat structures. Because managers in tall organizations have more control readily available to them and because almost everyone in the company is a specialist, authority in tall organizations is usually centralized at the top of the hierarchy. Only at that level are there individuals who deal with and understand all parts of the organization's operations.

Conversely, authority is more decentralized in relatively flat structures. This is because a manager with a broad span of control must grant more authority to his or her employees, as the manager is unable to keep up sufficiently with all developments to make the best decisions. Decisions are more likely to be made by the employee who is on the scene and is most familiar with the situation. As might be expected, employees in flat organizations are less specialized than those in taller ones.

Strategically speaking, both organizational types have certain advantages.[3] The relatively tall, centralized organization allows for better communication of the business's mission, goals, and objectives to all employees. It also enhances coordination of functional areas to ensure that each area works closely with the other functions and that all work together to attain the business's goals and objectives. Finally, in these organizations, planning and its execution are relatively easy to accomplish since all employees are centrally directed. Tall organizational structures are well suited for environments that are relatively stable and predictable.

Relatively flat structures also have their advantages. Administrative costs are usually less than those in taller organizations, because fewer hierarchical levels require fewer managers, which, in turn, means fewer secretaries, offices, and fringe benefits. A second advantage is that decentralized decision making allows managers at various levels to have more authority, which may increase their motivation to assume responsibility for their area's performance. Third, because of the greater freedom in decision making, innovations are encouraged. Flat structures, therefore, are appropriate for more dynamic environments.

For example, Alcoa, the world's largest producer of aluminum, recently flattened its structure in an attempt to lower costs and to speed up decision making in its increasingly competitive environment. The company eliminated two levels of top management—including the offices of president and three group vice presidents, and twenty-four staff positions—and granted considerable autonomy to its twenty-five business unit managers. Each business unit manager, for instance, now has authority to spend up to $5 million without higher-level approval, an increase of 400 percent over the previous spending limit, and reports directly to the chief executive officer (CEO) rather than to a group vice president.[4]

## ■ Horizontal Growth

Returning to our earlier illustration of a small business with an owner-manager, recall that success necessitates growth. This growth is not only vertical, as just discussed, but also horizontal. **Horizontal growth** refers to an increase in the breadth of an organization's structure. In Figure 8.1, the small business segmented itself horizontally into two departments—manufacturing and marketing. If the company continues to grow, it will eventually need specialists in such areas as personnel, accounting, and finance. Right now, the owner-manager is carrying out those functions, but with growth, his or her expertise will be increasingly needed for strategic management. Individuals will need to be hired to manage the personnel, accounting, and finance activities. Thus, with growth, the structure of an organization is broadened to accommodate the development of more specialized functions.

As an example, consider the comments of T. J. Rodgers, founder of Cypress Semiconductor Corporation. Using a niche-differentiation strategy, this enterprise grew to a $135 million company in five years by developing superfast memory chips. With such rapid growth, however, Rodgers quickly found himself overextended.

> At about $50 million in revenues, I felt I could run it. . . . I could name everybody in the company. But as it grew larger, I found myself stretched. One Friday night at 11 P.M., I realized that if there wasn't a change, I'd have to stop sleeping within six months to keep up the pace.[5]

In other words, a new business may originally have its owner-manager and its few employees performing multiple functions on a daily basis. With growth, however, each function expands so that ultimately no one individual can be intimately involved—either physically or intellectually—in all of the company's functions. This is the point at which various key functional areas are formally set apart as departments, and existing employees and new hires are each assigned to one of these newly formed functional units.

This functional structure, elaborated upon in the following section, is the way small businesses typically organize as they experience growth. This structure, of course, is not the only form available to management. After the functional structure is discussed, other forms are also presented. But, in all cases, growth involves both vertical and horizontal elaboration. It is the strategic direction of the firm that determines the specific type of structure that is most appropriate.

## ORGANIZATIONAL STRUCTURE

As an enterprise grows to become an established business, it will adopt one of a number of different organizational structures to implement its strategy. Over time, as its situation changes, the enterprise may shift to another structure. Many large, well-known companies change structures several times in a decade in order to carry out their strategy more effectively. This section discusses seven major types of structures that are available to organizations: functional, product divisional, geographic divisional, multidivisional, strategic business unit, matrix, and horizontal.

### ■ Functional Structure

As suggested in the preceding section, the initial growth of an enterprise often requires it to organize by functional areas. The **functional structure** is characterized by the simultaneous combination of similar activities and the separation of dissimilar activities on the basis of function. This structure is by no means limited to small businesses. Companies of any size that have a single product line or a few similar product lines are well suited to the functional organizational structure. Small businesses, however, are likely to have only a few functional departments; larger organizations may be quite differentiated, both horizontally and vertically. Figure 8.3 shows a large business that has experienced both vertical and horizontal growth.

**Figure 8.3**          **A Functional Structure with Vertical and Horizontal Growth**

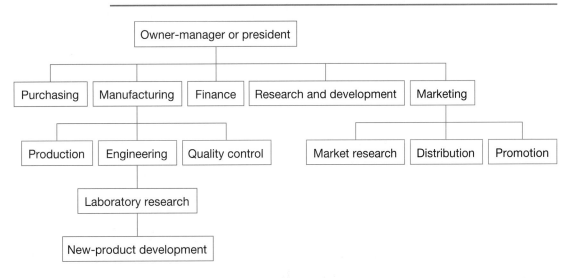

Comparing this business with the one shown in Figure 8.1, we can see that growth brings about more extensive horizontal expansion. Rather than simply dividing its employees into manufacturing and marketing functions, this organization has grown so that it also needs specialists in purchasing, finance, and research and development. Furthermore, its growth has resulted in vertical extensions. Manufacturing has become so complex that it has had to segment itself into the functions of production, engineering, and quality control. Engineering contains two additional levels—laboratory research and new-product development. Likewise, marketing has been divided into market research, distribution, and promotion functions.

A functional structure has certain strategic advantages and disadvantages. On the plus side, this structure emphasizes the functions that the organization must carry out. Specialization by function is encouraged, with the resulting benefits that specialization brings. For instance, when functional specialists interact frequently, they may realize synergies that increase their department's efficiency and effectiveness. Furthermore, their interaction can result in improvements and innovations for their functional area that may not have occurred had there not been a critical mass of specialists organized within the same unit. On the psychological side, working closely on a daily basis with others who share one's functional interests is likely to increase job satisfaction and, hence, contribute to lower turnover.

In addition, the functional organization facilitates the processes of planning, organizing, motivating, and controlling groups of personnel. Translating the organization's mission, goals, and objectives into action is easier when each functional area is activated to plan, organize, motivate, and control within its own boundaries. Finally, the training and development of personnel is often more efficient than in other structures because the training centers on standard types of functional skills.

This structure, however, is accompanied by some disadvantages. Because the business is organized around functions rather than around products or geographic regions, it is difficult to pinpoint the responsibility for profits or losses. If an organization's sales have declined, is the problem due to purchasing, research and development, manufacturing, or marketing? In a functional structure, such problem analysis can be quite ambiguous.

Along these same lines, a functional structure often creates a narrow perspective of the organization among its members. Marketing personnel, for instance, are likely to view the organization totally from a marketing perspective, because they have little experience with other functional areas. The same is true for employees in manufacturing, finance, and other functions. Problems and opportunities are perceived more in terms of the interests of each functional area than in the way they affect the overall organization. Consequently, different solutions to the same problem or different strategies to take advantage of an environmental opportunity are advanced as desirable by the various functional departments.

Finally, communication and coordination across functional areas are often difficult. For instance, employees in manufacturing view their function as central to organizational success and attribute operational problems to other functional areas. Marketing, meanwhile, views increased sales as primarily attributable to its efforts but sees slow sales as manufacturing's fault. It should be clear that as functional departments begin to proliferate, coordination becomes increasingly difficult. Functional differentiation presents management with the

## Removing the Blinders at Ford

One of the potential weaknesses in a functional structure is that it can encourage employees to take a narrow perspective of their organization. It is easy for functional managers and operative employees to look at problems from the standpoint of marketing or production or some other functional specialty rather than see them from the viewpoint of the company as a whole.

Ford Motor Company has devised a program to reduce this problem. In a $5\frac{1}{2}$-day session for middle managers, the managers are first grouped by their functional specialties. Then they are asked to "think about how their function works within the company, how others perceive it, and how it ought to work."

As they discuss their thoughts with managers from other functional areas, they begin to realize how narrow their perspective is. That is, they tend to view Ford primarily as a manufacturing company or a finance company or a company that specializes in personnel. As a result of the session, they learn to take a broader view of the organization, realizing that their particular function is only one of many interrelated activities that must be accomplished for Ford to attain its goals. Ford terms this process "chimney-breaking."

In a broader sense, Ford's strategic alliance with Mazda to develop several cars and sport-utility vehicles jointly has helped Ford engineers expand their perspective. Ford has learned to emphasize quality over price in purchasing parts. Mazda has learned how to better control emissions, measure noise and vibration, and improve its marketing skills. Both firms have improved their operations by taking a broader view of their organizations rather than focusing on functional activities in isolation of total organizational needs.

SOURCES: O. Suris, "Ford Hopes to Set Pattern for Contract with Union," *Wall Street Journal Interactive Edition,* 10 May 1996; D. K. Rigby and R. W. T. Buchanan, "Alliances the Corning Way," *Directors & Boards,* Winter 1994, p. 18; T. Sasaki, "What the Japanese Have Learned from Strategic Alliances," *Long Range Planning* 26(6) (1994): pp. 41–53; J. B. Treece, K. L. Miller, and R. A. Melcher, "The Partners," *Business Week,* 10 February 1992, pp. 102–107.

challenging task of coordinating disparate activities so that a unified, logical whole may be attained.

Whenever an organization begins to expand its product lines significantly or grow geographically, the functional structure begins to lose its strategic usefulness. Management then faces the issue of changing its organization's structure to one more appropriate to its strategy.

### ■ Product Divisional Structure

The product divisional structure is well suited for businesses with several product lines. Rather than organizing the firm around functions, the **product divisional structure** focuses on the company's product categories. Figure 8.4 illustrates this structure for a firm that manufactures and sells home appliances. Its activities and personnel are grouped into three product divisions: refrigerators and ranges, washers and dryers, and small appliances. Each product division will contain its own functional areas. The small-appliances division, for instance, may have its own manufacturing and marketing departments because the products that it makes and sells may require different manufacturing methods and channels of distribution from those of the other two divisions. Other functions, however, such as finance, may be centralized at the

**Figure 8.4**                    **Product Divisional Structure**

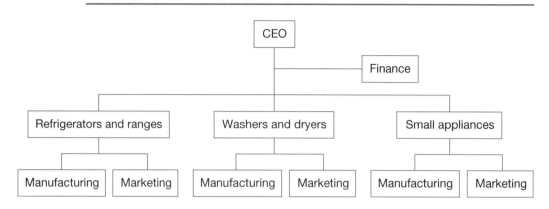

top of the organization because they benefit the organization as a whole and because economies can be realized. For example, the corporation as a whole can obtain more favorable interest rates when borrowing money than could the small-appliances division alone.

This structure is also widely used in nonmanufacturing organizations. For instance, supermarkets typically have a number of product managers (e.g., produce manager, meat manager, dairy manager, and bakery manager) who report to the store manager; and department stores are divided into product areas such as women's sportswear, men's shoes, children's wear, furniture, and appliances. Universities, being service organizations, are also usually organized by "product" divisions: history, mathematics, computer sciences, marketing, art, and so on.

The advantages of the product divisional structure are several. Rather than emphasize the functions that the organization performs, the structure emphasizes product lines. The result is a clear focus upon each individual product category and a greater orientation toward customer service. Also, the ability to pinpoint the responsibility for profits or losses is greatly enhanced, since each product division becomes a profit center to which profits and losses can be directly attributed. A **profit center** is an organizational unit charged with a well-defined mission and is headed by a manager accountable for the center's revenues and expenditures. Thus, it is clear to upper management which divisions are operating profitably and which are incurring losses. Furthermore, the product divisional structure is ideal for training and developing managers, since each product manager is, in effect, running his or her "own business." Hence, product managers develop general management skills—an end that can be accomplished in a functional structure only by rotating managers from one functional area to another.

Even relatively small companies can use a product divisional structure. A few years ago Stryker Corporation, with annual revenues of $281 million, converted from a functional structure to one with several semiautonomous product divisions. Now, Stryker employs a highly trained sales force for each division to market a specialized product—such as hospital beds, hip implants, medical video cameras, or surgical power tools—rather than use one companywide sales force to sell all of these products. As its president says, "It's achieving focus through decentralization."[6]

Of course, the product divisional structure also has its disadvantages. In some ways, it can be more expensive to operate than a functional structure, because more functional personnel may be required. In Figure 8.4, for example, because the firm has three manufacturing departments rather than only one, the total personnel expense for manufacturing is likely to be higher than if only one department were necessary. Such extra expenses raise the firm's break-even point. Second, the coordination of activities at headquarters becomes more difficult. Top management finds it harder to ensure that all of the firm's marketing personnel, for instance, are following the same policies and procedures when serving customers. This problem can become fairly significant when an organization has forty or fifty product divisions, which is fairly common among large firms. In addition, the customer can be confused by being called on by different sales representatives from the same firm. Third, because each product manager emphasizes his or her own product area, what may be in the best interests of the firm may be overlooked as product managers compete for resources such as money, physical space, and personnel.

In fact, disadvantages like these led Nestlé's U.S.-based subsidiary to convert its product divisional structure to a functional structure in 1991. By consolidating such product lines as Carnation, Stouffer Foods, Quik, and Taster's Choice under one manager, Nestlé saved at least $30 million in overhead and administrative expenses. It also allowed the business unit to benefit from increased scale economies.[7]

### ■ Geographic Divisional Structure

When a firm operates in various geographical areas, an appropriate structure may be the **geographic divisional structure,** in which activities and personnel are grouped by specific geographic locations. This structure may be used on a local basis (a city may be divided into sales regions), on a national basis (northeast region, mid-Atlantic region, midwest region), or on an international basis (North American region, Latin American region, Western European region, Middle Eastern region). Figure 8.5 illustrates a national company (at the top) and an international company (at the bottom) organized by geographic divisions.

There are a number of advantages to organizing geographically. First, products and services may be better tailored to the climatic needs of specific areas. For example, retailers may stock heavier clothing for their outlets in northern states and lighter clothes in southern stores. Second, a geographic divisional structure allows a firm to respond to the technical needs of different international areas. For instance, in many parts of the world, the electrical system is different from that in the United States; the geographic structure allows firms to accommodate these geographic differences. Third, producing or distributing products in different national or global locations may give the organization a competitive advantage. Many firms, for example, produce components in countries that either have a labor cost advantage or are located close to essential raw materials. The final product may then be assembled in still another location that is more appropriate for the advanced technology required or that is closer to the final consumer. Fourth, a geographic organization may better serve the consumer needs of various nations. For instance, the

**Figure 8.5**                    **Geographic Divisional Structures**

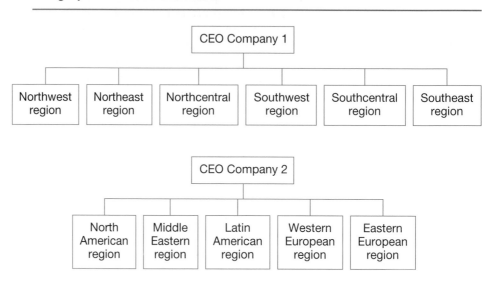

need for hair-grooming products differs from one society to another, and the geographic structure allows firms to respond to these differing needs. Fifth, organizing along geographic lines enables a company to adapt to varying legal systems. Automobile insurance companies within the United States, for example, often have a geographic division because no two states have the same insurance regulations. Finally, geographic divisions allow firms to pinpoint the responsibility for profits or losses, because each division is a profit center.

The disadvantages of a geographic divisional structure are similar to those identified earlier for the product divisional structure. Often, more functional personnel are required than would be the case for a functional structure, because each region has its own functional departments. Coordination of companywide functions is more difficult than in a strictly functional organization, and regional managers may emphasize their own geographic areas to the exclusion of a companywide viewpoint.

## ■ Multidivisional Structure

As a firm continues to expand by adding more and more product lines, it may outgrow all of the preceding structures. At this stage, firms with multiple product lines may adopt the **multidivisional structure,** in which the company is partitioned into several divisions, with each division responsible for one or more product lines.

Consider Maytag as an example. At one time in its history, this appliance firm had a fairly simple structure with three product divisions—gas range products, laundry products, and electric range products. But it continued to expand its product lines by acquiring Magic Chef (a producer of air conditioners, refrigerators, and furnaces), Toastmaster (a manufacturer of small appliances), and Hoover (a maker of vacuum cleaners and European major appliances).

**Figure 8.6**                              **Multidivisional Structure of Maytag**

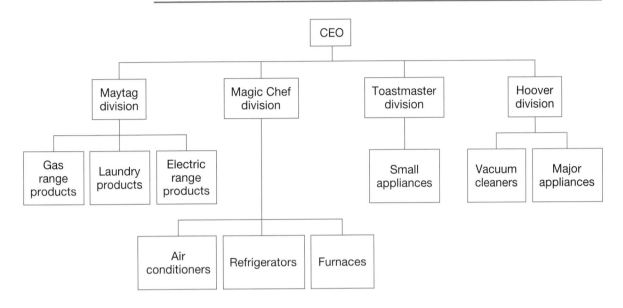

Maytag's current structure is depicted in Figure 8.6. As you can see, the multidivisional structure encompasses several divisions, with each division comprised of one or more product lines.

The multidivisional structure has several advantages. First, continued growth is facilitated. As new product lines are created or acquired, those lines may be integrated into an existing division or may serve as the foundation for a newly developed division. Second, since each division has its own top-level strategic managers, the workload of the CEO's headquarters staff is lightened. This gives the CEO more time to analyze each division's operations and to decide on resource allocations on the basis of the portfolio analysis techniques discussed in chapter 5. Third, authority is delegated downward to each division and, within each division, to each product line. This decentralization allows for a better alignment of each division and product line with its unique external environment. Fourth, accountability for performance can be logically evaluated at the product line level as well as at the divisional level.

As is true with each structure discussed, however, the multidivisional structure has certain disadvantages. First, the distribution of corporate overhead costs across the divisions is difficult and relatively subjective. Inevitably, the distribution results in some divisional managers feeling that their divisions have received too heavy an allocation. Second, dysfunctional divisional rivalries often emerge as each division attempts to secure a greater share of the firm's resources. Third, when one division makes components or products that another division needs, conflicts can arise in setting transfer prices. *Transfer pricing* refers to the price that one division charges another division for its products or parts. The selling division normally prefers to charge a relatively high transfer price to increase its profits, but the purchasing division prefers to pay a relatively low transfer price to lower its costs.

S T R A T E G I C    I N S I G H T

## ITW's Multidivisional Structure

Illinois Tool Works (ITW), headquartered in a Chicago suburb, is a low-profile manufacturer of 90 product lines and almost 100,000 products, including nails, screws, bolts, strapping, wrapping, valves, capacitors, filters, adhesives, tools and machines, plastic buckets, plastic loops that hold six-packs together, Zip-Pak resealable food packages, and Kiwi-Lok nylon fasteners. ITW is a member of the Fortune 200, with annual sales of about $3 billion and 17,000 employees. Its primary markets are the construction, automotive and truck, electronics, agricultural, and telecommunications industries. Half of its revenues come from foreign sales.

The company searches for market niches and often dominates those in which it operates. At the corporate level, the firm follows a growth strategy, with most of its business units pursuing a niche–low-cost/differentiation strategy.

In addition to focusing on internal growth, ITW pursues a strategy of horizontal integration and diversification by regularly acquiring smaller companies that complement ITW's core businesses. Its ninety product lines are grouped into nine divisions. ITW's businesses are relatively small, with about $30 million in annual revenue. Each product line manager controls manufacturing, marketing, and R&D. When a new product with commercial possibilities is developed, it is often split off to form a new business unit.

ITW seeks to keep costs as low as possible. Its largest division, the construction products group, generates $420 million a year but has only three headquarters employees: a president, a controller, and a shared secretary.

According to corporate chairman W. James Farrell, ITW's success is linked to its decentralized structure, enabling it to remain close to its customers and minimize costs. These efforts may explain why ITW has been noted for its unique ability to prosper during recessionary times. Its carefully formulated strategy and appropriate structure have helped ITW to rank consistently toward the top in the metals products industry in *Fortune's* annual survey of "Most Admired Corporations."

SOURCES: "Illinois Tool Names Farrell Chairman, CEO," *Dow Jones News Service,* 7 May 1996; H. S. Byrne, "A New Chapter," *Barron's,* 11 December 1995, p. 18; "Illinois Tool Works, Inc." *Wall Street Journal,* 8 August 1995, p. B2; C. Willis, "Wall Street," *Money,* April 1992, pp. 69–70; H. S. Byrne, "Illinois Tool Works," *Barron's,* 16 November 1992, pp. 51–52.

## ■ Strategic Business Unit Structure

Organizational growth may ultimately require that related product lines be grouped into divisions and that the divisions themselves then be grouped into strategic business units. This **strategic business unit structure** is particularly well suited to very large, diversified firms. An example of such a firm is illustrated in Figure 8.7.

The major advantage of the strategic business unit structure is that it reduces corporate headquarters' span of control. Rather than managers at the corporate level having to control many divisions, they need control only relatively few strategic business units. This reduction in span of control also lessens the chance that headquarters will experience information overload as the various organizational units report on their operations. Another advantage is that this structure permits better coordination among divisions with similar missions, products, markets, or technologies.

The strategic business unit structure, however, has a number of disadvantages. First, corporate headquarters becomes more distant from the division and product levels with the addition of another vertical layer of management. Second, rivalry among the strategic business unit managers for greater shares of corporate resources can become dysfunctional and can negatively affect the corporation's overall performance. Third, this structure complicates portfolio analysis. For instance, a strategic business unit may be considered a poor performer overall, but some of its divisions may be stars.

Note that it is important not to confuse the concept *strategic business unit* with that of *strategic business unit structure*. When we are discussing strategy formulation, the term *strategic business unit* may be used in more than one way.[8] A single company that operates within a single industry (e.g., a business that builds swimming pools) is a strategic business unit. But a product division or geographic division of a large multidivisional firm is also a strategic business unit. *Strategic business unit* may even be used to refer to the large firm's multidivisional level that combines several product divisions or geographic divisions. More specifically, a strategic business unit is an organization or a division, product line, or profit center of an organization that produces a set of products/services for well-defined markets or customers in competition with identifiable competitors.

When our reference point is strategy implementation, however, the term *strategic business unit structure* is used to identify the organizational structure type discussed in this section of the chapter. That is, a strategic business unit structure is one in which related product lines are grouped into divisions and those divisions are then grouped into larger entities referred to as strategic business units, as shown in Figure 8.7.[9]

### ■ Matrix Structure

Up until this point, each of the organizational structures discussed has possessed a single chain of command. That is, each employee in those structures reports to only one manager. The structure discussed in this section, however, is unique in that it possesses a dual chain of command. The **matrix structure** is

**Figure 8.7**   **Strategic Business Unit Structure**

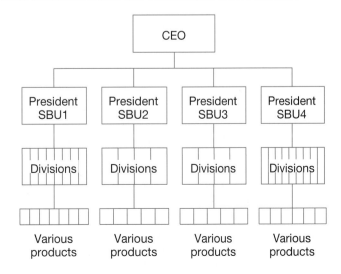

one in which both functional and project managers exercise authority over organizational activities. Hence, personnel within the matrix have two supervisors—a project manager and the manager of their functional department.

The matrix structure is most commonly used in organizations that operate in industries where the rate of technological change is very fast. For example, firms such as TRW and Boeing use a matrix structure. As shown in Figure 8.8, a matrix structure contains literally two organizations—a functional organization (shown horizontally across the top) and a project organization (shown vertically at the left of the chart). In project A, for example, the project manager has brought together some members of the organization's functional departments to work on a specific project. In a construction company, for instance, that project might be the building of a refinery in Thailand. When it is completed, the personnel in project A will return to their functional departments. As another example, in the computer industry, project A might be the development of a new, more powerful personal computer. During the time they are assigned to the project, the employees are accountable not only to the project manager but also to the manager of the functional department from which they came.

Some companies use a matrix even though the rate of technological change in their industry is not extremely fast. For example, Toyota used the matrix structure to develop the Lexus, its entry into the top-of-the-line luxury-car market. A number of engineering, marketing, research and development (R&D), and finance personnel were brought together to work on developing an automobile that would compare favorably with the best offered by the German, British, and U.S. automakers.[10]

A variation on the traditional project form of the matrix structure is reflected in Procter & Gamble's (P&G) use of this system. Although many people associate the matrix structure most closely with high-technology enterprises, P&G actually pioneered this form of organization in 1927. At P&G, rather than a project manager being in charge of a temporary project, each of

**Figure 8.8**                    **Matrix Structure**

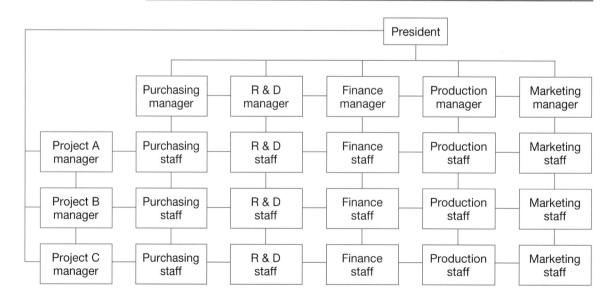

P&G's individual products has a brand manager. The brand manager pulls various specialists, as they are needed, from their functional departments. For instance, if a detergent, such as Tide, is experiencing slowing sales, the brand manager for Tide might call together members of the R&D department to develop a new additive, members of the advertising staff to create ads for "new, improved Tide," members of the packaging department to design a new container for the detergent, and so on. Each brand manager reports to one of twenty-six category managers, an individual who is in charge of all related products in a single category (e.g., detergents such as Tide, Cheer, and Ivory Flakes). It is this manager's responsibility to coordinate the advertising and sales of related products so that competition among the products is minimized.[11] As we can see, then, P&G uses a mixture of a matrix structure and a multidivisional (category) structure.

In whatever form it is used, the matrix structure offers certain advantages. First, by combining both the functional structure and the project (or product) structure, a firm can enjoy the advantages of both forms. Second, the matrix is a cost-efficient structure because project managers pay only for the services of functional personnel when they need them. The remainder of the time, these functional employees are working in their own departments and are not on the payroll of any particular project. By contrast, in a strictly project form of organization, the functional employees are employed full-time within a single project or product division.

Third, a matrix organization has considerable flexibility. Employees may be transferred with ease between projects, a flexibility that is greatly reduced in a more permanent form of structure. Fourth, a matrix permits lower-level functional employees to become intimately involved in a project. They are responsible for making and implementing many of the decisions at the project level. Hence, their motivation may be enhanced, and their job satisfaction is also likely to be relatively high.

Fifth, the matrix structure is an excellent vehicle for training and developing general managers. Each project manager, in a sense, is running his or her "own business." The skills developed at this level are essential skills for higher-level positions in the organization. Finally, top management in a matrix is freed from day-to-day involvement in the operations of the enterprise and is, therefore, able to concentrate on strategic problems and opportunities.

Although the matrix has numerous advantages, it is also accompanied by some significant disadvantages. First is the greater administrative cost associated with its operation. Because coordination across functional areas and across projects is so important, matrix personnel spend considerable time in meetings exchanging information. Although this communication is essential, it consumes valuable time that could otherwise be spent on actual project implementation. Second, matrix structures are characterized by considerable conflict, which takes two forms. One is conflict between project and functional managers over budgets and personnel. The other is conflict among the project managers themselves over similar resource allocation issues.

Finally, working in a matrix can be a source of considerable stress for some functional employees. Reporting to two managers can create significant amounts of role ambiguity and role conflict for an individual. As might be expected, some organizations, such as PepsiCo and Digital Equipment, have found managing a matrix to be so complicated that they have reverted to more traditional structures.

■ **Horizontal Structure**

As American firms have grown in size, many of them have also grown in their organizational layers, with ensuing increases in their bureaucracy. This has made some of them less efficient as well as less capable of meeting the needs and expectations of their customers. These problems have had to be confronted by management. Senior executives have ordinarily responded by instituting a more **horizontal structure**—one with fewer hierarchies.

Recall from chapter 4 that a phenomenon has been in vogue in the 1980s and the 1990s—corporate restructuring, which means changing the way work is done in organizations (changing activities and relationships). Throughout the 1980s and the 1990s, organizational restructuring has often involved forming a more horizontal structure through **downsizing,** which refers to two related changes.

The first is eliminating one or more hierarchical levels from the organization's structure. Most frequently, the levels eliminated are those staffed by vice presidents or other middle managers, although the headquarters' staff positions are also common targets. Additionally, some employees temporarily or permanently lose their jobs. The goal is to cut costs (and thereby improve the corporation's ability to compete) and to abolish some of the bureaucratic maze and red tape that invariably accompany multiple organizational layers.

The first change must necessarily be accompanied by the second: a pushing of decision making downward in the organization. That is, by removing one or more hierarchical levels, an organization reduces the number of individuals in the chain of command who must approve decisions. Because fewer levels result in a broader span of control for upper-level executives, more decisions must be made by lower-level personnel who are closer to the customer. Otherwise, continuing to refer most decisions upward would quickly overload top management.

What is anticipated from the horizontal structure through downsizing is the achievement of higher efficiencies as well as customer responsiveness. In some situations, as discussed in the previous chapter, substantial decision-making authority is transferred to cross-functional teams who are in charge of key processes.

The horizontal organization may take various unconventional forms. As shown in the top part of Figure 8.9, a horizontal organization may have a president and three vice presidents. Each vice president may be in charge of several key organizational processes. For instance, vice president 1 is in charge of process A and B. Each of these processes has its own manager whose group is comprised of cross-functional personnel.

As shown in the bottom part of Figure 8.9, a horizontal organization may be circular. Similar to Eastman Chemical's structure, the organization may have a president connected to various cross-functional teams. According to Ernest Deavenport, president of Eastman Chemicals, "Our organizational chart is now called the pizza chart because it looks like a pizza. . . We did it in circular form to show that everyone is equal in the organization"[12]

## ASSESSMENT OF ORGANIZATIONAL STRUCTURE

The key issue in this chapter is how an organization can implement its strategy by designing its structure appropriately. In this section, we wish to examine how managers can assess the effectiveness of their organization's current

**Figure 8.9**　　　　　**Horizontal Structure**

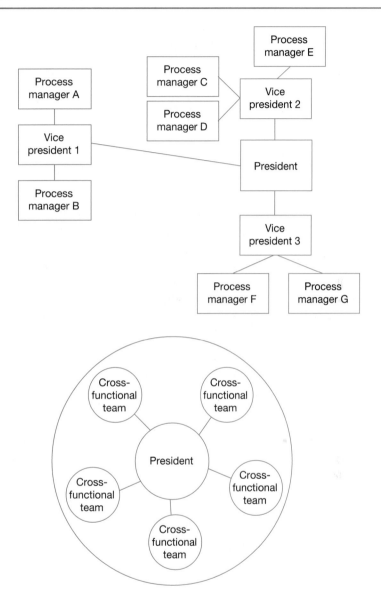

structure in that regard. There are, unfortunately, no hard-and-fast rules for evaluating the appropriateness of an organization's structure. However, the extent to which a structure is—and will continue to be—effective in helping the organization implement its strategy can be at least partially assessed by answering the following questions. These questions are highlighted in Table 8.1.

- *Is the structure compatible with the corporate profile and the corporate strategy?* Recall that at the corporate level, a firm may be in one business, several related businesses, or several unrelated businesses. Although the one-business company may effectively adopt the functional struc-

| **Table 8.1** | **Checklist for Determining Appropriateness of Organizational Structure** |
|---|---|

1. Is the structure compatible with the corporate profile and the corporate strategy?
2. At the corporate level, is the structure compatible with the outputs of the firm's business units?
3. Are there too few or too many hierarchical levels at either the corporate or business unit level of analysis?
4. Does the structure promote coordination among its parts?
5. Does the structure allow for appropriate centralization or decentralization of authority?
6. Does the structure permit the appropriate grouping of activities?

ture, this form of specialization may be inappropriate for one in multiple businesses. In the situation of a multiple business firm, a product divisional or multidivisional structure can more appropriately emphasize the corporation's products and services rather than its functions. Hence, an organization's structure should be compatible with its corporate profile.

Its structure should also be compatible with its corporate-level strategy. For instance, if the corporation intends to grow continuously, it may find its growth eventually stymied by a product divisional or geographic divisional structure. The reason is that horizontal expansion places an ever-increasing burden on corporate-level management owing to the widening span of control. At some point, it is not humanly possible to keep up with the activities of all of the firm's product or geographic divisions. Hence, continued growth may eventually require adopting the multidivisional or strategic business unit structure.

- *At the corporate level, is the structure compatible with the outputs of the firm's business units?* A product divisional structure, for instance, may be more appropriate than a geographic divisional structure for a corporation with business units that produce fasteners, cutting tools, and hand tools. The reason is that the demand for these products is based on their technical specifications and perceived quality. Each product division can, therefore, concentrate on producing and marketing its own product line. However, a geographic divisional structure may be better suited to a corporation with business units that sell retail clothing and shoes. These items are sold together, and demand for them will differ from one geographic region to another depending on climate, culture, and tradition. Hence, they can be marketed more effectively through specialization based on geographic location.

- *Are there too few or too many hierarchical levels at either the corporate or business unit level of analysis?* It is important that an organization's structure match the nature of the environment in which it operates. Normally, flatter organizations with relatively fewer hierarchical levels and wider spans of control may be better suited for dynamic, fast-changing environments than taller structures. Conversely, taller organizations with relatively more hierarchical levels and narrower spans of control may operate more effectively in stable, more predictable environments than flatter ones do. Recall that the trend has been to reduce the number of hierarchies in firms, although some organizations will remain taller relative to others even after they are downsized.

Corporate-level managers must also realize that the firm's business units need not necessarily have the same structures. Some business units may operate in relatively dynamic environments, and others may compete in relatively stable environments, necessitating differences in their structures.

Overall, in answering this particular question, a manager may find it helpful to compare the configuration of his or her organization with those of its competitors.

- *Does the structure promote coordination among its parts?* Varying degrees of coordination among an organization's parts may be necessary, depending upon the particular situation. For instance, firms with multiple unrelated business units that operate fairly autonomously may find that relatively little coordination among the business units' operations is required. However, within each business unit, management may find it essential to coordinate closely the activities of functional departments potentially through process management. Firms with multiple related businesses usually require greater coordination of their business units' activities, and companies that operate in only one business generally concentrate on coordinating their functional processes.

As a rule, the more complex an organization, the more difficult coordination is to achieve. This problem is especially evident in organizations with related businesses. Very complex businesses may have to establish special, permanent coordinating units that integrate, for example, the activities of research and development, production, and sales.

- *Does the structure allow for appropriate centralization or decentralization of authority?* The extent to which decision making should be systematically delegated downward in an organization depends upon a number of factors. One, obviously, is organizational size. In general, very large organizations tend to be more decentralized than very small ones, simply because it is difficult for the CEO of a very large company to keep up with all of the organization's operations.

Another factor is the number and type of businesses a firm is in. Firms with large numbers of unrelated businesses tend to be relatively decentralized, allowing the heads of the diverse business units to make most of the decisions affecting those units. In such cases, corporate-level management's primary responsibility is to determine the overall corporation's mission, goals, and strategy and to leave the actual operating decisions to those on the scene. By contrast, organizations in only one business can more easily be managed in a centralized fashion.

The type of environment affects the need for decentralization. Organizations in rapidly changing environments must be relatively decentralized so that decisions can be made quickly by those who are closest to the situation. At the other end of the spectrum, organizations in relatively stable environments can be managed effectively through centralized decision making, since change is relatively slow and fairly predictable. In such cases, the majority of decisions follow a routine pattern, and procedures can be established in advance for many decision-making situations.

- *Does the structure permit the appropriate grouping of activities?* The extent to which organizational activities are appropriately grouped affects how well strategy is implemented. For instance, related product lines should be grouped together. Customers are confused when they are called on by one sales representative for personal computers but have to contact another sales representative from the same company to purchase a printer for the computer. Likewise, some department stores insist on selling men's suits in one department, but ties and dress shirts in another department down the aisle. As another type of example, it is difficult to hold a product divisional manager fully responsible for sales of a product when he or she had no control over either the development or the production of the product.

## KEIRETSU AND OTHER POSSIBLE STRUCTURES

The organizational structures discussed so far are Western conceptions. A Japanese form of organization that has received increasing attention is the **keiretsu,** which represents a horizontally and vertically connected group of businesses with interlocking board members who are senior managers of member companies. The member companies also have mutual ownerships in each other. Keiretsu members often engage in joint ventures with each other and sign reciprocal purchase agreements. Some knowledgeable observers have argued that to compete effectively in the global economy may require forming European and American keiretsus in the future.[13]

The keiretsu normally includes twenty to forty-five businesses anchored to a major manufacturer or a bank. The businesses cooperate in research and development and share technological and market information with each other.

Some of today's Japanese keiretsus are capitalizing on the digitalization of technology, relating to each other what may have been previously unrelated businesses, according to Ferguson, an expert in high-technology industries. He asserts, with respect to keiretsus, that previously unrelated businesses—"cameras, computers, stereos, photocopiers"—are converting to form a related and "unified information technology sector, itself based on common digital components and standard interfaces."[14]

Other knowledgeable observers alternatively believe that the wave of the future will be a structure variously termed the "modular corporation," the "virtual corporation," or the "network pattern."[15] In this configuration, an organization "outsources," or contracts with other companies for all of its functions except for its core competencies. For instance, a company might concentrate on designing and marketing a product while letting other companies manufacture the product, deliver it, and bill customers for their purchases. Such a system allows a company to concentrate on those processes in which it possesses a particular competence, without having to divert its resources to other activities. The amount of capital investment is obviously much lower than it would be if the company itself handled all of the functions, and this lowered-investment level means that the company has considerable flexibility to change with its environment.

For instance, neither Reebok nor Dell Computer owns a manufacturing plant. Both outsource all manufacturing functions to contractors. This system, of course, has had precedence. Construction companies and publishing houses have been structured in this fashion for decades. But it is clear that organizations in other industries are increasingly interested in shedding fixed assets and gaining flexibility by adopting elements of a modular structure.

## A Structural Revolution at IBM

One of the world's largest and most successful firms of the past fifty years found itself floundering as it entered the 1990s. In 1991, IBM's sales dropped 6.1 percent, to $64.8 billion, its first decline in revenue since 1946. And, for the first time in its history, IBM incurred a loss—$2.8 billion. That loss grew to $5 billion in 1992.

Its problem? IBM was operating as it always had, but its environment had changed dramatically. The computer industry today is one of continually accelerating change. For instance, the life cycle of a notebook computer may be as short as three months. Many of IBM's competitors, moreover, are aggressive, flexible, and extremely quick, garnering the rewards that accrue to those who are first to the market with new technology.

At the center of this dynamic environment stood huge, bureaucratic, centralized IBM—a company still dominated by its mainframe computer division. As it always had, IBM required that all major decisions be made at corporate headquarters at Armonk, New York. Those decisions were guided by policies that virtually forbade any internal competition with the mainframe division, subjected new product plans to endless discussion, and kept IBM divisions from competing unfettered with their more nimble competitors. As a result, IBM introduced its personal computer four years after Apple did, entered the PC-compatible laptop market five years behind Toshiba, and followed Digital Equipment into the minicomputer market only after an eleven-year lag.

To turn the corporation around, top management unveiled an extensive structural reorganization. Some of the major changes being implemented are:

- The creation of semiautonomous business units, each with profit and loss responsibility, but also able to make its own manufacturing and pricing decisions. Every business unit manager must sign an annual contract with corporate management agreeing to goals and objectives in such areas as growth, profit, return on assets, quality, and customer satisfaction. Each business unit decides for itself how it will meet those goals and objectives.
- A drastic reduction in work force. After avoiding involuntary layoffs for more than 70 years, IBM has pruned its work force by 160,000 and its payroll by about 40 percent. Most—but not all—of this reduction has been accomplished by voluntary buyout and early retirement programs. By design, the majority of these cuts were primarily in managerial and staff positions.
- Reorganization of the research and development function. Insiders have complained that IBM takes too long to get products outside the door, testing them repeatedly and delaying delivery. As a result, top managers, engineers, and customer-service representatives worked together to create a leaner department that emphasizes speed and eliminates useless paperwork and excessive product testing.

Several obstacles to effective implementation of the restructuring remain. One is the ongoing attempt to change IBM's culture, which, historically, has not encouraged autonomy. A recent survey of many of the firm's top managers revealed that many still do not accept the need for changing the "old IBM." Another is the challenge to maintain high-quality standards while improving customer responsiveness and speed to market. IBM officials have always boasted that their products have always met or exceeded quality standards. But IBM must now pursue quality with speed.

SOURCES: B. Ziegler, "IBM Is Growing Again; 'Fires Are Out', Chief Says," *Wall Street Journal Interactive Edition*, 1 May 1996; L. Hayes, "Gerstner Is Struggling as He Tries to Change Ingrained IBM Culture," *Wall Street Journal*, 13 May 1994, pp. A1, A8 (quotation from p. A1); "IBM Will Raise Number of Jobs It Plans to Trim," *Wall Street Journal*, 11 February 1993; J. Main, "Betting on the 21st Century Jet," *Fortune*, 20 April 1992, pp. 102–117 (quotation from p. 102); D. Moreau, "From Big Bust to Big Blue: IBM and Its Vigorous Rebirth," *Kiplinger's Personal Finance Magazine*, July 1995, pp. 34–35.

# SUMMARY

Implementing strategy requires management to consider how the organization should be structured. In new, small companies, structure is fluid, with each employee often knowing how to perform more than one task and the owner-manager being involved in all aspects of the business. Success leads to growth, however—both vertical and horizontal. With growth comes a more permanent division of labor.

Vertical growth refers to an increase in the length of an organization's hierarchical chain of command. Organizations in stable, predictable environments often become relatively tall, with many hierarchical levels and narrow spans of control. Conversely, companies in dynamic, rapidly changing environments usually adopt flat structures with few hierarchical levels and wide spans of control.

Horizontal growth refers to the segmentation of the organization into departments or divisions. The first formal structure usually adopted by a growing business is the functional structure, an organizational type that forms departments along functional lines—manufacturing, marketing, finance, research and development, personnel, and so on. Its strengths are that it emphasizes the functions that the organization must carry out, which results in a number of advantages; it facilitates the processes of planning, organizing, motivating, and controlling; and it is an efficient structure for the training and development of personnel. Its weaknesses, however, are that it makes pinpointing the responsibility for profits or losses difficult; it creates a narrow perspective of the organization among its members; and it inhibits communication across functional areas and coordination of their disparate activities. Whenever an organization begins to expand its product lines significantly or grow geographically, the functional structure begins to lose its strategic usefulness.

The product divisional structure is well suited for a business with several product lines because the firm is structured around its product categories. This structure's strengths are that it emphasizes the firm's product lines; it makes coordination of functions easier because each product division has its own functions; it allows responsibility for profits or losses to be pinpointed since each product division is a responsibility center; and it encourages development of general managers. Its weaknesses are that it may be more expensive to operate than a functional structure because more functional personnel are required; it inhibits coordination of activities at the corporate level; and it creates dysfunctional competition among division managers for corporate resources.

The geographic divisional structure is used by firms that operate in various geographic areas. Structuring around location provides such advantages as tailoring products/services to climatic needs of specific areas, responding to the technical needs of different international locations, gaining a competitive advantage by producing or distributing products in different locations, serving the consumer needs of various nations better, adapting to varying legal systems, and pinpointing the responsibility for profits or losses. The disadvantages of this structure are the same as those for the product divisional structure.

As a firm adds more product lines, it may eventually adopt the multidivisional structure, in which similar product lines are organized into divisions. This structure facilitates continued growth, frees corporate management for strategic planning, decentralizes authority to individual divisions and product lines so that decision making is quicker, and enables management to pinpoint responsibility for profits and losses. Its unique weaknesses are that distribution of corporate overhead costs is subjective and difficult to make, dysfunctional divisional rivalries often occur, and transfer pricing from one division to another can become a source of contention.

Further growth may lead an organization to adopt the strategic business unit structure. In this case, divisions with similar missions, products, markets, or technologies are combined under a strategic business unit. This structure further reduces corporate headquarters' span of control and permits better coordination. However, it also distances corporate headquarters from the product level, can create dysfunctional rivalries among strategic business units, and complicates portfolio analysis.

The matrix structure is a combination of the functional structure and the product/project structure. The matrix enjoys the advantages of both structural types, it is cost-efficient for each individual project or product, it is flexible, it permits lower-level employees to become highly involved in projects, it helps train and develop general managers, and it frees top-level management for planning. But the matrix also is associated with greater administrative costs, greater conflict, and higher stress.

The horizontal structure has been developed in response to the increasing bureaucracy associated with growth of some firms. Throughout the 1980s and 1990s, organizational restructuring has involved forming a more horizontal structure through downsizing. Downsizing refers to the elimination of one or more hierarchical levels accompanied by a pushing of decision making downward in the organization.

To determine whether an organization's structure is appropriate for implementing the organization's strategy, a manager must analyze how compatible the structure is with such features as the organization's corporate profile, corporate strategy, business unit strategy, need for coordination, number of hierarchical levels, degree of decentralization, and grouping of activities. Other structures, such as the keiretsu and the "modular corporation," are structures that American firms may adopt in increasing numbers.

## TAKE IT TO THE NET

We invite you to visit the Wright page on the Prentice Hall Web site at:

**http://www.prenhall.com/wright**

for this chapter's World Wide Web exercise.

# KEY CONCEPTS

**Downsizing**   A means of organizational restructuring that includes the elimination of one or more hierarchical levels from the organization and a pushing of decision making downward in the organization.

**Flat organization**   An organization characterized by relatively few hierarchical levels and a wide span of control.

**Functional structure**   A form of organizational structure in which jobs and activities are grouped on the basis of function—for example, manufacturing, marketing, and finance.

**Geographic divisional structure**   A form of organizational structure in which jobs and activities are grouped on the basis of geographic location—for example, northeast region, midwest region, and far west region.

**Hierarchical chain of command**   The authority and accountability chain that links managers and employees in an organization.

**Horizontal growth**   An increase in the breadth of an organization's structure.

**Horizontal structure**   An organizational structure with fewer hierarchies designed to improve efficiency by reducing layers in the bureaucracy.

**Keiretsu**   A horizontally and vertically connected group of businesses with interlocking board members who are senior managers of member companies.

**Matrix structure**   A form of organizational structure that combines a functional structure with some form of divisional structure (usually product or project divisions). It contains a dual chain of command in which the functional manager and the project/product manager exercise authority over the same employees.

**Multidivisional structure**   A form of organizational structure that contains several divisions, with each division comprised of one or more product lines.

**Organizational structure**   The formal ways that tasks and responsibilities are allocated to individuals and the ways that individuals are formally grouped together into offices, departments, and divisions.

**Product divisional structure**   A form of organizational structure whereby jobs and activities are grouped on the basis of types of products or services—for example, automobiles, computer services, and electronics.

**Profit center**   An organizational unit charged with a well-defined mission and headed by a manager who is accountable for the unit's revenues and expenditures.

**Span of control**   The number of employees reporting directly to a given manager.

**Strategic business unit structure**   A form of organizational structure in which related product lines are grouped into divisions and those divisions are then grouped into larger entities referred to as strategic business units.

**Tall organization**   An organization characterized by relatively many hierarchical levels and a narrow span of control.

**Vertical growth**   An increase in the length of the organization's hierarchical chain of command.

# DISCUSSION QUESTIONS

**1.** Why does organizational growth require greater formalization of roles within the organization?

**2.** Why does organizational growth require both vertical and horizontal expansion?

**3.** Explain why a relatively tall organizational structure is not appropriate for a dynamic, rapidly changing environment.

**4.** Why is a functional structure often appropriate for small businesses?

**5.** As an organization that is structured functionally begins to add new products to its original product offerings, it often changes its structure to a product divisional form. Explain why.

**6.** What is the rationale underlying the geographic divisional structure?

**7.** Explain the difference between a multidivisional structure and a strategic business unit structure.

**8.** A matrix structure is a combination of which two forms of organizational structure? Explain.

**9.** Of all of the forms of organizational structure discussed—functional, product divisional, geographic divisional, multidivisional, strategic business unit, matrix, and the horizontal structure—which is the most flexible? Explain why.

# STRATEGIC MANAGEMENT EXERCISES

1. Assume that you have started a pizza restaurant in your town. Furthermore, assume that your restaurant has become very successful and that you eventually expand on a national basis. Draw an organization chart that portrays your business at the very beginning. Then, draw two more organization charts that show the vertical growth and the horizontal growth of your company as it grows to become a nationwide business.

2. Assume that you own a business that produces casual furniture. Draw a functional organization chart for your business. Now, assume that your business expands into furniture retailing. Draw a product divisional structure that encompasses your manufacturing and retailing operations.

3. Choose a company and examine its latest annual report. Sometimes, an explicit organization chart is contained in the report. Other times, a

summary chart is provided. In still other cases, there may be no structure depicted, but there is sufficient information for you to draw a rough sketch of the structure. Once you have determined the organization's structure, identify what type it is (functional, product divisional, geographic divisional, multidivisional, strategic business unit, matrix, or a combination of two or more of these). Explain your reasoning.

4. Select a business that has existed for at least ten years. Detail how its organizational structure has evolved over time. Explain why it changed from one structure to another at certain junctures. Or, if it has maintained the same structure during its life, explain why. Can you offer suggestions for improving its present structure?

5. From library research, identify an organization that is using a corporate growth strategy (discussed in chapter 4). Analyze how this organization's strategy has influenced its structure. Is its current structure the optimal structure for this enterprise? If not, what structure might be more appropriate?

6. From library research, identify an organization that is using a corporate retrenchment strategy (chapter 4). Analyze how this organization's strategy has influenced its structure. Is its current structure the optimal structure for this enterprise? If not, what structure might be more appropriate?

# NOTES

1. J. Hagel, "Fallacies in Organizing Performance," *The McKinsey Quarterly* 2 (1994): 97–108. Also see J. Child, *Organization: A Guide for Managers and Administrators* (New York: Harper & Row, 1977), p. 10.

2. Ibid., pp. 50–70.

3. P. R. Lawrence and J. W. Lorsch, *Organization and Environment: Managing Differentiation and Integration* (Homewood, Ill.: Irwin, 1969); R. Duncan, "What Is the Right Organizational Structure?" *Organizational Dynamics* 7 (Winter 1979): 59–80.

4. M. Schroeder, "The Recasting of Alcoa," *Business Week,* 9 September 1991, pp. 62–64.

5. J. A. Byrne, "Is Your Company Too Big?" *Business Week,* 27 March 1989, p. 90.

6. Z. Sawaya, "Focus Through Decentralization," *Forbes,* 11 November 1991, pp. 242–244 (quotation from p. 244).

7. Z. Schiller and L. Therrien, "Nestlé's Crunch in the U.S.," *Business Week,* 24 December 1990, pp. 24–25.

8. See C. W. Hoffer, "Toward a Contingency Theory of Business Strategy," *Academy of Management Journal* 18 (1975): 784–810.

9. R. P. Rumelt, *Strategy, Structure, and Economic Performance* (Cambridge: Harvard University Press, 1974).

10. A. Taylor, "Here Comes Japan's New Luxury Cars," *Fortune,* 14 August 1989, pp. 62–66.

11. B. Dumaine, "P&G Rewrites the Marketing Rules," *Fortune,* 6 November 1989, pp. 34–48; A. Swasy, "In a Fast-Paced World, Procter & Gamble Sets Its Store in Old Values," *Wall Street Journal,* 21 September 1989, p. 1; Z. Schiller, "No More Mr. Nice Guy at P&G—Not by a Long Shot," *Business Week,* 3 February 1992, pp. 54–56.

**12.** J. A. Byrne, "The Horizontal Corporation," *Business Week,* 20 December 1993, p. 81.

**13.** M. Anchordoguy, *Computers, Inc.: Japan's Challenge to IBM* (Cambridge: Harvard University Press, 1989).

**14.** C. H. Ferguson, "Computers Are the Coming of the U.S. Keiretsu," *Harvard Business Review ,* 68 p. 56 (1990).

**15.** S. Tully, "The Modular Corporation," *Fortune,* 8 February 1993, pp. 106–116; J. A. Byrne, R. Brandt, and O. Port, "The Virtual Corporation," *Business Week,* 8 February 1993, pp. 98–103; J. Wilson and J. Dobrzynski, "And Now the Post-Industrial Corporation," *Business Week,* 3 March 1986, pp. 64–71; and M. Piore and C. Sabel, *The Second Industrial Divide* (New York: McGraw-Hill, 1984).

# STRATEGIC MANAGEMENT MODEL

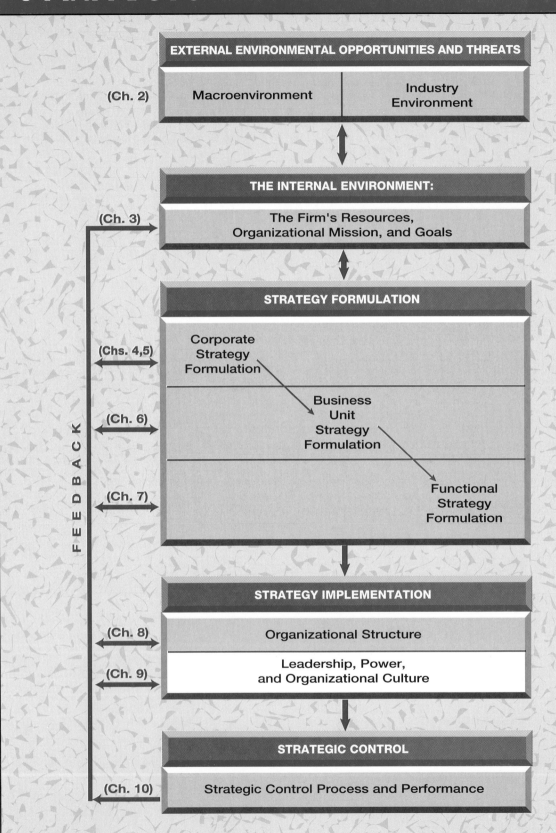

**EXTERNAL ENVIRONMENTAL OPPORTUNITIES AND THREATS**

(Ch. 2)

| Macroenvironment | Industry Environment |

**THE INTERNAL ENVIRONMENT:**

(Ch. 3)

The Firm's Resources, Organizational Mission, and Goals

**STRATEGY FORMULATION**

(Chs. 4,5) Corporate Strategy Formulation

(Ch. 6) Business Unit Strategy Formulation

(Ch. 7) Functional Strategy Formulation

FEEDBACK

**STRATEGY IMPLEMENTATION**

(Ch. 8) Organizational Structure

(Ch. 9) Leadership, Power, and Organizational Culture

**STRATEGIC CONTROL**

(Ch. 10) Strategic Control Process and Performance

# Strategy Implementation: Leadership, Power, and Organizational Culture

Any strategy, no matter how well conceived, is doomed to failure unless it is effectively implemented. The preceding chapter examined how an organization should be structured to carry out its strategy. This chapter analyzes implementation from another perspective. Our interest here is in how an organization's chief executive officer (CEO) as well as other top managers can use their office and influence to ensure that the organization's members are implementing strategies effectively.

The top management team has several means at its disposal to encourage managers and other employees to put their full efforts into strategy implementation. The first resource is leadership. The CEO is recognized as the organization's principal leader, one who sets the tone for the members of the firm. The second resource is power. By influencing the behavior of others through formal and informal means, the CEO and other top managers attempt to ensure that organizational members channel their efforts into appropriate directions. The third resource is organizational culture. All organizations have a culture; the key for the CEO and other top managers is to understand and manage the culture in such a way that it facilitates—rather than hinders—the firm's strategic actions.

## LEADERSHIP

Although some people equate *leadership* with *management*, the two concepts are not synonymous. For example, over time, a manager plays many roles. Several of them are not directly related to leadership. For instance, as a *resource allocator*, the manager determines the distribution of organizational resources such as money, time, and equipment. As a *monitor*, he or she receives information and analyses related to internal operations and external events. As a *disseminator*, the manager transmits information received from the external environment to members of the organization. All of these roles are part of the manager's job. Another role is that of *leader*.[1] A manager exhibits **leadership** when he or she secures the cooperation of others in accomplishing a goal. Hence, it is evident that the term *manager* is considerably broader than the term *leader*.

Although this chapter emphasizes the role of the CEO as the organization's leader, it is important not to overlook the fact that leadership is required at all organizational levels and in all functional areas. Strategies cannot be implemented through the CEO's efforts alone.

The need for organizational leadership has never been more important. As John P. Kotter, a management researcher, points out, in the relatively stable and prosperous 1950s and 1960s, the saying "If it ain't broke, don't fix it" prevailed. Under this axiom, it was clear that too much leadership "could actually create problems by disrupting efficient routines."[2] But as has been emphasized throughout this book, today's world is too dynamic and turbulent for an organization to compete effectively by simply continuing—no matter how efficiently—to do what it did in past years.

Our concern in this chapter is with strategic leadership, which differs from leadership at the middle-management and supervisory levels in a number of ways. **Strategic leadership** is concerned with both the external environment and with the firm's internal operations (rather than primarily with the latter); the process is characterized by greater ambiguity, complexity, and information overload; it involves the complicated task of integrating multiple functional areas rather than managing only one or a few functions; and it requires managing through others rather than directly supervising operations.[3] The job of strategic leadership is to establish the firm's direction—by developing and communicating a vision of the future—and to motivate and inspire organization members to move in that direction.[4] Not surprisingly, a review of leadership research concludes that top-level managers have a substantial impact on organizational performance.[5]

Just as strategic leadership is more important now than in past decades, it most surely will become even more essential in the coming years. Frequent environmental change and the growing complexity of organizations are trends that are likely to accelerate. Figure 9.1 portrays how external environmental changes and internal organizational complexity increase the importance of competent leadership.

It is important to remember throughout this chapter that good leadership is a necessary, but not sufficient, condition for organizational effectiveness. Although research demonstrates that leadership is an important determinant of organizational performance, it is clear that organizational effectiveness also depends on factors beyond the leader's control.[6] As we saw in chapter 2, such factors as economic conditions, industry structure, international developments, governmental policies, and technological innovations influence organizational results.

This section examines the concept of leadership. First, the formal role, or office, of the strategic leader is explored. Then the focus turns to the leader's style of leadership—the way the leader behaves in exercising authority and making decisions. Finally, how the leader works with other managers as a member of the top management team is analyzed.

**Figure 9.1**  **External and Organizational Changes that Present Challenges for Leadership**

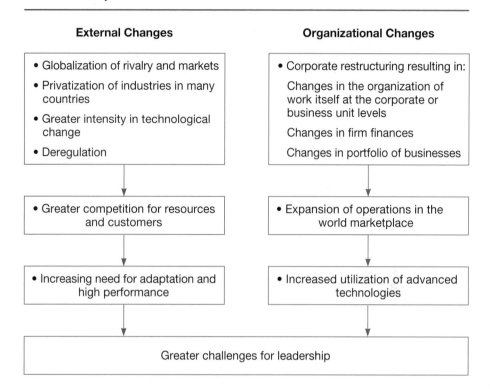

## The Office of the Leader

Anyone who occupies the office of the CEO has the right to influence the behavior of the organization's members. In the case of a corporation, the CEO has been granted **formal authority** by the board of directors to influence specific aspects of employees' behavior. In a small entrepreneurial company, the CEO's authority may stem from the ownership of the firm.

Why do employees follow the direction of the CEO? Their motivation may be "an internalized value, such as obedience to authority figures, loyalty to the organization, respect for law, reverence for tradition, or merely the recognition that submission to authority is a necessary condition for membership in the organization."[7]

In any case, the chief mechanism for wielding formal authority is through the CEO's control over resources and rewards. These elements can cover a broad spectrum, including pay and bonuses, career progress, budgets, delegation of authority and responsibility, formal recognition of accomplishments, and status symbols.[8] The effective leader ensures that the organization's reward systems are consistent with its strategic direction. For instance, a company that wants to emphasize product innovation must allocate sufficient budget resources to research and development personnel, reward risk-taking behaviors, and not reward actions that are designed to maintain the status quo. For example, at 3M, pay raises and promotions are tied to innovative results. Managers and employees simply are not rewarded for standing still.

## ■ The Style of the Leader

Every leader has a distinctive **leadership style**—the characteristic pattern of behavior that a leader exhibits in the process of exercising authority and making decisions. Some leaders are flamboyant; others are quiet and contemplative. Some seek broad-based participation when making decisions; others arrive at decisions primarily on their own with little input from others. Whatever the style, an organization's leader sets the tone for the firm's members. His or her style is a matter of considerable interest to employees at virtually all levels, and it is an important variable in determining how committed the employees are to the firm's mission and goals and how much effort they will put into implementing the company's strategies.[9]

The most appropriate leadership style is a matter of some controversy and, in any case, is partially constrained by the personality of the leader. Because the bulk of research in this area focuses upon the styles of leaders of relatively small groups, the usefulness of that research for our purposes is limited. Here, our concern is with leaders of entire organizations or business units. As we have already emphasized, upper-level leadership is qualitatively different from leadership at lower levels.[10] From this perspective, the most pertinent body of knowledge available is the recent work on transformational and transactional leadership styles.[11] These styles and how they are used in practice are discussed in the paragraphs that follow.

### Transformational and Transactional Leadership Styles

With **transactional leadership**, managers use the authority of their office, much as we just described, to exchange rewards such as pay and status for employees' work efforts. By contrast, with **transformational leadership**, managers inspire involvement in a mission, giving followers a "dream" or "vision" of a higher order than the followers' present reality. In effect, the transformational leader motivates followers to do more than they originally expected to do by stretching their abilities and increasing their self-confidence.[12] Organizational members are "transformed" by becoming more aware of the importance of their tasks and by being helped to transcend their own self-interest for the sake of the organization's mission.

Steven Jobs, the founder of Apple Computer, serves as an example of a transformational leader. In the company's early days, he was able to inspire his employees with his vision of making computing power accessible to a wide range of customers. Without his employees' willingness, and even enthusiasm, to put in long hours of work and to generate innovative ideas, Apple would never have been able to revolutionize the computer industry. By contrast, transactional leaders are less interested in inspiring followers than in ensuring that their organizations operate effectively and efficiently. The typical transactional leader is often concerned with increasing sales, market share, and profits incrementally rather than with "transforming" the organization.

Management researcher Bernard M. Bass proposes that most leaders exhibit both transactional and transformational styles, although they do so in different amounts.[13] Ultimately, the distinction between the two leadership styles is that leaders who are largely transactional continue to move their organizations in

## S T R A T E G I C   I N S I G H T

# *Leadership Style at Southwest Airlines*

Herb Kelleher has built Southwest Airlines into one of the most profitable and fast-growing airlines in the country through an emphasis on low-cost operations. In doing so, he has also managed to win the trust and respect of the personnel.

Now the nation's seventh-largest airline, Southwest has grown from a local carrier in Texas that specialized in no-frills flights between Dallas and Houston to one that offers service throughout the Southwest, Midwest, Southeast, and West Coast. It has expanded profitably even though it offers no on-board meals, no assigned seating, no interairline baggage transfers, and no listings on computer reservation systems. In some areas, standby tickets can be purchased through automated teller machines in convenience stores.

The market for this bare-bones service is short-haul passengers who desire low prices and frequent departures. To serve these passengers efficiently, Southwest's planes are able to arrive at an airport gate, unload baggage and passengers, load new baggage and passengers, and leave within ten minutes. How? By having employees who are considerably more productive than those in the rest of the airline industry. High productivity, combined with the airline's lack of frills, give Southwest a 43 percent cost advantage over the huge American Airlines. Under Kelleher's leadership, productivity, sales, and profits have soared in the 1990s. Some analysts have suggested that Kelleher may be America's best CEO.

Why are employees this dedicated? One pilot says that "it's not a Mary Kay-type atmosphere where we're all starry-eyed. It's mutual respect." This respect starts at the top with CEO Kelleher. He has established excellent rapport with the personnel and seems to be able to work out amenable agreements with which all sides are happy, unlike the bitter negotiations that have characterized labor contracts at several other airlines. Through profit-sharing plans, cross-utilization of workers, and Kelleher's concern for employees, the company has managed to forge an atmosphere of trust and loyalty.

Kelleher, for instance, is highly visible. He often takes Southwest flights and frequently visits the service areas where the planes are maintained. The visits are invariably upbeat and optimistic, with Kelleher dressing in a casual fashion (often in a Southwest Airlines shirt) and kidding with the crew. He knows individuals' names and sends birthday and Valentine's Day cards to each employee.

Most of all, though, he seems to care. As he puts it: "If you don't treat your own people well, they won't treat other people well." His actions support his words. He and all the other top managers of Southwest Airlines work at least once every three months as baggage handlers, ticket agents, and flight attendants. The point is to create an understanding of what each employee encounters on his or her job. As Kelleher explains, "When you're actually dealing with customers, and you've done the job yourself, you're in a better position to appraise the effect of some new program or policy."

His words are reinforced by the head of Southwest's mechanics and cleaners union: "How many CEOs do you know who come into the cleaners break room at 3 A.M. on a Sunday passing out doughnuts or putting on a pair of overalls to clean a plane?"

SOURCES: A. Q. Nomani, "Eastern Airports Are Still Out of Reach to Start-Ups," *Wall Street Journal Interactive Edition*, 25 April 1996; M. A. Verespej, "Flying His Own Course," *Industry Week*, 20 November 1995, pp. 22–24; "Southwest Airlines' Herb Kelleher: Unorthodoxy at Work," *Management Review*, 84(1) (1995):9–12; K. Labich, "Is Herb Kelleher America's Best CEO?" *Fortune*, 2 May 1994, pp. 44–52; P. O'Brian, "Southwest Airlines Is a Rare Air Carrier: It Still Makes Money," *Wall Street Journal*, 26 October 1992, p. A1 (source of fourth quotation); R. S. Teitelbaum, "Southwest Airlines: Where Service Flies Right," *Fortune*, 24 August 1992, p. 116 (source of second quotation); A. Farnham, "The Trust Gap," *Fortune*, 4 December 1989, pp. 56–78 (source of third quotation, p. 78); F. Gibney Jr., "Southwest's Friendly Skies," *Newsweek*, 30 May 1988, p. 49 (source of first quotation).

line with historical tradition, resulting in incremental improvements. Transformational leaders, however, lead their organizations toward a future that may result in significantly different processes and levels of performance.[14] This proposed difference is illustrated in Figure 9.2.

Note that transactional leadership is hypothesized to enhance an organization's performance steadily, but not dramatically. The proponents of transformational leadership, on the other hand, suggest that it can make significant changes in organizational performance. Also note that we propose that an organization's performance declines somewhat shortly after the transformational leadership process begins. Dramatic changes in the way an organization operates often result in short-term declines in performance, because organizational members may initially resist changing from the status quo and may experience difficulty in rising to the new expectations.

Both transactional and transformational leaders can exhibit all of the leadership styles identified in the well-known leadership theories. These include such commonly studied styles as task-oriented leadership (emphasizing task effectiveness) or relationship-oriented leadership (emphasizing the building of relationships with employees), as well as those styles that emphasize directing employees, encouraging employee participation in decision making, or setting goals. But even as these two types of leaders engage in the same style, their intent may be quite different. For instance, the transactional leader may delegate responsibility to an employee as a reward for fulfilling an agreement, but a transformational leader may delegate for the purpose of developing employee skills.[15]

### Leadership Style in Practice

When is a transactional style needed, and when might a transformational style be required? As we have already seen, most leaders will exhibit both behaviors, although one may predominate. In general, we can propose that organizations that are meeting or exceeding their objectives and that do not foresee signifi-

**Figure 9.2**          **Hypothesized Results of Transactional and Transformational Leadership Styles**

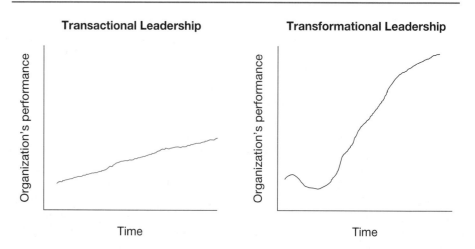

S T R A T E G I C     I N S I G H T

## Henry Ford: Transactional and Transformational Leadership

Henry Ford (1863–1947) illustrates a leader who combined both transactional and transformational leadership styles:

> In 1914, he made a deal that workers found hard to resist. He offered them the unusually high wage for that time of $5 a day in exchange for their accepting rigid control of their behavior both inside and outside the plant. No idle time was to be tolerated. Internal spies were employed to enforce disciplinary rules. Yet, it was this same Henry Ford who revolutionized the automobile industry, making possible the mass production of the cheap, affordable automobile for the mass market.

How did Henry Ford transform the automobile industry? The transformation began with an argument between Ford and his partner Alexander Y. Malcolmson in 1905. Ford wanted to produce a simple, inexpensive car, but Malcolmson favored a more expensive and exclusive line. Malcolmson lost the argument and subsequently sold his interest in the company, leaving Ford to concentrate on the Model T—a sturdy, black automobile with a four-cylinder, twenty-horsepower engine. Introduced in 1908, the car sold for $825.

The Model T clearly met the needs and the financial resources of American consumers. More than 10,000 cars were sold the first year. Within five years, annual unit sales reached about a half-million. When production of the car ceased in 1927, 15 million Model Ts had been sold by Ford Motor Company.

By concentrating on one type of affordable automobile, Henry Ford created a mass market for the Model T. In turn, the huge demand for the car gave rise to the use of assembly line production with standardized parts. The volume enabled Ford to reduce the price of the car without decreasing profits. By 1913, the car's selling price had dropped to $500. It fell to $390 two years later and sold for $260 in 1925. Meanwhile, the time required to produce the car declined from $12\frac{1}{2}$ worker-hours in 1912 to $1\frac{1}{2}$ worker-hours in 1914.

This single car literally transformed not only the automobile industry but also the lifestyle and work habits of an entire nation. The impact of Henry Ford's transformational leadership continues to this day.

SOURCES: Arthur M. Johnson, "Henry Ford," in *The Encyclopedia Americana, International Edition*, Vol. 11 (Danbury, Conn.: Grolier, 1990), pp. 566–567; Robert Sobel, "Henry Ford," in *The World Book Encyclopedia*, Vol. 7 (Chicago: World Book, 1990), p. 380; B. M. Bass, *Leadership and Performance Beyond Expectations* (New York: Free Press, 1985), p. 27 (source of quotation).

cant changes in their environment can be well led through a transactional style. Increasingly, however, because of the intensity of domestic and foreign competition and dramatic environmental changes, many organizations require transformational leadership. Even casual perusal of such publications as the *Wall Street Journal, Business Week,* and *Fortune* will illustrate the strategic difficulties that many firms are facing.

Consider, for instance, the different strategic directions taken by IBM and Canon when they entered the copier business in the 1970s. Pursuing a transactional style, IBM's top management concentrated on developing products that were similar to those of the market leader—Xerox—and they imitated Xerox's service, pricing, and distribution. IBM's efforts were such a failure that it withdrew from the copier market. By contrast, Canon's top management used a transformational approach. Rather than duplicating Xerox's strategy, Canon concentrated on smaller copiers and taught its sales force to make presentations directly to department managers and secretaries who desired decentralized copying facilities rather than a centralized copy center. This approach contrasted dramatically with the traditional route of selling to the head of the duplicating department. Today, Canon is a major player in the copier industry.

Because transformational leadership is of considerable importance and is likely to take on even more significance, we will examine the process in detail at this point. Researchers Tichy and Devanna, who studied twelve CEOs, propose a three-stage process of transformational leadership.[16] Each stage will now be described.

**Recognize the Need for Change.** First, the transformational leader must recognize the need for change and be able to persuade key managers in the organization of that need. This task may be difficult when changes in the environment are gradual and the organization is still meeting its objectives. As Peter F. Drucker, a management theorist and consultant, emphasizes, the best time to cast off the past is when the organization is successful—not when it is in trouble. When an organization is successful, its resources are allocated "to the things that *did* produce, to the goals that *did* challenge, to the needs that *were* unfulfilled."[17]

To overcome this tendency, Tichy and Devanna suggest that leaders measure the performance of their organizations against that of their competitors and not just against last year's performance. Additionally, measures of organizational performance must include more than the typical economic indicators, such as earnings per share, market share, and return on investment or assets. They should also include such measures as customer satisfaction, product quality as compared with competitors', new-product innovations, and other similar indicators.

Managers of troubled organizations more readily recognize the need for change. Increasingly, such firms are replacing their CEOs with managers from other corporations. For example, in recent years, Hughes Aircraft hired its CEO away from IBM, the CEO of Gulfstream Aerospace came from Xerox, and Campbell Soup's CEO was recruited from Gerber Products. An outsider can sometimes make the hard decisions, such as to initiate mass layoffs, that an insider might be reluctant to make. Outsiders, of course, also bring a fresh perspective to the firm and its problems. On the other hand, outsiders may have to spend months just learning the business and industry and trying to develop a network of contacts before they are able to take any decisive actions. Furthermore, hiring an outsider generally sends a message to the firm's vice presidents and other top managers that they were not considered worthy of promotion. For that reason, the act of hiring an outsider is often followed by an exodus of some of the company's top managerial talent.[18]

**Create a Shared Vision.** Once the need for change is recognized, the leader must inspire organizational members with a "vision" of what the organization can become. In entrepreneurial ventures, this vision may be developed by the leader; but in large corporations, the vision is more likely to evolve through a participative process involving the CEO and key managers in the firm.[19] But Andrall E. Pearson, former CEO of PepsiCo, makes it clear that it is the leader's role to "spearhead" this effort, not just preside over it.[20] He also emphasizes that no strategic vision is permanent: "Lasting competitive edges are hard to generate."[21] Therefore, the transformational process is ongoing and not a one-time event.

An important part of the vision is high performance standards. From observation, it is clear that transformational leaders stretch their followers' abilities. High-performing organizations rarely pursue moderate goals or performance standards. Pearson observes, "This doesn't mean arbitrary, unrealistic goals that are bound to be missed and motivate no one, but rather goals that won't allow anyone to forget how tough the competitive arena is."[22] In such cases, the CEO must provide a role model for the organization's members. Transformational CEOs must "set a personal example in terms of the long hours they work, their obvious commitment to success, and the consistent quality of their efforts."[23] Furthermore, their public behavior should reflect their own excitement and energy, and the more contact they have with employees at all levels, the more contagious their excitement is likely to be.[24]

Besides serving as role models, transformational leaders must communicate their vision clearly and completely to all members of the organization. Management researchers Warren G. Bennis and Burt Nanus reinforce the importance of this suggestion by stating that the lack of a clear vision is a major reason for the declining effectiveness of many organizations in recent years. Clear communication of a vision creates a focus for the employees' efforts, and it is important that this vision be repeated over and over and not be allowed to fade away.[25] Few suggestions are more timely. The consulting firm Booz, Allen & Hamilton has reported that only 37 percent of senior managers think that other key managers completely understand new organizational goals, and only 4 percent of the senior managers believe that middle managers totally understand those goals.[26]

The common conception of the transformational leader as a dynamic, charismatic personality is only occasionally true.[27] Many CEOs have effectively led their organizations through major transformations without being charismatic figures. Undoubtedly, charisma helps a leader influence others, but it is hardly a requirement for a transformational leader.

**Institutionalize the Change.** Finally, the transformational leader must institutionalize the changes that have been created. The CEO must first ensure that the change is proceeding as planned. David A. Nadler, a management researcher, points out that all too many CEOs have learned, to their chagrin, that the changes they ordered never occurred. The reason is usually a lack of feedback mechanisms. Those mechanisms that were effective during stable periods often break down during turbulent change periods. In such situations, top management must develop multiple and highly sensitive feedback devices.[28] Feedback through multiple channels is essential, because change programs, even though successful, often have side effects such as the creation of new problems.

The CEO must also realize that the institutionalization of significant change (i.e., making the new ways of behaving a regular and normal part of organizational life) takes time. Encouraging organizational members to work and interact in different ways requires a new reward system. Because people are likely to behave in ways that lead to the rewards they desire, rewards such as pay increases and promotions should be linked to the types of behavior that are required to make the organization change effective. Management researcher Aaron J. Nurick recommends that if the organization benefits financially from the change program, its members should share in the gains. The connection between organizational improvement and the employees' well-being thus becomes clear. Without such rewards, employees are unlikely to see involvement as worthy of their efforts.[29]

At all three of these stages identified by Tichy and Devanna, it is essential that the CEO have clear, accurate, and timely information. Bennis makes a number of suggestions, based on his own experience and research, for ensuring that such information reaches the CEO.[30] These suggestions include that the CEO not rely exclusively on his or her assistants and intimate associates for information. Thus, the CEO should be accessible to the members of the organization and to its customers and should read more than staff summaries for information on the environment. Second, he proposes that CEOs rotate their key assistants every two years to ensure continuing openness. He also recommends that these assistants be in contact with the organization's constituent groups so that they will understand their obligations and the limits of their power. Finally, he believes that CEOs should actively encourage their advisers to act as devil's advocates so that "groupthink" (the situation that results when group members emphasize the importance of solidarity over critical thinking) does not prevail.

## ■ The Leadership Team

Although this chapter focuses primarily upon the CEO, no single individual can possibly lead a complex organization alone. Therefore, most CEOs spend considerable amounts of time and effort developing a team of top-level managers. Typically, the **top management team** is headed by the CEO and is comprised of executives immediately below the CEO's level on the organization chart. However, such teams may also include middle managers, depending upon the desires of the CEO and the situation facing the particular company. A group of compatible managers who work well together and complement one another's abilities can provide a very powerful sense of direction for a company.

Why are many organizations today emphasizing team building at the top management level? There are a number of excellent reasons:[31]

- The CEO has a complex integrative task and cannot possibly be effective at that task without working closely with the individuals who are in charge of the organization's major activities (functions, products, regions, etc.).
- Subordinate managers usually possess greater expertise about the operating components of the organization and their own fields than the CEO does.
- The outcomes of a team's deliberations—versus the decisions of a single manager—are more likely to be innovative, because they come from a group of individuals possessing different skills, perspectives, and information.
- Team members, and their divisions or departments, should be more understanding and supportive of organizational decisions because they have a voice in shaping those decisions.
- Communication among top managers is enhanced because of their regular, frequent meetings.
- The lower-level managers on the team receive valuable developmental experience.

Furthermore, a recent study of top management teams in 460 midwestern banks revealed that technical and administrative innovations were more likely to occur when the team members represented diverse functional areas. Cross-functional communication was considered essential to organizational innovation.[32]

One well-known firm that has used its top management team advantageously is UAL Corporation. Chairman and CEO Stephen M. Wolf works closely on a daily basis with the executives in charge of such areas as finance, marketing, employee relations, public relations, and the legal department. The successful turnaround that UAL has achieved since Wolf took over in 1987 is partially attributed to his ability to assemble a talented top management team.[33]

Some corporations have gone even further, replacing their chief operating officer (COO) with an executive team—or committee—that reports directly to the CEO. For example, Xerox has a six-person executive team, Nordstrom (the Seattle-based department store) is run by four "co-presidents," and Microsoft's three-person "office of the president" reports directly to Chairman William Gates III. Such arrangements, of course, can sometimes prove unwieldy. Their success often depends upon the interpersonal compatibility of the executives and the extent to which each is willing to be a "team player."[34]

# POWER

To influence the behavior of others, a leader must possess power. This section examines the need to acquire power and then explores the ways a leader can use power to implement strategy.

### ■ The Role of Power

Although the popular conception of a CEO is of an individual who wields great amounts of power, this perception is far from correct. In fact, each time a manager climbs to a higher rung on the hierarchical ladder within an organization, he or she becomes more, not less, dependent upon other people.[35] In some sense, the CEO is the most dependent of the managers in an organization, because how well or how poorly the CEO (and, consequently, the organization) performs depends upon the performance of all of the organization's members. This is not to say that a CEO does not have formal authority to influence the behavior of employees, because he or she does. But we do wish to emphasize that trying to control the behavior of others solely through formal authority has its limitations.

The first of these limitations is that CEOs soon find out that not everyone in today's organizations passively accepts and enthusiastically carries out a constant stream of orders from above. Subordinates may resist orders, subtly ignore them, blatantly question them, or even quit. As Robert H. Miles, a management researcher, points out: "The raw use of power doesn't have the acceptance it did 25 years ago. People aren't willing to put up with it."[36]

Second, CEOs are always dependent upon some individuals over whom they have no formal authority.[37] Common examples include members of the board of directors, customers, and influential members of government regulatory agencies.

Hence, effective implementation of strategy requires the CEO to influence the behavior of others in ways that rely upon formal authority but also in ways that do not. In the latter sense, the CEO must acquire power over those individuals upon whom he or she is dependent. By **power** we refer to the ability—apart from formal authority or control over resources and rewards—to influence the behavior of other people. The following section explains how top managers can use power to implement strategies.

## ▪ Techniques of Using Power

Top managers can wield power in a number of ways, as illustrated in Figure 9.3. This section discusses these common techniques, which CEOs and other top-level managers employ to implement organizational strategies.

### Expertise

A major source of power for many top managers is expertise.[38] Managers generally establish this power base through visible achievement. The greater the achievement, the more power the manager is able to accumulate.[39]

**Expertise** refers to a manager's ability to influence the behavior of others because these individuals believe that their manager is more knowledgeable about a problem, an opportunity, or an issue than they are. Managers who reach the CEO's office by rising through the firm's ranks will often be viewed as experts because it is clear to the organization's members that their CEO mastered a variety of jobs on the way to the top and, hence, is familiar with the employees' tasks. An executive who is hired from outside the firm to become its CEO may or may not enter that job with expert power, however. If the individual is from a company in the same industry, though, he or she is more likely to be viewed as an expert.

For example, Lee Iacocca was probably perceived as an expert by Chrysler's employees when he was hired as that firm's CEO, because he had spent most of

---

**Figure 9.3**   **Techniques of Using Power**

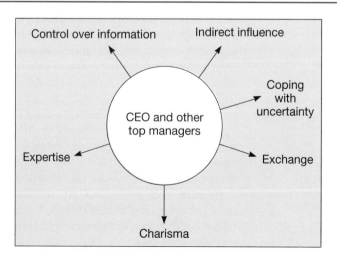

his career prior to that time at Ford, where he had successfully held a variety of jobs. On the other hand, when John Sculley became CEO of Apple Computer, his expertise was as a marketing whiz at PepsiCo. Although much of his marketing experience could be transferred to the personal-computer business, one could have predicted that his expert power would be constrained by his limited knowledge of computers. To overcome this constraint, Sculley attempted to learn all that he could about computers after being hired at Apple.

Management researcher Gary A. Yukl suggests that leaders who possess expert power must take care in how they communicate that expertise to others. He cautions such leaders to avoid acting superior to others who possess less expertise and not to speak in an arrogant, condescending manner. As he points out, sometimes expert leaders who are trying to sell their proposals to others "fire a steady stream of arguments, rudely interrupt any attempted replies, and dismiss any objections or concerns without serious consideration."[40]

## Control over Information

**Control over information** refers to a manager's access to important information and control over its distribution to others.[41] Henry Mintzberg's research indicates that the CEO is normally the single best-informed member of an organization. He or she is formally linked to all of the organization's key managers. Because each of these managers is a specialist relative to the CEO, the CEO is the person who best sees the totality of the organization and is most knowledgeable about its internal activities. He or she also has a number of external contacts—in other companies, in regulatory agencies, and so on—which provide excellent sources of information. Although the CEO may not know everything, he or she usually knows more than anyone else.[42]

Because the CEO has more information than anyone else, he or she is able to interpret information in order to influence the perceptions and attitudes of others.[43] If the leader's information is more complete than that of any other individual, no one will be able to question his or her decisions effectively. Even the board of directors may prove impotent, because its power, based on legal standing, can be overcome by the CEO's power of information and knowledge.[44]

## Exchange

The use of exchange as a power base is very common. In **exchange**, a leader does something for someone else and can then expect that person to feel a sense of obligation toward the leader. Hence, when the leader makes a special request of that person later, the person will usually feel obligated to carry out that request. CEOs may even develop friendships with others in terms of exchange, knowing that friendship carries with it certain obligations.

For instance, a top manager's relationship with the corporation's CEO or board of directors can add to—or detract from—the manager's power. As an extreme example, take the case of one COO who supported higher pay for his chairman, insisted that the chairman's country club dues be paid by the firm, deferred in public to the CEO, invariably addressing him as "Mr. Chairman," and even donated $250,000 in company funds to a university to honor the chairman. This manager, not surprisingly, was later named CEO by the chairman.[45]

Quite often, building reciprocal relationships with organizational members requires the ability to submerge one's ego. Those who set aside their status and power are more likely to be viewed favorably by those who are either above or below them in the organization's hierarchy. Such managers, of course, are more able to secure the enthusiastic cooperation of others.[46]

## Indirect Influence

Top managers can often get others to implement the organization's strategies through **indirect influence**—that is, by modifying the situation in which individuals work. One variation of this technique involves making permanent changes in the organization's formal reward systems. In such cases, only those individuals who correctly carry out the organization's strategy will receive bonuses, pay raises, or promotions. For example, each of the six persons on the executive team that runs Xerox has a specific area of responsibility. However, to encourage the executives to work closely together, Xerox's board of directors has developed a compensation system for the executive team members that rewards overall company results—not simply the results of each person's own area.[47] Carrying this concept further, a manager can modify the organization's structure or even the physical layout of offices and departments to weaken groups or individuals who oppose certain aspects of the strategy.

Opposition to an organization's strategy is not unusual. Strategic change often reduces the status and power of some individuals while enhancing that of others. Those who believe that their status will be diminished often oppose the new strategy, if not openly, then through delaying tactics and other quiet forms of noncompliance.

In another type of indirect influence, the CEO may place only those individuals who are supporters in responsible positions. A loyal supporter, for instance, can be placed in charge of an important task force or committee to ensure that the group's recommendation coincides with the strategic direction set by the manager. Obviously, this technique must be used with care. If the CEO is surrounded only by loyal supporters, strategic decisions can become characterized by groupthink, and questions and objections that should be voiced may never arise.

## Charisma

Another highly effective power base for influencing the behavior of others is charisma. **Charisma** refers to a leader's ability to influence others through his or her personal magnetism, enthusiasm, and strongly held convictions. Often, leaders are able to communicate these convictions and their vision for the future through a dramatic, persuasive manner of speaking.[48] As Yukl points out, charismatic leaders attempt to create an image of competence and success. Their aura of success and personal magnetism makes them role models for their employees. The more that followers admire their leaders and identify with them, the more likely they are to accept the leaders' values and beliefs. This acceptance enables charismatic leaders to exert considerable influence over their followers' behaviors.[49]

The more success the charismatic leader has, the more powerful he or she becomes. This combination of charisma and expertise can be extremely potent in influencing the behavior of others. Hence, charismatic leaders who set high standards of performance that are realistic are likely to have highly motivated and committed organization members.[50]

As some researchers have pointed out, charismatic leaders are most likely to be effective during periods of organizational crisis or transition.[51] Times of stress are more likely to encourage employees to respond to a leader who appears to have the answer to the problems that the organization is facing. If the leader's strategy results in early successes and if organizational performance begins to improve, the leader's power base will increase dramatically.

### Coping with Uncertainty

Every organization faces environmental contingencies; these may consist of various trends or developments, such as competition, governmental regulations or laws, cost pressures, new technologies, and so on. The relative importance of these many contingencies will vary from one organization and industry to another. But when a development or trend has an important implication for any particular organization at a specific time, it can be termed a **critical contingency**.[52]

For example, in the highly competitive and rapidly changing financial services industry, the critical contingency is developing new financial products. Those companies that are most effective at anticipating and meeting the market's needs are more likely to be profitable. Thus managers in those companies who create popular new financial products are able to amass significant amounts of power to influence organizational decisions. Likewise, in an industry whose critical contingency is efficiency/cost control—such as in the airline industry—managers who lower their organization's cost structure can gain considerable amounts of power.[53]

Relating these ideas to the business unit strategies presented in chapter 6, we can surmise that, in industries in which the critical contingency is external product/market trends or events, companies that adopt either the niche-differentiation strategy or the differentiation strategy are more likely to be profitable. In those companies, most of the power therefore will likely be held by managers in marketing, advertising, and/or product research and development (R&D). Similarly, in environments in which the efficiencies of processing or delivering products/services comprise the critical contingency, those businesses that adopt the niche–low-cost strategy or the low-cost strategy will be most effective. Hence, their operating decisions are most likely to be influenced by managers in accounting, production/operations, or process R&D. Finally, in environments in which both operating efficiencies and product/service differentiation are the critical contingencies, executives in any—or all—of these areas are likely to wield power.

## ORGANIZATIONAL CULTURE

**Organizational culture** refers to the values and patterns of belief and behavior that are accepted and practiced by the members of a particular organization.[54] Because each organization develops its own unique culture, even organizations within the same industry and city will exhibit distinctly different ways of operating. The following sections discuss the evolution of organizational culture, the impact of culture on an organization's strategy, and the methods leaders use to shape organizational culture.

## ■ The Evolution of Culture

The purpose of organizational culture is to enable a firm to adapt to environmental changes and to coordinate and integrate its internal operations.[55] But how do appropriate values, behaviors, and beliefs develop to enable the organization to accomplish these ends?

For many organizations, the first—and major—influence upon their culture is their founder. His or her assumptions about success form the foundation of the firm's culture.[56] For instance, the primary influence upon McDonald's culture was the fast-food company's founder, Ray A. Kroc, who died in 1984. His philosophy of fast service, assembly line food preparation, wholesome image, and devotion to the hamburger are still reflected in McDonald's operations today. Kroc's influence is the primary reason why McDonald's did not diversify outside the fast-food industry, did not specialize in made-to-order hamburgers, prohibited franchisees from being absentee owners, encouraged franchisees to experiment with new products, targeted advertisements and sales promotions to both adults and children, and opened Ronald McDonald Houses near major medical centers to provide low-cost housing to families of sick children.

As Yukl points out, the set of beliefs about the distinctive competence of the organization (i.e., what differentiates it from other organizations) is one of the most important elements of culture in new organizations. These beliefs directly affect organizational strategies and operations. For example, a company that owes its success to developing innovative products is likely to respond to a decline in sales with new-product introductions; a company that offers a common product at a low price would respond with attempts to lower costs even further.[57]

However, as time passes, Yukl notes, "segments of the culture that were initially functional may become dysfunctional, preventing the organization from adapting successfully to a changing environment."[58] McDonald's, for instance, has departed from some of Kroc's precepts in order to continue its success under changing conditions. As customers have become more interested in a diversified menu, McDonald's has expanded from hamburgers to fish and chicken sandwiches and even pizza. Increasing societal emphasis on healthy diets has led to new products such as salads, cereal, and low-fat hamburgers and yogurt as well as to modifications in the food preparation process. The company even made its first departure from fast food to take advantage of its strong brand name by licensing Sears, Roebuck & Company to sell children's clothing with the McDonald's name emblazoned on it.[59]

So, in general, we can say that the foundation of an organization's culture reflects the values and beliefs of its founder. But the culture is modified over time as the environment changes. Environmental change renders some of the firm's culture obsolete and even dysfunctional. New elements of the culture must be added as the old are discarded in order for the organization to maintain its success. But as Figure 9.4 illustrates, a given organization's culture may also change to reflect the powerful influence of a transformational leader other than the founder.[60]

**Figure 9.4**          **Evolution of Organizational Culture**

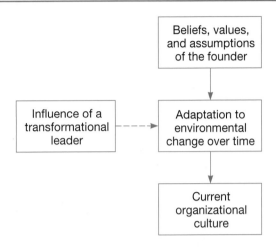

For example, in recent years, the culture of Walt Disney Company has changed significantly. The founder's influence on the conservative family entertainment company was such that for years after his death, executives would wonder "What would Walt have done?" before making decisions. As the company lost ground to its competitors by releasing an outdated line of family movies, its newly hired CEO, Michael Eisner, brought in a new team of managers who had never known Disney. By freeing its top management of the elements of the past, which had become dysfunctional, Eisner has produced the types of movies that are popular with today's moviegoers.[61]

## ■ Impact of Culture on Strategy

Organizational culture can facilitate or hinder the firm's strategic actions. One study showed that firms with "strategically appropriate cultures"—such as PepsiCo, Wal-Mart, and Shell—outperformed selected other corporations with less appropriate cultures over an eleven-year period. The successful firms experienced an average revenue increase of 682 percent (versus 166 percent for the other organizations), their stock prices rose by 901 percent (versus 74 percent), and growth in their net income outpaced the other firms by 756 percent to 1 percent. These successful firms had developed cultures that emphasized three key groups of stakeholders—customers, stockholders, and employees. Note that the point is *not* that these corporations have strong cultures, for many less successful firms—such as Sears, General Motors, and Citicorp—possess strong cultures. The point, rather, is that the culture of a successful firm must be appropriate to—and supportive of—that firm's strategy. Furthermore, the culture must contain values that can help the firm adapt to environmental change.[62]

## S T R A T E G I C   I N S I G H T

## Leadership and Organizational Culture at Wal-Mart

Wal-Mart's culture cannot be separated from the beliefs of its founder, Sam Walton, who died in 1992. During his career, "Mr. Sam" provided the guiding vision that took his company from a single store in Arkansas in 1962 to the position of world's largest retailer by 1990. This meteoric growth was not due simply to low prices or store location. Many retailers that offered low prices, such as Korvette's and Woolco, no longer exist; and, if location were the primary key to success, Sears and Macy's would be highly profitable. Rather, to a great extent, the biggest difference between Wal-Mart and other retailers was Sam Walton himself.

From the beginning, Walton realized that retailing begins with the customer. The concepts of customer service and customer satisfaction are ingrained into every one of Wal-Mart's 400,000 "associates" (the firm's term for employees). Each week, Wal-Mart's regional vice presidents follow in Walton's footsteps by spending three or four days visiting stores in their region, talking to customers and associates and comparing Wal-Mart's prices and merchandise with those of such competitors as Kmart. Each Saturday, all of Wal-Mart's top managers meet to compare findings and decide what changes are needed in their stores during the coming week. Some even say that the first lesson Walton instilled in his associates was a "bias for action," so that change in the stores is constant.

As the company grew, Walton realized that empowering associates was the most efficient way of keeping in touch with the customer. Hence, associates are kept informed weekly about their store's—and even their own department's—performance. All associates know their products' cost, markup, overhead, and profit. Walton believed that the more associates understand about their business, the more interested they'll be in serving their customers. Each department manager acts as an entrepreneur, running his or her own business, and each is encouraged to experiment. Those whose experiments are successful are invited to the Saturday meeting at company headquarters in Bentonville, Arkansas, to explain their ideas to top management.

Finally, Sam Walton realized that giving motivational speeches and leading associates in the "Wal-Mart cheer" ("Give me a W! Give me an A! Give me an L! Give me a squiggly! . . .") could only go so far in helping them identify with the organization. So, early on, he decided to make associates a real part of the company by making every associate who has been with Wal-Mart for at least a year eligible for profit sharing. Wal-Mart contributes about 6 percent of each associate's salary to the plan, and associates can take their share in cash or in Wal-Mart stock whenever they leave the company. As a typical example, one Wal-Mart truck driver related that, after driving for thirteen years, he received only $700 when he resigned. But, in nineteen years with Wal-Mart, he had already accumulated $707,000 in profit sharing.

CEO David Glass is continuing Walton's commitment to cost control, innovation, greater emphasis on the upscale market, and a customer-centered culture. He is convinced that there is no other company where 400,000 people work so closely together as true partners.

SOURCES: T. Agins, "Queen-Sized Women Find Fashion in Upscale Label," *Wall Street Journal Interactive Edition*, 8 May 1996; L. Lee, "Discounter Wal-Mart Is Catering to Affluent to Maintain Growth," *Wall Street Journal*, 7 February 1996, pp. A1, A8; R. Halverson, "David Glass," *Discount Store News*, 4 December 1995, pp. 55–56; T. Andreoli, "Bud Walton: Vision and Spirit: Wal-Mart's Co-Founder Dies at Age 73," *Discount Store News*, 3 April 1995, pp. 1–2; D. Longo, "New Generation of Execs Lead Wal-Mart into the Next Century," *Discount Store News*, 5 December 1994, pp. 45–48; A. Markowitz, "Wal-Mart Charts Future in Mexico, Canada," *Discount Store News*, 21 February 1994, pp. 1, 87; B. Saporito, "A Week Aboard the Wal-Mart Express," *Fortune*, 24 August 1992, pp. 77–84; S. Walton and J. Huey, *Sam Walton: Made in America* (New York: Doubleday, 1992).

Because culture reflects the past, periods of environmental change often require significant modification of the organization's culture.[63] It is essential that changes in strategy be accompanied by corresponding alterations in organizational culture; otherwise, the strategy is likely to fail. Conservative organizations do not become aggressive, entrepreneurial firms simply because they have formulated new goals and plans.[64]

A firm caught in changing environmental conditions may devise a new strategy that will make sense from a financial, product, or marketing point of view. Yet the strategy will not be implemented because it requires "assumptions, values, and ways of working" that are at variance with the organization's culture.[65] An organization can change its strategy and its structure, but may find its employees reverting to their prior ways of operating if it does not confront the assumptions underlying its culture.[66]

As an example of a company modifying both its culture and its strategy, consider Electronic Data Systems (EDS).[67] Founded in the early 1960s by H. Ross Perot, EDS exemplified a powerful "can-do, anything-is-possible" entrepreneurial spirit. Strongly nonunion, the company had an extremely stringent hiring process followed by a grueling trial and training period. Those who survived displayed unusually high morale and a devotion to doing whatever was required to accomplish the task. By the early 1980s, EDS possessed a culture that could be described as "gung ho."

But in the mid-1980s EDS was acquired by General Motors, and Perot left the company within two years. In a brief period of time, EDS found itself without its strong leader, without its independence, and with a work force that had expanded almost overnight from several thousand to 60,000 employees. To compound its identity crisis, EDS failed to win an important contract with Kodak, leading its top management to reassess both its strategy and its culture.

EDS is now undergoing some material changes under chairman and CEO Les Alberthal. His vision for EDS is that it be recognized "as the premier provider of information technology services based on its contributions to the success of its customers."[68] Toward that end, Alberthal emphasizes that EDS must help its customers succeed by understanding their needs. To accomplish that goal, EDS's structure is being transformed from that of a big company to an organization of many smaller companies (multiple business units with decentralized decision-making authority). Because each business unit focuses upon a specific segment of the market, this move puts EDS employees in closer contact with customers and their needs. At the same time, EDS is transforming its historical "trust us" type of customer service to one that is more characterized by listening and cooperation.

To support this strategy/structure transformation, EDS modified its culture. Employees are viewed as "volunteers" who may, if their needs are not fulfilled, leave EDS for other employment. Managers are evaluated not only on revenue and profit figures but also on the extent to which they motivate and empower their employees. Managerial training programs have been altered to help managers become more involved with their employees and to learn to serve as mentors to them. Overall, the manager's role has changed from that of "taskmaster" to one of "servant" to the employee. Alberthal saw these shifts as essential to attracting talented employees in an increasingly diverse work force.

**S T R A T E G I C    I N S I G H T**

## PepsiCo's Distinctive Culture

Surely one of the most distinctive U.S. corporate cultures is PepsiCo's. New managers are put through a rigorous training program likened to Marine Corps boot camp, with those who can't meet the standards washing out. Once through the program, each manager is given considerable freedom. Risk taking is encouraged, and second guessing is rare. Even after PepsiCo lost $16 million on its ill-fated Grandma's Cookies venture, the executive who designed the project was subsequently promoted.

An important value is winning. Not surprisingly, the typical managerial work week is sixty hours. In fact, when an internal survey revealed that some employees at headquarters were disturbed that they didn't have sufficient time to do their laundry at home, the company installed dry cleaning equipment rather than reduce the workweek.

PepsiCo may take management development more seriously than almost any other corporation. CEO Roger Enrico spends about half of his time reviewing the performance of the firm's top 600 managers. He also personally interviews all applicants for positions of vice president and president. He expects those below him to spend about 40 percent of their time on personnel development and performance evaluation.

The managers who survive the intense atmosphere are rewarded with first-class air travel, stock options, bonuses that can reach 90 percent of salary, fast promotions, and fully loaded company cars. Those who don't meet the firm's expectations are out.

These values are consistent with PepsiCo's strategic direction—growth. Managers are given considerable autonomy and are encouraged to "love change" and move quickly to take advantage of opportunities.

Capitalizing on growth opportunities is of paramount importance in consumer products and has made PepsiCo one of the premier firms in the world. When growth slows, PepsiCo is not afraid to change, as shown by its spin-off of its fast-food restaurants.

SOURCES: M. Wallin and D. Lytle, "PepsiCo Moves to Shore Up S. American Bottler," *Dow Jones News Service*, 9 May 1996; R. Frank, "Pepsi to Take Control of Latin American Bottler," *Wall Street Journal Interactive Edition*, 10 May 1996; P. Sellers, "PepsiCo's New Generation," *Fortune*, 1 April 1996, pp. 110–118; J. M. Graves, "Wayne Calloway's Gift and Curse," *Fortune*, 6 February 1995, pp. 14–15; S. Sherman and A. Hadjian, "How Tomorrow's Best Leaders Are Learning Their Stuff," *Fortune*, 27 November 1995, pp. 90–96; D. Anfuso, "PepsiCo Shares Power and Wealth with Workers," *Personnel Journal*, June 1995, pp. 42–48; M. Magnet, "Let's Go for Growth," *Fortune*, 7 March 1994, pp. 64–66; "Pepsi's Old Boy Wins Lead Post," *Marketing*, 27 January 1994; A. Rothman, "Can Wayne Calloway Handle the Pepsi Challenge?" *Business Week*, 27 January 1992, pp. 90–98.

### ■ How Leaders Shape Culture

CEOs other than the founder can be influential in shaping the organization's culture so that it becomes more appropriate for its present or anticipated environment. Transactional leaders are less likely to modify the firm's culture than transformational leaders. Bass points out: "The transactional leader works within the organizational culture as it exists; the transformational leader changes the organizational culture."[69]

How can a leader change the organization's culture? Management researcher Edgar H. Schein advocates five "primary embedding mechanisms" for altering culture.[70] The first mechanism is systematically paying attention to certain areas of the business. This goal may be accomplished through formally measuring and controlling the activities of those areas or, less formally, through the CEO's comments or questions at meetings. For instance, a top manager can direct the attention of organizational members toward controlling costs or to serving customers effectively. By contrast, those areas that the leader does not react to will be considered less important by employees.

The second mechanism involves the leader's reactions to critical incidents and organizational crises. The way a CEO deals with a crisis—such as declining sales, new governmental regulation, or technological obsolescence—can emphasize norms, values, and working procedures or even create new ones. For instance, some companies have reacted to declining profits by cutting compensation across the board; all employees, including top management, take the pay cut. This action emphasizes a belief that "we are a family who will take care of one another." Other firms, by contrast, lay off operative employees and middle managers, while maintaining (or even increasing) the salaries of top management. Nonadaptive cultures frequently reflect top management's values of arrogance and insularity. Self-interest takes precedence over concerns about customers, stockholders, or employees.[71]

The third mechanism is to serve as a deliberate role model, teacher, or coach. As we have seen earlier in the chapter, the visible behavior of the leader communicates assumptions and values to subordinates.

The way top management allocates rewards and status is a fourth mechanism for influencing culture. Leaders can quickly communicate their priorities by consistently linking pay raises, promotions, and the lack of pay increases and promotions to particular behaviors. For instance, General Foods found that the changing environment of the 1980s rendered its historical emphasis on cost control and earnings less effective. To redirect the efforts of managers toward diversification and sales growth, top management revised the compensation system to link bonuses to sales volume rather than only to increased earnings and began rewarding new-product development more generously.[72]

The fifth mechanism identified by Schein involves the procedures through which an organization recruits, selects, and promotes employees and the ways it dismisses them. An organization's culture can be perpetuated by hiring and promoting individuals whose values are similar to the firm's. By contrast, an organization attempting to alter its culture can accelerate that change by hiring employees whose beliefs and behaviors more closely fit the organization's changing value system.

In addition to these five primary embedding mechanisms, Schein identifies several "secondary reinforcement mechanisms."[73] These include the organization's structure, its operating systems and procedures, the design of its physical space, various stories or legends that are perpetuated about important events and people, and formal statements of organizational philosophy. These mechanisms are labeled *secondary* because they work only if they are consistent with the five primary mechanisms. The primary embedding mechanisms and secondary reinforcement mechanisms are summarized in Table 9.1 on page 250.

As an example of the secondary mechanisms, the belief that open communication and close working relationships are important is reflected in the open designs of the headquarters of companies such as Levi Strauss in California and Nike in Oregon.[74]

Schein emphasizes the critical linkage between leadership and organizational culture by stating that "the unique and essential function of leadership is the manipulation of culture."[75] Culture is created by the actions of leaders; it is institutionalized by leaders; and when it becomes dysfunctional, leadership is

**Table 9.1**                        **Mechanisms for Embedding and Reinforcing Organizational Culture**

*Primary Embedding Mechanisms*

1. What leaders pay attention to, measure, and control
2. Leader reactions to critical incidents and organizational crises
3. Deliberate role modeling, teaching, and coaching
4. Criteria for allocation of rewards and status
5. Criteria for recruitment, selection, promotion, retirement, and excommunication

*Secondary Articulation and Reinforcement Mechanisms*

1. Organization design and structure
2. Organizational systems and procedures
3. Design of physical space, facades, buildings
4. Stories about important events and people
5. Formal statements of organizational philosophy, creeds, charters

Source: E. H. Schein, *Organizational Culture and Leadership* (San Francisco: Jossey-Bass, 1985), Chap. 10.

required to change it. What a CEO needs most, according to Schein, is an understanding of how culture can help or hinder the organization in attaining its mission and the skills to make the appropriate changes.[76]

# SUMMARY

Top-level managers have a number of means to encourage organizational members to put their full efforts into strategy implementation: strategic leadership, power, and organizational culture. In today's dynamic and turbulent world, the importance of strategic leadership cannot be overemphasized. The firm's leaders must articulate the organization's mission and goals and then inspire, motivate, and support the firm's members as they work together to implement the organization's strategies.

The CEO, simply by virtue of the office, possesses the potential to influence the behavior of the organization's employees. This source of influence is termed *formal authority*. Through it, the CEO can control resources and rewards. Additionally, each CEO has a distinctive leadership style that sets the tone for the firm's members. Some leaders use a transactional style, exchanging rewards for employees' work efforts. This style can be effective in firms that are already performing well and do not anticipate significant environmental change, because it encourages employees to continue to engage in high performance.

In companies that are experiencing competitive difficulties or are undergoing environmental change, a transformational leadership style is preferable. A transformational leader inspires involvement in a mission, giving followers a "vision" of a higher order and motivating them to stretch their abilities. Such leadership is thought to make significant changes in organizational performance.

Because no single CEO, regardless of how talented he or she may be, can lead a complex organization single-handedly, most companies emphasize top management teams. Led by the CEO, such teams of executives are able to enhance the organization's coordinative activities, creativity, information flows, and strategy implementation.

In influencing the behavior of others, CEOs and other top managers have available, in addition to their formal authority and leadership style, various other techniques for wielding power. For instance, managers who are perceived as experts in their field often have significant influence over the behavior of others. They can also use their access to important information and control over its distribution to affect behavior. Leaders often use exchange as a power base, doing something for others to create a sense of obligation. Also, a manager can indirectly influence others by modifying the organization's structure, physical layout, or reward system. A manager who possesses charisma can also have a powerful impact upon followers. Finally, managers who deal successfully with critical environmental contingencies can acquire significant power.

Organizational culture refers to the values and patterns of belief and behavior that are accepted and practiced by the members of an organization. A given organization's culture reflects the influence of its founder, its experiences after the departure of its founder, and, at times, the powerful influence of a transformational leader other than the founder.

An organization's culture can facilitate or hinder the firm's strategic actions. Successful strategy implementation requires a "strategically appropriate culture"—one that is appropriate to, and supportive of, the firm's strategy. Moreover, that culture must contain values that can help the firm adapt to environmental change.

A leader can change the organization's culture through such mechanisms as paying systematic attention to certain areas of the business, serving as a deliberate role model, and allocating rewards and status. Leaders can also set an example for the firm's members through the way in which they react to organizational crises and through the processes the organization uses to attract, hire, and promote employees.

## TAKE IT TO THE NET

We invite you to visit the Wright page on the Prentice Hall Web site at:

### http://www.prenhall.com/wright

for this chapter's World Wide Web exercise.

## KEY CONCEPTS

**Charisma**   A leader's ability to influence the behavior of others through his or her personal magnetism, enthusiasm, strongly held beliefs, and charm.

**Control over information**   A situation in which a manager has access to important information and controls its distribution to others to influence their behavior.

**Critical contingency**    An environmental trend or development that has important implications for an organization. Managers who cope successfully with such contingencies acquire significant amounts of power.

**Exchange**    A situation in which a leader does a favor for someone so that he or she will feel a sense of obligation toward the leader.

**Expertise**    A manager's ability to influence the behavior of others because they believe that the manager possesses greater expertise or is more knowledgeable about a situation than they are.

**Formal authority**    The official, institutionalized right of a manager to make decisions affecting the behavior of subordinates.

**Indirect influence**    The influence on the behavior of others brought about by modifying the situation in which they work.

**Leadership**    The capacity to secure the cooperation of others in accomplishing a goal.

**Leadership style**    The characteristic pattern of behavior that a leader exhibits in the process of exercising authority and making decisions.

**Organizational culture**    The values and patterns of belief and behavior that are accepted and practiced by the members of a particular organization.

**Power**    The ability, apart from functional authority or control over resources or rewards, to influence the behavior of others.

**Strategic leadership**    The process of establishing the firm's direction—by developing and communicating a vision of the future—and motivating and inspiring organization members to move in that direction.

**Top management team**    A team of top-level executives, headed by the CEO.

**Transactional leadership**    The capacity to motivate followers by exchanging rewards for performance.

**Transformational leadership**    The capacity to motivate followers by inspiring involvement and participation in a mission.

# DISCUSSION QUESTIONS

1. Explain the difference between leadership and management. Give examples of each concept.

2. Delineate the relationship between an organization's reward system and its strategic decisions.

3. Explain transactional leadership, and give examples. Identify the conditions under which it is likely to be effective.

4. Explain transformational leadership, and give examples. Identify the conditions under which it is likely to be effective.

5. What is the role of clear, accurate, and timely information in each of the three stages of the transformational process?

6. Explain the concept of managerial dependency and why it requires the CEO to develop sources of power other than formal authority.

7. Give examples of leaders you have known who wielded power through expertise; through control over information; through exchange; through indirect influence; and through charisma.

8. Think of an organization with which you are quite familiar. Describe its culture. Explain how its culture may have evolved.

9. Give an example of an organization whose culture is appropriate for its strategy. Now, give an example of a firm whose culture has hindered its strategy.

10. Relate a story about an important event or a person that reflects elements of a particular organization's culture.

## STRATEGIC MANAGEMENT EXERCISES

1. Assume that you are the CEO of a commercial airline that competes with the low-cost strategy. Describe an appropriate organizational culture for your company.

2. Assume that your airline (Exercise 1) has now changed its strategy from low-cost to low-cost–differentiation. As CEO, what changes might you consider implementing in style of leadership, exercise of power, and organizational culture?

3. Find, in your library, an example of transformational leadership. Explain the situation fully: Who is the leader? What is the organization? Why was transformational leadership necessary? What characteristics and/or behaviors made the manager a transformational leader? What were the results of his or her attempts to transform the organization? (Particularly good sources for this exercise are the *Wall Street Journal*, *Business Week*, and *Fortune*.)

4. Strategies involving mergers and acquisitions are particularly vulnerable to cultural problems. Mergers between two organizations often are easier to accomplish on paper than in reality. Reality may reveal that the cultures of the organization fail to mesh as easily as corporate assets. From library research, identify a firm acquiring another or identify two companies that are currently merging or have engaged in a merger within the past few years. Learn as much as you can about each company's organizational culture. What problems are the two businesses having in combining their cultures? From your research, what other problems can you predict will occur in the future?

# NOTES

1. H. Mintzberg, *The Nature of Managerial Work* (New York: Harper & Row, 1973), Chap. 4.

2. J. P. Kotter, *The Leadership Factor* (New York: Free Press, 1988), p. 11.

3. D. C. Hambrick, "Guest Editor's Introduction: Putting Top Managers Back in the Strategy Picture," *Strategic Management Journal* 10 (1989): 6.

4. D. Tosti and S. Jackson, "Alignment: How It Works and Why It Matters," *Training* 31 (April 1994): 58–64; J. P. Kotter, *A Force for Change: How Leadership Differs from Management* (New York: Free Press, 1990), p. 5.

5. D. V. Day and R. G. Lord, "Executive Leadership and Organizational Performance: Suggestions for a New Theory and Methodology," *Journal of Management* 14 (1988): 453–464.

6. G. A. Yukl, *Leadership in Organizations*, 2nd ed. (Englewood Cliffs, N. J.: Prentice Hall, 1989), pp. 263–266; J. Pfeiffer, "The Ambiguity of Leadership," *Academy of Management Review* 2 (1977): 104–112.

7. S. Lahiry, "Building Commitment Through Organizational Culture," *Training & Development* 48 (April 1994): 50–52; J. R. Emshoff, "How to Increase Employee Loyalty While You Downsize," *Business Horizons* 37 (March/April 1994): 49–57; Yukl, *Leadership in Organizations*, p. 15.

8. Yukl, *Leadership in Organizations*, pp. 17–18.

9. G. Trumfio, "Managing from the Trenches," *Sales & Marketing Management* 146 (February 1994): 39; J. A. Parnell, & E. D. Bell, "A Measure of Managerial Propensity for Participative Management," *Administration and Society* 25: 518-530.

10. Day and Lord, "Executive Leadership and Organizational Performance: Suggestions for a New Theory and Methodology," p. 459.

11. This distinction was first made by J. M. Burns, in *Leadership* (New York: Harper & Row, 1978).

12. See D. T. Bastien and T. J. Hostager, "Jazz as a Process of Organizational Innovation," *Communication Research* 15 (1988): 582–602; C. Manz, D. T. Bastien, and T. J. Hostager, "Executive Leadership during Organizational Change: A Bi-Cycle Model," *Human Resource Planning* 14 (1993): 276–287.

13. B. M. Bass and B. J. Avolio, "Transformational Leadership and Organizational Culture," *International Journal of Public Administration* 17 (1994) p. 22.

14. B. M. Bass, "Leadership: Good, Better, Best," *Organizational Dynamics* 13 (Winter 1985): 26–40; N. M. Tichy and D. O. Ulrich, "SMR Forum: The Leadership Challenge—A Call for the Transformational Leader," *Sloan Management Review* 26 (Fall 1984): 59–68.

15. Ibid.

16. N. M. Tichy and M. A. Devanna, *The Transformational Leader* (New York: Wiley, 1986).

17. P. F. Drucker, *Managing in Turbulent Times* (New York: Harper & Row, 1980), p. 44.

18. J. S. Lublin, "More Companies Tap Industry Outsiders for Top Posts to Gain Fresh Perspectives," *Wall Street Journal*, 21 February 1992; J. Cole and P. B. Carroll, "GM's Hughes Division Hires Armstrong from IBM to Become Chairman, Chief," *Wall Street Journal*, 20 February 1992; B. Hager, L. Driscoll, J. Weber, and G. McWilliams, "CEO Wanted. No Insiders, Please," *Business Week*, 12 August 1991, pp. 44–45.

19. Tichy and Devanna, *The Transformational Leader*.

20. A. E. Pearson, "Six Basics for General Managers," *Harvard Business Review* 67, no. 4 (July–August 1989): 96.

21. Ibid., p. 97. Reprinted by permission of the *Harvard Business Review*. Excerpt from "Six Basics for General Managers," by Andrall E. Pearson (July–August 1989). Copyright © 1989 by the President and Fellows of Harvard College; all rights reserved.

22. Ibid., p. 95. Reprinted by permission of the *Harvard Business Review*. Excerpt from "Six Basics for General Managers," by Andrall E. Pearson (July–August 1989). Copyright © 1989 by the President and Fellows of Harvard College; all rights reserved.

23. Ibid. Reprinted by permission of the *Harvard Business Review.* Excerpt from "Six Basics for General Managers," by Andrall E. Pearson (July–August 1989). Copyright © 1989 by the President and Fellows of Harvard College; all rights reserved.

24. A. M. Mohrman Jr., S. A. Mohrman, G. E. Ledford Jr., T. G. Cummings, E. E. Lawler III, and Associates, *Large-Scale Organizational Change* (San Francisco: Jossey-Bass, 1989), p. 106.

25. W. Bennis and B. Nanus, *Leaders: The Strategies for Taking Charge* (New York: Harper & Row, 1985), pp. 27–33, 87–109.

26. S. Feinstein, "Labor Letter," *Wall Street Journal*, 1 May 1990.

27. P. Salz-Trautman, "Germany," *Management Today* (January 1994): 46.

28. D. A. Nadler, "Managing Organizational Change: An Integrative Perspective," *Journal of Applied Behavioral Science* 17 (1981): 294.

29. A. J. Nurick, "The Paradox of Participation: Lessons from the Tennessee Valley Authority," *Human Resource Management* 24 (Fall 1985): 354–355.

30. W. Bennis, *Why Leaders Can't Lead: The Unconscious Conspiracy Continues* (San Francisco: Jossey-Bass, 1989), pp. 140–141.

31. The first two reasons are based on Hambrick, "Guest Editor's Introduction: Putting Top Managers Back in the Strategy Picture," p. 6. The remaining reasons are based on R. A. Eisenstat and S. G. Cohen, "Summary: Top Management Groups," in J. R. Hackman, ed., *Groups That Work (and Those That Don't): Creating Conditions for Effective Teamwork* (San Francisco: Jossey-Bass, 1990), pp. 78–79. See also D. C. Hambrick and P. A. Mason, "Upper Echelons: The Organization as a Reflection of Its Top Managers," *Academy of Management Review* 9 (1984): 193–206.

32. K. A. Bantel and S. E. Jackson, "Top Management and Innovations in Banking: Does the Composition of the Top Team Make a Difference?" *Strategic Management Journal* 10 (1989): 111.

33. K. Kelly, "United Wants the Whole World in Its Hands," *Business Week*, 27 April 1992, pp. 64–68; K. Kelly, "He Gets By with a Lot of Help from His Friends," *Business Week*, 27 April 1992, p. 68.

34. D. J. Yang, "Nordstrom's Gang of Four," *Business Week*, 15 June 1992, pp. 122–123; A. Bennett, "Firms Run by Executive Teams Can Reap Rewards, Incur Risks," *Wall Street Journal*, 5 February 1992.

35. For a discussion of managers' dependence on others for power see D. Krackhardt and J. R. Hanson, "Informal Networks: The Company Behind the Chart," *Harvard Business Review* 71, no. 4 (July–August 1993): 104–111; J. P. Kotter, "Power, Dependence, and Effective Management," *Harvard Business Review* 55, no. 4 (July–August 1977): 125–136.

36. T. A. Stewart, "New Ways to Exercise Power," *Fortune*, 6 November 1989, p. 53.

37. Kotter, "Power, Dependence and Effective Management," p. 128.

38. J. R. P. French Jr., and B. Raven, "The Bases of Social Power," in D. Cartwright, ed., *Studies in Social Power* (Ann Arbor, Mich.: University of Michigan Press, 1959), pp. 150–167.

39. Kotter, "Power, Dependence and Effective Management," p. 130.

40. Yukl, *Leadership in Organizations*, p. 47.

41. A. Pettigrew, "Information Control as a Power Resource," *Sociology* 6 (1972): 187–204.

42. H. Mintzberg, *Power in and Around Organizations* (Englewood Cliffs, N. J.: Prentice Hall, 1983), pp. 121–122.

43. A. Kuhn, *The Study of Society: A Unified Approach* (Homewood, Ill.: Irwin, 1963).

44. Mintzberg, *Power in and Around Organizations*, p. 122.

45. J. Pfeffer, *Managing with Power: Politics and Influence in Organizations* (Boston: Harvard Business School Press, 1992), p. 107.

46. Ibid., pp. 182–185.

47. Bennett, "Firms Run by Executive Teams Can Reap Rewards, Incur Risks," p. 21.

48. D. E. Berlew, "Leadership and Organizational Excitement," in D. A. Kolb, I. M. Rubin, and J. M. McIntyre, eds., *Organizational Psychology: A Book of Readings*, 2nd ed. (Englewood Cliffs, N. J.:

Prentice Hall, 1974); R. J. House, "A 1976 Theory of Charismatic Leadership," in J. G. Hunt and L. L. Larson, eds., *Leadership: The Cutting Edge* (Carbondale, Ill.: Southern Illinois Press, 1977).

49. Yukl, *Leadership in Organizations*, p. 206.

50. P. Salz-Trautman, "Germany," p. 46.

51. Bass, *Leadership and Performance*, pp. 37–39; J. A. Conger and R. Kanungo, "Toward a Behavioral Theory of Charismatic Leadership in Organizational Settings," *Academy of Management Review* 12 (1987): 637–647.

52. D. J. Hickson, C. R. Hinings, C. A. Lee, R. E. Schneck, and J. M. Pennings, "A Strategic Contingencies Theory of Intraorganizational Power," *Administrative Science Quarterly* 16 (1971): 216–229.

53. G. R. Salancik and J. Pfeffer, "Who Gets Power—And How They Hold on to It: A Strategic–Contingency Theory of Intraorganizational Power," *Organizational Dynamics* 5 (Winter 1977): 5; D. C. Hambrick, "Environment, Strategy, and Power within Top Management Teams," *Administrative Science Quarterly* 26 (1981): 253–276.

54. C. D. Pringle, D. F. Jennings, and J. G. Longenecker, *Managing Organizations: Functions and Behaviors* (Columbus, Ohio: Merrill, 1988), p. 594.

55. E. H. Schein, *Organizational Culture and Leadership* (San Francisco: Jossey-Bass, 1985), p. 9.

56. E. H. Schein, "The Role of the Founder in Creating Organizational Culture," *Organizational Dynamics* 12 (Summer 1983): 14.

57. Yukl, *Leadership in Organizations*, pp. 215–216.

58. Ibid., p. 216.

59. For articles on McDonald's culture, see R. Henkoff, "Big Mac Attacks with Pizza," *Fortune*, 26 February 1990, pp. 87–89; R. Gibson and R. Johnson, "Big Mac, Cooling McDonald's Mystique," *Fortune*, 4 July 1988, pp. 112–116.

60. L. Nakarmi and R. Neff, "Samsung's Radical Shakeup," *Business Week*, 28 February 1994, pp. 74–76.

61. K. Kerwin and A. N. Fins, "Disney Is Looking Just a Little Fragilistic," *Business Week*, 25 June 1990, pp. 52–54; B. Dumaine, "Creating a New Company Culture," *Fortune*, 15 January 1990, p. 128.

62. M. A. Verespej, "Masters of Change," *Industry Week*, 7 March 1994, p. 9; J. P. Kotter and J. L. Haskett, *Corporate Culture and Performance* (New York: Free Press, 1992). For an analysis of cultural impact of related diversification or shareholder value, see S. Chatterjee, M. H. Lubatkin, D. M. Schweiger, and Y. Weber, "Cultural Differences and Shareholder Value in Related Mergers: Linking Equity and Human Capital," *Strategic Management Journal* 13 (1992): 319–334.

63. L. Hayes, "Gerstner Is Struggling as He Tries to Change Ingrained IBM Culture," *Wall Street Journal*, 13 May 1994, pp. A1, A8.

64. Pringle et al., *Managing Organizations: Functions and Behaviors*, p. 309.

65. Schein, *Organizational Culture and Leadership*, p. 30.

66. D. Tosti and S. Jackson, "Alignment: How It Works and Why It Matters," *Training* 31 (April 1994): 58–64; T. Brown, "The Rise and Fall of the Intelligent Organization," *Industry Week*, 7 March 1994, pp. 16–21; D. Lawrence Jr., "The New Social Contract Between Employers and Employees," *Employee Benefits Journal* 19, no. 1 (1994): 21–24.

67. This account is largely based on "The Transformation of EDS' Culture," *Open Line EDS* 11 (Spring 1990): 2–6; "Interview," *Open Line EDS* 11 (Spring 1990): 7–9; and, to a lesser extent, on Pringle et al., *Managing Organizations: Functions and Behaviors*, p. 310.

68. "The Transformation of EDS' Culture," p. 2.

69. Bass, *Leadership and Performance*, p. 24.

70. This discussion is based on Schein, *Organizational Culture and Leadership*, pp. 224–237.

71. J. B. Barney, L. Busenitz, J. O. Fiet, and D. Moesel, "The Relationship Between Venture Capitalists and Managers in New Firms: Determinants of Contractural Covenants," *Managerial Finance* 20 (1994): 19–30; Kotter and Heskett, Corporate Culture and Performance, p. 142.

72. "Changing the Culture at General Foods," *Business Week*, 10 February 1986, pp. 52–57.

73. Schein, *Organizational Culture and Leadership*, pp. 237–242.

74. M. Alpert, "Office Buildings for the 1990s," *Fortune*, 18 November 1991, pp. 141–142; T. R. V. Davis, "The Influence of the Physical Environment in Offices," *Academy of Management Review* 9 (1984): 273.

75. Schein, *Organizational Culture and Leadership*, p. 317.

76. Ibid., pp. 316–317, 320.

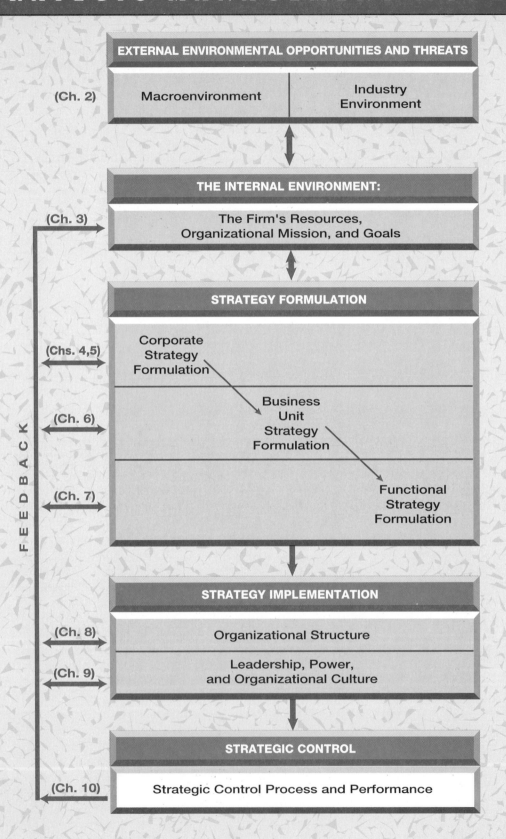

# STRATEGIC MANAGEMENT MODEL

**EXTERNAL ENVIRONMENTAL OPPORTUNITIES AND THREATS**

(Ch. 2)

| Macroenvironment | Industry Environment |
| --- | --- |

**THE INTERNAL ENVIRONMENT:**

(Ch. 3)

The Firm's Resources, Organizational Mission, and Goals

**STRATEGY FORMULATION**

(Chs. 4,5)    Corporate Strategy Formulation

(Ch. 6)    Business Unit Strategy Formulation

(Ch. 7)    Functional Strategy Formulation

FEEDBACK

**STRATEGY IMPLEMENTATION**

(Ch. 8)    Organizational Structure

(Ch. 9)    Leadership, Power, and Organizational Culture

**STRATEGIC CONTROL**

(Ch. 10)    Strategic Control Process and Performance

# 10 Strategic Control Process and Performance

The activities of formulating, implementing, and controlling are closely linked. Chapters 3, 4, 5, 6, and 7 focused on formulating or planning—establishing the organization's mission and goals and developing its corporate-level, business unit, and functional strategies. Then, implementing those strategies was discussed in chapters 8 and 9. We now turn to the task of control.

**Strategic control** consists of determining the extent to which the organization's strategies are successful in attaining its goals and objectives. If the goals and objectives are not being reached as planned, then the intent of control is to modify the organization's strategies and/or implementation so that the organization's capability to accomplish its goals will be improved.

Control, in the business administration sense, is most often discussed in the context of budgeting. It is important to understand that strategic control is much broader than this traditional usage of the term. In the control of budgeted expenditures, the focus is usually for a time span of a year or less; quantitative measurements are used to determine whether actual expenditures are exceeding planned spending; the emphasis is on internal operations; and corrective action is often taken after the budget period has elapsed. But in strategic control, the focal time period usually ranges anywhere from a few years to more than a decade, and qualitative as well as quantitative measurements are taken. Moreover, both internal operations and the external environment are assessed. The process is ongoing because intermittent corrective actions may be necessary to keep the organization on course. By the end of the focal period, it may be too late. These differences are summarized in Table 10.1.

**Table 10.1**                    **Differences Between Strategic Control and Budgetary Control**

| Strategic Control | Budgetary Control |
|---|---|
| Time period is lengthy—ranging from a few years to more than ten years. | Time period is usually one year or less. |
| Measurements are quantitative and qualitative. | Measurements are quantitative. |
| Concentration is internal and external. | Concentration is internal. |
| Corrective action is ongoing. | Corrective action may be taken after budget period has elapsed. |

## STRATEGIC CONTROL AND CORPORATE GOVERNANCE

As discussed in chapter 3, corporate governance refers to boards of directors, institutional investors, and blockholders, who monitor firm strategies to ensure managerial responsiveness. How effective these components of corporate governance are with respect to strategic control has been addressed by a number of authors.

Recall that, legally, boards of directors are authorized to represent the interests of the owners. They are also responsible for such aspects of corporate leadership as selecting or replacing the CEO, advising top management, and monitoring executive and firm performance. Although it is common for several top managers, such as the CEO and vice presidents, to also serve as board members, in some situations senior executives have comprised the majority of board membership. Moreover, in many instances CEOs have served as chairs of boards of directors. This lack of separation between top managers and their monitors, the board of directors, has been recognized as problematic. Harvard's Donaldson has suggested that management's role in formulating and implementing strategy "precludes it from also objectively evaluating the strategic path once it is in place."[1] Thus, when senior managers are numerous on the board, there may be a need to reduce their number while adding people from outside the firm to the board. Some authorities have argued that outsiders are further motivated to push for improved firm performance by their desire to build a reputation for effective board membership. Also, select scholars find that, with more outsiders as board members, CEO dismissal becomes more likely if corporate performance is poor.[2] In addition, some experts contend that outsiders are more inclined to exert pressure for corporate restructuring.[3]

This is not to say that insiders are always ineffective board members. An argument has been made that some insiders compete for succession to the position of CEO.[4] Thus, their sensitivity to the appearance of being beholden to the CEO may serve to strengthen their resolve to control strategy formulation and implementation effectively. A concern for legal liability may also encourage insiders to support board control. Indeed, one study finds that insiders are positively associated with board control.[5]

CEO duality may also influence board control. **CEO duality** refers to a CEO also serving as chair of the board. Various studies have shown mixed results regarding the desirability of CEO duality,[6] but one study has indicated that CEO duality may be detrimental.[7] In the context of our discussion, the implication may be that whether insider board members are willing to exert control could depend on whether there is CEO duality. Specifically, when the CEO is also chair of the board, the insider members may be reluctant to disagree with his or her predispositions. That is because the CEO largely determines the future career prospects as well as the monetary and nonmonetary rewards of the firm's senior executives. Additionally, the successive promotions of senior managers to their current position of authority may have been approved by the CEO. Consequently, it may be in the interest of each senior executive to support the decisions of the CEO, particularly in his or her presence. Thus, insider board members may be ineffective monitors of firm strategy when CEO duality exists.

In the absence of CEO duality, however, insiders may contribute to board control, sometimes in subtle and indirect ways so that their potential opposition to the CEO's decisions may escape documentation. For example, insiders with firm-specific knowledge may ostensibly present various sides of issues, while carefully framing the alternatives in favor of one that may be in opposition to the wishes of the CEO. Subtly contributing to effective board control may enhance the reputation of senior executives not only as valuable board members but as enlightened managers. Constructive contributions to board control may also lessen executives' anxiety over potential insider legal liability. Thus, whereas insiders may enhance board control in the absence of CEO duality, they may weaken board control when CEO duality exists. The implication is that strategic control will be enhanced if the chair of the board of directors is an outsider rather than the firm's CEO.

How effective institutional investors and blockholders are with respect to strategic control has also been addressed in a number of studies. Recall that institutional investors include pension and retirement funds, mutual funds, banks, and insurance companies, among other money managers. Blockholders are individuals, groups, or families who are significant shareholders. The premise that institutions and blockholders can effectively exert strategic control is intuitively persuasive. Blockholders as well as institutional investors ordinarily own substantial equity stakes; consequently, it is normally in their best interests to monitor firm strategies.

Although a number of empirical examinations document that institutional investors play effective monitoring roles, the impact of blockholders seems less certain.[8] Apparently, some blockholders are active monitors of firm strategy, whereas others tend to be passive investors. For instance, blockholders who are descendants of a firm's founder may be passive owners, but those whose profession is the management of investments may provide active monitoring.

As is evident from the preceding discussion, boards of directors, institutional investors, and blockholders can exert strategic control by monitoring top executive and firm performance. The CEO, along with senior executives, however, also exert strategic control. In the following paragraphs we discuss the strategic control process in the context of the role top managers should play.

**Figure 10.1**					**Steps Involved in Strategic Control**

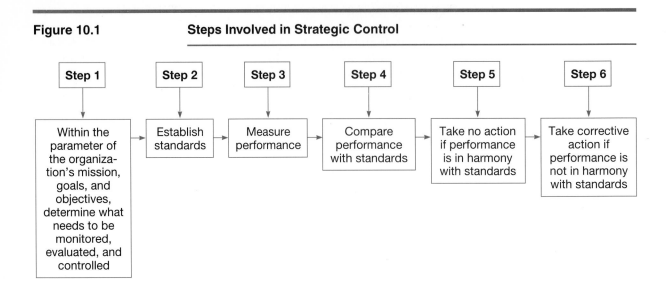

## THE STRATEGIC CONTROL PROCESS AND TOP MANAGEMENT

From the perspective of senior executives, the strategic control process consists of several steps. First, top management must decide what elements of the environment and of the organization need to be monitored, evaluated, and controlled. Then, standards must be established with which the actual performance of the organization can be compared. These first two steps will be strongly influenced by the organization's mission, goals, and objectives, which direct management's attention to certain organizational and environmental elements and to the relative importance of particular standards.

Next, management must measure or evaluate the company's actual performance. These evaluations will generally be both quantitative and qualitative. The performance evaluations will then be compared with the previously established standards. If performance is in line with the standards or exceeds them, then no corrective action is necessary. (When performance exceeds standards, management should consider whether the standards are appropriate and whether they should be raised.) However, if performance falls below the standards, then management must take remedial action. These steps are delineated in Figure 10.1.

## FOCUS OF STRATEGIC CONTROL

The focus of strategic control is both internal and external. Neither element can be examined in isolation, because it is top management's role to align advantageously the internal operations of the enterprise with its external environment. In fact, strategic control can be visualized as "mediating" the ongoing interactions between environmental variables and the company's internal dimensions. Relying upon quantitative and qualitative performance measures, top management uses strategic control to keep the firm's internal dimensions

**Figure 10.2**                    **Strategic Control as a Mediator**

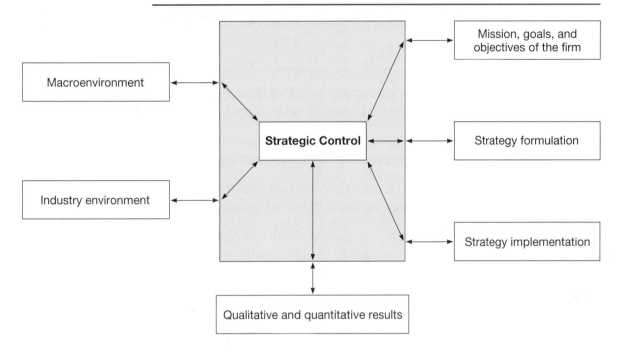

aligned with its external environment. The role of strategic control as a mediator is portrayed diagrammatically in Figure 10.2.

The following sections discuss three key areas that must be monitored and evaluated in the process of strategic control: the macroenvironment, the industry environment, and internal operations.

## ■ Macroenvironment

The first focus of the strategic control process is usually the organization's macroenvironment. Although individual businesses normally exert little, if any, influence over the forces in the macroenvironment, these forces must be continuously monitored. Changes or shifts in the macroenvironment have strategic ramifications for the company. Consequently, strategic control involves continuously examining the fit between the company and its changing external environment.

In this context, strategic control consists of modifying the company's operations to defend itself better against external threats that may arise and to capitalize on new external opportunities. For instance, during the economic downturn of the early 1990s, several discerning companies prospered by taking advantage of recession-induced opportunities. Campbell Soup, for example, reacted to the trend toward less expensive cook-at-home products by repackaging its high-end Gold Label cream of broccoli soup into the red-and-white can and marketing it as a base for meals that could be prepared at home. In slightly more than a year, consumers bought 55 million cans, making it one of Campbell's best-sellers ever.[9]

Another company that prospered during the economic rough times was Electronic Transaction Corporation. This relatively small business, which verifies checks written by customers, attracted 115 new clients in 1991, among them such retailing giants as Wal-Mart and Kmart.[10]

## ▪ Industry Environment

Strategic control also involves monitoring the industry environment. Again, the purpose is to modify the company's operations so that it can better defend itself against threats and better capitalize on opportunities. It is important to remember in this regard that environmental analysis—both at the macroenvironment and at the industry levels—is not confined to the past or present; top management also needs to estimate future environmental trends.

Take, for instance, the response of one car producer to escalating costs in the automobile industry. BMW, in expanding its manufacturing operations, decided to escape Germany's average 1992 hourly labor cost per car of $24.36 by locating its new plant in South Carolina. (U.S. average hourly labor costs per car were only $15.39; additionally, the average U.S. autoworker received twenty-three annual vacation days and holidays compared to forty-two days in Germany.) BMW hoped that this lowering of production costs would enable it to price its cars more competitively vis-à-vis such Japanese products as Lexus and Infiniti.

Through this decision, BMW is using strategic control to look toward the future. Its U.S. and Japanese competitors are becoming increasingly cost-efficient while continuing to improve product quality. As Nissan, Toyota, and Honda open manufacturing plants in Europe, and GM Europe continues to enjoy considerable success, BMW finds itself challenged on all sides. Hence, it wants to become more globally competitive by producing cars in the United States—the world's largest auto market. By reducing its manufacturing and shipping costs, BMW hopes to remain competitive in the United States as well as in other markets in Latin America.[11]

## ▪ Internal Operations

Strategic control also involves the internal operations of the business through monitoring and evaluating its strategy formulation and implementation. Corrective action may then be necessary. Monitoring and evaluating the company's operations involve viewing its present and future strategic posture. The bases for monitoring and evaluating are the qualitative and quantitative standards established by top management.

Qualitatively, the broad question asked is, How effective is our strategy in accomplishing our mission and goals? Consider the goal of product leadership, for instance. In evaluating its product leadership, an organization compares its products with those of competitors and determines the extent to which it pioneers in the introduction of new products and product improvements.

Note that pioneering is not enough. A company must also follow through. Xerox, for instance, introduced the first commercial fax machine in 1964, but today, its machines account for only 7 percent of U.S. fax sales. Likewise, Raytheon was the first company to market a microwave oven—in 1947—but today, 75 percent of all microwave ovens in U.S. homes are made in the Far East.[12]

In the broad quantitative sense, management will ask, How effective is our strategy in attaining our objectives? (Recall that objectives are specific, quantifiable versions of goals, which, in turn, are desired general ends toward which organizational efforts are directed.) For instance, management can compare the firm's 11.2 percent rate of return on investment over the past year with its stated objective of 10 percent and conclude that its strategy has been effective in that particular respect. Whether evaluating a strategy's effectiveness is undertaken relative to the best in the world, relative to the company's rivals, or relative only to itself, the point of strategic control is to take corrective action if negative gaps exist between intended and actual strategic results.

# STRATEGIC CONTROL STANDARDS

Evaluating an enterprise's performance may be accomplished in a number of ways. Management, for instance, often compares current operating results with those from the preceding year. A qualitative judgment may be made about whether the business's products or services are superior to, inferior to, or about the same as last year's. Several quantitative measures may also be used, including return on investment (ROI), return on assets (ROA), return on sales (ROS), and return on equity (ROE).

Confining control standards only to comparisons of current performance versus past performance, however, can be myopic, because it ignores important external variables. For example, assume that a business's ROI has increased from 8 to 10 percent over the past year. Management might consider that a significant improvement. But the meaning of this measure depends upon the industry in which the company operates. In a depressed industry, an ROI of 10 percent may be outstanding, but that same return in a growth industry will be disappointing, because the leading firms may earn 15 to 20 percent. An improvement in a company's ROI is less encouraging, then, if its past performance has been significantly behind that of its major competitors.

Often, strategic control standards are based on the practice of **competitive benchmarking**—the process of measuring a firm's performance against that of the top performers in its industry. After determining the appropriate benchmarks, a firm's managers set goals to meet or exceed the performance of the firm's top competitors. Taken to its logical conclusion, competitive benchmarking—if practiced by all of the firms in an industry—would result in increased industrywide performance. Increasingly, companies may be benchmarking against the best in the world (whether the best is inside or outside of the company's industry).

This section examines a variety of competitive benchmarking standards that can be used for strategic control. These standards can be based on data derived from the PIMS program, published information that is publicly available, ratings of product/service quality, innovation rates, and relative market share standings. Viewed broadly, these standards include both quantitative and qualitative information.

STRATEGIC INSIGHT

## Benchmarking at Xerox and Ford

Benchmarking is a process by which one organization may learn how other firms might perform specific activities more efficiently. The first major adopter of this technique was Xerox, a firm that was shocked in 1979 when Japanese competitor Canon introduced a midsize copier for a retail price that was below Xerox's *production costs*. At first, Xerox managers thought Canon was selling its copier below cost to capture market share, but investigation revealed that Canon was simply far more efficient than Xerox.

As a response, Xerox began a successful turnaround by studying not only how Canon achieved its cost efficiencies, but also how other firms performed certain functions. In one case, for instance, it observed the product shipping process at L. L. Bean (an outdoor clothing manufacturer and catalog retailer). Bean's order-filling system was similar to Xerox's in that both required employees to handle products that varied in shape and size, but Bean could fill orders three times as fast as Xerox. As a result of imitation, Xerox reduced its order-filling costs by 10 percent.

More recently, Ford learned that its strategic alliance partner, Mazda, was processing accounts payable with fewer than ten employees. Ford, which had 500 accounts-payable processing workers, studied Mazda's system carefully and ultimately reduced its staff by 75 percent. Ford has also learned how to design more exacting tolerances for its parts.

Companies can benchmark virtually any activity, but experts on competitive benchmarking emphasize that an organization must first understand its own processes in detail before studying those of other firms. And it is imperative that the individuals sent to observe those processes in other firms are the people who actually must implement the changes within their own organization. But they are cautioned that any changes they introduce into their own department or division are likely to also affect processes in other parts of the organization.

SOURCES: "Xerox Corp. Unveils Document Fax Centre Pro 735," *Dow Jones Business News*, 1 May 1996; O. Suris and N. M. Christian, "Will Consumers Respond to Ford's Recall Alert?" *Wall Street Journal*, 8 May 1996, pp. B1, B7; P. Eakin, "Quality You Can Bank On," *Quality*, January 1995, pp. 14–20; "Quality and Beyond," *Management Decision*, September 1994, pp. 22–23; T. Sasaki, "What the Japanese Have Learned from Strategic Alliances," *Long Range Planning*, 26, no. 6 (1994): 41–53; J. Carbone, "Benchmarking Corporate Operations—Like Purchasing," *Electronic Business Buyer*, October 1993, pp. 67–70; J. Main, "How to Steal the Best Ideas Around," *Fortune*, 19 October 1992, pp. 102–106.

### ▪ PIMS Program

A thorough evaluation of a business's performance may take into account the performance of its competitors or the best in the world (even if the best is outside of the industry). For that reason, the PIMS program was developed; the **PIMS (profit impact of market strategy) program** is a database that contains quantitative and qualitative information on the performance of more than 3,000 business units. It helps management of participating companies evaluate the performance of their organizations relative to the performance of other businesses in the same industry or other industries. When a company's results compare unfavorably, strategic control is typically required.

PIMS was developed as a result of General Electric's efforts to evaluate systematically the performance of its business units in the 1960s.[13] Using a program developed by Professor Sidney Schoeffler of Harvard University, GE's top managers and corporate staff began to assess business unit performance in a formal, systematic fashion. Subsequently, other companies were invited to join the project, and in 1975, Professor Schoeffler founded the Strategic Planning Institute to conduct PIMS research.

Each of the participating businesses provides quantitative and qualitative information to the program. Included are data on variables such as market share, product/service quality, new products and services introduced as a percentage of sales, relative prices of products and services, marketing expenses as a percentage of sales, value of plant and equipment relative to sales, and research and development expenses as a percentage of sales. Two profitability measures are used: net operating profit before taxes as a percentage of sales (ROS), and net income before taxes as a percentage of total investment (ROI) or of total assets (ROA).

Each of these variables may be used for strategic control purposes. For instance, if a business's product quality is consistently judged to be below average, then this information can be used to improve quality. Below-average profitability signals management that changes in strategy formulation or implementation may be necessary.

To take full advantage of PIMS, a business needs to be a participating member of the PIMS program. However, all businesses may broadly exert strategic control by comparing their situations with some of the PIMS principles.[14] PIMS, of course, is not the only source of strategic control data. A number of other information bases are discussed in the following section.

## ■ Published Information for Strategic Control

*Fortune* annually publishes the most- and least-admired U.S. corporations with annual sales of at least $500 million in such diverse industries as electronics, pharmaceuticals, retailing, transportation, banking, insurance, metals, food, motor vehicles, and utilities. Corporate dimensions are evaluated along the following eight lines:

- Quality of products/services
- Quality of management
- Innovativeness
- Long-term investment value
- Financial soundness
- Community and environmental responsibility
- Use of corporate assets
- Ability to attract, develop, and keep talented people

The most-admired companies are those that rank high on these variables. Although *Fortune*'s list consists of very large, publicly traded companies, the information in the listing may nevertheless provide valuable guidelines for the strategic control of smaller firms. In addition to *Fortune*, publications such as *Forbes*, *Industry Week*, *Business Week*, and *Dun's Business Month* evaluate the performance of companies in various industries.

Which particular measures of comparison to use, of course, must be determined by top management. But a number of competitive benchmarking variables are considered important for strategic control because they significantly affect performance. They are discussed in the following sections.

## STRATEGIC INSIGHT

## *Broadening a Myopic Perspective at General Motors*

In the 1960s General Motors (GM) developed a quantitative standard for measuring the quality of the automobiles it was manufacturing. On its scale, a score of 100 was perfect; each defect a new car contained lowered its score by one point. So a car with a score of 80 contained 20 defects. GM's management established a score of 60 as "passing."

But when too many cars failed to attain a passing grade, rather than take corrective action and improve the quality of its outputs, management decided to modify the standard. The new standard for perfection was raised from 100 to 145. As a result, a car with 41 defects that would have "failed" under the old standard now had a passing score of 104.

GM and other U. S. automakers, however, became increasingly serious about product quality as pressure from foreign competition steadily increased during the 1970s. But even by 1980, the quality of American-made cars was still suspect. A Detroit consulting firm, Harbour & Associates, reported that GM's 1980 cars averaged 7.4 defects per car, Chrysler's averaged 8.1, and Ford's averaged 6.7. Meanwhile, Japanese-made autos averaged only 2.0 defects.

American manufacturers continued to stress quality improvements throughout the 1980s and into the 1990s, however. By 1992, a GM factory in Oklahoma City produced the most defect-free cars (Buick Centuries and Oldsmobile Cutlasses) of any plant in North America—0.71 defect per car. Second was a Toyota plant in Ontario.

GM increasingly began to realize the role that customer service played in quality considerations. When 1,836 of its new Saturn sedans were recalled because they left the factory with improperly mixed antifreeze that would create holes in the cooling systems, GM took a large step forward in customer service. Rather than recall the cars for free repairs, the usual approach of automakers, GM offered to exchange each car with the defective coolant for a new Saturn.

This service-oriented approach, combined with Saturn's superb quality (it now has the same low defect rate as Honda), resulted in Saturn dealers selling an average of 115 cars per month—twice the sales/dealer rate of second-place Toyota.

SOURCES: R. Blumenstein, N. M. Christian, and O. Suris, "Local GM Labor Dispute Spins Out of Control," *Wall Street Journal*, 13 March 1996, pp. B1, B3; M. Darling, "GM's Saturn: Colossal Blunder?" *Journal of Commerce and Commercial Management*, 6 October 1995, p. 8A; S. Gabriella, "Saturn's Mystique is Endangered As GM Changes the Car and the Organization," *Wall Street Journal*, 27 July 1995, p. B1; M. Keller, *Collision: GM, Toyota, Volkswagen & the Race to the 21st Century* (New York: Doubleday, 1993); N. Templin, "GM's Saturn Subsidiary Is Fighting for Its Future," *Wall Street Journal*, 16 June 1993, p. B4; M. Keller, *Rude Awakening: The Rise, Fall and Struggle for Recovery of General Motors* (New York: Merrow, 1989), pp. 29–30.

### ■ Product/Service Quality

Interestingly, over the years there has been a positive relationship between the quality of products and services that companies produce and the financial performance of those firms. This relationship is illustrated by the *Fortune* listing just described. Recall that quality has two key aspects—the conformance of a product or service to the internal standards of the firm and the ultimate consumer's perception of the quality of that product or service. It is important to distinguish between these two aspects of quality, because a number of products that have conformed to internal standards have not sold well. So although conformance to standards is a necessary condition for a product's or service's success, it is not sufficient. Ultimately, a firm's outputs must be perceived as superior by the marketplace.[15]

To evaluate product quality, *Fortune* asks some 8,000 executives, outside directors, and financial analysts to judge the outputs of the largest firms in the United States. About 4,000 responses are usually received.[16] According to the results, those firms whose outputs are perceived to possess high quality are also the higher-performing companies.

Taking a different approach, the PIMS program assesses quality through judgments made by both managers and customers.[17] A meeting is held by a team of managers in each of the PIMS participating businesses. These managers identify product/service attributes that they believe influence customer purchases. They then assign a weight to each attribute. Finally, they rate the quality of each attribute of their company's outputs relative to those of the products/services produced by the leading companies. These ratings are augmented by survey results from customers who also rate the quality of the products produced by businesses in various industries. The results of the PIMS program suggest a strong positive correlation between product quality and business performance.

One publication, *Consumer Reports*, may be used by executives as a means for strategic control of output quality. Literally hundreds of products are evaluated by this publication annually. Because the evaluation by *Consumer Reports* is unbiased (it does not accept advertising), it is an excellent source of product quality information for competing businesses. Even if the products of a particular business are not evaluated by this publication, that company can still gain insight on its competitors' product quality.

Specific published information may also exist for select industries. Perhaps the best known is the "Customer Satisfaction Index" released annually by J. D. Power for the automobile industry. A questionnaire survey of 70,000 new-car owners each year examines such variables as satisfaction with eighty-one aspects of vehicle performance; problems reported during the first ninety days of ownership; ratings of dealer service quality; and ratings of the sales, delivery, and condition of new vehicles.[18]

Certainly, it is imperative that an enterprise, regardless of its size, engage in some means of assessing the relative quality of its products and services. If the quality of its outputs compares favorably with that of the competition, then no direct action may be necessary, although emphasizing high quality in future advertising might prove to be advantageous. If the company's outputs do not compare favorably with the competition's, then corrective action is essential.

## ■ Innovation

Innovation may be conceptualized, measured, and controlled in different ways. Many researchers have approached this subject by focusing on expenditures for product research and development (R&D) and process R&D.[19] These studies conclude that the more money spent on developing new or improved products and processes, the higher the level of innovation is likely to be.[20] This same approach is taken in the PIMS program.

Some firms plan and control their programs for innovation very carefully. 3M, for instance, has established a standard that 25 percent of each business unit's sales should come from products introduced to the market within the past five years. The standard is taken quite seriously by 3M managers, since "meeting the 25% test is a crucial yardstick at bonus time."[21] Currently, almost a third of 3M's sales come from products introduced within a five-year period.

Not surprisingly, 3M invests between 6 and 7 percent of its sales revenue in R&D, a figure that is double the average of U. S. industry.[22]

Some observers have suggested that the strategic control of innovation must emphasize incremental improvements in products and services rather than sweeping, fundamental innovations.[23] Several attribute the Japanese superiority over U. S. business performance in some industries to the Japanese emphasis on incremental innovations. A continuous series of incremental innovations means that each year the company's outputs improve as a result of small, but numerous and cumulative, innovations.[24]

### ■ Relative Market Share

A business's size and market share, relative to its largest rivals in the industry, are important in formulating and implementing strategy and in controlling the company's strategic direction. Recall from chapter 6 that both small and large market shares can lead to high performance. In large, leading companies, relative market share and growth in relative market share play important roles in managerial performance evaluations.[25] Managers at all levels in the organization are partially evaluated on their contributions to the company's gains in relative market share. Such gains, of course, also depend upon other strategic variables, such as product quality, innovation, pricing, and industry forces. Thus, changes in relative market share may serve as a strategic control gauge for both internal and external variables.

For instance, several years ago Johnson & Johnson chose to extend its product line of baby shampoo, baby powder, and baby oil to mail-order educational toys. But after a decade, its annual toy sales had still not exceeded $25 million, a very small share of the gigantic toy market. Chairman and CEO Ralph S. Larson made the strategic decision to divest the toy business. As he stated, "If a business doesn't have a reasonable prospect of achieving leadership, we have a responsibility to exit it."[26]

For successful smaller businesses, relative market share serves as a strategic control barometer in another way. The discussion in chapter 6 suggested that some businesses may strategically plan to maintain a low market share. In this event, the strategic control of market share may emphasize variables that do not promote market share growth. Such variables may include policies that encourage high prices and discourage sales events and price discounts. Empirical research has concluded that for certain companies in particular industries, emphasizing increases in relative market share is counterproductive.[27]

Strategic control actions for maintaining a small market share may include limiting the number of product/markets in which the company will compete. A small market share combined with operations in limited product/markets "enables a company to compete in ways that are unavailable to its larger rivals."[28]

## EXERTING STRATEGIC CONTROL

Strategic control may be exerted in a number of different ways to ensure that the organization is performing in accordance with its mission, goals, and objectives. Some of the more important ways are presented in this section.

## ■ Control Through Multilevel Performance Criteria

Strategic control through **multilevel performance criteria** may involve setting performance standards for individuals, functions, products, divisions, or strategic business units. In the first instance, controlling individual performance depends upon what the individual employee does. An office worker's performance might be monitored by measuring the number of orders processed per day; a factory worker's daily production could be evaluated; and a sales representative's monthly sales figures could be appraised. Some jobs, of course, are less subject to quantitative measurement. Examples include a research and development scientist, whose work might not show results for months or years; a corporate planner; and individuals who work in teams.

Control at the functional level may include controlling for the volume of production and defect rates incurred in the manufacturing function. In marketing, performance control might include evaluating sales volume and measuring the level of customer satisfaction through interviews or questionnaire surveys.

At the product, divisional, and strategic business unit levels, strategic control of performance may include evaluating productivity improvements, sales growth, and changes in market share. In a qualitative sense, performance control can also include judging how product, divisional, and strategic business unit executives cooperate with one another to attain synergy for the overall organization.

At all levels, from the individual to the strategic business unit, corrective action should be taken if actual performance is less than the standard that has been established. On the other hand, should performance in some area—such as a function, division, or strategic business unit—be far above the standard, management should attempt to ascertain the reasons for the excellent performance. In some cases, the methods that one unit is using to achieve above-standard performance can be transferred to other organizational units, thereby improving their performance as well.

## ■ Control Through Performance

Control through performance can take place by monitoring the company's ROI, ROE, or other measures of profitability that were mentioned earlier. These evaluations take the form of comparisons vis-à-vis the performance of others in the marketplace. The PIMS program, of course, evaluates performance in this manner. Growth in relative market share may also be evaluated for strategic control.

In addition to monitoring and evaluating the key areas discussed earlier in the chapter, top management monitors the price of the company's stock. Price fluctuations suggest how investors value the performance of the firm. Management is always very concerned over sharp price changes in the firm's stock. A sudden drop in price will make the firm a more attractive takeover target. Sharp increases may mean that an investor or group of investors is accumulating large blocks of stock to engineer a takeover or a change in top management. Hence, managers continuously monitor price changes in their firm's stock.

## ■ Control Through Organizational Variables

A final way that strategic control can be exerted is through organizational variables. Control can be effected directly through the formal organization or indirectly through the informal organization.

## The Formal Organization

The **formal organization**—the management-specified structure of relationships and procedures used to manage organizational activity—can facilitate or impede the accomplishment of the enterprise's mission, goals, and objectives. As we have already seen, the formal organization determines who reports to whom, how jobs are grouped, and what rules and policies will guide the actions and decisions of employees. Chapter 8 illustrated, for instance, how an organization's structure can become outmoded and no longer appropriate for its mission. At such times, strategic control will dictate a change from, say, a functional structure to a product divisional structure. That change will have to be accompanied by appropriate modifications in organizational reward systems so that the new forms of required behavior will be rewarded and older, less appropriate behaviors will not be.

For example, some organizations that have changed from functional or product divisional structures to matrix structures have experienced considerable difficulty. Such a dramatic change cannot be accomplished overnight, yet some top managers have evidently believed that by drawing a new organization chart and explaining it to their employees, new appropriate behaviors would naturally follow. But they do not. Employees must understand the compelling reasons underlying the change to a matrix structure to divorce them from their old ways of behaving, and they must then be trained extensively in the new types of behaviors that will be required. After this groundwork is laid, the change to the matrix structure must be accompanied by a new organizational reward system that encourages teamwork, frequent reassignment of personnel, greater participation, and open communication. Concomitantly, it should discourage loyalty to a functional area and to one supervisor.

The importance of clearly communicating the organization's values to all employees and establishing a rewards system that reinforces those values cannot be overemphasized. When management overlooks the key role that values and rewards play, or when the relationship among values, communication, and rewards is inconsistent, then informal organizational patterns develop to counterbalance the flaws and inconsistencies.

## The Informal Organization

The **informal organization** refers to the interpersonal interactions that naturally evolve when individuals and groups come into contact with one another.[29] These informal relationships can play destructive or constructive roles in helping the organization pursue its mission, goals, and objectives.

When it is obvious to everyone that what is valued by the organization is also what is actually rewarded, then the informal organization tends to promote the attainment of the organization's desired purposes. But when the organization's value system is ambiguous, or when inconsistencies exist between what is valued and what is rewarded, then the informal organization develops its own set of consistent values and rewards. For example, most organizations claim to reward high job performance. If, in fact, employees discern that most of the major promotions and pay raises actually go to individuals who have the greatest seniority, regardless of their level of performance, then this "informal value" is communicated throughout the organization. Managers' exhortations

## *Downsizing as Strategic Control*

One of the most common corrections in strategic control made by corporations during the 1980s and the 1990s has been *downsizing*—an aspect of which involves shrinking an organization's work force to make the firm more competitive. But two studies by consulting firms show that these results are not often attained.

Wyatt Company surveyed 1,005 firms, the majority of which had downsized during the preceding five years. Following the downsizing, only 46 percent of the firms achieved their goals of reducing expenses, only 32 percent increased profits as they had hoped, only 22 percent met their increased productivity goals, only 19 percent improved their competitive advantage as much as they desired, only 13 percent attained their sales goals, and only 9 percent reached their product quality goals.

A Mitchell & Company study of sixteen large firms in various industries revealed that, two years after downsizing, the stock prices of twelve of these sixteen corporations were trading in a range that was 5 to 45 percent below the stocks of comparable firms in their industries. What's wrong? Although the reasons vary from one corporation to another, one common problem seems to be that the changes in the formal organization created by downsizing result in dysfunctional consequences in the informal organization. As one downsizing consultant puts it:

> The numbers might be right, the forecasts might be right and the stock analysts might approve wholeheartedly, but if the human aspects aren't managed well, the effort can go into the tank.

All too often, unfortunately, the human aspects aren't managed too well. For instance, those employees who survive the cuts are often left stunned and wondering whether they'll be next. (They often are next, according to an American Management Association study that shows that companies that downsize once are more likely to downsize again in the future.) Obviously, such emotions are not usually associated with highly motivated, committed employees.

Work force reductions are made in various ways. Some firms simply cut, say, 10 or 15 percent of their employees, "across the board." In such cases, efficient departments lose employees just as do inefficient departments. Other firms attempt to minimize morale problems by offering early retirement to employees who have been with the firm for a certain number of years. Although this technique sounds more rational, these firms are often shocked to find that "a lot of training, experience, and skills [are] going out the door...."

Workers realize that their firms must reduce expenses. However, they resent cost-cutting programs that invariably affect employees first. They recognize that there are many reasons for high costs, and employees are only one of them. Yet they often seem to be the most expendable. But layoffs are no substitute for solving an organization's fundamental problems.

As is evident, downsizing can have detrimental effects on company morale. When Nynex Corporation entered a second round of cuts to trim its work force by 22 percent, managers became particularly bitter. Said one Nynex executive, "Two months ago, I would have said that morale is low and it couldn't go any lower. But I'd have to say it's even lower today."

Not all companies operate this way, of course. Some attempt to retain their human resources even during recessionary periods through such practices as implementing hiring freezes, retraining and deploying older workers, reducing pay temporarily, shortening the workweek, or simply never overstaffing in the first place. Critics charge that effective management at the outset can reduce or eliminate the need for downsizing in the future. In addition, there is increasing evidence to suggest that downsizing can increase costs in the long run.

*continued*

*Downsizing as Strategic Control*

SOURCES: A. Markels and M. Murray, "Downsizing to Reduce Costs Hurts Some Firms in Long Run," *Wall Street Journal Interactive Edition*, 14 May 1996; T. Petzinger Jr., "Downsizing Raises Questions about Management Skills," *Wall Street Journal Interactive Edition*, 11 May 1996; J. Nocera, "Living with Layoffs," *Fortune*, 1 April 1996, pp. 69–80; B. Bartosh, "Adventures in Downsizing: A Case Study," *Information Strategy: The Executive's Journal*, Winter 1995, pp. 47–52; G. A. Poole, "The New Idle Rich: How to Do Nothing in the Age of Downsizing," *Forbes*, 4 December 1995, pp. S32–35; D. C. Band and C. M. Tustin, "Strategic Downsizing," *Management Decision*, December 1995, pp. 36–45; "The Pain of Downsizing," *Business Week*, 9 May 1994, pp. 60–68 (source of third quotation); E. Lesly and L. Light, "When Layoffs Alone Don't Turn the Tide," *Business Week*, 7 December 1992, pp. 100–101; E. Faltermayer, "Is This Layoff Necessary?" *Fortune*, 1 June 1992, pp. 71–86 (source of second quotation, p. 72); A. Knox, "The Downside and Dangers of Downsizing," *Washington Post*, 15 March 1992 (source of first quotation).

to perform better will be largely ignored by employees, because they realize that the formally touted value of high performance is vacuous.

The informal organization cannot be directly controlled by management. It can, however, be influenced indirectly by ensuring that the formal organization is consistent in the sense that it clearly communicates its values and then rewards behaviors that are compatible with those values. It may also be influenced through the informal behavior of managers.

For instance, when managers interact with employees during the workday or off-hours, employees learn quickly whether their ideas are solicited, respected, and taken seriously. Informal bonds of mutual trust and respect are translated into loyalty to the organization and to the supervisor.

Managers may also communicate informally simply through their behavior. One manager commented on his CEO's work schedule as follows:

> He was the first one in the office. His car was in the lot by 7:00 every morning, and he never left before 6 P.M. That told people a lot about what he expected from us.[30]

In another case, the owner-manager of an amusement park asks different employees to walk with him through the park during their breaks. As they walk, the manager smiles and greets customers. If there is litter on the grounds, he picks the trash up and deposits it into receptacles. If customers ask questions or appear to need directions, he assists them. The message is very clear. The owner-manager values a clean amusement park and a friendly, courteous, customer-oriented staff.

# SUMMARY

Strategic control consists of determining the extent to which the company's strategies are successful in attaining its goals and objectives. If the goals and objectives are not being reached as planned, then the intent of control is to modify the enterprise's strategies and/or implementation so that the organization's ability to accomplish its goals will be improved. In strategic control, the focal time period usually ranges from a few years to more than a decade; qualitative and quantitative measurements are taken; both internal operations and the external environment are assessed; and the process is continuous.

Board of directors, institutional investors, and blockholders monitor firm strategies to insure managerial responsiveness. Moreover, on the basis of the organization's mission, goals, and objectives, top management selects what elements of the environment and of the organization need to be monitored, evaluated, and controlled. Then, standards are established to which the actual performance of the business will be compared. Next, management measures the company's actual performance—both quantitatively and qualitatively. If performance is in line with the standards or exceeds them, then no corrective action is necessary. However, if performance falls below the standards, then management must take remedial action.

The focus of strategic control is both internal and external. Top management's role is to align advantageously the internal operations of the business with its external environment. Hence, strategic control can be visualized as "mediating" the interactions between environmental variables (in both the macroenvironment and the industry environment) and the organization's internal operations.

Evaluating a company's performance may be accomplished in a number of ways. For instance, current operating results can be compared with results from the prior year, both quantitatively and qualitatively. However, management must also evaluate important external variables such as the performance of competitors. Several competitive benchmarks can be used, but chief among them are the focal company's relative product/service quality, its innovative ability to develop new products and services and to improve its production and customer service deliver processes relative to those of its competitors, and its relative market share.

Strategic control can be exerted by top management in a number of different ways. First, management can control performance at several different levels—individual, functional, product, divisional, and strategic business unit. Control can also focus on performance through monitoring key financial ratios and changes in the firm's stock price. Finally, strategic control can be exerted directly through the formal organization by clear communication of the organization's values and a determination that the company's reward system is consistent with those values; and it can be exerted indirectly through the informal organization by appropriate managerial behavior.

## TAKE IT TO THE NET

We invite you to visit the Wright page on the Prentice Hall Web site at:

**http://www.prenhall.com/wright**

for this chapter's World Wide Web exercise.

# KEY CONCEPTS

**CEO duality**   A situation in which the CEO also serves as chair of the board.

**Competitive benchmarking**   The process of measuring a firm's performance against that of the top performers in its industry.

**Formal organization**   The management-specified structure of relationships and procedures used to manage organizational activity.

**Informal organization**   Interpersonal relationships and interactions that naturally evolve when individuals and groups come into contact with one another.

**Multilevel performance criteria**   Performance standards that are established for each of the following levels: individual employee, function, product line, division, strategic business unit, and organization.

**PIMS program**   A database, termed the profit impact of market strategy (PIMS), that contains quantitative and qualitative information on the performance of more than 3,000 business units.

**Strategic control**   Determining the extent to which an organization's strategies are successful in attaining its goals and objectives.

# DISCUSSION QUESTIONS

1. Although strategic control and control in the more traditional budgetary sense are similar in some respects, they also differ significantly. Explain their similarities and differences.

2. What roles do the organization's mission, goals, and objectives play in strategic control?

3. Explain how strategic control mediates the interactions between the business's internal dimensions and its external environment.

4. In strategic control, management might compare the organization's performance this year with its performance in previous years. What are the strengths and weaknesses of this one comparison?

5. Explain how competitive benchmarking is used in strategic control. What are some commonly used competitive benchmarks?

6. What is the PIMS program? How can it aid in strategic control?

7. "If a business unit's performance is below standard, corrective action should be taken. If its performance is above standard, no managerial action is necessary." True or false? Why?

8. What is the relationship between strategic control and changes in the firm's stock price?

9. How are organizational values and rewards related to strategic control?

10. Give an example from your own experience of a manager who communicated organizational values through his or her informal behavior.

## STRATEGIC MANAGEMENT EXERCISES

1. On the basis of your own perceptions as a consumer, compare the relative quality of two competing products (other than automobiles) or services that you have purchased. How might your perceptions be used by the manufacturers or sellers of these products and services in strategic control?

2. Over the past decade, the U. S.-based automobile companies have attempted to improve the quality of their cars relative to those of Japanese manufacturers. One way U. S. executives can exert strategic control is through comparing the quality of their cars with the quality of Japanese automobiles. Assume that you are a top-level manager with one of the U. S.-based car companies. Refer to a recent *Consumer Reports* issue that evaluates cars. Determine how the quality of the American company's car(s) compares with that of its Japanese rival(s). From your strategic control assessment, would you say that the American car company should take corrective action? Justify your answer.

3. Select a company of your choice. From library research, what source or sources of information can you obtain that may assist the management of that company in making strategic control decisions? Describe the source(s), the information contained, and how the information might be used by management for strategic control.

4. Select an airline company. Conduct library research on your chosen company so that you can elaborate on how strategic control has affected the direction of the company. Recall that strategic control consists of modifying a company's operations to maintain a compatible fit between the company and the changing environment.

# NOTES

1. G. Donaldson, "The New Tool for Boards: The Strategic Audit," *Harvard Business Review* 73, no. 4 (1995): 103.

2. See B. Hermalin and M. S. Weisbach, "The Determinants of Board Composition," *Rand Journal of Economics* 19, 4 (1988): 589–605; E. F. Fama and M. C. Jensen, "Separation of Ownership and Control," *Journal of Law and Economics* 26, (1983): 301–325; M. S. Weisbach, "Outside Directors and CEO Turnover," *Journal of Financial Economics* 20 (1988): 431–460.

3. P. A. Gibbs, "Determinants of Corporate Restructuring: The Relative Importance of Corporate Governance, Takeover Threat, and Free Cash Flow," *Strategic Management Journal*, 14 (1993): 51–68.

4. M. S. Mizruchi, "Who Controls Whom? An Examination of the Relation Between Management and Boards of Directors in Large Corporations," *Academy of Management Review* 8 (1983): 426–435.

5. B. K. Boyd, "Board Control and CEO Compensation," *Strategic Management Journal* 15 (1994): 335–344.

6. See J. A. Alexander, M. L. Fennell, and M. T. Halpern, "Leadership Instability in Hospitals: The Influence of Board-CEO Relations and Organization Growth and Decline," *Administrative Science Quarterly* 38 (1993): 74–99; B. R. Baliga, R. C. Moyer, and R. S. Rao, "CEO Duality and Firm Performance: What's the Fuss?" *Strategic Management Journal* 17 (1996): 41–53; S. Finkelstein and R. A. D'Aveni, "CEO Duality as a Double-Edged Sword: How Boards of Directors Balance Entrenchment Avoidance and Unity of Command," *Academy of Management Journal* 37 (1994): 1079–1108.

7. M. Kroll, P. Wright, K. Barksdale, and A. Desai, "The Impact of Board Effectiveness, Large External Shareholders and CEO Rewards Ratio on Acquisition Performance Moderated by CEO Duality," working paper, University of Texas at Tyler.

8. See P. Wright, S. Ferris, A. Sarin, and V. Awasthi, "Impact of Corporate Insider, Blockholder, and Institutional Equity Ownership on Firm Risk Taking," *Academy of Management Journal* 39 (1996): 441–463; J. J. McConnell and H. Servaes, "Additional Evidence on Equity Ownership and Corporate Value," *Journal of Financial Economics* 27 (1990): 595–612.

9. J. Weber, W. Zellner, and Z. Schiller, "Seizing the Dark Day," *Business Week*, 13 January 1992, p. 27.

10. D. J. Yang and G. Smith, "Where Gloom and Doom Equal Boom," *Business Week*, 13 January 1992, p. 28.

11. W. Brown, "BMW to Build Car Assembly Plant in U. S.," *Washington Post*, 24 June 1992; P. Ingrassia and T. Aeppel, "Worried by Japanese, Thriving GM Europe Vows to Get Leaner," *Wall Street Journal*, 27 July 1992.

12. T. A. Stewart, "Lessons from U. S. Business Blunders," *Fortune*, 23 April 1990, p. 128.

13. C. H. Springer, "Strategic Management in General Electric," *Operations Research* 21 (1973): 1177–1182.

14. R. D. Buzzell and B. T. Gale, *The PIMS Principles* (New York: Free Press, 1987).

15. L. Dube, L. M. Renaghan, and J. M. Miller, "Measuring Customer Satisfaction for Strategic Management," *Cornell Hotel and Restaurant Administration Quarterly* (February 1994): 39–47; J. M. Groocock, *The Chain of Quality* (New York: Wiley, 1986).

16. P. Wright, D. Hotard, J. Tanner, and M. Kroll, "Relationships of Select Variables with Business Performance of Diversified Corporations," *American Business Review* 6, no. 1 (January 1988): 71–77.

17. Buzzell and Gale, *The PIMS Principles*, Chap. 6.

18. A. Taylor III, "More Power to J. D. Power," *Fortune*, 18 May 1992, pp. 103–106.

19. Buzzell and Gale, *The PIMS Principles*, Chap. 6; P. Wright, M. Kroll, C. Pringle, and J. Johnson, "Organization Types, Conduct, Profitability, and Risk in the Semiconductor Industry," *Journal of Management Systems* 2, no. 2 (1990): 33–48.

20. P. Fuhrman, "No Need for Valium," *Forbes*, 31 January 1994, pp. 84–85.

21. R. Mitchell, "Masters of Innovation: How 3M Keeps Its New Products Coming," *Business Week*, 10 April 1989, p. 61.

22. K. Kelly, "3M Run Scared? Forget About It," *Business Week*, 16 September 1991, p. 59.

23. R. Simons, "How New Top Managers Use Control Systems as Levers of Strategic Renewal," *Strategic Management Journal* 15 (1994): 169–189.

24. O. Port, "Back to Basics," *Business Week*, Special 1989 Bonus Issue, pp. 14–18.

25. Buzzell and Gale, *The PIMS Principles*, Chap. 5.

26. J. Weber and J. Carey, "No Band-Aids for Ralph Larsen," *Business Week*, 28 May 1990, p. 86.

27. W. E. Fruhan Jr., "Pyrrhic Victories in Fights for Market Share,"; and R. G. Hamermesh, M. J. Anderson, and J. E. Harris, "Strategies for Low Market-Share Businesses," in R. G. Hamermesh, ed., *Strategic Management* (New York: Wiley, 1983), pp. 112–125, 126–138.

28. Hamermesh, Anderson, and Harris, "Strategies for Low Market-Share Businesses," p. 135.

29. D. Krackhardt and J. R. Hanson, "Informal Networks: The Company Behind the Chart," *Harvard Business Review* 71, no. 4 (July-August 1993): 104–111.

30. J. Gabarro, "Socialization at the Top—How CEOs and Subordinates Evolve Interpersonal Contacts," *Organizational Dynamics* 7 (Winter 1979): 14.

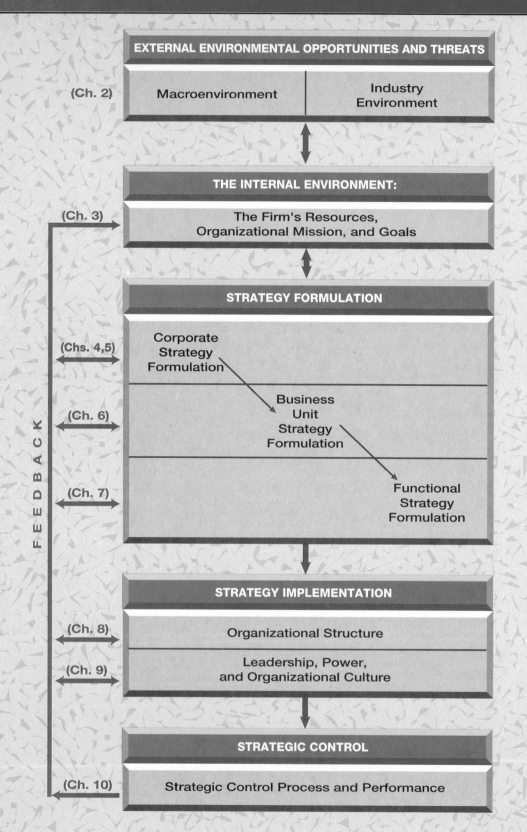

# STRATEGIC MANAGEMENT MODEL

**EXTERNAL ENVIRONMENTAL OPPORTUNITIES AND THREATS**

(Ch. 2)

| Macroenvironment | Industry Environment |
|---|---|

**THE INTERNAL ENVIRONMENT:**

(Ch. 3)

The Firm's Resources, Organizational Mission, and Goals

**STRATEGY FORMULATION**

(Chs. 4,5)

Corporate Strategy Formulation

(Ch. 6)

Business Unit Strategy Formulation

(Ch. 7)

Functional Strategy Formulation

**STRATEGY IMPLEMENTATION**

(Ch. 8)

Organizational Structure

(Ch. 9)

Leadership, Power, and Organizational Culture

**STRATEGIC CONTROL**

(Ch. 10)

Strategic Control Process and Performance

FEEDBACK

# 11 Strategic Management and the World Marketplace

Few businesses based in the United States can escape the impact of foreign competition. Besides widely publicized international competition in such industries as automobiles, motorcycles, steel, tires, and watches, American-made goods also compete head to head in their home markets with foreign firms in product lines such as fans, luggage, outerwear, jewelry, musical instruments, dolls, hand tools, consumer electronics, sporting goods, zinc, blouses, suits, semiconductors, and shoes. Among the home bases of the 500 largest industrial corporations in the world, 34 countries are represented, including Zambia and Panama. U.S.-based corporations still dominate the list with 161 companies, followed by Japan with 128 and Britain with 40.[1] In select areas, the United States is no longer at the top. In banking, for instance, the United States places only 4 banks in the world's top 50; Japan accounts for 20, Germany has 8, and 6 are based in France.[2]

Even though a company may choose to operate only within a confined local area, that choice does not necessarily exempt the business from foreign competition. Foreign firms conduct business in virtually every industry represented in the United States. Some American-based businesses, of course, choose to operate in other countries through one or more of the ways that this chapter discusses. But in any case, virtually every top manager must have an understanding of the issues involved in international strategic management.

## OVERVIEW OF WORLD OPERATIONS

This chapter focuses primarily on businesses that choose to operate worldwide. This involvement may range from limited activities such as purchasing from foreign sources or exporting to a foreign market to operating throughout the world as if there were no national boundaries. To give you some idea of the magnitude of international trade, we list some selected statistics on U.S. exports and imports in Table 11.1

Ordinarily, international operations evolve gradually. Most enterprises begin their involvement with foreign countries through importing or exporting products. If particular sites overseas possess attractive resources or markets, a business may become further involved through licensing select organizations in those countries to use its technology, production processes, or brand name. Alternatively, the enterprise may enter into partnerships or joint ventures with foreign companies as a means of penetrating certain markets. Gradually, the company may become more deeply involved by initiating direct investments in select countries. Such investments may include the company's starting its own operations abroad or buying portions or all of the ownership of foreign-based organizations. U.S. and foreign direct investments are shown in Table 11.2. Direct investment refers to investors in one country owning at least 10 percent of a private enterprise in another country.

In this chapter, business operations will be considered on three levels: international, multinational, and global. **International businesses** are those that are minimally or moderately involved in foreign operations.[3] They may purchase from foreign companies, export to other nations, enter into licensing agreements with foreign-based organizations, or conduct strategic alliances with foreign firms. **Multinational organizations** are companies that are heavily involved in overseas operations through direct investments abroad. They

**Table 11.1**

**U. S. Exports, Imports, and Balance of Trade (in billions of dollars)**

| Year | Exports | Imports | U. S. Balance of Trade |
|------|---------|---------|------------------------|
| 1970 | 42.7 | 40.0 | +2.7 |
| 1975 | 107.7 | 98.5 | +9.2 |
| 1980 | 220.6 | 244.9 | −24.3 |
| 1985 | 213.1 | 345.3 | −132.2 |
| 1990 | 393.6 | 495.3 | −101.7 |
| 1991 | 421.9 | 488.1 | −66.2 |
| 1992 | 447.5 | 525.1 | −77.6 |
| 1993 | 464.9 | 574.9 | −110.0 |
| 1994 | 512.4 | 663.8 | −151.4 |

*Source: Statistical Abstract of the United States*, 1992 (U.S. Department of Commerce, Bureau of the Census), p. 796; C. L. Bach, "U.S. International Transactions, Fourth Quarter and Year 1993," *Survey of Current Business*, March 1994, p. 44; *Statistical Abstract of the United States*, 1995, p. 815.

**Table 11.2** **U. S. and Foreign Direct Investment (in millions of dollars)**

| Year | U.S. Direct Investment Abroad | Foreign Direct Investment in the United States | Largest Targets of U.S. Direct Investments (1993) | | Largest Foreign Direct Investors in the United States (1993) | |
|---|---|---|---|---|---|---|
| 1970 | 75.5 | 13.3 | 1. United Kingdom | 96.4 | 1. Japan | 96.2 |
| 1975 | 124.1 | 27.7 | 2. Canada | 70.4 | 2. United Kingdom | 95.4 |
| 1980 | 215.4 | 83.0 | 3. Germany | 37.5 | 3. Netherlands | 68.5 |
| 1985 | 230.3 | 184.6 | 4. Switzerland | 32.9 | 4. Canada | 38.4 |
| 1990 | 430.5 | 394.9 | 5. Japan | 31.3 | 5. Germany | 34.7 |
| 1993 | 548.6 | 445.3 | | | | |

Source: Statistical Abstract of the United States, 1995 (U.S. Department of Commerce, Bureau of the Census), p. 806, 809; C. L. Bach, "U.S. International Transactions, Fourth Quarter and Year 1993," Survey of Current Business, March 1994, p. 44.

function on a country-by-country basis, with their subsidiaries operating independently of each other. **Global firms** are also heavily involved in foreign business and have made direct investments overseas, but their subsidiaries operate interdependently.[4] These distinctions are summarized in Table 11.3. Further elaborations on these differing levels of involvement are made in many of the following sections of this chapter. We begin with an examination of the international macroenvironment.

**Table 11.3** **Various Levels of Operations**

| Organization | Level of Involvement |
|---|---|
| Domestic organization | Chooses to operate totally within the confines of the United States. |
| International organization | Elects minimal or moderate international involvement. May purchase from foreign sources, export to other countries, license operations to foreign firms, or enter into strategic alliances with foreign-based companies. |
| Multinational organization | Chooses heavy international involvement. Makes direct investments abroad through starting its own operations in other countries or buying part or all of the ownership of foreign-based firms. Subsidiaries operate independently of one another on a country-by-country basis. |
| Global organization | Elects heavy international involvement. Makes direct investments abroad through starting its own operations in other countries or buying part or all of the ownership of foreign-based firms. Subsidiaries operate interdependently as a single, coordinated system. |

# MACROENVIRONMENT

As an organization's environment expands from domestic to international, management faces not only a larger number of environmental elements but also far greater environmental complexity. Chapter 2 suggested how certain macroenvironmental forces have strategic implications for top management. This section follows that same format but concentrates upon international forces in the macroenvironment: political-legal forces, economic forces, technological forces, and social forces.

## ■ Political-Legal Forces

All nations have their own particular laws and regulations that affect business activities. Some countries, for example, have rigid guidelines for hiring and firing employees; some require that a certain percentage of those employed by a foreign-owned business be citizens of the country in which the business operates; and some require that a portion of what is produced within their boundaries be exported to earn foreign exchange. These laws and regulations that are particular to each nation offer opportunities or pose threats to the business interested in operating across national boundaries. At times, the degree of opportunity or threat is influenced by major world political-legal trends.

The years between the end of World War II and the early 1980s can be characterized as a period during which the predominant political-legal trend was for the governments of industrialized countries to exert more influence over business operations. This trend was exhibited by governments in such countries as Great Britain, France, West Germany, Italy, Canada, and Japan. In some cases, governments even owned major manufacturers. For instance, Great Britain owned Jaguar and British Leyland, and West Germany owned Lufthansa. In France, the socialist government of Prime Minister François Mitterrand nationalized some major firms such as ITT-France and Honeywell-Bull in 1981. And Canadian legislation was passed requiring that energy companies operating within the borders of Canada be owned by Canadians.

This same trend also characterized the operations of businesses in less industrialized parts of the world. Communist governments, of course, permitted little, if any, free enterprise, preferring to run their economies through centralized state planning. In developing nations, key industries such as utilities, communications, steel, and raw materials extraction were generally owned by the government.

A second political-legal trend during this time period involved increased trade protection. Many countries increased the protection of their domestic industries through tariffs, import duties, and import restrictions. For example, in Latin American countries, import duties on a variety of products ranged from under 40 percent to more than 100 percent.[5] European and Southeast Asian nations also imposed heavy duties on imports. Even the United States imposed import fees on a variety of products, including food, steel, and cars. Furthermore, the United States convinced Japanese manufacturers to restrict "voluntarily" their exporting of cars to the United States. Likewise, European countries instituted import quotas on selected products such as Japanese stereos and watches.

## Entering the Japanese Auto Market

Much has been made of the barriers erected by the Japanese government to prevent foreign-made automobiles from being sold in Japan. And, in truth, many barriers exist. But aggressive automakers seem to find ways to compete on Japanese soil.

BMW, for example, viewed Japan as a growth market as early as a decade ago. It was able to enter the market by adapting its models to Japanese regulations and consumer needs, offering extended warranties, investing heavily in service facilities and parts inventories, conducting its own training for Japanese mechanics, and supervising its operations closely. Its commitment was unwavering; analysts estimated that BMW paid almost half a billion dollars alone for choice real estate on which to build showrooms in Tokyo. BMW has more than 125 outlets in Japan.

Other German companies, such as Volkswagen, Mercedes, and Audi, were following suit.

The result? In 1994, about two-thirds of the foreign-made cars registered in Japan were built in Germany. Mercedes and BMW each sold twice as many cars as GM, Ford, and Chrysler combined. Not coincidentally, both German automakers sold through their own dealers, whereas all three American companies continued to rely heavily on importers to sell their cars. It wasn't until late 1992 that some American products began arriving in Japan with steering wheels on the right, as the Japanese prefer.

The Germans' aggressive move into Japan could pay off for years to come. Japan is the world's second-largest automobile market, and Japanese car buyers have exhibited extreme brand loyalty. In fact, some analysts estimate that almost 70 percent of them buy from the same company—and often even from the same salesperson—every time they purchase a new car.

SOURCES: G. F. Adams, "The Impact of Japanese Auto VRAs on the U. S. and Japanese Economies," *Journal of Policy Modeling* (April 1994): pp. 147–164; J. Flint, "Japan and the J-Curve," *Forbes*, 14 March 1994, pp. 40–41; P. D. Ballew and R. H. Schnorbus, "The Impact of the Auto Industry on the Economy," *Chicago Fed Letter*, March 1994, pp. 1–4; W. Spindle, "Have You Driven a Ford Lately—in Japan?" *Business Week*, 21 February 1994, p. 37; "Foreign Car Sales in Japan," *Parade*, 22 March 1992, p. 16; P. Ingrassia, "Detroit's Big Three Are Trying to Conquer a New Market: Japan," *Wall Street Journal*, 19 November 1991; K. L. Miller, "What's This? American Cars Gaining in Japan?" *Business Week*, 22 July 1991, pp. 82–83; T. R. Reid, "U. S. Automakers Grind Gears in Japan," *Washington Post*, 23 September 1990; C. Rapoport, "You Can Make Money in Japan," *Fortune*, 12 February 1990, p. 92; B. Yates, "The Road to Mediocrity," *Washington Post Magazine*, 17 December 1989, p. 35; M. Berger, "How Germany Sells Cars Where Detroit Can't," *Business Week*, 9 September 1985, p. 45.

Protectionist measures not only involved the protection of home industries from foreign imports, but restrictions were also placed on exporting advanced technology to other countries. The United States, for instance, banned the export of certain electronic, nuclear, and defense-related products to many nations.

There were, of course, countervailing trends. To offset the impact of some of the protectionist measures, twenty-three countries entered into the cooperative General Agreement on Tariffs and Trade (GATT) in 1947. GATT has assisted in eradicating or relaxing quota and import license requirements, introducing fairer customs evaluation methods, opposing discriminatory internal taxes, and serving as a mediator between governments on trade issues. GATT membership has now reached ninety-five nations.

By the middle of the 1980s and into the 1990s, however, trends toward the reversal of trade protectionism and strong governmental influence in business operations were becoming evident. In the United States, new economic policies reduced, on the whole, governmental influence in business operations by deregulating certain industries, lowering corporate taxes, granting more generous depreciation allowances, and relaxing rules against mergers and acquisitions. A similar trend was evident in Great Britain. Jaguar, for instance, was sold to individual investors (and later purchased by Ford Motor Company), as was British Telecom. As the trend spread, France's insurance industry and previously nationalized banks and manufacturing businesses were sold to investors.

Furthermore, the countries of Europe banded together to develop a trade-free European Community. Today, Europe is moving gradually, but steadily, toward a single market of 340 million consumers. The European Economic Area, as it is called, is the largest trading bloc on earth, accounting for over 40 percent of the world's gross domestic product (GDP).[6] Meanwhile, across the Atlantic, the United States, Canada, and Mexico proposed a North American Free Trade Agreement to create a $6 trillion tariff-free market within a decade. Parenthetically, some experts have warned that with freer trade and during periods of political instability, Latin American investments in the United States may be increasingly motivated by capital flight.[7]

This trend toward less regulation even extended to the previous communist countries. As the nations of Eastern Europe overturned their governments, they began to permit free-enterprise operations and to invite foreign investment in their economies.[8] As a result of these developments, numerous firms worldwide have found a more receptive political-legal climate.

## ■ Economic Forces

Common economic indicators such as gross domestic product (GDP) can suggest opportunities for businesses when an economy is expanding or, conversely, can warn of threats when the economy is contracting. But the most challenging international economic variables for strategic planners are interest rates, inflation rates, and currency exchange rates.

For example, the cost of borrowing is very high in a number of Latin American countries, with annual interest rates sometimes exceeding 100 percent. These high interest rates are often accompanied by excessive rates of inflation. In small nations, like Bolivia, annual inflation has been as high as 26,000 percent.[9] But even larger and more industrialized countries, like Brazil, have experienced annual inflation rates of 2,700 percent.[10] Such common decisions as pricing products or estimating costs become almost impossible to make under such conditions. Furthermore, high inflation rates cause the prices of goods and services to rise and, hence, become less competitive in international trade.

Currency exchange rates present challenges because of their dramatic changes over time. For instance, the Mexican peso was devalued by about 75 percent relative to the world's major currencies during the 1980s. U.S. firms operating in Mexico received pesos for their products and services, and their pesos would buy far fewer dollars than before the devaluation. The devaluation, therefore, reduced their profits considerably. By the 1990s, however, wild fluctuations in exchange rates had moderated in other countries and their rate of inflation had declined. The value of the peso had a drop of more than 50 percent relative to the dollar between 1994 and 1995.

## ■ Technological Forces

Technology has a major impact on international business operations. For years, manufacturing firms in technologically advanced societies have sought plant location sites in countries with low labor or raw materials costs. Developing nations have generally welcomed such entrants. With them come an influx of financial resources, the opportunity for work force training, and the chance to acquire new technologies. In many cases, this interaction has benefited the developing country. Furthermore, some observers have even predicted that production technologies will be transferred from more advanced countries to such newly industrializing nations as Mexico, Brazil, Spain, Taiwan, Hong Kong, Singapore, and South Korea.[11] In this chapter, the term **technologically advanced nations** is used to refer to the United States, Canada, Japan, Australia, New Zealand, and the major industrial powers of Europe. The term **newly industrializing nations** refers to developing nations that have experienced rapid industrial growth over the past two decades. They were identified earlier in this paragraph. **Developing nations** is the term employed to refer to countries that have not yet experienced significant industrial development and includes any country not grouped under the two other categories.

However, the experiences of other developing nations have been quite disappointing. Although a firm's decision to operate in a foreign country is made for economic reasons, the host country often expects—but does not necessarily get—specific economic and social help in the form of assistance to local entrepreneurs, the establishment of research and development facilities, and the introduction of products relevant to its home market.[12] Such relationships do provide on-the-job training and improve the local economy, but the overall long-term contribution to the host country is questionable in the minds of some leaders of developing nations.[13]

Among the disappointments have been the results of technology transfer from the foreign firm to the host country:

> For example, firms such as Leyland Motors, General Electric, and Daimler-Benz have structured plants in various [developing nations]. The basic problem has continued to be the almost total dependence of the host countries on the multinationals for the provision of parts, motors, and product innovations.[14]

However, technology transfer is not the only source of disappointment for host countries. Their leaders also point to discontent with extractive industries:

> Whatever the raw material, it is argued, the nature of extractive industry constitutes a systematic depletion of the valuable national assets of the host country, while leaving little of enduring value. . . . All the training and technological transfer of this kind are highly specific to the nature of the industry. When bauxite, coal, and other ores are exhausted, the local people's gained knowledge can rarely be transferred to other national undertakings.[15]

Within this context, some of the leaders of developing nations have acquired negative attitudes toward foreign firms. Nevertheless, these countries will continue to need the expertise of the technologically advanced nations.[16] The key is for each party—the company and the host country—to develop an understanding of the wants and needs of the other. In an economic and technological sense, both parties need each other, and both can benefit significantly from a successful relationship.

### ■ Social Forces

Each of the world's countries has its own distinctive **culture**—that is, its generally accepted values, traditions, and patterns of behavior. Not surprisingly, these cultural differences interfere with the efforts of managers to understand and communicate with those in other societies. The unconscious reference to one's own cultural values—the **self-reference criterion**—has been suggested as the cause of most international business problems. Individuals become so accustomed to their own ways of looking at the world that they believe that any deviation from their perspective is not only wrong but also, perhaps, incomprehensible. But companies that can adjust to the culture of a host country will usually have the competitive edge. For instance, by adapting to local tastes rather than rigidly adhering to those of its U. S. customers, Domino's has found profitable business overseas through selling tuna and sweet corn pizzas in Japan and prawn and pineapple pizzas to Australians.[17]

Culture strongly influences the values that individuals hold. In turn, values influence the goals that individuals and organizations in a particular society set for themselves. The goals of managers in firms from technologically advanced countries, therefore, are likely to clash with the goals of the leaders of developing nations:

> On a macro-level, incongruencies in values have resulted in a major controversy over whether business unit goals should be influenced by market forces or by political priorities. The leaders of the multinationals have argued for market conditions influencing business decisions, whereas the developing nations have primarily sought corporate undertakings which benefit long-term social programs as well as business decisions which boost local employment.[18]

On a micro-level, managers of firms from technologically advanced nations often hold goals that are based on valuing mass production and efficient operations. However, mass production assumes certain worker-machine ratios, and efficient operations require particular worker-machine interfaces. Thus, these managers may demand behavior from local personnel that gives priority to productivity. The local employees, however, may resist these demands because they believe, on the basis of their own values, that business decisions should be secondary to social and religious norms. For instance, in some countries, it is customary to take a nap after lunch. In others, religious requirements call for taking several breaks during the workday to pray.[19]

It is clear that cross-cultural differences in norms and values require modifications in managerial behaviors:

> Doing business abroad often requires a great deal of patience and perseverance. In America, "getting down to business" and being efficient in pursuing and attempting to close sales agreements are considered desirable. . . . The U. S. businessperson is seen as displaying perseverance by quickly moving on to the next potential customer rather than by patiently pursuing an uninterested prospect. . . . Perseverance takes on a different connotation overseas. Whereas the American persists in certain large markets to make sales, successful foreign businesspersons are tenacious with select customers within those markets.[20]

In some countries, making the first business deal may take months or even years. The reason is that until personal friendships and trust develop between the potential buyer and seller, the people of those countries are unwilling to commit themselves to major business transactions.[21] After the first break-through, however, business transactions may become routine.

Social norms that are not well understood by outsiders often constrain business transactions. For instance, Japanese business executives expect their clients or suppliers to interact socially with them after working hours. These interactions can consume up to three or four hours an evening, several times a week. Westerners who decline to attend such social gatherings regularly are seriously handicapped in transacting business, because these social settings are requirements for serious business relationships.

Finally, managers of U.S.-based corporations operating abroad should remember that their firms have exceptionally high visibility because of their American origins. Hence, citizens of countries whose culture encourages strong political activism may disrupt the business operations of American corporations to send a political "message" to the U.S. government. For example, only two months after Euro Disneyland opened in France, hundreds of French farmers blocked its entrances with their tractors. The farmers wished to convey their displeasure with cuts in European Community farm subsidies that had been encouraged by the United States.[22]

---

### S T R A T E G I C   I N S I G H T

## *Tips for Doing Business in Asia*

- Realize that the Japanese rarely express negative emotions to foreigners. Hence, you can misread their intentions because they may smile even when angry.
- Exchange business cards with your hosts. Bilingual cards are especially appreciated. Show respect by carefully reading each card you receive.
- Control your physical gestures: Don't backslap, pat heads, or cross your legs. Even using your hands may make Japanese executives uncomfortable.
- Avoid jokes and conversation about politics.
- Always eat a bit of whatever food is offered; but never completely clean your plate, or you will be perceived as still being hungry.
- In Hong Kong, to signal your waiter to bring the check, pantomime a writing motion, using both hands. Never curl your index finger at anyone. That gesture is reserved for animals.
- Avoid giving flowers, since the wrong color or type can insult the recipient.

- Do not call on a company without an introduction. In Japan, particularly, meetings are taken very seriously.
- Don't employ the typical American "let's-get-to-the-point" negotiating style. The Japanese, in particular, want to get to know the people they are dealing with before doing business with them.
- Never bring your company's lawyer to a meeting before a deal is closed. Business relationships should be built on trust.
- Never brag—not even about your family. The Japanese, for instance, tend to be humble, even about their children's accomplishments.
- If you receive a compliment from a Chinese executive, deny it politely. Although the Chinese offer frequent compliments, they consider a "thank you" in response to be impolite.
- Never address South Koreans by their given names; that practice is thought to be rude.

SOURCES: A. Rashid, "South Asia: Out of the Shadow," *Far Eastern Economic Review*, 23 December 1993, p. 23; J. T. Yenckel, "Fearless Traveler: Sorting Through the Chaos of Culture," *Washington Post*, 20 October 1991; A. B. Stoddard, "Learning the Cultural Tricks of Foreign Trade," *Washington Business*, 18 June 1990, p. 11; F. H. Katayama, "How to Act Once You Get There," *Fortune, Special Issue: Asia in the 1990s*, Fall 1989, pp. 87–88; T. Holden and S. Woolley, "The Delicate Art of Doing Business in Japan," *Business Week*, 2 October 1989, p. 120.

## INDUSTRY ENVIRONMENT

The nature of industry competition in the international arena differs from one country to the next. In some nations, competing successfully may not necessarily depend on such familiar American concepts as bargaining power, the threat of new entrants, or substitute products. Rather, engaging in competition may be possible only if the company is willing to barter by trading the firm's products and services for goods from the host country. A number of Japanese companies, as an example, trade their products for oil in some markets of the Organization of Petroleum Exporting Countries (OPEC).

The industry environment is complicated by the potential for linkages between domestic and international competitive forces. For instance, when a strong overseas competitor enters the domestic market of a firm, the firm's most effective response may be to counter its foreign competitor's move by entering its domestic market:

> Effective counter-competition has a destabilizing impact on the foreign company's cash flows, product-related competitiveness, and decision making about integration. Direct market penetration can drain vital cash flows from the foreign company's domestic operations. This drain can result in lost opportunities, reduced income, and limited production, impairing the competitor's ability to make overseas thrusts.[23]

From a global perspective, industry analysis can be quite challenging. A firm, for instance, may produce its parts in one nation, assemble them in other countries, and sell the final product to another group of nations. As an example, RCA has located its business units in such diverse countries as Taiwan, Japan, Mexico, and Canada. The operations of these business units are coordinated with those of other RCA units located in the United States. Each business unit performs complementary manufacturing or support functions. Hence, one unit may manufacture components; others may perform subassembly work, warehousing, or distribution. Each business unit is an integral link in the overall strategy of RCA's world operations.[24] As might be expected, such industry forces as market position, bargaining power of suppliers and customers, and the threat of new entrants or substitute products have different ramifications for each of RCA's business units, even though, in unison, these units produce television sets.

The world's constantly improving communication networks have, in a sense, "shrunk" some global industries to the extent that a few corporations are able to use one television advertisement to promote their products or services. Cable News Network (CNN), for instance, is beamed into 78 million households in more than a hundred countries, and MTV Network reaches twenty-eight nations. Taking advantage of this "homogeneity," Levi Strauss, for example, produces one advertisement worldwide. It promotes its jeans through ads featuring American rock music and nonspeaking actors. As the director of MTV Europe states: "Eighteen-year-olds in Paris have more in common with 18-year-olds in New York than with their own parents. . . . They buy the same products, go to the same movies, listen to the same music, sip the same colas."[25] However, most firms must still customize the advertisements for their products along particular national or regional boundary lines.

## MISSION, GOALS, OBJECTIVES, AND S.W.O.T. ANALYSIS

An organization's mission, the reason for its existence, may be closely intertwined with international operations in several ways. For instance, a firm may need inputs from abroad. Wrigley, the chewing gum manufacturer, would be unable to produce its products without the gum base derived from trees in Southeast Asia. Virtually all of Japan's industries would come to a standstill if imports of raw materials from other nations were halted, since Japan's natural resources are quite limited.

Organizational mission and international involvement are also connected through the economic concept of **comparative advantage**. This concept refers to the idea that certain parts and products may be produced more cheaply or with higher quality in particular countries owing to advantages in labor costs or technology. Also, certain raw materials and natural resources may be extracted more economically in particular locales. For instance, the cost of drilling for oil is significantly lower and its availability is significantly greater in Saudi Arabia than in Europe. Because oil is the basic raw material for producing many chemical products, European chemical firms have sought joint ventures with oil companies in Saudi Arabia. For this reason, Japanese chemical companies are not major world competitors. Japan has no oil, and Japanese chemical firms have, to date, been unsuccessful in arranging joint ventures with firms in oil-producing countries.

Finally, some firms' missions require international connections for prestige reasons. The attempt to surround a perfume product, for instance, with a certain mystique seems to necessitate New York, London, and Paris connections. You may have noticed that the more prestigious brands of cosmetics and perfumes often have "New York, London, and Paris" conspicuously inscribed on their packages.

A firm's goals and objectives may also require global involvement. To reduce costs, for example, a firm may seek production sites in foreign countries. For political-legal reasons, organizations may need to locate manufacturing facilities abroad. For instance, establishing production facilities in selected countries can avoid problems with protectionist trade legislation. Finally, making products in other countries helps management understand the needs of foreign customers. Ford, for example, has twenty plants in Western Europe. Manufacturing there helped Ford engineers design windshield wipers for cars engaged in high-speed driving on the German autobahns.[26]

Remember that a firm's mission is defined within its external environmental opportunities and threats as well as in the context of its internal resource strengths and weaknesses. Top management, then, must evaluate the firm's internal resource strengths and weaknesses and the international environment's opportunities and threats. In the first part of the S.W.O.T. analysis, management can use the following questions as guidelines in evaluating the company's internal strengths and weaknesses:

- Does the firm have a strong market position in the countries in which it operates?
- Does the firm's product/service quality compare favorably with that of its world competitors?
- Does the firm have a technological advantage in the world regions where it operates its major businesses?

- Does the firm have a strong brand reputation in the countries in which it sells its products/services?
- Are the firm's managers and employees more talented than those of its major world competitors?
- Is the firm's financial position strong?
- Is the firm consistently more profitable than its world rivals?
- Are the firm's product and process research and development efforts likely to produce better results than those of its competitors?
- Are the firm's various world operations subject to unionization?

Answers to these questions may serve as a basis for evaluating the firm's strengths and weaknesses.

The following questions may guide management's thinking about the second part of the S.W.O.T. analysis, the opportunities and threats that exist in the firm's external environment:

- What threats and opportunities do political-legal forces present?
- What threats and opportunities are presented by economic forces?
- What threats and opportunities do technological forces present?
- What threats and opportunities are presented by social forces?
- What is the size of the industry(ies)?
- What are the growth rate and potential of the industry(ies)?
- Is the industry(ies) cyclical? If so, can the cyclicality be smoothed out across different world markets?
- Is the industry(ies) subject to fluctuations in demand because of seasonable factors? If so, can these seasonal factors be smoothed out across different world markets?
- How intense in world competition is the industry(ies)?
- What is the median industry(ies) profitability? What is its (their) potential profitability?
- Is the industry(ies) susceptible to unionization?
- What is the rate of innovation in the industry(ies)?

## CORPORATE-LEVEL STRATEGIES

In chapters 4 and 5, we saw that firms have available to them several corporate-level strategies: growth, stability, or retrenchment. Using growth strategies, many firms attempt to gain market share to reduce their unit costs of operations. Large increases in sales are sometimes available only through global expansion. Coca-Cola and PepsiCo realized many years ago that significant increases in sales were more likely to be achieved overseas than in the already saturated U. S. marketplace.

Likewise, Caterpillar has become one of the world's leading construction equipment makers because of its global involvement.[27]

> Two-thirds of the total product cost of construction equipment is in heavy components—engines, axles, transmissions, and hydraulics—whose manufacturing costs are capital intensive and highly sensitive to economies of scale. Caterpillar turned its network of sales in different countries into a cost advantage by designing product lines that use identical components and investing heavily in a few

large-scale, state-of-the-art component manufacturing facilities to fill worldwide demand.[28]

Corporate growth strategies may include strategic alliances, license agreements, or direct investments. **International strategic alliances** are partnerships of two or more firms from different nations that join together to accomplish specific projects or to cooperate in select areas of business. One of the best-known examples of an international strategic alliance is the automobile production facility in California that is owned jointly by General Motors and Toyota.

An **international license agreement** is the granting of permission by a firm in one country to a company in another nation to use its technology, brand name, production processes, or other operations. A fee is paid to the granting firm by the company being licensed. For example, pharmaceutical firms such as Merck and Upjohn have licensed organizations in other parts of the world to produce and sell their brands of drugs.

**International franchising** is a special type of licensing in which a local franchisee pays the franchisor, headquartered in another country, for the right to use the franchisor's brand names, promotion, materials, and procedures.[29] Examples may be found in hotels (Hilton), soft-drink bottling (Coca-Cola), and fast-food restaurants (McDonald's).

**Direct investments** may take place in one of two ways. A firm may engage in internal growth by establishing physical facilities and operations in another country. Many well-known companies, such as IBM and Citicorp, pursue this route. Alternatively, a company may grow externally by merging with or by acquiring all or part of the ownership of a foreign firm. For example, Electrolux of Sweden purchased U.S.-based Poulan/Weedeater.

Stability is a corporate strategy that a firm adopts when its goal is to maintain its current size and scope of operations in the world. Such a strategy obviously would not include engaging in new strategic alliances, license agreements, or direct investments.

When a firm's performance is disappointing, a corporate retrenchment strategy may be necessary. Retrenchment may involve revising products/markets in particular nations, pruning assets and work forces in other locations, selling or spinning off parts of world operations, selling the entire business, or—in the worst-case scenario—liquidating it. Firestone, for instance, attempted to reverse its poor performance in the early 1980s by selling its operations in five foreign countries and by reducing its ownership to a minority position in other foreign subsidiaries. Eventually, however, Firestone was sold to Bridgestone, a Japanese-based competitor.[30] Next we examine level of operations and market share.

## LEVEL OF OPERATIONS AND MARKET SHARE

As we saw earlier in this chapter, a business may be involved only in its domestic market or it may compete overseas at one of three levels: international, multinational, or global. Within the domestic, international, or multinational context, an enterprise may compete successfully with a high or low market share. However, firms that choose to compete at the global level usually operate effectively only through maintaining a high market share. The relationship between level of operations and market share is illustrated in Figure 11.1.

# STRATEGIC INSIGHT

## Strategic Alliances: A Popular Way to Enter Foreign Markets

Increasingly, American companies are looking to strategic alliances as efficient ways to enter foreign markets. For instance, U.S.-based firms have formed more than 2,400 strategic alliances with European companies since 1980. Such companies as Occidental Petroleum, Atlantic Richfield, Texaco, Xerox, and Coca-Cola have engaged in strategic alliances with firms in China since the mid-1980s.

Why the popularity of strategic alliances? Both partners often hope to achieve several ends: lower the costs (and the risks) of high-technology product development, increase sales so that greater economies of scale may be attained, broaden a firm's product line by joining with a company that makes complementary products, and gain a lookout post so that other competitors' moves may be more easily tracked.

### Sony's Venture with Apple Computer
A few years ago, the giant Japanese consumer electronics manufacturer, Sony, grew interested in the personal computer (PC) industry. During this same time, U.S.-based Apple Computer felt the need to expand its product line to include a small laptop computer. But Apple didn't have the required miniaturization skills. Because the PC industry is characterized by frequent product introductions and brief product life cycles, Apple's management believed that the company couldn't wait to develop internally the skills that were needed.

So Apple asked Sony to manufacture the laptop for them. The result was the Macintosh PowerBook 100, which quickly became a best-seller.

The two companies were an ideal match. For some years, Sony had produced some of the floppy disk drives, monitors, and power supplies used in Apple's larger Macintosh computers.

### Chrysler's AMC Venture with Beijing Automotive Works
Of course, some strategic alliances end in failure. After four years of on-again and off-again negotiations, American Motors Corporation (AMC), now a subsidiary of Chrysler, and the Chinese-owned Beijing Automotive Works agreed to produce Jeeps jointly. China offered not only a huge market but also low labor costs and an excellent location for exporting to all of Asia.

But problems arose quickly. Most fundamentally, the two partners could never agree on the nature of the Jeep to be produced. And U.S. executives learned too late that they did not have the right to convert their Chinese earnings into dollars—meaning that the venture often did not have enough hard currency to buy parts from Detroit, because most of its output was sold inside China. As the shaky partnership continued, American managers learned that Beijing Automotive Works was hoarding proceeds from Chinese sales at about the same time that China announced a hefty increase in duties on parts kits imported from Detroit. Shortly thereafter, U.S. managers departed from the country, leaving the Chinese to run the assembly line on their own. Although China still holds the controversial most favored nation trade status, Chrysler has made no attempt to reenter the partnership.

SOURCES: S. Weintraub, "Nafta Benefits Flow to Both Sides of Rio Grande," *Wall Street Journal Interactive Edition*, 10 May 1996; R. L. Rose, "For Whirlpool, Asia Is the New Frontier," *Wall Street Journal*, 25 April 1996, pp. B1, B4; "A Simpler Model of International Joint Venture Distributorships: The American-Kuwaiti Experience," *Omega*, October 1995, pp. 525–538; A. Yan and B. Gray, "Bargaining Power, Management Control, and Performance in United States-China Joint Ventures: A Comparative Case Study," *Academy of Management Journal* 37(6), 1994: 1478–1517; S. Wilhelm, "International Ventures Focus on Asia and Russia," *Puget Sound Business Journal*, 12 May 1995, p. 9A; C. Smith, "Investment: Neighbor's Keeper," *Far Eastern Economic Review*, 10 March 1994, p. 56; R. B. Egen, "The Health of Nations," *Journal of Business Strategy*, March-April 1993, pp. 33–37; B. R. Schlender, "Apple's Japanese Ally," *Fortune*, 4 November 1991, pp. 151–152; J. Mann, *Beijing Jeep* (New York: Simon & Schuster, 1990).

**Figure 11.1**               **Competing Domestically, Internationally, Multinationally, Globally, and Market Share Goals**

LEVEL OF OPERATIONS

|  |  | Domestic Organizations | International Organizations | Multinational Organizations | Global Organizations |
|---|---|---|---|---|---|
| **MARKET SHARE GOALS** | **High** | Domestic, high share | International, high share | Multinational, high share | Global, high share |
| | **Low** | Domestic, low share | International, low share | Multinational, low share | |

Some businesses may be involved only in their domestic market. In certain cases, they may not yet be subject to foreign competitive pressures. Some realty companies that compete only in local towns serve as examples. On a national basis, these companies operate with very small market shares. Other competitors, such as Century 21, sell real estate nationwide and have large market shares.

Moving outside the domestic market, some companies choose to be involved on an international basis. They operate in various countries but limit their involvement to importing, exporting, licensing, or strategic alliances. The act of exporting alone can significantly benefit even a small company. For instance, Vita-Mix Corporation, a small Ohio business ($15 million in annual sales), began exporting its blenders to such countries as Norway and Venezuela. Since that move, Vita-Mix has more than doubled its work force by hiring sixty-three new employees even though it is located in an economically depressed area and its overall market share is tiny.[31]

Still other companies are involved multinationally. They have direct investments in other countries, and their subsidiaries operate independently of one another. As an example, Colgate-Palmolive has attained a large worldwide market share through its decentralized operations in a number of foreign markets.

Finally, some firms are globally involved. They have direct investments abroad and operate their subsidiaries interdependently. Caterpillar is an example of such a firm. Some of its various world subsidiaries produce components in different countries, other subsidiaries assemble these components, and still other units sell the finished products. Caterpillar has achieved its low-cost position by producing its own heavy components for its large global market. If its various subsidiaries operated independently and only produced for their individual regional markets, Caterpillar would be unable to realize economies of scale.

Global firms normally attempt to gain a high market share. Coordinating an interdependent global system is extremely complex, and this complexity—and expense—can be justified only when a high market share is attainable and it is feasible to profitably coordinate the operations of multiple subsidiaries.

## BUSINESS UNIT AND FUNCTIONAL STRATEGIES

Business units may adopt any one of a number of generic strategies, as discussed in chapter 6. If low market share is the business unit's goal, then management may choose from among the strategies of niche–low-cost, niche-differentiation, or niche–low-cost/differentiation. These strategies are appropriate

### STRATEGIC INSIGHT

## *Coca-Cola: A Multinational Firm*

Almost half of all the soft drinks consumed in the world are made by Coca-Cola. (Its nearest competitor, PepsiCo, has less than one-fourth of the world market.) Its overseas business is quite profitable: About 68 percent of Coca-Cola's sales and 80 percent of its profits come from 170 countries outside the United States.

What's the secret behind Coke's international success? There may be several.

First, the firm's brand name has been well known across the globe since World War II. Second, Coke's management is patient. It spent several million dollars in China and waited fifteen years to make a profit. Third, the firm pays attention to the details. Coke considers no retail outlet too small to sell its products. In Japan, for instance, Coca-Cola has held seminars for owners of mom-and-pop stores on how to compete with larger outlets. Not surprisingly, Coca-Cola–Japan is Coca-Cola's largest profit center, even larger than Coke–U.S.

Fourth, Coca-Cola is consistent, unless the situation requires flexibility. In much of the world, Coke's package, logo, taste, and adver-

tising are the same. But in countries that are unfamiliar with soft drinks, Coke has modified the flavor of its products to conform more closely to local tastes.

Fifth, it enters new markets intelligently. For instance, to cut through red tape and speed up the entry process, Coke often offers bottling franchises to the nation's most powerful companies. Then to control the bottlers, it sometimes buys part of the firm. In the last decade alone, Coke invested more than $1 billion in bottling strategic alliances.

The future looks bright indeed. Although annual sales growth in the United States averages only 2 or 3 percent, yearly sales are increasing in such large markets as Mexico and Brazil by about 25 percent. Coca-Cola recently doubled its capacity in China, where it sells more than 100 million cases annually. The company is now moving aggressively into Vietnam.

Overall, Coca-Cola expects world sales to double between 1990 and the year 2000. According to insiders, Coke's biggest challenge today is keeping up with world demand.

SOURCES: "Russian Coca-Cola Site Opened by Inchape," *Wall Street Journal*, 11 September 1995, p. A8; E. DeMarco, "Troubles Worsen for Coke Joint Venture in India," *Atlanta Business Chronicle*, 7 July 1995, p. 15A; E. Beck, "Where West Faced East, Colas Now War; Coke is Ahead in Eastern Europe; Pepsi Fires Back," *Wall Street Journal*, 7 September 1995, p. A10; G. G. Marcial, "Two Reasons Why Coke Is It: China and Russia," *Business Week*, 7 March 1994, p. 106; K. Barnes, "On the '90s Ho Chi Minh Trail," *Advertising Age*, 7 February 1994, p. 4; "Lowe Gives Diet Coke Everyman Feel in New Ads," *Marketing*, 27 January 1994, p. 1; M. J. McCarthy, "As a Global Marketer, Coke Excels by Being Tough and Consistent," *Wall Street Journal*, 19 December 1989.

for domestic, international, and multinational enterprises. For instance, Rolls-Royce, an international company, uses the niche-differentiation strategy. It maintains a small market share internationally by selling its cars only to very wealthy buyers in particular nations.

On the other hand, if the goal of a business unit is to attain a large market share, it has available the low-cost, differentiation, low-cost–differentiation, or multiple strategies. These strategies may be adopted by domestic, international, multinational, and global companies. McDonald's is an example of an international company that has experienced success with the low-cost–differentiation strategy. Colgate-Palmolive serves as an illustration of a multinational firm that has successfully employed the low-cost–differentiation strategy. Caterpillar operates with success as a global firm using low-cost–differentiation.

No generic strategy can be successfully implemented without careful planning, execution, and coordination of each business unit's functional departments.[32] In formulating functional strategies, managers must be aware that functions are interrelated. Each functional area, in attaining its purpose, must mesh its activities with the activities of the other functional departments. The extent to which all of the business unit's functional tasks mesh smoothly determines the effectiveness of the unit's generic strategy.

For domestic, international, and multinational companies, the coordination of functional strategies may be undertaken independently within each business unit. Hence, international and multinational companies generally coordinate functional strategies on a country-by-country basis. Global firms, however, coordinate functional strategies across the firm's business units located in various countries, because their units' actions are interdependent.

## STRATEGY IMPLEMENTATION

Earlier, in chapters 8 and 9, we learned that structure and behavior are key aspects of strategy and implementation. Whatever organizational structure is adopted by a business that operates in two or more countries, the relationship between its headquarters and its subsidiaries may be either bilateral or multilateral.[33] International and multinational firms generally have bilateral, independent relationships between their headquarters and subsidiaries. This type of relationship, in which the headquarters interacts independently with each subsidiary, is depicted in Figure 11.2.

There are advantages to bilateral relationships. Take, for instance, the case of Bausch & Lomb, the maker of such optical products as Ray-Ban sunglasses and contact lenses. Headquarters sets the firm's overall strategic direction and then allows local management to make all other decisions. As a result of recently permitting managers on the scene to determine the design for sunglasses—so that the designs for the European and Asian markets are now quite different—Bausch & Lomb's international sales have increased from one quarter to approximately half of its total revenue, and the firm now controls 40 percent of the world market for sunglasses.

Global firms, on the other hand, usually maintain multilateral, interdependent relationships between their headquarters and subsidiaries. Figure 11.3 portrays this situation in which the operations of the subsidiaries are interdependent. The primary advantage of multinational relationships is that efficiencies

**Figure 11.2**    **Bilateral Relationships Between Headquarters and Subsidiaries of International or Multinational Organizations**

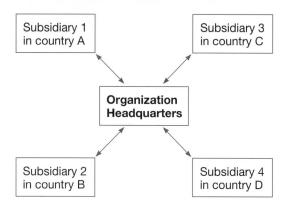

can be gained via specialization of operations in countries that are well-suited to particular operations.

Certainly, operating outside one's own country offers special challenges in areas such as leadership and maintaining a strong organizational culture. Some countries, for instance, resist innovation and radical new approaches to conducting business. Others, however, welcome such change. Swedish companies, for instance, have led the way in employing autonomous work groups that manage themselves.

Recall the dangers of the self-reference criterion. All too often managers believe that the leadership styles and organizational culture that worked in their home country should work elsewhere. But as we have seen, each nation has its own unique culture, norms, traditions, values, and beliefs. Hence, it should be

**Figure 11.3**    **Multilateral Relationships Between Headquarters and Subsidiaries of a Global Organization**

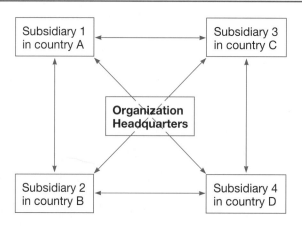

obvious—but often is not—that leadership styles, motivation programs, and organizational values and norms must be tailored to fit the unique culture of each country in which the organization operates.

# SUMMARY

This chapter focuses on businesses that choose to operate in the world marketplace. Ordinarily, such operations evolve gradually. Most companies begin their involvement with foreign countries through importing or exporting products. They may become further involved through licensing select organizations in other countries to use their technology, production processes, or brand names. Or they may enter into partnerships or strategic alliances with foreign companies as a means of penetrating certain markets. Still deeper involvement may be achieved by initiating direct investments in particular countries.

There are three levels of foreign business operations: international, in which a domestic company is minimally or moderately involved in foreign operations through importing, exporting, licensing, or conducting strategic alliances; multinational, in which the enterprise makes direct investments abroad and operates each of its foreign subsidiaries independently on a country-by-country basis; and global, in which the firm also makes direct investments abroad but operates its subsidiaries in an interdependent fashion.

Much as a domestic company does, the organization that chooses to engage in world commerce must analyze its macroenvironment and industry environment. The difference, of course, is that as an organization's environment expands from domestic to global, management faces not only a larger number of environmental elements but also far greater environmental complexity.

Within the organization, mission, goals, and objectives may be closely intertwined with world operations. Likewise, corporate-level strategies must take into account unique global considerations.

Enterprises that operate at the international or multinational level may compete successfully with either a high or a low market share, depending upon their particular mission and goals. Global firms, however, must usually maintain a high market share for effective operation.

At the business unit level, the generic strategies of niche–low-cost, niche-differentiation, and niche–low-cost/differentiation are appropriate for international and multinational businesses that desire to maintain a low market share. On the other hand, if the business unit's goal is to attain a high market share, it has available the low-cost, differentiation, low-cost–differentiation, and multiple strategies. These strategies may be adopted by international, multinational, and global companies.

In determining functional strategies, international and multinational businesses coordinate their functional activities on a country-by-country basis. Global firms, however, coordinate functional strategies across the firm's business units located in various countries, since their units' actions are interdependent.

As management implements its strategies, it must take into account the unique culture of each country in which its business operates. The leadership styles, motivation programs, and organizational culture that worked in the United States may need to be tailored to each individual international setting.

## TAKE IT TO THE NET

We invite you to visit the Wright page on the Prentice Hall Web site at:

**http://www.prenhall.com/wright**

for this chapter's World Wide Web exercise.

## KEY CONCEPTS

**Comparative advantage**   The concept that products or parts can be produced less expensively or with higher quality or that natural resources can be extracted more economically in particular geographic locations owing to advantages in labor costs, technology, or availability of such natural resources as minerals and timbers.

**Culture**   The generally accepted values, traditions, and patterns of behavior of a societal group.

**Developing nation**   A country that has not yet experienced significant industrial development.

**Direct investment**   When investors in one country own at least 10 percent of a private enterprise in another country.

**Global firm**   A firm, heavily involved in the world marketplace through direct investments, that operates its subsidiaries in an interdependent fashion.

**International business**   A business that is minimally or moderately involved in foreign operations. It may import or export goods, enter into licensing agreements with foreign-based organizations, or conduct strategic alliances with foreign companies.

**International franchising**   A special type of licensing in which a franchisee pays the franchisor, headquartered in another country, for the right to use the franchisor's brand names, promotion, materials, and procedures.

**International license agreement**   The granting of permission by an organization in one country to a company in another nation to use its technology, brand name, production processes, or other operations. A fee is paid to the granting organization by the company being licensed.

**International strategic alliance**   A partnership of two or more organizations from different nations that join together to accomplish specific projects or to cooperate in selected areas of business.

**Multinational organization**   An organization, heavily involved in overseas operations through direct investments, that functions on a country-by-country basis, with its subsidiaries operating independently of one another.

**Newly industrializing nation**   A developing nation that has experienced rapid industrial growth over the past two decades. This category includes Mexico, Brazil, Spain, Taiwan, Hong Kong, Singapore, and South Korea.

**Self-reference criterion**   The unconscious reference to one's own cultural values.

**Technologically advanced nation**   A nation that is grouped among the major industrial powers of the world. This category includes the United States, Canada, Japan, Australia, New Zealand, and the industrialized nations of Europe.

## DISCUSSION QUESTIONS

1. What businesses can you identify that are not directly affected by foreign competition?

2. Obtain the latest listing of the world's largest industrial corporations. How many U. S.-based firms are on the list? How does this figure compare with a listing from 1960 or 1970?

3. Explain how a domestic company, over time, expands to become a global firm. What are the normal stages in this process?

4. Discuss fully the differences between a multinational enterprise and a global firm.

5. What is the major distinction between an international enterprise and a multinational organization?

6. Forecast what future world political-legal trends might affect global business.

7. How do the goals of a multinational or global organization differ from those of the host country? Why do they differ?

8. Explain how the self-reference criterion can lead to problems for U. S. managers operating abroad.

9. Why might an organization's mission influence management to engage in world operations?

10. Explain the relationship between a business's level of operations and its market share goals.

## STRATEGIC MANAGEMENT EXERCISES

1. Select a well-known energy company. From your recollection of current events, what global opportunities and threats does the macroenvironment pose for this company? Identify several specific opportunities and threats for each of the following forces: political-legal, economic, technological, and social.

2. Identify a particular company in a well-defined industry, such as automobiles or computers. From your recollection of current events, analyze that company's industry environment from a world perspective. You may wish to use relevant sections of the "Industry Analysis Worksheet" from Worksheet 2 at the end of chapter 2 to guide your analysis.

3. Acquire the annual report of a firm that operates in more than two countries. Does its annual report specifically identify its mission and goals in global terms? What suggestions would you make to improve this company's mission and goal statements?

4. Using a global firm of your choice, determine what corporate-level and business unit–level strategies it has adopted. Give evidence to support your answers.

5. Assume that you are a member of the top management team of a food-processing company that follows a corporate growth strategy. Your company has decided to expand into both the western and eastern regions of the European continent. Specifically, which countries would you suggest as appropriate for licensing agreements? Why? In which would you prefer to make direct investments? Why?

# NOTES

1. "Fortune's Global 500," *Fortune*, 26 July 1994, pp. 188–234.

2. "Global Banking," *The Banker*, February 1994, pp. 49–52; "International Bank Scorecard," *Business Week*, 6 July 1992, p. 63.

3. Some firms initially enter into international business through a strategic alliance. See J. Bleeke and D. Ernst, "Is Your Strategic Alliance Really a Sale?" *Harvard Business Review*, 73 no. 1 (January-February 1995): 97–105. Other firms adopt a different mode of entry. See F. Robles, "International Market Entry Strategies and Performance of United States Catalog Firms," *Journal of Direct Marketing* 8, no. 1 (1994): 59–70.

4. See K. Ohmae, "Putting Global Logic First," *Harvard Business Review* 73 no. 1 (January-February 1995): 119–125. Also see P. Gray, "Productivity Through Globalization," *Information Systems Management* 11, no. 1 (1994): 90–91.

5. *International Financial Statistics Yearbook* (Washington, DC: International Monetary Fund, 1989).

6. C. Rapoport, "Europe Looks Ahead to Hard Choices," *Fortune*, 14 December 1992, p. 145.

7. J. A. King and J. D. Daniels, "Latin American and Caribbean Direct Investments in the U. S.," *Multinational Business Review* 2 (1994): 1–10.

8. F. M. E. Raiszadeh, M. M. Helms, and M. C. Varner, "How Can Eastern Europe Help American Manufacturers?" *The International Executive* 35 (1993): 357–365.

9. *International Financial Statistics Yearbook*, pp. 35–52.

10. C. S. Manegold and M. Kepp, "Elegant Armed Robbery," *Newsweek*, 2 April 1990, p. 30.

11. B. Schofield, "Building-and-Rebuilding—A Global Company," *The McKinsey Quarterly* 2, 1994: 37–45; R. B. Reich, *The Next American Frontier* (New York: Times Books, 1983).

12. A. R. Negandhi, "Multinational Corporations and Host Governments' Relationships: Comparative Study of Conflict and Conflicting Issues," *Human Relations* 33 (1980): 534–535.

13. P. Wright, D. Townsend, J. Kinard, and J. Iverstine, "The Developing World to 1990: Trends and Implications for Multinational Business," *Long Range Planning* 15, no. 4 (July–August 1982): 116–125.

14. Ibid., p. 119. Reprinted from *Long Range Planning*, Vol. 15, P. Wright et al., "The Developing World to 1990: Trends and Implications for Multinational Business," pp. 116–125, Copyright (1982), with permission from Pergamon Press Ltd, Headington Hill Hall, Oxford OX3 OBW, UK.

15. Ibid., p. 119. Reprinted from *Long Range Planning*, Vol. 15, P. Wright et al., "The Developing World to 1990: Trends and Implications for Multinational Business," pp. 116–125, Copyright (1982), with permission from Pergamon Press Ltd, Headington Hill Hall, Oxford OX3 OBW, UK.

16. J. B. Treece and K. L. Miller, "New Worlds to Conquer," *Business Week*, 28 February 1994, pp. 50–52.

17. M. J. Williams, "Rewriting the Export Rules," *Fortune*, 23 April 1990, p. 89.

18. P. Wright, "MNC—Third World Business Unit Performance: Application of Strategic Elements," *Strategic Management Journal* 5 (1984): 232.

19. P. Wright, "Doing Business in Islamic Markets," *Harvard Business Review* 59, no. 1 (January–February 1981): 34–40.

20. P. Wright, "Systematic Approach to Finding Export Opportunities," in D. N. Dickson, ed., *Managing Effectively in the World Marketplace* (New York: Wiley, 1983), pp. 338–339.

21. P. Wright, "Organizational Behavior in Islamic Firms," *Management International Review* 21, no. 2 (1981): 86–94.

22. "No Fun: Tourists Stranded As Farmers Cut Off 'Euro Disneyland' Site," *Harrisonburg* (Va.) *Daily News-Record*, 27 June 1992.

23. C. M. Watson, "Counter-Competition Abroad to Protect Home Markets," in D. N. Dickson, ed., *Managing Effectively in the World Marketplace* (New York: Wiley, 1983), p. 359.

24. P. Wright, "The Strategic Options of Least-Cost, Differentiation, and Niche," *Business Horizons* 29, no. 2 (March–April 1986): 22.

25. K. Wells, "Global Ad Campaigns, After Many Missteps, Finally Pay Dividends," *Wall Street Journal*, 27 August 1992.

26. T. Eiben, "U. S. Exporters on a Global Roll," *Fortune*, 29 June 1992, p. 94.

27. T. Hout, M. Porter, and E. Rudder, "How Global Companies Win Out," in D. N. Dickson, ed., *Managing Effectively in the World Marketplace* (New York: Wiley, 1983), pp. 188–191.

28. Ibid., p. 189.

29. P. Chan and R. Justis, "Franchise Management in East Asia," *Academy of Management Executive* 4 (1990): 75–85.

30. Z. Schiller, "Can Bridgestone Make the Climb?" *Business Week*, 27 February 1989, pp. 78–79; "Survival in the Basic Industries: How Four Companies Hope to Avoid Disaster," *Business Week*, 26 April 1982, pp. 74–76.

31. W. J. Holstein and K. Kelly, "Little Companies, Big Exports," *Business Week*, 13 April 1992, p. 70.

32. B. Parker and M. M. Helms, "Generic Strategies and Firm Performance in a Declining Industry," *Management International Review* 32 (1992): 23–29.

33. Wright, "MNC—Third World Business Unit Performance: Application of Strategic Elements," pp. 231–240.

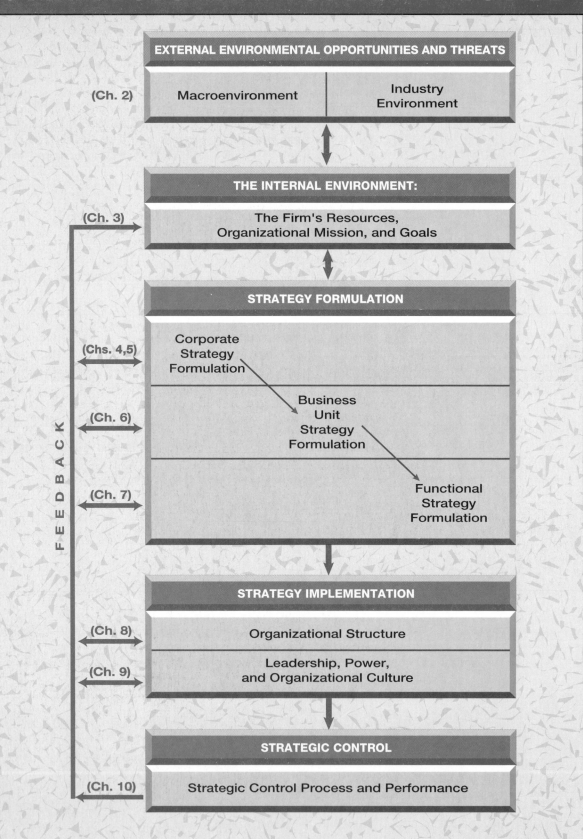

# STRATEGIC MANAGEMENT MODEL

**EXTERNAL ENVIRONMENTAL OPPORTUNITIES AND THREATS**

(Ch. 2)

| Macroenvironment | Industry Environment |

**THE INTERNAL ENVIRONMENT:**

(Ch. 3)

The Firm's Resources, Organizational Mission, and Goals

**STRATEGY FORMULATION**

(Chs. 4,5)

Corporate Strategy Formulation

(Ch. 6)

Business Unit Strategy Formulation

(Ch. 7)

Functional Strategy Formulation

**STRATEGY IMPLEMENTATION**

(Ch. 8)

Organizational Structure

(Ch. 9)

Leadership, Power, and Organizational Culture

**STRATEGIC CONTROL**

(Ch. 10)

Strategic Control Process and Performance

FEEDBACK

# Strategic Management in Not-for-Profit Organizations

T he basic principles of strategic management presented in this book are equally applicable to profit and not-for-profit organizations. It is important, for instance, that all organizations analyze their environment; formulate a mission, goals, and objectives; develop appropriate strategies; implement those strategies; and control their strategic direction. However, in a more specific sense, there are some distinct differences between profit and not-for-profit organizations that have significant strategic implications. This chapter examines those differences.

## TYPES OF NOT-FOR-PROFIT ORGANIZATIONS

Although not-for-profit organizations can be categorized in a number of ways, a basic classification consists of two groups: private not-for-profit organizations (which we will refer to as nonprofit organizations) and public not-for-profit organizations (which we will term public organizations). Some significant differences between business organizations and these two types of not-for-profit organizations are illustrated in Table 12.1.

**Nonprofit organizations** are entities that attempt to contribute to the good of society and are supported by private funds. Examples of such organizations include the following:

- Private educational institutions (e.g., Harvard University, the University of Chicago)
- Charities (e.g., Easter Seal Society, March of Dimes)

**Table 12.1** | **Some Differences Between Profit and Not-for-Profit Organizations**

|  | *Business Organization* | *Nonprofit Organization* | *Public Organization* |
|---|---|---|---|
| Ownership | Private | Private | Public |
| Funding | Sales of products and services | Membership dues, contributions from private and/or public sources, sale of products and services | Taxes and user fees |
| Types | Single proprietorship, partnership, corporation | Educational, charitable, social service, health service, foundation, cultural, and religious | Federal government, state government, local government |

- Social service organizations (e.g., Alcoholics Anonymous, Girl Scouts of the U. S.A.)
- Health service organizations (e.g., Houston's Methodist Hospital, Johns Hopkins Health System)
- Foundations (e.g., Ford Foundation, Rockefeller Foundation)
- Cultural organizations (e.g., Los Angeles Philharmonic Orchestra, Chicago's Field Museum of Natural History)
- Religious institutions (e.g., St. Patrick's Cathedral, Memphis's Bellevue Baptist Church)

**Public organizations** are those created, funded, and regulated by the public sector. They are largely synonymous with what we commonly term *government* and include agencies at all levels of government, such as the following:

- Federal government agencies (e.g., Internal Revenue Service, United States Navy, Environmental Protection Agency)
- State government agencies (e.g., University of Kentucky, Texas Department of Corrections, Pennsylvania Turnpike Authority)
- Local government agencies (e.g., Dallas Public Library, Dade County Sheriff's Department, New York City Transit Authority)

In the United States, almost 18.5 million people are employed in public organizations, more than the number employed in manufacturing jobs.[1]

Both nonprofit and public organizations are indispensable to maintaining a civilized society. Many of society's essential needs cannot be provided by for-profit organizations. For instance, most individuals could not afford to pay for private police protection, and each major city has one or more "charity" hospital where the indigent can receive medical care.

The products and services of businesses can be obtained only by those who pay for them, but the outputs of public organizations and those of many nonprofit organizations are available to virtually all members of society. For instance, anyone—even a tourist—can receive the protection of a city's police force; anyone can travel along a toll-free interstate highway; and any child with birth defects is eligible for help from the March of Dimes. Some nonprofit organizations, of course, restrict their goods or services only to those who pay for the cost of providing the outputs. Examples are private universities (which exist to provide the public with an alternative to secular or mass education) and some cultural organizations (which must sell tickets to cover their costs but also usually offer some special annual events that are free to the public at large).

# STRATEGIC ISSUES FOR NONPROFIT AND PUBLIC ORGANIZATIONS

This section examines some key strategic management issues in nonprofit and public organizations. First, we look at how environmental analysis may be conducted by these organizations. Then, we determine how they may develop their mission, goals, and objectives. We analyze next how they could formulate, implement, and control their strategies. Finally, we suggest some ways that not-for-profit organizations can increase their strategic management effectiveness.

## ■ Environmental Analysis

As the environment of not-for-profit organizations becomes increasingly dynamic, strategic management becomes more and more important. For example, nonprofit organizations have recently experienced reductions in federal aid and changes in tax laws that have reduced the incentive for corporations and individuals to make contributions. Simultaneously, competition for financial donations among nonprofits has increased with the rise of organizations dedicated to combating AIDS, Alzheimer's disease, child abuse, and drunk driving.[2]

Likewise, public organizations that once had a near monopoly in certain services, such as the U.S. Postal Service, are experiencing rapid change. Over the past few years, the Postal Service has felt increasing competitive pressure in express mail and the parcel business from such rivals as United Parcel Service and Federal Express. Additionally, in first-class mail, the Postal Service is losing business to a product substitute—the business-owned facsimile (fax) machine. Under such conditions, the necessity of planning well and operating effectively and efficiently becomes clear.

Two of the primary ways in which the environment of not-for-profit organizations differs from the environment of business organizations are in their sources of revenue and in the composition and concerns of their stakeholder groups. The following subsections explore these differences.

### Sources of Revenue

Although there are a number of differences between businesses and not-for-profit organizations, perhaps the chief distinction is the source of the organization's revenues. Business income is derived almost exclusively from a single source—the sale of its products and services to individuals or organizations. Not-for-profit organizations, however, may receive revenue from a number of sources: taxes, dues, contributions, and in some instances, sales of their products or services. These differences are illustrated in Figure 12.1.

**Figure 12.1**                    **Sources of Income for Profit and Not-for-Profit Organizations**

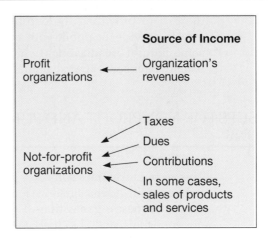

Some of the contributors of revenue to certain organizations may never use, at least in a direct sense, the organizations' outputs. For instance, consider a family violence center. The center's purpose is to provide a haven for women and their children from abusive spouses, but the center must rely on others, who may never use the center, for financial support. Another example is the local public school system. Public schools have been asked to shoulder increasing responsibilities as society has changed. They are being looked to as sources of prevention training for drug abuse and teenage pregnancy, as locations for after-school care for latchkey children, and as institutions that must increase the quality of education for children. The financial support for pursuing these goals must come from all of the school district's taxpayers—not just the parents of the students who attend the schools. Consequently, some taxpayers may be reluctant to support higher taxes for the public schools.[3]

Successful businesses know their customers and their needs. They recognize that satisfying their customers' needs is crucial for their existence. But not-for-profit organizations have a less direct relationship with their "customers." Those they serve are not necessarily those who contribute financially to their operations. Hence, their strategic planning must be twofold: planning for serving their clients or customers, and planning for securing the financial funding to provide those services.

The first type of planning—to serve customers—may sometimes have to be done with little or no input from the customers. For instance, agencies that handle the problems of the mentally ill or those that safeguard children can hardly survey their clients to ascertain their needs. In such cases, agencies often plan their services on the basis of discussions with professionals who have expertise in that particular field and of what similar agencies in other locales have done. The second type of planning—to acquire financial funding—may become quite political. A government agency, for instance, must compete against other agencies for the limited funds available; those that are most successful are often the ones that acquiesce to demands made of them by those who control the funds. Defense Department appropriations, for instance, often depend upon the department's compliance with congressional wishes.

## External Constituencies and Stakeholders

Strategic planning in business, as we have seen, involves taking into account the varying goals of the organization's stakeholders (e.g., its owners, employees, customers, creditors). The same is true for not-for-profit organizations, but the stakeholder groups and concerns are significantly different. This difference can best be seen in public organizations.

Although the managers of a government entity may engage in rational strategic planning, these plans may be ignored by political leaders who must respond to public pressure to win reelection. What may be rational in an economic sense may be politically unwise.

> Political leaders have learned that government often works only when a consensus forms to deal with a perceived crisis. The solutions may not conform with any plan, and governmental actions may be taken without regard to rational priorities. Nevertheless, the most important consideration may be that the actions are acceptable to the various constituency groups that are able to affect the decision. Since this occurs at all levels of government on a regular basis, it will be frustrating to managers who want government to function in an orderly manner. Government is not an orderly procedure because there are too many people with a variety of perspectives who are involved in reaching decisions.[4]

This greater number and diversity of stakeholders may result in less managerial autonomy for public agency managers than for managers in business. Because government agencies are "owned" by all citizens, their activities may often be more closely monitored by their constituents. This greater visibility means that managers' decisions are more public.

For example, Los Angeles County's Transportation Commission, a public agency, solicited bids from engineering firms a few years ago to build high-technology electronic trolley cars. Only two builders responded—Idaho-based Morrison Knudsen Corporation and Sumitomo Corporation, headquartered in Tokyo. When word leaked out that the Transportation Commission's construction unit would recommend awarding the contract to Sumitomo, the chairman of Morrison Knudsen attempted to get the decision reversed. Joining with him were various members of the public who strongly argued for a "Made in America" decision, politicians from both California and Los Angeles, and numerous lobbyists, lawyers, and political activists. As a result of the furor, the Transportation Commission reopened the bidding.[5]

In addition to being subject to public visibility, managerial actions are also scrutinized carefully by oversight agencies such as legislative bodies, courts, and executive groups. Hence, although managers of public organizations may not need to concern themselves with such business threats as hostile takeovers, foreign competition, or bankruptcy, they have a complicated environment in which to operate. They must serve customers or clients who may be separate from the organization's sources of funding. But the organization's operations must satisfy both the customers and the funding sources, as well as other constituencies and oversight agencies. This complexity is illustrated in Figure 12.2.

## ■ Mission, Goals, and Objectives

Not-for-profit organizations need clearly defined missions, goals, and objectives. This section explores this need and examines some reasons why clarity in organizational direction is sometimes lacking.

**Figure 12.2**                    **Stakeholder Constraints on Public Organizations**

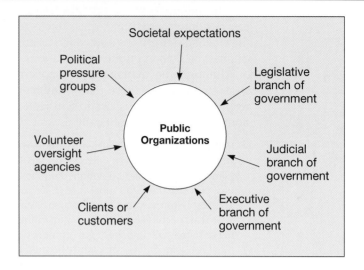

## *Mission*

Certainly, having a well-focused mission and clear goals and objectives is as important to not-for-profit organizations as it is to businesses. Management researcher and consultant Peter F. Drucker points out that "the best nonprofits devote a great deal of thought to defining their organizations' missions."[6]

As an example, consider the Girl Scouts of the U.S.A.[7] In 1976, Frances Hesselbein became national executive director of the organization, which was experiencing several problems. In a diverse society, it was comprised mostly of white, middle-class girls; scout leaders were becoming increasingly difficult to recruit as women entered the work force in growing numbers; the Boy Scouts of America were considering extending membership to girls; and membership in the Girl Scouts had declined steadily for eight years.

Hesselbein's first step was to examine the mission of the Girl Scouts. The organization's management considered these questions: "What is our business?" "Who is the customer?" "What does the customer consider as value?" They decided that the Scouts existed for one major reason: to help girls reach their highest potential. As Hesselbein explained:

> More than any one thing, that made the difference. Because when you are clear about your mission, corporate goals and operating objectives flow from it.[8]

This strong self-identity helped the Scouts reject pressures from women's rights activists to support their causes and from charities to act as door-to-door canvassers. Today, although Hesselbein is no longer president, the organization numbers 2.3 million girls (15 percent of them are from racial minorities); conducts market research to determine the needs of modern girls; awards the most popular proficiency badges for math and computer expertise instead of for good grooming and hosting a party; sports uniforms designed by Halston and Bill Blass; and publishes monographs on such issues as teen pregnancy, drug use, and child abuse.

In the public arena, as Congress attempts to reduce the federal deficit, efforts are being directed toward clarifying the respective missions of the Navy, Army, Air Force, and Marine Corps. For instance, critics have charged for decades that the United States has the only military with four air forces (all four branches of the service have their own airplanes and helicopters). Furthermore, both the Air Force and the Navy have bomber aircraft. As the defense budget shrinks, much thought is being given to reducing this expensive overlap by defining clearly just what the mission of each military branch should be.[9]

### Goals and Objectives

Although having a clearly defined mission and goals is essential to an organization's success, many not-for-profit organizations fail in this regard. Businesses, for instance, can easily measure sales, market share, profits, return on

---

## STRATEGIC INSIGHT

### A Nonprofit Organization's Mission: Howard Hughes Medical Institute

Once a tax shelter created by Howard Hughes, an important, but little known, nonprofit organization is the Howard Hughes Medical Institute. Founded in 1953 by the billionaire aviator-industrialist, the institute states its mission as follows:

- The primary purpose and objective of the Howard Hughes Medical Institute shall be the promotion of human knowledge within the field of the basic sciences (principally the field of medical research and medical education) and the effective application thereof for the benefit of mankind.

The institute is a scientific and philanthropic organization with the principal purpose of conducting biomedical research in five broad areas: genetics, immunology, neuroscience, structural biology, and cell biology and regulation. It accomplishes its scientific mission by funding research through laboratories located in some of the most prestigious academic medical centers, hospitals, universities, and other research institutions in the United States, Canada, Mexico, Australia, and New Zealand. Its philanthropic goals are attained by financially supporting various aspects of science education, from elementary school through postgraduate training.

In 1994, the institute had total assets of $7.8 billion, most of which is invested in equities, private partnerships, and nonequity securities. Earnings from this investment portfolio support the institute's operations. In 1994, the institute funded $280 million in medical research and support services and spent an estimated $50 million on science education. Unlike most foundations, Hughes does not dispense grants. Rather, it hires top researchers who go on working at their own medical schools, universities, or research centers. Without political and money pressures, they are free to set their own agendas.

How effective is Hughes' approach? So far in the 1990s alone, Hughes investigators at various locations have made scientific discoveries that are helping in the fights against colon cancer, cystic fibrosis, atherosclerosis, HIV, immune deficiencies, hypertension, and an inherited form of blindness.

SOURCES: M. B. Regan, "A Research Behemoth Gets Even Bigger," *Business Week*, 21 February 1994, p. 56; *Annual Report of the Howard Hughes Medical Institute 1993* (Bethesda, MD: Howard Hughes Medical Institute); P. Choppin, "Basic Medical Research," *Vital Speeches*, 15 June 1993, pp. 530–533.

investment, and so on. But not-for-profit organizations do not usually have such clear goals.

One of the reasons for this lack of clarity is that many of the goals are value-laden. Some states, for example, held fierce debates over mandatory seat belt laws. Was the goal to protect the lives of automobile drivers and passengers, or was it to protect the rights of those individuals to choose—or not to choose—to buckle up? Is the goal of a prison system rehabilitation of prisoners or punishment?

Second, not-for-profit goals often involve important trade-offs. This situation can be illustrated by the debate surrounding the potential closing of any military base. Its closing will reduce the federal deficit, but it will also harm the economy of the local area. Which is the more important consideration? During the 1992 presidential campaign, economist Herbert Stein emphasized the trade-off dilemma that any president faces: "He has to choose between assisting Russia, assisting urban ghettos in the U. S. and promoting aggregate growth in the American economy."[10] There is simply not sufficient funding available to accomplish all three goals.

Third, goals may often be deliberately vague, broad, and general, such as "protect our environment" or "help the homeless." Broad, general goals are more likely to secure the support of diverse stakeholders and provide inspiration for organization members. Also, vague goals are less likely to invite close scrutiny and debate than specific goals are and, hence, may avoid alienating potential supporters. Universities, for instance, often publicize their goal of offering a high-quality education. Few could argue with such a goal, and it helps skirt such issues as whether research or teaching is more important, how selective the university's admissions policies should be, and how much emphasis will be given to sports programs. Debates on any of these issues are almost certain to alienate some stakeholders, thereby reducing the flow of funds to the university.

Goals in public organizations are often vague because leadership is subject to frequent turnover. Changes in direction, for instance, can occur in a state where a Democrat replaces a Republican governor. Four years later, election results can alter the state's direction yet again. Vague goals, such as "operate the state for the benefit of all of its citizens," therefore, are likely to have more permanency and lend more of an aura of stability than very specific goals will.

Goals may sometimes not reflect the needs of the organization's "customers" as much as they reflect the wishes of the organization's financial donors. Church-affiliated universities, for instance, may make decisions that anger their students but conform to the wishes of the denomination that accounts for much of their financial backing. Some nonprofit organizations, in fact, may be reluctant to turn down substantial funding, even if the donor insists that the funds be used for a purpose outside the basic mission of the organization. Again, vague goals may appear more appropriate in such situations.

The question, of course, is whether these reasons for establishing vague goals are valid. In a number of situations we do not believe that they are. Although formulating goals and objectives is more challenging for not-for-profit organizations than for businesses, having clarity in direction is helpful if organizations are to operate effectively. Perhaps the major reason for our belief is that without clear goals, an organization has no way to measure its progress or its effectiveness.

Both nonprofit and public organizations might bring together their various stakeholders to hammer out a set of specific, measurable objectives. The process will not be smooth, because each stakeholder group may have its own agenda. Even so, without this process, these organizations may be unable to evaluate their performance.

Virtually every organization can define specific goals. Determining goal attainment may be undertaken through setting standards. For instance, the family violence center mentioned earlier could formulate a means of evaluating how effectively it is able to prevent its clients from suffering further abuse and how well it enhances its clients' self-esteem. Moreover, it also may define such performance ratios as expenditures per client day. Because such organizations typically cannot begin to help all of those who need their help, the more tightly they can control their costs, the more clients they can serve. Broad measures of costs per month or per year cannot help control costs as effectively as more specific ratios. Such standards act as a surrogate performance measure when profit figures are not applicable.

## ■ Strategy Formulation, Implementation, and Control

The processes of formulating, implementing and controlling strategy are often more complicated in not-for-profit organizations than in businesses. Some of those complications are examined next.

### *Strategy Formulation and Implementation*

In general, we can say that most of these not-for-profit organizations attempt to satisfy specific societal needs. For instance, the American Red Cross rushes to aid victims of natural disasters; the Salvation Army ministers to the physical and religious needs of homeless persons. The U.S. Navy keeps the sea lanes of the world open; the Army concentrates on ground defense. Within a state, some universities serve as major research and graduate institutions; others concentrate on teaching undergraduates.

Often, one of the features that distinguishes not-for-profit organizations from businesses is the presence of greater political constraints upon the strategic choices of not-for-profits. In public organizations, for instance, many decisions are subject to the approval of oversight agencies and the legislative and executive branches of government. These strategic decisions become even more politicized by their public visibility in the press. Several years ago, for example, the National Academy of Public Administration complained about the complexity of the controls and rules over managerial decisions in the federal government.[11]

Many functional strategies are also greatly constrained by rules governing such areas as purchasing and personnel. For instance, a General Accounting Office survey of federal government employees revealed that 5.7 percent of those surveyed were "poor performers." Although some of these employees improved their performance, voluntarily quit, or were removed from their jobs, almost 40 percent never improved and were not asked to leave. That group received more than $1 billion in annual salaries.[12] Finally, the frequent turnover of leadership, discussed earlier, may discourage employees from channeling much effort into support of the strategy, since they know that the current strategy may be short-lived.

Even if strategy could be formulated and unfettered by political considerations, implementation of the strategy can be a problem. Public managers have

## STRATEGIC INSIGHT

## *Strategies for Churches*

### Internal Growth Strategy

One of the nation's largest churches is Houston's Second Baptist Church. With a Sunday morning attendance of 12,000, the church complex covers thirty-two acres. In 1984, however, the church was simply a conventional church on a large plot of land. Its incoming pastor, H. Edwin Young, was familiar with the demographics of the area: thousands of young families and single people new to Houston. He sold his vision of a growing church to his congregation and persuaded them to pledge over $17 million needed for new physical facilities while the church borrowed over $26 million for additional construction costs.

Pastor Young dispatched church members to study office management techniques at Xerox and IBM and parking and people skills at Disney World. He varied religious services to fit particular needs. In addition to the traditional Sunday morning service, a Sunday evening service caters to a mostly singles crowd; on Wednesday nights, separate services are offered, one traditional and one with religious rock music.

Today, computers regulate mood lighting during church services; shuttle buses bring latecomers in from outlying parking decks; parking attendants empty the church's numerous parking lots every Sunday in half an hour; billboards and television ads invite people to visit this "Fellowship of Excitement"; an information desk is staffed with cheerful attendants; aerobics classes are held daily beginning at 6:00 A.M.; and a restaurant offers two types of menus: "saints" for those who prefer a low-calorie meal, and "sinners," for those who desire richer food.

### Turnaround Strategy

The U.S. Catholic Church, like many organizations, is trying to overcome stagnant revenues and steadily rising costs. Taking the lead in this fight is the Archdiocese of Chicago, which has taken the following steps:

- Sold assets of $6.2 million
- Restructured archdiocesan offices and laid off fifty employees to save $1.5 million
- Required all parishes to submit three-year budgets and quarterly financial reports
- Had each parish establish a local advisory council of business leaders
- Devised repayment plans for loans made to the parishes and began charging interest on these loans
- Increased tuition at parish schools
- Raised the assessment each parish pays the archdiocese from 6.5 to 10 percent of its annual revenues.
- Consolidated parishes and schools in the archdiocese
- Encouraged church members to increase their giving
- Began marketing the services of the church to new groups, such as young adults

Although some of the changes have met with resistance, Joseph Cardinal Bernardin maintains that there is little choice. He emphasized that to "fulfill our mission, we have to have the resources."

SOURCES: C. Y. Coleman, "Churches Preach a High-Tech Gospel," *Wall Street Journal*, 6 May 1996, pp. B1, B3; "Religion in America," *American Demographics*, March 1994, pp. 4–6; K. Kelley, "Chicago's Catholic Church: Putting Its House in Order," *Business Week*, 10 June 1991, pp. 60–65 (source of quotation p. 65); R. G. Niebuhr, "Megachurches Strive to Be All Things to All Parishioners," *Wall Street Journal*, 13 May 1991.

weaker authority over their subordinates than business managers do. Such decisions as pay, promotion, termination, and disciplinary action are often subject to rules rather than to managerial discretion. Employees who enthusiastically carry out the strategy of the organization may receive the same rewards as those who ignore the strategy to pursue their own ends. In one of the most flagrant examples of restrictive work rules, New York City public school custodians are required to sweep school floors only every other day and to mop them only three times a year. Furthermore, cafeteria floors need to be mopped only once a week. The average annual salary for such work in 1994 was $60,000.[13] In a similar case, the *Wall Street Journal* reported that restrictive work rules at Philadelphia's International Airport required three employees to change one lightbulb: a building mechanic to remove the light panel, an electrician to insert the new bulb, and a janitor to clean up the area.[14]

Because our political system is designed to ensure frequent turnover through regularly scheduled elections and through limitations on how long individuals can hold some offices, government leaders are encouraged to take a short-range approach to strategic management. Voters in the next election may be more likely to reelect officials who have benefited them during the past several months than those who have an excellent long-range plan but have demonstrated little in the way of immediate results.

Although nonprofit organizations may operate under fewer constraints than public organizations do, implementation of strategy can be constrained by those who oppose the strategy. For instance, public abortion clinics may be picketed by right-to-life advocates. More important, however, may be the constraints imposed by the nature of the work force in many nonprofit organizations. Often, the bulk of the workers are volunteers who receive no pay for their services. As long as the direction of the organization is consistent with their values and beliefs, they will cooperate in implementing strategic decisions. But should the agency's direction deviate from their values, they may quit the organization and even actively oppose its operations.

In fact, many nonprofit organizations develop their organizational culture around a cause. Often, the founder of the organization and the members exhibit the attitudes and behaviors of "true believers" who are willing to work long hours at little or no pay to further their particular beliefs and values. Many environmental groups as well as pro- and antiabortion organizations possess such powerful cultures. Few businesses are able to develop their culture around such powerful and emotional goals.

Another consideration is that businesses often have more attractive financial compensation packages than not-for-profit organizations. Individuals who are motivated by such considerations, therefore, will often seek employment in business organizations. This choice reduces the pool of talented workers from which public and nonprofit organizations can choose. In addition, the trend toward two-income families has certainly diminished the number of volunteers available to nonprofit organizations.

Not-for-profit organizations may also implement their strategies in a more centralized fashion than businesses.[15] As we saw in an earlier chapter, many businesses have responded to increasing environmental change by decentralizing their decision making. Although environments in many cases are equally dynamic for public and nonprofit agencies, the same trend has not occurred there. Because so many differing stakeholder groups must be considered when management implements strategy, often only the top managers are fully aware of how stakeholders' attitudes are changing.[16] For this reason, implementation decisions are made at the top levels of the organization. In addition, under the civil service system in public organizations, which primarily rewards seniority rather than merit, few employees are able to perceive a connection between their job performance and their compensation. Because incentives are not used to channel their behavior into the appropriate areas of strategy implementation, their behavior is instead controlled through an extensive network of rules and procedures, resulting in a bureaucratic configuration in which decision-making authority is centralized.

A further difficulty with implementation of strategy in some not-for-profit organizations is that these institutions are staffed largely by professional people who see themselves as committed to the profession rather than to the particular organization for which they currently work. For instance, physicians are said to be engaged in the practice of medicine (a profession) rather than working for a particular hospital. College professors are often referred to (and view themselves) as professors of physics or history rather than as employees of a specific university. In such cases, they "will probably publish more, spend less time on college committees, devote less time to teaching and students, attend more professional meetings, and be more willing to leave the college"[17] than the individual who identifies more with the organization than the profession. The problem that this perspective poses from the organization's viewpoint is that such persons may have primary loyalty to their profession rather than to the organization that employs them.[18] Therefore, strategic managers may need to persuade these persons to emphasize their responsibilities to the organization as well as to their profession.

## Strategic Control

Without clearly stated goals and objectives, strategic control becomes very difficult to achieve. For instance, the quality of education in public schools might be measured in several ways. One way is to determine how well students can solve problems and communicate those solutions, with the measurement taken once at the beginning of a period of time and again at the end of that time period. If the results are less than the school district has set as its goal, then corrective action must be taken. Likewise, a church that did not increase its membership as much as it desired during a particular year would have to take some corrective action, as would a police department that failed to meet its goal of solving 80 percent of the crimes committed during a twelve-month period.

Control is more difficult, obviously, when goals are not clear or when an organization has conflicting goals. Recall the example of the family violence center used earlier. The particular community in which it operates believes that it has been successful because its services are well publicized and fully used. However, it has very nearly gone bankrupt trying to help all who need its services, and its director argues that the center has just begun to scratch the surface!

In some cases, nonprofit organizations have literally had no objectives in certain key areas. The prestigious University of Chicago hospital, for instance, had no budgeting system to track its costs until 1989.[19] Without standards, the hospital's management could not determine the cost of a procedure, such as an appendectomy. Lack of both cost objectives and cost information made the control of costs virtually impossible.

Even under conditions in which the corrective actions that should be taken are clear, control may still not occur. For instance, in business, when a project or program is no longer contributing to a firm's profits, decisions are made either to rejuvenate the program, if appropriate and possible, or to terminate it. Hence, profit serves as a readily acceptable yardstick to help management determine the amount of resources that various programs should receive.[20]

This means of control is not available to not-for-profit organizations. In fact, only rarely are programs terminated, particularly in government. This fact can be demonstrated quickly by virtually any debate on how to reduce the federal deficit. Few individuals want their taxes raised, but any proposal to terminate a program (and, hence, lower expenditures) quickly brings an outcry from those stakeholders who will be adversely affected by the program's demise. As a result, governments at all levels continue to add programs that are needed but rarely end any of their ongoing programs. But strategic control requires that a manager make choices, because it is simply not possible to do everything well.[21] Even when a lack of funding makes it imperative to cut programs, the programs cut are not necessarily the ones least needed; often, the programs eliminated are the ones that are less likely to create a highly vocal protest from their constituents.

---

### S T R A T E G I C   I N S I G H T

## *Strategic Control at the Post Office*

The U.S. Postal Service faces increasing competition from air express companies, facsimile machines, long-distance telephone companies, electronic mail, and interactive cable television. While its revenue growth (about $47 billion a year) stagnates, its operating expenses continue to escalate. A 1992 General Accounting Office report revealed that, even though considerable automation of post office operations had occurred, operating expenses were $295 million more than expected. In fact, while the volume of mail delivered declined, the number of work hours increased.

As a result, major attempts at strategic control are under way. The first try, however, failed. Postmaster General Anthony Frank's request for a one-cent increase in first-class postage—which would have raised $800 million annually—was denied by the Postal Service Board of Governors. Although the vote was 6 to 3 in favor of the increase, a unanimous vote is required. Frank responded: "I'm the only CEO of a major corporation in America who doesn't have control over his own prices." Before leaving office, however, he managed to cap labor costs (which amount to 83 percent of operating expenses) and give management more flexibility in hiring temporary workers. He also announced an early-retirement plan designed to trim payrolls, hired a polling company to measure customer satisfaction, and extended window hours.

Frank was succeeded by Marvin Runyon, who continued the strategic control measures by eliminating—through early retirement—25 percent of the Postal Service's managerial positions. He restructured the organization, replacing its seventy-three regional divisions with two functional divisions: one for processing and distributing mail and one for customer services. In total, about 50,000 workers were laid off, and a budget surplus of $500 million was achieved in 1992. Runyon also made good on his promise not to increase postage rates through 1994.

SOURCES: W. Keenan Jr., "Can We Deliver?" *Sales & Marketing Management* (February 1994): 62–67; "General Delivery," *Sales & Marketing Management* (February 1994): 66; S. Barr, "Can the Postal Service Get Lean?" *Folio: The Magazine for Magazine Management*, 1 March 1993, pp. 63–64; W. R. Cummings, "Reinventing the Post Office," *Wall Street Journal*, 11 January 1993; R. Davis, "Postal Chief Wants Service That Delivers," *USA Today*, 10 August 1992; S. Rudavsky, "Postal Service Plans Sweeping Overhaul," *Washington Post*, 7 August 1992; "That Was Then, This Is Now," *Washington Post Magazine*, 14 June 1992, p. 11; M. Lewyn, "Pushing the Envelope at the Post Office," *Business Week*, 25 November 1991, pp. 56–57 (quotation is from p. 56).

Even charitable nonprofit organizations may behave in similar ways. For instance, sometimes the mission of an agency is actually accomplished or its environment changes so that its mission becomes unnecessary. Consider the Mothers' March of Dimes organization, which was originally established to support research that would lead to a cure for polio. With the widespread distribution of the Salk vaccine in the 1950s, polio ceased to be the threat it once was. But the March of Dimes did not go out of existence. Instead, it adopted a new cause—birth defects—in order to sustain itself.

## ■ Improving Strategic Management

Although some of the difficulties in implementing strategic management concepts in not-for-profit organizations are unlikely to disappear (e.g., the desire of elected officials to be reelected minimizes an emphasis on long-range planning), other problems can be overcome. The concepts of effective strategic management presented in this book are not limited to business institutions. Both nonprofit and public organizations can benefit significantly by analyzing their environmental opportunities and constraints and by formulating a mission and goals that allow them to fulfill the needs of some segment of society. They must then develop a strategy that relates their strengths and weaknesses appropriately to their environment and allows them to create a distinctive competence in their operating arena. An organization structure must be fashioned that enables the agency to deal effectively with its environmental demands; and a culture should be established that enhances—rather than interferes with—its operational effectiveness.

Some not-for-profit organizations are highly effective, of course. But for those that are not, these basic principles of strategic management can be most useful in increasing their ability to carry out their mission. In some of these situations, the culture may be such that improvement is virtually impossible without a major change. Strong transformational leadership may be required, along with a significant modification in policies, so that employees' attitudes and practices can be unfrozen and changed. Top management's commitment to the concept of change must be complete and highly visible. Concurrently, reward systems must be altered to encourage creativity, new ways of doing old things, and service to the agency's clients or customers.

Certainly, such change cannot occur overnight. One authority suggests that top management start gradually to chip away at detrimental cultural aspects and look for special opportunities to implement strategic management principles in narrow, well-defined areas. In this way, management can devote the resources and time that are required for success.[22]

Finally, we would be negligent if we did not emphasize the need for managerial training. In some nonprofit organizations, the top-level managers may be individuals who were sensitive to a particular need in our society and created an organization to serve that need. But even the best of intentions cannot serve society as effectively as good intentions combined with managerial skills. The most socially oriented of programs must, in the long run, use each of its dollars and the time of its employees as effectively and efficiently as it possibly can. Otherwise, all of those who are in need of its services may never receive them or may receive only partial care.

---

S T R A T E G I C   I N S I G H T

## Strategic Alliances for Public Organizations

An increasing number of public organizations are finding that strategic alliances with private industry can improve their operating effectiveness. In some cases, for instance, "privatizing" government functions can reduce costs and improve revenue flows.

Take, for example, Chicago's parking enforcement program. During the 1980s, $420 million of parking ticket fines went unpaid. That's because, after a ticket was written, it took an average of two years for the ticket to be recorded. But, in 1990, Chicago turned the recording process over to Dallas-based Electronic Data Systems (EDS). Now the 14,000 parking tickets written by police officers each day are electronically imaged and stored on optical disks by EDS personnel the very same day. Other parking tickets, written by meter monitors, are entered by the ticket writer directly into hand-held computers and are electronically transferred into EDS's computer. The city is now saving about $5 million a year in administrative expenses, ticket revenues are increasing substantially, and parking meter revenues are significantly higher.

In other developments, such states as California and New York are experimenting with contracting out some welfare functions to private companies. For instance, in New York, a welfare mother costs the state about $23,000 annually. But, in its contract with America Works (a private company), New York pays only $5,300. America Works and other similar firms, such as MAXIMUS and Lockheed IMS, can cut expenses by superior use of computer technology, a lack of restrictive work rules, and little bureaucracy. America Works is not only less expensive for the taxpayers, but it also succeeds at getting almost 70 percent of its clients off the welfare rolls.

Meanwhile, Baltimore has turned over the management of nine inner-city schools to a Minneapolis-based company—Education Alternatives. This company hopes to save money while reducing the student-teacher ratio and increasing the use of technology in these schools. Its profit will come from part of the savings.

Some government agencies are even forming strategic alliances with nonprofit organizations. Florida's prison system, for instance, paroles some of its first offenders into the custody of the Salvation Army. About two-thirds of these parolees become "permanently rehabilitated" (they are not indicted for another crime for at least six years).

As budget deficits mount at the federal, state, and local levels, government officials continue to search for creative ways to lower costs. Strategic alliances with private industry and nonprofit organizations show considerable promise in helping officials attain this goal.

SOURCES: J. Huey, "Finding New Hopes for a New Era," *Fortune*, 25 January 1993, p. 65; J. Mathews, "Taking Welfare Private," *Newsweek*, 29 June 1992, p. 44; A. Kotlowitz, "For-Profit Firms to Manage Public Schools in Baltimore," *Wall Street Journal*, 11 June 1992; P. F. Drucker, "It Profits Us to Strengthen Nonprofits," *Wall Street Journal*, 19 December 1991; R. Henkoff, "Some Hope for Troubled Cities," *Fortune*, 9 September 1991, p. 126.

# SUMMARY

Strategic management principles apply equally to businesses and not-for-profit organizations. But these two types of institutions differ in some important ways that have strategic implications.

Perhaps the chief distinction is their source of revenue. Businesses generate income in the form of sales revenue; not-for-profit firms may receive revenue from such diverse sources as taxes, dues, contributions, or even sales. But a business's revenue is derived directly from its customers—those who purchase its products or services. However, a not-for-profit's revenue often comes from individuals who may never even use the outputs of that organization. For instance, a public organization may provide welfare payments to families below the poverty level. However, the sources of those funds are taxes paid by income earners with relatively higher salaries. Similarly, a nonprofit organization such as a privately owned museum may allow the public to view its exhibits for no admission fee. But its revenues may be generated by the interest from an endowment created by a family many decades ago. Therefore, not-for-profit organizations must engage in two types of strategic planning—how to serve their clients or customers, and how to secure the necessary financial funding to provide those services.

A second distinction between businesses and nonprofits is that planning in some not-for-profit firms, particularly public organizations, may be complicated by political considerations, which are not relevant to businesses. The large number and diversity of stakeholders in a government agency means that its managers' decisions are more public than they are in other types of organizations. These decisions must be responsive to the wishes of varying constituencies, requiring management to engage in a difficult balancing act.

Although having a clear mission and goals is essential to an organization's success, many not-for-profit organizations fail in this area. Several reasons account for this shortcoming: Goals tend to be value-laden; they often involve important trade-offs; they may be deliberately vague, broad, and general; leadership is subject to frequent turnover, particularly in public organizations; and the goals may not reflect the needs of the organization's customers as much as they reflect the wishes of the organization's financial supporters. The problem, of course, is that vague goals cannot help management measure an organization's progress or its effectiveness.

Strategy implementation in not-for-profit organizations, particularly public agencies, is often highly visible and political. But even if strategies could be implemented in a rational fashion, public managers would still operate under another unique constraint. They have weaker authority in such areas as pay, promotion, termination, and disciplinary action than business managers have. By the same token, managers in private nonprofit firms must often supervise a work force comprised largely of volunteers, which poses a different set of constraints. Other distinctions exist as well. For instance, research shows that not-for-profit organizations implement their strategies in a more centralized fashion than businesses do, and they are sometimes staffed by professional people who may be more committed to their profession than to the organization for which they currently work.

Strategic control, of course, is difficult to achieve when goals are not clearly defined and measurable. It is made even more difficult by the fact that not-for-profit organizations, unlike businesses, cannot usually terminate programs even if they have outlived their usefulness. Just the threat of program termination quickly brings an outcry from those stakeholders who will be adversely affected by the program's demise, and they often wield sufficient political power to forestall termination indefinitely.

However, both nonprofit and public organizations can benefit significantly by following the principles presented in this book. They, as well as businesses, should analyze their environmental opportunities and constraints and formulate mission and goals that allow them to fulfill the needs of some segment of society. They should then develop a strategy that relates their strengths and weaknesses appropriately to their environment and allows them to create a distinctive competence in their operating arena. To implement their strategy, they must fashion an organization structure that enables them to deal with their environmental demands and a culture that enhances their organizational effectiveness. Cultures and reward systems that are too constraining must be altered to improve the organizations' operating efficiency and their long-term effectiveness.

## TAKE IT TO THE NET

We invite you to visit the Wright page on the Prentice Hall Web site at:

**http://www.prenhall.com/wright**

for this chapter's World Wide Web exercise.

## KEY CONCEPTS

**Nonprofit organization**   A form of not-for-profit organization that is supported by private funds and exists to contribute to the good of society.

**Public organization**   A form of not-for-profit organization that is created, funded, and regulated by the public sector.

## DISCUSSION QUESTIONS

1. Your text states that "nonprofit and public organizations are indispensable to maintaining a civilized society." Explain why.

2. Explain how not-for-profit organizations differ from businesses in the way that they derive their revenue. What are the implications of these differences for strategic management?

3. We have seen that the top managers of public organizations probably have less autonomy than do business CEOs because of the greater number and diversity of stakeholders in public organizations. Explain how multiple stakeholder interests can reduce managerial autonomy.

4. Why do not-for-profit organizations often have vague, general goals rather than clear, specific ones?

5. What are the disadvantages of vague, general goals?

6. Select a not-for-profit organization and describe the specific societal needs that it attempts to satisfy. Does it have any competitors? If so, who are they?

7. How does the implementation of strategy in not-for-profit organizations differ from that in businesses?

8. Why is strategy implementation more centralized in not-for-profit organizations than in businesses?

9. From a strategic perspective, what are the difficulties of managing professional employees? Volunteer employees?

10. Why do public organizations have more difficulty terminating programs than businesses have?

## STRATEGIC MANAGEMENT EXERCISES

1. Assume that you have the resources and backing to found a university. Formulate a mission statement for your university. Now, develop a set of goals for the university. How would you ensure that the needs of your university's "customers" are met through the goals that you have devised? (Note that customers would include employers of the university's graduates, graduate schools that accept your graduates, students, parents who pay tuition, etc.)

2. Use your own university to answer the following questions: What is your university's mission? What are it major goals? Base your answers on written documents, if they exist; otherwise, you will need to derive your answers from interviews and observation. After gathering information on your university, determine how it might formulate and implement appropriate strategies to serve its constituents and stakeholders better. Give specific examples.

3. The United Way of America is supposed to provide financial support for a wide variety of charitable causes. But in the early 1990s, news reports revealed that much abuse and fraud had taken place in its headquarters' organization. From library research of this scandal, suggest how the use of strategic control techniques might have prevented these problems from ever occurring at the United Way of America.

## NOTES

1. B. Vobejda, "In Job Strength, Manufacturing Eclipsed by Public Sector," *Washington Post*, 18 August 1992.

2. The demand for business executives to support nonprofits not only has increased for financial help but also for serving as consultants or board members. See W. G. Bowen, "When A Business Leader Joins a Nonprofit Board," *Harvard Business Review* 72, 1 (September-October 1994): 38–43; J. A. Bryne, "Profiting from the Nonprofits," *Business Week*, 26 March 1990, p. 67.

3. W. H. Newman and H. W. Wallender, "Managing Not-for-Profit Enterprises," *Academy of Management Review* 3 (1978): 24–31.

4. Reprinted from W. H. Eldridge, "Why Angels Fear to Tread: A Practitioner's Observations and Solutions on Introducing Strategic Management to a Government Culture," in J. Rabin, G. J. Miller, and W. B. Hildreth, eds., *Handbook of Strategic Management* (New York: Dekker, 1989), p. 329, by courtesy of Marcel Dekker Inc.

5. F. Rose, "How a U. S. Company Used Anti-Japan Mood to Help Reverse a Loss," *Wall Street Journal*, 22 April 1992.

6. P. F. Drucker, "What Business Can Learn from Nonprofits," *Harvard Business Review* 67, no. 4 (1989): 89.

7. Bryne, "Profiting from the Nonprofits," pp. 67, 70–74.

8. Ibid., p. 72.

9. J. Lancaster, "Hill Takes Aim on Duplication in Military Services," *Washington Post*, 8 August 1992.

10. P. D. Harvey and J. D. Snyder, "Charities Need a Bottom Line Too," *Harvard Business Review* 65, no. 1 (1987): 14–22.

11. National Academy of Public Administration, *Revitalizing Federal Management* (Washington, D. C.: National Academy of Public Administration, 1986).

12. D. Priest, "Study Ties Job Success to Bosses," *Washington Post*, 9 October 1990.

13. R. Flick, "How Unions Stole the Big Apple," *Reader's Digest*, January 1992, pp. 39–40.

14. "Philly Thinks Private," *Wall Street Journal,* 30 June 1992.

15. P. C. Nutt, "A Strategic Planning Network for Non-Profit Organizations," *Strategic Management Journal* 5 (1984): 58.

16. J. Ruffat, "Strategic Management of Public and Non-Market Corporations," *Long Range Planning* 16, no. 4 (1983): 75.

17. W. G. Bennis, N. Berkowitz, M. Affinito, and M. Malone, "Reference Groups and Loyalties in the Out-Patient Department," *Administrative Science Quarterly* 2 (1958): 484.

18. Newman and Wallender, "Managing Not-for-Profit Enterprises," pp. 24–31.

19. J. F. Siler and T. Peterson, "Hospital, Heal Thyself," *Business Week*, 27 August 1990, p. 68.

20. Eldridge, "Why Angels Fear to Tread: A Practitioner's Observations and Solutions on Introducing Strategic Management to a Government Culture," p. 329.

21. Ibid., p. 330.

22. Ibid., p. 335.

# Company Index

# Name Index

# Subject Index

# II. CASES IN STRATEGIC MANAGEMENT

# Strategic Management Case Analysis

Most of you are majoring in some aspect of business administration and are already familiar with case analysis. A case portrays a real organizational situation and requires you to analyze that situation and then develop recommendations for future action. The difference between the cases in strategic management and those in previous courses is that the cases here assume a broader perspective. Cases in finance have a financial orientation, and those in organizational behavior usually focus on individual or group behavior, but the cases in this book reflect a broad, companywide perspective. Each case presents a real organization, and organizations in a wide variety of industries and operating situations are represented.

You have probably already taken a series of courses that specialize in various functional areas, such as marketing, accounting, finance, and production/operations management. This knowledge can prove very useful to you when you begin working as a functional specialist (e.g., accountant, financial analyst, or sales representative). However, most successful business executives need strategic skills, particularly as they move up into general management positions. As this upward movement occurs, they typically encounter a very different set of problems from those that they dealt with as functional specialists. Unfortunately, their functional expertise is of limited assistance to them in either diagnosing or resolving these general management problems. Success in such activities requires the integration of knowledge in a wide variety of areas, both theoretical and functional. Hence, the goal of this textbook—and the course it accompanies—is to help you develop a general management capability by exposing you to a number of situations that require the integration of knowledge from different areas. The contents of this book provide the fundamental framework needed to bring together and integrate what you have learned in other courses so that you will be able to analyze these cases from a companywide perspective.

This introduction should help you to analyze the cases contained in this textbook and assist you in organizing and presenting your thoughts in written (or oral) form.

# READING THE CASE

Case analysis requires you to read the case carefully and to read it more than once. Some students read the case quickly to get an overview of the situation presented and then reread it slowly, taking notes on the important issues and problems. Subsequently, they begin to organize and analyze the case information. However, each person must develop his or her own approach to case analysis. No single technique works well for everyone.

Since cases reflect reality, it should not be surprising that some of the information is not well organized, that irrelevant information is presented, and that relevant information may be dispersed throughout the case. Information rarely comes to us in neatly tied packages. One of your first tasks, therefore, is to organize the information in the case. An outline that can help you organize the material is discussed in the following section, or your professor may provide you with his or her own guidelines for organizing the issues in the case.

Students often have questions about the time frame of a particular case. We have found it most efficient to assume that you are analyzing the case in the year(s) that the case covers. For instance, if the last year covered in the case is 1994, then you should not ordinarily analyze the case with information gathered since that date. In some instances, however, your professor may ask you to update the case, particularly if, at the case's end, significant pending problems and issues are still unresolved.[1]

# WRITING THE CASE ANALYSIS

The guidelines presented in the following subsections for the written analysis of cases are offered to help you organize and present your thoughts. (If your professor gives you a set of guidelines, by all means, use those.) As you read the case carefully, you may organize and analyze the information in the case under each of the headings used for the following subsections.

## ■ Macroenvironment

The macroenvironment, the broadest of all the sections in your analysis, is intended to help you decipher the macroenvironmental information you extract from the case and organize it selectively under such headings as "Political-Legal," "Economic," "Technological," and "Social," as shown in chapter 2. You should read the case for both explicit and implicit information in these categories. Outside research may be necessary to increase the information available in one or more of these areas. Then within each category, your task is to determine what opportunities and threats are presented to the firm featured in the case by the macroenvironmental force.

One way of accomplishing this end is to use headings and, under each heading, discuss how the external forces may act as opportunities or threats to management. Another way is to use brief, descriptive sentences for each heading's topic. For example, if the case is on General Motors (GM), the following "Economic" heading may be used with a brief sentence:

*Economic* (Opportunity) The relatively low recent value of the dollar (compared with its value in the early 1980s) versus foreign currencies has helped GM become more price competitive.

A threat or constraint may be noted as follows:

*Political-Legal* (Threat)   The U.S. government is demanding higher and higher fuel efficiency standards from U.S. automakers.

A number of different factors may be listed under each of the macroenvironmental headings, depending upon the range of information provided in the case and the extent of your research outside what's given in the case. Some cases may have many relevant factors under, for instance, the heading "Political-Legal" but few under "Technological."

## ■ Industry Environment

The industry environment section requires you to extract information from the case and from any other available source through your own research and then organize and analyze it under the five industry forces discussed in chapter 2: "Threat of Entry," "Intensity of Rivalry Among Existing Competitors," "Pressure from Substitute Products," "Bargaining Power of Buyers," and "Bargaining Power of Suppliers." You should use these headings to help you organize your analysis.

For example, assume that the case you are analyzing is on GM's automobile business units. Under the heading "Threat of Entry," you might mention that economies of scale act as a barrier to domestic companies that may seek to enter the U.S. automobile industry. However, more and more vehicle producers from abroad have entered the American market over the years. Thus, although the threat of new entry from U.S. sources is limited, the threat of foreign automakers' exporting their products to America and even building manufacturing facilities in the United States is certainly present.

Under "Bargaining Power of Suppliers," you might mention that most suppliers of automobile parts do not have strong positions relative to GM. For instance, the major U.S. steel companies are not working at full capacity and, hence, would be anxious to sell to GM.

This is not to say that suppliers generally have weak bargaining power. In certain industries, some suppliers possess relatively strong bargaining power relative to buyers. For instance, Monsanto's NutraSweet unit had a strong bargaining position as a supplier to the soft-drink producers until its patent for aspartame expired in 1992.

The point of analyzing the macroenvironment and industry environment, of course, is to relate the opportunities and threats in these two areas to the firm featured in the case. A review of chapter 2 should help you in this analysis.

## ■ The Firm's Resources, Mission, Goals, Objectives, Social Responsibility, and Ethics

Parts or all of the heading "The Firm's Resources, Mission, Goals, Objectives, Social Responsibility, and Ethics" may be used for your analysis. Sometimes, information is explicitly provided on these topics; other times, it is implicit, forcing you to read between the lines. One question that you might consider posing and analyzing is the following:

1. What are the firm's strengths and weaknesses?

As discussed in chapter 3, a firm's strengths and weaknesses reside in its resources. Consequently, you may wish to use the questions posed in chapter 3 regarding the firm's human, organizational, and physical resources to determine the corporation's particular strengths and weaknesses.

You might also pose the following:

2. Is there an explicit or an implicit statement of the firm's mission? Does it accurately portray the direction in which the firm is going, or are the firm's operations incompatible with its mission?

You may recall that in chapter 3, the mission of GM (to continue our example) is stated in the following way:

> The fundamental purpose of General Motors is to provide products and services of such quality that our customers will receive superior value, our employees and business partners will share in our success, and our stockholders will receive a sustained, superior return on their investment.

Unfortunately for GM, there has been a gap between its mission and its actual operating results. Surveys of car owners indicate that GM is not perceived as offering superior value to its customers.[2] In fact, a car produced by Toyota and sold under the GM brand (Geo Prism) has sales far below those of its "twin" product, Corolla, which is produced and marketed by Toyota.[3] Furthermore, GM has laid off large numbers of employees, and its stock has not been a top performer.

Another question you might consider:

3. Are the expressed or implied goals and objectives of the firm consistent with one another? Is there evidence that these goals and objectives are being attained?

In Chapter 3, we indicated that the goals of various stakeholders often differ. And Chapter 9 pointed out that compromise may be important in helping resolve these differences. Sometimes, however, compromise is not attainable, and the effectiveness of the firm suffers as a result. For example, in the middle to late 1980s, H. Ross Perot—head of Electronic Data Systems, a subsidiary of GM; a member of the GM board of directors; and a major stockholder in GM—desired a course of action for GM that differed significantly from the course favored by GM's top management. Because compromise was unattainable, GM's management purchased Perot's stock holdings for about $750 million, at a time when GM had just incurred a large quarterly loss.

Here is another question you might consider for your analysis.

4. Is the firm operating in a socially responsible manner? Are the decisions and actions of its managers ethical?

As we emphasized in chapter 3, analysis in the areas of social responsibility and ethics can be difficult because the guidelines are not always clear-cut. If the case contains these issues, you may have to formulate your own answer to dilemmas such as whether it is socially responsible to lay off employees to enhance a firm's competitiveness or whether social responsibility can be better served by keeping the employees on the payroll, even at the expense of the firm's profits and, perhaps, survival.

## ■ Corporate-Level Strategies

As we pointed out in chapter 4, a basic question facing top management at the corporate level is, In what particular businesses or industries should we be operating? The answer to this question depends upon the firm's particular resource strengths and weaknesses and the opportunities and threats in the external environment.

The next step is to answer the following questions: Which specific strategies has the firm adopted—growth, stability, or retrenchment? How effective have these strategies been? Some corporations have effectively adopted growth strategies, but others have been less successful. Some companies have grown by developing or acquiring businesses with a common core. General Electric, for example, has attained success through involvement in businesses that share a common technological core. As another instance, Philip Morris has been one of the world's largest consumer product firms, particularly with its tobacco and food businesses. However, Philip Morris was unable to transfer its expertise in consumer products to its marketing of 7-Up, which it eventually divested.

Some corporations or business units have effectively adopted the stability strategy. This strategy enables the corporation to focus managerial efforts on the existing businesses with the goal of enhancing their competitive postures. Top executives may also adopt this strategy if they perceive that the cost of adding new businesses is more than the potential benefits. At the business unit level, the stability strategy may be chosen for other reasons. For instance, some enterprises have decided not to expand because of concern that growth may reduce the quality of their products and services. In a number of industries, some large businesses may elect stability to avoid being prosecuted for engaging in monopolistic practices.

A strategy of retrenchment may be appropriate in certain situations. For instance, Tambrands diversified in the 1980s from a single-product company into such unrelated businesses as home diagnostics and cosmetics. These acquisitions, however, provided "little more than a stream of operating losses and management distraction that has hurt its basic tampon business."[4] In its retrenchment strategy, Tambrands sold both the diagnostics and cosmetics businesses at a loss. However, since pruning those operations, it has performed well by concentrating solely on its tampon business.

Your answer to the question—In what businesses or industries should we be operating?—may be made more specifically by examining the discussion in the next section.

## ■ Corporate Portfolio Management and Related Issues

Many firms operate multiple business units in various industries, as we saw in chapter 5. At the corporate level of such enterprises, the task is to use S.W.O.T. analysis to evaluate each business unit within a portfolio framework context. For example, a weak business unit that faces external threats would be placed in compartment H or I of our proposed S.W.O.T. framework. (Alternatively, this same business would be classified as a "dog" in the original BCG framework, would be placed in the "divest" compartment of the revised BCG framework, and would be considered an "unsuccessful business unit" in the GE framework.) Once the business unit is placed in the appropriate category in the portfolio framework, then the guidelines associated with its placement may be used to recommend corporate growth, stability, or retrenchment strategies. In the example we are using, the guideline in our S.W.O.T. framework is to turn-around, divest, or liquidate the business. (The original BCG, revised BCG, and GE frameworks recommend either liquidating or divesting the business.)

You may also wish to determine how involved corporate-level top management should get in formulating and implementing business unit strategies. Recall from chapter 5 that relatively centralized decision making may be appropriate for corporations with related businesses, while relatively more decentralization may be better for firms operating unrelated businesses. Finally, you may wish to explore such issues in the case as corporate returns and top management's motives for engaging in acquisitions.

## ■ Business Unit Strategies and Functional Strategies

If the case is about a corporation with individual business units, then the units may have adopted different generic business unit strategies. If the firm is in a single business, such as McDonald's or Tambrands, then its business unit and corporate-level strategies are the same. In either case, your task is to identify which business unit strategy the firm has adopted and to evaluate how appropriate that strategy is. Is it compatible with the firm's corporate strategies and with its objectives for market share? Does it enable the company to compete effectively? Here you will wish to refer to chapter 6 and review the seven generic strategies available to business units.

As discussed in chapter 7, business unit strategies influence functional strategies; conversely, the extent to which functional strategies are effectively formulated helps determine the success of the business strategies. In this section of your analysis, you will want to explore the consistency of the business unit strategies and the supporting functional strategies.

For example, if the corporation emphasizes scope economies and if the business unit has adopted a low-cost strategy, then it would be inconsistent for the business unit to formulate a marketing strategy with costly advertising and promotion. However, expensive promotional campaigns would be consistent with corporate scope innovations and the adoption of the differentiation strategy.

Your analysis may extend to other considerations as well. For instance, a firm that produces a high-priced luxury product with the niche-differentiation strategy should not pursue a goal of substantially increasing its production/operations capacity and market share. Consumers who purchase luxury products or services do so only as long as the items are perceived as exclusive.

## ■ Strategy Implementation

The actual implementation of corporate, business unit, and functional strategies is considered in this part of your analysis. Reference to chapter 8 will help you in evaluating the relationship of the firm's organizational structure to its strategies. Is this structure suitable for a firm with these strategies? Or has the firm outgrown the need for this structure?

Chapter 9 should assist you in determining whether the CEO's leadership style and use of power are appropriate for the firm's strategies. Also consider whether the organization's culture is supportive of the strategies that it is attempting to implement.

Note that some cases will give you considerable information on strategy implementation, organizational charts, organizational culture, and the CEO. Others will provide little data on these matters. If your professor encourages outside research, you can usually collect at least some information on these issues if the firm is a large, publicly held corporation.

## ■ Strategic Control

Although strategic control was discussed in chapter 10, the actual process involves every aspect of strategic management. That is, strategic control is a process that must occur in the analysis of the following aspects of the firm:

- Macroenvironment
- Industry environment
- Firm resources, mission, goals, objectives, social responsibility, and ethics
- Strategy formulation
- Strategy implementation

In this section of your analysis, you will want to determine which aspects of the case are in particular need of strategic control scrutiny and, if possible, attempt to bring them together to draw overall conclusions. It is helpful, as chapter 10 points out, to compare this year's results with those of the firm in previous years. Alternatively, strategic control may be examined by comparing the firm's qualitative and quantitative results with those of its rivals or other firms. If you have access to the Profit Impact of Market Strategies (PIMS) program, you may wish to use it for these comparisons.

Besides PIMS, there are other sources of data available for assessing strategic control. They include Dun & Bradstreet's *Industry Norms and Key Business Ratios* and various publications by Value Line, Standard and Poor's, Moody's, and Robert Morris Associates. Additional information can be gleaned from annual reports and 10-K reports of the firm's chief competitors. Recall that strategic control involves not only quantitative data but also qualitative information. Annual reports and industry analyses, such as those by Standard and Poor's and Moody's, are particularly rich in qualitative information.

You may also wish to analyze the financial aspects of the case. Financial information can be revealing. For instance, a top manager stated to one of the authors that his firm not only was "recession-proof," but also continuously faced an increase in market demand. Yet, the inventories of the firm had jumped dramatically during the previous three years.

Financial ratios may be used in your quantitative analysis. The idea is to discern trends by calculating certain key ratios and then comparing them with (a) the median ratios in the industry, (b) the ratios of the firm's major competitors, and (c) the firm's ratios in prior years. Exhibit 1 lists many of the most important ratios, shows how to calculate them, and indicates what they mean.

Although a firm's financial ratios are normally analyzed in relation to industry ratios, you may wish to allow for some flexibility in your analysis. For

**Exhibit 1**  **Financial Ratios**

| Ratios | Formula | What Ratios Represent |
|---|---|---|
| *Liquidity* | | |
| Current ratio | $\dfrac{\text{Current assets}}{\text{Current liabilities}}$ | This ratio is an indication of a firm's ability to meet current obligations. Ordinarily a ratio of 2 to 1 or better is desirable. |
| Quick ratio | $\dfrac{\text{Current assets} - \text{inventory}}{\text{Current liabilities}}$ | This ratio indicates how much of the current liabilities the current assets can immediately cover, excluding the inventory (since inventories may not be subject to immediate sale or may have a lower market value than book value). |
| Sales-to-receivables ratio | $\dfrac{\text{Net sales}}{\text{Trade receivables} - \text{net}}$ | This ratio measures the times trade receivables turn over during a year, indicating how frequently they are converted to cash. |
| Days in receivables ratio | $\dfrac{365}{\text{Sales/receivables ratio}}$ | This figure expresses the average time in days that receivables are outstanding. |
| Inventory turnover ratio | $\dfrac{\text{Cost of sales}}{\text{Average Inventory}}$ | This ratio measures the times the firm's inventory turns over during a year, indicating how efficiently inventory is being managed. |
| Days in inventory ratio | $\dfrac{365}{\text{Sales/inventory ratio}}$ | Dividing the inventory turnover ratio into 365 days yields the average length of time units are in inventory. Normally, the smaller this number is, the more efficiently inventories are being managed. |
| Cost of sales-to-payables ratio | $\dfrac{\text{Cost of sale}}{\text{Trade payables}}$ | This ratio measures the number of times trade payables turn over during the year, or how quickly the firm pays them. |
| Days in payables ratio | $\dfrac{365}{\text{Sales/payable ratio}}$ | Division of the payable turnover ratio into 365 days yields the average length of time trade debt is outstanding. Typically, a small number of days suggests the firm is paying its bills in a timely fashion. |
| Sales-to-working capital ratio | $\dfrac{\text{Net sales}}{\text{Net working capital}}$ | This is a measure of the firm's ratio of sales to working capital. The greater the number, the less adequate is the firm's working capital base relative to its sales. |
| *Coverage* | | |
| Times interest earned ratio | $\dfrac{\text{EBIT}}{\text{Annual interest expense}}$ | Measures the capability of the firm to make good on its yearly interest costs. |
| *Leverage* | | |
| Net fixed assets-to-tangible net worth ratio | $\dfrac{\text{Net fixed assets}}{\text{Tangible net worth}}$ | This ratio measures the extent to which the owner's equity has been invested in plant and equipment. |
| Debt-to-net worth ratio | $\dfrac{\text{Total liabilities}}{\text{Net worth}}$ | This ratio expresses the relationship between the capital contributed by creditors and that contributed by shareholders. |
| *Operating* | | |
| Percent of profits before taxes-to-net worth ratio | $\dfrac{\text{Profits before taxes}}{\text{Tangible net worth} \times 100}$ | This ratio expresses the rate of return on tangible capital employed by the firm. Normally, the larger this number is, the better the firm's performance. |
| Percent of profits before taxes-to-total assets | $\dfrac{\text{Profits before taxes}}{\text{Total assets} \times 100}$ | This ratio expresses the pre-tax return on total assets and measures the effectiveness of management in employing the resources available to the firm. |

**Exhibit 1 (continued)    Financial Ratios**

| Ratios | Formula | What Ratios Represent |
|---|---|---|
| *Operating* | | |
| Sales/net fixed assets ratio | $\dfrac{\text{Total sales}}{\text{Net fixed assets}}$ | This ratio measures the productivity of a firm's fixed assets by determining the number of times fixed assets turned over in the last year. |
| Sales/total assets ratio | $\dfrac{\text{Total sales}}{\text{Total assets}}$ | This ratio is a measure of a firm's ability to generate sales in relation to total assets. Normally, the larger the number, the more productive the firm is thought to be. |
| Percent of depreciation, amortization, depletion expenses-to-sales | $\dfrac{\text{Depreciation amortization depletion expenses}}{\text{Total sales} \times 100}$ | This is the measure of the amount of total sales absorbed by non-cash expenses. |
| Market-to-book ratio | $\dfrac{\text{Market price of firm's stock}}{\text{Book value per share}}$ | This ratio measures the securities market's expectations concerning the firm's future earnings. Any value greater than 1 suggests the securities market expects future return on equity to be greater than the firm's cost of equity capital. |
| Return on equity ratio | $\dfrac{\text{Net profit after taxes}}{\text{Stockholder's equity}}$ | This measures the rate of return on the book value of total stockholder's equity. |

example, a lower current ratio for some businesses may be less of a concern. As a case in point, Avon sells its cosmetics to consumers door-to-door for cash. Many of its rivals, however, sell cosmetics via retailers. Select retailers not only have the right to return unsold products, but also make payments over a period of weeks or even months (which is not as attractive as cash on delivery).

A less common ratio, market-to-book value, should also be calculated. Simply divide the firm's latest stock price by its book value per share; the result helps indicate whether investors view the firm's future positively. If the ratio is greater than 1, then investors forecast that the company's return on equity is expected to be greater than its required rate of return. If it is less than 1, then the firm's forecasted return on equity is less than its required rate of return. This ratio allows you to assess how favorably the stock market views the strategic direction of the firm.

## ■ Your Recommendations for Future Action

In the preceding sections of your analysis, you have probably identified issues, problems, and inconsistencies that need to be addressed. You may have made more specific suggestions in response to them—that is, in some cases, you may have stated that modifications be made in the firm's corporate-level or business unit strategies; in others, you may have suggested that one or several of the functional strategies be improved. Alternatively, you may have recommended that changes be made in the way that strategies are implemented. At this point, you might make broader recommendations, involving the overall firm.

**Exhibit 2**                    **Cross-Reference Information for Case Analyses**

| Section of Analysis | Textbook Chapter |
| --- | --- |
| Macroenvironment | Chapter 2, "External Environmental Opportunities and Threats" |
| Industry environment | Chapter 2, "External Environmental Opportunities and Threats" |
| The firm's resource, mission, goals, objectives, social responsibility, and ethics | Chapter 3, "The Internal Environment: The Firm's Resources, Organizational Mission, and Goals" |
| Corporate-level strategies | Chapter 4, "Corporate-Level Strategies" |
| Corporate portfolio management and corporate-level strategy related issues | Chapter 5, "Corporate Portfolio Management and Related Corporate-Level Strategy Issues" |
| Business unit strategies and functional strategies | Chapter 6, "Business Unit Strategies"; Chapter 7, "Functional Strategies" |
| Strategy implementation | Chapter 8, "Strategy Implementation: Organizational Structure"; Chapter 9, "Strategy Implementation: Leadership, Power, and Organizational Culture" |
| Strategic control | Chapter 10, "Strategic Control Process and Performance" |

Remember that a change that you recommend in one aspect of the organization's strategies or operations may affect several other parts of the company.

The recommendations should be addressed to the firm's top management and should be well organized and thought through. They also should be feasible in terms of human, organizational, and physical resources. Here, your ability to convince your instructor and classmates of the accuracy of your analysis and the power of your recommendations is of utmost importance.

We must emphasize that not all cases provide comprehensive information on all of the topics discussed in the previous pages. Some may focus only on specific areas, such as ethics or new product development. The framework presented here encompasses the total organization within its external environment. Consequently, you may or may not be able to use this entire set of topics in analyzing any particular case. However, in any case analysis, you may find the information in Exhibit 2 useful. This exhibit relates each section of your analysis to the corresponding chapter in this textbook. Before beginning your analysis, it may help to reread the discussion in the text regarding a particular issue.

## COURSEWORK SUGGESTIONS

We would like to conclude by offering you some suggestions on how to perform well in the strategic management course.

1. Be actively involved in the course. At a minimum, you should attend all classes and participate fully in the class discussions. Participation involves asking questions, expressing your views, providing relevant examples from your own experience or outside reading, and helping extend the discussion to other related issues. Of course, case discussions can be exciting only when you have prepared for each class by knowing the facts and understanding the issues in the case. Thorough preparation will enable you to convey your knowledge and understanding to others clearly and persuasively. These skills are of considerable importance to a practicing manager.

2. As you participate, remember that this is a broad-based course in strategic management. Regardless of your particular academic major, attempt to view the issues in the case more broadly than you ordinarily might from the more limited perspective of a marketing major or a finance major, for instance. Remember that the goal is an integrated set of recommendations to top management.

3. Do not approach class discussions with a closed mind. A good discussion can bring out many different facets in a case—probably more than you can generate through an individual analysis. Listen to the other members of the class and evaluate their contributions carefully.

4. Do not let yourself be intimidated by a bad experience. Eventually, everyone in class may make an inane comment, may panic and lose the train of thought in midsentence, or may realize as he or she is speaking that what is being said is incorrect. Do not let these experiences affect your willingness to participate in the future. Participation in case analysis is an excellent training ground for future business presentations and committee meetings.

5. Do not suggest the use of a consultant. You are the consultant and should have specific, detailed recommendations for top management.

6. Learn to work well within a group. Many professors form teams of students in the strategic management course. Teamwork adds realism to the study of cases since, in reality, groups of key executives deal with strategic planning in business organizations. Working in a group, however, presents a particular set of challenges. Hence, we offer these suggestions.

   - If you are allowed to select your group members, ensure that they have similar objectives for their grade in the course (if you are aiming for an A, do not join a group of students who wish to just squeak by, even if they are your best friends) and that you all have compatible schedules that permit you to meet outside of class.
   - Try to form a group of individuals with different academic majors. Synergy is more likely to occur when the group has students who are majoring in different fields, such as finance, accounting, information systems, human resource management, and production/operations management.
   - Do not divide the case into parts and assign an individual to each part. This technique will result in a fragmented, piecemeal, and disjointed analysis. Even if the primary responsibility for various parts of the case is assigned to specific individuals, every member of the group should be involved in all parts of the case analysis.
   - Cooperate closely with one another. Through cooperation and a free exchange of ideas, the team should be able to devise innovative solutions to case problems. But the only way to accomplish this is for

every member to participate fully during the team meetings. Ideally, only one person should talk at a time, while the others listen. One member should record all of the ideas expressed. If one person is particularly shy, others should encourage that person to talk by using such techniques as asking "What is your opinion on that issue?"

- Divide the work equitably. If one member is not doing his or her fair share, you must diplomatically, but quickly, inform that person that more is expected.

- Prepare thoroughly for the oral presentation. It is essential that you rehearse, as a group, several times. Ensure that each member knows his or her cue for speaking. Do not bring extensive notes and read from them. On the other hand, do not memorize your part word for word. Rather, prepare an outline of your part, and then let the key points on the outline guide your presentation.

- Be sure that your oral presentation fits neatly into the time allotted by your professor. It is not uncommon to see case presentations that either do not fully utilize the time allotted or run out of time before alternatives and recommendations can be thoroughly addressed. It is your responsibility to know the time allotment, to provide detailed analysis, and to set priorities so that key issues can be covered without rushing at the end.

- Get accustomed to speaking before people. Such presentations are routine in most aspects of the business world, so this course gives you an excellent opportunity to overcome your hesitancy to talk before a large group. If you have prepared well and have rehearsed several times, your presentation will be well received by your audience, even though you personally may feel a bit uncomfortable.

## SUMMARY

The remainder of this book contains cases. A case portrays a real organizational situation and requires you to analyze that situation and then develop recommendations for future action. To accomplish these ends, you will need to take a broad, companywide perspective.

After reading the case carefully several times, you will want to take notes to organize your analysis and presentation. We suggest that you analyze the case by using the following outline:

- Macroenvironment
- Industry environment
- The firm's resources, mission, goals, objectives, social responsibility, and ethics
- Corporate-level strategies
- Corporate portfolio management and related issues
- Business unit strategies and functional strategies
- Strategy implementation
- Strategic control
- Your recommendations for future action

Finally, we offer several suggestions for enhancing your performance in the strategic management course and for working within a group.

# NOTES

1. M.M. Helms and W.W. Prince, "Focused Library Instruction for Business Strategy Students and Strategy Practitioners," *Journal of Management Education* 17 (1993): 390–398.

2. R.L. Simon, D. Lavin, and J. Mitchell, "Tooling Along," *The Wall Street Journal*, 4 May 1994, pp. A1, A16; K. Kerwin, J.B. Treece, T. Peterson, L. Armstrong, and K.L. Miller, "Detroit's Big Chance," *Business Week*, 29 June 1992, pp. 82–90.

3. J.B. Treece, "Will Detroit Cut Itself Loose from Captive Imports?" *Business Week*, 4 September 1989, p. 34.

4. A. Dunkin, "They're More Single-Minded at Tambrands," *Business Week*, 28 August 1989, p. 28.

# Saturn Corporation: American Automobile Manufacturing in Transition

John A. Parnell, Texas A & M University Commerce

Michael L. Menefee, Purdue University

*Internet sites of interest:* **www.gm.com**
**www.saturncars.com**

## THE BIRTH OF SATURN

*"In 1985 when I joined the Saturn team, the auto industry in this country was undergoing some significant challenges. Today it is no different. We are being attacked from all sides. The competition is unrelenting in their pursuit of market dominance, if not subjugation. . . .These are challenging times for the heartiest of times, the most well established businesses. . . .These are not times for sissies or whiners in the closet. Rather, these are times when boldness is required from people who can see beyond today into the world of the future."*

ALAN G. PERRITON, VICE PRESIDENT, MATERIALS MANAGEMENT, SATURN CORPORATION

By the early 1980s, Asian imported vehicles had made significant inroads into the American automobile market. General Motors' response—the "J-Car" design introduced in 1982 as the Chevrolet Cavalier, Pontiac 2000, Oldsmobile Firenza, Buick Skylark, and Cadillac Cimarron—did nothing to slow its continued erosion in the small car market. Then CEO Roger Smith decided to start from scratch, considering the best production technology and labor-management techniques from around the world in pursuit of lost market share. In 1982, Smith initiated a project to innovatively design and manufacture small cars in the United States that were competitive with imported vehicles.

In 1984, 99 United Auto Workers (UAW) members, GM managers, and staff personnel from 55 plants joined to form the "Group of 99" to plan for the pursuit of this goal. Together, this group was charged "to identify and recommend the best approaches to integrate people and technology to competitively manufacture a small car in the United States."

Shortly thereafter, GM unveiled its first demonstration vehicle. In 1985, Saturn Corporation was formed as an independent, wholly owned subsidiary of

GM to continue the project under the direction of newly appointed president Joseph Sanchez. Sanchez served only 19 days until his death, succeeded for one year by William Hoglund, and then by current president Richard "Skip" LeFauve. Whereas most new organizations attempt to fight employee organization efforts, Saturn was created and organized with union involvement from the beginning.

In 1987, construction began on Saturn's manufacturing, assembly, and training and development operations facility, now covering 4 million square feet located on 2400 acres in Spring Hill, Tennessee, a small community 45 miles south of Nashville. By early 1988, Saturn began recruiting the first of 3000 workers for its Spring Hill plant from 136 GM/UAW facilities in the United States. Roger Smith and UAW President Owen Bieber drove the first Saturn vehicle off the final assembly line on July 30, 1990.

Today, Saturn's Spring Hill facility employs 8,200 people and is currently producing over 300,000 vehicles annually. Vehicle quality and satisfaction rates rival or exceed those of many of Saturn's Asian competitors. Saturn is seeking expansion, selling more cars, and contributing to GM's financial turnaround. Saturn has embarked on a distinctively different course for automotive success.

## ■ The Automobile Industry

The genesis of the automobile can be traced back to the development of steam engines, gasoline engines, and electric motors in the 1890s. By 1910, 187,000 automobiles were sold annually at approximately $750 each. Henry Ford's application of standardization, specialization, and mass production concepts contributed to Ford's emergence as industry leader. However, in the 1920s, Buick, Cadillac, Chevrolet, Oldsmobile, Delco, and Fisher Body came together to form General Motors. Unlike Ford, GM focused not on efficiency, but on product choice, offering a wide range of products updated annually to reflect engineering and styling innovations. GM secured industry leadership in 1931.

Imports began to challenge the domestic oligopoly in the late 1950s with smaller, more economical vehicles. However, weak dealer networks, parts availability, and service problems spelled failure for the imports. GM responded by producing larger, more expensive cars loaded with options. GM abhorred the slim margins of small cars and believed that the potential for such imports would remain insignificant. Meanwhile, Japanese automakers were back at the drawing board.

In the early 1970s, imported vehicles—particularly Japanese manufacturers—made a second surge into the domestic market. With cars more in tune to American preferences, improved quality, and a stronger dealer network, Japanese manufacturers carved out a sizable niche in the American market. By 1975, imports had secured one-fourth of the domestic automobile market.

Today, Japanese manufacturers account for approximately thirty percent of U.S. car sales. The Big Three auto makers consistently account for about 65%, with European manufacturers holding most of the remaining five percent of the market. Saturn's production increased from 280,002 cars in 1994 to 301,613 in 1995, improving its percentage of total U.S. production from 3.2 percent to 3.6 percent (see Exhibit 1).

Today, domestic production of automobiles is heavily concentrated among three firms: GM, Ford, and Chrysler. However, distinction between "domestic" and "import" can become blurred. In the 1980s, many Japanese manufacturers

**Exhibit 1**    **North American Car Production**

| Make | Car Sales 1995 | Car Sales 1994 | 1995 Share | 1994 Share |
|------|------|------|------|------|
| General Motors | 3,066,627 | 3,046,755 | 36.7 | 35.2 |
|   Chevrolet/GEO | 1,013,897 | 833,150 | 12.1 | 9.6 |
|   Pontiac | 622,851 | 653,936 | 7.4 | 7.6 |
|   Buick | 509,821 | 572,212 | 6.1 | 6.6 |
|   Oldsmobile | 390,964 | 481,326 | 4.7 | 5.6 |
|   Cadillac | 187,481 | 226,129 | 2.2 | 2.6 |
|   Saturn | 301,613 | 280,002 | 3.6 | 3.2 |
| Ford | 1,802,654 | 2,048,112 | 21.6 | 23.7 |
| Chrysler | 840,669 | 968,634 | 10.1 | 11.2 |
| Toyota | 733,568 | 618,970 | 8.8 | 7.1 |
| Honda | 657,896 | 607,018 | 7.9 | 7.0 |
| Nissan | 571,043 | 638,199 | 6.8 | 7.4 |
| All Others | 691,928 | 729,293 | 8.3 | 8.4 |
| TOTAL | 8,364,385 | 8,656,981 | 100.0 | 100.0 |

Based on data obtained from *Automotive News*, January 9, 1996.

Note: See the current issue of *Automotive News* for the most recent figures. Above figures do not include trucks or vehicles produced outside of the U.S.

constructed production facilities in the United States, including Honda (Marysville, Ohio), Nissan (Smyrna, Tennessee), Mazda (Flat Rock, Michigan), and Toyota (Georgetown, Kentucky). Joint ventures between "big three" firms and Japanese companies were also prevalent. The New United Motors Manufacturing, Inc. (NUMMI) project began producing vehicles in Fremont, California, in 1984 under a 50/50 GM-Toyota agreement. Diamond-Star Motors Corporation began production in Bloomington, Indiana, in 1988 under a 50/50 Chrysler-Mitsubishi agreement. Domestic auto manufacturers also hold significant ownership in Japanese manufacturers: GM owns 39% of Isuzu, Ford owns 30% of Mazda, and Chrysler owns 25% of Mitsubishi.

General Motors experienced moderate declines in the production of both cars and trucks as well as revenues in the late 1980s and early 1990s. Since GM's recorded loss in 1992, the company has posted modest and growing profits through 1995 (see Exhibits 2 & 3).

## SATURN CORPORATION: MISSION, PHILOSOPHY, & VALUES

As an independent, wholly-owned subsidiary of General Motors, Saturn drafted the following mission:

Market vehicles developed and manufactured in the United States that are world leaders in quality, cost, and customer satisfaction through the integration of

**Exhibit 2**                    **Consolidated Income Statements for General Motors**

|                                                              | 1995 | 1994 | 1993 | 1992 |
|--------------------------------------------------------------|------|------|------|------|
| Total Net Sales & Revenues                                   | $168,826.6 | $154,951.2 | $138,219.5 | $132,429.4 |
| Cost of Goods Sold                                           | 126,535.3 | 117,220.5 | 106,421.9 | 105,063.9 |
| Gross Margin                                                 | 42,291.3 | 37,730.7 | 31,797.6 | 27,365.5 |
| Expenses                                                     |      |      |      |      |
|   Selling, General, and Admin.                     | 13,514.7 | 12,233.7 | 11,531.9 | 11,621.8 |
|   Interest Expense                                 | 5,302.2 | 5,431.9 | 5,673.7 | 7,305.4 |
|   Depreciation Expense                             | 8,554.4 | 7,124.4 | 6,576.3 | 6,144.8 |
|   Amortization of Special Tools                    | 3,212.0 | 2,900.7 | 2,535.3 | 2,504.0 |
|   Amortization of Intangible Assets                | 255.3 | 226.2 | 330.4 | 310.2 |
|   Other Deductions                                 | 1,678.4 | 1,460.5 | 1,624.7 | 1,575.4 |
|   Special Provision for Scheduled Plant Closings and Other Restructurings | — | — | 950.0 | 1,237.0 |
|   Total Expenses                                   | 32,517.0 | 29,377.4 | 29,222.3 | 30,698.6 |
| Net Income (Loss) Before Taxes                               | 9,776.3 | 8,353.3 | 2,575.3 | ($3,333.1) |
|   Adjustments for credits and accounting changes   | (51.8) | (758.1) | — | (20,165.2) |
| Net Income (Loss)                                            | $9,724.5 | $7,595.2 | $2,575.3 | ($23,498.3) |

Dollars in millions

Source: *General Motors Annual Report, 1995.*

people, technology, and business systems and to transfer knowledge and experience throughout General Motors.

The Saturn team has also articulated the "Saturn Philosophy" to fulfill the mission:

We, the Saturn Team, in concert with the UAW and General Motors, believe that meeting the needs of Customers, Saturn Members, Suppliers, Dealers, and Neighbors is fundamental to fulfilling our mission.
To meet our customer needs:

- Our products and services must be world leaders in value and satisfaction.

To meet our members' needs:

- We will create a sense of belonging in an environment of mutual trust, respect, and dignity.
- We believe that all people want to be involved in decisions that affect them, care about their jobs and each other, take pride in themselves and in their contributions, and want to share in the success of their efforts.
- We will develop the tools, training, and education for each member, recognizing individual skills and knowledge.
- We believe that creative, motivated, responsible team members who understand that change is critical to success are Saturn's most important asset.

**Exhibit 3**       **Consolidated Balance Sheet for General Motors**

| | 1995 | 1994 |
|---|---:|---:|
| *Assets* | | |
| Cash and Cash Equivalents | $ 11,044.3 | $ 10,939.0 |
| Other Marketable securities | 5,598.6 | 5,136.6 |
|     Total Cash and Marketable Securities | 16,642.9 | 16,075.6 |
| Finance receivables | 58,732.0 | 54,077.3 |
| Accounts and Notes receivables | 9,988.4 | 8,977.8 |
| Inventories (less allowances) | 11,529.5 | 10,127.8 |
| Contracts in process | 2,469.2 | 2,265.4 |
| Net Equipment on operating leases (less accum. depreciation) | 27,702.3 | 20,061.6 |
| Deferred income taxes | 19,028.3 | 19,693.3 |
| Property | 37,739.8 | 34,780.6 |
| Intangible assets | 11,898.9 | 11,913.8 |
| Other assets | 21,392.1 | 20,625.5 |
|     Total Assets | $217,123.4 | $198,598.7 |
| *Liabilities* | | |
| Accounts Payable | $ 11,898.8 | $ 11,635.0 |
| Notes and loans payable | 83,323.5 | 73,730.2 |
| U.S., foreign, and other income taxes—deferred and payable | 3,231.6 | 2,721.0 |
| Postretirement benefits other than pensions | 41,595.1 | 40,018.2 |
| Pensions | 6,842.3 | 14,353.2 |
| Other liabilities and deferred credits | 46,886.6 | 42,867.3 |
|     Total Liabilities | 193,777.9 | 185,324.9 |
| Stocks Subject to Repurchase | — | 450.0 |
| Preference stocks | 1.2 | 2.4 |
| Common stock—$1-2/3 par value | 1,255.0 | 1,257.2 |
| Common stock—Class E | 44.3 | 26.8 |
| Common stock—Class H | 9.7 | 7.9 |
| Capital surplus | 18,870.9 | 13,149.4 |
| Net income retained for use in the business | 7,185.4 | 1,785.8 |
|     Subtotal | 27,366.5 | 16,229.5 |
| Minimum pensions liability adjustment | (4,736.3) | (3,548.4) |
| Accumulated foreign currency translation adjustments | 222.5 | 100.4 |
| Net unrealized gains on investments in certain debt and equity securities | 492.8 | 243.1 |
|     Total Stockholder's Equity | 23,345.5 | 12,823.8 |
|     Total Liabilities and Stockholder's Equity | $217,123.4 | $198.598.7 |

Dollars in millions
Source: *General Motors Annual Report, 1995.*

To meet our suppliers' and dealers' needs:

- We will strive to create real partnerships with them.
- We will be open and fair in our dealings, reflecting trust, respect, and their importance to Saturn.
- We want dealers and suppliers to feel ownership in Saturn's mission and philosophy as their own.

To meet the needs of our neighbors, the communities in which we live and operate:

- We will be good citizens, protect the environment, and conserve natural resources.
- We will seek to cooperate with government at all levels and strive to be sensitive, open, and candid in all our public statements.

The Saturn philosophy is founded on a unique approach to decision making and management of the organization known as "the partnership." Saturn is attempting to overcome many of the traditional management-labor problems that have for so long become synonymous with the United States automobile industry. The Saturn approach brings together leaders of Saturn management and the UAW to improve trust and efficiency in decision making. The memorandum of agreement is quite short in comparison to UAW agreements with other auto manufacturers. The model has worked well in practice. For instance, when GM and its suppliers laid off 20,000 workers in early 1996 in response to the strike at the Delphi Chassis Systems in Dayton, Ohio, Saturn kept its 8,200 workers on the payroll at a daily cost of $1.6 million. In return, the UAW agreed to work Easter, Memorial Day, and several additional Sundays to make up for lost production during the strike.

As in other organizations, management is responsible for securing resources, legal and regulatory matters, employee selection and promotion, and the formal dispersion of expenditures. Likewise, the UAW is primarily concerned with fulfilling its duty of fair representation (DFR). However, there exists a partnership arena where management and the UAW work together and share responsibilities. Activities in this arena include the mission, philosophy and values, memorandum of agreement, strategic and tactical planning, operational planning, and operational performance. The partnership does not eliminate conflict, but instead attempts to promote a less adversarial, more advocative means of problem resolution.

Within the management-UAW partnership, Saturn has also adopted five corporate values to support the commitment to be one of the world's most successful car companies:

- *Commitment to Customer Enthusiasm*: We continually exceed the expectations of internal and external customers for products and services that are world leaders in cost, quality, and customer satisfaction. Our customers know that we really care about them.
- *Commitment to Excel*: There is no place for mediocrity and half-hearted efforts at SATURN. We accept responsibility, accountability, and authority for overcoming obstacles and reaching beyond the best. We choose to excel in every aspect of our business, including return on investment.
- *Teamwork*: We are dedicated to singleness of purpose through the effective involvement of members, suppliers, dealers, neighbors, and all other stakeholders. A fundamental tenet of our philosophy is the belief that effective teams engage the talents of individual members while encouraging team growth.
- *Trust and Respect for the Individual*: We have nothing of greater value than our people! We believe that demonstrating respect for the uniqueness of every

individual builds a team of confident, creative members possessing a high degree of initiative, self-respect, and self-discipline.
- *Continuous Improvement*: We know that sustained success depends on our ability to continually improve the quality, cost, and timeliness of our products and services. We are providing opportunity for personal, professional, and organizational growth and innovation for all SATURN stakeholders.

# HUMAN RESOURCE STRATEGIES

The Saturn-UAW agreement necessitates that all Saturn team members be selected from a pool of employees from other GM plants for as long as laid-off UAW workers are available. In other words, Saturn is not free to hire local Tennesseans as long as there exist reasonably qualified unemployed UAW workers from other GM facilities. UAW officials praise this provision of the Saturn agreement, arguing that no GM facility should hire outside workers when other GM workers have been laid off and are jobless. Interestingly, this policy leads to a 100 percent geographically transplanted work force for the Spring Hill, Tennessee, plant.

Saturn promotes the utilization of self-directed, integrated teams of between six and fifteen members that manage their own work and are involved in decisions that affect them. Each team is led by a work unit counselor (WUC), who initiates group activities and represents the group. Decisions are not made by voting, but instead by consensus. The Saturn model does not require 100 percent agreement. Instead, teams seek at least 70 percent agreement and demand 100 percent support from all members.

Saturn applicants for team members must complete a detailed 12-page assessment that asks for specific information on skills, attitudes, and behaviors. For those who are selected, there are no time clocks, no privileged parking spots, and no private dining rooms at Saturn. Dress is casual, and all employees are on salary. Words such as "manager" and "executive" are not frequently used.

Training is an integral part of the Saturn human resource strategy. In 1992, 5% of a worker's salary is tied to the successful completion of 92 hours of approved training, on Saturn time.

# PRODUCTION & TECHNOLOGY STRATEGIES

The Saturn facility is a unique, vertically integrated manufacturing and assembly complex that boasts approximately 95% U.S. product content. The design and engineering processes are tackled by multidisciplinary teams that include product engineers, materials managers, financial managers, marketers, and representatives of the UAW. All of Saturn's in-house product design is done electronically using computer-aided design (CAD), computer-aided manufacturing (CAM), and computer-aided engineering (CAE) techniques.

Saturn's simultaneous engineering approach integrates people and automation to form a more efficient workplace. Saturn does not follow the conventional practice of dividing product development into separate tasks to be done sequentially. For example, the car frame and other components that are to be added meet at each work station. One goal of simultaneous engineering is to reduce in-process inventory between the engine component machining operations, engine assembly, the concurrent transmission assembly, and the final car assembly process. This creates an enormous potential for cost avoidance.

A key tenet of Saturn's strategic approach to vehicle production is the flexible assembly system. Flexible assembly plays its most important role in assembly of the engine and transmission, where heavy components can be readily rotated and repositioned for a variety of assembly operations. Flexible assembly systems are helping manufacturers cut production costs, improve quality, increase factory output, and build different versions of a product while on the same production line. Specifically, flexible assembly can save more than 40 percent of floor space.

Perhaps the most compelling example of how Saturn has utilized team member involvement in its operations design is the skillet system method of assembly. Under the traditional chain-and-drive system, workers move along the line to complete production tasks. A group of Saturn engineers and team members sought a more effective system, given four primary parameters: ergonomics, quality, member utilization, and cost-effectiveness. After two years of research, the skillet system was recommended. The skillet system can be described as a moving sidewalk; workers step on the skillet, perform their necessary operations, and step off when done. The vehicle continues to travel on the skillet to other workers. The result, according to Saturn officials, is a more user-friendly system that requires fewer team members and is consistent with Saturn's world-class quality mission.

Another waste-reduction technique employed by Saturn is lost foam casting. When using this form of casting the engine block, head, and other internal parts are formed from styrofoam. The foam is covered with ceramic and sand and placed into steel casts. The aluminum is then poured into the cast and is formed into the shape of the foam. The foam is then melted by the hot aluminum, eliminating substantial waste and much of the machine work involved in the normal casting process.

Thermoplastic body panels lower manufacturing costs while scrap materials can be reprocessed. These panels also make the car lighter, allowing for better gas mileage and higher performance with a smaller engine. This also allows Saturn to produce cars at a lower cost.

Saturn also seeks just-in-time (JIT) partnerships with suppliers to improve efficiency and reduce storage costs associated with excess inventories. JIT principles are also employed in the production facility, where the inventory created at any stage of production may supply the next stage for two hours or less. Hence, this approach creates a unique challenge for Saturn. Problems on the production line or with suppliers stop the entire production line throughout the complex.

## MARKETING STRATEGIES

The Saturn-retailer relationship is a focal point of Saturn's comprehensive approach to marketing its vehicles. Saturn's preference for the word "retailer" to "dealer" signifies its belief that retailers and customers should establish relationships, not make deals. Retailers sell only Saturns but get wide territories, so they compete with rival auto makers and not each other. In 1991, more cars were sold per dealer at Saturn retailers than those associated with any other manufacturer.

Saturn strongly encourages a bottom-line pricing approach to increase retailer-consumer trust. Customers entering a Saturn showroom are told exactly what each vehicle will cost up front. Saturn customers appear to appreciate the elimination of pressure, haggling, and negotiating at the retailers. And if a customer is not satisfied with the vehicle, he or she is free to return it within 30 days or 1500 miles for a full refund.

The automaker recently introduced a certification program for used vehicles, and Saturn retailers make a special effort to repurchase used Saturns for resale on their lots. Vehicles are "certified" if they meet quality standards for maintenance and performance. In early 1996, Saturn became the first automobile manufacturer in decades to use network media to promote used vehicles. Dealers began selling the certified used vehicles at no-haggle prices. Analysts see the move as an attempt to bolster the confidence in resale values of the vehicles as well as secure sales from an increasing market for used automobiles.

Saturn's marketing strategy also appears to be integrated with its approach to customer service and satisfaction. For example, upon discovering that faulty Texaco coolant had been placed in some of its vehicles, Saturn offered new cars, free rentals until they were delivered, and extra options at no extra charge to the 1836 affected customers. While some analysts noted the positive publicity received by Saturn as a result, Saturn officials maintain that the move was designed to take care of its owners.

Saturn aggressively targets the typical Asian vehicle purchaser: young to middle-aged, educated, family-oriented consumers with median incomes of around $50,000. Today, the average Saturn owner is 38 years old; 50% of owners have college degrees, compared to 38% for other domestic manufacturers. Seventy percent of Saturn customers named a non-GM vehicle as their second choice, and 45% said they would have purchased an Asian car if their Saturn choice were not available. Saturn is particularly interested in treating female consumers with the respect and integrity often perceived to be lacking at competitive dealerships.

Saturn marketing success depends on its ability to sway buyers who are already predisposed to a belief that facets such as dependability, durability, quality, and high resale value are paramount in Japanese vehicles. Indeed, Saturn's advertising efforts have been aimed at such persuasion. Marketing analysts have suggested that this feat depends on Saturn's ability to distance itself from General Motors. To date, Saturn has enjoyed some success in this arena. In one survey, only 26% of Saturn customers associated Saturn with GM. Saturn has also shunned traditional domestic car makers' approaches to advertising that primarily rely on themes of sex appeal, prestige, and excitement. Instead, advertising more resembles its Japanese counterparts, emphasizing "a different kind of car, a different kind of car company."

Saturn likes to view its customers as family. The company hosted the "Saturn Homecoming" in June 1994, mailing invitations to more than 600,000 Saturn owners. Festivities included plant tours, car shows, arts and crafts events, concerts, and a fireworks display. Approximately 40,000 people attended the event in Spring Hill, while another 100,000 owners attended Saturn retailer-sponsored events nationwide.

Saturn's sales account for approximately three percent of the U.S. car market. Further, J.D. Powers & Associates reported that Saturn customer satisfaction (score of 160) trailed only Lexus (179) and Infinity (167), while scoring ahead of industry leaders Acura (148), Mercedes-Benz (145), Toyota (144), Audi (139), Cadillac (138), and Jaguar (137), as well as the industry average (129).

## FUTURE CHALLENGES AT SATURN

Regardless of GM's estimated $3 billion investment, including $1.9 for the Spring Hill facility, Saturn's profit status is difficult to analyze because of the allocation of start-up expenses to the corporation at large. Saturn is believed to have lost $800 million in 1991, and GM reports that Saturn's first profit was generated in May 1993. Several analysts have charged that high profits will be difficult to sustain, saddled by labor charges in excess of $30 per hour and the huge Spring Hill investment.

There is a considerable amount of financial confusion surrounding Saturn. Mounting evidence suggests Saturn executives believe that greater volume is necessary to cover the high administrative and marketing expenses associated with the division. Critics charge that GM's investment in Saturn well exceeds $5 billion and the division has not yet achieved a profit. However, outsiders can only speculate since financial documents at the business level are not available.

The increase in profit pressure on Saturn has been accompanied by an increase in control exercised at the corporate level. As a result, Saturn is buying more GM-made parts, considering production of its vehicles at other GM facilities, and preparing to launch GM's electric vehicles in the coming decade. In effect, Saturn is becoming "General Motorized," and may fear the mystique or the "different kind of car company" is beginning to evaporate as the division becomes just another business unit within the GM bureaucracy.

Saturn produced its one-millionth car on June 1, 1995. Although there has been talk of a plant expansion in Spring Hill, Saturn has been hesitant to do so without assurances that quality will not decline. Production beyond 500,000 can only be accomplished with a major expansion at Spring Hill or the development of a second Saturn facility. If it chose to do so, Saturn could retool an older GM plant or build a new one from scratch.

Saturn officials have also expressed an interest in developing a larger Saturn model for the late 1990s. There are rumors that the carmaker will add a larger sedan based on the 1996 Adam Opel AG Vectra and build 200,000 annually by 1999 at a Wilmington, Delaware, plant scheduled to be idled. However, although larger cars typically bring heftier margins, an additional $1 billion would likely be required to develop the vehicle. In a recent survey, 94% of Saturn owners said they would likely repurchase a Saturn even if a larger option were not available. Further, the interest in smaller Saturns may continue to grow if gasoline prices rise substantially.

However, much of the impetus for a larger vehicle has come from the corporate level. Not only has GM decided that any larger vehicles will likely be remakes of existing cars, it has also suggested that the Spring Hill labor agreement would not be in force in the other plants that produce them. UAW officials have voiced opposition to the production of the Opel-clone.

The integration of Saturn's business level strategy with GM's corporate strategy remains a key concern. In some respects, Saturn is an extension of

General Motors, a model for other divisions to follow. Some analysts predict that Saturn will look more like other divisions in the future and less like the experiment which created it. However, many others also believe that the ultimate success of Saturn depends on its ability to disassociate itself from General Motors and remove the negative perceptions concerning inferior quality and poorly motivated workers. Even GM officials and dealers associated with other divisions—typically GM's largest division, Chevrolet—have begun to express some dissatisfaction with the high amount of perceived support given to Saturn. As Skip LeFauve put it, "We've got to earn our capital just like anyone else at GM. That's the way it should be." While Saturn's sales climb, Chevrolet's market share continues to decline from 20% two decades ago to 12% today. Competition with GM divisions for capital appears inevitable.

## REFERENCES

Bemowski, K. (1995). To boldly go where so many have gone before. *Quality Progress, 28*(2), 29-33.

Bennett, M.E. (1992). The Saturn Corporation: New management-union partnership at the factory of the future. *Looking Ahead, 8*(4), 15-23.

Carey, R. (1995). Five top coporate training programs. *Successful Meetings, 44*(2), 56-62.

Economist (1992). General Motor's Saturn: Success at a price. *Economist, 323*(7765), 80-81.

Dessler, G. (September 1995). Enriching and empowering employees—the Saturn way. *Personnel Journal*, p. 32.

*Direct Marketing* (November 1995). Saturn Corp. homecoming sparks interest. pp. 24-25.

Garfield, B. (1992). Old imagery powers old perceptions of Detroit cars. *Advertising Age, 63*(13), S20.

Geber, B. (1992). Saturn's grand experiment. *Training, 29*(6), 27-35.

Gelsi, S. (1995). Saturn slots upwards of $20M to bring used cars into marketing mix. *Brandweek, 36*(38), 4.

General Motors Corporation (1991). *Annual Report*. Detroit, MI: General Motors Corporation.

Holzwarth, F. (1992). Ten theses in pursuit of lean production. *Looking ahead, 8*(4), 10-13.

J.D. Power and Associates (1992). *The Saturn Way*. New York: J.D. Power and Associates.

Kilburn, D., & Halliday, J. (1995). Saturn chooses Japan shop. *Adweek, 36*(50), 2.

LeFauve, R.C. (1992). The Saturn Corporation: A Balance of people, technology, and business systems. *Looking Ahead, 8*(4), 14.

LeFauve, R.C., & Hax, A.C. (Spring 1992). Managerial and technological innovations at Saturn Corporation. *MIT Management*, pp. 8-19.

Manji, J.F. (1990). Saturn: GM fights back. *Automation, 37*(10), 28-30.

Morris, K. (1992). Sales: Saturn-GM. *Financial World, 161*(8), 48.

Moskal, B.S. (1989). Hybrid incubator hatches workers. *Industry Week, 238*(15), 27, 30.

O'Connor, L. (November 1991). Flexible assembly: Saturn's road to success. *Mechanical Engineering*, pp. 30-34.

O'Toole, J., & Lewandowski, J. (1990). Forming the future: The Marriage of people and technology at Saturn. *Stanford University Industrial Engineering & Engineering Management*, March 29, 1990.

Overman, S. (March 1995). Saturn teams working and profiting. *HRMagazine*, pp. 72-74.

Perriton, A.G. (March 18, 1992). A different kind of car—A different kind of company: A different materials management. *A.I.A.G. Presentation*.

Rickard, L. (1996). Saturn. Unpublished manuscript.

*Saturn Corporation* (1992). Saturn fact sheet and other company literature. Spring Hill, TN: Saturn Corporation.

Schlossberg, H. (1991). It's lift-off for Saturn. *Marketing News, 25*(8), 1, 29.

Serafin, R. (1990). GM's Saturn enters crucial period. *Advertising Age, 61*(10), 16.

Serafin, R., & Horton, C. (1992). Automakers focus on service. *Advertising Age, 63*(27), 3, 33.

Solomon, C.M. (1991). Behind the wheel at Saturn. *Personnel Journal, 70*(6), 72-74.

Taylor, A., III (1988). Back to the future at Saturn. *Fortune, 118*(3), 63-72.

Templin, N. (June 16, 1993). GM's Saturn subsidiary is fighting for its future. *Wall Street Journal*, B4.

Treece, J.B. (1990). Here comes GM's Saturn. *Business Week, 3153*, 56-62.

———— (1991). The planets may be perfectly aligned for Saturn's lift-off. *Business Week, 3184*, 40.

———— (1991). Getting mileage from a recall. *Business Week, 3215*, 38-39.

Vasilash, G.S. (1989). Business strategies: Nearing Saturn. *Production, 101*(6), 42-43.

*Ward's Auto World* (1995). Saturn is meeting 'financial targets.' Vol. 31, No. 12, p. 35.

Wetzel, J.J. (1991). Managing the interfaces for the success of the product, the customer, the company. University of Michigan 1991 Management Briefing Seminar, Traverse City, Michigan, August 8.

Winter, D. (1995). Saturn turns 10. *Ward's Auto World, 31*(7), 67-71.

Womack, J.P. (1992). The lean difference: An international productivity comparison and the implications for U.S. industry. *Looking Ahead, 8*(4), 3-9.

Woodruff, D. (1991). At Saturn, what workers want is . . . fewer defects. *Business Week, 3242*, 117-118.

———— (1992). Saturn. *Business Week, 3279*, 86-91.

———— (1992). What's this—Car dealers with souls? *Business Week, 3260*, 66-67.

# XEL Communications, Inc. (A)

Robert P. McGowan, University of Denver
Cynthia V. Fukami, University of Denver

As he was turning into the parkway that curves around his company's plant, Bill Sanko, President of XEL Communications, glanced at a nearby vacant facility that once housed a now-defunct computer manufacturer. Over the next few months, in May 1995, XEL would be moving into this building. While this move was a sign of how far XEL had come in the last ten years, Bill considered that they might have met the same fate as the previous tenant. He also wondered whether they would be able to sustain the same culture that enabled the company to succeed in a rapidly changing, highly competitive industry. At the same time, he realized that change could also create opportunities.

After parking and completing the short walk to his office, Bill grabbed a copy of that day's *Wall Street Journal*. One article which caught his attention was entitled, "Baby Bells Lobby Congress for Regulatory Freedom." As one of many suppliers of telecommunications equipment to the Regional Bell Operating Companies (RBOCs), this development posed some interesting issues for XEL Communications. If the RBOCs were allowed to pursue their own manufacturing (which they are currently prohibited from doing), how would this affect XEL's existing contracts? As telephone and cable companies develop more strategic alliances and partnerships, would this provide an opportunity for XEL? At the same time, it appeared that the telecommunications industry was now becoming a global industry in which developing countries allow outside companies to establish and maintain telecommunications services. What role could XEL play in this rapidly growing market?

# THE TELECOMMUNICATIONS INDUSTRY

A decade after the breakup of the telephone monopoly, the prospect of intense competition driving the telecommunications industry was creating some interesting scenarios.[1] The AT&T of old was the model for the telecommunications company of the future. "You're going to see the re-creation of five or six former AT&Ts—call them 'full-service networks'—over the next five years or more," said Michael Elling, first vice president at Prudential Securities. Marketing and capital-equipment dollars are invested more efficiently if distribution is centralized, he continued. "It could be that U S WEST, Time Warner, and Sprint get together. It could be that Bell Atlantic, Nynex, and MCI get together. It could be that GTE, AT&T, and a few other independents (local providers not affiliated with a regional Bell) get together."

The inevitability of such combinations was matched by the uncertainty over what form they would take. A business known for its predictability had suddenly found itself unpredictable. "I think you can't rule anything out in this industry anymore," says Simon Flannery, a vice president at J.P. Morgan Securities. "All the rules of the game are up for review."

In most cases, telecommunications systems transmitted information by wire, radio, or space satellite. Wire transmission involved sending electrical signals over various types of wire lines such as open wire, multipair cable, and coaxial cable. These lines could be used to transmit voice frequencies, telegraph messages, computer-processed data, and television programs. Another somewhat related transmission medium that had come into increasingly wider use, especially in telephone communications, was a type of cable composed of optical fibers. Here, electrical signals converted to light signals by a laser-driven transmitter carried both speech and data over bundles of thin glass or plastic filaments.

Radio communication systems transmitted electronic signals in relatively narrow frequency bands through the air. They included radio navigation and both amateur and commercial broadcasting. Commercial broadcasting consisted of AM, FM, and TV broadcasting for general public use.

Satellite communications allowed the exchange of television or telephone signals between widely separated locations by means of microwaves—that is, very short radio waves with wavelengths of 4 to 0.4 inches, which corresponded to a frequency range of 3 to 30 gigahertz (GHz), or 3 to 30 billion cycles per second. Since satellite systems did not require the construction of intermediate relay or repeater stations as did ground-based microwave systems, they could be put into service much more rapidly.

Not only had the mode of delivery changed, but also the content. Modern telecommunications networks not only sent the traditional voice communications of telephones and the printed messages of telegraphs and telexes, they also carried images—the still images of facsimile machines or the moving images of video in video conferences in which the participants could see as well as hear each other. Additionally, they carried encoded data ranging from the business accounts of a multinational corporation to medical data relayed by physicians thousands of miles from a patient.

The U.S. telecommunications services industry was expected to continue to expand in 1994.[2] Revenues were expected to rise about 7.7 percent, compared with a 6 percent increase in 1993. In 1994, revenues generated by international services increased about 20 percent, and local exchange telephone service was expected to rise by 3 percent. Sales of domestic long distance services were expected to grow more than 6 percent in 1994, depending on overall growth in the economy. Value-added network and information services were to climb an estimated 15 percent in 1994. Revenues from cellular mobile telephone services were to increase 39 percent in 1994; satellite service revenues in 1994 were to grow nearly 25 percent.

Local telephone services were provided by about 1,325 local telephone companies (telcos), including 7 Regional Bell Operating Companies (RBOCs), telcos owned by GTE, Sprint (United Telecom and Centel franchises), and independent local telephone companies. Many of these small, local companies operated as rural telephone cooperatives. Long distance service was provided by AT&T, MCI, Sprint, WilTel, Metromedia Communications, Litel Telecommunications, Allnet, and more than 475 smaller companies.

In 1993, the local exchange telephone companies were confronted with increasing competitive pressures in certain local services they had monopolized for decades. In response to these pressures, and to possible future competition from cable TV companies and others for local exchange telephone service itself, the RBOCs stepped up their campaign to obtain authority to enter the long distance and telecommunications equipment manufacturing businesses, and to offer video programming services.

The major long distance carriers, meanwhile, focused their attention on wireless technologies and made plans to work with or acquire companies in the wireless market. This would enable them to provide long distance services to cellular users and possibly to develop a more economical local access network to reach their own subscribers. Internationally, the large service providers continued to make alliances and seek out partners in efforts to put together global telecommunications networks and offer the international equivalent of the advanced telecommunications services available in the U.S. domestic market.

In terms of policy developments that affect the telecommunications industry, the Clinton Administration had focused its attention on the national telecommunications infrastructure, or the "information superhighway." Bills were introduced in both houses of Congress that addressed this and other key telecommunications policy issues. There was broad consensus that the Federal Government should not finance the construction of a national network. Rather, the Government was being urged to help promote competition in network access, advance interconnection and interoperability standards, see that customers would have access to new services provided over the digital infrastructure at reasonable rates, and support pilot projects for applications in education and health care. Under proposed legislation, the digital infrastructure would be extended to tap information resources at libraries, research centers, and government facilities. Congress was to consider major telecommunications legislation in the future and would then face how it would resolve the contentious issues involved that concerned so many large and powerful interests. There were also signs that some states would also open up their exchange and local service markets to competition.

Cable TV companies were likely to become another group of competitors the local telephone companies would face in the near future. Cable companies already had connections with 60 percent of U.S. households, and cable facilities extended into areas where another 30 percent of the households were located.

New digital and fiber optic technologies would allow them to provide telephone services over their networks, something cable companies already were doing in Britain.

## XEL COMMUNICATIONS: THE BEGINNING

XEL Communications was born not only with an opportunity but with a challenge as well. Bill Sanko started with General Telephone and Electronics (GTE) as a product manager after spending six years in the U.S. Army.[3] He was chosen in 1972 to help establish the GTE Satellite Corporation. After he was successful with this enterprise, GTE then selected Bill for another startup business called Special Service Products in 1980.

The Special Service Products division was established to manufacture certain telecommunications products to compete with small companies who were making inroads into GTE's market. These products ranged from voice and data transmission products to switches customized to specific business needs. After two previous failures, it was GTE's third (and perhaps final) try at starting such a division. Company officials granted Sanko almost full autonomy to build the division, including recruiting all key executives, establishing a location in Aurora, Colorado, a rapidly growing region east of Denver, and in designing the division's overall operating philosophy.

By 1984, the division realized its first year of break-even operations, but it wasn't enough to win over GTE executives. Despite its initial success and the prospect of a fast-growing market, SSPD found itself heading toward orphan status in GTE's long-range plans.[4] After divestiture in telecommunications, GTE opted to concentrate primarily on providing telephone service rather than hardware. (GTE has subsequently divested all of its manufacturing divisions.) "Even though we were doing the job expected of us in building the business," Sanko said, "GTE's and SSPD's strategic plans were taking different directions." They opted to close the division. Sanko lobbied and ultimately persuaded GTE to sell the division.

The result was an action as unlikely as it was logical. On July 3, 1984, appropriately one day before Independence Day, Sanko and fellow managers from SSPD signed a letter of intent to buy the division from GTE. Two months later, the bill of sale was signed and XEL Communications, Inc. became an independent company. Sanko gathered a group of managers and raised the money—some through second mortgages on homes. GTE loaned Sanko and his colleagues money, and the rest was supplied by venture capitalists. In fact, just before the new company was scheduled to begin operations, one of the banks backed out of the arrangement. According to Julie Rich, one of the co-founders and Vice President for Human Resources, "we didn't have any money lined up from September to December of 1984. Making the first payroll for a company of 180 employees was one of the major challenges. Christmas that first year was particularly lean."

The financing was eventually arranged, and XEL was underway. Sanko reflected on the perils and rewards of leaving the corporate nest to seek one's fortune: "In the end, it was the right thing to do, but it wasn't an easy decision to make. After 17 years with GTE, I had achieved vice president status; and I was more than a little nervous about leaving the corporation."[5]

## EARLY YEARS

One of the more interesting exercises in starting any new company is what to name it. John Puckett, Vice President for Manufacturing and also one of the original founders, recalled: "We did a lot of brainstorming about what to call this new company—including taking initials from the original founders' names and seeing what combinations we could come up with. Usually, they didn't make a whole lot of sense. We finally decided on XEL, which is a shortened version of excellence."

More than simply naming the company, one of the key concerns for XEL Communications was whether their customers would stay with them once they were no longer part of GTE—not that XEL has ever exactly been an abandoned child. GTE may have kicked XEL out the door in 1984, but it remains XEL's biggest customer, with GTE Telephone Operations accounting for about 35 percent of the company's total business. In fact, the relationship between the two companies continues to be close and mutually beneficial: Ever the proud parent, GTE recognized XEL as its Quality Vendor of the Year in both 1987 and 1988, and as a Vendor of Excellence in subsequent years.

At first, all XEL produced was a handful of products for GTE. Even so, the company showed a profit in its first year of independent operation. "We were off to a better start than you might expect, just because we had always had a certain independence," says Sanko. "We had our own engineers, we were a non-union shop (unlike most of the other divisions of GTE at the time), we had installed our own computer systems, and we were out here in Colorado, on our own. We were doing things differently from the start, and so we just continued."

Weaning itself from GTE was a corporate goal entirely dependent on new product development, and XEL spent over 10 percent of its revenues on R&D. That focus on development would not likely change: The XEL product line is custom manufactured and therefore constantly evolved and changed as customers' needs changed. "Running a small company has a lot of challenges," Sanko says. "But one of the major advantages is being able to respond to the market and get things done quickly. Here we can respond to a customer requirement."

## XEL'S PRODUCTS AND MARKETS

For example, XEL sold products that facilitated the transmission of data and information over phone lines. Driving the need for XEL's products was the fact that "businesses are more and more dependent on the transfer of information," as Bill Sanko noted. In addition, more businesses, including XEL, were operating by taking and filling orders, for example—through electronic data exchanges. Instead of dialing into inside salespeople, businesses often accessed databases directly.

XEL's products performed a number of functions that allowed businesses to incorporate their specific telecommunications needs into the existing telephone "network" functions such as data exchanges. XEL had a diverse product line of over 300 products that it manufactured. Some of its major products included:

Fiber Optic Terminal Products
Coaxial Business Access
Analog Voice Products
Analog Data Products
Digital Data Products
Digital Transmission Products
Telecom Maintenance Products

XEL's products would, for example, translate analog information into digital transmissions. Adapting electronic information for fiber optic networks was another area of emphasis for XEL, as was adapting equipment to international standards for foreign customers.

One of XEL's strengths was its ability to adapt one manufacturer's equipment to another's. Often, it was the bits and pieces of telecommunications equipment that XEL provided to the "network" that allowed the smooth integration of disparate transmission pieces. XEL also sold central office transmission equipment and a full range of mechanical housings, specialty devices, power supplies, and shelves.

"Business customers and their changing telecommunications needs drive the demand for XEL's products. That, in turn, presents a challenge to the company," said Sanko. Sanko cited the constant stream of new products developed by XEL—approximately two per month—as the driving force behind its growth. Industry-wide, product life cycle times were getting ever shorter. Before the breakup of the Bell System in 1984, transmission switches and other telecommunications devices enjoyed a 30-to-40 year life. In 1995, with technology moving so fast, XEL's products had about a three-to-five year life.

In terms of its customers, XEL sold to all of the Regional Bell Operating Companies as well as such companies as GTE and Centel. Railroads, with their own telephone networks, were also customers. XEL's field salespeople worked with engineers to satisfy client requests for specific services. Over a period of time, a rapport was built up with these engineers, providing XEL with new product leads.

With all the consolidations and ventures in telecommunications, one might suspect that the overall market would become more difficult, but Sanko believed "out of change comes opportunity. The worst-case scenario would be a static situation. Thus, a small company, fast to respond to customer needs and able to capitalize on small market niches, will be successful. Often, a large company like AT&T will forsake a smaller market and XEL will move in. Also, XEL's size allows it to design a product in a very short time."

Interestingly, Sanko was watching pending federal legislation proposing to open up local telephone services to companies other than the regional Baby Bells. Consequently, said Sanko, "we need to expand our market and be prepared to sell to others as the regulatory environment changes." Sanko believed legislation would be signed in the near future that would set the groundwork and timetables to open local telephone monopolies to competition. The recent joint venture between Time Warner and U S WEST also signalled that telephone and cable companies would be pooling their resources to provide a broader array of information services.

As for the future, Sanko saw "a lot of opportunities we can't even now imagine."

## THE XEL VISION

In addition to developing products and maintaining customer loyalty, XEL also had to deal with a number of important "people" issues. "We had good, sound management practices right from the beginning," Sanko said.[6] "We were competing with small companies who did not have the control systems, discipline, and planning experience that we had gained as part of GTE. Coming from a large arena, we could start from the top down and tailor the procedures to our needs, rather than, as many small businesses do, have to start developing controls from the bottom and then apply them—hopefully in time."

Yet, while bringing such experiences from GTE proved to be quite valuable, there were also a number of thorny issues which emerged. The first one involved people. As with any transition, there were those people that the owners wished to bring on to the new team and those whose future, for whatever reasons, was not with this new organization. "We were fortunate that personnel from GTE worked in tandem with us in this people transition phase," noted Julie Rich. "We spent a great deal of time talking people through it."

There were other critical human resource issues as well. One of the first ones was the design of the benefits package for the people. Under GTE, XEL had a traditional benefits package with little employee selection. To be competitive as well as cost effective, Julie needed to design a package that had to be reduced from 42% of overall payroll costs to 30%. She also wanted to create a package that was flexible and allowed the individual some latitude. "One approach we instituted was to allow individuals to have an allowance for total time off as opposed to so many days for sick leave, vacation, and the like. Its primary purpose was to bring down costs. And while it did succeed in this regard, we did have occasions in which people were coming to work sick rather than use this time."

Another approach was to institute a cafeteria plan of benefits in which the individual would select the specific benefits they would like to receive as part of an overall package. "The cafeteria approach was just beginning to be discussed by organizations at this time (1984)," noted Julie. "We felt there were a great deal of pluses to this approach; and it allowed the employee some discretion."

One critical issue that XEL wanted to address was developing a culture that would distinguish them from others and would also demonstrate that they were no longer a division of a large corporation. So, beginning in 1985 and carrying over into 1986, Julie Rich did a lot of reading and research on changing culture. By 1986, a first draft of these ideas and principles was developed (Exhibit 1). Julie reflected on this initial effort: "Once we developed 'XEL's Commitment to XEL-ENCE,' we printed up a bunch and hung them on the walls. However, nothing changed. You also have to realize that this company is largely comprised of engineers and technicians; and for them, a lot of this visioning was foreign."

By late 1986 and early 1987, the senior management team felt that a change agent was needed to help them deal with the issue of managing culture. An outside party was brought in; his philosophy was that corporate vision should be strategically driven. This approach was warmly received by Bill Sanko and through a series of monthly meetings, he worked with senior management.

**Exhibit 1**                    **XEL's Commitment to Excellence**

XEL Communications, Inc. is a customer-oriented supplier of high quality transmission system products and services to telecommunications service providers with emphasis on the effective application of emerging digital technologies.

XEL provides its customers with products which allow them to offer competitive special service features to the end users while improving system operating efficiencies.

To achieve our commitment to XEL-ENCE:

1. Our customers' needs shall always come first.

2. Profitability ensures a return to our investors, company growth, and team member rewards.

3. High ethical standards are maintained in all corporate relationships.

4. On-time individual commitments are a personal pledge.

5. Superior performance through teamwork achieves rewards and advancement.

6. Customers, employees, and suppliers are team members to be treated with respect and dignity at all times.

His first effort was directed at getting the team to determine what their core values were and what they would like the company to look like in five years. Bill made an effort to develop a first draft of such a statement. In addition, other members of the senior team made similar efforts. "It was interesting," Julie notes. "Even though we each had a different orientation and background, there was a lot of consistency among the group." The team then went off-site for several days and was able to finalize the XEL Vision statement (Exhibit 2). By the Summer of 1987, the statement was signed by members of the senior team and was hung up by the bulletin board. Again, Julie reflects: "The other employees were not required to sign the Vision statement. We felt that once they could really buy into it then they were free to sign it or not."

Julie then described their approach to getting the rest of the organization to understand as well as become comfortable with the XEL Vision:

"Frequently, organizations tend to take a combination top-down/bottom-up approach in instituting cultural change. That is, the top level will develop a statement about values and overall vision. They will then communicate it down to the bottom level and hope that results will percolate upward through the middle levels. Yet it is often the middle level of management which is most skeptical, and they will block it or resist change. We decided to take a "cascade" approach in which the process begins at the top and gradually cascades from one level to the next so that the critical players are slowly acclimated to the process. We also did a number of other things—including sending a copy of the vision to the homes of the employees and dedicating a section of the company newspaper to communicate what key sections of the vision mean from the viewpoint of managers and employees."

Unlike the first vision statement which was hung on the wall but not really followed, this new vision statement has sustained and reinforced a corporate culture. Julie believed that employee involvement in fashioning and building the statement made the real difference, as well as the fact that XEL made signif-

**Exhibit 2**                     **The XEL Vision**

**XEL will become the leader** in our selected telecommunications markets through in-novation in products and services. Every XEL product and service will be rated Number One by our customers.

**XEL will set the standards** by which our competitors are judged. We will be the best, most innovative, responsive designer, manufacturer, and provider of quality products and services as seen by customers, employees, competitors, and suppliers.*

**We will insist upon the highest quality from everyone in every task.**

**We will be an organization where each of us is a self-manager who will:**

- initiate action, commit to, and act responsibly in achieving objectives
- be responsible for XEL's performance
- be responsible for the quality of individual and team output
- invite team members to contribute based on experience, knowledge, and ability

**We will:**

- be ethical and honest in all relationships
- build an environment where creativity and risk taking is promoted
- provide challenging and satisfying work
- ensure a climate of dignity and respect for all
- rely on interdepartmental teamwork, communications, and cooperative problem solving to attain common goals**
- offer opportunities for professional and personal growth
- recognize and reward individual contribution and achievement
- provide tools and services to enhance productivity
- maintain a safe and healthy work environment

**XEL will be profitable and will grow** in order to provide both a return to our investors and rewards to our team members.

**XEL will be an exciting and enjoyable place to work while we achieve success.**

---

*Responsiveness to customers' new product needs as well as responding to customers' require-ments for emergency delivery requirements has been identified as a key strategic strength. There-fore, the vision statement has been updated to recognize this important element.

**The importance of cooperation and communication was emphasized with this update of the vision statement.

icant use of teams in all facets of its business, including decision making. For example, in 1990, XEL was experiencing some economic difficulties. The employees were brought into meetings and were told the business was in trou-ble, and were asked for ideas on how to deal with the downturn. The employ-ees discussed the problem and decided to try a four-day work week rather than lay off anyone. After a few months, the economic difficulties continued and the employees reluctantly decided to lay off 40% of the work force. The work teams were asked if they wanted to be involved in deciding who would be laid off. They declined to participate in these tough decisions, but were still clearly concerned about the decisions themselves. In fact, Julie recalls being visited by a number of production workers during this time. "There was one particular fellow who knew that a coworker had a family, and that he would suffer a great deal of hardship if he was to be laid off," Julie remembers. "This fellow came in to my office and asked that he be laid off instead of his coworker. That's when I knew the employees believed in and shared our vision." Eventu-ally, virtually all of the laid-off production workers were hired back.

In a strange way, the business crisis of 1990 moved the teams along more quickly than they might have developed in times of profit. Like many businesses using work teams and facing downsizing, XEL laid off a number of middle managers who were not brought back when business improved. When tough decisions needed to be made, the work teams no longer had managers to fall back on.

When teams, or managers, are making decisions, it is routine for the XEL Vision statement to be physically brought into the discussion, and for workers to consult various parts of the statement to help guide and direct decisions. According to Julie, the statement has been used to help evaluate new products, to emphasize quality (a specific XEL strategic objective is to be the top quality vendor for each product), to support teams, and to drive the performance appraisal process.

The XEL Vision was successfully implemented as a key first step, but it was far from being a static document. Key XEL managers continually re-visited the statement to ensure that it became a reflection of where they want to go, not where they have been. Julie believed this was a large factor in the success of the vision. "Our values are the key," Julie explains. "They are strong, they are truly core values, and they are deeply held." Along with the buy-in process, the workers also see that the statement is experimented with. This reflected the strong entrepreneurial nature of XEL's founders—a common bond that they all share. They were not afraid of risk, or of failure, and this spirit was reinforced in all employees through the vision itself, as well as through the yearly process of revisiting the statement. Once a year, Bill Sanko sat with all employees and directly challenged (and listened to direct challenges) on the XEL Vision. Since 1987, only two relatively minor additions have altered the original statement (see Exhibit 2).

## HUMAN RESOURCE MANAGEMENT AT XEL

Julie Rich was pleased as she scanned the recent article in *Business Week* which mentioned XEL's efforts to use team-based compensation.[7] It mentioned that since they instituted this system, average production time has been slashed from 30 days to 3, and waste as a percentage of sales has been cut in half. "We have certainly come a long way."

Julie was heavily involved in the development of XEL's first vision statement, and she chuckled about the reaction from others: "Being the non-engineer in an outfit that is predominantly made up of technical people, they looked at me like they thought I was crazy. This 'touchy-feely' vision and values statement was about as foreign to them as it could get. Yet, once they saw the linkage to XEL's strategy and direction, it began to catch on." In many ways, Julie was an unusual HR manager. Not only did Julie believe HR to be a strategic issue for XEL, Julie herself was one of the owners of the business. Where HR was often relegated to a "staff" function, Julie was clearly a "line" manager at XEL. Julie felt very comfortable working closely with technical managers, and carried the entrepreneurial spirit as strongly as her colleagues.

Once the vision statement had been finally developed, Julie and others soon turned their attention to the issue of managing the new culture within XEL. A key ingredient of this process was changing the mindset of the employees. In the GTE days, individuals had discrete jobs and responsibilities which were governed by specific policies and procedures. "We wanted to instill a sense of ownership on the part of employees," Julie noted. When asked when she knew that the culture was working, she replied, "One day, a work team was having a meeting. The team leader was agitated, and was speaking harshly to one of the team members. One of the other workers stood up and confronted the team leader, saying that his treatment of the worker was not consistent with The XEL Vision." The worker and her team leader still work on the same team at XEL.

The HR system at XEL was unusually well-integrated. The team-based work system created a great deal of intrinsic motivation, and opportunities for employee voice and influence were in abundance. The workers participated in hiring decisions, and XEL used a 360-degree performance appraisal system. Production workers were appraised by peers and also appraised themselves. The compensation system used a three-pronged approach: profit-sharing to encourage teamwork, individual and team-based merit to encourage quantity and quality of performance, and skill-based pay to encourage continuous improvement. In one quarter in 1994, the 300 production workers were paid an average of $500 each in profit-sharing. When workers mastered a new task, they had the opportunity to earn an additional 50 cents per hour. Finally, each unit shared a bonus based on meeting a quarterly goal, such as improving on-time delivery. The average reward was 4.5% of payroll, with top teams earning up to 10% and lagging groups getting nothing. Employee response to the compensation system was generally positive. "The pay system doesn't stand alone," said Julie. "It's only in support of the teams."[8]

Julie did a lot of background reading in the management literature as well as exploring what other companies were doing. Unfortunately, she found that there was little to go on. "That is when, in working with John Puckett, vice-president for manufacturing, we began to see that self-directed work teams could give them a distinct competitive advantage—resulting in better quality products that could be delivered in a timely manner."

A key step in the development of self-directed teams was to create an open organization. The first step was to take a look at the physical layout of the work environment. One experience remains vivid for Julie: "I remember that on one particular Friday, John was toying with the idea of how to better organize the plant. One worker approached John and told him to take the weekend off and go fishing. John, initially hesitant, decided to do so; and over one weekend, the workers came in and, on their own, redesigned the entire floor. On Monday, John returned and found that they had organized themselves in various work cells—each devoted to a particular product group. Teams were then organized around this cellular production and began to set their own production goals and quality procedures."

## XEL'S STRATEGIC PLANNING PROCESS

The business telecommunications market was rapidly changing and evolving in 1996—creating an ideal business climate for XEL.[9] Working with local telephone companies and others, XEL designed and manufactured equipment that "conditioned" existing lines to make them acceptable for business use.

**Exhibit 3**          **XEL Planning Cycle**

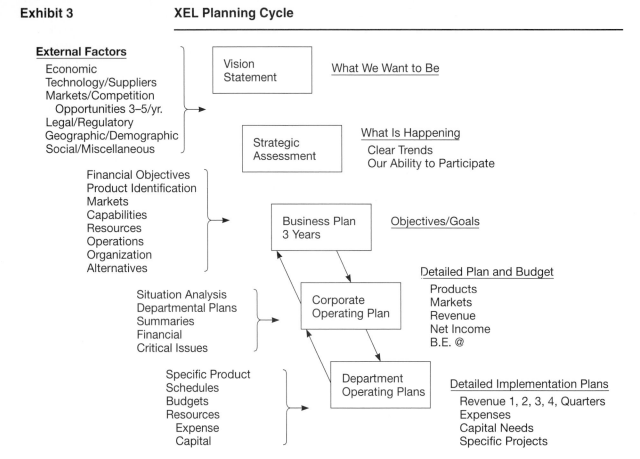

**External Factors**
Economic
Technology/Suppliers
Markets/Competition
    Opportunities 3–5/yr.
Legal/Regulatory
Geographic/Demographic
Social/Miscellaneous

Vision Statement — What We Want to Be

Financial Objectives
Product Identification
Markets
Capabilities
Resources
Operations
Organization
Alternatives

Strategic Assessment — What Is Happening
Clear Trends
Our Ability to Participate

Business Plan 3 Years — Objectives/Goals

Situation Analysis
Departmental Plans
Summaries
Financial
Critical Issues

Corporate Operating Plan — Detailed Plan and Budget
Products
Markets
Revenue
Net Income
B.E. @

Specific Product
Schedules
Budgets
Resources
    Expense
    Capital

Department Operating Plans — Detailed Implementation Plans
Revenue 1, 2, 3, 4, Quarters
Expenses
Capital Needs
Specific Projects

As a means of positioning themselves for products and markets in a rapidly changing environment, XEL engaged in a strategic planning process on an annual basis. Exhibit 3 provides an overview of this process. As Bill Sanko noted: "Since there are such rapid changes taking place and new products being constantly introduced, we needed to tie what we're doing back to the strategic elements—quality, responsiveness, cost."

The strategic planning process began in August of each year with the senior management team listing strategic issues and taking on key assignments. For Bill, his key assignment began with assessing key external factors. Taking on such an assignment provided him an opportunity to step back and look at the bigger picture.

"I hope that legislation pending will deregulate local telephone companies. This will open up local telephone services to companies other than the regional Baby Bell. At present, AT&T has an almost 60% hold in the market with respect to long distance but deregulation will allow the local companies to enter the global market. Major telephone companies have been downsizing in the recent past to cut down on costs by developing products and installing services that require less maintenance and, therefore, fewer people to maintain them. With this trend, we hope to get business from our present customers seeking help to develop such products for them."

Another key industry trend which was constantly monitored is technology. The pace at which the technology was moving had reduced the product life cycle from 40 years to less than 5 years. Bill noted the example of fiber optic products, which is a very hot area in today's market; XEL was trying to compete with other companies with respect to building fiber optic products. Other areas in which it was trying to find opportunities for a small company was the emerging personal communications systems market.

With the industry trend data as a beginning, the senior team then spent the ensuing months in developing plans around the key strategic issues. This would then entail capturing data on key competitors and assessing their strengths and weaknesses relative to XEL. "Some of these data are available due to public disclosure requirements," according to Bill Sanko," but data on private competitors are particularly difficult to get—due to the competitive nature of the business; we get a lot of information through trade show contacts."

Throughout this entire process, the XEL team needed to keep a focus on those critical success factors that would determine their performance. Essentially, they involved innovativeness, a skilled sales force, quality, investing in automation, effective pricing, and, above all, responsiveness.

Another key goal was to achieve a 20% improvement in margin by year end 1994 and to strive to reach 25% by December 1995 and 30% by December 1997. This goal is one that was particularly sensitive among the senior management team since it involved two critical variables: pricing coupled with achieving economies of scale in the manufacturing plant. Previously, achieving such a goal was parceled out among the respective groups: marketing and sales, operations, finance, and the like. Unfortunately, this activity was frequently tabled in the face of day-to-day activities. It was then decided that a cost reduction team needed to be formally structured to address this goal. As such, XEL decided to hire an engineer, a technician, and a buyer from outside the organization to constitute the team. Its primary responsibility was to examine the pricing of products and costs, and to target core products for the purpose of achieving 25% improvement in margin by December of 1995. The team reported primarily to the vice president of manufacturing, John Puckett.

In terms of overall financial performance, XEL has been profitable. Its revenues increased from $16.8 million in 1992 to $23.6 million in 1993 and $52.3 million in 1994—more than a three-fold increase in three years.

Another key issue that was identified in the strategic planning process was how much to invest in R&D—given the rapid pace of technology development that is taking place in this industry. XEL's goal was to invest 10% of its sales in R&D. "We have come to realize that we grew faster than last year's plan," according to Bill Sanko, "and we need to invest more in engineering as a means of keeping pace. Our goal is to have one-third of our revenue in any given year come from products introduced in the past two years." This would also involve investing its R&D efforts into new technologies as cable TV converges with telecommunications.

Aside from investment in new technologies, the other key strategic issue that was identified in the planning process was penetration into international markets. XEL was seeking to do business in Mexico in order to build data networks that are critical in upgrading Mexico's infrastructure. It has also looked for business opportunities in countries such as Brazil, Chile, Argentina, Puerto Rico, and the Far East. As a means of focusing responsibility for this effort, XEL tapped Malcom Shaw, a new hire of XEL who is fluent in Spanish and has prior marketing experience in South America, to lead this international expansion effort.

As all of the above issues indicate, the formal strategic planning process was a critical ingredient of XEL's way of doing business. "Strategic planning makes you think about how to invest for the future," Bill emphasized. "The role of the CEO is really to keep a viewpoint of the big picture—not to micro-manage the operation." To reinforce this last point, it should be noted that Bill Sanko had a personal tragedy in June of 1992, in which he was involved in a serious auto accident—the car in which he was traveling was broadsided by another auto. "Even while I was out of the office for an extended period of time," noted Bill, "the fact that we had a formal strategic plan and an annual operating plan gave us the guidance to continue business as usual." As the planning process moved forward, Bill's goal was to have their 1995 strategic plan ready for the November meeting of the Board of Directors. As Julie noted, "We don't just look for 'programs,' but for ideas for the longterm."

## XEL'S MARKETS

The marketing and sales functions for XEL closely reinforced the earlier emphasis on being responsive and oriented to customer's needs. Don Bise, vice president of marketing, came to XEL with diverse experience, having moved around in nine previous firms. "The culture here at XEL is much less structured than some other organizations where I worked before," Don reflected. "I feel much more comfortable in a stand-alone company as opposed to being a branch or subsidiary of a large firm."

Unlike many companies in which the marketing approach is to have product managers dedicated to certain product segments or accounts, XEL's sales managers worked closely with the engineers in addressing customer needs. "The difficulty with having the sales manager or the engineer working solely with the customer is that their particular perspective may differ," noted Don. "By having both the engineer and the sales manager working with the customer, we have cut down on the communications difficulties and have been able to develop a more realistic pricing and delivery schedule. At the same time, by having the engineer present, he is able to understand their specific needs or can steer them towards a reasonable solution to what they are trying to achieve. This has gone a long way to create great customer loyalty and repeat business. In addition, we have been able to manage our overall costs better. Our marketing expenses are typically 6-7% of sales, which is low compared to a number of companies."

In terms of XEL's marketing strategy, a number of external developments have reshaped its approach. "Traditionally, in a market as concentrated as the telecommunications industry, the customer has tremendous buying potential and tries to leverage this as much as possible. With more players coming into this market, coupled with downsizing on the part of the Regional Bell Operating Companies, we are trying to develop a portfolio approach to make us less dependent on a few key accounts. As a result, XEL must introduce new products for traditional as well as new accounts. This means that XEL must pay a great deal of attention to technology."

To meet this goal, marketing worked closely with the engineering group—not only in the sales area but also in new product development. Specific market opportunities included the convergence of telephony with cable, personal communication services based on radio expertise, and business access in developing countries. To reach these market segments, Don Bise noted that XEL was exploring several avenues.

One approach was the OEM (Original Equipment Manufacturer) market in which XEL built the product according to another's specification. GTE's Airfone, which allowed airline passengers to place and receive calls, was a three-way venture in which XEL manufactured the electronics for the phone and did final assembly and test. This venture was quite profitable for XEL; they shipped about 300 Airfones a day out of their plant in 1995. A second approach was to build customized units for voice and data transmission in the industrial market. Exhibit 4 provides an example of XEL's approach to this market.

A third avenue, one that offered a great deal of future potential, is the international market. This is an area that Don was particularly excited about: "Clearly the growth path is international as developing regions are looking to upgrade their telecommunications infrastructure to spur economic growth. To do this, both voice and data transmission are key. What XEL can do is take something that we are familiar with and use it in areas they aren't familiar with. For example, in one particular country, we found that we can take one of our channel units and plug it into their system—providing an instant upgrade to their current capabilities." Yet going international was not without its risks. "We would prefer to begin by developing a niche in international markets with our existing equipment. This would minimize some of the up-front risks. As the international side of the business begins to take off, we realize we will need to have a local in-country partner and will need to have some local manufacturing content."

To compete successfully in the future, Don felt that XEL should "go where they ain't." XEL needed to seek out niches where there was very little or no competition, keep its cost low, and price accordingly. He felt that their traditionally strong customer base, the major telephone companies, was using its buying power to telegraph the prices they would accept. At the same time, they were cutting down their list of vendors quite extensively.

## FINANCIAL CONSIDERATIONS

Turning from the ever-present spreadsheet on his desktop computer, Jim Collins, vice-president of finance, reflected on the key financial considerations facing XEL. "Coming from another company to XEL, I soon found out that the culture here is quite different. There is indeed a sense of empowerment and teamwork. People set their own goals, and the engineers make a serious commitment to the customer."

In addition to the formal strategic planning process, financial planning at XEL involved a 3-year top-down plan with input from the bottom up. According to Jim, "I interface a great deal with marketing and sales and develop costs. My goal is to ensure that there aren't a lot of surprises. We also tend to manage by percentages." Jim was asked whether XEL was experimenting with implementing some form of activity-based accounting. He noted that they reviewed it in 1993 and decided that they weren't ready. Yet, they do plan to implement a modified activity-based accounting system in 1995. "We tend to look at the major drivers of cost in this business. There is an overall operations review once a month among the senior management team in which there is open dialogue, and we explore a number of key operational issues."

Yet the financial picture for XEL has not always been rosy. "In addition to the costs associated with the separation from GTE, there were three years where we lost money—part of this was due to our dependency on GTE as it was going through its own consolidation as well as a new product introduction which didn't fly." Again, Jim Collins remarked: "Those two setbacks were a bitter pill to swallow. We now try to make our financial projections more realistic—even somewhat on the conservative side. We also set targets by market segments."

Although there was pressure to raise cash by going public, Jim felt that this wasn't realistic for XEL. "We really don't want analysts setting constraints for our business—rather we tend to look for cash infusions from strategic partnerships and alliances." Both Bill Sanko and Jim Collins were actively involved in negotiating these partnerships, particularly in the international arena. "Above all," Jim commented, "we need to stay focused, develop a plan, and get realistic input."

## QUALITY MANAGEMENT AT XEL

One of the critical success factors that was identified in the strategic planning process and was imbedded throughout XEL was the focus on responsiveness to customers. When XEL was in its initial stages, cycle time—the period from start of production to finished goods—was about six weeks. That left customers disgruntled and tied up money in inventory.[10] XEL's chain of command, moreover, had scarcely changed since the GTE days. Line workers reported to supervisors, who reported to unit or departmental managers, who reported on up the ladder to Sanko and a crew of top executives. Every rung in the ladder added time and expense. "If a hardware engineer needed some software help, he'd go to his manager," Sanko says. "The manager would say, 'Go write it up.' Then the hardware manager would take the software manager to lunch and talk about it. We needed everybody in the building thinking and contributing about how we could better satisfy our customers, how we could improve quality, how we could reduce costs."

Soon after XEL drafted its vision statement, John Puckett, vice president for manufacturing, redesigned the plant for cellular production, with groups of workers building whole families of circuit boards. Eventually, Sanko and Puckett decided to set up the entire plant with self-managing teams. By 1988, the teams had been established, and the supervisory and support staff was reduced by 30%.

The RIF (Reduction in Force) was achieved by a number of avenues. In 1990, there was a downturn in business and workers went to a four-day work week in order to avoid layoffs. Unfortunately, the downturn continued and production workers, supervisors, and support staff were laid off. Workers were asked for cost-saving ideas. Some workers moved to trainer roles. One worker was moved to Industrial Engineering while another became the manager of facilities.

Unlike other plans where workers are given incentives to provide cost-saving ideas and suggestions, there was no such direct financial incentive at XEL. As Julie recalled, "We were in a total survival mode—the only payoff was that the doors stayed open." Eventually, the teams and the quality strategy took hold and a turnaround was achieved. Virtually all laid-off production workers were rehired. The supervisory and support staff were not. This is a testament to the strength of the team system at XEL.

XEL rebuilt itself around those teams so thoroughly and effectively that the Association for Manufacturing Excellence chose the company as one of four to be featured in a video on team-based management. Dozens of visitors, from companies such as Hewlett-Packard, have toured through their facility in search of ideas for using teams effectively.

On the shop floor, colorful banners hung from the plant's high ceiling to mark each team's work area. Charts on the wall tracked attendance, on-time deliveries, and the other variables by which the teams gauge their performance. Diagrams indicated who on a team was responsible for key tasks such as scheduling.

Every week, the schedulers met with Production Control to review what needed to be built as well as what changes needed to be made. The teams met daily, almost always without a manager, to plan their part in that agenda. Longer meetings, called as necessary, took up topics such as vacation planning or recurring production problems. Once a quarter, each team made a formal presentation to management on what it had and hadn't accomplished.

As for results, XEL's cost of direct assembly dropped 25%. Inventory had been cut by half; quality levels rose 30% (Exhibits 5 and 6). The company's cycle time went from six weeks to four days and was still decreasing (Exhibit 7). Sales grew to $52 million in 1994, up from $17 million in 1992. Above all, according to John Puckett, these self-directed work teams must be guided by customer focus (Exhibit 8). In order to facilitate this, customers frequently came in and visited with the team. By clearly understanding their customers' needs the teams were

**Exhibit 4**          **XEL Communications, Inc.**
**Customer Returns, Component Level, All Causes**

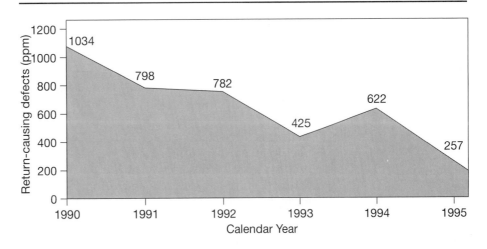

**Exhibit 5**

**XEL Communications, Inc.**
**Cycle Time Reduction, 1985-94**

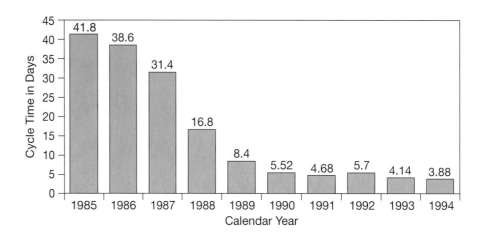

**Exhibit 6**

**XEL Communications, Inc.**
**WIP Annual Inventory Turns 1986-95**

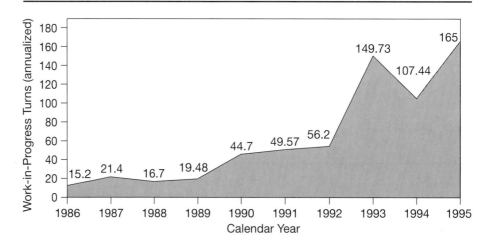

able to respond rapidly with a high quality product. At the same time, XEL team members went and visited with their key suppliers.

Another key issue for manufacturing involved establishing certain procedures while retaining a certain degree of flexibility. Part of this involved the strategic issue of entering global markets. As firms go global, meeting ISO 9000 standards for quality becomes critical. "To meet these standards, several things have to take place," John noted. "We have to have a structure that defines the process; then we need to document and have solid procedures in place." In addition, John felt that manufacturing for international markets would also mean building manufacturing capabilities closer to those markets, which entailed a host of environmental issues and labor laws. Developing alliances would also be critical since XEL could not afford to run it all.

**Exhibit 7**

**XEL Communications, Inc.
Productivity, 1991-95**

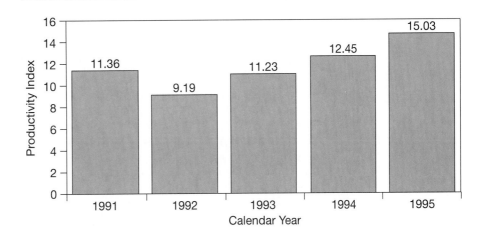

**Exhibit 8**

**XEL Communications, Inc.
Scrap/Rework (in $Thousands)**

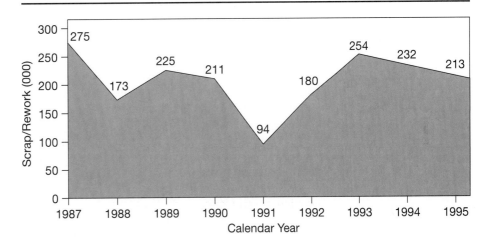

In terms of integration with other parts of XEL, John briefly sketched out the overall process. "Basically, most of manufacturing is driven off of the financial and market plan. We start with a three-year plan which is converted in terms of the demands on facilities. My staff then develops models which reflect product development and product mix. The budget then sets the baseline for new product development. Here, at XEL, we tend to plan on the low side and are fairly conservative. Currently, we target two new products per month and produce in low volume for beta testing. This allows us to carefully manage costs."

As for future issues, John was struggling with the XEL goal of improving margins by 25% by December of 1996. "This is going to be a real challenge for my operation since we have to maintain a short cycle time as the business grows without a lot of excess inventory. We instituted a just-in-time (JIT) system several years ago, and we are currently turning our inventory about 7 or 8 times, which is close to our benchmarks relative to the best in our business (Exhibit 9). Supply chain management is really critical for us."

Another issue John faced was maintaining the culture which had been instituted through the team-based training. "While the current teams have pretty much gelled in terms of feeling comfortable with setting their targets and self-managing, orienting new members becomes a challenge. We are exploring some form of built-in orientation which would involve two weeks of internal training."

John also faced an even greater concern: skilled workers. "I think one of the serious deficiencies in our current U.S. educational system is vocational and occupational education. People have simply not been prepared. There is a misconception that there is a shortage of jobs in this business. They are dead wrong. One of my difficulties is finding qualified workers. As a basic assembler, you aren't going to become rich and put down a deposit on a BMW. But it provides a nice steady income—particularly for two-wage-earning families." John felt that there needed to be a stronger work ethic for those entering the labor force. "We need to understand how to transfer those hard skills that are needed as well as the concept of holding a job. Part of this should involve more industry-level involvement in changing the overall mind-set of what is needed for today's workers. I would like to create an environment in which people really enjoy working here."

The strategic need for skilled workers drove XEL's involvement in a Work Place Learning Skills program, funded by the Department of Education. When XEL began training workers in quality tools, managers noticed that the training was not having as great an effect as it might have. Upon further investigation, the managers discovered that some workers were having difficulty not only in making calculations, but also in reading the training materials. Using the DOE grant, and working with Aurora Community College, which is located near the plant, XEL developed a basic skills training program which is now used as a template by DOE for worker training across the United States. The program, not surprisingly, was designed by an employee task force made up of managers and workers. The task force used a questionnaire to ask employees which courses they would be interested in taking. Participation in the program was not mandatory, but a measure of its success is that 50% of employees participated in the program on their own time. Courses were offered on site for convenience, and included "soft" skills such as communication and stress management. On December 1, 1994, XEL was awarded a three-year DOE grant to expand and continue the training, and to evaluate scientifically the effects of the training on such outcomes as productivity and ROI. Julie believed that these training programs were consistent with other Human Resource policies of XEL, such as skill-based pay. More than that, Julie stated, "The Work Place Learning Skills program is consistent with our XEL vision." As further testament to these efforts, XEL's overall workforce productivity continues to improve.

## MAINTAINING INNOVATION

In a climate that is constantly undergoing rapid change, staying ahead of the competition is the name of the game. For XEL, this meant that cross-functional

**Exhibit 9**          **XEL Communications, Inc.**
**Process Solder Defects**

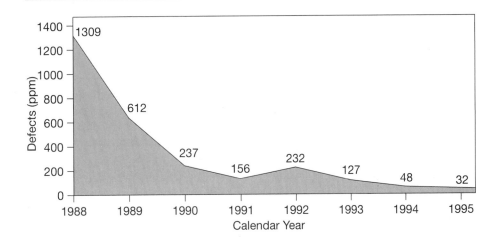

relationships were key. One critical link in this process was the role of new product development. Terry Bolinger, vice-president of engineering, described how this process worked: "Here at XEL, engineering is involved from start to finish. Rather than have a large marketing staff that is out there making calls or picking up new pieces of information, we deliberately have a small group. The engineers do a lot of traveling at XEL—going out in the field and working directly with the customers."

As for its commitment to innovation, XEL allocated approximately 10% to 12% of sales to R&D. Terry noted that, for the current year, he spent below this amount. When pressed why, he commented: "I guess I am hesitant to spend up to this amount since I don't want to grow my engineering group too fast. A few years back, we went through some cutbacks due to a number of factors, and I am somewhat gun-shy about that experience. I know we are running at about the 10% level, and Bill keeps pressing me about this. But I would rather proceed somewhat cautiously."

In order to create a climate to allow his people to innovate, Terry noted that he was careful not to create a management system that bogged everything down. "Our process of setting priorities is fairly free-form. While we are typically running 50 projects at one time, we don't do much formal scheduling. We went through a time in which a lot of formal planning and presentations were done. Unfortunately, we spent too much time in meetings and too little in what I considered the search and discovery process." While Terry was comfortable with this loose form of management, he laughed that others were not so at ease. "I see Bill Sanko stroll the office periodically, and I know that he is often perplexed with how this works—coming from his engineering background. I just say 'trust me' and he is pretty good at accepting it."

In addition to this loose form of project management, Terry tried to motivate his engineers in other ways. "I also try to give them interesting assignments which will challenge them. They are also allowed to work at odd hours—many come to work on weekends or at night. In a number of cases, I will simply send them to work at home where they can be relaxed. If they need some particular equipment, I will get it for them with little or no questions asked. Also, they periodically like to travel just to get out of the office; and field calls to customers or potential customers is a way of getting them charged up." There were also periodic in-house seminars with professors from various universities who would come and brief them on new technological advances. In a sense, Terry was trying to re-create the college environment within XEL.

As XEL continued to grow, Terry saw several issues that were critical for his group: "First is the issue of how do I improve time to market without sacrificing quality; second, how do I speed up product development; and third, how do I respond extremely fast to new technology developments?" As he prepared his departmental plan for the strategic planning meeting, he also shared some concern about the opening of the second building. While he clearly needed more space for his people, the ease with which an engineer could go over to manufacturing or marketing and sales if he or she had a question or needed some information would be hard to replace.

## XEL'S FUTURE

Ironically, the most serious current issue for XEL came from its own success, namely growth. XEL had increased its labor force by 50% and had doubled its revenues in the last year, and was experiencing some associated growing pains. Hiring sufficient workers was difficult, and assuring that the new workers will "fit" the XEL culture was hindered because of the pressures to add staff. The teams, who normally hired their own replacement workers, were less able to participate in the hiring process since they were under great pressure to produce and satisfy their customers.

Another example of the pressures of growth occurred in the skills training program. Originally, team members were scheduled to teach the classes. Unfortunately, as pressures for production increased, more and more team members canceled their training classes. As a solution, trainers were hired from local community colleges, and the team members acted as their partners to assure the course content was job-related.

Growth increased pressure to satisfy customer demands, increased pressure on the culture via the increased size and complexity, and created additional financial pressures. As a high-technology company, XEL faced the challenge of using technology to help the company be more effective. XEL would use its annual strategic planning process to determine its priorities, what measures it will use to assess its results, and which feet to hold to the fire.

Having finished reading the *Wall Street Journal* article, Bill Sanko made a note to have a copy made for the next managers' meeting, which was scheduled for every other Thursday. He also wondered what the new session of Congress would bring—now that the Republicans appeared to be in solid control.

Since XEL was in the process of beginning its annual strategic planning process, Bill thought that a useful exercise for the next managers' meeting would be to have everyone list and prioritize the key strategic issues facing XEL over the next three to five years. At the same time, he wondered whether it would be possible for XEL to maintain its entrepreneurial culture while it managed rapid growth.

# NOTES

1. *Financial World*, October 11, 1994.
2. 1994 University of Michigan Economic Forecast
3. *Denver Business Journal*, June 17, 1994, p. 12.
4. *Rocky Mountain Business Journal*, July 1, 1985.
5. *Colorado Business*, July 1990.
6. *Rocky Mountain Business Journal*, July 1, 1985.
7. *Business Week*, November 14, 1994, p. 62
8. *Ibid.*, p. 62.
9. *Denver Business Journal*, April 15, 1994.
10. *Inc.*, September 1993, p. 66.

# Tootsie Roll, Inc.

## Sharon Ungar Lane, Bentley College
## Alan N. Hoffman, Bentley College

## INTRODUCTION

*"Tootsie Roll's good for-tunes are an accumulation of many small decisions that were probably made right plus bigger key decisions, such as acquisitions, that have been made right, and a lot of luck."*

MEL GORDON, CEO
TOOTSIE ROLL, 1993

Tootsie Roll Industries, Inc., a niche candy maker, has often been voted one of *Forbes* magazine's "200 Best Small Companies of America." A top quality pro-ducer and distributor of Tootsie Rolls and other candy, Tootsie Roll Industries maintains a 50% market share of the taffy and lollipop segment of the candy industry, and sales have increased each year for the past nineteen years. The world's largest lollipop supplier, the company produces approximately 16 mil-lion lollipops and 37 million individual Tootsie Rolls a day.

## EARLY HISTORY

In 1896, Leo Hirschfield, a young immigrant from Austria, set up a small shop in Brooklyn, New York, to make candy from a recipe he had brought from Europe. As he rolled the sweet, chewy chocolate candies, his thoughts wan-dered to his young daughter, Clara "Tootsie" Hirschfield, and he named his new confection the "Tootsie Roll." He wrapped the Tootsie Rolls individually in paper to keep them clean and sanitary, and priced them at a penny each.

Hirschfield's Tootsie Rolls were an immediate success, and demand quickly outpaced supply. Hirschfield realized he would need more capital to promote and expand his business. After just one year, he merged his operation with a local candy manufacturer, Stern & Saalberg, which incorporated eight years later, and officially changed its name to the Sweets Company of America in 1917.

From 1922 to 1966, the Sweets Company of America set up manufacturing facilities around the United States to meet growing demand for Tootsie Roll products. Having captured America's sweet tooth with the Tootsie Roll, the company expanded its product line in the 1930s, developing a series of companion products such as the first soft-centered lollipop, the Tootsie Pop, which had a Tootsie Roll center and a hard candy outside.

In 1962, Ellen and Melvin Gordon took over as President / Chief Operating Officer and Chief Executive Officer / Chairman of the Board, respectively. In 1966, the Gordons changed the company name to Tootsie Roll Industries, Inc. and opened a large manufacturing facility in Chicago (which subsequently became the company's world headquarters). In the late 1960s, Tootsie Roll began exploring foreign markets, establishing a subsidiary in Mexico and licensing a firm in the Philippines to produce and distribute Tootsie Rolls. After a positive response in both these countries, the company expanded to Canada in 1971.

Amazingly enough, as the Tootsie Roll celebrates its 100th birthday in 1996, the candy still tastes exactly the same as it did when it was first hand-rolled by Leo Hirschfield. The company's success, as 19 consecutive years of record sales and 14 consecutive years of record earnings confirm, is based on strong consumer awareness of the Tootsie Roll brand name, and strategic acquisition of other well positioned and highly recognized brand names to leverage its existing operations. The Gordons own 66% of the voting rights and 47% of the company's stock, and continue to control the company, which remains exclusively a candy company making the very best quality candy for the market it knows best.

## THE CANDY INDUSTRY

The United States' largest manufacturing sector, the processed food and beverage industry, is composed of two primary divisions: lower value-added and higher value-added food processors. Higher value-added processors, such as candy manufacturers, make retail-ready, packaged, consumer brand name products which have a minimum of 40% of the industry shipment value added through sophisticated manufacturing. Candy is a $20 billion retail industry worldwide, and accounts for about one third of the dollar-value of the snack-food market (the largest segment of the higher value-added division). Tootsie Roll Industries occupies a niche market within the Standard Industrial Classification (SIC) code 2064 (candy and other confectionery products) which includes taffies, lollipops, and chewing gum. The U.S. confectionery market generates approximately $9.7 billion in annual sales.

Candy is not yet a "mature" industry in the United States. The compound annual growth rate for candy in the past ten years has been close to 6% a year, a very solid gain in an industry that is supposedly mature. In fact, within the chocolate confectionery subcategory, the United States ranks 11th in the world in per capita consumption and fifth in the world in growth since 1980. Based on current demographics, many analysts believe that there will be further growth for confectioneries. A "baby boomlet" is on the way, significantly increasing the teenage population. By the time the population bulge peaks in the year 2010, it will top the baby boom of the 1960s in both size and duration. According to government statistics, the percentage of children between the ages of 5 and 14 will rise during the 1990s, increasing from 14.2 percent of the population in 1990 to 14.5 percent in the year 2000. This trend will serve as a strong foundation for increasing consumption of confectionery products through the end of the century. Nevertheless, spending for food and drink as a percentage of all personal consumption is declining in the United States, and most manufacturers recognize that future opportunities lie in using profits from domestic sales to penetrate foreign markets.

Many U.S. producers now use complex processing methods and efficient, automated manufacturing operations which yield comparable quality at lower cost, and are finding a growing international market for their products. Despite recessionary economic conditions and reduced discretionary income, foreign consumers purchase U.S. higher value-added foods and beverages because U.S. products compare favorably with similar products made elsewhere, offering equal or better quality at a lower price. Today, the top five importers of U.S. products are: Japan, Canada, Mexico, South Korea, and the Netherlands. Foreign demand for U.S.-produced higher value-added products (including candy) has increased since 1993, thanks primarily to the rapid growth of the middle class in developing and emerging nations, and growth in the new markets of the former Soviet bloc nations.

However, the candy industry has recently faced several industry curbs. New nutritional labeling requirements were imposed by the Food and Drug Administration in 1990 to regulate serving size, health messages, and the use of descriptive terms such as "light" and "low fat." The Federal Trade Commission also developed stringent sale-date requirements and strict guidelines for documenting environmental claims on packaging. These new regulations were imposed under costly, disruptive, difficult-to-meet deadlines, and posed a particular threat to many foreign food and beverage processors, who are not accustomed to such extensive product analysis and disclosure. For Tootsie Roll, this major packaging revision was costly, and involved detailed laboratory analysis and package modification of every item the company produces.

Candy is still a treat for all ages. People who loved Tootsie Rolls when they were children often buy them for their children and thus the Tootsie Roll perpetuates itself. The baby boom generation grew up with Tootsie Roll products, therefore name recognition is very high among this group. While parental purchases may increase due to brand recognition, the baby boomers are becoming increasingly more concerned with their health and their children's diet. As a result, baby boomers are purchasing less candy for themselves and their children. Thus, as people become more health and weight conscious, their demand for sugar-based products decreases. Additionally, as this consumer group gets older, their concern for dental health becomes greater. Candy has been identified as a major cause of dental decay, and hard, sticky, or chewy snacks, such as Tootsie Rolls, cannot be eaten by people who have had various kinds of dental work. Also, some parents do not buy candy because they are concerned that sugar causes hyperactivity in some children.

Children are Tootsie Roll's primary target market, since children ages six to seventeen create the greatest demand for confectionery products. According to a study by the Good Housekeeping Institute, candy is the second most requested snack food among six to twelve year olds; only ice cream is higher in demand. This group (ages 6 to 17) spend $60 billion of their own money annually, with two-thirds of this spending on candy, snacks, and beverages.

# TOOTSIE ROLL—1996

Tootsie Rolls are unique, and occupy a niche of the candy market which includes taffies, lollipops, and chewing gum. Tootsie Roll Industries' competition is other candy and ready-to-eat snack food manufacturers. Tootsie Roll Industries commands 2–3% of the overall market as the eighth largest candy manufacturer following Hershey (27%), M&M Mars (25%), Nestle (10%), Brach (6%), Huhtamaki (4%), Storck (3%), and RJR Nabisco (3%). Although Tootsie Roll has captured only 2–3% of the total candy market, it continues to be the leader in its own segment, where it maintains a 50% market share. Tootsie Roll's strengths are brand loyalty, established shelf space, state-of-the-art manufacturing facilities, and the fact that there are fixed price ceilings for candy products. Also, as the United States becomes a more nutrition-oriented society, Tootsie Rolls have another advantage because they contain no cholesterol and have less saturated fat than other leading candy bars.

Tootsie Roll uses many suppliers for sugar, corn syrup, cocoa, and milk, and adapts to fluctuations in commodity prices by changing the formula and size of its products to keep total costs relatively constant. For example, Tootsie Roll can substitute corn syrup for some of the necessary sugar, thus decreasing its dependency upon a given commodity or supplier. Tootsie Roll also reduces and controls costs by owning its own refinery. The company can thus buy raw sugar and make, rather than buy, processed sugar, decreasing its dependence on processed sugar suppliers. When natural disasters affect the availability or price of one of its ingredients—for instance, sugar or cocoa—as did floods along the Mississippi River in 1993, the company usually decreases the size of its product to keep the selling price constant.

Tootsie Roll Industries' vertically-integrated structure supports its drive for competitiveness, keeping total costs down and maintaining its leading edge in technology. In addition to the sugar refinery, Tootsie Roll owns its own advertising agency, so that commissions flow back in to it. The company also makes the sticks for its lollipops, has a print shop for color printing, and owns a machine shop where new machinery is built and existing machinery rebuilt. Tootsie Roll Industries also constantly upgrades its manufacturing equipment to maintain the utmost efficiency.

Tootsie Roll's objectives, which have made it one of America's strongest companies, are, and have always been:

1. Run a trim operation
2. Eliminate waste
3. Minimize cost
4. Improve performance

To be competitive in the world candy market, where margins are limited, one must produce top-quality candy very efficiently. Tootsie Roll has spent millions of dollars on state-of-the-art expansion and automation of its five production facilities (Chicago, Massachusetts, New York, Tennessee, and Mexico). Much of its equipment is designed specifically for Tootsie Roll. As Mel Gordon, CEO and Chairman of the Board of Tootsie Roll Industries, explains: "Anybody can buy machinery and in that way become state-of-the-art, but if you develop your own adaptations to the machinery so that it runs faster and runs better for your products, or you develop in-house machinery that does what nobody else in the market can do, then you're ahead of state-of-the-art. We've strived in the last 15 years to be ahead of state-of-the-art." However, the one aspect of its operations the company has not been able to control is the power of its packaging material suppliers. Increased demand has led to dramatic price increases in paper, board, plastics, and foil. To insulate itself from price fluctuations, Tootsie Roll has, whenever possible, negotiated fixed price contracts with its packaging suppliers.

## ACQUISITIONS

Tootsie Roll Industries often generates more cash than it needs for internal growth, and can therefore consider complementary acquisitions. Following strict criteria, such as a strong brand name, and a preference for non-chocolate (such as hard candies and chewy candies) over chocolate so as not to compete in its own niche, Tootsie Roll has made several key acquisitions of proven brands to expand its product line, increase its shelf space, and spur growth. As President Ellen Gordon explains, "We add new lines only when it benefits our product in quality and efficiency."

Two of Tootsie Roll's earliest acquisitions (1972) were the Mason Division of Candy Corporation of America, which makes such well-known products as Mason Mints, Mason Dots, Mason Licorice Crows, and Mason Spice Berries; and the Bonomo Turkish Taffy Company. In 1985, Tootsie Roll acquired Cella's Confections, which makes chocolate-covered cherries; and in 1988, it acquired the Charms Company, thereby becoming the world's largest manufacturer of lollipops. Charms' principal product, the Blow Pop, a lollipop with a bubble gum center, makes a nice complement to the highly successful Tootsie Pop. Shortly after the acquisition of the Charms Company, Mel Gordon observed, "We specialize in hard candies such as Tootsie Pops and Blow Pops and all the flat pops that Charms makes. That's a big niche for us, to be the world's largest manufacturer of pops. Also, we're in chewy candy with the Tootsie Roll and the growing Frooties and Flavor Roll lines. We feel that in those two areas we have a certain dominance and we'd like to keep our expertise focused in those areas."

In November 1993, Tootsie Roll purchased the chocolate and caramel division of the Warner-Lambert Company, which makes the popular brands Junior Mints, Charleston Chew, Sugar Daddy, Sugar Babies, and Pom Poms. The acquisition of these new lines places Tootsie Roll Industries in more direct competition with other major chocolate manufacturers such as Hershey and M&M Mars, and provides it with a number of new products which clearly complement its "chewy" candy product lines. Over the years, Tootsie Roll has carefully and selectively acquired 17 popular candy brands, enlarging its niche in the candy and other confectionery segment of the higher value-added products market.

## DISTRIBUTION/ADVERTISING

Tootsie Roll Industries uses over 100 public and contract brokers to distribute its products to nearly 15,000 customers. To market the newly-acquired Warner-Lambert brands more effectively, Tootsie Roll created new packaging for them which resembled the packaging of its more established Tootsie Roll products and capitalized on the synergies of Warner-Lambert products with its existing lines.

In addition to using its distribution network to increase sales of Warner-Lambert products, Tootsie Roll is pushing those products generally associated with movie theaters, such as Junior Mints, into mainstream retail outlets: convenience stores, grocery stores, drug chains, and warehouse club stores. Convenience stores and supermarkets have traditionally been the dominant candy retailers, but have recently been losing sales to discount stores and drug store chains. Right now, all four venues share equally in confectionery sales. However, most candy purchases are impulse buys made while waiting in line at a store, and since many supermarkets have switched to candy-free aisles, these impulse sales have been reduced. As impulse sales opportunities are diminished, the customer must search for the product. A consumer is unlikely to undertake a search unless desire is heightened through advertising. Parents are the target market that advertisements must reach. However, marketing efforts often tend to focus on children, who are not always the purchasers. These eager consumers purchase through, and with the acceptance of, a parent.

Tootsie Roll has most recently focused its sales efforts on the more rapidly growing classes of trade such as warehouse clubs. In the candy industry it is difficult to gain shelf space, particularly when competing with large companies such as Hershey and M&M Mars. It appears that Tootsie Roll has begun to make progress toward this objective. Tootsie Rolls are beginning to appear in warehouse stores, such as Sam's, BJ's Warehouse, and COSTCO, with large packages of traditional Tootsie Rolls and bags of multi-colored Tootsie Roll pops.

Candy regularly shows the strongest gains from promotion and merchandising, clearly evident by the significant increases in candy sales during major holiday periods — Valentine's Day, Easter, Halloween, and Christmas. In fact, candy has shown a stronger response to promotions than any other snack category.

The third quarter has always been the strongest for Tootsie Rolls due to increased Halloween sales. However, Halloween is changing. Grocery retailers report that there is a noticeable shift in consumer behavior because of concern for child safety. In the last several years, Halloween celebrations have moved from the streets, with "trick or treating" door to door, to indoor parties sponsored by schools, churches, and, more recently, enclosed shopping malls, thereby reducing purchases for candy that used to be given to trick or treaters. Also, parents have been reluctant to purchase any products that could be easily tampered with, particularly at Halloween. The way Tootsie Roll products are packaged creates a potential concern. Individually wrapped, unsealed products can be tampered with and are thus negatively impacted by an event such as the 1982 Tylenol poisoning. In fact, Tootsie Roll sales suffered in the wake of that national scare.

While Tootsie Roll's 100-year history has contributed to its wide product recognition, a tradition of national advertising begun in the early 1950s on television programs such as "The Mickey Mouse Club" and "Howdy Doody" has successfully made "Tootsie Roll" a household word, establishing its domestic market; and schedules continue to be regularly placed in both electronic and print media. Although the Tootsie Roll and Charms brands are well known, as Ellen Gordon puts it, "It's important to keep them in front of the public." In Tootsie Roll's memorable 1970s advertising campaign, "How Many Licks?", a little boy asks a wise owl, "How many licks does it take to get to the Tootsie Roll center of a Tootsie Pop?" Consumers became actively involved as they tried to answer the question for themselves. Although the company has had several successful advertising campaigns since then, it currently spends very little on advertising (approximately 2% of sales, concentrated on television), relying instead on nostalgia and its 100-year-old brand. Internationally, however, aggressive advertising programs support the brands in Mexico as well as in the Pacific Rim markets and certain Eastern European countries.

# THE GORDONS

Tootsie Roll Industries, Inc. has been run since 1962 by the husband and wife team of Ellen Gordon, President and Chief Operating Officer, and Melvin Gordon, Chairman of the Board and Chief Executive Officer. The couple owns 47% of the company stock, most of which was inherited by Ellen Gordon, whose family has been Tootsie Roll's largest shareholder since the early 1930s.

Ellen and Melvin Gordon have been working together since the 1960s. They are quick to state that they have an open door policy, but often do not attend annual meetings, saying that they already know what has happened. Together with five other executives, they plan all of the company's marketing, manufacturing, and distribution strategies, but the Gordons alone determine Tootsie Roll's corporate vision by controlling strategic planning, decision making, and the setting of corporate goals. Ellen, 64, and Melvin, 75, have no immediate plans to retire, and insist they want to continue working, although on a number of occasions they have expressed the desire to have one of their four daughters (none of whom currently works for Tootsie Roll) take over the management of the company. "We hope that our children, or the management that we are building up in the company, will be able to run the company someday," the Gordons claim, but they have no definite strategic plan for passing on the succession.

Tootsie Roll's strong performance and superior balance sheet should make it a prime target for a takeover, but the Gordons' determination to maintain control over Tootsie Roll Industries may be one reason why Wall Street has shown little interest in the company. The majority of Tootsie Roll's voting stock, 66%, is controlled by the Gordons, and the couple says they have no intention of selling the company. Ellen Gordon explains: "We're busy making Tootsie Roll products and selling them. We're kind of conservative and we don't make projections."

Although Tootsie Roll does not intend to sacrifice long-term growth for short-term gains, its strategy has simply been to focus on making Tootsie Rolls, rather than on preparing forecasts or strategic planning. Over the years, several key acquisitions have enhanced Tootsie Roll's product line, but these acquisitions have generally been made as opportunities have presented themselves within its niche market, and not necessarily as part of a well thought out strategic plan. The Gordons remain arrogant in their view of the market, and Ellen Gordon repeatedly states, "No one else can make a Tootsie Roll."

Recently, Tootsie Roll Industries took advantage of an opportunity related to the location of its headquarters in Chicago. The lease on their 2.2 million square foot facility in Chicago was due to expire and the landlord was not willing to renew it. Tootsie Roll faced the possibility of relocating to a less expensive territory because, with a low ticket item like candy, every penny counts, but the company did not wish to relocate. At the same time, the city did not want Tootsie Roll Industries to leave because it feared the resulting rise in unemployment. Thus, Ellen Gordon was able to leverage the firm's 850 jobs into a lucrative package of incentives to stay headquartered in Chicago. The deal signaled a national trend: small companies are more likely to get big tax concessions and other perks as city economies increasingly depend on them. The Gordons' negotiations garnered $1.4 million in state and local tax exemptions over the next fifteen years, a $20 million low-interest-rate loan to buy the Tootsie Roll plant, $200,000 in job training funds, and the creation of a state enterprise zone located in the plant for tax breaks on machinery and utilities. In turn, the Gordons agreed to add 200 workers over five years and start a loan program for employees to buy homes in Chicago.

Tootsie Roll has remained an independent company for its 100-year history and Ellen Gordon feels that its independence has been a great strength: "As we have grown beyond a small entrepreneurial company we have been able to retain some of our entrepreneurial philosophy and way of doing business." The Gordons are determined to continue Tootsie Roll as an independent company "for generations to come," but Ellen claims, finally, that the key to its success is ". . . fun. Whenever I tell people I work in a confectionery company there's always a smile. That's very important—the magic of candy."

## GLOBAL OPPORTUNITIES

The United States accounts for 90% of Tootsie Roll's sales; the remaining 10% of Tootsie Roll products are sold in foreign markets. Mexico is Tootsie Roll's second largest market, and Canada is third. However, because U.S. consumer spending for food and drink as a percentage of all personal consumption is declining, Tootsie Roll and other candy manufacturers have begun to recognize that future growth opportunities lie in using domestic profits to penetrate foreign markets.

Tootsie Roll needs to increase its sales and distribution internationally in order to continue to grow as the U.S. market moves toward maturity. As trade barriers decrease, Tootsie Roll's opportunities to expand internationally are growing, especially because foreign demand for U.S.-produced higher value-added products, including candy, has increased significantly since 1993. The predicted reduction or elimination of the European Community confection tariffs and variable levies on ingredient composition may also facilitate export growth into Eastern Europe.

Tootsie Roll Industries has begun slowly and cautiously working toward worldwide market penetration, targeting export growth to the Far East and Europe, where per capita confectionery consumption is 40% higher than in the United States. Tootsie Roll currently holds licenses in several countries and regions including the Philippines, Colombia, Europe, the Far East, and Latin America. In addition, the company opened a sales office in Hong Kong in 1992 for sales to China, Korea, and Taiwan, and exports products to the Middle East, Eastern Europe, and Central and South America. However, this international activity remains a very small percentage of Tootsie Roll's total sales.

Since the Gordons are not getting any younger, the future of Tootsie Roll candy will depend on several key decisions they will make over the next few years. Perhaps the time has come for Mel and Ellen to think ahead while they are still on top.

# U.S. Electricar: Zero-Emissions Autos in the 1990s

Robert N. McGrath, Embry-Riddle Aeronautical University

During the 1996 Atlanta Olympics, the General Motors Corporation spent millions of dollars advertising the introduction of a two-seat passenger all-electric automobile called the EV-1, the first truly commercial, mass production electric car that had been announced for sale in decades. Unfortunately, what the TV commercial did not say, but what otherwise was common knowledge among industry followers, was that the car would be priced as high as some luxury automobiles yet travel less than 100 miles before it needed recharging—except, of course, on cold days or in conditions of frequent acceleration and deceleration, in which case the single-charge range could easily be cut in half. GM had created a special division for the design, development, and commercialization of this one automobile, which, despite much acclaim as the most technologically advanced automobile in the world, years of careful prototyping, and an unprecedented level of market testing and analysis, did not have a range much better than its technological brethren of a century before (*Autoweek*, December 13, 1993; *New York Times*, January 28, 1994; *Detroit News*, May 8, 1994).

The Ford Motor Company was either more cautious or farther behind, having in the advanced prototype stage a small, European-style delivery van of similar technology and performance characteristics as GM's passenger car (*Business Week*, May 30, 1994). Chrysler's approach was different still, having already started leasing, for over $100,000 per vehicle, an electric variant of the Chrysler Voyager minivan, which also could not travel more than a hundred miles or so on a charge (*New York Times*, May 6, 1994). Meanwhile, all of the major automobile manufacturers around the world, many of the smaller automobile manufacturers, and many small firms starting up or spilling over from other industries, were also scrambling to develop the best product of this kind that they could (*Automotive News*, June 7, 1993). For a list of the projects being pursued by major players in the industry, see Exhibit 1.

**Exhibit 1**        **Industry Incumbents' Electric Vehicle Programs Underway in 1993**

*Chrysler Corporation*
Program: 50 Dodge Caravan/Plymouth Voyager Electric
Battery: Nickel-Iron or Nickel-Cadmium
Range: 80 miles
Top Speed: 70 mph
Partners: Energy Power Research Institute, General Electric, SAFT America, Good-year.
Customers: Utilities

*Daihatsu Motor Co. Ltd.*
Program: 300 (per year) Hijet vans and Ruggers
Battery: Lead-Acid
Range: Hijet, 81 miles at 25 mph; Rugger, 125 miles at 25 mph.
Top Speed: Hijet, 50 mph; Rugger, 56 mph
Partners: Japan Storage Battery Co., Kansai Electric Power Co.
Customers: Government Units and Electric Power Companies

*Fiat Auto SPA*
Program: 400 Panda Elettras and Cinquecentros
Battery: Elettra, Lead-Acid; Cinquecentro, Lead-Acid and Nickel-Cadmium
Range: Elettra, 62 miles at 31 mph; Cinquecentro, 62 miles at 31 mph (Lead-Acid); 93 miles at 31 mph (Nicad)
Top Speed: Elettra, 43 mph; Cinquecentro, 50 mph (Lead-Acid); 53 mph (Nicad)
Customers: Utilities, Governments, Individuals

*Ford Motor Company*
Program: 80 EcoStar vans
Battery: Sodium-Sulfur
Range: 100 miles
Top Speed: 70 mph
Partners: Asea Brown Boveri, Silent Power Ltd., United Technologies Automotive Inc.
Customers: Utilities and governments in U.S., Mexico, Europe

*General Motors Corporation*
Program: 50 Impact prototype passenger cars
Battery: Lead-Acid
Range: 100 miles
Top Speed: 75 mph
Partners: Hughes Power Control Systems, Delco Remy
Customers: Internal use, contractors seeking defense department grants

*Honda Motor Company*
Program: planning a ground-up design
Battery: Lead-Acid
Partners: Advanced Lead-Acid Battery Consortium

*Isuzu Motors Ltd.*
Program: 8 1994 Elf Delivery vans
Battery: Lead-Acid
Range: 56 miles at 25 mph
Top Speed: 62 mph
Partners: Co-op Electric Vehicles Development Corp., Japan Storage Battery Co.
Customers: Local community groups, delivery companies, the Tama zoo

*Mazda Motor Corporation*
Program: 3 Eunos/Miata roadsters
Battery: Nickel-Cadmium
Range: 112 miles at 25 mph

**Exhibit 1 (continued)**    **Industry Incumbents' Electric Vehicle Programs Underway in 1993**

Top Speed: 81 mph
Partner/Customer: Chugoku Electric Power Co.

*Mitsubishi Motors Corporation*
Program: 28 Libero cargo vans
Battery: Lead-Acid and Nickel-Cadmium
Range: 102 miles at 25 mph (Lead Acid); 155 miles at 25 mph (Nicad)

*Nissan Motor Company*
Program: 52 1991 Cedric/Glora sedans
Battery: Lead-Acid
Range: 75 miles at 25 mph
Top Speed: 62 mph
Partner: Japan Storage Battery Co.
Customers: Local government units and corporations in urban areas

*PSA Group (Peugot and Citroen)*
Program: 600 Peugot and Citroen C25 vans
Battery: Lead-Acid
Range: 43 miles
Top Speed: 50 mph
Customers: 17 French cities, 8 European countries, Hong Kong

*Renault*
Program: 50 to 100 Master and Express vans
Battery: Lead-Acid and Nickel-Cadmium
Customers: Towns, major companies

*Suzuki Motor Co.*
Program: 1992 Alto, 86 Carry vans
Battery: Lead-Acid
Range: Alto, 80 miles at 25 mph; Carry, 75 miles at 25 mph
Top Speed: Alto, 62 mph; Carry, 47 mph
Partners: Japan Storage Battery Co.
Customers: Government units

*Toyota Motor Company*
Program: 40 Towne Ace vans
Battery: Nickel-Cadmium
Range: 99 miles at 25 mph
Top Speed: 68 mph
Customers: Governments/municipalities

*Volkswagen AG*
Program: 70 Jetta CityStromers
Battery: Lead-Acid
Range: 75 miles
Top Speed: 65 mph
Partners: RWE

Source: *Automotive News*, June 7, 1993.

In a more general sense, their aim was to produce an automobile that would not cause any pollution at all, or one that would cause "zero-emissions." Why? In 1990 the California legislature had adopted into law the requirement that, beginning in 1998, all automobile manufacturers which sold significant numbers of vehicles in the state must make available for sale zero-emissions vehicles, in numbers that would account for about 2% of total automobile purchases (Winn, 1994). This figure was grounded in some fairly rough analyses, made by California public officials, which noted that about 2% of all vehicles in the state were owned and operated by organizations with fleets of automobiles of various descriptions. The required percentage rose in the out-years, as California officials seemed resolved to begin, and then carefully nurture, a transition to clean automobiles that, as a bonus, also would not be dependent on imported foreign oil. Pressured by this deadline, most manufacturers decided that "zero-emissions" also meant "all-electric," and a resurrection of the kind of cars that competed fairly well with gasoline models until the invention of the electric starter in 1912. Few experts in the field foresaw the successful development of any other kind of technology as early as 1998.

The large automobile manufacturers faced a tough list of options. They could spend billions, collectively and in some cases individually, developing electric vehicles that virtually all industry officials "knew" would fail because of the ongoing consumer love affair with the performance and cost characteristics of gasoline-powered automobiles. Or, they could simply exit the California market altogether and avoid spending all those billions, but this would leave wide open 15% of the total U.S. automobile market, which was also well-known for its global marketplace leadership. Or, they could ignore the law and be fined $5,000 per vehicle they sold in California starting in 1998. Or, they could find less drastic and more innovative solutions, such as getting credit for zero-emission vehicle sales by licensing other small companies to design and develop zero-emission automobiles, and marketing them under their own names. Exhibit 2 provides a list of some of the recently-formed EV firms in the United States.

In most studies, the economics of production as well as the lack of marketplace acceptance forecast failure, except perhaps in some small niches. The *idea* of zero-emissions automobiles was very popular, of course, but when it came time to actually pay a steep price for an underperforming albeit clean car, consumers voiced reluctance (*J.D. Power Report*, May 1993; *Automotive News*, June 7, 1993; *Automotive News*, December 5, 1994). Worse still, the most environmentally-conscious individuals constituted a segment that in general could ill-afford luxury-priced automobiles. So the vision was appealing, but the reality was daunting.

# U.S. ELECTRICAR

## ■ Company History

U.S. Electricar was a fairly young company and, like many others, experienced a great deal of early change. The firm began in 1976 in Sebastopol, California, as Solar Electric Engineering, Inc., during an era when environmental and energy consciousness became important in the United States. Solar Electric became successful enough at developing solar-powered consumer products to go public in 1980 (*Battery & EV Technology*, May 1994). Later, by acquiring a company called California General Sun, Inc. in 1985, and through a joint venture with a company called Solar Electric Technology, the company found even greater success developing energy-related technologies such as advanced solar cells (*Moody's OTC Manual* 1995).

By the early 1990s it became apparent to management that in light of the California zero-emission statutes, it fortuitously already had some of the key

**Exhibit 2**          **Electric Vehicle Start-Ups**

*AC Propulsion Inc.* San Dimas, California.
Founded: 1991
1993 Revenue: $.7 Million          Employees: 6
Profile: AC was founded by Alan Coccioni, who was instrumental in designing the Impact before leaving GM. His expertise was in electric drivetrains.

*Ecoelectric Corp.* Tucson, Arizona.
Founded: 1992
1993 Revenue: not available          Employees: not available
Profile: Ecoelectric was founded by former race-car driver and computer software company owner Mary Ann Chapman; she was planning a Phoenix-to-Tucson courier service, conversion of small sedans and pickup trucks, the design of components, and EV consulting in maintenance and repair.

*Renaissance Cars Inc.* Palm Bay, Florida.
Founded: 1989
1993 Revenue: $0          Employees: 26
Profile: Renaissance was founded by President Bob Beaumont and was building a ground-up two seater named Tropica, a sporty, technologically-advanced roadster, but designed for warm climates and having no roof. Beaumont's first attempt at EVs was the Citicar, a 38 mph "glorified golf cart"; 2,253 sold from 1974 to 1976.

*Rosen Motors Corp.* Los Angeles, California.
Founded: 1993
1993 Revenue: not available          Employees: not available
Profile: Rosen Motors was founded by Ben Rosen, Chairman of Compaq Computer Corporation; he was planning a hybrid EV which included a gasoline turbine engine.

*Solectria Corp.* Arlington, Massachusetts.
Founded: 1986
1993 Revenues: $2 Million          Employees: 25
Profile: James D. Worden was President; Solectria converted GEO Metros and Chevrolet S-10 pickup trucks, and was also working on a ground-up EV called Sunrise.

*Unique Mobility Inc.* Golden, Colorado
Founded: 1967
1993 Revenues: $2.3 Million          Employees: 45
Profile: Unique was headed by Ray A. Geddes, was developing EV components, and had contracts with BMW, Ford, and others.

Source: *Business Week*, May 30, 1994; *Inc.*, May 1994.

skills that would probably be necessary to be successful in developing Electric Vehicles (EVs). In addition to consumer products, the firm had been producing on-road electric cars since 1983, and, in 1992, started developing custom-built, original equipment cars and vans (*Business Wire*, August 3, 1993). By 1993, the firm had sold more than 200 electric vehicles, and began promoting itself as the country's largest EV manufacturer.

In June of 1993 it was announced that the firm had selected Gates Energy Product's Genesis lead-acid battery as the featured power source for all of the electric vehicles it would subsequently produce, at a planned rate of 500 total vehicles a year. David Brandmeyer, Engineering Vice President and General Manager, said, "With Genesis batteries powering our EVs, Electricar can provide vehicles today that realize the full potential of existing EV technology. EVs are an affordable, environmental transportation alternative that are viable now within the appropriate operations setting" (*Battery & EV Technology*, June 1993). Also that month, Electricar secured exclusive distribution rights to an advanced electronic drivetrain developed by the Hughes Power Control Systems division of General Motors.

On July 30, 1993, Solar Electric acquired Nordskog Electric Vehicles, Inc. for $300,000 in cash and notes payable, $1,900,000 worth of common stock, and $1,000,000 in convertible notes payable. Nordskog had been producing industrial electric vehicles since 1946, and had produced over 55,000 such vehicles over the years. This acquisition gave Solar Electric immediate access to a network of 70 dealers, the largest EV production backlog in the industry, an 11-acre production site in Redlands, California, and the ability to produce a full spectrum of EVs, from in-plant industrial units to automobiles, trucks, vans, and 22-passenger buses.

On October 20th, Solar Electric acquired a Florida company called Consulier Automotive, which was known for its development of lightweight, high-tech materials for use in the construction of automobile bodies, and formed a wholly-owned subsidiary called U.S. Electricar Consulier, Inc. Eleven days later this subsidiary acquired, from a company called Mosler Auto Care Center, the assets it would need in order to develop composite integrated chassis and automobile body systems for lightweight cars. This acquisition was financed with $1,250,000 in shares of unregistered common stock. In November of the same year it acquired the Synergy Electric Vehicle Group, and in December it acquired the Livermore Research and Engineering Corporation. Each acquisition was made for approximately $250,000 in common stock.

## ■ A Commitment to EVs

On January 12 of 1994, the name U.S. Electricar was formally adopted. This decision was not merely symbolic; it reflected management's decision to devote all the firm's resources to the EV industry and divest all lines of business not dedicated to this purpose.

Four product groups were established: a commercial line which included utility, cargo, passenger, commercial delivery, and airport EVs; a bus group which would concentrate on 22-passenger EVs using existing designs; an Original Equipment Manufacturer (OEM) group which would concentrate on developing new designs for vans, trucks, buses, sedans, utility vehicles, and sports cars; and a mainstay "upfit" group which would concentrate on retrofitting Chevrolet S-10 pickup trucks and GM Geo Prizms with electric powertrains (*Battery & EV Technology*, May 1994). The primary distinction between the commercial, bus, and upfit group and the OEM group was one of how much the product would be produced internally versus externally. The commercial, bus, and upfit group were, to varying degrees, to retrofit other manufacturers' products, or use a lot of other manufacturers' existing designs and components. The OEM group was intended to develop products which would be all new U.S. Electricar design and manufacture. However, it was always assumed the divisions would share resources and work in concert with each other.

The upfit group was to become Electricar's bread-and-butter business, and the idea attracted a great deal of attention from manufacturers looking for short-term solutions to the California mandates. In particular, Ford was interested in supplying Electricar with what the industry termed "gliders": regular automobiles, but without the gasoline-engine components. The concept was simple. It was much easier to *fit* an existing model with electric components than it was to *retrofit* a fully-produced auto by first stripping out the gasoline engine. In this way Electricar could keep costs down, and Ford could get the credit for supplying zero-emissions vehicles in California. Ford was considering the Windstar minivan and Crown Victoria sedan for such a program, but had serious concerns about also being able to maintain the image for quality that it had struggled so hard to achieve. Ford was slow to commit until it could be sure that Electricar could meet the tough standards of being a "qualified vehicle modifier" (*Los Angeles Times*, November 16, 1994; *The Toronto Star*, November 26, 1994).

In any event, in conjunction with management's decision to commit to the EV industry was the establishment of its headquarters in Santa Rosa, California. By this time the firm owned a 14,650 square foot product development facility in Sebastopol, and leased 15,000 square feet of production space, 20,000 feet of warehouse space, and a 1,400 square foot sales office in Los Angeles. The company had about three hundred people on its payroll.

By the end of the year a great debate was underway regarding the California statutes and the EV issue in general. Fortunately, U.S. Electricar was faring well on all sides of the debate. An article in the December 1993 *Motor Trend* read, "Little credence has been given to small-time electric car manufacturers—and for good reason. Their wares have fallen short in too many ways."

Beyond mediocre performance and range, small-time ground-up EV efforts haven't offered the kind of fit and finish expected in new vehicles. Many production cars retrofitted to electric by converters have even failed to provide such basics as smooth and responsive steering, braking, shifting, and clutch operation. Crashworthiness of battery-laden EVs has also been suspect because barrier crash testing of these low-volume vehicles isn't required.

So how can an electric car company possibly overcome these problems? Perhaps by following the lead of Solar Electric Engineering of Sebastopol, California. For years, this company's niche was retrofitting year-old Ford Escorts and similar car models for electric propulsion, a business plan suitable only for small-time success. But significant corporate restructuring and several recent key acquisitions could change that.

Solar Electric's renewed vision began to unfold with the opening of its Electricar Los Angeles facility, the first in a series of planned satellite operations destined to serve regional EV markets. The company then signed with GM Hughes Electronics to buy variants of the high-tech electric powertrain developed for the GM Impact. It followed up with the acquisition of Nordskog Electric Vehicles, an established industrial EV manufacturer and recent electric bus developer, and then Consulier Automotive.

Each of these moves is individually noteworthy, but together they signify a unified plan for the production and sale of purpose-built electric vehicles. GMHE's advanced electric powertrains will provide a level of performance more in line with that of today's gasoline-powered cars. Consulier's expertise in automotive cored-composite technology—showcased in its ultra-lightweight, race-proven composite monocoque Consulier Intruder supercar—will provide advanced body/chassis technology for a ground-up vehicle. The Nordskog operation will supply an existing nationwide network of 70 service centers and potential sales outlets and yet another EV manufacturing site in California.

Much of the praise being given Electricar by the automotive establishment was no doubt deserved. In June of 1994, it was announced that the National Highway Traffic Safety Administration certified Electricar's light pickup truck under all Federal Motor Vehicle Safety Standards. As far as anyone could remember, this was the first EV to ever achieve this certification without exemptions or waivers. Boasted Ted Morgan, Electricar's CEO, "U.S. Electricar's new vehicle safety program establishes a new threshold for the electric vehicle industry comparable to the highest level of passenger car safety," and attributed much of the success to "virtual prototyping" on a special computer program (called DYNA3D) developed over a 15-year period at the Lawrence Livermore National Laboratory (LLL). Electricar had been using LLL's software in a collaborative agreement; in a sense, LLL was a pure R&D lab, and Electricar was a field test. Benefits of this software were similar to the benefits of tools generally called Computer-Aided-Design (CAD). LLL's software allowed much safety engineering to be done by computer simulation, making possible a drastic reduction in the number of actual crash tests needed, and a reduction in the time required to redesign imperfections. This innovation was certainly a coup, as small firms typically are too strapped for cash to fund extensive and massively expensive developmental tasks where complex technologies are involved (*Alternative Energy Network*, June 7, 1994).

On the other hand, there was still poor acceptance in the marketplace, even in the niches that Electricar was targeting. Though the characteristics of Electricar's products were probably best suited to the industrial fleet market, managers of industrial fleets were tough, pragmatic, sophisticated customers (*Automotive News*, April 26, 1993). While advocates could clearly see the advantages of EVs' low maintenance, energy efficiency, relative ease of refueling once a home base was wired for it, and relatively cheap electricity (the cost-per-mile of operating an EV was cheaper than the same measure for gasoline engine autos), they were dissuaded by the exorbitant initial price tags, short range, unproved reliability, service technician re-training costs, service-bay remodeling costs, low payload capacities, and battery replacement costs. Some of these worries presented a paradox for the industry, since EV manufacturers could not work out real-life bugs without first achieving the significant sales volumes that would bring desperately-needed experience. One fleet manager commented, "I tried to get someone from GM to give me a vehicle range. It varied by about 40 miles depending on who you talked to. Let's face it, 40 miles is a considerable distance to walk" (*Automotive News*, August 8, 1994).

In order to improve sales, on August 1, 1994, Electricar established its own credit corporation to help finance sales of EVs in creative ways. Leasing arrangements, for example, would allow potential buyers such as fleet managers the flexibility of trying EVs before (or without) committing to purchase (*Business Wire*, August 1, 1994).

But by the end of 1994 it was apparent that in order to continue to grow as the firm's management wished—in fact, in order to survive as a going concern—further arrangements and some restructuring of operations and financial liabilities would be required. It became obvious the firm needed additional capital, and more moves were necessary.

## ■ Global Alliances

In one important strategic move, Electricar established an arrangement with the Itochu Corp., which would bring in an immediate $15 million, but would give Itochu 3% of Electricar, and possibly another 5% if Itochu eventually opted to convert debt to equity. Itochu was a large Japanese trading company experienced in distributing automobiles for several Japanese automotive giants. This move was essentially the beginnings of a global alliance, and had associated risks and opportunities.

The deal included the formation of a Tokyo-based joint venture, the Japan Electricar Corporation (JEC), formed to develop EV products targeted at commercial fleet purchasers in that region. The immediate intention was for U.S. Electricar to export fleet vehicles specifically tailored to the Japanese market. JEC would essentially be the marketing arm and would have exclusive distribution rights in all of Asia. Also as part of the deal, Itochu would gain access to Electricar's vehicle designs.

Some critics were skeptical of Itochu's decision, as well as Electricar's long-term technology strategy. Despite Electricar's advances in areas such as manufacturing advanced composite materials and the impressive inroads made in engineering processes, Electricar's designs were still centered on lead-acid battery technology. Many experts seriously doubted that lead-acid technology was the viable, long-term propulsion technology needed to solve the EV range problem and really gain marketplace acceptance, except in very small niches. Its converted Chevrolet S-10s and GEO Prizms still had ranges of only about 60 to 80 miles, and sold (in lots of 30 or more) for about $33,000 and $29,000, respectively (*New York Times,* June 10, 1994). The first S-10 was only delivered to Florida Power and Light on May 31, 1994, however, so production economies were certain to improve. The short-term production goal was 400 conversions a month. Worse, EV subsystems such as the battery, electronic controller, and electric drive motors were so interrelated that the vehicles were centered on the technological characteristics of the battery. In short, Itochu was at risk of buying access to vehicle designs that might well become obsolete, given the likelihood of significant advances in other promising battery technologies (McGrath, 1996).

Nevertheless, the joint venture envisioned the sale of converted Grumman postal vehicles for distribution as light industrial delivery trucks in Japan—U.S. postal vehicles already had right-hand drive, required in Japan on all vehicles. Itocho would also be aided by a third party in the venture—Tokyo R&D, renowned in Japan for automotive design excellence and willing to provide technological services to the venture. Quipped an Itochu Executive Vice President, "We are just buying a ticket to see if it will hit the jackpot or not. . . . We hope we can get a major capital gain" (*Wall Street Journal,* June 10, 1994).

Soon Electricar would announce that much of the firm's production activities would be relocated to a site in Malaysia, due to the generally poor business climate for EVs in the United States. But this decision was no doubt encouraged by the fact that in industrializing Asian countries, one million cars had been sold in 1994—a figure which had doubled in only six years, and was expected to double again by the year 2000 (*World Trade,* August 1995).

Another important alliance was formed on October 6, when Electricar entered into a joint venture with Grupo Industrial Casa of Mexico City. Casa was Mexico's largest bus body manufacturer, and sold buses throughout Latin America. The venture aimed at developing, manufacturing, and marketing several thousand industrial EVs, especially small food delivery trucks and buses, for the heavily congested and polluted cities of North, Central, and South America. Mexico City seemed especially opportune, since a new law there banned gasoline delivery trucks six hours a day, three days a week. "The Mexican side of this venture was exuberant," said Casa's Chairman Ricardo Cornejo. "In the cooperative spirit of NAFTA [the North American Free Trade Agreement], this exciting venture follows a global business strategy to design and manufacture vehicles directly within the customer's market" (*United Press International*, October 6, 1994). Two jointly-owned corporations were planned, one based in the United States which would handle U.S. and Canadian operations, and one based in Mexico which would handle the remainder of the Western Hemisphere.

Next, a test-market of Electricar EVs was established in Hawaii, inaugurated by a two-year, $1.8 million contract from the Hawaiian Electric Vehicle Development Project. The project was matched by $3.4 million in Federal funds. A total of twenty-nine electric sedans would be furnished to indigenous electric utility companies as well as the U.S. Air Force and Navy (*U.S. Electricar News*, August 11, 1994). This project would serve as a feasibility test for entry into government fleets, which Federal law mandated must include "alternative fuel" vehicles (i.e., electric, propane, methanol, solar, hybrid, etc.) by 1996. Though alternative fuel vehicles were, technologically speaking, a much more inclusive category than all-electric vehicles, the law created the opportunity for as many as 500,000 EVs to be sold by the year 2000 (*Battery & EV Technology*, May 1994).

On November 21, Electricar announced that the U.S. Department of Commerce had awarded it funding for a five-year, $21.8 million program for the further development of a cost-effective composites manufacturing process. Electricar was to act as lead company in an extended effort to advance the technology involved in producing lightweight, high-quality, affordable, and safe EVs. The magnitude of the program was impressive: Electricar was commissioned to develop composites fit for use in EV components that would be recyclable, never require painting, and would be cost effective in production runs equivalent to making materials for 1,000 to 25,000 vehicles a year. This government subsidy was a significant step towards making mass-marketable EVs possible, and clearly positioned Electricar at the front. In a similar vein, on December 13, 1994, it was announced that Electricar and Kaiser Aluminum agreed jointly to develop advanced aluminum structures for EVs. The specific focus was improving the Electrolite urban delivery vehicle recently introduced by Electricar, which was intended for international markets. But certainly the knowledge gained would be transferable to other EVs and be useful to both firms.

In terms of actual production, between August 1994 and February 1995, U.S. Electricar produced 190 converted GEO Prizms and Chevrolet S-10 pickups, and seven electric buses. Additionally, it shipped several hundred off-road vehicles, such as forklift trucks and airport service vehicles. Financial data for U.S. Electricar can be found in Exhibits 3 and 4.

**Exhibit 3**          **Consolidated Income Account, years ended July 31 ($000)**

|                                                  | *1994*   | *1993*  | *1992*  |
|--------------------------------------------------|----------|---------|---------|
| Net Sales                                        | 5,787    | 863     | 1,220   |
| Cost of sales                                    | 6,372    | 802     | 848     |
| Gross margin                                     | (585)    | 61      | 372     |
| R&D                                              | 7,724    | 376     | 56      |
| Selling, general, and admin. expenses            | 11,805   | 1,936   | 777     |
| Interest expense                                 | 339      | 146     | 80      |
| Depreciation and amortization                    | 833      | 17      | 14      |
| Other expense (income)                           | 17       | 24      | (31)    |
| Loss on disposition of solar home                | —        | —       | 55      |
| Market development expense                       | 3,718    | —       | —       |
| Total other costs & Expenses                     | 24,436   | 2,499   | 951     |
| Income (loss) from continuing operations         | (25,021) | (2,438) | (579)   |
| Income (loss) from discontinued operations       | —        | (169)   | (203)   |
| Net Income                                       | (25,201) | (2,607) | (782)   |
| Previous retained earnings                       | (5,050)  | (2,443) | (1,661) |
| Retained earnings                                | (30,071) | (5,050) | (2,443) |
| Earnings on common shares                        | (1.67)   | (.45)   | (.20)   |
| Common shares: Year-end (000)                    | 15,518   | 5,839   | 4,393   |
| Average (000)                                    | 9,571    | 4,487   | 3,871   |

Source: *Moody's OTC Industrial Manual*, 1995.

## VIEWS FROM THE TOP

### ▪ Ted Morgan: CEO

Ted Morgan had been the President and CEO of Electricar since November of 1992 (Cronk, 1995). He came to the firm having already established himself as something of an expert at managing and financing growth ventures, developing niche strategies, and creating novel methods of distribution. He developed these skills working in sales and marketing positions in the Xerox Corporation for 14 years, and honed them through nurturing The Office Club superstore chain to an eventual merger with Office Depot in 1991, which created a $3 billion company.

From this experience Morgan had a strong appreciation for what institutional investors looked for in a growth company. He was much less expert at acquiring private financing, which was fueling most EV start-ups in the early nineties. The EV industry was fueled mostly by environmental concerns, not the opportunity for short-term gain. But technologies and other factors were evolving rapidly, and professional fund investors were beginning to take serious notice.

To attract large, professionally-managed blocks of funds, Morgan knew that establishing credibility was a critical factor. He believed in establishing

**Exhibit 4**          **Consolidated Balance Sheet, as of July 31 ($000)**

|                                                    | 1994     | 1993    | 1992    |
|----------------------------------------------------|----------|---------|---------|
| *Assets*                                           |          |         |         |
| Cash and equivalents                               | 5,327    | 617     | 57      |
| Accounts receivable                                | 1,551    | 625     | 26      |
| Inventory                                          | 6,716    | 1,086   | 214     |
| Other                                              | —        | —       | 20      |
| Prepaid and other current assets                   | 803      | 269     | —       |
| Total current assets                               | 14,397   | 2,597   | 317     |
| PP&E                                               | 4,945    | 2,809   | 54      |
| Intangibles, net                                   | 1,355    | 47      | —       |
| Other assets                                       | 609      | —       | —       |
| Total assets                                       | 21,306   | 5,453   | 371     |
| *Liabilities*                                      |          |         |         |
| Accounts payable and accrued expenses              | —        | —       | 267     |
| Accounts payable                                   | 5,314    | 534     | —       |
| Accrued payroll and related expenses               | 406      | 274     | —       |
| Accrued warranty expenses                          | 640      | 127     | —       |
| Other accrued expenses                             | 801      | 459     | —       |
| Customer deposits                                  | 1,769    | 154     | 204     |
| Notes payable & current portion of long-term debt  | 18       | 464     | —       |
| Notes payable, other                               | —        | —       | 165     |
| Notes payable, related parties                     | —        | —       | 129     |
| Total current liabilities                          | 8,948    | 2,012   | 765     |
| Long-term debt                                     | 9,980    | 1,020   | 30      |
| Royalties payable                                  | 773      | —       | —       |
| Series A preferred stock                           | 7,118    | 4,408   | —       |
| Notes receivable                                   | (1,094)  | (1,000) | —       |
| Common stock                                       | 25,652   | 4,063   | 2,019   |
| Retained earnings                                  | (30,071) | (5,050) | (2,443) |
| Total shareholder's equity                         | 1,605    | 2,421   | (424)   |
| Total liabilities & stock equity                   | 21,306   | 5,453   | 371     |
| Net current assets                                 | 5,449    | 585     | (448)   |
| Book value                                         | 0.02     | 0.41    | (0.10)  |

credibility upfront, by putting in place the strongest management team possible, not just at the top but down several layers of management, all the way to the point of purchase. Such a team should be capable of performing its own extensive marketing research and subsequently developing a sound, easily communicable strategy. He felt that the pronouncements made by environmentalists of the benefits of EVs were wild-eyed, and that the hundreds of millions of dollars of needed capitalization would never materialize unless the firm's plans could withstand the tough scrutiny of the venture capital community.

Key to becoming that one-in-ten choice of venture capitalists, then, was the development of a sound business plan. He felt sure that a company should never go to market prematurely. Otherwise a firm could easily wind up spending all its "easy" money foolishly and wastefully and then, after initial failures became evident, find it only that much more difficult to find subsequent investors. Being a small, public company had the advantage of being open to scrutiny, though such visibility was a double-edged sword.

In short, Morgan was a pragmatist and realist who felt unsure about blue-sky terms like "synergy," and felt uneasy about partnering relationships and alliances that did not show economic returns. The nature of the financial environment mandated remuneration to the owners. Hence Electricar had embarked on its acquisition spree when management realized what additional help it would need to succeed. Morgan knew that across-the-board reliance on in-house development of technologies would be too slow, but going outside the firm for help invited much trouble unless control was assured. Morgan felt that acquisitions, patenting, and licensing were viable approaches to keeping developments proprietary.

On the other hand, Morgan did not believe in being too focused, mostly due to the premature nature of so many key technologies. He felt that the "upfit" business was an appropriate entree to the EV industry and had huge national and international potential, but subsequent industry developments were much harder to foresee accurately. There were no rules to this industry yet and many paths were possible. "Fleet operators" was about as specific as he would define Electricar's potential niche, though of course he could cite endless examples of how rapid transit districts, public utilities, and corporations should be attracted to what he had in mind. Generally, Morgan envisioned an Electricar that leased fleets of vehicles and also provided maintenance, warranty, training, and other services. But "in the short term, [success depended on] the ability to raise capital. That's the measure of success. The only measure of success" (Cronk, 1995).

In contrast to the combined wisdom of the Big Three in Detroit, Morgan felt that the key to early success lay not so much in the performance of EVs as it did on price. He noted the obvious difficulty that Chrysler was having leasing its electric Voyager for up to $120,000 apiece. He felt that if volumes could be reached where converted Chevrolet S-10s could be leased for about $20,000, "every utility company in the country" would line up for them. Such an accomplishment might create a 3-to-5 billion dollar "niche," and several hundred million dollars of business by as early as 1997.

With numbers like these in mind, it was no wonder that Morgan rarely thought about the individual consumer, and saw little point in pursuing individual sales, which almost certainly would have to be done through layers of middlemen and independent dealers. He felt that Electricar did not have the capital, tools, and distribution network needed to really crack the mass market. Foreseeable per-unit margins were not nearly inviting enough: "Everybody is attempting to paint grandiose pictures of what's going on here. The reality is that the business-to-business transaction is the only transaction right now in the electric vehicle area. . . . We'll leave others to their dreams of building hundreds of thousands of electric vehicles" (Cronk, 1995).

## ■ John Dabels: Vice President for Sales

John Dabels was Vice President for Sales, Marketing, and Government Relations. He was fairly new to Electricar, having joined the firm in May of 1994. But from October 1990 to March of 1993, he had served as the Director of Market Development for General Motors' Impact program. Prior to that, he had been Director of Marketing for Buick since 1979.

Naturally, Dabels was intimately familiar with the individual automobile purchaser—the regular consumer. He felt that the 1990s rebirth of the electric automobile concept, constituent technologies, and other broad conditions were such that this time around, the EV was ready to become much more than a fad. He felt that EVs did make consumer sense for short trips in confined communities, for commuting where routes were predictable on a daily basis, for running kids around, for shopping trips, and so forth—EVs were not ready to be "first" cars, but were ready to take their place in many families as second or third cars. However, he too felt that price was a severe problem. But he also had a more encompassing and systematic view of what an automobile was and could be. In particular, he understood that when it came to cars, many people viewed the purchasing experience as obnoxious, and that this simple reality was an important obstruction to sales.

Hence, Dabels felt that the EV was less characteristically like a gasoline automobile than it was like a very large electric appliance or even personal computer, and that lessons could and should be taken from those industries. There, successful marketing innovations included the use of mail-order houses and home shopping networks; certainly, enough managerial ingenuity existed in the neophyte EV industry to adapt the wisdom developed in the electronics and computer industries. No one should be a slave to doing business anything like the way the established auto giants did business.

In fact, Dabels was generally skeptical about the major players' willingness or abilities to succeed in the much-different EV world: "I think there will be some guys wildly successful before the Big Three figure out what to do. . . . Today, if you're not a car guy you don't qualify in the auto industry. You've got to be a car engineer. Those guys hit such small, narrow markets that they have literally forgotten about the consumer. They'll come out with engineering ideas that are not well-executed. They have great disdain for marketing people" (Cronk, 1995).

## ■ Robert Garzee: Vice President of U.S. Electricar

Robert Garzee was a Vice President of U.S. Electricar, and President of the Synergy EV Group. He came to Electricar with the acquisition of Synergy, Inc., in 1993. There he learned the ropes of learning and profiting through partnering. For example, he was an original member of the CALSTART design team, a quasi-public consortium of several organizations devoted to making the EV movement happen in California. He had previously spent 12 years with IBM, eight in a marketing-management capacity.

Unlike CEO Morgan, Garzee was a big fan of strategic partnering. He had learned through experience that consortia could be extremely effective if the right people were involved and the management was good. At McClellan Air Force Base in California, home of the Air Force's R&D activities in developing advanced/special materials, he had brought together the Sacramento Municipal Utility District, the City of San Jose, California, the FMC Corporation, Pacific

Gas & Electric, and Nordskog in a successful program that advanced the state of the art of composite materials intended for use in buses and automobiles. When Electricar absorbed Synergy and Nordskog, this brought an important subset of this consortium under U.S. Electricar's control, also making it economically accountable for progress. The price for all this control, of course, included not only the costs of acquisition, but continuing administrative oversight.

In any event, Garzee also was committed to the fleet market, and felt that the Big Three would or could not respond well to that niche. Like Morgan, Garzee had a view that seemed pragmatic: " . . . people are buying industrial EVs not because they want to solve the pollution problem, but because it's the best way to solve a business problem. . . . If, for some reason, Detroit decides [to] back out, I [still] don't see the utilities saying that EVs don't make any sense. . . . EVs will cost about 15-20% more than their [gasoline] counterparts, but it doesn't take long to make up that percentage once in operation" (Cronk, 1995).

## ■ Scott Cronk: Director of Business Development

Scott Cronk was Director of Business Development at Electricar and led its strategic partnering activities. Cronk came to Electricar with a Big Three pedigree. General Motors had sponsored his engineering degree at the General Motors Institute in Flint, Michigan, and he joined GM in 1982. From 1988 to 1991 he managed an avionics product line in northern Europe for Delco Systems Operations, a division of GM. From 1991 to 1994 he worked at Delco Electronics headquarters, leading international business development and planning. He joined Electricar in 1994.

Where Morgan seemed to be the stern pragmatist on the team, Cronk seemed to be more abstract and philosophical. Cronk felt that in order to bring the EV idea to profitable fruition, a "new business theory" would be required—or at least a synthesis of business practices that at the time had not yet been pieced together in traditional American business circles. He felt that it was incumbent upon managers in the new industry to bring together four forces: environment, energy, economy, and education.

The environmental force was straightforward. It seemed imperative that the world find a way out of its dependence on oil, a limited resource and one that was draining the U.S. economy of massive amounts of money each year. But the more important issue was pollution, a problem that affected not only lifestyles but possibly the future of the planet. Managers in the new industry should root themselves in this idea.

The energy force referred not to oil, but to electricity. Industrialized society had created a massive infrastructure that was just as dependent on electricity as it was on oil, and overall capacity had been built to accommodate peak electric-load requirements. This was inefficient on a social scale—an extensive EV industry could absorb the excess, off-peak capacity, make the industry more efficient in the process, and reduce the unit cost of using electricity, which is obviously the energy resource of the future (however it might be generated).

In terms of economic forces, the early 1990s saw the economically painful transition from a defense-oriented, Cold War world economy to one that was market-driven and militarily peaceful in its basic character. The managerial and technical brilliance that won the technological battles of the Cold War was too important a national resource to underemploy; these skills could be applied to a new endeavor—the EV—that had a total potential that rivaled defense spending. Managers had a window of opportunity for acquiring much of this talent (especially in California) that would not stay open for very many years.

In terms of education, managers should feel it their responsibility to convert the environmental, energy, and economic forces into an overall consensus—by advocating EVs through such fundamental marketing and informational campaigns—that basic education was the prime goal. Across the board, grassroots movements needed help from the new industry which it spawned.

However, Cronk felt that a fifth "e"—enterprise structure—was probably the most crucial, since it would require the most ingenuity and effort from industry management. This was the essence of what he foresaw as the new, necessary business theory. He felt that it would be absolutely necessary for management in the EV industry to abandon the old automotive industry model. A century of development had evolved the automobile industry into a giant, hierarchical, oligopolistic structure, oriented towards technologies, not markets.

Cronk's alternative vision was difficult to describe, since what he had in mind had no fully-formed precedent. The "virtual corporation" model that developed in the computer industry was not exactly it, though networks of value-adding firms would be essential. The "lean production" model was incomplete, though production efficiency was a must. The Japanese *keiretsu*, or cluster of closely interconnected firms supplying the parent firm, was the closest single model Cronk could articulate, though he noted two problems: one, he felt that the Japanese model was excellent at developing emerging technologies, but did not make the transition well to a mature industry environment; two, some of the formal relationships found in *keiretsus* were deemed collusive in the U.S. legal system, and were illegal.

Cronk articulated his vision in this way:

> [The term "EV" should] refer to any vehicle which is focused on efficient use of energy predominantly through the use of lightweight structural materials and electric motors that drive the vehicle's wheels. It is important to define EVs in this way because at this time it is far from clear which types of energy storage devices will win out in the end. . . .
>
> New electric energy storage and delivery systems and new structural materials: this is what EVs are about. [This] moves the discussion away from 'the battery' and allows us to focus on a larger, more multidimensional set of challenges. . . . (Cronk, 1995; p.122)

## CONCLUSION

By 1995, management at Electricar decided to focus its resources on what had become core lines of business: electric transit shuttle buses and industrial/commercial vehicles. In order to accomplish this complete corporate conversion, however, some manufacturing operations had to be suspended and/or closed. Facilities in Redlands, California, were temporarily shut down, while operations in Los Angeles and Florida were permanently closed (but planned to be moved to the Redlands, California, facility.) During this moratorium, management looked scrupulously at the continued viability of its electric sedan and light truck conversion business, but in any eventuality decided to continue providing full services to previous purchasers of these wares. As a result of these decisions, the firm's work force was reduced by about 30%, with additional reductions foreseen.

By late 1994 and throughout 1995, the firm was still suffering losses. For the quarter ending October 31, 1994, Electricar reported net sales of $6.18 million, which was greater than its total revenues for all of fiscal year 1994 (Electricar's fiscal year ended on July 31)—but net losses amounted to $8.96 million, or $.54 per share. In the first quarter of fiscal year 1994, sales had been $1.12 million, which yielded a net loss of $1.26 million or $.21 per share. Through the first nine months of 1995, Electricar had suffered a $37 million loss on revenues of $11 million (*World Trade*, August 1995).

While the firm had a number of promising products and development contracts as of early 1995, the volumes were obviously inadequate to break even, much less achieve profitability. The management team now felt it had to attempt to define the direction it intended to go in marketing electric vehicles. They felt they had to anticipate, to the best of their ability, where the demand

---

**Exhibit 5**      **Automobile Ownership Costs**

|  | *1993 Ford Escort* | *Hypothetical EV* |
|---|---|---|
| Price | $11,387 | $11,900 |
| 6% sales tax | 683 | 0 |
| Acquisition cost | $12,070 | $11,900 |
| Per mile (cents): |  |  |
| Gasoline and oil | 4.8 | 0 |
| Electricity | 0 | 1.5 |
| Maintenance | 2.2 | 1.0 |
| Tires | .7 | .8 |
| Battery | 0 | 8.0 |
| Total | 7.7 | 11.3 |
| Dollars per year: |  |  |
| Insurance | $784 | $784 |
| License/registration | 147 | 100 |
| Depreciation | 2,412 | 1,179 |
| Finance charge | 527 | 517 |
| Total | 3,870 | 2,580 |
| (cents per mile) | 25.8 | 17.2 |
| Total (cents per mile) |  |  |
| Operation | 7.7 | 11.3 |
| Fixed | 25.8 | 17.2 |
| Operation cost per mile | 33.5 | 28.5 |

"Table compares costs for a 1993 Ford Escort against a mythical electric vehicle that would compete against it evenly as a choice for a household's second car, based on a four-year, 60,000 mile cycle."

Source: *Automotive News*, June 7, 1993.

for electric propulsion would grow over the next decade. They then needed the financing which would allow U.S. Electricar to take advantage of those opportunities.

# REFERENCES

*Alternative Energy Network,* "U.S. Electricar Announces FMVSS Certification of Volume Production Electric-Powered Truck." June 7, 1994.

*Automotive News,* "Key Players: Fleet Managers Take Lead Role in Cutting Costs, Testing Use of Alternative Fuels." April 26, 1993.

*Automotive News,* "California Dreaming." June 7, 1993.

*Automotive News,* "Electric Utility Fleet Managers Cast Wary Eye at Electric Vehicles." August 8, 1994.

*Automotive News,* "Conversions Generate Interest in EV Conversions." December 5, 1994.

*Autoweek,* "Plug In, Turn On, or Drop Out: A Debate Grounded in Reality." December 13, 1993.

*Battery & EV Technology,* "Electricar Selects Gates Energy Products' Lead-Acid Batteries." June 1993.

*Battery & EV Technology,* "Electricar Keeps Its Focus on the Road." May 1994.

*Business Week,* "Electric Cars: Will They Work? And Who Will Buy Them?" May 30, 1994.

*Business Wire,* "Solar Electric Acquires Nordskog Electric Vehicles." August 3, 1993.

*Business Wire,* "U.S. Electricar Establishes Credit Corporation to Offer Electric Vehicles Financing for Fleets, Dealers." August 1, 1994.

Cronk, S.A. 1995. *Building the E-Motive Industry: Essays and Conversations About Strategies for Creating an Electric Vehicle Industry.* Society of Automotive Engineers. Warrendale, PA.

*Detroit News,* "Why Big Three's Electric Car Strategy Backfired." May 8, 1994.

*Inc.,* "Charged Up: Electric Vehicles." May 1994.

*J.D. Power Report,* "Consumers Aren't Turned on by Electric Vehicles." May 1993.

*Los Angeles Times,* "Ford in Talks to Sell Frames for Electric Car Production." November 16, 1994.

McGrath, R.N. 1996. *Discontinuous Technological Change and Institutional Legitimacy: A Morphological Perspective.* (Doctoral Dissertation.) University Microfilms, Inc.

*Moody's OTC Industrial Manual,* 1995. New York: Moody's Industrial Services, Inc.

*Motor Trend,* "Trends: Environmental Report." December 1993.

*New York Times,* "Expecting a Fizzle, GM Puts Electric Cars to Test." January 28, 1994.

*New York Times,* "Chrysler, With Misgivings, Will Sell Electric Mini-Vans." May 6, 1994.

*New York Times,* "U.S. Electricar Announces a Venture With Itochu of Japan." June 10, 1994.

*The Toronto Star,* "Electric Gliders." November 26, 1994.

*United Press International,* "Electricar Pact in Mexico." October 6, 1994.

*U.S. Electricar News,* "U.S. Electricar, HEVDP to Offer EV Test Drives at Dedication Ceremony in Honolulu." August 11, 1994.

*Wall Street Journal,* "Itochu Agrees to Take Stake in Car Company." June 10, 1994.

*World Trade,* "Looking to the ASEAN Market for a Jump Start." August 1995.

Winn, J.L. 1994. "The Role of Government and Industry in the Development of The Electric Vehicle." Society of Automotive Engineers Technical Paper 941035.

# NTN Communications, Inc.— Interactive Television: The Future Is Now

Julie Driscoll, Bentley College
Alan N. Hoffman, Bentley College
Alison Rude, Bentley College
Carol Rugg, Bentley College
Bonnie Silveria, Bentley College

*Internet site of interest:* **www.ntn.com**

*"In the next five years, interactive television is going to take off. The whole industry is going to explode."*

DANIEL DOWNS, CO-FOUNDER, NTN COMMUNICATIONS, INC.

On June 28, 1994, Patrick Downs, Daniel Downs, and Don Klosterman met to decide the future strategic direction of NTN Communications. NTN's interactive television programming products, QB1 and Diamond Ball, designed to run on a variety of platforms including television and personal computers, were big hits. But the continual advent of new technologies, such as direct satellite communication, made it hard to stay current. The three principals needed to decide where to focus their efforts and resources in light of the veritable explosion of new technologies in the marketplace.

## QB1—INTERACTIVE FOOTBALL

QB1 is an interactive television game that allows patrons of hotels, taverns, and restaurants to play the role of quarterback during live television coverage of college and professional football games. Patrons watch a live football game on television and predict the quarterback's calls by punching their play of choice (pass, middle, deep is one option) on a portable playmaker box. Once the real action begins, their choices are locked in and beamed by satellite to NTN's Carlsbad, California, headquarters. Viewers win or lose points based on the accuracy of their predictions. Using sophisticated computers and software, the score of each QB1 competitor is tabulated instantaneously and bounced back via satellite to each game site. As the game progresses, QB1 players can track how they are doing against every single individual competing across the country as their scores and results are flashed on the television screen. "QB1 is definitely a game of skill; you cannot be successful at it if you approach it as a game of chance," says Dan Klosterman, co-founder of NTN Communications, who, together with NFL coaches Don Schula, Hank Stram, and Bill Walsh, collective winners of six Super Bowl games, developed QB1 for NTN.

## WHAT IS INTERACTIVE TELEVISION?

Interactive communication, a synthesis of television, games, education, and information systems, is potentially the "mega-industry" of the 1990s. Although interactive communication is popular with restaurant/bar owners, educators, business professionals, and home owners, there are many consumers who do not understand the concepts behind it, and some who are not even aware that interactive options exist.

Interactive communication is two-way (or more) communication between a viewer and a device, usually a television screen. A viewer may interact with a television program as if a dialogue were taking place between two people. For example, a person can play "Jeopardy" interactively by answering the questions on the show via a remote control device. While one viewer answers the questions, viewers at any number of other locations may also answer; thus all participating viewers compete against each other simultaneously, making for a more active and enjoyable viewing experience through interactive participation.

## THE HISTORY OF INTERACTIVE TELEVISION

The earliest form of interactive communication was the Morse code machine which made two-way communication possible via a transmitter and a receiver. Next, the telephone enabled virtually any two people to be linked; and now more than two people can communicate instantly via sophisticated teleconferencing technology. Companies such as AT&T, Picturetel, and Intel have also developed video-conferencing which enables participants from remote locations to see each other via satellite or long distance telephone lines while they talk. Universities also use video-conferencing to conduct classes for students in inaccessible locations. Now, the development of the "information highway" by companies such as America Online, Compuserve, and Prodigy allows users to communicate with a vast database of information, and with other users, via computer hook-up.

Interactive television is a natural development of current technology. The potential for interactive communications is so great that no single firm will be able to dominate all aspects of the industry. Consequently, many alliances are forming among cable, telephone, and computer firms to develop the necessary technology and infrastructure. Time Warner has joined forces with Silicon

Graphics to develop computer equipment for an interactive television network, and with US West to develop a full-service interactive system. In addition, the Federal Communications Commission has granted regional telephone companies permission to offer audiovisual services, and thus to compete directly with cable companies.

## COMPANY HISTORY

NTN was founded in 1983 by three sports executives: Donald C. Klosterman, and Patrick J. and Daniel C. Downs. Pat Downs was vice-president and business manager of the San Diego Padres baseball team from 1964 to 1969 and director of special projects for Time/Life Broadcast Properties in San Diego from 1970 to 1973. Dan Downs began his career in the early 1960s in the Los Angeles Dodgers' management training program. In 1966, he became stadium manager and director of sales for the Houston Oilers football team, and was later promoted to assistant general manager. His interest in interactivity dates back to those Houston Oilers days, when he and his boss, Don Klosterman, were working on ways to get more fans to the Astrodome to watch the Oilers play.

Pat and Dan Downs made ambitious plans, but more than once their interactive ventures teetered on the brink of financial ruin. Nevertheless, they persevered, marketing their first game, QB1, to restaurants and bars. After losing the financial backing of Time Inc.'s Home Box Office, they risked everything to build the interactive network themselves, going without pay for three years, even losing their homes. Still the Downs brothers never considered turning back, though many advised them to quit. "In retrospect, we were ahead of the times. But we hung on long enough to raise enough capital to keep going," said Dan Downs. "At times it felt really lonely out there. But we believed so much in what we were doing, we just kept going." Now people who scoffed at them years ago want to deal. "We've put ourselves in a position to succeed and that's what we intend to do," Pat says. "Deals with the big players (ABC, AT&T, and Sony) are in the works, and when the superhighway comes along, we will be ready to go."

NTN Communications, Inc., an international provider of interactive television games and educational programs, and a pioneer in developing interactive television, was formed from the merger of Alroy Industries, Inc. and National Telecommunicator Network, Inc. The company's revenues presently derive from three sources: broadcasting, the sale of interactive equipment, and the licensing of technology. NTN owns and operates the only interactive television network in North America that broadcasts 24 hours a day, every day of the week.

A number of games are now available through NTN's interactive network. The company began with sports games because it was their area of expertise, and have since broadened their product base to include Diamond Ball (baseball), Power Play (hockey), Passport (an interactive travel game), Spot Light (an entertainment game), and Playback (a music game). NTN's niche is public venues and special event productions such as the Superbowl, the Grammy Awards, the Academy Awards, all game shows on the ABC television network, and trade shows, sales conferences, and charity events. NTN has the capability to allow many people to participate at the same time through the use of their 200 unit playmaker system, which is perfect for large events, and the wide variety of their games is a strength because there is something for everyone.

## NTN'S TARGET MARKETS

The NTN network is currently marketed to group viewing locations such as bars and restaurants. There are approximately 700 location subscribers in the United States and 220 in Canada. All NTN network programming is produced at NTN corporate headquarters in Carlsbad, California, and transmitted to subscribers using multiple data transmission techniques including FM radio transmission, direct satellite broadcast, and television transmission via vertical blanking intervals. Using the same technology as that used for pay-per-view movies, NTN can provide simultaneous transmission of up to eight live events for interactive play, allowing the company to broadcast different programs to different geographic locations at the same time. The NTN feed is carried via satellite and each establishment has a decoder which enables it to receive advertisements and games designated specifically for that location.

Bars and restaurants are capitalizing on interactive trends by offering games tied to popular sporting events to increase traffic into their establishments and increase sales. However, observers have noted that the success of their interactive offerings is tied directly to the bar or restaurant's successful promotion of the event. For example, a pub in Chicago gets at least 30 extra people specifically to play NTN's QB1 game, while another bar down the street, although full, may have only a few people using the interactive game.

NTN currently services four domestic markets: the hospitality, home, education, and video games markets. For the hospitality market, NTN has joined with LodgeNet to provide over 14,000 hotel rooms nationwide with an interactive network of games which allows hotel guests to play along with live sporting events. For the home market, NTN has joined forces with Prodigy, AT&T ImagiNation Network, GEnie, and GTE's Main Street to offer interactive computer games. For the interactive education market, NTN provides surveys, academic competitions, and testing capabilities which can be performed within a single classroom at a particular site, or at several different locations, all with instantaneous feedback via satellite networks. And NTN's wholly-owned subsidiary, IWIN, Inc. is a full-service provider of interactive applications and transactions services for the interactive games industry.

NTN also operates internationally. In Canada, NTN has an exclusive license with NTN Interactive Network, Inc. NTN also has an agreement with TWIN, its licensee for Europe (owned by Whitebread Breweries, PLC, and BBC Enterprises) to license the rights to all of NTN's products and services throughout Europe. Australasia became an operational company in November 1993 with a broadcast facility in Sydney, Australia, and NTN is currently pursuing interactive education opportunities in Mexico, and has received some approval from the Mexican Ministry of Education.

## NEW PRODUCTS

In 1993, NTN formed a wholly-owned subsidiary, IWIN (I Win), to take advantage of the legalization of home betting on horses. IWIN is a full-service provider of interactive applications and transactions services to the worldwide gaming industry, and is currently testing a new pari-mutuel game called

"Triples" which allows cable TV subscribers in California to wager on the races at the Los Alamitos Race Course. NTN plans further expansion into the gaming industry using a vertical market strategy to break into the lottery and casino gaming markets in the near future.

In January 1994, NTN teamed up with Replica Corporation to offer Replica's interactive investment and Sports Fantasy Games through NTN's distribution system. The agreement boosts NTN's offerings, adding to its appeal to new target markets as well as current customers. In March of the same year, NTN cut a deal with Event Entertainment and Kingvision Pay-Per-View to form the NTN Event Network which will offer interactive boxing for 8-12 fights per year.

Interactive programming has many potential uses beyond allowing players to participate in games—for instance, enlivening training and education. To expand its capabilities in more markets, NTN formed an Interactive Education Division in 1993. Interactive education can provide rural or disadvantaged students with the same opportunities as those from wealthier school districts by allowing students to participate actively in the learning process and communicate with teachers at remote locations as if they were in the same classroom. At the same time, teachers effectively control the process by quickly monitoring student progress and providing instant feedback. NTN has had success in developing and licensing its interactive technology to KET, an education network in Kentucky. NTN has also developed the Interactive Learning System, a unique tool for teaching students in a more enjoyable environment. It operates via satellite and has been used for conducting surveys, academic competitions, and testing. The Interactive Learning System has been used in 19 states for more than five years and regional centers are currently being established in California and Arizona.

NTN is also working with the Mexican government to provide educational services. Field tests were conducted in which Mexican schools received a satellite broadcast transmitted from Mexico City. These tests were successful and NTN anticipates making a final agreement with the Mexican government to provide interactive educational services to approximately 3,000 schools in the near future. Under this arrangement, NTN will receive $695 per month, per system, for the next five years in addition to a one-time installation fee of $250 and a monthly maintenance fee of $150 per system. In addition to the 3,000 schools already targeted, there are 5,700 schools remaining which could benefit from NTN's services. However, NTN has not yet received a signed contract, and if the deal falls through NTN stands to lose millions of dollars in potential revenue.

NTN seeks to expand into the corporate world by using their products for corporate training, product knowledge testing, employee testing, and certification and technical training. They plan to market interactive training as a way to help companies cut their training and development costs by combining training with other branches of the company or by eliminating the need for an on-site trainer.

In 1995, NTN entered into an agreement with America Online to provide 24–hour access to NTN's popular interactive football game "QB1" and their new interactive trivia game "Countdown." NTN also entered into an agreement that will make NTN's interactive programming available to more than 285 TGI Friday's restaurants throughout the United States.

In February 1996, NTN debuted "QB1" on the Internet. NTN was granted early access to Microsoft's new Internet Explorer "Active X" technology to allow NTN more efficient delivery of its interactive games, play along sports, and trivia on the Internet's World Wide Web.

## NTN'S COMPETITIVE LANDSCAPE

The competition in the field of interactive television is fierce. Many new entrants are adept at using both current technologies such as television and telephone lines, and state-of-the-art technologies such as satellites, cellular networks, and personal computers. NTN's direct competitor in the interactive television home market is the Interactive Network, Inc. (IN). IN distributes their own interactive network whose programming is very similar to that of NTN. IN's subscriber-based service allows television viewers to play along in real time with televised sporting events, game shows, dramas, news, and talk show programming. Currently testing in Sacramento, California, and Chicago, Illinois, IN's system, like that of NTN, is designed to run on many different delivery platforms. The biggest threat IN poses to NTN, however, is that it is backed by Tele-Communications, Inc., Gannett Co., Cablevision, NBC, and A.C. Nielsen, large media investors with "deep pockets," all of whom are significant players in their respective industries.

Because NTN's services are designed to utilize various already existing delivery mechanisms, their competitors are diverse. Local and long distance telephone companies such as AT&T and Bell Atlantic are recent entrants into the interactive television marketplace, which can use their existing telephone infrastructure and a combination of both television and personal computers to deliver interactive programming.

Many cable-TV companies across the United States are also interested in interactive television both as a future programming alternative and as an opportunity to expand their revenue stream. The cable companies pose a real threat because they have large financial resources, their delivery infrastructure via cable networks is already in place, and they have access to a wide variety of programming possibilities.

In addition, online services such as Prodigy, CompuServe, and America Online pose a competitive risk to NTN. They have been in the interactive marketplace for over ten years; they have the infrastructure in place; and their products already provide high levels of interactivity through interactive chat and gaming capabilities.

As is characteristic of most growth industries, many new players will compete directly with NTN. The threat to NTN is real, especially because competition can take so many different forms. And, because there are so many ways a company wishing to compete can proceed, the current climate in the industry is volatile and unpredictable. In addition, there are no industry standards; thus, a company developing its own technology runs the risk of being side-tracked by an alternative technology. In addition, NTN relies on distribution networks, such as radio stations and telephone and cable companies, to supply their products to customers. Consequently, they are at the mercy of their distributors to get their products to clients. Mergers and alliances are one way to reduce this threat. Alternatively, a concerted effort to offer the best services (those most desired by consumers) would shift the balance of power in NTN's favor by outdoing the competition.

In the home and hospitality segments, NTN relies heavily on information providers (NHL, NFL, Trivia, the Academy Awards) to supply content for their products, which are, in turn, evaluated primarily on the basis of their association with major sporting events or game shows.

## THE INFORMATION SUPERHIGHWAY

Technological advances have given consumers access to many services without having to leave home, and it is interactive technology (the ability of the consumer to respond and communicate directly and interactively with a television or computer) that makes it all possible. Because it is so responsive to consumer needs, the growth potential for interactive technology is huge. Cable subscriptions currently represent approximately 61% of the total television household market, and are on the rise; and many consumers spend a significant portion of their time watching movies, playing video or electronic games, or watching sports programs.

Industry experts predict that television and cable services are still in their infancy, and that the near future holds a wider selection of cable channels, the ability to select and watch a movie on demand, and the ability to interact directly with the television. However, television is not the only medium competing for a share of the interactive market. A recent study revealed that the average household spends almost twice as much time using a computer as watching television. Some experts even predict that PCs will replace televisions as the household electronic appliance of choice and that the majority of homes will have a PC by the year 2000, despite the extra expense. Software and cable companies currently offer very similar products such as news services, home-shopping, and electronic games, suggesting that computer and video marketing are beginning to converge in a competition for the same consumers. Microsoft plans to capitalize on this trend by developing software that works with both platforms. The company is currently working on a network which will operate not only on phone networks but on cable-TV networks as well, which could have a tremendous impact on the interactive television segment. For example, Microsoft Baseball, a CD-ROM program which dials into an electronic service to retrieve daily scores, will eventually become a video update program which will allow consumers to scan for the baseball footage they missed the night before. In addition, Microsoft is forming alliances with Hollywood film studios and other software companies to combine computing and video technologies more effectively. As Microsoft's president Bill Gates puts it, "The PC industry has come a long way, but that's nothing compared with what's going to happen."

## THE FUTURE

The future of the information superhighway is promising, but uncertain. Because technology is constantly changing there are very few industry standards relevant to the development of interactive television. Companies developing a product must take all the risks and may very well end up with an already obsolete new product. A recent FCC ruling granting permission to telephone companies to offer audiovisual services opens even more doors for players intending to enter the market. However, because it is unclear which avenue or mode of technology will be the wave of the future, cable, telephone, and computer companies are forming alliances which not only combine technologies, but secure markets within the industry. Cable companies, for example, already enjoy concessions such as right-of-ways and legal easements for cable installations, and monopolies on particular service territories which prevent other cable companies from competing directly with them.

The future of the information superhighway becomes even more uncertain when satellite technology is factored in. As satellite technology advances, satellite dishes are becoming smaller and more inexpensive, and will soon be offering greater opportunities for interactive technology. In fact, satellites may very well supersede cable and telephone technology, which would tremendously benefit all involved. For instance, digging permits or right-of-way issues, a large source of aggravation and cost for cable companies today, would be eliminated. In fact, many businesses currently opt for satellite television services instead of cable because cable companies cannot provide access, either because of awkward location or building and right-of-way issues. There are, however, problems with satellite technology, especially with regard to the "line of sight" when satellite signals are obstructed by large buildings or other impediments.

## DEMOGRAPHIC TRENDS

One potential problem for NTN is the public's lack of product awareness. In a recent survey, 66% of the population stated they did not have much interest in or awareness of interactive television, although 22% indicated they were interested in subscribing to interactive television in their homes. However, the survey did reveal a rise in interest among consumers between 18 and 34; and as the income levels of those surveyed rose, so did interest in interactive services. Thus consumer education, especially education targeted to particular demographic markets, is crucial to the promotion of interactive products.

The elderly currently represent 13% of the U.S. population, and population growth statistics predict that the group of those over 65 will grow at a faster rate than any other age group between 1994 and 2000. Although the elderly population often have a great deal of leisure time, historically speaking they have not been comfortable with high-tech devices. While interactive television could offer useful services to this age group (e.g., at-home bingo, shopping), it is not clear there is sufficient interest among this demographic group.

The 0-15 age segment currently represents 23% of the total population and although this age segment shows slow growth within the next few years, it will continue to be, proportionately, the largest population segment in the United States through the year 2002.

## MARKETING

Within the interactive industry, NTN has positioned itself in an enviable niche: programming and programming distribution. NTN's ongoing marketing objectives include:

- attracting important new sponsors and advertisers
- forming new strategic alliances and securing new contracts
- entering into agreements that expand the distribution of their programs and services.

At the same time, the interactive industry is continually changing and NTN's marketing strategies must reflect this. In 1992, NTN repositioned itself as a leader in interactive communications, rebuilding its core product offerings and recasting NTN's marketing operation.

NTN's primary market focus is hospitality, especially restaurants, bars, and hotels. NTN's plan is to garner expertise in this segment before moving into the home market, their next growth segment. In North America alone, there are approximately 330,000 bars and restaurants NTN can target—a tremendous growth area. Some of NTN's subscribers include: Bennigan's, Steak and Ale, Hooters, TGI Friday's, Chili's, Ground Round, and Chi Chi's. In 1993, NTN added military bases, college campuses, hospitals, country clubs, fraternal organizations, and bowling centers to their list of subscribers. These subscribers are easy markets for NTN products because they can afford them, and it is not necessary to sell them television set-top boxes.

NTN entered the hotel segment of the hospitality industry through an agreement with LodgeNet Entertainment Corporation, which gave NTN access to 14,000 guest rooms. The full hotel segment potential is 250,000 guest rooms in major hotel chains such as Marriott, Hilton, ITT Sheraton, Radisson, Ramada, and Holiday Inn. Interactive marketing to the hospitality industry grew significantly since 1992, the subscriber base nearly quadrupling from 776 to 2,500 locations by the end of 1995. During 1995, the number of interactive participants has increased to 75 million. These increases mark significant growth and are considered reliable indicators of future industry growth.

Advertisers are also finding creative ways to take advantage of interactive television services. Infomercials are using interactive TV to review feedback about their products, and Ocean Spray has teamed up with NTN to create interactive advertisements which sponsor prizes for top-scoring customers. Indeed, the latest challenge for advertisers will be marketing their products effectively using interactive media. Anticipated trends include:

- more sponsor-oriented programs focused on specific interest groups
- product channels which allow for comparison shopping
- increased use of infomercials
- increased availability of commercial spots.

Currently, NTN has national advertisers such as Paddington, Seagrams, Miller Brewing, which has been a sponsor of NTN's game QB1 for the past three years, and American Express, which advertises on NTN's Passport game. Advertisers view the interactive network as a powerful medium and an effective way to target many different segments of their markets at the same time. In addition, advertising on this medium is more cost effective. The flexibility of interactive programming allows advertisers to tailor their product promotions to different geographical areas and age groups, especially the hard-to-reach 21-35 year olds. Advertisers are thus able to reach more than five million players each month, with a year-end 1995 estimate of eleven million per month, a major attraction for many corporate sponsors.

## FINANCIAL SITUATION

NTN's financial objectives are: increase shareholder value by reaching profitability; fund future growth from revenues generated by the Company; and contain costs. The company achieved its first objective of reaching profitability in the fourth quarter of 1993, realizing a profit of $160,000. However, NTN reported a consolidated net loss of $3.9 million for 1995 as compared to a consolidated net profit of $707,000 for 1994.

NTN's stock price has fluctuated from a low of 12 cents in 1990 to $11.50 in 1993. As of April 11, 1996, the price was $4.09. One of management's objectives is to "have a stock that can properly reflect both the current results, as well as future potential which entails expenses for which no financial benefits may be available for the short term."

NTN currently has a sale-lease back arrangement for its equipment, which allows for an off-balance sheet financing method. Under this arrangement NTN pays for the equipment, sells the assembled equipment to another company for a higher price to pay for it, then leases it back, an arrangement NTN found necessary because of insufficient working capital to finance the cost of the equipment itself. In the future, NTN will finance the equipment purchases by exercising the warrants and options.

In 1995, sales grew by 33%, a rise attributable to increases in sales of equipment, numbers of subscribers, and in retail sales of products. NTN's other sources of revenue include license fees and royalties from foreign licensees, and the advertising and sponsorship revenues from companies advertising on its games and shows.

## LEGAL ISSUES

The legal environment for interactive services is uncertain. The major obstacle to NTN's effort to provide an interactive betting service is that in many states home betting is illegal. Senate Bill 1431 legalizes home betting in California, but mandates blackout areas of 15 miles around satellite facilities and 30 miles around racetracks. The process for legalizing home betting in other states has been slower than expected, hindering penetration of the market. However, there are five states where betting is legal: Kentucky, Pennsylvania, Michigan, Ohio, and New York, making them potential candidates for a home betting service. This number will most likely increase as state governments seek additional revenue through gambling profits.

Other legal hassles include a patent infringement case with Interactive Network, Inc. (IN). The dispute involves NTN's royalty-free use of IN's patent to lock out responses from viewers during a live sports telecast. Under a partial settlement agreement, IN licensed NTN's QB1 trivia game for a fee, but the license expired on March 31, 1993, and has not yet been renewed. As of now, IN is the only other company developing a subscription-based interactive television service, and it has formed powerful alliances that could lock NTN out of certain key markets. For example, Cablevision, an affiliate of Rainbow Programming, Inc., currently services all of Boston, and a great deal of New York's residential and business market. However, NTN does not think that patent technology is key to their success in the interactive industry. Rather, it is NTN's corporate philosophy that they can maintain a competitive edge by differentiating their product and service offerings, and by fostering consumer loyalty.

Licensing arrangements, which are similar to patents, also act as barriers to new firms entering the interactive sports entertainment market, and may allow

NTN to gain a competitive advantage in the marketplace. In September 1995, NTN signed a new multi-year exclusive NFL licensing agreement. Under this arrangement, NTN can also sub-license the use of NFL games for interactive television to other cable service companies and delivery systems.

## STRATEGIC DIRECTION?

NTN is at a critical point in its life cycle. NTN faces several opportunities and challenges on the technological and competitive fronts. NTN must confront tremendous competitive pressures from other interactive service providers such as MSN (The Microsoft Network), Prodigy, Compuserve, and the World Wide Web, any of which could, from another perspective, provide opportunities for NTN to cultivate strategic alliances. Given NTN's limited resources, Patrick, Dan, and Don know they need to focus on a particular strategic direction for NTN and concentrate NTN's resources on one or two technologies, either cable, telephone, online, satellite, or wireless communication, if NTN is to survive and prosper in the long run.

## REFERENCES

Aho, Debra. "Miller Calls an Interactive Play." *Advertising Age,* October 11, 1993, p. 41.

Armstrong, Larry. "I Have Seen the Future and Its—Urp!" *Business Week,* January 24, 1994, p. 41.

Armstrong, Larry; Sager, Ira; Rebello, Kathy; Burrows, Peter. "Home Computers." *Business Week,* November 28, 1994, p. 88.

Bhattacharya, Sanjoy. "NTN Communications, Inc." *D. Blech and Company,* November 16, 1993, pp. 1-10.

Fawcett, A. W. "Interactive TV's Toughest Question." *Advertising Age,* October 11, 1993, pp. 39-40.

Hartke, James, Tarum Chandra, and Peter Kambourakis. "NTN Communications, Inc." *Laidlaw Equities, Inc.,* June 8, 1993, pp. 1-20.

Hunger, J. David, and Thomas L. Wheelan. *Strategic Management.* Reading: Addison-Wesley Publishing Company, 1993.

*Interactive Network.* Annual Report, 1993.

*Interactive Television Today and Tomorrow.* San Francisco: Interactive Services Association, July 18, 1994.

*NTN—At a Glance.* San Diego: Leedom's San Diego Stock Report, 1994.

*NTN Communications.* Annual Report, 1993.

*NTN Communications.* First Quarter Bulletin, 1994.

*NTN Communications.* Standard American Stock Exchange Stock Reports. New York: McGraw-Hill, Inc., 1994.

"NTN Communications is Teaming with Event Entertainment and Kingvision Pay-Per-View." *Broadcasting and Cable,* March 14, 1994, p. 12.

Quinn, James Brian. *Intelligent Enterprises.* New York: The Free Press, 1992.

Smith, Virginia. "The Consumer Market for Interactive Television: Today and Tomorrow." *AT&T Consumer Video Services,* July 18, 1994, pp. 1-9.

# KFC: Doing Chicken Right in the U.S. Fast-Food Industry

Jeffrey A. Krug, The University of Memphis
W. Harvey Hegarty, Indiana University

*Internet site of interest:* **www.kentuckyfriedchicken.com**

*"I think our most critical issue in the future will be our ability to handle change. We have a concept that, in the last two years, has moved us out of the 1960s to perhaps the late 1980s. Unfortunately, it's 1994, and we have a lot more changes that need to take place in our system. Our system is older in terms of facilities and product forms, and our attitudes still don't reflect the realities of our changing business environment.*

*"One of the great challenges at KFC is that there is a lot that needs fixing. It's like being a kid in a candy store—you don't know where to go first. I think one of the toughest challenges we have had is to stay focused. That is true on the menu side as well. People really see us as being the experts on chicken-on-the-bone. There is so much we can still do with products such as Rotisserie Chicken and different forms like that.*

*"We also have a significant service problem in a service-driven industry. I think we have got to figure out a way to meet our customer service expectations, which we don't meet today. They come to us really because they love our product in spite of our service. And you can't survive long-term on that trail."*

KYLE CRAIG, PRESIDENT, KFC BRAND DEVELOPMENT, APRIL 1994

Through 1994 and 1995, KFC remained the world's largest chicken restaurant chain and the world's third largest fast-food chain. It held almost fifty percent of the U.S. market in terms of sales and ended 1995 with over 9,000 restaurants worldwide. It was opening a new restaurant at a rate of roughly one per day worldwide and was operating in over 65 countries. One of the first fast-food chains to go international during the late 1960s, KFC has developed one of the world's most recognizable brands.

Craig found himself faced with a number of critical issues in 1994. Despite KFC's past successes in the U.S. market, much of KFC's growth was now being driven by its international operations, which accounted for 95 percent of all new KFC restaurants built in 1994. Additionally, intensified competition among the largest fast-food competitors had resulted in a number of obstacles to further expansion in the U.S. market. Further expansion of freestanding restaurants was particularly difficult. Fewer sites were available for new construction and those sites, because of their increased cost, were driving profit margins down. Profit margins were driven down further by the need to promote the brand more rigorously, consumer pressure to reduce prices, the high cost of bringing new products to market, and higher operating costs.

Through the late 1980s, most of KFC's competition was limited to other fried chicken chains such as Church's, Popeyes, and Bojangles. Today, KFC is faced with competition from non-fried chicken chains such as Hardee's and McDonald's, who have introduced fried chicken to their menus. With KFC's menu limited to chicken, it has lost business to chains which offer customers a greater variety of food items that cut across different food segments. In addition, a number of new, upscale chicken chains—for example, Kenny Rogers

Roasters and Boston Market—have entered the market. These new chains have focused on higher-income customers by offering non-fried chicken items. Because KFC is best known for its fried chicken products, these new entrants are reaching out to customer groups which KFC is only now beginning to tap. Even Pizza Hut, a sister company of PepsiCo, introduced buffalo wings to its menu in 1995.

KFC's early entry into the fast-food industry in 1954 allowed KFC to develop strong brand name recognition and a strong foothold in the industry. However, its early entry into the industry has also been the cause of many present-day problems. By the mid-1980s, many of KFC's restaurants had begun to age and were designed mainly for take-out. As a result, KFC had to expend significant financial resources to refurbish older restaurants and to add additional inside seating and drive-thrus, in order to accommodate customers' increasing demands for faster service.

KFC's major problem in 1994 and 1995 was how to transition the old KFC into a new KFC which appealed to consumer demands for more healthy food items at lower prices, greater variety in food selection, and a higher level of service and cleanliness in a greater variety of locations. In effect, this entailed greater reflection over its entire business strategy—its menu offerings, pricing, advertising and promotion, points of distribution, restaurant growth, and franchise relationships.

## THE U.S. FOOD SERVICE INDUSTRY

The concept of franchising became well-established by the early 1950s. Colonel Harland Sanders founded Kentucky Fried Chicken in 1954, Ray Kroc opened the first McDonald's restaurant in 1955, and Burger King quickly followed by opening its first restaurant in Miami, Florida. Other franchises founded in the 1950s were Chicken Delight, Burger Chef, Burger Queen, Carol's, and Sandy's. Today, the U.S. restaurant industry is made up of over 550,000 restaurants and food outlets, according to the National Restaurant Association (NRA). Standard & Poor's estimates that U.S. food service industry sales surpassed $289 billion in 1995. Exhibit 1 shows U.S. food service industry sales segmented into eleven categories. The fast-food segment continued to outpace all other segments, with estimated sales of $93.4 billion in 1995. This compared with an estimated $87.8 billion in sales in the full-service segment.

The U.S. food service industry as a whole grew at an estimated compounded annual growth rate of 4.2 percent from 1990 to 1995, compared with an annual growth rate of 5.1 percent in the U.S. gross domestic product. The fast-food segment of the food industry grew at a more healthy rate of 6.0 percent, outpacing all food categories except social caterers and vending, which grew only slightly more quickly. While eleven categories of restaurants make up the food industry, the top three—fast-food, full-service, and institutions—have maintained a constant share of about 73 percent of total industry sales. However, the share of industry sales controlled by the fast-food segment has risen by about 2.6 points over the last five years, mainly at the expense of full-service restaurants and institutions.

**EXHIBIT 1**                    **U.S. Food Service Industry Sales**

| ($ Billions) | 1990 | 1991 | 1992 | 1993 | 1994 | 1995 | 5-Year Growth Rate |
|---|---|---|---|---|---|---|---|
| Fast-Food | 69.8 | 73.6 | 75.6 | 81.4 | 87.1 | 93.4 | 6.0% |
| Full-Service | 75.9 | 79.2 | 80.3 | 83.0 | 85.3 | 87.8 | 3.0% |
| Institutions | 26.4 | 27.5 | 28.3 | 27.7 | 29.5 | 30.6 | 3.0% |
| Vending | 16.3 | 19.9 | 20.3 | 20.7 | 21.9 | 22.9 | 7.0% |
| Food Contractors | 14.1 | 15.0 | 15.5 | 16.0 | 16.4 | 17.1 | 3.9% |
| Lodging Places | 14.9 | 14.3 | 15.2 | 15.5 | 16.2 | 16.9 | 2.6% |
| Bars & Taverns | 8.7 | 8.6 | 9.2 | 8.9 | 9.1 | 9.4 | 1.6% |
| Cafeterias | 4.4 | 4.6 | 4.5 | 4.5 | 4.7 | 4.9 | 2.2% |
| Social Caterers | 2.3 | 2.4 | 2.5 | 2.7 | 2.9 | 3.1 | 6.2% |
| Ice Cream | 2.0 | 2.1 | 2.4 | 2.5 | 2.5 | 2.6 | 5.4% |
| Military | 1.0 | 1.1 | 1.1 | 1.1 | 1.1 | 1.1 | 1.9% |
| Total Sales | 235.8 | 248.3 | 254.9 | 264.0 | 276.7 | 289.8 | 4.2% |

Source: Standard & Poor's, Industry Surveys, 1996. 1994 and 1995 sales estimated.

## THE U.S. FAST-FOOD INDUSTRY

Financial and other data for the fast-food segment of the U.S. food service industry are most frequently reported for eight separate categories: sandwich chains, pizza chains, family restaurants, dinner houses, chicken chains, steak restaurants, contractors, and hotels. Exhibit 2 shows sales for the largest 100 U.S. fast-food chains over the last five years. The top 100 chains have grown at a compounded annual rate of 4.9 percent over the last five years. Only three of the nine food categories have grown at greater than a 6.0 percent annual rate: family chains (6.1 percent), dinner houses (12.7 percent), and chicken chains (6.8 percent). The growth in the chicken segment has, in recent years, suffered from the health trend away from fried foods. However, new entrants to the chicken segment such as Boston Market and Kenny Rogers Roasters, which have promoted non-fried chicken products—and the addition of non-fried chicken products to KFC's menu—have revived growth within the chicken segment.

Exhibit 2 indicates that the top four fastest growing categories within the fast-food industry control 69 percent of all fast-food sales. During the last six years, the market share held by these four categories has increased from 64.5 percent to 68.8 percent. The most significant improvement in sales has occurred in the dinner house segment. Eight of the fifteen major dinner houses registered double-digit sales growth in 1995, including Lone Star Steakhouse &

**Exhibit 2**                    **Top 100 Fast-Food Chain Sales By Food Segment**

| ($ Billions) | 1990 | 1991 | 1992 | 1993 | 1994 | 1995 | 5-Year Growth Rate |
|---|---|---|---|---|---|---|---|
| Sandwich Chains . . . .35.6 | 36.7 | 39.7 | 41.0 | 44.0 | 47.2 | 5.8% |
| Pizza Chains . . . . . . . .9.2 | 9.6 | 10.4 | 10.2 | 10.5 | 11.2 | 4.0% |
| Family Chains . . . . . . .6.4 | 7.0 | 7.7 | 7.6 | 8.0 | 8.6 | 6.1% |
| Dinner Houses . . . . . . .5.4 | 6.3 | 6.9 | 7.6 | 8.7 | 9.8 | 12.7% |
| Chicken Chains . . . . . .4.6 | 4.5 | 4.7 | 5.0 | 5.6 | 6.4 | 6.8% |
| Steak Chains . . . . . . . .3.4 | 3.5 | 3.3 | 3.0 | 3.0 | 3.2 | -1.2% |
| Food Contractors . . . .11.2 | 10.8 | 11.2 | 10.6 | 11.1 | 11.7 | 0.9% |
| Hotels . . . . . . . . . . . .5.3 | 5.4 | 5.5 | 5.7 | 5.8 | 6.0 | 2.7% |
| Other . . . . . . . . . . . . .6.7 | 6.7 | 6.7 | 6.8 | 7.2 | 7.5 | 2.4% |
| Total Sales . . . . . . . .87.8 | 90.5 | 96.1 | 97.6 | 104.0 | 111.7 | 4.9% |

Source: *Nation's Restaurant News*, National Restaurant Association.

Saloon (55.2 percent), Outback Steakhouse (49.7 percent), Fuddruckers (32.9 percent), Ruby Tuesday (22.6 percent), Hooters (18.6 percent), and Applebee's (15.0 percent).

Much of the improvement in sales among the dinner houses and family restaurant chains during the last decade is partially attributable to demographic trends in the United States. In particular, the number of young people as a percentage of the population is declining. Those in the 18–24-year age group, for example, are of particular importance to fast-food restaurants because they consume about five meals away from home weekly, compared to under four meals for all consumers. While this age group nearly doubled during the 1960–1980 period, it will drop by about 20 percent by the year 2000. Those over the age of 65 tend to eat out less often, about two times per week, and this group is the most rapidly growing age group in the country. Older individuals tend to spend more time eating their meal, prefer sit-down restaurants, and are more likely to choose more upscale restaurants such as dinner houses. The higher price of the average meal in a dinner house is offset by the fewer times that older individuals eat out each week.

The initial high growth rates in fast-food franchising in the United States during the late 1950s and 1960s made the fast-food industry attractive to new entrants. The lack of established market share leaders and brand loyalties meant that there were relatively few companies that could defend against new market entrants. During this period, a number of fast-food chains were acquired by larger, diversified firms. Some of the most notable acquisitions were Pillsbury's acquisition of Burger King, General Foods' acquisition of Burger Chef (which was later sold to Hardee's Food Systems in 1982), Ralston-Purina's acquisition of Jack in the Box, United Brand's acquisition of Baskin-Robbins (which it later sold in 1973), and Great Western's acquisition of Shakey's Pizza.

The acquisition of a number of fast-food franchises by larger, more established marketing firms intensified competition during the 1970s. Not only were many fast-food chains owned by larger companies with resources enabling them to promote and invest heavily in their respective chains, but consumers increasingly demanded more value for their dollar. This further intensified competition and a second wave of acquisitions followed during this period. PepsiCo acquired Pizza Hut in 1977 and Taco Bell in 1978. KFC, which was sold by Heublein to R.J. Reynolds Industries in 1982, was also acquired by PepsiCo, in 1986. Other notable acquisitions during this period were Hardee's acquisition of Roy Rogers, Popeyes' acquisition of Church's, Tennessee Restaurant Company's acquisition of Friendly's Ice Cream, and Gibbons, Green von Amerongen's acquisition of Jack in the Box. Many of these acquisitions were made in order to strengthen the parent company's position within the fast-food industry (e.g., PepsiCo's decision to diversify into fast-food by acquiring Pizza Hut, Taco Bell, and Kentucky Fried Chicken). However, another factor that led to many of these acquisitions was the deteriorating financial position of smaller competitors, brought about by a lack of resources to compete with the market share leaders. A number of chains, therefore, became attractive takeover targets.

An interesting characteristic of the fast-food industry is that, in almost all cases, the leader in each food segment controls a large relative market share when compared to the market shares of its nearest competitors. Exhibit 3 shows the market share leaders in the top six fast-food categories for the industry's leading chains. KFC controls 58 percent of the chicken segment, while McDonald's, Red Lobster, Ponderosa Steak House, Denny's, and Pizza Hut control 34, 19, 23, 21, and 48 percent of their respective segments.

Demographically, consumers became more and more demanding during the 1980s. In 1991, the National Restaurant Association conducted a survey to measure consumer attitudes toward fast-food and moderately-priced restaurants. Of those consumers who said they would rather go to a fast-food restaurant than any other type of restaurant under most circumstances, 48 percent mentioned being in a hurry, being busy, and wanting fast service as the major factor in their choice of a fast-food restaurant. Convenience, expense, "didn't feel like cooking," and quality were less important. This trend was further supported in a 1992 survey by the National Restaurant Association, which found that 66 percent of the respondents felt that their expectations of the value they received at fast-food restaurants for the price paid was generally met. Twenty-four percent of the respondents felt that value fell below their expectations.

By 1994, however, consumers had become more demanding. In addition to demanding faster service, consumers were increasingly demanding a greater variety of menu items, greater value for their dollar, and fast-food available at a greater number of non-traditional outlets, such as airports. This has resulted in a number of fast-food chains (such as McDonald's, Taco Bell, and Wendy's) offering combinations of food items ("value meals") at lower prices and several fast-food chains cutting across food segments by offering products not traditionally offered by other competitors in their food segment (for example, Hardee's offering fried chicken). The latter has affected KFC, which competes exclusively within the chicken segment.

**Exhibit 3**                    **Leading U.S. Fast-Food Chains (ranked by estimated 1995 sales, $000s)**

| Sandwich Chains | Sales | Share |
|---|---|---|
| McDonald's | 15,800 | 33.5% |
| Burger King | 7,830 | 16.6% |
| Taco Bell | 4,853 | 10.3% |
| Wendy's | 4,152 | 8.8% |
| Hardee's | 3,520 | 7.5% |
| Subway | 2,905 | 6.2% |
| Arby's | 1,730 | 3.7% |
| Dairy Queen | 1,185 | 2.5% |
| Jack in the Box | 1,082 | 2.3% |
| Sonic Drive-In | 880 | 1.9% |
| Carl's Jr. | 562 | 1.2% |
| Other Chains | 2,658 | 5.5% |
| Total | 47,156 | 100.0% |

| Family Restaurants | Sales | Share |
|---|---|---|
| Denny's | 1,810 | 21.1% |
| Shoney's | 1,277 | 14.9% |
| Big Boy | 1,010 | 11.8% |
| Cracker Barrel | 970 | 11.3% |
| Int'l House of Pancakes | 729 | 8.5% |
| Perkins | 688 | 8.0% |
| Friendly's | 656 | 7.7% |
| Bob Evans | 585 | 6.8% |
| Waffle House | 294 | 3.4% |
| Coco's | 279 | 3.3% |
| Marie Callenders | 261 | 3.1% |
| Total | 8,559 | 100.0% |

| Dinner Houses | Sales | Share |
|---|---|---|
| Red Lobster | 1,850 | 18.9% |
| Olive Garden | 1,250 | 12.8% |
| Applebee's | 1,012 | 10.4% |
| Chili's | 950 | 9.7% |
| T.G.I. Friday's | 870 | 8.9% |
| Outback Steakhouse | 822 | 8.4% |
| Ruby Tuesday | 545 | 5.6% |
| Bennigan's | 455 | 4.7% |
| Chi-Chi's | 340 | 3.5% |
| Ground Round | 305 | 3.1% |
| Other Dinner Houses | 1,366 | 14.0% |
| Total | 9,765 | 100.0% |

| Pizza Chains | Sales | Share |
|---|---|---|
| Pizza Hut | 5,400 | 48.1% |
| Little Caesars | 2,050 | 18.2% |
| Domino's Pizza | 1,973 | 17.6% |
| Papa John's | 450 | 4.0% |
| Sbarros | 420 | 3.7% |
| Round Table Pizza | 374 | 3.3% |
| Chuck E. Cheese's | 307 | 2.7% |
| Godfather's Pizza | 260 | 2.4% |
| Total | 11,234 | 100.0% |

| Chicken Chains | Sales | Share |
|---|---|---|
| KFC | 3,720 | 58.1% |
| Boston Chicken | 725 | 11.3% |
| Popeyes Chicken | 689 | 10.8% |
| Chick-fil-A | 507 | 7.9% |
| Church's Chicken | 501 | 7.8% |
| Kenny Rogers Roasters | 263 | 4.1% |
| Total | 6,405 | 100.0% |

| Steak Houses | Sales | Share |
|---|---|---|
| Ponderosa | 741 | 23.2% |
| Golden Corral | 629 | 19.7% |
| Sizzler | 625 | 19.6% |
| Ryan's | 562 | 17.6% |
| Western Sizzlin' | 349 | 10.9% |
| Quincy's | 287 | 9.0% |
| Total | 3,193 | 100.0% |

Source: *Nation's Restaurant News,* National Restaurant Association. See current issues for recent figures.

## THE CHICKEN SEGMENT OF THE FAST-FOOD INDUSTRY

Only about one-half of all chicken chains had established restaurants outside of the United States by 1995. In contrast, KFC opened its first restaurant outside of the United States in the late 1950s. KFC's early expansion abroad, its strong brand name, and managerial experience operating in international markets partially explains KFC's dominant market share. KFC also leads all chicken chains in sales and units in the U.S. market; however, it faces much stronger competition domestically (see Exhibit 4). During the last five years, KFC's sales have grown at a 2.7 percent annual rate, while the overall chicken segment has grown at an average annual rate of 7.1 percent. With the exception of Church's, Boston Market, Popeyes, Chick-fil-A, and Kenny Rogers have grown at significantly faster rates than KFC. Boston Market and Kenny Rogers, which have focused on non-fried chicken products, have been particularly successful. In addition, while KFC, Popeyes, and Church's have focused on unique fried chicken recipes served to customers in free-standing restaurants, Chick-fil-A serves pressure-cooked and char-grilled skinless chicken breast sandwiches to customers in sit-down restaurants located predominately in shopping malls.

### ■ Chick-fil-A

Chick-fil-A's relatively high growth rate during the last five years may at first appear surprising, considering the culture at Chick-fil-A and the management style of S. Truett Cathy, Chick-fil-A's founder, chairman, and chief executive officer. Cathy, a strongly religious man, keeps all Chick-fil-A stores closed on Sundays. He also refuses to take the company public, will not franchise, and does not aggressively advertise his product or concept. Cathy is also involved in a variety of community activities which take him away from the day-to-day operations of his business, and he contributes heavily to youth programs, charities, and scholarship funds.

Chick-fil-A's corporate culture and new distribution strategy, however, have helped it maintain a higher growth rate in sales over the last five years compared to the chicken segment as a whole. For example, Cathy is well-known for treating his employees like family members. This has resulted in low turnover rates among both managers and part-time workers. In addition, Cathy has taken the step to expand beyond shopping malls. As many malls have added food courts, often consisting of up to fifteen fast-food units competing side-by-side, shopping malls have become less enthusiastic about allocating separate store space to food chains. In addition to Chick-fil-A's original sit-down mall stores, it has begun opening smaller units in shopping mall food courts, freestanding units, restaurants in hospitals and colleges, and "Dwarf Houses" (full-service restaurants which offer hamburgers and steaks as well as chicken).

### ■ Church's and Popeyes

Much of the slow growth in sales and units in Popeyes and Church's is a function of financial problems during the last five years. In 1989, the San Antonio-based Church's Fried Chicken was acquired in a hostile takeover by

| **Exhibit 4** | | | **Top U.S. Chicken Chains** | | | | |
| --- | --- | --- | --- | --- | --- | --- | --- |
| *Sales ($ Millions)* | *1989* | *1990* | *1991* | *1992* | *1993* | *1994* | *1995* |
| KFC | 3,000 | 3,249 | 3,400 | 3,400 | 3,400 | 3,500 | 3,720 |
| Boston Market | N/A | N/A | N/A | 43 | 152 | 384 | 725 |
| Popeyes | 510 | 560 | 536 | 545 | 564 | 610 | 689 |
| Chick-fil-A | 264 | 300 | 325 | 356 | 396 | 451 | 507 |
| Church's | 466 | 445 | 415 | 414 | 440 | 465 | 501 |
| Kenny Roger's | N/A | N/A | N/A | N/A | 69 | 150 | 263 |
| Total U.S. Market | 4,240 | 4,554 | 4,676 | 4,758 | 5,021 | 5,560 | 6,405 |
| *Year-End Restaurants* | *1989* | *1990* | *1991* | *1992* | *1993* | *1994* | *1995* |
| KFC | 4,937 | 5,006 | 5,056 | 5,089 | 5,128 | 5,149 | 5,200 |
| Boston Market | N/A | N/A | N/A | 83 | 217 | 937 | 971 |
| Popeyes | 739 | 778 | 794 | 775 | 764 | 848 | 932 |
| Chick-fil-A | 411 | 441 | 465 | 487 | 545 | 534 | 825 |
| Church's | 1,111 | 1,059 | 1,021 | 944 | 932 | 592 | 702 |
| Kenny Roger's | N/A | N/A | N/A | 35 | 102 | 187 | 303 |
| Total U.S. Market | 7,198 | 7,284 | 7,336 | 7,413 | 7,688 | 8,247 | 8,933 |

Source: *Nation's Restaurant News*, National Restaurant Association.

Al Copeland, owner of Popeyes Famous Fried Chicken & Biscuits. The $400 million leveraged buy-out of Church's was financed through Merrill Lynch and the Canadian Imperial Bank of Canada. Most of the financing was achieved through the issue of junk bonds. Merrill Lynch and CIBC's fee was $58 million!

Copeland's strategy was two-fold: (1) to convert Church's restaurants into Popeyes restaurants and (2) to sell off several hundred Church's restaurants in order to cover interest and debt payments arising from the acquisition of Church's. Exhibit 4 shows that both sales and the number of Church's restaurants began to fall in 1990. Sales began to rise again in 1993. Popeyes achieved a five-year growth rate in sales of 4.2 percent, higher than the growth rate of KFC during this period. The growth of Popeyes units grew at a lower 3.7 percent annual rate. Much of this growth, of course, was achieved through the conversion of Church's units into Popeyes units. Church's units have fallen from 1,059 restaurants in 1990 to 702 in 1995, an annual decline of 7.9 percent. In a 1992 court battle, Copeland was forced out as owner of Popeyes and Church's, and the two units became divisions of America's Favorite Chicken Co., a subsidiary of the Canadian Imperial Bank of Canada and Copeland's major financial backer during the 1989 takeover of Church's.

A major issue facing Church's and Popeyes in 1996 is whether they can survive over the long term as they have been unable to make major market share gains over the last ten years. In addition, the chains have been burdened by large debt that accumulated as a result of Al Copeland's acquisition of Church's and subsequent financial problems, which ultimately led to Copeland's downfall. There is also some concern that Church's and Popeyes' current owner, the Canadian Imperial Bank of Canada, does not have the managerial know-how and expertise to operate Church's and Popeyes other than as autonomous units. The Canadian Imperial Bank's eventual takeover of Church's and Popeyes was a court-approved remedy for Al Copeland's inability to repay the bank for the bank's financial support of Copeland's acquisition of Church's. Therefore, there is little strategic fit or opportunity to transfer value from the parent to the newly acquired chicken chains.

### ▪ Boston Chicken

Through the early 1980s, all of the leading chicken chains focused on fried chicken products. However, by the mid-1980s, many fast-food chains began to recognize the need to introduce products which appealed to an increasingly health-conscious consumer. To address these needs, the major chicken chains added more healthful products to their menus, such as grilled chicken sandwiches and rotisserie chicken. However, they continued to emphasize what they did best—fried chicken-on-the-bone.

In 1985, a new restaurant called Boston Chicken was opened in Newton, Massachusetts. Instead of offering a wide range of fried and non-fried chicken products, Boston Chicken chose to build a concept around a single product: marinated, slow-roasted chicken. Part of Boston Chicken's strategy was to differentiate itself from other fast-food restaurants by emphasizing the "home-cooked" nature of its products. The menu was simple. Customers chose a quarter or half chicken, white or dark meat, and two side orders. Side orders were selected from a variety of food items in a delicatessen-like display case. Corn bread was included with every meal. In addition to its roasted chicken meals, the menu included chicken sandwiches, chicken soup, chicken salad, and chicken pot pie. All food items were made from scratch, further enhancing the restaurant's image for "home-cooked" rather than "fast" food. Units were simple and clean and the decor was designed to give the appearance of a delicatessen. While units were designed mainly for take-out, no drive-thrus were used. This further enhanced its delicatessen image. Prices were slightly higher than other chicken chains, but this fit with the "home-cooked" image of the restaurant and appealed to professionals and other higher income customers.

On November 9, 1993, Boston Chicken went public. From an initial offering of $20 per share, the price jumped to $48.50 by the close of the day, a 143 percent increase. According to NASDAQ, it was the largest first-day increase in stock price of any new stock in any industry in over two years. Total market capitalization was $18.6 million. Boston Chicken's first annual report for the year ended December 26, 1993, showed the company's first profit—net income of $1.6 million on revenues of $42.5 million. This represented a 413 percent increase in revenue from the previous year. Boston Chicken later changed its franchise name to Boston Market.

## KENTUCKY FRIED CHICKEN CORPORATION

### ▪ Parent-Subsidiary Relationship

When PepsiCo, Inc. acquired KFC from RJR-Nabisco in 1986, KFC's relationship with its parent company underwent dramatic changes. RJR-Nabisco ran

KFC as a semi-autonomous unit, satisfied that KFC management knew the fast-food business better than they. In contrast, PepsiCo acquired KFC in order to complement its already strong presence in fast food. After its acquisition of KFC, PepsiCo had the leading market share in chicken (KFC), pizza (Pizza Hut), and Mexican food (Taco Bell). However, rather than allowing KFC to operate autonomously, PepsiCo undertook sweeping changes. These changes included negotiating a new franchise contract to give PepsiCo more control over its franchisees, reducing staff in order to cut costs, and replacing KFC managers with its own. In 1987, a rumor spread throughout KFC's headquarters in Louisville that the new personnel manager, who had just relocated from PepsiCo's headquarters in New York, was overheard saying that there will be "no more home-grown tomatoes in this organization."

Such statements by PepsiCo personnel, uncertainties created by several restructurings which led to layoffs throughout the KFC organization, the replacement of KFC personnel with PepsiCo managers, and conflicts between KFC and PepsiCo's corporate cultures created a morale problem within KFC. Colonel Sanders' philosophy when he founded KFC was to create an organization with a relaxed atmosphere, lifetime employment, good employee benefits, and a system of relatively independent franchisees. In stark contrast to KFC's culture, PepsiCo's culture was characterized by a strong emphasis on performance. PepsiCo used its Taco Bell, Pizza Hut, and KFC operations as training grounds for its future top managers and rotated its best managers, on average, every two years among its KFC, Taco Bell, Pizza Hut, Frito-Lay, and Pepsi-Cola subsidiaries. Therefore, there was immense pressure for managers to continuously show their managerial prowess within short periods, in order to maximize their potential for promotion. However, KFC personnel were often chosen from outside the KFC organization or hired through executive consultants. This practice left many existing KFC managers with the feeling that they had few career opportunities with the new company. One KFC manager commented that a senior manager told him that "You may have performed well last year, but if you don't perform well this year, you're gone, and there are 100 ambitious guys with Ivy League MBAs at PepsiCo who would love to take your position."

PepsiCo., Inc., headquartered in Purchase, New York, has three major divisions: beverage, snack foods, and restaurants. The two business units within the beverage division, Pepsi-Cola North America and Pepsi-Cola International, are both located in Somers, New York. Frito-Lay, located in Dallas, Texas, is the sole business unit within the snack food division. The restaurant division contains four business units directed by PepsiCo Worldwide Restaurants (Dallas, Texas): Pizza Hut, Inc. (Dallas, Texas), Taco Bell (Irvine, Texas), KFC (Louisville, Kentucky), and PepsiCo Restaurants International (Dallas, Texas).

Officially, PepsiCo managers were given autonomy to make their own decisions. In reality, PepsiCo kept a tight reign on its units. This was partially the result of its policy of continuously evaluating managers for promotion. Accounting, MIS, and financial planning systems were dictated from PepsiCo and much of KFC's capital expenditures were allocated by PepsiCo from other PepsiCo units. In 1995, KFC accounted for a little over one percent of PepsiCo's consolidated operating profit but 9.2 percent of total capital spending. In contrast, Frito Lay accounted for 47.9 percent of PepsiCo's overall 1995 operating profit but 36.3 percent of capital spending.

Asked about KFC's relationship with its parent, Kyle Craig commented:

The KFC culture is an interesting one because I think it was dominated by a lot of KFC folks, many of whom have been around since the days of the Colonel. Many of those people were very intimidated by the PepsiCo culture which is a very high performance, high accountability, highly driven culture. People were concerned about whether they would succeed in the new culture. Like many companies, we have had a couple of downsizings which further made people nervous. Today, there are fewer old KFC people around and I think to some degree people have seen that the PepsiCo culture can drive some pretty positive results. I also think the PepsiCo people who have worked with KFC have modified their cultural values somewhat and they can see that there were a lot of benefits in the old KFC culture.

Even now, though, that is still not universally understood. PepsiCo pushes their companies to perform strongly, but whenever there is a slip in performance, it increases the culture gap between PepsiCo and KFC. I have been involved in two downsizings over which I have been the chief architect. They have been probably the two most gut-wrenching experiences of my career. Because you know you're dealing with peoples' lives and their families, these changes can be emotional if you care about the people in your organization. However, I do fundamentally believe that your first obligation is to the entire organization.

## ■ Financial Results

Exhibit 5 shows KFC's corporate sales since 1993. KFC corporate sales continue to grow at a healthy rate. Sales have grown at a compounded annual growth rate of 13.6 percent during the last five years. Sales were up 13.8 and 9.2 percent in 1994 and 1995, respectively, mainly because of new restaurant construction outside the United States, higher pricing in U.S. restaurants, and higher

| Exhibit 5 | **PepsiCo, Inc. Corporate Net Sales ($000s)** | | |
|---|---|---|---|
| | *1993* | *1994* | *1995* |
| Beverages | 8,638 | 9,687 | 10,548 |
| Snack Foods | 7,027 | 8,264 | 8,545 |
| Restaurants | 9,356 | 10,521 | 11,328 |
| Pizza Hut | 4,129 | 4,443 | 4,828 |
| Taco Bell | 2,901 | 3,431 | 3,609 |
| KFC | 2,326 | 2,647 | 2,891 |
| Total | 25,021 | 28,472 | 30,421 |
| | | | |
| Domestic | 18,309 | 20,246 | 21,674 |
| International | 6,712 | 8,226 | 8,747 |
| Total | 25,021 | 28,472 | 30,421 |

Source: PepsiCo, Inc. annual reports.

Note: Sales data include sales from company restaurants and royalties from franchises (sales from franchises are excluded).

**Exhibit 6**                              **KFC Worldwide Restaurant Growth**

| Year | U.S. Stores | New Builds | %Total | Int'l Stores | New Builds | %Total | Worldwide Stores | New Builds | %Total |
|------|-------------|------------|--------|--------------|------------|--------|------------------|------------|--------|
| 1986 | 4,720 | - | 71.8% | 1,855 | - | 28.2% | 6,575 | - | 100.0% |
| 1987 | 4,814 | 94 | 64.0% | 2,708 | 853 | 36.0% | 7,522 | 947 | 100.0% |
| 1988 | 4,899 | 85 | 63.1% | 2,862 | 154 | 36.9% | 7,761 | 239 | 100.0% |
| 1989 | 4,961 | 62 | 62.4% | 2,987 | 125 | 37.6% | 7,948 | 187 | 100.0% |
| 1990 | 5,006 | 45 | 61.1% | 3,181 | 194 | 38.9% | 8,187 | 239 | 100.0% |
| 1991 | 5,056 | 50 | 59.6% | 3,424 | 243 | 40.4% | 8,480 | 293 | 100.0% |
| 1992 | 5,089 | 33 | 58.3% | 3,640 | 216 | 41.7% | 8,729 | 249 | 100.0% |
| 1993 | 5,128 | 39 | 56.8% | 3,905 | 265 | 43.2% | 9,033 | 304 | 100.0% |
| 1994 | 5,149 | 21 | 54.7% | 4,258 | 354 | 45.3% | 9,407 | 373 | 100.0% |

Source: PepsiCo annual reports.

franchise royalty revenues. Foreign restaurants represented about 55 percent of KFC's net sales in 1994 and 1995. Exhibit 6 shows KFC's worldwide restaurant growth during the last nine years. Increasingly, most of KFC's new restaurant construction is outside of the United States. Of 373 new restaurants built in 1994, only 21 were constructed in the United States. While international restaurant construction has grown at a compounded annual rate of 10.9 percent, U.S. restaurant construction has grown at a low 0.7 percent annual rate.

Slower restaurant growth and lower profits in the United States reflect a variety of factors. First, new, upscale chicken chains, such as Boston Market and Kenny Rogers Roasters, have attempted to cut out a market niche by marketing non-fried chicken products to higher income consumers. Second, many sandwich chains have introduced fried chicken and chicken sandwiches to their menus. By widening their menus, sandwich chains have appealed to families who need to satisfy different family member preferences. Third, all competitors in the fast-food industry have been under pressure to lower prices while at the same time improving menu offerings and service. All of these factors have made it more difficult for individual KFC restaurants to increase sales from year to year.

## ■ Business Strategy

Before 1986, KFC's menu offerings were relatively limited. Its major product offerings were its Original Recipe and Extra Crispy fried chicken products. However, by the mid-1980s, slowing per-store sales and increased competition among fast-food competitors led KFC to aggressively develop new products to appeal to a wider variety of consumers. In 1987, Chicken Littles were introduced. Designed as a snack product, Chicken Littles consisted of a small chicken patty in a small bun. One year later, KFC introduced its full-size chicken filet burger. Both products, however, were only modestly successful and ultimately withdrawn from KFC's menu.

Between 1990 and 1993, KFC introduced a variety of products in an attempt to expand its consumer base to lunch and snacks. In 1990, Hot Wings and Spicy

Chicken were introduced. In 1992, Honey BBQ chicken, Oriental Wings, and Pop Corn Chicken were introduced as limited time offerings to attract new customers. And, in 1993, a full-size barbecue sandwich was introduced. All of these offerings were only modestly received. In October 1993, KFC introduced its Rotisserie Gold chicken nationally. The introduction of rotisserie chicken received a tremendous response. During the fourth quarter of 1993, KFC reported a ten percent increase in sales in restaurants which offered the new roasted chicken product. Rotisserie chicken, which was slow-roasted and sold in whole, half, or quarter sizes, was designed to compete with the roasted chicken product that served as Boston Market and Kenny Rogers' major menu item.

In response to competition from sandwich chains and the consumer trend toward increased value, KFC made the decision to test an all-you-can-eat buffet in one of its franchises in Arkansas in 1991. The buffet, which was offered for $4.99 (lunch) and $5.99 (dinner) (1995 prices), offers up to 30 food items including fried chicken, biscuits, a salad bar, vegetable bar, and Pepsi-Cola soft drinks. Ultimately, KFC plans to introduce the buffet into about one-half of its domestic restaurants.

KFC's image as a fried chicken chain and the older age of many of its restaurants led to a new campaign to upgrade its restaurants in the mid-1980s. By 1994, over three-fourths of all KFC restaurants in the U.S. had been refurbished. In addition, KFC outfitted many of its restaurants with additional seating and drive-thrus, in order to accommodate increased consumer demand for both indoor seating and faster take-out service. In 1986, about three-fourths of KFC's sales were take-out. Take-out sales had fallen to about one-third of all sales by 1988 and have continued to fall since that time. In order to help dispel KFC's image as a fried chicken chain, Kyle Craig made the decision in 1990 to change the restaurant chain's official logo from Kentucky Fried Chicken to KFC. While the old Kentucky Fried Chicken signs can still be seen in KFC's older restaurants, its newer restaurants have signs that carry only the initials "K F C" accompanied by the profile of Colonel Sanders, KFC's founder.

One of the most difficult problems for KFC in 1994/95 was distribution. Because KFC's domestic restaurant construction program has slowed during the last five years, KFC has searched for new ways to grow the KFC brand domestically. When asked how KFC planned to grow its brand in the future, Kyle Craig commented:

> You know that McDonald's is still building a couple hundred restaurants a year, but we are not building a lot of traditional (freestanding) restaurants. But the business is changing. It is very expensive to build today, for us it is about a million dollars per restaurant. The returns are not what they once were so as opposed to going in and building traditional million-dollar restaurants, we are saying, hey, does it make more sense to go into other types of distribution centers; does it make sense to set up a delivery unit that may be much less expensive a way to expand both our points of distribution and consumer access to our products? I think we will find much more financially viable ways to grow the brand and we are trying to do it both for ourselves and for our franchisees.

## ■ Franchising Problems

KFC's ability to expand its distribution base was limited by an on-going feud with its franchisees. Through the mid-1980s, KFC's franchisees had been allowed to operate with little interference from KFC management. This "hands-off" approach could be traced back to the 1950s when Harland Sanders sold his first franchise, and resulted mainly from the Colonel's lack of interest in franchise affairs. Over time, franchise independence became a deeply-rooted part of KFC's corporate culture. As a result of their independence, and the control they had over their day-to-day operations, KFC franchisees developed a strong devotion to both the Colonel and the KFC organization.

When PepsiCo acquired KFC in 1986, one of its first steps was to negotiate a new contract which would give it more control over franchises' menu offerings and operations, allow it to close unprofitable franchises, and allow it to take over franchises that were poorly managed. Such actions were viewed as critical to improving product and service consistency and improving KFC's QSCV (quality, service, cleanliness, value) image. In addition, KFC believed that future growth in the KFC concept would come from smaller KFC units in shopping malls, colleges, and hospitals. In many cases, this meant that KFC would have to build units within close proximity of existing KFC franchises.

The last contract between KFC and its franchisees, prior to KFC's acquisition by PepsiCo, was negotiated in 1976. This contract stipulated that KFC would not build any KFC unit within 1.5 miles of an existing franchise. This stipulation was designed to protect existing franchises from lost sales to new KFC units built within these 1.5 mile protection zones. The 1976 contract also gave franchises power over supplier sourcing and the right of automatic contract renewal. The new contract would eliminate the 1.5 mile protection zone, eliminate automatic contract renewal, and increase PepsiCo's control over supplier sourcing. In 1989, the Association for Kentucky Fried Chicken Franchises (AKFCF) sued KFC over its new contract. In December 1993, KFC guaranteed that they would adhere to the 1.5 mile limit for seven months and Kyle Craig personally pledged not to open new full-service restaurants, home delivery, or take-out units within 1.5 miles of an existing franchise. However, the law suit remained unresolved in a Kentucky federal court in early 1996.

## CONCLUSION

KFC faced a variety of problems and issues at the end of 1994 and in early 1995. Still the world's largest chicken chain and third largest fast-food chain, it continued to grow at a healthy rate worldwide. It also continued to control one-half of all chicken chain sales in the United States and had one of the world's most recognized brands. In addition, its new rotisserie chicken and buffet had been tremendously successful in those markets where they had been introduced. However, while prospects for continued growth internationally were bright, continued growth within the domestic market was threatened by a number of industry and societal trends. Competition from sandwich chains and new chicken chains, as well as consumer demand for a wider variety of menu offerings, forced KFC to reanalyze its product strategy. At the same time, KFC and other fast-food competitors were forced to improve product offerings and to serve their product faster and with better service to consumers who increasingly demanded greater value for their money. Asked to comment on KFC's situation, Kyle Craig responded:

> We are in a fairly complex business with lots of agendas. Our franchises want one thing done, PepsiCo wants something else done, and our field operators want

something done differently than the company [does]. There has to be a central location where key decisions are made and a vision for the business is established. I think I or another leader has to be that visionary. Our number one issue is our ability to handle change. We have introduced the Rotisserie product and that's given our franchises some confidence, but this franchise situation has been very difficult. If we can resolve that in the next year or two we really could operate as a unified system as opposed to 3000 franchise stores going one way and 2000 company stores going another way. People do see us now as doing a better job of meeting their variety needs and recognize that we are not solely dependent on fried chicken, but they don't yet see us as contemporary as we would like them to in the long term. This is particularly true of people who do not presently patronize KFC. Today's consumer is less loyal, more value driven, and much more information based. The only thing that I am sure of is that tomorrow's consumer is going to be even more demanding.

# Circuit City Stores, Inc.: Plugged Into Growth in a Saturated Market

Donald L. Lester, Union University
John A. Parnell, Texas A&M University
Commerce

C ircuit City Stores, Inc. is a specialty retailer of electronics and appliances headquartered in Richmond, Virginia. The company generated annual sales in fiscal 1994 of $4.13 billion from 294 outlets. Most of the firm's superstores, regular stores, and mall stores operate under the Circuit City name, with some mall stores under the Impulse name. Currently, Circuit City stores are located in twenty-two states. Circuit City is a public company traded on the New York Stock Exchange under the ticker CC.

The company has experienced rapid growth for almost two decades. The key challenge facing the top management team is how to continue that growth in light of the saturation of most major U.S. markets.

## BACKGROUND

Circuit City began operations in 1949 when its founder, Samuel S. Wurtzel, opened his first retail store in Richmond. Sam Wurtzel was a visionary who was able to anticipate what was to eventually be labeled the "Age of Consumerism" in America. He taught his employees that every customer contact was an opportunity to make a friend.

Sam Wurtzel also envisioned the growth of the consumer electronics industry. While having his hair cut in a barber shop in Richmond, he noticed the construction of a television station, the first to be built in the South. Deciding that television had a promising future, Wurtzel opened a retail television store named Ward's Company in the front half of a tire store. He also introduced his product to the public by hauling a two-hundred pound television set door-to-door, providing in-home demonstrations.

That same year, 1949, Abraham Hecht joined Ward's as a partner. For the next decade the two men expanded operations to four television and home appliance stores, all located in Richmond. By 1959, annual sales volume had reached approximately one million dollars.

Ward's Company's strategy changed in 1960 with the introduction of licensed departments (approximately 3000 square feet dedicated to electronics and/or appliances, operated by Ward's) in mass merchandising discount stores around the country. The four stores in Richmond continued to operate, but the new licensed departments represented the company's desire to grow. In 1961, the company made its first public offering of 110,000 shares at $5.375 per share. This capital provided seed money for future growth.

In 1962, Circuit City began to offer a new service plan to its customers. If a set could not be repaired in the home, Circuit City would loan the customer a television. This emphasis on service after the sale became an important competitive advantage. In 1964, the fifth television and appliance store was opened in Richmond.

## THE ACQUISITION GAME

The company decided to expand through acquisition in 1965 with the purchase of the Richmond Carousel Corporation, a subsidiary of T. G. Stores. This acquisition binge continued until 1970 when Franks Dry Goods was purchased. The following chart details the primary businesses acquired by Circuit City:

| Company | Primary Business | # of units | Date Acquired | Date Sold |
|---|---|---|---|---|
| Richmond Carousel | Mass Merchandisers | 1 | 1965 | 1975 |
| Murmic of Delaware | Hardware/Housewares | 6 | 1965 | 1975 |
| Custom Electronics (Dixie Hi-Fi) | Hi-Fi/Audio/Mail Order | 13 | 1969 | 1977 |
| The Mart | TV/Appliances | 4 | 1969 | 1975 |
| Certified TV | TVs | 3 | 1969 | 1972 |
| Zody's (Licensed Departments) | Department Stores | 100 | 1969 | 1983 |
| Woodville Appliance | TV/Appliances | 5 | 1970 | 1975 |
| Franks Dry Goods | TV/Appliances | 1 | 1970 | 1972 |

By 1970, Ward's was operating over 100 licensed departments and stores, with annual sales of $56 million.

## A DECADE OF RETRENCHMENT

Circuit City began a serious retrenchment from the acquisition game during the early 1970s. Alan Wurtzel, son of founder Sam Wurtzel, spearheaded a divestment program that included selling or closing most of the businesses acquired during the mid- to late-1960s. To replace the loss of sales represented by the acquired outlets, Circuit City began implementing a strategy of internal growth, some of which is outlined below.

In 1971, Circuit City opened two specialty audio stores in Richmond under the name of Sight 'N Sound. Five audio stores were opened in 1973 in Washington, D.C., Richmond, Va., Charlotte, N.C., Costa Mesa, Ca., and City of Commerce, Ca. The company also opened nine Dixie Hi-Fi discount audio stores and The Loading Dock, a 40,000 square-foot retail warehouse showroom displaying a vast selection of audio, video, and major appliance products.

In 1976, the company began replacing the Dixie Hi-Fi and Custom Hi-Fi discount stores with the new concept "Circuit City" stores. The first six stores opened in the Washington, D.C., market. This concept featured top brand names in audio and video products, an in-store service department, convenient product pick-up area and knowledgeable sales personnel in a 6,000 to 7,000 square foot Circuit City store. The Circuit City stores reflected a strategic planning program begun by Ward's in 1976, which called for a new type of store for the future and a redeployment of assets. Ward's had been involved in over a dozen different businesses due to the strong wave of acquisitions from the late 1960s, and the new strategic direction was designed to narrow its focus. Sales reached $111 million by 1979.

## A DECADE OF GROWTH

In 1981, Circuit City merged with Lafayette Radio Electronics Corporation, which operated eight consumer electronics stores in metropolitan New York. It also began expanding the Loading Dock concept in new markets under the name Circuit City Superstores. The first four superstores opened in Raleigh, Greensboro, Durham, and Winston-Salem, North Carolina. The Richmond Loading Dock stores were renamed Circuit City superstores in 1982. In 1984, the entire company was renamed Circuit City Stores, Inc.

The company also began replacing Circuit City stores with Circuit City Superstores. The first replacements were in Knoxville, Tenn., Charleston, S.C., and Hampton, Va. In 1986, all the remaining non-Circuit City operations, including Lafayette and Zodys licensed departments, were closed and resources diverted into building Circuit City Superstores. In 1987, Circuit City acquired a custom electronics design and manufacturing company—Patapsco Design, Inc., of Maryland—to serve as an in-house engineering firm. In 1988, the first Impulse stores in Baltimore, Md., Richmond, Va., and McLean, Va., were opened. These were operations within malls that handled small electronic gift ideas. In 1989, the advertising concept of "Circuit City—Where Service is State of the Art" was begun. A new graphic automation system was also installed to increase the effectiveness of print advertising.

## OUTSTANDING PERFORMANCE

Circuit City Stores, Inc. seeks to maintain a low price image, excellent product selection, and unparalleled commitment to customer service, while maintaining a leadership position in margin and commitment to continuous improvement to maintain its competitive edge.

From 1984 to 1988, Circuit City provided the highest return to investors of any company listed on the New York Stock Exchange. The major company investments leading to this performance included:

1. The point of sale information system;
2. The opening of three automated distribution centers;
3. The development of an intensive sales training program; and,
4. The establishment of a balanced management structure which shifted marketing responsibilities to the operating divisions near the customer and technical and logistical responsibilities in the home office.

Circuit City first reached $1 billion in sales in 1987. By 1990, sales had climbed to over $2 billion.

## NEW DIRECTIONS FOR THE NINETIES

Circuit City introduced a private-label credit card program by establishing the First North American National Bank in 1990. By 1996, this venture employed nearly 1,000 people and had expanded operations to include two call centers. In 1991, *Answer City*<sup>SM</sup>, a toll-free phone service that assists customers with questions about product installation and operations was opened. In fiscal year 1993, CarMax, a retailing venture selling used cars, was initiated, and a 15,000 square-foot prototype store design was introduced to serve areas too small to support a full superstore. The firm also expanded into the Boston and Chicago markets. In 1994, the company announced plans to open 180 Superstores over the next three years. This expansion plan would place Circuit City in every major metropolitan area in the United States, except New York.

However, the focus of expansion into the major metropolitan markets of the United States has been at the expense of the international arena. This has given the company substantial growth, but it has done so at the expense of smaller markets. Some of Circuit City's competitors have specifically focused on the smaller markets, similar to the strategy of Wal-Mart, and this strategy has allowed them to gain market share.

Circuit City has implemented a point-of-sale system that speeds the customer's shopping experience through automatic inventory checks as well as credit card and check approval. It also allows the customer to receive better service while dealing with one employee. Additionally, the company has a Customer Service Information System which keeps a historical record of individual customer transactions. This system is beneficial in helping customers with future purchases, in helping to ensure that new products can be integrated with existing products in the home, and in facilitating product returns and product repair—even when the customer has lost a receipt (Circuit City Annual Report, 1994).

Circuit City's point-of-sale system is linked to its automated distribution system. This allows the company to keep a close eye on inventories and to provide overnight replenishment of inventories (Annual Report, 1994). The system tracks the shipment of nearly every box traveling to company locations. It is reported that this system adds as much as one percentage point to Circuit City's pre-tax margin (Foust, April 27, 1992).

Throughout its growth, the company has emphasized the need for cost control. Organization of its distribution channel has been instrumental in maintaining a low-cost distribution system. Circuit City operates fully automated distribution centers that service the stores. Each store is less than a day's drive from a distribution center. Using the point-of-sale system, the centers can replenish inventories overnight. The centers utilize laser barcode scanners to reduce labor requirements, prevent inventory damage, and maintain tight inventory control.

Circuit City believes that developments in digital sound and video will generate higher industry growth as the decade progresses. Digital products are becoming popular, and direct broadcast satellite technology transmits digital signals to a variety of U.S. markets. Circuit City will be selling the hardware and programming for this new technology. It is anticipated that in the late 1990s, high-definition television with its clear theater-style screen will spark additional growth as consumers upgrade a variety of existing products to obtain digital quality (Annual Report, 1994). In addition, video CD players, unveiled in 1994, are designed to play both audio CDs and a new generation of video CDs (Gillen, 1994). Analysts believe that this recording system provides a higher quality picture with compact disc quality sound.

Circuit City's advertising layout focuses on a quality image. It emphasizes exceptional service and price guarantees. This focus has given Circuit City strong name recognition throughout its market and helps develop markets prior to stores being opened. In addition, Circuit City currently offers over 300 brands. Each of the product categories has many varying brands to choose from, with large selections within each brand.

Circuit City has also taken a proactive approach to human resource development. Each associate receives extensive training to ensure a thorough understanding of the products before being allowed contact with the consumer. The company has included training for the associates that enables them to offer "one-stop" shopping. This concept allows for the customer to complete the entire transaction with the sales counselor. Sales counselors can accept all forms of payment and process credit applications for Circuit City's private-label credit card. This approach simplifies the transaction for the buyer and has enabled the company to generate considerable labor savings by reducing the support staff at each store. This is a new concept for Circuit City. However, this aggressive sales approach has earned the firm's sales force a "pushy" reputation.

## FUTURE GROWTH IN A DIFFERENT INDUSTRY

Historically, top management appears to have demonstrated the strength to make decisions that negatively affect the stock price for the long-term good of the company. The company has also focused its strength of management, customer service, and operating control into the used car industry in a venture known as CarMax. The company feels the same skills it currently uses in the retailing of electronics and applicances can be transferred to the used car business.

Developed as a growth vehicle, CarMax opened its doors in Richmond, Virginia, in late 1993. Richard Sharp, current CEO of Circuit City, and Austin Ligon, senior vice president of corporate planning and automotive, placed the first showroom less than a mile from corporate headquarters. Other locations include Raleigh, Atlanta, and Charlotte.

Retail sales of previously owned vehicles total about $150 billion annually in the United States (Simison, 1996). Industry insiders speculate that the used car market will continue to grow, boosted by the price of a new car, $20,000 on average (Rudnitsky, 1995). During the past five years, the average price of a used car has increased from $6,000 to over $10,000 (Welles, 1996). In 1995, the average price of a used car sold by a franchise was $11,585, compared to $9,188 by independent dealers and $4,316 by private individuals (CNW, 1996). Consumers are finding used cars to be a better value since the typical new car depreciates 28% in the first year (Welles, 1996).

The supply of late model used cars is projected to rise as the popularity of leasing continues to grow. From 1991 to 1995, the percentage of new car acquisitions made under leasing arrangements rose from 15.4% to 31.5% (CNW, 1996). In 1995, 2.4 million leased cars were returned to the leasing company, many of which were resold at auctions (*Newsday*, 1996).

Currently, used auto retailing is a highly fragmented industry without a single market share leader. Used car sales in the United States are roughly split into thirds, with 36% coming from franchised dealers, 33% from independent dealers, and 31% from private parties (CNW, 1996). An estimated 35 million used cars between two and ten years old were sold in the United States in 1995 (McKesson, 1996). The typical used car dealer averages about $2 million in sales annually (Rudnitsky, 1995).

CarMax's offering is highly differentiated. Inventories are stocked with between 500 and 1200 vehicles, each less than five years old with fewer than 70,000 miles. Non-negotiable prices are clearly marked on each vehicle, and each car comes with a complete thirty-day warranty. There is a no-pressure sales philosophy, and consumers can operate the user-friendly computers in each showroom to find the locations of vehicles on the lot that match their make, model, price, and other preferences. CarMax buys its cars at auctions, and from consumers and fleet dealers, but all vehicles must pass a 110-point inspection before being offered for sale.

Circuit City has not publicized the financial results of its early years of used car operations, but Sanford Bernstein's Ursula H. Moran estimates that the Richmond operation turned over about 4,000 vehicles in 1994, for total sales of approximately $55 million (Rudnitsky, 1995). Competition is expected to intensify with the entrance of other used car superstore outlets. Autonation USA plans to open 25 outlets in South Florida and Texas by the end of the decade. CarAmerica has experienced success with its two concept stores in Wisconsin. Driver's Mart plans to open more than ten outlets per year in the late 1990s. Other competitors include HPR Automotive and Car Choice (Mohl, 1996).

CarMax is also looking at the new car industry, having recently signed a franchise agreement with Chrysler Corporation that will allow it to sell new Chryslers in Norcross, Georgia.

## KEY PERSONNEL

Chairman of the Board: *Alan L. Wurtzel*. Wurtzel, son of founder Sam Wurtzel, had joined the company in 1966 as vice president for legal affairs. He became President in 1969 and Chairman and Chief Executive Officer (CEO) in 1984. In 1984, he retired as President, and in 1986 he retired as CEO.

President and CEO—*Richard L. Sharp*. Sharp joined the company in 1982 as executive vice president. Sharp had been president of his own software company, and he is credited with the development of the point-of-sale system. In 1984, he was elected President of Circuit City, assuming the CEO duties in 1986.

Senior Vice President and Chief Financial Officer (CFO)—*Michael T. Chalifoux*. Chalifoux came to Circuit City in 1983 from public accounting. In 1989, he became the vice president and CFO. He became a member of the board in 1991.

The Board of Directors consists of ten individuals, including the three individuals already mentioned and a retired vice president. Of the remaining six, two are from the academic world, two are retired presidents of other corporations, one is an attorney, and one is the Executive Vice President of an advertising company.

# THE INDUSTRY

The specialty brand-name consumer electronics and major appliance industry in which Circuit City competes is currently faced with a variety of environmental changes. As the population ages, consumer electronics stores will need to determine the customer base they wish to serve and will have to market more aggressively to that target. Retailers will need to segment the data base and offer different promotions to different customers depending on purchase habits and behaviors or on demographics (Abrams, 1993).

As the consumer population becomes more informed about technological innovations and products, consumer electronic retailers will need to offer a more upscale product and improved customer service. Consumers will become more demanding as they spend a larger portion of their disposable income and will expect retailers to be on the same level or above.

Americans have always had an affinity for electronics and gadgets. This affinity has not decreased in the 1990s. The trend has always been to replace outdated electronics with newer models and to purchase add-on products. This trend will continue and consumer electronics retailers will be able to take advantage of this portion of the market.

The recession of the early 1990s provides the best picture of the effect tough economic times could potentially have on the electronics industry. While the industry as a whole has suffered, with Radio Shack closing over 175 stores and Highland Superstores, Inc. filing for Chapter 11 protection (Hewes, 1992), some segments of the industry, particularly the home-office and the television sector, have been extremely strong. However, when white-collar workers lost their jobs due to downsizing, many turned to freelancing or consulting from their homes, fueling a demand for equipment that until recently had been marketed primarily to businesses (Lavoie, 1992).

While worries about a sluggish economy have persuaded many consumers to forgo a trip or other luxury, they tend to adopt a recession mentality. Some buyers feel if they have to give up dinners out and expensive vacations in favor of nights at home, they will at least invest in a decent TV. Many consumers feel that television is an inexpensive way to entertain their families (Therrien, 1992).

Circuit City remained strong during the economic downturn of the early 1990s, maintaining its expansion plans and increasing its sales dramatically. In fiscal year 1992, Circuit City reported sales growth of 28% and earnings growth of 38%. Same-store sales increased by 3% in 1992 and 7% in 1993. Despite the the industry's problems, some of the strong are getting stronger. Circuit City and Best Buy were able to gain market share as other specialty retailers retrenched (Foust, 1992).

Circuit City is the industry leader in sales followed by Silo and Best Buy. Other competitors in the industry include Tandy, Highland, and REX. On the fringe of this industry are discount retailers (Wal-mart, K-Mart, and Target), wholesale clubs, regional chains, and mom-and-pop stores. Sales figures for each competitor for year end 1993 are presented in Exhibit 1. All sales figures are in millions of dollars.

## SILO

Reported sales for Silo in 1992 were $1 billion, and sales for 1993 were running 20% higher than those during 1992. President Peter Morris attributed the sales increase to four changes Silo implemented early in 1993: changes in sales' associates compensation so that it is based on gross margin dollars (rather than total sales), changes in store organization, a move to "every day low pricing" and a new emphasis of "every day low pricing" in its advertising (Pinkerton, August 1993).

## TANDY

Tandy includes Incredible Universe Superstores, Computer City, The Edge In Electronics, Radio Shack, McDuff Electronics, and Video Concepts. Tandy has a store of some type in literally every town in the United States with 5,000 people or more (Hartnett, May 1993).

Incredible Universe Superstores were designed to be destination stores with broad assortments, rather than convenient, neighborhood Radio Shack stores (Hartnett, May 1993). Computer City stores feature all brands of merchandise. The 5,000-item assortment includes personal computers, printers, telephones, fax machines, copiers, software, and furniture. The Edge in Electronics is Tandy's upscale retail chain.

**Exhibit 1**                   **Sales Figures for Competitors**

| Company | Sales—1993 (in millions) |
| --- | --- |
| Circuit City | $2,790 |
| Silo | 953 |
| Best Buy | 929 |
| Tandy | 703 |
| Highland | 575 |
| REX | $   202 |

Radio Shack stores are in convenient neighborhood locations with a unique product mix of gadgets and parts, all sold by a knowledgeable staff. It is estimated that one in four Americans will visit a Radio Shack in the next year.

The two successful consumer electronic superstores for Tandy are McDuff and Video Concept. The stores had estimated sales of $600 million, a 5% improvement over the previous year. All plans for expansion of the two chains are dependent on the performance of the Incredible Universe superstores (Gelfand, January 1993).

## BEST BUY CO.

Best Buy Co. recently announced aggressive plans to expand its number of stores by 41% in the next 18 months to 112, with stores in 14 states. The chain reported sales of $929 million for 1992. The no-commission policy it instituted may be the wave of the future for electronics stores, said Peter Hisey, senior editor of *Discount Store News*. Even though Best Buy might have incurred losses during the change, market share has grown consistently (Goerne, 1992).

Best Buy offers more than 2,000 products covering every imaginable category within video/audio equipment, home office equipment, major appliances, and entertainment software. Additionally, the company provides a wide range of customer services, including authorized warranty service on most products, extended service plans, revolving credit, in-home delivery, and installation.

## HIGHLAND SUPERSTORES

After peaking at 92 stores in 1991, Highland has been left with only 30 stores in the Great Lakes region and more than $100 million of debt. The chain is seeking a debt reorganization plan with its creditors through Chapter 11.

## REX STORES CORP.

REX Stores Corp. was formerly known as Audio/Video Affiliates, Inc. Buying in volume for 100-plus stores while slashing overhead has enabled the Dayton, Ohio-based company to keep its prices low as it targets smaller, less competitive markets (Pinkerton, August 1993). The company's goal is to have 50% more stores within the next two years. All this expansion is taking place in small- to mid-sized cities with populations averaging 50,000. Stores can currently be found in cities with populations ranging from 30,000 to 300,000.

## DISCOUNT RETAILERS, WHOLESALE CLUBS, REGIONAL CHAINS AND MOM-AND-POP STORES

According to industry observers, these stores sell consumer electronics, but their primary focus is on entry-level products. They carry step-up and more sophisticated products, but they don't sell them (Glasse, March 1993). For this reason, Circuit City has noted that these competitors exist, but does not feel that Circuit City competes directly with them in terms of products, customer service, service programs, and sales staff.

## CIRCUIT CITY'S FINANCIAL POSITION

Circuit City has been successful in achieving growth in its sales and profitability. The company's income statement is summarized in Exhibit 2.

Circuit City has consistently increased its sales and profitability through internal expansion and the continued success of its existing stores. While the company's gross margin has decreased resulting from prices being driven down by competition and the company's more recent sales of lower margin computer/home-office products, Circuit City has been able to keep its operating margin and its net profit margin stable by operating more efficiently. This has been achieved by automating the company's distribution and point-of-sale functions.

**Exhibit 2**      **Income Statement for Circuit City**

| (In $000s) | FYE93 | % | FYE94 | % | FYE95 | % |
|---|---|---|---|---|---|---|
| Sales | $3,269,769 | 100.0 | $4,130,415 | 100.0 | $5,582,947 | 100.0 |
| Gross Profit | 923,720 | 28.3 | 1,105,656 | 26.8 | 1,385,000 | 24.8 |
| Operating Income | 179,070 | 5.5 | 213,791 | 5.2 | 278,630 | 4.9 |
| Net Profit | $ 110,250 | 3.4 | $ 132,400 | 3.2 | $ 167,875 | 3.0 |

**Exhibit 3**      **Statement of Fixed Charges**

| (In $000s) | FYE 92 | FYE 93 | FYE 94 |
|---|---|---|---|
| Net Profit | $ 78,223 | $110,250 | $198,457 |
| +Depreciation | 117,929 | 145,742 | 198,457 |
| +Interest Expense | 9,033 | 3,820 | 4,791 |
| =Cash Available for Fixed Charges | 205,185 | 259,812 | 335,648 |
| Interest Expense | 9,033 | 3,820 | 4,791 |
| +Current Maturities of Long-Term Debt | 1,927 | 1,828 | 1,819 |
| +Lease & Rent Expense | 59,996 | 72,175 | 89,579 |
| Total Fixed Charges | $ 70,956 | $ 77,823 | $ 96,189 |
| Fixed Charge Coverage (%) | 2.89 | 3.34 | 3.49 |

Circuit City's financial performance should be analyzed on its own merit, since the direction of the company and that of its industry are opposites. While most of the major players in the industry are in retrenchment, Circuit City is growing.

The most important ratio for banks when considering the financial viability of a company is a typical debt service coverage ratio or a fixed charge coverage ratio, depending on the circumstances. Circuit City has substantial lease and rental expenses since the company has sale-leaseback agreements on many of its stores. Exhibit 3 presents Circuit City's ability to meet its fixed charges.

Circuit City's cash flow is strong, as evidenced by the fixed charge coverage of 3.49 in 1994. Further evidence includes the repayment in 1994 of $60 million in subordinated debt. Exhibit 4 presents Circuit City's consolidated balance sheet.

| Exhibit 4 | Consolidated Balance Sheet for Circuit City | | |
|---|---|---|---|
| **Assets** | *1995* | *1994* | *1993* |
| Cash & cash equivalent | $ 46,962 | $ 75,194 | $ 141,412 |
| Net accts & notes receivable | 264,565 | 188,890 | 120,448 |
| Merchandise inventory | 1,035,776 | 721,348 | 515,771 |
| Deferred income taxes | 25,696 | 26,700 | — |
| Prepaid expense & other assets | 14,162 | 11,476 | 13,270 |
| Total current assets | 1,387,161 | 1,023,708 | 790,901 |
| Property & equipment net | 592,956 | 438,096 | 370,791 |
| Deferred income taxes | 5,947 | 78,688 | 87,588 |
| Other assets | 17,991 | 14,172 | 13,650 |
| Total assets | 2,004,055 | 1,554,664 | 1,262,930 |
| Liabilities | | | |
| Current inst of long-term debt | 2,378 | 1,819 | 1,828 |
| Accounts payable | 576,578 | 419,037 | 278,348 |
| Accrued expenses & other liabilities | 113,631 | 86,826 | 66,487 |
| Accrued income taxes | 13,533 | 38,582 | 26,310 |
| Total current liabilities | 706,120 | 546,264 | 372,973 |
| Long-term debt excluding current ins | 178,605 | 29,648 | 82,387 |
| Deferred rev & other liabilities | 241,866 | 268,360 | 232,054 |
| Total Liabilities | 1,126,591 | 844,272 | 687,414 |
| Common stock | 48,238 | 48,040 | 47,835 |
| Cap in excess of par value | 72,639 | 64,485 | 54,540 |
| Retained earnings | 756,587 | 597,867 | 473,141 |
| Total stock equity | 877,464 | 710,392 | 575,516 |
| Total liabilities & stock equity | 2,004,055 | 1,554,664 | 1,262,930 |
| Net current assets | $ 681,041 | $ 477,444 | $ 417,928 |

# ORGANIZATIONAL STRATEGY

Circuit City seeks *growth*. Over the life of the company, growth has been and continues to be its major driving force. Through mergers, acquisitions, and opening new types of stores the company has grown to 294 retail outlets in twenty-one states. Over the next three years the company's plans are to open 180 new stores, representing a 61% increase. This expansion will put them in every major metropolitan market area in the United States, except New York.

Circuit City attempts to distinguish itself from the competition through the strength of its merchandising assortment and by consistently delivering exceptional customer service. To maintain margin and not give market advantage to discount competitors, Circuit City has adopted a marketing approach that includes some lower-priced initiatives along with stepped-up advertising and promotions in highly competitive areas. The overall goal remains to differentiate the consumer offer through an outstanding merchandise selection and exceptional customer service. A customer service information system, developed in 1992, maintains an online history of all customers and their purchases.

The company has also adopted an internal strategy of high quality and low cost service to the stores. The point-of-sale computer information system handles the total sales transaction with one associate, maintains detailed records of all purchases, and keeps inventory levels adequate at each store.

# THE FUTURE

Circuit City presently has a variety of growth options should it seek to continue to pursue this strategy. The firm could continue rapid expansion plans to reach all major metropolitan markets. Continued growth would allow the company to further improve its market share and increase its sales revenue. In addition, continued expansion into the major markets will give the company the ability to fully utilize the experience and technology it has developed over the past years.

However, growth cannot be pursued without a price. The rate at which the company is presently growing will place burdens on the management to maintain the control it currently has. Many competitors before Circuit City have run into this problem and faced retrenchment to remain viable. As the company opens new stores the infrastructure of the company must expand to handle the increased demand. With the emphasis the management has placed on customer service, the threat of reduced service levels to the stores is possible with rapid expansion. Further, the strain on the financial sources, especially during downturns in the economy, can be damaging.

Circuit City could slow expansion plans and concentrate on maximizing profit in current markets. This would allow the company to emphasize the return to the company from the current markets and absorb the new markets and work them into the system. It would also allow the company to have a feel for what the new market will be like for the company. Slowing expansion will allow management to insure that proper controls are in place and the infrastructure of the company can handle the new markets. If there are problems, they can be addressed with more problems building up.

However, slowed expansion might allow competitors to make inroads into the new markets. This will make it more difficult to enter these new markets once the competition has set up. As this happens, competitors will begin to gain market share on the company. In addition, because the company uses a national advertising campaign, not having stores in every market will not give them full utilization of their ads. The full advertising has helped introduce Circuit City to new markets, and could leave consumers confused as to where their stores are. Circuit City could also lose some of its clout with suppliers. Being in the number one slot with rapid expansion gives the company a strong position with the suppliers. If this is abandoned, suppliers may view this as an indication the company is in trouble.

Circuit City could focus on expansion into Canada. Canada's proximity allows the company to utilize the current operations, while its market is not vastly different from the United States and will allow the company to expand internationally without major problems. However, cross-cultural expansion—even into Canada—requires the learning of a new culture, including such factors as political, legal, and currency differences. This could slow the expansion process and possibly create a learning curve challenge for operations and management.

Circuit City could continue diversification plans into the $150 billion used car market (Lavin, 1994). By gaining only a small part of this market, revenues of the company could increase significantly. However, as the energy is invested to learn the new business, the focus on the core business may suffer. Management will have to balance the resources of the company in the two industries, further straining capital resources.

Chief Financial Officer Mike Chalifoux described the Circuit City executives perspective of their business succinctly: There is not one "right" strategy for a business; there is only a strategy that is right for its time. To that end, the Superstore concept is continually scrutinized and updated, always being redesigned to fit the current merchandising and aesthetic standards of the day. Chalifoux relates that Circuit City's top management team decided in the early 1980s to focus on doing one hundred things 1% better than its competitors, rather than trying to do one thing 100% better.

The company's recent foray into banking and used car sales represents an attempt to capitalize on its retailing, marketing, and management strengths. Chalifoux says there are no plans for global expansion of the Superstore concept.

## REFERENCES

Abrams, Judith. "The Power of Private Label Plastic." *Dealerscope*, September 1993, pp. 74-76.

Circuit City Stores, Inc., Richmond, Virginia, *1994 Annual Report*.

CNW Marketing Research Spreadsheet. "At-a-glance data and quick analysis of used car trends." *Used Gold Newsletter*, February 1966, p. 3.

Foust, Dean. "Circuit City's Wires are Sizzling." *Business Week*, April 27, 1992, p. 76.

Gelfand, Michael. "Consumer Electronics Superstores." *Discount Merchandiser*, January 1993, pp. 60-66, 70.

Gillen, Marilyn A. "CES Reflects Industry's Forward Focus." *Billboard*, January 22, 1994, pp. 11, 96.

Glasse, Jennifer. "Speaking Out on Keeping Up." *Dealerscope*, March 1993, pp. 10-11.

Goerne, Carrie. "Customer Friendly Sales Reps Get Tryout." *Marketing News*, October 26, 1992, pp. 1, 3.

Hartnett, Michael. "New Path for Tandy." *Stores*, May 1993, pp. 20-26.

Hewes, Ken. "Weak Economy Makes Hard Times for Hard Lines." *Chain Store Age Executive*, August 1992, pp. 29A-31A.

Lavoie, Francis J. "Spotty Outlook Ahead for Consumer Electronics." *Electronics*, January 1992, pp. 40-42.

Lavin, Douglas. "Cars Are Sold Like Stereos By Circuit City." *Wall Street Journal*, June 6, 1994, pp. B1, B6.

McKesson, Mike. "CarMax concept draws attention of potential customers." *Lafayette Business Digest*, January 8, 1996, p. 3.

Mohl, Bruce. "Superstores move in on used cars." *Boston Globe*, February 19, 1996.

*Newsday*. "Newer vehicles drive growth of used cars in American market." *Newsday, Money & Careers*. February 4, 1996, p. 1.

Pinkerton, Janet. "Mining the Boondocks." *Dealerscope*, August 1993, pp. 50-53.

Rudnitsky, Howard. "Would you buy a used car from this man?" *Forbes*. October 23, 1995, pp. 52-54.

Simison, Robert L. "New-car dealers form alliance to sell used vehicles in trendy superstores." *Wall Street Journal*, February 7, 1996, p. A3.

Therrien, Lois. "Recession, Hell—Let's Buy Another TV." *Business Week*, October 19, 1992, p. 35.

Welles, Edward. Show and sell, VirtuMall, Internet Resource.

# Four Seasons Regent Hotels and Resorts

Angela R. Lanning, University of Guelph
Robert C. Lewis, University of Guelph

I n March of 1995, the Four Seasons Regent (FSR) corporate marketing team had reviewed their plans for the remainder of the year. Collectively, the team agreed that their plans and objectives should remain intact, that their strategies were working, and that Four Seasons Regent would continue to strengthen its domination in the luxury hotel market.

Individually, however, each member of the team had unresolved questions about the past, present, and future of the company. Things had been so hectic over the past two years that nobody had really had time to analyze the effectiveness of past marketing strategies. There were indications that the consolidation of Regent and Four Seasons had been successful, but was there anything that had been overlooked? Were they making legitimate, informed, and realistic decisions in their 1995 Marketing Plan? Were there any potential threats to their position as the leading luxury hotel chain that they had not yet considered?

Perplexed by many of these issues, members of the marketing team wondered to themselves ". . . can we wait until next year to think about it—nobody has time for this right now."

It was at that point that John Richards' secretary interrupted the meeting to ask him to take an urgent phone call from John Sharpe, Executive VP of Operations. "Have you seen today's *Wall Street Journal?*" said Sharpe. "No," said Richards. "Then listen," said Sharpe.

"Ritz-Carlton Hotels has been 49% acquired, with a right to buy the rest, by a group of investors, including Marriott International Inc., which intends to transform it into a high-growth international chain. Richard Rainwater, a Texas millionaire and one of the investors, is quoted as saying, `With the additional capital and the potential for efficiencies provided by Marriott, this company could be five to ten times the size it is today in five to ten years.'"

"Well folks," said Richards, as he hung up the phone. "In light of this new development, it would be a good idea for us to re-evaluate all our corporate strategies. Let's start thinking about how this will affect our competitive situation. Does anyone have any thoughts on this?"

## ■ Background

In May of 1993, Isadore Sharp, Chairman and President of Four Seasons Regent Hotels and Resorts, concluded his oration at the annual shareholders meeting:

> The last two years have been extraordinarily difficult and all these difficulties are not yet behind us. We have every confidence that we have invested wisely, consolidating our leadership and assuring our future. We have only to keep our focus to continue to improve what we are already doing well, and profits and shareholder equity will rise with our reputation.

The acquisition of Regent Hotels in mid-1992 had been a great source of turmoil for Four Seasons Hotel Company. The integration of the two luxury hotel chains and the high debt load resulting from the transaction had left the company in a strained financial position. The global economic downturn that began in 1990 had also been a significant obstacle and had affected profits throughout the tour and travel industry. It wasn't until the end of 1993, however, that indications of an economic recovery finally appeared.

All of this had presented an enormous challenge for John Richards, Senior Vice President of Marketing. By the end of 1994, however, there were indications that the efforts of the corporate marketing team were paying off. Cost efficiencies were being realized and there were noticeable improvements in occupancies and average room rates for many of the Regent properties.

In light of these trends, preparation of the 1995 marketing plan appeared elementary. Four Seasons Regent management saw itself as able to maintain its leadership in the luxury hotel market by continuing to focus on its long-time principal marketing objectives.

The key objectives that would continue to drive the company's marketing initiatives for 1995 had been established:

1. Leverage the Four Seasons Regent combination,
2. Increase individual business worldwide, and
3. Improve global sales network efficiencies.

John Richards had wondered, however, if it was as simple as all that or whether more strategic thinking and direction were necessary from the corporate level before the marketing plan was actually developed. And now there was this Ritz-Carlton thing!

## COMPANY BACKGROUND

Four Seasons Regent Hotels and Resorts, headquartered in Toronto, Canada, was the world's largest luxury hotel operator. Founded in 1960 by Isadore Sharp, the company in 1995 managed 39 medium-sized luxury urban and resort hotels in 16 countries under management contracts with their owners, containing approximately 13,000 guest rooms, and had 11 other management contracts on properties under construction or development in nine countries. Four Seasons Regent held a minority equity interest in 20 of these hotels. Exhibit 1 shows a list of hotels operated by Four Seasons Regent, its equity interest, some occupancy details, and their hotel locations—many of which would be virtually impossible to duplicate.

## ■ The Founder

In 1992, honored for being the driving force behind the international success of Four Seasons, Isadore (Issy, pronounced Izzy) Sharp received the prestigious Canadian award of CEO of the Year. An article in *The Financial Post* (Toronto) attributed the growth of Four Seasons to largely the result of one man's vision. "Isadore Sharp has created a company that friends and foes alike agree is a model for how Canadian companies compete globally in an increasingly inter-connected world economy."

Issy Sharp completed his studies in architecture in 1952 and immediately joined his father in the construction business. His hotel empire began with a small motel he built in a seedy downtown area of Toronto. Its doors opened in 1961 and its rapid success inspired Issy to continue in the hotel business but only in the upscale end of it. After four hotels, he decided to go public with Four Seasons as a way to finance his expansion plans.

Four Seasons first went public with a 25% ownership offering on the Toronto Stock Exchange during a new issue boom in the late 1960s. The original investors, all of whom were still members of the board of directors in 1995, maintained 75% ownership. Due to the instability and high discounting of the stock, they repurchased and took the company private again in 1978. Philosophically, Issy didn't want to sacrifice his long-term quality objectives for quarterly results that would please short-term investors.

Four Seasons went public again in 1985 but, to ensure that fractional ownership would not delete his singular vision, Issy maintained 80% control of the voting shares. His absolute control of the company was considered an asset by market analysts because it meant that Issy would be able to maintain the culture of Four Seasons.

## ■ The Regent Acquisition

In August 1992, wishing to expand quickly in the Far East, Four Seasons completed a (US) $122 million deal to acquire the luxury Regent Hotels Company from its Hong Kong owners. The transaction included the addition of 15 management contracts (including four hotels under construction), the Regent International Hotels trademark and trade names, and a 25% ownership interest in the Regent Hong Kong hotel. The purchase was financed by a combination of existing working capital lines, additional bank indebtedness, and a (Cdn) $58.5 million new equity issue (in early 1995, one Canadian dollar equalled approximately 72 U.S. cents). The structure of the company underwent significant changes after the acquisition, resulting in a complicated web of holding companies designed to satisfy the interests of all parties involved in the agreement.

Some of the benefits and risks associated with the acquisition were identified in the *Four Seasons Regent 1992 Annual Report*:

**Exhibit 1**          **Properties Managed by Four Seasons Regent Hotels and Resorts (1994)**

| Hotel and Location | Date of Opening Change/latest renovation in Yield | Equity Interest | Number of Rooms | Term to Initial Expiration of Management Contract (years from 1993) | 1993 Occupancy | Change from 1992 |
|---|---|---|---|---|---|---|
| *North America* | | | | | | |
| Austin, Texas Four Seasons Hotel | 1986 +0 to 10% | 19.9% ** | 292 | 18 | high 70s | up |
| Beverly Hills, CA Regent Hotel | 1927/1990 +11 to 20% | 0 | 295 | 31 | mid 60s | up |
| Boston, MA Four Seasons | 1985/1992 +11 to 20% | 15% ** | 288 | 16 | high 70s | up |
| Chicago, IL Ritz-Carlton | 1975/1991 +0 to 10% | 25%* | 429 | 31 | mid 70s | up |
| Chicago, IL Four Seasons Hotel | 1989 +11 to 20% | 7.7% | 343 | 30 | low 80s | up |
| Dallas, Texas FS Resort & Club | 1979/1994 +0 to 10% | 0 | 357 | 8 | high 70s | up |
| Houston, Texas Four Seasons Hotel | 1982/1992 +0 to 10% | 0 | 399 | 23 | high 60s | down |
| Los Angeles, CA Four Seasons Hotel | 1987 +11 to 20% | 0 | 285 | 48 | mid 70s | up |
| Mexico City, Mexico Four Seasons Hotel | 1994 N/A | 0 | 239 | 20 | N/A | N/A |
| Nevis, West Indies Four Seasons Resort | 1991 Over 20% | 15% | 196 | 27 | mid 60s | up |
| Newport Beach, CA Four Seasons Hotel | 1986/1994 +11 to 20% | 0 | 285 | 22 | high 60s | up |
| New York, NY Four Seasons Hotel | 1993 N/A | 14.9% | 367 | 19 | N/A | N/A |
| New York, NY The Pierre Hotel | 1981/1991 +0 to 20% | 19.9% | 205 | 18 | mid 70s | up |
| Palm Beach, FL FS Resort Ocean Grand | 1989 N/A | 0 | 234 | 40 | N/A | N/A |
| Philadelphia, PA Four Seasons Hotel | 1983/1993 +0 to 10% | 5% | 371 | 19 | mid 60s | up |

**Exhibit 1 (continued)   Properties Managed by Four Seasons Regent Hotels and Resorts (1994)**

| Hotel and Location | Date of Opening Change/latest renovation in Yield | Equity Interest | Number of Rooms | Term to Initial Expiration of Management Contract (years from 1993) | 1993 Occupancy | Change from 1992 |
|---|---|---|---|---|---|---|
| San Francisco, CA Four Seasons Hotel | 1976/1990 +0 to 10% | 0 | 329 | 12 | high 60s | down |
| Santa Barbara, CA FS Biltmore Resort | 1929/1988 +0 to 10% | 10% | 234 | 18 | low 70s | down |
| Seattle, Washington FS Olympic Hotel | 1982/1992 +0 to 10% | 3.4% | 450 | 46 | mid 70s | flat |
| Wailea, Maui, HI Four Seasons Resort | 1990 +11 to 20% | 0 | 380 | 16 | low 60s | up |
| Washington, DC Four Seasons Hotel | 1979 +11 to 20% | 15% | 196 | 15 | low 80s | up |
| Minaki, Ontario Four Seasons Resort | 1986 N/A | 100%** | 142 | 18 | N/A | N/A |
| Toronto, Ontario Four Seasons Hotel | 1974/1992 +11 to 20% | 19.9% | 380 | 18 | high 60s | up |
| Toronto, Ontario FS Inn On The Park | 1963/1985 +0 to 10% | 19.9% | 568 | 18 | high 40s | up |
| Vancouver, BC Four Seasons Hotel | 1976/1990 +0 to 10% | 19.9% | 385 | 18 | mid 70s | up |
| Montreal, Quebec** Le Quatre Saisons | 1976 N/A | 0 | 300 | 10 | N/A | N/A |
| *Asia* | | | | | | |
| Bangkok, Thailand Regent Hotel | 1983/1994 +0 to 10% | 0 | 400 | 1 | mid 50s | up |
| Chiang Mai, Thailand Regent Hotel | 1995 N/A | 0 | 67 | to 2024 | N/A | N/A |
| Hong Kong Regent Hotel | 1980/1993 +0 to 10% | 25% | 602 | 6 | mid 70s | down |
| Jakarta, Indonesia Regent Hotel | 1995 N/A | 5% | 384 | to 2015 | N/A | N/A |
| Kuala Lumpur, Malaysia Regent Hotel | 1989 Behind | 0 | 469 | 15 | mid 70s | up |

**Exhibit 1 (continued)   Properties Managed by Four Seasons Regent Hotels and Resorts (1994)**

| Hotel and Location | Date of Opening Change/latest renovation in Yield | Equity Interest | Number of Rooms | Term to Initial Expiration of Management Contract (years from 1993) | 1993 Occupancy | Change from 1992 |
|---|---|---|---|---|---|---|
| Singapore Four Seasons Hotel | 1994 N/A | 0 | 257 | to 2014 | N/A | N/A |
| Singapore Regent Hotel | 1982/1991 +10 to 20% | 0 | 441 | 14 | mid 60s | up |
| Taipei, Taiwan Regent Hotel | 1990 Behind | 0 | 553 | 4 | high 70s | up |
| Tokyo, Japan Four Seasons Hotel | 1992 +11 to 20% | 0 | 286 | 8 | mid 60s | up |
| *South Pacific/ United Kingdom/Europe* | | | | | | |
| Auckland, New Zealand Regent Hotel | 1985/1995 Behind | 0 | 332 | 12 | high 50s | down |
| Bali, Indonesia Four Seasons Resort | 1993 N/A | 0 | 147 | 19 | N/A | N/A |
| Melbourne, Aust. Regent Hotel | 1981/1986 Behind | 0 | 363 | 1 | low 60s | down |
| Nadi Bay, Fiji Regent Hotel | 1975/1993 +10 to 20% | 18% | 294 | 18 | high 60s | up |
| Sydney, Australia Regent Hotel | 1982/1990 Behind | 0 | 594 | 29 | mid 50s | down |
| London, England Four Seasons Hotel | 1970/1991 +0 to 10% | 50% | 227 | 17 | low 60s | down |
| London, England Regent Hotel | 1992 N/A | 0 | 309 | 17 | N/A | N/A |
| Milan, Italy Four Seasons Hotel | 1993 N/A | 19.9% | 98 | 19 | N/A | N/A |
| *Under Construction or Development* | | | | | | |
| Aviara, CA Four Seasons Resort | Unknown | 5% | 337 | to 2085 | | |
| Berlin, Germany Four Seasons Hotel | 1996 | 23% | 204 | to 2071 | | |

**Exhibit 1 (continued)  Properties Managed by Four Seasons Regent Hotels and Resorts (1994)**

| Hotel and Location | Date of Opening Change/latest renovation in Yield | Equity Interest | Number of Rooms | Term to Initial Expiration of Management Contract (years from 1993) | 1993 Occupancy | Change from 1992 |
|---|---|---|---|---|---|---|
| Bombay, India Four Seasons Hotel | 1997 | 0 | 300 | N/A | | |
| Cairo, Egypt Four Seasons Hotel | 1997 | 0 | 105 | N/A | | |
| Goa, India Four Seasons Hotel | 1997 | 0 | 295 | N/A | | |
| Hualalai, Hawaii Four Seasons Resort | 1996 | 0 | 250 | to 2066 | | |
| Istanbul, Turkey Four Seasons Resort | 1996 | 0 | 65 | N/A | | |
| Prague, The Czech Republic Four Seasons Hotel | 1997 | 0 | 185 | to 2072 | | |
| Punta Mita, Mexico Four Seasons Hotel | N/A | 20% | 100 | N/A | | |
| Royal Sentul Highlands, Indonesia Regent Hotel | 1996 | 0 | 171 | N/A | | |
| Riyadh, Saudi Arabia Four Seasons Hotel | 1998 | 0 | 231 | N/A | | |

*The 25% ownership in the Ritz-Carlton Chicago is the result of an arrangement that was made with the owners of the hotel at the commencement of the management contract. The details of this agreement are unknown, but it has no significance to this case.

**Interest sold or management contract terminated as of December 31, 1994, or early 1995 (San Francisco).

*Sources:* Occupancy and yield figures from Deacon Barclays de Zoete Wedd Research Ltd. All other information is excerpted from the FSR 1993 Annual Report. Four Seasons Regent defines yield as occupancy times average rate.

## ■ Benefits

1. Geographic diversification of the company's revenue sources, which helps to moderate the effects of regional economic downturns.
2. Leveraging the Corporate cost base by utilizing the existing base of management to oversee a significantly larger business.
3. Enhanced marketing opportunities through the integration of distribution networks, resulting in a more cost-effective organization.
4. The elimination of a direct luxury hotel competitor in both present and future locations.

## ■ Risks

1. The potential of owner conflicts regarding breaches of radius restriction in their management contract related to the acquisition. Namely, The

Regent Singapore, The Regent Taipei, and the Four Seasons Los Angeles properties are predisposed to strained relationships between the owners and Four Seasons for this reason.

2.  Foreign currency matters, e.g., Regent earns fees from hotels operating in ten different countries thus increasing the element of risk associated with the rapid fluctuation of international exchange rates.

3.  In 1997 the Chinese government [took] control of Hong Kong. The effects that this event will have on the Hong Kong business community are difficult to predict.

After considering a number of options, the corporation decided to maintain the head office of Regent in Hong Kong, and to continue to operate Regent as an independent subsidiary. Initially, Four Seasons planned to flag the entire chain of hotels under the Four Seasons trade name to establish the worldwide presence of a single brand. After further consideration, however, it was decided that the newly acquired hotel management contracts would be kept under the Regent trade name, but any new developments would be flagged as Four Seasons hotels, regardless of geographical location. This decision led to the designation of their new developments in New York, Bali, and Milan as Four Seasons hotels.

FSR management subsequently reviewed this approach and decided that new hotels in Asia and the South Pacific would be more successful with the Regent brand name because of higher customer awareness in those markets. Apart from a few major international destinations, new developments in North America and Europe would continue to be flagged as Four Seasons.

The decision of how to flag a new hotel was also influenced by the owners of the hotel properties. The owner's choice of brand name was often a stipulation of new management contracts. This added another element of complexity to the branding issue.

## ■ Getting Out

In June of 1994, Issy Sharp announced plans to relinquish his controlling interest in Four Seasons Regent. The announcement stunned the hotel world and his own staff. Recognizing the inevitability of change in the ownership of the company, Mr. Sharp, then 62, said that he wanted to control the process and commit his personal involvement and leadership to achieving a smooth transition over a period of 3 to 5 years. "Every good leader should know when to step down and how to ensure the continuing good health of the company. It's tempting to stay on too long, but at Four Seasons Regent I believe the time to act is now."

One of the many implications associated with the possible sale of Four Seasons Regent was the fact that many of the existing management contracts provided that they could be terminated by the owners in the event of a change in control of the company. Putting the company up for sale clearly jeopardized many properties in the portfolio of hotels under FSR management.

On November 10, 1994, a partnership was commenced with Prince Al-Waleed Bin Talal Bin Abdulaziz Al Saud, an international investor with previous heavy investments in EuroDisney and Fairmont Hotels of San Francisco, other companies needing a capital infusion. The Prince bought 25% of Four Seasons' shares for (Cdn) $165 million from Issy and other shareholders. Issy Sharp's voting stake dropped to about 65 percent from his previous 80 percent. Referring to the investment as a "long-term strategic alliance," the Prince said that "It is consistent with my strategy to invest significant amounts of capital with superior management teams throughout the world." In addition to his investment, the Prince was working closely with the company to identify opportunities to acquire and develop luxury hotels for Four Seasons Regent to manage. He had allocated $100 million to this program. As a first step, Four Seasons Regent would manage a luxury hotel being developed by the Prince in Riyadh, Saudi Arabia.

Analysts said there was some disappointment that the offer wasn't for 100 percent of the shares. But the deal solved a critical problem for Sharp. "If something happens to me, my estate doesn't have to act. They'll have adequate liquidity because of this transaction." Sharp also said that he was not considering stepping down for at least three years. Further, Sharp indicated there was plenty of management depth ready to continue his leadership and management agenda as most in the corporate office had been with the company for many years.

## THE INDUSTRY

The hotel industry was generally divided into five categories: budget, economy, mid-price, upscale, and luxury. In the U.S. market, luxury hotels, which included Four Seasons, had the brightest outlook for 1995 with forecasted occupancies as high as 75% according to Smith Travel Research, an industry research firm. Projected operating performance figures for the U.S. market are presented in Exhibit 2.

The World Travel and Tourism Council reported in 1993 that travel and tourism was the world's largest industry, accounting for more than 6% of Gross Domestic Product (GDP) and 13% of consumer spending worldwide. Travel growth, according to Boeing's 1993 Current Market Outlook (an industry newsletter), was expected to increase an average of 6% per year through the year 2000. Travel to, from, and within Asia accounted for 25% of world air travel but, by the year 2010, was expected to account for 42% of travel growth (Four Seasons Annual Report, 1993).

The World Tourism Organization tracks the arrivals and tourism receipts for six regions. The preliminary findings for 1994 indicated that Asia was the dominant growth leader in tourism. These findings are presented in Exhibits 3a, 3b, and 4 along with the 1994 average occupancies and room rates for Asia's top five destinations.

Growth of hotel supply was slow to moderate in most parts of the world, while GDP in all markets was expected to grow. Other reports, however, drew different conclusions. It was generally agreed that east and southeast Asia would remain the focal point of economic growth over the next several years, as well as the fastest growing area of travel, fueled primarily by intra-regional activity which was not necessarily in the luxury category.

At the same time, there were new trends apparent in the luxury market: While luxury segments were increasing demand, it was on a different scale than before the recession. What complicated the rebirth of upscale hotels was price. For example, in the U.S., room rates were averaging around $113 in the luxury segment and $77 in the upscale segment—lower than they should be to support replacement costs.

While the hotel industry as a whole was operating at 65% of replacement costs, the luxury market was trading at 45%. In addition, 70% of all hotels were

**Exhibit 2**                    **Projected Operating Performance Figures for the U.S. Hotel Market (1994-1995)**

| Occupancy Percent | 1995 | 1994 | % Change |
|---|---|---|---|
| Price Level | | | |
| Luxury | 75.3 | 72.2 | 4.3 |
| Upscale | 69.2 | 67.9 | 1.9 |
| Mid-price | 65.5 | 65.1 | 0.6 |
| Economy | 63.4 | 62.1 | 2.1 |
| Budget | 62.4 | 61.3 | 1.8 |
| Location | | | |
| Urban | 69.1 | 67.1 | 3.0 |
| Suburban | 67.1 | 65.3 | 2.8 |
| Airport | 72.8 | 70.6 | 3.1 |
| Highway | 63.5 | 62.4 | 1.8 |
| Resort | 69.7 | 68.3 | 2.0 |
| **Average Rate (US$)** | **1995** | **1994** | **% Change** |
| Price Level | | | |
| Luxury | 113.49 | 109.88 | 3.3 |
| Upscale | 77.58 | 74.25 | 4.5 |
| Mid-price | 59.31 | 56.79 | 4.4 |
| Economy | 46.33 | 44.04 | 5.2 |
| Budget | 35.98 | 34.00 | 5.8 |
| Location | | | |
| Urban | 93.79 | 89.42 | 4.9 |
| Suburban | 59.86 | 57.57 | 4.0 |
| Airport | 66.61 | 63.61 | 4.7 |
| Highway | 47.10 | 45.40 | 3.7 |
| Resort | 96.95 | 94.04 | 3.1 |

Source: *Four Seasons Regent*

profitable in 1994, but only 50% of luxury hotels were in the black that year. Most industry experts predicted it would be several years before more upscale brands traded at a profitable rate. They also agreed that the current business climate was all part of a natural pattern: a segment gets overbuilt, overfinanced, debt is restructured, and properties get repositioned.

Significant trends were also occurring in the luxury resort market. To meet growing customer demand for "enrichment" holidays, resort hotels were moving from "service providers" to "experience managers" where guests become alumni. MRA, a hospitality industry consulting firm based in Philadelphia, cited five major shifts in tourists' motivation that were causing resorts to shift focus to organized, interactive programs of "experiential learning."

**Exhibit 3a**                **1994 Tourism Arrivals and Growth Rate by Region**

| Region | Arrivals (millions) | % Total | % Change (from 1993) | Receipts (billions) | % Total | % Change (from 1993) |
|---|---|---|---|---|---|---|
| World | 528.4 | 100.0 | 3.0 | $321.5 | 100.0 | 5.1 |
| Europe | 315.0 | 59.7 | 1.9 | 153.3 | 47.7 | 0.6 |
| Americas | 108.5 | 20.5 | 4.1 | 97.4 | 30.3 | 8.9 |
| East/Asia/ Pacific | 74.7 | 14.1 | 7.6 | 59.0 | 18.3 | 14.0 |
| Africa | 18.6 | 3.5 | 1.5 | 5.7 | 1.8 | -4.0 |
| Middle East | 7.9 | 1.5 | -4.0 | 3.7 | 1.1 | -12.0 |
| South Asia | 3.7 | 0.7 | 7.0 | 2.4 | 0.8 | 11.2 |

Source: 1994 Tourism arrivals from *Tourism in 1994 Highlights (January 1995),* World Tourism Organization, Madrid.

**Exhibit 3b**                **1994 Occupancy and Room Rates at Asia's Top Destinations**

| City | Occupancy Percent | Avg. Room Rate (US$) | Type of Hotel |
|---|---|---|---|
| Bangkok | 61 | 75 | 4-Star |
|  | 50 | 139 | 5-Star |
| Beijing | 73 | 92 | 4-Star |
| Hong Kong | 82 | 130 | 4-Star |
|  | 72 | 239 | 5-Star |
| Singapore | 82 | 130 | 4-Star |
|  | 70 | 128 | 5-Star |
| Tokyo | 69 | 200 | 4-Star |
|  | 67 | 280 | 5-Star |

Note: Rates based on 1994 year-end exchange rate. Rating based on international standard.
Source: 1994 occupancy and room rates from *Travel Business Analyst, Hong Kong,* February 1995.

In Asia, Four Seasons was exploring the fertile fields of Thailand and Indonesia to make its mark on the hottest luxury segment: boutique hotels. Their newest, with 67 suites, was the Regent, Chiang Mai, Thailand. Meanwhile, in the Americas, Situr and its partner Grupo Plan, a Mexican development firm, had teamed up to start Hoteles Bel-Air Mexico, a chain of posh boutique hotels along Mexico's Pacific Coast.

Reports out of the U.S. showed resorts were showing steady improvement as Americans emerged from the recession with pent-up desires to get away.

Analysts assessed what resort travelers wanted:

- Vacationers favored shorter trips closer to home.
- They showed preferences toward all-inclusive pricing that included transportation, transfers, lodging, meals, and recreations.

**Exhibit 4**                    **Hotel Market Business Cycles, 1995**

| Downturn | Slump | Recovery | Growth |
|----------|-------|----------|--------|
| *Asia Pacific* | | | |
| Seoul | Jakarta | Shanghai | Brisbane |
| Melbourne | Kuala Lumpur | Beijing | Sydney |
| Taipei | Bangkok | Bali | Tokyo |
| | Manila | | Hong Kong |
| *Europe* | | | |
| Hungary | Austria | Spain | United Kingdom |
| Poland | Germany | Italy | Turkey |
| Czech Republic | Belgium | Switzerland | Greece |
| | Netherlands | Sweden | |
| | France | Norway | |
| | | Denmark | |
| *United States* | | | |
| | Honolulu | Los Angeles | Atlanta |
| | San Diego | Miami | Houston region |
| | | Orlando | New Orleans |
| | | Washington, DC | Denver |
| | | Boston | Phoenix |
| | | New York | Las Vegas |
| | | Chicago | |
| *Canada* | | | |
| | Montreal | Halifax | Vancouver |
| | | Edmonton | |
| | | Calgary | |
| | | Toronto | |
| | | Ottawa | |
| *Central, South America and the Caribbean* | | | |
| | Venezuela | Peru & Mexico beaches | Colombia |
| | Bahamas | Brazil | Chile |
| | US Virgin Islands | Other Caribbean islands | Costa Rica |
| | | Argentina | Nevis & St. Kitts |
| | | Aruba | Puerto Rico |
| | | | Mexico's commercial markets |
| *Middle East and Africa* | | | |
| | Egypt | Kenya | South Africa |
| | | Jordan | United Arab Emirates |
| | | Saudi Arabia | |
| | | Morocco | |
| | | Bahrain | |
| | | Tunisia | |

Source: *Hotels*, January 1995, p. 29.

- They were interested in fitness programs and amenities geared to children.
- They included companies, which are turning to resorts as places to combine business with a vacation retreat for executives and their families.

Knowing the resort industry was improving, if not set to soar, international chains including Radisson, ITT Sheraton, and Hilton were preparing for the millennium.

Gaining a share of the resort market was key to the global strategies of many upscale chains, which needed elegant resorts to complement more well-known city hotels. "The luxury market is clearly headed toward resorts with more privacy and exclusivity," according to John Richards. "You will not see big single-style buildings in this segment nor will you see boutique hotels built in the U.S. or Hawaii," he said. Labor is just too costly to build and run small resorts in these areas. Instead, Four Seasons is looking at Asia and also at Mexico, areas where construction and labor costs are dramatically lower, to build its boutiques.

# FOUR SEASONS CORPORATE STRATEGY

Four Seasons Regent had a clear set of corporate objectives that was driven by two primary goals: to be the first choice as manager of luxury hotels and resorts world-wide, and to operate the finest hotel or resort in each destination where it locates by creating a positive experience for its guests. Four Seasons' annual reports consistently referenced a set of key objectives that had been adopted as part of its core mission:

1. Market Leadership: to achieve and maintain leading market share in major markets;
2. Operational Strength: to operate the finest urban hotel or resort in each destination;
3. Motivated people: to maintain the industry's most motivated employee group, a factor inextricably linked to building customer value;
4. Earnings growth: to increase trend line EPS by 10% to 15% per annum from the fiscal 1985 base—the year prior to becoming a public company; and
5. Leverage: to achieve a long-term targeted debt-to-equity ratio, net of cash, of 1:1.

A long-range strategy was to improve the company's earnings by concentrating on hotel management rather than on the ownership of hotels. This permitted expansion without assuming significant additional capital risks. The company's stated position was to have no more than a 10% to 20% equity interest in any of its projects. Future growth expansion was planned only in locations that satisfied Four Seasons Regent's objectives of better servicing the travel needs of its existing customer base and attracting new international business travelers. Management expected that future expansion would focus on Europe, China, and Southeast Asia.

## ■ Financial Performance

Four Seasons Regent earned revenues from hotel management and hotel ownership operations. Management revenues were derived from a combination of fee categories, the terms of which are listed in Exhibit 5. Earnings from hotel ownership were derived from cash flow participation and the realization of capital appreciation upon the sale of the ownership interest.

**Exhibit 5**

**Hotel Management Contracts—Fees and Terms**

*a) Basic management fee and other related fees*
Percentage of annual gross operating revenue of the hotel or percentage of defined profit, calculated and payable monthly, or, in one case, a lump-sum amount payable annually.

*b) Incentive Fees*
Percentage of defined profit or of annual net cash flow of the hotel after specified deductions, payable monthly, quarterly, or semi-annually, subject to adjustment at year-end, or payable annually, or, in one case, a lump sum payable annually.

*c) Pre-opening development and purchasing fees*
Negotiated amounts, payable in monthly installments prior to the opening of the hotel.

*d) Centralized purchasing fees*
Percentage of cost of purchases of food and beverage inventories, operating supplies and furniture, fixtures and equipment.

*e) Refurbishing fees*
Percentage of total cost of approved refurbishing programs or negotiated amounts.

*f) Corporate sales and marketing charge and corporate advertising charge*
Percentage of annual budgeted gross operating revenue or gross rooms revenue of the hotel, payable monthly and calculated on the basis of the cost of providing the services, or a flat charge.

*g) Centralized reservation service charge*
Monthly charge per hotel room, calculated on the basis of the number of hotel rooms or the number of reservations made, or a flat charge.

Source: *Four Seasons 1994 Annual Report*

Financial results for hotel management operations and hotel ownership operations, from 1990 to 1994, as well as pro forma results for 1995 to 1997, are shown in Exhibit 6. Exhibit 7 shows consolidated balance sheets for 1993 and 1994.

## ■ 1992 and 1993 Financial Summary

Approximately 75 percent of the total fees for both 1992 and 1993 were basic management fees and other related fees, and 25 percent were from a combination of the other six fee categories. Of the fee revenues generated by Four Seasons Regent in 1993, 52 percent were attributable to hotels in which Four Seasons Regent owned an equity interest, exactly half of the hotels at that time.

Fee revenues from hotel management operations increased 42 percent in 1993. Of the $17.8 million increase in fee revenues, $10.8 million related to the 11 Regent hotels acquired and operating in 1993 as opposed to those earned in 1992 from the date of acquisition on August 14. The balance of the increase resulted from the growth in fees from newly opened properties in New York, Milan, Bali, Nevis, and London and from the growth in incentive fees earned at several other properties.

Operations of all Four Seasons Regent's North American hotels improved their financial performance in 1993, with an average growth in gross operating profit of more than 25 percent. This was primarily the result of increases in occupancies and room rates; the average yield rose by over 11 percent in 1993.

**Exhibit 6**      **Four Seasons Regent Hotels Statement of Earnings 1990-1997[*]**
**(In thousands of Canadian dollars except per share amounts)**

| | 1990 | 1991 | 1992 | 1993 | 1994 | 1995[*] | 1996[*] | 1997[*] |
|---|---|---|---|---|---|---|---|---|
| Total Revenues of *Managed Hotels* | | | | | | | | |
| Four Seasons | 66092 | 631023 | 728000 | 916700 | 1188708 | 1296886 | 1437750 | 1563200 |
| Regent | 0 | 0 | 151000 | 435200 | 509447 | 523595 | 569125 | 614655 |
| Total | 66092 | 631023 | 879000 | 1351900 | 1698155 | 1820481 | 2006875 | 2177855 |
| Hotel Management Ops. Fee Revenues | | | | | | | | |
| Four Seasons | 37820 | 34849 | 35600 | 42500 | 58315 | 60305 | 67574 | 74252 |
| Regent | 0 | 0 | 6900 | 17779 | 21569 | 21467 | 23334 | 25201 |
| Total | 37820 | 34849 | 42500 | 60279 | 79884 | 81772 | 90908 | 99453 |
| General & Admin. Exps. | (22820) | (20763) | (23865) | (32359) | (34000) | (35676) | (37460) | (39333) |
| EBITD Mgt. Ops. | 15000 | 14086 | 18635 | 27920 | 45884 | 46096 | 53448 | 60120 |
| Hotel Ownership Ops. Revenues | 157214 | 137365 | 93099 | 38019 | 43093 | 53500 | 56000 | 59000 |
| Dist. from Hotel Investments | 0 | 0 | 1845 | 3839 | 6795 | 5000 | 5000 | 5000 |
| Cost of Sales | (136069) | (136945) | (97736) | (33675) | (34464) | (44940) | (46760) | (49265) |
| Fees to Management | (6878) | (5539) | (3501) | (1021) | (1271) | (3300) | (3300) | (3300) |
| EBITD Ownshp. Ops. | 14267 | (5119) | (6293) | 7162 | 14153 | 10260 | 10940 | 11435 |
| **Total EBITD** | **$29,267** | **$8,967** | **$12,342** | **$35,082** | **$60,037** | **$56,356** | **$64,388** | **$71,555** |
| Investment Income | 3494 | 2021 | 3202 | 4770 | 510 | 0 | 0 | 0 |
| Depreciation/Amort. | (8138) | (10830) | (12840) | (13216) | (15702) | (14250) | (15000) | (15325) |
| Interest Expense | (1208) | (40) | (8604) | (17855) | (27239) | (19900) | (16900) | (15000) |
| Provision for Loss from Disposed Hotels | (2240) | | (13789) | (110000) | | | | |
| Provision for (Loss)Recovery on Mortgages Receivable | | | 12906 | (17000) | (6828) | ** | | |
| Tax (Expense)/Recovery | | | | | | | | |
| Current | (225) | 125 | 875 | (1482) | (2297) | (2500) | (3800) | (3000) |
| Deferred | (3614) | 2514 | 13662 | 468 | (459) | (831) | (1073) | (1284) |
| **Net Profit** | **$17,336** | **$2,757** | **$7,754** | **($119,233)** | **$8,022** | **$18,875** | **$27,615** | **$36,976** |
| EPS ($) | .84 | 0.13 | 0.32 | (4.30) | 0.29 | 0.68 | 1.00 | 1.27 |
| Cash Dividend/Share | .11 | .11 | .11 | .11 | .11 | | | |
| Share Price Year-end | 16.00 | 17.50 | 19.38 | 13.00 | 16.25 | | | |
| Common Stock Outstanding (Millions) | 20.1 | 22.2 | 27.7 | 27.8 | 28.4 | 27.8 | 27.6 | 29.1 |
| Debt, Net of Cash | 60.7 | 121.3 | 290.2 | 345.6 | 299.2 | | | |
| Shareholders' Equity | 112.4 | 139.6 | 247.8 | 126.8 | 140.5 | | | |
| Debt-to-equity Ratio, Net of Cash | .5 | .9 | 1.2 | 2.7 | 2.13 | | | |

Source: 1992-1994 Four Seasons Annual Reports and, projections for 1995-1997, RBC Dominion Securities

[*]Regent revenues only August 14-December 31.

[**]Costs associated with sale of shares. Investment banking costs primarily to Goldman Sachs, engaged to seek a strategic investor.

The term "yield," as defined by Four Seasons Regent, is hotel occupancy multiplied by achieved room rate. A substantial loss was reported, however, for 1993. This was due to a decision to dispose of interest in seven hotel properties

**Exhibit 7**          **Consolidated Business Sheets, 1993-1994**
**December 31, 1994 and 1993 (In thousands of Canadian dollars)**

|  | 1994 | 1993 |
|---|---|---|
| *Assets* | | |
| Current Assets | | |
| Cash and short-term investments | $9,436 | $11,926 |
| Receivables | 39,182 | 25,975 |
| Inventory | 814 | 750 |
| Prepaid expenses | 1,440 | 1,795 |
| Total Current Assets | 50,872 | 40,446 |
| Notes and mortgages receivable | 25,098 | 37,475 |
| Investments in hotel partnerships | 151,256 | 171,873 |
| Fixed assets | 68,052 | 72,606 |
| Investment in management contracts | 116,486 | 114,323 |
| Investment in trademarks and trade names | 64,238 | 65,889 |
| Other assets | 21,534 | 20,288 |
| **Total Assets** | **$497,536** | **$522,900** |
| *Liabilities and Shareholders' Equity* | | |
| Current Liabilities | | |
| Bank indebtedness | $ - | $825 |
| Accounts payable and accrued liabilities | 44,904 | 36,253 |
| Long-term debt due within one year | 876 | 3,821 |
| Total Current Liabilities | 45,780 | 40,899 |
| Long-term debt | 307,721 | 352,898 |
| Deferred income taxes | 3,530 | 2,316 |
| Shareholders' equity | | |
| Capital stock | 175,729 | 169,810 |
| Contributed surplus | 4,784 | 4,784 |
| Deficit | (38,076) | (43,007) |
| Equity adjustment from foreign currency translation | (1,932) | (4,800) |
| Total Shareholders' Equity | 140,505 | 126,787 |
| **Total Liabilities and Shareholders' Equity** | **$497,536** | **$522,900** |

Source: *Four Seasons Regent 1994 Annual Report*

and a provision of $110 million on possible real estate loss and $17 million on the company's loan portfolio on their prospective sales.

The average total management fee revenues received by Four Seasons Regent from each hotel group, per available room, was expected to increase significantly through 1997. This was primarily due to the additional rooms added or to be added in the resort and Asian markets, which have higher average revenues per room.

## ▪ 1994 Financial Summary

The strong recovery in occupancies and room rates, combined with effective cost control measures implemented since 1992, resulted in an increase of over 45 percent in 1994 in the average gross operating profit of managed hotels. Operating earnings from hotel management increased 64 percent while hotel ownership earnings increased 98 percent, from 1993 levels, reflecting strong recovery in the London, Hong Kong, and Chicago markets which generated virtually all the revenues and earnings from hotel ownership operations, from the company's equity interests. This improvement positively affected growth in the company's management incentive fee revenues, which were tied to the profitability of certain managed hotels. Incentive fees represented 15 percent of total management fee revenues for 1994 as compared to ten percent in 1993.

Four Seasons hotels that opened in 1994 included Mexico City and Singapore, plus assumption of the management contract at The Ocean Grand in Palm Beach, Florida. One management contract, for Le Quatre Saisons property in Montreal, was discontinued on January 1, 1994.

New hotels opened in 1993 (Milan, London, New York, Bali) made a strong contribution to overall improvements in 1994. The Four Seasons Boston, Regent Sydney, and Regent Hong Kong also had strong performances in 1994. Average rooms performance figures for Four Seasons and Regent hotel groups are presented in Exhibit 8.

Significant gains in room revenues were realized in many Four Seasons and Regent hotels between 1993 and 1994. Fourteen properties had yield performance gains greater than ten percent, five of which were Regent hotels.

In November 1993, the company implemented a disposition program to sell seven of its significant real estate interests with the objective of substantially eliminating its hotel ownership segment and reducing debt levels by approximately one-third ($120 million). This would also allow the company to reduce its exposure to future real estate cycles and to reduce ongoing capital and operational funding requirements. As of December 31, 1994, it had completed the sale of its interest in three hotels (Austin, Minaki Lodge, and Boston) and used $51.7 million generated from these sales for debt reduction. The company continued to manage the Austin and Boston hotels under long-term management agreements. Notes receivable related to the hotel in San Francisco were sold in early 1995 and

| Exhibit 8 | **Rooms Performance** | | | |
|---|---|---|---|---|
| | | *Occupancy %* | *Average Rate* | *Yield* |
| **Four Seasons** | | | | |
| 1993 Actual | | 68.7% | $183.58 | $126.12 |
| 1994 Actual | | 70.2% | $208.16 | $146.13 |
| **Regent** | | | | |
| 1993 Actual | | 66.0% | $152.96 | $100.95 |
| 1994 Actual | | 71.4% | $162.23 | $115.83 |

Source: *Four Seasons Regent Hotels*

the management contract terminated. Other hotels in the program were in Santa Barbara, Vancouver, Toronto, and London. Sale of these interests was expected to generate about $50 million in 1995 after asset-related debt payments.

# CORPORATE MARKETING

The overall marketing strategy of the corporation was to serve the luxury segment of the market for business and resort travel worldwide. The corporate office was responsible for the development of overall sales and marketing strategies. These included establishing broad international awareness for both Regent and Four Season brands, as well as developing local market potential for specific hotels.

Four Seasons also provides an international corporate advertising program which develops and places advertising for the Four Seasons hotels and oversees the individual hotel's programs. Regent coordinates the advertising programs for the individual Regent hotels. In 1994, Four Seasons Regent implemented a standard policy of identifying Four Seasons Regent Hotels and Resorts with all corporate and hotel advertising programs.

The corporate marketing staff of Four Seasons Regent also oversees the planning and implementation of hotel marketing programs, and organizes the training and development programs for local sales and marketing staff. The local marketing strategy concentrated on developing rooms and food and beverage business for hotels locally and regionally, and promoting the hotel as a center of community activity with a view to developing local revenues, particularly from catering. Four Seasons Regent generally recovered the costs associated with providing all of these services.

## ■ Sales Mix

The corporation estimated that business travel and leisure travel represented approximately 66 percent and 34 percent, respectively, of Four Seasons and Regent's combined occupancy. Approximately 37 percent of occupied rooms at the seven resort properties were sold to vacationers. Other major markets for resorts were corporate groups and incentive groups, representing 29 percent and 16 percent, respectively, of all occupied rooms. Approximately 40 percent of urban business and virtually all of resort business was booked through travel agents.

Forty-nine percent of hotel revenue, overall, was derived from the sale of guest rooms and 41 percent from the sale of food and beverages. The other ten percent was attributable to the sale of other services to hotel guests. Asian hotels generally had a higher contribution of food and beverage sales than North American hotels. Food and beverage business for the Four Seasons Tokyo, for example, represented approximately 65 percent of total revenues. This was typical of upscale Asian hotels, especially in Japan.

## ■ Worldwide Reservations Systems

As a further means of more effectively securing global business, Four Seasons Regent upgraded its international reservations network in 1992. This system provided reservation services in the local language at a total of 22 locations worldwide in major European and Asian cities. Separate toll-free reservations telephone numbers were designed to preserve and enhance the individual Four Seasons and Regent brand identities, while integration enabled the reservations network for each hotel group to sell the other hotel group in cities or countries where its hotel group did not operate, or to sell rooms at a second hotel in the same city if one hotel was full. Central systems booked 35-40 percent of individual reservations for the company.

### ■ Sales Office Network

Four Seasons Regent operated 13 worldwide sales offices to develop group and corporate business for hotels. Since the 1992 acquisition of Regent, sales operations had been integrated worldwide to provide larger and more diversified sales and marketing coverage for both brands.

## COMPETITION

Competition from large hotel chains was vigorous in all Four Seasons Regent markets and was primarily comprised of the Ritz-Carlton, Peninsula, Mandarin, Shangri-La Westin, Inter-Continental, and Hyatt hotel chains. Four Seasons management strategically considered these five hotel chains to be their only real competition at or near their level of quality. Other major international hotel chains such as Sheraton, Marriott, Le Meridien, and Kempinski of Germany, were considered secondary competition as most properties were not at the same luxury level. Individually owned luxury hotels were also a source of competition in certain markets.

Ritz-Carlton was considered the leading competitor, with seven city hotels positioned in direct competition with Four Seasons or Regent hotels in 1995. Ritz-Carlton hotel locations are shown in Exhibit 9.

Peninsula, Shangri-La, and Mandarin Oriental were located in virtually all major Asian destinations. Westin and Hyatt were present in major cities and resort destinations worldwide. Inter-Continental hotels were located in most major world capitals and gateway cities. Most of the other chains mentioned were in just about all Four Seasons Regent locations. Most of Four Seasons Regent competitive analysis was based on comparisons with Ritz-Carlton.

Ritz-Carlton, after three years of endeavor, had received in 1992 the prestigious Malcolm Baldrige National Quality Award, which recognized American companies for their commitment to service, consistency, and reliability. Four Seasons and Regent hotels, however, have individually gathered more accolades than Ritz-Carlton hotels.

## THE OUTLOOK FOR 1995

Performance projections for 1995 suggested 11.5 percent and 6.9 percent yield increases for Four Seasons and Regent Hotels, respectively (see Exhibit 10). In light of continuing performance improvements throughout the company, the marketing team decided to focus on the same priorities:

**Exhibit 9**          **Ritz-Carlton Hotel Locations**

| *United States* | *Hawaii/Pacific/Asia* | *Europe* | *Mexico* |
|---|---|---|---|
| Boston | Double Bay, Australia | Barcelona | Cancun |
| New York | Kahana, Maui | | |
| Pentagon City (DC) | Big Island of Hawaii | | |
| Philadelphia | Sydney | | |
| Tysons Corner (DC) | Hong Kong | | |
| Washington, DC | Seoul | | |
| Amelia Island, FL | Bali, Indonesia | | |
| Atlanta | Osaka, Japan | | |
| Buckhead, GA | | | |
| Naples, FL | | | |
| Palm Beach, FL | | | |
| Cleveland | | | |
| Dearborn, MI | | | |
| Kansas City | | | |
| St. Louis | | | |
| Houston | | | |
| Phoenix | | | |
| Aspen | | | |
| Pasadena, CA | | | |
| Rancho Mirage, CA | | | |
| Marina del Rey, CA | | | |
| San Francisco | | | |
| Laguna Niguel, CA | | | |

- Growing individual business worldwide
- Improving the quality and nature of group business
- Striving for greater marketing efficiencies
- Strengthening individual brands and hotels
- Leveraging the Four Seasons Regent combination
- Focusing on special situations
- Focusing on *'Unique Service = Value = Worth More'* as the main communications message throughout the world

From these priorities, three collective objectives were identified as the main focus of marketing efforts in 1995.

## *Growing individual business worldwide.*

The company identified this market as its greatest opportunity to support its growing international portfolio. While the majority of group sales take place relatively close to a hotel's location, and require heavy local sales involvement, individual travel decisions can be made anywhere and can be effectively influenced by the efforts of a worldwide sales organization, regardless of location.

**Exhibit 10**    **1995 Budgeted Hotel Performance**

|  | Four Seasons | Regent |
|---|---|---|
| **Occupancy %** | 73.4% | 72.2% |
| **Average Rate** | $221.81 | $169.83 |
| **Yield** | $162.81 | $122.62 |

Source: Four Seasons Regent Hotels

Four Seasons introduced three company-wide initiatives to influence and attract global individual business travel:

1. A hotel guest recognition program to provide basic information to each hotel on the top 100 individual customers for all other properties. According to the 1995 Marketing Plan, this focus was on what was believed to be the primary need for the high-end individual traveler—that of recognition during a first stay in a Four Seasons or Regent hotel.

2. Development of a promotional database to sell and communicate directly with individual customers who voluntarily were willing to be contacted. This would also allow for increased cooperation with promotional partners who wished to cross-market with Four Seasons Regent.

3. Reshaping of direct sales efforts in the North American sales offices to focus more on individual travel segments. In the past, worldwide sales offices had focused on the lucrative group and incentive markets but, now that the company portfolio ranged across many continents, sales efforts would have to be diversified to support growth in both individual and group-travel segments.

### Leveraging the Four Seasons Regent Combination.

Four Seasons Regent planned to continue to ensure that "cross-selling" of the Four Seasons and Regent brands was the rule rather than the exception. Given the increasingly global nature of both the competition and target customers, Four Seasons Regent was committed to using combined human resources and systems to represent the entire company regardless of brand or location.

### Improving Global Sales Network Efficiencies.

Two primary initiatives were put in place to facilitate faster and more cost-effective communications.

1. Wherever possible, individual hotels would soon be electronically linked to worldwide reservations systems, allowing each hotel to communicate directly and easily with reservations outlets.

2. By mid-1995, 17 Four Seasons and 8 Regent hotels would have a database software program for the management of group rooms and function space. The next objective was to link up the individual hotels to worldwide sales offices, allowing for more consistent timely information on key accounts and eliminating the manual/voice exchange of information.

## LOOKING TO THE FUTURE

Continued improvement from existing operations as a result of the worldwide economic recovery, combined with additional fee income from recently opened hotels and hotels opening in Chiang Mai, Thailand (mid 1995), Jakarta (mid 1995), Istanbul and Royal Sentul Highlands, Indonesia (mid 1996), and Berlin (mid 1996) were expected to contribute to further increases in the company's operating margins in 1995 and 1996.

Four Seasons Regent would continue to serve the luxury segment of the market for business and leisure travel and intended to maintain and improve upon the standards established in existing properties, as well as those in the hotels and resorts presently under development or construction. Four Seasons Regent would continue to review opportunities to manage newly constructed and existing hotels and resorts. They planned to seek development opportunities aggressively worldwide and their goal was to have a combined portfolio of 50 hotels and resorts within five years.

The corporate marketing team's discussion continued for many hours as it contemplated the issues that the Ritz-Marriott marriage had introduced. Many questions were still left unanswered. Would Ritz-Carlton stay exclusively in the luxury market? Would the Ritz-Carlton name be enhanced or jeopardized by their association with a worldwide mid-market hotel chain? Would Marriott put its name on Ritz-Carlton hotels? Should Four Seasons Regent position against Ritz-Carlton, Marriott, or both? What if Marriott started stealing Four Seasons Regent employees for its Ritz-Carlton operations? Most of all, how will any of these issues affect Four Seasons Regent and should Four Seasons Regent devise strategies to deal with any of these eventualities?

Richards pondered the possibilities. If strategies needed to be devised, what would they look like? Do we respond to the threat, do we preempt, fortify, defend? When, and at what point? How does the Regent acquisition fit into this? Are we in a better or worse position? Do we have the right organization to handle this?

"It looks like we all have quite a lot to think about tonight" said Richards as the conversation came to a tiresome end. "Let's meet again tomorrow to prepare our contingency plans."

Shortly after this incident, John Sharpe, a 20-plus-year veteran of Four Seasons was named President of the company and heir apparent to Issy Sharp. John Richards, among others, was promoted to Executive Vice President.

# Dakota, Minnesota & Eastern Railroad: A Light at the End of the Tunnel

Paul Reed, Sam Houston State University

John C. "Pete" McIntyre caught himself shaking his head as he thought back over his almost nine years as President of the Dakota, Minnesota & Eastern Railroad (DM&E). Pete remembered the railroad's first days in 1986: no working capital, track and roadbed that had not been properly maintained in 20 years, old locomotives, and a lack of freight cars. Over the years, droughts, blizzards, wild fire, record rains, and subsequent flooding had contributed to DM&E's woes. To add to the company's problems was an unfriendly Chicago & NorthWestern Railroad (C&NW), the DM&E's major customer and supplier.

The DM&E had been a survivor, Pete thought. Over time, $60 million had been put into track rehabilitation, locomotive purchase, and freight car leasing. The railroad was now better prepared to meet the uncertainty of the elements. Even the C&NW had loosened, somewhat, its stranglehold on the DM&E.

Most of the events of the past year appeared to bode well for the DM&E. In July 1994, the railroad refinanced its long-term debt at considerable savings. In March 1995, the State of South Dakota had agreed to issue $35 million in state revenue bonds to finance the rebuilding of the western 266 miles of the railroad. In April 1995, the powerful, and hopefully more friendly, Union Pacific Railroad (UP) purchased the C&NW. Pete knew that the next few years would be all important to the DM&E. When and how the railroad would get to the light at the end of the tunnel would occupy Pete's thoughts for some time.

## INDUSTRY BACKGROUND

In the 160-year history of railroading in the United States, the industry traveled through some of its most profound changes during the past 25 years. The combination of deregulation in the transportation arena, basic changes in the nature and output of American heavy industry, the loss of local business, the use of Continental United States as a bridge for cargo that formerly passed through the Panama Canal, and the dramatic increase in long-distance coal movement for power generation have caused the railroads of today to be far different from the traditional railroads of yesterday. In essence, railroads were once responsible for hauling almost everything and everybody into and out of every city and village, and accounted for 75 percent of all United States intercity freight ton-miles in 1929.[1] The volume of freight handled by today's railroads is some 260 percent of that of 1929, although modal share has been lost to trucks, river carriers, and pipelines. In 1993, railroads handled 38 percent of all freight ton-miles.[2] Thus, railroads have evolved from general freight carriers to specialized freight carriers primarily handling large-volume bulk commodities, oversized or bulky loads, and general products and merchandise when combined into container or trailer-sized lots (intermodal).

The Interstate Commerce Commission (ICC) classifies all of the common carrier railroads operating within the United States into one of three categories based primarily on annual operating revenue. The major rail freight carriers are defined as Class I railroads and must meet an adjustable revenue threshold for a period of three continuous years. In 1993, this threshold was $253.7 million. Regional railroads are those carriers that operate at least 350 miles of track and/or earn revenue between $40 million and the Class I threshold. The DM&E is classified as a regional railroad, the second largest of 34 such mid-sized carriers in the United States. Local railroads are all those that fall below the regional railroad criteria and include Switching and Terminal railroads. A comparison of these three types of railroads is shown in Exhibit 1.

## THE BEGINNINGS

During the 1970s and into the 1980s, the railroad industry in the upper Midwest had felt drastic changes stemming from the deregulation of both trucking

---

**Exhibit 1**        **Types of Railroad in the United States: 1994**

| Type of Railroad | Number | Miles Operated | Employees | Annual Revenue ($000,000) |
|---|---|---|---|---|
| Class I | 12 | 123,738 | 189,086 | $27,990 |
| Regional | 34 | 21,581 | 11,642 | 1,543 |
| Local | 463 | 23,645 | 12,530 | 1,241 |
| **Totals** | **509** | **168,964** | **213,258** | **30,774** |

Source: Association of American Railroads, *Railroad Facts: 1994*, p. 3

and railroads, the decline of heavy industry, the loss of local railroad business, the growth of coal traffic, and mergers. During this period, many lines merged, were downsized, or disappeared with pieces purchased by former competitors or, in many cases, entrepreneurs desiring to operate their own railroad.

The C&NW was particularly active during this time frame, purchasing and then abandoning major portions of competitors—Chicago GreatWestern (1,450 miles) and Minneapolis and Saint Louis (1,300 miles)—plus acquiring the Minneapolis-Kansas City line of the Rock Island (600 miles). By the late 1980s, the C&NW had also sold or abandoned some 4,500 miles of its own trackage. Included in this downsizing was the vast majority of its lines in Minnesota and South Dakota.

Most of the trackage of what is now the DM&E (Exhibit 2) was unprofitable for the C&NW for several years. In 1983 and again in 1985 the C&NW petitioned to abandon the line from five miles west of Pierre to Rapid City. This action would leave South Dakota with no centrally located east-west rail transportation. C&NW's requests were met with unusually strong opposition from the State and U.S. Senator Larry Pressler, R-South Dakota. Realizing that abandonment was no longer a wise move, the C&NW was faced with either continued operations or sale. All parties agreed that the former was not feasible and therefore the C&NW initiated actions to find a buyer.

Lengthy negotiations ended in September 1986, with the sale of what is now the DM&E to a group of investors. The $26 million agreement was heavily leveraged, with Westinghouse Credit Corporation the primary lender and the C&NW assuming a $4 million subordinated note.

**Exhibit 2**          **DM&E Dakota, Minnesota & Eastern Railroad**

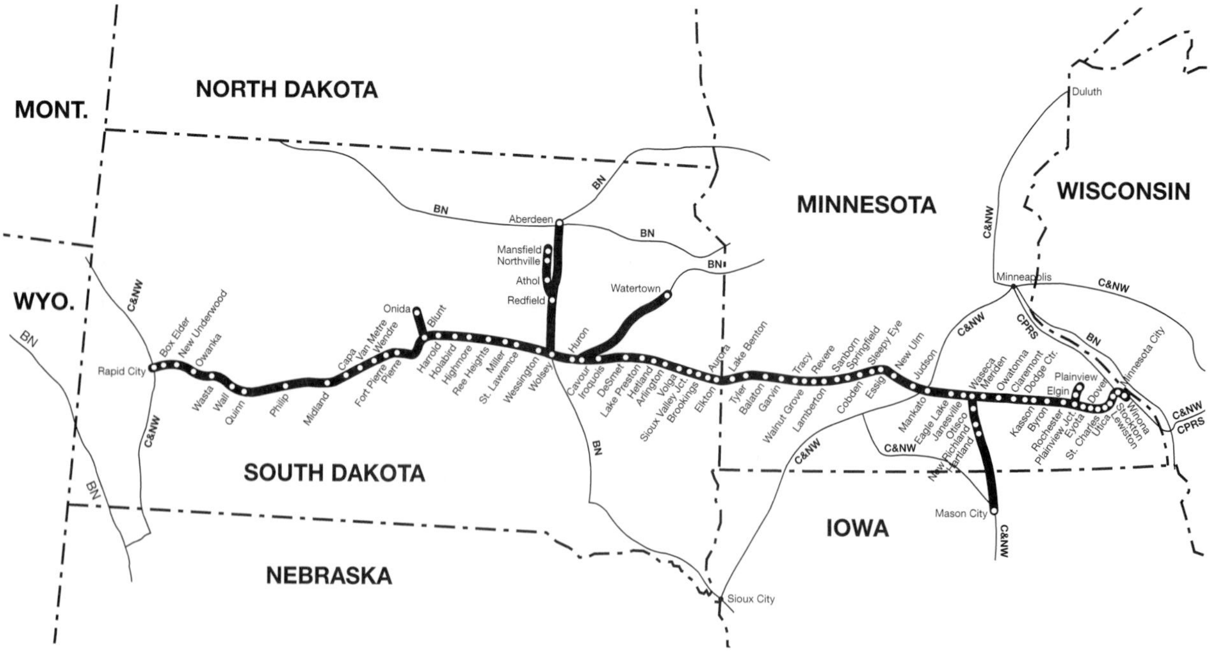

The buyers acquired 826 miles of track and rights to operate on an additional 139 miles. Included were 18 C&NW locomotives, averaging 35 years old, and maintenance and repair equipment. The C&NW retained ownership of the tracks at the DM&E's main interchanges at Winona and Mankato, MN, Mason City, IA, and Rapid City, SD. It also could exercise veto power over DM&E's rates and route proposals or any changes in existing financing. The new line also had to agree to pay substantial monetary penalties unless 89 percent of DM&E's originated traffic was loaded in C&NW freight cars.[3]

Of additional concern to newly hired President "Pete" McIntyre were the assumptions others had used in entering the purchase agreement, and the agreement itself. Traffic projections had been overstated. The physical condition of track was far worse than estimated. Revenue projections were based on an unrealistic level of business. The DM&E was seriously undercapitalized. Many were of the opinion that the C&NW had been paid far too much for the property. Also, the negotiators had, in effect, severely limited McIntyre and his subordinates' ability to operate the road efficiently by agreeing to the aforementioned C&NW restrictions.

# INTERNAL ENVIRONMENT

## ■ Description of the Railroad

The DM&E is headquartered in Brookings, SD, and operates mainly in South Dakota and Minnesota. A 69-mile branch line serves Mason City, Iowa. Exhibit 3 shows that the Winona-Rapid City main line and the trackage to Mason City carry the greatest freight tonnages. It also indicates that most traffic is

**Exhibit 3**          **DM&E Railroad 1994 Freight Density Map Shown in Million Gross Tons per Mile (no scale)**

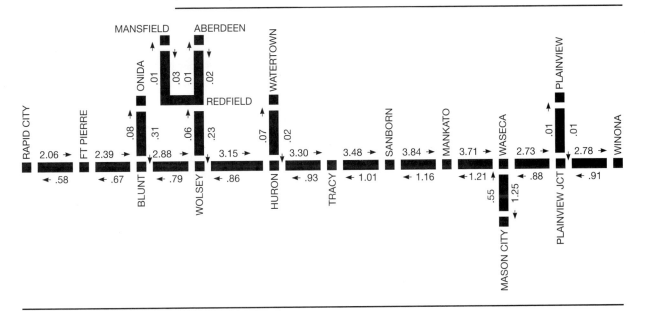

east-bound. West-bound trains consist mainly of empty cars being returned for loading. Track conditions on most of the line prevent freight train speeds in excess of 25 mph and approximately 40% of the line can only support 10 mph.

The DM&E serves the main line with a minimum six day per week commercial train (See Glossary) service between Rapid City and Winona. A similar schedule handles freight between Waseca, MN, and Mason City. During peak months (June-October) two trains per seven day week are often scheduled. Extra trains also originate at points between Pierre and Waseca to handle grain and other tonnage. Branch lines see trains on an as-needed basis. Local freights provide service to many on-line customers, thus relieving commercial trains from making numerous stops between Rapid City and Winona.

Freight cars are sorted and blocked at the division points at Waseca and Huron, S.D. The DM&E must turn over most of its traffic to the UP(C&NW) at its four principal gateways. This forces the DM&E to pay the UP(C&NW) switching charges in excess of $100 per car or share revenue on all through traffic. Exhibit 4 indicates the size of the largest cities (1990 Census) along the DM&E route and the ownership of the trackage.

The company owns and operates car and locomotive repair shops at Huron. Major repairs and overhauls are performed on the road's 59 locomotives. Similar services are provided, on an as-needed basis, to freight cars of other railroads. All active locomotives have been rebuilt or received major overhaul since start-up. The availability rate for locomotives is over 96 percent and approaches 100 percent during the winter months, when many units are stored due to lower traffic requirements. During the summer-fall season, the DM&E is often required to lease a few locomotives to handle increased traffic.

Grain and grain-derived products make up 45 percent of the DM&E's carloads. Grain shipments include South Dakota wheat and corn and soybeans

---

**Exhibit 4**                **Largest Cities and Track Ownership**

| State | City | Size | Track Ownership |
|---|---|---|---|
| Minnesota | Winona | 47,828 | UP(C&NW) |
| | Rochester | 70,745 | DM&E |
| | Owatonna | 19,386 | UP(C&NW) |
| | Waseca | 18,079 | DM&E |
| | Mankato | 31,477 | UP(C&NW) |
| Iowa | Mason City | 29,040 | UP(C&NW) |
| South Dakota | Brookings | 16,270 | DM&E |
| | Huron | 12,448 | DM&E & BN |
| | Watertown | 17,592 | BN & DM&E |
| | Aberdeen | 24,927 | BN & DM&E |
| | Pierre | 12,906 | DM&E |
| | Rapid City | 54,523 | UP(C&NW) |

Source: U.S. Government—1990 Census

from eastern South Dakota and the western two-thirds of Minnesota. The second major item of traffic is bentonite clay (used in foundry operations, oil drilling, iron ore pelletizing, and cat litter) which is turned over by the UP(C&NW) at Rapid City for delivery by DM&E to its lines farther east. Other major traffic sources include industrial sand, cement, wood chips, lumber, and kaolin clay (used in the manufacturing of cement). Exhibit 5 shows the traffic mix.

## ■ Mission

In the words of President Pete McIntyre, to provide rail users in the upper Midwest with consistent, damage-free, on time, wholesale and retail transportation service with the intent of moderate growth and profitability, recognizing its employees as valuable assets and with the aim of being customer driven.[4]

## ■ Senior Management

The DM&E maintains a lean organization throughout its entire structure. Senior management appears relatively young, well qualified, and highly motivated.

John C. McIntyre—Director, President, and Chief Executive Officer. His thirty-seven year railroad career includes 29 years with the C&NW where he advanced from clerk to Assistant Vice President and Division Manager—Chicago. McIntyre also has an equity position in the railroad.

Lynn A. Anderson—Director, Vice-President of Marketing and Public Affairs. He is responsible for marketing, pricing, sales and serves as liaison to various federal, state, and local governments. Spent 15 years with the C&NW,

| Exhibit 5 | Historical Carloadings by Category (1989-1994) | | | | | |
|---|---|---|---|---|---|---|
| **Categories of Traffic** | **1989** | **1990** | **1991** | **1992** | **1993** | **1994** |
| Wheat | 6,664 | 8,949 | 10,532 | 9,883 | 11,319 | 10,353 |
| Bentonite Clay | 740 | 6,756 | 9,054 | 9,666 | 9,545 | 10,737 |
| Woodchips | 3,450 | 3,768 | 3,232 | 3,353 | 2,369 | 2,359 |
| Corn | 8,436 | 10,443 | 8,045 | 8,469 | 4,281 | 4,601 |
| Cement | 3,321 | 1,976 | 2,171 | 2,853 | 2,581 | 2,514 |
| Industrial Sand | 4,055 | 5,040 | 2,369 | 3,407 | 3,040 | 3,276 |
| Lumber/Boards | 109 | 825 | 656 | 546 | 458 | 454 |
| Soybeans | 1,902 | 2,915 | 2,766 | 2,973 | 1,921 | 2,275 |
| Kaolin Clay | 0 | 663 | 1,036 | 1,295 | 2,321 | 466 |
| Soybean Oil | 1,458 | 1,566 | 1,969 | 1,971 | 2,231 | 2,005 |
| Wheat Flour | 434 | 966 | 974 | 930 | 891 | 1,124 |
| All Others | 9,644 | 8,721 | 8,658 | 9,814 | 9,813 | 10,429 |
| **Totals** | **40,024** | **52,588** | **51,462** | **55,160** | **51,040** | **50,593** |

Source: Company records

rising to the position of general manager of grain marketing and pricing. Anderson also has an equity position on the railroad.

Robert F. Irwin—Vice-President Transportation. He is responsible for scheduling, train operations, dispatching, personnel (engineers, conductors, and brakemen) and division point operations. Irwin spent 22 years with the C&NW where he held various operating positions in the Midwest.

James H. Appleman—Chief Mechanical Officer. He oversees providing operational maintenance for locomotive and freight cars so that the DM&E can meet projected traffic levels and customer service requirements. He spent 20 years with CONRAIL, where he rose from welder to Manager of Yards & Productivity.

Kurt V. Feaster—Chief Financial Officer. He is involved in finance, personnel, accounting, and computer information activities. Has served in various financial capacities for three different railroads during the past 25 years. Last served as Chief Financial Officer for the Wheeling & Lake Erie Railway.

Douglas G. DeBerg—Chief Engineer. He is responsible for upgrading and maintaining the railroad infrastructure, including track, bridges, signals, and buildings. Has spent over 30 years working in various engineering capacities for five different railroads. DeBerg joined the DM&E July 1, 1995.

## ■ Corporate Philosophy

DM&E has made a long-term commitment to provide reliable freight service and not diversify into nonrail efforts. Overall, DM&E believes in strengthening its position as a rail freight carrier in the upper Midwest by making its existing system more efficient and serving its present territory better. Accordingly, DM&E increased revenues by enlarging its market share of freight shipped by existing customers, by regaining customers who had shifted to trucks when the railroad was operated by previous owners, by serving new shippers in its territory, and by improving relations with other railroads. The railroad continues to employ a strategy of strengthening its existing traffic base and increasing its market share within the territory it serves rather than expanding much beyond South Dakota and Minnesota. The DM&E has also shown great interest in better controlling its main traffic interchanges such as the UP(C&NW) Colony Line that delivers over 20,000 cars a year to the DM&E at Rapid City. Also, ownership of UP's (C&NW) Winona freight yard would permit direct interchange with Mississippi River barge traffic and the Canadian Pacific Railroad (CP).

## ■ Marketing

The DM&E has the freedom to set rates within a relevant range of pricing and has aggressively gone after traffic from both large and small shippers. It has initiated long-term agreements with large shippers to stabilize its traffic base; given eight to 10 percent discounts to grain shippers who make unit train shipments of 25 cars or more; and has initiated pricing and service packages to provide South Dakota and Minnesota farmers markets in Texas, the Eastern United States, the Pacific west coast, and the gulf coast via the Mississippi River. The DM&E adds or reschedules train service and has opened a computerized Customer Service Center to improve rail-customer interface.

The DM&E knows the importance of the customer and has done considerable research and planning to identify customer needs and packaging services to satisfy them. Marketing V.P. Lynn Anderson feels that the Customer Service Center has enabled the DM&E to better determine customer expectations in terms of car supply, transit times, loss or damage, billing, switching, car tracing, response time, etc.[5] While DM&E's innovative ideas affect shippers and receivers of all categories of traffic, the marketing of grain is of particular interest. The DM&E took advantage of the Winona end of track on the Mississippi River by developing a rail-barge service that opened up new markets to shippers and receivers at prices that took advantage of cheaper barge rates. Going in the opposite direction, DM&E has been dispatching unit grain trains to the Pacific Northwest via the Burlington Northern Railroad (BN). In March 1995 alone, the DM&E originated eleven 54 car grain trains.

The DM&E has also been successful in gaining some new industry along its lines. For example, a new soybean processing facility in Volga, S.D., will add approximately 1,500 carloads annually.

DM&E's innovative efforts, however, are often offset by the weather. The rains and floods of 1993 greatly reduced corn and soybean production and resulted in the DM&E moving 4,500 fewer carloads in 1993 and 1994. High water closed down the Winona rail-barge operation for several weeks in both years. Conversely, 1994 was an excellent year for all crops and the DM&E anticipates large shipments of all types of grain in 1995.

Lynn Anderson's department also faces other challenges: the demographics of the DM&E service area limit the size and nature of the railroad's target markets; occasional freight car shortages, particularly during peak demand; some difficulty in interchanging traffic with the UP(C&NW); and prior agreements precluding car interchange with the CP at Winona impact on shippers, receivers, and the DM&E itself.

## ■ Transportation

Providing accident-free, timely service that meets customer needs is a never-ending challenge to the DM&E. Poor track, interchange difficulties, lack of adequate passing sidings to permit train meets, locomotive and train crew shortages, and the weather have too often equated to high operating costs, train derailments, and unsatisfied customers. The DM&E inherited trackage that, in the main, had not received adequate maintenance in 20 to 30 years. A great portion of the line west of Huron, for example, is the original 72 pound (per yard) rail laid in the early 1900s. Eighty odd years of pounding have made the track and the supporting grade increasingly unable to support 100 ton railcars moving at speeds much above 10 mph.

DM&E tracks end short of the yards at Mason City, Rapid City, and Winona and, as a result, entry, car switching, and exit are controlled by the UP(C&NW). DM&E trains were often forced to idle for several hours waiting for the C&NW(UP) yard crews to put outgoing trains together or clear tracks for incoming cars.

Lack of adequate sidings (6,000 ft.) often causes one DM&E train to wait several hours for a meet with a train coming from the opposite direction. Additional time is lost when there is a shortage of rested train crews or a lack of locomotives.

The weather adds its toll. Winter may cause trains to take 120 hours to make the Rapid City-Winona trip rather than the ideal 60 hours. Heavy rains result in unstable track and, coupled with deferred maintenance, ultimately causes 80 percent of the derailments that annually cost the DM&E $3 million. (Individual derailment costs varied from a few thousand dollars to over $1 million.)

Some or all of the above factors cause train crew overtime, extra crews, higher freight car rental expenses, and increased locomotive fuel and maintenance costs. These items can easily add $1 million to operating expenses. Vice President Bob Irwin and his Transportation Department continually fight to improve service while lowering costs. Yard engine crews now assemble trains, conduct air tests, and often take the train a mile or two out of town. All the commercial train crew has to do is climb aboard and depart. This division of duties saves the commercial crew two to three hours, thus reducing overtime and improving transit time. Irwin also has added three local freight trains that pick up and deliver freight cars to the many grain elevators and businesses along the line. This enables the commercial train to travel from Rapid City to Winona or Mason City without performing switching duties.

In December 1994, Bob Irwin and his C&NW(UP) counterpart reached agreement on improving the interchange of traffic. The C&NW(UP) began expediting yard switching in Winona by adding a second engine crew, increased emphasis on timely delivery of traffic to the DM&E at Rapid City, and moved the congested Mason City interchange north to Albert Lea, MN. This move now permits a DM&E train crew to complete the traffic interchange in six hours. Before, this operation often required in excess of 12 hours and a second train crew.

As Vice President of Transportation, Irwin leads a team of 61 locomotive engineers and 32 conductors plus a management and administrative staff of 15. The DM&E trains its own conductors and has a 70 day cross-training program, in conjunction with the Santa Fe Railroad, where senior conductors are qualified as engineers. This dual qualification has added job stability by permitting conductors to serve as engineers during peak season and return to their former duties during slack time. The increased number of operating crews and the addition of nine locomotives has given the DM&E needed flexibility in train make up and scheduling.

## ▪ Engineering

This department has the Herculean task of maintaining track, bridges, and other physical plant in a safe condition commensurate with DM&E requirements. This charge includes cross-tie replacement, rail replacement, rock ballasting, surfacing (cleaning, leveling, and smoothing of track), sub-grade and bridge improvements.

As mentioned earlier, the DM&E inherited a poorly maintained railroad. Added to these woes was the discovery that the native clay (Pierre shale) subgrade on the Pierre-Rapid City (PRC) section would prove very unstable during periods of heavy rains. In effect, the water becomes trapped between wet clay and track structure and the wet clay itself often proves unable to support the weight of 100 ton car trains. Frequently, the end result is that water, clay, ballast, etc., are squeezed to both sides of the railbed, thus causing the track to sink. Some of these soft spot areas extend for 500 feet. Unseasonably wet weather in four of the last five years has played havoc on the PRC section and by late June 1995 had washed out roadbed in eastern South Dakota and at many places across Minnesota. Repair costs for the "flood of 1993" approximated $2.1 million and were paid for by a Federal emergency relief grant. The

| Exhibit 6 | Dakota, Minnesota & Eastern Railroad Corp. Capital Expenditures ($000) | | | | | | |
|---|---|---|---|---|---|---|---|

| Capital Expenditures | 1987-89 | 1990 | 1991 | 1992 | 1993 | 1994 | Total |
|---|---|---|---|---|---|---|---|
| SD Track—West of Pierre | $5,629 | $2,614 | $955 | $2,221 | $1,421 | $2,019 | $14,949 |
| SD Track—East of Pierre | 5,843 | 3,429 | 219 | 1,120 | 797 | 2,216 | 13,624 |
| Total SD Track | $11,562 | $6,043 | $1,174 | $3,341 | $2,218 | $4,235 | $28,573 |
| MN Track | 6,250 | 2,969 | 1,374 | 1,713 | 3,811 | 4,350 | 20,467 |
| Total All Track | $17,812 | $9,012 | $2,548 | $5,054 | $6,029 | $8,585 | $49,040 |
| Locomotive & All Other | 2,618 | 1,410 | 1,267 | 1,454 | 2,280 | 3,803 | 12,832 |
| Total | $20,430 | $10,422 | $3,815 | $6,508 | $8,309 | $12,388 | $61,872 |
| Funded by | | | | | | | |
| SD Grant (FRA Funds)* | 626 | 0 | 0 | 89 | 264 | 467 | 1,446 |
| SD Grant (State Funds) | 1,502 | 345 | 278 | 567 | 0 | 0 | 2,692 |
| SD State Loan | 0 | 0 | 75 | 0 | 0 | 0 | 75 |
| SD Industry | 346 | 0 | 48 | 76 | 0 | 0 | 470 |
| SD FRA Loan | 4,870 | 2,720 | 60 | 0 | 0 | 0 | 7,650 |
| MN Grant (FRA Funds) | 228 | 70 | 21 | 49 | 868 | 494 | 1,730 |
| MN Grant (State Funds) | 1,301 | 408 | 334 | 509 | 0 | 0 | 2,552 |
| MN State Loan | 3,161 | 967 | 5 | 0 | 1,833 | 1,229 | 7,195 |
| MN Industry | 465 | 210 | 0 | 40 | 361 | 200 | 1,276 |
| DM&E Cash | 7,931 | 5,702 | 2,994 | 5,178 | 4,983 | 9,998 | 36,786 |
| Total | $20,430 | $10,422 | $3,815 | $6,508 | $8,309 | $12,388 | $61,872 |

*FRA—Federal Rail Administration

Source: Company records

costs associated with the wet spring of 1995 have yet to be totaled but will add up to several hundred thousand dollars.

The DM&E had spent in excess of $49 million on track and bridge-related capital projects by the end of 1994. Over 59 percent of this was from cash generated from operations and the remainder came from federal and state loans and grants plus loans from customers. The DM&E also performs normal maintenance and maintenance-support activities that are not included in capital expenditures. Exhibit 6 shows capital expenditures for 1987–1994.

Budgeted capital track expenditures for 1995 approximate $7.2 million. Included are installation of 59,000 cross ties, 150,000 tons of rock ballast (2,000 car loads), surfacing 270 miles of track, installing 13 miles of longitudinal drain plastic pipe, upgrading 12 bridges, replacing 780 feet of wooden bridging with culvert and earthen fill, constructing a 6,000 ft. passing track near Wendte, S.D., and installing five miles of continuous welded rail west of Wolsey, S.D.

The railroad has long recognized that a targeted main line average speed of 25 mph will never be attained until a solution is found to the PRC subgrade problems, and replacement of the lightweight rail between Wolsey and Pierre, S.D. After extensive study, the DM&E determined that those two projects would require an estimated $35 million to accomplish. Included in the project are replacement of 96 miles of 72 lb. rail, 85 miles of ditching, surfacing of the entire 170 mile PRC subdivision with a total of 6,800 cars of ballast, and installation of 35 miles of waterproof fabric between ballast and clay. Also, over 4,500 perforated lateral drain pipes and 20 miles of perforated longitudinal piping will be used to remove trapped pockets of water.

The need for the upgrading of this section of the DM&E and the resultant benefits to the state resulted in the signing of legislation authorizing the issuance of up to $35 million in revenue bonds. Under terms of the bill, South Dakota will acquire ownership of the western 266 miles of track, leasing it back to the DM&E on an exclusive basis until the bonds are paid off by the railroad. At that time, ownership will revert to the DM&E. The Wolsey to Pierre section will require $20 million and take approximately three years to finish. The PRC will need $15 million to complete and will take an additional three years. There are several underwriters interested in handling the bond offering and a nine or 10 percent interest rate is expected. The DM&E hopes to receive the proceeds for the Wolsey to Pierre portion in late fall 1995.

The Engineering department is staffed with 30 section personnel who are equally spread along the 10 sections of 850 mile owned rail. Each three-man section is responsible for maintaining a safe railroad across its section. The department's other 37 non-management personnel install and maintain signals, repair bridges, inspect track, and operate a variety of equipment. This 67 man base work force is augmented by temporary hires in the spring and summer. Also, the railroad uses contractors for all major capital projects.

## ■ Mechanical

This department is tasked with maintaining the DM&E locomotive fleet, repairing all on-line railcars owned by other railroads, and providing similar service to nearly 300 newly-leased covered hoppers. James Appleman's 36-member department has the equipment and expertise to perform almost any type of maintenance or repair requirement. The fact that locomotive availability remains 96 percent or higher with units manufactured between 1952 and 1974 and averaging 39 years in age is a testament in itself. The department is currently covering 100 percent of its entire budget from foreign railcar (i.e., railcars owned by others) repairs.

## ■ Human Resources

Human Resources Management (HRM) is not centrally administered. Hiring and training are done at the department level, while pay, benefits, performance appraisal, and administrative recordkeeping are performed by the Finance and Accounting Department. Human resources, however, take a back seat to no functions on the DM&E. President Pete McIntyre continually stresses the importance of all employees, both as people and as the real cause of the railroad's success.[6] Most key managers seem to echo this philosophy, though some seem to have difficulty adjusting from the too typical railroad confrontational leadership style.

## Communications

Pete McIntyre schedules "Employee Appreciation Dinners" in the summer and during the Christmas season at major locations. The employees seem to enjoy the "give and take" during these festivities and many feel relatively free to express their views. McIntyre and other rail officials get out on the line as often as possible but acknowledge that their hectic jobs keep them from getting needed feedback.[7] Face-to-face communication is supplemented by a quarterly newsletter *DM&E Enroute*, which keeps employees, customers, and supporters informed of current operations and future plans. One innovation is an open invitation to employees to phone McIntyre direct, or in his absence, leave a message. Overall, employees have a positive attitude toward these efforts, although some feel they need more one-on-one contact and a few wonder if they are really listened to.

## Stable Work Force

The DM&E recognizes the importance of job security to employee morale, turnover, and possible increased productivity. The use of temporary employees and contract labor serve to minimize layoffs greatly in the seasonal transportation, engineering, and mechanical departments. In addition, cross training affords flexibility needed to move employees efficiently where needed.

## Pay

The DM&E pays its craft, clerical, and non-union employees very competitively versus local rates. The DM&E has admitted from the beginning that it could not match the train crew pay of unionized Class I railroads. Rates of pay are 15 to 25 percent below comparable wages on the C&NW(UP). Extensive overtime on the DM&E plus profit sharing and year-round employment (Class I railroads often have winter layoffs) undoubtedly narrow this gap.

The DM&E also uses bonus and merit pay to reward non-union employees further. Bonuses for all non-managerial employees averaged $1,700 in 1990, $2,200 in 1991, $2,700 in 1993, and $2,300 in 1994. All but operating United Transportation Union (UTU) non-managerial employees are eligible to receive performance appraisal-based merit pay. This incentive averaged 3 percent in 1990, 2 percent in 1991, 3 percent in each year from 1992 to 1994, and 4 percent in 1995. In addition, this category of employees received 3 percent across the board increases in 1990, 1992, and 1993.

## Benefits

The benefits package offered DM&E employees equals or exceeds those provided by the major union railroads. Exhibit 7 gives a sample comparison.

## Unions

Although the initial DM&E work force was comprised, in large part, of former union members, there was little sentiment for unionization. Many employees knew that for the railroad to survive in the short run, all costs had to be kept to a minimum. Also, some employees blamed the union for the loss of their former jobs with major Class I carriers and were willing to forgo some wages just to get

**Exhibit 7**

## Sample Benefits Comparison

| Benefit | DM&E | Unionized National Railroad Plan |
|---|---|---|
| Life Insurance | $50,000 | $10,000 |
| Accidental D&D | $50,000 | $8,000 |
| 401(K) | Yes | Not Provided |
| Profit Sharing | Yes | Not Provided |
| Maximum Medical | $1,000,000 | $500,000 |
| Deductible | $100-each individual | $100-each individual |
| Maximum out-of-pocket | $500-individual<br>$1,000-family | $2,000-each person covered |

Source: DM&E Benefits Brochures

back in their profession. The DM&E remained non-union until June 1990 when train crew, railcar repairmen, and electricians began being represented by the UTU. One of the major complaints against the DM&E was its failure to improve wages as compared to major railroads.

The American Train Dispatchers Association attempted to organize the dispatchers in 1989 but failed. The UTU attempted to organize engineering employees in 1991 but was rejected by a vote margin of 2 to 1. In August 1992, the car repairmen voted to decertify the UTU and formed their own local union. In November of 1992, the International Association of Machinists (IAM) failed in their attempt to organize the Mechanical Department. The IAM has renewed its organization efforts and an election is upcoming.

### Morale

Employee attitudes are generally good across the various categories of workers. Turnover is within limits and a "can do" spirit seems fairly prevalent. The lack of scheduled time off for train crews, however, appears to be an unsolvable problem for both union and management. Train crews often find themselves called back to work 10 hours after completing a trip, or spending a day away from home waiting for a train to complete the round trip. This leaves little time with family, and planned outings are a rarity. Some consideration had been given to a six-day-on, two-off work cycle but variables in demand, schedule interruptions, and the unwillingness of many to lose overtime pay have made this proposal impractical. Many train crew members use vacation or "sick" time for days off.

### ■ Summary of Financial Performance 1992–1995

The DM&E has continued to improve its financial condition since start-up and particularly from 1992 to date. The railroad generated $40.4 million in operating revenues in 1992, while traffic volume was 55.1 thousand carloads. Operating revenues for 1993 were $41.9 million and traffic volume 51 thousand carloads, a 3.7 percent increase in revenues and a 7.5 percent decline in carloads. In 1994, operating revenue was $43.3 million while carloads stood at 50.6 thousand, an increase of 3.3 in revenue and a .07 percent decrease in carloads over comparable 1993 levels. Dur-

**Exhibit 8**

### Dakota, Minnesota & Eastern Railroad Income Statements 1992–1994 ($000)

| | 1992 | 1993 | 1994 |
|---|---:|---:|---:|
| **Revenues** | | | |
| Freight | 40,377 | 41,969 | 43,283 |
| Other | 577 | 454 | 715 |
| Net Revenue | 40,954 | 42,423 | 43,998 |
| **Operating Expenses:** | | | |
| Car Hire & Car Leases | 5,723 | 6,308 | 6,439 |
| Fuel | 3,381 | 3,492 | 3,606 |
| Accident Expense + Insurance | 3,831 | 3,559 | 4,354 |
| Transportation | 7,288 | 8,232 | 8,174 |
| Maint. of Way (Inc. Prop. Tax) | 3,515 | 3,711 | 3,849 |
| Maint. of Equipment | 1,952 | 1,959 | 1,964 |
| Total Operating Expenses | 25,690 | 27,261 | 28,386 |
| Gross Profit | 15,264 | 15,162 | 15,612 |
| **General & Admin. Expenses:** | | | |
| Wages & Benefits | 2,049 | 2,113 | 2,284 |
| Professional Fees (Inc. Audit) | 599 | 1,400 | 984 |
| Other | 382 | 186 | 151 |
| Other Expenses (Income) | (164) | (689) | (366) |
| **EBITDA** | 12,398 | 12,152 | 12,559 |
| Adjustments | (1,029) | 0 | 7,484 |
| **Adjusted EBITDA** | 11,369 | 12,152 | 20,043 |
| Depreciation & Amortization | 3,314 | 3,482 | 3,945 |
| **EBIT** | 8,055 | 8,670 | 16,098 |
| Interest-Revolver(net of int. income) | (10) | 108 | 92 |
| Interest-Westinghouse | 2,319 | 1,924 | 823 |
| Interest-CNW | 991 | 1,350 | 742 |
| Interest-Government Loans | 249 | 273 | 207 |
| Interest-First Bank/Tifco/Etc. | 148 | 151 | 175 |
| Interest-New Debt | 0 | 0 | 1558 |
| **EBT** | 4,358 | 4,864 | 12,501 |
| Income Tax | 895 | 1,800 | 4,715 |
| **Net Income** | 3,463 | 3,064 | 7,786 |
| Less Preferred Dividends-Reg | 186 | 187 | 187 |
| Net Income Available to Common | 3,277 | 2,877 | 7,599 |

Source: Company records

ing the first five months of 1995, operating revenues were $16.7 million or $72,000 over budget. At the same time, carloadings increased slightly over the same period in 1994.[8] Exhibit 8 presents income statement data for years 1992–1994.

## Revenues

Traffic volume during 1992–1994 decreased in seven of 12 commodity groups with an overall decrease of 8.3 percent. The largest increases were in bentonite clay, wheat, wheat flour, woodchips, and soybean oil. Major decreases in corn and soybeans are attributable to weather and market conditions rather than to loss to other transportation modes. Higher gross revenues were due to increased traffic in commodities that command higher per car charges such as bentonite clay, lumber, wheat, and wood chips.

## Operating Expenses

These expenses rose 10.4 percent between 1992 and 1994. Increased traffic coupled with roadbed problems increased expenses in all six categories. Expenses during the first five months of 1995 exceeded budget by $600,000. This overrun was due to accident costs.[9]

## Liquidity and Capital Resources

Cash generated from operations is the DM&E's primary source of liquidity and is used principally for debt service, capital expenditures, and working capital requirements. The DM&E was highly leveraged at start-up and has been forced to ask continually for federal, state, and local financing to assist in roadbed maintenance. Governmental loans are at approximately three percent and have a delayed principal payment feature. The July 1994 private placement of 13 year 10.13 fixed rate senior secured notes totaling $32 million enabled the DM&E to refinance older senior obligations, some carrying a 13 percent interest rate. The DM&E recorded a gain of $4,660,813 net of tax on this transaction and it is carried as an extraordinary item in the 1994 income statement. The DM&E continues to pay down its senior debt and as of April 1, 1995, had reduced its debt to equity ratio to 2.4 to 1. The ideal railroad debt to equity ratio is 2 to 1. The South Dakota revenue bond issue requires the DM&E to not exceed a 3 to 1 debt to equity ratio. See Exhibit 9 for balance sheet information for 1992–1994.

# EXTERNAL ENVIRONMENT

## ▪ Competition

The DM&E's operations are subject to competition from railroads and trucks.

## Rail

There are several local and three major railroads that have lines in or near the DM&E service area.

**C&NW.** As mentioned earlier, the C&NW has played a sort of Jekyll and Hyde role during most of DM&E's existence. One of the most unusual twists in

**Exhibit 9**

**Dakota, Minnesota & Eastern Railroad
Balance Sheets 1992–1994 ($000)**

|  | *1992* | *1993* | *1994* |
|---|---|---|---|
| *Assets* | | | |
| Cash | 1,231 | 575 | 5,316 |
| Accounts Receivable | 6,555 | 8,582 | 7,530 |
| Materials & Supplies Inventory | 417 | 590 | 1,634 |
| Prepaid Expenses | 574 | 1,043 | 888 |
| Total Current Assets | 8,777 | 10,790 | 15,368 |
| PP&E-Net | 53,369 | 56,545 | 63,848 |
| Capitalized Leases-Net | 0 | 0 | 0 |
| Deferred Fin. & Other Assets | 1,062 | 4,579 | 3,167 |
| Total Assets | 63,208 | 71,914 | 82,383 |
| *Liabilities and Stockholders' Equity* | | | |
| Accounts Payable-Trade | 1,834 | 2,522 | 1,210 |
| Accts Pay-Intnl+Contract Allow | 1,158 | 1,664 | 1,618 |
| Car Hire Payable | 591 | 985 | 890 |
| Notes Payable | 286 | 257 | 257 |
| Wages & Benefits Payable | 1,519 | 1,835 | 1,946 |
| Interest Payable | 495 | 252 | 1,560 |
| Other Accrued Liability | 2,858 | 2,401 | 2,497 |
| Total Current Liabilities | 8,741 | 9,916 | 9,978 |
| Deferred Income Tax Liability | 4,784 | 6,450 | 10,904 |
| Revolving Loan | 2,000 | 2,000 | 2,650 |
| Westinghouse Term Loans | 16,105 | 12,849 | 0 |
| CNW Term Loan | 7,388 | 8,947 | 0 |
| Government Loans-Net | 10,652 | 13,930 | 7,317 |
| First Bank | 313 | 435 | 220 |
| New Debt | 0 | 0 | 33,393 |
| Other Liabilities | 874 | 1,972 | 258 |
| Total Liabilities | 50,857 | 56,499 | 64,720 |
| Preferred Stock | 2,025 | 2,212 | 2,399 |
| Senior Preferred Stock | 0 | 0 | 0 |
| Common Stock | 3,290 | 3,290 | 2,758 |
| Retained Earnings | 7,203 | 10,080 | 12,673 |
| Treasury Stock | (167) | (167) | (167) |
| Total Stockholders' Equity | 12,351 | 15,415 | 17,663 |
| Total Liab. & Stockholders' Equity | 63,208 | 71,914 | 82,383 |

Source: Company Records

this saga occurred in July 1992 when the C&NW unexpectedly backed out of an earlier agreement to sell the "Colony Line" to the DM&E for $6.3 million.

A possible reason for C&NW's action took place a month later when UP requested Interstate Commerce Commission (ICC) approval to acquire ownership of the C&NW. The addition of the most powerful railroad in the United States to the C&NW equation would, in the DM&E's opinion, severely restrict its already limited operational freedom. As a result, the DM&E intervened in the ICC proceedings requesting:[10]

1. Enforcement of the sale of the Colony Line.
2. Removal of interchange restrictions at Winona, Mankato, Owatonna, and Mason City.
3. Allowing direct service to shippers at Winona and access to shippers via reciprocal switching agreement at the other three cities.
4. Modifying the car supply agreement which requires the DM&E to use C&NW cars while at the same time not requiring the C&NW to furnish them. The DM&E could use cars from any source without C&NW penalty.

Later DM&E-C&NW negotiations resulted in an agreement whereby the C&NW relinquished its financial investment in the DM&E, thus enabling DM&E to refinance under more favorable terms; guaranteed all "Colony Line" traffic would be turned over to the DM&E; relaxed interchange restrictions in Mason City and agreed to the establishment of a committee to resolve operating disputes. Unresolved problems would be subject to binding arbitration. There would be monetary penalties if DM&E trains were unduly delayed operating over C&NW track. Lastly, DM&E would retain right of first refusal should the "Colony Line" be offered for sale. Also, C&NW would be given preference in any proposed sale of DM&E.[11] As a result of this December 1993 agreement, DM&E withdrew its opposition to UP gaining control of C&NW.

Subsequent ICC approval led to UP's purchase of C&NW on April 1995 and the beginnings of a new relationship for DM&E. A late May meeting between the two roads went well and UP promised to honor the agreements that C&NW had made with DM&E. The topic of future line sales to DM&E was discussed. UP has traditionally avoided owning lines that were separated from the rest of its rail system. This fact may enhance the DM&E's chances of buying the Colony Line and the former C&NW railyard in Winona. These purchases would give the DM&E ownership of both ends of its rail line and permit better control of soliciting, scheduling, and routing of freight. Resultant revenue increases would be substantial. McIntyre feels that there will be no quick resolution to these line purchases.[12]

**Other.**  Conversely, as major carriers continue selling off ancillary lines, there remains the opportunities for smaller railroads to pick up complementary trackage. The UP(C&NW)'s Minneapolis-Sioux City Iowa branch (277 miles), the CP's corn lines across southern Minnesota (112 miles) and northern Iowa to the Mississippi River (253 miles), and BN's Sioux City to Aberdeen, South Dakota, route (265 miles) may fit this category for the DM&E.[13]

## Trucks

Trucks carry a greater share of intercity traffic than do railroads. Their innate flexibility, relatively low capital requirements, and huge network of tax-supported highways gives them great advantage in smaller volume and under

500-mile shipments. Railroads are very competitive in bulk shipments over long distances. Intermodal shipments (truck or container on rail flatcar) often offer the advantages of both modes to shippers.[14] The DM&E faces the strongest truck competition in Minnesota.

## ▪ Weather

DM&E's location in the upper Midwest will always subject the railroad to weather extremes. While the "flood of 1993" caused extensive crop damage, the moderate temperatures and rainfall in 1994 resulted in bumper crops in both South Dakota and Minnesota. The spring of 1995 was the wettest on record for South Dakota. As planting deadlines for small grains such as wheat and oats passed, farmers switched planting plans to include more corn and soybeans. Given a normal growing season with no early frost, harvest yields are expected to be average.[15] While the DM&E does not expect the level of traffic that resulted from the 1994 crop, they do not anticipate a significant decrease in traffic revenue due to the wet spring.

## ▪ Economic

### South Dakota

Agriculture remains the economic mainstay of the state, while agribusiness, processing of forest products, and mining make significant contributions. Due to this industry mix combined with the absence of a strong manufacturing base, South Dakota's economy tends to be affected less than the national average during times of both economic upswings and downturns. Per capita personal income percent change in 1993–94 found South Dakota, at 9.5%, to be one of the fastest growing states. Although per capita personal income is growing, at $19,577 in 1994, it remains below the national average of $21,809. Increases in both farm and nonfarm income were near or above average and the state enjoyed above average increases in earnings in both durables and nondurables manufacturing.[16] Noteworthy is that although the state had the number one increase in average annual pay in 1994, it continues to rank last in overall average annual pay.[17]South Dakota is forecasted to experience the region's fastest job growth in 1995, due primarily to gains in manufacturing, business, and financial services.[18]

### Minnesota

Minnesota is a leading agricultural state with a strong industrial base. It is becoming increasingly urban and is considered the commercial center of the upper Midwest. The state's economy revolves around a steady flow of products from factories, forests, and farms, supplemented by income from mining and marketing.[19] Per capita personal income percent change in 1993–94 found Minnesota, at 7.0%, to be one of the fastest growing states. The average per capita personal income in 1994 was $22,453, above the national average of $21,809. Increases in both farm and nonfarm income were near or above average, and the state enjoyed above average increases in earnings and in both durables and nondurables manufacturing.[20]

## ■ Legal/Political

The DM&E is subject to various federal, state, and local laws and regulations pertaining, in varying degrees, to almost every phase of its operations.

### Federal

Government programs and policies which influence the strength of the dollar, export enhancement, crop support prices, and interest rates greatly affect the agricultural sector of the economy and therefore the DM&E. Major federal legislation aimed specifically at rail industry enhancement includes:

1. The 1976 Railroad Revitalization and Regulatory Reform Act (4Rs)—freed the railroads of 75 year old regulations that may have been appropriate before the coming of the truck and airplane. Railroads were permitted greater flexibility in rate making, abandonments, mergers, and line sales. Federal funds were provided through state agencies to rehabilitate needed rail trackage. Individual states were required to become involved in rail planning.

2. The Staggers Rail Act of 1980 furthered the work of the 4R's Act. It further streamlined the mechanics of restructuring the physical rail system and rail rate structure. It allowed railroads either to increase net revenues on unprofitable branchlines or to redirect traffic and abandon them.

3. Rural Rail Infrastructure Act of 1995 has been introduced by South Dakota Senator Pressler. The act would mandate $25 million a year in matching fund grants to the states and provide for $500 million in funded loan guarantees. These monies are aimed principally for secondary rail lines like the DM&E.

Other pertinent federal legislation is:

1. Highway Trust Fund—Has subsidized truck use of the highway network. Over $125 billion is to be spent exclusively on highways over the next five years while railroad support under the 4R's Act is running at $8–10 million a year.

2. Federal Employees' Liability Act—Is a form of workers' compensation mandated for the railroad industry. Unlike workers' compensation, it is an adversarial system rather than no-fault. As a result, average cost per employee hour worked is $1.51 for railroads and $0.27 for the rest of American industry.

3. Railroad Retirement Act—Requires larger contributions from railroads than from employers under the social security system.

4. Safety User Fees—Railroads must fund federal safety inspections of their track and equipment ($32 million in 1992) while truck and barge competitors do not have this requirement.

### South Dakota

The state has a history of support for the rail industry. In 1973, the governor appointed a task force to recommend changes in state taxation and regulation of railroads in order to lessen their financial plight. It was hoped this would reduce the need for branch line abandonment. The state later used 4R's Act funding to help rehabilitate critical branch lines. In 1979, the state legislature moved rail regulatory authority to the Department of Transportation and authorized the use of state funds to purchase rail properties from private companies. The state subsequently purchased over 1,000 miles of track of what became known as the state core system. Since then, several hundred miles have been sold to BN or leased to local rail operators. The BN is under contract to operate the 368 miles remaining in the state core system.

The DM&E has used state 4R's Act funding to refurbish the RedfieldMansfield branch and 12 miles of the Huron to Watertown line. The DM&E enjoys strong political support in both states. In South Dakota, the governor's office, state senators, and representatives have all taken a positive and active role. The 1995 act authorizing $35 million of state revenue bonds has been mentioned elsewhere. U.S. Senator Pressler is a powerful advocate at the federal level.

## Minnesota

Minnesota has been politically supportive, particularly monetarily through its Rail Service Improvement Program. The State Rail Plan is the principal legislative vehicle for supporting the rail industry. This plan uses the 4R's Act and state funds to assist in the acquisition and rehabilitation of rail lines and subsidization of continued rail service. The state has used over $25 million of its own monies to supplement 4R's Act grants. Funds are distributed to approved rail rehabilitation projects via the Minnesota Rail Service Improvement Program. Project funding is as follows:

| | | |
|---|---|---|
| 70% | State Funds | (Some of which are federal dollars. This is a low-interest loan program. Typical is 3% interest, 10 year payback.) |
| 10% | Shippers | (Loan—no interest, negotiable payback. DM&E bases payback on number of carloads shipped. A 3-4 year payback period is typical. Shippers are paid back first, then the state.) |
| 20% | Railroad | (Is the minimum they must contribute—it may be the balance of the project, in the case of cost overruns.) |

The DM&E used over $6.3 million to fund projects through 1990. During 1993–1995, it will utilize an additional $5.7 million for track rehabilitation.

## ■ Planning For The Future

Pete McIntyre's day was soon filled with the normal business of a busy executive. He spent several hours gathering and dispersing information, making decisions, and checking on the progress of previous ones. It was late afternoon before he got back to his earlier thoughts of the railroad's future. Pete reached in his lower left drawer, pulled out his copy of the 1995 DM&E Strategic Audit and Plan, and began searching for a pencil.

## GLOSSARY

**Bridge route** A railroad that serves as a connection that joins two or more noncontiguous rail lines.

**Car hire** The renting of freight cars from another railroad. Charges are computed on a daily basis.

**Commercial trains** DM&E terminology for thru freights. A thru freight is a train that makes infrequent stops along its assigned route. Such stops are normally for changing operating crews.

**Gateway** A rail center where freight cars from connecting railroads are interchanged.

**Intermodal** Freight that is moved by differing modes of transportation enroute to its destination.

**Local traffic** Freight that originates and terminates on the trackage of the same railroad.

**Local freight** A train that services customers along the rail line. Such service includes the delivery and pick up of empty or loaded freight cars. This type of train relieves the commercial or thru freight of such duties.

**Originating traffic** Freight that originates on one railroad but is interchanged with another in order to reach its final destination.

**Overhead traffic** Freight received from one railroad for delivery to a second railroad.

**Sort and block** The arranging of freight cars so they will be in order for delivery to individual customers, destinations, or connecting railroads.

**Terminating traffic** Freight that is received from another railroad for delivery to its final destination.

**Trackage rights** A right to use the tracks of another railroad. A rights fee is normally charged.

**Waybill** A document, prepared by the carrier of freight, that contains details of the shipment, route, and charges.

# REFERENCES

1. Association of American Railroads, *Railroad Facts: 1994 Edition*, Economics and Finance Department, Washington, D.C., p. 32.
2. *Ibid.*, p. 32.
3. "DM&E Seeks Access to C&NW Track," *DM&E Enroute*, May 1993, p. 1.
4. Interviews with President John C. "Pete" McIntyre, Dakota, Minnesota & Eastern Railroad Corporation, May-June 1995.
5. Interviews with Vice President Marketing Lynn A. Anderson, Dakota, Minnesota & Eastern Railroad Corporation, May-July 1995.
6. McIntyre, Interviews, May-June 1995.
7. Interviews with numerous DM&E officials, August 1992, May-June 1993, May-June 1995.
8. "DM&E Meets Revenue Goal, Expense Up," *DM&E Enroute*, June 1995, p. 2.
9. *Ibid.*, p. 2.
10. "DM&E and NorthWestern Face Off," *Trains*, August 1993, p. 18.
11. "DM&E, C&NW Sign Colony Line Pact," *DM&E Enroute*, January 1994, p. 1.
12. McIntyre, Interviews, July 1995.
13. South Dakota Bureau of Finance and Management, *Economic and Revenue Forecast*, February 9, 1993, p. 1.

14. Helming, Bill. "The U.S. and Global Economy Outlook," prepared for the Annual Agricultural/Commercial Credit Conference Meeting of the South Dakota Bankers Association, April 7, 1995.

15. South Dakota Bureau of Finance and Management, *Economic and Revenue Forecast*, February 15, 1995, p. 2.

16. Bureau of Economic Analysis, "Per Capita Personal Income Growth in 1994," Economics and Statistics Administration, US Department of Commerce News, April 27, 1995, p. 3.

17. "Business Climate Rated: South Dakota's Economy Gets Average Grades," *Brookings Register,* May 25, 1995, pp. A1-2.

18. South Dakota Bureau of Finance and Management, *Economic and Revenue Forecast*, February 15, 1995, p. 2.

19. Bureau of Economic Analysis, "Per Capita Personal Income Growth Picked Up in 44 States in 1992," Economics and Statistics Administration, US Department of Commerce News, April 27, 1993, Table 2.

20. Bureau of Economic Analysis, "Per Capita Personal Income Growth in 1994," Economics and Statistics Administration, US Department of Commerce News, April 27, 1995, p. 1.

# HealthSouth Corporation

W. Jack Duncan, University of Alabama at Birmingham

Peter M. Ginter, University of Alabama at Birmingham

Michael D. Martin, HealthSouth Corporation

Kellie F. Snell, HealthSouth Corporation

Richard M. Scrushy, chairman and CEO of HealthSouth Corporation, was not surprised by many things when it came to his business. The April 22, 1996, issue of Forbes magazine, however, surprised even him. Forbes listed HealthSouth as the nation's fourth-largest company in market value growth in 1995, and as the two hundred thirty-third largest U.S.-based company in terms of market value. HealthSouth grew by 298 percent in market value in 1995,162 surpassed only by Ascend Communications, U.S. Robotics, and FORE Systems. Scrushy stated that he "was just surprised because I would have thought there would be more than three companies that outgrew us in market value growth." He was elated that the company he founded only thirteen years ago was now on lists with "big conglomerates we've known about our entire life."

HealthSouth Corporation was the nation's largest provider of outpatient and rehabilitative health care services, as well as the largest ambulatory surgery center provider. The company changed its name from HealthSouth Rehabilitation Corporation to HealthSouth Corporation (HC) to indicate clearly that it was not just a rehabilitation company anymore. HealthSouth, listed on the New York Stock Exchange, was second only to Columbia/HCA in the health care industry. At the close of 1995, HealthSouth operated over 700 locations throughout the United States and Canada. Its goal was simple: "To be the dominant outpatient health care provider in the nation's top 300 cities with 100,000 or more population."

HealthSouth Corporation was one of the most successful business ventures in modern health care. The Corporation's growth can be described as nothing less than "explosive" since its acquisition of National Medical

Enterprise's rehabilitation business in December 1993. Yet, growth involves its own challenge and explosive growth involves even greater challenges. As Scrushy reviewed selected operating results at the end of 1995 (Exhibits 1-3), and reflected on the company's position as it neared the end of its first decade of growth, he wondered about HealthSouth's future.

The ultimate direction of health care reform remained uncertain. Would there be significantly more competition in the rehabilitation market? Scrushy realized that, to sustain growth, continued hard work was even more necessary than during the startup period. Additionally, he realized that some key strategic decisions would have to be made: What was the optimum mix of businesses for HealthSouth Corporation? How far should HealthSouth go with its integrative "virtual hospital" model? What pitfalls lie ahead? Can success continue?

## BEGINNING OF SUCCESS

HealthSouth Rehabilitation Corporation was organized in 1983 as AMCARE, Inc., but in 1985 changed its name to HealthSouth Rehabilitation Corporation (HRC). The company was founded by a group of health care professionals, led by Scrushy, who were formerly with LifeMark Corporation, a large publicly held, for-profit health care services chain that was acquired by American Medical International (AMI) in 1984.

In 1982, Richard Scrushy reflected on how he first recognized the potential for rehabilitation services: "I saw the TEFRA (Tax Equity and Fiscal Responsibility Act) guidelines and the upcoming implementation of Medicare's prospective payment system as creating a need for outpatient rehabilitation services. It was rather clear that lengths of stay in general hospitals would decrease and that patients would be discharged more quickly than in the past. It became obvious to me that these changes would create a need for a transition between the hospital and the patient's home." Medicare provided financial incentives for outpatient rehabilitation services by giving comprehensive outpatient rehabilitation facilities (CORFs) an exemption from prospective payment systems, and allowed the services of these facilities to continue to be reimbursed on a retrospective, cost-based basis.

"I also saw that LifeMark, my current employer, would suffer significant reductions in profitability as the use of the then-lucrative ancillary inpatient services was discouraged under the new reimbursement guidelines. I discussed my concerns about the upcoming changes in Medicare with Life-Mark management and proposed that we develop a chain of outpatient rehabilitation centers. I saw that the centers I proposed were LifeMark's chance to preserve its profitability under PPS, and when they rejected my proposal, I saw cutbacks and a low rate of advancement in the future," Scrushy confirmed.

"I repeated my proposal for AMI's management when it acquired LifeMark, but AMI could not implement the program immediately after such a major acquisition. I resigned and founded HealthSouth Rehabilitation Corporation in conjunction with three of my colleagues from LifeMark."

**Exhibit 1**

## HealthSouth Corporation and Subsidiaries
### Consolidated Balance Sheets

| Assets | December 31, 1994 ($000) | December 31, 1995 ($000) |
|---|---|---|
| Current Assets: | | |
| Cash & Cash Equivalents | $ 73,438 | $ 104,896 |
| Other Marketable Securities | 16,628 | 4,077 |
| Accounts Receivable, Net of Allowances for Doubtful Accounts & Contractual Adjustments of $147,435,000 in 1994 and $212,972,000 in 1995 | 246,983 | 336,818 |
| Inventories | 27,398 | 33,504 |
| Prepaid Expenses & Other Current Assets | 69,092 | 70,888 |
| Deferred Income Taxes | 3,073 | 13,257 |
| Total Current Assets | 436,612 | 563,440 |
| Other Assets: | | |
| Loans to Officers | 1,240 | 1,525 |
| Other | 41,834 | 60,437 |
| Property, Plant, and Equipment—Net | 872,795 | 1,100,212 |
| Intangible Assets—Net | 426,458 | 734,515 |
| Total Assets | $ 1,778,939 | $ 2,460,129 |
| **Liabilities & Stockholders' Equity** | | |
| Current Liabilities: | | |
| Accounts Payable | $ 88,413 | 90,427 |
| Salaries & Wages Payable | 34,848 | 59,540 |
| Accrued Interest Payable & Other Liabilities | 57,351 | 58,086 |
| Current Portion of Long-Term Debt | 19,123 | 27,913 |
| Total Current Liabilities | 199,735 | 235,966 |
| Long-Term Debt | 1,032,941 | 1,253,374 |
| Deferred Income Taxes | 9,104 | 15,436 |
| Other Long-Term Liabilities | 9,451 | 5,375 |
| Deferred Revenue | 7,526 | 1,525 |
| Minority Interests-Limited Partnerships | 15,959 | 20,743 |
| Commitments & Contingent Liabilities | | |
| Stockholders' Equity: | | |
| Preferred Stock, $.01 Par Value—1,500,000 Shares Authorized; Issued and Outstanding—None | | |
| Common Stock, $.01 Par Value—150,000,000 Shares Authorized; Issued 78,858,000 in 1994 and 97,359,000 in 1995 | 789 | 974 |
| Additional Paid-In Capital | 388,269 | 740,763 |
| Retained Earnings | 138,205 | 208,653 |
| Treasury Stock, At Cost (91,000 Shares) | (323) | (323) |
| Receivable from Employee Stock Ownership Plan | (17,477) | (15,886) |
| Notes Receivable from Stockholders | (5,240) | (6,471) |
| Total Stockholders' Equity | 504,223 | 927,710 |
| Total Liabilities & Stockholders' Equity | $ 1,778,939 | $ 2,460,129 |

**Exhibit 2**

**HealthSouth Corporation and Subsidiaries**
**Consolidated Statements of Income**
**(in thousands except for per share amounts)**

|  | December 31, 1994 | December 31, 1995 |
|---|---|---|
| Revenues | $ 1,274,365 | $ 1,556,687 |
| Operating Expenses: | 930,845 | 1,087,554 |
| Operating Units Corporate General & Administrative | 48,606 | 42,514 |
| Provision for Doubtful Accounts | 27,646 | 31,637 |
| Depreciation & Amortization | 89,305 | 121,195 |
| Interest Expense | 66,874 | 91,693 |
| Interest Income | (4,566) | (5,879) |
| Merger & Acquisition Related Expenses | 6,520 | 34,159 |
| Loss on Impairment of Assets | 10,500 | 11,192 |
| Loss on Abandonment of Computer Project | 4,500 | — |
|  | 1,180,230 | 1,414,065 |
| Income Before Income Taxes & Minority Interests | 94,135 | 142,622 |
| Provision for Income Taxes | 34,778 | 48,091 |
|  | 59,357 | 94,531 |
| Minority Interests | 8,864 | 15,582 |
| Net Income | $ 50,493 | $ 78,949 |
| Weighted Average Common & Common Equivalent Share | 86,461 | 94,246 |
| Net Income Per Common and Common Equivalent Share | $ 0.58 | $ 0.84 |
| Net Income Per Common Share Assuming Full Dilution | $ 0.58 | $ 0.82 |

■ **Early Development**

HealthSouth Corporation began operations in January 1984. Its initial focus was on the establishment of a national network of outpatient rehabilitation facilities supported by a rehabilitation equipment business. In September 1984, HC opened its first outpatient rehabilitation facility at Little Rock, Arkansas, followed by another one at Birmingham, Alabama, in December 1984. Within five years, the Company was operating twenty-nine outpatient facilities located in seventeen states throughout the Southeastern United States. By the end of 1995, HealthSouth operated in more than 700 locations—from California to New Hampshire, from Florida to Wisconsin, and into Canada. Business was booming. In June 1985, HC started providing inpatient rehabilitation services with the acquisition of an 88-bed facility in Florence, South Carolina. During the next five years, the company established eleven more inpatient facilities in nine states, with a twelfth under development.

**Exhibit 3**

**HealthSouth Corporation and Subsidiaries
Consolidated Statements of Stockholders' Equity**

| | Common Shares | Common Stock | Add. Paid-In Capital | Retained Earnings | Treasury Stock | Receivable ESOP | Notes Received from Stock-holders | Total Stock-holders' Equity |
|---|---|---|---|---|---|---|---|---|
| Balance - December 31, 1994 | $ 78,767 | $788.6 | $ 388,269 | $ 138,205 | $(323) | $ (17,477) | $(5,240) | $ 504,223 |
| Adjustment for ReLife Merger | 2,732 | 27.3 | 7,114 | (3,734) | 0 | 0 | 0 | 3,407 |
| Proceeds from Issuance of Common Shares | 14,950 | 149.5 | 330,229 | 0 | 0 | 0 | 0 | 330,379 |
| Proceeds from Exercise of Options | 819 | 8.2 | 8,499 | 0 | 0 | 0 | 0 | 8,507 |
| Income Tax Benefits Related to Incentive Stock Options | 0 | 0 | 6,653 | 0 | 0 | 0 | 0 | 6,653 |
| Reduction in Receivable from Employee Stock Ownership Plan | 0 | 0 | 0 | 0 | 0 | 1,591 | 0 | 1,591 |
| Increase in Stockholders' Notes Receivable | 0 | 0 | 0 | 0 | 0 | 0 | (1,231) | (1,231) |
| Purchase of Limited Partnership Units | 0 | 0 | 0 | (4,767) | 0 | 0 | 0 | (4,767) |
| Net Income | 0 | 0 | 0 | 78,949 | 0 | 0 | 0 | 78,949 |
| Balance - December 31, 1995 | $ 97,268 | $ 973.6 | $ 740,764 | $ 208,653 | $ (323) | $ (15,886) | $ (6,471) | $ 927,710 |

■ **South Highlands Hospital**

A key development in HealthSouth's growth strategy was the December 1989 acquisition of the 219-bed South Highlands Hospital in Birmingham, Alabama. Although South Highlands had been marginally profitable, its inability to obtain financing meant that it was unable to meet the needs of its physicians, particularly James Andrews and William Clancy, both world-renowned orthopedic surgeons. As Scrushy noted: "My immediate concern was to maintain the referral base that Drs. Andrews and Clancy provided. HC had benefited from the rehabilitation referrals stemming from the extensive orthopedic surgery performed at South Highlands. The surgeons needed a major expansion at South Highlands to practice at maximum effectiveness and Drs. Andrews and Clancy would seek the facilities they needed elsewhere if something wasn't done. On the surface our acquisition of South Highlands was defensive."

The purchase of South Highlands Hospital for approximately $27 million was far from a defensive move. Renamed HealthSouth Medical Center (HMC), this hospital was developed into a flagship facility. HC immediately began construction of a $30 million addition to the hospital. Even during construction, referrals continued to flow from HMC to other HC facilities. The construction created interest in the medical community, which in turn created business. The emergency facility at HMC eliminated the necessity of delaying evaluation and treatment of athletic injuries that could be quickly transferred to the facility through HC's extensive linkages with 396 high school and college athletic programs.

The acquisition of additional medical centers is an outgrowth of Health-South's rehabilitative services. The medical centers provide general and specialty health care services emphasizing orthopedics, sports medicine, and rehabilitation. In each market where a medical center has been acquired, HealthSouth enjoyed well-established relationships with the medical communities serving the facility. Following each acquisition, it has been HealthSouth's goal to provide resources for improving the physical plant and expanding services through the introduction of new technology. All HealthSouth medical centers are JCAHO accredited and participate in the Medicare prospective payment system. At the end of 1995, the company's inpatient facilities achieved an overall bed utilization rate of just over 70 percent.

## ■ Surgery Centers

As the result of the acquisition of Surgical Health Corporation (SHC), Sutter Surgery Centers, Inc. (SSCI), and Surgical Care Affiliates, Inc. (SCA), Health-South became the largest operator of outpatient surgery centers in the United States. At the end of 1995, HC operated over 100 free-standing surgery centers, with others under development. Most of these facilities were located in markets served by the company's outpatient and rehabilitative service facilities, creating the potential for significant synergies through cross-referrals between surgery and rehabilitative facilities as well as centralization of administrative services. The entry of the outpatient surgery market provided an important ingredient in the realization of HealthSouth's integrated service model illustrated in Exhibit 4. In light of developments in managed care, this integrated service model offered payers convenience and cost-effectiveness because they could deal with a single provider for a variety of services (one stop shopping). With this model, Scrushy noted: "We are laying the foundation for Health-South to be the health care company for the twenty-first century. We are establishing the platform on which we will build. Health care in the next century will not be based on the traditional hospital model. Rather, the emphasis will be less intrusive surgical interventions, more efficient diagnostic procedures, and less restrictive environments." According to Scrushy, "Health care in the future will develop around the virtual hospital—an integrated service delivery model that replaces many of the functions of the acute-care hospital with lower-cost outpatient facilities."

**Exhibit 4**                    **Integrated Service Model**

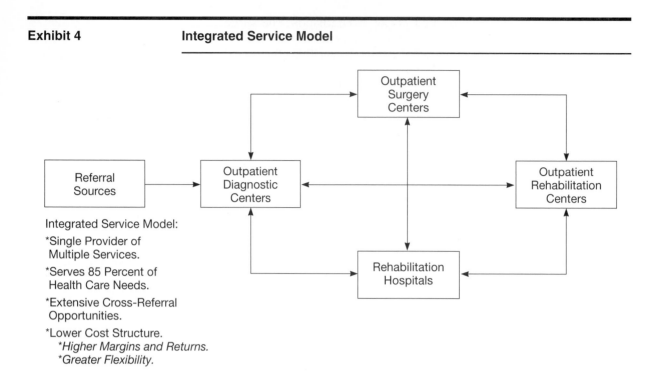

Integrated Service Model:

*Single Provider of
 Multiple Services.

*Serves 85 Percent of
 Health Care Needs.

*Extensive Cross-Referral
 Opportunities.

*Lower Cost Structure.
  *Higher Margins and Returns.
  *Greater Flexibility.

# INDUSTRY OVERVIEW

Every year more than 4 million people need rehabilitative health care services as the result of automobile and industrial accidents, sports and recreational injuries, crime and violence, or cardiac, stroke, and cancer episodes. It is estimated that at any particular time, 13 percent of the U.S. population and almost one-half of Americans over 75 years of age require some form of rehabilitative health services. With the population aging, this suggests even higher demand for rehabilitative health services in the future.

Medical rehabilitation involves the treatment of physical limitations through which therapists seek to improve their patients' functional independence, relieve pain, and ameliorate any permanent disabilities. Patients using medical rehabilitation services include the handicapped and those recovering from automobile, sports, and other accidents; strokes; neurological injuries; surgery; fractures and disabilities associated with diseases; and conditions such as multiple sclerosis, cerebral palsy, arthritis, and heart disease. Over 80 percent of those people receiving rehabilitative health care services return to their homes, work, schools, or active retirement.

## ■ Rehabilitation Services

Medical rehabilitation provider services include inpatient rehabilitation in dedicated freestanding hospitals and distinct units of acute-care hospitals; comprehensive outpatient rehabilitation facilities; specialty rehabilitation programs (such as traumatic brain injury and spinal cord injury); pediatric rehabilitation; occupational and industrial rehabilitation; and rehabilitation agencies.

The availability of comprehensive rehabilitation services was limited in the United States. Provision of rehabilitation services by outpatient departments of acute-care hospitals was fragmented because services were provided through several departments, and private practice therapists rarely provided a full-range of comprehensive rehabilitation services. Often, patients requiring multidisciplinary services would be treated by different therapists in different locations, which could result in uncoordinated care.

Comprehensive inpatient rehabilitation services were provided by freestanding rehabilitation hospitals, distinct units in acute-care hospitals, and skilled nursing facilities. Analysts with Solomon Brothers estimated that the rehabilitation services segment of the health care industry in the United States would grow at a rate of 13 to 15 percent in 1996 and that HealthSouth Corporation should increase its earnings per share by 20-22 percent over the next three years, therefore significantly outperforming the rehabilitation market in general. A number of factors would drive industry growth and ultimately affect HC's performance.

The incidence of major disability increases with age. Improvements in medical care have enabled more people with severe disabilities to live longer. Data compiled by the National Center for Health Statistics showed that, in 1995, 35 million people in the United States (one out of every seven people) had some form of disability. The National Association of Insurance Commissioners pointed out that seven out of ten workers would suffer a long-term disability between the ages of 35 and 65. Increases in leisure time among the middle age population resulted in more physical activity and thus more sports injuries, a major portion of HealthSouth's business. At the same time, the greater proportion of the population in the elderly age group increased the demand for rehabilitation services associated with the elderly, such as treatments for strokes and amputations. As a direct result of improved technology, three million people a year survive automobile crashes, sports injuries, strokes, and heart attacks and require rehabilitation services to restore normal functions.

Purchasers and providers of health care services, such as insurance companies, health maintenance organizations, businesses, and industry were seeking economical, high-quality alternatives to traditional health care services. Rehabilitation services, whether outpatient or inpatient, represented such an alternative. Often early participation in a disabled person's rehabilitation prevented a short-term problem from becoming a long-term disability. Moreover, by returning the individual to the work force, the number of disability benefit payments was reduced, thus decreasing long-term disability costs. Independent studies by companies such as Northwestern Life have shown that of every dollar spent on rehabilitation a savings of $30 occurred in disability payments. Insurance companies generally agreed that every rehabilitation dollar spent on patients with serious functional impairments saved from $10 to $30 in long-term health care costs such as nursing care.

As noted previously, inpatient rehabilitation services, organized as either dedicated rehabilitation hospitals or distinct units, were eligible for exemptions from Medicare's prospective payment system. Outpatient rehabilitation services, organized as comprehensive outpatient rehabilitation facilities or rehabilitation agencies, were eligible to participate in the Medicare program under cost-based reimbursement. Inpatient and outpatient rehabilitation services were typically covered for payment by the major medical portion of commercial health insurance policies. Moreover, Medicare reimbursement and the policies of private insurance companies encouraged early discharge from acute care hospitals, thereby providing opportunities for outpatient rehabilitation, home health, and long-term-care facilities.

Advances in medical science and trauma care made it possible to save the lives of numbers of victims of accidents, greater violence, and serious sports injuries. These victims were provided with therapeutic options that offered opportunities for inpatient and outpatient rehabilitation facilities. Although HealthSouth is no longer simply a rehabilitation company, rehabilitative services remained the core of its integrated systems model. Expansion into medical centers and outpatient surgery augment and capitalize on the company's reputation and relationships in the markets it served.

## ■ Rehabilitation and Outpatient Surgery

At the close of 1992, HealthSouth's primary rehabilitation services competitors were National Medical Enterprises, Inc., Continental Medical Systems, ReLife, NovaCare, and AdvantageHealth. By the beginning of 1996, HealthSouth had acquired all of these competitors except CMS. It is estimated that HealthSouth presently controls about 40 percent of the rehabilitation beds and approximately 12 percent of the outpatient rehabilitation beds.

Within one year of entry into the market, HealthSouth became the industry leader in ambulatory surgical centers. According to Alex Brown & Sons, of the roughly 2,100 freestanding ambulatory surgery centers approximately 75 percent were single-site and physician owned. This market, in other words, was highly fragmented and represented a major opportunity for HealthSouth. The company owned about ten percent of the freestanding surgical centers.

As illustrated in Exhibit 5, HC's operating units were located in forty-two states, the District of Columbia, and Canada and consisted of 15 medical centers, 15 diagnostic centers, 497 outpatient clinics, and 112 outpatient surgery centers. The competition faced in each of these markets was similar although unique aspects did exist, arising primarily from the number of health care providers in specific metropolitan areas. The primary competitive factors in the rehabilitation services business were quality of services, projected patient outcomes, responsiveness to the needs of the patients, community and physicians, ability to tailor programs and services to meet specific needs, and the charges for services.

HealthSouth's rehabilitative facilities competed on a regional and national basis with other providers of specialized services such as sports medicine, head injury rehabilitation, and orthopedic surgery. Competitors and potential competitors included hospitals, private practice therapists, rehabilitation agencies, and so on. Some of the competitors had significant patient referral support systems as well as financial and human resources. HealthSouth centers competed directly

Exhibit 5

## Location of HealthSouth Facilities as of January 1, 1996

| State | Outpatient Centers | Inpatient Centers | Medical Centers | Surgery Centers | Diagnostic Centers |
|---|---|---|---|---|---|
| Alabama | 19 | 9 | 1 | 5 | 4 |
| Alaska | 0 | 0 | 0 | 1 | 0 |
| Arizona | 17 | 3 | 0 | 2 | 0 |
| Arkansas | 2 | 1 | 0 | 2 | 0 |
| California | 46 | 1 | 0 | 18 | 0 |
| Colorado | 21 | 0 | 0 | 4 | 0 |
| Connecticut | 1 | 0 | 0 | 0 | 0 |
| Washington, DC | 1 | 0 | 0 | 0 | 1 |
| Delaware | 4 | 0 | 0 | 0 | 0 |
| Florida | 47 | 8 | 2 | 20 | 1 |
| Georgia | 8 | 3 | 0 | 4 | 1 |
| Hawaii | 3 | 0 | 0 | 0 | 0 |
| Idaho | 0 | 0 | 0 | 1 | 0 |
| Illinois | 46 | 0 | 0 | 2 | 0 |
| Indiana | 13 | 1 | 0 | 2 | 0 |
| Iowa | 3 | 0 | 0 | 0 | 0 |
| Kansas | 3 | 0 | 0 | 0 | 0 |
| Kentucky | 2 | 1 | 0 | 2 | 0 |
| Louisiana | 2 | 1 | 0 | 1 | 0 |
| Maine | 2 | 0 | 0 | 0 | 0 |
| Maryland | 15 | 1 | 0 | 5 | 3 |
| Massachusetts | 1 | 0 | 0 | 1 | 0 |
| Michigan | 1 | 0 | 0 | 1 | 0 |
| Mississippi | 3 | 0 | 0 | 0 | 0 |
| Missouri | 30 | 4 | 0 | 6 | 0 |
| Nebraska | 2 | 0 | 0 | 0 | 0 |
| Nevada | 2 | 0 | 0 | 0 | 0 |
| New Hampshire | 7 | 1 | 0 | 0 | 0 |
| New Jersey | 18 | 2 | 0 | 2 | 0 |
| New Mexico | 3 | 1 | 0 | 1 | 0 |
| New York | 12 | 0 | 0 | 0 | 0 |
| North Carolina | 13 | 1 | 0 | 3 | 0 |
| Ohio | 24 | 0 | 0 | 1 | 0 |
| Oklahoma | 9 | 1 | 3 | 1 | 0 |
| Ontario, Canada | 1 | 0 | 0 | 0 | 0 |
| Pennsylvania | 19 | 8 | 5 | 0 | 0 |
| South Carolina | 6 | 5 | 2 | 0 | 0 |
| Tennessee | 13 | 6 | 0 | 6 | 1 |
| Texas | 42 | 13 | 1 | 14 | 3 |
| Utah | 1 | 1 | 0 | 1 | 0 |
| Virginia | 10 | 3 | 1 | 1 | 1 |
| Washington | 23 | 0 | 0 | 1 | 0 |
| West Virginia | 1 | 4 | 0 | 0 | 0 |
| Wisconsin | 1 | 0 | 0 | 4 | 0 |
| Total | 497 | 79 | 15 | 112 | 15 |

**Exhibit 6**                    **HealthSouth Corporation Market Share**

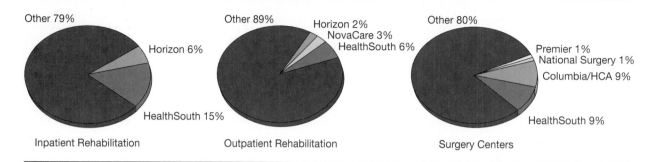

Inpatient Rehabilitation Services acquisitions include NME, RELife, NovaCare, and Advantage.
Outpatient Rehabilitation Services include Caremark and Advantage Acquisitions.
Surgery Center includes Surgical Care Affiliates, Sutter, and Surgical Health Acquisitions.

with local hospitals and various nationally recognized centers of excellence in orthopedics, sports medicine, and other specialties.

HealthSouth's surgery centers competed primarily with hospitals and other operators of free-standing surgery centers in attracting patients and physicians, in developing new centers, and in acquiring existing centers. The primary competitive factors in the outpatient surgery business were convenience, cost, quality of service, physician loyalty, and reputation. Hospitals had a number of competitive advantages in attracting physicians and patients.

The company faced competition every time it initiated a certificate of need project or sought to acquire an existing facility. The competition would arise from national or regional companies or from local hospitals that filed competing applications or that opposed the proposed CON project. Although the number of states requiring CON or similar approval was decreasing, HC continued to face this requirement in several states. The necessity for these approvals, which was somewhat unique to the health care industry, demanded that organizations planning to open new facilities or purchase expensive and specialized equipment convince a regulatory or planning agency that such facilities or equipment were really needed and would not merely move patients from one provider to another. They served as an important barrier to entry and potentially limited competition by creating a franchise to provide services to a given area.

The market for outpatient rehabilitation services was estimated to be approximately $7.9 billion. In-patient rehabilitation services were estimated to be another $7.7 billion, and the market for outpatient surgery centers was estimated at approximately $6 billion. HealthSouth's estimated market share in each of these markets is shown in Exhibit 6.

## ■ Reimbursement

Aggressive acquisition and managed care marketing efforts have radically altered the payer mix of HealthSouth over the past five years. Reimbursement for services provided by HC were divided into four distinct categories: commercial or private pay including HMOs, PPOs, and other managed care plans; workers' compensation; Medicare; and "other," which included a relatively insignificant amount of Medicaid. The percentage of each varied by business segment and facility. As illustrated in Exhibit 7, commercial or private pay-

**Exhibit 7**          **HealthSouth Corporation Revenue Sources**

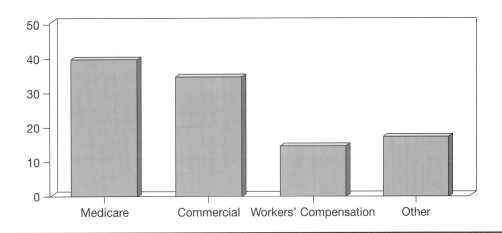

ment represented about 34 percent of total company receipts, Medicare accounted for 41 percent of overall HC revenues, workers' compensation comprised 11 percent of overall revenues, and all "other" sources accounted for 14 percent.

## ■ Commercial or Private Pay

Approximately 80 percent of the population under age 65 had medical insurance coverage. The extent of the coverage varied by location. Generally, charges for inpatient rehabilitation were completely (100 percent) reimbursed under general hospitalization benefits, and outpatient rehabilitation was reimbursed 100 percent similar to other outpatient services. Studies conducted by the Life Insurance Marketing and Research Association found that more than 70 percent of the employers in their sample provided some financial assistance for employees who participated in company-approved rehabilitation programs. Northwestern National Life Insurance Company reported that complete rehabilitation was possible in 66 percent of the light-industry injuries and in 62 percent of heavy-industry injuries. Of particular significance is the fact that HealthSouth's size and leadership made possible an aggressive managed care contracting strategy. In 1993, for example, HC had 265 managed care contracts. In 1995 the number increased to 1,200. Almost two-thirds of all HC's commercial revenues were under managed care contracts compared to only one-third in 1995.

## ■ Medicare

Although the rehabilitation services market had grown significantly, it continued to represent a relatively small portion of Medicare expenditures. Since 1983, the federal government had employed a prospective payment system as a means of controlling general acute-care hospital costs for the Medicare program. In the past, the Medicare program provided reimbursement for reasonable direct and indirect costs of the services furnished by hospitals to beneficiaries, plus an allowed return on equity for proprietary hospitals. As a result of the Social Security Act Amendments of 1983, Congress adopted a prospective payment system to cover the routine and ancillary operating costs of most Medicare inpatient hospital services.

HC is generally subject to PPS with respect to Medicare inpatient services. However, as of 1995, Medicare continued to pay certain defined units, freestanding rehabilitation facilities, and certified outpatient units on the basis of "reasonable costs" incurred during a base year (the year prior to being excluded from Medicare's prospective payment system or the first year of operation) adjusted by a market basket index. As a result, PPS has benefited the rehabilitation segment of the health care industry because the economic pressure on acute-care hospitals to discharge patients as soon as possible with the resulting demand for increased outpatient rehabilitation services which are currently exempt from PPS. Even inpatient rehabilitation units in acute-care facilities can obtain exemption from PPS upon satisfaction of certain federal criteria.

## ▪ Workers' Compensation

Increasingly, managed care attempts to include workers' compensation into seamless products. About 40 percent of the costs associated with workers' compensation claims are medical costs and many of these can be reduced through discount purchasing, utilization management, and outcomes-based treatment programs. Much of HealthSouth's expansion over the past several years has been motivated by the need to attack managed care as an opportunity rather than retreat from it as a threat. By becoming the largest rehabilitation services provider and building a network of inpatient and outpatient facilities nationwide, HC has been able to sign national contracts with payers, gain market share, and offset any erosion in margin. At the present time, workers' compensation is estimated to be about 15 percent of HC's rehabilitation business.

## ▪ Regulation

The health care industry was subject to regulation by federal, state, and local governments. The various levels of regulatory activity affected organizations by controlling growth, requiring licensure or certification of facilities, regulating the use of properties, and controlling the reimbursement for services provided. In some states, regulations controlled the growth of health care facilities.

Capital expenditures for the construction of new facilities, addition of beds, or acquisition of existing facilities could be reviewed by state regulators under a statutory scheme, usually referred to as a *CON program.* States with CON requirements placed limits on the construction and acquisition of health care facilities as well as the expansion of existing facilities and services.

Licensure and certification were separate but related regulatory activities. The former was usually a state or local requirement, and the latter was a federal requirement. In almost all instances, licensure and certification would follow specific standards and requirements set forth in readily available public documents. Compliance with the requirements was monitored by annual on-site inspections by representatives of various government agencies.

To receive Medicare reimbursement, each facility had to meet the applicable conditions of participation set forth by the U.S. Department of Health and Human Services relating to the type of facility, equipment, personnel, and standards of medical care, as well as compliance with all state and local laws and regulations. In addition, Medicare regulations generally required entry into such facilities through physician referral.

# HEALTHSOUTH TODAY

HealthSouth's primary objective is to be the provider of choice for patients, physicians, and payers for outpatient and rehabilitative health care services throughout the United States. Its growth strategy is based on four interrelated elements: (1) implementation of the Company's *integrated service model* in appropriate markets; (2) successful marketing to managed care organizations and other payers; (3) provision of high-quality, cost-effective health care services; and (4) expansion of its national network.

- *Integrated Service Model.* HealthSouth attempts to offer an integrated system of health care services including outpatient rehabilitative services, inpatient rehabilitative services, ambulatory surgery services, and outpatient diagnostic services. The Company believes that such an integrated model offers patients and payers convenience and offers substantial referral opportunities. HealthSouth estimates, for example, that one-third of its outpatient rehabilitative patients have had outpatient surgery, virtually all inpatient rehabilitation patients will require some form of outpatient rehabilitation, and almost all inpatient rehabilitation patients have some type of diagnostic procedure.

- *Marketing to Managed Care Organizations and Other Payers.* For almost 20 years HealthSouth has focused on the development of contractual relationships with managed care organizations, major insurance companies, large regional and national employers, and provider alliances and networks. The Company's documented outcomes with thousands of patients and its reputation for quality have given it a competitive advantage over smaller competitors.

- *Cost-Effective Services.* An important corporate goal is to provide high-quality, cost-effective health care services. The Company has developed standardized clinical protocols which resulted in "best practices" techniques throughout all HealthSouth facilities. The Company's reputation for its clinical programs is enhanced by its relationship with major universities and its support of clinical research facilities. The Company believes that outpatient and rehabilitative services are inherently less expensive than comparable services delivered in an inpatient environment. To this end HealthSouth is committed to the "virtual hospital" or "hospital without walls" concept, whereby services are delivered more cost-effectively without the heavy overhead burden of the acute-care hospital.

- *Expansion of National Network.* As the largest provider of outpatient and rehabilitative health care services in the United States, HealthSouth is able to realize economies of scale and compete successfully for national contracts with national payers and employers while retaining the ability to respond to the unique needs of local markets. The national network offers payers the convenience of dealing with a single provider, to utilize greater buying power through centralized purchasing, to achieve more efficient costs of capital and labor, and to recruit and retain physicians more efficiently.

# FUNCTIONAL CONSIDERATIONS

HC's management was a group of young energetic professionals. In 1995, HealthSouth was formally organized around four operating divisions, each with its own president. All presidents reported to Scrushy, who remained as chairman of the board and chief executive officer. The operating divisions were HealthSouth Inpatient Operations, HealthSouth Outpatient Centers, Health-South Surgery Centers, and HealthSouth Imaging (diagnostic) Centers (see Exhibit 8). The average age of the executive officers was 43 years, with a range from 55 to 36. Despite the relative youth of the executive officers, the team as a whole had an average tenure with the company of slightly over eight years. The range is one year to 12 years. Four of the 12 executive officers had been with HealthSouth from the time of its inception.

The corporate climate was characterized by a sense of urgency that was instilled in all of HealthSouth's employees directly by the chairman and CEO. Scrushy founded HealthSouth at the age of 32. As with many entrepreneurs, he was a visionary, but had the ability to make things happen. He worked virtually 365 days a year, 16 to 20 hours a day for the first five years, waiting until 1989 before taking his first vacation. His pace remained furious, working over 75 hours a week.

As a result of Scrushy's "hands-on" style, HC was run; it did not drift. This was not likely to change with the operating divisions reporting directly to the chairman and CEO. One of the company's most effective tools was a weekly statistical report, compiled every Thursday and distributed on Friday. The report included weekly statistics and trends such as payer mix, census, and revenue. It was reviewed over the weekend; and, if there was a negative trend, it was corrected. Thus, any problem was short lived. In this manner the management team was focused on real and developing problems.

Another tool was effective communications. Every Monday morning at 7:00 A.M. there was a meeting of the company's officers that included personnel from operations, development, finance, and administration. In this meeting each employee made a presentation, detailing what he or she accomplished in the previous week and what was planned for the current week. Questions were answered and problems were resolved. One additional benefit was that each employee was held accountable for his or her actions. Although this could be perceived to be overkill, it was believed to be necessary and helpful to the participants. At one time the meetings were stopped for about six weeks. After the company experienced a slight dip in performance and coordination, the meetings were immediately reinstated.

## ■ Staffing and Compensation

Unlike many other health care companies, HealthSouth had not experienced staffing shortages. Clinicians were in short supply, but HC was able to recruit and maintain excellent personnel. The ability to offer a challenging environment was a key factor. A HealthSouth inpatient facility in a metropolitan location typically competed favorably against other hospitals and nursing homes for the skills of new therapists. HealthSouth's outpatient facilities offered an attractive alternative to the clinician by offering eight-hour workdays with weekends and holidays off.

**Exhibit 8**                  **HealthSouth Corporation Operations**

| Outpatient Rehabilitation | Medical Centers (not an operating division) | Surgery Centers | Inpatient Rehabilitation | Diagnostic Centers |
|---|---|---|---|---|
| *Services Include:* | *Services Include:* | *Services Include:* | *Services Include:* | *Services Include:* |
| Aquatic therapy | Cardiology | ENT | Aquatic therapy | Computed tomography |
| Audiological screenings | Day surgery | Gastroenterology | Amputee | Electromyography |
| Biofeedback | Diagnostic imaging | General surgery | Arthritis | Magnetic resonance imaging |
| Driving assessments | Dial-a-nurse | Gynecology | Brain injury | Mammography |
| Family education | Emergency room | Lithotripsy | Burns | Nerve conduction velocity |
| Foot and ankle | Foot and ankle | Ophthalmology | Cardiac | Nuclear medicine |
| Functional capacity evaluations | Gastroenterology | Oral surgery | Cerebral palsy | Radiographic fluoroscopy |
| General orthopedics | General surgery | Orthopedics | Community re-entry | Ultrasound |
| Hand therapy | Hand surgery | Pain management | General rehabilitation | |
| Headache | Joint replacement | Plastic surgery | Joint replacement | |
| Injury prevention | Lithotripsy | Podiatry | Multiple sclerosis | |
| Neurology | Neurological sciences | Urology | Neurobehavioral | |
| Neuropsychology | Occupational health | | Orthopedics | |
| Occupational therapy | Oncology | | Orthotics/ Prosthetics | |
| Pain | Orthopedics | | Pain management | |
| Physical therapy | Pain management | | Pediatrics | |
| Speech therapy | Plastic surgery | | Pulmonary | |
| Spine rehabilitation | Spine | | Renal dialysis | |
| Sports therapy | Sports medicine | | Spinal injury | |
| Urinary therapy | Urology | | | |
| Vision therapy | | | | |
| Work hardening | | | | |
| WCA/FCA | | | | |

All of the company's employees were competitively compensated. One compensation tool used was employee incentive stock options, which were granted to key corporate and clinical personnel. The options required a vesting period of four years with 25 percent of the amount being vested annually. If the employee left for another job, the options were lost. With the tremendous success of the company, the stock options had created "golden handcuffs." Some employees had options that could be exercised at prices less than $18 a share. Although HC stock was trading for $29 per share in December 1995, throughout 1995 it traded in a range of $16 to $32 per share. Additionally, in 1991 the company created an employee stock ownership plan (ESOP) for the purpose of providing substantially all employees with the opportunity to save for retirement and acquire a proprietary interest in the company.

## ■ Development

In order to realize these objectives, HealthSouth initiated an aggressive acquisition strategy. During 1995, HealthSouth finalized pooling-of-interest mergers with Surgical Health Corporation (37 outpatient surgery centers in 11 states) and Sutter Surgery Centers, Inc. (12 outpatient surgery centers in three states), as well as stock purchase acquisitions of the rehabilitation hospitals division of NovaCare, Inc. (11 inpatient rehabilitation facilities, 12 other health care facilities, and two CONs in eight states), and Caremark Orthopedic Services, Inc. (120 outpatient rehabilitation facilities in 13 states). In addition, the company entered into agreements to acquire Surgical Care Affiliates, Inc. (67 outpatient surgery centers in 24 states) and Advantage Health Corporation (150 inpatient and outpatient rehabilitation facilities in 11 states). Advantage Health is a particularly important acquisition not only because of its size but because it was the largest provider of rehabilitation services in the Northeast.

## ■ Marketing

The company's marketing efforts were similar for each business segment. The demand was controlled by physicians, workers' compensation managers, insurance companies, and other intermediaries. HC administrators and clinicians were all involved in the marketing effort. The company hired a number of individuals who were formerly case managers with local intermediaries, such as insurance companies and HMOs. Every outpatient clinic had its own marketing director.

HC entered into contracts to be the exclusive provider for rehabilitation services directly to industry. Firms such as General Motors were excellent targets because they had many employees in various markets that HealthSouth served. In such cases, significant new business could be generated and in return HealthSouth could afford to discount its charges. HC expanded its marketing efforts to include a focus on national contracts with large payers and self-insured employers.

HealthSouth established a national marketing effort with training programs, national account managers, case managers, and a carefully developed marketing plan for each facility based on a number of factors, including population demographics, physician characteristics, and localized disability statistics. The objective was to put into place a consistent sales methodology throughout HealthSouth and take advantage of its national system of rehabilitation facilities. This national coverage enabled HealthSouth to provide services for national as well as regional companies.

Marketing programs were directed toward the development of long-term relationships with local schools, businesses and industries, physicians, health maintenance organizations, and preferred provider organizations. In addition,

HC attempted to develop and enhance its image with the public at large. One example was the company's joint promotional arrangement with the Ladies Professional Golf Association, whereby HC provided and staffed a rehabilitation van for the players while they were on tour.

HealthSouth's pricing was usually lower than that of the competition. However, this was not used as a major selling point, but rather a bonus. HealthSouth focused mainly on quality of services and outcomes as the best marketing tool.

## ■ Financial Structure

HealthSouth's growth was funded through a mix of equity and debt. The company raised $13 million in venture capital before going public in 1986. Because of the company's startup nature in its early years, commercial banks were reluctant to lend significant funds for development. After the company's initial public offering, commercial bankers were more responsive to financing growth plans. HC continued to use a conservative mix of equity and debt and believed its cost of capital was the lowest in the health care industry. A decision to give up ownership was an easy one. The founders understood that a smaller percentage ownership of a larger company would be worth more and would not carry as much risk.

Earnings increases were significant, with compounded earnings growth of 416 percent from 1986 to 1990. During the 1990 to 1993 period growth rates declined, as expected, but remained impressive by industry standards. Operating revenues for 1995 increased about 22 percent over 1994. Revenues are estimated to grow between 10-15 percent from 1996-1999. The large ($7.9 billion) outpatient rehabilitation market is fragmented and HC is one of the few providers that has the ability to develop a powerful network. In 1995 it was estimated that HC's outpatient revenue grew about 32 percent (34 percent in visits and two percent in pricing). Surgery center growth is expected to be about 15-20 percent, which should result from a combination of continued acquisitions and same-store volume and price increases. Inpatient services will continue to be the cash cow for HC. Currently, inpatient rehabilitation and specialty medical centers account for about 46 and 11 percent of 1995 revenues, respectively. The outlook for these businesses remains encouraging.

# WHERE DOES HEALTHSOUTH GO FROM HERE?

Richard Scrushy was reviewing company projections for the continued success of HealthSouth Corporation. He could not help but wonder if it were possible for HC to continue such rapid growth. All the questions raised earlier were in his thoughts. What will I need to do to make it happen? Are there things we should be doing differently? How can I ensure that HealthSouth does not outgrow its resources (capital and management)? Does the market provide ample opportunity to grow at 20 to 30 percent per year? What external factors do we face? What should we do to ensure that medical rehabilitation continues to be favorably reimbursed? What is the real number of facilities needed, and how many acquisition targets are there? Are our current strategies what they should be?

Scrushy focused on answering the questions. He knew that he could formulate a plan to ensure HealthSouth's success. In fact, in a probing interview in *Rehabilitation Today* (May 1991), Scrushy was careful to state that he would consider any acquisition where he believed "value could be added" and dismissed the possibility that the company's "regional name" implied that his aspirations were regional. Clearly, he was willing to go anywhere, anytime he believed opportunities existed. To date, nothing had changed his mind.

# REFERENCES

Sources used for quotes and information to supplement public documents of HealthSouth include the following.

Brown, Alex & Sons, Inc. Research Report, Health Care Group, December 28, 1995.

Brown, Alex & Sons, Inc. Research Report, Health Care Group, February 16, 1996.

Hansen, Jeffrey. "HealthSouth Finishes Deal Doubling Size." *Birmingham News* (January 6, 1994), pp. 6D and 10D.

"HealthSouth Wins Notice of *Forbes,* Wall Street," *Birmingham News* (April, 19, 1996), pp. 1E-4E.

Hicks, W. G., M. Willard, K. Miner, and M. Sullivan. "Consolidation Steamroller Continues to Move Ahead." *Gowen Perspectives* (February 28, 1996).

Securities and Exchange Commission. HealthSouth Corporation. Form 10-K. Washington, DC, March 15, 1996.

United States Equity Research. *Health Services.* Solomon Brothers. March 13, 1996.

U.S. Investment Research. *Healthcare Services.* "Trailblazing into the Northeast." Morgan Stanley. January 2, 1996.

Wilder, Marvin. "The Powerhouse Behind HealthSouth." *Rehabilitation Today* (May 1991), pp. 22-31.

# Compass Bancshares, Inc.

Douglas L. Smith, University of Alabama
at Birmingham

John Noland, University of Alabama
at Birmingham

Patrick Asubonteng Rivers, University
of Alabama at Birmingham

Dr. Woodrow D. Richardson, University
of Alabama at Birmingham

Three and a half months of stress and anxiety in Bill Swan's life would hopefully come to an end today. Today, April 11, 1995, was the annual shareholders' meeting of Compass Bancshares, where Bill, age 27, had been an employee for 5 years. Many employees would be at the annual meeting because a major issue was up for vote. Most employees were shareholders because they participated in a payroll deduction stock purchase plan offered by the bank. Bill had participated in the plan since he first came to work and owned 350 shares with a market value of approximately $9,100. Like most employees, Bill viewed his stock investment as a nest egg for retirement.

The major issue revolved around a battle which had been going on for several months between Harry Brock, the founder and retired CEO of the bank, and Paul Jones, the present CEO. The stockholders would vote on whether the bank appointed three new directors who supported a merger with a larger bank or directors who supported remaining independent.

As Bill got dressed to attend the meeting, he picked up the two proxy cards off his dresser. White proxy cards from Compass and blue cards from Brock's Committee to Maximize Shareholder Value had been mailed to all shareholders. Bill could not decide which way to vote, so instead of mailing his card, he planned to take them to the annual meeting. He was still not comfortable with how to vote. Should he vote for a group of directors who will most assuredly take action to sell the bank, or should he vote for directors who favor remaining independent? He began to think back over the events of the last three and one-half months.

# THE CURRENT SITUATION

Although Harry Brock retired as CEO of Compass Bancshares in 1991, he was still on the board of directors and continued to be interested in the performance of the bank. He also was aware of the changes looming on the horizon in the banking industry. In the summer of 1994, Brock communicated to Jones that the bank should merge with another bank. Brock informed the board that he would, on his own, investigate potential buyers, with both Brock and the board realizing that he did not have the authority to finalize an offer. He found a buyer in First Union for $30.70 a share and brought the offer to the board for consideration. Jones did not support the proposal and asked the board for permission to contact First Union and terminate any idea of a sale. Jones and the majority of the board of directors disagreed with Brock and felt the bank should remain independent. This matter was confined to private board discussion until January 1995. At that time, Brock publicized that he wanted the bank to merge with a larger bank to take advantage of national interstate banking. The battle between Jones and Brock became a public spectacle. At one point, Brock was actually evicted from his Compass office and had to find other office space from which to run his operation. Brock felt so strongly about his position that he, along with two other board members, formed a committee labeled the "Committee to Maximize Shareholder Value" to pursue the merger idea.

Along with most other Compass employees, Bill first heard about the battle in January and was initially shocked to hear that Mr. Brock wanted to sell the bank. Bill's reaction was to side with Jones because he thought not selling the bank would preserve his job. Then Bill heard that Jones was talking about selling the bank to Regions, a large bank in town. Maybe Brock's plan would result in fewer jobs lost because an out-of-town purchaser would want to retain most of the employees; however, Regions might want to eliminate duplicate jobs in Birmingham. So, what is the best answer for Bill personally?

Under Brock's leadership, the "Committee to Maximize Shareholder Value" started a proxy fight to elect a board of directors who would support the merger. He produced a videotape to "set the record straight," including clipped excerpts of Jones' court depositions that indicated Jones had personal motives for power and greed and had been in contact with Regions to discuss a potential merger. Brock's rationale was that "nationwide banking" would bring great changes to the banking industry. He stated that the competition heretofore had been minimal by saying "if we think we have had competition in the past, it has been a picnic compared to the future." Brock was successful in involving Compass in statewide banking. He felt that consolidation was going to be fast paced and that the best thing to do was "pick your partner first" to get maximum advantage for the stockholders and protection for employees. A March 28 Birmingham News article reported that "Jones said in his testimony that he and Stanley Mackin, CEO of Regions Financial, had a 'wide ranging conversation about a number of issues,' including the possibility that he might succeed Mackin as the CEO of the merged banks."

Jones stated that he disagreed with Brock's idea and that he did not think the time was right. He said that a merger with a larger bank could cost the local Birmingham area anywhere from 850 to 1,000 jobs. Jones had also produced a video for employees to calm their fears about the possible merger when the information became public. He attempted to discredit Brock's rationale about the benefits of a merger. In his comments to employees, Mr. Jones stated that in the three-year business plan adopted by the board, there was no plan to sell the bank, but instead the plan was for the bank to remain independent. Bill was not knowledgeable about all the workings of the board, but he was confused about some of the statements. He wondered why the company plan was for only three years. He also wondered about the relationship between Jones and Stanley Mackin, CEO of Regions Financial. Jones' court deposition stated that Mackin was planning to retire in two or three years and that Jones might be the CEO of the merged banks.

Since January, Bill had not known what to do. His uncertainty related to two questions: 1) should he be looking for another job since long-term employment at Compass may be uncertain, and 2) how to vote his shares. He was getting reports from Bloomberg Investment Services every day and talking to his co-workers. Rumors that some executives were sending out their resumes accentuated the stress of the situation. He also wondered if the bank would be sold after the three-year pledge elapsed, thereby resulting in job losses. His boss had been to some information meetings and had suggested that employees vote for Jones and support the board. Was she just saying that to please the executives or did she really feel that way? Bill also heard that voting for employee shareholders who are investing through the monthly investment plan will not be confidential, so executives will know how he votes. Managers are jokingly saying there will be a list of those who vote a certain way.

The infighting had an impact on the public's view of the company. The price of the stock increased from $22 a share, prior to the Brock public announcement of his proxy fight plans, to as high as $28 on March 2. The day before the board meeting the stock closed at $26.63. The normal trading volume for the stock on the Nasdaq was less than 100,000 shares a day. However, since the public announcement, the volume had been much higher, reaching as high as 1.9 million shares a day. At least one major investment firm, which provided services for several hundred institutional investor clients, recommended a vote for Jones' position. Institutions held about 20% of Compass' shares. Employees, like Bill, owned approximately 30% of the shares.

Key events related to the current tense situation are described in Exhbit 1.

## THE PROXY PROCESS

Compass will hold its annual meeting on April 11, allowing shareholders to vote for board members who will determine the company's future. Three board members up for election—Jones, Charles Daniel, and George Hansberry (see Exhibit 2 for a list of Compass' Board of Directors)—were supportive of maintaining Compass' independent status.

In publicly held companies, a proxy process is utilized to obtain votes from shareholders on issues to be handled at the annual meeting. Compass used this process for its April 11 meeting. However, unlike the normal process, Harry Brock and his group of supporters also implemented a proxy process to solicit support for their list of nominees for directors. The steps taken by the Committee, as stated in the proxy statement, were "because it is their strong feeling that directors of the company owe an obligation to you, the stockholders of the Company, to maximize your investment in every way." It further stated that

| Exhibit 1 | Prelude to a Proxy Fight |
|---|---|
| Summer 1994 | Compass Bank founder Harry B. Brock Jr. tells his successor, Chairman and CEO D. Paul Jones Jr., that Compass should merge with a larger bank. His rationale is that under the new legislation which allows interstate branching, Compass will face intense competition. They should take advantage of the situation and merge with a larger bank, realizing a good stock sale price for shareholders. |
| Sept. 26 | Brock says he plans to contact regional banks to gauge their interests in Compass. Jones replies that Brock does not speak for the board of directors. |
| Sept.-Oct. | Brock contacts several banks about a merger, including (1) Sun Trust in Atlanta, (2) Wachovia in Winston-Salem, N.C., (3) Barnett in Jacksonville, Fla., and (4) First Union in Charlotte, N.C. |
| Oct. 17 | Brock tells Compass board that he has a merger proposal from First Union Corp., which is a bank with assets of $72.3 billion. The offer is for $1.14 billion. |
| Dec. 1 | Compass hires CS First Boston as its investment adviser. |
| Jan. 1995 | Jones privately visits J. Stanley Mackin, chairman and CEO of Regions Financial Corp., to discuss a possible merger of their banks. |
| Jan. 27 | Brock announces proxy fight to elect a board of directors that favor merging Compass with a larger regional bank. Two Compass directors, G.W "Red" Leach and Stanley M. Brock, align with Brock. |
| Jan. 30 | Compass directors Charles W. Daniel, Marshall Durbin Jr., and Goodwin L. Mryrick announce they are backing Jones. |
| Jan. 31 | Compass director Tranum Fitzpatrick announces his support for Jones. |
| Feb. 13 | Compass board of directors adopts three-year strategic plan based on CS First Boston's recommendation that Compass remain independent. |
| Feb. 25 | Compass director Thomas D. Jernigan, who favors a merger, resigns from Compass' board, leaving the board with 11 directors. Two more directors, John S. Stein and William E. Davenport, publicly back Jones. |
| Mar. 1 | Compass announces it will hold its annual meeting on April 11. Proxies mailed to shareholders of record. |
| Mar. 17 | Compass' biggest shareholder, the Daniel Foundation, backs Jones. Brock files a civil suit against Compass, accusing Jones of securities rules violation to sway shareholders. The accusation revolved around the mailing of proxy materials before rules permitted and not giving more than 20 days' notice of the annual shareholders' meeting. |
| Mar. 24 | Institutional Shareholder Services Inc. recommends to its clients that they vote for Jones' position. |
| Mar. 28 | Federal Judge Sam Pointer rules in Compass' favor, dismissing Brock's lawsuit. A Court deposition disclosed that Jones held discussions in January with Regions Financial to discuss a possible merger. Jones dismissed the meeting as "very tentative," although Jones admitted he was being considered as the head of the new merged company. Regions is the parent of First Alabama, a major bank in Alabama. |
| Apr. 3 | Coal magnate Garry N. Drummond, a Compass director, throws his support to Brock. Four directors have announced support for Brock, while seven have announced support for Jones. |
| Apr. 11 | Stockholders' meeting. |

Source: Rupinski, *Birmingham Post-Herald.*

"the members of the Committee and their nominees intend to take other appropriate steps to maximize the value of the company's stock." Brock also stated that it is the opinion of the committee that directors should act independently of the CEO, keeping the interests of stockholders in mind. Steps to this end would include "soliciting offers or proposals from suitable potential merger

**Exhibit 2**

**Board of Directors**

| Name | Dir. Since | Shares Held | Occupation |
|------|------|------|------|
| *Nominees to serve until 1998:* | | | |
| D. Paul Jones Jr. | 1978 | 512,911 | Chairman of the Board, CEO, and President, Compass Bank. Age 52. |
| Charles W. Daniel | 1982 | 197,445 | President, Dantract, Inc. (real estate investments). Age 54. |
| George W. Hansberry | | 15,214 | Physician. Age 67. |
| *Directors to serve until 1996:* | | | |
| William Eugene Davenport | 1993 | 20,121 | President and CEO, Russell Lands, Inc. (resort land development). Age 54. |
| Marshall Durbin Jr. | 1971 | 591,407 | President of Marshall Durbin & Company, Inc. (poultry processing). Age 63. |
| Tranum Fitzpatrick | 1989 | 148,447 | Chairman of Guilford Company, Inc. and President of Guilford Capital and Empire-Rouse, Inc. (real estate investment and development). Age 56. |
| Goodwin L. Myrick | 1988 | 915,014 | President and Chairman of the Board of Alabama Farmers Federation, Alfa Corporation, Alfa Insurance Companies, and Alfa Services, Inc. (agriculture and insurance), and a dairy farmer. Age 69. |
| John S. Stein | 1989 | 43,758 | President and CEO of Golden Enterprises, Inc. (snack food and metal fastener production and distribution). Age 57. |
| *Directors to serve until 1997:* | | | |
| Harry B. Brock Jr. | 1970 | 789,829 | Retired since March 31, 1991, as Chairman of the Board, CEO, and Treasurer of the Corporation and Compass Bank. Age 68. |
| Stanley M. Brock | 1990 | 171,866 | Attorney. Age 44. |
| Garry N. Drummond Sr. | 1990 | 64,872 | CEO of Drummond Company, Inc. (coal and coke production, real estate investment). Age 56. |

partners. This is the reason the members of the Committee have undertaken to solicit proxies to elect three new and independent directors." The proxy statement was sent to shareholders on March 16. Brock and "Red" Leach also submitted Shareholder Proposals through proxy statements, recommending addition of the following proposals, which would:

1. require the Company, within 10 days after its receipt of certain proposals for the purchase of the assets or stock of the Company or for the merger of the Company, to mail to the stockholders of the Company the details of such proposal.

2. require prior approval by the holders of a majority of the shares of the Company's Common Stock before any of the following plans or agreements with "principal officers" of the Company may be agreed to : (1) any employment contract for a principal officer in excess of one year; (2) any "golden parachute" contract providing for severance pay or continued compensation in excess of one year's salary; (3) any non-qualified stock option agreement or supplemental retirement plan for a principal officer; and (4) any other plan or agreement providing for post-retirement benefits for a principal officer greater than would be payable under agreements now in effect.

This process was most assuredly confusing to shareholders. For example, Compass issued a proxy which contained white cards to be marked and submitted by shareholders. Brock's proxy contained blue cards for shareholders to mark and submit. Each side reported spending $500,000 on soliciting support for their plan. Both sides sent follow-up and replacement proxies which inundated Bill with piles of paper and added to the uncertainty of the situation. With each package he received, more negative information about the opposing side was included which caused him to feel he could trust neither Jones nor Brock.

## THE COMPANY AND ITS BUSINESS

Compass Bancshares Inc. was a multi-state bank holding company with headquarters in Birmingham, Alabama. The company had assets of $9.1 billion as of Dec. 31, 1994, with 204 bank offices in Alabama, Texas, and Florida, employing 4,100. Performance in 1994 included profits of $99,671,000 or $2.68 per share, compared with $89,718,000 or $2.37 per share in 1993. The company was publicly owned, with 37,940,000 shares outstanding. Exhibit 3 contains financial results for Compass from 1992–1994.

Compass Bancshares and Compass of Texas were multi-bank holding companies, as defined by the Banking Holding Company Act (BHC Act) and were registered with the Federal Reserve. Under the BHC Act, a bank holding company was required to obtain prior approval of the Federal Reserve before it acquired all the assets or ownership of any bank.

Alabama, Florida, and Texas, where Compass Bancshares operated its banking subsidiaries, each had laws relating to acquisitions of banks, bank holding companies, and other types of financial institutions. Compass Bank, organized under the laws of the State of Alabama, was regulated by the Alabama State Banking Department. Compass Bank-Florida was regulated by the Florida Department of Banking and Finance. Compass Bank-Dallas and Compass Bank-Houston were regulated by the Department of Banking of the State of Texas and the Federal Deposit Insurance Corporation (FDIC). All these banks, except the Texas banks, are members of the Federal Reserve System.

Since the time Bill had come to work at Compass, one of the things he had enjoyed was the feeling among employees of being part of a family. For example, employees were recognized for achievements, given Thanksgiving dinner, and publicized in company newsletters. This past closeness of employees had made the current turbulent environment even more unsettling for Bill.

**Exhibit 3**  **Financial Highlights ($000, except per share data)**

|  | 1994 | 1993 | 1992 |
|---|---|---|---|
| *Period End Balances:* | | | |
| Assets | $9,123,253 | $7,333,594 | $7,004,506 |
| Loans, net of unearned income | 5,761,511 | 5,197,464 | 4,627,530 |
| Earnings assets | 8,381,434 | 6,842,111 | 6,466,511 |
| Deposits | 7,062,404 | 5,625,097 | 5,349,279 |
| Shareholders' equity | 600,613 | 545,584 | 506,426 |
| *Average Balances:* | | | |
| Assets | $8,019,343 | $7,047,256 | $6,737,664 |
| Loans, net of unearned income | 5,355,755 | 4,889,217 | 4,227,721 |
| Earnings assets | 7,420,117 | 6,514,959 | 6,197,150 |
| Deposits | 6,209,041 | 5,417,890 | 5,095,987 |
| Shareholders' equity | 574,549 | 533,526 | 477,891 |
| *Income/Expense:* | | | |
| Net interest income | 331,368 | 329,013 | 313,334 |
| Provision for loan losses | 3,404 | 36,306 | 52,885 |
| Noninterest income | 85,631 | 103,186 | 95,613 |
| Noninterest expense | 261,966 | 257,703 | 242,262 |
| Pre-tax income | 151,629 | 138,190 | 113,800 |
| Net income | 99,671 | 89,718 | 75,390 |
| *Per Common Share Data:* | | | |
| Net income | $ 2.68 | $ 2.37 | $ 2.01 |
| Cash dividends declared | 0.92 | 0.76 | 0.67 |
| Book value | 16.25 | 14.93 | 13.28 |
| *Profitability Ratios:* | | | |
| Return on average assets | 1.24% | 1.26% | 1.12% |
| Return on average common shareholders' equity | 17.35 | 16.90 | 16.12 |
| Noninterest expense to average assets | 3.27 | 3.62 | 3.60 |
| Net yield on average earning assets | 4.46 | 5.00 | 5.06 |
| Net yield on average earning assets—taxable equiv. | 4.54 | 5.11 | 5.19 |
| *Asset Quality ratios:* | | | |
| Allowance for loan losses to net loans | 1.86% | 2.13% | 1.80% |
| Loan loss provision to average net loans | 0.06 | 0.74 | 1.25 |
| Net charge-offs to average net loans | 0.15 | 0.22 | 0.59 |
| Nonperforming loans to loans | 0.21 | 0.37 | 0.61 |
| Nonperforming assets to loans and ORE | 0.33 | 0.77 | 1.41 |
| *Asset Structure Ratios:* | | | |
| Shareholders' equity to total assets | 6.58% | 7.52% | 7.23% |
| Total qualifying capital | 13.06 | 13.23 | 11.61 |
| Net loans to total deposits | 81.58 | 92.40 | 86.51 |
| Average net loans to average total deposits | 86.26 | 90.24 | 82.96 |

Source: *Compass Bancshares Annual Report.*

# GOVERNMENT REGULATION

The banking industry had been highly regulated for many years, mainly to protect the economy from bank failures. Controls included the interest rates charged customers, plus the cost and quantity of money available to banks from the Federal Reserve System. The most significant early legislation included The McFadden Act of 1927, which prohibited expansion of banks across state lines, and The Glass-Steagall Act of 1933, which put in place many tight restrictions, including inhibiting interstate branches and limits on consolidations. A summary of banking legislation is shown in Exhibit 4.

Because states had much authority in banking operations, a group of ten states in the southeast formed a "regional compact" in the early 1980s to allow regional banks to do business across state lines among the ten states. This effort was an attempt to avoid any future interstate activity by powerful banks from large financial centers such as New York. The compacts were challenged in the U. S. Supreme Court but upheld, thus allowing banks to merge across state lines.

The Interstate Banking Bill of 1987 further opened up competition in the industry by allowing interstate banking on a national basis. Under this bill, approval by the individual states was still required. Recently, President Clinton signed into law the Riegele-Neal Interstate Banking and Branching Efficiency Act of 1994 (Interstate Act), which went into effect in 1996 and permitted bank holding companies to acquire banks located in another state without regard to whether the transaction is prohibited under state law.

The Federal Reserve Act imposed certain limitations on extensions of credit and transactions between banks that were members of the Federal Reserve System. Banks that were not members of the Federal Reserve System were also subject to these limitations. Federal law prohibited a bank holding company from engaging in certain arrangements in connection with any credit or sale of property. Generally, federal and state banking laws and regulations governed all areas of the operations of the bank. Federal and state banking regulatory agencies also had the general authority to limit the dividends paid by insured banks and bank holding companies if such payments were deemed to constitute an unsafe and unsound practice.

# COMPETITIVE ENVIRONMENT

The Alabama banking industry consisted of five dominant banks: AmSouth Bancorporation, SouthTrust Corporation, Regions Financial Corporation, Compass Bancshares, Inc., and Colonial BancGroup. Exhibit 5 compares Compass' financial performance to the other dominant Alabama banks. Over the past few years, these banks have grown primarily through acquisitions. Each of these entities is discussed in the following paragraphs.

### ■ Amsouth Bancorporation

In 1995, AmSouth was the largest bank holding company in the State of Alabama. Headquartered in Birmingham, Alabama, AmSouth had 369 offices in Alabama, Florida, Tennessee, and Georgia. AmSouth had grown significantly

**Exhibit 4**  **Summary of Legislative Activity**

| Year | Regulation Activity | Content |
|------|---------------------|---------|
| 1913 | Federal Reserve Act of 1913 | Imposed limitations on the extension of credit and other transactions by and between banks which are members of the Federal Reserve System. |
| 1927 | The McFadden Act of 1927 | Prohibited bank expansion across state lines. Gave states authority to set branching standards for banks in their jurisdiction. |
| 1933 | The National Banking Act of 1933 (Glass-Steagall Act) | Essentially excluded U.S. banks from non-Treasury securities markets. Banned affiliation between commercial and investment banking functions. Inhibited interstate branch operations, limited consolidation of banks. Prohibited banks from paying interest on demand deposits and placed ceilings on rates of other accounts. "Regulation Q" fixed prices for deposits and gave thrifts a slight advantage in rates they could pay. |
| 1956 | Bank Holding Company Act of 1956 (The BHC Act) | Required a bank holding company to obtain prior approval of the Federal Reserve before it can acquire substantially all the assets or ownership or control of voting share if afterwards it would direct or control > 5% of the voting shares of such bank. To restrict single and multibank holding companies by prohibiting acquisitions of banks in other states, unless other states' laws allow so. A 1975 Act closed the loophole that actually encouraged the growth of BHCs. |
| 1977 | The Community Reinvestment Act of 1977 (The CRA) | Encouraged regulated financial institutions to help meet the credit needs of their local community, including low and moderate income neighborhoods. |
| 1980 | The Depository Institution Deregulation and Monetary Control Act of 1980 (DIDMCA) | The first to allow increased competition in banking environment. Interest rate ceilings phased out by 1986, interest-bearing checking allowed, thrifts' lending power expanded. |
| 1980 | Congressional Acts (various) | Phased out interest rate ceilings, lessened the regulatory differences between banks and non-banks, reduced some regulatory burdens. |
| 1982 | Bank Holding Company Act | Major deregulation left banks free to set own rates in interest-bearing accounts and charge as desired for services. |
| 1982 | Depository Institutions Act | Authorized money market accounts, expanded thrifts' lending powers, made provisions for aiding failing thrifts, interest rate differentials paid by banks and thrifts to be phased out by 1984. |
| 1984–1985 | Supreme Court Actions | 1984: Upheld acquisitions of discount brokerage firms by banks. 1985: Upheld constitutionality of the regional interstate banking pacts, allowing states to enact interstate banking legislation, usually in the form of reciprocal agreements - and merge. This negated the 1933 McFadden Act. |
| 1986 | DIDMCA (continued) | Final provisions of 1980 Act enacted. Minimum balance requirements on money market accounts eliminated. Interest rate ceilings on passbook savings accounts lifted. |
| 1987 | Interstate Banking Bill of 1987 | Allowed for reciprocal banking between states. |
| 1991 | Federal Deposit Insurance Corporation Improvement Act of 1991 | Recapitalized the Bank Insurance Fund and Saving Association Insurance Fund. Required federal banking agencies to take prompt action concerning banks that fail to meet minimum capital requirements; mandated new disclosure rules, tougher auditing and underwriting standards. |
| 1993 | National Depositor Preference Statute | Losses will fall more completely on unsecured, non-deposit general creditors, and both insured and uninsured domestic depositors will receive preference in claims against a receivership estate over the creditors of the bank. |
| 1993 | Federal Reserve System overhaul (pending) | Proposed increasing accountability of the central bank. |

**Exhibit 4 (continued)**     **Summary of Legislative Activity**

| Year | Regulation Activity | Content |
|------|---------------------|---------|
| 1994 | Bankruptcy Reform Act of 1994 | Altered the Bankruptcy Code to include creation of Bankruptcy Review Commission to evaluate the bankruptcy system. |
| 1994 | Riegle-Neal Interstate Banking & Branching Efficiency Act of 1994 (The Interstate Banking Act) | Permitted bank holding companies to acquire banks located in any state without regard to whether the transaction is prohibited under any state law, however, states may establish the minimum age of a local bank subject to acquisition by an out-of-state holding company. Minimum age is limited to maximum of 5 years. Law passed 1995; commenced July 1996. |

over the past decade through an aggressive acquisitions strategy and offered extensive consumer, trust, and investment services. For example, in July 1993, AmSouth announced its intent to take over Florida Bank of Jacksonville, Florida. In keeping with its tradition of offering bids up to two times book value, AmSouth offered Florida Bank 1.81 times its book value. In August 1993, AmSouth announced plans to purchase First Federal Savings Bank of Calhoun, Georgia, for $14 million in stock. AmSouth chose First Federal because of its strategic location between its Chattanooga offices and the Georgia State Bank of Rome, which AmSouth was also in the process of acquiring. Also, in August 1993, AmSouth announced plans to acquire Citizens National Corporation of Naples, Florida, for $48.8 million in stock, giving AmSouth $289.6 million more in Florida assets. AmSouth's offer was 2.74 times the adjusted book value of the thrift, but was seen as justified because of its attractive location in the southwest Florida area. In September 1993, AmSouth filed a plan with the SEC to issue $300 million in debt to help pay for some of its recent acquisitions throughout Florida. In December 1993, AmSouth completed its acquisition of First Sunbelt Bancshares, which also owned Georgia State Bank of Rome. This merger was achieved through a stock swap. In total, AmSouth added 145 banking offices in 1993, a 70 percent increase in assets. This expansion continued in 1994 with five acquisitions in Florida, Tennessee, and Georgia.

## ■ Southtrust Corporation

The second largest bank in Alabama, SouthTrust was considered the most aggressive of the group. The retail leader had substantially out-branched the other banks, competing head-to-head with small community banks across the state. As soon as Alabama law allowing interstate banking went into effect in mid-1987, SouthTrust began seeking growth through out-of-state acquisitions. It was the first of Alabama banks to branch into the Florida panhandle. In 1988, SouthTrust bought banks in South Carolina and Tennessee and moved into Georgia in 1989. In 1990, SouthTrust bought banks in central Florida and moved northeast with purchases in North Carolina (Cantrell, 1992).

In 1991, SouthTrust expanded its presence in Atlanta and central Georgia with its purchase of 22 former Fulton Federal Savings & Loans offices. In 1992, SouthTrust purchased First American Bank of Georgia, which boosted its presence in Atlanta to a total of $2 billion in assets with some 70 offices in 11

**Exhibit 5**

**Performance Indicators for the Five Largest Alabama Banks (1990–1994)**

| Bank | 1990 | 1991 | 1992 | 1993 | 1994 |
|---|---|---|---|---|---|
| SouthTrust Corporation | | | | | |
| EPS | 1.71 | 2.13 | 2.49 | | |
| DPS | 0.46 | 0.48 | 0.52 | 0.60 | |
| NI | 69,708 | 90,006 | 114,246 | 150,535 | |
| AmSouth Bancorporation | | | | | |
| EPS | 1.97 | 2.07 | 2.51 | 3.10 | 2.25 |
| DPS | 0.94 | 0.98 | 1.07 | 1.22 | 1.43 |
| NI | 75,000 | 83,000 | 108,000 | 146,720 | 127,290 |
| Regions Financial Corporation | | | | | |
| EPS | 1.91 | 2.16 | 2.60 | 3.01 | |
| DPS | 0.84 | 0.87 | 0.91 | 1.04 | |
| NI | 68,894 | 78,256 | 95,048 | 112,045 | |
| Compass Bancshares, Inc. | | | | | |
| EPS | 1.51 | 1.74 | 2.01 | 2.37 | 2.68 |
| DPS | 0.53 | 0.59 | 0.67 | 0.76 | 0.92 |
| NI | 52,605 | 63,374 | 76,003 | 89,718 | 99,671 |
| Colonial BancGroup | | | | | |
| EPS | 1.19 | 1.45 | 1.97 | 2.35 | 2.74 |
| DPS | A=0.60 | A=0.63 | A=0.67 | A=0.71 | A=0.80 |
| | B=0.20 | B=0.23 | B=0.27 | B=0.31 | B=0.40 |
| NI | 9,143 | 10,430 | 13,793 | 18,709 | 27,671 |

EPS = Earnings per Share

DPS = Dividends per Share

NI  = Net Income ($000)

counties in central Georgia. Through acquisitions, SouthTrust's assets more than doubled by 1992 and were in excess of $17.6 billion at the end of 1994. In 1995, SouthTrust owned 396 banks in Alabama, Florida, Georgia, North Carolina, South Carolina, and Tennessee.

## ■ Regions Financial Corporation (First Alabama Bancshares, Inc.)

First Alabama, one of the South's most conservative banks, had increased its earnings and dividends consecutively for the past 21 years. First Alabama's growth had occurred primarily through acquisitions when J. Stanley Mackin assumed control in 1990 with a strategy intended to build market share through the purchase of savings and loans throughout Alabama and then move into neighboring states. In 1993, the parent company changed its name from First Alabama Bancshares to Regions Financial Corporation in recognition of its expansion outside of Alabama. Banks outside Alabama operated under the name of Regions Bank, while those within Alabama retained the First Alabama name. Mackin's five-year profitability goals included raising

Region's return on equity (ROE) to 15% and its asset base to $12 billion by 1995. As a result of Mackin's strategy, Region's ROE was up to 15 % by the end of 1992 and up to 16.6 percent by the end of second quarter 1993, with operations expanding into Florida, Georgia, Louisiana, Mississippi, South Carolina, and Tennessee.

### ■ Colonial Bancgroup

Colonial was established in 1981 with one bank and $166 million in assets. Colonial was the fifth largest bank holding company in Alabama. Through acquisitions, Colonial had grown to a $2+ billion bank holding company with 100 offices across the Southeast. Colonial's strategy was to build market share by acquiring other financial institutions, add profitable new lines of business or product, and expand to other growth markets. In 1994, Colonial purchased two banks in Alabama, Brundidge Banking Company and Colonial Mortgage Company.

## HISTORY OF COMPASS BANK

Harry B. Brock Jr., 69, co-founded Central Bank & Trust Co. in Birmingham, Alabama, in 1964. His background was primarily in sales, which resulted in his aggressiveness in pursuing other markets. He initiated state-wide branching, expanding the bank outside its home county. He was also responsible for the bank's entrance into the Texas market, which was unique in that the bank skipped over several neighboring states to pursue a new market. Following his retirement in 1991, he continued as a director until 1997. Exhibit 6 presents a list of key events in the history of Compass Bancshares, Inc., formerly Central Bank & Trust Co. Under Brock's leadership, Central Bank enjoyed continuously improving performance and was recognized as a fast-growing company. It was also a low-cost producer, having an efficiency ratio, as measured by noninterest expenses relative to net operating revenues, lower than any of the other major Alabama banks.

Brock's past actions had instilled a strong sense of loyalty in employees. They had come to trust his decisions based on performance results. While employees felt that Brock had the best interests of the bank in mind, they were also worried about the consequences of a bank merger on their future with the company.

## COMPASS AND PAUL JONES

Upon Brock's retirement in 1991, his handpicked successor, D. Paul Jones, took the reins of Compass as President and CEO. Jones joined Compass Bank in 1978 at the request of Brock. Jones, a lawyer by background, was with the firm which handled legal matters for Compass. Since taking over as CEO of Compass in 1991, Jones, 52, had continued the record of increasing profits and earnings per share. Under his leadership, Compass has also further expanded into new markets in Texas and Florida.

| Exhibit 6 | **Brief History of the Rise of Compass Bank** |

| | |
|---|---|
| 1964 | Harry B. Brock Jr. co-founded Central Bank & Trust Co. in Birmingham, Alabama. |
| 1971 | Bank acquires the larger State National Bank in Decatur, becoming one of the first Alabama banks to move beyond its home county. |
| 1972 | D. Paul Jones Jr., an attorney with the Birmingham law firm of Balch & Bingham, becomes Central's legal counsel. |
| 1973 | Central Bancshares of the South Inc. becomes the new name for the bank holding company. |
| 1977 | *American Banker* ranks Central as one of the country's fastest growing banks. |
| 1978 | Jones leaves Balch & Bingham, joining Central as a senior vice president, general counsel, and a member of the board of directors. |
| 1980 | Brock, with Jones' assistance, is instrumental in pushing the Statewide Bank Merger Bill through the Alabama Legislature. It allows banks to branch across county lines. Jones is named executive vice president. |
| 1981 | Statewide branch banking takes effect. |
| 1984 | Jones is named vice chairman, with responsibility for financial, human resources, trust, legal, and credit departments. |
| 1987 | Central skips across several Southern states to acquire its first out-of-state bank in Houston. In later years it acquires more banks in Houston, Dallas, and San Antonio, eventually getting 69 banking offices in the state. Central moves its administrative operations to the newly built Brock Center on Birmingham's Southside. |
| 1989 | Jones is named Central's president and chief operating officer. |
| 1991 | Brock retires as Central's chairman and chief executive officer and is succeeded by his handpicked choice, Jones. Later in the year, Central buys its first bank in Florida. |
| 1993 | Central Bank of the South changes its name to Compass Bank to reflect its expansion in all directions. |

Source: Rynecki, *Birmingham Post-Herald.*

In July 1991, Central entered the Florida market with the acquisition of Citizens & Builders Federal Savings Bank, Pensacola. In 1987, Central became the first out-of-state bank to enter the Texas market with the purchase of a Houston bank. At that time, the Texas economy had taken a severe beating from collapsing oil and real estate prices. In May 1993, Central signed an agreement to purchase Spring National Bank in Houston, Texas, which was holding $75 million in assets and $67 million in deposits. This increased Central's assets in Texas to $1.8 billion. During this same period, Central also announced its intent to purchase First Federal Savings Bank of Northwest Florida for $14.4 million. This was Central's third acquisition in the Fort Walton Beach, Florida, area, increasing its Florida asset base to $223 million. In August of 1993, Central signed an agreement to purchase First Performance National Bank in Jacksonville, Florida, Central's first expansion into the northeastern region of Florida.

On November 8, 1993, Central changed its name to Compass Bancshares, Inc. in order to make the bank more marketable outside the State of Alabama.

**Exhibit 7**

## Compass Bank Mergers & Acquisitions (1991–1994)

| Acquisitions | Date Acquired | Assets Acquired (In 000s of Dollars) |
|---|---|---|
| Plaza National Bank<br>Dallas, Texas | 1-31-91 | 50,000 |
| River Oaks Bancshares, Inc.<br>Houston, Texas | 3-28-91 | 427,000 |
| Gleneagles National Bank<br>Plano, Texas | 5-9-91 | 20,000 |
| Bank of Las Colinas, N.A.<br>Irving, Texas | 5-9-91 | 30,000 |
| Citizens & Builders Federal Savings, F.S.B.<br>Pensacola, Florida | 7-12-91 | 39,000 |
| Promenade Bancshares, Inc.<br>Dallas, Texas | 7-31-91 | 170,000 |
| Ameriway Bank, N.A.<br>Houston, Texas | 12-11-91 | 40,000 |
| Interstate Bancshares, Inc.<br>Houston, Texas | 6-18-92 | 66,000 |
| City National Bancshares, Inc.<br>Carrollton, Texas | 10-28-92 | 62,000 |
| FWNB Bancshares, Inc.<br>Plano, Texas | 12-22-92 | 161,000 |
| Cornerstones Bancshares, Inc.<br>Dallas, Texas | 1-19-93 | 239,000 |
| First Federal Savings Bank of Northwest Florida<br>Ft. Walton Beach, Florida | 10-14-93 | 101,000 |
| Peoples Holding Company, Inc.<br>Ft. Walton Beach, Florida | 10-21-93 | 43,000 |
| Spring National Banking<br>Houston, Texas | 11-3-93 | 75,000 |
| First Performance National Bank<br>Jacksonville, Florida | 12-7-94 | 278,000 |
| Security Bank, N.A.<br>Houston, Texas | 5-1-94 | 76,000 |
| Anchor Savings Bank<br>Jacksonville, Florida | 5-12-94 | 100,000 |
| First Heights Bank, F.S.B.<br>Houston, Texas | 10-1-94 | 68,000 |

Source: *Compass Bancshares Annual Report*

All offices throughout Alabama, Florida, and Texas were united under one name. Compass was the name chosen for Central's Texas offices because another Texas bank was already operating under the name of Central Bank. Central also chose the name "Compass" because of its compatibility with the company's already established logo.

Compass had been expanding into the Florida and Texas markets, which were both growing faster than the Alabama market. By 1994, Compass had one-fourth of its assets based in these markets. Because Compass was a low-cost provider, it was able to offer very competitive prices on its products and services targeted at small business and consumer niches. Even with all the acquisitions made during the last few years, Compass consistently increased its return on equity.

In November 1993, Compass signed an agreement to purchase Security Bank of Houston, increasing its assets in Texas to $2 billion and its banking offices from 3 to 39. Compass completed the purchase in May 1994, and began to acquire First Heights Bank of Houston, giving Compass 22 more offices in the Houston area, $885 million in deposits, and $47 million in consumer loans. This was Compass' largest Texas transaction.

From 1991 to 1994, Compass acquired 18 financial institutions in Florida and Texas. A list of the mergers and acquisitions completed from 1991 to 1994 with their asset size and closing dates is shown in Exhibit 7.

## THE ISSUE

As Bill thinks about the situation, he tries to determine his options. Is Harry Brock rationally motivated to want to sell the bank, or is he just trying to regain control of a company he founded? Even if he loses this battle, Brock will still have other opportunities to raise other issues since he will still be serving on the Board of Directors for two more years. Jones seems to believe that a higher price for the shareholders could be realized when stock prices are not so depressed. Bill would like to know the future as to mergers in the industry.

The employees, as shareholders, will heavily influence the outcome of this battle when they vote today. As Bill enters the door of the Birmingham-Jefferson Civic Center at 9:15 A.M., the questions are still swirling in his mind. What should he do?

## REFERENCES

"Brock's Review and Critique of His Lawsuit Against Compass Bancshares, Inc." Videotape.

Cantrell, W. (July 1992). "Bama's Big Four Are Booming." *Bank Management*, 68: 36–43.

Compass Bancshares, Inc. Annual Report, 1994.

Rupinski, Patrick, "End of fight will be relief for Jones," *Birmingham News*, April 11, 1995, p. A1, A3.

Rynecki, David, "Shootout at the Compass corral," *Birmingham News*, April 12, 1995, p. F1, F5.

# Southwest Airlines Company

John J. Vitton, University of North Dakota
Charles A. Rarick, Transylvania University
Ronald P. Garrett, United States Air Force

*Internet site of interest:* **www.iflyswa.com**

W all Street was stunned when Southwest Airlines announced fourth-quarter earnings for 1994 that were far below analysts' expectations! Financially, the 1990s had been devastating for the domestic passenger airline industry. Southwest was the sole exception among the major air carriers, having rung up 22 years of consistent profitability, while other carriers hemorrhaged red ink. It was the only major carrier to achieve net and operating profits in 1990, 1991, and 1992. Yet here in black and white, Southwest stated in its 1994 annual report that it experienced a 47 percent decline in earnings in 1994's fourth quarter as compared to fourth quarter 1993. Also, as compared to 1993 levels, load factors and passenger revenue yields were depressed. Load factors, which measure an airline's percentage of seats occupied by paying passengers, fell to 57.8 percent in January 1995, down from 63.1 percent for January 1994.

Harassed by low fares offered by newly aggressive carriers such as United's "U2" and Continental's Lite, Southwest responded by slashing its already ultra-cheap fares. Southwest was particularly provoked by United's apparent targeting of the California market with "U-2," a Southwestern style, low-cost, no-frills operation. Gary Kelly, Southwest's Chief Financial Officer, "noted that intra-California traffic accounts for 10-15% of Southwest's total business." He also stated that "Since we're already on a competitive stance with United, we'll simply confine our efforts, particularly our long-haul service to markets where United dominates."[1] These fare wars came at a rather inopportune time, when Southwest was digesting the acquisition of Salt Lake City-based Morris Air. While the acquisition gave Southwest a presence in the Pacific Northwest, the one-time acquisition cost of $10 million and the conversion of the Morris operation into that of the parent company hurt Southwest's bottom line. Southwest's 13% increase in capacity in 1994 was also provoking a competitive response.

Herb Kelleher, Southwest's ebullient CEO, was identified as "Commander-in-Chief" in the aircarrier's first-ever national TV ad campaign. Speaking from a mocked-up war room, with "Wild Blue Yonder" playing in the background, Herb said: "It's not a gimmick, it's not a promotion with us. It's something we believe in with all of our fiber. It's every seat, every flight, everywhere we fly. Other airlines try to copy Southwest, but they're just facsimiles of the real thing. Southwest is THE low-fare airline. If there's a fare war, they're gonna get nuked."[2]

# COMPANY HISTORY

The Southwest Airline operation is truly a Horatio Alger story! During a 1967 luncheon meeting, Herbert D. Kelleher, a young San Antonio lawyer, was discussing with his client Rollin King, a Texas entrepreneur and pilot, the bankruptcy of a small air carrier, which had served small Texas towns. Later in the meeting, King broached the concept of a low-fare, no-frills, short haul airline with frequent flights between major Texas cities. Three points of a napkin were labeled—Dallas, Houston, and San Antonio.

Initially skeptical and later intrigued by King's plan, Kelleher raised $560,000 to back the venture. An application was filed with the Texas Aeronautics Commission in November 1967; however, starting up an airline was very difficult as the airline industry was heavily regulated. The burden of proof was on King and Kelleher to convince the Texas regulators that a new airline was needed. In February 1968, the Commission approved and issued a certificate to Air Southwest Company to fly from Love Field, Dallas, to Houston and San Antonio. Braniff, Continental, and Trans Texas obtained a restraining order to block Southwest's certificate from taking effect, claiming that the Texas market could not possibly support another air carrier. Investors urged Kelleher to give up the fight after losing the first two of three courtroom battles. Kelleher persevered and won the third battle when the Texas Supreme Court ruled in Air Southwest's favor. This allowed the airline to begin service with a fleet of three aircraft. Lamar Muse was hired to run the airline, which was renamed Southwest Airlines. Muse, as the former president of several airlines, brought extensive airline knowledge to the new company. His initial actions included buying four 737-200 aircraft and hiring veterans from Braniff, American Airlines, and Trans Texas to help mold and create an innovative approach to operations which is still prevalent today.[3] On June 18, 1971, the first Southwest flight took off from Love Field in Dallas headed for Houston.

In 1971, one-way Southwest fares were $20 for the flights from Dallas to San Antonio and from Dallas to Houston. The company lost $3.7 million in its first eleven months in operation. Southwest added a fourth plane to its fleet in September 1971, and two months later opened service on the third leg of the triangle, Houston to San Antonio. On February 1, 1973, Braniff initiated price wars on the flights between Dallas and Houston and Southwest countered by offering half-fare tickets. Despite fare wars, Southwest proudly proclaimed 1973 as its first profitable year.[4] The airline also announced that it was expanding its routes into the Rio Grande Valley (Harlingen), Texas.

There were more battles to be fought, however. A hearing was held in U.S. District Court on whether Southwest would be allowed to remain at Dallas Love Field, or be forced to move with other airlines to the new Dallas-Fort Worth Regional Airport. Judge W.M. Taylor Jr. ruled in April 1973 that Southwest could operate out of Love Field as long as it remained open as an airport.[5] Southwest gained a virtual monopoly position at Love Field, which was much closer to downtown Dallas than the Dallas-Forth Worth airport. This monopoly proved to be limiting, however, when the Wright Amendment became law in 1979. This law, championed by Texas U.S. representative James Wright, who later was forced out of office for misuse of funds, prevented airlines operating out of Love Field from providing direct service to states other than those neighboring Texas. Southwest's customers could fly from Love Field to Arkansas, Louisiana, New Mexico, and Oklahoma, but had to buy new tickets and board different Southwest flights to points beyond.

Braniff was fined the maximum of $100,000 on December 27, 1978, for using illegal tactics designed to force Southwest Airlines out of business. As a result of this settlement, Southwest was able to add to its Boeing fleet.

The Airline Deregulation Act of 1978 allowed Southwest to enter markets outside the state of Texas. This expansion will be described in the Operations Section.

In the 1980s, Southwest's annual passenger traffic count tripled. Nearly bankrupt Muse Air Corporation, founded by one-timer Southwest Executive, Lamar Muse, was sold to Southwest in 1985, which operated that Houston-based airline as TranStar. TranStar was liquidated in 1987 when profits fell, due to competition from Houston-based Continental Airlines.

*Air Transport World* magazine named Southwest the 1992 "Airline of the Year," stating that "Southwest has demonstrated excellence over the years in disciplines required for safe, reliable, and fairly priced air transportation."[6] The airline also won the first annual Triple Crown for the best on-time performances, best baggage handling record, and best customer satisfaction in 1992 and repeated again in 1993.

In 1994, Southwest expanded its service into the Northwest and California by acquiring Salt Lake City-based Morris Air on December 31, 1993.

# THE AIRLINE INDUSTRY

The dawn of U.S. commercial aviation occurred on January 1, 1934. Passengers could fly one-way between Tampa and St. Petersburg, Florida, for $5.00 in a open-cockpit Benoist flying boat. The day-long trip by land took only 20 minutes by air. Financial troubles resulted in bankruptcy for the airline only four months later.[7]

The formative years and even the more mature stage of the airline industry life cycle were characterized by heavy government regulation of private carriers. Economists frequently identify protection of a fledgling industry from destructive competition and national defense as two of the primary justifications for governmental intervention in a market-driven economy. Regulation by the U.S. government of the airline industry began with a series of air mail acts beginning with the Kelly Act of 1925, which authorized airmail contracts between the U.S. Post Office and private carriers and made the postmaster general "the czar of the industry without competitive bidding."[8] Air mail contracts were extremely important to the fledgling airlines to supplement meager passenger revenue. The Air Mail Act of 1934 severed aircraft manufacturers' linkage to the airline industry. Boeing had to divest itself of United Airlines, Pratt & Whitney engines, and Sikorsky helicopter. General Motors sold its stock in Eastern and Western airlines, AVCO gave up American, and North American Aviation sold its TWA holdings. The Post Office, Interstate Commerce Commission, and Department of Commerce were all involved in developing weather information, navigational aids, and airport facilities. Also, in 1934, the nation's 24 domestic airlines were placed under the Railway Labor Act.[9]

By 1936, airline income from passengers surpassed that from airmail. The stretched-out, incredibly strong DC-3, designed by Jack Northrup, increased the speed and comfort of air travel. It operated reliably and profitably, and made the Ford Trimotor obsolete. Pan American pioneered Pacific flights in 1935, spanning the sea in Clipper Ships that pampered their passengers in airborne grand hotels.

By 1938, the airline industry was in critical financial shape and several major airlines faced bankruptcy. In response, Congress passed the McCarren-Lea Act (better known as the Civil Aeronautics Act) in 1938, which superseded all previous civil aviation legislation. The new Act created the Civil Aeronautics Board (CAB) to administer the Act. The CAB set fares, awarded domestic airline routes, and also determined which airlines would fly them. The Board also approved mergers, and forbade any airline from operating without being certified by CAB. This in effect established barriers to entry and curbed destructive competition. The Act also enabled the CAB to determine subsidy levels, write consumer regulations concerning overbooking, establish lost luggage policies, and regulate air safety.

In 1956, the jet age was ushered in by the 600-mph Boeing 707 and Douglas DC-8, which marked the end of an era of propeller-driven airliners such as the DC-4 and the pressurized Lockhead Constellation. That same year a TWA Super Constellation and a United DC-7 collided over Grand Canyon, killing 128 people. This led to a reorganization of governmental regulatory agencies. The Civil Aeronautics Act was superseded in 1958 by the Federal Aviation Act, which established the Federal Aviation Agency (FAA) as the watchdog of air safety. The FAA responsibilities were for safety rules, use of navigable air space, and development of air navigation facilities. The CAB was left intact to administer airline pricing and routing policies and was responsible for accident investigations. In 1967, Congress created the Department of Transportation (DOT) and abolished the Federal Aviation Agency. Safety came under the Department of Transportation's jurisdiction within the Federal Aviation Administration.

While real gross national product grew by 3.6 percent between 1949 and 1980, constant dollar domestic airline passenger revenue increased by 9.0 percent per annum. . . . Domestic air passenger miles rose by 11.4 percent annually from 1949 to 1980. During the same period, intercity rail and bus passenger counts were declining by 1.8 percent a year. Air transport volume exceeded the rail and bus total in 1964 and by 1981, 65 percent of the U.S. adult population had flown at least once.[10]

Air carrier profits plummeted during the recessionary period 1957–58 and the CAB approved domestic price increases on passenger rates. From 1962 through 1968, "the price of an average airline ticket declined by more than 13 percent. . . . By 1968 productivity gains began to be outpaced by rising costs—

of labor, landing fees, and interest charges. The CAB approved of several small increases but in 1970, the airline industry recorded the largest loss in its previous history. Fuel costs soared during the 1970s, rising from 13 percent of airline operating expenses to 31% by 1980, due to OPEC cartel pricing policies in 1974 and again in 1979."[11]

The deregulation movement began in 1974. Many economists and consumer advocates, such as Ralph Nader, cited the lower fares of the unregulated intrastate air carriers in California and Texas (22-26% lower than interstate carriers) and called for the abolishment of the CAB. In 1974, the airline industry could be described as an oligopoly with the "Big Four" being American, Eastern, Trans World, and United. In earlier years, the airlines established fares at approximately the level of standard railroad passenger fares plus Pullman car charges. Under the CAB, airline management did not have to manage finances carefully, as the CAB would allow a 10-12% return on assets (ROA) to be tacked on to labor, fuel, and other costs. This was then passed on to customers in the form of higher prices. Many also felt that the economies of jet aircraft were not reflected in lower prices to the customer.

The Airline Deregulation Act was passed by Congress on October 24, 1978. The CAB was phased out in a "twilight zone" with domestic routing decisions coming under the jurisdiction of the airlines. The CAB lost authority over domestic rates and fares on January 1, 1983, and the CAB was out of existence on December 31, 1984. On January 1, 1985, the CAB's authority over foreign air transportation matters was transferred to the Department of Transportation in consultation with the Department of State. The CAB's authority over mergers, intercarrier agreements, and antitrust immunities for foreign transport was turned over to the Department of Justice. However, in the twilight years, DOT was given approval over mergers. Safety responsibilities remained with DOT's Federal Aviation Administration.

Immediately after the Deregulation Act of 1978, the second OPEC oil shock hit the aviation industry with hurricane force. This was followed by the illegal strike by the Professional Air Traffic Controllers Organization (PATCO). Eleven thousand FAA controllers, who had signed an employment oath not to strike against their government, went out on strike and were subsequently fired after a warning by President Reagan to return to work within 48 hours. Despite soaring interest rates, the 1979-1982 recession, and escalating oil prices, more than 120 new airlines appeared, with most being small commuter lines.[12] As of 1988, over 200 airlines went bankrupt or had been acquired in mergers since deregulation; only 74 carriers remained.[13] Among the casualties since 1978 were Braniff, Eastern, Pan American, Peoples Express, Air Florida, Midwest, Frontier, and a host of smaller carriers.

Major airlines, unshackled from the North-South or East-West air routes required by CAB edicts, have gone to a hub-and-spoke flight structure which uses feeder aircraft operating on the spokes to consolidate passengers at the hubs. In 1988, "450 million passengers boarded commercial airlines, compared to 275 million in 1978. However, with nine of ten airline passengers traveling on some sort of discounted fare, the average cost of travel on an airliner has dropped 13 percent over the last decade if inflation is taken into account, according to the Transportation Department."[14]

The airline industry recently chalked up its greatest growth: 56% more passengers crammed aboard its planes in 1990 than a decade before. The 1980s was a time of heady expansion, of billion-dollar aircraft orders, and rapid addition of international routes. Horizontal mergers were allowed and eight carriers swallowed 11 others. Economists viewed the industry as a highflier across a business landscape marred by the declining auto, steel, and energy industries.[15]

"In the ten years (1978-1988) since deregulation, the Department of Transportation presided over 21 mergers. During that era, the ten largest airlines controlled 93 percent of the domestic market, compared with 89 percent in 1977, in part as a result of major airlines gobbling up regional and other smaller carriers."[16] Two of the Department of Transportation mergers, Northwest/Republic and USAir/Piedmont, were challenged by the antitrust division of the Department of Justice to no avail.

In 1988, at last count, the eight largest airlines had gained effective control over 48 of the 50 largest regionals. The Department of Transportation allowed the major airlines to acquire numerous commuter airlines. Alfred Kahn, now a Cornell University professor and formerly the chairman of the Civil Aeronautics Board, was the principal architect of airline deregulation. Noting the flurry of mergers and acquisitions, Kahn stated that "consumers are more likely to be exploited."[17]

In the early 1990s, the airline industry was confronted with a bath of red ink, excessive leverage often twice what is considered prudent, and a business turndown that reduced revenue. More than 100,000 airline employees have been laid off since 1989. Many others have taken pay cuts. In addition, the U.S. Justice Department has been investigating airline price fixing. The concern involves anticompetitive price signaling using the computerized reservation systems. Also, computer bias—giving an advantage to the computer owner's by listing their flights prior to leasee flights—and other "dirty tricks," such as computer screens showing competitor's flights filled when they were not, were other concerns.

Deep discount for the discretionary (leisure) traveler, while the business traveler pays higher fares, created another problem area. In 1993, 92% of airline passengers bought their tickets at a discount, paying on average just 35% of full fare. Frequent flyer programs are extensively used to promote customer loyalty.

High concentration, resulting in a few airlines controlling landing slots and gates, is a major concern at many hub airports. Some studies have shown the routing through hubs has increased air fares rather than reducing them.

Major airlines are concerned that weak competitors in Chapter 11 bankruptcy are permitted to disregard creditor short-term claims and their subsequent low prices make competition destructive. Between 1989 and 1993, the industry lost $12 billion and Southwest alone showed a profit.[18] Air safety is at an all-time high. The industry is heavily unionized but has been cutting costs through layoffs, reduction in food items offered, and two-tier pay schemes. Delta, United, American, US Air, and Northwest were the leading firms in an industry confronted with huge losses.

By 1995, the airlines recovered from their financial swoon, with Northwest and others registering significant profits. "Low cost airlines generated about $1.4 billion in revenue in 1994, up from $450 million in 1992 and next to nothing in 1989," according to Paul Karos, an airline analyst at CS First Boston. John Dasburg, Northwest Airlines CEO, says that the new low cost, short haul carriers "are viable products, they will endure, for the same reason Motel 6 endures. This product will be defined. It will be located in the top hundred markets that are 750 nautical miles or less from each other."[19]

# HUMAN RESOURCES

## ■ Management

Herbert D. Kelleher is Chairman of the Board, President, and Chief Executive Officer and the driving force behind Southwest's success. Son of a Campbell Soup Company manager, Herb Kelleher's formative years were spent in Haddon Heights, New Jersey. Herb was star athlete and student body president at Haddon Heights High School. He graduated from Wesleyan University in Connecticut where he studied English literature. Later, he attended New York University Law school. Herb and his wife moved in 1961 to San Antonio, Texas, where he entered his father-in-law's law firm. During Southwest's early years, Kelleher served as general counselor and director of the firm. When Lamar Muse, Southwest's president, resigned in 1978 because of differences with Rollin King, Kelleher became president. Three years later Kelleher took over as CEO and president of Southwest Airlines Company.

Herb is a 62-year-old Irishman, a workaholic, who smokes five packs of cigarettes a day and is considered to be one of the zaniest CEOs in America. He loves to party and drink and has been known to sing "Tea for Two" while wearing bloomers and a bonnet at a company picnic. One Easter, he walked a plane's aisle clad in an Easter bunny suit and on St. Patrick's day, he dressed as a leprechaun.[20] Behind all of this is a leader who works 14-hour days, seven days a week, and leads by example. His management style— referred to as "management by insanity"—is far from any textbook style and it has worked extremely well. He has made work at Southwest fun for its employees and customers. He encourages flight attendants to organize trivia contests, delivering instructions to customers in rap fashion and awarding prizes to customers with the biggest holes in their socks.[21] Kelleher uses the "Management By Walking Around" (MBWA) concept. He regularly helps flight attendants serve drinks and peanuts when he flies. Every quarter, Kelleher and other top managers work a different job within the company for a day.[22] They have been observed doing tasks ranging from serving as counter agents, to loading baggage, to serving drinks. Southwest has fostered the practice of trying to breed leaders, not managers or administrators. Kelleher's span of control was reduced from 13 executives earlier to only four or five to free him up to monitor long-term developments, promote growth, and also to maintain good employee and customer relations. Some critics claim Kelleher holds power very tightly and he is the only one who makes major decisions. Some of the decisions were not so good, such as the acquisition of Muse Air. Others say Herb is the type of manager who will drink at a bar in the early hours of the morning with a mechanic just to find out what is wrong. Then he will fix the problem.

Until 1991, Southwest was the only major airline without an incentive stock-option plan for management personnel. There are no other management perks and executives receive the same percentage of pay increases as other employees. Southwest officers, with the exception of Kelleher, are in the 35- to 48-year-old bracket. On March 23, 1993, Herb Kelleher was appointed to a highly visible congressional commission entitled the National Commission to Ensure a Strong Competitive Airline Industry.

## ■ EMPLOYEES

Herb Kelleher proudly proclaimed that "The people who work here don't think of Southwest as a business. They think of it as a crusade."[23]

Southwest's personnel department is called the "University of People," to reflect top management's attitude toward its employees. Southwest generally recruits only in cities into which it flies in order to obtain employees who are familiar with Southwest. Recruiters are looking for that "Southwest Personality" of friendliness, warmth, and kindness. They search for people who are extroverts with a sense of humor. Recruiters ask prospective employees questions such as: "Tell me how you recently used your sense of humor in a work environment" and "Tell me how you used humor to defuse a difficult situation." Job candidates who can't answer these questions satisfactorily are automatically disqualified. Only one in ten applicants fits the company's image and is hired. Southwest looks for extroverts with a team attitude. One flight attendant played "The Eyes of Texas" on his harmonica over the loudspeaker after touchdown and sang cautions about remaining seated until coming to a full stop at the terminal. A customer reported the attendant received "three ovations from the passengers and would have had a standing ovation except that the seat-belt sign was on." Southwest does not hire anyone from other airlines as it does not want to inherit their problems.[24] The motto at Southwest is: "Do it right, but keep it light."

Levering and Moskowitz also found that "Southwest also put a lot of money into training. Its University for People, located in a terminal building at Dallas's Love Field, not far from the corporate headquarters, runs quarterly leadership training programs that are required for all supervisors and managers. Customer-care programs are run by line-level employees. For example, flight attendants teach other flight attendants. Pilots get customer-care training, a very rare practice in the airline industry. This is in keeping with Herb Kelleher's answer to the question why his low-fare carrier had been posting profits: 'We dignify the customer.'"

Training is emphasized in part because Southwest promotes from within. The airline fills roughly 80 percent of higher-level jobs through internal promotion.

While almost 90% of Southwest's employees are unionized, they do not exhibit the adversarial roles found in many major corporations. Contract agreements allow very flexible work rules. Pilots and flight attendants are often seen cleaning the aircraft between flights.[25] New contracts have been signed recently with the Southwest Airlines Pilot Association; the Teamsters, which represents mechanics, aircraft cleaners, and stock clerks; the IAM, which represents customer-service and reservations employees; the Ramp, Operations, and Provisioning Association and Southwest Airlines Professional Instructors Association. In January 1995, Standard & Poor's noted that Southwest Airlines took a major step to reinforce its market share when it reached an innovative, ten-year agreement with its pilots. The contract maintains current pay rates for five years, with 37% raises in three of the final five years. Stock options are offered in lieu of pay increases.

With an average salary of $47,000, Southwest's work force is among the airline industry's best paid and its productivity is also higher than the industry's average.[26] Southwest was the first carrier to offer a profit-sharing plan to employees (1973) and some early participants have become millionaires. Employees can collect only when they leave. Other benefits include unlimited space-available travel for employees and their families and fully transferable passes for accomplishments such as perfect attendance. Southwest also offers a flexible health-benefit program under which employees can choose coverage suitable to their individual circumstances, and a stock-purchase plan under which employees can acquire stock at 90% of market value via payroll deductions.[27] Employees own about 10% of the company's outstanding shares.

Kelleher has delegated to the lowest level the authority to make decisions on the spot without having to wade through layers of management and waste valuable time. Says Kelleher: "The bigger we get, the smaller I want our employees to think and act." The 1993 edition of *The 100 Best Companies to Work For In America* chose Southwest as one of the ten best. "Last year, Southwest's turnover was about 7% including retirements—half the industry average."[28] In 1990, when fuel prices skyrocketed, one-third of the Southwest employees contributed $130,000, unbeknownst to upper management, to offset some of the increased operating costs.

Herb Kelleher, in the company's 1991 annual report, attributed the airline's success to its business strategy and "because our people have the hearts of lions, the strength of elephants, and the determination of water buffaloes."

## OPERATIONS

Southwest runs one of the most impressive operations in the airline industry. Its 203 aircraft make over 1,900 flights a day. In 1994, Southwest generated 624,476 flights, carrying 42,742,602 customers in perfect safety to their destinations. (SWA, 1994 Annual Report)

Southwest's gates average 10.5 departures a day, whereas the industry average is only 4.5 departures. Southwest's aircraft are airborne for an average of eleven hours and ten minutes per day, compared to the industry average of only eight hours. The airline's philosophy is that it can make money only when the aircraft are in the air. Seventy percent of the time, Southwest is able to off-load a group of passengers, service the aircraft, and board a new group of passengers in 15 minutes (see Exhibit 1).[29] Ten percent of the turnarounds are under ten minutes. Most airlines require an hour's ground time to turnaround a flight. This feat is made possible by "guaranteeing seats" but not reserving them with only one class of seat. Groups of thirty are given plastic chips at the gate and board in a first come, first on board operation. Not having to load meals onboard also speeds up the turnaround as does aircrew help in cleaning the aircraft (See Exhibit 1). In 1994, only 0.86 percent of the airline's flights were canceled or delayed due to mechanical incidents. (SWA, 1994 Annual Report, p. 8)

Operating only Boeing 737 series jet aircraft, Southwest simplifies its training, maintenance, and inventory costs. The company's fleet of aircraft averaged only 7.7 years of age at the end of 1994. "At year's end 1994, Southwest owned 97 of the 199 aircraft in the fleet. Of the remaining 102 aircraft, 72 were operated pursuant to long-term leases with various renewal and purchase options at the end of the lease periods and 30 of the older 737s were under short-term leases expiring over the next several years."[30] Southwest contracts out all heavy engine maintenance plus most component work to firms that can do the work for less than doing it in-house. Almost 75 percent of Southwest's fleet have Stage 3 engines which are quieter and more fuel efficient. Twenty-five

**Exhibit 1**

### Anatomy of a 15-Minute Turnaround

| | |
|---|---|
| 7:55 | Ground crew chat around gate position. |
| 8:03:30 | Ground crew alerted, move to their vehicles. |
| 8:04 | Plane begins to pull into gate; crew moves toward plane. |
| 8:04:30 | Plane stops; jetway telescopes out; baggage door opens. |
| 8:06:30 | Baggage unloaded; refueling and other servicing underway. |
| 8:07 | Passengers off plane. |
| 8:08 | Boarding call; baggage loading, refueling complete. |
| 8:10 | Boarding complete; most of ground crew leaves. |
| 8:15 | Jetway retracts. |
| 8:15:30 | Pushback from gate. |
| 8:18 | Push-back tractor disengages; plane leaves for runway. |

On a recent weekday a Southwest Airlines flight arrived at New Orleans from Houston. The scheduled arrival time was 8:00 A.M., and departure for Birmingham, Alabama, was 8:18 A.M. *Forbes* clocked the turnaround, half-minute by half-minute.

Source: "Hit'em Hardest with the Mostest," *Forbes*, September 16, 1991.

737-300 aircraft are scheduled for delivery in 1997, 16 in 1998, and ten in 1999. Between 1997 and 2001, 63 Boeing 737-700 aircraft will be delivered to Southwest. This series is more fuel efficient, easier to maintain, and is expected to be quieter.

In 1989, Southwest became a major airline when it exceeded the billion dollar revenue benchmark. The airline has grown to become the sixth largest U.S. air carrier in terms of domestic customers it transported. Southwest flies to 45 cities in 22 states. (SWA, 1994 Annual Report)

Southwest's strategy is to provide high-frequency, short haul, point-to-point, not hub-and-spoke—low-fare flights. All of Southwest's flights are under two hours in flying time and under 750 nautical miles. Airports near city centers are used whenever possible—e.g., Dallas' Love Field, Chicago's Midway, Detroit Municipal Airport, etc. In an interview with a *Forbes* reporter in 1991, a Southwest executive defended Southwest's slow growth, saying "We attack a city with a lot of flights, which is another form of aggression in the airline industry. We don't go in with just one or two flights—we'll go in with ten or twelve. That eats up a lot of airplanes and capacity, so you can't open a lot of cities. Call it a kind of guerrilla warfare against bigger opponents. You hit them with everything you've got in one or two places instead of trying to fight them everywhere."[31] (See Exhibit 2.) Southwest held a 65% market share in its top 100 markets, as of second quarter 1994, and its passenger load factor was 67.3 percent.

Southwest's rock-bottom fares are often a third below those of its competitors. For example, "In the first quarter of 1991, Southwest's fares were 15% lower than those of its nearest competitor, American West, 29% lower than Delta's, 32% lower than United's, and 39% lower than US Air's."[32] To promote those remarkably low ticket prices, Southwest has to control costs tightly. Its operating costs per available seat mile were 2.3 percent lower in 1994 than in

**Exhibit 2**    **Airline Efficiency Measures**

|  | Airline Passengers Per Employee | Cost Per Available Seat - Mile (Cents) |
|---|---|---|
| AMR | 863 | 8.25 |
| Delta | 1,181 | 9.26 |
| Northwest | 1,015 | 9.51 |
| Southwest | 2,523 | 7.20 |
| UAL | 837 | 9.30 |
| USAir | 1,141 | 11.09 |
| Continental | 850 | 7.91 |
| TWA | 731 | 9.64 |

Source: Commercial Aviation Report, 1993 Data, "Southwest's New Deal," *Fortune*, January 16, 1995, p. 94.

1993. Labor and fuel costs are the most significant, with each ranging as high as 35% of costs. Travel agent fees range between 8% and 14%, with an average of approximately 10%.

As of 1994, Southwest Airlines operated eight reservation centers located in Albuquerque, Chicago, Dallas, Houston, Little Rock, Oklahoma City, Phoenix, and Salt Lake City. "Southwest in recent months (July 1994), was dropped by the major computer reservation systems owned by competitors such as United, US Air, and Continental, which have been hurt by Southwest's expansion into East Coast markets. The reservation system owners maintained that since Southwest refused to pay fees for having its flights listed in their systems, it should not enjoy the same benefits as paying carriers. Southwest has refused to pay these fees, and is listed now only on American Airline's Sabre system." Travel agents currently sell 80% of U.S. airline tickets. Their commissions ranged from 12.96% (1990), 14.08% (1991), 14.31% (1992), to 14.36% (1993). To counter these escalating fees, Southwest is using ticketless systems. Passengers are given confirmation numbers over the telephone for their flights and present identification to airline personnel at airport gates. Also, the growth of on-line systems, which provide access to travel-related information, is causing a growth spurt in personal computer sales. Southwest has added more agents and new reservations centers to iron out the problems that still exist in its overloaded reservation system.

# MARKETING

From the beginning, Southwest has been dedicated to offering point-to-point service in short haul markets with low fares; frequent, conveniently timed flights; and friendly, reliable customer service. This market niche strategy has helped the airline become the sixth largest, and one of the strongest. It has heavily promoted these benefits to consumers. Until recently, Southwest was the only airline of this type. As Donald Valentine, Southwest's Vice President of Marketing and Sales, states, "While we make no pretense at being every-thing for everyone, we constantly strive to improve our convenient, depend-able service for travelers who want to get to their destinations on time, inexpensively—with no hassles." As a result of its marketing strategy, South-west has consistently ranked first in market share in more than 90 percent of its top 50 city-pair markets and is currently holding an overall market share exceeding 65 percent. (SWA, 1994 Annual Report)

Southwest established an innovative frequent flyer program which is based on trips flown, not total miles. Valentine orchestrated this plan to appeal to business and other short haul customers. Passenger contests are held in flight with winners obtaining frequent flyer miles and vacations.[33] The unique frequent flyer program is called "Company Club." After membership is attained with ten round-trip flights, Southwest awards a free trip to the club member and from then on, it takes only eight round-trip flights for each additional free trip. It is the only program by a major airline that rewards a person for short trips.

Southwest does answer the 1,000 or so letters it receives each week with a personal response. It takes up to 1,500 man-hours a week from 45 employees and two departments. Kelleher believes that the letters are the best system he has found to monitor airline performance.

The *product* Southwest Airlines Company is trying to sell can be described as follows, according to the 1991 Southwest Airlines Annual Report: "Southwest is the nation's low fare, high customer satisfaction airline. We primarily serve short haul city pairs, providing single class air transportation which targets the business commuter as well as leisure traveler." Air transportation is the prod-uct that can be served or sold to two types of travelers, business and leisure (discretionary).

Southwest's *prices* are purposefully low because its principal competition in short haul markets is often ground transportation. The airline wants to make flying more cost effective than driving a car or taking a train between two points. According to Southwest's annual report, it recognizes that the leisure market, which is highly price sensitive, is very large and can be stimulated with low fares. As a result, Southwest tends to grow its own markets, often stimulating traffic three- and four-fold versus traffic levels previously existing. "As is typical for Southwest when it's battling for market share, its fares are cheap. For instance, the airline said tickets for any intra-California routes will cost $69 each. Two types of discount fares are offered. The average fare nation-wide for a Southwest ticket is $58. Southwest's fares are approximately one-third lower than the prices of its competitors."[34]

Southwest has the lowest operating costs in the industry. This enables the air carrier to offer low fares which are vital to the short haul customer. One reason Southwest's operating costs are so low is because of its point-to-point travel system, compared to the hub-and-spoke systems other airlines use. This gives Southwest the ability to provide high frequency flights between city-pairs. This results in lower ticket fares compared to competitors. South-west would like an average of ten or more trips per day along these routes, each averaging two hours of flight time or less. For example, Southwest used this strategy in the highly traveled California market. As a result, Southwest is able to offer the lowest fares along any major route, getting travelers (business as well as pleasure) out of their cars and into Southwest jets. Major airlines such as United or American are either forced out of the market or have to compete on Southwest's terms. Competitors often call Southwest's niche strategy the "through-the-legs philosophy," avoiding head-on competition with the giants by going around them.[35]

The fact that Southwest Airlines does not have a reserved seating system is another reason operating costs are low. A potential traveler calls the airline directly for a reservation or can use one of Southwest's innovative ticket machines at the airport to purchase a ticket. This reduces the cost of a reservation system and also makes it more convenient for the customer.

Finally, Southwest has only one type of aircraft in its fleet. The Boeing 737 is the principal aircraft. This significantly simplifies maintenance, flight operations, and training activities. The 737 has been recognized as one of aviation's most successful aircraft. It is attractive, comfortable, and is cost-effective to operate in the short- to medium-range markets.

Southwest Airlines uses a variety of *promotions* to market its *product* to the flying public. Southwest will sponsor major sporting events such as the Southwest Conference basketball tournament or competitive athletic teams, using its logo as an attraction. The airline promotes its frequent flyer program. Southwest rewards customers with the shortest route to free trips—a frequent flyer program based on a few short trips, not long mileage. Southwest will also sponsor many charity events in an effort to help those who are less fortunate. In an effort to celebrate its partnership with Sea World of Texas and California, Southwest painted three of its aircraft to look like Shamu, the famous whale at Sea World. The airline also painted an aircraft with the Texas State Flag on it in tribute to its home state of Texas. Southwest was also the official airline for San Antonio's "Viva Fiesta 1993."

Southwest makes it a point to give customers the most flights available to destinations so they can better plan their schedules. This, coupled with Southwest's use of convenient downtown airports, makes flying easier and—most importantly—cost-effective for its customers.

The *place* portion of the marketing mix is very important to Southwest. Currently, Southwest operates 203 planes flying to 45 cities in the midwestern, southwestern, and western regions of the United States. Southwest tends to stay away from areas in which its short turnaround times would be in jeopardy. This makes flights along the New York, Boston, and Washington, D.C., corridors nearly impossible to penetrate. Southwest also wants to fly in areas where it doesn't have to go head-to-head with the major carriers. For example, airlines such as American and United used to fly frequent routes along the Dallas, San Antonio, and Houston triangle. But, this market was prime for Southwest's short haul, low cost philosophy. As a result, Southwest, with its no-frills approach compared to the full service approach of the other carriers, was able to carve its own niche in this market and go around the competition. Currently, Southwest has the largest market share in the Texas, California, and Phoenix regions due to this philosophy.

## FINANCE

Southwest's 21 years of continued profitability began in 1973, the airline's second full year of operation. Only two quarters have been marred by red ink. In 1987, the first quarter loss was attributed to Southwest's ill-fated 1985 acquisition of Muse Air. By 1987, Muse was draining $2 million a month from South-west, so Kelleher shut down the operation. Its $4.6 million, 1990 fourth-quarter net loss was only the second in 71 quarters.[36]

In 1989, Southwest's annual operating revenues exceeded $1 billion. This made Southwest a major airline, according to Department of Transportation definitions. Only ten domestic carriers presently earn revenues of over $1 billion annually. Southwest Airlines has one of the strongest financial statements in the airline industry. It continues to have the highest profit margins, the lowest operating costs, and a high credit rating. The absence of a huge debt load sets it apart from other major airlines. At a time when other airlines have up to 275% of their assets financed, Southwest has approximately 54%.

In 1990, Salomon Brothers ranked Southwest second among the major airlines in financial strength. Only two U.S. major carriers posted 1990 operating profits, with Southwest racking up $81.9 million and American $68 million. Net profits were generated by only two airlines. United's net income was $95.8 million and Southwest's $47.1 million in 1990. Gary Kelly, the Vice President of finance for Southwest, stated, "We emphasize cost controls, sound marketing, and growth at a reasonable rate. That makes the finance official's job easy." Southwest has never missed a dividend payment since dividends were initiated in 1976.

Between 1991 and 1992, Southwest's passenger revenues increased 28.3%, its freight revenues jumped 25.5%, and other revenues rose 46.6%. Even more impressive, Southwest's net income increased from $27 million in 1991 to $91 million in 1992, and its cash position was $303.1 million. On the other side of the coin, operating expenses increased 20.1% from 1991 to 1992. The primary factors contributing to the increases were the addition of seventeen 737 aircraft, higher travel agency commissions, increased contributions to profit sharing, higher aircraft leasing charges, and increased maintenance costs. (SWA Annual Reports) According to Kelleher, "Hard times come on a regular basis. Our secret is that we manage in good times as if it were hard times, and then we are ready for hard times."[37]

Because of the company's astute leadership, conservative expansion, and sound financial condition, it is able to access the capital markets to acquire new aircraft, expand operations, and continue the patient development of new short haul city pairs. Southwest has an impressive unrestricted, revolving credit of $250 million from a number of domestic banks. For further financial information see the Consolidated Balance Sheet (Exhibit 3) and the Consolidated Statement of Income (Exhibit 4).

## THE FUTURE

Wall Street analysts, institutional investors, and financial reporters are standing by to hear "the rest of the story!" Will Southwest reverse the 1994 plunge in earnings of 47%? Will load factors improve? Has Southwest expanded too rapidly and will it enter bankruptcy as did Braniff, in the years following enactment of the Airline Deregulation Act? Can Southwest maintain its distinctive culture as it grows? With the delivery of the new Boeing 737-x aircraft set for 1997, will Southwest make good on its threats to offer transcontinental flights?

# Exhibit 3

**Southwest Consolidated Balance Sheet**
**(in thousands except/share and per share amounts)**

| | Years Ended December 31, | | | |
| | 1995 | 1994 | 1993 | 1992 |
|---|---|---|---|---|
| *Assets:* | | | | |
| Current assets: | | | | |
| Cash and cash equivalents | $ 317,363 | $ 174,538 | $ 295,571 | $ 437,989 |
| Accounts receivable | 79,781 | 75,692 | 70,484 | 57,355 |
| Inventories of parts and supplies, at cost | 41,032 | 37,565 | 31,707 | 30,758 |
| Deferred income taxes | 10,476 | 9,822 | 10,475 | — |
| Prepaid expenses and other current assets | 24,484 | 17,281 | 23,787 | 15,792 |
| Total current assets | 473,136 | 314,898 | 432,024 | 541,894 |
| Property and equipment, at cost | | | | |
| Flight equipment | 3,024,702 | 2,564,551 | 2,257,809 | 1,874,085 |
| Ground property and equipment | 435,822 | 384,501 | 329,605 | 294,458 |
| Deposits on flight equipment purchase contracts | 323,864 | 393,749 | 242,230 | 214,584 |
| | 3,784,388 | 3,342,801 | 2,829,644 | 2,383,127 |
| Less allowance for depreciation | 1,005,081 | 837,838 | 688,280 | 559.034 |
| | 2,779,307 | 2,504,963 | 2,141,364 | 1,824,093 |
| Other assets | 3,679 | 3,210 | 2,649 | 2,869 |
| | $ 3,256,122 | $ 2,823,071 | $ 2,576,037 | $ 2,368,856 |
| *Liabilities and Stockholders' Equity* | | | | |
| Current Liabilities: | | | | |
| Accounts payable | $ 117,473 | $ 117,599 | $ 94,040 | $ 82,023 |
| Accrued liabilities | 348,476 | 288,979 | 265,333 | 208,357 |
| Air traffic liability | 131,156 | 106,139 | 96,146 | 65,934 |
| Income taxes payable | — | — | 7,025 | 6,744 |
| Current maturities of long-term debt | 13,516 | 9,553 | 16,068 | 16,234 |
| Total current liabilities | 610,621 | 522,270 | 478,612 | 379,292 |
| Long-term debt less current maturities | 661,010 | 583,071 | 639,136 | 735,754 |
| Deferred income taxes | 281,650 | 232,850 | 183,616 | 136,462 |
| Deferred gains from sale and leaseback of aircraft | 245,154 | 217,677 | 199,362 | 224,645 |
| Other deferred liabilities | 30,369 | 28,497 | 21,292 | 13,167 |
| Commitments and contingencies | | | | |
| Stockholders' equity | | | | |
| Common stock, $1.00 par value: 500,000,000 shares authored; 143,255,795 shares issued and outstanding in 1994 and 142,756,308 shares in 1993 | 144,033 | 143,256 | 142,756 | 96,047 |
| Capital in excess of par value | 162,704 | 151,746 | 141,168 | 177,647 |
| Retained earnings | 1,120,581 | 943,704 | 770,095 | 605,928 |
| Less treasury stock, at cost (2,904 shares in 1992) | — | — | — | 879,586 |
| Total stockholders' equity | 1,427,318 | 1,238,706 | 1,054,019 | 879,622 |
| | $ 3,256,122 | $ 2,823,071 | $ 2,576,037 | $ 2,368,856 |

**Exhibit 4**  **Southwest Consolidated Statement of Income**
**(in thousands except for share amounts)**

| | Years Ended December 31, | | | |
| | 1995 | 1994 | 1993 | 1992 |
|---|---|---|---|---|
| Operating Revenues: | | | | |
| Passenger | $ 2,760,756 | $ 2,497,765 | $ 2,216,342 | $ 1,623,828 |
| Freight | 65,825 | 54,419 | 42,897 | 33,088 |
| Charter and other | 46,170 | 39,749 | 37,434 | 146,063 |
|     Total operating revenues | 2,872,731 | 2,591,933 | 2,296,673 | 1,802,979 |
| Operating Expenses: | | | | |
| Salaries, wages, and benefits | 867,984 | 756,023 | 641,747 | 512,983 |
| Fuel and oil | 365,670 | 319,552 | 304,424 | 257,481 |
| Maintenance materials and repairs | 217,259 | 190,308 | 163,395 | 122,561 |
| Agency commissions | 123,380 | 151,247 | 144,941 | 113,504 |
| Aircraft rentals | 169,461 | 132,992 | 107,885 | 77,472 |
| Landing fees and other rentals | 160,322 | 148,107 | 129,222 | 105,929 |
| Depreciation | 156,771 | 139,045 | 119,338 | 101,976 |
| Other operating expenses | 498,373 | 437,950 | 382,945 | 317,269 |
| Merger expenses | — | — | 10,803 | — |
| Total operating expenses | 2,559,220 | 2,275,224 | 2,004,700 | 1,609,175 |
| Operating Income | 313,531 | 316,709 | 291,973 | 193,804 |
|   Other Expenses (Income): | | | | |
| Interest expertise | 58,810 | 53,368 | 58,460 | 59,084 |
| Capitalized interest | (31,371) | (26,323) | (17,770) | (15,350) |
| Interest income | (20,095) | (9,166) | (11,093) | (10,672) |
| Nonoperating (gains) losses, net | 1,047 | (963) | 2,739 | 3,299 |
|     Total other expenses | 8,391 | 17,186 | 32,336 | 36,361 |
| Income Before Taxes and Cumulative Effect of Accounting Changes | 305,140 | 299,523 | 259,637 | 157,443 |
| Provision For Income Taxes | 122,514 | 1120,192 | 105,353 | 55,816 |
| Income Before Cumulative Effect of Accounting Changes | 182,826 | 179,331 | 154,284 | 101,627 |
| Cumulative Effect of Accounting Changes | — | — | 15,259 | 12,538 |
| Net Income | $ 182,626 | $ 179,331 | $ 169,543 | $ 114,165 |
| Per Share Amounts: | | | | |
| Income before cumulative effect of accounting changes | $ 1.23 | $ 1.22 | $ 1.05 | $ .71 |
| Cumulative effect of accounting changes | — | — | .10 | .09 |
| Net Income | $ 1.23 | $ 1.22 | $ 1.15 | $ .80 |

Gary Kelly, Southwest's Chief Financial Officer, expects that "Some of South-west's difficulties will take the first half of '95 to get fully sorted out."[38]

"Long-range planning is a thing of the past at Southwest Airlines, where Kelleher approvingly quotes Klausewitz: 'No battle plans survive contact with the enemy.' Southwest sets its basic construct, niche, and adopts new tactics everyday."[39]

Michael Boyd, an aviation systems research analyst, believes United, saddled with higher costs, is likely to lose any head-to-head battle with Southwest. Aaron Gellman, director of the Transportation Center at Northwestern University, admires how Kelleher manages to stay ahead of his rivals and said: "Whatever other airlines do, Herb is going to eat them up in ways they haven't even thought of. The hardest thing for rivals to copy seems to be Kelleher's secret weapon—the trust and respect of his employees."

## REFERENCES

1. McKenna, James T., "Southwest to Raise Ante in United Markets," *Aviation Week & Space Technology,* July 18, 1994, p. 22.

2. Garfield, Bob, "Commander Kelleher Eyes Future in New Southwest Ads, "*Advertising Age,* Vol. 65, No. 42, October 3, 1994, p. 3.

3. "The Southwest Story," Southwest Airlines Company, Dallas, Texas, 1990, p. 2.

4. Southwest Airlines Annual Report, Southwest Airlines Company, Dallas, Texas, 1990, p. 6.

5. "The Southwest Story," Southwest Airlines Company, Dallas, Texas, 1990, p. 6.

6. Southwest Airlines, "Fact Sheet," 1992.

7. Wells, Alexander T., *Air Transportation: A Management Perspective,* Wadsworth Publishing Company, Florence, Kentucky, Third Edition, 1994, p. 38.

8. Kane, Robert, and Allan Vose, *Air Transportation,* Kendall & Hunt Publishing Company, Dubuque, Iowa, 1971, p. 25.

9. Clark, Lindley H., "Airlines and Railroads: A Weird Marriage," *The Wall Street Journal,* Wednesday, March 15, 1989, p. A16.

10. Biederman, Paul, *The U.S. Airline Industry: End of an Era,* Prager Publishers, 1982, p. xiii.

11. Hamilton, Martha M., "Airline Mergers to Land on Other Desks," *Washington D.C. Post,* December 22, 1988, Section One, p. A23.

12. Wells, p. 302.

13. Ibid, pp. 76-77.

14. Ibid.

15. Ibid.

16. Hamilton, Martha M., p. A23.

17. Rose, Robert L., "Major U.S. Airlines Rapidly Gain Control Over Regional Lines," *The Wall Street Journal,* Wednesday, February 17, 1988, p. A-1.

18. Smith, Timothy K., "Why Air Travel Doesn't Work," *Fortune,* April 3, 1995, p. 46.

19. Ibid., pp. 49-50, & 56.

20. Levering, Robert, and Milton Moskowitz, *The 100 Best Companies To Work For In America,* Doubleday Press, 1993, p. 413.

21. Woodbury, Richard, *"Prince of Midair,"* Time, January 25, 1993, p. 55.

22. Jaffe, Charles A., "Moving Fast by Standing Still," *Nation's Business,* October 1991, p. 59.

23. Teitelbaum, Richard S., "Where Service Flies Right," *Fortune,* August 24, 1992, pp. 115.

24. Levering and Moskowitz, p. 412.

25. Chakravarty, Subrata N., "Hit'em Hardest With The Mostest," *Forbes,* September 16, 1991, p. 50.

26. Wells, Edward O., "Captain Marvel," *Inc.,* January 1992, p. 46.

27. Henderson, Danna K., "Southwest Luvs Passengers, Employees, Profits," *Air Transport World,* July 1991, p. 32.

28. Zeller, Wendy, et al., "Go-Go Goliaths," *Business Week,* February 13, 1995, p. 69.

29. Chakravarty, p. 50.

30. Southwest Airlines Annual Report, Southwest Airlines Company, Dallas, Texas, 1994, p. 8.

31. Chakravarty, p. 49.

32. Ibid., p. 50.

33. Lawrence, Jennifer, "Don Valentine Is At The Heart of Southwest's Success," *Advertising Age,* January 25, 1988, p. 57.

34. Teitelbaum, p.115.

35. Zeller, Wendy, and Eric Schine, "Striking Gold in the California Skies," *Business Week,* March 30, 1992, p. 48.

36. Kelly, Kevin, "Southwest Airlines: Flying High with 'Uncle Herb,'" *Business Week,* July 3, 1989, p. 83.

37. Donlan, Thomas G., "The State Bird of Texas, Southwest Airlines' Herb Kelleher Has The Right Stuff"' *Barrons,* October 19, 1992, p. 10.

38. O'Brian, Bridget, "Southwest Air Says First-Half Results Are Likely To Be Hurt by Competition," *The Wall Street Journal,* February 13, 1995, p. A2.

39. Donlan, p. 14.

# Cuchara Valley Ski Resort

Gary Bridges, University of Southern Colorado

Donna M. Watkins, University of Southern Colorado

William D. Chandler, University of Southern Colorado

"This is not going to be an easy job," Gary White muttered to himself as he began to spread out worksheets, financial statements, snowfall reports, and other data. He had been associated with Cuchara Valley Ski Resort in a variety of capacities for about 10 years and had witnessed all of its ups and downs. Gary was currently a professor at the business school of a nearby university. His roles at the ski resort had included two stints as controller, informal consultant, ski instructor, member of the ski patrol, owner and operator of three base area shops, and a home owner in the ski area's residential neighborhood. Now, as a consultant for another prospective buyer, he was being asked to give an opinion on whether the resort could ever be financially viable, and if so, to recommend specific actions.

Gary had made some hard decisions in his life—as an Air Force pilot and in his prior corporate position as an auditor. He had moved his family to this rural, mountain area 10 years ago in the hope that this lifestyle would be better for raising a family. They had become involved in community, church, and school activities, and were as much "locals" as outsiders could be. He had watched the valley residents band together and provide the support services that the ski area needed. But more times than anyone was willing to admit, the result had been disappointment and even financial ruin for some of the residents. Yet, every year carried a new hope that the ski area would open and provide much-needed jobs to the valley.

Gary thought back to when the resort first opened. Located in the southern part of Colorado, Cuchara Valley Ski Resort (CVSR) was a small ski area tucked away in the Sangre de Cristo mountain range in the shadows of the towering Huajatallos (known locally as the Spanish Peaks). Two miles away was the unincorporated village of Cuchara, Colorado. The resort was developed by local entrepreneurs and Texas developers, and opened in December 1981 under the name Panadero Ski Resort. (The name had been changed as the result of a dispute between one of the original developers and a new owner.)

The resort property covered 335 acres. The ski trails and terrain covered about 50 acres, 90 percent of which was public land for which the resort had acquired a use permit from the U.S. Forest Service. Because of the resort's distance from major lodging facilities, five different sets of condominiums had been built early in the ski area's history. In addition, approximately 37 acres of the original land had been sold as individual half-acre lots at an average price of $30,000. Twenty homes had been built; the average value of these homes was $500,000. Except for the ten acres that had been designated as green space, the remaining land was available for further development as single- or multi-family dwellings.

Because of its Southern Colorado location, Cuchara Valley Ski Resort had always been attractive to skiers from Texas, Oklahoma, and Kansas, especially those who drove. It was much closer than other Colorado ski areas and didn't require crossing any mountain passes (see Exhibit 1).

**Exhibit 1**          **CVSR Distances to Major Cities**

Even before the ski resort was built, the area had attracted visitors at other times of the year. The Cuchara area had been a popular summer resort for many years, with many of its summer residents being from this same market. Summer visitors enjoyed fishing, camping, horseback riding, and hiking. In the fall, visitors would come to see the brilliant color changes of the valley's spectacular aspen forests. Hunters from many states also came in search of the area's wildlife—bear, mule deer, elk, and mountain lion.

An additional draw to the area was an 18-hole, championship golf course, Grandote, which was located approximately 14 miles from the ski resort in the community of La Veta. The golf course normally operated from May through September and had been recognized as one of the 10 best golf courses in Colorado by a national golf publication. Despite its excellent design, the golf course seemed to flirt constantly with financial disaster; it was currently plagued by litigation, IRS liens, and a duel between past and present owners.

Until 1986, the CVSR partnership/management group had stayed basically intact, but, as Gary was fond of saying, the owners now changed as often as the fall leaves. The itinerant ownership was partly the result of considerable uncertainty in the Texas investment community brought about by the collapse of oil prices in the early 1980s. Collectively, the owners' lack of experience in ski resort management resulted in well-intentioned but often inappropriate expectations. During the 1985-86 ski season, the resort's Texas lender (Summit Savings) balked at advancing more money for operations. In a fit of brinkmanship, the resort's owners closed the resort in mid-February, a full six weeks ahead of schedule. The early closure left area businesses struggling to dispose of excess inventory. The resort's early and sudden closure badly damaged its reputation as several out-of-state church groups and other guests with confirmed reservations for Spring Break had to scramble to make last-minute arrangements.

The lender began foreclosure proceedings and the owners sued. Gary, along with the resort's mountain manager, was asked to work with a court-appointed receiver who supervised the 1986 summer maintenance operations. Eventually, the parties reached a settlement whereby the partners escaped financial liability and the lender took possession of the resort in the fall of 1986.

The loan to develop and open the ski resort amounted to approximately $22 million. Appraisals done shortly after foreclosure estimated a total value of between $8 million and $10 million. The lender/owner realized that the value of a ski resort resided in a business that was operating and generating revenue rather than in the assets themselves; so Summit Savings agreed to provide operating funds for the 1986-87 ski season while it tried to sell the resort.

The 1986-87 ski season saw the most snowfall in the resort's history but because of the prior year's early closure, the slow start in advertising, and a general uncertainty about the resort's future, the skier count was disappointing.

Not long after the 1986-87 season ended, the lender (Summit Savings) was merged with seven other marginal S&Ls in Texas, as part of a restructuring effort known as the Southwest Plan. The newly formed S&L was called Sunbelt Savings. From Gary's perspective, this turned out to be an "unholy alliance" as it resulted in yet another top management group: Soon after Sunbelt Savings was formed, a different group of S&L executives in Texas assumed responsibility for the Cuchara Valley Ski Resort. Their first action was to hire a management company called Club Corporation of America (CCA) from Dallas, Texas, to operate the ski area for the 1987-88 ski season. Gary remembered the local residents questioning the reasons for hiring an out-of-state management group. Their fears were confirmed when they learned that CCA's expertise was managing golf courses.

The organization chart of CVSR's ownership/management became even more complicated when the Resolution Trust Corporation (RTC) assumed control of this S&L behemoth (Sunbelt Savings). Now, all decisions had to be cleared through RTC officials. After dismissing CCA in 1988, the new and improved RTC-managed S&L, Sunbelt Savings, agreed to fund Cuchara's operations for the 1988-89 ski season, during which they attracted the third highest skier count (25,055) in Cuchara's operating history. Despite this relatively successful season, Sunbelt Savings decided that it would not provide operating funds for the 1989-90 season nor for the foreseeable future. They made this announcement three weeks before the scheduled opening. Sunbelt retained a skeleton crew to answer telephones and to show the property to prospective buyers.

The resort remained closed for three seasons (89-90, 90-91, and 91-92). During this time, local resort management entertained an array of "lookers" professing their desire to buy the ski resort. Finally, in 1991, a Texas businessman who owned a summer home in Cuchara began serious negotiations with the RTC. The sale was finalized in 1992 with the RTC financing a little over half of the purchase price.

Gary had liked the new owner and felt that he started his ownership with the best interests of the resort and the surrounding area in mind. The new owner believed that with the relatively low cash investment, CVSR could generate positive cash flow in the short term and eventually become profitable

After two seasons (1992-93 and 1993-94), it was clear that the owner's expectations were overly optimistic. At the end of a slower-than-expected 1993-94 season, during which the owner had to provide additional cash for operations, he accepted a new investor's offer to assume financial and operating responsibility for the ski operations for the 1994-95 ski season.

Had someone been telling this story to Gary, he knew he would have laughed out loud and said "preposterous" to what happened next. But he had been there and he knew it was all true: The new investor ran out of money before the first snowfall and never opened the resort. He not only failed to open the resort for business, but he also made off with the funds from pre-season ticket sales and left many employees and local merchants unpaid for their services. With legal help, the earlier Texas owner regained full control; but doing so took several months, and the 1994-95 ski season was over by then. It was safe to say that it had not been a good winter for the valley.

## ■ Snow and Water

Cuchara's southern location had to be considered a mixed blessing in that its snowfall was always consistently inconsistent. The original developers realized this and constructed a snow-making system which, in theory, could cover 75 percent of the skiable terrain with man-made snow. But because of faulty installation, occasional unseasonably warm temperatures during the ski season, and technological advances, the snow-making system was, although operable, inefficient and bordering on obsolescence. Nevertheless, man-made snow had been what kept the resort open during its frequent dry periods (see Exhibit 2).

Snow-making was almost always done at night when the temperatures were colder; effective snow-making required temperatures below 28 degrees

**Exhibit 2**                **CVSR Snowfall in Inches 1985-86 to 1995-96**

| Season | Sept | Oct | Nov | Dec | Jan | Feb | Mar | Apr | May | Total |
|--------|------|------|------|------|------|------|-------|-------|------|--------|
| 1985-86 | 2.50 | 10.00 | 25.00 | 10.00 | 18.00 | 21.00 | 41.50 | 47.00 | 15.00 | 190.00 |
| 1986-87 | 1.50 | 16.75 | 33.74 | 21.00 | 39.50 | 74.75 | 126.10 | 30.50 | 21.25 | 365.09 |
| 1987-88 | 0.00 | 0.00 | 50.00 | 36.00 | 29.50 | 19.00 | 83.25 | 25.00 | 18.00 | 260.75 |
| 1988-89 | 1.00 | 0.00 | 33.75 | 32.50 | 35.75 | 52.75 | 12.00 | 14.75 | 0.00 | 182.50 |
| 1989-90 | 3.00 | 20.00 | 7.00 | 39.50 | 30.25 | 43.00 | 33.00 | 35.75 | 22.25 | 233.75 |
| 1990-91 | 0.00 | 25.25 | 36.00 | 30.25 | 17.75 | 32.25 | 70.00 | 37.00 | 2.50 | 251.00 |
| 1991-92 | 0.00 | 15.50 | 74.50 | 7.00 | 27.75 | 59.50 | 40.75 | 3.50 | 0.00 | 228.50 |
| 1992-93 | 0.00 | 5.75 | 85.50 | 39.75 | 13.00 | 47.50 | 55.25 | 56.00 | 19.00 | 321.75 |
| 1993-94 | 6.75 | 19.88 | 31.75 | 31.25 | 28.00 | 22.00 | 66.00 | 70.50 | 5.00 | 281.13 |
| 1994-95 | 0.25 | 14.50 | 27.25 | 10.50 | 21.25 | 16.50 | 47.50 | 113.00 | 10.75 | 261.50 |
| 1995-96 | 16.00 | 1.00 | 14.25 | 24.75 | 24.25 | 22.25 | 58.25 | 10.00 | 0.00 | 170.75 |
| Avg | 2.82 | 11.69 | 38.07 | 25.68 | 25.91 | 37.32 | 57.60 | 40.27 | 10.34 | 249.70 |
| Min | 0.00 | 0.00 | 7.00 | 7.00 | 13.00 | 16.50 | 12.00 | 3.50 | 0.00 | 170.75 |
| Max | 16.00 | 25.25 | 85.50 | 39.75 | 39.50 | 74.75 | 126.10 | 113.00 | 22.25 | 365.09 |

Fahrenheit. Snow-making systems rely on a system of pumps and compressors to move the water great distances up very steep terrain and then spray it through guns (actually high-pressure nozzles with fan blades) under pressure. Cuchara's system was all electrical and operated off a separate electric meter. Each night (eight to ten hours) of snow-making operation cost approximately $1,500 in electricity usage.

Management usually started making snow in November, well before the resort opened, so as to have a sufficient base for the resort's traditional mid-December opening. December's natural snowfall alone usually was not sufficient to accommodate skiing. It was extremely important to have good snow (a 30" to 45" base was considered adequate) at Christmas because December and March were always the biggest months of the season.

Temperature and utility costs were critical determinants of the resort's snow-making strategy, but the most limiting constraint to short-term snow-making ability and long-term planning had always been the availability of water. Baker Creek flowed from a source high in the peaks of the Sangre de Cristo range and was the resort's only source of water for snow-making and domestic use (homes, condos, and restaurants). The resort owned water rights under Colorado water law allowing it to divert a specified volume (measured by cubic feet per second) out of Baker Creek. Water for domestic use was pumped to a 100,000 gallon storage tank. In addition, the resort stored approximately one-and-a-half acre-feet (1 million gallons) of water in a small pond.

Without this pond as a storage facility, it would have been impossible to make snow. Heavy snow-making would empty the pond in about eight hours and it took twelve hours to refill under most conditions. The County Water Commissioner would constantly monitor the metered usage of snow-making water to ensure that the resort did not use more than its legal entitlement.

Water rights represent the "right" of the owner to divert water from a stream, in this case Baker Creek, or a river for agricultural use (irrigation) or commercial use (watering the golf course or making snow). The water rights concept is fairly rare and occurs only in the Western states. It is based on historical and original usage of the respective waterway which may date back to the original settlement of the state.

Gary felt that additional water (and storage) was a must. Snow-making needed expanding and, eventually, additional housing would be required if CVSR were to become a true destination resort. He knew that water rights could be bought and sold on an open market basis, with higher priority rights (lower numbers) costing more than lower priority rights (higher numbers). Each residential unit required the water right for one Equal Quantity Ratio (EQR) or enough water to supply the annual needs of a typical family of four (estimated at about 88,000 gallons). This arbitrary unit of water right sold for between $1200 and $2000. Since CVSR already used its entire allotment of 347 EQRs, the resort would need to buy additional EQRs (which it then would make available to homeowners or hotel developers) if it hoped to develop additional lots. EQRs for another 50 units could cost as much as $100,000.

"Of course," Gary thought, "owning the rights and actually getting the water could be two different things." He knew that owning the water rights to a stream such as Baker Creek would not guarantee that the actual volume of water in that stream (determined by snowfall) would be enough to fulfill an owner's legal water rights, especially the demand a fully developed resort might create. Could Mother Nature be counted on to ensure that Baker Creek would always have enough water to meet the resort's growing needs? Gary had never seen Baker Creek dry, but beyond that, he didn't have an answer. He made a note to recommend a water resource expert.

## ▪ Resort Services

Next Gary took a look at the resort's services. He wanted to present a clear picture of what the resort had to offer skiers. "Good people" was the first item he wrote down. Most of the employees were year-round valley residents, and they had always done their best to be friendly and helpful to resort visitors. The resort's wages had always been below the Colorado ski industry's averages, though, and it was getting harder and harder to lure quality, skilled employees back for the see-saw ride.

## ▪ Skiing Terrain

The skiing terrain at CVSR was considered moderate, with 40 percent beginner, 40 percent intermediate, and 20 percent expert runs. The U.S. Forest Service had recently allowed Cuchara to open an additional 45 acres of expert terrain called The Burn, but it was ungroomed and was not served by a lift (see Exhibit 3).

## ▪ Lift Tickets, Ski Rental, and Ski School

The resort's moderate ticket prices, ranging from $15 to $25, placed Cuchara near the lowest of Colorado's and New Mexico's lift ticket prices (see Exhibit 4).

**Exhibit 3** **Resort Credentials**

| Ski Resort | Elevation Top | Elevation Base | Number Lifts | Vertical Drop | Number of Trails |
|---|---|---|---|---|---|
| Cuchara | 10810 ft | 9248 ft | 4 | 1562 ft | 24 |
| Monarch | 11900 ft | 10790 ft | 4 | 1160 ft | 54 |
| Taos, N.M. | 11819 ft | 9207 ft | 11 | 2612 ft | 72 |
| Wolf Creek | 11775 ft | 10350 ft | 6 | 1425 ft | 50 |

Ski rentals were available at the base area and in the village of Cuchara. The equipment was acceptable, although not in top-notch shape. Prices were standard for the industry.

The ski school offered basic group and private lessons. As with rentals, ski school prices were competitive. Ski instructors were typically local residents who knew the mountain well.

### ■ Food and Lodging

At the base area, CVSR had available a snack bar, the Warming Hut, where skiers could purchase food and drinks from morning until late afternoon. A full service dining facility, Baker Creek Restaurant, was also located in the base area and served lunch and dinner. A limited number of other restaurants and bars were located in the village of Cuchara and in La Veta.

Although cabins and condos were located within the resort's "borders," none was currently owned by CVSR. Consequently, resort employees reserved lodging for all overnight skiers through local property managers who had contracted with the owners of condos and cabins to provide reservation and cleaning services. When the resort was busy, especially during Christmas vacation and Spring Break, the housing on the resort property would be filled; the resort would then direct overnight guests to the limited local hotels in Cuchara and La Veta. Almost all of the ownership groups had recognized the need for more beds in the resort, but no one had the money to build additional facilities.

CVSR did not provide transportation to and from Cuchara or La Veta. Gary knew that the larger ski areas in the state had ski-in/ski-out lodging adjacent to their slopes. At CVSR, skiers could drive from the condos to the base area in a matter of minutes, although slippery, steep roads and limited base area parking might be considered by some to be problematic. Other resorts had

**Exhibit 4** **Selected Lift Ticket Prices**

| Resort | Adult Full Day | Child Full Day | Adult Half Day |
|---|---|---|---|
| Cuchara | $25 | $15 | $18 |
| Monarch | $27 | $16 | $22 |
| Taos, N.M. | $37 | $22 | $24 |
| Wolf Creek | $31 | $19 | $22 |

solved such problems by providing bus service from the lodging facilities to the base area; Cuchara had no transportation services within the resort property. Was lodging a problem for CVSR? Gary wondered if the lack of rooms near the base area should be considered a major constraint on the resort's long-term viability.

### ■ Other Services

CVSR tried to behave as much like a larger resort as it could. A few times during the season there would be a dance band or a concert at the restaurant or the Warming Hut. Outside of these typically peak periods, the base area was closed down at night except for the restaurant.

The base area had a small shopping area with six retail spaces open during the day that sold T-shirts, sweatshirts, and ski-related gear such as goggles, gloves, etc. Child care could also be arranged for either the day or night.

## MARKET DATA

### ■ Target Customers

Cuchara's management had consistently marketed the resort to families and groups (mostly church groups) who were beginner and intermediate skiers and who typically drove to Colorado. Gary remembered meeting a chaperone for a group from Texas who told him that somewhat isolated places were, in her mind, a great destination for middle school and high school kids. She had said that it was much easier to "chaperone" when you didn't have to worry about the kids out walking up and down the streets of an unfamiliar ski town. Gary was not sure that was the "marketing theme" the resort wanted to use.

In fact, Gary's years of watching the numbers had led him to the conclusion that church groups were usually break-even business at best and were often loss leaders, at least where lift tickets, ski rentals, and ski lessons were concerned, because of the sizable discounts given. However, management generally felt that at least during slower periods (January and February), groups helped pay the bills until March. Because Spring Break schedules were not as standardized as Christmas vacation dates, the resort was generally busy throughout the month of March. There was also a glimmer of long-term strategic thinking that members of these groups would return with their families or in smaller groups and pay the regular prices.

CVSR did not totally ignore the southeastern Colorado market. The resort focused on the same beginner/intermediate skier, especially those who might want to "try out" skiing but didn't necessarily have the money or want to spend the money to go to the larger ski areas or destination resorts such as Aspen or Vail. In fact, it was typical of skiers in this market to arrive in the morning and drive home after a day's skiing, thereby avoiding the cost of lodging.

### ■ Location

Gary got out a map and began to look at various distances. CVSR was 114 miles south of Colorado Springs, the closest airport with substantial commercial air service. Pueblo was 35 miles closer but it was served only by commuter service that connected in Denver. La Veta, located 15 miles from CVSR, had an unattended runway that could accommodate small jets but had no scheduled air service and had no instrument landing capability.

The resort was 31 miles west of Interstate Highway 25, Colorado's only north-south interstate. Residents of large cities in Texas, Kansas, and Oklahoma could drive to Cuchara in eight to ten hours (see Exhibit 1).

## ■ Competition

The nearest competitors to Cuchara were Wolf Creek Ski Area, a Colorado ski area approximately three hours' driving time west; Monarch Ski Area, a Colorado ski area approximately three hours' driving time north and west; and Taos Ski Area, a New Mexico ski area approximately two hours' driving time west and south. Getting to any of these three ski areas from any eastern or southeastern destination required not only additional hours on the road but also substantial mountain driving over high mountain passes. For someone who was not used to this kind of driving, snow-packed or icy mountain roads could be most unnerving.

As Gary sifted through the industry data and brochures he had on these competitors, he noted that ticket prices were anywhere from $1 to $12 higher than those at Cuchara (see Exhibit 4). But if a group were coming from outside the state, would a few dollars a day per person really matter? Gary wasn't sure. Ski rental and ski school prices weren't an issue: Unless you went to Aspen or one of the other destination resorts, prices for rentals and ski lessons were about the same everywhere.

Next he took a look at the terrain and snowfall. All of the competitors had more skiable terrain than did Cuchara. Each also had considerably more expert runs. Since Gary and his family had been skiing for years, that was especially appealing to him. Then he looked at the snowfall charts. "No comparison," he thought. All three competitors had more snowfall than Cuchara had. In fact, Wolf Creek typically received more snowfall than any other ski area in Colorado.

And what about the night life, the restaurants, and all those other things skiers liked to do when they weren't skiing? Gary thought that, in general, the competing ski areas were as isolated as Cuchara. None had significant development surrounding the base area as some of the destination resorts did. But Gary had to admit that each of the competitors had larger towns and more entertainment within 20 to 30 miles.

The last thing that Gary considered was off-season activity. Most large ski areas in the state had found ways to use the slopes or other facilities during the summer. Some resorts had installed alpine slides. An alpine slide was a concrete bobsled-like path that was placed on the slopes; visitors rode to the top on the ski lifts and then came down the concrete slide on a cart with wheels that had limited steering and braking capability. Some resorts groomed their trails for mountain biking and let biker and bike ride the ski lifts up the mountain. Concerts, fairs, and other types of gatherings were also typical. These types of activities were supported, of course, by the resorts' abundance of lodging and shopping.

CVSR and its competitors did not typically have summer activities. Summer activity in Taos was certainly big because of its Native American influence and its artist community. But most of this activity occurred in the city of Taos, not at the ski area. Gary thought that CVSR probably had the most potential of the four ski areas because of the lodging that was reasonably close to the base area and because of the well-established summer resident/visitor clientele that had been visiting the Cuchara Valley annually for many years. Throughout the changing ownership of CVSR, Gary had seen various events organized such as both classical and popular music concerts, art shows, etc. Attendance had been acceptable for first-time events, but none had been continued from year to year so as to build a reputation.

## MARKETING ACTIVITIES

Gary knew that Cuchara primarily used direct mail to reach previous guests and group leaders. In addition, management had occasionally put employees on the road to make direct contact with church groups in Texas, Oklahoma, and Kansas.

For the southeastern Colorado market, CVSR usually bought TV and radio spots in Pueblo and Colorado Springs which emphasized low prices and no lift lines. The resort would also sell discount tickets to the military and through various retail outlets such as convenience stores and supermarkets. For skiers from Pueblo and Colorado Springs, it was about the same distance away as Monarch Ski Resort.

Gary had learned from resort employees who had worked at other ski areas that ski shows were generally an important marketing tool in that travel agents attended them and could provide important group business. He knew that shows were held in Wichita, Kansas; in Dallas and Amarillo, Texas; and, of course, in Denver. Typically, two or three attractive and enthusiastic marketing representatives from each ski resort would attend these shows and set up attractive booths highlighting their resorts' strengths. CVSR's attention to ski shows has been spotty at best.

From what Gary knew, it cost only between $125 and $200 to set up a booth at one of these shows, and it seemed to him that traveling to regional shows would be cheaper than visiting individual groups and would result in far more contacts. But what about personal service? Gary knew that the friendliness of the valley people was an appealing feature of Cuchara. Traveling to cities and making personal visits with church groups was a nice touch. Unfortunately, no data had been kept on these issues. So Gary could not determine if direct mail, personal visits, or ski shows resulted in the most "bang for your buck."

## COLORADO SKI INDUSTRY

Gary thought he had better have a look at the big picture also. He found that data from Colorado Ski Country USA showed the Colorado ski industry to be maturing; it had increased its skier visits only .5 percent in the 1993-94 season and then had suffered a similar percentage decline in the 1994-95 season (see Exhibits 5 & 6). A skier visit or skier day represents one skier buying one lift ticket on a given day; if a particular skier skis more than one day, the skier is counted each of these days. The larger Colorado ski resorts had been attacking the stagnant growth by expanding their skiable terrain and adding high speed

**Exhibit 5**                    **Cuchara and Colorado Skier Days 1981-82 to 1994-95**

| Season | Colorado | Cuchara |
|---|---|---|
| 1981-82 | 7,616,699 | 12,567 |
| 1982-83 | 8,200,442 | 22,263 |
| 1983-84 | 8,617,318 | 35,337 |
| 1984-85 | 9,052,345 | 31,232 |
| 1985-86 | 9,110,597 | 12,998 |
| 1986-87 | 9,453,359 | 16,495 |
| 1987-88 | 9,557,002 | 16,383 |
| 1988-89 | 9,981,916 | 25,055 |
| 1989-90 | 9,703,927 | Closed |
| 1990-91 | 9,788,487 | Closed |
| 1991-92 | 10,427,994 | Closed |
| 1992-93 | 11,111,290 | 22,775 |
| 1993-94 | 11,011,290 | 17,203 |
| 1994-95 | 11,105,106 | Closed |

Source: Information for Colorado obtained from Colorado Ski Country, USA.

lifts and other amenities. In fact, Colorado ski resorts had spent $44.5 million on capital improvements during 1992-93 and $43.5 million during 1993-94.

While the statewide skier visit count was holding its own, summer and winter vacation air travel into Denver International Airport (DIA) had declined. In addition, winter overnight lodging figures in the ski areas were down. Industry experts had interpreted this to mean that many of the skiers were coming from the Front Range (Boulder, Denver, Colorado Springs, etc.). Gary knew that for several years these Front Range cities had been experiencing a significant population migration from other states. Perhaps that increase had created a set of new Colorado residents who were interested in skiing.

Other data showed that tourism (winter and summer visitors) in Colorado was becoming more of a regional activity. The number of visitors statewide that arrived by car had increased significantly.

## FINANCIAL DATA

The final item on Gary's list was the financial data. He knew that Cuchara earned revenue from lift ticket sales, ski equipment rentals, ski lessons, child care, and food service. First he looked at the revenue and expense data for the two seasons (1992-93 and 1993-94) the resort had been operating under the current owner (see Exhibits 7 and 8). The owner had given the ski shop to a local resident rent free. In return, the shopkeeper had stocked a small amount of CVSR merchandise as well as the merchandise she sold. The shopkeeper's only

**Exhibit 6**

## Colorado Skier Visits

| Destination Resorts | 1993-94 | 1994-95 |
|---|---|---|
| Aspen Highlands | 106,197 | 159,288 |
| Aspen Mountains | 359,848 | 329,535 |
| Buttermilk | 172,948 | 168,439 |
| Crested Butte | 530,088 | 485,840 |
| Cuchara Valley | 17,300 | Closed |
| Howelson Hill | 16,171 | 14,095 |
| Monarch | 158,148 | 162,982 |
| Powderhorn | 61,202 | 80,241 |
| Purgatory | 302,103 | 382,839 |
| Ski Sunlight | 88,251 | 93,952 |
| Snowmass | 814,852 | 767,509 |
| Steamboat | 1,021,149 | 1,013,606 |
| Telluride | 300,388 | 301,748 |
| Wolf Creek | 140,456 | 157,995 |
| Total | 4,089,101 | 4,118,069 |
| *Front Range Destination Resorts* | | |
| Arapahoe Basin | 257,358 | 262,240 |
| Arrowhead | 23,721 | 28,641 |
| Beaver Creek | 504,516 | 538,897 |
| Breckenridge | 1,215,013 | 1,227,357 |
| Copper Mountain | 842,210 | 770,973 |
| Keystone | 1,095,857 | 1,042,171 |
| Silver Creek | 93,516 | 92,547 |
| Vail | 1,527,698 | 1,568,360 |
| Winter Park | 1,008,040 | 986,077 |
| Total | 6,567,929 | 6,517,263 |
| *Front Range Resorts* | | |
| Eldora | 145,011 | 145,370 |
| Loveland Basin | 295,000 | 258,000 |
| Ski Cooper | 67,193 | 66,404 |
| Totals | 507,204 | 469,774 |
| Grand Totals | 11,164,234 | 11,105,106 |
| Number Increase/Decrease | 52,942 | -59,128 |
| Percent Increase/Decrease | 0.48 | -0.53 |

Source: Colorado Ski Country USA.

CUCHARA VALLEY SKI RESORT

**Exhibit 7**        **Cuchara Valley Ski Resort Financial Summary**

| Season | Skier Count | Revenue | | | | | | Totals |
|--------|-------------|---------|---------|-----------|----------|---------|--------|
| | | Lift Tickets | Ski School | Ski Rental | Baker Creek | Warming Hut | |
| 1981-82 | 12,567 | Unknown | Unknown | Unknown | Unknown | Unknown | |
| 1982-83 | 22,263 | Unknown | Unknown | Unknown | Unknown | Unknown | |
| 1983-84 | 35,337 | $312,696 | $32,679 | 0 | $ 85,304 | $73,921 | $504,600 |
| 1984-85 | 31,232 | 315,264 | 34,666 | 65,880 | 139,035 | 96,397 | 651,242 |
| 1985-86 | 12,998 | 113,946 | 21,771 | 62,766 | 53,239 | 59,589 | 311,311 |
| 1986-87 | 16,495 | 145,442 | 17,918 | 52,727 | 29,783 | 52,704 | 298,574 |
| 1987-88 | 16,383 | 114,848 | 17,689 | 50,031 | 35,162 | 48,247 | 265,977 |
| 1988-89 | 25,055 | 260,660 | 52,960 | 106,696 | 0 | 76,178 | 496,494 |
| 1989-90 | Closed | 0 | 0 | 0 | 0 | 0 | 0 |
| 1990-91 | Closed | 0 | 0 | 0 | 0 | 0 | 0 |
| 1991-92 | Closed | 0 | 0 | 0 | 0 | 0 | 0 |
| 1992-93 | 22,775 | 323,053 | 41,140 | 97,646 | Closed | Leased | 461,839 |
| 1993-94 | 17,300 | $195,305 | $54,898 | $ 94,397 | $ 67,528 | $57,998 | $470,126 |

obligation was to remit sales dollars from the resort's merchandise to the resort.

Gary also noted that during the first season (92-93), the restaurant had been closed and the Warming Hut had been leased out. Only a rent amount was collected. In the following season, both food establishments had been operated by the resort.

Overall, the report showed a small profit in the neighborhood of $36,000 over the two-season period. At least that's what it said on paper. But Gary knew that the spreadsheet covered only the two seasons, the four months each year during which skiers could use the mountain. It didn't reflect the expenses of the other eight months of each year. Summer maintenance of the equipment and lifts was required, and someone had to be around to answer the phones. In addition, the fall months (usually beginning in October) always saw a flurry of activity as the resort geared up for the coming season. Marketing activities increased markedly, equipment was readied, and employees were hired and trained.

Next he looked at the list of assets (see Exhibit 9). Some of these assets were "the originals"—snow cats, chair lift motors and assemblies, etc. Some major replacements were due. While depreciation amounts had always been included in expense records, he knew that no real cash existed to make the kind of capital improvements that were going to be necessary in the near future.

Exhibit 8

# Cuchara Valley Ski Resort Summary of Earnings 1992-93 and 1993-94

|  | Dec 92 | Jan 93 | Feb 93 | Mar 93 | Dec 93 | Jan 94 | Feb 94 | Mar 94 | Total |
|---|---|---|---|---|---|---|---|---|---|
| **Ski Operations** | | | | | | | | | |
| Revenue | 58649 | 102397 | 3328 | 96578 | 78555 | 21479 | 49695 | 54478 | 465159 |
| Expenses | 61603 | 76731 | 37157 | 37157 | 70494 | 69414 | 45184 | 32267 | 430007 |
| Profit/Loss | **-2954** | **25666** | **-33829** | **59421** | **8061** | **-47935** | **4511** | **22211** | **35152** |
| **Ski School** | | | | | | | | | |
| Revenue | 6907 | 18108 | 544 | 18405 | 25197 | 4981 | 13239 | 12034 | 99415 |
| Expenses | 13467 | 23099 | 1332 | 1332 | 9082 | 14128 | 9448 | 17412 | 89300 |
| Profit/Loss | **-6560** | **-4991** | **-788** | **17073** | **16115** | **-9147** | **3791** | **-5378** | **10115** |
| **Ski Rental** | | | | | | | | | |
| Revenue | 18756 | 37417 | 1068 | 36758 | 33433 | 10672 | 23179 | 28904 | 190187 |
| Cost of Sales | 0 | 0 | 0 | 0 | 658 | 0 | 0 | 0 | 658 |
| Gross Margin | 18756 | 37417 | 1068 | 36758 | 32775 | 10672 | 23179 | 28904 | 189529 |
| Expenses | 9006 | 14606 | 4406 | 4406 | 18720 | 10767 | 6148 | 8964 | 77023 |
| Profit/Loss | **9750** | **22811** | **-3338** | **32352** | **14055** | **-95** | **17031** | **19940** | **112506** |
| **Ski Merchandise** | | | | | | | | | |
| Revenue | 3245 | 3805 | 249 | 0 | 3898 | 1628 | 2362 | 4516 | 19703 |
| Cost of Sales | 3630 | 3492 | 149 | 0 | 1652 | 6996 | 1777 | 886 | 18582 |
| Gross Margin | -385 | 313 | 100 | 0 | 2246 | -5368 | 585 | 3630 | 1121 |
| Expenses | 0 | 0 | 0 | 0 | 326 | 0 | 0 | 0 | 326 |
| Profit/Loss | **-385** | **313** | **100** | **0** | **1920** | **-5368** | **585** | **3630** | **795** |
| **Food & Beverages** | | | | | | | | | |
| Revenue | 2151 | 2448 | 2134 | 0 | 41746 | 22087 | 30711 | 27642 | 128919 |
| Cost of Sales | 0 | 0 | 0 | 0 | 24953 | 12049 | 13006 | 5561 | 55569 |
| Gross Margin | 2151 | 2448 | 2134 | 0 | 16793 | 10038 | 17705 | 22081 | 73350 |
| Expenses | 1249 | 2296 | 2121 | 2121 | 40750 | 23356 | 12345 | 12777 | 97015 |
| Profit/Loss | **902** | **152** | **13** | **-2121** | **-23957** | **-13318** | **5360** | **9304** | **-23665** |
| **Property Management** | | | | | | | | | |
| Revenue | 3945 | 12422 | -6 | 1224 | 9340 | 54342 | 28701 | 22447 | 132415 |
| Cost of Sales | 0 | 0 | 0 | 0 | 325 | 44276 | 15157 | 36841 | 96599 |
| Gross Margin | 3945 | 12422 | -6 | 1224 | 9015 | 10066 | 13544 | -14394 | 35816 |
| Expenses | 0 | 0 | 0 | -15500 | 9394 | 3819 | 3243 | 4099 | 5056 |
| Profit/Loss | **3945** | **12422** | **-6** | **16724** | **-379** | **6247** | **10301** | **-18493** | **30761** |
| **General & Administrative** | | | | | | | | | |
| Expenses | 6988 | 10038 | 6134 | 322 | 12214 | 15233 | 7443 | 6390 | 64762 |
| **Marketing** | | | | | | | | | |
| Expenses | 9692 | 15576 | 3087 | 583 | 11929 | 8766 | 8041 | 6237 | 63911 |
| Total Revenue | 93653 | 176597 | 7317 | 152965 | 192169 | 115189 | 147887 | 150021 | 1035798 |
| Total Cost of Sales | 3630 | 3492 | 149 | 0 | 27588 | 63321 | 29940 | 43288 | 171408 |
| Total Gross Margin | 90023 | 173105 | 7168 | 152965 | 164581 | 51868 | 117947 | 106733 | 864390 |
| Total Expenses | 102005 | 142346 | 54237 | 30421 | 172909 | 145483 | 91852 | 88146 | 827397 |
| Total Profit/Loss | **-11982** | **30759** | **-47069** | **122544** | **-8328** | **-93615** | **26095** | **18587** | **36993** |

**Exhibit 9**            **CVSR Assets as of August 1, 1994**

| Assets | Cost |
|---|---|
| **Warming Hut** | |
| Equip | $55,574 |
| Improvements | 10,193 |
| Total | 65,767 |
| **Vehicles** | 9,428 |
| **Operations Equipment** | 207,761 |
| **Snow-Making Equipment** | |
| Compressor Line | 172,903 |
| Improvements | 2,267 |
| Total | 175,170 |
| **Lifts** | 212,766 |
| **Rental Equip** | |
| Skis, Boots & Poles | 10,294 |
| Bindings | 24,964 |
| Skis | 31,168 |
| Total | 66,426 |
| **Baker Creek** | |
| Kitchen Equip | 13,582 |
| Cooler | 6,150 |
| Improvements | 2,050 |
| Cash Registers | 5,114 |
| Total | 26,896 |
| **Office Equip** | 20,216 |
| **Grand Total** | $784,430 |

# CONCLUSION

Gary decided that the key to preparing a financial pro-forma was a good estimate of skier visits. Unfortunately, the frequent closures and erratic marketing efforts and inconsistent snow made this a daunting task. He felt that the large corporate-owned ski areas would continue to spend heavily on expansion plans to increase market share and there were even rumors of major consolidations. Gary also remembered the fate of a small ski area called Conquistador, located at Westcliffe, Colorado, about 60 miles from Cuchara. Conquistador had almost mirrored Cuchara's experience and its most recent owners had

**Exhibit 10**                **CVSR Ticket Sales 1993-94 by Type**

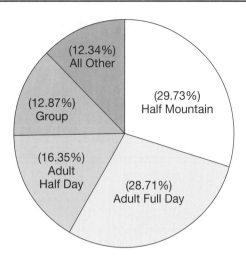

decided to sell off all of its assets and abandon efforts to operate a ski area. Was Cuchara doomed to this fate? On the other hand, Wolf Creek and Monarch ski areas had experienced growth in their skiers during 1994-95, 3 percent and 12 percent, respectively. Gary felt that an increase in lift ticket prices was certainly appropriate and he realized that promotional discounts and the variety of less-than-full price tickets sold reduced the average revenue per lift ticket to something less than the price charged for an adult, full-day ticket. He believed that an increase to $28 for an adult, full-day ticket was warranted. Using historical data (Exhibit 5), he could determine an average revenue-per-skier for each of the departments including lift tickets. This would be a starting point for estimating future revenues.

# Beloit Poland S.A.

Zbigniew Malara, Technical University of Wroclaw, Poland

Mark Kroll, The University of Texas at Tyler

John Holm, The University of Texas at Tyler

## INTRODUCTION

On June 4, 1989, the Polish Communist system was abolished and Poland held its first truly democratic parliamentary elections in 50 years. The mere broadcast of election returns over national television captivated the population, most of which had never experienced the power of democracy. That day also represented the beginning of a great experiment—the Polish people's attempt to transition their very tightly controlled, centrally planned economy into a market-driven one in which individuals are free to pursue their own dreams of economic prosperity.

It was inevitable that the transition process was going to be very difficult. The Nationalization Act of 1946 transferred ownership of all businesses with more than 50 employees to the central government. Forty-three years later, the Polish economy was comprised of about 15,000 state-owned enterprises, each of which had been operated under extremely tight regulations and controls. Heretofore, enterprise managers essentially responded to directives from government and Communist Party officials who were far removed from the enterprise. The management of these organizations received orders from central planners, tried to meet expectations, and continuously fed their higher-ups streams of reports and documentation justifying their activity. Suddenly, however, the directives, detailed instructions, and purchase orders ceased, and the enterprise managers and their workers found themselves on their own.

Managers were immediately faced with both the opportunities and threats a free market holds. Without guaranteed demand for their products, many failed immediately. Unemployment rose dramatically. Within a few months three million workers were unemployed, representing about fifteen percent of the workforce, and the situation was not about to improve. The unemployment rate was calculated at 13.5, 16.7, and 14.7 percent in 1992, 1994, and 1995, respectively.

However, many organizations prospered. Despite the many business failures, others—especially those with long histories—were determined to survive and prosper in their new environments. One such business was the century-old State Paper-Making Machine Factory (known as FAMPA), located in the southwestern city of Jelenia Góra (see Exhibit 1). FAMPA was the only firm in the former communist bloc capable of producing a full line of paper and paper board manufacturing equipment. Before the transition, FAMPA employed about a thousand people. FAMPA was an important employer in the city of 100,000 and one of the few firms in the area which had exported throughout the communist world.

## HISTORY OF THE COMPANY

FAMPA was founded in Jelenia Góra in 1854 as Fullner Werke and was managed and owned exclusively by the Fullner family for about 90 years. From the company's founding until the end of the Second World War the city of Jelenia Góra

**Exhibit 1**       **Geographical location of Beloit Poland S.A.**

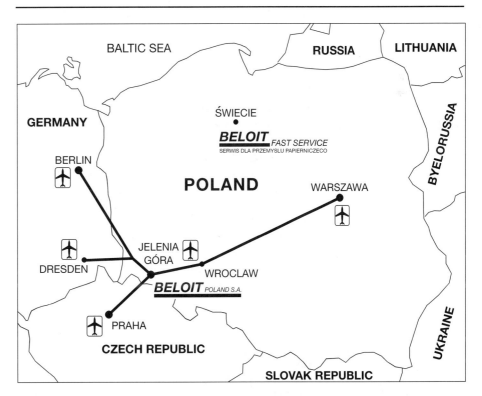

was a part of Germany, just across the southwest border from Poland. After the war, this land was ceded to Poland, and the firm came under the control of a newly Soviet-installed, centralized Polish communist government. The name was changed to the Factory for Paper-Making Machinery, (FAMPA).

Under the direction of the firm's new government-appointed management, the early post-war years were spent rebuilding the plant and training workers using pre-war documentation and pre-war technology. Later, efforts were made to update the company's technology and modernize its procedures. One constant however was the firm's mission, that of making specialized equipment for use in the paper and cellulose industries both in Poland and abroad.

Since Europe's manufacturing base—including the paper industry—was in ruin after the war, there was plenty of work for FAMPA. During the period from 1946 to 1964 FAMPA manufactured and installed equipment for 36 complete paper mills. Additionally, FAMPA completed modernizations and rebuilds of several existing plants which had a combined capacity of 400,000 tons a year. In 1964 FAMPA entered a technology licensing agreement with Beloit Walmsley, Ltd., the British subsidiary of the U.S.-based Beloit Corporation. With access to new technology FAMPA installed 100 new paper plants in 25 countries from 1964 to 1991. From 1946 to 1990 FAMPA had refurbished or installed enough paper mill capacity to produce three million tons of paper annually.

## INTO THE UNKNOWN

In December 1989, the Polish government set out principles by which state-owned firms could engage in joint venture projects with foreign investors. In July 1990, the Privatization of State-Owned Enterprises Act outlined the process Poland's state-owned firms would follow in their conversion to privately-owned firms. Both of these steps engendered a certain amount of excitement in the ranks of the younger members of state-owned enterprises' engineering and management teams.

On September 27, 1990, FAMPA was restructured into a state-owned joint-stock company. Although shares were initially owned by the state, they were expected to be distributed to the employees and joint venture partners (if any) in the near future. The new president of the board of directors was Miroslaw Miroslawski, who was very much a representative of the younger, change-oriented element of FAMPA. As the transition proceeded, Miroslawski recognized the need to undertake immediate steps to stabilize the company. One of the major problems FAMPA faced was tremendous overstaffing. Under Communist control, excess employment was acceptable. FAMPA now had to prepare to meet the competition in the international papermaking machinery market, which required a thorough analysis of costs and break-even points.

Miroslawski and the board came under tremendous pressures from the trade unions when the firm began to lay off workers who were not needed or not willing to change. The unions charged that pursuit of the best interests of stockholders—some of whom would be the employees—was not inherently bad, but that long-term employees should not be sacrificed in the process. They questioned whether the pursuit of lower costs, higher sales, and profits would really benefit union memberships.

However, not everyone resisted the change, believing instead that FAMPA must change in order to survive. To them, Miroslawski became something of a latter-day Moses, leading the new company on its perilous journey into the unknown. For his part, Miroslawski simply recognized the extent of the over-staffing problem in every part of the firm. This made the firm a "colossus on clay feet" in terms of its ability to respond to change and compete. Between 1988 and 1994, the workforce shrank from about 1500 to about 500.

Miroslawski had come to understand some of the fundamentals of strategic planning, and recognized that to chart its course effectively, the company needed to define its mission, objectives, and goals. He was also painfully aware of the goal conflict that existed among various FAMPA employee groups, among both the management and non-managerial ranks. While older managers wanted to take a go-slow, status quo approach, the younger managers were eager to pursue rapid change. These conflicting goals were manifest on the board of directors, with substantial divisions between groups of board members.

The president also recognized that his firm was going to be making its transition in a very unstable political and economic environment. The new demo-cratically elected government was very unstable, with annual changes in prime minister. Although the electorate and the politicians knew change was neces-sary, the pain of the transition to a free market economy was proving to be very severe for many who had relied on the old system for so long. The political instability in turn led to changes in social and economic policy and regulatory instability.

Meanwhile, inflation was rampant in Poland, running at an annual rate of 170 percent in 1990. Coupled with the increase in unemployment, it became clear that the government would have to control its own spending and the expansion of the money supply it was using to pay for it. However, to do so would require balanced budget discipline, necessitating deep cuts in spending and/or higher taxes on an economy which had little ability to pay more. The government would also have to adopt a sound monetary policy which, at least in the short run, would cause significant additional unemployment.

Miroslawski also recognized that his market environment—especially the competitive nature—would be quite different from the past. Both its domestic and foreign sales were controlled by bureaucrats in Poland and in the Soviet Union. Domestic sales consisted of simply receiving orders from central plan-ners. Sales to other Soviet Bloc nations were made through ministries, and did not require a substantial marketing effort. Now the company would have to meet Western competitors head on. He wondered how it would be possible to attract the capital and technological infusion his firm so desperately needed. He was also quite concerned how the firm would mount an effective marketing effort with little or no expertise in this area.

With little money, antiquated technology, no marketing expertise, a host of new competitors to deal with, and the great expectations of his firm's work-force, Miroslawski recognized the absolute necessity for the board to integrate the expectations of FAMPA's stakeholders around some common goals. He knew in the end that the firm would have to emerge committed to providing quality products at competitive prices and high levels of customer support, pro-duction without high pollution, opportunities for its current workforce and the economy of Poland, and a reasonable return for its shareholders. He thought the task at first overwhelming, but FAMPA had no choice but to proceed.

## ■ Beloit Corporation's New Polish Subsidiary

In 1991, 80 percent of FAMPA's common stock was put up for sale in an open bidding process. Most of the world's major manufacturers of paper-making equipment submitted bids. The winning bid was submitted by the Beloit Corporation, parent of FAMPA's long-time partner Beloit Walmsley and one of the three largest firms in the industry. Beloit is 80 percent owned by Harnischfeger Industries (a U.S.-based firm) and 20 percent owned by Mitsubishi Heavy Industries (a Japanese-based firm). In 1995, Beloit had sales of approximately $970 million which accounted for about 45 percent of Harnischfeger Industries' total sales. In addition, Beloit had units in virtually every region of the world. Financial statements for Harnischfeger Industries are provided below, as well as information on the firm's papermaking segment. Exhibit 2 provides a list of Beloit's operating units, Exhibit 3 lists the locations of its facilities around the world, and Exhibit 4 provides a map of these locations.

The twenty percent of FAMPA's stock purchased by the employees was purchased at one-half the per-share price paid by Beloit. Employees were allowed to purchase whatever quantity of shares they wished. Because Beloit's parent Harnischfeger Industries' stock is traded on the New York Stock Exchange and only 20 percent of Beloit Poland's shares are now publicly held, they are not traded on the new Polish National Stock Exchange. Hence, employees wishing to trade shares must do so on an informal basis.

Beloit's winning bid for 80 percent of FAMPA's common stock was $7 million. Beloit also committed to a $15 million investment over the ensuing seven years. The new owners immediately changed the name of the firm to Beloit Poland S.A. (S.A. designating an incorporated entity in Poland) and it became one of a family of Beloit subsidiaries. Beloit planned to refocus its new division's sales efforts from that of being a global competitor to serving primarily the Central and Eastern European markets, leaving other regions to Beloit's

| Exhibit 2 | **Beloit Subsidiaries** |
|---|---|

| Subsidiary | Location |
|---|---|
| Beloit Corporation | Delaware |
| Beloit Canada Ltd./Ltee | Canada |
| Beloit Industrial Ltda. | Brazil |
| Beloit Poland S.A. | Poland |
| BWRC, Inc. | Delaware |
| Beloit Asia Pacific Pte. Ltd. | Singapore |
| Beloit Italia S.P.A. | Italy |
| Beloit Lenox GmbH | Germany |
| Beloit Walmsley Ltd. | United Kingdom |
| J&L Fiber Services, Inc. | Wisconsin |
| Optical Alignment Systems and Inspection Services, Inc. | New Hampshire |
| Sandusky International, Inc. | Ohio |

**Exhibit 3**                    **Beloit's Worldwide Facilities**

| Plant and Location | Floor Space (Sq. Ft.) | Principal Operations |
| --- | --- | --- |
| Beloit, Wisconsin | 928,000 | Papermaking machinery and finished product processing equipment |
| Beloit, Wisconsin | 230,000 | Castings, pattern shop |
| Waukesha, Wisconsin | 57,000 | Castings, pattern shop, and finished product processing |
| Waukesha, Wisconsin | 76,000 | Refiner plate machining, finished product processing and warehousing |
| Rockton, Illinois | 469,000 | Papermaking machinery, finished product processing equipment and R&D center |
| South Beloit, Illinois | 163,000 | Castings |
| Dalton, Massachusetts | 277,000 | Stock and pulp preparation equipment and specialized processing systems |
| Lenox, Massachusetts | 127,000 | Winders |
| Pittsfield, Massachusetts | 36,000 | Research and development facility and pilot plant for process simulation |
| Aiken, South Carolina | 92,000 | Rubber and polymeric covers for rolls; rubber blankets; rubber and metal roll repairs |
| Columbus, Mississippi | 133,000 | |
| Federal Way, Washington | 55,000 | |
| Neenah, Wisconsin | 77,000 | |
| Clarks Summit, PA | 88,000 | |
| Renfrew, Canada | 145,000 | |
| Kalamazoo, Michigan | 23,500 | Filled rolls for supercalenders and specialty rolls |
| Portland, Oregon | 41,000 | Bulk materials handling and drying systems |
| Rochester, New Hampshire | 15,650 | Specialty services provide principally to the paper industry |
| Pensacola, Florida | 7,250 | Specialty services provide principally to the paper industry |
| Sandusky, Ohio | 254,000 | Centrifugal castings |
| Glenrothes, United Kingdom | 56,000 | Centrifugal castings |
| Campinas, Brazil | 202,000 | Papermaking machinery and finished product processing equipment; stock and pulp preparation equipment; woodyard and pulp plant equipment |
| Bolton, United Kingdom | 465,400 | Papermaking machinery and finished product processing equipment; stock and pulp preparation equipment |
| Pinerolo, Italy | 517,400 | |
| Jelenia Góra, Poland | 522,000 | |
| Świecie, Poland | 37,000 | Components and parts for papermaking machinery equipment |
| Cernay, France | 35,200 | Roll-covering service |

other divisions. Where it could, Beloit Poland would participate with other company units in filling international orders. For Beloit Poland the acquisition meant it could access the latest technology available and its parent's financial resources.

The financial and technological resources of Beloit are considerable. Sales of the parent company, Harnischfeger Industries, exceeded $1.5 billion in 1991. In addition, the company had a history of investing heavily in research and development, injecting about $30 million annually. This has resulted in Beloit

**Exhibit 4**       **Worldwide Beloit Group Locations**

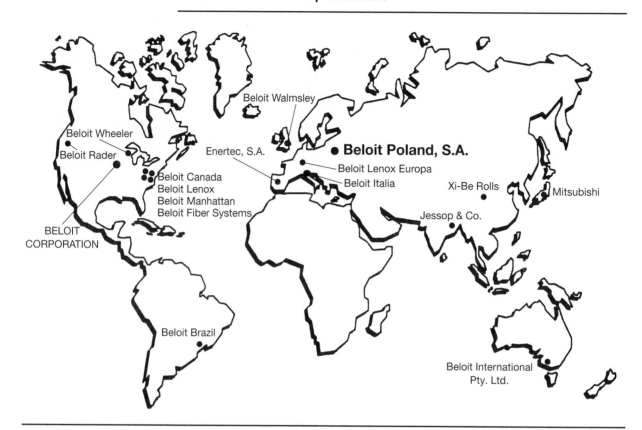

enjoying patented technological advantages in an industry in which they are critical.

The papermaking machinery segment of Harnischfeger had sales of $970 million in 1995, a thirty-six percent increase over 1994. Foreign sales accounted for about 41 percent of total sales. The market for this kind of equipment is cyclical and currently demand is slowly rising. Beloit earned a profit of $87.5 million in 1995. Exhibits 5a, 5b, and 5c provide financial information on Harnischfeger and its various business segments.

Beloit Poland fell under the terms of Poland's new Polish Commercial Code, enacted in June 1991. Under this code, Beloit Poland would be designated as a joint-stock company which, for the most part, possessed the same legal rights and responsibilities as corporations in Western nations. As it was considered a joint-stock company headquartered in Poland, it would be required to work under Poland's labor, taxation, and penal codes.

## THINKING GLOBALLY, ACTING LOCALLY

The market for papermaking equipment involves very large capital commitments and highly sophisticated technology; an average-sized paper plant costs $25 million to equip. Beloit is the largest of a three-firm oligopoly, also includ-

**Exhibit 5a**

## Harnischfeger Industries, Inc. Consolidated Statement of Income (000)

| | Year Ended October 31, 1995* | 1994** |
|---|---:|---:|
| **Revenues** | | |
| Net sales | 2,152,079 | 1,551,728 |
| Other income | 61,865 | 23,301 |
| Total | 2,213,944 | 1,575,029 |
| Cost of sales | 1,671,932 | 1,195,851 |
| Product development, selling and administrative expenses | 330,990 | 279,016 |
| Operating income | 211,022 | 100,162 |
| Interest expense – net | (40,713) | (47,366) |
| Income before Joy merger costs, provision for income taxes and minority interest | 170,309 | 52,796 |
| Provision for income taxes | (59,575) | (13,979) |
| Minority interest | (7,230) | (2,224) |
| Income from continuing operations before Joy merger costs | 103,504 | 36,593 |
| Joy merger costs | (17,459) | — |
| Income taxes applicable to Joy merger costs | 6,075 | — |
| Income from continuing operations after Joy merger costs | 92,120 | 36,593 |
| Income (loss) from and (net loss) on sale of discontinued operations net of applicable income taxes | (31,235) | (3,962) |
| Extraordinary loss on retirement of debt, net of applicable income taxes | (3,481) | (4,827) |
| Cumulative effect of accounting change, net of applicable income taxes and minority interest | — | (81,696) |
| Net income (loss) | 57,404 | (53,912) |
| **Earnings (loss) per share** | | |
| Income from continuing operations before Joy merger costs | 2.23 | 0.84 |
| Income from continuing operations after Joy merger costs | 1.99 | 0.84 |
| Income (loss) from and (net loss) on sale of discontinued operations | (0.67) | (0.09) |
| Extraordinary loss on retirement of debt | (0.08) | (0.11) |
| Cumulative effect of accounting change | — | (1.87) |
| Net income (loss) per share | 1.24 | (1.23) |
| Average shares outstanding | 46,218 | 43,716 |

 * FY 1995 amounts reflect Joy Environmental as a discontinued operation.

** FY 1994 amounts are restated to include the results of Joy Technologies Inc. and to reflect Joy Environmental as a discontinued operation.

**Exhibit 5b**         **Harnischfeger Industries, Inc. Condensed Balance Sheet (000)**

|  | *October 31, 1995* | *October 31, 1994\** |
|---|---|---|
| Assets | | |
| Current assets: | | |
| Cash and cash equivalents | 239,043 | 196,455 |
| Accounts receivable - net | 499,953 | 421,871 |
| Inventories | 416,395 | 357,847 |
| Net current assets of discontinued operations | — | 20,047 |
| Other current assets | 57,999 | 47,181 |
| Total | 1,213,390 | 1,043,401 |
| Property, plant and equipment - net | 487,656 | 490,237 |
| Intangible assets | 214,739 | 213,628 |
| Investment in Measurex Corporation | — | 66,347 |
| Noncurrent assets of discontinued operations | — | 43,251 |
| Other assets | 124,982 | 125,089 |
| Total Assets | 2,040,767 | 1,981,953 |
| Liabilities and Shareholders' Equity | | |
| Current liabilities: | | |
| Short-term notes payable, including current portion of long-term obligations | 22,802 | 16,540 |
| Trade accounts payable | 263,750 | 237,618 |
| Employee compensation and benefits | 100,041 | 75,679 |
| Advance payments and progress billings | 154,401 | 121,212 |
| Accrued warranties | 43,801 | 33,529 |
| Other current liabilities | 138,508 | 127,498 |
| Total | 723,303 | 612,076 |
| Long-term obligations | 459,110 | 568,933 |
| Liability for postretirement benefits | 101,605 | 118,610 |
| Deferred income taxes | 34,805 | 20,751 |
| Other liabilities | 73,057 | 73,648 |
| Minority interest | 89,611 | 85,570 |
| Shareholders' equity | 559,276 | 502,365 |
| Total Liabilities and Shareholders' Equity | 2,040,767 | 1,981,953 |

\*FY 1994 amounts are restated to include Joy Technologies Inc.

**Exhibit 5c**

**Harnischfeger Industries, Inc. Business Segment Summary
for the Year Ended October 31, 1995 (000)**

| | Net Sales | | Operating Profit | |
| --- | --- | --- | --- | --- |
| | 1995* | 1994** | 1995* | 1994** |
| Papermaking Machinery and Systems | 970,418 | 712,778 | 85,719 | 32,195 |
| Mining Equipment | 941,779 | 729,521 | 122,116 | 82,541 |
| Material Handling Equipment | 239,882 | 109,429 | 22,850 | 12,094 |
| Total Business Segments | 2,152,079 | 1,551,728 | 230,685 | 126,830 |
| Corporate Administration | — | — | (19,663) | (26,668) |
| Interest Expense - Net | — | — | (40,713) | (47,366) |
| Income before Joy Merger Costs, Provision for Income Taxes and Minority Interest | — | — | 170,309 | 52,796 |

| | Orders Booked | | Backlog at End of Period | |
| --- | --- | --- | --- | --- |
| | 1995* | 1994** | 10/95* | 10/94** |
| Papermaking Machinery and Systems | 1,016,273 | 795,888 | 679,625 | 633,770 |
| Mining Equipment | 972,419 | 703,354 | 221,540 | 190,900 |
| Material Handling Equipment | 263,649 | 137,689 | 130,879 | 107,112 |
| Total Business Segments | 2,252,341 | 1,636,931 | 1,032,044 | 931,782 |

*FY 1995 amounts reflect Joy Environmental as a discontinued operation.

**FY 1994 amounts are restated to include the results of Joy Technologies Inc. and to reflect Joy Environmental as a discontinued operation.

ing the German firm Voith Sulzer Papertech and the Finnish company Valmet Paper Machinery, Inc. These two firms each control a percentage of the market slightly smaller than that held by Beloit. In 1993 and 1994, Beloit won judgments for patent infringement against both of its major competitors for copying its paper drying process, a critical component in paper production.

Valmet is the world's second leading supplier of printing paper machines, accounting for more than fifteen percent of the world's paper output. Since 1858, more than 1200 machines have been delivered around the world, including recent deliveries to Korea, South Africa, and the U.S. Printing and specialty paper plants are located in Finland and Canada, pulp drying lines are made in Finland, and paper finishing machines are manufactured in Finland, Italy, France, and the U.S. Demand for paper is strong in North America, Asia, and Great Britain, contributing significantly to Valmet's success.

**Exhibit 6**          **Annual Sales for FAMPA/Beloit Poland (in millions of dollars)**

| Year | Sales |
| --- | --- |
| 1990 | 10.7 |
| 1991 | 14.5 |
| 1992 | 8.7 |
| 1993 | 15.1 |
| 1994 | 12.5 |
| 1995 | 34.0 |

Like Beloit, Valmet places a great emphasis on research and development. The company has seven research centers, each of which specializes in a different area of the papermaking process. Other segments of Valmet include an automotive division which manufactures the Saab Cabriolet and the Opel Calibra as well as other vehicles; an aviation division which maintains the aircraft and engines of the Finnish Air Force; and Valmet Power Transmissions, a manufacturer of gears, couplings, and mechanical drives.

## BELOIT'S INITIAL RESPONSE

It was clear to the Polish management team that in order to be competitive, Beloit would not only have to utilize an initial $15 million injection from its parent firm effectively, but would also have to streamline the organization in order to be responsive to the market. The strategic goal agreed to by the Polish team and Beloit was for the plant's capacity to rise from $20 million in annual sales to $35 million within two years and $50 million by the year 2000. This would raise Beloit Poland's capacity to a level sufficient to produce the equipment needed to furnish two typical paper mills annually. Exhibit 6 lists annual sales figures for FAMPA and Beloit Poland from 1990–1995.

Beloit also inserted its own people into two key management roles. While Miroslawski remained the president of the board of directors, Richard Endicott was named general manager. A new outside financial director, Mark McFarland, was also added to the management team. The firm was reorganized into what was essentially a functional structure, illustrated in Exhibit 7. Aside from the Americans holding senior positions, the rest of the management team remained Polish. The 500 employee level achieved after the restructuring was expected to meet the company's needs for the foreseeable future, with no major additions or layoffs anticipated.

Both Beloit's $15 million infusion and its plans for rapid sales growth assuaged many of those who had opposed FAMPA's sale to a foreign firm. The initial fear was that Beloit was buying FAMPA to obtain its market share and would reduce or close FAMPA's operations and supply its former customers from other Beloit units. However, after the investment and growth plans were initiated, such anxieties disappeared.

Beloit Poland S.A. was to specialize in supplying equipment capable of manufacturing paper and paper board sheet up to twenty feet wide and tissue up to twelve feet wide. It would remain responsible for marketing turn key installa-

**Exhibit 7**

**Organizational structure of Beloit Poland S.A.**

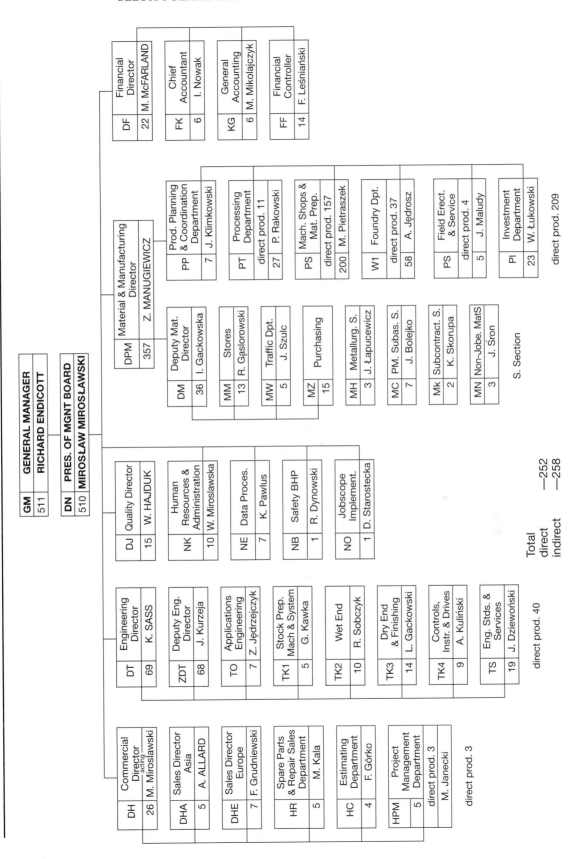

| GM | GENERAL MANAGER |
|---|---|
| 511 | RICHARD ENDICOTT |

| DN | PRES. OF MGNT BOARD |
|---|---|
| 510 | MIROSŁAW MIROSŁAWSKI |

Total
direct —252
indirect —258

tions, involving design of a new facility's equipment to meet the customer's production requirements, manufacture of the equipment, installation of the entire production process at the customer's plant site, conducting test runs, trouble-shooting problems and making final adjustments, and servicing the equipment after the sale. This process also involves licensing the use of the technology by the customer. Much of the Beloit technology is proprietary and an effort is made to protect it.

Beloit normally provides training for production technicians before and during startup, as well as planning assistance to the customer throughout the process to insure the customer's specifications will result in a plant which actually meets the customer's needs. Beloit also provides consulting services in the areas of construction engineering of the plant, and plant management. Beloit usually supplies its customers with spare parts, specialty supplies, and maintenance following the sale.

## BELOIT POLAND'S PRESENT STRATEGY AND POSITION

By 1994 Beloit Poland had not reached its anticipated targets, but was generating sales of about $12.5 million, two-thirds of which were exports. However, after losing money each year since the acquisition, Beloit Poland turned its first profit on sales of $35 million in 1995, an accomplishment widely attributed to its association with Beloit. Total employment has grown to slightly more than the original 500 figure. Employees generally feel circumstances have improved during the last few years, having received pay raises in excess of the rate of inflation and other newfound benefits, such as one-hour lunch breaks.

In many ways, the firm's goals and objectives remain unchanged:

1. to grow the firm and modernize it so it can continue to be a world-class competitor,
2. to continuously improve the quality and technical sophistication of the product,
3. to win new markets for its products and services, and
4. to diversify its activities by entering new, but related, fields.

These were the intentions behind privatization of FAMPA, as pursuing these goals allowed the business to survive and even prosper.

However, as a division of a much larger organization, in addition to the goals of the past, Beloit Poland must continue to focus its efforts toward integrating with the parent organization. For instance, rather than being a global competitor, Beloit Poland is expected to focus on that region of the world not adequately served by Beloit's other divisions. Beloit Poland must also learn to capitalize on the capabilities of its sister units and outsource those products and services it is not in a position to offer, or represent a strategic weakness when it attempts to compete alone. Beloit's various global units normally market its products within the geographic region they are designated to serve. However, Beloit USA maintains centralized marketing and financing units which also pursue global opportunities and coordinate the work of various divisions when especially large orders are involved.

Additionally, Beloit Poland faces a much more dynamic market environment than when under Communist control. During that period, sales were made at predetermined, relatively constant exchange rates and profit was not an issue. Now both the Polish currency as well as the currencies of the neighboring countries in which it sells float in terms of their relative values. Additionally, as Eastern European countries move toward free-market economies, they become subject to the same kinds of economic cycles as occur in the West. Such volatility results in significant changes in the relative attractiveness of Beloit Poland's products. For instance, while Germany was attempting to incorporate East Germany, its economy cooled dramatically, resulting in a 30 percent decline in Beloit Poland's sales.

A major competitive advantage Beloit Poland has is its entrée into a host of formerly state-owned paper manufacturers in what used to be the Soviet Bloc. These firms, many of which are no longer state-owned, are familiar with Beloit's products, and switching costs in this industry are typically high as the components of papermaking systems sold by suppliers are not typically compatible with competitors' equipment. Beloit Poland has recently been working very hard to maintain and expand its market share in the former Soviet Republics, especially Russia and the Baltic States.

Beloit Poland has also been working closely with Beloit USA to enter the Turkish, Korean, Southeast Asian, and Chinese markets. All of these nations are expanding their paper and cellulose products production in step with their relatively rapid economic growth rates. In the Korean, Southeast Asian, and Chinese markets, Beloit faces high-quality competition from Japanese and European firms but has enjoyed good market penetration in these areas. Unfortunately, Beloit has lacked capacity to meet the demand in these emerging markets. It is hoped Beloit Poland will be able to meet some of the unsatisfied demand. Beloit USA manages bid preparation and marketing efforts and usually helps arrange financing in these more distant markets.

Additionally, Beloit's parent, Harnischfeger Industries, hopes Beloit Poland might provide an opening for products of its other major divisions: Harnischfeger Heavy Equipment Group and Joy Manufacturing. These divisions produce materials handling equipment, construction and excavation cranes and draglines, and underground mining and surface mining equipment. Perhaps it is thought that it might be possible for Beloit Poland to grow through diversification into these product areas. As Poland's economy expands, its consumption of energy in the form of coal will likely increase, thereby expanding its need for mining equipment. As the economy expands, Poland's need for construction and materials handling equipment will also likely grow.

Other possibilities Beloit Poland is exploring include the application of its technical expertise and production capacity to new, related, select product-markets in Poland. Areas of interest include equipment used in agricultural and food products processing. FAMPA and Beloit Poland both produced parts used by manufacturers in both of these industries, although such sales have always been a minor part of the firm's total volume. Beloit Poland is presently exploring the possibility of forward integration and expansion into these markets. The firm's management knows little about the total demand for these products other than they are expected to grow as Poland's economy expands and consumers demand more processed foods and more energy is consumed. Even so, it is important to the management of Beloit Poland, especially the Polish management, to grow the firm and create opportunities for people in the local community.

Beloit Poland has also invested considerable energy in its efforts to achieve the same level of product and service quality for which Beloit USA has become known. The firm's quality motto has become "Quality gained now is a guarantee for the future of the firm and its employees." Beloit Poland's workforce is encouraged to see each new order as a challenge to be met and an opportunity to ensure future orders.

The quality assessment and assurance program at Beloit Poland is a complex but coherent mosaic of activities which revolve around three basic tenets. First, individual employees' efforts are concentrated and integrated to achieve high quality. Each employee is to become a true master at the job he/she performs and do it right the first time, while recognizing and working to ensure his/her individual efforts will flow efficiently toward the completion of each contract. Second, Beloit Poland emphasizes implementation of consistent quality assessment programs which are not unduly burdensome and costly. Finally, the company seeks to create an environment in which high levels of product quality can be achieved to ensure customers that no other competitor could have delivered the quality of products and services provided by Beloit Poland. Hence, management must work to develop an environment in which the pursuit of quality is reinforced, not discouraged, and that employees understand the firm's commitment to product quality. As evidence, both ISO 9000 and ISO 9001 certifications were achieved in 1993, covering design, construction, production, assembly and installation, and services.

## LOOKING BACK AT THE TRANSITION

The state-owned enterprise FAMPA in Jelenia Góra was one of the first firms in Poland to enter the hazardous path to privatization. At that time, confusion and uncertainty were high as neither the government nor the management of FAMPA really knew what they were doing and how the transition was to unfold. As one of the first East Bloc nations to undertake the transition, there were few if any tested models for converting an economy from one which was centrally planned to one based at least in large part on free-market principles. No one had any experience at dismantling the inefficiencies originally integrated into the system when centralized planning began.

# The Euro Disney Case: Early Debacle

## Albert J. Milhomme, Southwest Texas State University

*Internet site of interest:* **www.disney.com**

## INTRODUCTION

On an early February morning in 1994, a mix of rain and snow was falling over the Euro Disney Theme Park. . . . Ten thousand miles away, sitting comfortably in his chair, Michael Eisner, the 53-year-old chairman of The Walt Disney Company, was feeling a strange but undeniable desire to lock his office door and hide for the rest of the day. "Wouldn't it be nice if someone else could take care of the mess!" he thought. . . . Euro Disney was at the agony stage.

Events began to flash back and forth in Eisner's mind: his studies at Denison University (Ohio) where he majored in drama and literature in 1950; his first job as an usher at NBC; then his shift to CBS, with a technician's job, before landing at ABC, where he was in charge of Saturday morning programming. Under his control, ABC went from last to first place on Saturday morning, a success which propelled Eisner into primetime where he oversaw the development of an impressive roster of big hits including *Happy Days*, *Barney Miller*, *Laverne and Shirley*, *Rich Man, Poor Man*, and *Roots*. In the late 1970's he left television to join Paramount and his former ABC boss Barry Diller; during eight years together they teamed to produce several box office smashes.

### ■ Joining The Walt Disney Company

At Roy Disney's request, Eisner received his golden opportunity to join The Walt Disney Company as chairman of the board in 1984. The management contract put a lot of incentives on profit, and favored short-term profitability over the long-term flexibility, safety, and independence of the firm. But this was not his problem. He signed the contract. (Eisner's 1993 earnings of $203,010,590 ranked him as number one among the top-paid chief executives.)

Eisner thought about the history of Disney. When Walt Disney died in December 1966, he left his company at the pinnacle of its success up to that date. Walt's brother Roy took over management of the company and supervised the building of Walt Disney World.

## WALT DISNEY WORLD

The first step in the plan had been to purchase a huge tract of land outside Orlando, Florida. Disney had not liked the situation that had developed outside Anaheim after the opening of Disneyland. There the Disney company owned only the area on which the theme park and its parking lot are built. As a result, development around the park proceeded unchecked, and the surrounding area became overgrown with hotels and motels which detracted from the Disney image. Moreover, the profits earned by businesses in the vicinity of the park were vastly greater than the revenues that the company received from park attendance.

Determined to prevent the same outcome in Orlando, Roy arranged through subsidiary companies the purchase of 28,000 acres of undeveloped land, an area of 34 square miles, large enough to hold a multitude of hotels and amusement parks. When Disney made the announcement of the park in 1965, the value of the land increased dramatically overnight. In 1984, however, chains such as Hyatt and Hilton were opening luxury hotels at the borders of Disney World. Potential Disney revenues were, once more, lost to these chains, and the situation which had developed at Disneyland was indeed recurring in Orlando, in spite of the three Disney-owned hotels with over 2,000 rooms.

Eisner remembered going against the conventional wisdom that higher prices would reduce attendance, and he raised the admission prices substantially. The result was a small drop in attendance and a huge increase in revenues. Essentially, Eisner had discovered that the Disney theme parks have a captive audience and a price inelastic demand. When Eisner raised the admission price by 45% in two years, the increase in theme-park price caused a 59% growth in company revenues and accounted for fully 94% of earnings growth in 1986.

Eisner realized that what was needed was more kinds of attractions and more rides inside existing theme parks, as well as additional theme parks or "gates," which would have new collections of attractions and new sources of fees. Disney looked for new "gate" ideas to capture tourists' imaginations. The Disney-MGM park opened to enthusiastic crowds in 1989.

In the effort to wrest tourist dollars from the Orlando competition, Disney did not ignore shopping and night-time entertainment. At night, many Disney guests used to leave the park to eat and play in the entertainment district of Church Street Station in Orlando. To keep patrons on the site, Disney built Pleasure Island, an entertainment complex featuring restaurants and night clubs. Also, the company looked at the food concession business. Eisner realized that the food concessions represented another source of revenue loss; as leases expired, the Disney company began to take over all the food operations at the theme parks.

Meanwhile, new attractions were constantly announced. In developing attractions, Eisner and his team had other money-making ventures in mind. Disney's guests needed somewhere to stay. Here was the opportunity. Disney got into the hotel business on a large scale by building luxury hotels, each of which offered a different kind of experience to Disney guests. Disney found the ideal formula for building hotels without putting a financial debt burden on the company. Management arranged limited partnerships to finance the hotel-building program and the convention centers.

### ■ Eisner's Midas Touch

The company's earnings jumped by more than 500% during his first four years. Jim Henson, the creator of the Muppets, sold his library of characters to Disney. Kermit and Miss Piggy became part of the Disney family, helping the company to move forward exponentially. Everything was going great; an article in the September 4th, 1989, *Adweek's Marketing Week* had a headline that read "Everything Eisner Touches Turns to Gold." "Eisner's sense of what will and won't work might have been tied to his nature. He is a tremendous evaluator," said journalist Betsy Sharkey.

## TOKYO DISNEYLAND

When Eisner joined Disney in 1984, Tokyo Disneyland was completing its first year of operations. After Disney's agreement with the Oriental Land Company in Japan, it took five years of planning and construction. More than 10 million people (9% from other Asian countries) visited the park that year, spending $355 million. This was $155 million more than had been expected, and was partially attributed to the average expenditure per visitor being $35, rather than the estimated $21. Thus, Tokyo Disneyland quickly became profitable. Growth continued, and by 1990 more than 14 million people visited the park, a figure slightly larger than the attendance at Disneyland in California and about half the attendance at Walt Disney World in Florida. The timing of the Tokyo Disneyland opening coincided with a rise in income and leisure time among the Japanese. A Disney executive said that a similar rise in income and leisure had contributed to the successful opening of the first park near Los Angeles.

The Tokyo park was in some ways a paradox. Tokyo Disneyland is nearly a replica of the two parks in the U.S. Signs are in English, and most food is American style. The Oriental Land Company demanded this because it wanted visitors to feel they were getting the real thing, and because they had noted that franchises such as McDonald's had enormous success in Japan as Japanese youth embraced American-style culture. That the park is nearly identical to the ones in the U.S. masks the fact that there have been numerous operational adjustments. Some changes were necessary, such as the addition of a Japanese restaurant. Where Disney uses its own staff to prepare advertising in the U.S., it has relied on outside agencies in Japan to adapt to cultural differences.

Though Disney was not a financial partner in the Tokyo venture, it was reaping the profit from its franchisee (10% royalty from admission and 5% from merchandise and food sales). At last, Disney had in hand the perfect global product, and had to take advantage of it quickly.

# EURO DISNEY

Eisner remembered that the dream to expand this perfect global product started in 1984, a few months after his arrival at Disney, with his decision to create a Disney Resort in Europe. Two teams began to work: one to select the ideal location, the other to design the most exciting park ever imagined. In 1985, Disney announced that it had narrowed its locational choice to two countries, Spain and France.

## ■ France or Spain?

The park was scheduled to open in 1992 at either location. Since the park was estimated to provide about 40,000 permanent jobs (a gross exaggeration; 12,000 jobs have been created up to now) and would draw large numbers of tourists, the two countries courted Disney. Disney openly played one country against the other in an attempt to get more incentives. Spain offered two different locations and 25% of the construction cost, and claimed it could attract 40 million tourists a year! The French claimed that they could attract 12 million customers a year, a number Disney estimated as the break-even point, and agreed to extend the Paris subway to the park's location and to create a station for the high speed train connecting the Benelux countries to the Mediterranean shores, at a cost of about $350 million. In addition, the French government offered 4,800 acres of land at about $7,500 per acre (a bargain price for the area), loaned 22 percent of the funds needed, and accepted a decrease of the value-added tax on the entrance fees from 18.6% to 7%.

If Disney opted for a Spanish location, the park would be like the ones in the U.S., where visitors are outside for almost all amusements. However, Disney had learned from the Tokyo experience that colder weather does not necessarily impede attendance. The colder climate in the Paris area would require more indoor shows, strategically located fireplaces, a glass dome over the teacup ride, and some protected waiting lines.

## ■ Paris Selection

After three years of discussions with land planners, lawyers, and government officials, the search culminated with the selection of a site at the heart of Europe: Marne-la-Vallée, France. Euro Disney was officially born. The negotiations resulted in Disney's agreement to own at least 16.7%, but no more than 49%, of Euro Disney, which includes satellite investments around the park for hotels, shopping centers, a campground, and other facilities. The total investment by 1992 was estimated at between 2.4 to 3.0 billion U.S. dollars. Disney, through EDL Holding Company, a wholly owned indirect Disney subsidiary, opted for a 49% stake in Euro Disney S.C.A. (Société en Commande par Action), a master limited partnership. Euro Disney S.A., another wholly owned indirect Disney subsidiary, was created to manage Euro Disney S.C.A. Remaining shares of Euro Disney S.C.A. were sold through an international syndicate of banks and securities dealers, with 50% going to investors in France, 25% in Britain, and the remainder elsewhere in Europe.

## ■ Shareholders' Equity and Liabilities

The share capital was FF1,700,000,000, the equivalent of about $300,000,000 at FF5.67/$1 rate of exchange. Shares were acquired by Disney at their face values, namely FF10, but sold without difficulty to other investors at FF72, creating a share premium (goodwill) of more than FF4,878,000,000, a large contribution to the shareholders' equity.

Euro Disney S.C.A. developed and financed the Euro Disneyland theme park as phase 1A of the project, and six hotels as phase 1B of the project. The theme park was then sold to Euro Disneyland S.N.C. (17% Disney, 83% French companies) and the hotels to six financing companies.

Euro Disney S.C.A., with Euro Disney S.N.C., was one of the "Owner Companies" provided for in the "Agreement on the Creation and the Operation of Euro Disneyland in France" signed in 1987, but indeed Euro Disney S.C.A. was not keeping many fixed assets in its books. Euro Disneyland S.N.C. (a type of general partnership) will own the "Euro Disney Theme Park" and lease it back to Euro Disney S.C.A.; ultimately, it will resell the theme park at a predetermined nominal price, 30 years after. Euro Disneyland S.N.C. is also managed by a wholly owned indirect Disney subsidiary corporation named "Société de Gérance d'Euro Disneyland S.A." The six financing companies which own the hotels will lease the land on which these hotels are built from Euro Disney S.C.A. and will lease the hotels back to six wholly owned Euro Disney S.C.A. subsidiary corporations. These hotels will be managed by E.D.L. Service S.A., a wholly owned Euro Disney S.C.A. subsidiary corporation (see Exhibit 1).

Disney's confidence was due in large part to the fact that 2.5 million Europeans visited the U.S. parks in 1990. It was also due to the fact Disney believed that it was at last, in the position to capture all the dollars in theme park related entertainment activities, a monopolistic situation often searched for, but never achieved by Walt or Roy. Michael Eisner will be the first one to apply the "magic" formula: "If someone can make a living at it, so can we!"

Euro Disney was indeed at the threshold of two formidable coups: first, a long-term real estate coup, the French government having sold to the firm some very expensive land at a bargain price; second, a short-term profit coup, with the potential earnings from the management contract being tremendous (see Exhibit 2). France was in full economic crisis. Job creation was the number one priority, and Disney was taking advantage of this crisis. No one considered the possibility of Disney falling prey to the same crisis . . . no one thought about it. As Euro Disney Chairman Fitzpatrick said, "Disney was determined to change Europe's chemistry."

## ■ Construction's Excitement

In 1988 the Disney "Imagineers" completed their design and construction began. Four million cubic meters of earth were moved to create a landscape of lakes, rivers, and hills. Most of 1989 was spent underground—laying foundations for the attractions and hotels, putting in place miles of conduit and cable, and preparing an infrastructure which could serve a city of 200,000 people.

By 1990, contractors, manufacturers, and suppliers had been mobilized across Europe. In a dozen different countries, show sets, ride vehicles, and

**Exhibit 1**                    **Euro Disney's Organizational Web**

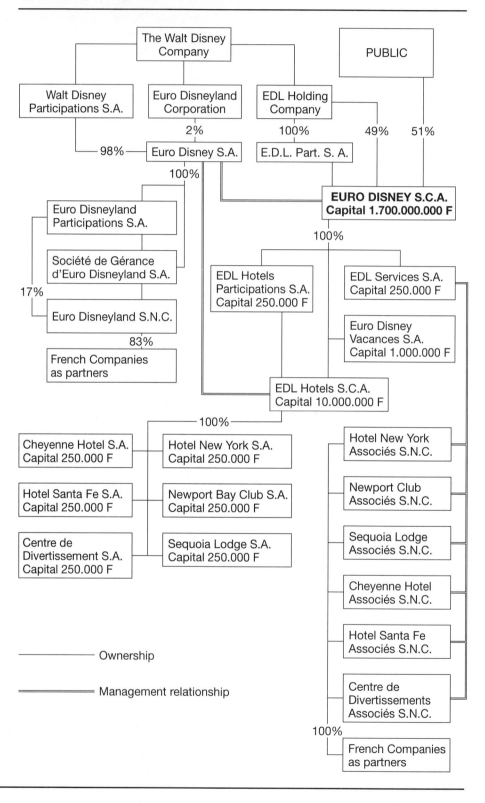

---

**Exhibit 2**                    **Management Incentives**

---

**Royalties (30-year agreement), paid directly to Walt Disney Company**

10% of gross revenues generated by ticket sales,

  5% of gross revenues from food, beverage, and merchandise sales,

10% of fees due from participants who sponsored some rides,

  5% of gross revenues of theme hotels.

**Base Fee, paid directly to EDL Participations S.A., a corporation wholly-owned by Walt Disney Company through EDL Holding Co. S.A.**

3% of the Euro Disney S.C.A.'s total revenues in a year, less 0.5 percent of the S.C.A.'s net after-tax profits, until the later of 1) the expiration of five financial years of operations, or 2) the end of the financial year in which the company satisfied certain financial tests under the bank-loan agreement.

Thereafter, the base fee would be 6% per year, less the 0.5% of the S.C.A.'s net after-tax profits.

This base fee is part of the operating expenses.

**Incentive Fee paid to EDL Participations**

0.5% of Euro Disney S.C.A.'s net after-tax profit.

35% of any pre-tax gain on sales of hotels.

If the Operating Cash Flow (OCF) exceeds FF1.4 billion, Disney will collect:

   30% of the OCF in the FF1.4-2.1 billion range,

   40% of the OCF in the FF2.1-2.8 billion range,

   50% of the OCF above FF2.8 billion range.

---

Audio-Animatronics figures were being fabricated. Trees were being tagged and transplanted, and the first costume designs were being sent to the manufacturers. On the site, more than 80 cranes reached over bare steel and raw concrete to bring the Resort's structures out of the ground.

In 1991, all efforts converged. More than 10,000 workers from 900 European companies were on the site and the Resort and Theme Park began to take on its definitive character and personality. At the Hotel New-York, one of the park's hotels, the silhouette of Manhattan emerged along the waterfront and the Hotel Cheyenne almost looked like a scene from "High Noon." In the Park, carpenters aged the rough-hewn storefront of Frontierland, turn-of-the-century cobblestones were laid along Main Street, and gold-leaf was applied to the sixteen turrets of the Château de la Belle au Bois Dormant. Over 30,000 props, 4,000 different signs and graphics, and 7,000 specially designed light fixtures were installed. The largest wardrobe in Europe was stocked with a half million costumes. The final phase of preparations had clearly begun.

## ▪ Cultural Adjustments

In spite of the economic benefits that the park was expected to bring, many people in France feared that the park would be just one more step toward the replacement of the French culture with that of the U.S. Critics called Euro Disney "a cultural Chernobyl." Eisner was pelted with eggs in Paris, and a magazine, *Le Nouvel Observateur*, showed a giant Mickey Mouse stepping on the rooftops of Parisian buildings.

# THE DREAM BECOMES REALITY

The Euro Disney cast had grown to 2,555 when Euro Disney opened the Casting Center on September 2, 1991. Each day, out of the 500 to 700 candidates interviewed, 60 to 70 were selected for their commitment to quality service, their enthusiasm, and their genuine liking of people, in addition to their professional skills. Eisner recalled the beginning of his marketing campaign with the Rendez-Vous au Château on October 12, 1991: "Over two-thousand journalists and guests joined us as we unveiled the Château de la Belle au Bois Dormant." The result was a great leap in awareness of the Euro Disney Resort throughout Europe.

This event served as the kick-off not only for the marketing and sales efforts, but also for the complete Pan-European promotional campaigns. Simultaneously, the Sales Division began ambitious programs to inspire European families to mark the Euro Disney Resort on their vacation agendas. The sales division established a strong presence in all major markets through special partnerships with leading companies in the travel industry. P & O European Ferries, the SAS Leisure Group, and Belgian Rail joined Disney as Travel Alliance Partners. Agreements with more than twenty tour operators had made the Euro Disney packages available in travel agencies throughout Europe. Disney also launched a tour subsidiary, Euro Disney Vacances, to promote the Resort throughout France, Germany, Italy, and the Netherlands.

## ■ Inauguration

On April 12, 1992, Euro Disney hosted the biggest event in Disney history, the official opening of the Euro Disney Resort. After five years as a design and construction company, Euro Disney became an operating resort management company literally overnight. The dream became a reality. But the overall cost did not remain within the FF22 billion budget. Instead, it reached FF23.7 billion.

Eisner remembered Disney's letter to the shareholders in the first annual report, saying that ". . . 1992 was a year of satisfaction, challenge, and change. First, satisfaction at having met the objectives. The Euro Disney Resort opened on the day planned. An extraordinary theme park, six splendid hotels, a campground, and Festival Disney came alive with guests from all over Europe. Satisfaction because Euro Disney hosted 7,000,000 guests in its first six months of operation and achieved an average hotel occupancy of 74%. The overwhelming majority of our guests stated their intent to make a return visit and to recommend Euro Disney to their family and friends."

It went on to say, "Satisfaction, as well, because of the tribute paid to the creation of Euro Disney by the French state, when Prime Minister Pierre Beregovoy bestowed the insignia of Chevalier de la Légion d'Honneur to Michael Eisner. Challenge, because the financial results were not as strong as hoped. During the first six months of operation, fear of giant traffic jams and RER strikes for Parisians, truckers blockading the highways of France for foreign tourists, and especially the very difficult economic environment contributed to not meeting the more ambitious objectives."

To build greater awareness of the product, Eisner remembered, the sales-marketing teams moved aggressively to develop new campaigns and to define new agreements with tour and travel operators. The entertainment team had created a multitude of special shows and festivities so that the Euro Disney Resort was an ever-changing celebration for each season and holiday. Disney also had new attractions planned for 1993, which, when combined with seasonal events, were designed to encourage repeat visits.

The Company was also actively pursuing phase 2 of development of the Euro Disney Resort with the French public parties. Given the sluggishness of the real estate market, Euro Disney had proposed reductions in the scale of the Second Detailed Program. It did postpone office development to concentrate on the core of the business—providing the best leisure facilities in Europe— and planned to add a second theme park, the Disney MGM Studios-Europe, and a water park. This expansion would have attracted a substantial number of additional visitors, and greatly increased the guest length of stay on Disney property. Disney was so optimistic that they were simultaneously negotiating a separate agreement which would have ensured the possibility of creating a third theme park at the beginning of the next century.

The financial structure of Euro Disney was extremely elaborate (see Exhibit 1). The leverage effect resulting from a large amount of borrowed money and a small amount of equity was at its center. This strategy would have been workable if the park was generating a return on investment above the mean interest rate on the debt, but it would be a disaster if the return on investment could not reach that level.

## WHEN THE DREAM TURNED INTO A NIGHTMARE

Disney had disastrous financial results for the first two years ($36 million in losses in 1992, and more than $900 million in 1993; see Exhibits 3 and 4)— although two-thirds of that was a write-off of pre-opening costs and a change in the accounting procedures. After these disastrous results, the financial restructuring of Euro Disney was under consideration, with the stockholders' equity melting down like snow in sunshine. The gravity of the situation became apparent when attendance in 1993 was down by 15% from the previous year. The share's value was really plunging (see Exhibit 5). Disney was taking a lot of heat for making what appeared to be some hasty marketing decisions.

### ■ Reactive Management Decisions

A series of price adjustments was made from the very beginning. A premium pricing strategy was initially employed. However, as soon as August 1992, three months after the inauguration, the 1,098-room Newport Bay Club Hotel was downgraded from first class to moderate category and in October 1992, was closed until the summer of 1993. Peak season, when highest prices apply, was shortened by a full month. Two other 1,000-room hotels were then demoted from first class to moderate. The park admission fee cost U.S. $40 for an adult and $26 for a child under 11, a price about 30% higher than the corresponding Disney World price. When the first financial results became known (October 1992), Disney decided to increase the entrance fee from FF225 to FF250. The U.S. Disney park's formula in terms of price elasticity of demand did not apply and the demand fell sharply (a 15% decrease in attendance for a 10% increase in price). Attendance figures were kept secret, but this approach

**Exhibit 3**         **Euro Disney S.C.A. Group Financial Statements 1990,1991,1992, and 1993**

*Condensed Consolidated Statement of Income (Millions of French Francs)*

|  | 9/30/93 | 9/30/92 | 9/30/91 | 9/30/90 |
|---|---|---|---|---|
| Revenues | 5725 | 8463 | 6201 | 3241 |
| Theme park and Resorts | 4874 | 3819 | 0 | 0 |
| Construction sales | 851 | 4644 | 6201 | 3241 |
| Costs and Expenses | 7542 | 9145 | 6215 | 3385 |
| Cost of Construction Sold | 846 | 4644 | 5826 | 3235 |
| Other Operating Expenses | 3382 | 2427 | 0 | 0 |
| Operating Income before Fixed and Administrative Expenses | 1497 | 1392 | 375 | 6 |
| Depreciation allowance | 227 | 316 | 48 | 21 |
| Lease rental expense | 1712 | 716 | 0 | 0 |
| Royalties | 262 | 197 | 0 | 0 |
| General and Administrative | 1113 | 845 | 341 | 129 |
| Operating Income | (1817) | (682) | (14) | (144) |
| Financial Income | 719 | 541 | 521 | 457 |
| Financial Expense | (615) | (307) | (115) | (75) |
| Income before Exceptional Income and Income Taxes | (1713) | (448) | 392 | 237 |
| Exceptional Income | (3624) | 109 | 4 | 144 |
| Income before Taxes | (5337) | (339) | 396 | 381 |
| Income after Taxes | (5337) | (188) | 249 | 381 |

*Condensed Consolidated Statements of Cash Flows (Millions of French Francs)*

|  | 9/30/93 | 9/30/92 | 9/30/91 | 9/30/90 |
|---|---|---|---|---|
| Cash Flows from Operations | (716) | 1228 | 1984 | (754) |
| Cash Flows from Investment | 974 | (4484) | (2213) | (1236) |
| Cash Flows from Financing | 608 | (474) | 2660 | 4451 |
| Change in cash | 1082 | (3730) | 2431 | 2461 |

*Condensed Consolidated Balance Sheet (Millions of French Francs)*

| Assets | 9/30/93 | 9/30/92 | 9/30/91 | 9/30/90 |
|---|---|---|---|---|
| Intangible Assets | 173 | 1491 | 79 | 34 |
| Tangible Assets | 5111 | 4788 | 2722 | 1297 |
| Long-term receivables | 5223 | 3988 | 1564 | 7 |
| Total Fixed Assets | 10507 | 10267 | 4365 | 1338 |
| Construction in-progress |  |  |  | 587 |
| Deferred Charges | 510 | 2001 | 1716 | 1075 |
| Inventories | 221 | 387 | 42 | 485 |
| A/R Financing Companies |  | 585 | 1915 | 1394 |
| A/R Trade | 313 | 456 | 11 | 953 |
| A/R Other | 966 | 1248 | 1903 |  |

| Exhibit 3 (continued) | Euro Disney S.C.A. Group Financial Statements 1990,1991,1992, and 1993 | | | |
|---|---|---|---|---|
| *Assets* | *9/30/93* | *9/30/92* | *9/30/91* | *9/30/90* |
| Short-term Investments | 861 | 1726 | 5947 | 3569 |
| Cash | 343 | 560 | 69 | 16 |
| Total Current Assets | 2704 | 4962 | 9887 | 5932 |
| Total Assets | 13721 | 17230 | 15968 | 8933 |
| *Liabilities* | *9/30/93* | *9/30/92* | *9/30/91* | *9/30/90* |
| Capital | 1700 | 1700 | 1700 | 1700 |
| Share Premium | 4880 | 4880 | 4878 | 4884 |
| Retained earnings | (5063) | 447 | 636 | 389 |
| Shareholders' equity | 1517 | 7027 | 7214 | 6973 |
| Deferred Income Tax | | | 151 | 5 |
| Deferred Revenues | 160 | 316 | 265 | 152 |
| Long-Term Debt | 8278 | 6222 | 4226 | |
| A/P to Related Companies | 1525 | 796 | 421 | 361 |
| A/P Accounts Payable | 1640 | 2869 | 3691 | 1442 |
| Current Liabilities | 3766 | 3665 | 4112 | 1803 |
| Total Equity Liabilities | 13721 | 17230 | 15968 | 8933 |

reinforced the belief that even in terms of attendance, the objectives were not being reached. Thousands of discounted tickets were issued for many organizations. Free passes were even offered to many officials.

Eisner recalled the letter to the shareholders prefacing the 1992 Annual Report. In it, Robert Fitzpatrick, the Euro Disney chairman, said "that looking at the future, Euro Disney had two primary objectives: to achieve profitability as quickly as possible, and to better integrate Euro Disney into its European environment while reinforcing our greatest asset—our Disney heritage."

## ■ Who Is Guilty?

As Michael Eisner stated in an interview with Larry King (11/11/93), "Everybody is giving us 42 reasons why we've made a mistake, because we have financial problems. The fact of the matter is, I am totally confident we made the right decision." Then he went on to say: "I am an inveterate salesman—can't help myself. I am sure we made the right decision geographically. Paris is a great city for tourism. Of course, it has not been a great city for tourists with families and kids, because it's been more an adult place. But we will overcome this obstacle."

Then in another interview Eisner said "I don't believe that the Company can reproach its management for the terrible recession (see Exhibits 6, 7, and 8) that is hurting Europe, and which is, to a greater extent, at the origin of today's situation. We are responsible for neither the real estate crisis nor the high French interest rate, which are dreadfully penalizing us. Not a single manager, whomever he be, could manage so many uncontrollable forces."

**Exhibit 4**          **Forecast and Reality**

|  | 3/31/93 forecast | 3/31/93 reality | 3/31/94 forecast | 3/31/94 reality | 3/31/95 forecast |
|---|---|---|---|---|---|
| *Revenues* | | | | | |
| Magic Kingdom | 4,246 | 3,800 | 4,657 | 3,100 | 5,384 |
| Second Theme Park | 0 | 0 | 0 | 0 | 0 |
| Resort & Property Dev. | 1,236 | 1,813 | 2,144 | 1,462 | 3,520 |
| *Total Revenues* | 5,482 | 5,613 | 6,801 | 4,562 | 8,904 |
| *Expenses* | | | | | |
| **Operating Expenses** | | | | | |
| Magic Kingdom | 2,643 | 3,745 | 2,836 | 3,371 | 3,161 |
| Second Theme Park | 0 | 0 | 0 | 0 | 0 |
| Resort & Property Dev. | 796 | | 1,501 | | 2,431 |
| General & Adm. Expenses | | 1,427 | | 961 | |
| Start-up Cost First Park | 0 | 340 | 0 | 340 | 0 |
| *Total Operating Expenses* | 3,439 | 5,512 | 4,337 | 4,672 | 5,592 |
| **Total Operating Income** | **2,043** | **101** | **2,464** | **(110)** | **3,312** |
| **Other Expenses** | | | | | |
| Royalties | 302 | 290 | 33 | 239 | 387 |
| Pre-Opening Cost Amortization | 341 | 125 | 341 | 300 | 341 |
| Depreciation | 255 | 258 | 263 | 238 | 290 |
| Interest Expenses | 567 | 650 | 575 | 937 | 757 |
| Interest Income | (786) | (986) | (788) | (564) | (768) |
| Lease Expenses | 958 | 1,603 | 950 | 1,545 | 958 |
| Management Incentive Fees | 55 | 0 | 171 | 0 | 477 |
| *Total Other Expenses* | 1,692 | 1,940 | 1,545 | 2,695 | 2,442 |
| Exceptional Income | 0 | 179 | 0 | (2,740) | 0 |
| Profit Before Taxation | 351 | (1,660) | 919 | (5,545) | 870 |
| Taxation | 147 | 0 | 389 | 0 | 366 |
| **Net Profit** | **204** | **(1,660)** | **530** | **(5,545)** | **504** |

### ■ Euro Disney Rescue Package Wins Approval

On March 15, 1995, Walt Disney Co. agreed to spend about $750 million to bail out its 49%-owned and fully-operated Euro Disney S.C.A. affiliate, apparently ending the threat that the gates of the troubled Magic Kingdom in France would close forever. A preliminary deal struck with representatives of Euro Disney's lead banks will cut the park's debt in half and is aimed at making Euro Disney profitable in its fiscal year ending Sept. 30, 1995, far earlier than many analysts had expected. The banks would kick in about $500 million and make other concessions.

**Exhibit 5**                     **Euro Disney: Evolution of Share Value**

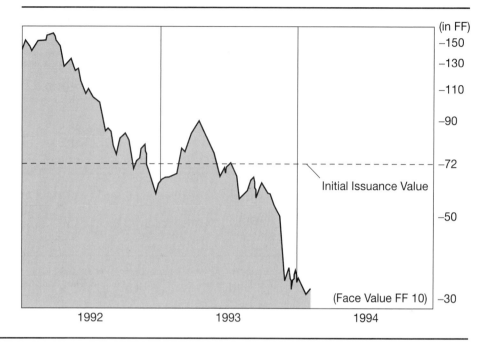

The plan calls for a rights offering of six billion francs, or about $1.02 billion. Such an offering consists of rights to purchase shares, usually at below-market prices, to existing shareholders, in the same proportion as their present owner-ship. Disney will spend three billion francs, or about $508 million, to buy 49% of the offering. The company also agreed to buy certain park assets for 1.4 bil-lion francs, or about $240 million, and lease them back on terms favorable to Euro Disney.

The plan would halve Euro Disney's debt to about 10 billion francs, or $1.69 billion, from the current 20 billion francs. The banks agreed to forgive 18 months of interest payments and will defer all principal payments for three years. Analysts estimated that the elimination of the interest payments will save Euro Disney about 1.9 billion francs.

The banks will also underwrite the remaining 51% of the rights offering that Disney is not buying. The offering is structured to maintain Disney's existing ownership interest in Euro Disney. "This will ensure that the resort, which has been the best-received park ever in Europe, will operate on a sound financial basis as well," said Eisner, who called the restructuring "fair and economically sensible." The agreement, endorsed by Euro Disney's lead banks, now must be accepted by all 63 creditor banks and the public shareholders.

As part of the package, Disney said it would eliminate for five years the lucrative management fees and royalties (Exhibit 2) it receives on ticket sales and merchandise. The royalties will be reintroduced at lower levels gradually over an unspecified period of time. Disney will still receive an "incentive fee" based on any profit made by the Euro Disney resort, which cost $3.68 billion to build. Disney and the banks said that prior to the rights offering, there will be a reduction in the capital of Euro Disney by reducing the par value of the

**Exhibit 6**

**Adjusted Gross Domestic Product, Using Purchasing Power Parity by Country, from 1985 to 1991 (dollar per capita)**

|  | 1985 | 1989 | 1990 | 1991 |
|---|---|---|---|---|
| Belgium | 11,805 | 15,194 | 16,301 | 17,454 |
| France | 12,875 | 16,310 | 17,301 | 18,227 |
| Germany | 13,525 | 17,020 | 18,307 | 19,500 |
| Italy | 11,585 | 15,046 | 16,012 | 16,896 |
| Luxembourg | 13,703 | 18,657 | 19,923 | 21,372 |
| Netherlands | 11,949 | 14,821 | 15,951 | 16,530 |
| Spain | 7,953 | 10,880 | 11,738 | 12,719 |
| Switzerland | 15,884 | 19,111 | 21,020 | 21,747 |
| United Kingdom | 11,473 | 15,177 | 15,866 | 15,720 |
| United States | 16,786 | 20,920 | 21,866 | 22,204 |

Sources: *Statistical Abstract of the United States 1994. The National Data Book,* p. 864, table no.1370. U.S. Department of Commerce. Economics and Statistics Administration. Bureau of Census.

**Exhibit 7**

**Discount and Currency Rates**

**Central Bank Discount Rates**

|  | U.S. | France | Germany | Italy | Netherlands | U.K. |
|---|---|---|---|---|---|---|
| 1985 | 7.50 | 9.50 | 4.00 | 15.00 | 5.00 | 10.78 |
| 1990 | 6.60 | 9.50 | 6.00 | 12.50 | 7.25 | 14.68 |
| 1991 | 3.50 | 9.50 | 8.00 | 12.00 | 8.50 | 11.75 |
| 1992 | 3.00 | 9.50 | 8.25 | 12.00 | 7.75 | 9.55 |
| 1993 | 3.00 | 9.50 | 5.75 | 8.00 | 5.00 | 5.60 |
| 1994 | 3.00 | 5.00 | 4.50 | 7.25 | 4.50 | 12.00 |

**Foreign Exchange Rate: Average National Currency Units/One dollar**

|  | France | Belgium | Italy | Netherlands | Spain | Switz. | Germany | U.K. |
|---|---|---|---|---|---|---|---|---|
| 1988 | 5.95 | 36.78 | 1.302 | 1.97 | 116.52 | 1.46 | 1.75 | .561 |
| 1989 | 6.38 | 39.40 | 1.372 | 2.12 | 118.44 | 1.63 | 1.88 | .610 |
| 1990 | 5.44 | 33.42 | 1.198 | 1.82 | 101.96 | 1.43 | 1.61 | .560 |
| 1991 | 5.64 | 34.19 | 1.241 | 1.87 | 104.01 | 1.43 | 1.66 | .565 |
| 1992 | 5.29 | 32.14 | 1.232 | 1.75 | 102.38 | 1.40 | 1.56 | .566 |
| 1993 | 5.66 | 34.58 | 1.573 | 1.85 | 127.48 | 1.47 | 1.65 | .665 |
| 1994 | 5.54 | 33.42 | 1.611 | 1.81 | 133.88 | 1.36 | 1.62 | .652 |

Sources: *Statistical Abstract of the United States 1994. The National Data Book,* p. 881, table 1402, and p. 882, table 1404. U.S. Department of Commerce. Economics and Statistics Administration. Bureau of Census.

**Exhibit 8**        **Selected International Economic Indicators 1980 to 1993**

### Gross National Product Growth Rate

|      | U.S   | France | Germany | Italy | Netherlands | U.K.  |
|------|-------|--------|---------|-------|-------------|-------|
| 1980 | − 0.5 | 1.6    |         | 4.1   | 0.9         | − 2.2 |
| 1985 | 3.2   | 1.9    |         | 2.6   | 2.6         | 3.8   |
| 1990 | 1.2   | 2.5    |         | 2.1   | 4.1         | 0.4   |
| 1991 | − 0.7 | 0.8    | 1.0     | 1.3   | 2.1         | − 2.2 |
| 1992 | 2.6   | 1.2    | 2.1     | 0.7   | 1.4         | − 0.6 |
| 1993 | 3.0   | − 1.0  | − 1.2   | − 0.7 | 0.2         | 1.9   |

### Ratio of Savings to Disposable Personal Income

|      | U.S | France | Germany | Italy | Netherlands | U.K. |
|------|-----|--------|---------|-------|-------------|------|
| 1980 | 7.9 | 17.6   |         | 21.9  | 11.0        | 13.1 |
| 1985 | 6.4 | 14.0   |         | 18.9  | 13.1        | 10.7 |
| 1990 | 4.2 | 12.5   |         | 18.4  | 16.5        | 8.6  |
| 1991 | 4.8 | 13.1   | 13.8    | 18.6  | 12.5        | 10.1 |
| 1992 | 5.3 | 13.9   | 13.9    | 18.7  | 13.2        | 12.3 |
| 1993 | 4.0 | 14.2   | 13.2    | –     | –           | 11.5 |

### Ratio of Gross Fixed Capital Formation to G.D.P.

|      | U.S  | France | Germany | Italy | Netherlands | U.K. |
|------|------|--------|---------|-------|-------------|------|
| 1980 | 20.4 | 23.0   |         | 24.3  | 21.6        | 17.9 |
| 1985 | 19.4 | 19.3   |         | 20.7  | 19.7        | 17.0 |
| 1990 | 16.8 | 21.4   |         | 20.3  | 20.9        | 19.4 |
| 1991 | 15.4 | 21.1   | 23.2    | 19.7  | 20.5        | 16.8 |
| 1992 | 15.5 | 20.0   | 23.4    | 19.2  | 20.4        | 15.5 |
| 1993 | 16.0 | 18.9   | 22.7    | 17.1  | 19.7        | 14.9 |

Source: *The National Data Book*, No. 1369, p. 863.

company's shares. While the price of the offering will be set later, the parties said it is currently estimated to be close to the present par value of Euro Disney stock, or about 10 francs a share.

The new agreement also calls for the banks and Disney to subscribe to bonds with 10-year warrants to purchase Euro Disney shares at 40 francs a share. That could raise up to 2.8 billion francs for the resort company. Disney also agreed to arrange for a 1.1 billion franc standby line of credit at market rates to provide for Euro Disney' s liquidity. "If the markets are strong enough to absorb three billion francs of new equity, then it is a good long-term fix," said Jack Hersch of MJ Whitman in New York. "But officials close to the talks say the real work is now in persuading creditor banks to agree to the deal. And approval by Euro Disney shareholders is not a foregone conclusion."

**Exhibit 9**        **Long-term Borrowings and Interest Rates**

| Currency FF in millions | Interest rate | 1993 | 1992 |
|---|---|---|---|
| 10-year Convertible Bonds [a] | 6.75% | 4,327 | 4,343 |
| Caisse des Dépôts Loan [b] | 7.85% | 1,442 | 1,442 |
| Phase 1A Credit Facility [c] | 9.75% | 2,071 | |
| Credit Foncier Loan [d] | 10.04% | 35 | 35 |
| Others | | 104 | |
| | | 7,979 | 5,820 |

At September 30, 1993, and 1992, total borrowings include accrued interest of FF 358 million and FF 368 million, respectively.

[a] 10-year convertible bonds: 6.75% fixed rate redeemed on October 1, 2001, at 110% of their principal amount, unless converted, redeemed, or purchased by the Company.

[b] Caisse des Dépôts loan: 40% is senior debt, 60% is subordinated debt, maturing 20 years from the drawing date. This loan bears interest at a weighted average rate of 7.85%. Principal repayments begin six years from the drawing date.

[c] Phase 1A Credit: Euro Disney S.C.A. borrowed in December 1992 FF 1,025 million at PIBOR plus 1%, and FF 270 million at fixed rate 8.35%. Principal repayments begin in 1998 through 2006. In March 1993, new borrowing at PIBOR plus 1.1%. Principal repayments begin in 1997 through 2006.

[d] Credit Foncier loan: originated in June 1992, bears interest at a rate of 3-month PIBOR minus 0.3%. Principal repayments begin in 1994 through 2017.

Nevertheless, things went smoothly.The Euro Disney resort was renamed Disneyland Paris. The rescue plan was approved by the shareholders on June 8, 1994. Offset of accumulated losses of approximately FF 4,863 million at September 30, 1993, against existing share premium provided by the small shareholders was approved by the shareholders.

Reduction of the stated capital of the company by 50% was also approved. Each initial shareholder holding two shares was allowed to subscribed to seven new shares at 10 francs a share. Euro Disney raised 5.79 billion francs through the rights offering, but this did not decrease the company's indebtedness by half, but only by 23%, from 21 to 16 billion francs. The equity increase brought a major new shareholder, Saudi Prince Alwaleed Bin Talal Abdulaziz Al Saud, who now holds 24.6% of the theme park. The ownership of Disney in Euro Disney was decreased from 49% to 39%, a sign that Disney did not believe it had a winner on its hands.

The lenders waived aggregate interest charges having a net present value of FF 1.6 billion (discounted at a rate of 7.5% to October 1, 1993) (see Exhibit 9). The waivers will result in estimated reductions of aggregate financial charges to the Group and the Financing SNCs of FF 400 million, FF 600 million, FF 450 million, and FF 220 million in fiscal years 1994, 1995, 1996 and 1997, respectively. The lenders also deferred payments of principal on all outstanding loan indebtedness of the Group and the Financing SNCs for three years from the time that each payment was originally due. This deferral will result in reductions of approximately FF 13 million, FF 50 million, FF 90 million, and FF 220 million in payments under the Group's financial leases in 1995, 1996, 1997, and 1998, respectively.

Royalties, which in fiscal year 1993 totaled FF 262 million, were being waived from October 1, 1993, to September 30, 1998, then reduced to 50% of their pre-restructuring levels thereafter until October 1, 2003. Base management fees were being waived from October 1, 1993, to September 1998. Management fees for fiscal years 1992 and 1993 for FF 113 million and FF 145 million, respectively, which were previously deferred, were waived permanently as well as accrued fees (FF 45 million) for fiscal year 1994.

The Walt Disney Company cancelled receivables due from Euro Disney of approximately FF 1.2 billion for services rendered in connection with the second phase of development of the Resort which was put on hold. At the end of the 1994 fiscal year, in spite of all the concessions, the net losses amounted to 1.8 billion francs, or $346.7 million. Operating revenue fell 16%. The number of visitors dropped from 9.8 million in 1993 to 8.8 million in 1994.

It was announced that the target break-even year is now 1996. Commenting on the financial results, new Euro Disney Chairman Philip Bourguignon said "1994 has been a difficult year. . . . But we still aim to break even by 1996."

At the end of fiscal 1995, for the first time in its history, Euro Disney proudly announced a small profit, resulting mostly from some exceptional gains. But this is hardly a definitive victory when one remembers that the company is temporarily not charged for any interest on its huge debt. Disneyland Paris has a long way to go, and it cannot continue its downward spiral in attendance.

# REFERENCES

Bancroft, Thomas, and Tatiana Pouschine. "Why not buy the real thing?" *Forbes* 1 October 1990: 208.

Benson, Tracy E. "America's best CEOs." *Industry Week* 2 December 1991: 28-29.

"Bonjour, Mickey." *Fortune* 20 January 1986: 8.

Cohen, Roger. "Euro Disney in danger of shutdown." *The New York Times* 23 December 1993, late ed.: D3.

Cohen, Roger. "Mickey lacks a soupçon of charm." *The New York Times* 11 July 1993, national ed.: E2.

Cohen, Roger. "When you wish upon a deficit." *The New York Times* 18 Jul. 1993, national ed.: H1.

Coleman, Brian, & Thomas R. King. "Euro Disney Rescue Package Wins Approval." *The Wall Street Journal* 15 March 1994, A3, A5.

Daniels, Bill. "Eisner outlines Disney decade of growth and soothes concerned stockholders." *Variety* 28 February 1990: 9.

Drozdiak, William. "Cheers, Jeers Greet Disney Debut in Europe." *The Washington Post* 13 April 1992: A1.

Drozdiak, William. "Euro Disney posts loss of $900 Million." *The Washington Post* 11 November 1993: B11.

Drozdiak, William. "L'Etat C'est Mouse." *The Washington Post* 2 March 1992: A12.

"Euro Disney adding alcohol." *The New York Times* 12 June 1993, late ed.: 42.

"Euro Disney affirms it will remain open for winter." *The New York Times* 25 August 1993, late ed.: D3.

"Euro Disney posts deficit." *The New York Times* 14 August 1993, late ed.: 35.

"Euro Disney Annual Report Fiscal Year 1991."

"Euro Disney Annual Report Fiscal Year 1992."

"Euro Disney Annual Report Fiscal Year 1993."

"Euro Disney S.C.A. Offering of 85,880,000 Shares of Common Stock." Prospectus. October 1989.

"Euro Disney S.C.A. Offering of 595,028,994 Shares of Common Stock." Prospectus. 17 June 1994.

"France, Disney ink $2-bil contract to construct Euroland." *Variety* 25 March 1987: 156.

Freedland, Jonathan, & Peter Clarke. "Mighty Mouse in Magic Kingdom." *The Guardian* 31 January 1994: 10-11.

Galbraith, Jane. "Farm Near Paris Picked As Site Of Euro Disneyland; Disney Co. Plans To Be Equity Investor." *Variety* 25 December 1985: 8.

Green, Peter. "Euro Disneyland nails construction for 1st phase; gets $1.3 billion in credit." *Variety* 13 July 1988: 61.

Grover, Ronald. "Thrills and chills at Disney." *Business Week* 21 June 1993: 73-74.

Gumbel, Peter. "Euro Disney Posts Wider 1st-Period Loss as Creditors Hold Inconclusive Talks." *The Wall Street Journal* 3 February 1994: A10.

Ilott, Terry. " Disney defers payment to help ED stock price." *Variety* 19 October 1992: 54.

Jaffe, Thomas. "Euro FantasyLand." *Forbes* 2 April 1990: 204.

Kamm, Thomas. "Euro Disney's Loss Narrowed in Fiscal 1994." *The Wall Street Journal* 4 November 1994: A10.

Kindel, Stephen. "Michael Eisner; at Walt Disney, the boast is, 'You ain't seen nothing yet.'" *FW* 3 April 1990: 76.

Lawday, David. "Where all the dwarfs are grumpy: Euro Disneyland may give Paris a run for the money." *U.S. News & World Report* 28 May 1990: 50-52.

Martin, Mitchell. "Mob pelts Disney chiefs." *The Washington Post* 6 October 1989: D2.

"Mickey goes to the bank." *The Economist* 16 Sep. 1989: 78-79.

"Mickey hops the pond." *The Economist* 28 Mar. 1987: 75.

Milhomme, Albert J. "Pricing Strategy at Euro Disney." *Advances in Marketing* Spring 1993: 302-307.

Milhomme, Albert J. "Culture, Economic Anthropology, and Theme Parks." *Journal of International Marketing* Vol. 2 No. 2, 1994: pp 11-21.

Oster, Patrick. "Vive Le Mouse!" *The Washington Post* 24 January 1993: E1-E5.

Riding, John. "Banks clear way for Euro Disney rescue." *Financial Times* 20 May 1994: 19.

Schwartz, Amy E. "Good, Clean . . . Flop?" *The Washington Post* 18 August 1993: A21.

Shapiro, Stacy. "Disney risk management learns French." *Business Insurance* 30 October 1989: 32-33.

Sharkey, Betsy. "Michael Eisner: Disney's big thinker is free of guile." *Adweek's Marketing Week* 4 September 1989: 3-4.

Toy, Patrick. "The mouse isn't roaring." *Business Week* 24 August 1993.

Toy, Patrick. "Is Disney Headed for the Euro-Trash Heap?" *Business Week* 24 January 1994: 52.

Thomas, Dana. "Mickey Mouse's School of Manners." *The Washington Post* 11 August 1992: B1.

Tully, Shawn. "The real estate coup at Euro Disneyland." *Fortune* 28 April 1986: 172.

Vaughan, Vicki. "Euro Disney designers work to avoid culture clash." *Journal of Commerce and Commercial* 2 May 1991: 1B.

Waxman, Sharon. "In Europe, can Mickey be the mouse that soared?" *The Washington Post* 14 August 1993: B1.

Waxman, Sharon. "The key to the Magic Kingdom." *The Washington Post* 13 October 1992: C1.

Will, George F. "In Europe, Mickey Mouse." *The Washington Post* 16 April 1992: A23.

Williams, Michael. "Eisner calls Euro Disney estimates 'Aggressive.'" *Variety* 21 October 1991: 58.

# First International Bank of California[1]

Julius S. Brown, Loyola Marymount University

Mary Mulligan, Loyola Marymount University

S taring out the window of his office, overlooking the city of Los Angeles after a long day, Manuel Cruz, President of First International Bank of California (Bancal), was contemplating the success that he had attained in life at such a young age. Born in Guadalajara,[2] the youngest of four children, Cruz spent the first eighteen years of his life in Mexico. Guided by the direction of his parents, who stressed the importance of education, Cruz was a diligent student, with an impressive academic record. His scholastic achievements earned him entrance into Harvard University in 1975, at the age of eighteen. There, he earned his bachelor's degree as well as his MBA.

Upon graduation, Cruz received an offer to work at the New York office of Bancal, a well-known United States commercial bank, headquartered in Los Angeles, with assets amounting to $45 billion. He began his career as a bank administrator, using his analytical skills to make decisions concerning the credit and investments of the bank and its customers. Having familiarized himself with the operations of Bancal, and having established a variety of contacts, it was decided that Cruz would travel to Los Angeles, where he would be groomed to assume the role of controller. It was in this capacity that Cruz served Bancal for seven years.

His ability to control the company's finances did not go unnoticed. Additionally, what set Cruz apart from his colleagues was the way in which he

---

[1] Note: This case is illustrative of financial analysis as of 1995.

[2] Guadalajara, with three million people, was the second largest city in Mexico and a strong commercial center.

---

interacted with other employees. Cruz seemed to gain the respect of his co-workers, strengthening relationships that he made with fellow employees as he climbed the corporate ladder. No doubt, it was his intellectual capabilities coupled with his excellent "people skills" that made Cruz the top contender for President of Bancal nearly three years ago. At the age of thirty-nine, Manuel Cruz, was one of the youngest Presidents that ever operated Bancal.

As the sun set over the city of Los Angeles, Cruz realized that his past successes would help him to face the new challenges ahead. Specifically, his main concern was addressing the Board of Directors' request that Bancal consider expansion into Mexico. Clearly, their interest was a result of the recent passage of the North American Free Trade Agreement. Additionally, it was a well-known fact that Cruz had a well-established contact in Guadalajara, Luis Ramirez, managing director of Grupo Turismo S.A. de C.V., one of the nation's leading tourist operator/developers. Ramirez, who was a longtime friend of Cruz's father, had expressed his interest in establishing a working relationship with Bancal, in the event that NAFTA was ratified. He explained that his company needed working capital in dollars, which was in short supply. Further-

---

**Exhibit 1**          **Guadalbank Balance Sheet 12/31/94 ($1.00 U.S. = M. Pesos 4.925)**

| Assets (U.S. dollars) | |
|---|---|
| Cash and Equivalents | 87,384,333 |
| Securities | 352,092,333 |
| Real Estate Loans | 126,085,691 |
| Commercial & Individual Loans | 629,191,642 |
| Farm Loans & Other | 89,000,000 |
| Real Estate and Other Assets | 12,328,333 |
| Total Assets | $1,296,082,332 |
| | |
| Liabilities and Capital | |
| Demand Deposits | 233,659,000 |
| Time Deposits | 397,586,666 |
| Other Deposits | 56,899,333 |
| Long-Term Liabilities | 303,264,000 |
| Loss & Revaluation Reserves | 168,103,333 |
| Equity Capital | 136,570,000 |
| Total Liabilities and Capital | $1,296,082,332 |
| | |
| Outstanding Shares | 150,000,000 |
| Book Value Per Share | $0.91 (M. Pesos 4.48) |
| Market Price Per Share (?) | $1.00 |
| Return on Equity | 20.6% |

$100,000,000 would purchase more than the necessary controlling interest if the buy decision is implemented.

more, he pointed out that if Bancal developed a strong relationship with Grupo Turismo, there was a possibility that the other members of the conglomerate would make capital commitments with Bancal. He also noted that Bancal could potentially benefit from locating in Guadalajara, where a strong American presence had not yet been established in the banking sector, as U.S. banks typically looked to Mexico City. Cruz was also pleased to find out that there was a possibility that Bancal could buyout an existing Mexican bank, known as Guadalbank. Cruz was able to obtain a copy of the bank's balance sheet and earnings summary, as illustrated in Exhibits 1 and 2. Consequently, since the passage of the trade agreement, expansion into Mexico had been an area of interest for Bancal.

Although Cruz was excited about the possibility of entering into the Mexican banking market, he realized that he must proceed with caution. Bancal had not had any previous working relationships in Mexico. Moreover, the bank was not very familiar with the banking sector in Mexico, as well as the new laws that govern the industry, since NAFTA had passed. As a result, Cruz decided to turn to two of his subordinates, Sandra Mireles, Vice-President of Marketing for Bancal, and Steve Brown, Vice-President of Finance.

Cruz was pleased to find that Mireles, a California native and the offspring of Mexican parents, was fluent in Spanish. A graduate of Wellesley, with an MBA from Harvard, Mireles had just been promoted to her new position. Previously, she was employed as a manager of commercial lending. Her predecessor at Bancal was dismissed because he had a habit of not fully researching Cruz's proposals. Thus, since this was Mireles' first assignment as the new Vice-President of Marketing, she knew that she must assume the task of gathering *all* of the pertinent information on the banking industry in Mexico, the implications of NAFTA on banking, and Grupo Turismo—a promising, potential large-scale customer for Bancal.

| Exhibit 2 | **Guadalbank Earnings Summary 12/31/94**<br>**(In U.S. Dollars; $1.00 U.S. = M. Pesos 4.925)** | |
|---|---|---|
| | Interest Income | $137,461,336 |
| | Less Interest Expense | 40,903,739 |
| | Net Interest Income | 96,557,597 |
| | | |
| | Miscellaneous Income | 10,844,903 |
| | Total Income | $107,402,500 |
| | | |
| | Provision For Loan Losses | 35,893,000 |
| | Personnel/Operating Expenses | 21,053,000 |
| | Total Expenses | $56,946,000 |
| | | |
| | Income Before Taxes | $50,456,500 |
| | Taxes | 22,273,900 |
| | Net Earnings | $28,182,600 |
| | Earnings Per Share | $0.1879 |

# THE HISTORY OF THE BANKING INDUSTRY IN MEXICO

Mireles' research had turned up the following information: The banking sector in Mexico had experienced significant changes over the past decade. The history of the banking system could be broken down into three major phases, beginning in 1982 with the nationalization of banks in Mexico.

- *Phase 1:* During this time, the government took over ownership of the banks and appointed its own presidents to replace the existing officers. Additionally, control was exercised via regulations. Thus, the government imposed restrictions on the banks in such a way that its interests were satisfied. For instance, at the same time that the banks were nationalized, the government budget deficit was large, amounting to as much as 16% of the gross domestic product.[3] As a result, restrictions were put in place, in efforts to reduce the government's cost of financing. Included were interest rate controls, selective portfolios, and required reserve ratios.

  Eventually, however, as the deficit shrank, the borrowing needs of the government also diminished. As a result, the government was not benefiting, as it had in the past, by the restrictions, and thus sought to reduce them.

- *Phase 2:* The second phase was a transitional period, during which emphasis shifted from public sector to private sector interests. The government was willing to shift its emphasis to the private sector because it no longer experienced the benefits of the restrictions as it had when the government deficit was high. The idea was to allow banks to operate in an arena in which banks could effectively serve the needs of the private sector. In addition, in 1985, the government began to sell minority shares in commercial banks. Clearly, these actions laid the groundwork for the privatization of the Mexican banks.

- *Phase 3:* 1991 marked the end of the deficit that plagued Mexico. This was made possible by cuts in government spending coupled with the low cost of financing the deficit (made possible by the government imposed restrictions). At the same time, it signaled the beginning of a major privatization program. Thus, banks were returned to the private sector by means of government auctions. Interestingly, banks were sold for 2.5 to 5.3 times their book value, indicating the importance of commercial lending for the private sector. Obviously, these banks, having made sizable investments, were doing everything that they could to recover their initial investment and to make substantial profits.

Profits during the first eleven months of 1992 rose 64%. At the same time, however, the fall of the Mexican stock market, coupled with an economic slowdown, made it difficult for banks to raise capital. Consequently, only the strongest banks were emerging viable under the recent privatization program. The most notable players included: Banco Nacional de Mexico (more commonly referred to as Banamex), Bancomer, and Banca Serfin. In 1991, the three combined held approximately 62% of the total banking assets in Mexico. After the devaluation in 1994, this figure dropped to 50%. A breakdown of their markets is shown in Exhibit 3.

---

[3] Gross Domestic Product (GDP) is the total value of goods and services produced by a country in a year, less net income sent or received from abroad.

**Exhibit 3**    **Asset Distribution of Earnings**

|  | Commercial | Mortgages | Credit Cards | Other consumer loans |
|---|---|---|---|---|
| Banamex | 60 | 26 | 11 | 3 |
| Bancomer | 58 | 28 | 8 | 6 |
| Serfin | 81 | 16 | 2 | 1 |
| Others | 83 | 11 | 5 | 1 |

# MEXICAN BANKS . . . WHERE THEY STAND IN TODAY'S COMPETITIVE ENVIRONMENT

Realizing that efficiency was the key to success, Mexican banks tried to identify areas in their operations in which they needed to make improvements. For instance, there were not enough skilled risk analysts in the Mexican banking sector. Furthermore, as the number of loans was expected to grow some 20%, the need for capable analysts became increasingly important. Also, Mexico lacked the state-of-the-art technology that provided many of its U.S. neighbors with a unique competitive advantage. Thus, Mexican banks had to address these key issues.

In addition to the aforementioned concerns, Mexican banks' primary focus had to be on the most recent developments surrounding the passage of the North American Free Trade Agreement—considering that this agreement would have profound effects on the Mexican banking sector.

# THE NORTH AMERICAN FREE TRADE AGREEMENT . . . WHAT IT MEANT TO THE BANKING SECTOR

The ratification of NAFTA was expected to have a direct effect on the banking sector in Mexico. Additionally, the financial services chapter of NAFTA establishes the rules that define the treatment by each NAFTA country, of the other's financial firms, investments in the financial sector, and cross-border services. Specifically, the agreement declares that "each country agrees to allow financial institutions of other countries to establish and operate in its market through subsidiaries." Consequently, U.S. banks will be able to set up subsidiaries in Mexico that can compete with Mexican banks. Previously, foreign banks were allowed to operate only representative offices, with the exception of the large New York bank, Citibank. Operating in Mexico since the early 1930's, Citibank was the only U.S. bank with branches in Mexico. Clearly, Citibank reaped the benefits of larger lending limits and lower funding costs, as it was allowed to open branches.

Although Mexico was opening up the banking sector to its U.S. neighbors, Mexico was making sure that U.S. banks proceeded slowly. There was a limit on the amount of market share that American subsidiaries could control. Initially, U.S. banks were restricted to an aggregate market share of 8%, and by the year 2000, this figure will increase to 15%. However, Mexico reserved the right to intervene if the market share of U.S. banks rose too quickly, until the year 2007, when restrictions end.

Specifically, individual U.S. banks will be limited to 1.5% of the total market share. In addition, during this transition period, U.S. banks can acquire Mexican banks, so long as they do not exceed the 1.5% limit. Following this period, in the year 2000, banks will be allowed to make acquisitions amounting to 4% of total market share. Subsequent expansion beyond this point will only be possible via internal growth, which includes capital received from the parent. Acquisition will no longer be an option.

Originally, eighteen foreign competitors had received charters to enter into the Mexican banking sector. It was estimated that these banks made $3.25 billion in new loans available in 1995. In addition, Mexico's financial sector was expected to grow 10% a year for the next three to five years. This figure is double the annual growth rate of Mexico's gross national product.[4] At the end of 1994, the banking industry was made up of institutions with assets amounting to $200 billion, compared to the $3.5 trillion industry in the U.S. While there was one bank for every 4,000 people in the United States, there was one bank per 18,000 people in Mexico. Given these figures, analysts claimed that Mexico was "underbanked" and that as the Mexican economy recovered, there would be a large demand for financial services provided by banks.

Although Mexico expected that competition from the U.S. was inevitable, it was extremely difficult for those who paid large sums of money to acquire the recently privatized banks to see U.S. banks receive permission to compete head-to-head with them. In addition, Mexican banks were feeling the impact of the sluggish economy, the lack of state-of-the-art technology, as well as the lack of adequate credit rating services. Not surprisingly, the profitability of most Mexican banks had decreased substantially. Even the three largest banks have suffered with a combined decrease in profits amounting to 44.5%.

## GRUPO TURISMO . . . A POTENTIAL CUSTOMER

One of the *main* reasons for Manuel Cruz's interest in establishing a subsidiary in Mexico was the fact that he had a powerful and influential Mexican contact, Luis Ramirez. Having taken advantage of the petrodollars circulating in Mexico in the 1970's, Ramirez started his own company, Estrella, which built and marketed upscale condominiums. Then, in 1987, he sold his company to the well-known conglomerate Grupo Amarillo, which operates in the steel, tourism, and retail markets. Ramirez then became involved in the tourist division of Amarillo, known as Grupo Turismo, and held the position of managing director.

---

[4] Gross National Product (GNP) includes production by a country's facilities abroad.

In order to get a better sense of Turismo's interest and potential commitment in establishing a relationship with Bancal, Mireles booked a flight to Guadalajara to meet with Ramirez.

# THE MEETING

Upon arriving in Guadalajara, Mireles met with Ramirez, who, like the typical Mexican businessperson, took the time to acquaint Mireles with the city, followed by lunch at the "Guadalajara Grill." The lunchtime conversation was spent recounting the stories about Ramirez's recollections of Manuel Cruz as a child growing up in Guadalajara, since Ramirez was a close friend of Cruz's father, Antonio. Fortunately, with Mireles' upbringing, she knew that business discussions would have to be postponed until a relationship was established between the two. The following day, the two began to discuss the idea of Bancal entering into Mexico. But first, Ramirez needed to tell Mireles more about Grupo Turismo.

Ramirez began, noting that tourism was Mexico's third largest single source of revenue, right behind maquiladoras[5] and oil. In addition, Grupo Turismo represented the tourism division of Grupo Amarillo. Basically, Turismo could be classified as a tourist operator/developer, although as Ramirez continued his explanation, it appeared as though Turismo was involved in a number of other industries. For instance, the primary area in which Turismo was involved was site development. Turismo developed land for what it called "megadevelopments." Other companies within the group operated hotels and built holiday homes. In fact, Grupo Turismo was the largest owner of hotels in Mexico. Thus, Turismo was a major real estate developer and tourism company with annual revenues of 1.7 billion new Mexican pesos (about $340 million at current exchange rates).

Additionally, as Turismo penetrated the Mexican market, it was beginning to look to other countries, such as Costa Rica. Specifically, the plan was to develop hotels, a marina, and a golf course, spanning 2,225 acres along the Costa Rican coast. No doubt, this would allow Grupo Turismo to diversify its business and to increase its profit margins.

After establishing the business in which Turismo operated, the discussion naturally shifted to finance. Specifically, Grupo Amarillo's assets totaled about $1 billion, with Turismo's assets amounting to roughly $600 million. (A consolidated balance sheet and income statement for Grupo Amarillo are provided in Exhibits 4a and 4b.) Ramirez continued, noting that Grupo Turismo had an $80 million initial public offering in December of 1992. Each share sold for 3,100 pesos (as of July 1993, the exchange rate was approximately 3,300 pesos/$), and each American Depository Share (ADS), representing ten shares, sold for $10.10. By mid-January, the share price increased to 3,300 pesos.

Growing at an annual rate of 15–20%, Turismo was investing heavily in new megadevelopments, and was in need of capital. Thus, the company was particularly interested in any new opportunities that NAFTA could provide, in the form of competitive commercial bank loans from new U.S. entrants.

[5] Maquiladoras enable manufacturers to ship machinery, raw materials, and components into Mexico for processing, assembly, and packaging. Products are then shipped back to the U.S.

**Exhibit 4a**      **Grupo Amarillo—Consolidated Income Statement—Year Ended Dec. 31, 1994**

|  | (In 000's of Mexican New Pesos) | (In 000's of U.S. Dollars)* |
|---|---|---|
| Net Sales | 1,436,726 | $291,721 |
| Other oper. inc. | 133,013 | 27,008 |
| Total Revenues | 1,569,739 | 318,729 |
| Other oper. exp. | 880,732 | 178,829 |
| Sell., gen., & admin. costs | 302,724 | 61,467 |
| Tot. cost of financing | 7,483 | 1,519 |
| Costs & expenses | 1,190,939 | 241,815 |
| EBT & profit sharing | 378,800 | 76,914 |
| Income Taxes | 29,075 | 5,904 |
| Emp. Profit Sharing | 2,349 | 477 |
| Inc. Tax & empl. profit shar. | 31,424 | 6,381 |
| Net Consol. Earnings | 347,376 | 70,533 |
| Net earn. of minor stk | 99,162 | 20,134 |
| Net earn. of majority stk | 248,214 | 50,399 |
| Yr end shares oustg | 402,193 | 81,664 |

*Note: Converted to U.S. dollars at Dec. 31, 1994, spot rate: P 4.9250/$1

# COUNTRY RISK ANALYSIS

In addition to the considerations given to the potential customer in Guadalajara, it was necessary to conduct a comprehensive country risk analysis of Mexico, in efforts to determine the feasibility of establishing a subsidiary. To begin the process, Mireles decided that it was necessary to gather general background information on Mexico.

# MEXICO AT A GLANCE

Mexico is a democratic, representative, and federal republic, comprised of 31 states and a federal district. Each state is free and sovereign in all internal affairs but is united in a federation established according to the principles of the Constitution.

In terms of its economic situation, Mexico's GDP increased by 6.5% annually between 1965 and 1980 but only 0.5% yearly by 1988. Weak oil prices, rising inflation, a foreign debt exceeding $100 billion, and worsening budget deficits added to the nation's economic problems in the mid-1980s, although the economy began to improve at the end of the decade. In the late 1980s the GDP was $176.7 billion (about $1,760 per capita). The World Bank estimated that

**Exhibit 4b**

**Grupo Amarillo—Consolidated Balance Sheet—Year Ended Dec. 31, 1994**

| | (In 000's of Mexican New Pesos) | (In 000's of U.S. Dollars)* |
|---|---|---|
| Assets: | | |
| Cash & equivalents | 126,647 | $ 25,715 |
| Receivables | 732,601 | 148,751 |
| Inventories | 393,433 | 79,885 |
| Integrated Resort Complexes | 400,356 | 81,290 |
| Prepaid Expenses | 17,908 | 3,636 |
| | | |
| Current Assets | 1,670,945 | 339,278 |
| Long-Term Receivables | 336,186 | 68,261 |
| Integrated Resort Complexes | 430,063 | 87,322 |
| Prop. Plant & Eq., net | 2,494,216 | 506,440 |
| Investments | 38,314 | 7,779 |
| Other Assets | 42,457 | 8,621 |
| Total Assets | 5,012,181 | 1,017,702 |
| | | |
| Liabilities: | | |
| Current Liabilities | 1,109,448 | 225,269 |
| Long-Term Debt | 1,166,640 | 236,881 |
| Other Liabilities | 362,737 | 73,652 |
| Minority Stockholders | 193,814 | 39,353 |
| Shareholder's Eq: | | |
| Majority Stk. Eq. | 1,373,987 | 278,982 |
| Minority Stk. Eq. | 805,555 | 163,564 |
| Total Shareholders' eq. | 2,179,542 | 442,547 |
| | | |
| Total Liabil & sh' eq. | 5,012,181 | 1,017,702 |
| Net current assets | 561,497 | 114,010 |

*Note: Converted to U.S. dollars at Dec. 31, 1994, spot rate: P 4.9250/$1

Mexico's gross national product, measured at average 1989–1991 prices, was $252.4 billion U.S. dollars, equivalent to $2,870 per person. Over the period from 1980 to 1991, it was estimated that GNP increased in real terms at an average annual rate of 1.5%, although GNP per capita declined by .5% per year, due to population growth.

Generally speaking, the standard of living in Mexico is low compared to the U.S. In addition, recent political turmoil has severely hampered the country's economic progress. Specifically, in efforts to stimulate the economy, the Zedillo administration had developed a plan to remove many restrictions on foreign investment, and had continued an extensive privatization program started by the previous administration of Carlos Salinas de Gortari.[6] Moreover, important restrictions have been replaced with competitive tariffs to encourage foreign participation in the Mexican market.

In spite of the government's efforts, Mexico's economy has been stagnating, at times even posting negative growth. The situation prompted government officials to increase spending and to lower interest rates. This resulted in a substantial weakening of the peso against the dollar. In late 1994, the Zedillo administration made a bold move, allowing the peso to float. As a result, in just one day, the peso lost more than 20% of its value, the largest drop against the dollar in a decade. Clearly, the devaluation had a direct impact on investor confidence in Mexico. The U.S. government had initially guaranteed an $18 billion line of credit. However, the entire bailout package, which was arranged by the United States in conjunction with the Bank for International Settlements (BIS), the International Monetary Fund (IMF), and commercial banks, totaled $50 billion. Specifically, the monetary aid was used to stabilize the peso. In addition, it was necessary to use some of the funds to pay approximately $6.78 billion in tesebonos—short-term, dollar-denominated debt instruments.

As a result of the devaluation the Mexican economy plunged. Additionally, since December about 2,000 workers in the banking sector lost their jobs. Thus, domestic consumption fell drastically as the purchasing power of local citizens diminished. GDP is expected to shrink at least 2% in 1995. Consequently, the government is relying on exports to trigger growth, with exports accounting for one quarter of the total GDP. In addition, inflation, according to Finance Minister Guillermo Ortiz, is expected to drop dramatically. The peso is expected to float, and the finance ministry, in efforts to improve the economy, is looking to provide tax incentives to promote long-term investments.

## POLITICAL AND FINANCIAL RISK

Mireles began her risk analysis (illustrated in Exhibit 5) with the identification of the political and financial variables that she believed posed a significant potential threat to Bancal as it contemplated entering into the Mexican market. Next, she assigned a risk rating to each of the variables, based on a scale of 1–10 (10 being the most risky). A weight, representing the importance of each variable, was also assigned, such that the sum of the weights totaled 100%. Finally, she considered the importance of each dimension, resulting in an overall country risk rating.

## POLITICAL RISK ANALYSIS

Beginning with the political risk factors, Mireles cited political tensions as a notable risk. That is, recent events had clearly shown that the electoral process could be quite a destabilizing force. For example, tensions grew in the past election, as the leading Presidential candidate, Luis Donaldo Colosio, was

[6]Both Ernesto Zedillo and Carlos Salinas de Gortari obtained their Ph.Ds in Economics from American universities.

**Exhibit 5**    **Country Risk Analysis For Mexico—Sandra Mireles***

| | Rating assigned by co to factor (Range is 1-10) | Wt assigned by co to factor based on importance | Wtd Value Factor |
|---|---|---|---|
| Political Risk Factors | | | |
| Political Tensions | 7 | 40% | 2.8 |
| Turmoil | 6 | 30% | 1.8 |
| Attitude of Host Gov't | 2 | 30% | 0.6 |
| | | 100% | 5.2=political risk |
| | | | |
| Financial Risk Factors | | | |
| Inflation | 6 | 40% | 2.4 |
| Credit Risk | 7 | 40% | 2.8 |
| Unfavorable Gov't Policies | 4 | 20% | 0.8 |
| | | 100% | 6.0=political risk |

| | Rating as Determined Above | Wt assigned by co to each risk category | Weighted Rating |
|---|---|---|---|
| Category | | | |
| Political Risk | 5.2 | 60% | 3.1 |
| Financial Risk | 6.0 | 40% | 2.4 |
| | | 100% | 5.5=overall country risk rating |

*Format adopted with permission from Jeff Madura, Florida Atlantic University. See: J. Madura, *International Financial Management* (St. Paul: West Publishing Company, 1992), p. 577.

assassinated. In addition, such political upheaval tends to have several ramifications for businesses, often resulting in capital flight. Specifically, in light of the aforementioned incident, the peso dropped in value. Translating this risk into a quantifiable figure, Mireles chose to rate political tensions a "7" and assigned a 40% weight.

In addition to political tensions, Mireles cited turmoil, or the threat of uprising, as yet another factor to consider. Once again, recent events had indicated the potential for insurrection. For instance, in 1994, conflict occurred in the state of Chiapas. The campesinos, the farmers of Southern Mexico, turned to armed conflict in protest against the government's decision to allow foreigners to purchase farmland. Thus, the threat of internal warfare was real and could seriously impact businesses that operate in the country. Mireles assigned a risk of "6" to this variable, and weighted it 30%.

Rounding out the political factors was the attitude of the host government. Although there are guidelines that the NAFTA countries must abide by, Mexico did reserve the right to intervene in the event that it felt that market share was rising too quickly. Clearly, this appeared to be a subjective judgment that is contingent upon the attitude of the host government. Moreover, the major banks in Mexico were already worried by the competition that they were facing from the U.S. Consequently, the U.S. banks that establish subsidiaries in Mexico must strive to maintain strong, positive relations with the Mexican government. Based on her calculations, Mireles assigned a risk of "2" and a weight of 30%.

# FINANCIAL RISK ANALYSIS

After determining the political risks, Mireles assessed the financial risks of opening a subsidiary. First, she looked at inflation, exchange, and interest rates. In terms of the inflation rate, Mireles' findings showed that Mexico had the highest inflation rate of the three NAFTA countries, which affected the purchasing power of its people. Thus, the Zedillo government has had to intervene from time to time in attempts to keep the inflation rate down.

Along with the inflation rate, Mexico has experienced exchange-rate as well as interest-rate fluctuations, which often are clearly a function of the stability of the country. High interest rates can slow the growth of the economy and inevitably reduce consumers' purchasing power, just as changes in exchange rates can influence demand. Clearly, these fluctuations can lead to translation and transaction gains/losses for subsidiaries, which may present a formidable risk. Mireles assigned a risk of "6" and a weight of 40%.

The risk of default, or credit risk, must also be considered. This is already a problem for banks operating in Mexico, as approximately 4.5% of the total loans are overdue. The December 31, 1993, figures for Banamex and Bancomer's past-due loans as a percentage of total loans amounted to 7.35% to 7.42%, respectively.[7] Clearly, Bancal must seriously contemplate this risk. Mireles rated it a "7" with a 40% weight.

Finally, Mireles tried to analyze the threat of unfavorable government economic policies. There was the previous government's nationalization of the banks to consider. Additionally, the policies of the administration during the period of nationalization, imposing unfavorable requirements such as interest-rate controls, selective portfolios, and required reserve ratios, because it was in the self-interests of the government, needed to be considered. More recently, the new administration was accused of a double cross when it went on record that it would not change its policy regarding a fixed dollar exchange rate only to later float the peso, shocking both investors and the citizens of Mexico.

In addition, Mexico was tightening the rules for the financial sector, after the recent reports of alleged fraud at two Mexican banks. Nevertheless, under NAFTA, the Mexican government may be more likely to implement favorable policies as they seek to uphold the free trade agreement. In fact, there was even speculation that the Mexican government might consider easing market share restrictions, permitting U.S. banks to increase their presence in Mexico, given Mexico's economic woes resulting from the devaluation of the peso. Based on her findings, Mireles rated this a "4" with a weight of 20%.

After rating and weighing the various political and financial variables, Mireles assigned an overall weight of 60% to the political risk and 40% to the financial risk. Her results, displayed in the exhibit, show a political risk of 5.2, a financial risk of 6.0, and an overall country risk rating of 5.5, indicating moderate risk.

---

[7]The industry average for past-due loans for the first nine months of 1993 was 9%.

## THE RETURN HOME

As the plane landed at LAX, Sandra Mireles began to think of the work that awaited her. Within the next week she would have to seriously analyze the collective data that she gathered on the banking industry, NAFTA, Grupo Turismo, and Mexico. She had to look at all aspects of Cruz's proposed idea of opening a subsidiary in Mexico. In addition, Mireles knew that the presentation she would make to Cruz would be a true test of whether she was the right person to replace her predecessor.

## A SECOND OPINION

While Mireles was returning from her stay in Guadalajara, Steve Brown was making preparations for his departure to Mexico. Brown, Vice-President of Finance for Bancal, was asked to assess the risk of entering into Mexico. Cruz believed that it was essential to have a finance as well as a marketing person make independent analyses.

Brown, a native of Massachusetts and a graduate of Boston College, was beginning his twentieth year with Bancal. A member of the finance department since he started with the company, Brown knew little about the Mexican culture. He was chosen for the assignment based on his seniority and his strong financial background.

## BROWN'S VISIT WITH OFFICIALS IN GUADALAJARA

Prior to his departure, Brown was quickly briefed by Mireles on the banking industry in Mexico, NAFTA, and Grupo Turismo, so as to prepare Brown for his analysis. Mireles also gave Brown a list of the political and financial risk factors that she evaluated, though she withheld her numbers.

Relying on the translation of an interpreter, Brown met with government officials the morning of his first day in Guadalajara to discuss the political ramifications of NAFTA, the financial policies of the new administration, in light of the recent devaluation of the Mexican peso, and to try to develop an idea of the government's sentiments regarding the entrance of foreign firms into Guadalajara. Also, he met with the Director of Finance for Grupo Turismo, Ricardo Silva, who discussed with Brown the desire of Grupo Turismo to start a working relationship with Bancal.

## BROWN'S POLITICAL RISK ANALYSIS

Brown's findings are summarized in the country risk analysis provided in Exhibit 6. Using the same factors that Mireles evaluated, Brown began with his assessment of the political risk factors. Beginning with political tensions, he noted, much like his colleague Mireles, that political upheaval had been on the rise in Mexico. Assassinations and protests were not uncommon and these

| Exhibit 6 | Country Risk Analysis for Mexico—Steve Brown* | | |
|---|---|---|---|
| | Rating assigned by co to factor (Range is 1-10) | Wt assigned by co to factor based on importance | Wtd Value Factor |
| Political Risk Factors | | | |
| Political Tensions | 10 | 35% | 3.5 |
| Turmoil | 9 | 35% | 3.2 |
| Attitude of Host Gov't | 7 | 30% | 2.1 |
| | | 100% | 8.8=political risk |
| Financial Risk Factors | | | |
| Inflation | 10 | 40% | 4.0 |
| Credit Risk | 10 | 30% | 3.0 |
| Unfavorable Gov't Policies | 9 | 30% | 2.7 |
| | | 100% | 9.7=political risk |

| | Rating as Determined Above | Wt assigned by co to each risk category | Weighted Rating |
|---|---|---|---|
| Category | | | |
| Political Risk | 8.8 | 30% | 2.6 |
| Financial Risk | 9.7 | 70% | 6.8 |
| | | 100% | 9.4=overall country risk rating |

*Format adopted with permission from Jeff Madura, Florida Atlantic University. See: J. Madura, *International Financial Management* (St. Paul: West Publishing Company, 1992), p. 577.

events tend to have a direct impact on businesses operating in Mexico. With this in mind, he assigned a risk of "10" and a weight of 35%.

The second factor—turmoil—was assessed by Brown and given a rating of "9" and a weight of 35%. He believed that the Chiapas incident was still a real threat that the Mexican government had to contend with, and that such events could shake investors' confidence. In addition, he was concerned with the role of drug traffickers, especially in light of the March 24, 1993, assassination of Cardinal Juan Jesus Posadas Ocampo outside of the Guadalajara airport. Posadas' death was said to have been the result of the outspoken position that he took in response to the drug problem in Mexico. According to officials, Joaquin Guzman and Hector Luis Palmer Salazar, known for their ties to drug cartels, were arrested in connection to the cardinal's death.

Finally, Brown analyzed the attitude of the host government. He noted that the government officials with whom he met appeared to be extremely supportive of Bancal. They tried to assure Brown that everything would go well for the bank, as long as the market share restrictions were not violated. Nevertheless, Brown knew that the Mexican banks were already feeling the pressure from

U.S. banks since the passage of the North American Free Trade Agreement and might eventually appeal to the government for assistance. Keeping this in mind, Brown assigned a risk of "7" and a weight of 30%.

## FINANCIAL RISK ANALYSIS

Turning to the financial risk factors, Brown evaluated the risk of the inflation, exchange, and interest rates. He did so in light of the substantial devaluation of the peso. That is, he noted the effect of the fallen peso on the banking industry in Mexico. Specifically, the central bank might have to increase the amount of money in circulation, which could contribute to inflationary problems for the country. Also, banks that made dollar-denominated loans would have to account for a possible increase in bad debt expense, as the devalued peso would make it increasingly difficult for banks' customers to repay their loans.

Interest rates are likely to remain high if U.S. investors are skeptical, and move their investments out of Mexico. Additionally, rates are likely to increase further, as those investors who stay in the Mexican market and bear the risk will demand such an increase in the returns on their investments. Currently, consumer interest rates are quoted at 30%, and after the devaluation this figure is likely to increase as prices and wages rise. Thus, interest rates might continue to increase, hindering economic growth. Based on his findings, Brown rated the risk of the inflation, exchange, and interest rates a "10" and gave it a weight of 40%.

When evaluating the credit risk, Brown looked at the past-dueloan figures for the banking industry, as Mireles had done in her analysis. Brown also took into account the fact that, given the current financial woes that plague Mexico, the risk of default is likely to increase. Brown assigned a risk of "10" and a weight of 30%.

Finally, Brown evaluated the risk of unfavorable government policies. Like Mireles, he noted the restrictions imposed by the government when the banks were nationalized, which were clearly unfavorable for banks operating in Mexico. Brown was also concerned by the government's reversal of the "peso policy,"which would have an impact on all businesses operating in Mexico. Thus, Brown assigned a rating of "9" and a 30% weight. As Exhibit 6 illustrates, the overall political risk is "8.8" while the financial risk is "9.7." Brown weighted the political risk factor 30% and assigned the financial risk a weight of 70%. Brown's overall country risk rating is 9.4.

## CRUZ PREPARES FOR THE RESULTS

While his subordinates were making their analyses in Guadalajara, Cruz gave serious thought to his plan to enter into Mexico. Cruz was determined to take a long-range view. His belief was that, given the current economic situation in Mexico, few ventures would appear to be attractive in the short/run. Nevertheless, as the country recovered, foreign investment would be critical.

Cruz was particularly intrigued by the opportunity to obtain Grupo Turismo as its first customer. Ramirez and Cruz had a longstanding relationship. Over the years, Luis watched his friend's son grow up to be a successful businessman. Now, thirty years later, they had an opportunity to work together for the mutual benefit of Bancal and Grupo Turismo. Above all, Cruz knew that he could trust Ramirez, and the camaraderie that existed between the two was essential to the success of any deal that Bancal would make in Mexico.

The initial thought was to open one branch in Guadalajara, with an initial outlay of $100 million. Further expansion would be feasible only based upon the success of the first Bancal office. Additionally, it was anticipated that Bancal would be able to attract other large accounts, once word was out that Grupo Turismo was working with Bancal. This was the proposition that Cruz was thinking of presenting to the Board of Directors, but only after hearing from the direct reports of Mireles and Brown.

## MIRELES AND BROWN PRESENT THEIR FINDINGS

Three weeks later, the day had finally come. Fraught with anxiety yet appearing to be in control, Mireles entered into the President's office and proceeded to submit her final recommendation. . . . Brown was scheduled to give his opinion that afternoon.

# Cemex: A Rock Solid Company

John Holm, University of Texas at Tyler

Mark Kroll, University of Texas at Tyler

Walter Greene, University of Texas Pan American

*Internet site of interest:* **www.cemex.com**

I n late December 1994, the Mexican government decided to let the value of the peso float. As a result, its value in dollar terms immediately fell by more than fifty percent. This sudden and unexpected devaluation led to a financial crisis and a drastic downturn in the economy of a country that was also having political problems. The ensuing recession lasted through 1995 and the economy will probably not stabilize until 1996.

During these troubled financial times, it was expected that most Mexican businesses would suffer, as often happens during a recession. However, one company actually thrived and experienced continued success throughout 1995 and 1996—Cementos Mexicanos, or Cemex. Cemex is the fourth largest producer of cement in the world. It is based in Monterrey, Mexico, but owns cement plants in Spain, Venezuela, Panama, the Caribbean, and the United States. It is these international plants that are helping Cemex become a strong Mexican company that is not being pulled down by the Mexican recession. Currently, almost two-thirds of Cemex's sales come from its foreign operations (see Exhibit 1).

For the past ten years, the CEO of Cemex has been Lorenzo Zambrano, the grandson of the founder. He has embarked on an aggressive growth strategy which has made Cemex an industry leader with operations in 26 countries (Smith 1995). Zambrano has embarked on a policy of entering foreign markets "whose economic cycles are not linked to that of Mexico" (*Cemex 1994*).

What has made Cemex such a strong and growing company? Cement is pretty much the same no matter from where or from whom it is purchased, so cement manufacturers must differentiate themselves in ways other than the

**Exhibit 1**                **Cemex's 1995 Sales (breakdown by country)**

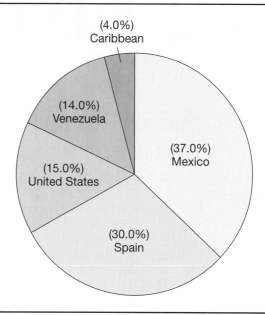

*Source:* Cemex 1995 Annual Report

physical product. For Cemex, one such way of achieving this kind of competitive advantage is through its foreign operations, which give it the ability to ship from low-cost manufacturing facilities to markets where demand is strong and prices are relatively high. The ability to produce and ship from and to various markets allows Cemex to compete with the other major cement producers in Europe such as Switzerland's Holderbank and France's Lafarge Coppée.

## THE HISTORY OF CEMEX

Cemex began operations in 1906 with the founding of Cementos Hidalgo in Mexico. Growth and development were achieved by entering international markets and maintaining a product line that was primarily cement. In 1931 Cementos Hidalgo and Cementos Monterrey, a rival firm, merged, creating what is now known as Cementos Mexicanos, or Cemex. Throughout the 1960s and 1970s, Cemex built new plants and acquired other cement manufacturers in Mexico. It began exporting in the late 1970s, which helped keep the company going during the contraction of the Mexican economy at that time. Acquisitions continued to increase and more new plants were brought on line. In 1989, Cemex acquired Cementos Tolteca, with seven plants and an annual capacity of 6.8 million tons. A major period of international expansion began in 1992 when Cemex bought two large cement producers in Spain, Valenciana, and Sanson. Vencemos, a Venezuelan cement firm, and Cemento Bayano in Panama were acquired in 1994. In 1995, a plant in New Braunfels, Texas, was acquired and another plant in Mexico began operations. Total production capacity is now at 55.8 million metric tons per year.

# INDUSTRY

Portland cement is the most common type of cement used in construction. It is made up of a combination of quarried limestone, clay (or shale or kaolin), and sand. These components are ground and mixed together by either a wet or dry process. The wet process involves mixing the limestone and clay with water to form slurry, which is then heated in a kiln to form a hard substance called clinker. In the dry process, which is more fuel-efficient, the original materials are not turned into slurry, but are directly heated to form clinker. After either process, the clinker is mixed with gypsum and ground into a fine powder called cement. When mixed with water, sand, and stone, the mixture forms concrete or mortar (*Lafarge 10K*).

The cement industry is growing rapidly, due in part to increased demand in the construction industries in both less-developed countries and industrialized nations. This has provided opportunities for many cement companies to establish plants in different regions around the world, resulting in global competition between the leading firms. Cement producers must now, more than ever, concentrate on their internal strengths to distinguish themselves from their competitors. Consumers no longer have to depend on one supplier but now can be selective and choose which cement producer can provide quality goods at the best prices.

Since cement is a commodity, the growth of the cement industry depends largely on construction and economic growth in the world economy. If someone wants to build factories or houses, they need cement. Third World and developing countries are where the most growth is projected and Cemex already has a head start.

From 1991 to 1994, cement consumption grew by more than nineteen percent ("Set" 1995). In 1994, global consumption of cement was 1.4 billion tons, or $80 billion, and was growing at an annual rate of 3.6% a year (Lenzler 1994). In Latin America and Asia, the consumption of cement is growing at twice the rate of the local economies (ibid). In many of these countries, European cement producers such as Switzerland's Holderbank and the United Kingdom's Blue Circle Industries have already entered the market. Even in the U.S., approximately two-thirds of cement production is from non-U.S. producers, including Cemex.

# INTERNAL STRENGTHS

Cemex sees itself as having five core competencies which have allowed it to become successful: low-cost operations, use of technology, management competence, market positioning, and financial strength. Cemex prides itself on its low-cost operations. Its Spanish plants have some of the highest productivity levels of any cement plant worldwide. Technologically, Cemex is also very current, with a computer network system which "links all of Cemex's offices in Mexico and abroad via a network of satellite dishes, leased lines, and microwave communications" (Smith 1995). Zambrano uses this system to obtain information on any of Cemex's worldwide plants at any time and allows him to react quickly to rapidly changing market conditions.

For Cemex, going "global" was not just a matter of buying overseas plants and suppliers. They had to improve internally as well. Zambrano once said that Cemex had to "improve faster than any other cement company in the world" (*Chief Executive*). He wanted the employees of Cemex to learn new ways to be productive. To do this, he went straight to the employees and asked them what they thought the barriers to an improved Cemex were. He asked them to imagine what the Cemex of the future would be like. The employees were shown how their performance, even at the lowest level, influenced Cemex's overall profits. They identified effective and ineffective practices in the company. The top managers would set goals and let the employees, working in teams, figure out solutions. These teams have redesigned such areas in Cemex as maintenance management and inventory systems, as well as human resources. The result was an increase in productivity of 25 percent and they identified $40 million in savings that could go to the bottom line (ibid).

# ACQUISITIONS

In the early 1990's, senior management at Cemex decided to develop an international presence and increase the company's share in markets that did not have economies linked to Mexico. This strategy would reduce dramatic fluctuations in cash flows since revenues would be obtained from countries with growing economies even when the Mexican economy is in recession. Prior to its global expansion, Cemex had made acquisitions primarily in the U.S. and Mexico. In the 1980's, it acquired Cementos Anahuac and Empresas Tolteca, its two largest competitors in Mexico, increasing its market share to approximately three times that of its closest competitor (Peagan 1995). Cemex's first major international acquisitions occurred in 1992 when it bought two Spanish cement plants, Valenciana and Sanson, for $1.84 billion. This acquisition surprised many investors who thought Cemex was just content to stay in Mexico where it had been performing quite well (Fink 1992). The stock price sank, as often happens to an acquiring company. However, the acquisition gave Cemex a foothold in Europe, where many of the world's other large cement producers are located. The two companies were combined to form Valenciana de Cementos, Spain's largest cement producer.

In April 1994, Cemex purchased a 60% stake in Vencemos, a Venezuelan cement producer, for $320 million. The results from this operation were consolidated in the 1995 financial statements. Also in 1994, Cemex purchased Cemento Bayano, a Panamanian plant giving Cemex a 50% market share in Panama. Cemex also bought its first production facility in the U.S., a cement plant in Texas purchased from one of Cemex's competitors, Lafarge Coppée of France. Previously, Cemex was involved in the U.S. market only through ready-mix concrete plants owned by its subsidiaries.

Cemex's international operations have contributed a great deal to the company's profits. Operating profits from the plant in Spain have risen from $37.7 million in 1993 to $95.5 million in 1994 and $200 million in 1995. Exports from the Venezuelan plant doubled to 2 million tons in 1995 and operating profits were $120 million. The operating margin at the Panamanian plant is 25 percent and all the revenues there are denominated in dollars.

# MARKET POSITION

Cemex's policy on market positioning is to "achieve a leading market share in each geographical area in which [it] has production operations" (*Cemex 1994*). Currently, Cemex is the market leader in Mexico, Spain, Venezuela, and Panama and has a dominant position in the Caribbean. Cemex is a growing presence in the United States with one cement plant in Texas and several ready-mix concrete plants operated through Sunbelt Corporation, its subsidiary in California, Arizona, Texas, and Florida.

Cemex has achieved a leading share in most of the markets in which it operates through a continuous focus on the cement business and a selective yet ambitious international expansion plan. In Mexico, the company has capitalized on its market leadership position by becoming a low-cost vendor concentrating on productivity maximization and cost reduction. Long-term growth in the domestic markets for housing and public infrastructure in Mexico is expected to grow by an average of 7.0% per year for the next five years. In the Mexican cement market 78% of the cement is sold in bags to retailers for use in small-scale construction. Five percent of sales are to industrial customers and seventeen percent of sales are to ready-mix concrete producers. This is in contrast to the U.S., where 80% of cement sales are in the ready-mix concrete segment (Peagam 1995). Cemex has increased its ready-mix business in recent years with 167 ready-mix plants operating in 50 Mexican cities (ibid).

In the U.S., Cemex strengthened its position in the cement market by increasing productivity and reducing costs. Most of Cemex's plants in the U.S. are part of its subsidiary Sunbelt Corporation. Prior to 1994, Sunbelt was mainly involved in the ready-mix concrete business as well as the trading and distribution of building materials. However, it acquired a cement plant in Texas, making it Cemex's first cement plant in the U.S. The regional headquarters for U.S. operations were recently moved to Houston, Texas. Cemex is continuously evaluating its operations in America to keep them in line with the overall long-term objectives of the company.

Cemex has continued to keep up with local demand in the various countries in which it has made acquisitions and has some of the highest production levels per workers for cement plants in the world. In Spain, Cemex is the largest cement producer, with a 28% market share, and has 11 cement plants, 133 ready-mix concrete plants, and 7 marine terminals. Demand for domestic cement is increasing around 5.5%–7% per year. With its acquisition of Vencemos in 1995, Cemex was able to achieve a leading market share in Venezuela. Currently Cemex accounts for 50% of the domestic market share for cement and 30% of the ready-mix cement market. In Venezuela, it operates 4 cement plants, 4 marine terminals, and 22 ready-mix concrete plants. The company hopes to capitalize on the long-term growth prospects for the country's building industry. With its acquisition of Cemento Bayano, one of Panama's leading cement companies, in September of 1995, the company established a large presence in the Central American market. In Panama, Cemex is benefiting from being the country's lowest-cost cement producer. Finally, Cemex has been in the Caribbean since 1991, and recently has strengthened operations there through strategic alliances and joint ventures. These decisions have resulted in the company producing about 80% of the region's traded cement.

## PRODUCTION CAPABILITIES

Cemex's production capability in Mexico was 27.8 million metric tons per year in 1995, an increase of 3.2 million metric tons over the previous year due in part to the building of its nineteenth plant in Mexico. In Spain, Cemex has a production capability of 11.8 million metric tons per year, which includes the joint capacity of the Valencia and Sanson plants. Cemex used to produce only concrete aggregates in the U.S., but with its recent acquisition of a cement plant in Texas, its U.S. production capabilities have increased from 2.9 million to 3.8 million combined tons of cement and aggregates per year. Production capabilities in Venezuela are at full capacity, producing 3.2 million tons per year. The Caribbean region is an area with high potential for growth. In 1994, Cemex acquired 100% ownership of a terminal in Freeport, Bahamas, with a 600,000 metric ton capacity, and 51% of another terminal in Nassau, Bahamas. Also in the same year, it acquired a 20% ownership in Trinidad Cement Limited, a company that has the capability of producing 500,000 metric tons of cement per year. Cemex's recent acquisition of Cemeto Bayano in Panama has increased Cemex's overall production capacity by 363,000 metric tons per year (*Cemex 1994*).

## DISTRIBUTION

One of the reasons why Cemex is able to distribute more than 44 million metric tons per year worldwide is because it is able to produce at a lower cost. For example, Cemex can produce a metric ton for $25, well below the industry average of $35 per ton. Cemex's strategic locations in different countries and low production costs have enabled it to fully utilize its productive capacity and sell the excess production in other countries such as Guatemala, Brazil, Ecuador, and Peru. Currently Cemex has 19 cement plants, 167 ready-mix concrete plants, and 3 marine terminals in Mexico. Cemex operations in the U.S. include one cement plant, 16 marine terminals, and 65 ready-mix concrete plants. In the Caribbean, Cemex operates 2 cement plants and 9 marine terminals and it operates a commercial office in Hong Kong (*Cemex 1994*).

Five percent of the world's cement consumption is traded through imports. Cemex has an extensive trading system which accounted for 8 million tons of cement and clinker in 1995. It has trading relations with 54 countries. Cemex has direct operations in Mexico, the U.S., Venezuela, Hong Kong, Brazil, and several Caribbean nations. It has trading relations with Panama, Honduras, Costa Rica, El Salvador, Denmark, Greece, France, Holland, Ireland, Nigeria, Peru, Taiwan, and several islands in the Caribbean.

Cemex's exports have increased dramatically in recent years. Exports from Mexico increased 196% between 1994 and 1995 (see Exhibits 2 and 3). One of the reasons for this is the weak state of the Mexican economy. Cemex took this opportunity to establish new trading relationships with the Far East including Indonesia, Malaysia, and the Philippines.

## MARKET POTENTIAL

The market potential for Cemex in each of its six major demographic locations is excellent, with the industry growing in each of the last few years. Mexico and Spain have averaged about 7 percent growth in demand per year in their cement

**Exhibit 2**

**Cemex's Mexican Exports in 1995 (percentage of total volume exported)**

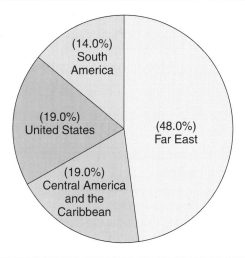

*Source:* Cemex 1995 Annual Report

**Exhibit 3**

**Cement Exports (million metric tons)**

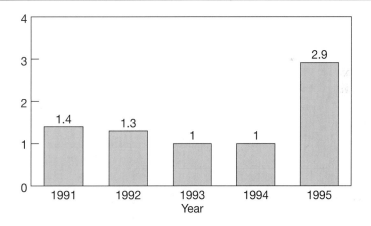

*Source:* Cemex 1995 Annual Report

industries. The southern regions of California, Texas, and Florida have averaged around 10 percent growth for the past three years. In 1995, Venezuelan officials introduced drastic plans to reverse falling economic activity, and Cemex is in a great position to reap the benefits of the inevitable industry upswing. The Panamanian government has committed itself to major public sector development projects which will extend past the year 2000, and this plan has already stimulated construction sector growth to over 20 percent of last year's level.

As Cemex continues to expand globally, its growth potential increases. Potential markets for the cement industry can be found throughout developing countries where there is a need to import concrete and cement products. Cemex has been aware of this for many years and continuously attempts to increase market share in these areas. Most recently, the company has been focusing on markets in Asia and the Pacific rim. Cemex's Hong Kong office is studying several ventures in China. Zambrano says, "We will be there one way or another in the next two years" (Smith 1995).

## OTHER OPERATIONS

While Cemex is mainly in the cement and ready-mix business, it is also involved in the tourism industry. Cemex's Marriot CasaMagna hotels in Puerto Vallarta and Cancun are among the leading hotels in those areas, which, in 1994, ranked first and second in local occupancy rates respectively. With the peso devaluation in December, the purchasing power of foreign currency has increased, thus strengthening the prospects for an increased number of foreign visitors. Exhibit 4 features the structure of Cemex.

## FINANCIAL INFORMATION

With the rapid pace of Cemex's acquisitions comes worries among investors about the amount of debt Cemex is taking on. The price of Cemex stock dropped from $9.40 in November 1994 to $3.33 in February 1995. Does this mean that the frenzied pace of acquisitions is adversely affecting Cemex in terms of its stock price? Many investors seem to think so. Recently, the stock price has gone up to around $7.50 but with all the recent acquisition activity that Cemex is promoting as being beneficial to the company, why hasn't the price gone up significantly? When Cemex recently announced the proposed acquisition of two Colombian cement companies for $600 million, its share price dropped 4 percent. Cemex's P/E ratio is also low at 6 compared to other Mexican cement firms which have P/E's of 15.

While the number and size of Cemex's acquisitions are impressive, the amount of debt it is taking on is even more impressive. Prior to making its Spanish acquisition, Cemex issued $1 billion in debt, the largest issue ever for a Latin American company. Investors were somewhat apprehensive, but the issue received an investment grade from Moody's and Standard and Poor's. Cemex remains confident in its ability to handle its debt (Smith 58). It had even made moves in anticipation of a peso devaluation. A $400 million convertible bond was issued at 4.25 % to "recycle short-term debt to a more manageable three-year maturity" (ibid). Cemex's CFO, Gustavo Caballero, has slowly extended the company's debt maturity time frame from two years to four and a half. He is also discussing a deal with Citibank and J.P. Morgan & Co. to roll over $350 million in swap loans backed by Cemex shares (Smith 59). Cemex has a total of $3.2 billion in dollar-denominated debt out of a total of $3.9 billion. Seventy-eight percent of Cemex's debt is long term. Exhibits 5 and 6 contain Cemex's 1995 income statement and balance sheet.

**Exhibit 4**                    **Cemex Structure**

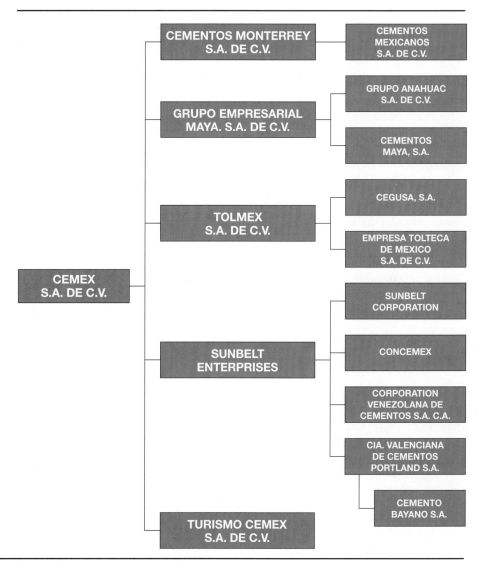

*Source:* Cemex 1995 Annual Report

## EXTERNAL ENVIRONMENT

The external environment in each of the countries in which Cemex operates varies. In the U.S., fluctuating interest rates and the anti-dumping order concerning the imports of Mexican cement have hindered sales, but large demand in America for cement has kept private-sector spending strong and created an urgency to reach an agreement concerning laws which prevent cement importation.

Mexico's economic status is the principal reason why Cemex has engaged in its international diversification strategy. The Mexican economic outlook remains uncertain at present. Public and private sector spending have been severely reduced as a result of the peso devaluation, and the government's

Exhibit 5

**CEMEX, S.A. DE C.V. and Subsidiaries—Consolidated Balance Sheets
(thousands of constant Mexican pesos as of December 31, 1995)**

| | December 31 | |
| --- | :---: | :---: |
| | *1995* | *1994* |
| Assets | | |
| Current Assets | | |
| Cash and temporary investments | $ 2,741,139 | 3,729,917 |
| Trade accounts receivable, less allowance for doubtful accounts of $379,143 in 1995 and $353,713 in 1994 | 2,969,375 | 2,964,942 |
| Other receivables | 1,180,995 | 1,202,417 |
| Inventories | 2,614,667 | 2,129,217 |
| Other current assets | 847,513 | 977,872 |
| Total current assets | 10,353,689 | 11,004,365 |
| Investments and Noncurrent Receivables | | |
| Investments in affiliated companies | 1,599,276 | 5,278,324 |
| Other investments | 265,954 | 423,276 |
| Other accounts receivable | 1,182,348 | 29,087 |
| Total investments and noncurrent receivables | 3,047,578 | 5,730,687 |
| Property, Machinery, and Equipment | | |
| Land and buildings | 16,315,240 | 14,496,371 |
| Machinery and equipment | 55,015,31 | 41,204,087 |
| Accumulated depreciation | (33,961,654) | (27,374,852) |
| Construction in progress | 805,426 | 3,192,051 |
| Total property, machinery, and equipment | 38,174,323 | 31,517,657 |
| Deferred Charges | | |
| Excess of cost over book value of subsidiaries and affiliated companies acquired | 12,641,905 | 11,270,083 |
| Other deferred charges | 2,347,136 | 2,885,050 |
| Accumulated amortization | (1,863,224) | (1,627,263) |
| Total deferred charges | 13,125,817 | 12,527,870 |
| Total Assets | $ 64,701,407 | 60,780,579 |
| Liabilities and Stockholders' Equity | | |
| Current Liabilities | | |
| Bank loans Notes payable | 3,535,801 | 2,388,081 |
| Current maturities of long-term debt | 2,388,822 | 1,095,208 |
| Trade accounts payable | 1,203,010 | 1,031,305 |
| Other accounts payable and accrued expenses | 2,088,794 | 2,110,830 |
| Total current liabilities | 10,019,721 | 8,127,892 |
| Long-Term Debt | | |
| Bank loans | 7,224,282 | 5,294,357 |
| Debentures | 48,750 | 222,256 |
| Notes payable | 18,566,015 | 19,569,355 |

**Exhibit 5 (continued)**     **CEMEX, S.A. DE C.V. and Subsidiaries—Consolidated Balance Sheets (thousands of constant Mexican pesos as of December 31, 1995)**

| | December 31 | |
| --- | --- | --- |
| | 1995 | 1994 |
| Current maturities of long-term debt | (2,388,822) | (1,095,208) |
| Total long-term debt | 23,450,225 | 23,990,760 |
| Other Noncurrent Liabilities | | |
| Pension plan and seniority premium | 528,011 | 453,656 |
| Deferred income taxes | 1,074,498 | 57,674 |
| Other liabilities | 379,678 | 276,182 |
| Total other noncurrent liabilities | 1,982,187 | 787,512 |
| Total liabilities | 35,452,133 | 32,906,164 |
| Excess of book value over cost of subsidiaries acquired | 129,771 | 132,284 |
| Stockholders' Equity | | |
| Majority interest: | | |
| Common stock—historical cost basis | 45,222 | 40,838 |
| Common stock—accumulated inflation adjustments | 1,367,526 | 1,367,526 |
| Additional paid-in capital | 6,374,826 | 3,318,849 |
| Excess (deficit) in equity restatement | (7,756,821) | 127,751 |
| Retained earnings | 16,349,515 | 14,058,611 |
| Net income | 5,868,907 | 2,893,114 |
| Total majority interest | 22,249,175 | 21,806,689 |
| Minority interest | 6,870,328 | 5,935,442 |
| Total stockholders' equity | 29,119,503 | 27,742,131 |
| Total Liabilities and Stockholders' Equity | $ 64,701,407 | 60,780,579 |

budget reductions have hurt infrastructure spending. Overall construction activity dropped by 22% in 1995. Cement demand has also fallen. The economy of the U.S. is growing but not as fast as in the past. Construction activity is expected to increase by only 2% in 1996. Construction spending has also increased around 4% per year across southern regions. Increased residential and commercial property developments resulting from lower long-term interest rates in the U.S. will be beneficial to Cemex. In Spain, the development of residential units has remained strong because government subsidies have helped to increase levels of cement consumption.

The Venezuelan government began a new economic recovery plan in 1994 to reverse some of the hardships faced by that country. So far, their efforts have indirectly and dramatically improved the cement demand in Venezuela and benefited Cemex in 1995 and 1996. However, the economy is still very slow. Forty-six percent of Cemex's products made in Venezuela were exported. Even so, the market share increased from 47% to 49%. The Venezuelan government is currently trying to stimulate building industry growth with the "settlement

| Exhibit 6 Income | Cemex, S.A. DE C.V. and Subsidiaries—Consolidated Statements of (thousands of constant Mexican Pesos as of December 31, 1995) | |
|---|---|---|

| | Years ended on December 31 | |
|---|---|---|
| | 1995 | 1994 |
| Net sales | $ 19,821,210 | 16,176,647 |
| Cost of sales | (12,088,257) | (9,329,364) |
| Gross profit | 7,732,953 | 6,847,283 |
| Operating expenses: | | |
| Administrative | (1,987,702) | (1,410,202) |
| Selling | (1,012,548) | (1,094,394) |
| Total operating expenses | (3,000,250) | (2,504,596) |
| Operating income | 4,732,703 | 4,342,687 |
| Comprehensive financing income (cost): | | |
| Financial expenses | (5,038,987) | (2,766,632) |
| Financial income | 561,313 | 2,692,595 |
| Foreign exchange loss, net | (2,823,440) | (1,105,527) |
| Monetary position gain | 11,682,191 | 1,055,786 |
| Net comprehensive financing income (cost) | 4,381,077 | (123,778) |
| Other expenses, net | (1,251,416) | (1,025,269) |
| Income before income tax, business assets tax, employees' statutory profit sharing and equity in income of affiliates | 7,862,364 | 3,193,640 |
| Income tax and business assets tax, net | (1,275,104) | (75,666) |
| Employees' statutory profit sharing | (13,349) | (65,323) |
| Total income tax, business assets tax, and employees' statutory profit sharing | (1,288,453) | (140,989) |
| Income before equity in income of affiliates | 6,573,911 | 3,052,651 |
| Equity in income of affiliates | 136,609 | 187,122 |
| Consolidated net income | 6,710,520 | 3,239,773 |
| Minority interest net income | 841,613 | 346,659 |
| Majority interest net income | $ 5,868,907 | 2,893,114 |

of public debt to contractors, the granting of easy-term housing loans, and the reactivation of infrastructure projects, including the building of railroads, dams, and a subway in Valencia. In addition, the creation of concessions under which the private sector would be allowed to participate in public infrastructure projects continues to be discussed" (*Cemex 1994*).

Panama has been an active market for Cemex for many years. Although its economy has slowed down somewhat, Cemex's plants have been performing very well. Cemex's market share increased to 51% and the company will be involved in a $336 million highway from Colon to Panama City to begin construction in 1996. Finally, the Caribbean region, with over 20 countries and 33 million people, is an area with high potential for growth in its economy and in the demand for cement. Because of fast development rates, there are many opportunities for construction and building material companies, particularly in Haiti and the Dominican Republic, with increased domestic and foreign spending. Cemex had a plant in Cuba as a joint venture between Mexico and Cuba, but recently pulled out after a request from the U.S. State Department that foreign companies not use confiscated American property.

## THE ANTIDUMPING CONTROVERSY

Everything is not perfect at Cemex, though. Along with other Mexican producers of cement, it has been engaged in an ongoing battle with the United States for several years over claims by the U.S. that Mexico is dumping its cement on the U.S. market. Some U.S. cement producers claim that Mexican companies are selling their cement at a cheaper price in the U.S. than in Mexico.

The controversy began in May 1990, when the Department of Commerce (DOC) put antidumping duties on Mexican cement. Some U.S. cement producers had claimed that certain parts of the cement industry, in particular those in the South and Southwest, were being injured by the dumping of Mexican cement. They petitioned the DOC to impose duties on imported cement. This petition was unusual in that it claimed injury to only a certain segment of the U.S. cement industry. Antidumping petitions normally involve an entire industry because if an import duty is imposed, it goes into effect at all ports of entry, not just in the injured area (Lande 1994). The Mexican producers complained and appealed to GATT using this reasoning and in 1992, a GATT panel sided with the Mexican producers, giving the reason that the American claims were coming only from regional cement producers and were not industry wide ("Set" 1995). However, the U.S. chose not to abide by the GATT ruling. The import duty on Mexican cement was raised from 43% to 62% of its imported price in May 1995 (ibid). Some Americans think the duty is too low, since Cemex, they claim, had not been giving them enough information concerning its costs and prices. However, with its international operations, Cemex can get around the antidumping duty by exporting to the U.S. from its Spanish plant.

## COMPETITORS

Cemex is the dominant producer of cement in Mexico and has high market shares in many of the other countries in which it has plants. However, it is not the biggest cement company in the world and must compete with other cement producers both on a global basis and within Mexico. The two largest competitors are Holderbank, located in Switzerland, and Lafarge Coppée, located in France. In addition, there are many cement producers in the United States and the Caribbean with which Cemex must compete for market share.

## HOLDERBANK

The world's largest producer of cement is headquartered in Switzerland. Holderbank is a holding company which engages in the production and sale of cement, ready-mix concrete, and other concrete products. It first began to expand in the 1950's when it entered markets in Brazil, Chile, Colombia, Costa Rica, Mexico, Peru, Venezuela, and Argentina (Lenzler 1994). It also has plants in Vietnam, Australia, and New Zealand. Holnam, the largest cement company in the U.S., was formed by merging Holderbank's U.S. assets with those of Ideal Basic Industries (ibid).

Apasco, Mexico's second largest cement company, is a subsidiary of Holderbank and competes directly with Cemex. Apasco operates 6 cement and 84 ready-mixed concrete plants in 40 cities in Mexico (McDermott 1994). Like Cemex, Apasco has a satellite communications system which it uses to keep track of the various operations of its plants. As Holderbank already has companies in Canada and the U.S., Apasco competes with Cemex only in the Mexican cement market. Both companies are planning increases of production and capacity, but the Mexican recession could put their plans on hold for now. Apasco had sales of $650 million in 1993, an 18% increase over the previous year. Holderbank also competes with Cemex through its cement plant in Venezuela.

## LAFARGE COPPÉE

This French corporation is the second largest producer of cement in the world. It owns cement plants all over the world. Sixty percent of its sales are in Europe. It must compete with Cemex in Spain through its subsidiary Asland S.A. Lafarge Coppée competes in the U.S. cement market through its subsidiary Lafarge Corporation, which operates plants mostly in the upper midwest. It controls approximately nine percent of the U.S. cement market (*Lafarge 10K*). Lafarge does not directly compete with Cemex in the U.S. since most of Lafarge's plants are in the northern half of the U.S. and Cemex competes primarily in the southern states. Lafarge used to have some plants in Texas as well as ready-mix terminals, but sold them to Cemex, which gave Cemex its first U.S. cement plant.

## OTHERS

In the Caribbean market, Cemex competes with Devcon International, one of the largest manufacturers of cement and cement products in the region. The company makes ready-mix concrete, crushed stone, concrete block, and asphalt and distributes bulk and bagged cement (*Devcon 10K*). It distributes its products to the U.S. Virgin Islands, Antigua, Barbuda, St. Maarten/sSt. Martin, Dominica, and the British Virgin Islands. It is a well-established company and will be a challenge for Cemex with Cemex's new facilities in the Caribbean and Cuba.

## CONCLUSION

While the future of Mexico's economy remains uncertain, Cemex's future appears bright. Almost one-third of their revenues are denominated in U.S. dollars which is helping to lessen the tremendous debt burden it is under.

Thanks to Zambrano's international expansion plans, Cemex has become one of the largest cement producers in the world and is continuing to grow. Having cement plants in many different parts of the world, from the Caribbean to Europe, has given Cemex an edge over its competition. However, Cemex must be careful in its acquisitions strategy. While the company's capacity has dramatically increased over the past five years, its stock price has not. Some investors are skeptical about the prices Cemex is paying for these acquisitions. Cemex also must look to other markets, primarily in Asia, and continue to work to decrease its debt.

# BIBLIOGRAPHY

"Cementos Mexicanos (CEMEX)." *Euromoney (Emerging Issues Supplement)*, Sep. 1993, 34.

"CEMEX: A New Foundation." *Chief Executive (CEO Brief)*, Jul/Aug. 1995, 10-12.

*Cemex 1994 Annual Report.*

"Cemex Wows Market With $1bn Blockbuster." *Euroweek*, 28 May 1993, 1.

"The Children With the Magic Powder." *The Economist*, 21 May 1994, 76-77.

*Devcon 10-K 1995.*

Fink, Ronald. "Cemex: The Spanish Acquisition(s)." *Financial World*, 27 October 1992, 21-22.

Heaney, Kathleen, and Mark Stockdale. "Cement (domestic); Cement (international)." *Institutional Investor*, Jun. 1993, SS14-SS15.

*Lafarge 10-K 1995.*

Lande, Stephen. "Dumping on Cement Dispute." *Business Mexico*, Sep. 1994, 44-46.

Lenzler, Richard. "Set In Concrete." *Forbes*, 18 July 1994, 42-43.

Marray, Michael. "Cemex Confounds the Sceptics." *Euromoney (Worlds; Best Credits Supplement)*, Sep. 1993, 37.

McCarthy, Joseph L. "Lorenzo Zambrano." *Chief Executive*, Sep. 1993, 27.

McDermott, Terry. "Laying the Foundation." *Business Mexico*, Jul. 1994, 39-40.

Peagam, Norman, and Michael Marray. "Cemex: Foreign Ambitions." *Euromoney*, May 1993, 137-138.

"Set In Concrete." *The Economist*, 3 June 1995, 28-29.

Smith, Gail, and John Pearson. "Cemex: Solid As Mexico Sinks." *Business Week*, 27 February 1995, 58-59.

Vogel, Jr., Thomas T. "Mexico's Cemex, Hurt by Peso's Fall, Gets Financing From Citibank, J.P. Morgan." *Wall Street Journal*, 27 Jan. 1995, A3.

# A League of His Own

Daniel O. Lybrook, Purdue University

Michael L. Menefee, Purdue University

As Mark Dimmich sat in his darkened office and rehashed the events that led to the current state of affairs, he wondered if owning a minor league baseball team was all it had been cracked up to be. The local media was on him, criticizing him for not being a better General Manager. The President of the Parks Board that had once given promises of help was criticizing him in the public media and undermining him behind his back. Local industry had not lived up to their promised support. The whole affair was simply a lot different than expected. What a mess! Should he just drop the whole thing? Or should he try again next year and go it alone, correcting his mistakes as he saw fit? Would a shared ownership design ease the burdens?

## HISTORY

Jim Gonzales, the previous year's general manager, had started working toward a new beginning for the Lafayette Leopards independent baseball team before the dust had settled from the failed experiment of its participation in the Great Central League last year. Though he had not secured financial backing, he really felt that minor league baseball could make a go of it in Lafayette.

Jim felt like he had learned from last year's experiences. Current common knowledge said that it takes a few years for independent baseball to turn a profit. After only one year of being in existence, Jim felt about a minor league franchise like Ray Kinsella in the movie *Field of Dreams*—"Build it and they will come." So he was very upbeat about trying again in Lafayette. He would try to build and organize the league himself without Dick Jacobsen, the former league President.

# THE ENVIRONMENT

The city of Lafayette, Indiana, is situated in the mid north region of Indiana, 60 miles northwest of Indianapolis and 120 miles southeast of Chicago. Tippecanoe County, of which Lafayette is the county seat, has a year round population of approximately 125,000 permanent residents. The major population centers in the county are Lafayette, with about 45,000 people, and West Lafayette, with about 25,000 people. These sister cities are self governed as is the surrounding county. During the fall to spring school year, an additional 30,000 students live in the area and attend Purdue University in West Lafayette. In the summer, the students at Purdue number about 8000.

The county is the business and industry center of this region of Indiana. The local Chamber of Commerce boasts a membership of close to 1000 businesses. Other than Purdue, which is the area's largest employer with over 12,000 employees, there are several large manufacturing concerns operating within the county. Wabash National (a truck trailer manufacturer), Eli Lilly (a drug manufacturer), Fairfield Manufacturing, Rostone Corp., Alcoa, Caterpillar, Subaru-Isuzu, TRW, and Landis Gyr all have facilities in the county.

To attend a professional baseball game, the closest major league teams are the Cubs and White Sox; 2 1/2 hours travel by car to Chicago. Recent surveys have stated that to attend a major league game costs a family of four around $100 not counting the transportation. With a driving time from Lafayette of seventy minutes, the closest minor league teams in the area were the Class AAA Indianapolis Indians and the Class A Danville, Illinois, club. Fort Wayne and South Bend also have minor league teams, but the drive from Lafayette is more than two and one half hours.

Indiana is legendary for basketball fanaticism and every boy at some time in his formative years dreams of playing for his favorite school, whether it be a secondary school or university. The area has also traditionally been very strong in youth baseball and youth baseball interest. There is a very strong summer youth program supported by the Parks and Recreation Department in Lafayette. Organized baseball starts with five year olds with T-ball leagues and continues up to American Legion ball for 17 and 18 year olds. This affords participation opportunities to a large percentage of those interested. This is carried over into the county through various township recreation boards. Of the five high schools in the county, three have played in an Indiana state baseball championship game in the last ten years, which speaks well of the interest and caliber of play in the area. Lafayette Jefferson has won the title twice and most recently played for the title just ten years ago. The county high schools, Harrison and McCutcheon, have each been in the title game in the last three years. Harrison won this year, and McCutcheon came in second two years ago. There is plenty of baseball competition and interest at the high school level.

Purdue is a member of The Big Ten athletic conference and plays a very competitive brand of baseball in the spring of each year. They will play approximately 25-30 home games each year and will draw crowds of 400-500 fans. This is close to the capacity of the Purdue baseball field. Their season ends in early June. An average of two to three players each year are drafted by major league organizations.

Lafayette also plays host to the international Colt World Series each summer. This tourney is played in the first two weeks of July. The format is a double elimination tournament for 14 and 15 year old players. There are eight teams that qualify from as far away as Puerto Rico and Hawaii. The tournament schedules two games per night over its two week venue and routinely draws over 1500 fans to Loeb Stadium Baseball Field for each session.

## LOEB STADIUM

Loeb Stadium is a 2400 seat capacity ballpark operated by the Lafayette Parks and Recreation Department. It is located in a corner of the 600 acre facility called Columbian Park. Within this park are tennis courts, a large swimming pool, the city zoo, three meeting facilities, an outdoor amphitheater, a playground, various rides, and concessions. Parking for approximately 120 cars is available in a lot next to the ballpark. This lot also serves as parking for the zoo and for general park use and is free of charge.

The ballpark has recently been renovated with major alterations to update the restrooms, dressing rooms, and general appearance. It is as good a facility as you will find in a city the size of Lafayette. Bill German, the head of the Parks Department, was the linking pin between the city government and the baseball team. Bill agreed to give this year's edition of the Leopards the rate of $3000 for the rental of the ballpark for the season—30 games—with an option for the next season. This rate covers electricity for the lights and maintenance on the field. The Leopards were responsible for their own personal liability insurance.

## PHOENIX FROM THE ASHES—A NEW START

Jim Gonzales felt that last season was a learning experience in what NOT to do. It was marked by a trail of unpaid bills and eventual lawsuits against the combination team and league owner, Dick Jacobsen. When the original general manager of the Leopards had gone unpaid for the initial two months of the season, he quit and Jim Gonzales—then the manager of the baseball team—took over to try to finish the season. The Leopards had won the title but the league, The Great Central League, had disintegrated at the conclusion of the season.

Jim was and is a baseball man and he felt that the problems had been primarily Jacobsen's. So he wanted to try again. Almost immediately upon the conclusion of the last season, Jim Gonzales and Bill German, Director of the Lafayette Parks Department, started to contact local businesses to try to garner financial support for the 1995 team. One potential investor, Brad Cohen, was quoted in the *Lafayette Journal and Courier*, the local newspaper: "We want to do everything we can to make sure that this team comes back. But baseball is like any business. You've got to impress your customers to bring them back. You've got to find a few people who can put in $1000 or $2000 and not expect to get it back. You can't expect someone to get a ten percent return on their money after the first year or two. It's an investment in the heart."

Jim felt that one of the important issues was to maintain the name of the team to build on the name recognition earned in the initial season and to establish continuity for the future. A potential problem was that if Jacobson had copyrighted the name, this year's version of the Leopards might have to pay for the name or—at the worst—not be able to use it. This would be a blow to his goal of continuity through identification. Upon checking, Jim found that

Jacobsen had overlooked this copyrighting detail. So the Leopards name was the new organization's for the taking.

Among Gonzales' objectives for the Leopards:

- an operating budget of $120,000
- season ticket sales of at least 700; these would be priced at $100 each
- a board of directors to include a team representative and community member from each city in a six team league, with teams based in Richmond, Anderson, Lafayette, and Terre Haute in Indiana, and two teams in the Chicago area. The Great Central League had four teams located in Minneapolis, Minnesota, Mason City, Iowa, Champaign, Illinois, and Lafayette, Indiana.

## A FINANCIAL ANGEL COMES FORTH

Jim eventually was contacted by Mark Dimmich who owned a local paint and body shop. Mark was interested in supporting baseball in the community because he and his family had attended some games and had enjoyed the Leopards the previous season. Mark felt that a night at the ballpark was a quality family experience and contributed to positive personal values. He especially liked the alcohol free environment of the ballpark. In March, he agreed to provide the necessary financial support for 1995. Mark and Jim prepared a trial budget based on the previous year's expenses and revenues to try to minimize any surprises that Mark might encounter (see Exhibit 1). The Leopards were in business again. Jim became very involved in getting the new league operating. Mark felt that hiring a full time general manager was more of an expense than he wanted to incur. Plus it was an expense that had not been included in the trial budget. So Mark was left with the Leopards general manager's hat as well as his other personal business to run. Jim was more interested in the formation of the league now that Dimmich had agreed to support a team and he eventually abandoned the promotional aspect of the Leopards. In addition, Jim was not adept at promotion. He was a baseball man. It was left to Mark to do the best that he could. At this point, there were two months left before the start of the season. Richmond opted to join a different independent league—The Frontier League—and negotiations with potential owners in Terre Haute broke down. Jim had firm commitments from three teams, but had trouble lining up a fourth. Then East Chicago came in and the league started the season with four teams: the Merrillville Muddogs, East Chicago Conquistadors, Lafayette Leopards, and Anderson Lawmen.

The initial agreement called for each team to pay the league $15,000. This money would go toward three major objectives: contract a sports statistical service to keep league records, pay for game baseballs (which the fans were allowed to keep if a foul ball was caught, as a promotional plus), and to pay for umpires. A sixty game schedule was worked out, with each team having 20 single game home dates and 5 doubleheaders. The league scheduled the start of play on June 13. Because of the heavy demands on Loeb Stadium for the Colt World Series the first two weeks in August and the American Legion Sectional and Regional, the Leopards schedule was unbalanced. It was skewed, with the majority of home games scheduled early in the season. In August, the Leopards had five home dates with ten road dates. The season was scheduled to end in late August with two rounds of playoffs.

---

**Exhibit 1**        **Trial Budget for the Lafayette Leopards**

| | |
|---|---:|
| Revenues: | |
| Gate | — |
| Concessions (15% of Gross) | — |
| Souvenirs | — |
| Ballpark Advertising | — |
| Program Ads/Sales | — |
| Expenses: | |
| Ballpark Rent | $3,000 |
| Administrative (1.5 Staff) | 25,500 |
| League Fees | 15,000 |
| Player Salaries | 36,000 |
| Liability Insurance | 2,000 |
| Travel Expenses | 15,000 |
| Laundry | 2,000 |
| Game Promotions | 10,000 |
| Marketing | 15,000 |
| Insurance for Promotions | 500 |
| Total | $124,000 |

---

The first round of the playoffs would be August 22–25. Mark felt that he did not get a very high priority when it came to scheduling these games. He said that if Lafayette really wanted professional baseball, the Park Board would have to give the team a higher spot in the pecking order. Instead of supporting the Leopards, the Park Board and the city administration gave either no support at all, or second class citizen status at best. It seemed the Colts came first, then American Legion baseball, and finally the Leopards. Mark was left on his own to try to make this experiment work.

## THE PARK BOARD

The Park Board is made up of seven members. The primary responsibility is to administer the physical facilities and programs of Lafayette city parks. There are seven of these spread around the city, with Columbian Park being the largest. The yearly budget for the park system is seven figures. Bill German is the head of Lafayette Parks Department, an appointed position. He sits as a member of the board as well as being responsible for administration of year round recreation.

Jim Gonzales had a good relationship with Bill German and the board. But Jim's background was in baseball, not business. Mark Dimmich thought that the Leopards would have to be run more professionally. The Park Board was leery of the Leopards because the previous owner had bounced two months of rental checks for the ballpark and had left a trail of unpaid bills around town. The board was suing for the money, plus damages, from the previous owner. The board had taken some heat for this from local business, who also supported the summer programs with sponsorships and advertising.

Largely because of this, the relationship between Mark and the board was strained. They were afraid of getting burned again and Mark wanted the Leopards to succeed and needed a sweetheart deal to enable this to happen. Mark never received this.

Bill German became openly critical of Mark's marketing strategies, being quoted in the local newspaper saying that Mark should put more emphasis on getting people to the ballpark instead of emphasizing outfield fence advertising. Bill felt that the Leopards needed to sell tickets and then try to get the fans to come back to more games, accentuating the municipal park attractions and working more in tandem with the overall park system. But he also became critical in private conversations around town.

## GETTING STARTED

The Leopards, by virtue of being the only one of these four teams to field a team last year, had a head start in filling their eighteen man roster. By early June, Jim had seventeen players signed for the season, six of whom had played for the Leopards the previous year. Jim Gonzales had been a college coach in Texas before coming to the Lafayette team and had numerous Texas connections. Many of the signees came from recommendations from college coaches in Texas, where the quality of college ball is excellent. On June 4, an open tryout camp was held locally at Loeb Stadium. A $10 registration fee was charged for each prospect. Twenty-three potentials showed for the tryout. One of the players said it best—"It would be a dream. There's nothing better than that. It's what every kid wants to do. There's nothing better than putting a baseball uniform on." Although that particular player was not signed for the team, the roster was filled with a recent Purdue grad who had not been drafted by the major league clubs. Each player signed for between $500 and $750 a month depending on experience and skill level. The season was scheduled to last two and a half months, including the playoffs. Jim started the season with ten position players and eight pitchers.

## LEOPARDS REVENUES

Minor league baseball teams garner revenue from four primary sources—gate receipts, concessions, parking, and advertising. Gate receipts cannot be accurately predicted, but some preseason operating revenues could be garnered from season ticket sales. Season tickets were priced at $100 for adults and $70 for retirees and children under 12. Concessions and the sale of Leopards logo items would largely depend on the attendance at the games. Advertising would depend on the local market's perception of what the individual business would be getting for their advertising dollar. Parking revenues were nonexistent because of the location of the ballpark.

Single game tickets were priced at $5 per game for adults and $3 per game for retirees and children under 12. A change from the year before was the fact there were no reserved seats so the ticket buyer could sit anywhere he or she chose. Season ticket sales were actually sold as a block of twenty-five tickets for a $1 discount per ticket. The tickets were not dated for any specific game and could be used at any game. With the purchase of a season ticket, you could use one or five or ten, etc., at any game that you chose. Total season ticket sales before the season started numbered 40.

Mark contracted with a local caterer to provide concessions at the games. The menu featured Polish sausage for $2, hot dogs and popcorn for $1, chili dogs for $1.50, nachos for $2.50, Pepsi products for $1, and O'Douls nonalcoholic beverage for $3. To get concessions, a fan had to go to a stand under the bleachers. There were no vendors. Alcoholic beverages are not permitted to be sold at Loeb. This is a policy set by the Parks Board and there is some sentiment on the board to alter that policy in the future. Mark, a non-drinker, supported the non-alcoholic policy because he felt that alcohol would cause more problems than it would be worth and perhaps tarnish the reputation of the events, impacting attendance. The Leopards received fifteen percent of the gross concession sales from the caterer. The average fan spent about $4 a game on concessions at Loeb.

The three most readily available sources of advertising revenue for a baseball team are yearbooks, programs, and ballpark advertising. The game program, which retailed for $1 each, was a four page, 8 1/2 by 11, two color, traditionally laid out baseball program with a Leopards roster insert. It featured a score card on the inside pages with ads purchased by local businesses. There were ten 1/8 page ads, three 1/4 page ads and one full page ad, with the balance taken up by the Leopards and the scoresheet. Rates for the season were $300 for an eighth page, $500 for a quarter page, and $1500 for a full page. These rates were for the full season, but Mark would prorate them if that is what it took to sell out the program.

There were a number of promotions at the games tied to program purchases based on the program numbers. A fan had to buy a program to be included in these. The Leopards did not print a yearbook.

The other advertising revenue—ballpark billboards—became a very interesting scenario. On the outfield fence at Loeb were thirty-four advertising signs paid for by local businesses to the Parks Department with the money earmarked for the summer youth baseball program. If the Leopards were going to generate any revenue from these, Mark would have to resell the signs. He tried to resell them for $1000 each but found few takers. The common sentiment among the advertisers was that they had already paid for the ads and they would be visible at the park even if they did not ante up again. In order to generate advertising revenue, Mark spent $2000 for tarps. He hired a local fan to drape the tarps over the existing advertising on game days. Mark was then able to sell advertising on the tarps. He sold three ads and took one, for his business for a total of four. (Pepsi, the only soft drink sold at Leopard games, took one, the local TV cable company took one, a local bank took one, and Mark's business had one.) Mark felt that it was not ethical to give advertisers different rates. If Pepsi had paid X dollars for its ad then any prospective advertiser should also pay that rate, a yearly take it or leave it approach. Two thirds of the way through the season, he changed his tune and a local industry agreed to pay for a sign as part of a company night promotion.

The parking at Columbian Park was free to the public. The lot next to the ball-park holds about 120 cars. This lot is used by all visitors to the park and there is no mechanism to charge for parking. Therefore, his parking revenues were zero.

## PROMOTIONS

The players appeared at a few youth baseball league outings but on the whole did not participate widely in community events. Jim seemed very reluctant, almost intimidated, to ask them to do much more than show up for practices and games.

Mark tried to get some help from local business and industry and knocked on doors all over town. He sold tickets to companies for the reduced rate of $3 in quantity. Fairfield Athletic Association bought a couple of hundred tickets that they distributed free to workers and their families. Staley bought some and sold them to their workers for $1. Cat bought some and resold them for $3 to employees. Cat had a night at Loeb and bought an outfield ad. Purdue, Lilly, and Wabash National stayed out of any promotion, though they were all approached.

## THE SEASON

The Leopards started the season by winning at home in front of 800 fans. But the overall play was sloppy and two games into the season, a Leopard was released by Gonzales for attitude reasons. Another infielder was signed to take the spot. A pitcher was released because he lived two and a half hours away and could not make every game because of a conflict with his financial analyst job. Another pitcher was signed to replace him. This type of personnel activity is more the norm than the exception in these types of independent leagues.

At the end of the first week of play, the Leopards were last in the league in attendance, averaging 650 fans a game. Merrillville was first with an average of over 1300 a game.

## BALL GAME PROMOTIONS

It is a promotional adage that you must turn minor league sports into a carnival atmosphere to draw fans. Some say the zanier the better. One famous story concerns dressing a person up as a taco and having the food item race a small child around the bases. When the child wins, the young fan gets a free ticket. The spectacle is intended to turn fans into repeat attenders.

The Leopards also featured a number of promotions during the games. Each game program was numbered. Between the top and bottom of the second and third innings a program number would be drawn. The first number would win an O'Doul's cap and T-shirt. The second winner received a coupon for a pizza from a well-known franchise.

In the middle of the fourth, two fans were selected by the Leopard mascot, Blooper. Both were given a bat which they stood up with the head of the bat touching the ground and the contestant's nose touching the handle. The first participant to complete ten rotations around a bat and run to first base won a pair of tickets to a future game. Blooper was a person dressed in a Leopard suit who walked around the park during the game, followed by an attendant to keep young children from pulling Blooper's tail.

Another program number was drawn in the middle of the fifth. This lucky fan stood at home plate and tried to throw a baseball into a trash can laying on its side on second base. If the ball went in the can AND stayed, the fan won $100. Sound simple? No one won the $100 during the entire season.

If your ticket number was selected in the seventh inning and a Leopard hit a grand slam home run OUT of the ballpark in the bottom of the seventh, that lucky recipient won $10,000. It would have been great publicity if someone had been able to collect this, but no Leopard connected for a grand slam and no fan was able to collect in this contest.

On the back of every ticket was a coupon which, when presented at the ice cream stand across from the park, got the holder a free extra scoop of ice cream with the purchase of a regular cone. There were fewer than five hundred of these redeemed.

The other promotion during games was a 50/50 drawing. Before the game, fans could purchase tickets, one for a dollar or three for two dollars. During the eighth inning, a number was drawn and the lucky person split the pot 50/50 with the ball club. On one memorable occasion late in the season, the lucky winner's split totaled ten dollars!

There were a number of promotions during the early part of the season. But as the season wore on and revenues started going south for Mark, these were stopped as a cost-cutting measure.

On June 24, an Elvis Presley impersonator performed before 550 fans for an hour after the game. After five games Lafayette still ranked last in the league in attendance with an average of 493 fans per game. Jim Gonzales said, "I won't say we have been disappointed in the crowds. We have played on a couple of nights where we had conflicts, like Harrison playing in the state finals."

On July 3, the Leopards swept a doubleheader and moved into first place for the first time all season. Three hundred and forty fans attended the games. After ten home games the Leopards were averaging 427 fans a game. The local newspaper polled fans in a highlighted box on the front sports page and asked "If you have gone to a game, what made you decide to attend? If you haven't seen them play, what has kept you away?"

Following are some of the comments that were received:

"You've got to get more local players. That would help ticket sales."

"The Leopards only have three other opponents. When there's so much local interest in youth baseball, that is a limiting factor."

"Paying $5 to watch them play another team 20 times is not appealing."

"I went because I want to support them. But they also had an Elvis impersonator and my eight year old son likes Elvis."

"We never know when the games are."

# THE MEDIA

The local paper gave favorable coverage to the Leopards, covering all home games with a staff reporter. The paper ran a Leopard schedule nearly every day on page two of the sports section with starting times prominently displayed.

Away games were covered with line scores and phoned in stories. Updates of player statistics were printed weekly. All in all, the local paper provided a positive marketing opportunity. Sports columnists regularly wrote about the team and issues surrounding the team. The need for aggressive marketing was extolled in many of these. The paper also published letters from fans who supported the team.

The Leopards also received TV coverage with short clips shown on the 6:00 or 11:00 p.m. news along with the game results. Not much human interest was included in their coverage. The Leopards did not receive any radio coverage.

## THE SECOND HALF

At the All Star break, the Leopards were still in first place by percentage points. They were still last in the league in attendance, averaging 372 fans. Just five games exceeded 400. The two home games prior to the All Star break drew 245 and 118 fans. Gonzales stated, "As far as an entire organization, I'm a little disappointed in the attendance. Mark Dimmich has put his neck on the line to keep the ball club here in town, and I thought more people would support that because he's a local person."

Mark said on July 22, "The amount of money I lose is going to depend on how the rest of the season goes. I probably need a lot more promotional stuff. But all that takes money. I knew I could never do as much as I wanted to. But as far as costs go, I have done this about as cheaply as I could to minimize my losses. A team in a town like this would have to draw 500 to 800 fans a game to make this worthwhile."

On August 13 a crowd of 58 fans showed for a day game between the league's top two teams, Lafayette and Anderson. It was played in the afternoon as a rain makeup but could not be played at night because of schedule conflicts with the Colt World Series.

The season was winding to a close. The playoff format had been changed twice in the previous two weeks. On August 15, the integrity of the league was jeopardized when the East Chicago team walked off the field during a game with the Leopards. The core of the team had been experiencing a series of personality conflicts that culminated in their decision to quit after an inning and a half. They forfeited the game and told the Leopards that they were through for the year. This team had been in turmoil because their management had been extremely unstable from the beginning. The Anderson owner assumed responsibility of the East Chicago team to try to finish the league's first year. The Conquistador players returned after two days and in fact did finish the season after the one game hiatus.

Dimmich was extremely concerned because he was the only owner to have paid the $15,000 league fee as of August 15. Mark was keeping the league office open by paying the rent himself. He had signed a one year lease for $975 a month. Of this the league was paying $450 a month, which was coming from his ante. Dimmich stated, "I would like to keep a team here next year, but I can't see myself being fully involved in it. It's certainly been a lesson."

The season further unraveled on August 18 when Jim Gonzales announced he was quitting at the end of the season. He cited lack of community support, as evidenced by the average attendance of 350 fans per game. He said, "I look at this, and I say, I've done everything I really think I could possibly do and nothing has changed in the two years. Maybe they need someone else in here to do something different. I think Mark Dimmich kind of looks at it the same way."

On August 20, the Leopards beat East Chicago 12-2 to clinch the league championship for the second year in a row. At the completion of the game, Jim Gonzales said the season was over and there would be no playoffs. Two of four teams had honored their $15,000 dues commitment, which was enough for the league to break even. If everyone had paid, the league would have had $30,000 to prepare for 1996. Gonzales said, "We just got to the point where we felt that we were being real honorable with the things we were doing, and a couple of teams weren't. We just said that we needed to stand up and make a decision." Dimmich said that playoffs would not enhance revenues or lessen his losses and could increase losses. Mark said, "I hated to quit without playing the league championship but I felt like I had to make a statement to the other team owners." Gonzales said, "There was talk about playoffs but I don't think any good would come out of it. They would be counterproductive. Our hearts were not in it. I don't know if we could play for another week. It got to the point where it was not any fun to come to the ballpark." And so the 1995 season was over. Mark estimated his 1995 losses at over $20,000.

Now Mark is sitting in his darkened office. He is left with $1500 worth of Leopards souvenir items, an option for the next year at Loeb Stadium, a copyrighted team name, a mascot suit, and a concept for a professional baseball team for Lafayette. What should he do?

# Church's Chicken in "Navajoland"

Jon Ozmun, Northern Arizona University

Casey Donoho, Northern Arizona University

Mike Nelson watched from his table as a Navajo family stood at the counter and ordered fried chicken, mashed potatoes, gravy, and biscuits. As they moved away from the order taker, a young couple made their order and a line started to form behind them. It was the beginning of the lunch "rush" at the Church's Chicken Restaurant in Window Rock, Arizona. "It's going to be another good day selling drumsticks in 'Navajoland'," Mike thought to himself.

Nelson was the owner of the Church's Chicken Restaurant (CCR) in Window Rock. The business had been started in 1991 and had been a success almost from the first day. Fast food was as popular on the Navajo Reservation as it was in the rest of the country, and fried chicken seemed to be preferred over hamburgers, tacos, and pizzas by the Native American consumers.

The success of the Window Rock restaurant had prompted Nelson to consider expansion into other population centers of the Navajo Reservation. His first choice for the next Church's Chicken Restaurant was Tuba City, Arizona. Nelson preferred this location because it was one of the largest communities on the reservation and because he was already established in the community with other two retail businesses—a Tru-Value Hardware and a V&S Variety store. As Nelson watched the restaurant begin to fill with the lunch crowd, he wondered if Tuba City was the right location choice for his next "drumsticks" business.

# BACKGROUND

Michael Nelson, a Navajo, was born and raised on the Navajo Indian Reservation. He attended Bureau of Indian Affairs (BIA) boarding schools from the first through the twelfth grades. Nelson attended the BIA high school in Ft. Wingate, New Mexico, where he played on the "Bears" football and basketball teams. After graduating from high school, Nelson enrolled at Fort Lewis College in Durango, Colorado, and graduated with a BS in Business Administration.

After graduation, Nelson worked three years for the Farmers Group Insurance Company. For the next six years, he worked at the Office of Navajo Economic Opportunity as budget and office manager and business research assistant. He left this position to become a Community Economic Industrial Planner for the Phoenix Regional Small Business Administration, working with representatives of manufacturers, distributors, franchisers, banking and investment institutions, and municipal and civic leaders on and off Indian reservations. Nelson held this position for three years. He then rejoined the Navajo Tribe as an Economic Planner in the Navajo Economic Planning Office developing feasibility studies and business plans for Tribal programs.

In 1971, Nelson formed Michael Nelson & Associates, Inc. (MNA). During the years which followed, he received numerous awards and honors for his contributions to the Navajo business community. Nelson received the Small Business Administration's Incentive Award in 1970. In 1984 he was named the "Outstanding Indian Business Person of the Year" by the U.S. Organization of Indian Businesses. In 1985 Nelson was named "Outstanding Businessman" by the Minority Business Enterprises in the USA.

# MICHAEL NELSON & ASSOCIATES

MNA was incorporated in the State of Arizona in October 1971. Nelson's first business venture was a clothing store in Window Rock—Navajo Westerners Store. He later added the V&S Variety Store in Tuba City, convenience stores in Dilkon and Teesto, Arizona, and Tru-Value Hardware stores in Window Rock, Kayenta, and Tuba City. The most recent addition to Nelson's small retailing "empire" was the Church's Chicken Restaurant in Window Rock in 1991. All businesses of MNA are located on the Navajo Reservation.

MNA's retail stores have combined assets of over $2 million. In fiscal 1994, MNA profits exceeded $200,000 on sales revenues of over $6 million. MNA employs a work force of 70 Navajos in its operations. MNA annually contributes over $800,000 to the Navajo Reservation economy through salaries and wages alone.

# CHURCH'S CHICKEN RESTAURANT—WINDOW ROCK

In 1990, Nelson obtained a franchise from Church's Chicken Restaurants, Inc., for the purpose of opening a restaurant in Window Rock, Arizona. In the process, he obtained exclusive rights to Church's Chicken Restaurants in the Arizona portion of the Navajo Indian Reservation. Window Rock is the capital of the Navajo Nation and, according to the 1990 U.S. Census, had a population of 6,187. The Window Rock market area population was 11,718 (1990 U.S. Census).

For his CCR location, Nelson leased space in the newly constructed Window Rock Plaza Shopping Center. For an annual payment of $36,000, the Navajo Tribe provided Nelson a new 3,000 square foot facility finished to his specifications. Nelson opened the restaurant in 1991 and it made a $23,000 profit the first year. Sales revenues and profits grew steadily each year and during 1994, Nelson realized a net profit of $78,000 on sales of $710,000 (see Exhibit 1).

From the onset in Window Rock, Nelson had faced strong competition for the customers' business. There were ten different restaurant choices available to the customer, including two popular franchises—Kentucky Fried Chicken (KFC) and Lotta Burger. Nelson chose to compete directly with KFC for three reasons. First, fried chicken was the "right" product. Nelson's experience convinced him that his target market had a strong preference for fried food. Second, he believed that the Church's franchise offered distinct advantages over KFC: CCR prices were about 10% lower and portions were larger (CCR cut a chicken into six pieces while KFC cut the chicken into seven pieces.). CCR also allowed the flexibility to add items to the regular franchise menu and this was not possible with KFC. Third, he believed that the Window Rock KFC had a few very good employees, but overall the franchise was poorly managed and the physical facility was over twenty years old and poorly maintained.

Nelson's analysis of the competitive situation in Window Rock proved to be correct. The KFC franchise was especially vulnerable to the newer, better managed CCR. Nelson later learned some specifics from Carla Yazzie, one of the day managers at the KFC whom he hired during CCR's third year of operation. Yazzie told Nelson that revenues at the KFC dropped dramatically as soon as the CCR opened for business. Yazzie indicated that by the end of the first year of direct competition, KFC's revenues were down substantially, from about $500,000 in 1990 to about $250,000 in 1991. In the next two years, KFC's revenues recovered slowly to approximately $450,000.

| Exhibit 1 | **Historical Financial Statements—Church's Chicken Restaurant—Window Rock, Arizona (in thousands of dollars)** |

|                          | *1994* | *1993* | *1992* | *1991* |
|--------------------------|-------:|-------:|-------:|-------:|
| Revenues                 | $712   | $664   | $594   | $457   |
| Cost of Sales            | 250    | 235    | 232    | 174    |
| Gross Profit             | 462    | 429    | 362    | 283    |
| Lease Expense            | 36     | 36     | 36     | 36     |
| Other Operating Expense  | 306    | 286    | 274    | 201    |
| Total Operating Expense  | 342    | 322    | 310    | 237    |
| Depreciation             | 11     | 18     | 27     | 16     |
| Interest                 | 11     | 4      | 6      | 3      |
| Before Tax Profit        | 98     | 85     | 19     | 27     |
| Income Tax               | 20     | 17     | 3      | 4      |
| Net Profit               | $ 78   | $ 68   | $ 16   | $ 23   |

## THE TUBA CITY OPTION

Starting a new restaurant in Tuba City was a complex undertaking, but Nelson was convinced that it could be very successful. For a physical facility, a new building was to be constructed on land controlled by Nelson and adjacent to one of his existing businesses, the V&S Variety Store. The location was on the corner of two major traffic arteries, State Highway 264 and Navajo Boulevard. Nelson had employed an architect in Flagstaff, Arizona, to develop plans for the building and following this had obtained a firm bid for the cost to construct the building. After including the additional costs for equipment, fixtures, and installation, the total cost for the physical facility ready to do business was $700,000.

Tuba City had a larger retail trade sector than Window Rock. There were eleven restaurants, including a 7-year old, successful KFC (operating out of a clean, attractive facility), plus a McDonald's, a Taco Bell, and a Dairy Queen. The proposed location of the Church's Chicken Restaurant was between the KFC and McDonald's and across the street from Taco Bell and Dairy Queen. The restaurants were located within one-half mile of each other on Highway 264.

Nelson had already met with Jennifer Simpson, a Commercial Loan Officer at Norwest Bank in Prescott, Arizona, and indicated that he wanted to finance the new business with a combination of internal and external funds (see Exhibit 2). Nelson had an excellent record in his business relations with Norwest. They had provided the bulk of the financing for his CCR at Window Rock and he was current on his loan repayments. Simpson was receptive to the idea for providing funding to Nelson provided that the new business venture met their loan criteria.

Norwest's loan request package included five years of pro forma income and cash flow statements (see Exhibit 3—Letter from Norwest Bank). Based on his experience with Norwest Bank in obtaining financing for the CCR in Window Rock, Nelson knew that the Loan Officer would require detailed substantiation

---

**Exhibit 2**        **Capital Requirements and Sources Summary Church's Chicken Restaurant—Tuba City, Arizona**

| Requirements | |
|---|---|
| Design and Construct Facility | $500,000 |
| Fixtures, Furniture & Equipment | 200,000 |
| Inventory | 10,000 |
| Beginning Cash | 40,000 |
| Total Requirements | $750,000 |
| Sources | |
| Cash from Michael Nelson | $100,000 |
| Norwest Bank - Loan | 650,000 |
| Total Sources | $750,000 |

**Exhibit 3**          **Letter from Norwest Bank**

Mr. Michael Nelson
Church's Chicken Restaurant
Window Rock, Arizona 86887

Dear Mr. Nelson,

It was a pleasure to meet with you last week and discuss the proposal to open a new Church's Chicken Restaurant in Tuba City. Norwest Bank would appreciate the opportunity to provide the financing for this business venture. We invite you to submit a loan application for this proposal at your earliest convenience.

The major categories to be addressed in your loan proposal are:

1. An assessment of the market to be served including demographics, economic factors, and present and anticipated competition.
2. A description of the marketing strategy to be employed.
3. A management plan including the identification of key personnel and their responsibilities.
4. A financial plan including pro forma annual income and cash flow statements for the first five (5) years of operations.

As I noted in our conversation, it is very important that you generate a sales forecast that is based on a reliable methodology and is not overly optimistic. The traffic count model you mentioned, using information from your Window Rock restaurant, together with sales estimates from the Kentucky Fried Chicken restaurant in Tuba City and justifiable growth projections should satisfy our requirements in this area. Our loan review committee will accept cost estimates that are based on your experience with the Window Rock operation.

The loan amortization schedule for your pro forma income and cash flow statements should be based on the following information:

Interest rate:   9.75%

Term of loan:   Seven years (84 months)

Principal and interest payments would begin as soon as the restaurant opens for business and would be due monthly.

I hope to receive your loan application in the near future.

Sincerely,

Jennifer Simpson

Commercial Loan Officer

---

for his projected revenues and costs. The proposed business must also be able to show a positive net income by the third year and a cumulative positive net income for the five-year period. Finally, the proposed business must show positive pro forma cash flows over the period; that is, it must be able to meet its annual cash requirements without the need for additional cash infusions.

As he watched the customers come and go, Nelson went over in his mind the information required for the loan application. Firm, reliable estimates of the costs for the physical facilities at Tuba City had been made. Historical income statements were available from the Window Rock restaurant to use in estimating the costs for the new restaurant. The major tasks remaining were the development of a five year sales revenue forecast and subsequent pro forma financial statements.

## THE SALES FORECAST

Prior to his meeting with Ms. Simpson at Norwest Bank, Nelson had met with a business consultant regarding several financial aspects of the proposed restaurant, including the sales forecast. The consultant had advised Nelson to build a base level (first year) sales forecast using his experience at the Window Rock restaurant together with traffic count information from Window Rock and Tuba City. This base level sales forecast could then be adjusted each year for expected growth in his target market. When this sales forecasting technique had been discussed with Simpson, she was willing to use it.

Traffic counts would be taken at both the CCR in Window Rock and the KFC in Tuba City. These counts would be obtained during an identical time frame on the same days. Based on his experience in Window Rock, Nelson knew that weekdays were busier than weekends, so he decided to collect hourly traffic counts on a Tuesday and Saturday of the same week. In addition, sales revenues would be collected on an hourly basis at the CCR in Window Rock. The traffic count data had two uses: first to compare the size of the markets in Window Rock and Tuba City, and second to estimate the revenues of the KFC in Tuba City. With this information and Nelson's experience in competing directly with KFC in Window Rock, a base level sales forecast could be made. The traffic counts and revenue data were completed on January 28, 1994, and the results are shown in Exhibit 4.

Once the base level sales forecast was developed, forecasts for the remaining four years could be made using a "growth model" approach. Using this approach, the second year's revenues would be based on the base year; the third year's based on the second year; and so forth. The adjustment for growth would be based on either Nelson's experience at CCR in Window Rock or the expected retail sales growth in the Tuba City market. To facilitate this step, Nelson had gathered information on income and population growth in Arizona, the Navajo Nation, and Tuba City. This data is summarized in Exhibit 5.

## THE PRO FORMA FINANCIAL STATEMENTS

Nelson planned to complete the pro forma income statements by using the sales forecasts together with information from the historical income statements at the CCR in Window Rock. To generate the pro forma cash flow analysis, he intended to use a procedure he had learned while developing an earlier loan proposal. During the five-year period of analysis, he did not plan to vary inventory substantially from its beginning level of $10,000. Therefore, cash flow generated annually from operations could be estimated by the following calculation:

Cash Flow = Net Income + Depreciation - Principal Payment

If this calculation was positive, "cash flow" would be positive. Alternatively, if the calculation was negative, this indicated a negative "cash flow," requiring an infusion of additional capital to the business.

**Exhibit 4**  **Traffic Counts and Sales Data**

*Location:* Kentucky Fried Chicken—Tuba City, Arizona

*Dates:* Tuesday, January 24, and Saturday, January 28, 1995

| | | | Customers | | | |
| | Traffic | | Walk-ins | | Drive-ins | |
| | *1-24* | *1-28* | *1-24* | *1-28* | *1-24* | *1-28* |
|---|---|---|---|---|---|---|
| *Time Period* | | | | | | |
| 10–11AM | 975 | 192 | 13 | 3 | 5 | 2 |
| 11–Noon | 1125 | 789 | 50 | 14 | 11 | 5 |
| Noon–1PM | 1386 | 878 | 74 | 36 | 32 | 7 |
| 1–2PM | 758 | 803 | 62 | 18 | 12 | 8 |
| 2–3PM | 615 | 492 | 38 | 21 | 13 | 8 |
| 3–4PM | 819 | 643 | 19 | 21 | 11 | 7 |
| 4–5PM | 691 | 511 | 36 | 5 | 8 | 4 |
| 5–6PM | 1085 | 728 | 36 | 18 | 14 | 6 |
| 6–7PM | 702 | 803 | 13 | 67 | 14 | 10 |
| 7–8PM | 706 | 945 | 28 | 40 | 19 | 9 |
| 8–9PM | 380 | 783 | 20 | 46 | 9 | 14 |
| 9–Close | — | 363 | — | 24 | — | 7 |
| Totals | 9242 | 7930 | 389 | 313 | 134 | 87 |

*Location:* Church's Chicken Restaurant—Window Rock, Arizona

*Dates:* Tuesday, January 24, and Saturday, January 28, 1995

| | | | Customers | | | | | |
| | Traffic | | Walk-ins | | Drive-ins | | Sales | |
| | *1-24* | *1-28* | *1-24* | *1-28* | *1-24* | *1-28* | *1-24* | *1-28* |
|---|---|---|---|---|---|---|---|---|
| *Time Period* | | | | | | | | |
| 10–11AM | 186 | 320 | 11 | 10 | 8 | 2 | $ 93 | $ 40 |
| 11–Noon | 248 | 851 | 18 | 36 | 12 | 9 | 188 | 154 |
| Noon–1PM | 1311 | 813 | 62 | 21 | 10 | 2 | 399 | 107 |
| 1–2PM | 608 | 404 | 34 | 16 | 9 | 10 | 162 | 123 |
| 2–3PM | 1083 | 973 | 79 | 30 | 12 | 12 | 138 | 152 |
| 3–4PM | 507 | 762 | 26 | 26 | 14 | 10 | 120 | 156 |
| 4–5PM | 668 | 761 | 53 | 20 | 8 | 3 | 201 | 100 |
| 5–6PM | 1071 | 836 | 31 | 28 | 16 | 14 | 174 | 182 |
| 6–7PM | 801 | 615 | 35 | 30 | 24 | 16 | 248 | 206 |
| 7–8PM | 768 | 468 | 34 | 24 | 20 | 14 | 189 | 148 |
| 8–9PM | 1405 | 534 | 36 | 33 | 14 | 9 | 301 | 255 |
| 9–Close | 523 | 620 | — | 6 | — | 10 | — | 125 |
| Totals | 9179 | 7957 | 419 | 283 | 147 | 111 | $2213 | $1748 |

**Exhibit 5**                 **Demographic Data**

### Market Area Populations - Current and Forecast

|  | Census 1990 | Forecast 1995 | Forecast 2000 |
|---|---|---|---|
| Window Rock | 6187 | 6806 | 7487 |
| Window Rock Market Area | 11718 | 12890 | 14179 |
| Tuba City | 7983 | 8901 | 9924 |
| Tuba City Market Area | 8983 | 10002 | 11141 |

### Population and Personal Income Growth Rates (%)

|  | 1990 | 1991 | 1992 | 1993 | 1994 | 1995 | 1996–2000 |
|---|---|---|---|---|---|---|---|
| Arizona Population Growth | 2.3 | 2.1 | 2.4 | 2.4 | 2.5 | 2.5 | 2.6 |
| Personal Inc. Growth | 5.6 | 4.5 | 6.6 | 7.0 | 8.1 | 8.3 | 8.0 |
| Per Capita Inc. Growth | 3.3 | 2.1 | 4.2 | 4.6 | 5.6 | 5.8 | 5.4 |
| Navajo Nation Per Capita Income Growth | 1.9 | 0.6 | 2.7 | 3.1 | 4.1 | 4.3 | 3.9 |
| Tuba City Population Growth |  |  |  |  |  | 2.2 | 2.2 |

Source: U.S. Census 1990 - Population and Housing Characteristics of the Navajo Nation

## THE DECISION

Nelson was scheduled to meet with the Norwest Commercial Loan Officer in two weeks. The project would either move ahead or be aborted based on the pro forma financial statements.

Nelson refocused his attention to the activity at the restaurant. He noticed that the lunch "rush" was about over and most of the booths were now empty. Two employees, Navajo youths of high school age, were busy tidying up the facility. Glancing outside, he observed a slow but steady stream of drive-in customers arriving and departing with their "drumsticks." "I will sure be excited to get started on my next restaurant," Nelson thought to himself.

# Kovacs Farms: The Flue-Cured Tobacco Business in Ontario

David R. Frew, Gannon University

S teve Kovacs arrived at Vanderbilt University as a freshman in the tumultuous 1960's. The culture of the middle south, the music, and the intellectual climate were new and exciting, wildly different from his home in Southern Ontario. Steve had grown up on a tobacco farm and learned an incredible work ethic. Tobacco farming was (and still is) backbreaking manual labor, and Steve, eldest of three sons, had been an exemplary son. He responded to his family's needs by learning to rise early, often working for several hours before the school bus came.

Steve's family was proud when their son won an academic scholarship to the prestigious American university. Even though it was hard to say goodbye in 1964, they wished him the best, hoping that pre-med studies would propel him toward a better life than he could have had "on the farm."

Steve excelled academically. What he lacked in scholastic preparation was more than compensated for by discipline, energy, and a farm-born work ethic. During his four undergraduate years he managed to graduate cum laude in microbiology and impress the faculty with his hands-on growing skills. He was a favorite in the university horticultural labs, learning to graft plants with success that the best faculty could only envy.

Vanderbilt also taught Steve two other important lessons. The first was that he did not want to be a physician. He became cynical about medical practice as a pre-med student and began to think that he would be happier in business or dealing with people (he had talent in both areas). Second, and more important, Steve met his soul mate and wife-to-be Connie. She was the most beautiful girl in freshman biology and it wasn't long until they were an item.

After graduation Steve and Connie moved to Toronto where he went to work for a public accounting firm as an auditor. His farming background had taught him a lot about business and Steve's work ethic and people skills made him a natural with clients. Steve's boss encouraged him to enroll in the University of Toronto's MBA program as a part time student and by 1975 he had earned his MBA, completed the tests to become a Registered Public Accountant (Canadian CPA), and settled into professional life in the city. By this time he and Connie were married and had two children.

# THE CALL OF THE FARM

But something was nagging inside Steve, telling him that he was in the wrong line of work. He was a success and had made lots of money. He and Connie had purchased a house in the suburbs for $80,000 which was appreciating rapidly, and they had managed to save almost another $100,000 through a self-designed investment plan. In the fall of 1975 Steve and Connie's oldest child began school and Steve began to develop an appreciation for the lack of teachers in the public school systems. As he worked with the Parents' Association and spent time in school he struck up a relationship with the principal. One day at an accidental meeting, his son's principal said, "Steve, if I had a faculty of persons like you, with a variety of experiences and enthusiasm, this would be a truly great school!"

That evening Steve and Connie talked about their life. They had plenty of money and security but Steve was growing frustrated with his job. The accounting firm had taken advantage of his enthusiasm, using him on the most challenging assignments. Meanwhile as Steve's career progressed he spent less time with his family. More importantly his work was becoming stale. After several year-end audits and tax preparations, there was not much to learn.

At Christmas time Steve asked his son's principal if he was serious about the teaching offer. Shortly after the first of the year, he had become a middle school teacher instructing 7th through 9th grade Business, Biology, and Geography. The principal loved him almost as much as the kids since he could teach almost any subject: bookkeeping, math, biology, chemistry, history and more. And at first Steve loved it too. He had more time with his family. He drove his kids to school each day and had an opportunity to see them at lunch. He enrolled in evening graduate classes in a program which was paid for by the Toronto Regional School System, earning a Master's Degree in Education in 18 months.

By 1980 external circumstances would have suggested that Steve's career transition was a success. His family was happy, he and Connie had adjusted to their lower income, their cash savings still allowed them to live well (especially for a teacher), and his teaching was regarded as exceptional. But the sleepless nights returned. This time, however, Steve and Connie were talking about the work ethic (or lack thereof) of his students. Steve was deeply troubled by his observation that most students were sleepwalking through high school. He wondered if any of them would be able to work hard and become a success as he had at Vanderbilt. He also worried about his own children. What was he teaching them by bringing them up in this urban environment? Would they have the advantages of understanding practical things and being able to work hard (as he had on the farm in Walsingham, Ontario)? The tobacco farm was beginning to look better and better.

In December, Steve took his family to Walsingham after Christmas to celebrate the holidays with his family. His parents, now in their mid 60's, were still running two of the family farms, and his brothers had never left the area. This year, however, things were not as festive as usual. After dinner, Steve's brothers asked him to go for a walk. Once they passed the barn their discussion grew serious.

Tobacco farming is intense work and the elder Kovacs had grown tired of the day-to-day demands. Earlier that year he had announced to Steve's brothers that he was selling out of the tobacco business and going into a new line of work on the farm. A Hungarian immigrant, Mr. Kovacs was an avid hunter and had always dreamed of owning a wild boar hunting farm. Northern Europeans value boar as a holiday treat (as North Americans love turkey) and he decided to build a boar raising business. His plan was to fence in a farm with its uncleared woods and use the barn as the epicenter of a guided hunting operation. He would purchase breeding stock, raise it in the barn where he had once raised chickens and cows, and then allow the boar to roam the fenced-in woods.

Hunters would come to the farm to hunt boar for a fee, or if they preferred, Mr. Kovacs would slaughter and ship the meat on demand. Steve's brothers were concerned that the idea was foolish and would risk family finances. "He has finally lost it Steve," exclaimed Joe Kovacs. "He thinks that all of his old Hungarian and Dutch cronies are going to come here and pay big bucks to shoot wild pigs!" "Most of Dad's friends are living in old people's homes and eating canned Christmas turkey with dentures," added Steve's youngest brother Mat. "You have to talk him out of this!"

Pondering the dilemma, Steve gave his brothers the answer that his father had given him years earlier about going to Vanderbilt. "Dad is a smart successful businessman and he has worked all of his life. He deserves to follow his dreams. And after all he made a success out of a crazier venture, like tobacco, hasn't he!" That evening, as Steve's dad outlined his plans, Steve nodded approval, offering a toast. Connie added that it was time for the parents to take it a little easier and have some fun. On the drive back to Toronto, however, Steve shared his concerns with Connie. He was secretly worried about his dad and about the boar farm venture.

## THE ONTARIO TOBACCO INDUSTRY

Most people are shocked to learn of the tobacco business in Southern Ontario. The tobacco belt there is a 1000 square mile area just north of Central Lake Erie extending 15 to 20 miles south of the lake shore. The retreat of the Wisconsin glacier from Central Lake Erie (just west of Long Point) deposited a sandy soil mixture which, in combination with the high rainfall and moderate temperatures caused by proximity to the lake, created perfect tobacco growing conditions.

The first growers were the local Indians. The tobacco grown in the region was an important source of trade and commerce among Native Americans prior to the arrival of the Europeans. When settlers migrated to the north shore of Lake Erie (today's Ontario), the crop was growing in the wild.

The primary thrust in the growth of the business was an expansionist move by a North Carolina based tobacco company (The American Tobacco Company) which decided to experiment with farming and processing near Leamington, Ontario (80 miles west of today's tobacco belt). The first experiments with burley (cigar) type tobacco were a success. In a few short years a steady stream of southerners was emigrating north to Canada to join the new tobacco business.

By the 1920's cigarettes began to replace cigars in the North American market. But the transition from burley to the flu-cured (cigarette) tobacco did not work well in Leamington. Gradually farmers shifted east toward the central portion of Lake Erie until they came to the "Norfolk Sand Plain" (today's tobacco belt) where soil conditions were perfect. By the 1940's they had developed agricultural strategies which differed slightly from those of the Carolinas but were quite efficient, resulting in plant quality equal to that of the south.

Farmers in Ontario begin production by planting seeds in sterilized soil inside greenhouses. As sprouts develop they are carefully cultivated in heated conditions and climatized by systematically removing glass from the greenhouses. By mid May the greenhouses are open to the elements and the heartiest of the plants are culled out for transplantation to the fields. By early June all of the young tobacco shoots are planted in neat rows in the fields. The crop is then tended just as it would be in the south. In the fall plants are individually picked, tied on stakes, and hung in out-buildings (called kilns) for drying. The kilning (drying) process is an art. Doors and windows are alternately opened and closed, heat is added, and the stakes of plants themselves are rotated in order to achieve optimum drying.

Drying success is so critical to the ultimate quality (and market value) of the product that most farmers hire a Carolina-based professional kilner to orchestrate the process. The kilner makes strategic decisions relative to how long to leave the crop in the drying building, when to move it up and down (within the kiln) for best effects, and when and for how long to open windows or add artificial heat. Once dry, plants are moved to the main barn for sorting, bailing, and storage but during the critical kilning process the tobacco is in the absolute control of the kilner, who is to tobacco approximately what the old German brew master was to beer.

In 1957 a tobacco cooperative called the "Ontario Flue-Cured Tobacco Marketing Board" was formed in the tobacco belt and settled in Tillsonburg. The organization, which was drawn together to help give Ontario's industry a competitive advantage on the world market, soon evolved into an economic force. Today's "Marketing Board" includes a headquarters building, a tobacco museum, and three organized annual tobacco auction sites (Aylmer, Delhi, and Tillsonburg) which operate in the Dutch style (beginning at a high price and bidding down). The Dutch system results in fast transactions (900 metric tons per day). The tobacco board meets each year to establish market price minimums which insure each farmer a reasonable economic reward for the year's crop. They also broker relationships between buyers and the eight registered Canadian processors who in turn process, package, and ship the crop either domestically or overseas. Perhaps their most important annual duty, however, is the estimation of the following year's market size. This figure, in combination with each farmer's quota, governs the amount of tobacco which can (legally) be sold.

The system works like this: The Marketing Board annually announces to the tobacco farmers the percentage of the total Ontario quota which will be grown and sold the next year. The Marketing Board controls 323 million pounds of tobacco quota. Thus if, during a particular year, the potential import and export market is estimated to be 60% of that (323 million pound) total, farmers are instructed to grow 60% of their individual quotas. As might be expected, the farmers wait with anticipation to hear this figure each year. This has been even more true recently since growing efficiencies have created excess farm capacity.

# TOBACCO, SIN TAX, AND HEALTH CARE

The tobacco industry in Southern Ontario grew steadily during the post-war period. When demand for cigarettes began to falter in the late 1970's as a result of negative publicity regarding smoking, European and Asian demand picked up dramatically. For tobacco farmers the only discernable change was in the country of origin of the purchasers at the auctions. Since 50.1% (1992) of Canadian tobacco is exported, domestic demand for cigarettes has not been an issue. Within Canada itself, the number of new smokers is declining in Ontario, but increasing in Quebec.

The biggest changes in the industry came about as a result of political processes. In the late 1970's pressures grew in Canada to develop a national health plan. While each province was left to the design details, the final programs which were presented to the Canadian public were all similar. Best known of these is the Ontario Health Insurance Program (OHIP) which has been cited by many Americans as a model plan (OHIP was the basis for much of the Clinton initiative).

Even though OHIP managed to eliminate insurance and litigation as component parts of the health care costs, the Ontario plan promised to be quite expensive. The plan promised "womb to tomb" coverage and it extended health care benefits to every member of society. Politicians were pleased with the potential benefits of OHIP and the elimination of private insurance and litigation costs, but worried about program funding. Just as they were entering discussions, the media was beginning to exclaim the terrible health hazards of smoking. There was a social concern that somehow the tobacco industry should be made to pay the health care bill since so many diseases were linked to smoking.

It did not take long for Ontario (and other provincial) legislators to conclude that the way out of the funding dilemma was to tax tobacco. In a round of what now looks to have been "magical thinking," the architects of OHIP projected that a schedule of slowly increasing taxes on cigarettes, levied both at the farm and consumer levels, could be used to fund health care. It was reasoned that tax revenues could be specifically targeted at health care costs associated with smoking as well as public health programming aimed at convincing Canadians to stop using tobacco products. Legislators reasoned that the decreasing stream of cash resulting from reduced smoking (and subsequent tax revenues) would coincide with the end of smoking by the general public. This would be accompanied by an eventual decrease in health care costs associated with the cessation of the treatment of smoking-related health problems.

The economics of the situation, however, proved to be quite different. Cigarette advertising (especially in U.S. based media) increasingly seemed to attract new (young) smokers, and the demand for cigarettes proved to be inelastic. As prices went up, the quantity of cigarettes smoked per consumer did not change. To exacerbate the situation the systematic linkage between cigarette taxes and the cost of health care (which rose dramatically during the 1980's) continued to drive up the cost of a package of Canadian cigarettes relative to U.S. prices. By 1990 a Canadian pack cost $6.00 as compared to the US. price of $1.50. The tax differential created a natural opening for smuggling, offering an immediate advantage of $4.50 per pack (or $40.00 per carton). Given the fact that the Canadian/U.S. border is some 4000 miles long and mostly unpatrolled, the opportunities were too good to be ignored.

Visionaries among the early architects of OHIP had recognized the potential for cigarette smuggling and other tobacco tax avoidance manipulations and decided to design a new grower control system. Prior to 1975, each individual tobacco farm was restricted to 50 acres of crop. Farmers generally produce 2200 to 3000 pounds per acre. A bale of tobacco weighs approximately 48 pounds and results in roughly 125 cartons of cigarettes (at 200 cigarettes per carton).

In 1976 a new quota system was introduced in which tobacco farmers owned "shares," granting the right to sell tobacco. At the onset of this system the number of shares granted to each existing farmer was based statistically upon the number of farms that were operated and the amount of tobacco that had been produced in the recent past. The original share system was based upon a per share par value which was established for each share. To grow and market a pound of crop legally, a farmer had to own a share of quota. Tobacco shares were valued at $1.00 and placed on the commodity market. The shares soon developed a financial life of their own, however, and values rocketed from their original ($1.00) designated value to $2.20 by 1980. Private investors were selling and buying tobacco shares in anticipation of shifts in the world market. A number of farmers noticed that the market value of their quota (shares) was far in excess of potential crop profits. A farmer who had been cultivating 100 acres of crop, for example, might have 250,000 shares which could be converted instantaneously to $550,000.00

Farmers began to cash out and retire, leaving vacant 100 acre tobacco farms for sale. The problem for potential entrants into the business was that the market value of the shares had risen to the point where it was impossible to get started in the business. The uncertainties in the financial market along with general turbulence in the industry sent tobacco growing into a tail spin, with total Ontario sales falling from 209 million pounds in 1975 to a low of 110 million pounds in 1987. In response to this trend share values fell to $1.00 in 1986, $.65 in 1987, and a record low of $.25 in 1989 (by 1994 the share value had risen to $1.05).

## THE NEW PROHIBITION

As the 1980's wore on more and more Canadians began to "dabble" in contraband cigarettes. There had been plenty of impetus for this kind if activity in the 1930's when the U.S. enacted its prohibition against liquor. Canadians from along the borders (especially in the Lake Erie and St. Lawrence River areas) had made millions during those adventuresome years running alcoholic beverages to welcoming American "gangsters." For Canadians, who were legally allowed to manufacture and sell booze, rum running was almost considered an honorable profession. Consequently the folk lore of smuggling (which was still alive and well as cigarette problems began to emerge) made Canadians more inclined to dabble in shady enterprises.

Tax avoidance mechanisms took a number of different turns during the 1980's. Natives, for example, purchased cigarettes on a tax-free basis acting from treaty rights. They then sold them at slightly less than market values, enjoying huge profits. Organized smugglers used more extreme measures. These ranged from secreting thousands of cartons of cigarettes (purchased in the U.S.) in trucks and sneaking them across Buffalo's Peace Bridge or the Ambassador Bridge in Detroit. In general, customs officials are too busy handling traffic to catch anyone. In 1993 a lumber truck carrying plywood was found to have all but the top layers of wooden panels hollowed out and containing thousands of cartons of cigarettes. In 1992 a series of tanker trucks were found to have false panels installed in the tanks and loads which proved to contain thousands of cartons of cigarettes instead of fuel oil. Customs officials estimate that they are catching only 10 to 15 percent of this kind of traffic.

Store owners or their suppliers are known to drive across the bridges in passenger cars, purchase hundreds of cartons of cigarettes, and recross the borders into Canada claiming that they have nothing to declare. The chance of getting caught this way has been estimated to be well below 5%.

The most "romantic" smuggling goes on in the spirit of the old rum runners with American boats transferring huge loads of cigarettes (purchased in the U.S.) to Canadian vessels which simply do not report to customs. During the summer of 1993 this kind of activity was so rampant in the St. Lawrence River that the U.S. Coast Guard announced it would no longer perform night time rescues. There was so much smuggling activity in the river after dark that they were afraid of being fired upon by cigarette smugglers who were overzealous about protecting their stock. In the early winter of 1994, the RCMP reported a gunfight in which police officers set off in pursuit of smugglers in snowmobiles running loads of cigarettes across the frozen St. Lawrence.

For tobacco growers there is another more pressing avenue for contraband sales, the "illegal" sale of non-quota crop. Most of the farmers who have purchased the rights to sell quota actually produce more than their allowable quota. This is because they don't want to take the risk of having too little to bring to market. For the average farmer this overage is usually in the neighborhood of 8 percent of quota. When the selling season is over it is not unusual to have 100 or more bales of tobacco left in the barn. It is not legal to sell that tobacco, but since Canada enacted its GST (a value added tax), many citizens have complained that their income, sales, and other taxes (compared to those of the U.S.) are unreasonable. Many Canadians feel that the existing quotas and taxation systems are obstacles to be avoided, and have reacted by developing an increasingly troublesome "black market economy."

In this environment it is not surprising that small entrepreneurs travel the tobacco belt stopping at farms to inquire about "extra" bales of tobacco. They are willing to pay well over the fixed market price for a bale on a "cash basis." These black market entrepreneurs take tobacco home, dry it in homemade equipment, and process it into cigarettes (using commercially available rolling machines). These are packaged in innocuous "generic type packages" given counterfeit tax stamps and sold to retail outlets. There is growing concern among farmers that a large amount of product is being sold that way and if they do not take advantage of this opportunity, they are simply missing the "boat."

In February 1994 the Premier of Quebec announced that he was going to take steps against the growth of cigarette smuggling by lowering taxes. Bob Rae, Premier of Ontario, objected, stating that this action would put his province in a terrible predicament. Ontario was increasingly dependent upon revenue from cigarette taxation and he was unable to lower taxes, but there was no way (legal or otherwise) to stop cigarettes from moving between provinces. The Quebec policy change would both stimulate existing tax avoidance schemes in Ontario and begin an inflow of the product from Quebec. To put the taxation problem in perspective, in 1993 an average bale of tobacco netted the farmer $80 and the government $3700. As the farmers complained that they were being squeezed out of business by taxes, smuggling, and government mishandling, Canada was becoming increasingly dependent upon tobacco tax revenues.

## THE 1980 BOAR FARM

To escape the craziness of the turbulent tobacco business elder Kovacs cashed in some of his tobacco quota in 1980, purchased a vacant farm, and began his boar shooting farm. His timing in cashing out shares was exquisite. The paper transaction generated cash which allowed for the purchase of a new (fourth) farm with buildings, restoration of the house on that farm into a lodge for the hunters, and the conversion of a number of outbuildings into bed and breakfast accommodations. In addition, breeding stock was purchased and a number of vehicles were added to transport hunters around the area. The farm was fenced in, a barn was converted for boar raising with a butchering facility, and the necessary licenses were obtained.

The first hunting season was reasonably successful. Everyone had heard of the venture and their long-time allegiance with the Kovacs family inspired them to at least visit if not take a stab at boar hunting. At year end Mr. Kovacs was happy to tell his family that he had come within $20,000 of breaking even. Steve and his brothers were growing concerned.

The second year, Mr. Kovacs grew discouraged when business worsened. Steve's brothers' fears seemed to be coming true. Modern Canadians were simply not interested in eating boar meat. To make matters worse elder Kovacs fell in late December and broke a leg. During his recovery in early January, Steve's mother had a heart attack.

In February Steve and his brothers had a conference with the family physician. "You have to talk him into retiring, Steve," suggested Doc Peterson. "They're just too old to be starting such a wild new business venture. People their age should be living in condominiums and going to Florida for the winter." "You're the only one who can do it," added his brothers. "He listens to you!"

In early March, Steve visited his father's banker to ask for financial details. The elder Kovacs' farm holdings now included 4 farms (600 total acres) with a total of 11 houses. Three of the farm houses were used by Mr. Kovacs and Steve's two brothers. One was rented and the others were either vacant or dedicated to the bed and breakfast operation at the Boar Farm. The estimated market value of all of this property (with buildings) was only $387,000 because of the current high cost of tobacco quota and the fact that there were many vacant farms in the region.

Steve's youngest brother Mat had lost interest in farming. He lived in one of the houses but commuted to a job in Simcoe. His interest in the situation was simply concern for his father and mother. The next older brother, Joe, was actively farming. He had not, however, been able to save much money since he had never really done anything but work for his father on the farm.

After speaking to his brothers and mother Steve developed a plan and went back to Toronto to discuss it with Connie. His old accounting firm helped with the legal problems, and Steve's principal granted him a leave as of March break to go home to square things away on the farm. In late March, Steve approached his father with the following proposal.

Two separate corporations would be drawn up. The first would be a land holding corporation which would own all of the farm lands and buildings except those lived in by the family. This corporation (consisting of Mr. and Mrs. Kovacs (one share), Steve, and his two brothers) would lease the farmland to a second corporation consisting of Steve and Connie. Steve's farming brother would be a salaried employee of the farming corporation. The farming corporation would buy the main farmhouse, barn, kilns, tobacco quota (of 150,000 shares) and surrounding 10 acres from elder Kovacs for $300,000. This would include all of the supplies, stock in process, and farming equipment, as well as the equipment purchased for the Boar Farm.

The three brothers (including Steve) would keep the houses where they were currently living and each would own 10 acres of land immediately surrounding their houses. Steve's two brothers were to pay an agreed upon market value for their individual farm houses in the form of a monthly payment (annuity) to their parents. Steve agreed to pay his brother an annual salary of $35,000 (approximately what his parents had been paying him).

The land-holding corporation agreed to lease the land to Steve for the nominal fee of $1000 per year for five years and then for 10% of farm operation profits over the next 8 years. It was agreed that the question of land rental fees would be reevaluated after that time. Under Canadian tax law the Land Holding Corporation is independent from the Farm Corporation.

## STEVE AND CONNIE'S TOBACCO FARM

At first, elder Kovacs objected. But after family persuasion, and his growing sense of Steve's enthusiasm for the new venture, he agreed, signing the official papers in April of 1982. Steve and Connie told the kids that they would be moving to Walsingham. Steve was looking forward to a life style where he and Connie could work together, and involve their children in their dream.

Back in Toronto, Connie sold their home and a car. Coupled with the most liquid parts of Steve's investment portfolio and his teacher's pension, they were able to raise $307,000. Steve paid his parents $150,000 and placed the remaining cash in the farm bank, receiving a $250,000 line of credit. Steve's parents purchased a condominium in Port Rowan, some 20 miles away, for $90,000 and vacated the main farm house making space for Connie and the kids when school ended that spring.

As Steve and his brother worked the farm that first year, his accountant's mind began to think in terms of diversification. Even with his considerable growing skill, and his ability to digest and learn the latest scientific support information from the Marketing Board and its research station in Delhi, he recognized the inherent risk in having all of his "financial eggs" in one basket. He had a healthy line of credit and felt confident of his relationship with the bank but still a few bad years could cripple him. Tobacco farmers generally use Mexican Mennonites to do much of the manual labor and the wages paid to them are not great, but could he withstand a crop failure? Long-term statistics suggested that the average farmer would lose a crop once in 12 years. Steve hoped that if this eventuality came to be, it would be in the 10th or 11th year, if at all.

As the last of 1982's tobacco plants were being transplanted to the fields and the rush of spring planting was ending, Steve developed his first diversification strategy. He was lying in bed with Connie one night talking about his ideas when she reminded him of his Vanderbilt days. "It's too bad you're through with the greenhouses, Steve," she remarked. "That was your favorite part of college." "Wow," he replied, "I should think of something to do with those greenhouses between May and March, shouldn't I?" The next week a truck backed up to the barn and dropped off several thousand ornamental tree cuttings, mostly evergreen types. By the end of the month the cuttings were growing happily in the main greenhouses, being jump-started in the rich tobacco soil.

The landscape tree business represented Steve and Connie's first major diversification. The plan was to accelerate the normal growth of these trees by greenhousing them for the first summer. In early spring, before tobacco planting, the trees are moved to the fields where they are cultivated into commercial landscape type plants selling for $100 or more, depending upon type. As Steve concentrated on growing, Connie studied decorating and landscaping trends, in an attempt to predict the kinds of trees which would be in demand in 6 to 10 years. By the third year they identified a lucrative substrategy. In late November, Steve would walk the fields looking for stunted trees which did not seem to have optimum growing potential. These would be marked, cut, and sold as Christmas trees.

At the first annual meeting of the landholding corporation, Steve's dad suggested that the various outbuildings, the lodge from the boar farm, and two unused farmhouses be actively rented or offered as bed and breakfasts. Steve's mom, who was feeling quite well by now, offered her services in the reclamation, redecorating, and management. There were 11 buildings in total plus the lodge, which could accommodate up to four families. In the second year of operation, the lodge and five of the smaller outbuildings were listed as a part of Ontario's "Farm Vacation" program and business grew. By the third year Steve and his brother had renovated three of the other buildings and converted the remaining three to permanent housing. The rental income as well as the bed and breakfast business provided a flow of cash for the land-holding corporation.

The first three crop years were successful beyond Steve's expectation. The marketing board established average percentage bases of over 50% and Steve's growing skills resulted in production excesses of 18%. The fourth year, 1986, was a disaster. Steve's crop was infected with blue mold and he lost almost 70% of the total. That fall was a depressing time for Steve and Connie. They spent a lot of time riding the back acres (land not used for tobacco) in their truck talking and worrying, wondering if they could withstand another bad crop.

As they rode one sunny November afternoon, Connie commented on the beauty of the back acres and the fact that no matter what, they could always depend on their rental incomes. "I have an idea!" Steve blurted out. "Let's develop some residential lots. We're already in the business. We own the land, and we have most of the equipment. What do we have to lose?" That afternoon Steve and Connie used their tractor to mark the proposed locations of several roads leading to the first of 30 lots which they marked off on a map of the farms. They selected non-tillable wooded land, within sight of streams and close to roads. They quickly realized that this idea would create a second major diversification. And with changes in the housing market and suburban sprawl, Walsingham (considered rural in the 1970's) was fast becoming the outreaches of suburbia for residents of Simcoe, Port Dover, and Delhi.

Following a good crop year in 1987, Steve observed that the value of his tobacco quota had fallen to $.32 (from a high of $2.20). In a move motivated as much by land acquisition for his real estate venture as it was by the potential to buy more quota or to price average, he purchased another 120 acres with a house, barn, and 100,000 shares of quota. The $74,000 farm was owned by the land holding corporation, while the quota ($32,000) was purchased by Steve and Connie.

In 1988 he planted tobacco on the new farmlands, adding to his old crop totals (his enlarged quota was 250,000). Providentially 1987 was a good market year, with total Ontario sales rising from 110 to 130 million pounds and the grower's quota percentage increasing from 28.6% to 37.3%. The quota rose again in 1989 but fell in 1990, sending a wave of discouragement through the grower's community. By the end of 1992 (even though quota percentages had risen again to about 47%), Steve and many of his fellow tobacco farmers were increasingly concerned with the politicization of the tobacco business and the role of tobacco in the Free Trade Agreement. In the U.S., content restriction legislation was passed which threatened exports ($20 million in 1992) to America. The farmers complained that they were not being protected under Free Trade and that the federal government was underrepresenting their export needs as they worried about NAFTA.

In 1991 Steve launched a new (financially based) diversification which was associated with his real estate development project. He had begun to recognize that a large number of persons were having a difficult time securing financing for purchasing the homes that he was building. In his view many "good risks" were turned down for mortgage loans. After two exceptionally good crop years, Steve had accumulated a relatively large reserve of cash which was languishing in low-interest bank accounts. Steve organized a consortium of five fellow farmers in similar situations and convinced them to begin a business of loaning mortgage funds to individuals who were having difficulty securing loans to buy his houses. He reasoned that even if a few defaulted, he would be in control of their property and able to resell it. In the first year they each invested $200,000 and incorporated in an organization which is financially independent from the farm operations. They are loaning funds at 11 to 14% to home buyers and have had no defaults to date.

## GINSENG AND THE FUTURE

But this diversification was not the total answer to insecurities in the tobacco market. By this time the Marketing Board had gathered powerful statistics to indicate the extent and seriousness of the contraband tobacco market. Their data suggested that the entire industry could be heading toward a financial crisis.

As tobacco farmers throughout the region watched the wild gyrations of the market they increasingly turned to the Marketing Board for advice. The laboratories at Delhi had preached diversification (as a risk minimization strategy) but had found little success with raising other crops in the sandy tobacco soil. In the late 1980's, however, the marketing board began to suggest the production of ginseng. There was (and still is) a surplus world demand for ginseng root and the crop is easily adapted to the conditions of Southern Ontario's tobacco belt.

The difficulty with growing ginseng lies in the extreme cost of production (estimated at 45 to 50 thousand dollars per acre) in combination with the relative lack of information about growing technologies and disease prevention. Ginseng is harvested as a root. It is grown under a cheesecloth canopy (simulating its natural habitat at the floor of mature forests) which is supported by a network of stakes placed at three foot intervals. It takes three to four years to bring a crop to harvest, and tobacco farmers worry that several kinds of unpredictable calamities could occur during that time. A 10-acre diversification into ginseng, for example, would cost approximately $500,000, creating the potential for financial disaster. There is also a concern that if a large number of farmers begin production, there could be an oversupply.

On the positive side, Ontario's earliest ginseng farmers report that they are harvesting between 2200 and 2600 pounds per acre and selling at prices ranging from $55 to $70 per pound. Top-end production could result in potential profits of $132,000 per acre per three year growing cycle. This would mean $1.3 million for a ten acre crop. There is an added concern, however, that the profit potential could stimulate interest in British Columbia and other provinces, thus further risking an oversupply.

As the 1994 crop season approaches Steve and Connie are puzzling over the dilemma of how to plan the next several years for their business. Tobacco is still highly profitable and one simple solution to the future might be to hold steady on existing diversifications and try to ride out the decade by maximizing attention to the tobacco crop. As they approach 50 years of age, however, they wonder how much longer they can keep up the work pace demanded by the tobacco business. Their two children are in high school now, and if the crop holds out until the year 2000 they will both have graduated from college, allowing Steve and Connie to ease their work pace and go into semi-retirement. The increased politicization and changes in the externals of the tobacco business, however, are more than troubling to Steve and Connie, and they are concerned that the industry could self-destruct.

As they consider the strategy of working hard for 5 to 10 more years and then retiring, however, they are concerned about their family. The land holding partnership has thrived since Steve developed it, but it has done so through the shepherding and success of Steve and Connie's initiatives. If they were to withdraw, the elder Kovacs (now in their 70's) and Steve's two brothers could be left in a tenuous position with regard to making a living. Steve and Connie also wonder if their own children might not be interested in returning to the farm after college. Given employment prospects these days, it might be useful for them to keep things going at the farm until such time as their two sons can return to take over the farm.

If they were to diversify, Steve and Connie wonder how much emphasis they should place in each of the individually incorporated ventures. Should they reduce their risk by adding ginseng production to tobacco, and continuing with real estate development? Lately they have been wondering about the construction of multi-unit dwellings in either condominium or apartment formats. Given the economy in North America, these kinds of units might be the easiest to sell over the next decade, and maintaining ownership or managership of them would insure a continuous cash flow. A diversification strategy of some sort would help insure against the potential financial problems of another crop failure, such as the blue mold experienced across Southern Ontario 1986.

Steve and Connie are also concerned about the fate of the land holding corporation with respect to its agreement to lease farm lands at 10% of the tobacco crop profits (before corporate taxes). In recent years, Steve's brothers, who have been surprised at the profit which Steve has been able to make, have expressed some concern that the land holder's share of profits has been too low. If the family votes to take a significantly higher percentage of pre-tax profits, the relative value of profits from other diversifications may increase. There is also some concern that the family land holding corporation will vote to take a percentage of the landscape tree profits. At first this venture seemed an innocuous sideline, but as Steve's brothers noted his success they have been questioning why these profits (from a crop also grown on the leased land) should not also be shared.

When Steve began to develop real estate, he was sensitive to this issue. Consequently he negotiated a deal to buy real estate development lands outright from the land holding corporation at the rate of $1000 per half acre lot. This price will be up for discussion in 1995, as well, and Steve and Connie wonder how the conclusion of that issue will affect their real estate activities. Another impending family matter relates to Steve's youngest brother, Mat. Things have not gone well for him in his job, and he has been discussing either "buying into" the business or joining his other brother as a salaried employee of the farm operations. Over the years Steve has increased Joe's salary by an average of 5% per year and paid Mat on a per diem basis for work which needed to be done. Mat's interests and skills lie more in the area of construction and repair than farming. One possible use for Mat would be to have him take over operations of the bed and breakfast business now that Steve's parents are reaching their mid 70's.

In any event, Steve and Connie are looking to slow down their frenetic pace. During the early years they often found themselves working 80- to 100-hour weeks. They feel that this has often been at the expense of their family as well as the overall quality of their life together. There are lull times in the business, and they have been able to take winter vacations to places like Florida, the Bahamas, and Europe, but they are soon hoping to slow their "everyday" pace so that they can enjoy life and their beautifully remodeled farmhouse a bit more.

## TECHNICAL NOTES ON THE TOBACCO INDUSTRY

The following data represent recent developments, industry statistics, and the position of the industry in the provincial and national economy.

1. Contraband cigarettes represent the most visible problem in the industry, from both grower and government perspectives. It is projected that

by 1996, contraband consumption will exceed legal consumption. Black market shoppers save as much as $35 per carton. Criminals can earn as much as $25 per carton.

2.  There are two general sources of contraband, domestic and foreign. Current trends indicate that the foreign sources are growing more rapidly than domestic, thus hurting both the farmer and the government. In 1992, the domestic totals were 8,640,000 pounds while foreign contraband totalled 15,744,000 pounds. In 1993, these totals grew to 20,213,000 pounds (domestic) and 13,475,000 pounds (foreign).

3.  The revenue loss in taxes to the federal government is estimated to be between $1.3 and $2.0 billion. Without consideration of the (spinoff effect) multiplier this is estimated to have cost the Canadian economy $5.6 billion in 1993.

4.  It was originally argued that increased taxation would reduce smoking. With consideration of the contraband totals this is clearly not the case. Some economists have argued that the availability of reduced price contraband product has, in fact, stimulated smoking behavior.

5.  In 1992 an export tax was initiated which made sales to nondomestic sources (a growing component of the Canadian Tobacco Industry) far less profitable. In addition this export tax opened doors to black market source tobacco.

6.  Enforcement agencies have had little success at either catching smugglers or deterring the use of counterfeit tax-paid labels.

7.  Ontario tobacco constitutes 93% of Canadian crop totals. There are 1,642 individual owners of production quota who are organized into 1,483 production units. There are an estimated 58,400 acres planted.

8.  The average domestic price of a pound of tobacco is $1.70. Exported product averaged $1.50. The 1992 minimum price was $1.40.

9.  The four major importers of Canadian tobacco include United Kingdom, United Stares, Germany, and Hong Kong. The minor importers (but growing) include Zimbabwe, Holland, Czechoslovakia, Hungary, Poland, Yugoslavia, Romania, Turkey, Ukraine, Russia, and Bulgaria.

10. In March 1984 the retail price of Ontario cigarettes fell by almost $2.00 per pack as a result of federal and provincial tax roll-backs. The tax adjustment was said to be a temporary measure to allow in-depth study of taxation versus contraband.

# Presque Isle State Park (Is This Place for the Birds?)

David R. Frew, Gannon University

C. Louise Sellaro, Youngstown State University

Harry Leslie was a legendary windsor knot tier, but tonight he was not having much luck. As he struggled in front of the bedroom mirror his wife called from the kitchen to remind him of his 7:00 p.m. meeting. "Better hurry it up Harry, it's almost 6:15 and you said that you were going to get there early!" "OK, OK," he muttered, "I'm almost ready." As she kissed him on his way out, neither acknowledged the tension that Harry felt. He hadn't mentioned it often as the fateful evening approached, but tonight's community information meeting had the unsettling potential to threaten his job. And this was, indeed, Harry's dream job: Chief Superintendent of Presque Isle State Park.

Harry closed the door carefully as he stepped out of the lighthouse that was home to his family (see Exhibit 1). The structure was old (1892) and a gust of November wind could easily rip the massive door from its hinges. It was a cold, clear night and the surf was pounding the beach near the lighthouse. As he bent his 220-pound frame into his car, Harry savored his family's living quarters. They lived in a working lighthouse on the north beach of a beautiful state park. His children had a magical existence with a beach at the back door and woods near the front entrance.

While he was driving the seven miles of deserted beach road toward the park gates and the city, a park police cruiser pulled next to him, waved, and motioned to the two-way radio. "Good luck boss, you're going to need it," chuckled officer Brandon. "Thanks, but I don't think it will be all that bad," replied Harry. "People are basically reasonable when it counts!"

As he left the park and headed toward the university where the public forum was to be held, Harry hoped that these had not been empty words. His

**Exhibit 1**

Presque Isle State Park

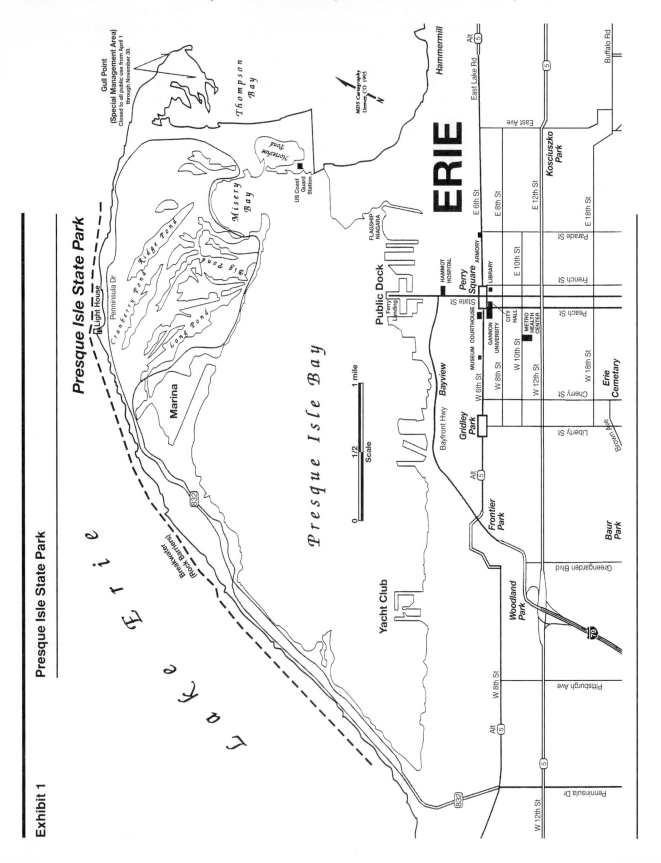

predecessor had caused himself political difficulties by making what he had considered "reasonable" changes at the park. Ultimately, however, community turmoil over those changes had helped to initiate his transfer to the political offices of Pennsylvania's Department of Environmental Resources (DER) in Harrisburg, a fate which didn't interest Harry. He was an outdoor person, not a bureaucrat or politician, and loved living in the park, being involved in day-to-day problems and using a hands-on approach. If a tree fell in a windstorm, Harry might be first at the scene, setting up warning signs and cutting away branches with his chain saw. He was less political and more practical than the previous park chief, and the park staff loved that about him.

The public meeting had been announced four weeks ago and was to be an information session. Harry and his staff had worked hard to develop a park management plan, an attempt to balance the diverse interests of the park and its constituency groups. The dilemma concerned how to juggle the various needs of the community and fit them into a strategic plan that would be acceptable to the various stakeholders who had concerns about how the park was to be used "for the public good."[1] He was also aware of the political "noise" that any of these factions could make if they didn't get their own way. But his plan was a reasonable one. It split the difference between commercial interests in the park and the concerns of the environmentally-oriented groups.[2]

Harry's hope for the meeting was that there would be a group of understanding individuals in attendance and that he could orchestrate a compromise. He believed that somehow all of the involved individuals and groups would have an important common interest: the well-being of Presque Isle.

It was 6:35 as Harry steered his car onto university grounds and threaded his way between people walking along the narrow campus road. He was amazed at the congestion. There were hundreds of people walking the narrow road to the parking lot, and cars were illegally parked on the lawn. Approaching the parking area, Harry's heart almost stopped as he realized what was actually happening. The parking lot was full and the crowd was streaming toward the lecture hall and *his* meeting!

Suddenly someone in the crowd recognized Harry's state vehicle, and a voice from the crowd yelled, "There's Leslie, the guy who's trying to ruin our park!" "Great," he thought to himself, "my career is ruined and I get a parking ticket all in the same evening."

# PRESQUE ISLE STATE PARK[3]

Presque Isle State Park (see Exhibit 1) is a sand spit peninsula which extends seven miles into Lake Erie. The peninsula joins the mainland just west of Erie, Pennsylvania, creating a sheltering arm that forms a beautiful natural harbor. The city of Erie is located near the center of Lake Erie's southern shore, and the peninsula has historically been critical to the development of the area. The population of Erie itself has stabilized at approximately 115,000, but the surrounding suburbs have been growing steadily. Combined, the areas have reached a population of 250,000.

The peninsula is one of central Lake Erie's two major sand spits, and is a unique geological and biological preserve. Presque Isle, along with its mirror image twin Long Point across the lake on the north shore, create a hydrodynamic lake effect which is said to be critical to the health of the entire lake. The eastward flowing waters pass between the points over a relatively deep water trench and increase in depth and velocity as they flow into Lake Erie's eastern basin. At the line which connects the tips of the two peninsulas, the average width of Lake Erie changes from forty-five to twenty-seven miles.

Presque Isle is a biologist's dream, and a classic example of secession forestation. The secession process, which is essential to the continued health and structural integrity of the peninsula, is activated at its eastern tip, an area called Gull Point. Secession is driven by a combination of natural forces. In late summer, water levels drop and winds calm. Sand, carried by westerly winds, comes to rest along the peninsula's north beaches just east of Gull Point, causing a series of sculpted sand bars. In the fall there are always several strong storms from the northeast (nor'easters). The winds tend to push the sandbars back (southwesterly) toward Gull Point creating parallel beach lines some thirty or forty feet east of the original beach.

Over the winter, water levels fall again. The effect on the beach looks as though nature is creating a double water's edge (two beaches). In the spring, cottonwood trees, common along freshwater beaches and the quintessential species on Presque Isle, pollinate by releasing fluffy air-driven seed balls. As spring winds freshen and water levels rise, these cottonwood balls are blown into the water. The cottonwood seeds float back onto Gull Point, and become lodged on the previous year's newly formed sand ridge. Over the summer the seeds root along the outer sand bar, forming a structure covered with scrub brush near the newly developing beach.

Assuming that this new ridge survives the next year's storms and water level shifts (which it does approximately thirty percent of the time), Presque Isle will have grown to the east by the width of the new parallel beach line. This (secession) is the process which has systematically driven Presque Isle eastward. A helicopter view of Presque Isle's eastern tip shows a series of arch-shaped rows of cottonwood trees. From the water's edge moving westward, rows grow further apart and the trees get taller. As the cottonwoods mature, organic materials build up near their bases and the curved rows of trees develop ridge lines to go with them. The older the secession line, the higher the ridge. Between the easternmost ridges, which are tiny compared to their westerly cousins, there are ponds formed by the water which is trapped between the parallel ridges.

As the ridge lines mature and grow taller (moving east to west), the pond structures between them also change. The eastern ponds are bottom-water fed, clearwater repositories with fish (trapped by secession) and limited plant growth. The second tier of ponds (to the west) usually develops a variety of marine algae and other plant life. As the ponds along Gull Point age, they change to marshy areas and finally rich soil which separates and nourishes the organic materials between the mature ridge lines.

From an ecological perspective, Presque Isle represents a rare environment where climax forest secession can be studied in a compact area. As a further bonus, the variety of structures provided by the secession environment makes a productive home for a vast array of birds and mammals. Presque Isle and Long Point create an important bird flyway. The area is registered as a National Natural Landmark, and the process of plant and animal succession is a source of both research and educational interest. Researchers, college professors, and students from across the U.S. and Canada have been engaged in the study of birds at both Presque Isle and Long Point for decades.

## BUSINESS AND LOCAL INTERESTS

To the local recreational and business communities, the easterly growth of the peninsula and the scientific interests of academics are more of a threat than a benefit. The regional economy has always been fueled by tourism rather than science.[4] Since the park was established in 1921 and a roadway built to its popular bathing beaches and picnic groves, millions of people have flocked to Erie and Presque Isle.

Since the demise of the local industrial base in the 1970's, tourism has taken on even more importance to the regional economy.[5] By 1990, economic data suggested that tourism, anchored by visits to Presque Isle, was the number two component of the regional economy. Attendance at Presque Isle has consistently been greater than that of Yellowstone National Park. By 1990, a wall of motels, restaurants, fishing tackle shops, bike rental centers, and other amusements had built up near the park entrance. Regional chambers of commerce estimate that the summer population of the Erie area is 160% of its winter totals.

For the tourist-based economy, any threat to the use of the peninsula is a potential business crisis, and there have been many threats over the years. In the 1950's, there was concern that the narrow western arm of the peninsula might wash away due to erosion. The continuous eastward motion of wind and water tends to wash sand from the western beaches toward Gull Point. Thus the natural process which causes secession threatens the peninsula's narrow western arm, beaches, and park entrance.

Since before the 1950's it was common for storm waters to break through the western arm, making the peninsula into an island. As a result, it was not unusual for visitors to be unable to exit the park. This problem was tackled by the U.S. Army Corps of Engineers which launched a rebuilding program in the late 1950's, adding dredged beach sand to the western arm of the peninsula. At the same time, an improved roadway system was built, solving the problem of weekend traffic congestion.

The Corps of Engineers has long suggested that, if left to its own devices, Presque Isle would ultimately separate from the mainland, becoming an island and continuing its relentless eastward migration away from Erie. Since the major rebuilding of the western arm, the Corps has continuously trucked sand to the peninsula to protect the bathing beaches.

This ongoing renewal plan had a multimillion-dollar price tag, so to save money, the Corps made a decision in the early 1980's to replenish the beaches with sand from quarrys south of Erie. Quarry sand is much coarser and less aesthetically pleasing than the dredged sand used in the early days of beach nourishment. But the coarser sand is less expensive, and it has been therefore argued that its heavier consistency will help hold the beaches in place.

During the middle 1980's, high water levels in combination with several severe fall storms did significant damage to the beaches. As in the 1950's, lake waters overflowed the peninsula, closing roads and reminding the public of the fragile nature of Presque Isle. Therefore, in a "final" move to stabilize the peninsula, the Army Corps announced a new program using parallel rock mound barrier reefs which were to run parallel to the north beach at a distance of approximately 500 yards from shore.

Theoretically the rock mound reefs would attenuate wave action from either prevailing southwesterlies or the fall/spring nor'easters. The movement of sand from west to east would be slowed to a manageable rate and only a small amount of material would have to be added to beach fronts to ensure stabilization. The final project was completed at a cost of more than twenty-three million dollars over a three and one half-year period.

As the last of an immense flow of federal and state tax dollars was spent for this project, a low water cycle began on the lake and it was beginning to appear that the threat of the loss of Presque Isle, or its roadways, had subsided and that the Army Corps had overreacted. Investment in tourism at the entrance to the park accelerated once more with two new bars, a restaurant, a windsurfing/rollerblading center, condominiums, and a scuba diving shop.

# PARK ADMINISTRATION

Erie's first settlers were attracted to the natural harbor formed by Presque Isle. They generally came via water, arriving by schooner or bateaux in the late 1700's. They settled on the creek inlets which emptied into the sheltered bay. As the town developed in the 1800's, the peninsula became a harbor barrier and a wilderness area utilized by citizens for hunting, fishing, and recreation. The federal government (whose needs decreased after hostilities with Canada and the War of 1812 ended) and the City of Erie both saw the land mass as an important strategic acquisition.

In 1921, while city and federal governments quibbled over ownership, the state of Pennsylvania negotiated a complex political deal in which the federal government could use an area for a Coast Guard station, but the State owned the peninsula. Meanwhile, the city was assured that a park would be developed for the well-being of the local population, and the city's water supply infrastructure (on the peninsula) would remain under the jurisdiction of the city of Erie.

Thus began a long history of state administration and the controversies which were to arise in later years. In the first and possibly most significant of all developments, it was determined that a roadway system would span the length of the park. In prior years a crude road ran from the mainland for the first few miles along the north beaches. Governor Fisher's proposed roadway was to loop around the eastern end of Presque Isle and encourage "motoring." Citizens could tour with automobiles to view flora, fauna, and wildlife.

Between 1938 and 1994, however, the volume of traffic grew at rates beyond the imagination of early park architects. Weekend totals reached astronomical numbers and the extension of park driving hours during summer months resulted in a constant stream of automobiles circling Presque Isle's fourteen-mile roadway system.

Over the first decades of development several personnel additions were needed in park administration, which now reports to Pennsylvania's Department of Environmental Resources. By 1982, the staff consisted of the superintendent, administrative staff, maintenance, a police department, the marina staff, and a lifeguard organization. (Later review of the Park personnel revealed the lack of a full-time naturalist position. An on-site individual was needed to continuously assess and monitor park preservation activities.) A number of superintendents were involved in the development of Presque Isle, but the greatest growth occurred between 1956 and 1986 under the direction of long-time Superintendent Michael Wargo. During the Wargo regime the park matured, a 473-boat marina was constructed, tourism grew, and the Corps of Engineers initiated and completed major renovations.

Upon Wargo's retirement, the state, which was beginning to sense the potential for both growth and political controversy, appointed Eugene Giza to the post. Giza was young and ambitious and understood the park's growth potential. He was also politically astute and sensed that there might be a linkage between park use and funding. The budget had undergone cuts in the early 1980's, and Giza developed activities which would encourage visitation and rationalize more funding. Unfortunately, budget cuts continued.[6]

Under the Giza administration the following developments occurred:

1. Old-fashioned "hole in the ground" outhouses were replaced with modern lavatory facilities. These featured an above-ground sand mound leach bed (similar to a septic system) and did not have to be emptied on a regular basis.

2. An all-purpose black top trail was built along the south (bayside) edge of the park. This encouraged hiking, running, biking, and rollerblading.

3. Winter activities such as festivals and carnivals were initiated.

4. A cross-country ski trail system was developed and an entrepreneur was given concession rights.

5. Running and bike races were encouraged in the park.

6. A Citizen's Advisory Committee was formed to shepherd the park.

## THE ENVIRONMENTAL BACKLASH

As early as the Wargo administration, an environmentalist reaction against peninsula policies began to build. Local groups such as the Audubon Society and the Birdwatchers began raising objections to park projects. The most significant blow to the continuity of tourist-related developments came when Presque Isle's own Citizen's Advisory Group began to lean toward environmental issues.

In summary, the environmental position was that too many park decisions were designed simply to increase use. This subsequently threatened the delicate environment, plants, animals, and water quality. An example was the early decision to place a roadway around the park and encourage motoring. Environmentalists argued that the delicate sand spit could not tolerate this volume of carbon-spewing gasoline engines. From an environmental posture it would have been preferable to make park visitors leave their automobiles at the park gates and hike or bicycle to the eastern portions of the park, or to operate an electric tram service to the eastern beaches and picnic areas.

Using this early decision as an example, business and tourist interests argued that the accessibility of park roads kept a constant stream of people (sightseers, swimmers, picnickers, hikers, and fishermen) traveling to the park. Any constraint to free access represented a threat to business. The increasingly vocal environmentalists cited examples of abuses of the park by motorists who crowded the roads. They polluted the air, parked cars in unauthorized areas, and disturbed plant life. This posed a threat to animals such as deer and foxes by changing their natural patterns of behavior, frightening them during late evening drives, and even hitting them with automobiles.

Some more reasonable environmental voices understood that old practices, like allowing automobile access, were not likely to be reversed. These ongoing threats to the park's environment, it was argued, created a special responsibility for park administration to be careful of the environmental implications of new decisions. As the Giza administration began its efforts to increase usage (and hopefully the budget allocation from Harrisburg), seeds of the final conflict were firmly sown.

Superintendent Giza explained to the environmental groups that his usage-driven decisions would ultimately be in the best interests of the park. Increased funding, he argued, could be used to safeguard the park's fragile geology and ecology. With more funding he could hire a full-time naturalist and initiate programs of public environmental awareness. And many of his ideas—for example, 10K races and biking—would be easy on the environment. But as defects in decisions began to emerge, various groups began to lose patience and take public stands against new programs.

While a number of these new plans which were perceived as a threat to the park were not actually the inventions of Giza, he began to take the administrative heat for them. During the final years of his administration the following issues came to the attention of the public:

1. **The Presque Isle Marina** opened in 1962, grew to 473 slips, and added underground fuel tanks as well as sewage treatment facilities.

2. **The Lagoon System** was connected to the marina lake, and a continuous navigable loop was created. This action joined two previously separate wetland and pond areas, and allowed plant life from the two areas to invade each other.

3. **Parking Lot and Pavilion Construction** continued through the 1980's, taking a toll on mature trees.

4. **The All-Purpose Trail** was built in 1984 to allow hikers and bikers access to the south waterfront, but wetlands had been violated and endangered plant species were compromised.

5. **Lyme Disease** was reported in the park and linked to mismanagement (oversupply) of the whitetail deer herd.

6. **Sand Mound Toilets,** constructed along the entire length of the park, had replaced the older pit toilet outhouses. The new design, viable in other (primarily mountainous) regions, proved to be inappropriate for a sand spit peninsula.

7. **Beach Replenishment** shifted from the use of dredged Lake Erie sand to quarry sand in order to save money.

8. **Rock Mound Barrier Reefs** were constructed between 1989 and 1992 to solve the problem of sand replenishment by slowing erosion. It was argued that these structures were not aesthetic and would lead to water pollution in the stagnant areas behind them.

9. **Beach Closings** occurred due to fecal coliform and other contaminants. Closings were beginning to occur at the same general time the sand mound toilets and the barrier reefs were installed.

While most of the environmental issues fell on deaf ears with respect to the business community and the general public, the beach closings were another matter. What would a closed beach, or even the rumor of a closed beach, do to tourism, business, and the public view of the park? This dilemma quickly raised a previously altruistic issue to the level of a real problem.

## THE GULL POINT CONTROVERSY

The "mother of all controversies" however, was the Gull Point issue. Gull Point, the 319-acre eastern tip of the peninsula had become a popular summer congregating point for local boaters. The natural curves of the point provide protection from prevailing southwesterly winds. The pristine beach, located miles away from public beaches and roadways, creates a sanctuary for boaters. Generations of persons had grown accustomed to anchoring, picnicking, and swimming at the tip of the point.

Boating season in Erie begins in early May and lasts through October, although there are a few hearty souls who push both extremes of the season. As the summer months progress, an increasing number of boaters is attracted to the Gull Point anchorage. The waters to the east of Gull Point and its sand spits offers protection from all but easterly winds. The many odd-shaped inlets of the developing sand spit tip, as well as the secession sand ponds, serve as an additional attraction, especially to boaters in shallow draft vessels. By early July a typical weekend finds hundreds of sail and power boats anchored at Gull Point. Sooner or later, boaters would find their way onto the fragile tip of the point where they participate in a variety of seemingly innocent activities: picnicking, sunbathing, hiking, exploring, and Frisbee.

Boaters knew that this area of Presque Isle was officially declared a bird sanctuary in 1957, and most Gull Point visitors perceived themselves as being careful about their usage of the area. They would yell at their children for throwing rocks at birds and go out of their way not to put a beach blanket on a nest. They thought they were being good citizens.

In the early days of the bird sanctuary, park police were unlikely to enforce the issue of the bird sanctuary. After all, many boaters reasoned, Gull Point is 319 acres and we are simply using the edge of the beach! What harm could that possibly do?

By the end of the 1980's, however, a storm of protests arose from environmental groups. They pointed to the huge list of endangered bird species which needed to make use of the peninsula. They further noted the critical nature of the water's edge to many of these migratory birds. A number of species reach the safe haven of Gull Point in a weakened condition, desperately needing respite at the water's edge to gather food and regain strength so they can continue their migration. Even episodic (weekend) disturbances by boaters could spell doom for these birds.[7] Other species used Gull Point for the express purpose of raising young, and episodic boat traffic could threaten the breeding process. The environmental groups were demanding that boaters, as well as hikers, stay away from Gull Point.

In and around Erie, the piping plover became the symbolic "poster child" of the Gull Point movement. This diminutive shore bird had become rare on Gull Point, almost in synchrony with the increase in the recreational boating industry. By the early 1990's, environmental groups were pointing to the fact that the endangered creature was no longer able to nest on Gull Point and asked if this might be the first of a long series of birds that would cease to exist as a result of lenience granted to suit the whims of boaters.

## GUNFIGHT AT THE OK CORRAL

As Harry stepped through the doorway of the lecture hall, the crowd grew quiet in anticipation. This was clearly a revisitation of Wyatt Earp, badge and all, trying to settle things between the forces of good and the forces of evil. "Folks," he began, "my name is Harry Leslie and the important thing is that we do what is right for future generations and for Presque Isle!" As he presented the main points of the park's new management plan, Harry began to realize that the question period might not go as smoothly as he had hoped. His plan included a variety of objectives: increasing park visitor capacity, limiting the number of approved duck blind locations, and prohibiting access to Gull Point from April 1 to November 30. It also included an additional 200 pages of meticulous detail: history, definitions, lists, and more. This was clearly the finest piece of systematic work ever produced in the name of planning for Presque Isle.

But the members of the audience wanted specific assurances. "Do you mean to tell me that I can't take my family to Gull Point in my boat any more?" "Who appointed you the king of the peninsula?" commented a second. "Are you going to refund the money that I spent for my boat?" asked a third. "What do you mean increased visitor capacity?" questioned a birdwatcher. "There are already too many people in the park!" "How come boaters can't disturb seagulls, but hunters can shoot ducks?" asked an irate sailor. "Typical liberal commie type," retorted a row of duck hunters who owned grandfathered rights to duck blinds within the Gull Point bird sanctuary.

As the session with the overflow crowd grew more agitated and ugly, Harry's stomach began to hurt. Many of these folks were the wealthy, the influential and elite forces of the community, and they acted like the fans at a professional wrestling match. As he struggled to answer questions, maintain order, and explain his environmental management plan, his thoughts turned to his children, sleeping in their lighthouse home. Would he really be able to maintain the lifestyle that had become such an important part of their family life? Or was his dream rapidly disintegrating into a nightmare?

## END NOTES

1. Presque Isle State Park operates under the Pennsylvania Bureau of State Parks. This division of the Department of Environmental Resources sets forth strategic management direction for all the Commonwealth's park areas. Management at Presque Isle incorporated this framework into its 1993 Strategic Management Publication. Agency goals must be developed within the context of these planning documents.

2. The mission of Presque Isle State Park is to conserve the park's natural and historic resources for current and future generations and to provide educational and recreational activities. Presque Isle's goals are set up to achieve the overall mission of the park. These goals are to manage park attendance while maintaining the fragile ecosystem and preserving the natural historical resources.

   The *Resource Management Plan* compiled and published by park management details key activities and strategically critical tasks that provide a foundation for the organization's structure and direction.

3. The Pennsylvania Legislature formed the Pennsylvania State Park and Harbor Commission in 1921 under Act 436. This Commission was given authority to acquire, develop, and operate Presque Isle State Park, which was formerly known as the Pennsylvania State Park at Erie.

4. Tourism now brings in approximately $80 million per year to the Erie area; this is mainly a function of visitor attraction to Presque Isle State Park. This industry has historically been viewed as a renewable, resource-based industry, and under this perspective tourists are perceived to *view* area attractions, but do not *consume* them. However, an increased recognition of the fragility surrounding the environment and its natural resources has now begun to change this perception, and for Presque Isle, tourism is perceived as competing for scarce resources and capital. The perception is based on an increasing awareness that a different type of tourist-consumption is occurring in the form of deleterious effects on the ecosystem.

5. The demise of Erie's industrial base during the late 1970's and early 1980's had a great impact on Presque Isle and the tourist economy. Massive layoffs and plant closings had resulted from revolutionary changes in the steelmaking and shipping industries which were the area's primary economic base. In a short time, tourism was a strong component of the local economy.

   An analysis of Presque Isle State Park attendance records suggests that during periods of economic downturn, people are more inclined to take comparatively inexpensive trips to a local state park. Travel is dependent on the course of the U.S. economy and visits to the park may be viewed as an alternative to longer, more expensive trips. Since competition for discretionary spending becomes intense in a sluggish economy, park visitation and tourism take on additional importance for the financial health of the local community.

6. Presque Isle's status as a state-controlled entity makes if vulnerable to threats not shared with the private sector. Its operating budget is solely funded by the Department of Environmental Resources, which must allocate a shrinking budget to over 100 parks. Presque Isle is not permitted to spend all the revenue it generates, as those funds are turned over to the state for allocation among all the state parks.

7. In 1937 the Park and Harbor Commission was supported by special legislation which gave the Commission jurisdiction over the waters up to 500 feet off the shores of Presque Isle, including the waters of Misery Bay. This was done to prevent encroachment by moored houseboats; today this code enables the park to prohibit water-skiing within the 500 feet of coastal waters surrounding the Park.

# Lord Nelson at Trafalgar

Mark Kroll, University of Texas at Tyler

On August 15, 1815, Napoleon Bonaparte sailed into permanent exile on board the Royal Navy ship the *H.M.S. Bellerophon*. Two months earlier he had been defeated by England and its allies at the Battle of Waterloo. That battle represented the last chapter in a tumultuous and bloody period in European history, the end of the Napoleonic Wars which had bled Europe for 15 years. Though no one knew it at the time, it also represented the last battle fought between England and France. Previously, from the time of the Norman conquest of the British Isles in 1066 until Waterloo, the English and French had been periodically at war.

The victory at Waterloo of course represented the culmination of the brilliant military career of Sir Arthur Wellesley, the Duke of Wellington. However, as is true for most great successes in warfare as well as commerce, the precursors which allowed Wellington to achieve his great victories over Napoleon were essential to its attainment. One, if not the most important, precursor to Wellington's success took place ten years before Napoleon's defeats in a great sea battle which was just as tumultuous and strategically important. That was the Battle of Trafalgar. The results of Trafalgar provided England undisputed supremacy of the seas for over 100 years, insured that Napoleon could never threaten an invasion of England, and made it possible for Britain to send its armies, such as the one led by Wellington, abroad without fear of those armies being destroyed in route in naval action.

At Trafalgar the Royal Navy was commanded by England's most celebrated naval officer, Vice Admiral Lord Viscount Nelson K.B. Lord Nelson's role at Trafalgar was very eloquently assessed by U.S. Navy Rear Admiral A.T. Mahan, who commented: "Rarely has a man been more favored in the hour of his appearing; never one so fortunate in the moment of his death."

# THE GEOPOLITICAL AND MILITARY SITUATION IN 1805

England and France had been at peace from 1783 to the rise to power of Napoleon Bonaparte. As Napoleon's intentions for conquest both in Europe and abroad became clear, England once again found itself at odds with its old nemesis. Given his quick success at being able to dominate the European Continent, he began to contemplate conquests off the continent. His first major expedition was his successful invasion of Egypt. However, Napoleon's success in Egypt was quickly rendered pointless when the British under Lord Nelson destroyed the French fleet supporting the invasion in 1798. This victory effectively marooned the French expeditionary force and Napoleon in Egypt. This British victory followed one off Portugal known as the Battle of St. Vincent, which was just as devastating to the French and materially weakened the French Navy.

On the heels of these naval defeats, the possibility of invading England and ridding himself of a constant source of frustration must have periodically entered Napoleon's mind. It does not appear to have ever become so important as to prevent him from planning other conquests, but by 1804 he was seriously entertaining invasion plans. However, once again the major constraint was sea power, or the lack thereof. To invade England successfully the invader must be able to get its army across the English Channel without its being destroyed in the process. This required in 1804 at least temporary naval control of the Channel. The problem for Napoleon was that throughout this period the English maintained a very powerful fleet off the northwest coast of France, guarding the entrance to the English Channel.

Napoleon began assembling an invasion force in the northern French coastal city of Boulogne in 1803. By 1805 he was ready to invade, but was still no closer to gaining naval supremacy in the English Channel. So in that same year he decided upon a plan to at least temporarily gain control of the Channel and mount an invasion. Having brought Spain into the war on his side, he had at his disposal both the French and Spanish fleets. The problem for Napoleon was that his navy was spread among various squadrons which were either bottled up in ports by British blockade, or in remote locations. If he was to clear the Channel he would have to concentrate all of his naval forces into a single fleet, and then attack the British fleet guarding the Channel. In 1805 he devised a plan which seemed very workable for a soldier, but proved very ineffective when applied to naval forces.

On the face of it the plan was simple, and seemed doable to Napoleon. He would order all of his admirals and their squadrons to break out of the various ports in which they were located, and sail to Martinique in the West Indies. Martinique was France's strongest outpost in the Caribbean. After the various squadrons rendezvoused in the West Indies, they would sail under the combined command of French Vice Admiral Pierre Villeneuve for the English Channel. Once in the Channel they would either do battle with the British fleet, or alternatively, draw them away from the Channel so the crossing could be accomplished (see Exhibits 1 and 2).

While the plan made great sense to a general, the admirals had their doubts. Fleets at sea in those days had no way of communicating with each other. It was quite possible for one fleet to sail within a relatively small distance of another and never meet, especially when sailing at night. Second, when forced

**Exhibit 1**                    **European Theater 1805**

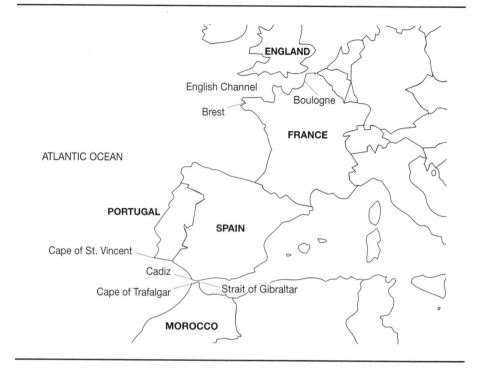

to rely on wind for propulsion, the chances of fleets being able to keep schedules were impossible. Finally, Napoleon did not count on Admiral Nelson's dogged pursuit of the largest of the fleets under the command of Admiral Villeneuve to the West Indies, which forced him back to Spain before the plan could be hatched. As a result, by the time the Battle of Trafalgar was fought Napoleon had given up on his navy and his invasion plans, and was marching his army south. The British had no way of knowing this and saw the destruction of the greater portion of the French-Spanish fleet as the only means of insuring the safety of England from invasion. Such a destruction was the British Admiralty's primary goal in 1805, and they saw Lord Nelson as the commander who could achieve it.

The combined French-Spanish fleet, having failed to link up with other French squadrons, sailed back to the west coast of Spain, having heard Nelson's fleet was closing on them. This was in spite of the fact Nelson's fleet at that time was only half the size of the combined fleet. When they reached the Spanish coast the combined fleet was attacked by a British squadron and suffered the loss of two ships. From there they made their way to the Spanish port of Cadiz, where they were to resupply and rethink their plans. Upon entering Cadiz, the British Mediterranean fleet quickly took up blockade positions. Not long after, Nelson's fleet arrived to join the blockade. It was readily apparent to the officers and men of the combined French-Spanish fleet that in all likelihood they could not leave Cadiz without a fight with the Royal Navy.

**Exhibit 2**

**Fleet Movements Before Trafalgar**

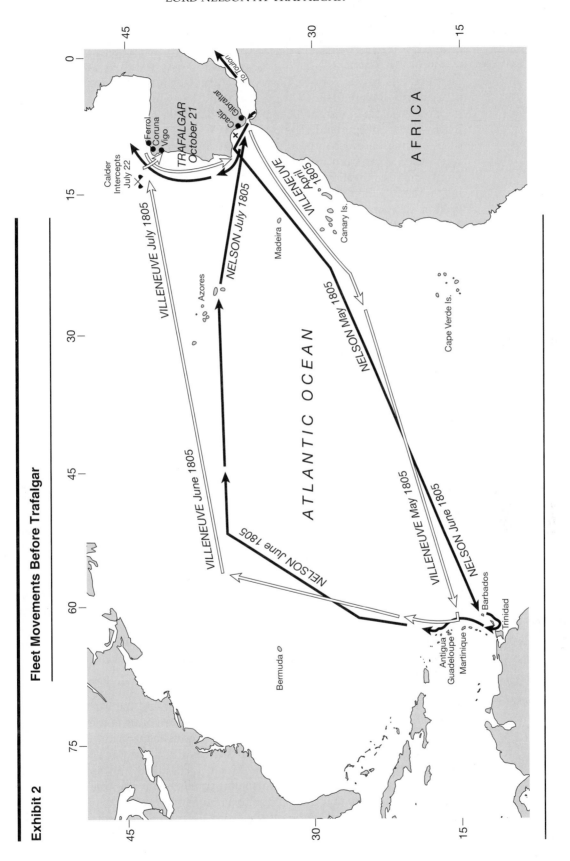

## THE COMMANDERS: NELSON VERSUS VILLENEUVE

Horatio Nelson was born in 1758, one of eight children and the third of five sons, to the Reverend Edmund Nelson and his wife Catherine Nelson. His father was pastor of the Anglican parish at Burnham Thorpe, a small village on the east coast of England. The day after Christmas in 1767 Catherine Nelson died, leaving her husband and their eight children. The family was not destitute, but was far from wealthy. The family had, through Catherine Nelson's family, some connections to the landed aristocracy which had secured Edmund his present position. More important to Horatio's future was Catherine's older brother Captain Maurice Suckling, who had distinguished himself in battle against the French in the Caribbean.

As a boy Horatio became fascinated by the sea and sailing. As Burnham Thorpe lay among the estuaries and ports on England's North Sea coast, Horatio was exposed early to sailing and maritime life. He was also formally schooled in his early years at the Royal Grammar School in Norwich and the Paston School in North Walsham. As the son of a parson who, though formally educated at Cambridge, had neither position nor wealth, there were two primary avenues for Horatio to pursue. He could, as did his father and elder brother, attend Cambridge and hope to secure a comfortable assignment after ordination, or pursue a military career. Given Horatio's fascination with the sea and the exploits of his uncle Maurice, he longed for a career in the Royal Navy.

In 1770 the Spanish captured the Falkland Islands from the British. Most considered them not worth a fight, but British honor was at stake, so the Navy was mustered. Horatio's uncle Maurice was recalled to command the 64-gun *Raisonnable*. Horatio saw this as his opportunity and beseeched his father to request his uncle Maurice take him to sea as a midshipman. With that the small, thin 12 year old began his naval career. From 1771 to 1777 Nelson served on both merchant and Royal Navy ships. During these years he participated in voyages to the West Indies, the East Indies, and the Arctic.

In 1777, at the age of 19, he passed the examination to become a lieutenant and was immediately assigned to the frigate *Loweswift*, which was ordered to Jamaica. As is unfortunately often the case, military careers flourish best during war. Such was the case with Nelson's. At the time of his first posting England was at war with its American colonies, which required significant naval support. In 1778, when the French and later the Spanish entered the war as American allies, the potential for advancement in the Royal Navy became all the better. So, by 1779, at the age of 21, Horatio Nelson was made post-captain and given command of the frigate *Hinchinbroke*. Attaining such rank made his eventual promotion to flag officer a matter of seniority.

From 1779 through the end of the American Revolution he was given various assignments in Central America, the Baltic Sea, and the West Indies. The end of the war found him in command of the frigate *Boreas* in the West Indies. While in the Caribbean he met Fanny Nisbet, whom he married two years later. In 1787 he sailed with his bride to England. Shortly thereafter he entered perhaps the most difficult period of his career, for in 1788 he was sent back to Burnham Thorpe on half pay. It is also unfortunately the case that peace is perhaps the worst thing that can happen to a military career.

The years 1788 to 1793 were difficult for Nelson as he did not see himself in any other role than that of a naval officer. Other officers often turned to other professions which they enjoyed, or came out of the war with enough prize money from captured enemy ships to live comfortably. Neither was the case with Nelson. He spent these years using whatever connections and sources of influence that were available to him to secure a command. However, as had previously been the case, it took the threat of war to return him to service. England began to muster its naval forces following the French Revolution and the ascent to power of Napoleon Bonaparte. On January 6, 1793, Nelson returned to active duty and was away at sea almost continuously until his death at Trafalgar in October 1805.

In terms of who Lord Nelson was as a person, as with any bright and capable person, it is a difficult question to answer with complete satisfaction. However, there are some consistent themes in his personality and view of the world and his place in it. First of all, he was utterly fearless. By all accounts of those who served with him, Nelson consistently exposed himself to every bit as much danger if not more than he asked any subordinate to face. In evidence of this fact one need only know that by the time the Battle of Trafalgar occurred he had lost his right arm and virtually all the use of an eye, and then lost his life at Trafalgar at age 47.

His courage might have come from another theme which seems consistent— Nelson was a very fatalistic man. He appears to have believed in providence and that he had a fate which he must see through. This belief in divine intervention in the lives of men was common in the 19th century. He likely believed that his fate, a fate ordained by God, was to accomplish for his nation great victories at sea, only to be killed in the process. Just prior to the beginning of action at Trafalgar he was bidding farewell to one of his captains, Henry Blackwood, who reported their last conversation as follows:

> He [Lord Nelson] then again desired me go away [to Blackwood's ship]; and as we were standing on the front of the poop, I took his hand, and said, 'I trust, my Lord, that on my return to the *Victory* [Nelson's flagship], which will be as soon as possible, I shall find your Lordship well, and in possession of twenty prizes.' On which he made this reply: 'God bless you, Blackwood, I shall never speak to you again.'

It has been suggested Nelson had a death wish at Trafalgar, on account of the tremendous danger to which he exposed himself and his flagship. It is just as likely he believed that it was his destiny to die in such a battle and there was little he could do to prevent it.

As was also characteristic of many in the Royal Navy, Lord Nelson's allegiances were very clear to him—to king and country. He appears to have had an unshakable belief in England's destiny to be a great power and that the rightful head of state was King George III, who was not even English, but German. However, Nelson also believed that the ultimate power to govern did and should reside in Parliament. In fact he had contemplated a political career. He was an active participant in the House of Lords upon his being given title. While the divine right of kings had been rejected in America and France, it still lived in the mind of Lord Nelson.

Another curious feature of Nelson's was his vanity. How much of his success was owing to a need to be admired and exalted cannot be measured, but it is clear glory, and the position and status it brought, were very important to Nelson. In his reports and written correspondence he rarely shies from making clear his own contributions to whatever successes he had to report. Those who met him report his inclination to make it known to all involved who he was and what he was. It is of course possible such displays of vanity were a reflection of an insecure man of humble birth attempting to create an identity for himself when immersed in the English aristocracy.

Regardless of Nelson's concern for his own prestige, it is also true that he was most generous with praise of his colleagues and subordinates. He consistently took pains to make sure those who had earned credit got their full measure. In addition, he worked to see that those who had served him well were looked after to the extent it was in his power to do so. His fellow officers and subordinates, as a result, seem to have been able to see past Nelson's vanity and find a faithful friend and superior who they knew they could count on.

In terms of leadership style, one would have to conclude he was not the martinet many British officers of his era were. An incident occurred in the hours just before battle was joined at Trafalgar which illustrates Nelson's style. A common seaman was wetting down some stowed canvas hammocks with a bucket so they would not catch fire. A Royal Marine officer was splashed with some of the water the sailor had thrown, and began cursing the sailor. Nelson saw the incident, came over, and told the officer the sailor was doing his job and that he was in the way, and that he should have gotten the whole bucket full for not being more careful. On the other hand, he did enforce Royal Navy regulations fully. For instance, he had two crew members hanged when it was determined they were homosexuals. He had high expectations for his officers and crews, but they all knew he held himself to a standard every bit as high as the one he held them to. A common theme throughout his career as an admiral was a willingness to trust subordinate officers and rely on their individual initiative in executing his plans. This undoubtedly grew out of his own willingness as both an admiral and a captain to deviate from orders when he perceived greater advantage could be gained by following another course of action.

In terms of tactics, Lord Nelson was perhaps the most innovative commander the Royal Navy had at the time. Most European naval officers of the era were schooled in a very regimented approach, normally involving engaging the enemy in a parallel fashion in line of battle. In fact, the large warships which were built to engage in major sea actions were referred to as "sail-of-the-line." In his two most important victories prior to Trafalgar Nelson had improvised tactics quite different from this traditional approach. This willingness to innovate was something both his superiors in the Admiralty and his subordinates admired in him and counted upon. The French, including Admiral Villeneuve, anticipated Nelson would, in the coming battle, depart from traditional tactics. What Nelson would do they had no idea. Villeneuve often dismissed Nelson's methods as rash and impulsive in discussions with subordinates, but there is no question the fact that they were facing Nelson weighed heavily on Villeneuve and his men.

Additionally, Nelson was not above playing mind games with his opponents. For instance, prior to the battle at Trafalgar the Royal Navy had been blockading the port of Cadiz, in which the combined fleet was anchored. Admiral Collingwood, who was Nelson's second in command, had taken up blockade positions within clear view of the port, as was customary in such situations. This was done while Nelson made a quick trip to London to clarify with the Admiralty what he had done and why, and what his plans were for facing the combined fleet. Upon Lord Nelson's return, he ordered his fleet to back off over the horizon and out of view of the enemy. He left only one or two fast-sailing frigates on watch. In this way his enemy knew only that the Royal Navy was present, but in what strength and how close they were left to guess.

Trafalgar was not the first occasion in which Admiral Pierre Villeneuve faced Lord Admiral Nelson. In 1798 Villeneuve had been involved in what became known as the Battle of the Nile, fought in Aboukir Bay off the coast of Egypt. The battle had been Nelson's first major success as a flag officer, resulting in the Royal Navy capturing or destroying all but two of the 13 French sail-of-the-line in the battle. One British sailor recounted it as being an awful sight, with the bay filled with the burned, naked bodies of the enemy. Admiral Villeneuve managed to escape the British with his flag ship and one other sail-of-the-line. As one would imagine, it left an indelible impression on Admiral Villeneuve.

Pierre Charles Jean Silvestre de Villeneuve was born in 1763 in Valensole, France, to an aristocratic family. He graduated from the French Royal Naval Academy, and from there entered the French Royal Navy. France was not long after plunged into revolution and the resulting political upheaval. During the administration of the National Convention which organized France's first Republic, Villeneuve achieved the rank of captain in 1793. Because of political purges and turnover in French naval leadership, Villeneuve advanced rapidly and by 1796, at the age of 33, was a rear admiral.

His first major action as a flag officer was the Battle of the Nile, which, as mentioned earlier, was a devastating defeat for the French Navy. The defeat also resulted in Napoleon's Middle Eastern campaign being frustrated and his expeditionary army being marooned in Egypt. While Villeneuve survived the battle and managed to save the only ships to escape British capture, upon his return to France Napoleon erroneously accused him of being largely responsible for the defeat. The charge was without foundation, and later Napoleon not only promoted Villeneuve to Vice Admiral, but made him commander-in-chief of the combined French-Spanish fleet. To his credit, Villeneuve had opposed the Egyptian campaign. Even so, Napoleon appears to have never had a great deal of confidence in Villeneuve or any of his naval commanders. So at age 41, with little combat experience and having never successfully led a naval attack against the British, Admiral Villeneuve was sent out by Napoleon to face Lord Nelson.

Whether or not Villeneuve had confidence in his own ability to command is an interesting question. Given he had not been able to successfully engage the British prior to Trafalgar, and did everything he could to avoid a fight with Nelson on previous occasions, it might be concluded he lacked confidence in his own tactical skills. What is quite clear is he had little confidence in either his French subordinates or his Spanish allies. His assessment was that accuracy in timing of maneuvers was very important, and French admirals were not always efficient at it and Spaniards were worse. In fairness to Villeneuve, his lack of confidence in his subordinates was at least to some extent justified and shared by Lord Nelson, who essentially counted on poor leadership and seamanship in his planning for Trafalgar. No doubt owing to this lack of confidence, Villeneuve did not think much of Napoleon's plan to have the French and Spanish fleets rendezvous in the West Indies and then attack the British fleet in the English Channel. It was only Napoleon's insistence that he sail that sent Villeneuve to the West Indies. After the attempt to combine various French and Spanish fleets failed to work, Villeneuve saw his role primarily as preserving the combined fleet.

Villeneuve's lack of experience in tactical skills showed at Trafalgar as Nelson's experience paid off. One area in which he showed his lack of skill was in his use of his frigates for reconnaissance. Frigates at that point in naval warfare were the eyes of a fleet. They, being smaller and much faster than capital ships, were used by Nelson as forward observers, messengers, and scouts. As mentioned earlier, during his vigil outside of the port of Cadiz waiting for the French, he kept his sail-of-the-line over the horizon and out of site of Villeneuve. Even so, he always knew what the combined fleet was doing as he used his frigates as forward observers. When there was news to report, the frigates would signal the main fleet. This allowed Nelson to stay far enough out to sea to keep the enemy guessing as to his strength, position, and maneuvers. When the combined fleet did sail out of Cadiz, Nelson's frigates were able to tell him their course, disposition, and position. With such intelligence, Nelson was able to stage the battle to his design.

In contrast, Villeneuve kept his frigates in port with his fleet. When he left Cadiz and sailed to meet Nelson, his frigates were to the land side of his fleet, rather than being deployed as forward observers in a position to ascertain Nelson's intentions. Villeneuve only knew what Nelson's intentions were when the British fleet was within clear view, and it was too late to respond with any kind of countertactics.

## THE COMPARATIVE ADVANTAGES OF THE ROYAL NAVY

It was reported that during his conveyance by the Royal Navy into exile on St. Helena, Napoleon commented to the captain of the *Bellerophon* that "In all my plans I have always been thwarted by the British Fleet." While his remark was a bit of an exaggeration, made by a man who was the captive of others, it did reflect the deep respect the former emperor had for the Royal Navy. It was also true that during his imperial reign Napoleon kept a bust of Lord Nelson in his official chambers. He is said to have sat carefully studying it from time to time. On his trip to St. Helena, his captors later reported he was very quizzical about what it was that made the Royal Navy such a formidable force.

While Napoleon was indisputably the master of Europe from 1800 to 1814, he was indeed frustrated on many occasions by England, and especially the Royal Navy. The struggle between England and France in fact has been likened to that of a fight between an elephant and a whale. Both are very large and powerful animals, but are very dissimilar in terms of preferred circumstance in which to operate. The elephant threatened more than once but could never master the narrow strip of sea between France and England. On the other hand, the whale eventually came on land, and, with some help, defeated its nemesis (Warner, 1971: 150).

By the time the Battle of Trafalgar was fought, the Royal Navy had achieved a decided superiority over its opponents. This superiority was not so much in numbers of ships, though in numbers the Royal Navy was somewhat larger than the combined French-Spanish Navy allied against it. Rather the Royal Navy enjoyed advantages which were largely intangible, such as seamanship, leadership, morale, cohesiveness, and determination to decide the issue regardless of the costs.

England had not been one of the early nations to send forth its ships on voyages of discovery, as had the Portuguese and Spanish in the 15th century. However, from the time of the English privateers during the reign of Elizabeth I, the sea had been one of the few avenues for advancement in what was otherwise a very class-conscious society. A young man willing to endure the hardships and perils of sea could improve his lot in either the merchant fleet or in the Royal Navy. This became even more the case as England became a colonial power with possessions spread around the globe. Good sailors who could bring home trade goods successfully, or capture enemy prize ships in actions with the Royal Navy, were essential to England's economic vitality. Not surprisingly, therefore, while most European nations worshipped their generals, England worshipped its famous sailors. England possessed, by the time Nelson was a boy, a maritime culture which prized seamanship. Napoleon himself might have summed it up best when reflecting on his ultimate defeat while in exile on St. Helena when he observed "there is a specialization in this profession [seamanship] which blocked all my ideas. They always returned to the point that one could not be a good seaman unless one was brought up to it from the cradle." Lord Nelson, his officers, and sailors had in fact been raised to go to sea.

For largely the same reasons as the quality of its general seamanship, the Royal Navy enjoyed an officer corps which was accomplished, confident, and determined. From childhood future English navy officers had legends which they idolized and sought to emulate. In Lord Nelson's case, his heroes when he joined the Royal Navy as a midshipman at age 12 were Admiral Lord Rodney and Admiral Lord Hood, who had made their own fame against the French. The Royal Navy had in its midshipmen corps an apprenticeship system which insured a continuous flow of young men who had practical experience to induct into its officer corps as lieutenants. While achieving entry into the officer corps and advancing to the rank of post-captain was certainly subject to political influence, it was also influenced by individual merit. An adolescent of modest background, such as Nelson, could, with the help of an uncle who was a navy captain, enter the service as a midshipman and achieve rapid advancement through skill, daring, and determination. In fact, the Navy was one of the few avenues for upward mobility open to a child of a rural parson, such as Nelson; a route to high position if he was prepared to take the risks.

Promotion above the rank of captain in the Royal Navy in the 18th and early 19th centuries was strictly by seniority. However, the realities were that those who had demonstrated initiative and ability were given important commands, while those less accomplished stayed home on inactive status, even if they were senior in rank. This was the result of a curious arrangement whereby officers both with and without command were still considered serving officers. However, if an officer did not have an assignment he was sent home on half pay. He could remain on that status the rest of his life if he did not receive another command. He would continue to rise in rank as his seniority lengthened, but if the admiralty had decided he was not worthy of command, he might stay on half pay at home for the rest of his career. On the other hand, an officer who was valued would be given major commands even though there might be a number of officers of higher rank growing old at home. Such was the case with Lord Nelson, who at Trafalgar held the rank of Vice Admiral, about half way up in the ranks of admirals, though he was commander of an entire theater of operations. So while political connections and influence might put an officer on the track to the rank of flag officer, it was performance that got him commands with full pay and the opportunity to win prizes in battle.

The reason the Royal Navy had an arrangement by which it furloughed active officers on half pay for extended periods of time was that, as with any nation, during peace time the need for officers declined. However, by retaining officers in the service rather than retiring them, the Royal Navy could quickly staff its ships with experienced officers when war broke out. Nelson himself was "dry docked" this way from 1787 to early 1793. Quite often officers had two professions, one which they pursued in peacetime and the other during war. Such an arrangement provided the Royal Navy with a certain measure of continuity; as the ranks of its seamen would change from conflict to conflict, the officer corps remained intact. For example, Vice Admiral Cuthbert Collingwood, Nelson's second in command at Trafalgar, first met Nelson in the West Indies when they were both young officers, and they remained friends for life.

In contrast the French Navy and its officer corps had experienced a great deal of turmoil in the late 18th and early 19th centuries, owing to the political upheavals which had plagued the country from the time of the French Revolution to the final exile of Napoleon. Those officers with long naval careers which predated the Revolution fell from favor while young officers who had been appropriately groomed by the Revolutionary Government rose through the ranks quickly. Admiral Villeneuve, the combined fleet commander at Trafalgar, achieved flag rank at 33, and was considerably younger than Nelson at the time of the battle. His second in command, Rear-Admiral Dumanoir le Pelley, was 35 at the time of the battle. Both men had seen limited action during the course of their careers.

The English also had a considerable advantage over the combined fleets of France and Spain in the cohesion and esprit de corps of its officers and sailors. The English shared a common culture, both in terms of the society in which they had been brought up and in the Navy they served. In contrast, the French and Spanish officers who commanded at Trafalgar were at best somewhat suspicious of each other. Spain, to a certain extent, was a reluctant ally pulled into the war by the French. Don Federico Gravina, the senior Spanish flag officer at Trafalgar, had requested he be relieved of his command when he was placed under the French Admiral Villeneuve. He was convinced to stay on by the Spanish government, but he was not enthusiastic about doing so. In an action with another British fleet just prior to the combined fleet's arrival at Cadiz, two Spanish ships were lost while no French ships were lost. This fact engendered a feeling among the Spaniards, likely unfounded, that their ships had been sacrificed to protect the French.

Further evidence of the disaffection which existed between the two sides can be found in the reception the French received upon arriving in Cadiz, Spain. The city's authorities were initially unwilling to provide any supplies or stores for the combined fleet. Only after being specifically ordered by the Spanish government in Madrid to cooperate was help forthcoming. This is in contrast to the reception the British received following the Battle of Trafalgar. Following the battle it was necessary for a British party to visit Cadiz, from which the combined French-Spanish fleet had sailed, in order to deal with prisoner exchanges. The British reported that during their visit they could not have been treated more hospitably nor could their reception have been warmer. In fact, within a few years the Spanish were engaged in a civil war in which much of the population sought to overthrow a Spanish monarchy being supported by Napoleon. In this effort they were aided by the British Army under Sir Arthur Wellesley, later Duke of Wellington.

As a result of the less than complete confidence the two parties in the French-Spanish alliance had in each other, and owing to what can only be described as a lack of confidence in themselves, the combined fleet approached the battle at Trafalgar with great trepidation. The Spanish in fact felt that in the coming battle they would be sacrificed by the French who commanded the combined fleet.

Perhaps just as debilitating for the combined fleet crews was a general sense of unease and pessimism about the coming engagement with the Royal Navy. This pessimism started at the top with Napoleon, who had little confidence in his Navy's chances against the Royal Navy, and filtered down through the ranks. And there was good reason for morale being low. Neither the Spanish nor the French had been able to win major engagements with the British throughout the careers of those involved at Trafalgar. The British had many heroes who had won many great victories, but those victories had come mostly at the expense of the French. This apprehension was heightened by the fact the combined fleet knew they were facing Lord Nelson, a commander who had badly beaten the French before and was spoiling for a final showdown now. In fact the French admiralty's anxieties were so great about fighting the Royal Navy that it was their fondest hope that they could somehow lure the British fleet guarding the English Channel away from its station and allow Napoleon to cross his army, without ever actually having to fight the British. The anxiety that pervaded the combined fleet existed despite their outnumbering the British fleet at Trafalgar 33 sail-of-the-line to the Royal Navy's 27.

The fact that a sense of foreboding existed in the combined fleet should not be confused with cowardice. There is plenty of evidence of bravery and gallantry on the part of both French and Spanish crews. One French ship, the *Aigle*, lost two-thirds of its ship's company at Trafalgar. French Admiral Lucas' ship sustained 490 deaths and 81 wounded. The *Algeciras*, French Admiral Magon's flagship, had 77 killed and 142 wounded in the battle, and Admiral Magon was himself killed while directing action. Spanish forces likewise fought gallantly, but paid heavily in lives lost. On the *Santissima Trinidada*, flagship of Admiral Cisneros, 200 men were killed in the battle. Nor was the pre-battle anxiety owing to any doubts about the worthiness of their ships. Both French and Spanish ship construction was in fact much admired by members of the Royal Navy, and if anything, considered superior to their own.

In terms of tactics, both navies (save for Lord Nelson) followed a time-honored doctrine in terms of how a naval battle was to be fought. That doctrine called for the warring fleets to each form a line of battle as though both were strands of beads laid side-by-side. The two lines of ships would then determine the issue in such an array. One of Nelson's major contributions to naval warfare was his willingness to depart from traditional tactics. The French likewise recognized the limitations of conventional tactics. Admiral Villeneuve in fact expressed dismay at how uninspired French fleet tactics were. However, he also viewed Nelson's tactics as reckless, though there was no denying the successes Nelson had achieved in earlier engagements. Nelson's stunning victory over the French in the Bay of Aboukir off the Egyptian coast in 1798, which stranded Napoleon and the French Army in Egypt, was the result of Nelson flying in the face of naval convention. All his superiors, subordinates, and opponents came to expect the unexpected from Nelson. "The Nelson touch," as it was referred to, appears to have inspired members of the Royal Navy and created a sense of dread in his opponents.

One final intangible which undoubtedly influenced events at Trafalgar was the eagerness of the British for a fight with the combined French-Spanish fleet, which would decide the issue of naval supremacy once and for all. From Nelson down to the ordinary seaman, worn out by years of blockading French and Spanish ports or chasing the French and Spanish fleets throughout the Mediterranean, the Atlantic, and the Caribbean, a decisive battle was much desired. Prior to Trafalgar, Nelson had spent over two years chasing the French fleet through the Mediterranean, across the Atlantic to the West Indies, and back across the Atlantic for the purpose of engaging it. This was in spite of the fact that throughout his pursuit, as was the case at Trafalgar, the French fleet held numerical superiority over the British. An officer on one of the British sail-of-the-line commented in his diary how members of his crew had chalked "victory or death" on their guns just prior to Trafalgar. Lord Nelson himself perhaps summed up the British attitude in an entry in his diary during the pursuit of the enemy before Trafalgar when he wrote:

> The business of an English Commander-in-Chief being first to bring the Enemy's fleet to battle on the most advantageous terms to himself (I mean that of laying his ships well on board the Enemy's as expeditiously as possible), and secondly to continue  them there without separating until the business is decided . . . if the two fleets are both willing to fight, but little maneuvering is necessary; the less the better: a day is soon lost in that business. . . .

## THE BATTLE OF TRAFALGAR

Having failed to combine the various elements of the French and Spanish Navies into a single force in the West Indies with which to attack the British in the English Channel, having been chased out of the West Indies by Lord Nelson, and then having been on the losing end of an engagement with an English fleet under Sir Robert Calder off the Spanish coast, Villeneuve and the combined fleet retired to Cadiz, Spain, on August 20, 1805. There, the British Mediterranean fleet under Vice Admiral Cuthbert Collingwood took up blockade station outside the port of Cadiz and waited. Nelson, having spent the previous years blockading and then chasing the combined fleet across the Atlantic, returned to England to report to the admiralty. His fleet joined Collingwood's off Cadiz.

By the time Villeneuve had taken refuge at Cadiz, Napoleon had, for all practical purposes, given up on crossing the English Channel, as he realized his navy would never gain him any kind of window during which to cross the channel in force. He then decided to turn his attentions to his Austrian and Russian adversaries, and relegate his navy to playing whatever supporting role it might in the Mediterranean, or making life miserable for the British in the West Indies.

On September 28, 1805, Lord Nelson rejoined the British fleet off Cadiz. His fleet consisted of 27 sail-of-the-line, 4 frigates, a schooner, and a cutter. The British faced a combined fleet of 33 sail-of-the-line. For perhaps the first time in three or four years, both Nelson and the British Admiralty were on the same page as to what his purpose was—to blockade the combined fleet at Cadiz until such time as the French commander-in-chief chose to do battle or attempt an escape. They believed, correctly, that in Nelson they had the leader who could destroy the French fleet. For his part, Nelson was determined that battle would be joined and the combined fleet destroyed. Such a victory would make an invasion of England virtually impossible and give the British free reign in terms of sending its armies overseas. Neither Nelson nor the Admiralty had yet discovered Napoleon had given up on his plans for invasion.

## ■ Lord Nelson's Battle Plan

As mentioned earlier, conventional wisdom called for an attacking fleet to approach its opponent in a single line of sail which would be brought alongside the enemy's line and battle be joined. Nelson rejected this strategy for several reasons. First, he was very concerned that given all the time it would take to maneuver his fleet into such a formation and then alongside the combined fleet, the enemy might escape or manage to get back into the port at Cadiz. Second, given his confidence in his officers and men, he was sure that the quicker he could get his individual ships joined in battle with the enemy, the more damage would be incurred and the greater the victory. Finally, he wanted to confound the enemy and confuse them as to his intent. As a result, Nelson resolved to attack the enemy's fleet in two separate columns, attacking in a perpendicular direction, as two wedges going through the single line of enemy ships (see Exhibit 3). One column would attack the enemy's line about a third of its length from the front, while the second column would attack the line about a third of a way from its rear. What was Nelson's intended result? To quote him, "I think it will surprise and confound the enemy. They won't know what I am about. It will bring forward a pell-mell battle, and that is what I want." He wanted a "pell-mell battle" because he was convinced that in a scrambled set of one-on-one engagements, superior English seamanship, gunnery, and leadership would carry the day.

In keeping with Nelson's inclination to expose himself to hazardous situations, his own flagship, *H.M.S. Victory*, would spearhead the column attacking the front of the enemy line, with his career-long friend Collingwood leading the other column aboard the *H.M.S. Royal Sovereign*. The one major problem with Nelson's plan was that it exposed the ships at the heads of the columns to tremendous enemy fire for a significant period of time before they could bring their own guns to bear. In addition, the first ships to reach the enemy line would likely find themselves initially engaged with multiple enemy ships. As a result, it was anticipated the damage and casualties sustained by the lead ships would be the worst suffered by any Royal Navy ships in the battle. In contrast, by the time the ships at the rear of the columns joined the battle the issue could very well be decided. Subordinate officers suggested Nelson's ship at least fall back to the second position in the column, but Nelson would have none of that.

While Nelson's plan was simple, it was reported to have sent an "electric shock" through the fleet owing to its departure from orthodoxy and its boldness. Likewise, simply having Nelson in command seems to have added to the fleet's confidence level and eagerness for the coming battle.

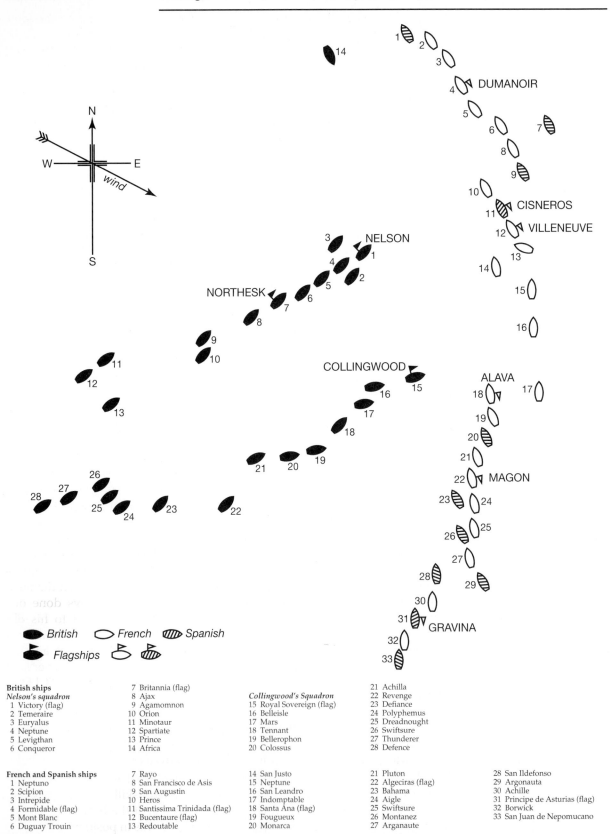

British ● French ○ Spanish ◧

Flagships ◖ ◗ ◖

**British ships**
*Nelson's squadron*
1 Victory (flag)
2 Temeraire
3 Euryalus
4 Neptune
5 Levigthan
6 Conqueror

7 Britannia (flag)
8 Ajax
9 Agamomnon
10 Orion
11 Minotaur
12 Spartiate
13 Prince
14 Africa

*Collingwood's Squadron*
15 Royal Sovereign (flag)
16 Belleisle
17 Mars
18 Tennant
19 Bellerophon
20 Colossus

21 Achilla
22 Revenge
23 Defiance
24 Polyphemus
25 Dreadnought
26 Swiftsure
27 Thunderer
28 Defence

**French and Spanish ships**
1 Neptuno
2 Scipion
3 Intrepide
4 Formidable (flag)
5 Mont Blanc
6 Duguay Trouin

7 Rayo
8 San Francisco de Asis
9 San Augustin
10 Heros
11 Santissima Trinidada (flag)
12 Bucentaure (flag)
13 Redoutable

14 San Justo
15 Neptune
16 San Leandro
17 Indomptable
18 Santa Ana (flag)
19 Fougueux
20 Monarca

21 Pluton
22 Algeciras (flag)
23 Bahama
24 Aigle
25 Swiftsure
26 Montanez
27 Arganaute

28 San Ildefonso
29 Argonauta
30 Achille
31 Principe de Asturias (flag)
32 Borwick
33 San Juan de Nepomucano

## ■ Admiral Villeneuve's Plans

Admiral Villeneuve's strategy upon leaving the port at Cadiz was to sail westward toward the Cape of Trafalgar, and then south, and then eastward into the Mediterranean. In this way he hoped to elude the British fleet which he assumed was positioned just over the horizon out of Cadiz. However, he and his officers recognized the chances of getting away without a fight were not great. In light of that fact, there was strong reluctance on the part of some French and virtually all the Spaniards to leave Cadiz. They felt their men needed additional training, the weather appeared threatening, and the British could only grow weaker the longer they had to remain at sea in blockade.

Villeneuve likely recognized these very good reasons for staying in port. However, despite all the misgivings, Villeneuve ordered the fleet would put to sea on October 18th. This was likely in response to news he had received from friends at the French Ministry of Marine that Napoleon had appointed a new commander for the combined fleet, and he was on his way to take over. Villeneuve, in what might have been a vain attempt to salvage his career, decided to put to sea and perhaps at some point in the future achieve a victory which might restore his career.

## ■ The Battle

The battle unfolded more or less as Lord Nelson had envisioned it. The one feature of such engagements which may seem odd to the 20th century reader is the snail's pace at which events unfolded. While Villeneuve ordered his fleet out of Cadiz on October 18, it was not until the 21st that the battle was joined. Huge, lumbering sail-of-the-line moved very slowly and maneuvered very clumsily. As a result of this fact, once an admiral had committed his fleet to a particular strategy, his ability to make major alterations in terms of deployment of his fleet was very limited. In addition, given these ships were propelled by sail, things rarely went completely according to plan due to wind speed and direction. Once committed, an admiral had to rely upon the initiative of his individual captains and ships, something Nelson felt very good about doing.

One of the most notable actions Nelson took just prior to the engagement was to send a signal to the British fleet which subsequently became famous: "ENGLAND EXPECTS EVERY MAN WILL DO HIS DUTY." Though it sounds very patriotic and inspiring, it did not necessarily have that effect on the fleet. Many responded with comments such as "Have we not always done our duty?" His second in command, Admiral Collingwood, reacted to his old friend's signal with the response that everyone in the fleet knew what was expected of them that day. Nevertheless, cheers went up from the fleet, and the signal became the stuff of legend. The next signal was the last Nelson ever sent his fleet, and remained atop the *Victory* until it was shot away: "CLOSE ACTION AND KEEP IT UP."

A little before noon on October 21st, 1805, Collingwood's flagship *Royal Sovereign* came under fire about half an hour before the *Royal Sovereign* could open up. However, when it did the results were devastating. One of Collingwood's trademarks was being able to deliver three well-placed broadsides in less than five minutes. It was something Collingwood drilled hard at, as did other commanders in the Royal Navy. At Trafalgar this gunnery skill proved very effective. At 12:24 Lord Nelson's flagship *H.M.S. Victory*, at the head of the other column, came under fire, and 15 minutes later it too was in position to open up with broadsides from its starboard guns. From that point on the lead ships of both columns were engulfed in a vortex of cannon fire, smoke, and flame as they closed with the ships of the combined fleet.

Nelson's own behavior is worth a comment. When he came to his position on the quarter deck just prior to the action he was joined by Captain Hardy, his flagship commander, Captain Blackwood, the frigate commander, John Scott, his secretary, Alexander Scott, the ship's chaplain, and Dr. William Beatty, the ship's surgeon. Captain Blackwood encouraged his Lordship to accompany him to his frigate, which would be safer and would offer a better view. Nelson declined. Both Dr. Beatty and Captain Hardy suggested that perhaps his Lordship might not wear his customary uniform, which had four very distinctive stars of orders embroidered on the left breast, as it would make him a marked man for French snipers stationed high up in the riggings. Nelson agreed it was probably not the best idea to be wearing such a coat, but said it was too late to change it.

The battle became more or less the pell-mell, close-action, ship-to-ship fight Nelson had sought. Though, as mentioned earlier, the French and Spanish did not want for courage, after a couple of hours of fighting it became clear who was going to carry the day. By four o'clock the combined fleet had been for the most part either captured, destroyed, or forced to flee. Of the 33 sail-of-the-line which had left Cadiz, 11 made it back to Cadiz, four made for the Straits of Gibraltar, and 17 were demasted, of which 13 were in the hands of the British and one was ablaze. It had been the most successful afternoon in the history of the Royal Navy.

Shortly after the *Victory* engaged the enemy Nelson's secretary, who was standing near him, was decapitated by cannon fire, then Hardy was wounded in the foot. At about 1:15 in the afternoon, during the most severe fighting the *Victory* saw in the battle, Lord Nelson was still pacing the quarter deck with Captain Hardy. At that time a French sniper's bullet entered the upper left breast of Lord Nelson, traveling downward through his lung and breaking his spine. He was taken below where it was determined his wounds were mortal. The *Victory's* log book contained the following entry by its commander: "Partial firing continued until 4:30. When a victory having been reported to the Right Honourable Lord Viscount Nelson, K.B. and Commander-in-Chief, he then died of his wounds."

## THE BATTLE'S CONSEQUENCES

In the days following October 21st additional British fleet action led to additional enemy ships being captured, and the totality of the Royal Navy's success was made all the greater. The results gave Britain undisputed supremacy at sea, which lasted into the 20th Century, when it was supplanted by the U.S. Navy. England and France never again fought a major sea battle, and Napoleon's range of operations was thereafter confined to the continent of Europe. In 1808, three years after Trafalgar, Spain became embroiled in a popular uprising against its monarchy which was installed by Napoleon. The British sent troops to Spain under the command of Sir Arthur Wellesley, later Duke of Wellington, to support the rebels. The French also sent in troops. Napoleon, having given up on any conquests off the European continent, went on to defeat the Russian-Austrian alliance and then invaded Russia in 1812. He was forced to retreat from Russia and, after several years of fighting, Wellesley evicted the French from Spain and launched an attack on France. In 1814 Britain, along with its allies Austria, Russia, Prussia, Sweden, and Portugal, defeated Napoleon under Sir Arthur Wellesley. Napoleon escaped from exile on the island of Elba and returned to France to attempt a comeback. Wellesley, then Duke of Wellington, and his allies again defeated Napoleon at Waterloo, and he was once again sent into exile.

For the commanders at Trafalgar, the battle represented closure of both men's lives. Lord Nelson's remains returned to London for one of the most elaborate state funerals in England's history. The body was taken from the *Victory* and transported up the Thames River by a column of barges. When it reached the Admiralty, the body lay in state overnight. On January 9, 1806, Nelson's coffin, made from the wood of the mast of a captured French ship, was borne in a processional so long that its head reached St. Paul's Cathedral before its end departed the Admiralty. Over 10,000 soldiers marched along with over 30 flag officers and 100 captains of the Royal Navy. At the end of the four-hour service, as the coffin was being lowered into its crypt in St. Paul's, Sir Isaac Heard recited the various titles held by Lord Nelson, and then concluded "the hero who in the moment of victory fell, covered with immortal glory."

For Admiral Villeneuve, the results were quite different. He and his flagship were captured at Trafalgar. He was taken to England as a prisoner of war, but was allowed to attend Nelson's funeral. In the spring of 1806 he was paroled and returned to France. On April 22, 1806, anticipating court martial, he committed suicide in Rennes, France.

As might be expected, in the decades following Trafalgar tacticians of various navies have studied the battle for lessons which might have general application. However, the lesson which emerges is that Lord Nelson knew his ships and men, knew his enemy, and designed a strategy which was likely to work in only that one moment in history. His genius in all his battles was recognizing the uniqueness of the circumstances and acting accordingly. Perhaps Nelson's only lasting contribution to naval warfare was to recognize there were no strategies which were always appropriate.

# REFERENCES

Aldington, Richard. *The Duke: Being an Account of the Life and Achievements of Arthur Wellesley, First Duke of Wellington*. New York: Viking Press, 1943.

Aubry, Octave. *Napoleon: Soldier and Emperor*. New York: J. B. Lippincott Company, 1938.

Ballard, Colin R. *Napoleon, An Outline*. New York: Books for Libraries Press, 1971.

Carr, Albert. *Napoleon Speaks*. New York: Viking Press, 1941.

Castelot, Andre. *Napoleon*. New York: Harper and Row Publishing, 1968.

Corbett, Julian Stafford, Sir. *The Campaign of Trafalgar*. New York: Longmans, Green, 1910.

Fournier, August. *Napoleon I, Volume I*. New York: Henry Holt and Company, 1913.

Pocock, Tom. *Horatio Nelson*. London: Pimlico, 1994.

Walder, David. *Nelson*. New York: The Dial Press, 1978.

# Dow Corning Corporation: Marketing Breast Implant Devices

Todd E. Himstead, Georgetown University

N. Craig Smith, Georgetown University

Andrew D. Dyer, Georgetown University

In December 1991, a federal court jury in California awarded a $7.3 million payment against Dow Corning to Mariann Hopkins, a silicone gel breast implant wearer who claimed injury to her autoimmune system.[1] The recipient was just one of thousands of women who had undergone breast implant surgery over the past twenty-five years. Throughout the 1980's there had been considerable questioning of the safety of these implants. The federal court judgment was seen as a landmark victory by the plaintiff's lawyers. Dow Corning and other breast implant manufacturers now were facing the possibility of substantial litigation from women claiming to be harmed by silicone gel implants. With perhaps as many as two million breast implant operations completed, the potential existed for thousands of lawsuits to be filed against the manufacturers.[2]

As it entered 1992, Dow Corning's exposure to product safety issues with silicone gel implants became more apparent. On January 6, 1992, the Food and Drug Administration (FDA) requested that breast implant producers and medical practitioners halt the sale and use of silicone gel breast implants, pending further review of the safety and effectiveness of the devices.[3] As a precautionary measure, Dow Corning retained former attorney general Griffin Bell on January 10, 1992, to conduct a complete investigation of the company's development, production, and marketing of silicone gel breast implants. On February 3, 1992, Dow Corning took a pretax charge of $25 million to earnings in 1991 to cover costs associated with frozen inventories, dedicated equipment, and other related costs.[4]

On February 10, 1992, Dow Corning's board elected Keith R. McKennon chairman and CEO. McKennon was a career Dow Chemical employee. His previous role was president of Dow Chemical USA. Having managed two previous product crises for Dow Chemical (including Dow's Agent Orange pesticide crisis) now he was charged with the decisions of what to do with the silicone gel implant product line and how to manage the legal, regulatory, and public relations challenges facing Dow Corning. Since breast implants represented less than 1% of total 1991 revenues,[5] McKennon might have been tempted to question whether Dow Corning should even continue with the implant products, despite the benefits to women resulting from their use in reconstructive and cosmetic surgery.

# DOW CORNING

Dow Corning Corporation was founded in 1943 with a mission to develop the potential of silicones. Silicones were new materials, unlike anything found in nature or previously manufactured. They were based on silicon, which was an element refined from quartz rock, a form of silica. The resulting chemical compounds were the basis for an infinite range of versatile, flexible materials that ranged from fluids thinner than water to rigid plastics, each with unique properties.

Dow Corning was established as a 50/50 joint venture by The Dow Chemical Company of Midland, Michigan, and Corning Glass Works (now Corning Inc.) of Corning, New York. Corning provided the basic silicone technology while Dow Chemical supplied the chemical processing and manufacturing know-how. Both companies provided initial key employees and maintained their ownership of Dow Corning from the outset.

The Dow Corning venture became successful in developing, manufacturing, and marketing silicone-based products. It grew steadily from 1943 in revenues, profits and employees and by 1991 generated revenues of $1.85 billion and income of $152.9 million, with some 8,300 employees.[6] In 1991, it was ranked 241 in the Fortune 500.[7] (For a five-year summary of Dow Corning's financial statements, see Exhibit 1.) In addition to developing silicone products, it had expanded development to related specialty chemical materials, poly-crystalline silicon, and specialty health care products. With some 5000 products, Dow Corning served a wide range of industries including aerospace, automotive, petrochemicals, construction, electronics, medical products, pharmaceuticals, plastics, and textiles. It had become a global enterprise with 33 major manufacturing locations worldwide, R&D facilities in the U.S., Japan, France, Germany, Belgium, and the U.K., and over 45,000 customers from countries including the U.S., Europe, Canada, Latin America, Japan, Australia, Taiwan, and Korea.

In the early 1990s, Dow Corning was seen as a model corporate citizen. It was a pioneer in corporate ethics, renowned for its Business Conduct Committee. The committee comprised six managers, who performed an ethics audit of every business every third year and reported results to the Audit & Social Responsibility Committee of the Dow Corning board. In October 1990 the committee audited Dow Corning's implant operation. It found no substantial ethical problems related to implants.

**Exhibit 1**    **Dow Corning Corporation: Five-Year Summary of Selected Financial Data**

### Consolidated Balance Sheets (in millions of dollars)

| Year ended: | 12/31/91 | 12/31/90 | 12/31/89 | 12/31/88 | 12/31/87 |
|---|---|---|---|---|---|
| **Assets** | | | | | |
| *Current Assets* | | | | | |
| Cash and cash equivalents | $7.9 | $9.1 | $4.1 | $36.9 | $10.8 |
| Short-term investments | 0.4 | 1.9 | 3.3 | 5.1 | 3.0 |
| Accounts and notes rec. | 334.1 | 336.3 | 293.4 | 289.6 | 258.8 |
| Inventories | 358.7 | 281.2 | 251.8 | 242.2 | 242.1 |
| Other current assets | 110.0 | 84.7 | 64.5 | 53.5 | 57.2 |
| Total current assets | 811.1 | 713.2 | 617.1 | 627.3 | 571.9 |
| *Property, plant, equipment* | | | | | |
| Land and land improvements | 107.4 | 95.8 | 92.5 | 88.6 | 80.1 |
| Buildings | 391.3 | 354.3 | 276.1 | 241.0 | 214.6 |
| Machinery and equipment | 1,533.9 | 1,272.3 | 1,109.7 | 1,066.3 | 1,000.5 |
| Construction-in-progress | 179.4 | 235.9 | 242.6 | 140.3 | 56.7 |
| | 2,212.0 | 1,958.3 | 1,720.9 | 1,536.2 | 1,351.0 |
| Less accumulated depr. | (1,000.1) | (846.6) | (740.3) | (705.2) | (630.2) |
| | 1,211.9 | 1,111.7 | 980.6 | 831.0 | 721.7 |
| *Other Assets* | 96.9 | 97.5 | 80.4 | 70.5 | 67.6 |
| | $2,119.9 | $1,922.4 | $1,678.1 | $1,528.8 | $1,361.2 |
| **Liabilities & Shareholders' Equity** | | | | | |
| *Current liabilities* | | | | | |
| Commercial paper payable | 41.4 | – | – | – | $39.7 |
| Notes payable | $59.3 | $104.0 | $23.6 | $13.0 | 7.3 |
| Current portion of long-term debt | 4.0 | 13.2 | 0.5 | 5.4 | 30.9 |
| Trade accounts payable | 135.3 | 121.0 | 107.3 | 114.2 | 90.3 |
| Income taxes payable | 28.2 | 26.0 | 36.8 | 29.2 | 42.7 |
| Accrued payrolls and employee benefits | 52.4 | 43.3 | 31.2 | 33.2 | 30.9 |
| Accrued taxes, other than income taxes | 15.8 | 16.3 | 18.9 | 19.7 | 12.3 |
| Other current liabilities | 113.6 | 70.3 | 68.2 | 79.4 | 71.5 |
| | 450.0 | 394.1 | 286.5 | 294.1 | 325.6 |
| *Long-term debt* | 286.8 | 267.7 | 274.3 | 200.4 | 95.7 |
| *Other Liabilities* | 198.5 | 196.9 | 190.4 | 183.9 | 183.7 |
| *Minority interest in consolidated subsidiaries* | 77.1 | 65.3 | 54.8 | 54.1 | 48.7 |
| *Stockholders' equity* | | | | | |
| Common stock, $5 par value—2,500,000 | | | | | |
| shares authorized and outstanding | 12.5 | 12.5 | 12.5 | 12.5 | 12.5 |
| Retained earnings | 1,028.8 | 953.4 | 853.8 | 758.0 | 668.5 |
| Cumulative translation adjustment | 66.2 | 32.5 | 5.8 | 25.8 | 26.5 |
| Stockholders' equity | 1,107.5 | 998.4 | 872.1 | 796.3 | 707.5 |
| | $2,119.9 | 1,922.4 | $1,678.1 | $1,528.8 | $1,361.2 |

---

**Exhibit 1 (continued)    Dow Corning Corporation: Five-Year Summary of Selected Financial Data**

---

*Consolidated Statements of Operations and Retained Earnings (in millions of dollars except per share amounts)*

| Year ended: | 12/31/91 | 12/31/90 | 12/31/89 | 12/30/88 | 12/31/87 |
|---|---|---|---|---|---|
| Net Sales | $1,845.4 | $1,718.3 | $1,574.5 | $1,476.8 | $1,303.0 |
| Operating costs and expenses: | | | | | |
| Manufacturing cost of sales | 1,195.5 | 1,105.2 | 1,000.8 | 954.4 | 842.1 |
| Marketing and administrative expenses | 380.8 | 351.6 | 314.2 | 293.3 | 263.8 |
| Implant costs | 25.0 | – | – | – | – |
| Special Items | 29.0 | – | – | – | – |
| | 1,630.3 | 1,456.8 | 1,315.0 | 1,247.7 | 1,105.9 |
| Operating income | 215.1 | 261.5 | 259.5 | 299.1 | 197.1 |
| Other income (expense) | 10.4 | (0.5) | 6.9 | 5.8 | 15.4 |
| Income before income taxes | 225.5 | 261.0 | 266.4 | 234.9 | 212.5 |
| Income taxes | 58.3 | 80.1 | 94.6 | 75.3 | 74.1 |
| Minority interests' share in income | 14.1 | 9.8 | 9.2 | 9.1 | 3.4 |
| Net income | 153.1 | 171.1 | 162.6 | 150.5 | 135.0 |
| Retained earnings at beginning of year | 953.2 | 853.8 | 758.0 | 668.5 | 587.5 |
| Cash dividends | (77.5) | (71.5) | (67.0) | (61.0) | (54.0) |
| Retained earnings at end of year | $1,028.8 | $953.2 | $853.6 | $758.0 | $668.5 |

Source: Dow Corning 10K Filings.

In 1991, Dow Corning was headed by John Ludington as chairman and Larry Reed as president and CEO. The organization was divided into two primary line organizations, Area Operations and Business Organization. Area Operations was responsible for sales and service of Dow Corning products around the world and was grouped into the U.S., Inter-America (Canada & Latin America), Europe, and Asia. The Business Organization was responsible for the development and manufacturing of Dow Corning's products and was organized on a product line-of-business approach.

Dow Corning's product line in 1991 included gasket sealants and windshields for the aerospace industry; silicone rubbers for the automotive industry; adhesives and sealants for the building trade and for consumer home improvement; and fluids, emulsions, and transdermal patches for the pharmaceutical industry, as well as a variety of medical products, such as tubing, adhesives, and surgical implants.

### ■ Dow Corning Wright

In 1991, Dow Corning Wright Corporation, a wholly owned subsidiary, manufactured and sold silicone gel breast implants for Dow Corning. It also manufactured and marketed metal orthopedic implants for Dow Corning. Dow

Corning Wright was headquartered in Arlington, Tennessee, and was headed up by chairman Bob Rylee and president and CEO Dan M. Hayes, Jr. It reported to Dow Corning's Business Organization and was considered a stand-alone line of business. Dow Corning Wright was established in 1978 when Dow Corning acquired Wright Medical, a small manufacturer of orthopedic hips and knees. Dow Corning then transferred all of its medical devices manufacturing and sales to this new subsidiary, including the breast implants. Dow Corning Wright 1991 revenues were approximately $80 million.[8]

## ■ Breast Implant Devices

Various options to achieve breast augmentation had been tried since the sixteenth century. Materials such as ivory, glass, and paraffin had been used for contour enhancement (by applying these materials to the breast externally). The first augmentation mammaplasty was accomplished in the late nineteenth century. Following this operation, a variety of non-silicone materials were injected or implanted to cosmetically alter or reconstruct breasts. The most successful implant device, developed during the 1950s, was a product with an outer sack made of polyurethane foam or silicone and filled with saline.

The next breakthrough came in 1962, when Dow Corning was approached by two plastic surgeons who wanted help in further developing breast implants for mastectomy and congenital deformity victims. The surgeons had designed an implant and had begun limited production, but looked to Dow Corning to apply its silicone gel and manufacturing expertise. In 1964, as a result of this request, Dow Corning developed a product based on an envelope of silicone elastomer (a rubber-like elastic substance) filled with silicone gel. The product was touted to be superior in terms of its look and feel for the recipients and was less likely to migrate over time through body and muscle tissue that surrounded the breast, compared with saline fluid-filled implants. Silicone gel breast implants became the market leader from that time on.

The advantage of silicone gel implants was that the silicone could hold its shape. This was particularly important for reconstructive patients, where there was little or no foundation to build on. Saline implants (made with salt water contained in a silicone envelope) were "water-like" and were unable to hold any shape by themselves. As a result, they were much less effective in providing either an enhanced figure or a complete reconstruction.

From 1965, when Dow Corning launched the first silicone gel breast implants, demand for the product was consistently high. Other manufacturers entered the market and the company became one of seven manufacturers in the U.S. producing the silicone gel product. Dow Corning introduced new models over time, with improvements in gel texture and envelope characteristics. The implants were available in a variety of sizes and contours. During the period 1965 to 1992, Dow Corning sold approximately 600,000 implants, 45% of them outside the US.[9] Dow Corning's market share of breast implants never exceeded 25% (once the industry had become established). In 1991, chairman Bob Rylee admitted that the breast implant line had sustained five consecutive years of financial losses, but the company continued selling them because millions of women were "counting on them."[10] Dow Corning also supplied silicone to the other implant manufacturers. During the 1980s, Dow

Corning's focus on medical devices moved to knee implants, and breast implants were not viewed as a strategic product. In 1991, Dow Corning's market share of breast implant sales was approximately 18%. It was the third largest supplier behind McGhan and Mentor.

### ■ Sales Agents

Dow Corning Wright's medical devices were sold by independent agents who had contracts to sell the products in specified geographic areas. They were paid a commission on sales and were reimbursed for expenses. In 1991, Dow Corning had some 70 medical device agents across the United States who were managed by a Dow Corning national sales manager, supported by two marketing staff. Some of the more senior agents also coordinated or supervised other agents regionally.

Some independent agents also sold non-Dow Corning products, though typically these products did not compete with Dow Corning's line. The agents relied on their strong relationship with the surgeons to make sales and maintained that relationship by providing quality products and good service. Of the 70 independent agents operating in 1991, two relied heavily on Dow Corning's breast implants, with some 50% of their sales derived from Dow Corning implants. For the remaining agents, their primary focus was hip and knee implants, with between 5% to 25% (an average of 10%) of their sales coming from breast implants.[11]

Geography was the major contributor to variations in volume, with certain regions having a higher demand for implants than others. The Pacific region was the site of the most (approximately 25%) breast augmentation procedures in the early 1990s, followed by the South Atlantic region with 21%, according to the American Society of Plastic and Reconstructive Surgeons (ASPRS). New England had the fewest procedures, with only 1.5%. California represented 19% of the total, Florida 12%, Texas 10%, and New York 4%.[12]

## MEDICAL DEVICES INDUSTRY

Breast implant products were considered part of the medical devices industry, an industry that was generally fragmented, with 97% of manufacturers employing 500 employees or less and 70% of manufacturers employing 50 employees or less.[13] Medical devices (also known as surgical appliances and supplies) included crutches, wheelchairs, orthopedic devices and materials, surgical implants, bandages, hearing aids, and protective clothing. In 1991, the U.S. manufactured and shipped some $10.7 billion worth of medical devices, growing 6.4% from 1990. The industry employed an estimated 89,500 people in 1991, up 3% from 1990; 58,300 of these employees were engaged as production workers. U.S. exports of medical devices also grew in 1991 by 18% to $1.4 billion, the fourth consecutive year of double digit growth.[14] The principal export items included respiratory products, orthopedic equipment and supplies, as well as artificial joints and internal fixation devices.

The principal manufacturers of breast implants in 1991 were: Baxter Healthcare Corporation (Deerfield, IL), Bioplasty Inc. (St. Paul, MN), Cox-

Uphoff (Carpinteria, CA), Dow Corning Corporation (Midland, MI), McGhan Medical Inc. (Santa Barbara, CA), Mentor (Santa Barbara, CA), Porex Technologies (Fairburn, GA), and Surgitek (Racine, WI).

## ■ Regulation

When Dow Corning first sold implants in 1965, the medical devices industry was not subject to specific government regulation. The Food and Drug Administration unit of the U.S. Department of Health and Human Services was given the responsibility to regulate all medical devices and device establishments on May 28, 1976, following the Medical Device Amendments to the Federal Food, Drug, and Cosmetic Act of 1938. Its goal was to ensure that the medical devices consumed by the public were safe and effective by regulating the industry, by analyzing product samples, and by researching the risks and benefits of those products. The 1976 amendments directed the FDA to issue regulations to set up an approval process for new devices and classify existing ones into Class I, II, or III, depending on the degree of testing necessary to provide reasonable assurance of the safety of the device.

At that time, the FDA classified breast implants as "Class II" devices, a rating that did not demand testing as a condition for remaining on the market. While an advisory panel was formed in 1977 to look at cosmetic implants, the lack of conclusive studies and the panel members' own positive experience with breast implants allowed the implants to be classified as "safe" with no more research necessary. Some FDA scientists disputed this finding, based on feedback from doctors who claimed that the implants could break or leak. A new panel in 1982 voted that there was insufficient evidence to establish the product's safety and efficacy. It went on to recommend that silicone gel–filled breast implants be placed at the top of the FDA's list for review. But the lack of consumer complaints lowered the priority on implants, as the FDA screened its huge backlog of other devices. John Vilforth, the FDA's medical devices division manager during the 1980's, commented during a later interview that few of the million or more women with implants had complained to the FDA and that the longer term effects allegedly occurring in 1991 had not been observed in the previous decade. The FDA took no action on implants between 1982 and 1988.

In January 1989 the FDA reclassified breast implants as "Class III," and on April 10, 1991, required all manufacturers (including Dow Corning) to submit, within 90 days, implant safety and effectiveness data in pre-market approval applications (PMAAs) for the FDA's evaluation. According to its 10-K filing, on July 8, 1991, Dow Corning submitted 30,000 pages of documentation along with its PMAA, detailing silicone gel breast implant manufacturing processes, product design and labeling, and 30 years of safety studies. After previewing the PMAAs, on September 25, the FDA ordered manufacturers to provide more implant risk data to the physicians who inserted them, while the FDA continued its review. In November 1991 the FDA's Advisory Panel, after hearing testimony, recommended keeping implants on the market, noting that the psychological benefits outweighed the health risks. It was up to FDA Commissioner David Kessler to make the final decision, however, and on January 6, 1992, Kessler requested that producers and physicians halt the sale and use of breast implants for 45 days. Dow Corning voluntarily suspended shipments on that day.

# PLASTIC SURGERY

## ■ Background

The plastic surgery profession began to formalize in the 1930's, although it had been practiced for centuries. Plastic surgeons were qualified surgeons who specialized in surgery either to reconstruct a human deformity or to enhance or modify a human feature. In 1992, there were over 5,000 certified plastic surgeons in the U.S. In the early 1990's, these plastic surgeons performed over 1.5 million procedures a year, with average fees ranging from $100 to over $6,000 per procedure.[15]

Plastic surgeons typically specialized in certain procedures and/or parts of the anatomy. For example, they would specialize in procedures such as skin grafts or nose surgery (rhinoplasty) or could specialize in a certain body part such as the hands or face. Plastic surgeons performing breast implant surgery typically became specialized in that procedure, and would average one implant operation per week. For these plastic surgeons, breast implant procedures represented from 20 to 40% of their income.[16]

## ■ Types of Plastic Surgery

The two main categories of plastic surgery were general reconstructive and cosmetic:

### General Reconstructive Plastic Surgery

Over one million reconstructive procedures were performed yearly by plastic surgeons in the early 1990's in the U.S. Reconstructive surgery was performed on abnormal structures of the body caused by birth defects, developmental abnormalities, trauma or injury, infection, tumors, or disease. It was generally performed to improve the patient's function, but may also have been done to approximate a normal appearance. Reconstructive surgery met the needs of two different categories of patients: those who had congenital deformities (known as birth defects) and those with developmental deformities (resulting from an accident, infection, disease, or aging). In the early 1990's, tumor removal was the leading procedure, constituting almost half of all reconstructive plastic surgery. Breast reconstruction was one of the top ten procedures. In 1990, 30,000 women received breast implants for reconstruction. Approximately 20% of all implant operations between 1965 and 1991 were for reconstructive surgery after undergoing a mastectomy operation.[17] In 1992, according to ASPRS statistics, 1% of reconstructive patients were under 19, 11% were between 19 and 34, 54% were between 35 and 50, 29% were between 51 and 64, and 5% were over 64. The average surgeon's fees for a breast reconstruction procedure using implants was $2,340 in 1992.[18]

### Cosmetic Plastic Surgery

Cosmetic surgery was performed to reshape normal structures of the body to improve the patient's appearance and self esteem. In 1990, 120,000 women received breast implants for cosmetic reasons. It was the leading cosmetic plastic surgery procedure. Other popular procedures included eye-lid surgery, nose reshaping, liposuction, collagen injections, and facelifts. Approximately 80% of all breast implant operations between 1965 and 1991 were cosmetic augmentations.[19] In 1992, according to the ASPRS, 3% of the breast augmentation (cosmetic) patients were under the age of 19, 60% were between 19 and 34, 34% were between 35 and 50, 3% were between 51 and 64, while none were over 64.[20] ASPRS estimated that its members billed $330 million a year for breast implant procedures in the early 1990's.[21] In 1992, the average surgeon's fees for a breast augmentation procedure using implants was $2,754.[22]

## ■ Surgeon Selection of Medical Devices

In buying medical devices such as breast implants, plastic surgeons looked pri-marily at four criteria in making their selection:

### Quality

The quality of the products had to be uniform and consistent. The surgeon could only inspect the product at the time of the operation, when the product was removed from its packaging. A faulty product would cause the operation to be delayed or postponed while backup supplies were sought.

### Service

Product availability was mandatory at the time of surgery, and had to meet the schedule of the surgeon. Successful suppliers therefore had to ensure very high service levels and were subject to high inventory carrying costs as a result.

### Price

Price, while not the dominant factor in the purchase decision, needed to be con-sistent with alternatives and enable the procedure to be affordable for the patient.

### Relationship

The relationship between the sales agent and the surgeon was critical. The sur-geon relied on and trusted the agent to provide the best and latest products together with quality service. Without such a relationship, it was unlikely that a medical device manufacturer could sell its products to a surgeon regardless of how well it scored in the other three criteria above.

Dow Corning felt that its strongest attributes were quality and relationships. Dow Corning generally had very strong credibility with the plastic surgeons, based on its leadership and innovation of new products. Dow Corning's scien-tists and physicians were highly regarded by the plastic surgeons and were constantly researching and publishing on key areas of interest. The indepen-dent agents were well connected to the plastic surgeons and provided an effec-tive channel for Dow Corning's products.

### ■ Patient Selection of a Plastic Surgeon

Patients requiring or requesting plastic surgery were either referred by their physician to a plastic surgeon or selected their plastic surgeon directly. The latter was especially the case for cosmetic surgery, where the costs were not covered by health insurance. In selecting a plastic surgeon, patients used a number of steps to decide which surgeon would be best:

- Gathering names of plastic surgeons from friends, family doctor, nurses, hospitals, advertisements, and directories (e.g., the Plastic Surgery Information Service, state and city directories of certified plastic surgeons).
- Checking the credentials of the surgeons, such as their training, board certification (i.e., certified by the American Board of Plastic Surgery), hospital privileges (i.e., approved to perform the specific procedure at an accredited hospital), and experience and membership of professional societies (e.g., ASPRS, which required certification by the American Board of Plastic Surgery together with a peer review, adherence to a strict code of ethics, and continuing education to maintain membership).
- Consulting and interviewing the surgeon to compare personalities and obtaining opinions on the type of surgery and approach. Typically, the interview also included discussion of the surgeon's fees and an assessment of the way the surgeon answered questions and described the risks involved. Generally, patients would pay a fee for this consultation and thus would have narrowed down the list of potential surgeons to two or three by this stage.

According to a pamphlet prepared by the ASPRS and distributed in plastic surgeons' offices, a good plastic surgeon should exhibit some or all of the following qualities:[23]

- Has been recommended by a friend who has had a similar procedure
- Has been recommended by a family doctor or operating room nurse
- Is listed by the American Society of Plastic and Reconstructive Surgeons
- Is board-certified by the American Board of Plastic Surgery
- Has completed a residency in a specialty related to (your) procedure
- Has answered all (your) questions thoroughly
- Has asked about the patient's motivations and expectations of the surgery
- Has offered alternatives, where appropriate
- Has welcomed questions about professional qualifications, experience, cost, and payment policies
- Has clarified the risks of surgery and the variations in outcome
- Has made sure that the final decision to undergo surgery is the patient's decision.

## CONSUMER NEED FOR IMPLANTS

Reconstructive breast surgery patients had usually contracted a form of breast cancer, but also could be accident victims, or women with a congenital deformity. The most common reconstructive surgery took place after a patient had undergone a mastectomy (surgical removal of one or both breasts). Augmentation surgery patients desired an increase in breast size to enhance their appearance (known as augmentation mammaplasty).

### ■ Reconstructive Surgery

Without plastic surgery, reconstructive surgery consumers faced spending the rest of their lives with one or both breasts removed. The silicone gel breast implant operation provided them with a solution to regain their original physical appearance. Hence, the availability of breast implants was a major breakthrough for women suffering from breast cancer. In the early 1990's, about one woman in nine developed breast cancer in the U.S. It was the most commonly occurring cancer in women, accounting for more deaths than cancer of any other part of the body except the lungs. It was the leading cause of death among U.S. women aged 40-55.[24]

Before implants were available, some women refused to undergo a mastectomy, opting for lumpectomy (surgical removal of the breast tumor) or radiation or no action at all. While a lumpectomy or radiation abated the cancer's growth, neither treatment necessarily eliminated the breast cancer and, if unsuccessful, the patient could face a painful and premature death. Women refusing mastectomies were either afraid of the operation or were concerned with the permanent disfiguration and their perceived inability to be accepted back into society.

But with breast implants available, women were more accepting of the mastectomy operation. During the February 1992 FDA Advisory Panel hearing into breast implant safety, breast implant recipient Elaine Sansom testified:

> My mother's fear of losing her breast kept her from an early diagnosis, which allowed her cancer to spread before her mastectomy. She lived horribly from that point on, going through the rounds of chemo [therapy] and radiation; having a tumor eat through her first vertebra, ending up in a halo vest with bolts in her head . . . Being diagnosed with breast cancer [myself] was devastating . . . The choice to have implants was life-saving for me. Because I'm a diabetic, I wasn't a candidate for other types of reconstruction. If silicone gel breast implants had not been available at that time, my decision would have been a different one.[25]

In a letter to the *Washington Times* on January 31, 1992, another silicone breast implant recipient wrote:

> Since the FDA's moratorium on silicone breast implants has occurred, I would like you to hear the other side (the majority)—from satisfied recipients. I am one of nearly 2 million . . . These lifelike implants have helped the majority of women to recover faster physically and psychologically by restoring their femininity. I would rather die than be denied the option of having to go through life horribly disfigured. The alternative saline implants are a poor substitute, and they, too, are surrounded by silicone . . . Just give us the facts—we will decide, along with our doctors. Don't legislate my life anymore.[26]

### ■ Breast Augmentation Surgery

Breast augmentation surgery consumers were women who wished to enlarge their breasts for appearance reasons. The images portrayed by fashion models and "sex symbols" had created certain perceptions regarding the size of women's breasts. As a result, clothing sizes and designs, as well as male expectations, centered around the "appropriate" size for a woman's breasts. However, normal variations in humans resulted in a wide variation in breast sizes and some women developed smaller breasts than others. Breast augmentation surgery offered an approach for these women to artificially enlarge their breasts permanently to a size that they felt was perceived as being more suitable for their figure and lifestyle.

Given the breast implant controversy, many examples were reported of women who had undergone augmentation surgery and their reasons why. Carol Lachnit, journalist with the *Los Angeles Times*, wrote:

> Back in 1991, Patricia Fodor was a newlywed with "a cute little figure" and the belief that silicone gel breast implants would enhance it. It was "a self esteem issue," she said. Because she worked in a doctor's office, Fodor even got a discount on the procedure.
>
> . . . Catherine, a 64-year-old Orange County woman . . . [received] her implants in 1987, when she was 58. "I was one of those women who didn't get everything some women have," she said. "I have poor hair, fine, thin hair. I can't do much about my hair, but for my bust, I thought this would be great. I was so thrilled." Catherine immersed herself in the world of ballroom dancing. She had gowns made to show off her new figure. She made friends and "everyone commented on how good I looked," she said.[27]

Other comments from breast augmentation surgery patients were included in an article in the *Washington Times*, January 29, 1992:

> "I just wanted to be average," sighs Janet, 34, of Alexandria, Virginia. Having her breasts enlarged from a "boyish" 32 A to a "beautiful" 36 C has improved Janet's self-image and outlook. She says she can shop in half the time, buy clingy clothing on sale and doesn't feel at all self-conscious. "You wouldn't look at me on the street and say, 'There goes a busty woman,'" says the 5-foot-4-inch, full-time mother. "I look just right."
>
> "Look, there's a pressure on women for physical beauty," says Janet, who does aerobics regularly. "Models can get three times their salary when they get implants, and if that doesn't tell you something about our society. . . . " She calls it an "unfair, idealized image of beauty," but Janet subscribes to it.
>
> . . . . And Jacki Buckler, 26, credits her new 36 C breasts—"very round, very full"—with giving her the confidence to go back to the University of Maryland to finish her degree in oceanography. "I'm pushing myself now," the part-time Giant cashier and waitress says . . . "I did this [the surgery] for myself, for no one else," Miss Buckler says. She paid for the $3,500 procedure in monthly $600 installments and says she hasn't regretted the expense or the pain of surgery for a minute.[28]

## CONSUMER PROBLEMS WITH THE PRODUCT

By 1985, some 1.3 million implant operations had been completed.[29] Already, though, complaints were being received by the manufacturers and the FDA from customers citing painful hardening lumps and seepage of the silicone gel into the body after the implant bag had ruptured. Concerns began to arise about the potential of implants to rupture, the tightening of scar tissue that often formed around implants, causing the breast to harden, and the possible seepage of silicone, which was alleged to be responsible for generating a host of immune-system disorders that were painful, debilitating, and untreatable.

Over the next seven years, consumer activists in Washington, D.C., began to challenge the product's safety, while plastic surgeons and some women's groups lobbied to defend implants.

A variety of documents began to be released by Dow Corning and other manufacturers revealing that medical studies performed as early as the 1970's had warned of possible problems with implants.[30] Consumer activists criticized the manufacturers for "hiding" the information, the plastic surgeons for not questioning the safety of the implants, and the government for being negligent and not acting on the studies earlier. Leading the charge was Public Citizen's Health Research Group (Public Citizen), an organization founded by Ralph Nader and Dr. Sidney Wolfe to represent consumer interests in health-related matters. Public Citizen became actively involved in the implant controversy in 1988 after it obtained internal Dow Corning and FDA documents that suggested silicone gel implants were not safe for human use. It continued to lobby Congress and the FDA and also provided information packets to consumers and acted as a clearinghouse for plaintiff attorneys.

With growing legal activity and media attention, implants eventually assumed a higher priority on the FDA's agenda. FDA action increased by the end of the 1980's, when the FDA forced several implant products off the market after it was discovered that the foam covering the silicone slowly disintegrated at body temperature. This disintegration allowed a chemical known as TDA to be released, which in very high doses developed cancer in rats. By 1991 and the FDA's request that manufacturers provide evidence of research on the safety of implants, Public Citizen had begun selling $750 kits of evidence to trial lawyers interested in filing suits on behalf of disgruntled customers. The Command Trust Network, a nationwide educational network of 8,000 "implant victims," raised $30,000 and gave interviews to hundreds of reporters.[31]

The ASPRS, meanwhile, dedicated $1.3 million to lobby for the continued use of implants. In October 1991 it orchestrated a Washington "fly in," during which it paid for 400 women to travel to Capitol Hill and lobby congress to keep implants a viable choice for women. Simultaneously, it placed newspaper ads and organized a letter-writing campaign of 20,000 letters to the FDA.[32] In November 1991, the FDA hearings were given the report by its Advisory Panel, which concluded that the psychological importance of the implants outweighed the medical risks.

In December 1991 the verdict in the case of *Mariann Hopkins vs. Dow Corning* was announced, awarding Ms. Hopkins $7.3 million in damages, based on claims of damage to her autoimmune system.[33] Following the court's decision, Mariann Hopkins' lawyer, Dan C. Bolton, wrote to FDA Commissioner Dr. David A. Kessler about concerns with silicone breast implants. An extract from this letter appears as Exhibit 2.

The verdict was followed by the FDA moratorium on the sale of all silicone gel breast implant devices until such time as the agency received evidence to allay fears of any links to disease. Canada followed the U.S. by placing a similar ban, however the U.K. and France allowed implants to remain on the market. The moratorium, which prevented the sale of silicone gel implants unless their installation was clinically supervised (i.e., a study sponsored by the manufacturer and the FDA), sparked strong reaction from plastic surgeons and feminist groups. The plastic surgeons stood by the product and their surgical procedures, while the feminist groups claimed that women were being deprived of the right to make their own medical decisions.

| | |
|---|---|
| **Exhibit 2** | **Excerpt of Letter from Mariann Hopkins' Attorney Dan C. Bolton to FDA Commissioner David Kessler, December 30, 1991** |

I am writing to express my serious concerns relating to the dangers of silicone breast implants and the conduct of a principal manufacturer of breast implants, Dow Corning Corporation, in engaging in a consistent pattern of corporate deceit and dishonesty relating to the safety of implants . . .

Mariann Hopkins . . . underwent breast reconstruction with silicone gel–filled breast implants manufactured by Dow following a bilateral mastectomy for fibrocystic disease in 1976. A bilateral rupture of the implants was discovered in February 1986. Mrs. Hopkins suffers from mixed connective tissue disease, an immune disorder, caused by her exposure to silicone gel.

On December 13, 1991, the jury unanimously rendered a verdict in the amount of $840,000 for compensatory damages, and $6,500,000 for punitive damages . . . the jury found that Dow's silicone breast implants were not properly designed and manufactured, that Dow had failed to warn of risks associated with implants, that Dow had breached implied and expressed warranties relating to its product and that Dow had committed fraud. The jury also found by "clear and convincing evidence" that Dow's fraud, in addition to its "malice" and "oppression," warranted the imposition of punitive damages. Under California law, "malice" means conduct that is "intended by the defendant to cause injury to the plaintiff or despicable conduct which is carried on by the defendant with a willful and conscious disregard of the rights and safety of others." "Oppression" requires a finding by the jury that the defendant has engaged in "despicable conduct that subjects a person to cruel and unjust hardship in conscious disregard of that person's rights."

Considerable evidence was presented at trial that Dow was aware of the risks of silicone as early as the 1960's, and continued to market a medical device intended for long-term use despite the absence of any studies demonstrating the long-term safety of silicone in the human body. Dow's conduct is especially unconscionable in light of the fact that Dow's own product literature represented that breast implants were safe for long-term use by women.

. . . the time has come to hold implant manufacturers, such as Dow, accountable for the safety of their product. I urge you to take appropriate steps to ensure that women do not continue to be victimized by irresponsible companies that are more concerned with their financial well-being than the health and safety of consumers . . . Dow's corporate response to the increasing numbers of women injured by its dangerous and defective implants was to issue a warranty program in the mid-1980's. This program provides partial reimbursement for the medical expenses incurred in removing implants because of rupture or immune sensitization so long as the physician extracts a release from the patient extinguishing all of her legal rights against Dow. This conduct is not only legally questionable but morally indefensible.

---

A lawsuit filed after this moratorium by an augmentation surgery patient was reported in the *San Diego Union-Tribune*, January 30, 1992:

> A woman who was given Dow Corning Corp.'s silicone gel breast implants to improve her figure has sued the company, claiming they made her ill and accusing the company of ignoring safety warnings about the devices, her attorney said . . . Stanley Rosenblatt said yesterday the Dade County woman, identified only as "Jane Doe," is in her 30's and received the breast implants in 1985 to enhance her figure. She is seeking $100 million in damages. The lawsuit, filed in Dade County Circuit Court, claims the woman was in perfect health before the operation but has since suffered "recurrent flu, recurrent strep throat, infections, excessive hair loss, constant fatigue, excruciating joint pain, rashes across her face and a constant low-grade fever." The woman has been bedridden "for months at a time" because of systemic lupus erythematosus, a disorder of the immune system, the suit claims . . . Dow Corning ignored warnings from its own employees about implant defects and concealed the information from doctors, patients, and federal regulators, the lawsuit alleges. "Plaintiff is a victim of an incredible 'con' perpetrated upon the public at large and women in particular," the lawsuit said. It accused Dow Chemical of constructing a "vast experiment" on 2 million women that should have been performed on laboratory animals instead . . . The surgeon is not being sued because Dow Corning convinced him the implants were safe, Rosenblatt said. The woman still has the implants but is deciding whether to have them

removed, he said. The lawsuit alleges an internal company memo shows Dow Corning salespeople misled surgeons by washing "the often greasy gel implants before showing them to physicians, with full knowledge that the product was dangerous to women."[34]

Pamela Johnson filed a lawsuit against another implant manufacturer. The following extract from the *Houston Chronicle* explains her complaint:

> Johnson's first set of breast implants, manufactured by MEC, [were] surgically implanted in 1976. O'Quinn [her attorney] said the company led Johnson's doctor to believe the implants had been tested and engineered so that the outer shell would contain the silicone gel, that the gel was cohesive and would not run if the shell ruptured, and that, if the gel did escape the shell, it would not harm human tissue. The doctor was told [that] the product would last a lifetime, O'Quinn said . . . In 1989, Johnson's implants ruptured. Her doctor, believing the product's problems had been solved, then inserted a new set of silicone gel implants . . . The second set was removed that same year, and another implant done, with a product made by a different manufacturer. Those implants were removed [in early 1992].[35]

Despite these suits, Dow Corning defended its product. Bob Rylee, Dow Corning Wright's chairman, stated that implants represented less than 1 percent of Dow Corning's $1.8 billion in revenues and the true risk with implants was less than 1 percent.[36]

## ■ Ongoing Investigations

The FDA Advisory Panel was scheduled to reconvene on February 18, 1992, to reconsider implant PMAA's. In addition to the FDA studies, another probe into Dow Corning's breast implants was launched on January 30, 1992, by the Los Angeles County district attorney's office, under its Corporate Criminal Liability Act.[37] The investigation was to determine whether Dow Corning sold the breast implants without fully disclosing health risk information required by law. District attorney Ira Reiner had requested that Dow Corning provide substantial information about the product, including laboratory data, internal memoranda, and copies of informational and promotional material about the implants (Exhibit 3 provides Dow Corning's implant package insert). L.A. County's Corporate Criminal Liability Act makes it a felony for corporate managers to fail to provide regulatory agencies with written notification of a "serious concealed danger" associated with a product and penalties included up to three years' imprisonment and fines up to $1 million.

At the same time, Dow Corning had hired Griffin Bell, a former U.S. attorney general and a circuit court judge, to investigate the company's development and marketing of the implants. He planned to select independent scientific and medical experts to assist his investigation, with free access to all of Dow Corning's records, resources, and employees. Bell's final recommendations would be made available to the FDA and the public. Dow also announced on January 29, 1992, that it would make public internal memoranda and other information by the week of February 10.

Lawyers and Public Citizen criticized the delays in having the documents released, claiming that the documents had been locked up for years and that, if the FDA had been given earlier access to the information, breast implants would have been off the market a long time ago.[38] Dow Corning disputed this view, stating that the FDA had possession of the relevant documents for many

| Exhibit 3 | Outline of Package Insert for Dow Corning's 1985 SILASTIC II Brand Mammary Implant H.P. Package Insert (with excerpts) |

## Description

### Specific Advantages

"Envelopes have greater tear propagation resistance."

"A special silicone layer within the envelope provides a barrier to significantly reduce gel bleed."

"Generally recognized as having acceptable level of reactivity."

### Indications

"Criteria for patient selection must be the responsibility of the surgeon."

### Contraindications

"A mammary implant may not be well tolerated in any patient who exhibits certain types of psychological instability, e.g., does not want implants, displays a lack of understanding, or inappropriate motivation or attitude."

"These are general, relative contraindications and each individual patient must be evaluated by her surgeon to determine the specific risk/benefit ratio."

### Precautions and Warnings

"SILASTIC brand medical-grade silicone elastomers made exclusively by Dow Corning are among the most non-reactive implant materials available."

### Possible Adverse Reactions and Complications

"Thousands of women per year have had cosmetic or reconstructive surgery with implantation of mammary prostheses. A number of patients are reported to have significant complications or adverse reactions. Typically, a patient undergoing a surgical procedure is subject to unforeseen intra-operative and post-operative complications. Each patient's tolerance to surgery, medication, and implantation of a foreign object may be different. Possible risks, adverse reactions, and complications associated with surgery and the use of the mammary prosthesis should be discussed with and understood by the patient prior to surgery. The adverse reactions and complications most likely to occur with the use of this product are listed below. IT IS THE RESPONSIBILITY OF THE SURGEON TO PROVIDE THE PATIENT WITH APPROPRIATE INFORMATION PRIOR TO SURGERY."

1. *Capsule Formation and Contracture*

2. *Sensitization*

"There have been reports of suspected immunological sensitization or hyperimmune system response to silicone mammary implants. Symptoms claimed by the patients included localized inflammation and irritation at the implant area, fluid accumulation, rash, general malaise, severe joint pain, swelling of joints, weight loss, arthralgia, lymphadenopathy, alopecia, and rejection of the mammary prosthesis. Such claims suggest there may be a relationship between the silicone mammary implant and the reported symptoms. Materials from which this prosthesis is fabricated have been shown in animal laboratory tests to have minimal sensitization potential. However, claims from clinical use of the silicone prosthesis in humans suggest that immunological responses or sensitization to a mammary prosthesis can occur. If sensitization is suspected and the response persists, removal of the prosthesis is recommended along with removal of the surrounding capsule tissue. This procedure is recommended to minimize the amount of residual silicone that may be left at the implant site."

3. *Implant Rupture Gel Extravasation*

"Dow Corning is not responsible for the integrity of the implant should such techniques as closed capsulotomies (manual compression) be used."

"As reported in the literature, when an implant ruptures gel may be released from the implant envelope despite the cohesive properties of the gel. If left in place, complications such as enlarged lymph nodes, scar formation, inflammation, silicone granulomas, and nodule formation may result."

"These potential consequences should be understood by the surgeon and explained to the patient prior to implantation."

"In the event of a rupture, Dow Corning recommends prompt removal of the envelope and gel. The long-term physiological effects of uncontained silicone gel are currently unknown."

"The patient should be informed that the life expectancy of any implant is unpredictable."

---

**Exhibit 3 (continued)**      **Outline of Package Insert for Dow Corning's 1985 SILASTIC II Brand Mammary Implant H.P. Package Insert (with excerpts)**

---

4. *Infection*

5. *Hematoma*

6. *Serous Fluid Accumulation*

7. *Interruption in Wound Healing*

8. *Skin Sloughing/Necrosis*

9. *Incorrect Size, Inappropriate Location of Scars, and Misplacement or Migration of Implants, etc.*

10. *Palpability of Implant*

11. *Asymmetry*

12. *Ptotic (Drooping) Breast*
"It is important that this possibility be discussed with the patient."

13. *Nipple Sensation*
"This should be discussed in detail with the patient."

14. *Microwave Diathermy*

15. *Implant Gel Bleed*

16. *X-ray Pre-Operative & Post-Operative*
"Post—Some physicians state an implant may pose difficulties in detecting tumors in certain locations in the breast via xeromammography."

17. *Calcification*

18. *Absorption of Biologicals By Implants*
*References to Carcinogenesis*
"During the past twenty years of clinical use, the medical literature indicates that the silicone mammary prosthesis is not carcinogenic."

**Instructions for Use**

1. *The surgeon should discuss possible risks, consequences, complications, and adverse reactions associated with the surgical procedure and implantation of the mammary prosthesis with the patient prior to surgery.*

2. *Surgical Procedures*
"Prior to use, the prosthesis should be carefully examined for structural integrity."

3. *Packaging*

4. *Recommended Procedure for Opening Package—Sterile Product*

5. *To Clean and (Re)Sterilize Mammary Implants*

**References**

**Warranty**

"Dow Corning warrants that reasonable care in selection of materials and methods of manufacture were used in fabrication of this product. Dow Corning shall not be liable for an incidental or consequential loss, damage, or expense, directly or indirectly arising from the use of this product."
"Dow Corning neither assumes nor authorizes any other person to assume for it any other or additional liability or responsibility in connection with this product. Dow Corning intends that this mammary implant product should be used only by physicians having received appropriate training in plastic surgery techniques."

---

years. Dow Corning also claimed to have performed some 900 studies into the safety of the implants, none of which concluded that implants would cause harm to the recipient.[39] Plaintiff lawyers, keen to obtain any new information surrounding implants, estimated that there were as many as 1,000 suits filed or about to be filed alleging that the implants had caused cancer, immune system disorders, or connective tissue disease.[40]

## NEW APPROACH REQUIRED

The seriousness of the implant issue had now escalated. On February 10, 1992, the same day Keith McKennon was appointed to chairman and CEO of Dow Corning, the company yielded to public pressure and disclosed 100 potentially embarrassing company documents that came to light in the Hopkins trial and more recently had been leaked to the press.[41] McKennon had been asked by the board to personally assemble Dow Corning's strategy and action plan to resolve conclusively the implant situation.

With many stakeholders to satisfy and ethical issues to deal with, the problem was going to be complex to solve. His first step was to understand what caused the implant controversy in the first place and to decide whether Dow Corning should continue to market this sensitive product. McKennon also had to assess the validity of the customer complaints, estimate the financial and legal exposure from future customer litigation, respond to the FDA's moratorium announcement, and determine the potential damage to Dow Corning's brand name and reputation.

## REFERENCES

1. Marcotty, Josephine, "Implant Lawsuits: Floods of Litigation Possible Because of Health Problems with Silicone Gel," *Star Tribune*, 30 January 1992, p. D1.

2. Appleson, Gail, "Court Orders Kept Breast Implant Data Secret for Years," *Reuters*, AM cycle, 30 January, 1992.

3. Ressberger, Boyce, "Silicone Gel Data Faked, Firm Says," *Houston Chronicle*, 3 November, 1992, p. A7.

4. Dow Corning Corporation, Form 10-K, 31 December, 1991.

5. Marcotty, op. cit., p. D1.

6. Dow Corning Corporation, Form 10-K, December 31, 1991.

7. *Fortune*, 20 April, 1992.

8. *Ward Business Directory of U.S. Private and Public Companies*, 1992.

9. McMurray, Scott, and Thomas M. Burton, "Dow Corning Plans to Quit Implant Line," *Wall Street Journal*, 19 March, 1992, p. A3.

10. Burton, Ghomas M., Bruce Ingersoll, and Joan E. Rigdon, "Dow Corning Makes Changes in Top Posts," *Wall Street Journal*, February 11, 1992, p. A3.

11. Gary E. Anderson, Executive Vice President, Dow Corning Corporation, interview, January 7, 1994.

12. American Society of Plastic Reconstructive Surgeons (ASPRS), *1992 Statistics*, Arlington Heights, IL, 1992.

13. According to the U.S. Food and Drug Administration.

14. U.S. Department of Commerce, *U.S. Industrial Outlook 1993* (Lanham, MD: Bernan Press).

15. ASPRS, op. cit.

16. Pisik, Betsy, "Dangerous Curves; For Many Women, Rewards of Breast Implants Worth Risks," *Washington Times*, 29 January, 1992, p. E1.

17. Lachit, Carroll, "Controversy That Won't Go Away," *Los Angeles Times*, 7 October, 1993, p. E1.

18. ASPRS, op. cit.

19. Lachit, op. cit.

20. Ibid.

21. Ibid.

22. ASPRS, op. cit.

23. ASPRS, "How To Choose a Qualified Plastic Surgeon" (Arlington Heights, IL: ASPRS, 1992).

24. U.S. Department of Commerce, *Statistical Abstract of the United States*. Bureau of the Census, Washington, D.C., 113th edition, 1993.

25. Samson, Elaine, National Organization for Women with Implants, FDA Panel Hearing, February 1992.

26. *Washington Times*, "FDA Chief David Kessler Joins the Hysteria Over Silicone," 31 January, 1992, p. F2.

27. Lachit, op. cit.

28. Pisik, op. cit.

29. Drew, Christopher, and Michael Tackett, "Access Equals Clout: The Blitzing of FDA," *Chicago Tribune*, 8 December, 1992, p. C1.

30. Byrne, John A., "The Best Laid Ethics Programs," *BusinessWeek*, 9 March, 1992, p. 69.

31. Ingersoll, Bruce, "Industry Mounts Big Lobbying Drive Supporting Implants," *Wall Street Journal*, 14 February, 1992, p. A5.

32. Drew, op. cit.

33. Cooper, Clair, "Thousands Await Decision as Implant Suit Hits Appeals Court," *Sacramento Bee*, 19 June, 1993, p. A6.

34. United Press International, "Dow Sued Over Breast Implants," *San Diego Union-Tribune*, 30 January, 1992, p. A9.

35. Piller, Ruth, "Trial Starts in Lawsuit Against Maker of Silicone Gel Implants," *Houston Chronicle*, 11 December, 1992, p. A33.

36. Marcotty, op. cit.

37. Steinbrook, Robert, and Henry Weinstein, "County Will Investigate Maker of Breast Implants," *Los Angeles Times*, 31 January, 1992, p. zB1.

38. Appleson, op. cit.

39. Anderson, op. cit.

40. Appleson, op. cit.

41. Burton et al., op. cit.